CASES AND MATERIALS ON
CALIFORNIA COMMUNITY PROPERTY LAW

MARRIAGE, PROPERTY, CODE

Eleventh Edition

■ ■ ■

Jo Carrillo

Professor of Law
University of California, Hastings College of the Law

AMERICAN CASEBOOK SERIES®

WEST ACADEMIC PUBLISHING

American Casebook Series is a trademark registered in the U.S. Patent and Trademark Office.

Printed in the United States of America

ISBN: 978-0-314-28372-6

To my parents,

my son,

and my whole team,

with love.

PREFACE

How intimate partners organize their lives together is a fascinating and important legal subject.

In this 11th edition, I introduce an emerging understanding of California community property law as a marital property *system*. The system holds that the formalized intimate partnership is made up of two equal partners. Material equality is built into the partnership by the concept of community property itself; relational equality by how the system holds the spouses to partnership fiduciary duties. Together, these aspects of the California community property system protect the parties, third persons who transact with them, and society at large.

Legislative statistics show that most married persons do not dissolve their marriage through litigation. Therefore, by necessity, the code-based California community property system must be and is meticulously maintained by the California Legislature. That said, litigation does occur. And when it does, it all too often illustrates how legal equality gets thwarted by daily life and social hierarchies.

The materials in this casebook present the living law. Code sections state the rules. Cases apply them. Cases also allow readers into the private lives of couples whose marriage has ended. Embedded in these endings are dramatic moments from which readers can develop their own perspective on how the community property system works and why.

Generations of law students have learned about community property law through this casebook. Some went on to lead California through key legal and social transitions.

The casebook derivation: The law of intimate partnership has changed since 1952 when Harold E. Verrall mimeographed his teaching notes for classroom use. Verrall called his notes CASES AND MATERIALS ON CALIFORNIA COMMUNITY PROPERTY. In 1960, West published the first formal edition of Verrall's notes; that edition was called CASES AND MATERIALS ON CALIFORNIA COMMUNITY PROPERTY LAW. West produced subsequent editions of Verrall's casebook in 1966 (Verrall), 1971 (Verral and Sammis), 1977 (Verrall), 1983, 1988, 1994 (Verrall and Bird), 1999, 2003, 2008 (Bird), 2011 (Bird and Carrillo), and now 2016 (Carrillo).[1]

Over the sixty-five years that CASES AND MATERIALS ON CALIFORNIA COMMUNITY PROPERTY LAW has been used in the classroom, huge social and legal transitions have occurred. Male management to equal

---

[1] DOUGLAS W. LIND, BIBLIOGRAPHY OF AMERICAN LAW SCHOOL CASEBOOKS, 1870–2004 134–140 (2006).

management. Fault divorce to no-fault dissolution. The adoption of a comprehensive Family Code to address property, custody, and domestic violence prevention. The rise of alternative dispute resolution. The necessity for disclosure. These changes (alone and together) have altered the institution of marriage. The changes have also brought nonmarriage into relief as a viable personal choice. The law of community property has morphed, in other words, from a lackluster explicitly gender-biased, fault-based set of Civil Code statutes that got away with opposing marriage and property as unrelated concepts *into* the comprehensive, gender-neutral if not gender-fair, no-fault, property-aware Family Code that exists today. For that reason, I add a new subtitle—MARRIAGE, PROPERTY, CODE—with the intent to underscore that the California community property system is law, yes. But more than that, it is a code-based, hybrid civil law slash common law system that legislates a relationship between marriage and property.

Original research: The 11th edition is based on original scholarship and presents state of the art information throughout.

Updated statutes and cases: Statutes are up to date, with accurate derivations. Recent relevant cases appear throughout the text and notes. Cases are cited by judicial district so as to identify the geographic origin of the dispute in a state that is large but not monolithic.

Statutory derivations: I've retained and updated derivations after each statute. I regard derivations as a concise legislative history of the code provision itself. Some statutes were enacted a very long time ago; hence I occasionally retain a historical derivation to indicate the longevity of the statutory provision. Many statutes were continued over from the Family Law Act of 1969 into the current Family Code of 1992. The derivation of a *continued* statute typically indicates that the statute was enacted in 1992 or 1993, operative 1994. Other statutes were added after the adoption of the Family Code; the statutory derivation for an *added* statute will indicate the year of adoption (*Added by Stats. . . .*).

Additionally, the California Legislature has undertaken to make every statute gender-neutral on its face. In 2015, references to "husbands" and "wives" were replaced with references to "spouse" and "spouses." Thus a recent derivation of 2016 typically means that the statute has been made gender-neutral on its face.

Additions and amendments on date of separation become operative on January 1, 2017.

Organized for ease of adoption: For the convenience of adopters and their students, the pattern of earlier editions has been continued in the 11th edition. Each chapter starts with a brief textual overview of the area, followed by statutes and cases. Cross-references to the current California Family Code are included in all excerpted cases. Footnotes have been omitted from the text and from the principal cases without so specifying. Notes to the cases follow.

Notes expand, illustrate, and contextualize the law.

A complete statutory Appendix appears at the back of the casebook (Appendix A).

Multilayered for ease of reading: There are multiple handles to make the casebook accessible to the reader.

Standard tools, of course, are the *Table of Contents* and *Table of Cases*, which can be used to pinpoint where a particular case is discussed in the text. *Statutes* under discussion appear in the text for context, a practice carried over from previous editions. *Notes* explore the main topic, as discussed above. The *italicized note headings*, if read sequentially, provide an abbreviated version of the casebook. *Text boxes* are used to highlight and abstract general points. The *Index* offers abbreviated outlines of each subject, as well as page number references. Appendix A compiles a *statutory appendix* to all statutes referenced in the text, plus additional statutes. Appendix B includes key *Judicial Council Forms* for illustration and ease of reference. Appendix C introduces students to *business broker valuation benchmarks*.

New material: Chapter 1 introduces California community property law as a public system. California is the most populous and diverse state in the U.S. It has the sixth largest economy in the world. Therefore, in my view, placing the community property system in the context of information about the state of California is a useful point of orientation.

Chapter 2 covers the community property principle. New material on special presumptions and particularly on bank accounts and sums is included. The material on accounts clarifies for students the ubiquitous practice of using deposit accounts (whether they be traditional or electronic). California adopted the California Multiple-Parties Account Law (CAMPAL for short) in the early 1980s and continued the law in the state Probate Code in the early 1990s. Included within CAMPAL is a community property presumption for sums on deposit in any covered deposit account of a (living) married person. The special presumption supersedes any other community property presumption as to sums on deposit in the account, making it an important element of the California community property system. The special presumption is discussed as a presumption in Chapter 2; particularized rebuttal rules are discussed in Chapter 5.

Chapter 3 introduces new material on gifts and personal injury claims and settlements. Chapter 3 also includes newly added California Family Code Secion 70, which abrogates *Marriage of Davis*, 61 Cal.4th 846, 352

P.3d 401 (2015) and *Marriage of Norviel,* 102 Cal.App.4th 1152, 126 Cal.Rptr.2d 148 (6th Dist. 2002).

Chapter 4 includes new information on the limits of the California community property system. The chapter also includes the most recently enacted and amended Family Code sections on the rights of putative spouses, as well as new information about the rights of nonmarital intimate partners.

Chapter 5, 7, 8, and 9 provide clear, updated coverage of commingled assets, dissolution, postdissolution set-aside petitions, and the distribution of property on the death of a spouse. New disclosure rules added to the Family Code to prevent coercion and fraud are discussed throughout Chapter 7 (dissolution) and Chapter 8 (set-aside motions for final dissolution judgments). Collaborative law and alternative dispute resolution are covered as well. Chapter 9 also provides the reader with expanded coverage on nonprobate assets.

Chapter 6 introduces students to the different categories of property management and control that are available for use by spouses during the course of a marriage. Chapter 6 includes—for the first time ever in the history of this casebook—contemporary, California-specific materials on domestic violence prevention. The new material discusses how domestic violence prevention statutes relate to community property rights. I attribute the inclusion of the material on domestic violence prevention to published scholarship of mine on the relationship between property, coercion, economic violence, and financial interpersonal violence.

Thoroughly updating the 10th edition of this casebook has taken me on a long journey. Many people have assisted, supported, and encouraged me along the way. Thank you to one and all. A special thanks to my family.

I would also like to acknowledge with gratitude: the Chip Robertson Scholarly Publications Fund; the University of California Hastings College of the Law for summer stipend support; Divina Morgan for excellent assistance in all things UC Hastings; the students who shared presence, comments, questions, and unique perspectives in the classroom; the University of Michigan Law Library for kindly allowing me access (as an unaffiliated visitor) to its collection; the people at West who are a pleasure to work with; and last, but certainly not least, Rade Vranesh, who assisted me with production at every step and stage of the project.

JO CARRILLO

San Francisco, California
September 12, 2016

SUMMARY OF CONTENTS

_____

PREFACE V

TABLE OF CASES XIX

PART I. AN OVERVIEW OF THE CALIFORNIA COMMUNITY PROPERTY SYSTEM

Chapter 1. An Overview of the California Community Property System 3
Section 1. The Sharing Principle 3
Section 2. Equal, Fair, and Just 3
Section 3. Marriage as a Partnership 6
Section 4. Comparing Common Law Title and Community Property Systems 13
Section 5. The California Community Property System 20
Section 6. The Tracing Principle 29
Section 7. The Equality of Interest Principle 31
Section 8. The Contract Modification Principle 33
Section 9. Chapter Summary 76

PART II. THE CHARACTERIZATION OF PROPERTY

Chapter 2. Community Property 81
Section 1. The Significance of Characterization 82
Section 2. The Community Property Principle 84
Section 3. Community Property Presumptions 89
Section 4. Onerous or Lucrative Titles 147
Section 5. Chapter Summary 155

Chapter 3. Separate Property 157
Section 1. State Constitutional Protection for Separate Property 157
Section 2. Separate Property Defined 157
Section 3. Personal Injury Claims, Money, and Property 170
Section 4. Earnings and Accumulations While Living Separate and Apart 185
Section 5. Chapter Summary 194

Chapter 4. Limits of the California Community Property System 197
Section 1. Property Outside the California Community Property System... 198
Section 2. Persons Outside the System 233
Section 3. Constitutional Limitations 279
Section 4. Chapter Summary 320

Chapter 5. Commingled Assets...**323**
Section 1. General Definitions and Rules...................................... 323
Section 2. Demand Deposit Accounts.. 325
Section 3. Purchases from a Commingled Deposit Account 336
Section 4. Commingled Credit Acquisitions.................................. 353
Section 5. Separate Property Business Profits.............................. 376
Section 6. Work Benefits.. 399
Section 7. Chapter Summary 421

PART III. MANAGEMENT AND CONTROL

Chapter 6. Community Property Management and Control............**427**
Section 1. Equal Management and Control..................................... 428
Section 2. Community Personal Property 448
Section 3. Community Real Property.. 463
Section 4. Transactions Between the Spouses 477
Section 5. Creditors' Claims 496
Section 6. Primary and Exclusive Management and Control of
     Community Property... 508
Section 7. Chapter Summary 524

PART IV. AT MARRIAGE'S END

Chapter 7. Division of Community Property at Dissolution **529**
Section 1. Dissolution, Legal Separation, Nullity........................ 529
Section 2. Division by Marriage Settlement Agreement 537
Section 3. Division by Court Order 558
Section 4. Chapter Summary 621

Chapter 8. Postdissolution Remedies.......................................**623**
Section 1. The Importance of Disclosure at Dissolution.............. 623
Section 2. Money Sanctions in an Ongoing Dissolution Proceeding............. 633
Section 3. Postjudgment Set-Aside Orders.................................... 655
Section 4. Grounds to Set Aside a Final Judgment of Dissolution 658
Section 5. Chapter Summary 710

Chapter 9. Distribution of Community Property at Death................**713**
Section 1. Community and Quasi-Community Property............................. 714
Section 2. Basics of Nonprobate Transfers 730
Section 3. Basics of Intestate Distribution and Administration.................. 751
Section 4. Allocating Debt/Creditors' Rights................................ 758
Section 5. Chapter Summary 788

Appendix A. Statutory Appendix..**791**

Appendix B. Judicial Council Forms.......................................**879**

Appendix C. Example Business Valuation Materials **887**

INDEX.. 897

TABLE OF CONTENTS

PREFACE V

TABLE OF CASES XIX

PART I. AN OVERVIEW OF THE CALIFORNIA COMMUNITY PROPERTY SYSTEM

Chapter 1. An Overview of the California Community Property System..3
Section 1. The Sharing Principle.. 3
Section 2. Equal, Fair, and Just... 3
Section 3. Marriage as a Partnership 6
    Notes 12
Section 4. Comparing Common Law Title and Community Property Systems 13
    Notes 15
Section 5. The California Community Property System 20
Section 6. The Tracing Principle 29
    Notes 30
Section 7. The Equality of Interest Principle 31
Section 8. The Contract Modification Principle 33
    A.   Premarital Agreements.. 34
        1.   Formalities 36
        2.   Postdissolution Spousal Support Waivers 36
        3.   General Contract Enforceability.............................. 37
            Notes.. 40
    B.   Transmutations 44
        Estate of Bibb 46
        Marriage of Valli.. 53
        Notes.. 67
        Marriage of Steinberger 71
        Note 75
Section 9. Chapter Summary 76

PART II. THE CHARACTERIZATION OF PROPERTY

Chapter 2. Community Property 81
Section 1. The Significance of Characterization 82
Section 2. The Community Property Principle 84
    A.   California Community Property and Quasi-Community Property.. 84
    B.   The "All . . . Except" Format of the Basic Community Property Statute.. 86

C. "All Property, Real or Personal, Wherever Situated . . . " 87
D. Community Property Appreciation and Rents, Issues, and
   Profits 88
E. A Principle Rather than a Definition 88
Section 3. Community Property Presumptions 89
A. The General Community Property Presumption 89
   Wilson v. Wilson 90
   Notes... 92
   Fidelity & Casualty Company v. Mahoney...................................... 97
   Notes... 100
   Marriage of Ettefagh 103
   Notes... 111
B. The Statutory Joint Form Title Community Property
   Presumption 115
   1. Early Twentieth-Century Case Law on Property Purchased
      with Community Property but Titled in Joint Tenancy......... 119
   2. Mid-Twentieth-Century Legislative Attempts at a Statutory
      Joint Title Community Property Presumption 122
   3. Current Legislation: California Family Code Sections 2580
      and 2581 124
      Note 126
      Marriage of Lucas 127
      Notes.. 128
C. The Statutory Community Property Presumption for Sums on
   Deposit in Any Account of a Married Person.................................. 132
   1. Basic Terms: Money, Cash, Sums on Deposit, Loan
      Proceeds... 132
   2. CAMPAL: Uniform Legislation on Demand Deposit
      Accounts... 134
D. Borrowed Funds Acquired During Marriage Are Presumptively
   Community Property... 137
   Marriage of Grinius.. 140
   Notes... 145
Section 4. Onerous or Lucrative Titles 147
   Estate of Clark... 148
   Notes 150
   Downer v. Bramet 151
   Notes 154
Section 5. Chapter Summary 155

Chapter 3. Separate Property 157
Section 1. State Constitutional Protection for Separate Property................ 157
Section 2. Separate Property Defined.. 157
A. Exceptions to the Community Property Principle......................... 157
   1. Property Owned Before Marriage... 158
   2. Property Acquired During Marriage by Gift.......................... 159

3.   Separate Property Appreciation Distinguished from Rents,
Issues, and Profits of Separate Property 161
George v. Ransom 164
Notes 165
Section 3. Personal Injury Claims, Money, and Property 170
A.   Personal Injury Claims 171
B.   No Imputed Contributory Negligence as a Matter of Law 172
C.   Personal Injury Settlements: Money and Property 176
D.   Tracing Personal Injury Settlements 177
Marriage of Devlin 178
Notes 181
E.   Personal Injury Claims Against the Other Spouse 183
Section 4. Earnings and Accumulations While Living Separate and
Apart 185
A.   The Bare Statute 185
B.   Perception, Intention, Conduct—The *Hardin-Manfer* Test 188
C.   Living Apart as Roommates: Applying California Family Code
Section 70 189
Notes 190
Section 5. Chapter Summary 194

**Chapter 4. Limits of the California Community Property
System** **197**
Section 1. Property Outside the California Community Property System ... 198
A.   Education That Substantially Enhances Its Holder's Earning
Capacity 199
Notes 201
Notes 206
Marriage of Graham 207
Marriage of Watt 210
Note 214
B.   The Hunt for a Colorful Month: Talent 215
Marriage of McTiernan & Dubrow 215
Notes 228
Section 2. Persons Outside the System 233
A.   Valid, Void, and Voidable Marriage 234
Notes 238
B.   Intimate Nonmarried Cohabitants 253
Vallera v. Vallera 254
Note 257
Marvin v. Marvin 258
Notes 271
C.   The Domicile Requirement 274
Rozan v. Rozan 275
Note 276
Grappo v. Coventry Financial Corporation 277
Notes 279

Section 3. Constitutional Limitations 279
    A.   The Due Process and Privileges and Immunities Clauses 280
        Addison v. Addison 281
        Notes 286
    B.   Retroactivity Problems 288
        Marriage of Bouquet 288
        Marriage of Heikes 295
    C.   The Supremacy Clause 305
        Wissner v. Wissner 305
        Notes 310
        Boggs v. Boggs 312
        Notes 319
Section 4. Chapter Summary 320

Chapter 5. Commingled Assets **323**
Section 1. General Definitions and Rules 323
Section 2. Demand Deposit Accounts 325
    A.   Account Access: The Contract of Deposit 325
    B.   Beneficial Ownership of Sums on Deposit 330
    C.   "Net Deposits" and the Family Expense Presumption 332
    D.   Confirming Sums and Purchases as Separate Property 333
    E.   Statutory Reimbursement Rights Compared with Excess
        Withdrawal Claims 334
Section 3. Purchases from a Commingled Deposit Account 336
    A.   The Exhaustion Method: Rebutting the General Community
        Property Presumption 337
        See v. See 339
        Notes 343
    B.   The Direct Tracing Method of Rebuttal for the General
        Community Property Presumption 345
        Marriage of Mix 346
    C.   Standard Bank Records Insufficient for Rebuttal 349
        Marriage of Frick 350
        Notes 352
Section 4. Commingled Credit Acquisitions 353
    A.   Credit Acquisitions During Marriage 354
        Marriage of Aufmuth 355
        Notes 358
    B.   Credit Acquisitions Before Marriage 358
        Vieux v. Vieux 359
        Notes 362
        Marriage of Moore 363
        Notes 367
        Marriage of Marsden 368
        Note 371
        Marriage of Frick 371
        Marriage of Geraci 373

Section 5. Separate Property Business Profits............................. 376
    A.   Substantial Justice: *Pereira* or *Van Camp*?..................... 376
        Pereira v. Pereira 379
        Notes.. 381
        Van Camp v. Van Camp... 383
        Notes.. 385
    B.   A Separate Property Business Distinguished from an Income
        Stream.. 388
        Austin v. Austin.. 388
        Notes.. 392
    C.   The Minimum-Plus Labor Standard 393
        Beam v. Bank of America... 394
        Notes.. 398
Section 6. Work Benefits.. 399
    A.   Deferred Earnings 399
        Notes.. 401
        Marriage of Green 403
    B.   Signing Bonuses and Client Books................................ 409
        Marriage of Finby 409
        Notes.. 421
Section 7. Chapter Summary 421

PART III. MANAGEMENT AND CONTROL

Chapter 6. Community Property Management and Control **427**
Section 1. Equal Management and Control.................................... 428
    A.   Property Ownership in Relation to Management and Control 429
    B.   Non-Statutory Claims Arising from the Property Right 429
        Wilcox v. Wilcox.. 430
        Note 431
        Meinhard v. Salmon 432
        Notes.. 436
    C.   A Right to Destroy? 441
        People v. Kahanic 441
        People v. Wallace 445
Section 2. Community Personal Property 448
    A.   The Managerial System 449
    B.   The Right to Avoid... 450
        Spreckels v. Spreckels 452
        Notes.. 454
    C.   Reimbursement Rights 458
    D.   The "Other than Testamentary" Limitation................... 460
        Tyre v. Aetna Life Insurance Co.................................. 461
        Notes.. 463
Section 3. Community Real Property.. 463
    Lezine v. Security Pacific Financial Services, Inc........................ 465
    Note 476

Section 4. Transactions Between the Spouses 477
   A.   Fiduciary Duties 477
   B.   Disclosure Without Demand 479
   C.   Impairment Claims 482
        Note 484
        Marriage of Rossi 485
        Notes 491
Section 5. Creditors' Claims 496
   A.   During Marriage 498
   B.   After a Date of Separation 499
   C.   Contract Debts for Non-Support Related Expenses 500
   D.   Tort Judgment Creditors 500
   E.   Liability of Quasi-Community Property 501
   F.   Liability of Quasi-Marital Property 501
   G.   Liability of Community Real Property Located in Another
       State 502
   H.   Liability for Premarital Debts 502
   I.   Liability for Premarital Support Obligations 502
Section 6. Primary and Exclusive Management and Control of
Community Property 508
   A.   One Spouse Has Exclusive Access to a Sole Bank Account 509
   B.   One Spouse Operates or Manages a Community Property
       Business 509
   C.   One Spouse Has a Conservator, the Other Spouse Has Legal
       Capacity 510
   D.   One Spouse Obtains a Court Order 511
      1.   Ex Parte Restraining Orders During Dissolution 512
      2.   Domestic Violence Prevention Act Restraining Orders 514
      3.   Obtaining Exclusive Management and Control to Prevent
         Financial Abuse 516
      4.   Economic Abuse 518
         Notes 522
Section 7. Chapter Summary 524

PART IV. AT MARRIAGE'S END

Chapter 7. Division of Community Property at Dissolution **529**
Section 1. Dissolution, Legal Separation, Nullity 529
   Notes 534
Section 2. Division by Marriage Settlement Agreement 537
   A.   Mediation, Arbitration, Disclosure Standards, and Support
       Modifications 538
       Elden v. Superior Court 539
       Marriage of Hufford 549
       Notes 556
   B.   Collaborative Law 558

Section 3. Division by Court Order 558
   A.   Powers of the Court to Divide and Dispose of Property 559
   B.   Jurisdiction to Divide Property 563
        Gionis v. Superior Court 564
        Robinson v. Robinson 566
        Notes.. 567
        Muckle v. Superior Court.. 568
        Note 577
   C.   Power to Defer Sale of the Family Home.................................. 577
        Marriage of Stallworth 577
        Notes.. 584
   D.   The Equal Division Requirement for Litigated Decisions 586
        Marriage of Tammen... 587
        Note 589
        Marriage of Eastis 590
        Notes.. 591
   E.   The Valuation Requirement for Litigated Divisions.................... 593
        Marriage of Micalizio.. 594
        Note 599
   F.   Confirmation and Assignment of Liabilities............................. 600
        Note 602
   G.   Tax Consequences of Division 602
        Marriage of Harrington.. 603
        Note 606
   H.   Omitted Assets 607
        Henn v. Henn.. 607
        Notes.. 611
        Aloy v. Mash 613
        Note 621
Section 4. Chapter Summary 621

Chapter 8. Postdissolution Remedies.................................... **623**
Section 1. The Importance of Disclosure at Dissolution 623
Section 2. Money Sanctions in an Ongoing Dissolution Proceeding............ 633
        Marriage of Feldman... 634
        Notes 652
Section 3. Postjudgment Set-Aside Orders....................................... 655
Section 4. Grounds to Set Aside a Final Judgment of Dissolution 658
   A.   The Pre-Statutory Doctrine 658
        Marriage of Baltins 659
        Notes.. 672
   B.   The Current Statutory Framework.. 674
        Marriage of Varner 675
        Note 687
        Marriage of Kieturakis.. 689
        Note 700

C.   Timely Filing... 700

        Marriage of Georgiou & Leslie..................................... 700

Section 5. Chapter Summary 710

Chapter 9. Distribution of Community Property at Death **713**

Section 1. Community and Quasi-Community Property 714

    A.   Probate Code Basics 714

    B.   The Surviving Spouse's Exalted Status 718

        Estate of Ben-Ali.. 720

        Note 729

Section 2. Basics of Nonprobate Transfers 730

    A.   Joint Tenancy at the Death of a Spouse 730

        Estate of Levine 731

        Notes... 733

    B.   Nonprobate Transfers at the Death of a Former Spouse 736

        Life Insurance Company of North America v. Ortiz 739

        Notes... 748

Section 3. Basics of Intestate Distribution and Administration 751

Section 4. Allocating Debt/Creditors' Rights 758

    Dawes v. Rich 765

    Notes 774

    Collection Bureau of San Jose v. Rumsey...................... 776

    Note 788

Section 5. Chapter Summary 788

Appendix A. Statutory Appendix... **791**

Appendix B. Judicial Council Forms.. **879**

Appendix C. Example Business Valuation Materials **887**

Franchise Business Valuation Examples 888

Law Firm Business Valuation Example....................................... 893

INDEX.. 897

TABLE OF CASES

The principal cases are in bold type.

In the editor's text *In re Marriage of* ___ captions are generally abbreviated to read *Marriage of* ___ for the first citation, and then the parties' names for all subsequent mentions.

Aarons v. Brasch, 200
Abrams, In re Marriage of, 637
Ackerman, In re Marriage of, 413
Addington v. Texas, 110
Addison v. Addison, **281**, 293, 294
Ades, Estate of, 341
Adkins, In re Marriage of, 671
Aheroni v. Maxwell, 697
Alford v. Pierno, 290
Aloy v. Mash, **613**
American Home Assurance Co. v. Société Commerciale Toutélectric, 637
Anderson v. Lemon, 434
Anderson, Estate of, 245
Andrade Development Co. v. Martin, 472
Andresen, Marriage of, 577
Angelia P., In re, 109
Aquino v. Superior Court, 724
Arstein, Estate of, 341
Ashodian, In re Marriage of, 107
Askew v. Askew, 537
Aspinall v. McDonnell Douglas Corp., 272
Atherley, Estate of, 258, 267
Aufmuth, Marriage of, 109, 142, 201, 217, **355**, 369
Austin v. Austin, **388**
Aylesworth, In re Marriage of, 553
Babbitt v. Babbitt, 262
Bagdasarian v. Gragnon, 588
Bagnall, In re Guardianship of, 307
Bailey v. Taaffe, 680
Baldwin, Estate of, 568
Ballinger v. Ballinger, 262
Baltins, Marriage of, **659**, 696
Bank of America Nat. Trust & Savings Ass'n v. Mantz, 308, 767, 769
Bank of America, etc. v. Bk. of Amador Co., 588
Bank of California v. Connolly, 455
Barber v. Barber, 278
Barneson, In re Marriage of, 50, 51, 52, 61
Barrett v. Franke, 361
Bazzell v. Endriss, 308

Beam v. Bank of America, 141, **394**
Beckman v. Mayhew, 258, 267
Bell, Marriage of, 494
Beltran, Marriage of, 494
Ben-Ali, Estate of, **720**
Benson, In re Marriage of, 56, 59, 61, 62, 70
Ben-Yehoshua, Marriage of, 288
Bergen v. Wood, 271
Bias v. Ohio Farmers Indemnity Co., 221, 224
Bibb, Estate of, **46**
Biddle, Marriage of, 232
Blethen v. Pacific Mut. Life Ins. Co., 462
Boggs v. Boggs, **312**
Bonds, Marriage of, 34, 63, 693, 696
Bono v. Clark, 106
Boseman, In re Marriage of, 578, 579
Bouquet, Marriage of, **288**, 299, 302
Boyd v. Boyd, 262
Boyd v. Oser, 283, 294
Bragg v. City of Auburn, 291
Branco v. UFCW-Northern California Employers Joint Pension Plan, 401
Branco, In re Marriage of, 374
Brandes, Marriage of, 510
Braud, Marriage of, 585
Bray, Estate of, 456
Brennan, In re Marriage of, 665, 671, 683, 685
Brewer & Federici, Marriage of v. Federici, 93, 687, 697, 704, 705, 706
Brewer v. Brewer, 307
Brink v. Brink, 493
Britton v. Hammell, 470
Brockman, In re Marriage of, 666
Brooks & Robinson, In re Marriage of, 59, 60, 65, 66
Brookwood v. Bank of America, 94
Brown v. Newby, 680
Brown, Marriage of, 414, 416, 419, 421, 609, 616
Buckley v. Chadwick, 291
Buie & Neighbors, In re Marriage of, 59, 60

Bullock's, Inc. v. Security-First Nat. Bk., 588
Buol, Marriage of, 124, 297, 298, 299, 301
Burdette, Estate of, 726
Burgard, In re Marriage of, 637
Burger King Corp. v. Rudzewicz, 573
Burkle v. Burkle, 58
Burkle, Marriage of, 40, 653
Burnham v. Superior Court, 571, 573, 575
Burquet v. Brumbaugh, 523
Bush v. Rogers, 457
Byrne v. Laura, 273
Cademartori, Marriage of, 129
Caldwell v. Methodist Hospital of Southern California, 685
Caldwell v. Odisio, 265
California Employment Stabilization Commission v. Payne, 292
California Teachers Assn. v. Governing Bd. of Rialto Unified School Dist., 782
California Trust Co. v. Bennett, 49
Campbell, In re Marriage of, 59
Cann, Estate of, 727
Carroll v. Puritan Leasing Co., 610
Cary, In re Marriage of, 258, 263, 266
Cecala, Estate of, 726
Ceja v. Rudolph & Sletten, Inc., 241
Chapman v. Chapman, 239
Cheryl E., In re, 669
Children's Hospital & Medical Center v. Bonta, 651
Clark v. Lesher, 609
Clark, Estate of, **148**
Clark, In re Marriage of, 606
Clifton, People v., 442
Coats v. Coats, 238
Cochran, Marriage of, 126
Cohen, Marriage of, 319
Collection Bureau of San Jose v. Rumsey, 776
Conrad v. Conrad, 750
Cook v. Cook, 742, 748
Cooke v. Cooke, 308
Cooper, Marriage of, 402, 584
Corker v. Corker, 262
Craig, In re Marriage of, 304
Credit Bureau of E. Idaho, Inc. v. Lecheminant, 167
Cross, In re Marriage of, 59, 60
Cudworth, Estate of, 352
Czapar, In re Marriage of, 468
Dairy Dale Co. v. Azevedo, 414
Dale v. Dale, 492, 493
Davies, In re Marriage of, 605, 606
Davis v. Damrell, 616, 617, 620
Davis, Marriage of, 27, 186, 188, 568

Dawes v. Rich, **765**, 780, 781, 784
Dawley, In re Marriage of, 261
De Buono v. NYSA-ILA Medical and Clinical Serv. Fund, 317
De Witt v. San Francisco, 119
DeBoer v. DeBoer, 75
Delamour v. Roger, 256
Delaney, Marriage of, 131
DePasse, Estate of, 244
Devlin, Marriage of, **178**
Deyoe v. Superior Court, 268
Diefendorff v. Hopkins, 384
DiGenova v. State Board of Education, 289
Doherty, In re Marriage of, 412, 419
Dorn v. Solomon, 734
Dorris, Marriage of, 567
Douglas Aircraft Co. v. Byram, 221, 224
Downer v. Bramet, **151**
Droeger v. Friedman, Sloan & Ross, 465, 466, 470
Duffy, Marriage of, 478, 484
Duke, In re Marriage of, 578, 584
Eastis, Marriage of, **590**
Economou, In re Marriage of, 572
Edwards v. Centex Real Estate Corp., 493
Elden v. Sheldon, 272
Elden v. Superior Court, **539**
Elkins, In re Marriage of, 609
Elkus v. Elkus, 18
England, Estate of, 734
Enovsys LLC v. NexTel Communications, 232
Epstein v. Resor, 291
Epstein, Marriage of, 343, 592, 605, 606, 668, 669
Eriksen, In re Estate of, 273
Esserman v. Esserman, 551, 554
Estrada, In re, 290, 292
Estudillo v. Security Loan etc. Co., 697
Ettefagh, Marriage of, 54, 62, **103**
Evans, Marriage of, 653
Fabian, In re Marriage of, 108, 109, 296, 297, 298, 299, 300, 301, 303, 304
Fait v. New Faze Development, Inc., 708
Feldman, Marriage of, 492, **634**
Fell, Marriage of, 674
Fenton, In re Marriage of, 225, 227, 414, 599
Ficke, Marriage of, 585
Fidelity & Casualty Company v. Mahoney, **97**
Fidelity Fed. Sav. & Loan Assn. v. de la Cuesta, 314
Fields v. Michael, 430, 460

Finby, Marriage of, 409
Fink, Marriage of, 276, 565, 589
Fithian v. Fithian, 618
Fithian, Marriage of, 310, 614
Fitzgerald & King, In re Marriage of, 571, 572
Flanagan v. Capital Nat. Bank, 255, 264
Fletcher, Estate of, 724
Folb, Marriage of, 381
Fonstein, In re Marriage of, 416, 417, 598, 605, 669
Forcum, In re Marriage of, 554, 555
Ford, Estate of, 109
Forgy v. Forgy, 551
Fort Halifax Packing Co. v. Coyne, 315
Fortier, Marriage of, 201, 230
Foss, People v., 443
Fossum, Marriage of, 491
Foster, Marriage of, 223, 224, 230, 414
Frankel v. Boyd, 767, 768, 773
Fransen, Marriage of, 287
Frederick, In re Marriage of, 619
Freeman, In re Marriage of, 650
Freese v. Hibernia Sav. etc. Soc., 108
French v. French, 614, 616, 617, 620
Frick, Marriage of, 350, 371
Friedman, In re Marriage of, 695, 697
Fukuzaki v. Superior Court, 553, 554, 556
Gade v. National Solid Wastes Management Assn., 315
Gagan v. Gouyd, 107
Gapsch v. Gapsch, 365
Garcia, Marriage of, 459
Garfein v. Garfein, 412, 419, 420
Gauze, People v., 446
George v. Ransom, 164
Georgiou & Leslie, Marriage of, 700
Geraci, Marriage of, 373
Gerst, Estate of, 726
Gillmore, In re Marriage of, 617
Gilmore v. Gilmore, 390
Ginns v. Savage, 698
Gionis v. Superior Court, 564
Golden v. Golden, 219, 223
Golub v. Golub, 231
Gonzalez, In re Marriage of, 667
Gordon v. Gordon, 455
Gorman v. Gorman, 610
Gould v. Fuller, 767, 768, 770, 773
Graham, Marriage of, 203, 207
Grappo v. Coventry Financial Corporation, 277, 571
Gray, Marriage of, 403, 572
Green, Marriage of, 403, 413
Greg F., In re, 709
Gregory v. Gregory, 673, 681, 682

Greiner v. Greiner, 430
Griffis, In re Marriage of, 300
Griffith v. Bank of New York, 666
Grimm v. Grimm, 55, 308, 462, 744
Grinius, Marriage of, 140
Grissom, In re Marriage of, 683
Grolemund v. Cafferata, 449, 459
Gudelj v. Gudelj, 75, 142
Guidry v. Sheet Metal Workers Nat. Pension Fund, 317
Guye v. Guye, 361
Hafner, Estate of, 245, 248
Haines, In re Marriage of, 52, 58, 64, 105, 109, 413, 693, 699
Hamilton v. Regents of the University of California, 285
Hannam, Estate of, 669
Hanrahan v. Sims, 365
Hansen v. Hansen, 681
Hardin, Marriage of, 186, 188
Harrington, Marriage of, 603
Harris v. Harris, 430, 454, 456
Harris v. King, 493
Harrod v. Pacific Southwest Airlines, Inc., 272
Hattis, In re Marriage of, 573, 576
Hawkins, In re Marriage of, 551
Haws v. Haws, 279
Head v. Crawford, 767
Hearst, Estate of, 541
Heggie, Marriage of, 688, 696
Heikes, Marriage of, 123, 295
Heintz v. Brown, 361
Henn v. Henn, 607
Henry V., In re, 724
Herrmann, In re Marriage of, 578, 579, 589
Hewitson, In re Marriage of, 596, 597, 599
Hicks v. Hicks, 141, 144, 347
Hilke, Marriage of, 296, 297, 301, 751
Hill & Dittmer, Marriage of, 35
Hill v. Estate of Westbrook, 269
Hill v. Hill, 545
Hillerman, Marriage of, 319
Hines v. Lowrey, 308
Hirsch, In re Marriage of, 495
Hisquierdo v. Hisquierdo, 311, 313, 317
Hodson v. New York City Employees' Retirement System, 307
Hokanson, In re Marriage of, 638
Holtemann, Marriage of, 69
Hopkins & Axene, In re Marriage of, 300
Hopkins, Marriage of, 456, 589
Horowitz, In re Marriage of, 580
Hufford, Marriage of, 549
Hull v. Superior Court, 565

Hyman v. Hyman, 269
Interinsurance Exchange v. Ohio Cas.
    Ins. Co., 289
International Shoe v. Washington,
    571, 573
Iredale and Cates, In re Marriage of,
    225, 227
Irwin v. Irwin, 609, 611
Jacobs, In re Marriage of, 606, 681
Jacobson, Marriage of, 287
Jafeman, In re Marriage of, 366
Johnson v. National Surety Co., 430
Jolly's Estate, In re, 100
Jones, In re Marriage of, 639
Jordan-Lyon Productions, Ltd. v.
    Cineplex Odeon Corp., 543
Juick, In re Marriage of, 587, 593
Jurcoane v. Superior Court, 12, 194
Kahanic, People v., 441, 446
Katz, Marriage of, 585
Keene v. Keene, 264, 265, 268
Kelley v. Kelley, 609
Kenney v. United States, 602
Kent, Estate of, 726
Kerr v. Kerr, 191
Kershman v. Kershman, 352
Keslar v. Pabst, 173
Khan v. Superior Court, 573, 652
Kieturakis, Marriage of, 689
Kilbourne, In re Marriage of, 233
Kilkenny, In re Marriage of, 552
King v. Goetz, 221
King, In re Marriage of, 223, 227, 230
Kinney v. Vallentyne, 469
Klug, In Marriage of, 613
Kraemer v. Kraemer, 282
Kuehn v. Kuehn, 687
Kulchar v. Kulchar, 682
Kulko v. Superior Court of California,
    573
Lackner v. North, 727
Lafferty v. Wells Fargo Bank, 704
Lahey, Estate of, 749
Landry v. Berryessa Union School
    Dist., 53
Lange, In re Marriage of, 693
Laure, Marriage of, 593
Lavine, In re, 291
Layton, Estate of v. Pulliam, 749
Lazzarevich v. Lazzarevich, 264
Lehman, In re Marriage of, 406, 408,
    413, 419
Leslie, Estate of, 244, 246
Leversee, Marriage of, 131
Levin v. Ligon, 612
Levine, Estate of, 731
Lewis v. Johns, 31
Lewis v. Superior Court, 609, 610

**Lezine v. Security Pacific
    Financial Services, Inc., 465**, 769,
    770
Lico, Marriage of, 69
Life Ins. Co. of N. Am. v. Cassidy, 740,
    745, 747
**Life Insurance Company of North
    America v. Ortiz, 739**
Lister, In re Marriage of, 468
Lockyer, People ex rel. v. Shamrock
    Foods Co., 724
Logan v. Forster, 381
Lontos, In re Marriage of, 571, 575,
    576
Lopez, In re Marriage of, 219, 587, 599
Los Angeles Airways, Inc. v. Hughes
    Tool Co., 671
Los Angeles Fire & Police Protective
    League v. City of Los Angeles, 456
Lowenschuss v. Selnick, 740
Lucas v. Hamm, 615, 619
Lucas, Marriage of, 54, 65, 66, 122,
    127, 295, 298, 369
Lusk, In re Marriage of, 565, 566
Lynam v. Vorwerk, 135
Lynch v. United States, 308
Lynn v. Herman, 430
Lyons, In re, 219
Macchi v. La Rocca, 255
MacDonald, Estate of, 48, 49, 50, 51,
    52, 55, 67
Machinists and Aerospace Workers,
    AFL-CIO v. Wisconsin Employment
    Relations Comm'n, 317
MacKay v. Darusmont, 457
Maglica v. Maglica, 274
Mahoney v. Mahoney, 203
Makeig v. United Security Bank &
    Trust Co., 191
Malcolm, United States v., 308
Manchester, Estate of, 725
Manfer, Marriage of, 186, 188
Manhattan Life Ins. Co. v. Barnes,
    742, 748
Mannheim v. Superior Court, 289
Mansell v. Mansell, 319
Maria P. v. Riles, 652
Maricle, In re Marriage of, 604
Mark v. Title Guar. & Trust Co., 471,
    472
Marriage Cases, In re, 11
Marsden, Marriage of, 193, **368**
Marsiglia v. Marsiglia, 668
Martin v. Hall, 617
Marvin v. Marvin, 258
Mason, Marriage of, 182, 612
Massachusetts v. Morash, 316
Mathews, In re Marriage of, 693, 697
Matuz v. Gerardin Corporation, 272

Maynard v. Hill, 12
McAlvay v. Consumers' Salt Co., 430, 431
McCarty v. McCarty, 311, 617, 618
McCreadie v. Arques, 670
McCulloch v. Maryland, 308
McDaniel, Estate of, 748
McFadden v. Santa Ana, O. & T. St. Ry. Co., 173
McGee v. International Life Ins. Co., 575
McHugh v. McHugh, 621
McKay v. Lauriston, 430
McTiernan & Dubrow, Marriage of, 215, 412, 413, 417
Mechanical Contractors Assn. v. Greater Bay Area Assn., 651
Meherin v. Meherin, 741, 745
Meinhard v. Salmon, 432
Mejia v. Reed, 687
Melton, In re Marriage of, 682, 709
Merchants' Ad-Sign Co. v. Sterling, 218
Merkel v. Merkel, 365
Metropolitan Bank v. St. Louis Dispatch Co., 218, 219
Meyer v. Kinzer, 148
Micalizio, Marriage of, 594
Milhan v. Milhan, 618
Milhan, Marriage of, 310, 618
Milian v. De Leon, 272
Miller, In re, 283
Mintz v. Rowitz, 457
Mitchell v. Mitchell, 555
Mitchell v. Moses, 430
Mitchell v. Read, 434
Mix, Marriage of, 54, 127, **346**, 356
Modnick, In re Marriage of, 666
Moll v. Moll, 414
Moncharsh v. Heily & Blase, 543, 544
Monti, Marriage of, 241
Moore v. UC Regents, 170
Moore, Marriage of, 363, 369, 370, 457, 653
Morris, Marriage of, 182
Moyer v. Workmen's Comp. Appeals Bd., 556
Muckle v. Superior Court, 568
Mueller v. Mueller, 226
Mundt v. Connecticut Gen. Life Ins. Co., 98, 308
Murphy, Estate of, 127, 345
Nadkarni, Marriage of, 522
Nakamura v. Parker, 522
Navistar Internat. Transportation Corp. v. State Bd. of Equalization, 221
Neal, Marriage of, 131
Nelson, Marriage of, 599

New York Life Ins. Co. v. Bank of Italy, 462
Newark Morning Ledger Co. v. United States, 226
Ney, Estate of, 386
Niccolls, Estate of, 107
Nichols, In re Marriage of, 225, 227
Nickson, Estate of, 108
Nielsen, In re Marriage of, 550, 552, 556
Niroo v. Niroo, 415
Nizenkoff, Marriage of, 319
Norman v. Baltimore & Ohio R. Co., 308
Norris v. Vaughan, 377, 399
Norviel, In re Marriage of, 186, 188
Norviel, Marriage of, 189
O'Brien v. O'Brien, 202
O'Connor, Estate of, 282
O'Neil v. Spillane, 666, 667
Oakley v. Oakley, 264, 265
Obergefell v. Hodges, 8
Odone v. Marzocchi, 430
Olivo v. Olivo, 406
Olson v. Olson, 63
Omer v. Omer, 269
Orange Unified School Dist. v. Rancho Santiago Community College Dist., 782, 783
Outfitter Properties, LLC v. Wildlife Conservation Bd., 709
Owen v. Cohen, 439
Pacific Gas & Electric Co. v. Zuckerman, 596
Pacific Palisades Bowl Mobile Estates, LLC v. City of Los Angeles, 708
Packard v. Arellanes, 767
Page v. Page, 439
Paley v. Bank of America National Trust & Savings Association, 287
Pancoast v. Pancoast, 149
Pangburn v. Pangburn, 415
Patrick v. Alacer Corp., 378
Patterson v. Patterson, 108, 109
Pendleton & Fireman, Marriage of, 34
Pepper, Estate of, 384
Pereira v. Pereira, 376, **379**, 384, 391, 395
Perkins v. Benguet Consolidated Mining Co., 573
Peters, Marriage of, 110, 191
Petersen, Estate of, 52
Petropoulos, In re Marriage of, 637, 650
Pimentel v. Conselho Supremo De Uniao Portugueza Do Estado Da California, 742, 748
Piscopo v. Piscopo, 231
Pitcairn, Estate of, 724, 725, 727

Planck v. Hartung, 273
Postema v. Postema, 202
Prentis-Margulis & Margulis, Marriage of, 491
Quay, In re Marriage of, 650
Ramirez, Marriage of, 242
Recknor, In re Marriage of, 244, 456
Reilley, In re Marriage of, 669
Reiss v. Reiss, 415
Reuling, Marriage of, 495, 683
Rice v. Santa Fe Elevator Corp., 317
Rich & Whillock, Inc. v. Ashton Development, Inc., 667
Rich v. State Board of Optometry, 291
Riddle v. Harmon, 128
Rives, In re Marriage of, 217, 596
Robertson v. Willis, 468
Robinson v. Grossman, 651
Robinson v. Robinson, 566
Robles v. Robles, 113
Rodriguez v. Menjivar, 517
Roeder v. Roeder, 668
Roesch, Marriage of, 286
Rojas v. Superior Court, 694, 695
Roosevelt v. Ray, 320
Rosan, Marriage of, 556, 597, 599
Rose v. Rose, 317
Rosen, In re Marriage of, 225, 227
Rosevear, Marriage of, 688, 696, 697, 705
Rossi, Marriage of, 485, 638, 707, 708
Rossin, In re Marriage of, 413, 418
Rowell, Estate of, 597
Roy v. Roy, 567
Rozan v. Rozan, 275, 276, 279
Rubenstein v. Rubenstein, 94, 492, 704, 705, 706
Ruddy v. Rossi, 308
Russell v. Russell, 219
Ryan, Estate of, 290
S.P. Mill Co. v. Billiwhack etc. Farm, 588
Sackett v. Spindler, 588
Saeta v. Superior Court, 693
Sail'er Inn, Inc. v. Kirby, 290
Salveter v. Salveter, 430, 431
Samuels v. Mix, 782, 783
Sanders, Estate of, 666
Sanguinetti v. Sanguinetti, 265
Santa Clara, County of v. Vargas, 778
Santa Cruz, City of v. Pacific Gas & Electric Co., 724
Sato v. Hall, 292
Sausalito, City of v. County of Marin, 290
Schindler v. Schindler, 733
Schlaefer v. Schlaefer, 307
Schneider v. Schneider, 240

Schwab v. Southern California Gas Co., 697
Scott v. Austin, 99
See v. See, 127, 142, 298, **339**, 347, 351, 355, 592
Select Base Materials v. Board of Equal., 49
Seltzer, Estate of, 597
Semaan, People v., 63
Severtson v. Williams Construction Co., 543
Shamblin v. Brattain, 671
Shelton, Marriage of, 352
Siberell v. Siberell, 119
Siegel, Marriage of, 577
Simmons, Estate of, 247
Simon v. Simon, 611
Simonian v. Dinoian, 161
Skaden, In re Marriage of, 407, 416, 418
Slater, In re Marriage of, 599
Slivka, In re Marriage of, 212, 226
Smalley v. Baker, 667
Smaltz, Marriage of, 460
Smethurst, In re Marriage of, 613
Smiley, In re Marriage of, 551, 555
Smith v. Bull, 223, 225, 226
Smith v. Lewis, 615, 616, 617, 619
Smith v. Lombard, 668
Smith v. Pust, 537
Smith v. Smith, 148, 612
Smith, In re, 402
Smith, Marriage of, 557
Snyder v. Snyder, 746
Sobiek, People v., 443, 444
Sonne, In re Marriage of, 405, 407, 408
Sousa v. Freitas, 265
Spahn v. Spahn, 567
Speers, Estate of, 727
Spengler, In re Marriage of, 414
Spreckels v. Spreckels, 190, 280, 283, 285, **452**, 462
Spring Valley W.W. v. Schottler, 218
Stallworth, Marriage of, 458, **577**
Stanford, People v., 444
Starkman, In Marriage of, 68
Steinberger, Marriage of, 57, 60, **71**
Stephenson, Marriage of, 454
Stevenot, In re Marriage of, 665, 667, 682, 698, 699
Stewart v. Preston Pipeline Inc., 695, 696
Stewart v. Stewart, 32
Stratton v. Superior Court, 468
Summers, In re, 59, 60
Sutphin v. Speik, 610
Swalm, People v., 444
T.L. James & Co. v. Montgomery, 316

Tammen, Marriage of, 587
Tannehill v. Finch, 273
Tarvin v. Tarvin, 573, 611
Taylor v. Polackwich, 271
Teel, In re, 319
Teitelbaum Furs, Inc. v. Dominion Ins. Co., Ltd., 609
Tejada, Marriage of, 243
Tharp, Marriage of, 634
Thomasset v. Thomasset, 107, 341
Thorne & Raccina, In re Marriage of, 709, 710
Thornton, Estate of, 269, 282, 283, 284, 285
Thorp v. Randazzo, 740, 744, 747
Titan/Value Equities Group, Inc. v. Superior Court, 543
Tobin v. Galvin, 191
Todd v. Todd, 200, 219
Todhunter v. Smith, 609
Tomaier v. Tomaier, 119, 275, 278, 279
Toomer v. Witsell, 286
Travelers Casualty & Surety Co. v. Superior Court, 693
Trimble v. Trimble, 262, 293
Trutalli v. Meraviglia, 260
Tully v. Tully, 307
Tyler, Estate of, 726
Tyre v. Aetna Life Insurance Co., 55, **461**
Union Oil Co. v. Stewart, 194
Vai v. Bank of America, 460
Valle, Marriage of, 459
Vallera v. Vallera, 248, **254**, 255, 260, 264, 266, 267
Valli, Marriage of, 53
Valsan Partners Limited Partnership v. Calcor Space Facility, Inc., 544
Van Camp v. Van Camp, 377, **383**, 390, 395
Van Maren v. Johnson, 32
Van Sickle, In re Marriage of, 565
Vargas, Estate of, 244, 247, 265
Vargas, People v., 782, 783
Varner, Marriage of, 493, **675**, 697, 705, 706
Velez v. Smith, 252
Vieux v. Vieux, 146, **359**, 364, 369
Vons Companies, Inc. v. Seabest Foods, Inc., 573, 574
Vryonis, Marriage of, 241
W.B. Worthen Co. v. Thomas, 308
Waite v. Waite, 617
Walker, Marriage of, 485
Wall, Marriage of, 194
Wallace, People v., 445
Walrath, Marriage of, 344, 413
Walton, Marriage of, 534

Ward-Chandler Bldg. Co. v. Caldwell, 219
Warner, In Estate of, 279
Warren, Marriage of, 592
Washburn v. Washburn, 202
Watson v. Peyton, 120
Watt, Marriage of, 210
Watts, Marriage of, 224, 387, 414, 643, 669
Weak v. Weak, 266
Weaver, In re Marriage of, 106
Weinberg v. Weinberg, 381, 396, 459
Weiner v. Weiner, 206
Weiss, Marriage of, 36
Wendland, Conservatorship of, 109
Wendt v. Wendt, 18
Wilcox v. Wilcox, 430
Williams v. Paxton, 167
Williams v. State of North Carolina, 284, 294
Williams, Estate of, 609
Wilson v. Wilson, 63, **90**, 276
Wipson, In re Marriage of, 670
Wissner v. Wissner, **305**, 616
Wolfe, In re Marriage of, 565
Wood, Estate of, 727
Woodby v. Immigration Service, 110
Woolsey, Marriage of, 654
Worth, Marriage of, 231, 320
Xia Guo and Xiao Hua Sun, Marriage of, 241
Yuba River Power Co. v. Nevada Irr. Dist., 223
Zaentz, In re Marriage of, 233
Zagorski v. Zagorski, 112
Zaragosa v. Craven, 173
Zierenberg, Marriage of, 571
Zschernig v. Miller, 317

CASES AND MATERIALS ON
CALIFORNIA COMMUNITY PROPERTY LAW

MARRIAGE, PROPERTY, CODE

Eleventh Edition

PART I

AN OVERVIEW OF THE CALIFORNIA COMMUNITY PROPERTY SYSTEM

∎ ∎ ∎

CHAPTER 1

AN OVERVIEW OF THE CALIFORNIA COMMUNITY PROPERTY SYSTEM

■ ■ ■

The California community property system is a highly developed and innovative body of rules that govern the business of marriage and registered domestic partnership. These rules are influential the world over.

At the heart of the system is *the sharing principle.*

The policies of the system are to effect equal, fair and just outcomes between married partners during their marriage and in the event of dissolution; to provide third-parties with confidence to deal with married persons; and to protect and further the public interest.

The concept behind the California community property system is that marriage is a partnership, a business organization for intimate partners, for which the California Family Code provides the default rules. The parties are free to modify most but not all of the default rules by contract.

SECTION 1. THE SHARING PRINCIPLE

Property acquired by two persons during marriage is owned by them together, by halves.

SECTION 2. EQUAL, FAIR, AND JUST

The sharing principle is heart of any community property system. The California community property system is constructed around the sharing principle, with three key principles: tracing, equality of interest, and the right to modify the community property system by contract. Globally, California is within the majority of marital property systems. Domestically, California law has created the "majority approach" to U.S. community property law.

In a traditional community property system the community comes into existence on the date of marriage. Property ownership is by vested right at acquisition. Dissolution is negotiated by the parties against the backdrop of the equal division rule. Only if the spouses cannot reach a marriage settlement agreement will a court step in to divide their inventoried community property assets equally between them.

There are nine U.S. community property states. Eight are traditional community property systems. They are Arizona, California, Idaho, Louisiana, Texas, Nevada, New Mexico, and Washington. Wisconsin is a community property system by adoption of the Uniform Marital Property Act, discussed below. Each one of these nine states has its own system; therefore each state's system builds itself around the sharing principle in a unique way.

Forty-one U.S. states are called "common law separate title states." During marriage, ownership is determined by the asset's title or else by the ownership of the funds that were used to acquire the asset. Separate ownership is the rule in these states, meaning that the spouse whose name is on title has the exclusive right to manage and control the titled asset during marriage. Spouses can opt into joint title if they want concurrent ownership and control as to any particular asset, but undivided concurrent ownership—sharing—is definitely the exception to the general rule. At dissolution, all forty-one states follow the equitable distribution (or division) approach. Forty of these states replicate traditional community property system outcomes at dissolution with an equitable distribution statute. Mississippi has no such statute, but it has adopted the equitable distribution doctrine by case law. A majority of equitable jurisdictions have incorporated one or more aspects of California law into their marital dissolution jurisprudence.

Alaska is a separate title equitable distribution state (ownership of marital assets is determine by title record). However, Alaska legislation also allows married persons with significant ties to the state to opt for a community property regime for one, some, or all of the assets of a marriage. Married persons opt in by contract or by settling a community property trust. Management and control is title based even for community property, unless the contract or trust states otherwise. Non-residents may use a community property trust so long as they name a qualified trustee, defined as an Alaska resident, an Alaska trust company, or an Alaska bank. ALASKA STAT. § 34.77.010 through § 34.77.995 (2014).

Tennessee is a separate title equitable distribution state that, as of 2010, allows married persons to opt into community property by use of a trust. There is no requirement that the parties be domiciled in the state, only that a qualified trustee manage the trust. Management and control rights are determined by the terms of the trust. Dissolution of community property occurs when an asset is distributed from the trust. TENN. CODE ANN. § 35.17.101–35.17.108 (2015).

Puerto Rico is a traditional community property jurisdiction that tends to follow California law closely in one or more areas. What distinguishes the Puerto Rican community property system from the other U.S. state systems is that in Puerto Rico marriages, called conjugal partnerships, are liquidated, not dissolved. This is a fine distinction, but one that can make a significant difference to creditors of the community. When a marriage is dissolved creditors can reach the community property as well as the separate property of the debtor spouse and sometimes, as in California, of the nondebtor spouse as well. When a marriage is liquidated, by comparison, creditors of the partnership are limited to reaching property owned by the conjugal partnership.

There are many differences between a traditional (*ganancial*) community property system and an equitable distribution system. Three key differences are listed below.

One, in a community property system immediate shared ownership occurs on the date an asset is acquired regardless of which spouse's name appears on title. In an equitable distribution system property ownership and control during marriage are determined by title.

Two, in a traditional community property system the sharing principle goes into effect on the date of marriage. In an equitable distribution system the sharing principle only goes into effect, if it does, at the end of a marriage.

Three, in a community property jurisdiction property ownership is by right; more specifically, the spouses have vested and equal ownership rights to any and all community property assets, typically on an asset-by-asset basis. In an equitable distribution system it takes a judge to recognize and confirm an equitable property right, which can be problematic since the judicial act of vesting one spouse with an equitable property interest requires divesting the titled spouse of the same.

One last word: I have heard it said that community property dissolution is simple: Just divide everything in half. In my opinion, only a misinformed view would or could suggest that marital property dissolution is a simple matter of dividing everything in half. Any community property system makes marital property dissolution, in any given case, potentially straightforward, but straightforward doesn't necessarily mean simple. Changes in asset values, changes in earning potentials over the course of the marriage, gifts, expectations about the gifts and other type of properties, title forms, the parties' intentions and skill set for management and control of assets, the degree of transparent disclosure (or obscurity) that the parties have practiced during their marriage, a history of intimate partner violence—these and other factors can and do make marital dissolution far from simple even if the ultimate outcome is to split everything equally. Add to that the complex quickly shifting clouds of human emotion made up of loss, sadness, regret, fear, anger, rage, betrayal, relief, indifference, despair, greed, personal growth, or whatever else it is that has brought one or both parties to the point of seeking dissolution, and one can begin to understand why it is that legal tools (and not just a calculator) are useful if not necessary to effect a fair and just dissolution of an intimate partnership.

Just divide it in half? Sounds Solomonic. But when it comes to property partition, the "divide in half" methodology can be distortedly simplistic, especially when it comes to two persons who do not wish to or cannot bring themselves to emotionally continue on with each other as concurrent owners of property, at least not if they are to move forward with their lives. In other words, equal, fair and just in the context of a marital dissolution are not arithmetical concepts, they are legal concepts. As such they encourage judges and other decision makers to be sensitive to the uniqueness of the marital partnership that the parties before them have created. Certainly in California, advising partners who are contemplating marriage, happily married, or seeking dissolution requires a working knowledge of the ever-revised California Family Code. What is equal, fair and just to the parties? What is fair and just to third parties who change their position in reliance on the marriage? What is fair and just from a societal perspective?

These are the questions that make up the terrain of the course.

SECTION 3. MARRIAGE AS A PARTNERSHIP

The idea of the California community property system is that marriage is a partnership. More specifically, marriage is a business partnership between two persons who are intimate with each other. What distinguishes the partnership of two persons who are married from that of two persons who are not married is the existence of a license. A valid marriage license (formalizes) the intimate partnership, just as a partnership agreement formalizes the business form of a general partnership. A valid marriage provides the intimate partners with access to a wide array of default rules for starting, operating, maintaining, and dissolving their partnership. The parties may contract out of nearly all of these default rules. Two rules cannot be waived. The spouses' mutual obligation of support during marriage, and the duty of good faith. Intimate partners who choose not to marry, by comparison, must either construct the details of their partnership agreement in accordance with the laws of contract, partnership, trust, and so on, or else accept that title documents will control property rights of assets acquired during the relationship.

This book is a study of the default California community property rules.

There are so many historical moments in which to begin the story of the California community property system.

One could begin with the northern European tribespeople, who followed the sharing principle in ancient times. One could begin with the

Visigoths, who carried the community property sharing principle with them from northern Europe, east into Eurasia, then west to Europe, and south to the Iberian Peninsula (what is today Spain), where they maintained their own lawways against the Romans. One could begin with Spanish law, which is the first body of law to codify the sharing principle.

In the Western hemisphere, one could begin with the 1848 Treaty of Guadalupe Hidalgo, or the 1849 California Constitution, or the 1850 California Organic Act. If we wanted to consider only twentieth century changes to California law, we might begin with the year 1927, when the California Legislature decided once and for all that the community property right was not contingent until dissolution, but rather vested at acquisition—the codification of equality of right principle was a major step forward for the rights of married women. The year 1970 is significant as the year that California adopted no-fault dissolution. The no-fault movement is important because it is the moment when California community property veers toward being a version of business organization law. The no-fault transition allowed married persons to decide that a marital partnership is over because the parties cannot reconcile their personal differences; and the equality of right principle guaranteed that once a petition for dissolution is filed, parties are entitled to assert ownership rights to one-half of the community property assets. Parties may ultimately decide to negotiate specific offsets and tradeoffs to reach a marital settlement agreement; but at the start of the dissolution process, their negotiation ideally commences with the knowledge that each is entitled to an arithmetic fifity-fifty vested right to community property as of the date of acquisition.

The year 1975 is the year that the state transitioned from male management and control to an equal management and control rule. Male management gave a married man the sole legal right to manage community personal property. Equal management and control recognized spouses as equal actors during marriage, either with the absolute right to manage and control community personal property as if it were that spouse's separate property. Equal management and control, and problems attendant to it, ultimately led to the adoption of the state Corporations Code into the Family Code. That adoption occurs in the early 1990s, and it brings with it an entirely new set of default rules on disclosure between spouses.

There are also many conceptual points at which we could start the story of California community property. Any one of those starting points rests on the premise that in California marriage is a civil contract, not a religious event. Marriage is a contract between two adult partners, both of whom must evidence their consent to the marriage contract, the default terms of which are set out in the California Family Code. On the date of marriage, a community comes into existence. That community is a property acquiring and holding entity. It begins to develop a distinct legal personality during marriage, thus allowing the partners to retain their individual identities as to property and liabilities. The partnership, not the individual partners, owns the "community property." By default, each partner has an equal right to manage and control the community property as a partnership fiduciary would; and each is constitutionally entitled to exercise exclusive management and control over their own separate property. In the event that the marriage ends by dissolution or death, each spouse owns a one-half vested interest in any and every community property asset as of the date of its acquisition.

A course in community property is relevant to every person, whether they are married or not, hope to be married or do not, believe in marriage or not. Perhaps it is useful to think of this course as a business organization course. The material can be technical. It is about how intimate partners can and do organize their property rights relative to each other during and at the end of their relationship. For that reason, it is also personally relevant and, I hope, ultimately instructive if not empowering. This is a course on how not to and therefore ultimately on how to manage, protect and, if necessary, dissolve an intimate partnership.

Students sometimes mistake a course in community property for a course in general family law. Child custody rights are not a matter of community property law, even though child custody issues are governed by the Family Code. Likewise paternity or parental rights are not part of the course in community property, even though those issues are also governed by the Family Code. Children are most definitely not community property, irrespective of some misinformed law review discussions to that effect. A course in California community property law is a specialized family law course. It is about the business of the marital partnership.

The legal concept of marital property presupposes the existence of marriage as a legal institution. Again, critiques of marriage or sociological arguments about the (many) limitations of marriage as an institution are outside the scope of this particular casebook. We are not concerned here with who marries or whether particular persons should marry as a sociological matter or whether marriage as an institution is class or race biased. Instead, we assume the fact of marriage, and—after the decision in *Obergefell v. Hodges*, 135 S.Ct. 2584, 192 L.Ed.2d 609 (2015)—we understand that marriage is an institution (or a business organization, if you will) that is open to any two persons. Marriage is a protected Constitutional right for all. From there we move on to study how the marital partnership is formed, how it acquires property, how it manages property, and how it dissolves property.

Finally, it is important to understand that the California community property law is a marital property *system* that, like marital property systems more generally, develops against the backdrop of three fundamental policy goals. One, a marital property system furthers the state's compelling interest in marriage. Two, a marital property system provides married persons with a default marital contract that comes into existence on the date of the marriage; the terms of the default contract are found in the state family code. Three, a marital property system gives third parties confidence in their transactions with married persons.

If a marital property system protects the public interest, the married persons, and third-party creditors, what motivates the partners themselves to marry?

Again, there are many answers depending on where one starts. Here is a list of some undercurrents that prevail throughout the casebook.

Happiness. Novelist Jane Smiley said, sixteen years ago, "we marry to make ourselves happy." Even though when we do marry, "we mostly don't know what will make us happy. Happiness is a multiple-choice test: Steady companionship? Lots of stuff? A nice place to live? Children? Plenty of sex? Good health? Freedom to do what we want? . . . ." Jane Smiley, *Why Do We Marry?* June 2000 HARPER'S MAGAZINE, reprinted at September–October 2000 UTNE READER 58. Many people today choose to be happy without the institution of marriage. Still, Smiley's observation remains relevant: marriage is an important way to express commitment to and the desire to co-create happiness with another person.

Wealth. George A. Akerlof and Robert J. Shiller might argue that marriage is a partnership that is critical to the continued development of the economy. If so, they would also recognize that it is an institution that is keenly susceptible to uncertainty caused by emotional events. As an economic institution, marriage reduces contracting problems between two persons who want to form an intimate partnership. Default contract terms, especially if the partners can be assured that the rules are fair, free up partner time to focus on the economic life of the firm. GEORGE A. AKERLOF AND ROBERT J. SHILLER, ANIMAL SPIRITS: HOW HUMAN PSYCHOLOGY DRIVES THE ECONOMY, AND WHY IT MATTERS FOR GLOBAL CAPITALISM, (2009).

Personal empowerment. Legal scholar Leigh Goodmark writes about the serious intimate partner violence rates in the United States. Goodmark correctly argues that historically marriage was an incredibly risky, if not dangerous, endeavor for women. She goes on to discuss how dominance feminism, over the past forty years, has legislated rules that hold perpetrators accountable for the violence and financial chaos they cause in the home. And yet, intimate partner violence does not abate. Goodmark's project is to move law and policy toward anti-essentialist feminist changes. By "anti-essentialist feminism," Goodmark means that in addition to current laws that address intimate partner violence, Goodmark would like to see family law rules that empower intimate partners to treat each other more fairly within the partnership. LEIGH GOODMARK, A TROUBLED MARRIAGE: DOMESTIC VIOLENCE AND THE LEGAL SYSTEM (2012). Goodmark's work to move the law toward an anti-essentialist response to domestic violence is one that I share. Indeed, anti-essentialism is what brought me to the study of community property law in the first place. What I discovered is that in California, an immensely complex state, the Family Law seeks to give married persons tools of empowerment relative to the marriage decision. The idea is that with fairer default laws about property rights, parties can make better and ultimately more productive choices for their partnership and for themselves and their families. When it comes to marriage, ignorance is not bliss. Parties today, for example, may bring educational debt to the marriage, or child support obligations, or they may have adult children who have certain expectations about family wealth. Whatever the case, parties are well advised to choose to educate themselves about the law from its source, not to leave their fate to popular culture conceptions about what marriage is or is not. Just because people do not choose to marry does not insulate them from acquiring property together. Or unfortunately, from breaking up. Therefore, my advice to Cinderella as well as to the royalty she marries is to become informed about the laws of intimate partnerships before taking the leap.

Marriage as a start-up. I think of marriage as a start-up. How that start-up gets organized, what sort of crusty cultural assumptions it disrupts when it starts to be profitable for the persons who work on its behalf—all of these issues and more are within the partners' powers of co-creation. Yes, there is a society. And yes, we live in society. But no, we are not powerless. We can make choices that allow us to develop and grow as human beings.

Marriage as an existential unknown. As we move through the California community property laws, it is not necessary to decide once and for all what marriage is or how it works. At this point in our study, the operating premise is simple: marriage is a partnership that allows its two partners a high degree of flexibility of organization relative to each other and the community property they will acquire together.

Fidelity. Often people imagine that sexual fidelity is the most important aspect of marriage. As far as law codes go, I would say that the most important aspect of marriage is financial fidelity. Personal fidelity (keeping one's word) and financial fidelity (accurately and truthfully disclosing one's activities to one's partner) go hand in hand of course, no matter how the parties' understand or practice their sexuality. In a survey conducted by the Pew Research Center in 2007, participants ranked *fidelity* as the most important factor, not necessarily sexual fidelity. Fidelity was followed by a happy sexual relationship, the sharing of domestic chores, adequate income, good housing, shared religious, spiritual, motivating beliefs, shared interests, children, and agreement on politics. The survey also found that by a margin of nearly three to one, respondents indicated that the main purpose of marriage is the "mutual happiness and fulfillment" of adults rather than the bearing and raising of children. *As Marriage and Parenthood Drift Apart,* pewresearch.org/pubs/526/ marriage-parenthood, (July 1, 2007).

Public ritual. Finally, the marriage partnership has long been commenced by ritual. The wedding attire. The wedding party. The wedding cake. The wedding feast. The engagement and wedding gifts. The wedding expenses. For many prospective spouses the engagement ring is key to negotiating the start-date of the legal marriage. All of these rituals signal to the partners, their family and their friends that a new community has come into legal existence.

On marriage becoming a gender-fair institution. The requirements for a valid marriage are found at Family Code Section 300, reproduced here.

WEST'S ANNOTATED CALIFORNIA FAMILY CODE

§ 300.   Consent; issuance of license and solemnization; marriage license and marriage certificate

(a) Marriage is a personal relation arising out of a civil contract between two persons, to which the consent of the parties capable of making that contract is necessary. Consent alone does not constitute marriage. Consent must be followed by the issuance of a license and solemnization as authorized by this division, except as provided by Section 425 and Part 4 (commencing with Section 500).

(b) For purposes of this part, the document issued by the county clerk is a marriage license until it is registered with the county recorder, at which time the license becomes a marriage certificate.

(Stats. 1992, c. 162 (A.B. 2650), § 10, operative Jan. 1, 1994. Amended by Stats. 1993, c. 219 (A.B. 1500), § 88; Stats. 2006, c. 816 (A.B. 1102), § 1, operative Jan. 1, 2008; Stats. 2014, c. 82 (S.B. 1306), § 2, eff. Jan 1. 2105.)

———

In 2015, the Legislature undertook to omit gender references in the Family Code. *In re Marriage Cases*, 43 Cal.4th 757, 76 Cal.Rptr. 3d 683, 183 P.3d 384 (2008) legalized same-sex marriage in the state. After *Obergefell*, *supra*, the California Legislature interpreted *In re Marriage Cases*, *supra*, to hold that the language "between a man and a woman" is unconstitutional because it violates equal protection (Const. Art. 1, Sec. 7.5). Notice, as you read the Family Code sections in this casebook, that a wave of amendments took place in 2014, effective January 1, 2015. They are intended to insure that the Family Code language is gender neutral.

The premise allows for nonbinary considerations of gender, which allows for a fuller development of the California community property system.

Law most obviously can usher in social change, just as social change can usher changes in the community property system. In an early United States Supreme Court opinion, *Maynard v. Hill*, 125 U.S. 190, 8 S.Ct. 723, 31 L.Ed. 654 (1888), the court drew an important distinction between religious and secular conceptions of marriage: a marriage is created by contract; but once the contract is executed, marriage becomes a status designation. This was a startling statement in favor of secularization in a world where marriage was widely considered a religious bond, not a contractual arrangement.

Parties who are married are legally recognized partners with each other, and their relationship is based on a formal contract. As such, they are entitled to a wide array of protections embedded in the Family and Probate Codes of the state. While a party can only be in one legal marriage at a time, a party can be married and living with someone else as an intimate nonmarried cohabitant (Chapter 4). When that happens, only the valid marriage comes with the default protections reserved for the legal spouse. We rely on the legal foundation of *Maynard v. Hill, supra*, in every chapter of this casebook when we comprehend that a final dissolution judgment serves two functions. One it terminates the parties' status as married partners, thus returning each party to the status of a single person. Two, it dissolves the parties' property rights and liabilities as to each other.

NOTES

1. *Laws governing marriage.* "Unquestionably [in California], the Legislature has full control of the subject of marriage and may fix the conditions under which the marital status may be created or terminated, as well as the effect of an attempted creation of that status." *Jurcoane v. Superior Court,* 93 Cal.App.4th 886, 113 Cal.Rptr.2d 483 (2d Dist. 2001).

2. *Restrictions on contracting a valid marriage.* Age limitation, consanguinity limitations, and a minimal mental capacity are required to contract marriage. See California Family Code Section 301 (defining the age of consent as 18 years of age), Section 352 (prohibiting the grant of a marriage license to those who lack capacity or are under the influence of "an intoxicating liquor or narcotic drug"), Section 2200 (providing that an incestuous marriage is void), and Section 2201 (providing that subsequent marriages are void unless the former marriage was dissolved) (Chapter 4).

SECTION 4. COMPARING COMMON LAW TITLE AND COMMUNITY PROPERTY SYSTEMS

Marital property law in the United States is traceable to two primary sources: the English common law and the civil law system that historically prevailed on the continent of Europe in general and Spain in particular.

The two types of marital property systems differ in how they regard the married persons during the existence of their marriage.

In the common law system—sometimes called the separate property system or the separate property title system—the spouses are regarded as individual economic actors. Each spouse owns the property he or she acquires during marriage. The spouses can opt into joint title form as to particular assets. The idea that each spouse is an individual economic actor sounds appealing in the abstract. But the shine wears off quickly if one spouse retires from the labor force for whatever reason. In that situation, a disparity of wealth may begin to characterize the marriage. If assets are acquired in the earning spouse's name alone, that partner begins to own most of the property. The other partner, the one without an income, becomes increasingly impoverished as compared to his or her spouse. The wealth difference between married persons can make for an arithmetically uncomfortable if not unfair marital dissolution, one that affects the individuals and society alike. The wealthy spouse exits the marriage with the benefit of ownership but no obligation as to dividing property for the other spouse's support. The impoverished spouse is left to seek family or public support. In other words, after a long term marriage it is possible for the impoverished partner to be ejected from the partnership with no means of support, leaving his or her future well being to third parties.

In a community property system the spouses own vested one-half shares in property they acquire during their marriage. An individual spouse can opt out of the community property system as to a particular asset, although this takes planning and record keeping. Separate property interests must be proved; they are not presumed. Instead, the community gets the systemic benefit of any property ownership. Moreover, just as in a business firm, a managing partner—in this case the housekeeper—is recognized as making a valuable contribution to the family. That contribution is quantified as a matter of law and protected through evidence. The legal quantification is the property rule that upon acquisition of an asset each spouse acquires a fifty-fifty vested ownership share. The evidentiary protection is the community property presumption that any asset acquired during marriage is more likely than not to be community property in character.

As discussed above, the majority of American jurisdictions adopted the common law marital property system from England. Like their predecessor, the American systems did not recognize the husband and wife as a marital partners. Instead, the husband and wife were a unity in which the husband was an individual and the wife was under his protection. The wife had two key legal disabilities with respect to property. One, she could not contract with third parties or with her husband. Two, she could not acquire property during the marriage except by inheritance. If a wife inherited property, she had access to courts of equity. But for women without an inheritance wealth disparity was built into the concept of marriage.

Beginning in the mid-nineteenth century, American common law jurisdictions enacted married women's property acts. The major effect of these statutes was to separate the spouses into two legal persons by restoring the wife's capacity to contract and thus to acquire, own, and manage property during marriage. The reforms ultimately resulted in a *title system to marital property*. The common law or "title system" is the idea that each spouse is theoretically entitled to ownership and control of all property that he or she acquires during marriage in his or her name alone. The title document, in other words, determines the married person's rights to the titled asset during the continuance of the marriage. Of particular importance is the right to management and control: title in one person's name alone gives the title holder the legal right to exclusive management and control, even during the marriage.

Largely due to early Spanish and French influences, eight American jurisdictions continued or adopted some version of the traditional Spanish *ganancial* community property system. The Spanish system was and still is a civil law system. It recognizes the spouses as forming a marital partnership—a community estate—while also retaining their identity as separate legal persons. In the U.S., each community property system gave husbands the power to manage community property. The period, known as the male-management era, lasted until the mid-1970s. Despite male-management by law, during marriage each spouse was deemed a co-owner of property as of the point of its acquisition and regardless of the monetary value of his or her actual contribution to the acquisition. In the 1970s, each community property system in the United States transitioned to the equal or dual management approach (Chapter 6). Where the United States systems fall short today, relative to civil law systems in the European Union for example, is that U.S. community property systems protect the rights of a married person to property, and especially to separate property, rather than the greater economic rights of the family as a whole.

The community property system was (and continues to be) a code based classification-based system. All assets owned by married persons are classified as either community or separate property. The definition of community property is property acquired during marriage while domiciled in the state. The definition of separate property is property owned prior to marriage, acquired during marriage by gift or inheritance, or otherwise excluded from the community property system by law.

The dividing line between the common law marital property system and the community property system has become blurred at divorce in recent years. The blurring is due to the adoption of the equitable division concept by all forty-one U.S. common law (title system) states. Equitable division, whether it be instituted by statute or decisional law, creates a deferred community property system at divorce. The equitable distribution doctrine generally provides that (certain) assets owned during marriage are subject to equitable (not equal) division upon dissolution. This determination is typically based on factors such as time (length of marriage) and contribution to purchase (how much did the spouse whose name is not on a title document help the owning spouse acquire the asset?) Contributions to acquisition can be monetary or labor based. A vibrant analytic philosophical debate exists about whether to quantify and monetize the housekeeper's contribution in equitable distribution states. Does putting a price on household labor diminish the qualitative value of the housekeeper's contribution? Does not putting a price on the housekeeper's contribution minimize its economic or quantitative value? *See*, Katharine B. Silbaugh, *Commodification and Women's Household Labor*, 9 YALE L.J. & FEM. 81 (1997).

Equitable distribution systems fall into two general categories. In some jurisdictions the divorce courts have the power to divide all property owned by either or both spouses regardless of its source. In these states courts exercise a broad discretion so as to to "do equity" between the parties at divorce. In other jurisdictions, the divorce court has limited discretion to divide (only) the "marital property," a term that parallels community property systems by how it excludes premarital acquisitions and gifts, as well as property that traces back to either. What constitutes an "equitable distribution" varies among the common law (title system) states. The key point here is that an equal (fifty-fifty) division of the marital property is not the same as an equitable (fair) division based on a spouse's contribution and need. The American Law Institute in its PRINCIPLES OF THE LAW OF FAMILY DISSOLUTION (2002), recommends a very strong equal division presumption, with very narrowly drawn exceptions; but that recommendation is still aspirational in most U.S. common law states.

NOTES

1. *Community property and deferred community property systems are in use around the world.* The English common law marital property system underwent similar reforms and modifications in common law jurisdictions outside the United States.

Judge McCall of the Family Court of Western Australia states that following the enactment of married women's property legislation in the late nineteenth century, a system of separation developed in both Australia and New Zealand. Under this "separation system," each spouse retains the property owned before marriage and each retains separately the property acquired by him or her during marriage. Upon breakdown of the marriage, however, this separation system is replaced by a statutory equitable distribution mechanism: "In exercising this power the court redistributes the property in accordance with what it currently considers necessary to achieve justice between the parties. It is with the exercise of this power that it is possible to say that there is, in a broad way, a principle of an embryo deferred community of property or equalization of assets system emerging." McCall, *Dissolving the Economic Partnership of Marriage,* 14 U.W. Australia L. Rev. 365, 377 (1982). In other words, an equitable distribution system effects a deferred community property system at divorce.

2.   *A deferred community property system compared to an immediate shared ownership system: the example of Wisconsin.* The Uniform Marital Property Act: National Conference of Commissioners on Uniform State Laws has promulgated the Uniform Marital Property Act (UMPA) for consideration by state legislatures. The UMPA is essentially a community property proposal which allows a common law state to adopt the "immediate shared ownership concept" like that used by the community property states. *Commentary, UMPA: The Uniform Marital Property Act,* 10 COMMUNITY PROPERTY JOURNAL 279, 286 (1983). Under the UMPA, property acquired during marriage is classified as "marital property" in which each spouse has a present undivided one-half interest. Property acquired prior to marriage or by gift or inheritance is classified as "individual property," meaning property owned wholly by the acquiring spouse.

Wisconsin was the first and is still the only common law state to adopt the UMPA; for that reason Wisconsin is today regarded as the ninth community property jurisdiction in the U.S. See Freed & Walker, *Family Law in the Fifty States: An Overview,* 19 FAMILY LAW QUARTERLY 331, 355 (Table IV) (1986); Winter, *UMPA Fights for Recognition,* 70 ABA JOURNAL 76 (1984).

In a prior generation of legal actors, the UMPA met with resistance in common law jurisdictions. The President of the Indiana Bar Association, for example, asserted that the "UMPA goes far beyond the recognized inequalities and would create far more problems than any it can solve. The side effects of this medicine make the cure worse than the disease." Grayson, *UMPA—The Bad Penny Comes Back,* 33 Res Gestae 573 (June, 1990). No evidence was offered in support of this medicalized mixed metaphor of an assertion.

3.   *Unpaid housework and career facilitation work: a look at California, Connecticut, and New York.* In the California system, the housekeeper's contribution is presumed to be a valuable contribution to purchase. That understanding is built into the community property principle as a matter of law: community property is any property acquired by the married persons during their marriage while domiciled in the state. The nonconclusive presumption that all property acquired during marriage is community

property further allows persons to make decisions about all aspects of their intimate partnership, including whether one or both spouses should stay home to care for children. In common law separate title systems, by comparison, it is far more difficult for two married persons to predict the ownership of property during marriage and, more to the point, in the event of dissolution.

The saga of Gary and Lorna Wendt of Connecticut (an equitable distribution jurisdiction) illustrates the risk that a spouse in a common law title jurisdiction assumes by staying out of the paid labor force so as to care for the home and facilitate the other spouse's career. But first let me (very briefly) address the inevitable critique of class bias inherent in a case that involves involve high net worth individuals. Lorna Wendt had the financial resources to take her argument to the Connecticut state supreme court. The issue she raised is not whether the spouses of wealthy CEO's deserve half. The issue she raised is whether a contribution made by one spouse to the other spouse's career has a value to the family. And if it does—because of course it does—how should that value get accounted for at dissolution? In California, it is not uncommon for high net worth individuals to appeal their dissolution outcomes. Appellants do all of us a service by raising important issues about gaps or potential gaps in a carefully maintained community property system.

Gary and Lorna Wendt divorced in 1997 after thirty-two years of marriage. They first met in high school and married shortly after graduation from college. Gary attended Harvard Business School, with the costs of tuition funded by his parents. Both spouses were employed while Gary was a student. Lorna worked as a public school music teacher until the couple's first child was born. Thereafter, she was not formally employed, but gave private music lessons until 1989. Over the course of their marriage, Gary rose to the position of CEO of GE Capital Systems, the largest division of General Electric Corporation (think Jack Donaghy in *Thirty Rock*). Lorna served as a homemaker, raising the couple's two daughters and entertaining her husband's business associates. Lorna characterized her homemaking effort as a tool that facilitated and thus directly contributed to Gary's career success. By the time the Wendt's sought marital dissolution, the marital inventory listed $100 million in assets presumably titled in Gary's name alone. Gary proposed a settlement offer to Lorna of $8 million, together with alimony of $250,000 per year.

Lorna refused. Instead, she sought equal division of the marital property on the theory that she and Gary were partners during their marriage.

The trial judge awarded Lorna $20 million, 20%, of the $100 million in assets at issue, plus $250,000 alimony per year. The trial judge opined that marriage should not be commercialized, and that "the attempt to value investments in human capital pushes the institution of marriage from a relationship based on love and obligation toward one based on self interest." The judge's view neatly summarized the analytic philosophical debate mentioned above.

Lorna appealed. But she lost her case again.

The reviewing court affirmed the lower court judgment: "Allowing the plaintiff's argument to persuade us would be, in effect, to write a community property presumption by judicial fiat. . . . [T]here is no presumption of an equal property distribution in Connecticut. . . . 'An equitable award does not require that the marital estate be divided equally.'" *Wendt v. Wendt,* 59 Conn.App. 656, 757 A.2d 1225 (2000). The summary underscores a key difference between community property and a majority of common law title system states.

In the end, Lorna exited the marriage with just a sliver of the total wealth that she and Gary had co-created as an economic unit. That was the ruling in Connecticut; and no matter how it gets rationalized, the state's operative premise is that unless a person "contributes" to the contribution of wealth already acquired in their marriage, that person no legal basis to petition for an equitable ownership interest. (The definition excluded significant retirement benefits that Gary would receive after leaving his corporate post.) This may be a useful rule when the married partners marry later in life, bringing substantial wealth (or poverty) to their marriage with them. But is the rule useful for partners who marry at the start of their work lives? How relevant in today's society is a rule that turns housework, homemaking, career facilitation, child care, and other caring activities into unpaid labor? Lorna and Gary created their life together from a young age. Why should Lorna's efforts be categorized as free labor "donations" to the family rather than as "contributions" to Gary's career?

In California, by sharp contrast, because Gary and Lorna were relatively penniless when they married it would be clear that their community partnership acquired wealth during their marriage in the amount of $100 million. The law recognizes that spouses acquire wealth together. Legally and philosophically that justifies the rule that both spouses get equal ownership rights to the wealth that their partnership creates, unless they contract otherwise. The default rules of the spouses' partnership agreement can be found in the California Family Code. So can the formalities and other requirements for contracting out of the default rules. The parties retain every right to change those default rules by contract, but if they choose not to, a nonconclusive community property presumption codifies the state's compelling interest in marriage and in fair dissolutions. In the Wendt marriage, such a presumption would treat Gary's earnings as Gary's and Lorna's community (partnership) earnings; and Gary's stuff (accumulations) as Gary and Lorna's stuff (community property). From a partnership perspective, fair is fair. Gary and Lorna would have known the community property sharing principle from day one of their marriage; and they would have had thirty two years to get very specific with each other about whether they wanted their partnership to adhere to the default rules of the community property system or not.

In *Elkus v. Elkus,* 169 A.D.2d 134, 572 N.Y.S.2d 901 (1991), a similarly high net worth couple sought dissolution after seventeen years of marriage. In *Elkus,* the high earner was the female spouse, opera star Frederica von Stade. At issue in the New York marital property system was whether one spouse's celebrity status and the derivative income streams it produces are marital property subject to equitable division upon divorce per N.Y. Domestic Relations Law Section 236 (McKinney Supp. 2009), which provides:

"[T]he court shall consider: . . . (6) any equitable claim to, interest in, or *direct or indirect contribution* made to the marital property by the party not having title, *including joint efforts* or expenditures and contributions *and services as a spouse*, *parent*, wage earner and *homemaker*, and to the *career* and *career potential* of the other party [and] * * * (9) the impossibility or difficulty of evaluating any component asset or any interest in a business, corporation or *profession*." (Italics added.)

According to the *Elkus* court:

"While it is true that the plaintiff was born with talent, and while she had already been hired by the Metropolitan Opera at the time of her marriage to the defendant, her career, at this time, was only in the initial stages of development. During the course of the marriage, the defendant's active involvement in the plaintiff's career, in teaching, coaching, and critiquing her, as well as in caring for their children, clearly contributed to the increase in its value. Accordingly, to the extent the appreciation in the plaintiff's career was due to the defendant's efforts and contributions, this appreciation constitutes marital property.

In sum, we find that it is the nature and extent of the contribution by the spouse seeking equitable distribution, rather than the nature of the career, whether licensed or otherwise, that should determine the status of the enterprise as marital property. *Id.* at 904–905.

In other words, a spouse who is actively involved in the other spouse's career contributes to the development of that career. Similar facts to *Wendt* except that the contributing spouse in *Wendt* was female while the contributing spouse in *Elkus* was male.

Is gender dispositive?

In California, to finish up the comparison, gender would not (and should not) determine the outcome in a case such as *Wendt*. All property acquired by the parties during the marriage would be characterized as community property and subject to equal division upon dissolution. The parties could contract out of that projected outcome (Chapter 1). Talent and education would be excluded from the community property principle (Chapter 4) because it is personal to its holder. Otherwise, all earnings and accumulations traceable to the working spouse's efforts would be subject to equal division at the end of the marriage, whether by divorce (Chapter 7) or death (Chapter 9).

SECTION 5. THE CALIFORNIA COMMUNITY PROPERTY SYSTEM

The California community property system is one of the most developed community property systems in operation today. It can be considered a public institution that regulates the economic rights and duties of married persons during and at the end of marriage.

The California community property system continued the Spanish *ganancial* community property system, but has since become *sui generis*.

The California system is organized around the sharing principle, as discussed above. To operationalize immediate shared ownership during marriage, three foundational principles come into play at dissolution.

The tracing principle.

The equality of interest principle.

The contract modification principle.

Many of the problems and tensions inherent in our present-day community property system are more easily understood when viewed in the context of how the system evolved. Key to understanding the system is coming to terms with the fact that the community property system is not of common law origin. It is a civil law system.

Being a civil law system does not make the California community property system a backwater, as common law trained jurists sometimes imply. It makes it part of the global majority. The civil law community property system is widely used around the world, and California is part of that majority. It might also be said, however, that the California community property system is a *hybrid* civil law-slash-common law system both because of its origins and the way in which California law early on adopted so-called "Americanized" rules to modify the civil law *ganancial* system. In the end, it is accurate to say that California continued the community property system, as it was treaty bound to do, but it subsequently made that system its own over the course of nearly two hundred years.

At the time California was annexed to the United States, the marital property law of the area was the Spanish-Mexican community property system. The 1848 Treaty of Guadalupe Hidalgo negotiated continuation of the community property system as part of the greater effort to protect the vested property rights of Mexican citizens who would be effected by the territorial transition. The California Constitution of 1849 put the treaty into effect by continuing the Spanish-Mexican system by making it the original marital property law of the new state. In actuality the Spanish-Mexican system was more Spanish (in code provisions) than Mexican; the reason being that during the Mexican era marriage was a local affair dealt with by *alcaldes*, or local judges. Alcaldes effectively applied what would have been Spanish law to local customs. Additionally, in the Spanish colonial world, Albuquerque and Santa Fe, New Mexico, were legal centers. San Francisco was merely a far out hub of nowhere. It was not until gold was discovered that San Francisco became a central port as well as a destination for immigrants from all around the world. At that point, the population increased overnight, a state was carved out of a territory, a state constitution was signed, a legal system mushroomed into being, and the 1850 California Organic Act was passed as a guide for the new jurists.

The 1849 California Constitution guaranteed the separate property of a married woman and directed the legislature to pass laws more clearly defining the rights of married women in "separate" and "common" property. The first legislature of the State of California codified the basic principles of the community property system. It also expressly provided that the common law of dower and curtesy should not be part of California common law. The husband was recognized by statute as the sole and exclusive agent for the management and control of all property during marriage, including the wife's separate property. By adopting the community property system but maintaining the common law restriction on a married woman's right to own property the seeds for hybridity between civil and common law approaches were planted.

CALIFORNIA CONSTITUTION

1849 Art. XI, Sec. 14

All property, both real and personal, of the wife, owned or claimed by her before marriage, and that acquired afterwards by gift, devise, or descent, shall be her separate property; and laws shall be passed more clearly defining the rights of the wife, in relation as well to her separate property, as to that held in common with her husband. Laws shall also be passed providing for the registration of the wife's separate property.

CALIFORNIA CONSTITUTION

1879 Art. XX, Sec. 8

All property, real and personal, owned by either husband or wife before marriage, and that acquired by either of them afterwards by gift, devise, or descent, shall be their separate property.

CALIFORNIA CONSTITUTION, AMENDMENT

1974, Art. I, Sec. 21

Property owned before marriage or acquired during marriage by gift, will, or inheritance is separate property.

THE CALIFORNIA ORGANIC ACT OF APRIL 17, 1850

AN ACT *defining the rights of Husband and Wife*

Passed April 17, 1850

The People of the State of California, represented in Senate and Assembly, do enact as follows:

§ 1.   All property, both real and personal, of the wife, owned by her before marriage, and that acquired afterwards by gift, bequest, devise, or descent, shall be her separate property; and all property, both real and personal, owned by the husband before marriage, and that acquired by him afterwards, by gift, bequest, devise, or descent, shall be his separate property.

§ 2.   All property acquired after the marriage by either husband or wife, except such as may be acquired by gift, bequest, devise, or descent, shall be common property.

§ 3.   A full and complete inventory of the separate property of the wife shall be made out and signed by the wife, acknowledged or proved in the manner required by law for the acknowledgment or proof of a conveyance of land, and recorded in the office of the Recorder of the county in which the parties reside.

§ 4.   If there be included in the inventory any real estate lying in other counties, the inventory shall also be recorded in such counties.

§ 5.   The filing of the inventory in the Recorder's office shall be notice of the title of the wife, and all property belonging to her, included in the inventory, shall be exempt from seizure or execution for the debts of her husband.

§ 6.   The husband shall have the management and control of the separate property of the wife, during the continuance of the marriage; but no sale or other alienation of any part of such property can be made, nor any lien or [e]ncumbrance created thereon, unless by an instrument in writing, signed by the husband and wife, and acknowledged by her upon an examination separate and apart from her husband, before a Justice of the Supreme Court, Judge of the District Court, County Judge, or Notary Public, or if executed out of the State, then so acknowledged before some Judge of a Court of Record, or before a Commissioner, appointed under the authority of this State to take acknowledgment of deeds.

§ 7.   When any sale shall be made by the wife of any of her separate property, for the benefit of her husband, or when he shall have used the proceeds of such sale with her consent in writing, it shall be deemed a gift, and neither she nor those claiming under her shall have any right to recover the same.

§ 8.   If the wife has just cause to apprehend that her husband has mismanaged or wasted, or will mismanage or waste, her separate property, she, or any other person in her behalf, may apply to the District Court for the appointment of a trustee, to take charge of and manage her separate estate: such trustee may, for good cause shown, be from time to time removed by the Court, and another appointed in his place. Before entering upon the discharge of his trust, he shall execute a bond, with sufficient surety or sureties, to be approved by the Court, for the proper performance of his duties. In case of the appointment of a trustee for the wife, he shall account for and pay over to the husband and wife, or either of them, the income and profits of the wife's estate, in such manner and proportion as the Court may direct.

§ 9.   The husband shall have the entire management and control of the common property, with the like absolute power of disposition as of his own separate estate. The rents and profits of the separate property of either husband or wife shall be deemed common property.

§ 10.   No estate shall be allowed to the husband as tenant by curtesy upon the decease of his wife, nor any estate in dower be allowed to the wife upon the decease of her husband.

§ 11.   Upon the dissolution of the community by the death of either husband or wife, one half of the common property shall go to the survivor, and the other half to the descendants of the deceased husband or wife, subject to the payment of the debts of the deceased. If there be no descendants of the deceased husband or wife, the whole shall go to the survivor, subject to such payment.

§ 12.   In case of the dissolution of the marriage, by the decree of any Court of competent jurisdiction, the common property shall be equally divided between the parties, and the Court granting the decree shall make such order for the division of the common property, or the sale and equal distribution of the proceeds thereof, as the nature of the case may require.

§ 13.   The separate property of the husband shall not be liable for the debts of the wife contracted before the marriage, but the separate property of the wife shall be and continue liable for all such debts.

§ 14.   In every marriage hereafter contracted in this State, the rights of husband and wife shall be governed by this Act, unless there is a marriage contract, containing stipulations contrary thereto.

§ 15.   The rights of husband and wife, married in this State prior to the passage of this Act, or married out of this State, who shall reside and acquire property herein, shall also be determined by the provisions of this Act, with respect to such property as shall be hereafter acquired, unless so far as such provisions may be in conflict with the stipulations of any marriage contract.

§ 16. All marriage contracts shall be in writing, and executed and acknowledged or proved, in like manner as a conveyance of land is required to be executed and acknowledged or proved.

§ 17. When a marriage contract shall be acknowledged or proved, it shall be recorded in the office of the Recorder of the County in which the parties reside, and also in the office of the Recorder of every County in which any real estate may be situated, which is conveyed or affected by such marriage contract.

§ 18. When any marriage contract is deposited in the Recorder's office for record, it shall, as to all property affected thereby, in the county where the same is deposited, impart full notice to all persons of the contents thereof.

§ 19. No marriage contract shall be valid, or affect any property, except between the parties thereto, until it shall be deposited for record with the Recorder of the County where the parties reside, and if it relates to real estate in other counties, with the Recorder of the County wherein such property is situated.

§ 20. A minor, capable of contracting matrimony, may enter into a marriage contract, and the same shall be as valid as if he was of full age: Provided, it be assented to, in writing, by the person or persons whose consent is necessary to his marriage.

§ 21. A marriage contract may be altered at any time before the celebration of the marriage, but not afterwards.

§ 22. The parties to any marriage contract shall enter into no agreement, the object of which shall be to alter the legal order of descent, either with respect to themselves in what concerns the inheritance of their children or posterity, or with respect to their children between themselves, nor derogate from the rights given by law to the husband, as to the head of the family, or to the surviving husband or wife, as the guardian of their children.

§ 23. No stipulation of any marriage contract shall be valid, which shall derogate from the rights given by law to the husband, over the persons of his wife and children, or which belong to the husband, as the head of the family, or to the surviving husband or wife, as the guardian of their children.

————

Legislators, judges and lawyers schooled in the common law tradition have been responsible for the modification and interpretation of the California community property system since its adoption in 1849, and they have not always shown an understanding of the basic tenets of the community property concept. Additionally, legal academics tend not to familiarize themselves with the California community property system; the result is that some if not most theoretical work on marital property rights is marred by a misinformed tendency to lump California in with common law systems. This tendency is particularly noticeable in articles written by scholars who are based outside of California; but it may be observable even in the work of scholars who are based in the state itself. Articles tend to include California within the scope of their discussion—since the state is the most populous state in the U.S.—but without demonstrating the necessary understanding of how different the law of say, New York or Florida, is from the law of California. What is perhaps most aggrieving for its lack of global perspective is the academic declaration that California law is a backwater, a holdover from the past.

This is the part of the text where I get to say a few words about the state that I call home. I no longer know whether I adopted California or California adopted me, but to quote Tupac Shakur, "California knows how to party."[1] And here are some reasons why.

Somewhere around 38.8 million people (or 12.2% of the U.S. population) are domiciled in the state of California, which makes it the most populous state in the U.S. The community property system applies to married persons who are domiciled in the state.

California has the sixth largest economy in the world. Its current state capital is Sacramento. California is an immensely beautiful state; it draws seventeen million tourists from around the world on an annual basis[2].

The California court system is the largest court system in the U.S.

According to the California Courts website, http://www.courts.ca.gov, the linguistic complexity of the state is unrivaled in the U.S. There are over 200 languages and dialects spoken in the state, with forty percent of residents speaking a language other than English in the home, and seven million residents having a proficiency in a language other than English. Heretofore declared "dead" indigenous languages and dialects are spoken on a daily basis in the state proving that those languages are very much alive if not well.[3] At this printing, English, Chinese (both dialects), Tagalog, Korean, and Vietnamese are protected languages in the state market economy pursuant to California Civil Code Section 1632 and 1632.5. *See,* Jo Carrillo, *In Translation for the Latino Market Today: Acknolwedging the Rights of Consumers in a Multilingual Housing Market*, 11 HARVARD LATINO L. REV. 11 (2008).

Multiple languages are interpreted in the courts every day: from July 2009 to June 2013, for example, there were one million total interpreter

---

[1] TUPAC SHAKUR, CALIFORNIA LOVE (Death Row.Interscope 1995).

[2] *See generally*, http://www.ca.gov and http://www.courts.ca.gov.

[3] *Id.*

service days provided by the courts. At this printing, languages certified for court interpreters number fifteen. They are: Arabic, Eastern Armenian, Western Armenian, Cantonese, Japanese, Khmer, Korean, Mandarin, Portuguese, Punjabi, Russian, Spanish, Tagalog, Vietnamese, and American Sign Language. Farsi is scheduled to be added in late 2016. Nothing about the state, including its community property system, is or can be fairly dismissed as a backwater.

California has fifty-eight counties. The least populated of which is Alpine County, in the high Sierra Nevada Mountains, with 1,110 residents. The most populated county is Los Angeles County, with 10,170,292 residents. The geographically smallest county is also one of the original 1850 counties; it is, of course, San Francisco County, which boasts a hilly 47 square miles of foggy fun and a population of 837,432 as of the 2013 census. The largest county in the state and in the U.S. was established in 1853; it is San Bernardino County, and it boasts a massively impressive 20,105 square miles of desert, wind, and sun with a population of 2,088,000 residents as of the 2013 census.

The California state senate and assembly is made up of one hundred and twenty (120) elected members who hail from every part of the geographically and culturally diverse state, as well as from every walk of life. The senate and assembly comprise the body of law makers who enact and amend the statutes you will read in this casebook.

California is a leader in the advance of the civil rights of LGBT persons within and without its borders. California has a statute that offers its impressive Family Code to same-sex couples, anywhere in the world, who live in a county that does not recognize same-sex marriage (Chapter 7). I call this the sanctuary statute. The state otherwise keeps its Family Code available only to those who are domiciled in the state. Yet, California is a jurisdiction that is quick to recognize that so much more progress is needed to ensure the civil rights of persons, no matter their sexual or gender identity or orientation. *Governor Brown Issues Proclamation Declaring June LGBT Pride Month, June 2, 2016.*

California is complicated, diverse, and its laws are under nearly constant review by one or another branch of government. This is particularly true for the California Family Code. Therefore, any academic argument that is not also technical is of limited use to understanding how an idea is implemented or operationalized in the day-to-day workings of the California community property system.

The California courts consist of Superior Courts, Courts of Appeal and the California Supreme Court. Superior courts are trial courts; they are located in each of the fifty-eight counties in the state. There are 2,024 judicial officers in the trial courts. The Family and Juvenile division is part of the state trial court system, as is the Collaborative Law Court System.

The Collaborative Law Court System offers parties an opportunity to work problems out together; these courts hear different types of cases, including domestic violence petitions.

The Family and Juvenile court system hears dissolution, legal separation and nullity of marriage petitions, with 138,968 filings in the past year. The Family Court also hears petitions for support and domestic violence, with 242,518 filing in the past year. For these petitions, trial judges have a broad grant of discretion, but that discretion is carefully exercised within the bounds of the law that you will study in this course. On appeal, California Courts of Appeal generally give discretion to trial court findings of fact by application of the substantial evidence standard of review. The de novo standard of review is reserved for questions of law.

The Courts of Appeal have 105 authorized positions for justices. Today there are six appellate districts in the state, some with multiple divisions. The state began with three judicial appellate districts, created by Constitutional amendment in 1904. In 1966, two additional districts were created. In 1984, the Sixth Appellate District was created. There were 20,198 filings last year, and 22,172 dispositions.

In citing cases throughout this casebook I have retained information about the judicial district in which the case arose. My intention is to orient the reader geographically.

The Court of Appeal for the districts are located as follows:

The First District is located in San Francisco.

The Second District has eight Divisions, seven in Los Angeles, one in Ventura.

The Third District is located in Sacramento

The Fourth District has three Divisions, in San Diego, Riverside, and Santa Ana

The Fifth District is located in Fresno.

The newest Sixth District, which includes Silicon Valley, is located in San Jose.

The Supreme Court employs one Chief Justice and six Associate Justices. There were 7,907 filings last year, with 85 written opinions. In the area of community property law, once the Supreme Court writes an opinion, practitioners in the field may bring pressure on the Legislature to consider the wisdom of that opinion. For example, recently the Legislature abrogated the opinion in *Marriage of Davis*, 61 Cal.4th 846, 352 P.3d 401 (2015). There were many reasons for abrogating *Davis*, some historical, some theoretical. But the primary and final reason cited by the Legislature is that the *Davis* majority opinion sought to draw a bright line rule in an area—marital dissolution—where bright line rules can be and often become a source of injustice. With that rationale, the Legislature ratified the current practice of empowering trial court judges with a broad grant of discretion.

A document called Court Statistics Reports is filed on an annual basis and available on the court website in PDF form. Current information about the community property system is also found under *Families and Children* on the court website.

There are twenty-nine California Codes. The California Family Code was added in 1992, effective 1994. The Family Code, as are other codes, is divided into Divisions, Parts, Chapters, Sections, Subsections, and Paragraphs. The Family Code is comprised of a total of nearly twenty thousand and fifty (20,050) numbered code sections, each with a derivation that gives the section's concise legislative history. (Some code sections have been repealed, so an occasional gap can be found in the numbering system.)

The Family Code is a comprehensive stand-alone collection of statutes that govern three broad topics: marital property issues, support and child custody issues, and domestic violence. Of these three topics, only property statutes are limited to persons in a valid or putative marriage. Otherwise, the custody and domestic violence sections apply to married and nonmarried persons alike.

The Family Code incorporates by reference one or more sections from at least the following state Codes: the Civil Code, the Civil Procedure Code, the Corporations Code, the Evidence Code, the Financial Code, the Government Code, the Insurance Code, Penal Code, the Probate Code, the Revenue and Taxation Code. Codes are interpreted in combination with the federal and state constitutions, federal and state case law, and the California Code of Regulations. Unlike the Civil Code, which is sometimes described as a restatement of the common law, the Family and Probate Codes displace the common law altogether. The Family Code continues the civil law *ganancial* community property system adopted by the 1849 Constitution and the 1850 Organic Act, but it makes that system entirely unique to contemporary California circumstances. The general idea is that because Family and Probate Code provisions reflect the Legislature's intent, they should be interpreted as such. The California Family Code is highly regarded in community property systems around the world, which means that California Supreme Court cases also tend to be followed far and wide.

The California system, like any other community property system, is built around the ancient sharing principle, an idea whose origin traces back to the Visigoths (eastern Germanic tribes) and their even more ancient Norse tribal ancestors. While the origins of community property are ancient, the contemporary California community property system may be ascribed in large part to the vigilant efforts of the California Legislature.

It is the job of the California Legislature to operationalize the sharing principle in a meaningful way by adapting and applying three basic principles to nearly every case.

The first of these basic principles is *the tracing principle* whereby property acquisitions are traced back to their original source.

The second basic principle is *the equality of interest principle*, which recognizes that both spouses have equal vested rights to community property, on an asset-by-asset basis, as of the date of acquisition.

The third basic principle is *the contract modification principle*, which allows parties to modify default community property rules by enforceable written contract.

These three underlying principles are introduced next in serial order. Their application is evident in every chapter.

SECTION 6. THE TRACING PRINCIPLE

A first basic idea underlying the community property system is the tracing principle.

Tracing is the idea that property of one character—community or separate—produces rents, profits, and issues of its same character. The statutes establishing and defining the California community property system indicate that a married person can hold property either as community or as separate, and that different rules govern the acquisition, management and distribution of the two types of property. It is therefore during marriage and especially at dissolution that it becomes necessary to characterize property within the system.

The drafters of the 1849 California Constitution, in adopting the community property system, saw fit to define only separate property. Property not within the ambit of that definition is by implication community property. The 1850 Organic Act statutes implementing the constitutional provision take a similar approach.

Today, the conceptual rubric is flipped. The Family Code starts with the principal of community property found at California Family Code Section 760. From there is creates general exceptions to that principle at California Family Code Section 770 and 771. Specific exceptions also appear throughout the Family Code (Chapter 3).

WEST'S ANNOTATED CALIFORNIA FAMILY CODE

§ 760.   **Community property defined**—*infra* at 85.

§ 770.   **Separate property of married person**—*infra* at 158.

§ 771. Earnings and accumulations during period of separation—
infra at 185.

———

Note that the statutory definitions of separate property include the "rents, issues and profits" of such property. This was not always the case. The original California statute, in accordance with the Spanish *ganancial* system (hereinafter the civil law system), provided that the rents, profits and income of separate property were to be characterized as community property during the marriage. Thus under the original 1850 California statute the spouses contributed to the community their time, energy and skill during marriage as well as an income from separate property, by usufruct.

In the case of *George v. Ransom*, reproduced below (Chapter 3) the California Supreme Court rejected the traditional rule that gave the community use of separate property rents, issues and profits. Instead it held that separate property continues to be separate property despite changes in form. The corollary of this rule is that separate property streams of income are also separate property. Therefore, to follow property through changes of form or to its various income streams, tracing became a necessary tool.

George v. Ransom gave rise to the so-called "American" rule of separate property rents, issues, and profits. By "American," commentators really meant common law. The tracing rule is a common law rule that derives from the law of trusts. *George v. Ransom* effectively incorporated that common law rule into the civil law community property system; the purpose for doing so was to identify separate property rents issues, and profits. Prior to the holding in *George v. Ransom*, separate property rents issues, and profits were characterized during marriage as community property by usufruct. After *George v. Ransom*, separate property income streams were characterized as separate property by right.

NOTES

1. *Tracing is an important part of every U.S. community property system.* The holding in *George v. Ransom* was criticized in the 1980s by family law commentators on the ground that the court confused "the civil law regime of community property with common law property notions" of ownership. Carol S. Bruch, *The Definition and Division of Marital Property in California: Towards Parity and Simplicity*, 33 HASTINGS L.J. 769, 779–81 (1982). The court was also accused of ignoring the legal history of California as well as that of Texas and Louisiana, which had similar statutes. Raymond August, *The Spread of Community Property to the Far West*, 3 WESTERN LEGAL HISTORY 35, 53 (1990).

Despite these criticisms, the tracing rule has long been and still remains a critically important rule in every community property system. The rule encompasses changes in form, such as when something is sold for cash or exchanged for something else. It encompasses rents, profits or other forms of income derived from property of either character.

The rule of *George v. Ransom* subsequently codified at California Family Code Section 770(a)(3) above is now the law in Washington, Nevada, Arizona and New Mexico. Texas vascillates about whether to treat separate property rents, issues, and profits as separate property or not.

"These states struck out on a quite different path toward development of basic principles of community property law from that followed generally in the states adhering to the Spanish rule." William A. Reppy, Jr., *Major Events in the Evolution of American Community Property Law,* 23 Family Law Quarterly 163, 172 (1989).

2. *Commingled assets.* The basic rule is that community property and separate property retain their character even when commingled. A general statement of the tracing rule holds that separate property produces separate property and community property produces community property. Tracing allows for the different characters to be apportioned between the owning estates. The community gets the benefit of the doubt in the form of an evidentiary presumption. The burden of rebuttal is always on the spouse who claims to own a separate property interest. A successful rebuttal requires proof, which typically involves tracing the property in whole or part back to a separate property asset (Chapter 4).

Suppose that one spouse owns a farm as separate property. The other spouse carries on farming operations that produce a crop. The crop is sold. Are the proceeds of the crop sale community property or separate property? And who owns the farm? *Lewis v. Johns*, 24 Cal. 98, 85 Am.Dec. 49 (1864).

SECTION 7. THE EQUALITY OF INTEREST PRINCIPLE

The equality of interest principle is a property rule. It provides that spouses own vested one-half shares in community property as of the date of acquisition. The equality of interest principle is a primary tenet of the civil law *ganancial* system, as such it is recognized by all U.S. community property jurisdictions today.

Most acquisitions of community property involve the direct contribution of the time, energy, and skill of married persons or may be traced to such a contribution. In addition, the spouses contribute equally to the acquisitions by performing what I shall call "family managerial activities." In the community property system, a managing partner's contribution is not only quantifiable, it is as valuable as a wage earning partner's contribution.

Rules of management and control did not always coincide with concepts of equal ownership in the California community property system. The statutes adopting the community property system placed the husband in control and management of the community property, as discussed above. He had the power to possess and exploit the property whereas his wife had no such rights. Male management was explained by California judges of the nineteenth century in guardian/ward terms. The husband was said to have "practical ownership" of the community property, the wife merely a "protected expectancy." *Van Maren v. Johnson*, 15 Cal. 308 (1860) posited that title of the community property "is in the husband, and he can dispose of the same absolutely, as if it were his own separate property. The interest of the wife is a mere expectancy, like the interest which an heir may possess in the property of his ancestor."

In *Stewart v. Stewart*, 199 Cal. 318, 249 P. 197 (1926) the wife argued that early twentieth century statutory changes limiting the husband's ability to make gifts of community property or conveyances of community real estate should be deemed to create, from the moment of acquisition, a vested interest in the wife's undivided one-half of the community property. The California Supreme Court rejected the argument, reasoning that the legislature did not plainly state any purpose to create a vested interest in the wife. Shortly thereafter, the California Legislature did speak plainly. It decreed that the interests of the spouses in the community property are "present, existing and equal," thus abrogating the decision in *Stewart*.

The equality of interest provision was the first codified in 1927. Today it appears at California Family Code Section 751.

WEST'S ANNOTATED CALIFORNIA FAMILY CODE

§ 751.   Community property; interests of parties

The respective interests of each spouse in community property during continuance of the marriage relation are present, existing, and equal interests.

(Stats. 1992, c. 162 (A.B. 2650), § 10, operative Jan. 1, 1994. Amended by Stats. 2014, c. 82 (S.B. 1306), § 14, eff. Jan. 1, 2015.)

———

With respect to community property vested after 1927, the courts no longer use the expressions "practical ownership," "mere expectancy," or "protected expectancy."

The 1927 statute had the effect of qualifying the wife as a party plaintiff in quiet title actions. It also produced several changes in the rules of procedure. Even so, the effect of the 1927 statute was less than sweeping.

It is not too surprising that California courts had difficulty recognizing the equality of ownership principle, given the fact that many of the major incidents of ownership—the rights to possession, management, and control—were vested by statute in the husband until 1975. Piecemeal limitations on the husband's rights to manage and control community property were added to the California Family Code over the years.

In 1975, the state rejected the male-management rule in favor over an array of management and control rules (Chapter 6).

Equal management and control became the default rule for community personal property.

Dual management and control remained the rule for consequential community real property transactions.

Primary management and control was the rule for community property businesses managed by one spouse alone.

Exclusive management and control was permitted by contract over sole bank accounts (but not over the sums on deposit in the account); where one spouse had a conservator and the other spouse retained legal capacity; and by court order to prevent the dissipation of community property assets during dissolution or because of domestic violence (Chapter 6).

SECTION 8. THE CONTRACT MODIFICATION PRINCIPLE

This section covers the third major tenet of the California community property system: the principle of contractual modification. The right to contract with an intimate partner allows a couple to execute a contract to modify, customize, or limit most, but not all, default rules of the community property system.

A contract that purports to modify mutual obligations of support during marriage is unenforceable as a matter of public policy. Otherwise, a contract modifying or altogether waiving postseparation and postdissolution spousal support rights does not violate public policy *per se*.

WEST'S ANNOTATED CALIFORNIA FAMILY CODE

§ 720.   Mutual obligations

Spouses contract toward each other obligations of mutual respect, fidelity, and support.

(Stats. 1992, c. 162 (A.B. 2650), § 10, operative Jan. 1, 1994. Amended by Stats. 2014, c. 82 (S.B. 1306), § 11, eff. Jan. 1, 2015.)

§ 1500. Effect of premarital agreements and other marital property agreements

The property rights of spouses prescribed by statute may be altered by a premarital agreement or other marital property agreement.

(Stats. 1992, c. 162 (A.B. 2650), § 10, operative Jan. 1, 1994. Amended by Stats. 2014, c. 82 (S.B. 1306), § 19, eff. Jan. 1, 2015.)

A. PREMARITAL AGREEMENTS

The CaliforniaOrganic Act of 1850 specifically provided that the system would be subject to premarital and marital contractual modification. That longstanding principle is codified at California Family Code Section 1500, reproduced above.

In 1984, the National Conference of Commissioners on Uniform State Laws approved the Uniform Premarital Agreement Act (UPAA). In 1985, California adopted the UPAA in large part, effective January 1, 1986 (hereinafter the CPAA 1985). The 1984 UPAA did not define voluntariness, but it did state a new rule that spouses-to-be could waive post-divorce spousal support. Like the 1984 UPAA, the CPAA 1985 did not define voluntariness. But unlike the 1984 UPAA, the CPAA 1985 was silent about whether parties could modify postdissolution spousal support rights and obligations by premarital contract.

The gap between the UPAA and the CPAA 1985 led to two widely followed decisions by the California Supreme Court. *Marriage of Pendleton & Fireman,* 24 Cal.4th 39, 99 Cal.Rptr.2d 278, 5 P.3d 839 (2000) and *Marriage of Bonds*, 24 Cal.4th 1, 99 Cal.Rptr.2d 252, 5 P.3d 815 (2000).

Marriage of Pendleton & Fireman held that the silence in the CPAA 1985 on the issue of postdissolution spousal support waivers changed the prior rule. Under the old rule, postdissolution spousal support waivers were categorically unenforceable as a matter of public policy. The new rule lifted the ban on postdissolution spousal support waivers for contracts executed on or after January 1, 1986. The new rule provided that a postdissolution spousal support waiver was enforceable if it was executed by mature, sophisticated persons, who were self-sufficient in property and earning ability, and who had the advice of counsel.

Marriage of Bonds considered how the premarital contracting law should strike the balance between the parties' right to modify the community property system by contract, on one hand, and their right to Family Code protections on the other hand. The CPAA 1985 did not define voluntariness. It did, however, place the burden of proving coercion on the party against whom contract enforcement is sought. *Bonds* specifically ruled that the CPAA 1985 supersedes general burden shifting laws on the issue of voluntariness. (The Civil Code shifts burdens of proof upon evidence of coercion.) Therefore, after *Bonds* the burden to prove that a premarital contract is the product of coercion is and remains on the party who seeks to challenge the enforceability of the premarital contract. In other words, a premarital contract that meets statutory formalities is presumptively enforceable unless and until the party against whom enforcement is sought can prove that it was the product of coercion either because it was unconscionable at execution or involuntarily executed.

In response to the decisions the Legislature amended the CPAA in 2001, effective 2002. The CPAA 2001 codifies *Marriage of Pendleton & Fireman* and *Marriage of Bonds* at California Family Code Sections 1612 and 1615.

Legal Transitions

Contracts executed before or on December 31, 1985 are governed by the pre-CPAA decisional law.

Contracts executed between January 1, 1986 and December 31, 2001 are governed by the CPAA 1985, as well as by *Marriage of Pendleton & Fireman* on the issue of postdissolution spousal support waivers, and *Marriage of Bonds* on the issue of voluntariness.

Contracts executed on or after January 1, 2002 are governed by the CPAA 2001, *infra* at 41–44.

Premarital contracts are executed before the marriage. By comparison amendments to premarital contracts are executed when parties are married to each other. After marriage the parties have transitioned from prospective spouses, with no marriage-based fiduciary duties to each other, to spouses who owe each other mutual obligations and marriage-based fiduciary duties. Spouses are subject to obligations under the Family Code, including California Family Code Section 721, one of which is that a spouse cannot take any unfair advantage of the other in a transaction between them (Chapter 6). An allegation of any unfair advantage made by an adversely affected spouse raises a presumption of undue influence in favor of that spouse. Undue influence is equated with constructive fraud in family law decisions. Therefore, a spouse who signs a contract that adversely affects him or her at the expense of the other spouse is presumed to have been unduly influenced by the benefitted spouse. This leaves it to the benefitted spouse to rebut the presumption of undue influence with proof that the adversely affected spouse signed the agreement voluntarily and based on full and accurate disclosure. See for example *Marriage of Hill & Dittmer*, 202 Cal.App.4th 1046, 136 Cal.Rptr.3d 700 (2d Dist. 2011).

Likewise, even though a contract meets basic CPAA formalities (it is in writing and signed by both parties) at execution, changed circumstances during the marriage can raise a presumption of undue influence under California Family Code Section 721 (Chapter 6). Here again, when a party neglects to update a premarital agreement to his or her advantage a rebuttable presumption of undue influence can be raised on behalf of the adversely affected party. The burden of rebuttal falls on the benefitted spouse.

1. Formalities

California Family Code Section 1611 sets out basic formalities for an enforceable premarital contract. The idea is to enhance the enforceability of premarital contracts by informing prospective spouses about the bare basic requirements for execution.

A premarital contract (or synonymously a "premarital agreement") is defined as "an agreement between prospective spouses made in contemplation of marriage and to be effective upon marriage." A premarital contract does not require consideration to be enforceable. California Family Code Section 1610.

California Family Code Section 1612 lists specific subject areas about which prospective spouses may contract. Spouses-to-be may contract over any species of property, present or future, legal or equitable, vested or contingent, real or personal, income or earnings. The list includes property matters; management and control matters; contingent dispositions (how property will be disposed of in the event of separation, dissolution, death, or the occurrence or nonoccurrence of any another event); testamentary matters; life insurance matters; choice of law matters. Property matters are most suitable for premarital contracting; precatory matters are predictably unenforceable.

The mutual obligations in California Family Code Section 720 cannot be waived by contract during marriage (Chapter 6). The same obligations can be waived, however, after a period of separation or postdissolution. Therefore, postseparation and postdissolution spousal support waivers are not *per se* unenforceable so long as the party against whom enforcement is sought was represented by independent counsel when signing the waiver and the waiver, at enforcement, is not unconscionable, as discussed further below.

For precatory terms, see for example *Marriage of Weiss*, 42 Cal.App.4th 106, 49 Cal.Rptr.2d 339, (2d Dist. 1996), rehearing denied, review denied, certiorari denied 117 S.Ct. 509, 519 U.S. 1007 (1996), a case in which a term was deemed unenforceable because it purported to require that any children of the marriage be brought up in a specific religion.

2. Postdissolution Spousal Support Waivers

California Family Code Section 1612(c) permits parties to contract over "[a]ny other matter, including their personal rights and obligations, not in violation of public policy or a statute imposing a criminal penalty."

The right to receive and the obligation to pay post dissolution spousal support are personal in nature. As such, subsection (c) codifies the new rule that a provision in a premarital contract that modifies or waives a postdissolution spousal support obligation is enforceable, but only if the following two elements are met.

One, the party against whom enforcement is sought—the party who waives spousal support rights if the contract is enforced—was represented by counsel when the waiver was signed.

A few words about element one: the absence of independent counsel, without more, is sufficient to presume coercion by the party who seeks enforcement—the party who is relieved of having to pay postdissolution spousal support if the waiver is enforced. Typically, spousal support waivers are mutually executed, meaning that each prospective spouse agrees to waive postdissolution spousal support rights relative to the other prospective spouse. As an abstract matter, each prospective spouse agrees to the same waiver of rights. And since it is unknown at marriage who will (or will not) request spousal support in the event of dissolution, it must be assumed that either party might. Therefore mutual spousal support waivers necessitate that both parties be represented by independent counsel when the waiver is signed if either waiver is to be enforceable in the future. The requirement of independent counsel reflects the state's compelling interest in postdissolution spousal support and in modifiable spousal support decisions (Chapter 7).

Two, notwithstanding representation by counsel at execution (signing), the waiver is enforceable if it is "not unconscionable" at enforcement (dissolution). A spousal support waiver is deemed unconscionable at enforcement—meaning fundamentally unfair at dissolution—if the waiver would make the party against whom enforcement is sought eligible for public assistance. There may be other situations in which a postdissolution spousal support waiver is deemed unconscionable.

Nevertheless the general rule is clear: an unconscionable spousal support waiver is unenforceable as a matter of public policy.

An unenforceable spousal support waiver is severed from the premarital contract.

Dssolution agreements that disallow spousal support modification are not *per se* unenforceable (Chapter 7).

3. General Contract Enforceability

General contract enforceability depends on disclosure and voluntary consent.

Generally, the absence of independent counsel, standing alone, is not sufficient to support a judgment of coercion as to any terms in the contract that are not postdissolution spousal support waivers. This rule is reversed for purposes of postdissolution spousal support waivers, as discussed above, but the rule clearly stands for all other terms in the premarital contract. In other words, the general rule is that independent counsel is not required to execute a premarital contract that does not contain a spousal support waiver. Signing a premarital contract without the benefit of legal counsel is a risky maneuver, to be sure; and it is risky precisely because the contract, which may effect important legal rights, might be deemed enforceable.

For example, assume that prospective spouses Barry and Sun decide to sign a premarital contract with one key term: all property earned during the marriage will be the separate property of the spouse who earns it. Barry is a professional baseball player; Sun is a sometimes employed hairdresser. The premarital contract does not waive spousal support rights, therefore, independent counsel at execution is not a prerequisite to its enforceability. But if this contract is enforceable ten years down the road, what effect will it have on the parties financial circumstances?

Premarital agreements are signed before marriage, at a time when the prospective spouses are not yet in a confidential relationship as a matter of law. Therefore, what the CPAA offers is protection for intimate partners who negotiate a marital contract before they are fully protected by the California Family Code. As *Bonds* brilliantly explained, intimate partners contract at arm's length, but they contract as people who know, trust, and expect to continue to trust each other. If they were already married, outcomes would be determined by Family Code conceptions of fairness. But because the parties are not yet married, contracting outcomes are determined by the relative bargaining strength of the parties. It bears rephrasing such an important point: when prospective spouses sign the premarital contract they have every intention of getting and staying married; but given the possibility that any particular marriage can end in divorce, the parties' relative bargaining strength is empirically relevant to the negotiation process whether the parties believe it to be or not. If the long parade of premarital agreement cases teaches anything, it is that people want to trust the person they intend to marry. They do not expect to be taken advantage of, especially at the start-up phase of the relationship. And so, they waive important rights confident that *their* marriage will never end, and, therefore, that *their* premarital contract will therefore never see the light of a courtroom.

California Family Code Section 1615(a) states that a premarital contract is not enforceable if the party against whom enforcement is sought can prove either of the following:

- The party did not execute the agreement voluntarily; or

- The agreement was unconscionable when it was executed.

The definition of unconscionability is codified in California Family Code Section 1615(a)(2). The definition of voluntariness is codified in California Family Code Section 1615(c).

California Family Code Section 1615(a)(2) provides that an agreement is unconscionable when executed if all three (paraphrased) elements are established.

- Section 1615(a)(2)(A): Before the premarital agreement was signed, the party who seeks enforcement did not fairly, reasonably, and fully disclose what they owned and what they owed to the party against whom enforcement is sought; and

- Section 1615(a)(2)(B): Before the premarital agreement was signed, the party against whom enforcement is sought did not waive the right to disclosure; and

- Section 1615(a)(2)(C): Before the premarital agreement was signed, the party against whom enforcement is sought could not have had reasonably discovered what the other party owned or owed.

California Family Code Section 1615(b) codifies the rule that "[a]n issue of unconscionability [financial disclosure] of a premarital agreement shall be decided by a court as a matter of law."

The above sections can be summarized like this: a fair contract is one for which there is disclosure. Parties cannot agree to financial terms if important financial facts are not revealed. If a party decides that certain financial facts are not relevant to the negotiation, that party can waive the right to disclosure as to those facts.

As mentioned above, California Family Code Section 1615(c) defines voluntariness.

The party against whom enforcement is sought is deemed to have voluntarily signed the contract if a court finds "in writing or on the record [paraphrased] all of the following."

- Section 1615(c)(1): The party against whom enforcement is sought was represented by independent counsel. Or, alternatively, that party was advised to seek independent counsel and expressly waived representation, in a writing separate from the premarital agreement; and

- Section 1615(c)(2): The seven day rule was met, meaning the party had not less than seven days to review a (presumably final or near final) draft of the contract; and

- Section 1615(c)(3): Assuming the party waived representation, that party was informed of the basic terms and effect of the agreement, of any rights and obligations he or she was waiving by signing the premarital agreement, and that information was presented in a writing separate from the premarital agreement in a language that the receiving party was at the time proficient in; and

- Section 1615(c)(4): There are no allegations of coercion in the form of duress, fraud, or undue influence, and the parties did not lack capacity to enter into the agreement; and

- Section 1615(c)(5): "Any other factors the court deems relevant." Factors like, for example, a history of intimate partner violence on or around the time the agreement was signed.

NOTES

1. *How is an amended premarital contract different from a contract executed during marriage for the first time?* California Family Code Section 1613 defines a premarital contract as one that becomes effective upon marriage. California Family Code Section 1614 permits amendments and revocations to such a contract. Does this mean that the CPAA 2001 continues to apply to amendments of a premarital contract made during marriage?

The CPAA 2001 does not speak to or otherwise govern contracts that are entered into for the first time during marriage. That said, the legislation is often used by attorneys as a template for documenting fairness and voluntariness.

In *Marriage of Burkle,* 139 Cal.App.4th 712, 43 Cal.Rptr.3d 181 (2d Dist. 2006), for example, the parties' negotiated a reconciliation contract during marriage (Chapter 6). The Burkles were not executing a premarital agreement, they were executing an entirely new contract during their marriage. Still, because they were living separate and apart, it appears that each spouse's team of attorneys (plural) agreed to use the CPAA 2001 as a model for executing the reconciliation contract. Disclosure was made and independent counsel assured that each spouse voluntarily entered into the contract.

2. *What is the difference between a contract executed during marriage and a transmutation?* Transmutations are defined as changes to the character of property made during marriage. Transmutations can be by bargained for exchange or by gift. Transmutations do not require consideration to be enforceable, but the absence of consideration raises a presumption of undue influence to protect the spouse was was adversely affected by the transmutation.

3. *Are premarital agreements recorded?* In order to give third parties constructive notice, parties may opt to file a premarital agreement in the public

record. If the subject of the agreement is real property, the agreement must be recorded to be enforceable against third parties, and it must be recorded in the county where the real estate is situated.

WEST'S ANNOTATED CALIFORNIA FAMILY CODE

§ 1600. Short title

This chapter may be cited as the Uniform Premarital Agreement Act.

(Stats. 1992, c. 162 (A.B. 2650), § 10, operative Jan. 1, 1994.)

§ 1601. Effective date of chapter

This chapter is effective on and after January 1, 1986, and applies to any premarital agreement executed on or after that date.

(Stats. 1992, c. 162 (A.B. 2650), § 10, operative Jan. 1, 1994.)

§ 1610. Definitions

As used in this chapter:

(a) "Premarital agreement" means an agreement between prospective spouses made in contemplation of marriage and to be effective upon marriage.

(b) "Property" means an interest, present or future, legal or equitable, vested or contingent, in real or personal property, including income and earnings.

(Stats. 1992, c. 162 (A.B. 2650), § 10, operative Jan. 1, 1994.)

§ 1611. Form and execution of agreement; consideration

A premarital agreement shall be in writing and signed by both parties. It is enforceable without consideration.

(Stats. 1992, c. 162 (A.B. 2650), § 10, operative Jan. 1, 1994.)

§ 1612. Subject matter of premarital agreements

(a) Parties to a premarital agreement may contract with respect to all of the following:

(1) The rights and obligations of each of the parties in any of the property of either or both of them whenever and wherever acquired or located.

(2) The right to buy, sell, use, transfer, exchange, abandon, lease, consume, expend, assign, create a security interest in, mortgage, encumber, dispose of, or otherwise manage and control property.

(3) The disposition of property upon separation, marital dissolution, death, or the occurrence or nonoccurrence of any other event.

(4) The making of a will, trust, or other arrangement to carry out the provisions of the agreement.

(5) The ownership rights in and disposition of the death benefit from a life insurance policy.

(6) The choice of law governing the construction of the agreement.

(7) Any other matter, including their personal rights and obligations, not in violation of public policy or a statute imposing a criminal penalty.

(b) The right of a child to support may not be adversely affected by a premarital agreement.

(c) Any provision in a premarital agreement regarding spousal support, including, but not limited to, a waiver of it, is not enforceable if the party against whom enforcement of the spousal support provision is sought was not represented by independent counsel at the time the agreement containing the provision was signed, or if the provision regarding spousal support is unconscionable at the time of enforcement. An otherwise unenforceable provision in a premarital agreement regarding spousal support may not become enforceable solely because the party against whom enforcement is sought was represented by independent counsel.

(Stats. 1992, c. 162 (A.B. 2650), § 10, operative Jan. 1, 1994. Amended by Stats. 2001, c. 286 (S.B. 78), § 1.)

§ 1613. Effective date of agreements

A premarital agreement becomes effective upon marriage.

(Stats. 1992, c. 162 (A.B. 2650), § 10, operative Jan. 1, 1994.)

§ 1614. Amendment or revocation of agreements

After marriage, a premarital agreement may be amended or revoked only by a written agreement signed by the parties. The amended agreement or the revocation is enforceable without consideration.

(Stats. 1992, c. 162 (A.B. 2650), § 10, operative Jan. 1, 1994.)

§ 1615. Unenforceable agreements; unconscionability; voluntariness

(a) A premarital agreement is not enforceable if the party against whom enforcement is sought proves either of the following:

(1) That party did not execute the agreement voluntarily.

(2) The agreement was unconscionable when it was executed and, before execution of the agreement, all of the following applied to that party:

(A) That party was not provided a fair, reasonable, and full disclosure of the property or financial obligations of the other party.

(B) That party did not voluntarily and expressly waive, in writing, any right to disclosure of the property or financial obligations of the other party beyond the disclosure provided.

(C) That party did not have, or reasonably could not have had, an adequate knowledge of the property or financial obligations of the other party.

(b) An issue of unconscionability of a premarital agreement shall be decided by the court as a matter of law.

(c) For the purposes of subdivision (a), it shall be deemed that a premarital agreement was not executed voluntarily unless the court finds in writing or on the record all of the following:

(1) The party against whom enforcement is sought was represented by independent legal counsel at the time of signing the agreement or, after being advised to seek independent legal counsel, expressly waived, in a separate writing, representation by independent legal counsel.

(2) The party against whom enforcement is sought had not less than seven calendar days between the time that party was first presented with the agreement and advised to seek independent legal counsel and the time the agreement was signed.

(3) The party against whom enforcement is sought, if unrepresented by legal counsel, was fully informed of the terms and basic effect of the agreement as well as the rights and obligations he or she was giving up by signing the agreement, and was proficient in the language in which the explanation of the party's rights was conducted and in which the agreement was written. The explanation of the rights and obligations relinquished shall be memorialized in writing and delivered to the party prior to signing the agreement. The unrepresented party shall, on or before the signing of the premarital agreement, execute a document declaring that he or she received the information required by this paragraph and indicating who provided that information.

(4) The agreement and the writings executed pursuant to paragraphs (1) and (3) were not executed under duress, fraud, or undue influence, and the parties did not lack capacity to enter into the agreement.

(5) Any other factors the court deems relevant.

(Stats. 1992, c. 162 (A.B. 2650), § 10, operative Jan. 1, 1994. Amended by Stats. 2001, c. 286 (S.B. 78), § 2.)

§ 1616. Void marriage, effect on agreement

If a marriage is determined to be void, an agreement that would otherwise have been a premarital agreement is enforceable only to the extent necessary to avoid an inequitable result.

(Stats. 1992, c. 162 (A.B. 2650), § 10, operative Jan. 1, 1994.)

§ 1617. Limitations of actions; equitable defenses including laches and estoppel

Any statute of limitations applicable to an action asserting a claim for relief under a premarital agreement is tolled during the marriage of the parties to the agreement. However, equitable defenses limiting the time for enforcement, including laches and estoppel, are available to either party.

(Stats. 1992, c. 162 (A.B. 2650), § 10, operative Jan. 1, 1994.)

§ 1620. Contracts altering legal relations of spouses; restrictions

Except as otherwise provided by law, spouses cannot, by a contract with each other, alter their legal relations, except as to property.

(Stats. 1992, c. 162 (A.B. 2650), § 10, operative Jan. 1, 1994. Amended by Stats. 2014, c. 82 (S.B. 1306), § 21, eff. Jan 1, 2015).

B. TRANSMUTATIONS

A transmutation is a change in the character of property.

Community property and separate property are defined by statute as default rules. Once married, however, the principle of contractual modification allows spouses to decide for themselves how their property will be characterized for purposes of marriage and dissolution. California has no policy preference for how married couples should hold property.

Whereas premarital agreements are "enforceable" (or not), transmutations are either "valid" (or not) as of the date they are made.

California Family Code Section 850 allows a married couple to transmute, or change the character of, "community property to separate property . . . separate property of either spouse to community property . . . and separate property of one spouse to separate property of the other spouse."

A transmutation is subject to fiduciary standards set out in California Family Code Section 721.

Prior to 1985 (the so-called easy transmutation era), the California courts were willing to find and enforce implied-in-fact transmutations. Today, transmutations are governed by: California Family Code Sections

850–853; California Family Code Section 721(b); and state and federal laws governing fraudulent transfers.

California Family Code Section 852(a) requires that a transmutation, whether of real or personal property, be made "in writing by an express declaration that is made, joined in, consented to, or accepted by the spouse whose interest in the property is adversely affected." Failure to meet the basic statutory formalities invalidates the transmutation attempt. A void transmutation has no effect on the character of the subject property.

WEST'S ANNOTATED CALIFORNIA FAMILY CODE

§ 850.   Transmutation by agreement or transfer

Subject to Sections 851 to 853, inclusive, married persons may by agreement or transfer, with or without consideration, do any of the following:

(a) Transmute community property to separate property of either spouse.

(b) Transmute separate property of either spouse to community property.

(c) Transmute separate property of one spouse to separate property of the other spouse.

(Stats. 1992, c. 162 (A.B. 2650), § 10, operative Jan. 1, 1994.)

§ 851.   Transmutation subject to fraudulent transfer laws

A transmutation is subject to the laws governing fraudulent transfers.

(Stats. 1992, c. 162 (A.B. 2650), § 10, operative Jan. 1, 1994.)

§ 852.   Requirements

(a) A transmutation of real or personal property is not valid unless made in writing by an express declaration that is made, joined in, consented to, or accepted by the spouse whose interest in the property is adversely affected.

(b) A transmutation of real property is not effective as to third parties without notice thereof unless recorded.

(c) This section does not apply to a gift between the spouses of clothing, wearing apparel, jewelry, or other tangible articles of a personal nature that is used solely or principally by the spouse to whom the gift is made and that is not substantial in value taking into account the circumstances of the marriage.

(d) Nothing in this section affects the law governing characterization of property in which separate property and community property are commingled or otherwise combined.

(e)   This section does not apply to or affect a transmutation of property made before January 1, 1985, and the law that would otherwise be applicable to that transmutation shall continue to apply.

(Stats. 1992, c. 162 (A.B. 2650), § 10, operative Jan. 1, 1994.)

§ 853.   Characterization of property in will; admissibility in proceedings commenced before death of testator; waiver of right to joint and survivor annuity or survivor's benefits; written joinders or consent to nonprobate transfers of community property

(a)   A statement in a will of the character of property is not admissible as evidence of a transmutation of the property in a proceeding commenced before the death of the person who made the will.

(b)   A waiver of a right to a joint and survivor annuity or survivor's benefits under the federal Retirement Equity Act of 1984 (Public Law 98–397) is not a transmutation of the community property rights of the person executing the waiver.

(c)   A written joinder or written consent to a nonprobate transfer of community property on death that satisfies Section 852 is a transmutation and is governed by the law applicable to transmutations and not by Chapter 2 (commencing with Section 5010) of Part 1 of Division 5 of the Probate Code.

(Stats. 1992, c. 162 (A.B. 2650), § 10, operative Jan. 1, 1994. Amended by Stats. 1993, c. 219 (A.B. 1500), § 100.)

§ 721.   Contracts with each other and third parties; fiduciary relationship—*infra* at 478.

———

Estate of Bibb illustrates the concept of transmutation by deed. It is not uncommon for people to believe that a deed settles all disputes. Deeds are important. But a deed can also raise more questions than it answers on its face.

ESTATE OF BIBB
87 Cal.App.4th 461, 104 Cal.Rptr.2d 415 (1st Dist. 2001)

Walker, J.

Family Code section 852, subdivision (a), provides: "A transmutation of real or personal property is not valid unless made in writing by an express declaration that is made, joined in, consented to, or accepted by the spouse whose interest in the property is adversely affected." The issues we address in the published portion of this opinion are: (1) whether a grant deed signed by a husband transferring his separate property interest in real property to himself and his wife as joint tenants satisfies the "express declaration" requirement of section 852, subdivision (a); and (2) whether an unsigned computer printout, entitled "DMV Vehicle Registration Information," reflecting that an automobile, which was previously registered in the husband's name alone, was reregistered in the names of the husband *or* the wife, satisfies the requirements for a valid transmutation under section 852, subdivision (a). * * *

FACTS AND PROCEDURAL BACKGROUND

Decedent, Everett L. Bibb, Jr. (Everett), and his first wife, Ethel Bibb (Ethel), had one child, Dozier Bibb (Dozier), appellant herein. During his marriage to Ethel, Everett purchased a lot in Berkeley, California, and constructed an apartment building thereon. Ethel died on November 25, 1977.

Everett began dating Evelyn Bibb (Evelyn), respondent herein, in 1988 or 1989. On January 29, 1991, Everett purchased a Rolls Royce automobile, and registered it in his name alone. After their marriage, the Rolls Royce was reregistered in 1995 in the names of Everett *or* Evelyn. * * * Everett married Evelyn in December of 1992. Evelyn testified that, after their marriage, money was used from a joint account to pay the man from whom Everett had purchased the Rolls Royce and to pay for maintenance and repairs on the vehicle.

In the latter part of 1994, Everett applied for a $225,000 loan, which was to be secured by the Berkeley property and was to be used, in part, to renovate the apartment building located thereon. Everett was unable to qualify for the loan with his own credit. In order to qualify for the loan based upon his wife's good credit, Everett signed a grant deed on January 24, 1995, conveying the real property from himself to himself and Evelyn, "his wife as joint tenants." Evelyn signed the note secured by a deed of trust on the subject property.

After having suffered a stroke in February of 1995, Everett died intestate on September 6, 1995. After Everett's death, Evelyn reregistered the Rolls Royce in her name alone, and, by signing an affidavit terminating joint tenancy, took title to the Berkeley property in her name alone.

Evelyn filed a petition for probate of Everett's estate on January 27, 1999. On November 15, 1999, Dozier filed a petition to establish the estate's ownership of the Berkeley property [and] the Rolls Royce * * * contending that the property had not been validly transmuted from Everett's separate property under section 852, subdivision (a). * * *

On July 13, 2000, Dozier filed a timely notice of appeal from the trial court's July 11, 2000 judgment denying his petition to establish the estate's ownership of the subject property.

Discussion

I. *The Real Property*

Relying on *Estate of MacDonald* (1990) 51 Cal.3d 262, 272, 272 Cal.Rptr. 153, 794 P.2d 911 (*MacDonald*), Dozier contends that the grant deed purporting to transmute Everett's separate interest in the Berkeley property into an interest owned as joint tenants by Everett and Evelyn does not satisfy the "express declaration" requirement of section 852, subdivision (a), because it does not contain language " 'expressly stat[ing] that the characterization or ownership of the property [was] being changed.' " Evelyn responds that the real property is presumed to be held in joint tenancy, as described in the grant deed, and, therefore, is excluded from probate under Probate Code section 6600, subdivision (b)(1).

The "express declaration" requirement for a valid transmutation of property under section 852, subdivision (a), was construed by the Supreme Court in *MacDonald, supra,* 51 Cal.3d 262, 272 Cal.Rptr. 153, 794 P.2d 911. The property at issue in *MacDonald* was the $266,557.90 disbursement from the husband's community property pension plan. (*MacDonald, supra,* at p. 265, 272 Cal.Rptr. 153, 794 P.2d 911.) Those funds were placed into three IRA accounts, which were opened in the husband's name alone, with the designated beneficiary of each a revocable living trust that left the bulk of the corpus to his children from a prior marriage. (*Ibid.*) Under "consent paragraphs," the IRA account agreements required the signature of a spouse not designated as the sole primary beneficiary to consent to the designation. (*Ibid.*) Mrs. MacDonald signed the consent paragraphs for all three IRA accounts. (*Ibid.*) Because the consent paragraphs were signed by Mrs. MacDonald, there was no dispute that the documents satisfied the requirements of a writing that was "made, joined in, consented to, or accepted by the spouse whose interest in the property is adversely affected." (§ 852, subd. (a); *MacDonald, supra,* at pp. 267–268, 272 Cal.Rptr. 153, 794 P.2d 911.) Thus, the specific issue addressed by the court in *MacDonald* was whether the consent paragraphs "constitute 'an express declaration' for the purposes of section [852, subdivision (a)]." (*MacDonald, supra,* at p. 268, 272 Cal.Rptr. 153, 794 P.2d 911.)

The court, in *MacDonald, supra,* 51 Cal. 3d at p. 268, 272 Cal.Rptr. 153, 794 P.2d 911, found that "[i]t is not immediately evident from a reading of section [852, subdivision (a)] what is meant by the phrase 'an express declaration.' Examination of the words of the statute and their arrangement reveals only that the 'express declaration' called for is to be one 'by' which '[a] transmutation of real or personal property' is 'made.' The statute does not state what words such an 'express declaration' must include, what information it must convey, or even what topics it should discuss." Because it found that the "express declaration" language of the statute is unclear and ambiguous, the *MacDonald* court turned to the legislative history and the historical circumstances of the statute's enactment, in order to "ascertain the intent of the Legislature so as to effectuate the purpose of the law." (*Select Base Materials v. Board of Equal.* (1959) 51 Cal.2d 640, 645, 335 P.2d 672; *MacDonald, supra,* 51 Cal.3d at p. 268, 272 Cal.Rptr. 153, 794 P.2d 911.) In this regard, the court found that, prior to the enactment of section 852, it was "quite easy for spouses to transmute both real and personal property; a transmutation [could] be found based on oral statements or implications from the conduct of the spouses." (Recommendation Relating to Marital Property Presumptions and Transmutations, 17 Cal. Law Revision Com. Rep. (1984) (Commission report) p. 213; *MacDonald, supra,* at p. 269, 272 Cal.Rptr. 153, 794 P.2d 911.) The prior rule of "easy transmutation" was found to have caused extensive litigation in dissolution proceedings and to encourage spouses to "commit perjury by manufacturing an oral or implied transmutation." (Commission report, *supra,* at p. 214; *MacDonald, supra,* at p. 269, 272 Cal.Rptr. 153, 794 P.2d 911.) Based on this history, the Supreme Court concluded that section 852, subdivision (a), was intended "to create a writing requirement which enables courts to validate transmutations without resort to extrinsic evidence and, thus, without encouraging perjury and the proliferation of litigation." (*MacDonald, supra,* at p. 272, 272 Cal.Rptr. 153, 794 P.2d 911.)

The court in *MacDonald, supra,* 51 Cal.3d at pp. 271–272, 272 Cal.Rptr. 153, 794 P.2d 911, determined exactly what type of writing the legislature intended to require by use of the phrase "express declaration." To aid in this determination, the court referred to its previous construction of a similar writing requirement in Civil Code section 683, subdivision (a) which requires that the creation of a joint tenancy be "expressly declared." (*MacDonald, supra,* at pp. 271–272, 272 Cal.Rptr. 153, 794 P.2d 911; see *California Trust Co. v. Bennett* (1949) 33 Cal.2d 694, 204 P.2d 324 (*Bennett*).) In *Bennett, supra,* at p. 699, 204 P.2d 324, the high court observed: "It is well settled that where a statute requires the formality of a writing for the creation of an interest in the property, it must contain words *indicating an intent to transfer* such interest, * * * " (Italics added.) Under this principle, Civil Code section 683 was interpreted so as to ensure "that a court need not look beyond the face of the proffered writing to determine *whether its writer intended to create* a joint tenancy." (*MacDonald, supra,* at p. 272, 272 Cal.Rptr. 153, 794 P.2d 911, italics added.) Explicitly following the approach elucidated in *Bennett, supra,* at p. 699, 204 P.2d 324, the court, in *MacDonald, supra,* at p. 272, 272 Cal.Rptr. 153, 794 P.2d 911, concluded that a writing signed by the adversely affected spouse is not an "express declaration" for purposes of section 852, subdivision (a), "*unless* it contains language which expressly states that the characterization or ownership of the property is being changed." (Italics in original.)

In *MacDonald, supra,* 51 Cal.3d at pages 272–273, 272 Cal. Rptr. 153, 794 P.2d 911, the court held that the IRA account consent agreements did not satisfy the express declaration requirement of section 852, subdivision (a), because they did not contain language characterizing the property assertedly being transmuted, it was impossible to tell from the face of the documents whether Mrs. MacDonald was "aware that the legal effect of her signature might be to alter the character or ownership of her interest in the pension funds," and there was no language expressly stating that she was effecting a change in the character or ownership of her interest. In arriving at its holding, the court clarified that a valid writing under the subject statute need not include "the term 'transmutation' or any other particular locution." (*MacDonald, supra,* at p. 273, 272 Cal.Rptr. 153, 794 P.2d 911.) In fact, the court held that the paragraph signed by Mrs. MacDonald would have been sufficient under section 852, subdivision (a), had it included an additional sentence reading: " 'I give to the account holder any interest I have in the funds deposited in this account.' " (*MacDonald, supra,* at p. 273, 272 Cal. Rptr. 153, 794 P.2d 911.)

As with the requirements for the creation of a joint tenancy under Civil Code section 683, the requirements for a valid transmutation under Family Code section 852, subdivision (a), can be divided into two basic components: (1) a writing that satisfies the statute of frauds; and (2) an expression of intent to transfer a property interest. Based upon the *MacDonald* court's interpretation and application of section 852, subdivision (a), as well as its reliance upon its prior construction of the express declaration requirement in Civil Code section 683, we understand the Supreme Court to have interpreted the express declaration language of section 852, subdivision (a), to specifically require that a writing effecting a transmutation of property contain on its face a clear and unambiguous expression of intent to transfer an interest in the property, independent of extrinsic evidence. (See *In re Marriage of Barneson* (1999) 69 Cal.App.4th 583, 593, 81 Cal.Rptr.2d 726 (*Barneson*) ["The *MacDonald* test * * * requires only a clear demonstration of a change in ownership or characterization of the property at issue"].)

As with the consent paragraphs in *MacDonald, supra,* 51 Cal.3d at p. 268, 272 Cal.Rptr. 153, 794 P.2d 911, there is no dispute in this case that the grant deed, which was signed by Everett, is a writing that was "made, joined in, consented to, or accepted by the spouse whose interest in the property is adversely affected." (§ 852, subd. (a).) Thus, we need only determine whether the deed, independent of extrinsic evidence, contains a clear and unambiguous expression of intent to transfer an interest in the property. The grant deed on the Berkeley property states that Everett, as surviving joint tenant, granted the property to himself and Evelyn as joint tenants. [The grant deed states: "For a valuable consideration, receipt of which is hereby acknowledged, E. L. Bean as surviving joint tenant hereby grant(s) to E. L. Bibb and Evelyn R. Bibb, his wife as joint tenants the following described real property in the City of Berkeley, County of Alameda, State of California: Legal description attached hereto."] The deed is drafted in the statutory form required for expressing an intent to transfer an interest in real property. (See Civ.Code, §§ 1091, 1092). Since the *MacDonald* court held that the consent paragraphs would have been adequate for a valid transmutation had they said, " 'I *give* to the account holder any interest I have * * * ,' " and since "grant" is the historically operative word for transferring interests in real property, there is no doubt that Everett's use of the word "grant" to convey the real property into joint tenancy satisfied the express declaration requirement of section 852, subdivision (a). (*MacDonald, supra,* at p. 273, 272 Cal.Rptr. 153, 794 P.2d 911, italics added.) Thus, the Berkeley property was validly transmuted into property held in joint tenancy, became Evelyn's separate property upon Everett's death, and was properly excluded from the probate estate. (§ 852, subd. (a); Prob.Code, § 6600, subd. (b)(1).)

II.   The Rolls Royce

The document purporting to evidence the transmutation of the Rolls Royce in this case is a computer printout entitled "DMV Vehicle Registration Information," which reflects that, as of October 5, 1995, the vehicle, which had been previously registered in Everett's name alone, was reregistered in the names of Everett *or* Evelyn. No signature of any party appears on the document. As with the real property, Dozier contends that the DMV printout does not satisfy the "express declaration" requirement of Family Code section 852, subdivision (a), because it does not contain language "expressly stat[ing] that the characterization or ownership of the property [was] being changed." (*MacDonald, supra,* 51 Cal.3d at p. 272, 272 Cal.Rptr. 153, 794 P.2d 911.) Evelyn responds that, because title to the automobile was held in joint tenancy, it is excluded from probate under Probate Code section 6600, subdivision (b)(1). Evelyn further argues that the transfer of title on the Rolls Royce is exempt from the requirements of section 852, subdivision (a), because the property was "commingled or otherwise combined" with marital property, as described in subdivision (d) of the subject statute.

Vehicle Code sections 4150.5 and 5600.5 effectively create a presumption that a vehicle "registered in the names of two (or more) persons as coowners in the alternative by use of the word 'or' " is held in joint tenancy. However, the Supreme Court's "interpretation of the 'express declaration' language in section 852, subdivision (a), can [also] be viewed as effectively creating a 'presumption' that transactions between spouses are not 'transmutations,' rebuttable by evidence the transaction was documented with a writing containing the requisite language." (*Barneson, supra,* 69 Cal.App.4th at p. 593, 81 Cal.Rptr.2d 726.) The court in *Barneson* addressed the conflict in the presumptions created by Family Code section 852, subdivision (a), and Evidence Code section 662, which provides that "[t]he owner of the legal title to property is presumed to be the owner of the full beneficial title." *Barneson* held that, because the Supreme Court's interpretation of section 852, subdivision (a), was based in part on a policy of " 'assuring that a spouse's community property entitlements are not improperly undermined,' " the general presumption under Evidence Code section 662 should not be used to negate the more specific requirements of section 852, subdivision (a). (*Barneson, supra,* at p. 593, 81 Cal.Rptr.2d 726; see *MacDonald, supra,* 51 Cal.3d at pp. 268–272, 272 Cal.Rptr. 153, 794 P.2d 911.) Following the principle enunciated in *Barneson,* the more general form of title presumption created by Vehicle Code sections 4150.5 and 5600.5 should not be used to negate the requirements of section 852, subdivision (a), which assure that a spouse's separate property entitlements are not undermined. (*MacDonald, supra,* at pp. 268–272, 272 Cal. Rptr. 153, 794 P.2d 911; see also *In re Marriage of Haines* (1995) 33 Cal.App.4th 277, 301–302, 39 Cal.Rptr.2d 673 [in case of conflict, the more specific presumption of undue influence in transactions between married persons under Fam. Code section 721 prevails over the more general presumption of ownership from title under Evidence Code section 662].)

Although the DMV printout may comply with the requirements for a presumption of joint tenancy under Vehicle Code sections 4150.5 and 5600.5, there is nothing on the face of the document evidencing that the change in the form of title was "made, joined in, consented to, or accepted by" Everett, the spouse whose interest in the property was adversely affected. (Fam. Code § 852, subd. (a).) Moreover, the document does not contain a clear and unambiguous expression of Everett's intent to transfer his interest in the subject property, as required by section 852, subdivision (a). (*MacDonald, supra,* 51 Cal.3d at pp. 271–273, 272 Cal.Rptr. 153, 794 P.2d 911; see *Estate of Petersen* (1994) 28 Cal.App.4th 1742, 1754–1755, 34 Cal.Rptr.2d 449 [designation of joint tenancy on account statement does not satisfy the requirement of an express written declaration pursuant to section 852, subd. (a)].) Thus, the Rolls Royce was not validly transmuted from Everett's separate property.

We are unpersuaded by Evelyn's argument that the Rolls Royce is exempt from the requirements of section 852, subdivision (a). Subdivision (d) of section 852 provides that "[n]othing in this section affects the law governing characterization of property in which separate property and community property are commingled or otherwise combined." As discussed above, application of section 852, subdivision (a), dictates that the Rolls Royce, which was owned separately by Everett prior to his marriage to Evelyn, maintain its character as Everett's separate property. In arguing that the Rolls Royce was somehow commingled or otherwise combined with marital property, Evelyn fails to cite any law governing the characterization of commingled or combined property, under which the vehicle should be characterized as something other than Everett's separate property. Since Evelyn fails to cite any law that conflicts with section 852, subdivision (a), there is no basis to conclude that the statute is inapplicable. (See *Landry v. Berryessa Union School Dist.* (1995) 39 Cal.App.4th 691, 699–700, 46 Cal.Rptr.2d 119 ["When an issue is unsupported by pertinent or cognizable legal argument it may be deemed abandoned and discussion by the reviewing court is unnecessary"].)

In short, because the Rolls Royce was not validly transmuted under section 852, subdivision (a), it remained Everett's separate property. Thus, the trial court erred in excluding it from the probate estate.* * *

DISPOSITION

Reversed with respect to the Rolls Royce. Affirmed in all other respects. Parties are to bear their own costs on appeal.

MCGUINESS, P.J., and PARRILLI, J., concur.

————

The next case is about a life insurance policy. The policy had a cash value as well as a term. And it was purchased by one spouse from a third party in the other spouse's name alone.

A bit of background: the general rule for term life insurance policies is that a life insurance policy is characterized identically to the funds that purchase the premium. If the premiums are paid with community property, then the term component of the policy is community property. Each spouse has a one-half interest in community property policy proceeds notwithstanding a pay on death beneficiary designation to someone who is not a spouse. Additionally, if the community property policy has a saving component, that benefit is characterized proportionally by the funds that contributed to the saved amount. The tracing principle, in other words, applies.

Is a life insurance policy purchased with community property funds and titled in one spouse's name alone a transmutation of the policy itself? A long history of cases has dealt with this exact issue in the context of real estate (Chapter 2). But in the recent case of *Valli*, the question arises in the far more intangible context of contractual benefits.

MARRIAGE OF VALLI
58 Cal.4th 1396, 171 Cal.Rptr.3d 454, 324 P.3d 274 (2014)

KENNARD, J.

During a marriage the husband used community property funds to purchase an insurance policy on his life, naming his wife as the policy's only owner and beneficiary. Upon dissolution of the marriage, is the life insurance policy community property or the wife's separate property? We conclude that, unless the statutory transmutation requirements have been met, the life insurance policy is community property. Because the Court of Appeal reached a different conclusion, we reverse that court's judgment.

I

After a 20-year marriage, Frankie Valli (husband) and Randy Valli (wife) separated in September 2004. Their three children were minors at the time of separation but have since become adults. Before the separation, in March 2003, husband used community property funds from a joint bank account to buy a $3.75 million insurance policy on his life, naming wife as the sole owner [of the insurance policy] and beneficiary [of the life insurance proceeds]. Until the parties separated, the policy premiums were likewise paid with community property funds from a joint bank account.

At the marital dissolution proceeding, wife testified that she and husband, while he was in the hospital for "heart problems," had talked about buying a life insurance policy. Wife said that husband and their business manager, Barry Siegel, told her that they would make her the policy's owner. Husband testified that he "put everything in [wife's] name, figuring she would take care and give to the kids what they might have coming" and that he had no plans to separate from wife when he bought the policy.

The trial court ruled that the insurance policy was community property because it was acquired during marriage with community funds. The court awarded the policy to husband and ordered him to buy out wife's interest in the policy by paying her $182,500, representing one-half of the policy's cash value at the time of trial. The Court of Appeal reversed, holding that the insurance policy was wife's separate property.

II

In a marital dissolution proceeding, a court's characterization of the parties' property—as community property or separate property—determines the division of the property between the spouses. * * * Property that a spouse acquired before the marriage is that spouse's separate property. (Fam.Code, § 770, subd. (a) (1).) Property that a spouse acquired during the marriage is community property (*id.*, § 760) unless it is (1) traceable to a separate property source (*In re Marriage of Lucas* (1980) 27 Cal.3d 808, 815, 166 Cal.Rptr. 853, 614 P.2d 285; *In re Marriage of Mix* (1975) 14 Cal.3d 604, 610, 612, 122 Cal.Rptr. 79, 536 P.2d 479), (2) acquired by gift or bequest (Fam.Code, § 770, subd. (a)(2)), or (3) earned or accumulated while the spouses are living separate and apart (*id.*, § 771, subd. (a)). A spouse's claim that property acquired during a marriage is separate property must be proven by a preponderance of the evidence. (*In re Marriage of Ettefagh* (2007) 150 Cal.App.4th 1578, 1591, 59 Cal.Rptr.3d 419. * * *)

Here, as mentioned earlier, husband during the marriage took out a $3.75 million insurance policy on his life, designating wife as the policy's sole owner and beneficiary. The parties do not dispute that the policy was purchased with community property funds from a joint bank account. What they do dispute is the policy's characterization. Husband argues that the policy is community property because it was purchased during the marriage with community funds. (See *Tyre v. Aetna Life Ins. Co.* (1960) 54 Cal.2d 399, 402, 6 Cal.Rptr. 13, 353 P.2d 725 ["A policy of insurance on the husband's life is community property when the premiums have been paid with community funds."]; *Grimm v. Grimm* (1945) 26 Cal.2d 173, 175, 157 P.2d 841 [same].) Wife argues that the policy is her separate property because husband arranged for the policy to be put solely in her name, thereby changing the policy's character from community property to separate property.

Married persons may, through a transfer or an agreement, transmute—that is, change—the character of property from community to separate or from separate to community. (Fam.Code, § 850.) A transmutation of property, however, "is not valid unless made in writing by an express declaration that is made, joined in, consented to, or accepted by the spouse whose interest in the property is adversely affected." (*Id.,* § 852, subd. (a).) To satisfy the requirement of an "express declaration," a writing signed by the adversely affected spouse must expressly state that the character or ownership of the property at issue is being changed. (*Estate of MacDonald* (1990) 51 Cal.3d 262, 272, 272 Cal.Rptr. 153, 794 P.2d 911.) The "express declaration" requirement "does not apply to a gift between the spouses of clothing, wearing apparel, jewelry, or other tangible articles of a personal nature that is used solely or principally by the spouse to whom the gift is made and *that is not substantial in value taking into account the circumstances of the marriage.*" (Fam.Code, § 852, subd. (c), italics added.)

Here, husband contends that because the express written declaration requirement was not satisfied, his act of placing the life insurance policy in wife's name did not transmute the policy, which was purchased during the marriage with community funds, into a separate property asset of wife. Wife argues that the transmutation requirements apply only to transactions between spouses, and not to one spouse's acquisition of property from a third party. Here, she argues, the only transaction was between husband and the insurance company issuing the policy. Because there was *no interspousal transaction,* in her view the transmutation requirements do not apply.

The Legislature adopted the statutory transmutation requirements in 1984 upon a recommendation of the California Law Revision Commission. (*Estate of MacDonald, supra,* 51 Cal.3d at p. 268, 272 Cal.Rptr. 153, 794 P.2d 911.) In its report to the Legislature, the commission observed that under then existing law it was " 'quite easy for spouses to transmute both real and personal property' " because a transmutation could be proved by evidence of an oral agreement between the spouses or by " 'implications from the conduct of the spouses.' " (*Id.* at p. 269, 272 Cal.Rptr. 153, 794 P.2d 911.) This " 'rule of easy transmutation * * * generated extensive litigation in dissolution proceedings' " where it encouraged spouses " 'to transform a passing comment into an 'agreement' or even to commit perjury by manufacturing an oral or implied transmutation.' " (*Ibid.*) As this court has concluded, therefore, in adopting the statutory transmutation requirements the Legislature intended "to remedy problems which arose when courts found transmutations on the basis of evidence the Legislature considered unreliable." (*Ibid.*; accord, *In re Marriage of Benson, supra,* 36 Cal.4th at p. 1106, 32 Cal.Rptr.3d 471, 116 P.3d 1152 [the transmutation statute "blocks efforts to transmute marital property based on evidence—oral, behavioral, or documentary—that is easily manipulated and unreliable"].)

The distinction that wife here urges us to draw between interspousal property transactions (which are subject to the transmutation statutes) and property acquisitions from third parties (which would not be subject to those statutes even when it has the claimed effect of changing community property funds to a separate property asset or vice versa) bears no relation to these legislative concerns, and it produces arbitrary and irrational results that the Legislature could not have intended. A few hypothetical examples illustrate this point.

Suppose a husband, shopping at a jewelry store, uses community funds to buy a particularly expensive diamond necklace that is "substantial in value taking into account the circumstances of the marriage" (Fam.Code, § 852, subd. (c)), intending to give it to his wife a few days later as a birthday present. Because of the particular necklace's value in comparison to the particular couple's financial situation, the gift exception does not apply. Under the analysis urged here by wife, the transmutation statutes would not apply to the necklace *purchase* because it was a third-party transaction with the jewelry store. But because the husband used community funds to buy the necklace and did not immediately transfer title or possession to the wife, the purchase itself did not cause any transmutation, and the necklace would be community property at least until the wife's birthday. On that day, the husband's act of giving the necklace to the wife, together with the wife's act of accepting the husband's gift, would be an interspousal transaction to which the transmutation requirements would apply even under the analysis urged here by wife. Absent an express written declaration, therefore, the necklace would remain community property even after the wife received it as a birthday gift from the husband.

Next, suppose that instead of buying the necklace for his wife before her birthday, the husband, on his wife's birthday, promises to buy a diamond necklace of her choice. They go to a jewelry store, the wife selects a particular necklace that is "substantial in value taking into account the circumstances of the marriage" (Fam.Code, § 852, subd. (c)), the husband pays for it with community funds, and they leave the store with the wife wearing the new jewelry. In this scenario, there would appear to be a single transaction, the jewelry store purchase. Under the analysis urged here by wife, the transmutation statutes would not apply to that single transaction because it was a purchase from a third party, and thus no "express declaration" would be required to transmute the community property funds to the wife's separate property asset.

For purposes of the transmutation statutes, it is difficult to conceive any justification for treating these two hypothetical scenarios differently. Under either scenario, the husband could present evidence, in a later dissolution proceeding, that he and the wife had discussed the advantages of diamonds as an investment, that they had orally agreed the necklace would eventually be passed on to their daughter, and that it was therefore understood between them that although this very expensive necklace would be the wife's to wear on special occasions, it would remain a community asset. To rebut the husband's evidence, the wife could deny having any conversation with the husband about investing in diamonds or purchasing jewelry as a family legacy, and she could present evidence of a contrary understanding that the necklace was to be hers alone. If the transmutation statutes did not apply, and in the absence of a writing expressly memorializing the parties' understanding and intent, the trial court in the dissolution proceeding would be obliged to base its decision regarding the necklace's character as community or separate property on a difficult assessment of the spouses' credibility as witnesses. (See, e.g., *In re Marriage of Steinberger* (2001) 91 Cal.App.4th 1449, 1456, 111 Cal.Rptr.2d 521.) Putting the trial court in such a position is what the transmutation statutes were enacted to prevent.

One could argue, perhaps, that the second hypothetical scenario, like the first, can and should be viewed as two transactions—a purchase from a third party *and* an interspousal giving of a gift—that are legally distinguishable even though they occurred simultaneously. Adopting that approach, one would conclude that the interspousal gift transaction was subject to the transmutation statutes in the second scenario just as in the first. But if the second jewelry gift scenario can be parsed into two simultaneous but legally separable transactions, then so here could husband's purchase of the life insurance policy, with title taken in wife's name. If, as wife here claims, the effect of the policy purchase with money from a joint bank account was to convert community property funds into her separate property asset, then the purchase necessarily involved a gift from husband to wife because wife has never maintained that she gave husband anything in exchange for his community interest in the purchase money. If the policy was a gift by husband to wife, then the giving and receiving of that gift was an interspousal transaction to which the transmutation statutes apply. (Cf. *Burkle v. Burkle* (2006) 141 Cal.App.4th 1029, 1036, fn. 5, 46 Cal.Rptr.3d 562 [the elements of a gift include "'delivery, either actual or symbolical'" and "'acceptance, actual or imputed'"].)

This point can be further illustrated by another hypothetical. Suppose in this case husband had initially taken title to the insurance policy jointly in his and wife's names, and then on a later date, after receiving estate planning advice and discussing the matter with wife, he had instructed the insurer to transfer the title to wife's name alone. In that situation, where wife acquired sole title to the policy sometime after the policy's purchase, it appears that wife would concede the transmutation statutes' applicability to any claim by her, in a marital dissolution proceeding, that the change in title changed the character of the policy from community to separate property. Therefore, under the analysis urged here by wife, whether the transmutation statutes apply to the insurance policy depends upon the entirely fortuitous circumstance of when she acquired sole title to the insurance policy, whether during the purchase or after the purchase of the policy. We are unwilling to conclude the Legislature intended application of the transmutation statutes to turn on such fortuitous distinctions.

We recognize that some court decisions have stated that a transmutation requires an interspousal transaction and that one spouse's acquisition of an asset from a third party is therefore exempt from the statutory transmutation restrictions. Those decisions are unpersuasive, however.

The notion that third-party transactions cannot be transmutations may be traced to the Court of Appeal's 1995 decision in *In re Marriage of Haines, supra,* 33 Cal.App.4th 277, 39 Cal.Rptr.2d 673. There, the Court of Appeal said that a transmutation is "an interspousal transaction or agreement which works a change in the character of the property." (*Id.* at p. 293, 39 Cal.Rptr.2d 673.) Referring to the wife's signing of a quitclaim deed conveying the family residence to the husband during the marriage, the court concluded that this was a transmutation subject to the statutory express declaration requirement. (*Ibid.*) The court did not consider whether any other transaction was a transmutation, and in particular it did not consider whether one spouse's purchase of property from a third party could be a transmutation.

The statement that a transmutation is "an interspousal transaction or agreement" (*In re Marriage of Haines, supra,* 33 Cal.App.4th at p. 293, 39

Cal.Rptr.2d 673) was later repeated in the Court of Appeal decisions in *In re Marriage of Campbell* (1999) 74 Cal.App.4th 1058, 1062, 88 Cal.Rptr.2d 580 and *In re Marriage of Cross* (2001) 94 Cal.App.4th 1143, 1147, 114 Cal.Rptr.2d 839 (*Cross*). But neither decision exempted a third-party transaction from the transmutation requirements on the basis that it was not "interspousal." Indeed, *Cross* said that the transmutation statutes address situations such as "where a wife buys a car for her husband with community property funds" (*Cross,* at pp. 1147–1148, 114 Cal.Rptr.2d 839), a typical third-party transaction. (See also *In re Marriage of Buie & Neighbors* (2009) 179 Cal.App.4th 1170, 1173–1175, 102 Cal.Rptr.3d 387 [applying transmutation statutes to a husband's purchase of a car for himself using the wife's separate funds].) In 2005, this court likewise stated that a transmutation is an "interspousal transaction" (*In re Marriage of Benson, supra,* 36 Cal.4th 1096, 1100, 32 Cal.Rptr.3d 471, 116 P.3d 1152), but we did not consider whether this definition excludes spousal purchases during the marriage from third parties with community funds.

The first decision to hold that a spousal purchase from a third party during a marriage was not subject to the statutory transmutation requirements was *In re Summers* (9th Cir.2003) 332 F.3d 1240, which was a bankruptcy proceeding rather than a marital dissolution proceeding. There, the federal appellate court was attempting to construe and apply California law "to determine whether the requirements of California's transmutation statute * * * must be met when realty is transferred from a third party to spouses as joint tenants." (*In re Summers,* at p. 1242.) Relying on the statement by the California Court of Appeal in *Cross* that a transmutation is an " 'interspousal transaction or agreement' " (*Cross, supra,* 94 Cal.App.4th at p. 1147, 114 Cal.Rptr.2d 839), the federal court concluded "that the transmutation requisites had no relevance to the conveyance in this case." (*In re Summers,* at p. 1245.)

The year 2008 saw the first decision by a California state appellate court exempting from the transmutation requirements a spousal purchase from a third party: *In re Marriage of Brooks & Robinson* (2008) 169 Cal.App.4th 176, 86 Cal.Rptr.3d 624. In that marital dissolution proceeding, the husband and the wife disputed ownership of residential property they had purchased during the marriage, taking title solely in the wife's name. (*Id.* at pp. 179–180, 86 Cal.Rptr.3d 624.) On appeal, the husband argued, among other things, that the purchase of the property in the wife's name alone was an attempted transmutation that was invalid because it did not comply with the statutory transmutation requirements. (*Id.* at p. 191, 86 Cal.Rptr.3d 624.) Rejecting the husband's argument, the Court of Appeal stated that there were "no facts suggesting a transmutation, valid or otherwise" because the property "was acquired in [the wife's] name in a transaction with a third person, not through an interspousal transaction." (*Ibid.*)

As mentioned earlier, these last two decisions (*In re Summers, supra,* 332 F.3d 1240; *In re Marriage of Brooks & Robinson, supra,* 169 Cal.App.4th 176, 86 Cal.Rptr.3d 624) are not persuasive insofar as they purport to exempt from the transmutation requirements purchases made by one or both spouses from a third party during the marriage. Neither decision attempts to reconcile such an exemption with the legislative purposes in enacting those requirements, which was to reduce excessive litigation, introduction of unreliable evidence, and incentives for perjury in marital dissolution proceedings involving disputes regarding the characterization of property. Nor does either decision attempt to find a basis for the purported exemption in the language of the applicable transmutation statutes. Also, these decisions are inconsistent with three Court of Appeal decisions stating or holding that the transmutation requirements apply to one spouse's purchases from a third party during the marriage. (*In re Marriage of Buie & Neighbors, supra,* 179 Cal.App.4th at pp. 1173–1175, 102 Cal.Rptr.3d 387; *Cross, supra,* 94 Cal.App.4th at pp. 1147–1148, 114 Cal.Rptr.2d 839; *In Re Marriage of Steinberger, supra,* 91 Cal.App.4th at pp. 1463–1466, 111 Cal.Rptr.2d 521.)

Our examination of the statutory language leads us to reject the purported exemption for spousal purchases from third parties. As we have said (*ante,* 171 Cal.Rptr.3d at p. 457, 324 P.3d at p. 276), the transmutation statutes provide an express exemption for gifts of relatively inexpensive personal items. (Fam.Code, § 852, subd. (c).) Because spouses most often use community funds to purchase such gifts for each other, the statutory exemption necessarily implies that gifts not qualifying for the exemption (because they are "substantial in value" or because they are not items "of a personal nature") *are* transmutations subject to the express declaration requirement, notwithstanding that a great many, if not most, involve purchases from third parties.

As mentioned, the Court of Appeal here concluded that the transmutation statutes were "not relevant to this case" because the disputed life insurance policy "was acquired from a third party and not through an interspousal transaction." After stating that conclusion, which we have determined to be erroneous, the court added: "Moreover, [wife] did not contend in the trial court, and does not contend on appeal, that the policy is her separate property through transmutation. Instead, [wife] contends that the policy is her separate property by operation of the form of title presumption." Referring to Evidence Code section 662, which states that "[t]he owner of the legal title to property is presumed to be the owner of the full beneficial title," the Court of Appeal here asserted that "because the form of title presumption applies * * * a transmutation theory is not involved."

This reasoning by the Court of Appeal, we also conclude, is erroneous. We need not and do not decide here whether Evidence Code section 662's form of title presumption ever applies in marital dissolution proceedings. Assuming for the sake of argument that the title presumption may sometimes apply, it does not apply when it conflicts with the transmutation statutes. (See *In re Marriage of Barneson* (1999) 69 Cal.App.4th 583, 593, 81 Cal.Rptr.2d 726.)

For the reasons we have given, the transmutation requirement of an express written declaration applies to wife's claim [in this proceeding] that the life insurance policy husband purchased during the marriage with community funds is her separate property. Wife does not contend that she presented evidence at trial sufficient to satisfy the express declaration requirement, nor does our examination of the record disclose such evidence. Husband never expressly declared in writing that he gave up his community interest in the policy bought with community funds. Accordingly, we agree with the trial court's characterization of the insurance policy as community property.

Because it concluded that the trial court had erred in characterizing the policy as community property, the Court of Appeal did not reach wife's contentions "that the trial court erred in awarding ownership solely to [husband] at the policy's cash value and that it abused its discretion in failing to maintain [wife] as a beneficiary on the policy as spousal support." The Court of Appeal will address those contentions by wife on remand.

DISPOSITION

The Court of Appeal's judgment is reversed and the matter is remanded to that court for further proceedings consistent with CONCURRING OPINION BY CHIN, J.

Concurring Opinion by CHIN, J.

I agree with the majority opinion, which I have signed. I write separately to discuss a threshold question that has been the primary focus of the briefs of the parties and amici curiae: What role, if any, does a common law rule codified in Evidence Code section 662 (section 662) have in determining, in an action between the spouses, whether property acquired during a marriage is community or separate?

Family Code section 760 provides: "Except as otherwise provided by statute, all property, real or personal, wherever situated, acquired by a married person during the marriage while domiciled in this state is community property." Family Code section 802 refers to the "presumption that property acquired during marriage is community property." In combination, these statutes provide a presumption that property acquired during the marriage is community property. (*In re Marriage of Benson* (2005) 36 Cal.4th 1096, 1103, 32 Cal.Rptr.3d 471, 116 P.3d 1152.) (I will sometimes refer to this presumption as the section 760 presumption.) It appears this presumption can be overcome by a preponderance of the evidence. (*In re Marriage of Ettefagh* (2007) 150 Cal.App.4th 1578, 59 Cal.Rptr.3d 419.)

Although the section 760 presumption is rebuttable, not just any evidence can overcome the presumption, but only evidence showing that another statute makes the property something other than community property. "By its own terms, the definition of community property in section 760 applies '[e]xcept as otherwise provided by statute.' It therefore exempts property defined as separate under other provisions. (E.g., [Fam.Code,] §§ 770 [property acquired by gift or inheritance], 771 [earnings and accumulations while living separate and apart].)" (*In re Marriage of Benson, supra,* 36 Cal.4th at p. 1103, 32 Cal.Rptr.3d 471, 116 P.3d 1152.) Thus, the general rule is that property acquired during marriage is community unless the preponderance of the evidence establishes that a specifically enumerated statutory exemption applies to make it something else.

As applied here, this presumption means that the life insurance policy is presumed to be community property, but that wife can overcome that presumption if she can show, by a preponderance of the evidence, that some other statutory provision makes it her separate property. There is, or should be, nothing particularly complex or difficult about this rule.

But wife, in arguing that the policy is her separate property, and the Court of Appeal, in so concluding, rely heavily on a different presumption found in the Evidence Code. Section 662 provides: "The owner of the legal title to property is presumed to be the owner of the full beneficial title. This presumption may be rebutted only by clear and convincing proof." Because legal title in the policy was in wife's name, wife argues, and the Court of Appeal found, the policy is presumed to be her separate property, a presumption rebuttable only by clear and convincing evidence.

Obviously, both presumptions cannot be given effect. The life insurance policy cannot both be presumed to be community property (because acquired during the marriage) and to be wife's separate property (because placed in her name). One statutory presumption must yield to the other.

In my view, as in the view of all amici curiae to appear in this case—law professors and attorneys specializing in the field—the section 760 presumption controls in characterizing property acquired during the marriage in an action between the spouses. Section 662 plays no role in such an action. The detailed community property statutes found in the Family Code, including section 760, are self-contained and are not affected by a statute found in the Evidence Code. I explain why.

California is, and always has been, a community property state. "The community property system originated in continental Europe, came to Mexico from Spain, and became California law through the treaty of 1848."

* * * "From the inception of its statehood, California has retained the community property law that predated its admission to the Union and consistently has provided as a general rule that property acquired by spouses during marriage, including earnings, is community property." (*In re Marriage of Bonds* (2000) 24 Cal.4th 1, 12, 99 Cal.Rptr.2d 252, 5 P.3d 815.) "The general theory is that the husband and wife form a sort of partnership, and that property acquired during the marriage by the labor or skill of either belongs to both." * * *

The presumption, now codified in the Family Code, that property acquired during the marriage is community, is perhaps the most fundamental principle of California's community property law. " 'This presumption is fundamental in the community property system and is an integral part of the community property law not only of this state but of other states and countries where the system is in operation.' " (11 Witkin, Summary of Cal. Law, *supra,* Community Property, § 15, p. 542, quoting *Wilson v. Wilson* (1946) 76 Cal.App.2d 119, 126, 172 P.2d 568.)

Section 662 may not nullify this fundamental presumption whenever, as is often the case, the contested property is in the name of one of the spouses. I agree with the amici curiae that, as the brief of the Northern California chapter of the American Academy of Matrimonial Lawyers and the Association of Certified Family Law Specialists puts it, "section 662 has no place in the characterization of property in actions between spouses." As that brief further states, applying section 662 to disputes between spouses "would subvert basic tenets of California family law."

* * * The statutes governing California's community property law are found in the Family Code; a statute outside of the community property law, such as Evidence Code section 662, cannot nullify those statutes. This circumstance was recognized when section 662 was enacted. (Stats.1965, ch. 299, § 2, p. 1297.) The Law Revision Commission comment to that section states that it "codifies a common law presumption recognized in the California cases." (Cal. Law Revision Com. com., 29B pt. 2 West's Ann. Evid.Code (1995 ed.) foll. § 662, p. 210.) But California's community property law has no common law roots. It derives from the European continent, not England. In its comment, the Law Revision Commission cited *Olson v. Olson* (1935) 4 Cal.2d 434, 49 P.2d 827. (See *People v. Semaan* (2007) 42 Cal.4th 79, 88, 64 Cal.Rptr.3d 1, 163 P.3d 949 [recognizing "that § 662 codifies the rule of *Olson v. Olson*"].) But that case indicates the common law presumption does not apply in the marital context: "The deed of gift, a written instrument, signed and acknowledged by appellant, *and unimpaired by any presumption of undue influence arising out of a marital relation between the parties* [the parties were not married at the critical time], was entitled to the full credit given to it by the trial court * * * ." (*Olson v. Olson,* at p. 438, 49 P.2d 827, italics added.) Neither the common law rule nor section 662, which codified that rule, ever applied to characterizing property acquired during marriage in actions between the spouses.

Section 662's purpose is to promote the public policy in favor of "the stability of titles to property" (Evid.Code, § 605; see *In re Marriage of Haines* (1995) 33 Cal.App.4th 277, 294, 39 Cal.Rptr.2d 673 (*Haines*).) That policy is largely irrelevant to characterizing property acquired during the marriage in an action between the spouses. *Haines* is instructive. The *Haines* court held that section 662 "must yield to" another presumption within California's community property law—"the presumption arising from the requirement that a husband and wife occupy a confidential relationship in their transactions with each other." (*Haines,* at p. 283, 39 Cal.Rptr.2d 673; see Fam.Code, § 721.)

Haines explained that section 662's "presumption is based on promoting the public 'policy * * * in favor of the stability of titles to property.' (See [Evid.Code,] § 605.) 'Allegations * * * that legal title does not represent beneficial ownership have * * * been historically disfavored because society and the courts have a reluctance to tamper with duly executed instruments and documents of legal title.' [Citation.] [¶] Section 662 is concerned primarily with the stability of titles, which obviously is an important legal concept that protects parties to a real property transaction, as well as creditors. Here, however, our focus is on characterization of marital property as effected by a transmutation by quitclaim deed. The issue is how property should be divided between spouses upon dissolution. This case does not involve third parties nor does it place at risk the rights of a creditor. * * * Thus, concerns of stability of title are lessened in characterization problems arising from transmutations that do not involve third parties or the rights of creditors." (*Haines, supra,* 33 Cal.App.4th at pp. 294–295, 39 Cal.Rptr.2d 673, fn. omitted.)

The presumption of undue influence exists to protect married persons. (*Haines, supra,* 33 Cal.App.4th at p. 301, 39 Cal.Rptr.2d 673.) "[A]pplication of section 662 in such situations can significantly weaken protections the Legislature intended to provide for spouses who are taken advantage of in interspousal transactions. This cannot be in keeping with the intent of the Legislature. * * * Application of section 662 would * * * in effect * * * abrogate the protections afforded to married persons under" what is now Family Code section 721, subdivision (b). (*Haines,* at p. 301, 39 Cal.Rptr.2d 673.) Accordingly, the *Haines* court "conclude[d] that application of section 662 is improper when it is in conflict with the presumption of undue influence. * * * Any other result would abrogate the protections afforded to married persons and denigrate the public policy of the state that seeks to promote and protect the vital institution of marriage." * * *

What *Haines* said about the presumption regarding undue influence applies just as much, if not more so, to the more fundamental presumption that property acquired during the marriage is community. Section 662 may not abrogate the more fundamental presumption just as it may not abrogate the less fundamental presumption. Much property acquired during marriage is in the name of one of the spouses, such as salaries, stock options, retirement benefits, and the like. Applying section 662 to all such property—and concluding that it is separate property unless shown to be otherwise by clear and convincing evidence—would largely nullify the presumption that property acquired during marriage is community.

In concluding that section 662 applies, the Court of Appeal relied heavily on two cases: *In re Marriage of Lucas* (1980) 27 Cal.3d 808, 166 Cal.Rptr. 853, 614 P.2d 285 (*Lucas*) and *In re Marriage of Brooks & Robinson* (2008) 169 Cal.App.4th 176, 86 Cal.Rptr.3d 624 (*Brooks*). Neither case supports the conclusion.

In *Lucas,* this court was concerned primarily with deciding "the proper method of determining separate and community property interests in a single family dwelling acquired during the marriage with both separate property and community property funds." (*Lucas, supra,* 27 Cal.3d at p. 811, 166 Cal.Rptr. 853, 614 P.2d 285.) Most of the opinion concerns the characterization of a house in which title was in the form of joint tenancy. Although it discusses presumptions at length, *Lucas* never cites section 662 even though that section had been enacted long before the opinion. Rather, it discusses two statutory presumptions, both of which used to be found in Civil Code former section 5110 and are now found in two separate sections of the Family Code. (Fam.Code, §§ 760, 2581.) One is the familiar presumption that property acquired during marriage is community property. (*Id.,* § 760.) The other is a presumption, found in a statute within the community property law and fully consistent with the general presumption, that specifically governs real property designated as a joint tenancy. (*Lucas,* at p. 814, 166 Cal.Rptr. 853, 614 P.2d 285.) As quoted in *Lucas,* that statute provided: " 'When a single-family residence of a husband and wife is acquired by them during marriage as joint tenants, for the purpose of the division of such property upon dissolution of marriage or legal separation only, the presumption is that such single-family residence is the community property of the husband and wife.' " (*Id.* at p. 814, fn. 2, 166 Cal.Rptr. 853, 614 P.2d 285, quoting Civ. Code, former § 5110 [see now California Family Code § 2581].) Both of these presumptions favor a finding of community property, and thus they are compatible.

Significantly, the statutory presumption regarding property in the form of joint tenancy applies "[f]or the purpose of division of property on dissolution of marriage." (Fam.Code, § 2581; see Civ. Code, former § 5110.) This language suggests that rules that apply to an action between the spouses to characterize property acquired during the marriage do not necessarily apply to a dispute between a spouse and a third party.

Thus, the form-of-title presumption the *Lucas* court discussed is a specific statutory presumption found within California's community property law, not the more general presumption found in section 662. That this is so is made clear later in the opinion when the court stated that certain "evidence and findings are insufficient to rebut the presumption arising from title *set forth in Civil Code section 5110* [i.e., current Fam.Code, § 2581]." (*Lucas, supra,* 27 Cal.3d at p. 815, 166 Cal.Rptr. 853, 614 P.2d 285, italics added.) *Lucas* does not address section 662's role in an action between the spouses.

Brooks also did not present this question. At the appellate level, the dispute in *Brooks, supra,* 169 Cal.App.4th 176, 86 Cal.Rptr.3d 624, did not involve an action between the spouses. Rather, on appeal, the sole dispute was between a *third party,* to whom the wife had sold certain real property, and the husband, who claimed an interest in the property and sought to set aside the sale. The wife did not even appear in the appeal. The Court of Appeal used section 662 to help resolve the dispute in favor of the third party, whom the trial court found to be a bona fide purchaser who had purchased the property without knowing of any community property claim the husband might have had. The Court of Appeal noted that the trial "court did not expressly determine whether the Property was a community property asset." (*Brooks,* at pp. 182–183, 86 Cal.Rptr.3d 624.) Rather, the trial court had merely held that the third party was a bona fide purchaser and, as such, " 'takes it[s] title free of any unknown community property claim [the husband] may have with respect to the Property.' " (*Id.* at p. 183, 86 Cal.Rptr.3d 624.) The Court of Appeal agreed with this conclusion. It emphasized section 662's purpose of promoting the stability of titles to property. (*Id.* at p. 185, 86 Cal.Rptr.3d 624.) Unlike in the case of an action between the spouses, this policy *does* play a role in a dispute between a spouse and an innocent third-party purchaser.

The *Brooks* court stressed that the appeal "does not involve a division of the community estate between [husband and wife]. Whether [the wife] might be obligated to reimburse [the husband] for his contributions to the Property was not before the trial court and is not an issue on appeal." (*Brooks, supra,* 169 Cal.App.4th at p. 188, 86 Cal.Rptr.3d 624.) * * *

In short, the statutes in the Family Code governing community property, including the section 760 presumption, are sufficient unto themselves. Evidence Code section 662's common law presumption does not nullify the community property statutes. *All* property acquired during the marriage is presumed to be community property. Evidence that certain property is in the name of one spouse might, depending on the circumstances, be relevant to help overcome the presumption if and only if it demonstrates that one of the statutory exemptions to the presumption applies. But that evidence does not itself reverse the presumption. Future courts resolving disputes over how to characterize property acquired during the marriage in an action between the spouses should apply the community property statutes found in the Family Code and not section 662.

WE CONCUR: CORRIGAN, and LIU, JJ.

NOTES

1. *The Civil Code presumption of title is inapplicable in dissolution proceedings.* The Family Code sets forth the default terms of the marriage contract; not the Civil Code. Justice Chen's concurrence explains why.

2. *A valid transmutation is made by express declaration.* California Family Code Section 852 appears to put an end to implied-in-fact transmutation agreements. Once valid, the transmutation occurs as of the date that the written express declaration is made, joined in, consented to, or accepted by the spouse whose interest in the property is adversely affected.

3. *The phrase "express declaration" is defined by case law. Estate of MacDonald*, 51 Cal.3d 262, 272, 272 Cal.Rptr. 153, 794 P.2d 911 (1990) defines the phrase as the present intent to change the character of property. "I hereby transmute" is present tense. "I will transmute," or "I plan to transmute," or "I'd like to someday transmute" are all future intent expressions that have no legal effect on the character of property. In *MacDonald*, it was decided that a nonprobate beneficiary consent form, without more, is not a transmutation.

So for example, assume that Alpha and Zed, who are married to each other, own a life insurance policy insuring Alpha's life. Alpha names Zed as Alpha's beneficiary—this type of beneficial designation is called a *spousal* pay on death beneficiary designation. At Alpha's death, Zed would own one-half of the policy proceeds, plus Zed would succeed to Alpha's one-half of the policy proceeds, leaving Zed with 100% of the policy proceeds.

But assume that Alpha decides to benefit Beta, a child from a previous marriage, instead of Zed. Alpha removes Zed's name as the policy beneficiary. Subsequently, Alpha names Beta—this type of beneficial designation is called a *nonspousal* designation, and as such it requires spouse Zed's consent.

By asking Zed to sign the consent form, Alpha is not asking Zed to give away Zed's one-half community property interest in the policy proceeds. Rather the consent form merely shows that Zed understood (on a certain date) that Alpha was naming Beta as the beneficiary of Alpha's one-half interest in the policy proceeds. The idea behind a consent form is to reduce the likelihood of litigation between Zed and Beta over the insurance proceeds in the event of Alpha's demise. The point here is that a consent form without an express declaration cannot effect a valid transmutation.

In order to effect a valid transmutation of Zed's one-half of the policy (and eventually the policy proceeds) from community property to Alpha's separate property, Zed (not Alpha) must follow the statutory formalities set out at Family Code Section 852(a). Zed's express declaration (*I, Zed, give to Alpha my one-half community property interest in the life insurance proceeds as Alpha's separate property*) can be included in the four corners of the consent form, thereby effecting a valid transmutation of Zed's one-half of the policy proceeds (assuming of course that it is voluntary). In such a case, a transmutation would make Beta the beneficiary of 100% of the insurance proceeds upon Alpha's death.

Some confusion has arisen in cases where the parties effect a transmutation as part of an estate planning process. In part the confusion stems from not underscoring for the client the difference between an estate plan and a transmutation. An estate plan is revocable; a valid transmutation is irrevocable. Nevertheless, the following question has come before the courts more than a few times: if a transmutation is part of a revocable estate plan, and the parties revoke the estate plan, is the transmutation also revoked? The courts have answered no. A transmutation is valid once the formalities are met. Therefore, once a valid transmutation takes effect there are only two ways to reverse it. The first method requires a subsequent (second) transmutation to undo the first transmutation. The second method requires a court order to avoid the transmutation on the ground that the express declaration was the product of coercion. (Chapter 6).

In *Marriage of Starkman,* 129 Cal.App.4th 659, 28 Cal.Rptr.3d 639 (2d Dist. 2005) the court held that a vague provision in a revocable community property trust agreement did not meet the express declaration requirement. The community property trust was part of a revocable estate plan that called for husband Christopher Starkman (heir to the U.P.S. fortune) to fund the trust with his separate property shares of U.P.S. stock. Christopher transferred the shares of stock into the community property trust; and the community enjoyed full use of the stock dividends. At dissolution, Christopher and spouse Christine revoked the trust. Christopher requested return of his shares of stock. Christine argued that the U.P.S. shares had been transmuted by the trust document as well as by their placement into the trust. The court analyzed the trust agreement. It found that the vague term in the trust was a vacuum cleaner clause (meaning a clause that sucks any and all property into the trust), and as such it did not constitute an express declaration under California Family Code Section 852(a). The effect of the court's ruling was that the disputed U.P.S. shares of stock remained Christopher's separate property. Moreover, because the vacuum cleaner clause was not an express declaration as to the stock dividends, any dividends that had been generated by Christopher's separate property stock and any purchases that had been made with those dividends were also Christopher's separate property.

The court stressed that one strong policy underlies California Family Code Section 852(a): *a person cannot fall into a transmutation by accident.* The court of appeal also noted that the purpose of the Starkman community property trust was not to transmute property; it was to avoid probate as to the assets in the trust (in the event that the marriage had ended by death rather than by dissolution).

Some family law practitioners warned that *Starkman* could present serious issues for estate planning attorneys insofar as it would be necessary for each asset intended to be transmuted to be (first) transmuted in a document extrinsic to the trust and then (second) transferred into the trust. Other practitioners expressed the contrary view that while two sets of documents might be necessary to effect a transmutation, it is not uncommon for the legislature to require documents that are extrinsic to trust or account documents. The rationale is to require that the party who stands to be adversely affected by a transmutation take as clear action as is possible to expressly (in writing) declare (make a clear and present tense statement) their intent to effect a transmutation of the identified asset(s). Vague statements cannot and should not be permitted to transmute property. Either way, the stakes can be relatively high if one considers that there are cases for which a failure to effectuate a valid transmutation could give rise to significant income tax liability for a surviving spouse on the death of the other spouse (Chapter 9). *See e.g.*, CALIFORNIA LAW MONTHLY (Sept. 2005).

Starkman was a dissolution case. Would the same result have obtained if the husband had died and the wife had sought to establish the community character of the trust assets?

In *Marriage of Holtemann*, 166 Cal. App.4th 1166, 83 Cal.Rptr.3d 385 (2d Dist. 2008) a similar issue arose on a smaller net worth scale. Husband Frank executed a revocable estate plan that included a very clear transmutation of his entire separate property estate to community property. Frank and wife Barbara sought dissolution just a few years later. At that time Frank revoked his estate plan thinking that the transmutation also would be automatically revoked. In the dissolution process, Barbara sought her one-half community property share of the disputed property. She based her claim of right on the transmutation agreement that Frank voluntarily signed. Frank contested the characterization of "his" property as "their" community property. The court found that the transmutation document was proof of Frank's express declaration, as signed by the adversely affected spouse, Frank. It met the formality requirements of California Family Code Section 852(a) and 721(b). The transmutation took effect on the date that Frank signed the express declaration document.

Holtemann is reminder that a transmutation can occur on an asset by asset basis or on an estate wide basis. In *Holtemann*, Frank transmuted everything he owned with one fell swoop of a signature to a quarter-page long document that made its effect clear.

4.   *Even if transmutation formalities are met, the transmutation must be voluntary.* The full analysis for a transmutation considers two issues, formalities and voluntariness. *Marriage of Lico*, 2012 WL 1560450 (1st Dist.), an unpublished opinion, explains why. Even if California Family Code Section 852(a) formalities are met, it is also necessary to analyze the transmutation

under California Family Code 721(b), which prohibits a spouse from taking "any unfair advantage" of the other spouse in a transaction between them (Chapter 6).

Burkle, supra, adds a piece to the analytical puzzle. There, the court decided that when parties negotiate an arithmetically unfair agreement, each represented by independent counsel, there is no basis for a finding of "any unfair advantage." Fairness does not mean arithmetically equal outcomes; it means negotiation based on full disclosure and consent.

5.   *Reliance, part performance, and estoppel are not incorporated into California Family Code Section 852(a).* The formalities for transmutation validity are mandatory. The traditional statute of frauds (found at California Civil Code Section 1624) admits of several exceptions or defenses, including full performance, partial performance, and estoppel. Should these exceptions be applicable to the writing requirement of California Family Code Section 852?

The California Supreme Court undertook to answer this question in *Marriage of Benson*, 36 Cal.4th 1096, 32 Cal.Rptr.3d 471, 116 P.3d 1152 (2005): Husband Douglas claimed that he had conveyed to wife Dianne his community property interest in their home in exchange for her oral promise to waive her community property interest in his retirement plan. The house was originally purchased by a trust set up for Dianne by her father (Diane's trust). Dianne's father wanted to ensure that the house would be entirely Dianne's separate property, through the trust, so he asked Douglas to sign a quitclaim deed conveying his interest in the house to Diane's trust. Douglas did so with the understanding that Dianne, in turn, had orally waived her interest in his retirement account. Dianne never reduced that waiver to writing. At dissolution, Douglas argued that the doctrine of partial performance exempted Dianne's oral agreement from the special statute of frauds of California Family Code Section 852. The lower courts agreed, reasoning that Douglas had substantially changed his position by conveying his community interest in the house in reliance on Dianne's promise to waive her community property interest in his retirement fund, which was of significantly lesser value.

The California Supreme Court reversed. After a review of the legislative history behind California Family Code Section 852, the California Supreme Court ruled that the Legislature did not intend to incorporate the traditional statute of frauds exceptions into the written transmutation requirement. The court observed that the absence of exceptions to the express written declaration requirement was evidence that the legislature intended to create "a standard from which married couples could not freely depart." The court noted that Douglas did not seek to undo an unfair transmutation that was the product of undue influence under California Family Code Section 721(b), but instead sought to establish the validity of a transmutation that failed to comply with the requirements of California Family Code Section 852(a).

A transmutation of sums on deposit in an account of a married person (Chapter 5) must meet the requirements of California Family Code Section

852(a). Hence, moving sums on deposit from one account to another, or changing them from one form to another, without more, is not enough to effect a valid transmutation.

Tangible interspousal gifts of a personal nature are exempt from California Family Code Section 852(a) formalities. The gift exemption appears at California Family Code Section 852(c). Gifts that qualify for the exemption are transmuted by operation of law when the qualifying gift is manually delivered to the donee spouse.

Not all gifts qualify for the Section 852(c) exemption. For example, one spouse's anniversary gift to the other spouse of 100 shares of stock in the donee's favorite company will not qualify for transmutation by operation of law under Section 852(c). Shares of stock are intangible personal property, as such they do not qualify for the exemption. Copyrights, patents, and trademarks must likewise be transmuted in accordance with California Family Code Section 852(a) requirements since they too are intangible personal property. Cash does not qualify for the Section 852(c) gift exemption because while cash is tangible personal property, it is not property of a personal nature. I would suggest that a car is not exempt because although it is tangible and personal, it is not clothing, wearing apparel, jewelry, or other tangible articles of a personal nature, as are the items listed in the exempting statute.

———

Suppose that as a twenty-fifth wedding anniversary gift, one spouse, using earnings, purchases a $10,000 diamond necklace for the other spouse. Shortly thereafter both spouses execute reciprocal wills, each containing the provision that "all property standing in the name of either spouse is community property." A few years later, the spouses petition to dissolve the marriage. The spouse who purchased the necklace contends that the necklace was purchased as a community property investment; the spouse who received the necklace contends that the necklace is separate property. What result?

The next case comes from the state's newest judicial district, the Sixth Appellate District, which was established on November 12, 1984. The Sixth District, includes Santa Clara County, home to Silicon Valley. A factoid about the Sixth Appellate District, e-filing is now mandatory.

MARRIAGE OF STEINBERGER
91 Cal.App.4th 1449, 111 Cal.Rptr.2d 521 (6th Dist. 2001)

COTTLE, P.J.

After a court trial in a marital dissolution action, the court entered judgment regarding the character and disposition of certain property of the parties. On appeal, the husband contends that the trial court erred with regard to wife's severance pay, certain stock options, and a diamond ring.

We find no error by the trial court with regard to wife's severance pay and the stock options, but reverse the judgment with regard to the diamond ring. * * *

Petitioner Buff Jones and defendant James Mark Steinberger were married on April 30, 1988. They separated on June 14, 1997, after a marriage of 9 years and 1.5 months. The parties have one minor son, born in January of 1996. A status-only dissolution of marriage was filed on December 28, 1998. Later, some of the parties' financial issues were handled by agreements reflected in a stipulated judgment filed on August 13, 1999. Other issues were handled in a court trial, which included the testimony of both parties and other witnesses. The trial was concluded on February 5, 1999, and the resulting judgment was filed on September 2, 1999. The judgment included provisions regarding * * * a diamond ring. James has filed a timely appeal focusing on these issues. * * *

A little more than five years after the marriage, the parties bought a loose diamond with community funds. James later set it in a ring and presented it to Buff after their fifth anniversary with a card referring to the five years, and also congratulating Buff on her recent promotion.

Buff testified that she considered it a gift. It was a woman's ring and only she had worn it since receipt. When James was asked at trial whether he presented the ring to Buff as a gift, he stated: "Ah, it was as a gift and as an investment, something that we both could enjoy." James also testified that it was not his intent to give her a fifth year anniversary ring, and that the most expensive gift he had given Buff during the marriage was a Christmas gift that had cost a few hundred dollars. * * *

After the trial testimony and briefing and argument by the parties, the trial court determined that the entire salary paid during the year after Buff's departure from Compuware should be awarded to Buff as her separate property. Regarding the stock options, the court adopted the calculation set forth in Buff's trial brief, Exhibit D, as the correct calculation. The court also reserved jurisdiction to consider further evidence on the tax consequences of this decision. The court found that the diamond ring was unilaterally given to Buff at or about the time of their fifth wedding anniversary as a gift, and that it was therefore Buff's separate property. * * *

The * * * issue on appeal is the court's ruling regarding the diamond ring. It is undisputed that the diamond was purchased approximately five years after the marriage with community funds. The parties' dispute concerns the application of Family Code section 852 (section 852). That section provides, in pertinent part: "Requirements (a) A transmutation of real or personal property is not valid unless made in writing by an express declaration that is made, joined in, consented to, or accepted by the spouse whose interest in the property is adversely affected. * * * [and] (c) This section does not apply to a gift between the spouses of clothing, wearing apparel, jewelry, or other tangible articles of a personal nature that is used solely or principally by the spouse to whom the gift is made and that is not substantial in value taking into account the circumstances of the marriage."

At trial, James argued that the ring was community property, because it was substantial in value taking into account the circumstances of the marriage, and because no valid written transmutation (as required by Family Code section 852) had been made. Buff argued that a written transmutation was not required for gifts of jewelry, and that as a result of the gift, the ring became her separate property.

The trial court found that the ring was Buff's separate property. The trial transcript includes the trial court's finding that the ring was substantial in value taking into account the circumstances of the marriage. In its statement of decision, the trial court stated as follows: "[James] purchased a diamond of substantial value using community funds and unilaterally gave it [to Buff] at or about the time of their fifth wedding anniversary as a gift, with a card announcing his congratulations. Prior to the presentation of this gift, [James] had the stone mounted in a gold setting configured in a ring for [Buff] to wear. [Buff] understood the ring and stone to be a gift to her and accepted it as such. [James] never, prior to separation, stated that the ring and stone were purchased as an investment, rather than a gift, as he now contends. On this issue, the court finds the testimony of [Buff] credible and the testimony of [James] not to be credible. Furthermore, there was no evidence that [Buff] was involved in the purchase or setting of the stone and ring. [¶] The credible evidence here was that the stone was put in a women's ring and used exclusively by [Buff], consistent with both the statute and the intent described above. Although the writing accompanying the gift did not satisfy the requirement of Family Code § 852(a), the court nevertheless finds that the ring was a 'true gift' and as such, it is the separate property of the recipient, Family Code § 770(a)(2) and § 850, and 852; cases cited in Hogoboom & King, California Practice Guide: Family Law (The Rutter Group, 1999)."

On appeal, James argues that the trial court erred, because "the plain meaning of section 852 is that if the gift between spouses consists of a substantial asset, it is not going to [be] held to be a gift unless there is a written expressed declaration transmuting the property from community to separate. There was not, in this case, such a sufficient writing."

We agree with James's interpretation of the statute. The statute specifically provides that a transmutation is "not valid unless" there is a sufficient writing. (Fam. Code, § 852, subd. (a).) The trial court found that the writing here (a card presented to Buff) was not sufficient. The statutory exception for jewelry applies only to a gift that is "not substantial in value taking into account the circumstances of the marriage." In her appellate brief, Buff has not argued that the evidence was insufficient to support the trial court's finding that the ring was substantial in value taking into account the circumstances of the marriage, or that the trial court's factual finding was erroneous. With regard to a substantial gift, the statute simply does not provide for implied or oral transmutations made without a sufficient writing.

We recognize that this statute, with its bright-line test regarding transmutations, may seem harsh in light of the informal, everyday practices of spouses making gifts during a marriage. In enacting section 852, however, the Legislature made a policy decision balancing competing concerns. When the rule now codified in section 852 was being considered, the Law Revision Commission stated as follows: "California law permits an oral transmutation or transfer of property between the spouses notwithstanding the statute of frauds. This rule recognizes the convenience and practical informality of interspousal transfers. However, the rule of easy transmutation has also generated extensive litigation in dissolution proceedings. It encourages a spouse, after the marriage has ended, to transform a passing comment into an 'agreement' or even to commit perjury by manufacturing an oral or implied transmutation. The convenience and practice of informality recognized by the rule permitting oral transmutations must be balanced against the danger of fraud and increased litigation caused by it. The public expects there to be formality and written documentation of real property transactions, just as it expects there to be formality in dealings with personal property involving documentary evidence of title, such as automobiles, bank accounts, and shares of stock. Most people would find an oral transfer of such property, even between spouses, to be suspect and probably fraudulent, either as to creditors or between each other. California law should continue to recognize informal transmutations for certain personal property gifts between spouses, but should require a writing for a transmutation of real property or other personal property. In the case of personal property 'gifts' between the spouses, gifts of most items such as household furnishings and appliances should be presumed community and gifts of clothing, wearing apparel, jewelry, and other tangible articles of a personal nature should be presumed separate (unless large or substantial in value). These presumptions most likely correspond to the expectations of the ordinary married couple." (Recommendation Relating to Marital Property Presumptions and Transmutations, 17 Cal. L. Revision Comm'n Reports 205, 213–214 (1984) [footnotes omitted].)

Section 852, as enacted, makes it clear that the Legislature chose to balance the various policy concerns (allowance for convenience and informality within marriages, while preventing or minimizing disputes, fraud and perjury) by enacting a clear, bright-line test regarding transmutations of property. In light of the Legislature's decision and the clear language of the statute, it would be inappropriate to hold that a transmutation of jewelry that was substantial in value taking into account the circumstances of the marriage occurred here without the writing required by section 852.

The trial court apparently relied in part on a section in the treatise, Hogoboom & King, California Practice Guide: Family Law (The Rutter Group, 1999). Section 8.510 of that treatise states: "Gifts between spouses: Either spouse can, by making a gift to the other, convert his separate property or interest in community property into the other spouse's separate property. [¶] (1)[8:511] Formalities: If the issue is one of post 1984 transmutation, an 'express written declaration' stating characterization or ownership is being changed will be required [citation]. Presumably, however, true 'gifts' can still be proved by evidence of the ordinary elements of a gift—i.e., *delivery* and *donative intent*. [See, e.g., *DeBoer v. DeBoer* (1952) 111 Cal.App.2d 500, 244 P.2d 953; *Gudelj v. Gudelj* (1953) 41 Cal.2d 202, 259 P.2d 656]." (Hogoboom & King, Cal. Practice Guide: Family Law (The Rutter Group) ¶¶ 8:510–511, p. 8–134.1.)

In light of the clear language of section 852, this comment is only partially correct. The cases cited are not persuasive with regard to gifts of jewelry that are substantial in value taking into account the circumstances of the marriage, because they precede the enactment of the rule now codified as section 852. Under the clear statutory provision of section 852, gifts of personal property that are substantial in value taking into account the circumstances of the marriage will not be considered converted to separate property without the writing required by section 852.

Because no valid written transmutation was made in this case, the trial court erred in holding that the diamond ring was Buff's separate property. Pursuant to section 852, the ring should be considered community property.

Disposition

In light of our conclusion that the diamond ring should be considered community property, the judgment is reversed, and the matter is remanded for the limited purpose of reconsidering the division of the parties' community property. Each party shall bear his or her costs on appeal.

BAMATTRE-MANOUKIAN and WUNDERLICH, JJ., concur.

NOTE

Transmutation occurs by operation of law when the following elements are met. The gift is made between the spouses. The gift is of an item such as clothing, wearing apparel, jewelry, or any other tangible article of a personal nature. The gift is going to be used solely or principally by the donee spouse.

And perhaps the most important requirement: the gift is not substantial in value taking into account the circumstances of the marriage.

The policy underlying the value limitation is to prevent the dissipation of the community estate by the manual delivery of a single item.

SECTION 9. CHAPTER SUMMARY

- The California community property system was continued from the Spanish territorial law by the 1849 California constitution and the 1850 California Organic Act. Today the parameters of the California community property system appear in California Family Code and related cases.

- The Family Code is based on the idea that marriage is a partnership that is functional and "self-governing."

- The California Family Code incorporates by reference many sections from a wide array of other California Codes.

- California trial courts have a broad grant of discretion in dissolution, separation, and nullity proceedings.

- California Courts of Appeal generally apply the substantial evidence standard of review, which gives discretion to trial court findings of fact. The de novo standard of review is reserved for questions of law; it is especially used when the law is at issue or when there is no reason for the appellate court to be deferential to the trial court findings of fact. The some evidence standard is available for use, as is the abuse of discretion standard.

- The marital partnership exists in the private sphere. Marriage is created by contract, and yet it is also a status designation. The principle of economic noninterference applies to marriage. Parties have the right to decide how they will proceed as a community. Even so, the marriage contract is infused with substantial state interest. Therefore, some decisions made by a spouse relative to the other spouse are reversible. Some are actionable. And some may even be deemed criminal within the provisions of the California Penal Code.

- The marriage contract incorporates current and future law.

- The three foundational principles of California community property system are:
  o The tracing principle: community property traces to community property; separate property traces to separate property.

- o The equality of interest principle: married persons obtain a vested one-half interest in community property as of the date of acquisition.

- o The contract modification principle: the Family Code sets the default rules of the marriage contract, but the married partners have the right to modify nearly all of those default terms by contract. The only two terms that cannot be modified or waived are the duty of mutual obligations during marriage and the duty of good faith.

- Before marriage, prospective spouses may execute a premarital agreement that modifies one, some, or nearly all of the default Family Code rules.

  - o To be enforceable, a premarital contract must be in writing, signed by both prospective spouses, fair, and voluntarily entered into.

  - o Postdissolution spousal support waivers are enforceable if the waiving party was represented by independent counsel when the contract was signed and if the waiver is not unconscionable when the contract is enforced.

  - o In terms of general contract enforceability: disclosure and voluntariness are defined by statute effective 2002. Disclosure is a question of law. Voluntariness is a question of fact.

- During marriage, parties may change the character of property.

  - o To be valid, a transmutation must be in writing and voluntary. The change in character is effected as of the date of the transmutation.

  - o Interspousal gifts of a personal nature are exempt from transmutation formalities. Exempt property is transmuted by operation of law upon delivery of the gift.

PART II

THE CHARACTERIZATION OF PROPERTY

. . .

CHAPTER 2

COMMUNITY PROPERTY

∎ ∎ ∎

There are two characters of property in the California community property system: community property and separate property.

California Family Code Section 760 states the sharing principle, which is that *community property* is any property acquired during marriage while domiciled in the state. The corollary *equality of interest principle* holds that spouses obtain vested one-half interests upon acquisition of a community property asset (Chapter 1). Date of acquisition determines inception of title, a legal concept important to the characterization of property as community or separate.

A valid marriage is a prerequisite to owning community property. An exception is made for a putative spouse who opts to dissolve an intimate partnership under the Family Code by reference to *quasi-marital property.*

Domicile in the state is required for a community property characterization. Even so, in a dissolution or probate proceeding, property acquired out of state by effort during marriage while domiciled out of state also can be included within the larger community estate as *quasi-community property.*

A *general community property presumption* is implied in California Family Code Section 760, reproduced below. The general presumption is nonconclusive. It is raised by proof of acquisition during marriage.

Special community property presumptions can be adopted by statute or by case law. Generally special presumptions supersede the general community property presumption as to the covered asset.

For nonconclusive community property presumptions, the burden of rebuttal falls on the spouse who seeks to confirm an asset as separate property.

This chapter covers the following topics:

- The basic community property principle;

- The general community property presumption;

- A superseding statutory community property presumption for any joint form title during a dissolution proceeding;

- A superseding statutory community property presumption for sums on deposit in any account of a married person; and

- Loan proceeds transferred by a lender to a third party on behalf of one or both spouses, or to one or both spouses.

SECTION 1. THE SIGNIFICANCE OF CHARACTERIZATION

In a community property system community property and separate property are mutually exclusive categories. Community property is property acquired during marriage by effort. Separate property is anything owned before marriage, received during marriage by gift, and the rents, issues, and profits of either.

To "characterize" property is to determine the relative ownership rights of the spouses. During marriage the spouses can use community property law as a financial planning tool. In a dissolution proceeding the parties use community property law to reach a negotiated marital settlement (Appendix B). In a probate proceeding community property rights determine intestacy rights.

The California community property system is one in which the character of an asset depends upon several factors. For property to be characterized as community property the following elements must be established.

On the date of acquisition:

- The parties were married. Only married persons can own community property.

- The property was acquired during marriage.

- The property was acquired by effort.

- One or both spouses are domiciled in California when the property is acquired.

A judge (or referee) has discretion to raise a rebuttable evidentiary presumption in favor of a community property characterization. The presumption is raised upon proof of acquisition (not just possession) during marriage. The burden of rebuttal is on the spouse who seeks to confirm the property as all or part separate.

Interests in money and property acquired during a marriage are governed by the law of the domicile at the time of acquisition. This applies even to money or property acquired in another state while domiciled in California. Out of state real property interests are characterized as California community property so long as the marriage, effort, and in-state domicile requirements are established (Chapter 7).

A petition for dissolution filed in a California superior court gives a judge jurisdiction to characterize property. Jurisdiction is over community and quasi-community property. Additionally, a separate property owner can consent to a court's exercise of jurisdiction over one, some, or all separate property assets.

Characterizing and dividing property raise different legal issues.

To "characterize" property is to determine whether it belongs to the community or to one of the spouses alone.

To "divide" property is to determine the spouses' arithmetic shares in community or commingled property. Division can be by agreement between the parties. If the parties fail to reach an agreement, the judge shall divide the property according to its character and in line with the equal division mandate (Chapters 1 and 7).

In California, as in any other community property state, title does not control ownership. What title documents do determine, however, is which community property presumption governs.

An asset acquired during marriage and titled in one spouse's name alone raises *the general community property presumption*. So too does an untitled asset. The general presumption is rebuttable by tracing the asset back to a separate property source, or by an enforceable agreement. The general presumption applies to borrowed funds that are transferred by the lender to the spouses or a third party on their behalf. In the case of borrowed funds, the lender's intent determines the character of the loan proceeds (Section C below).

Any statutory presumption is a special presumption that applies to an identified type of asset or assets. Special presumptions supersede the general community property presumption unless otherwise noted in the language of the special presumption itself.

Assets that are acquired during marriage and titled in both spouses' names raise a statutory community property presumption. *The special joint form title community property presumption* is limited to dissolution proceedings. Moreover, rebuttal is limited to an agreement between the spouses the contents of which make clear that despite the joint form title one spouse is to retain a separate property interest in the titled asset in the event of dissolution (Section 3B below).

In California there is *a special statutory community property presumption for sums on deposit in any account of a married person*. The presumption is possession-based. Rebuttal is either by an agreement between the spouses that specific sums on deposit in a specific account are not to be community property, or by tracing specific sums on deposit back to a separate property source (Section 3C below).

Community property presumptions allow for the likelihood that the divorcing spouses may recall generally when an asset was acquired (during marriage or not), even if they cannot prove the exact date of acquisition. Presumptions assist the parties, lawyers, and the judge by starting the characterization process.

To sum up, upon proof of acquisition during marriage the general rule is that property is presumed to be entirely (100%) community property unless proven otherwise.

ACQUISITION TIME LINE FOR PURPOSES OF CHARACTERIZATION

Before marriage (ABM)--------*During* marriage (ADM)-------*After* date of separation (ADS)
Individual property (SP)-------Presumptively CP-------------------------SP

- Property owned on the date of marriage is separate property
- Property acquired during marriage is presumed to be community property
- Property owned before marriage, acquired by gift during marriage, or the rents, issues, and profits of such property is separate property.
- "Earnings and accumulations" acquired after the date of separation are the earning spouse's separate property.

A community property presumption—whether general or special—is an evidentiary leniency; as noted above it gives the community the benefit of the doubt. In the California community property system, presumptions are nonconclusive, which is to say that they (only) can be rebutted by contradicting evidence. The standard of rebuttal is generally the lowest preponderance of the evidence standard. *Marriage of Ettefagh*, below, explains.

An asset titled in one spouse's name alone does not divest the unnamed spouse. Instead the unnamed spouse is a hidden owner ("hidden" because his or her name is absent from the title) of a vested one-half community property interest in the asset.

SECTION 2. THE COMMUNITY PROPERTY PRINCIPLE

California Family Code Section 760 is the core statute of the California community property system. It states a principle, not a definition.

A. CALIFORNIA COMMUNITY PROPERTY AND QUASI-COMMUNITY PROPERTY

The basic statute covers a lot of conceptual and legal ground. Its key issues are date of acquisition and domicile. Property acquired during marriage by effort while domiciled in the state is California community property. So too is property that traces back to a community property source.

WEST'S ANNOTATED CALIFORNIA FAMILY CODE

§ 760.   Community property defined

Except as otherwise provided by statute, all property, real or personal, wherever situated, acquired by a married person during the marriage while domiciled in this state is community property.

(Stats. 1992, c. 162 (A.B. 2650), § 10, operative Jan. 1, 1994.)

––––––––

Out of state property acquired while domiciled in a different state can be brought into the California community property system as quasi-community property, but only for purposes of dissolution. Property acquired in a different jurisdiction does not become quasi-community property on the date that one or both spouses establish domicile in California. Rather it is the filing of a petition for dissolution in a California superior court that establishes state jurisdiction to characterize any out of state property (that was acquired while domiciled out of state) as quasi-community property.

There are two nearly identical quasi-community property definitions. One, found at California Family Code Section 125, reproduced below, applies in a dissolution proceeding (Chapter 7). The other, found at California Probate Code Section 66, *infra* at 715, applies in a probate proceeding (Chapter 9). Jurisdiction to divide community and quasi-community property is discussed in Chapter 7.

WEST'S ANNOTATED CALIFORNIA FAMILY CODE

§ 125.   Quasi-community property

"Quasi-community property" means all real or personal property, wherever situated, acquired before or after the operative date of this code in any of the following ways:

(a) By either spouse while domiciled elsewhere which would have been community property if the spouse who acquired the property had been domiciled in this state at the time of its acquisition.

(b) In exchange for real or personal property, wherever situated, which would have been community property if the spouse who acquired the property so exchanged had been domiciled in this state at the time of its acquisition.

(Stats. 1992, c. 162 (A.B. 2650), § 10, operative Jan. 1, 1994.)

B. THE "ALL . . . EXCEPT" FORMAT OF THE BASIC COMMUNITY PROPERTY STATUTE

The standard format for a basic community property statute is "all . . . except . . . " By this linguistic structure community property is *all* property acquired during marriage *except* separate property (Chapter 3).

Community property and separate property are mutually exclusive categories. When the two characters get mixed together in one asset, the asset is said to be "commingled." An important subsidiary rule of the California community property system is that the act of commingling does not change the character of the contributing property. A spouse has the right to request an equitable accounting to determine the proportional character ownership of a commingled asset. The right to an accounting has its origin in the property right itself, as well as in specific state civil and family codes.

California law requires parties to inventory assets at the end of a marriage. Divorcing spouses are free to reach a dissolution agreement on an asset-by-asset basis. If they cannot agree about how to divide their property, California law directs the factfinder to characterize assets one at a time, on an "asset-by-asset" basis. Some states permit characterization on a "hotchpot" basis; in these states, assets are put into one lot of property (a "hotchpot") which is then divided between the spouses as a single unit.

General property law doctrine dictates that inception of title to an asset occurs on the date that an enforceable legal interest is acquired. Community property law dictates more specifically that a person's marital status on the date of acquisition decides the character of an asset or accumulation. *A single person* acquires individual property during an intimate relationship. *Married persons and registered domestic partners (RDPs)* acquire community property during marriage. *A person who is separated from his or her spouse* acquires earnings and accumulations as separate property during the period of separation.

Acquisition can be established by creation, purchase, title, color of title, claim of right, gift, transfer or any other method that gives or may give rise to an ownership or superior possessory right in one or both spouses.

California spouses have the statutory right to transmute property from community property to separate property, from separate property to community property, or from the separate property of one spouse to the separate property of the other spouse. Not every U.S. community property state is as permissive. Some states—Texas being an example—restrict the transmutation of property from community to separate as part of a policy to protect the marital household. The character of a transmuted asset changes on the date of a valid transmutation (Chapter 1).

C. "ALL PROPERTY, REAL OR PERSONAL, WHEREVER SITUATED . . . "

The California Family Code is neutral about how spouses should hold property during marriage, and in what character. Such decisions are left to the spouses.

California Family Code Section 760 includes the phrase "all property," which signals that spouses may hold and acquire community property in any form. "All property" is broadly defined to include real, personal, tangible, intangible, present, future, vested or contingent interests. "All property" also includes any interest that is reducible to property by a private declaration. Presumably it also includes leaseholds, pre-possessory interests, and any other transferable interest upon which a legal claim can be based. Some interests are excluded (Chapter 4).

The California Civil Code classifies property as either real or personal. *Real property* refers to land, structures on land, and any personal property affixed to structures. *Personal property* is defined as anything that is not real property. Property that is not real property is a broad category that includes so much more than the usual type of personal property. Personal property can be tangible or intangible. Past, present or future. Vested or contingent. Personal or proprietary. For now, however, the more typical range of personal property is reduced to the list provided by the state for parties on FL 160 (Appendix B).

Property acquired in another jurisdiction while married and domiciled in California may be community property depending how the property is acquired. Property "wherever situated" that is acquired while the acquiring spouse is domiciled in California is California community property. And, by the tracing principle, property that is acquired with the proceeds of California community property is characterized by California Family Code Section 760 as California community property.

California Family Code Section 751 is a companion statute to California Family Code Section 760. California Family Code Section 751 codifies the equality of interest principle to ensure that each spouse owns a *vested* one-half community property interest in any community property asset as of the date of its acquisition. The equality of interest principle allows a spouse to know, as of any given date, what he or she owns relative to the other spouse. Community property ownership rights are not contingent upon dissolution. Rather, community property rights come into existence at acquisition, which is to say during the marriage.

An asset is property. But more abstractly an asset is generally defined as a probable future economic benefit obtained as a result of a past transaction. An asset—as an underlying property—can appreciate or depreciate over time. It can produce rents, issues, or profits. Appreciation and rents, issues, and profits are distinct from each other. Each is also distinct from the underlying asset that it traces back to.

D. COMMUNITY PROPERTY APPRECIATION AND RENTS, ISSUES, AND PROFITS

California Family Code Section 760 implicitly characterizes the appreciation (or depreciation) of community property identically with the underlying asset.

All property acquired during marriage by effort while domiciled in the state is community property.

The appreciation of community property is community property by the tracing principle. Likewise depreciation.

The rents, issues and profits of community property are community property by application of the tracing principle.

E. A PRINCIPLE RATHER THAN A DEFINITION

The concluding example below is far from comprehensive. Nevertheless, it shows the range and limits of California Family Code Section 760 as a nexus point in the Family Code.

Assume that one spouse agrees to house sit a neighbor's house. That act—because it requires labor—is an onerous effort. If the neighbor pays the housesitting spouse, the compensation comes into the marriage as community property. If the neighbor fails to pay the housesitting spouse, a breach of contract claim arises. A claim based on contract is proprietary in nature, not personal, which means that any damages obtained to settle the claim enter the marriage as community property.

Assume also that the neighbor is adjudged the proximate cause of a personal injury to the housekeeping spouse.

In the California system, a personal injury claim is not proprietary and thus not subject to characterization as community property. The theory is that a personal injury claim is just that: personal. The claim arises to address a harm to the body. Therefore it is not tradeable or subject to characterization as property. That said, a fine distinction separates the personal injury claim from money or other property received to settle it. Money or property received to settle a personal injury claim that arose during marriage is property, and as such it falls within the community property system (Chapter 3).

The basic statute starts the above analysis. The proprietary housesitting contract falls within the community property system and, more specifically, within basic principle of California Family Code Section 760. Any claim on that contract would also fall within the system, and within the basic principle. The personal injury claim falls outside of the community property system. However, because the personal injury claim arose during marriage, if it is settled during marriage for money or property, that money or property would fall within the community property system, but under a different (specialized) community property statute (California Family Code Section 780) that mandatorily assigns the personal injury settlement to the injured spouse in a dissolution.

The simple contract scenario hints at how much conceptual ground the concept of a community property system can cover.

The basic community property statute is broad in scope. It tends toward over-inclusivity rather than under-inclusivity. Even so, it does not include every acquisition or accumulation. Hence the basic statute is best understood not as a rigid definition, but as a general principle.

SECTION 3. COMMUNITY PROPERTY PRESUMPTIONS

There are three main community property presumptions in the California system. They provide a basic level of protection for the community. In order of historical appearance, the presumptions are:

- The general community property presumption.

- A statutory community property presumption for joint form titles acquired during marriage.

- A statutory community property presumption for sums on deposit in an account during marriage.

A. THE GENERAL COMMUNITY PROPERTY PRESUMPTION

The general community property presumption has its source in California Family Code Section 760. The general presumption applies to all assets that are not otherwise governed by a more specific (and thus superseding) community property presumption. Practically speaking the general presumption applies to untitled assets and to assets titled in one spouse's name alone.

Any community property presumption is an evidentiary leniency in favor of the community. As such it is a legal protection for the community estate, which is to say the marital partnership.

The general community property presumption holds that property acquired during marriage is probably community property absent actual proof otherwise. Rebuttal is permitted on an asset-by-asset basis. The standard of proof for rebuttal is preponderance of the evidence. Proportional rebuttal is permitted. The court has discretion to raise (or not) the general community property presumption upon proof of acquisition during marriage.

The two cases that follow—*Wilson v. Wilson*, reproduced below, and *Fidelity & Casualty v. Mahoney*, also reproduced below—illustrate the relationship between the general community presumption and the concept of judicial discretion.

Wilson is a dissolution case. It involves a dispute over the character of a house titled in the husband's name alone. At dissolution, the trial court raised the general presumption on the wife's evidence that the house had been acquired during marriage. The husband sought to rebut with proof that community income over the course of the marriage was less than family expenses for that same period. He asked the court to draw the inference that community funds were therefore insufficient to buy the house during the marriage, making the house his separate property by default. Despite the husband's evidence the court characterized the house as community property. The husband appealed. The court of appeal affirmed the trial court's exercise of discretion.

Wilson illustrates the basic approach for using the general community property presumption. The trial court has discretion to raise the general presumption on proof of acquisition during marriage. Once the general presumption is raised, the trial court also has discretion to decide if the presumption is rebutted. Additionally, if left unrebutted, the general community property presumption is sufficient, as a matter of law, to support a final characterization of community property for purposes of dissolution.

WILSON V. WILSON
76 Cal.App.2d 119, 172 P.2d 568 (1st Dist. 1946)

PETERS, PRESIDING JUSTICE.

Defendant appeals from an interlocutory decree of divorce granted to his wife after an extended and bitterly contested trial. * * *

The parties were married in New York on January 15, 1931. Shortly thereafter they established their domicile in San Francisco, and resided here until they separated on December 28, 1940. They have no children. This action was filed by the wife on January 19, 1942. * * *

The trial court found that the residence of the parties in San Francisco was community property and awarded the plaintiff a one-half interest therein, together with the exclusive right of use and occupancy. * * *

The testimony in reference to the residence is not as clear as might be desired, but this condition of the record was caused by defendant's failure to be frank and fair with the trial court. Admittedly the house was purchased in 1938, some seven years after the marriage, and admittedly title was taken and still stands in defendant's name. Admittedly the house cost $20,000. Defendant testified that he paid for the house in cash and that the funds used for the purchase were the accumulations of dividends from property owned by him before marriage. Based on this evidence defendant urges as his principal contention on this appeal that it was error to find that the house was community property. In this connection he argues that since he testified that his sole community income was $6,000 a year, and since his wife testified that she estimated their living expenses at $3,500 to $4,000 per month, obviously the community funds were more than exhausted in paying the living expenses, and therefore the house must have been purchased with his separate funds. * * *

The defendant, however, was in a much better position to know the exact living costs of the parties because he paid most of the household bills in cash. He testified that his wife's testimony as to their living expenses was "absolutely false" (R.T. 515) and that actually it cost them $300 to $800 a month for living expenses. (R.T. 516.) Obviously, if the $300 figure was believed by the trial court there was a substantial part of the $6,000 a year salary that could have been used to buy the house. The trial court was entitled to disbelieve the defendant's testimony as to the source of the funds, but to believe his testimony as to their living costs. It was entitled to disbelieve his testimony in part or in toto. Moreover, there is substantial evidence that after marriage, plaintiff, who is an artist, sold some of her art creations for substantial sums, and that the money so received was treated as community property. There is, therefore, in the record some evidence, weak though it may be from which it may reasonably be inferred that community funds were used to buy the house. This testimony, without the necessity of relying on presumptions, supports the challenged finding.

In addition the finding is supported by the strong presumption that all property acquired [during] marriage. * * * is community property. This presumption is fundamental in the community property system and is an integral part of the community property law not only of this state but of other states and countries where the system is in operation. * * * Coupled with this presumption is the elementary but fundamental rule that the burden rests upon the person asserting that the property is separate to establish that fact. * * *

The presumption is, of course, a rebuttable one. But whether the evidence adduced to overcome the presumption is sufficient for the purpose is a question for the trial court. As in other cases of presumptions, the rule is that the presumption may outweigh the evidence adduced against it and that notwithstanding controverting testimony the presumption alone will support a finding in accordance therewith. * * *

Counsel for defendant, while giving lip service to these well settled rules, contends that they have no application here for at least two reasons—first, that the evidence controverts the presumption as a matter of law, and, secondly, that the presumption has no place in the present case at all. So far as the first contention is concerned, little need be said. Obviously, whether defendant's evidence rebutted the presumption was a question for the trial court. In view of what has already been said about defendant's testimony, obviously the trial court was justified in disregarding his testimony on this issue and finding in accordance with the presumption.

Defendant's second argument is that evidence that the house was bought in 1938 after marriage was not sufficient to raise the presumption— that in addition plaintiff was under a duty to show that the funds used in the purchase were acquired after marriage. In the absence of such evidence, says defendant, there is no evidentiary basis for the presumption. There is no such limitation on the rule—if there were, there would be but little room for the operation of the presumption. Obviously, if a litigant had to trace the funds used in each purchase to funds acquired after marriage there would be few cases indeed to which the presumption could apply. The true rule is that the burden is on the party asserting the separate character of the property, and that the presumption applies when the one claiming that the property is community offers evidence that property was acquired after marriage. * * *

NOTES

1. *Burden of proof, evidentiary standard, and standard of review.* The general community property presumption is fair insofar as it tends to serve one (if not all) of the following functions. It reflects the fact that the parties do not negotiate at arm's length given that they are in an intimate, confidential relationship. It reflects the probability of outcome: property acquired during marriage is more likely than not community in character. It reflects the parties' relative access to the evidence. And it furthers an identifiable state policy of encouraging marriage by protecting the community.

More technically, the general presumption protects the community by giving the benefit of the doubt to the community proponent. In the California community property system, the burden of rebuttal is on the separate property proponent. The evidentiary standard of rebuttal is preponderance of the evidence in nearly all cases, as mentioned above. The standard of review on appeal is typically the substantial evidence standard. In cases where a question of law arises the de novo standard applies.

2. *Conclusive versus nonconclusive presumptions.* In the community property context, a conclusive presumption would be a property rule. By contrast a nonconclusive presumption would function as a rebuttable evidentiary leniency. So, for example, defining the housekeeper's contribution

as a gainful activity as a matter of law (as California Family Code Section 760 implicitly does) constitutes a *conclusive* presumption that functions to a vest a one-half community property interest in both spouses on the date an asset is acquired.

By comparison the *non*conclusive general community property presumption is an evidentiary leniency that allows the factfinder to begin the analysis about the character of property if records are absent or uncertain.

3.   *Tracing and financial disclosure.* The separate property proponent can only rebut the general presumption with actual proof. Often that proof comes in the form of financial records. Sometimes proof comes in the form of corroborating testimony or circumstantial evidence. Today, California has enhanced Family Code disclosure standards (Chapters 7 and 8) to support the policy of cooperative (rather than adversarial) discovery in dissolution proceedings.

4.   *The need to update* Wilson. *Wilson* was decided in 1946, a legal period known as the male-management era (Chapter 6). Under male management, the husband, by statute, was the sole legal manager of the community property. As exclusive manager the husband was legally able to obtain and keep records and to access information, especially about acquisition and valuation; the wife was not. And yet, in that era a husband had no legal duty to disclose financial information to the wife. Starting with the enactment of the Family Code and more precisely with amendments in 2001 (effective January 1, 2002), disclosure duties were enhanced for purposes of dissolution (Chapter 8). The duties come into play at dissolution, but they incorporate California Family Code Section 721 duties, which come into existence on the date of marriage. Thus under the California Family Code, spouses are in a confidential fiduciary relationship from the start of marriage through dissolution. With respect to any particular asset, duties continue until the asset or liability is definitively assigned at dissolution to one spouse or the other.

Even though the husband in *Wilson* had no duty to keep records or to disclose financial information to the wife, the trial court declined to accept his argument that the house was separate property because the community income was insufficient to make the purchase. Instead, the court looked to date of acquisition: it was during marriage; the general presumption was raised; and that presumption was a sufficient basis upon which to decide the character of the house. *Wilson*-like arguments appear decade after decade in the California reports. Most often they are made without corroborating financial records.

5.   *Updating* Wilson *with legislation passed in the original Family Code and amended thereafter: California Family Code Sections 721, 1100, and 2102. Marriage of Brewer & Federici v. Federici*, 93 Cal.App.4th 1334, 113 Cal. Rptr.2d 849 (2d Dist. 2001), (also discussed in Chapter 8), goes part of the way toward updating *Wilson*. In 1980, Janess Brewer, a vice-president of National Broadcasting Company (NBC), married Ovidio Federici, an artist. They separated seventeen years later, in 1997. The parties reached a negotiated

marriage settlement agreement, or MSA. Importantly, the MSA was negotiated in 1998, several years after California Family Code Section 721 was enacted (Chapter 6) and after the original version of California Family Code Section 2100 et seq. went into effect (Chapter 8).

Janess and Ovidio cooperated with discovery. Janess was represented by an attorney; Ovidio negotiated the MSA on his own, although he twice consulted with attorneys. The MSA awarded to Janess her NBC retirement plan (singular), the value of which she listed as "unknown." Months after the final judgment of dissolution was issued, Ovidio filed a motion to set aside the property division and ultimately the MSA. The factual basis for Ovidio's set aside motions was mistake: specifically Ovidio argued that he mistakenly believed that Janess only had one retirement plan when in fact she had two— he pointed out that since the original MSA awarded only one retirement plan to Janess, the second retirement plan was an omitted asset (Chapter 8). Janess countered that the Civil Code imposed the legal duty to identify and value the pension plans on Ovidio; she cited California Civil Code Section 1577 for the principle that a mistake of fact cannot be "caused by the neglect of a legal duty on the part of the person making the mistake."

The trial court set aside the final judgment. Brewer appealed. Applying the abuse of discretion standard, the court of appeal relied on California Family Code Sections 721(b), 1100(e) and (the original version of) 2102—not on the California Civil Code Sections cited by Janess. Under those California Family Code Sections the court said, the correct legal approach, which was not codified at the time *Wilson* was decided, is to recognize that marriage creates a fiduciary relationship between the spouses. In the context of negotiating a MSA, as the parties are still married. The legal relevance of the parties' marital status is that the negotiations are not arm's-length; rather, they are "negotiations between fiduciaries required to openly share information." (*Brewer & Federici, supra* at 1344). The court went on to say that Brewer did not meet her disclosure requirements when she valued her NBC pension as "unknown."

When it comes to disclosure and financial records, the court wrote:

"[T[he Family Code imposes fiduciary obligations on both parties. One obligation is to make full, accurate, and complete disclosure, including the continuing duty to update and augment information. (Fam. Code, §§ 1100, subd.(e), 2100, subd. (c), 2102; *Rubenstein v. Rubenstein*, 81 Cal.App.4th 1131 at pp. 1150–1151.) It reasonably follows that a spouse who is in a superior position to obtain records or information from which an asset can be valued and can reasonably do so must acquire and disclose such information to the other spouse. (Compare with *Brookwood v. Bank of America*, (1996) 45 Cal.App.4th 1667, 1673–1674 [53 Cal.Rptr.2d 515] [discussing unilateral mistakes in arm's length transactions]." *Id.* at 1348.

6.   *The general community property presumption is a protection for the community.* As a way of marking inception of title the general community

property presumption looks not to the title records, but to date of acquisition. As such it is an acquisition based statute. Anything acquired during marriage is presumptively community property subject to proof otherwise. Date of marriage is easily confirmed. So too is date of acquisition, at least for titled assets. Additionally, domicile is not often at issue but, if it is, domicile is relatively easy to establish. By comparison, requiring proof about who contributed to a purchase, and how much they contributed would produce potentially far more complicated legal proceedings. The house in *Wilson* was acquired during the parties' marriage, while the parties were domiciled in the state. Therefore, the trial court was well within its discretion to raise the California Family Code Section 760 general community property presumption.

A community property interest vests as of the date of acquisition in equal one-half shares. The community property presumption is an important, but rather mechanical, protection for the community; by comparison disclosure requirements protect the community in a more nuanced way. Disclosure especially prevents impairment of the community property in a case like *Wilson* where one spouse is unwilling to provide financial information to the other spouse.

To reiterate an important framework: in the absence of specialized disclosure rules a community property presumption protects the community in at least three ways. One, the general presumption gives the community an evidentiary leniency as to either spouse's acquisitions so long as those acquisitions are made during marriage while domiciled in the state. Even out of state purchases become community property under this protection. Two, the general presumption places the burden of rebuttal on the spouse who seeks to confirm the property as their's alone. This is notice to the separate property claimant, as of the date of acquisition, that in the event of divorce, the claimant will be required to present actual proof to rebut any applicable community property presumption. Three, since rebuttal requires actual proof, even without specialized disclosure rules, rebuttal often anticipates the free exchange of financial information.

Overprotection is systemically guarded against by the exercise of judicial discretion. It is within the factfinder's discretion to raise the general presumption (or not) and to decide if that presumption has been rebutted (or not). The evidentiary standard for rebuttal is the low preponderance of the evidence standard, as discussed in *Ettefagh*, below). The standard of review on appeal is most typically the substantial evidence standard. (By contrast the standard of review for the granting (or denying) of a motion to set aside a final dissolution judgment is abuse of discretion.) The preponderance of the evidence standard for rebuttal prevents the factfinder from (unintentionally or intentionally) effectuating a fault-based property determination in a dissolution proceeding, as a fault-based division is against state public policy (Chapter 7). And the substantial evidence standard of review instructs the appellate reviewer to defer to the factfinder's findings.

7. *Title by creation.* In *Wilson*, the wife created valuable untitled artwork during the marriage, which she sold for cash. There is no necessity for the appellate court to discuss copyright issues, but it does point out with approval that the trial court treated "the money so received [during marriage from the sale of the art] . . . as community property."

8. *The housekeeper's contribution during marriage.* In California the married housekeeper's contribution is conclusively presumed to be a benefit to the community. In the nine U.S. community property states, the actual amount and quality of spouse's housekeeping is irrelevant and inadmissible on the issue of property characterization at dissolution. By comparison, in the forty-one U.S. states that trace their marital property law back to English common law, the housekeeper's contribution is a matter of proof. In those states, the quantity and quality of "housekeeping efforts," whether broadly or narrowly defined, may be and typically are relevant in deciding property rights at dissolution (Chapter 1). For a definition of what evidence gives rise to an equitable right to property acquired by one's spouse during marriage, see e.g. N.Y. DOMESTIC RELATIONS LAW § 236 (2010).

———

What happens when a marriage ends after just a short time? Is property possessed by a spouse still presumptively community property? Is possession a reliable proxy for date of acquisition? If it is, is proof of possession during a short marriage sufficient to raise the general community property presumption? *Fidelity & Casualty Company v. Mahone,* reproduced below, addresses these questions.

The spouses in *Fidelity* were married for two months when the husband died in a plane accident. Immediately before boarding the fatal flight, the husband purchased an accident life insurance policy with an unknown sum of change that the court deems to have been one dollar ($1). The accident policy named the husband as the owner and the insured; it named the husband's child from a prior marriage as the sole pay-on-death beneficiary. When the husband died a dispute between the husband's child and his surviving wife arose over the policy proceeds.

The child produced the insurance contract naming him as the pay-on-death (P.O.D.) beneficiary. The surviving spouse produced evidence of her marriage to the decedent; she also relied on the fact that the decedent was in possession, during his marriage, of the one dollar he used to buy the policy, thus making it more likely than not that the one dollar was community property in character. The surviving spouse did not introduce financial or salary records into evidence.

The trial court declined to raise the general community property presumption based on the fact that the decedent used money in his possession to purchase the policy. Without evidence of acquisition during marriage, the court confirmed the accident policy as separate in character, thus recognizing the decedent's son as the rightful owner of the entirety of the policy proceeds. The surviving spouse appealed.

Fidelity is yet another case underscoring the idea that the principle of community property found at California Family Code Section 760 is not possession based, it is acquisition based. A fine distinction, perhaps. But proof that a spouse is in possession of an asset during marriage is not the same as proof that the asset was acquired during marriage. Possession and acquisition are distinct concepts. A particular factfinder may exercise her discretion to rule that possession is circumstantial evidence of acquisition in a long term marriage, but possession necessarily loses its evidentiary weight in a short term marriage.

FIDELITY & CASUALTY COMPANY V. MAHONEY
71 Cal.App.2d 65, 161 P.2d 944 (2d Dist. 1945)

WOOD, J.

On June 28, 1943, in Louisville, Kentucky, J. B. Mahoney, Sr., a resident of Los Angeles, purchased an airplane-travel accident insurance policy from the plaintiff insurance company and mailed it to the beneficiary named therein, J. B. Mahoney, Jr., of Los Angeles, his sixteen-year-old son by a former marriage. Soon after the policy was purchased, the insured boarded an airplane for the purpose of going to Los Angeles, and within an hour thereafter the airplane fell in Kentucky and as a result thereof he was killed.

Patricia Mahoney and the insured had been married about two months preceding the airplane accident, and at all times during their marriage they were domiciled in California. She made a demand on the insurance company for one-half the proceeds of the policy on the ground that the policy was purchased with community property.

The insurance company filed this action in interpleader, and upon stipulation an interlocutory decree was entered wherein it was ordered that upon deposit in court by the insurance company of $4,989.50 (being the amount of the policy less $10.50 for costs) it would be released from liability under the policy, and it was further ordered that J. B. Mahoney, Jr., and Patricia Mahoney litigate between themselves to determine who was entitled to receive the amount so deposited. The insurance company made the deposit.

Defendant Patricia Mahoney alleged, among other things, that she was the widow of J. B. Mahoney, deceased; that the premium on said policy was paid by J. B. Mahoney from community property funds owned by him and her; and that as his widow she was entitled to one-half of said $5,000.

Defendant J. B. Mahoney, Jr., alleged, among other things, that he was the beneficiary named in the policy; that the $5,000 was not community property; that Patricia Mahoney had no right, title or interest in said $5,000; and that the policy was purchased with the separate property of the deceased J. B. Mahoney.

The court found that the $5,000 was not community property; that Patricia Mahoney had no right, title or interest therein; and that the policy was purchased with the separate property of deceased J. B. Mahoney. The court concluded that J. B. Mahoney, Jr., was entitled to a judgment ordering that the funds deposited with the court be paid to his guardian. The judgment was that J. B. Mahoney, Jr., by his guardian, recover judgment as against defendant Patricia Mahoney, and that he, by his guardian, was entitled to the sum of $2,494.75 deposited in court by plaintiff. Defendant Patricia Mahoney appeals from the judgment, and contends that the findings of fact are not supported by the evidence.

In the statement on appeal it is recited: "There is no evidence as to the nature or extent of the decedent's estate, whether separate or community, except that it is shown the decedent earned a gross monthly salary in an undetermined amount during the period of his second marriage and that he had a bank account in his own name. There was no evidence on behalf of either of the defendants as to whether or not the premium paid for said policy of insurance came from the separate estate or the community estate of the decedent." The record does not show what amount was paid for the policy, but since it was stated in the written opinion of the trial judge and in the briefs that the amount was $1.00, it will be assumed herein that $1.00 was the amount of the premium.

Appellant's theory is that the insurance premium was paid by the insured from community funds, that such payment was a gift by the husband [to his son as beneficial designee] of community funds, and that such gift, being without her written consent, was a nullity under the provisions of section 172 of the Civil Code [replaced by California Family Code 1100(b)] as to her one-half interest in the premium money, and therefore she is entitled to one-half the proceeds of the policy.

Section 172 of the Civil Code provides: "The husband has the management and control of the community personal property, with like absolute power of disposition, other than testamentary, as he has of his separate estate; provided, however, that he cannot make a gift of such community personal property * * * without the written consent of the wife." [Replaced by California Family Code Section 1100(a)] If the insurance premium was paid from the husband's separate funds the wife was not entitled to any part of the proceeds of the policy, it being provided in section 157 of the Civil Code [replaced by California Family Code Section 752] that "Neither husband nor wife has any interest in the property of the other. * * *" In *Mundt v. Connecticut Gen. Life Ins. Co.*, (1939), 35 Cal. App. 2d 416, wherein the husband had paid the premiums on his life insurance policy from community funds without the wife's consent, the question was whether the wife, who was not the named beneficiary, was entitled to one-half the proceeds of the policy. In that case the court said " * * * the only test applied to this problem has been whether the premiums (on a policy issued on the life of a husband after coverture) are paid entirely from community funds. If so, the policy becomes a community asset and the nonconsenting wife may recover an undivided one-half thereof. * * * " The court was required to find whether the money used in paying the premium was paid from community funds. As above shown, there was no oral or documentary evidence as to whether the money used in paying the premium was community property or separate property. As to appellant's contention that the findings were not supported by the evidence, she argues that, since there was no evidence to the contrary, the presumption, under section 164 of the Civil Code [replaced by California Family Code Section 760] that property acquired after marriage (other than by gift, devise, or descent) is community property, is determinative that the money used to pay the insurance premium was community property. There is a presumption that property acquired after marriage, other than by gift, devise, or descent, is community property. * * * Where the marriage relation has existed a short period of time the presumption that property acquired after marriage is community property is of less weight than in the case of a long-continued marriage relation. There is no presumption, however, as to when property was acquired. (*Scott v. Austin*, 57 Cal. App. 553, 556.) The marriage relation had existed about two months. The husband had a bank account in his own name. It was not shown at the trial whether his bank account was large or small or whether the bank account had been in existence a long or short time, and it was not shown whether his monthly salary was large or small. It would seem that proof of such matters was available. Such proof would have been of material assistance to the trial court in determining whether the $1.00 used in paying the premium was acquired before or after the marriage, especially in view of the short time of marriage and in view of the small amount of the premium. The appellant had alleged in her answer that the premium was paid from community funds, but she did not allege that it was paid without her consent. Even if the premium had been paid from community funds, the gift of the $1.00 would not be invalid unless it was made without her consent. Although she was in the best position to know and to prove whether she had so consented, she offered no evidence as to whether she had consented to such payment. She was the one who was asserting an interest in the proceeds of a policy wherein she was not a named beneficiary. The $5,000 was not property which had been in actual possession of the husband or wife. In the transaction whereby the husband expended $1.00 and acquired the accident insurance policy he did not dispose of property in possession of the value of $5,000 or of any value in excess of $1.00. If the $1.00 was community property, and if the payment of it was an invalid gift because she had not consented thereto, her only interest therein during his lifetime would have been a one-half interest in the cash surrender value of the policy, namely, some amount less than fifty cents. There was no evidence that it had any surrender value. It was only upon the death of the insured that the expenditure of the $1.00 became the basis of a fixed right to recover $5,000. The appellant was not entitled to a portion of the $5,000 unless, as above stated, the premium was paid from community funds, and unless she had not consented to such payment. It was necessary therefore to determine the source of the $1.00 used in paying the premium. The burden was upon appellant to prove that the $1.00 premium was paid from community funds. Also the burden was upon her to prove that she did not consent to the payment of the premium. She failed to carry the burden in both respects.

As above indicated, only one-half of the amount deposited in court was in dispute. Before judgment was rendered, counsel stipulated and the court ordered that the other half of the amount deposited in court be paid to defendant, J. B. Mahoney, Jr.

The judgment is affirmed.

NOTES

1.   *Acquisition versus possession.* There is early twentieth century case law that property possessed by either spouse at the time of dissolution, without more, may be sufficient to meet the substantial evidence standard for purposes of raising the general community property presumption. See e.g., *In re Jolly's Estate*, 196 Cal. 547, 238 P. 353 (1925). However, *Jolly* predates many important changes in California family law, including the idea that the community property interest is vested, not contingent. For that reason, *Jolly's Estate* is not strong precedent.

The Texas Family Code includes two general community property presumptions, as does the Louisiana Civil Code. In Texas, an acquisition-based general presumption is implied in the state's general statute which provides that property *acquired* during marriage is community property. Rebuttal is by preponderance of the evidence. A second possession-based presumption is expressly stated in the Texas code as well; it provides that property *possessed* by either spouse during or upon dissolution of the marriage is presumed to be community property, with rebuttal being by clear and convincing evidence. TEX. FAM. CODE ANN. § 3.002 (West 2006).

2.   *The general community property presumption can be raised only if no superseding presumption applies.* Superseding community property presumptions are enacted at California Family Code Section 2581 and at California Probate Code Section 5305(a), both of which are discussed below.

3.   *Cash is classified as tangible personal property, as such it is governed by the general community property presumption.* See Section 3C below.

4.   *Sums on deposit in an account are intangible personal property.* Sums on deposit in an account are governed by a superseding special community property presumption found at California Probate Code Section 5305(a), discussed below. Sums on deposit are not cash and hence they are not covered by the general presumption. Nor are they inseparable from the account, which means that title to the demand account in which the sums are deposited does not necessarily determine the ownership of sums on deposit in that account.

Sums on deposit in a demand deposit account (savings and/or checking account) are classified as a debt for which the depositor is the creditor and the financial institution the debtor. Sums on deposit may be withdrawn by the depositor at a teller's window, with an ATM card, a check, or an electronic transfer to a third party. Sums on deposit come into the account owner's actual possession if and only if they are withdrawn in the form of cash. Sums on deposit are discussed in Section 3C below. Demand deposit accounts are discussed in Chapter 5.

5.   *Does the general community property presumption apply to all property?* Should it? Does it apply, for example, to biological materials like sperm, ova, or embryos? Does it apply to rent controlled leaseholds? Does it apply to patents? To income generated from patents? Artwork? To income obtained from the sale of the artwork? Does it apply to military pensions? See Chapter 4.

6.   *Rebuttal by tracing.* The general presumption can be rebutted in one of two ways. It can be rebutted by tracing the disputed asset back to a provable separate property source. Or it can be rebutted by an agreement between the spouses, in which case the terms of the agreement decide the ownership of the asset. When tracing is used, ownership shares are calculated by using the following ratios.

REBUTTAL BY TRACING:
THE BASIC FORMULA

$$\frac{\text{CP contribution to purchase}}{\text{Purchase Price}} = \text{CP\% of ownership}$$

$$\frac{\text{SP contribution to purchase}}{\text{Purchase Price}} = \text{SP\% of ownership}$$

- **Step 1:** Net character contribution to purchase are divided by the purchase price of the asset to obtain proportional ownership shares. The legal necessity of using an historic purchase price as the denominator is explained in Chapter 5, Section 4B.

- **Step 2:** Net character contributions to purchase are reimbursed, without interest.

- **Step 3:** Proportional ownership shares are multiplied by asset appreciation (or depreciation), if any. Applicable, rents, issues and profits (if any) are also apportioned by reference to ownership percentages.

What standard of proof applies to a rebuttal claim? Citing *Wilson*, courts in other community property states began to discuss the California Family Code Section 760 general presumption as a property rule rather than as an evidentiary leniency. *Marriage of Ettefagh*, reproduced below, corrects that misunderstanding by clarifying that, as a legal matter, any credible evidence can be used to overcome the general community property presumption.

In *Ettefagh, infra,* valuable real estate was acquired during marriage by the husband Vahid, who titled the real estate acquisitions in his name alone. Upon dissolution, Vahid and wife Semrin disagreed about the characterization of the real estate. Both parties stipulated to the joinder of Vahid's father, Hashem, to the proceedings. Hashem testified that Vahid acted as his (Hashem's) agent in the purchase of the real estate, using Hashem's funds. The trial court judge exercised its discretion to raise the general community property presumption as to each of the disputed real estate parcels. Finding Hashem's testimony credible by a preponderance of the evidence, the court subsequently rebutted the general community property presumption on a parcel-by-parcel basis. Wife Semrin appealed; she argued that the evidentiary standard for rebutting the general community property presumption should be the higher clear and convincing standard, as only that higher standard was consistent with the fiduciary duties that spouses owe each other during marriage.

The First District Court of Appeal applied the substantial evidence standard to the trial court's factual findings. It applied the de novo standard to the legal question of which evidentiary standard to use—the lower preponderance of the evidence or the higher clear and convincing evidence? Ultimately, Justice Simons decided that the low preponderance of the evidence standard was the correct one to use in the context of a dissolution proceeding. The rationales given were that the lower standard furthers the goals of the California no-fault community property system and promotes the equality of interest principle by equally distributing the *risk of judicial error* between the spouses.

MARRIAGE OF ETTEFAGH

150 Cal.App.4th 1578, 59 Cal.Rptr.3d 419 (1st Dist. 2007)

SIMONS, ACTING P. J.

On appeal from a judgment of dissolution, Semrin Ettefagh [Semrin] challenges numerous property and support rulings issued by the trial court. In the published portion of our Family Code section 760 that property acquired by either spouse during marriage is community property. The parties agree that the presumption is rebuttable, affects the burden of proof and is overcome by sufficient evidence that the property was a gift to one of the spouses. The parties divide, however, on the quantum of evidence required. Semrin claims that the trial court erred in holding that the presumption of section 760 could be rebutted if her former husband, Vahid Ettefagh [Vahid] established by a preponderance of the evidence that the contested property was a gift to him. She asserts that clear and convincing evidence of a gift is required to rebut the community property presumption. We conclude, however, that the trial court applied the correct standard of proof. In the unpublished portion of the opinion, we reject a number of other arguments raised by Semrin and affirm.

FACTUAL AND PROCEDURAL BACKGROUND

The Parties

As a teenager, she moved with her family to Los Angeles, where, in 1971, she met Vahid, a native of Iran. The couple married in August 1972. Both attended college in the United States, after which they moved to Iran in 1977. The parties had two children, one of whom, Jehan, was a minor at the time of trial. Semrin and Vahid separated in 1996. Semrin later returned to California and filed a petition for dissolution of the marriage on August 28, 1997. After the petition was filed, the parties stipulated to the joinder of Vahid's father, Hashem Ettefagh [Hashem] as a claimant in the proceedings.

Properties in Controversy

At trial, one of the principal contested issues was the characterization of four parcels of California real estate (collectively the California properties). The first parcel acquired was referred to as "Santa Ana Court" in Tiburon and was deeded to "Vahid Ettefagh, an unmarried man," on May 4, 1987. This recital in the deed is obviously incorrect, since Vahid had been married to Semrin for over a decade at the time the property was deeded. Hashem testified at trial that he provided the funds for the purchase of this property. Vahid testified that he invested neither his personal funds nor any funds from his family's textile corporations in the Santa Ana Court property. Vahid later conveyed the property to Hashem on March 8, 1994.

The parties refer to the second parcel as the "Larkspur Shopping Center property." On April 27, 1990, the Southern Pacific Transportation Company transferred this property to Vahid and his sister, Maryam Ettefagh, granting each an undivided one-half interest. This deed also erroneously refers to "Vahid Ettefagh, an unmarried man." Again, Hashem testified that he contributed funds used to purchase the property, but that Vahid did not. Vahid testified that he contributed neither personal nor corporate funds to its acquisition. On March 8, 1994, Vahid conveyed this property to Hashem.

The third and fourth properties are both located in Santa Rosa. The parties refer to them as "Santa Rosa large" and "Santa Rosa small." On August 5, 1992, Vahid's sister, Shahla Ettefagh, conveyed a 50-percent interest in the "Santa Rosa small" property to "Vahid Ettefagh, a married man as his sole and separate property." Hashem's testimony was that he used money from his Bank of America account for the downpayment on this property and that Vahid paid no money for the property when it was purchased. Vahid also testified that none of his funds were used for the purchase. Vahid conveyed his interest in this property to Hashem on March 8, 1994.

Hashem granted an undivided one-half interest in the fourth parcel, the "Santa Rosa large" property, to Vahid on January 23, 1989. Vahid testified that his funds were not used to purchase the property. By grant deed dated March 8, 1994, Vahid conveyed his interest in this property to Hashem.

In addition to the properties in California the parties also had significant real property holdings abroad, including several pieces of real property in Iran and Turkey. These included an interest in a residential property on Anaherta Street in Tehran, parcels of property identified as "Golnar," an apartment referred to as "Lavasoon," a ski chalet in Shemshak, Iran, seaside apartments located in Ayvaluk, Turkey, and parcels of land referred to as Shomal 1, 2 and 3.

The Trial Court's Decision

After an 18-day trial, on January 19, 2005, the trial court issued a 20-page statement of decision, making a number of dispositions regarding the parties' real and personal property, and awards of spousal and child support. We summarize only those aspects of the statement of decision relevant to the issues on appeal.

After reviewing the testimony concerning the California properties, in which Semrin claimed a community property interest, the trial court noted that "[g]enerally, these properties were either purchased by Hashem with his own funds and then title placed in that of his son Vahid in order to assist him in obtaining a green card and entry into the United State[s], *or,* Vahid sent money he had earned during the marriage from Iran to his father in California so that his father could purchase property and invest for Vahid." The parties agreed that these properties were presumed to be community assets under section 760 because they were acquired during the marriage. Despite the presumption, the trial court found that the California properties were Vahid's separate property. It explained there was no documentary evidence supporting Semrin's claims that the funds used to purchase these properties came from her husband. In addition, the trial court appears to have credited Hashem's testimony that he purchased these properties with his own funds and simply placed title in Vahid's name.

In reaching its decision concerning the California properties, the trial court expressly rejected Semrin's contention that the community property presumption of section 760 can only be overcome by clear and convincing evidence. Citing *In re Marriage of Haines* (1995) 33 Cal.App.4th 277, 39 Cal.Rptr.2d 673, the trial court concluded that a party seeking to overcome the presumption established by section 760 must establish the separate nature of the property by a preponderance of the evidence. Since section 760 is not a title presumption, "virtually any credible evidence" could be relied upon to overcome it. The court determined that the presumption had been rebutted because "the evidence demonstrates that Vahid acquired interests in the California properties as gifts from his father Hashem. There is insufficient testimony and no written documentation to the contrary." * * *

I. The Community Property Presumption of Section 760

Semrin's principal contention on appeal is that the trial court applied the wrong standard of proof in ruling that the California properties were Vahid's separate property. Because the properties were acquired during the marriage, Semrin correctly notes that they are presumed to be community property under section 760. She argues that Vahid was required to produce clear and convincing evidence to rebut this presumption and that the trial court erred in accepting "any credible evidence" to overcome the presumption. We disagree; nothing in the constitutional, statutory, or decisional law of this state requires a higher standard of proof than preponderance of the evidence.

A.   Standard of Review

We review the trial court's factual findings regarding the existence and character of the parties' property under the substantial evidence standard. The trial court's selection of what legal principles to apply is subject to de novo review. (*Bono v. Clark* (2002) 103 Cal.App.4th 1409, 1421, 128 Cal.Rptr.2d 31.) This includes the choice of the applicable standard of proof, which is a question of law that we review de novo. (See *In re Marriage of Weaver* (1990) 224 Cal.App.3d 478, 488–489, 273 Cal.Rptr. 696.)

B.   The Standard of Proof Required to Overcome the Presumption in Section 760 is Preponderance of the Evidence

1.   The Legal Context

Before addressing Semrin's first claim, it is helpful to review certain statutory rules that necessarily guide our decision. Two different Family Code sections are relevant to our inquiry. Section 760 states the presumption that, except as otherwise provided by statute, all property acquired during marriage is community property. On the other hand, section 770, subdivision (a)(2) provides, "(a) Separate property of a married person includes all of the following: * * * (2) All property acquired by the person after marriage by gift, bequest, devise, or descent."

"A presumption is an assumption of fact that the law requires to be made from another fact or group of facts found or otherwise established in the action. A presumption is not evidence." (Evid.Code, § 600, subd. (a).) Presumptions are either conclusive or rebuttable, and rebuttable presumptions are divided into two categories, those affecting the burden of producing evidence and those affecting the burden of proof. (Evid.Code, § 601.) The parties do not dispute that Family Code section 760 is a rebuttable presumption affecting the burden of proof, but argue over the standard of proof necessary to prove a fact, like gift, that overcomes the presumption.

The Legislature has directed that the standard of proof will generally be by a preponderance of the evidence. Evidence Code section 115 states that "[e]xcept as otherwise provided by law, the burden of proof requires proof by a preponderance of the evidence." As used in this section, the word " 'law' includes constitutional, statutory, and decisional law." * * * The preponderance of the evidence standard is the "default standard of proof" in civil actions in this state. * * * While clear and convincing proof is occasionally required by case law, "it remains an *alternative* to the standard of proof by a preponderance of the evidence." * * *

In this case, no party has cited, and we have not found, any constitutional or statutory provision that would require a burden of proof other than preponderance of the evidence to rebut the community property presumption. Semrin's claim that the community property presumption may be overcome only by the production of clear and convincing evidence rests instead on case law. * * * An examination of the relevant case law reveals a host of decisions with inconsistent statements regarding the requisite burden of proof. These cases often lack any consideration of contradictory rulings or substantial analysis of the issue. In evaluating these cases, we are guided by the Supreme Court's admonition that " 'judicial expressions purporting to require clear and convincing [or clear and satisfactory] evidence must be read in light of the statutory provision for proof by a preponderance of the evidence." * * *

2. *The Case Law*

Semrin relies on four cases to argue that the community property presumption may be overcome only by clear and convincing evidence. In *Estate of Niccolls* (1912) 164 Cal. 368, 371, 129 P. 278, the court stated, "the burden of overcoming the [community property] presumption by clear and satisfactory evidence rests upon the party claiming that the property is separate." *Gagan v. Gouyd* (1999) 73 Cal.App.4th 835, 843, 86 Cal.Rptr.2d 733 concluded that the contesting spouse "has the burden of proving by clear and convincing evidence that the property is separate, not community." *In re Marriage of Ashodian* (1979) 96 Cal.App.3d 43, 48, 157 Cal.Rptr. 555 stated that postnuptial acquisition of property "is presumed community unless proven otherwise by clear and convincing evidence." Finally, *Thomasset v. Thomasset* (1953) 122 Cal.App.2d 116, 123, 264 P.2d 626 noted "expressions in the decisions to the effect that the separate character of property acquired after marriage is to be established by 'clear and convincing evidence,' 'clear and decisive proof,' [and] 'clear and satisfactory proof.' "

A careful examination of these cases is revealing, however. For example, in *Estate of Niccolls, supra,* 164 Cal. 368, 129 P. 278, the Supreme Court's statement that "clear and satisfactory evidence" is needed to overcome the community property presumption (*id.* at p. 371, 129 P. 278) was dictum, unnecessary to the court's decision. In the very same paragraph, the court related that the evidence regarding the acquisition of the subject property was "without substantial conflict" and that "it pointed *indisputably* to the conclusion that the house and lot in controversy were not community property." * * *

In *Gagan v. Gouyd, supra,* 73 Cal.App.4th 835, 86 Cal.Rptr.2d 733, though the court noted that the wife had "the burden of proving by clear and convincing evidence that the property is separate" * * * , it held there was *no evidence* that the wife's interest was her separate property. * * *

Thus the wife's proof would have failed under either standard. Moreover, *Gagan* relied on *Ashodian* as support for the proposition that clear and convincing evidence is needed to rebut the community property presumption. *Ashodian,* however, concerned the distinct property presumption attaching to a wife's pre-1975 acquisitions of property by an instrument in writing (§ 803, subd. (a)), and is therefore inapposite. * * *

Thomasset acknowledged "expressions in the decisions to the effect that the separate character of property acquired after marriage is to be established by 'clear and convincing evidence,' 'clear and decisive proof,' [or] 'clear and satisfactory proof' " * * * , but went on to declare that "[t]he decision of the trier of fact must be according to the *preponderance of evidence.* * * *" Later cases have interpreted *Thomasset* in this fashion. (See *In re Marriage of Fabian* (1986) 41 Cal.3d 440, 446, 224 Cal.Rptr. 333, 715 P.2d 253 [citing *Thomasset* for the proposition that "[t]o overcome the community property presumption the spouse asserting a separate property interest must establish *by a preponderance of the evidence* that the parties had a contrary agreement" (italics added)]; *Patterson v. Patterson* (1966) 242 Cal.App.2d 333, 341, 51 Cal.Rptr. 339 [noting that community property presumption "may be overcome by a preponderance of the evidence" and citing *Thomasset* as support].) Though relied upon by Semrin, *Thomasset* undermines her position.

Semrin also relies on Witkin as support for her claim that clear and convincing evidence is required to overcome the community property presumption. (1 Witkin, Cal. Evidence (4th ed. 2000) Burden of Proof and Presumptions, §§ 38, 39, pp. 187–189.) But Witkin relies primarily on *Estate of Nickson* (1921) 187 Cal. 603, 203 P. 106 (*Nickson*), which is questionable authority for this proposition. In *Nickson,* the court recognized that "the presumption is one which can only be overcome by 'clear and satisfactory proof' or * * * by 'clear and convincing evidence,' " but, the court went on to say, "we are still required to determine the scope and meaning of [those] terms." * * * *Nickson* then relied on *Freese v. Hibernia Sav. etc. Soc.* (1903) 139 Cal. 392, 73 P. 172, to conclude " '[t]he property is merely considered as the property of the community until the contrary is shown by legal proof, and legal proof would seem to be a preponderance of the testimony under all the facts and circumstances of the particular case." * * * We are of the opinion that it is incumbent on the party seeking to overcome the presumption of community property to do no more than to produce such legal evidence as, under all the circumstances of the particular case, would ordinarily produce conviction in an unprejudiced mind, and that in the face of such evidence the naked presumption, unsupported by any testimony, must fall.' " (*Nickson,* at p. 606, 203 P. 106, quoting *Freese,* at p. 395, 73 P. 172 * * *)

Thus, *Nickson* defined "clear and convincing" evidence to mean, simply, a preponderance. But, the high court's seeming embrace of both standards makes it weak authority for either.

Several cases have recognized that a mere preponderance of the evidence is sufficient to overcome the community property presumption. (See, e.g., *In re Marriage of Fabian, supra,* 41 Cal.3d at p. 446, 224 Cal.Rptr. 333, 715 P.2d 253 ["To overcome the community property presumption the spouse asserting a separate property interest must establish by a preponderance of the evidence that the parties had a contrary agreement." (dictum)]; *In re Marriage of Haines, supra,* 33 Cal.App.4th at p. 290, 39 Cal.Rptr.2d 673 ["The burden of proof for the party contesting community property status is by a preponderance of the evidence."]; *In re Marriage of Aufmuth* (1979) 89 Cal.App.3d 446, 455, 152 Cal.Rptr. 668 ["This presumption is rebuttable [citation], and it may be overcome by a preponderance of the evidence."]; *Patterson v. Patterson, supra,* 242 Cal.App.2d at p. 341, 51 Cal.Rptr. 339 ["A presumption arises that the post-marital property is community but this presumption may be overcome by a preponderance of the evidence."].) None of these cases cite *Nickson,* or distinguish the cases relied upon by Semrin, or provide any analysis to buttress their conclusion. Examining the policy factors that should determine the burden of proof selected for any particular fact strongly supports the preponderance standard.

3.   *An Analysis of the Interests at Risk*

As our Supreme Court has observed, the selection of a standard of proof reflects the significance our society attaches to a given issue. " 'The function of a standard of proof * * * is to "instruct the factfinder concerning the degree of confidence our society thinks [the factfinder] should have in the correctness of factual conclusions for a particular type of adjudication." * * * The standard serves to allocate the risk of error between the litigants and to indicate the relative importance attached to the ultimate decision.' " * * * The standard of proof required in a given situation "may depend upon the 'gravity of the consequences that would result from an erroneous determination of the issue involved.' " * * *

When the preponderance of the evidence standard applies, the parties to an action share the risk of an erroneous determination more or less equally. * * * " 'Any other standard expresses a preference for one side's interests' " * * * , and the clear and convincing standard is imposed in those cases in which particularly important individual interests or rights are at stake. (See, e.g., *Estate of Ford* (2004) 32 Cal.4th 160, 172–173, 8 Cal.Rptr.3d 541, 82 P.3d 747 [proof of equitable adoption]; *Conservatorship of Wendland, supra,* 26 Cal.4th at pp. 546–548, 110 Cal.Rptr.2d 412, 28 P.3d 151 [withdrawal of artificial nutrition and hydration from conservatee]; *In re Angelia P.* (1981) 28 Cal.3d 908, 922, 171 Cal.Rptr. 637,

623 P.2d 198 [termination of parental rights]; see also *Addington v. Texas, supra,* 441 U.S. at pp. 425, 432–433, 99 S.Ct. 1804 [commitment to mental hospital]; *Woodby v. Immigration Service* (1966) 385 U.S. 276, 285, 87 S.Ct. 483, 17 L.Ed.2d 362 [deportation].)

To determine whether the clear and convincing standard of proof is appropriate in this case, we look to the interests of the spouses as defined by the Legislature in the Family Code. * * * Section 760 provides that property acquired during marriage is community property, while section 770 creates an exception for gifts to either spouse. No evident societal interest would seem to favor either provision, and the effect of these two statutes has been stated as a single rule: "Generally, property acquired during marriage by either spouse, other than by gift or inheritance, is community property." * * * A determination of how the property in question was acquired—by gift or by purchase with community funds affects only the classification of the property as either separate or community. * * * The interests of husband and wife in *community* property are "present, existing, and equal" (§ 751), but neither spouse, ordinarily, has any interest in the *separate* property of the other (§ 752).

Peters [52 Cal.App.4th 1487, 1491, 61 Cal.Rptr.2d 493 (3d Dist. 1997)] is instructive. In that case, the court reviewed the trial court's determination of the date of separation. Section 771 provides, "The earnings and accumulations of a spouse * * *, while living separate and apart from the other spouse, are the separate property of the spouse." This section will, in some cases, make the date of separation significant in the property allocation. The *Peters* court determined that the "date of separation is proven by a preponderance of the evidence rather than by clear and convincing evidence." * * * It concluded that imposing the higher burden of proof reflects a preference for the interests of one of the parties and occurs only when interests " 'more substantial than mere loss of money' " are at stake. * * * Because the "date of separation affects only the classification of property" and each spouse has identical economic interests at risk in disputing the date of separation, the equal distribution of risk requires application of the preponderance standard. * * *

In this case, as in *Peters,* only money is at stake and both spouses share an equal risk that the court may err in classifying the property. If the trial court determines that the property was acquired by gift, then the property will be the receiving spouse's separate property, and the other spouse will lose the half interest in it to which he or she would otherwise be entitled under section 760. If, on the other hand, the trial court were to determine that the property was acquired with community funds (or that the contesting spouse had failed to overcome the community property presumption), then the property will be community property, and the receiving spouse will lose a half interest in it by operation of section 760. "Which spouse loses this economic interest depends on the trial court's determination. * * * The interests of the parties are inverse but equal. Since both parties have identical economic interests at risk in contesting [the method of acquisition], it would otherwise be appropriate to apply the preponderance standard on the issue because of its roughly equal distribution of the risk of error." * * *

In sum, the case law is inconclusive and the nature of the parties' interests at risk in this dispute are purely economic and relatively equal. Thus, we conclude the trial court correctly selected the preponderance of the evidence standard.

DISPOSITION

The judgment is affirmed. Respondents shall recover their costs on appeal. * * *

We concur. GEMELLO and NEEDHAM, JJ.

NOTES

1. *Only money?* Is money all that is at stake in a case like this? Was husband Vahid required to disclose to wife Semrin the fact that he was purchasing property during marriage not for the community but for his father? As between Vahid and Semrin, who was in the superior position to obtain records as to the source of funds that purchased the property? See *Brewer & Federici, supra.*

2. *Management and control.* Does a party who asserts a separate property interest in an asset also concede that he or she exercised exclusive management and control rights over that asset during the marriage? If so, what (if anything) excuses the party from having to produce financial documentation, like bank statements, at dissolution? In other words, a property owner has the right of exclusive control over a separate property asset. Does this right includes the right not to keep records to an asset whose character will most certainly be disputed in a dissolution?

3. *Disclosure of business and investment opportunities. Ettefagh* was decided five years after enhanced dissolution disclosure standards went into effect, and yet the court treats the case as a simple characterization issue. The case involved valuable appreciating assets, specifically residential and commercial real estate in expensive Northern California. The family home and some commercial properties were located in Marin County; other commercial real estate holdings were located in Sonoma County. So, in addition to characterization questions, disclosure questions loomed, but were left unaddressed in the court opinion. Assuming Vahid kept important financial information from Semrin (as it seems he did), should Semrin's attorney have raised the issue of nondisclosure from the outset? If Vahid's acts of nondisclosure were established, what remedy might Semrin have, if any? What remedy should she have?

Secrets are typically the basis of deception and coercion. Coercion is a factual basis for fraud. Assuming the real estate parcels that Vahid purchased were acquired during marriage while the parties were domiciled in California, as the court does, then one can deduce from Semrin's claims that Vahid failed to inform her that he was acting as his father's purchasing agent by using funds deposited into his (Vahid's) account by his father (Hashem) to buy real estate. California Family Code Section 721 imposes fiduciary standards on spouses as well as disclosure standards. For properties purchased during the marriage, did Vahid take unfair advantage of the marriage, and hence of Semrin, by not disclosing the financial facts behind the transaction? Did he take unfair advantage of Semrin's trust?

What about benefits that arose from the date of separation to the date of divorce? Pursuant to California Family Code Section 2102 (Chapter 8), to prevent fraud (among other wrongs) from the date of separation forward, written disclosure is required of "any investment opportunity, business opportunity, or other income-producing opportunity that presents itself after the date of separation, but that results from any investment, significant business activity outside the ordinary course of business, or other income-producing opportunity of either spouse from the date of marriage to the date of separation, inclusive." The disclosure must be made with enough time for the other spouse to decide if he or she (wife Semrin in this case) wants to "participate in the opportunity." If such written disclosure is not made "the division of any gain resulting from that opportunity" is treated as an omitted asset and subject to the continuing jurisdiction of the court (Chapter 8).

4. *Corroborating evidence and rebuttal standards.* What if financial documents are unclear, unpersuasive, or missing, should the separate property claimant be required to introduce corroborating evidence of his or her separate property claim? If a community property system uses the lower preponderance of the evidence standard for community property presumptions, as California's system does, should one corroborating witness be sufficient to rebut the general community property presumption? Two? Three? Should the witness's relationship to the separate property claimant weigh against permitting the witness to testify as a corroborating witness for purposes of rebuttal?

Vahid's testimony, as an interested party in the dissolution proceeding, was corroborated by his father Hashem, who claimed to be the true owner of the parcels. On appeal the issue was solely whether there was substantial evidence for the trial court to have found that the general community property presumption was rebutted by a preponderance of the evidence. The appellate court upheld the trial court judgment based on the testimony of one credible, but interested, witness.

In *Zagorski v. Zagorski*, 116 S.W.3d 309, 317 (Tex. Civ. App. 2003), a dispute arose over $2,057,524.20 that husband Anthony received by wire transfer during marriage from a foreign bank account. Wife Lori argued that the deposit was income received during marriage and therefore community in character. She argued that the money had been loaned by Anthony, before marriage, to various foreign business entities that then repaid him with interest, during marriage, at his request. Lori also argued that Anthony had opted to repatriate the money for his personal use, and to that end he deposited the $2,057,524.20 into an account where it became commingled to the point of confusion with (other) community property sums on deposit. In response Anthony introduced inception of title evidence based on documents and corroborating testimony. After a nine-day bench trial, the Texas trial court raised a general possession-based presumption of community property as to the $2,057,524.20, but then ruled that because Anthony had rebutted the presumption by clear and convincing evidence the $2,057,524.20 was Anthony's separate property. Lori appealed. The Texas Court of Appeal applied the substantial evidence standard to affirm the trial court. Anderson J. explained that even though Anthony's documentary evidence of inception of title was not as specific as it could have been, the trial court nevertheless found that it had been corroborated by the testimony of three credible witnesses. The testimony of each of the three witnesses met the clear and convincing standard of proof required to rebut the community property presumption found at TEX. FAM. CODE ANN. § 3.003 (West 1998). *Zagorski* distinguished *Robles v. Robles*, 965 S.W. 2d 605, 616 (Tex. Civ. App. 1998), writ denied, as standing for the principle that the "*un*corroborated testimony of [an] interested party does not conclusively establish a fact even when uncontradicted." (Italics in the original.). *Id.* at 317.

How would *Ettefagh* be decided under Texas law?

5. *If any evidence can be accepted to rebut the general community property presumption, can the same be said for proof of disclosure?* Do you agree that the trial court's exercise of discretion to rebut the community property presumption as to the disputed properties met the substantial evidence standard on appeal? The trial court found Hashem to be a credible witness, but should the trial court have also required Vahid to provide financial documentation to support his claims that he accepted money from his father to act as his father's purchasing agent? Would it make a difference if Vahid accepted the money by a wire transfer into his bank account? If he had accepted cash? If he had deposited his father's check into his and Semrin's joint deposit account?

The First District Court of Appeal found that the uncorroborated testimony of an interested party (Hashem) was substantial evidence to rebut the general community property presumption. It also held that the correct rebuttal standard was the low preponderance of the evidence standard. In light of questions about disclosure, financial records, the parental relationship between the third-party and the separate property claimant, are you satisfied that a judicial error was minimized in *Ettefagh*?

More on standards of proof as instruments of state policy: is it good policy to rebut an acquisition-based community property presumption with a low preponderance of evidence standard? A possession-based community property presumption with a higher clear and convincing standard of proof? Or, is the higher clear and convince evidence standard a fairer choice no matter the type of community property presumption applied? Which review standard better protects the spouses as individuals? Which better protects the community? Which is consistent with statutory disclosure duties?

Dicta in earlier California cases suggested that a clear and convincing standard might be a fairer standard to use in a dissolution proceeding than the low preponderance of evidence standard. Those cases are superseded, however, by the ruling in *Ettefagh*.

6.   *Sums on deposit in an account.* California Probate Code Section 5305(a), discussed below, creates a special community property presumption for sums on deposit in any account of a married person during marriage. The special presumption is raised by evidence of sums on deposit in the account, which is to say that it is raised on the basis of possession. The presumption for sums on deposit is consistent with prior case law.

Ettefagh was decided in 2007, nearly fourteen years after the special presumption for sums on deposit in an account went into effect. If Vahid deposited his father's money into a bank account, he commingled those funds with community funds. But without financial records, the question of sums on deposit was not raised. How difficult is it to produce financial records for a bank accounts? Even if the records are not character specific (Chapter 5), when money is used to purchase appreciating assets, might it not be necessary to require disclosure of account records as part of normal disclosure and cooperative discovery (Chapter 8)?

7.   *Community property presumptions in relation to a* former *spouse's estate.* A former spouse whose ex-spouse dies more than four years *after* a final dissolution judgment is not entitled to use community property presumptions in the ex-spouse's probate proceeding. The former spouse must prove his or her claim as any other nonspousal claimant would.

Commingled accounts, fiduciary duties, disclosure, and negotiating marriage settlement agreements are discussed in Chapters 5, 6, 7, and 8.

WEST'S ANNOTATED CALIFORNIA FAMILY CODE

§ 802.   Property acquired during marriage terminated by dissolution more than four years prior to death

The presumption that property acquired during marriage is community property does not apply to any property to which legal or equitable title is held by a person at the time of the person's death if the marriage during which the property was acquired was terminated by dissolution of marriage more than four years before the death.

(Stats. 1992, c. 162 (A.B. 2650), § 10, operative Jan. 1, 1994.)

B. THE STATUTORY JOINT FORM TITLE COMMUNITY PROPERTY PRESUMPTION

California Family Code Section 2581 states a special community property presumption that applies only in a dissolution proceeding, and then only to assets that are titled in joint form. The special presumption supersedes the general community property presumption. Rebuttal is determined by the statute, which requires that a separate property proponent show evidence that the parties agreed, despite the joint form title, that the property was not to be community property in the event of dissolution. Proof can come in the form of a clear statement in the title document. Or it can come in the form of an extrinsic written agreement between the spouses that the property is not to be community property in the event of dissolution.

The special joint form title community property presumption cannot be rebutted by tracing.

If rebuttal fails the asset is entirely (100%) community property. In that case, tracing can be used to establish a statutory reimbursement amount (Chapter 5).

The California community property system permits spouses and registered domestic partners to choose from among four available concurrent title forms:

- Joint tenancy,
- Tenancy in common,
- Community property, and
- Community property with the right of survivorship.

WEST'S ANNOTATED CALIFORNIA FAMILY CODE

§ 750. Methods of holding property

Spouses may hold property as joint tenants or tenants in common, or as community property, or as community property with a right of survivorship.

(Stats. 1992, c. 162 (A.B. 2650), § 10, operative Jan. 1, 1994. Amended by Stats. 2001, c. 754 (A.B. 1697), § 2; Stats. 2014, c. 82 (S.B. 1306), § 13, eff. Jan. 1, 2015.)

———

A joint interest is defined by California Civil Code Section 683, originally enacted in 1872.

WEST'S ANNOTATED CALIFORNIA CIVIL CODE

§ 683. Joint tenancy; definition; method of creation

(a) A joint interest is one owned by two or more persons in equal shares, by a title created by a single will or transfer, when expressly declared in the will or transfer to be a joint tenancy, or by transfer from a sole owner to himself or herself and others, or from tenants in common or joint tenants to themselves or some of them, or to themselves or any of them and others, or from [spouses], when holding title as community property or otherwise to themselves or to themselves and others or to one of them and to another or others, when expressly declared in the transfer to be a joint tenancy, or when granted or devised to executors or trustees as joint tenants. A joint tenancy in personal property may be created by a written transfer, instrument, or agreement.

(b) Provisions of this section do not apply to a joint account in a financial institution if Part 2 (commencing with Section 5100) of Division 5 of the Probate Code applies to such an account.

(Enacted 1872. Amended by Stats. 1929, c. 93, p. 172, § 1; Stats. 1931, c. 1051, p. 2205, § 1; Stats. 1935, c. 234, p. 912, § 1; Stats. 1955, c. 178, p. 645, § 1; Stats. 1983, c. 92, § 1, operative July 1, 1984; Stats. 1989, c. 397, § 1, operative July 1, 1990; Stats. 1990, c. 79, (A.B. 759), § 1, operative July 1, 1991.)

———

The *joint tenancy* and the *tenancy in common* have their origins in early modern English common law. The title forms are still in widespread use in the U.S. today, although some states do not permit the joint tenancy form between spouses.

In California the joint tenancy and the tenancy in common title forms may be used by unmarried and married persons. The key component of the joint tenancy is the right of survivorship, which is an agreement between the title holders that upon the death of one, the survivor(s) will step into ownership of the whole without the necessity of probate. Tenancy in common property, by contrast, does not pass by right of survivorship; rather, the decedent's share of the property passes through the decedent's estate.

The *community property* title form is the default community property title in U.S. community property jurisdiction. In California the use of a community property title form is available to married persons and registered domestic partners, but not to unmarried partners. The traditional community property title does not include a right of survivorship; therefore upon the death of a spouse, his or her one-half interest in the community property asset passes by probate. A married person has the free right of devise as to his or her one-half community property interest. Many spouses devise their one-half interest to each other, but no rule requires that outcome. If a married person dies intestate, without a valid will, the decedent's one-half of the community property descends to the surviving spouse, who already owns one-half. The intestacy rule, therefore, effectively leaves the surviving spouse with a 100% interest in any community property asset (Chapter 9).

Community property with the right of survivorship is a recent community property title form authorized as of July 1, 2001 by the enactment of California Civil Code Section 682.1(a). Its use is restricted to married persons and registered domestic partners. The community property with the right of survivorship title form is a hybrid community property-slash-joint tenancy title. It is community property for purposes of characterization at death; and it includes a right of survivorship so that when the one spouse dies first, the surviving spouse steps into ownership of the whole without the necessity of probate.

One important benefit of both types of community property title forms is that the surviving spouse is eligible for a valuable double step-up in basis for purposes of calculating the surviving spouse's income tax liability when the asset is eventually sold.

In 1983, California Civil Code Section 683 was amended to add subdivision (b). The change is intended to "make clear that this section does not apply to a joint account in a credit union or an industrial loan company." 16 Cal.L.Rev. Comm. Reports 129 (1982); 83 S.J. 3245. What applies instead is the California Multiple-Party Accounts Law found in California Probate Code Sections 5100 through 5407. In 1989, California Civil Code Section 683 was amended to reflect the expansion of the California Multiple-Party Accounts Law to a wider array of demand deposit accounts.

In 1990, California adopted an updated Probate Code. The former Probate Code was replaced by a new code that took effect on July 1, 1991. Included within the newly enacted Probate Code is the California Multiple-Party Accounts Law, CAMPAL (Chapter 5). Included within CAMPAL, more particularly, is a specialized community property presumption discussed in Section 3C below.

WEST'S ANNOTATED CALIFORNIA CIVIL CODE

§ 682.1. Community property of [spouses]; subject to express declaration in transfer documents; application and operation of section

(a)   Community property of [the spouses], when expressly declared in the transfer document to be community property with right of survivorship, and which may be accepted in writing on the face of the document by a statement signed or initialed by the grantees, shall, upon the death of one of the spouses, pass to the survivor, without administration, pursuant to the terms of the instrument, subject to the same procedures, as property held in joint tenancy. Prior to the death of either spouse, the right of survivorship may be terminated pursuant to the same procedures by which a joint tenancy may be severed. . . .

(b) This section does not apply to a joint account in a financial institution to which Part 2 (commencing with Section 5100) of Division 5 of the Probate Code applies.

(c) This section shall become operative on July 1, 2001, and shall apply to instruments created on or after that date.

(Added by Stats. 2000, c. 645 (A.B. 2913), § 1, operative July 1, 2001.)

––––––––

Cross references to the above code section locate the general community property presumption in California Family Code Section 760.

The need for California Civil Code Section 682.1 was summarized in the Legislative Committee reports as follows:

> "Although it may be commonly understood that property acquired by the spouses during marriage which is held in joint tenancy form is presumed to be community property, less understood is that this presumption applies only for the purposes for division of property upon dissolution or legal separation. If one party dies, the language of how title is held in the deed is controlling, not the community property presumption. . . . People are often under the misperception that because they acquired a home during marriage, the home will be treated as community property, with the tax advantages that accrue to community property upon the death of a spouse, regardless of the form of title. This is simply not the case. . . .

> Historically, spouses in California have been told that in order to avoid probate, they should hold their property in joint tenancy. . . . Often, however, taking title in joint tenancy may not be the most desirable option for tax reasons. Spouses nevertheless frequently wish to provide for an automatic right of survivorship for their community property, which cannot be altered by will, and which need not pass through probate. This [statute] creates that new form of title—community property with right of survivorship—which the parties may elect if they so choose. . . . This [legislation] does not affect, in any way presumptions regarding title to real property. Rather, it works on a prospective

basis, defining a new form of property which will avoid future confusion regarding title."

Editor's note: if you are interested in the events that led to the passage of the California special joint form title community property presumption or if you are analyzing a case in which the marriage ended by death, read on. Otherwise, skip to Sections 1 and 2 below. Start reading again at Section 3 below for a discussion of the most current legislation.

1. Early Twentieth-Century Case Law on Property Purchased with Community Property but Titled in Joint Tenancy

The early case law continues to apply when a marriage ends by death (Chapter 9). For that reason, it is useful to know the debate that early cases generated.

Important reminder: In a dissolution proceeding, the early case law discussed below is *superseded* by California Family Code Section 2581 and, where applicable, California Probate Code Section 5305(a).

Prior to the passage of the special joint form title community property presumption buying property with community property dollars but then taking title to that property in joint tenancy was considered a difficult to decipher message. Was the property community property because of the source of purchase funds? Or, was it separate property because the use of a common law title form raised a title presumption that, if left unrebutted, had the effect of transmuting the community property purchase funds into separate property?

Two legal rules arose to deal with the situation. One rule was expressed in *Siberell v. Siberell*, 214 Cal. 767, 773, 7 P.2d 1003 (1932). A contrary rule was expressed in *Tomaier v. Tomaier*, 23 Cal.2d 754, 146 P. 2d 905 (1944).

Siberell instructs on the nature of the joint tenancy title, and the relationship between common law titles and community property titles in the California community property system. Citing *De Witt v. San Francisco*, 2 Cal 289, 297 (1852), *Siberell* explains:

> " 'Joint tenancy is a technical feudal estate, founded like the laws of primogeniture, on the principle of the aggregation of landed estates in the hands of a few, and opposed to their division among many persons. For the creation of a joint tenancy, four unities are required, namely, unity of interest, unity of title, unity of time, unity of possession.' " *Id.* at 771.

The court goes on to state:

" . . . from the very nature of the estate, as between husband and wife, a community estate and a joint tenancy cannot exist at the same time *in the same property.*" (Italics added.) *Id.* at 773.

Notwithstanding its deference to the factfinder's decision, *Siberell* announced that the use of a joint tenancy deed transmutes community property purchase funds as of the date of acquisition. The court reasoned that the joint tenancy deed reflected the parties' agreement to avoid the complications of probate law for the titled asset, but their agreement was enforceable even if the marriage ended by dissolution. (This part of the *Siberell* opinion is superseded by California Family Code Section 2580 et. seq. reproduced and discussed below.) *Siberell* justified its approach by likening the joint tenancy deed to a binding (first) agreement between the parties:

"[T]he use of community funds to purchase the property and the taking of title thereto in the name of the spouses as joint tenants is tantamount to a binding agreement between them that the same shall not thereafter be held as community property but instead as a joint tenancy with all the characteristics of such an estate. It would be manifestly inequitable and a subversion of the rights of both husband and wife to have them in good faith enter into a valid engagement of this character and, following the demise of either, to have a contention made that his or her share in the property was held for the community, thus bringing into operation of the law of descent, administration, rights of creditors and other complications which would defeat the right of survivorship, the chief incident of the law of joint tenancy." *Id.* at 773.

Five years later, in *Watson v. Peyton*, 10 Cal.2d 156, 73 P.2d 906 (1937), the spouses used community property funds to acquire a house in joint tenancy. When their marriage ended by dissolution rather than death, the community property proponent argued that the "first binding agreement" rationale stated in *Siberell* should not apply in a dissolution proceeding. The community property proponent conceded that she had been the one to suggest that the spouses take title as joint tenants for purposes of avoiding probate complications. But, she argued, the spouses agreed only to what might happen if the marriage ended by death; they never discussed dissolution. *Watson* followed the general rule stated in *Siberell* that a joint tenancy title is a first binding agreement between the spouses to transmute community property purchase funds into the concurrently owned separate property asset. But the court decided—in light of the evidence that the parties had not discussed dissolution when they bought the property—that the community property proponent would be permitted to rebut the first agreement (established by the joint tenancy title) with a second agreement that the asset was to be community property in the event of a dissolution.

Watson was decided in an era when the California community property system permitted oral transmutations (Chapter 1). Against this backdrop, *Watson* cited *Siberell* (a joint tenancy deed is a binding first agreement to transmute community property purchase funds to separate property); but rather than treat the first agreement as a valid transmutation of community property purchase funds to separate property realty, the court treated it as a presumption rebuttable by a second agreement. In *Watson* there was no substantial evidence of a second agreement (undisclosed intentions do not rise to the level of an agreement for purposes of rebutting a title presumption). The wife was therefore estopped from "defeating her act [of taking joint tenancy title] by testimony of a hidden intention not disclosed to the other party at the time of the execution of the document."

Tomaier, involved two parcels of real estate—one in California and one in Missouri—two trials, and two appeals, one of which went all the way to the California Supreme Court. Each parcel was acquired with community property funds with title was taken in joint tenancy form. The first trial court applied *Siberell* to hold that taking title in joint tenancy community property transmuted the purchase funds, but it overlooked *Watson* when it excluded the husband's rebuttal evidence. The husband appealed. The question on appeal was whether the joint tenancy title transmuted community property purchase funds into separate property on the date of acquisition (the *Siberell* transmutation theory) or merely raised a presumption of transmutation that could be rebutted by a second agreement that the property was not as stated in the title (the *Watson* presumption theory).

Ultimately, *Tomaier* accepted the *Siberell* explanation of common law titles as separate property in character, but it ruled that *Watson* was the better statement of law. Thus in the context of a dissolution proceeding, the rule became that a joint tenancy title raised a presumption of separate property that was rebuttable with evidence of a second binding agreement to treat the titled asset as community property for purposes of dissolution.

Tomaier was decided before the adoption of the special joint form title community property presumption currently found at California Family Code Section 2580 et seq., below. In light of the legislation, *Tomaier* is superseded for purposes of a dissolution proceeding, but still serves as precedent in the context of probate. Thus in a probate proceeding, the rule in *Tomaier* is that a joint tenancy or tenancy in common title form is presumed to be the character stated in the title document: common law titles are separate property in character; community property titles are community property in character; and rebuttal rests with the party who challenges the title character (Chapter 9).

In the intervening years between *Tomaier* (1944), and the year that the first statutory joint form title presumption went into effect (1965), dozens of conflicting decisions were handed down. Some accepted the *Siberell* transmutation by deed approach. Others relied on the *Tomaier* rebuttable presumption approach. Few if any of these cases adequately addressed the empirical soundness of the first-agreement rationale. That theory is questionable since attorneys do not ordinarily assist in routine residential real estate transactions in California.

Case after case illustrated dissolution traps that uninformed but otherwise good faith spouses might fall into by the simple act of using community property funds to buy an asset whose title was taken in joint tenancy form. The flood of cases revealed the legal fiction on which *Siberell* and *Tomaier* rest, namely that when spouses buy property they do so with full knowledge of how common law joint titles (joint tenancy and tenancy in common) and community property joint titles operate within the context of the California community property system.

2. Mid-Twentieth-Century Legislative Attempts at a Statutory Joint Title Community Property Presumption

In 1965 the California Legislature enacted a special community property presumption the effect of which was to overrule *Siberell* and supersede *Tomaier*. The 1965 legislation provided that "for the purpose of the division of such property upon dissolution of marriage or legal separation only, the presumption is that such single family residence is the community property of the husband and wife." The 1965 legislation was limited on its face to dissolution proceedings and to "a single family residence of a husband and wife acquired by them during marriage as joint tenants. . . ." In 1969, effective 1970, the California Family Act was passed; the legal transition repealed the 1965 legislation for purposes of the Civil Code, but subsequently continued it in the Family Act.

The legislation did not speak to rebuttal methods. Thus, in 1980, *Marriage of Lucas*, 27 Cal.3d 808, 166 Cal.Rtpr. 853, 614 P.2d 285 (1980), excerpted below, was decided. The issue was how, as a matter of law, the 1965 special presumption could be rebutted. The Lucases were married from 1964 to 1976, during which time they purchased a single family residence with a separate property down payment (belonging to the wife) and a community property loan. The spouses took title to the residence as joint tenants to avoid probate. Their marriage ended by dissolution instead.

Under the legislation (then California Civil Code Section 5110) the disputed Lucas family residence was presumptively characterized as community property. The trial court permitted the separate property contributor to rebut the special joint title presumption by tracing the down payment back to her separate property trust funds. The community property proponent appealed. The California Supreme Court reversed, saying that there was no substantial evidence of a second rebuttal agreement. The court relied on the *Tomaier* rationale. In the absence of a second agreement, the house remained entirely (100%) community property, notwithstanding the fact that a separate property down payment was used to purchase the house. *Lucas* went on to hold that the separate property contribution to purchase was presumed to be a gift made by the separate property owner to the community property estate absent evidence to the contrary. The gift rationale part of the *Lucas* decision was repealed by California Family Code Section 2640, discussed below, a move that raised retroactivity issues (Chapter 4).

The rebuttal rationale in *Lucas* was codified in 1983 by an amendment to the 1965 legislation that took effect on January 1, 1984. Former Civil Code Sections 4800.1 and 4800.2—the 1984 legislation—accomplished three goals. One, it applied to any asset acquired during marriage and titled in joint tenancy or tenancy in common. Two, it specified that rebuttal was to be by a second written agreement either in the title or in a separate document. Three, it recognized a statutory right of reimbursement for traceable separate property contributions that are made to the purchase of an entirely (100%) community property asset.

Litigation soon identified that the 1983 legislation contained two errors. The first error was that the language of the statute inadvertently omitted from its reach the concurrent title form known as "community property". Civil Code Sections 4800.1 and 4800.2. Because of this error the 1983 anti-Lucas amendment was limited on its face to property titled in joint tenancy and tenancy in common. (The concurrent title form of "community property with the right of survivorship" had not yet been created by the Legislature.) The second error, a consequence of the first error, was that divorcing spouses who produced a joint tenancy title could only rebut it with a written agreement, whereas those who produced a community property title could rebut with either a written or an oral agreement. The unintended consequences of the 1984 amendment was that it protected couples who relied on common law titles from the risk of judicial error caused by indeterminate oral rebuttal evidence, but it left couples who relied on community property titles exposed.

The 1983 oversight was corrected in 1986, effective January 1, 1987. From January 1, 1987 on, the special joint form title community property presumption applies to *any* asset in *any* joint form title, no matter the date of acquisition.

Application of the special joint form title presumption to pre-1987 acquisitions was held constitutional in *Marriage of Heikes*, 10 Cal.4th 1211,

44 Cal.Rptr.2d 155, 899 P.2d 1349 (1995). On the issue of rebuttal: *from 1984 on*, proof of a written agreement between the spouses is required to rebut the special community property presumption for concurrent common law titles (joint tenancy and tenancy by the entirety). However, because vested property interests are at stake, it is only *from 1987 on* that a written agreement becomes necessary to rebut the special presumption for property titled in community property form.

A distinct legal issue can arise if the rebuttal agreement is also a transmutation. In such a case, the rebuttal agreement may be subject to the California Family Code Section 852(a) transmutation formalities as well as to California Family Code Section 721(b). See *Marriage of Buol*, 39 Cal.3d 751, 218 Cal.Rptr. 31, 705 P.2d 354 (1985) (in bank).

Transmutations are covered in Chapter 1. Fiduciary duties are covered in Chapter 6.

3. Current Legislation: California Family Code Sections 2580 and 2581

Today, the legal transition from the pre-1965 decisional law to the 1965 legislation to the 1984 anti-Lucas legislation to the 1987 post-*Lucas* corrective legislation appears to be complete. The corrected Family Act statute, moreover, has been continued in the Family Code as California Family Code Sections 2580 and 2581, reproduced below.

Additionally, California Family Code Section 2640 clearly creates a statutory right of reimbursement when funds of one character are used to contribute to the purchase of an asset of an entirely different character. Reimbursement is without interest and may be subject to value limitations.

California Family Code Section 2581, which continues former Civil Code Section 4800.1, creates a special *community property* presumption to supersede *Siberell* and *Tomaier*. The special presumption applies to any asset in joint form, but application is limited to a dissolution proceeding only. Rebuttal is by evidence of a clear statement in the title document, or by an (enforceable) second agreement between the spouses. Tracing is not permitted to effect a rebuttal.

In the case of a successful rebuttal, proportional shares are determined by the subsequent (second) agreement.

If the rebuttal effort is unsuccessful, then the disputed asset is deemed entirely (100%) community property in character. In that case, California Family Code Section 2640(b), reproduced below, allows the separate property contributor to trace contributions to purchase to calculate any reimbursement due.

WEST'S ANNOTATED CALIFORNIA FAMILY CODE

§ 2580. Legislative findings and declarations; public policy

The Legislature hereby finds and declares as follows:

(a) It is the public policy of this state to provide uniformly and consistently for the standard of proof in establishing the character of property acquired by spouses during marriage in joint title form, and for the allocation of community and separate interests in that property between the spouses.

(b) The methods provided by case and statutory law have not resulted in consistency in the treatment of spouses' interests in property they hold in joint title, but rather, have created confusion as to which law applies to property at a particular point in time, depending on the form of title, and, as a result, spouses cannot have reliable expectations as to the characterization of their property and the allocation of the interests therein, and attorneys cannot reliably advise their clients regarding applicable law.

(c) Therefore, a compelling state interest exists to provide for uniform treatment of property. Thus, former Sections 4800.1 and 4800.2 of the Civil Code, as operative on January 1, 1987, and as continued in Sections 2581 and 2640 of this code, apply to all property held in joint title regardless of the date of acquisition of the property or the date of any agreement affecting the character of the property, and those sections apply in all proceedings commenced on or after January 1, 1984. However, those sections do not apply to property settlement agreements executed before January 1, 1987, or proceedings in which judgments were rendered before January 1, 1987, regardless of whether those judgments have become final.

(Added by Stats. 1993, c. 219 (A.B. 1500), § 111.6. Amended by Stats. 1993, c. 876 (S.B. 1068), § 15.2, eff. Oct. 6, 1993, operative Jan. 1, 1994.)

§ 2581. Division of property; presumptions

For the purpose of division of property on dissolution of marriage or legal separation of the parties, property acquired by the parties during marriage in joint form, including property held in tenancy in common, joint tenancy, or tenancy by the entirety, or as community property, is presumed to be community property. This presumption is a presumption affecting the burden of proof and may be rebutted by either of the following:

(a) A clear statement in the deed or other documentary evidence of title by which the property is acquired that the property is separate property and not community property.

(b) Proof that the parties have made a written agreement that the property is separate property.

(Added by Stats. 1993, c. 219 (A.B. 1500), § 111.7.)

§ 2640. Contributions to the acquisition of the property; waivers; amount of reimbursement

(a) "Contributions to the acquisition of property," as used in this section, include downpayments, payments for improvements, and payments that reduce the principal of a loan used to finance the purchase or improvement of the property but do not include payments of interest on the loan or payments made for maintenance, insurance, or taxation of the property.

(b) In the division of the community estate under this division, unless a party has made a written waiver of the right to reimbursement or has signed a writing that has the effect of a waiver, the party shall be reimbursed for the party's contributions to the acquisition of property of the community property estate to the extent the party traces the contributions to a separate property source. The amount reimbursed shall be without interest or adjustment for change in monetary values and may not exceed the net value of the property at the time of the division.

(c) A party shall be reimbursed for the party's separate property contributions to the acquisition of property of the other spouse's separate property estate during the marriage, unless there has been a transmutation . . . or a written waiver of the right to reimbursement. The amount reimbursed shall be without interest or adjustment for change in monetary values and may not exceed the net value of the property at the time of the division."

(Stats. 1992, c. 162 (A.B. 2650), § 10, operative Jan. 1, 1994. Amended by Stats. 1993, c. 219 (A.B. 1500), § 114.5; Stats. 2004, c. 119 (S.B. 1407), § 1.)

NOTE

Tracing establishes a prima facie statutory right of reimbursement in a dissolution action dividing an entirely community property asset. See *Marriage of Cochran*, 87 Cal.App.4th 1050, 104 Cal.Rptr. 2d 920 (4th Dist. 2001), as modified on subsequent appeal 2006 WL 2412798, unpublished.

———

Lucas remains important for educational purposes. Specifically useful is Justice Manuel's public policy discussion, which delineates between the general presumption and the special joint form title presumption.

MARRIAGE OF LUCAS

27 Cal.3d 808, 166 Cal.Rptr. 853, 614 P.2d 285 (1980)

MANUEL, J.

[T]he presumption arising from the form of title is to be distinguished from the general presumption * * * that property acquired during marriage is community property. [This is because a joint form title] is an affirmative act of specifying a form of ownership in the conveyance of title that removes such property from the more general presumption. * * * It is because of this express designation of ownership, that a greater showing is necessary to overcome the presumption arising therefrom than is necessary to overcome the more general presumption that property acquired during marriage is community property. In the latter situation, where there is no written indication of ownership interests as between the spouses, the general presumption of community property may be overcome simply by tracing the source of funds used to acquire the property to separate property. (*See In re Marriage of Mix* (1975) 14 Cal.3d 604, 608–612, 122 Cal.Rptr. 79, 536 P.2d 479; *Estate of Murphy* (1976) 15 Cal.3d 907, 917–919, 126 Cal.Rptr. 820, 544 P.2d 956; *See v. See* (1966) 64 Cal.2d 778, 783, 51 Cal.Rptr. 888, 415 P.2d 776.) It is not necessary to show that the spouses understood or intended that property traceable to separate property should remain separate.

The rule requiring an understanding or agreement comes into play when the issue is whether the presumption arising from the form of title has been overcome. It is supported by sound policy considerations, and we decline to depart from it. To allow a lesser showing could result in unfairness to the spouse who has not made the separate property contribution. Unless the latter knows that the spouse contributing the separate property expects to * * * acquire a separate property interest, he or she has no opportunity to attempt to preserve the joint ownership of the property by making other financing arrangements. The act of taking title in a joint and equal ownership form is inconsistent with an intention to preserve a separate property interest. Accordingly, the expectations of parties who take title jointly are best protected by presuming that the specified ownership interest is intended in the absence of an agreement or understanding to the contrary. * * *

In the present case there is no evidence of an agreement or understanding that [the separate property claimant] was to retain a separate property interest in the house. Nor is there any finding by the trial court on the question. The only findings in this regard are that neither party intended a gift to the other. Such evidence and findings are insufficient to rebut the presumption arising from title set forth in Civil Code section 5110, [current California Family Code 2581]. The trial court's determination must therefore be reversed. * * *

BIRD, C.J., and TOBRINER, MOSK, CLARK, RICHARDSON and NEWMAN, JJ., concur.

NOTES

1.   *Apportionment.* The apportionment aspects of the *Lucas* decision are considered in Chapter 5.

2.   *Unilateral creation and severance are allowed, but subject to challenge by a nonjoining spouse.* Common law joint title forms can be created and severed unilaterally under California Civil Code Section 683, reproduced above. Unilateral creation occurs when one spouse grants property to him or herself and the other spouse as joint owners, as when Spouse 1 conveys *"to Spouse 1 and Spouse 2 as joint tenants." Riddle v. Harmon*, 102 Cal.App.3d 524, 162 Cal.Rptr. 530 (1st Dist. 1980) did away with the common law strawperson requirement for severing a joint tenancy. *Riddle* says that unilateral severance occurs when one joint tenant conveys joint tenancy property to herself, as when O and A own property as joint tenants and O conveys *"to O."* O's conveyance breaks the unity of title, the effect being that title between O and A defaults to a tenancy in common.

Unilateral creation and severance by a spouse is subject to challenge under California Family Code Section 1102(a). Part of the management and control provisions, California Family Code Section 1102(a) protects spouses and third parties by requiring that spouses join (sign) in any conveyance of community real property. Failure to do so gives the nonjoining spouse a right to avoid the transaction for which joinder is missing. Since any joint form title is presumptively community property at dissolution, it is probable if not likely that California Family Code Section 2581 modifies, if not supersedes, *Riddle,* for purposes of characterizing property in a dissolution proceeding. If so, California Family Code Section 1102 would give the nonjoining spouse a basis upon which to challenge the other spouse's unilateral action to sever a joint title. Additionally, in a probate proceeding, severance of the right of survivorship must have been recorded to be effective as against the nonjoining spouse (Chapter 9).

3.   *Rebuttal versus reimbursement.* Tracing is a species of unilateral conduct. Tracing means that one spouse offers proof that funds for the purchase of an asset trace back to a provable separate property source. An agreement, by contrast, is a species of bilateral conduct. An agreement shows that both spouses consent to a certain outcome or outcomes in the event of a dissolution.

4.   *Substantial evidence.* In *Lucas,* the court found no evidence to rebut the community property presumption. What was needed, at a minimum, was a second agreement between the parties that a separate property contribution retained a separate property interest in the jointly titled asset.

Practice problem: X and Y acquire a house during marriage with community property funds. They take title as joint tenants. The house costs

$100,000. X contributes $25,000 of provable separate property funds to the purchase of the house in the form of a down payment. The community property contributes $75,000 to the purchase of the house. No additional agreements are entered into between the spouses on the date of acquisition. Assume that at dissolution, the house has a fair market value of $200,000. What is the character of the house? How much is each party entitled to from the sale proceeds?

- The joint form title raises the California Family Code Section 2581 community property presumption as to the house. The house is presumed to be entirely (100%) community property for purposes of dissolution.

- Rebuttal would require X—the separate property contributor— to produce a second agreement between X and Y that X is to retain a separate property interest in the house— notwithstanding use of a joint title form (joint tenancy)—in the event of dissolution.

- No rebuttal agreement exists in this case, meaning that the house is entirely (100%) community property.

- California Family Code Section 2640(b), which applies to the division of entirely community property assets, entitles X to a reimbursement, without interest, for X's $25,000 separate property down payment. This reimbursement can take the form of a lien against the property.

- When the house is sold for $200,000:

  o X is *reimbursed* $25,000 for the separate property down payment; payment releases X's lien;

  o The community is *reimbursed* $75,000 for its contribution to the purchase of the house.

- Appreciation belongs to the community since the underlying asset (the house) is entirely (100%) community property. Appreciation is divided in equal one-half shares between X and Y at dissolution.

- Transaction costs are borne entirely by the community, with each spouse responsible for one-half of the transactions costs.

5. *Commercial property. Lucas* was extended to commercial property in *Marriage of Cademartori*, 119 Cal.App.3d 970, 174 Cal.Rptr. 292 (1st Dist. 1981). In that case, spouse John sold real property in 1966. He invested the proceeds in a warehouse, taking title as "John P. Cademartori and Sandy Cademartori, his wife." The reviewing court held that the use of a joint title form indicated that the spouses had a first agreement to characterize the commercial property as community property for purposes of dissolution. That first agreement could only be rebutted by a second agreement that the warehouse was not to be community property in the event of a dissolution.

Unlike its 1965 predecessor statute, California Family Code Section 2581 applies at dissolution to *any* asset taken in *any* of the four available joint title forms, whether that asset is a single family residence, a vacation home, an investment property, a car, or any other asset. The special joint title form presumption protects the spouses' expectancy interest in the event of dissolution.

6.   *Retroactive application of California Family Code Section 2580 and 2581.* California Family Code Section 2580 states that, effective January 1, 1984, the legislation is to apply in dissolution proceedings regardless of date of acquisition.

Parsing out the special joint title community property presumption in California Family Code Section 2581: any asset that is held in any joint form title is presumed to be community property for purposes of a dissolution proceeding, as discussed above. The date of purchase (before or during marriage) is not relevant for purposes of applying the special community property presumption. The use of the special joint title form presumption does not affect vested property rights; it simply gets the dissolution proceeding off to an evidentiary start.

Turning to the rebuttal subsections in California Family Code Section 2581(a) and (b): prior to the enactment of California Family Code Section 2580 and 2581 parties could orally agree to rebut any presumption raised by a joint form title, and, as *Lucas* points out, in some judicial districts parties could rebut by tracing.

Still with the rebuttal subsections: from January 1, 1984 on, only a *written* second (rebuttal) agreement is admissible to rebut the California Family Code 2581 special community property presumption as to common law joint form titles (the joint tenancy and the tenancy in common). From January 1, 1987 on, only a *written* second (rebuttal) agreement is admissible to rebut the California Family Code 2581 community property presumption as to community property joint form titles (the community property title and the community property with the right of survivorship).

The necessity for different dates is the result of a legislative oversight in the original drafting. (Community property title forms were omitted from the original legislation. It took a couple of years to add them in.)

Current standards impose the additional requirement of producing a written agreement on a separate property contributor who expects to rebut the joint form community property presumption. For that reason, rebuttal methods can raise a retroactivity issue.

7.   *Retroactive application of California Family Code Section 2640 may affect vested property rights.* The retroactive application of California Family Code Section 2640 to pre-January 1, 1984 acquisitions was held unconstitutional by the California Supreme Court in a series of cases starting with *Buol, supra.*

On or before December 31, 1983, a separate property contribution made to an entirely (100%) community property asset is presumed to be a gift to the community absent evidence of a reimbursement agreement between the spouses.

California Family Code Section 2640(b) establishes a new rule by reversing the gift presumption to create a statutory right of reimbursement.

Hence from January 1, 1984 on, a separate property contribution to the purchase of an entirely (100%) community property asset is presumed to be a (no-interest) loan from the separate property estate to the community. The loan presumption is rebuttable by evidence that the separate property contributor intended to make a gift to the community.

Anytime a reimbursement is justified under Section 2640 it is made without interest.

8. *2004 Amendments to California Family Code Section 2640.* Effective January 1, 2005, the amended version of California Family Code Section 2640 includes a new subsection (c), which is reproduced above. Subsection (c) extends the right of reimbursement to cover separate property contributions to the other spouse's separate property.

9. *Acquiring an asset in joint title form* before *marriage.* How should property be characterized for purposes of dissolution if a couple acquires property in joint tenancy *before* marriage, but then makes loan payments with community property funds *during* marriage? *Marriage of Leversee*, 156 Cal.App.3d 891, 203 Cal.Rptr. 481 (1st Dist. 1984) interprets California Family Code Section 2581 to apply only to acquisitions that are made in joint title form during marriage.

10. *Transferring an asset owned as separate property before marriage into joint ownership during marriage.* Is property owned by one spouse in sole title before marriage but then transferred into joint title during marriage "acquired during marriage" by the community? If so, is it property within the meaning of California Family Code Section 760 and thus governed by California Family Code Section 2581?

The appellate courts have conflicting views on the issue. *Marriage of Neal*, 153 Cal.App.3d 117, 200 Cal.Rptr. 341 (1st Dist. 1984) suggests that the California Family Code Section 2581 presumption applies in such a case. Disapproved on other grounds in *Buol*, (at 751, 763 n. 10 and by subsequent case law). *Marriage of Delaney*, 111 Cal.App.4th 991, 4 Cal.Rptr.3d 378 (1st Dist. 2003) is skeptical because "the acquisition of property during marriage by a purchase or a gift is clearly different from an interspousal transmutation of property *already* owned by one or both spouses." In other words, when a spouse owns property in sole title but then transfers that property into joint title during marriage, the transaction is properly understood as a transmutation (Chapter 1). Does understanding such a transaction as a transmutation better protect the adversely affected spouse? Does California

Family Code Section 721(b) apply to prevent one spouse from taking any unfair advantage of the other in the transaction between them (Chapter 6)?

11. *Nonmarried intimate partners.* California Family Code Section 2581 does not govern the rights of unmarried intimate partners. Their rights are governed by contract; or, in the absence of a contract by the California Civil Code and state common law (Chapter 4).

C. THE STATUTORY COMMUNITY PROPERTY PRESUMPTION FOR SUMS ON DEPOSIT IN ANY ACCOUNT OF A MARRIED PERSON

At this stage in the course, understanding the spouses' property rights in money depends on grasping two basic points. The first is a working definition of money. The second is a working understanding of the basic forms that money can take.

1.   Basic Terms: Money, Cash, Sums on Deposit, Loan Proceeds

Money is a general term, defined here in line with the extensive legal-economic literature on money as a mechanism of exchange. *See e.g.*, DAVID FOX, PROPERTY RIGHTS IN MONEY 7–8 (2008) for a list of citations that historicize the concept of money back through the early nineteenth century.

Money, as a general term, represents a "thing" because it can be and is used in an exchange transaction. Money—the thing—can purchase other things—a computer, a suit, a TV, a bike, and so on. Money can be used to obtain a service (Internet) or shelter (rent). It can be used to acquire an asset for which the state keeps a record of title (a house, a car, or a boat are examples) or it can be used to purchase an asset whose income must be reported to the Internal Revenue Service (shares of stock, bonds, a business). Money can be used to discharge a debt (a credit card principal payment or a mortgage principal payment) or to create a contract debt, as with a demand deposit account.

The exchange of money is not considered barter. The reason being that money is itself a commodity, not a form of labor. Money, in other words, is a thing that people want. Money is sometimes described as a commodity that labor can produce. Money can take the form of coins, bills, banknotes, electronic balances or transfers. *Coins* (pennies, nickels, dimes, quarters, and so on) and *paper bills* are tangible in nature, as are banknotes (meaning paper checks). *Paper checks* represent I.O.U.s that give the named payee a right to access the amount of sums indicated in writing on the check. Because the payee must actually cash a check in order to receive payment from the payor, the sums indicated on the check remain in the account until the check is cashed.

Cash is a more specific term that signifies paper notes and coins. Cash is tangible asset. Cash is an untitled asset. As such cash is governed by the general community property presumption. Cash gives its bearer full rights of use, subject only to the claims of someone who can prove a superior legal right to the cash. Another thing about cash is that it is highly fugitive. To test out this assertion: leave a $20 bill in a public space and see how quickly it disappears. Or take a look at http://www.wheresgeorge.com and other popular cash-tracking websites.

Sums on deposit in a bank are possessed via an independently titled asset called an account. Sums on deposit are governed by a special community property presumption found in the California Probate Code, discussed below. Intangible electronic balances move through a deposit account on any given day; they represent a debt that is enforceable by a named person or entity on a deposit contract—the account owner—against the financial institution that holds the deposits—the bank. In this scenario, the depositor is the creditor; the bank is the debtor. The depositor calls on the debt by withdrawing sums on deposit (electronic impulses) from an account that the depositor has contractual access to. Assuming sufficient funds, the depositor's calls are payable upon demand.

Electronic fund transfers from a bank to a third party on behalf of the account owner are drawn from the account owner's sums on deposit. As such, EFTs are made from sums that are in possession of the account owner(s).

Direct transfer of loan proceeds occurs when a lender transfers money to a seller (typically) on behalf of a buyer. In this scenario the buyer is the borrower. The borrower does not come into possession of the transferred funds. Rather the transfer is a loan, issued from the lending institution's general account. In the case of a direct loan transfer, the bank is the creditor that promises, by contract with the borrower-buyer, to transfer funds on behalf of the borrower-buyer to a named third-party seller. Funds transfer directly from the bank to the named third-party seller.

Some loans are *unsecured*. When a person opens a credit card account, for example, the bank agrees to transfer the purchase funds to the seller in exchange for the credit card holder's promise of repayment. In the ordinary course of business, instead of asking the credit card holder to secure the account with collateral (like real estate or an existing bank account), the credit card company uses monthly time tables, fees for late payments, credit reporting services, and credit balance adjustments to collect the debt.

Other loans are *secured* by collateral.

In a dissolution or probate proceeding, money, in any and every form, can take on an emotional value—positive, negative, or mixed. Among its positives money can represent care, trust, planning, thoughtfulness, love, respect, honor, family, and other more or entirely personal value points. Among its negatives money might represent loss, greed, predation, rejection, breach of trust, oppression, waste of time, abuse through excessive control, to name only a few.

Physical possession typically determines rights to cash.

Contract rights determine a person's right to access sums on deposit in a demand deposit account.

Sums on deposit in an account go up or down depending on deposits and withdrawals made to and from the account on a specific day.

Net deposits (actual contributions minus withdrawals) determine an unmarried person's beneficial right to sums on deposit in an account.

Net character contributions (net character deposits minus family expenses) determine a married person's beneficial right to sums on deposit in an account.

Generally, all deposits in any account of a married person are presumed to be community property, by operation of California Probate Code Section 5305(a).

2.   CAMPAL: Uniform Legislation on Demand Deposit Accounts

In 1990, effective July 1, 1991, California repealed its former Probate Code and enacted a Revised Probate Code. The revised code includes the California version of the Uniform Multiple-Party Accounts Law, a general law that applies to the accounts of married and unmarried persons.

The California Multiple-Party Accounts Law, CAMPAL for short, enhances the uniform multiple-party accounts law in several respects. Most relevant here is that CAMPAL includes within it a special community property presumption that specifically governs any account of married person. The CAMPAL community property presumption is found at California Probate Code Section 5305(a), reproduced below.

California Probate Code Section 5305(a) supersedes the general community property presumption (Chapter 2), the California Family Code Section 2581 joint form title community property presumption (Chapter 2), and the general provisions of CAMPAL. Additionally, CAMPAL supersedes California Civil Code Section 683 as to bank accounts. CAMPAL is discussed further in Chapter 5.

As between spouses, California Probate Code Section 5305(a) governs sums on deposit in any account owned by a married person (or registered domestic partner) during the marriage (or registered domestic partnership) or at death. The special presumption applies in a dissolution proceeding, an equitable accounting, a probate proceeding, and any other proceeding in which a claim to sums on deposit is asserted by one or both spouses.

By operation of California Probate Code Section 5305(a) sums on deposit in any account of a married person are presumptively community property. The presumption is nonconclusive. Rebuttal is by tracing or by agreement as to the specific sums on deposit in a specific account. Any rebuttal agreement as to the character of funds must be in writing and signed by both spouses (Chapters 2 and 5).

California Probate Code Section 5305(a) is consistent with prior case law. For example, in the textbook case of *Lynam v. Vorwerk*, 13 Cal.App. 507, 110 P. 355 (1st Dist. 1910), the spouses opened a bank account in 1899. Each signed a bank deposit agreement that gave either access to the sums on deposit in the account during their joint lifetimes; the agreement did not specify a right of survivorship. The husband died first in 1903. At that time the wife decided not to probate his estate. Instead, she continued to withdraw money from the account without keeping any special track of deposits. When the wife died in 1907, the husband's estate sued the wife's estate for an accounting.

The husband's estate (the plaintiff) argued that the sums on deposit on the date of the husband's death were community property since the account was not a joint tenancy account with right of survivorship. The wife's estate (the defendant) countered that the spouses intended to create a joint tenancy. The court ruled in favor of the husband's estate. Its rationale was that even though both spouses had access to the account during their lifetimes, they did not specify a right of survivorship. Therefore, on the day of the decedent's death he owned a one-half interest in the account deposits.

Next the *Lynam* court took up the issue the character of the sums on deposit on the date of the husband's death. The husband's estate argued that because the sums were possessed during the long marriage they were more likely than not community property in character. The wife's estate sought to confirm the sums on deposit as her separate property. The trial court had raised the general community property presumption as to any sums on deposit on the date of the husband's death. The appellate court affirmed, explaining that ordinarily community property is acquired during marriage, but given the type of property (sums on deposit in an account) and the long term nature of the marriage (decades), the trial court acted within its discretionary power to raise the general presumption upon proof of possession of the sums on deposit rather than upon proof of date of acquisition.

CAMPAL is consistent with *Lynam*. CAMPAL names the community property account as the default account for married persons (even though it names the joint tenancy with the right of survivorship account as the default account for nonmarried persons). Additionally, due to the nature of the property (sums on deposit), the CAMPAL community property presumption is possession-based, not acquisition-based.

The existence much less the full reach of CAMPAL has been overlooked in community property casebooks, treatises, workbooks, and study aids. CAMPAL is in the Revised Probate Code, as it was passed when the legislature was considering Uniform Probate Code issues. As the Law Commissioners made clear, CAMPAL, including the special community property presumption for sums on deposit, governs issues that can arise during life or at death.

Here is the special CAMPAL community property presumption for sums on deposit in any demand deposit account of a married person:

WEST'S ANNOTATED CALIFORNIA PROBATE CODE

§ 5305. Married parties; community property; presumptions; rebuttal; change of survivorship right, beneficiary, or payee by will

(a)   Notwithstanding Sections 5301 to 5303, inclusive, if parties to an account are married to each other, whether or not they are so described in the deposit agreement, their net contribution to the account is presumed to be and remain their community property.

(b)   Notwithstanding Sections 2581 and 2640 of the Family Code, the presumption established by this section is a presumption affecting the burden of proof and may be rebutted by proof of either of the following:

(1)   The sums on deposit that are claimed to be separate property can be traced from separate property unless it is proved that the married persons made a written agreement that expressed their clear intent that the sums be their community property.

(2)   The married persons made a written agreement, separate from the deposit agreement, that expressly provided that the sums on deposit, claimed not to be community property, were not to be community property.

(c)   Except as provided in Section 5307, a right of survivorship arising from the express terms of the account or under Section 5302, a beneficiary designation in a Totten trust account, or a P.O.D. payee designation, may not be changed by will.

(d)   Except as provided in subdivisions (b) and (c), a multiple-party account created with community property funds does not in any way alter community property rights.

(Stats. 1990, c. 79 (A.B. 759), § 14, operative July 1, 1991. Amended by Stats. 1992, c. 163 (A.B. 2641), § 131, operative Jan. 1, 1994; Stats. 1993, c. 219 (A.B. 1500), § 224.7.)

CAMPAL applies to borrowed funds if the funds are deposited into the account of a married person. However, CAMPAL does not apply to borrowed funds if the funds have been directly transferred by the lender to a third party on behalf of the married person, as for example in a real estate purchase. Instead the general presumption applies to the transferred funds. The next section introduces the lender's intent test as a rebuttal method.

D. BORROWED FUNDS ACQUIRED DURING MARRIAGE ARE PRESUMPTIVELY COMMUNITY PROPERTY

If a lender extends credit to a married person, how are the loan proceeds characterized? Is a spouse's creditworthiness to obtain a loan characterized? Are the borrowed funds characterized? If so, how?

Borrowed funds (loan proceeds) acquired during marriage are presumptively community property under California Family Code Section 760. On the issue of presumptions: whether borrowed funds are governed by the general community property presumption or by the California Probate Code Section 5305(a) depends on the form in which the funds are held by the debtor spouse(s). Both presumptions are community property presumptions. What differs about them is how they may be rebutted

Borrowed funds can be distributed as cash (coins and bills) or as a tangible paper check (I.O.U.) made out *by* the financial institution *to* the borrower. Alternatively, they can be distributed to a third party on behalf of the borrower. A paper check can be exchanged for cash, which is an untitled asset. Or, a paper check can be deposited into an account. If so, the loan proceeds (now in the form of sums on deposit) implicate the special CAMPAL community property presumption found at California Probate Code Section 5305(a).

In a retail real estate transaction, it is not uncommon for a financial institution to transfer loan proceeds directly to an intended third-party recipient. A purchase contract may require the buyer's mortgage lender to transfer the purchase money loan proceeds directly to the seller's financial institution or—if the transaction is a loan refinance—to the borrower's current mortgage holder. When funds are directly transferred by a lender directly to a third party on behalf of the borrower, the proceeds do not come into the borrower's possession. In point of fact, the sums belong to the lender; they are transferred by the lender to a third party on the debtor's behalf, upon the debtor's promise to repay the lender for the amount transferred. In the event that married debtors dissolve their marriage, they will be obligated to pay the lender for the debt. Therefore, accounting equities require that the community be credited for any community property loan proceeds.

Hence, the general rule is that borrowed funds obtained by the spouses during marriage are presumed to be community property. And the corollary of that rule is that borrowed funds are credited to the community as a contribution to purchase even if the loan has not yet been repaid.

It is possible to obtain a separate property loan during marriage. Funds obtained by one spouse are separate property upon proof that the lender solely intended to rely on that spouse's separate property in agreeing to extend the loan. This legal test allows a lender to decide whether it wants to bring its ownership claims (in the event of default) against the community or (solely) against the separate property owner.

To decide which community property presumption governs the disposition of loan proceeds, three scenarios help delineate the issues.

Scenario 1: Cash. Assume that borrowed funds are distributed by the lender to one or both spouses in the form of *cash.* In this case, the general presumption applies because cash is an untitled asset. Rebuttal is by tracing the cash back to a separate property loan or by producing an enforceable written agreement between the spouses that the cash was not to be community property. Because the cash originates from a loan obtained during marriage, the separate property trace requires proof that the lender solely relied on separate property in extending the loan. The lender's intent test is mapped out below.

Scenario 2: Loan proceeds are delivered to a married borrower for deposit in a bank account to which one or both spouses have access. Assume the funds are *deposited* by the lender into one or both spouses' bank account(s). The CAMPAL community property presumption found at California Probate Code Section 5305(a) applies as long as the loan proceeds remain on deposit in the account. Sums on deposit are held in a titled asset (the bank account) in the form of intangible (electronic) sums. Rebuttal of sums on deposit proceeds by California Probate Code Section 5305(b) unless the sums on deposit in a specific bank account are traced back to a separate property source. Because the sums on deposit in this scenario originate from a loan that was obtained during marriage, the separate property trace will require application of the lender's intent test, which is to say proof that the lender solely relied on separate property in extending the loan.

Scenario 3: Loan proceeds are transferred by the lender directly to a third party on behalf of one or both spouses. Assume that the spouses want to buy a house. They deliver to the seller $x of their work savings in the form of a cash down payment. The spouses also obtain financing to pay for the remainder of the purchase price. The seller promises to deliver marketable title to the house to the spouses when their lender *transfers* $y to the seller on their behalf.

In this scenario, the cash down payment ($x) represents a contribution to the purchase of the house. So too do the loan proceeds ($y). In any proceeding between the spouses the loan (even though it may be outstanding), is treated as an actual community property contribution to purchase. Rebuttal is possible upon proof that the lender solely intended to rely on one spouse's separate property in originating the loan.

THE LENDER'S INTENT REBUTTAL

The general community property presumption applies to loan proceeds obtained during marriage.

Rebuttal, at the very least, requires proof of both of the following elements:

    (a) The lender intended to rely *solely* on the separate property claimant's separate property in originating and closing the loan; and

    (b) The lender did in fact rely solely on separate property in extending the loan.

Rebuttal may also require proof that the separate property character of the loan was disclosed to the other spouse as required by California Family Code Section 721 (Chapter 6.)

The lender's intent test has practical significance in terms of creditors' rights because if loan proceeds are community in character, an institutional lender can reach all community and separate property assets in the event of default. But if the loan proceeds are separate property in character, the lender must must first satisfy the default with the debtor spouse's separate property assets (including the asset secured by the loan) before turning to available community property assets. Marshaling separate property before community property may reduce the efficiency with which the lender might otherwise satisfy a debt, but ultimately it does not necessarily reduce the scope of property that the lender can reach (Chapter 6).

The lender's intent test acknowledges a market reality: during the origination of a loan, the property that a lender expects to be able to reach first corresponds with the characterization of the loan proceeds. Thus to the degree that the lender relies on income, the lender expects to be paid from community property if the borrower defaults. But if a lender intends to rely solely (only) on one spouse's separate property information and collateral in extending the loan, then that lender understands that it must exhaust the debtor spouse's separate property before turning to any community property. Credit acquisitions, creditors' rights, and tax implications at dissolution are covered in more detail throughout this casebook.

Marriage of Grinius, reproduced next, illustrates, explains, and acknowledges California's adoption of the lender's intent test.

MARRIAGE OF GRINIUS

166 Cal.App.3d 1179, 212 Cal.Rptr. 803 (4th Dist. 1985)

WORK, ASSOCIATE JUSTICE.

Factual and Procedural Background

Victor and Joyce Grinius were married the same day they signed an antenuptial agreement which listed their separate assets and stated "all property owned by [either spouse] at the time of the marriage and all property coming to [either spouse] from whatever source during the effective term of this Agreement shall be the separate property of [the respective spouse.]" Victor listed common stock in two companies, $2,500 in a profit sharing plan, improved San Diego real property, and unimproved real properties in Florida. Joyce listed only her car and miscellaneous household furnishings.

The antenuptial agreement also provided:

"This Agreement shall be binding upon the parties during the first six years of marriage only. Thereafter, the terms of this Agreement may be renegotiated by the mutual agreement of both parties or, in the alternative, the parties may choose not to renegotiate its terms and to allow it to entirely lapse. In such latter event, each party shall immediately have, upon expiration of said first six years of marriage, all rights and obligations with respect to each other and with respect to property which are provided by law. Such rights and obligations shall be retroactive to the date of marriage without regard to the provisions otherwise contained in this paragraph."

However, even after a lapse, the parties' premarital separate property was to retain its separate character.

Shortly after marriage Victor resigned his job so he and Joyce could open a restaurant. Joyce apparently had worked in a restaurant for a number of years before marriage. They located a suitable building, costing $60,000. The purchase money was obtained from two sources: (1) a $20,000 downpayment from an $80,000 Small Business Administration (SBA) loan guaranty lent by California First Bank (hereafter referred to as SBA loan) and (2) $40,000 loaned by Home Federal Savings and Loan. Although only Victor signed the SBA loan guaranty, both Victor and Joyce signed the promissory note from California First Bank. Victor alone signed the Home Federal Savings and Loan promissory note. The SBA loan was secured by both community and separate property. Both Victor and Joyce negotiated the original purchase offer. However, without Joyce's knowledge, Victor placed title to the property in his name alone.

Victor and Joyce used the remaining $60,000 of the SBA loan to remodel the building, buy equipment, and pay their living and restaurant expenses. These funds were disbursed through the restaurant's checking account on which Victor and Joyce were the signators. Indeed, during the course of the marriage all personal and restaurant expenses were paid from this joint account.

Victor and Joyce both worked in the restaurant in several different capacities and continued to do so during the course of their marriage. Their community earnings were placed in the restaurant checking account; however, from time to time Victor also deposited funds received from his separate property into the account to prevent overdrafts.

Monthly payments on the purchase money loans were made from the joint restaurant checking account. In 1975 Victor also used $30,098.00 and $39,821.93 of his separate property funds to pay on the SBA and Home Federal loans, respectively. Again, in 1978 Victor paid $33,818 of separate property funds to retire the SBA loan. That same year, Victor and Joyce signed a $63,000 installment note in favor of San Diego Trust and Savings, secured by a trust deed on the restaurant property. From these proceeds, $42,000 was used to pay the outstanding balance on the Home Federal promissory note.

Victor and Joyce separated in April of 1980. Before trial, Victor stipulated the restaurant business was community property and the business was sold. Victor and Joyce and their respective counsels were each granted $5,000 from the sale proceeds. The trial court found all of the contested assets, except the restaurant real property, to be community property. The restaurant real property, worth $340,000, was determined to be Victor's separate property.

The Separate Property Characterization of the Restaurant Real Property Is Not Supported by Substantial Evidence

I

A trial court's findings regarding a property's separate or community character is binding and conclusive on review when supported by substantial evidence (*Beam v. Bank of America,* 6 Cal.3d 12, 25, 98 Cal.Rptr. 137, 490 P.2d 257; *Hicks v. Hicks,* 211 Cal.App.2d 144, 149, 27 Cal.Rptr. 307), even though evidence conflicts or supports contrary inferences. (*Beam v. Bank of America, supra,* 6 Cal.3d at p. 25, 98 Cal.Rptr. 137, 490 P.2d 257. * * *) However, substantial evidence is not synonymous with "any" evidence. * * * It must have ponderable legal significance and " 'must be reasonable in nature, credible, and of solid value; it must actually be "substantial" proof of the essentials which the law requires in a particular case.' " * * *

We review the evidence supporting the trial court's characterization of the restaurant property as Victor's separate property.

Property bought during marriage by either spouse is rebuttably presumed to be community property [Section 760]; *See v. See, supra,* 64 Cal.2d 778, 783, 51 Cal.Rptr. 888, 415 P.2d 776; *In re Marriage of Aufmuth,* 89 Cal.App.3d 446, 455, 152 Cal.Rptr. 668, . . .), and typically the spouse asserting its separate character must overcome this presumption. Victor relies on [an] antenuptial agreement to support his separate property claim. * * * It lapsed six years after the date of marriage and reinvested the spouses with all communal rights retroactive to the date of marriage. Therefore, at trial the agreement had no effect on the presumption of community acquisition.

Victor next traces the source of payments for the restaurant property to overcome the fundamental community presumption. Specifically, he argues the purchase money loans were separate property and the restaurant real property, thus acquired, maintains the same character. * * *

"The character of property as separate or community is determined at the time of its acquisition. [Citations.]" * * * Here, the restaurant property was acquired shortly after marriage and is presumed to be community property. [Section 760] However, the character of credit acquisitions during marriage is "determined according to the intent of the lender to rely upon the separate property of the purchaser or upon a community asset." * * *

While the California courts have consistently and uncritically applied the intent-of-the-lender rule, they have inconsistently espoused the applicable test. (See generally Young, *Community Property Classification of Credit Acquisitions in California: Law without Logic?* (1981) 17 Cal.Western L.Rev. 173 (hereafter cited as *Classification of Credit Acquisitions*).) In early cases, the Supreme Court required a showing the lender relied *entirely* on the existing separate property of a spouse in extending the loan to characterize the loan proceeds as separate property. . . . The more modern and oft-cited formulation found in *Gudelj v. Gudelj,* 41 Cal.2d 202, 259 P.2d 656, apparently relaxes the standard: "In the absence of evidence tending to prove that the seller *primarily* relied upon the purchaser's separate property in extending credit, the trial court must find in accordance with the [Section 760] presumption." * * * The *Gudelj* opinion cited no authority for this apparent change and had no opportunity to apply the standard since no evidence of lender reliance on separate property was proffered. Later cases have been decided on seemingly different standards. Courts have found evidence of lender's intent in: (1) reliance on or hypothecation of separate property * * * , (2) sole reliance on separate property * * * ; and (3) extension of the loan on the faith of existing property belonging to the acquiring spouse. * * * Nonetheless, in all of the above cases, loan proceeds were characterized as a spouse's separate property *only* when direct or circumstantial evidence indicated the lender relied solely on separate property in offering the loan.

With the above review in mind, we restate the applicable standard: Loan proceeds acquired during marriage are presumptively community property; however, this presumption may be overcome by showing the lender intended to rely *solely* upon a spouse's separate property and did in fact do so. Without satisfactory evidence of the lender's intent, the general presumption prevails (italics added).

Victor presented no direct evidence of lender intent and instead offered circumstantial evidence to prove lender reliance on his separate property. * * * He argues the "SBA loan guaranty was premised solely on [his] posting of collateral consisting of his entire separate property." However, a review of the SBA loan conditions outlined on the loan guaranty authorization refutes this contention. The SBA required nine separate conditions, only two of which necessitated hypothecation of Victor's separate property. Specifically, loan approval required: (1) a second deed of trust on the restaurant property and improvements, (2) Joyce's signature on the promissory note and all instruments of hypothecation, (3) a first lien on the restaurant machinery, equipment, furniture and fixtures presently owned and later acquired with the loan proceeds, (4) acquisition and assignment of an $80,000 life insurance policy on Victor, (5) purchase of hazard insurance on the restaurant property, (6) a third deed of trust on Victor's improved real property in San Diego, already subject to prior liens totaling $107,000, (7) assignment of 3100 shares of Victor's separate property stock, (8) the furnishing of the restaurant's quarterly balance sheets and profit and loss statements, and (9) the use of the SBA's management assistant services "as deemed necessary by SBA or Bank."

The primary collateral for the loan was the restaurant property. Alone, this hypothecation provides no inference of lender intent; to argue otherwise is to rely on circular reasoning. The requiring of Joyce's signature on the note and instruments of hypothecation does suggest the lender did look toward community assets for security. However, Joyce's signing of the documents, without more, does not compel a finding in favor of the community. * * * Moreover, given the effect of the antenuptial agreement at the time of the loan, Joyce arguably had few, if any, existing community interests to pledge. Conditions three through five clearly suggest reliance on community interests. Both insurance policies and the restaurant equipment were purchased from the joint restaurant account and were presumptively community property. Indeed, Victor stipulated to the community nature of the restaurant business. Yet, some of the same loan proceeds challenged here were used for operating capital for the restaurant and were specifically earmarked for the purchase of trade fixtures and the liquor license, assets unquestioningly found to belong to the community. This inconsistency clearly contradicts Victor's contention.

Victor nonetheless relies on *Hicks v. Hicks, supra,* 211 Cal.App.2d 144, 27 Cal.Rptr. 307, to bolster his argument. In *Hicks,* the trial court made an "implied finding that the proceeds from the loans * * * were the separate property of [husband]." (*Id.,* at p. 153, 27 Cal.Rptr. 307.) Affirming, the Court of Appeal stated: "The trial court was entitled to conclude that the original bank loans were made to the [husband] on the credit of his separate property as, at the time they were obtained, he had been married less than a year and his community earnings were not then of paramount significance, whereas his separate property approximated $500,000 in value." (*Id.,* at p. 155, 27 Cal.Rptr. 307.) However, the court in *Hicks* did not point to any evidence of the lender's actual intent and, indeed, *specifically refrained* from detailing the basis for its conclusion. (*Id.,* at p. 153, 27 Cal.Rptr. 307.) Thus, *Hicks* provides no guidance in determining lender intent in a mixed collateral situation. As one commentator has noted, "Although the *Hicks* case may seem to have been reasonably and correctly decided, in truth it stands as an unfortunate example of an improper assumption regarding a critical factual issue which the *Gudelj* Rule addressed: Whether the lender (or credit seller) *in fact primarily relied* upon separate property of a spouse or upon the general credit of the spouse when credit was extended to that spouse." (*Classifications of Credit Acquisitions, supra,* at p. 216.)

Loan conditions eight and nine demonstrate the SBA's concern about the operation and management of the restaurant business. This interest is wholly consistent with the stated purpose of the SBA:

> "For the purpose of preserving and promoting a competitive free enterprise economic system, Congress hereby declares that it is the continuing policy and responsibility of the Federal Government to use all practical means and to take such actions as are necessary, consistent with its needs and obligations and other essential considerations of national policy, to implement and coordinate all Federal department, agency, and instrumentality policies, programs, and activities in order to: foster the economic interests of small businesses; insure a competitive economic climate conducive to the development, growth and expansion of small businesses; establish incentives to assure that adequate capital and other resources at competitive prices are available to small businesses; reduce the concentration of economic resources and expand competition; and provide an opportunity for entrepreneurship, inventiveness, and the creation and growth of small businesses." * * *

In granting these small business loans, the SBA is constrained by statute and policy considerations. Many of these loan guidelines are outlined in Chapter 1 of Title 13 of the Code Federal Regulations. Section 120.2, subdivision (c)(1), of Chapter 1 specifically provides: "No financial assistance shall be extended unless there exists reasonable assurance the loan can and will be repaid pursuant to its terms. Reasonable assurance of repayment will exist *only* where the past earnings record and *future prospects indicate ability to repay the loan and other obligations.* It will be deemed not to exist when the proposed loan is to accomplish an expansion which is unwarranted in light of the applicant's past experience and management ability, or when the effect of making the loan is to subsidize inferior management." (Italics added.) Accordingly, in the absence of evidence the SBA acted contrary to their official duties in this instance * * * , we find the loan was extended on both the ability of the community to repay the note and to manage the restaurant. Therefore, the SBA loan funds are a community asset, not Victor's separate property.

The second purchase money loan from Home Federal Savings and Loan was secured by a first deed of trust on the restaurant property. Victor presents no evidence to rebut the community presumption and, indeed, concedes the Home Federal Loan was likely extended in reliance on the interest in the restaurant property already acquired with the SBA loan funds. Thus, this loan must also be seen as an asset of the community. * * *

In sum, Victor has failed to present sufficient evidence to rebut the presumption that property acquired during marriage is community property. Therefore, the restaurant property and all rents, issues and profits thereof are properly characterized as community property. * * *

NOTES

1.   *For an historicized criticism of the lender's intent test* see *Perlman, A Reappraisal of California's Intent of the Lender Rule,* 37 UCLA L.R. 389, 407– 408 (1989). Perlman conducted a survey of the lending practices of institutional lenders in southern California. She found that the lenders rarely, if ever, rely solely on separate property in extending credit to a married person, and that if a lender in fact did so, it would be unlikely to admit that fact in the case of a default since such an admission could work to its detriment. By this analysis, without careful planning, it is practically impossible for a spouse to rebut the presumption that borrowed funds (i.e., the loan proceeds that were acquired during marriage) are community property.

Where the lender relies on one or both spouses' ability to repay the loan with earnings, it is relying on community property information. Another reason why most loans obtained during marriage are community property.

So how to understand the lender's intent test?

One function of a community property system is macroeconomic. Third parties need encouragement and confidence to deal with married persons; to the degree a marital property system gives lenders that confidence it serves a social good by keeping credit available for purchases like homes, vehicles, and other consumer items.

Another function is to protect the partnership and the individuals within that partnership. The lender's intent test puts spouses on notice that loan proceeds obtained during marriage are presumptively community in character. If a spouse plans or intends a separate property loan, he or she—at the very least—has the burden to obtain documentary proof that the lender has intended to rely *solely* on that spouse's separate property in extending the loan. It may also be necessary under California Family Code Section 721(b) for a spouse who intends to obtain a separate property loan to give the other spouse notice of the plan (Chapter 6).

Creditworthiness is an analysis of a person's credit history and a prediction that future earnings from paid work and other assets will be sufficient to repay a loan. Traditional algorithms that determine creditworthiness tend to be proprietary, exceedingly sensitive to data, and subject to change. New algorithms are often introduced into the market by the tech industry. Still, the broad elements that informed lenders in the past continue to be used today: credit history; employment history; current earnings as a predictor of future earnings; debt-to-income ratio; timeliness of payment.

Does California Family Code Section 760 govern a married person's financial information?

2. *Repaying a separate property loan with community property (earnings)*. *Vieux v. Vieux*, 80 Cal.App.222, 251 P. 640 (2d Dist. 1926) sets out the so-called American rule that repaying a separate property loan with community property earnings gives the community a pro tanto, proportional, interest in the asset. *Vieux* gave two rationales for recognizing pro tanto ownership, one contract based and one property based. An (implied) contract rationale presumes that the parties agreed that the community would acquire an ownership interest in the property in exchange for the use of community funds to pay the down the separate property loan secured by the property. The property rationale allows a court to exercise its discretion to recognize a pro tanto ownership interest in the community as a way of protecting the community's expectation that contributing to the pay down of mortgage principal will result in the acquisition of a pro tanto property interest.

The benefit of the American rule is that it entitles the community to share in appreciation of the underlying asset as of the date of the community's first contribution to purchase. The community becomes an investor in the property on that date. (Sometimes this is referred to as the "buy in" approach.) The drawback is that the community is exposed to the consequences of default and depreciation (Chapter 5).

The civil law rule differs from the American rule in how it characterizes property at inception of title. If a separate property loan is used to acquire property before marriage, for example, then the asset is confirmed as separate property. If the community subsequently helps repay the separate property loan that is secured by the property, the community is entitled to a (mere) reimbursement, not to an ownership share. The community's reimbursement can be computed at sale, but more often than not it is computed at dissolution. The incentives under the civil law rule are exactly opposite of what they are under the American rule; the community is not entitled to a share of appreciation, but neither is it exposed to the consequences of default or asset depreciation.

3. *Loan contracts signed during marriage.* In *Grinius*, the trial court (incorrectly) characterized the apparently struggling restaurant business as community property, while confirming the underlying real estate as the record title holder's separate property. The result was that husband Victor was given full ownership of real estate that was purchased during marriage ($60,000) with a community property loan. This in turn gave him the asset appreciation as well ($280,000).[1] The trial court was persuaded by Victor's argument that he alone signed the loan documents, which made the mortgage proceeds his separate contribution to the purchase of the real estate. The court of appeal reversed, finding that there was no evidence to rebut of the community property presumption as to the real estate. The court was not persuaded that the fact that the lender had presented the contract to Victor alone to sign was evidence of the lender's intent to rely solely on Victor's separate property.

The *lender's intent test* focuses on the lender's intent in originating the loan, not on the spouse's intent in signing a promissory note. On a parallel issue, a contract debt incurred during marriage by either spouse obligates the community property. Therefore, since the community property is liable for the loan, it is only fair that the community property also should get credit for that loan in any apportionment proceeding.

SECTION 4. ONEROUS OR LUCRATIVE TITLES

In the Spanish *ganancial* system, property acquired during marriage through direct or indirect exploitation of either spouse's labor was said to be *onerous*, meaning acquired by effort or consideration. Whereas property acquired gratuitously, by a gift or windfall, was deemed to be *lucrative*, meaning acquired without effort or by gift.

Because an onerous title has its source in labor, California Family Code Section 760 applies.

---

[1] Appreciation is determined by subtracting the purchase price ($60,000) from the fair market value of the asset at dissolution ($340,000):

$$\$340{,}000 \text{ FMV at sale} - \$60{,}000 \text{ purchase price} = \$280{,}000 \text{ appr.}.$$

California Family Code Section 770(a)(2) defines gifts received during marriage as separate property. This definition governs lucrative acquisitions.

Where is the line between onerous and lucrative drawn?

Estate of Clark, below, involves a will contest brought by a parent (in two jurisdictions) against his adult child's estate. The parent (Major Clark) was the child's sole intestate heir; the child died leaving a substantial estate to his friend. Shortly after the son's death, Major Clark got married. During that marriage Major Clark brought legal actions to contest his son's will.

Major Clark won the will contest action in an Oklahoma probate court. The son's will beneficiary appealed. Under Oklahoma practice a trial de novo was had in the district court and the will was deemed valid. Major Clark appealed. While the appeal was pending in Oklahoma, Major Clark reached a settlement agreement with his son's executor. Major Clark was paid one-half the value of his child's estate, about $150,000. Three years later, Major Clark died. His surviving spouse inventoried the $150,000 settlement money as community property. Major Clark's other relatives objected.

The trial court characterized the settlement as separate property of Major Clark. It reasoned that the money traced back to Major Clark's separate property cause of action, namely—the will contest in the matter of his son's estate. Major Clark's widow appealed. The court of appeal affirmed. The $150,000 settlement was confirmed as Major Clark's separate property. The court did not address the fact that Major Clark exerted effort to prosecute his legal claims.

ESTATE OF CLARK
94 Cal.App. 453, 271 P. 542 (2d Dist. 1928)

CRAIL, JUSTICE PRO TEM.

The Supreme Court has construed the definition of separate property * * * to include "property taken in exchange for, or in the investment, or as the price of the property so originally owned or acquired." *Meyer v. Kinzer*, 12 Cal. 247, 73 Am.Dec. 538; *Smith v. Smith*, 12 Cal. 216, 73 Am.Dec. 533.

In case the will was held to be invalid, Major Clark was the sole heir of his son, and his right to contest the will was cast upon him immediately upon the death of his son. He claimed that his son's will was not a valid will. In this contention he had been sustained by the county court of Noble County, Okla. By way of compromise, however, he consented to the dismissal of his contest and to the admission of the will to probate. The terms of the compromise contemplated, however, that in consideration of withdrawing his contest, Major Clark should receive the half of his son's estate. It is this property and the profits thereof which are involved in this litigation. Had the will been rejected, he would have received all of his son's estate, and beyond doubt it would have been his separate property. The question is whether what he did receive is any the less his separate property because it came to him through the compromise that was effected. It would not be questioned that if, instead of acquiring a clear title to half of his son's estate by withdrawing his contest to the will, Major Clark had adopted the method of having the appeal dismissed and the will denied probate, and then transferring to the legatees and devisees one-half of the property, this property would be his separate property.

Did Major Clark transfer to the devisee under the will a property interest in return for that which was received by him under the terms of the compromise? * * *

The right of an heir to transfer his inheritance, even though there is a will or purported will in existence, is recognized by our courts. At the instant of his son's death Major Clark had a property right which he could assign or transfer or surrender for a consideration acceptable to him, and also the statutory right, which of itself is a property right, to contest his son's will. * * * This right was a right vested in him prior to his marriage, and therefore was his separate property. The property involved in this litigation came to Major Clark in exchange or in payment for such property, and was likewise his separate property. * * *

While the mere expectancy of an heir is not usually regarded as property, the moment the ancestor has died, that expectancy is changed into a vested interest in property. It becomes thus vested by virtue of the death.

Much reliance is placed by appellant upon the case of *Pancoast v. Pancoast*, 57 Cal. 320. This case involved a situation where a man, before his marriage, intruded, without any right, on certain land, and after his marriage made a deed and gave up possession of a portion of the same to the rightful owner, in consideration whereof the owner conveyed to the trespasser the rest of the tract in fee. In this case the court held that as the trespasser had nothing before marriage except the mere ability to give trouble and cause expense to the true owners, the title which the latter conveyed to him after his marriage was something wholly new and did not fall within any of the classes of new acquisitions enumerated in the statute as being separate property, and was in law community property. There are some features of the case which are similar to the instant case; but there is this difference: That in the *Pancoast* case the occupation does not appear to have been founded on any claim of right at all, but was a naked trespass, and the court refused to recognize a mere trespass as property; whereas Major Clark's claim to his son's estate was made in good faith on a bona fide contention that his son's will was invalid, and the Oklahoma court approved the settlement and found that it was free from fraud and duress and was for the best interest of the proponents of the will. In other words, that the contest was brought on probable cause. But above the good faith and above the probable cause, as steadfast as the rock of Gibraltar, stands out this element of differentiation—that his contest was the assertion of a statutory right amounting to property.

It is the contention of appellant that the will was declared to be a valid will by the Oklahoma court, and that it was therefore a valid will ab initio. The facts are that at the time of the settlement the will had not yet been declared to be a valid will; that it was the subject of a contest brought by Major Clark, a contest which the statute specifically authorized him to bring; that the will was an unnatural will in that it excluded by its provisions the only person who was the natural object of the bounty of the decedent; that the contest had been successful in the county court, and it was only by the prosecution of an appeal that the executors and legatees would have been able to obtain anything out of the estate; that no order of a probate court of Oklahoma had yet been entered admitting the will to probate; and that a will may be ever so valid, but until it is admitted to probate it is of no value as evidence of title. . . . Thereafter the will was admitted to probate after the only person who was adversely interested had withdrawn his contest. * * *

It is true that the property in litigation was acquired by Major Clark during the time he was married to appellant, but it was acquired by way of the compromise of a statutory right which was in itself property and which he owned prior to his marriage. Property acquired by compromise is separate property if the right compromised is separate. The right compromised is the consideration for the property obtained by the compromise, and the principle is the same as where property is purchased with separate funds. * * *

Judgment affirmed.

NOTES

1.   *A property cause of action is transferable.* A property cause of action is an intangible asset. If acquired during marriage, it may be subject to the rules of community property. Major Clark's will contest was a property cause of action against his son's testamentary estate, which made the claim lucrative separate property. Additionally, the cause of action accrued before Major Clark's marriage, which made it separate property on the basis of date of acquisition. California Family Code Section 770 (Chapter 3).

During his marriage, Major Clark put substantial effort into pursuing his legal claims. Should the court have addressed the issue of Major Clark's onerous effort as a community property contribution to settling the estate claim?

If it had, would the $150,000 be community property? Part community property? Or separate property subject to the community's right of reimbursement for Major Clark's labor?

2. *Tracing, agreement, and the married person's labor contribution to claim settlement.* Today, California Probate Code Section 5305(a) would apply to any sums that Major Clark might have deposited into his account during his marriage. Those sums would be presumed to be community property absent rebuttal evidence. Could Major Clark's estate rebut the special community property presumption for sums on deposit by tracing the $150,000 on deposit back to his probate related settlement? To the probate claim? Alternatively, could Major Clark rebut the special community property presumption as to sums on deposit by entering into an agreement with his spouse that some or all of the estate settlement was not be community property? Would such an agreement better allow Major Clark and his spouse to negotiate over how best to value Major Clark's (community property) labor contribution to the $150,000 settlement?

The next case involves an former spouse who sought to set aside a final dissolution judgment. Today California Family Code Section 2121 governs this issue (Chapter 8). The former spouse alleged that the husband deceived her by not inventorying, as community property, a ranch that he acquired from his employer in lieu of retirement benefits. At the time of the dissolution the ex-husband's conservator argued, the (then) husband considered the ranch a gift (separate property). The trial court dismissed the plaintiff's complaint. The court of appeal reversed and remanded on the issue of the ranch's character.

DOWNER V. BRAMET

152 Cal.App.3d 837, 199 Cal.Rptr. 830 (4th Dist. 1984)

KAUFMAN, ASSOCIATE JUSTICE.

Plaintiff Gloria Alice Bramet Downer (hereinafter referred to as former wife) appeals from a judgment of nonsuit on her complaint for the determination of her rights in certain property and for fraud. She claims a community property interest in the proceeds of sale of a one-third interest in a ranch conveyed to her former husband George Keith Bramet by his employer after the parties separated. At the close of former wife's case, former husband moved for nonsuit. The motion was granted and judgment entered accordingly.

Facts

The parties were married in 1953, and separated in 1971. Former husband was an accountant and a tax expert. He worked for Chilcott Enterprises before, during and after the marriage, beginning in 1943. Chilcott Enterprises consisted of several businesses and corporations owned and operated by Edward Chilcott and his wife. Former husband was an officer of several of the corporations and acted as secretary-treasurer, accountant and record keeper for all of the Chilcotts' operations. Mr. Chilcott considered former husband his "righthand man."

Chilcott Enterprises had no retirement program of any kind for its employees. According to former wife's testimony, sometime in the mid-1960s former husband told her that Mr. Chilcott was going to give to him and two other employees a ranch in Oregon in lieu of retirement benefits. Nothing further was thereafter said about the ranch.

The parties separated in November 1971. In December 1972, after some exchange of drafts between the parties and their counsel, a marital settlement agreement was executed. The agreement, which was later incorporated in the judgment of dissolution, provided that all income and earnings of former husband or former wife after March 4, 1972, should be the separate property of the acquirer and that each party released any claim to such earnings or after acquired property. However, the agreement also contained a warranty "that neither party is now possessed of any property of any kind or description whatsoever, other than the property specifically mentioned in this Agreement" and a provision reading: "If it shall hereafter be determined by a Court of competent jurisdiction that one party is now possessed of any community property not set forth herein . . . such party hereby covenants and agrees to pay to [the other on demand an amount equal to one-half of the then] or present fair market value of such property, whichever is greater."

In August 1972, before the parties executed the agreement, but after the March 4 date specified in the settlement agreement, the Chilcotts deeded the W-4 Ranch in Oregon to former husband and two other employees. Former husband did not mention his interest in the ranch at the time he executed the settlement agreement in December 1972.

Former husband continued working for Chilcott Enterprises after the dissolution until he became disabled after suffering a stroke in 1976. In 1978, the ranch was sold for over $1,350,000 and former husband's interest in the sale proceeds was turned over to his conservator. This action was instituted in 1980 shortly after former wife learned of the conveyance of the ranch to former husband and the other employees.

Mr. Chilcott testified in essence that the conveyance to the three employees was a gift—the reason he deeded the ranch to the three employees was that he did not need the money and he just felt like giving it away.

Additional facts will be included in the discussion of the propriety of the nonsuit. * * *

The Nonsuit

A nonsuit may be granted only when, " ' * * * disregarding conflicting evidence and giving to plaintiff's evidence all the value to which it is legally entitled, herein indulging in every legitimate inference which may be drawn from that evidence, the result is a determination that there is no evidence of sufficient substantiality to support a verdict in favor of the plaintiff if such a verdict were given.' " * * * The question is thus whether there was substantial evidence that would have supported a verdict in favor of former wife on the issue of her interest in the ranch (or, more correctly, the proceeds from the sale of the ranch).

Former wife contends there was substantial evidence the transfer of the ranch interest to former husband was in lieu of pension benefits, and is therefore community property. Former husband contends there is no substantial evidence the ranch constituted a retirement benefit and argues the transfer of the ranch interest was a gift, and thus, separate property pursuant to Civil Code section 5108 [now Family Code section 770]. The trial court agreed with former husband that the transfer of the interest in the ranch to him was a gift and concluded therefore that it was his separate property.

We agree with the trial court and former husband that the Chilcotts' transfer of a one-third interest in the ranch to former husband was legally in the form of a gift. Civil Code section 1146 defines a gift as "a transfer of personal property, made voluntarily, and without consideration." The evidence establishes that that is precisely what was done in the case at bench. There is no evidence the ranch was transferred pursuant to a legal obligation to do so on the part of the Chilcotts. There is no evidence of any bargained-for contractual obligation nor of any detrimental reliance by former husband sufficient to invoke the doctrine of promissory estoppel. There is nothing to show, for example, that former husband was induced to stay in the Chilcotts' employ by the statement assertedly made by Mr. Chilcott that the ranch was going to be conveyed to the three employees in lieu of a pension program. There being no evidence of any legal obligation to convey the ranch, its conveyance can only have been a gift.

However, the conclusion the conveyance was legally a gift does not resolve the ultimate question of the characterization of the ranch interest or the proceeds of its sale as community or separate. Although Civil Code section 5108 [now Family Code section 770] provides that property acquired by the husband after marriage by gift is his separate property, the language of section 5108 must be read in the context of the entire marital property scheme. Earnings or property attributable to or acquired as a result of the labor, skill and effort of a spouse during marriage are community property. * * * Even though the transfer of the ranch interest was legally a gift, there is substantial, indeed strong, evidence the gift was made by former husband's employer in recognition of former husband's devoted and skillful services during his lifelong employment at Chilcott Enterprises.

The evidence shows former husband began working for Chilcott Enterprises in 1943. He became Mr. Chilcott's righthand man, did all the accounting for the various Chilcott operations, was responsible for all the tax planning, advice, and filing of returns, handled sales contracts and recordkeeping, served as officer in several of the corporate entities and supervised the ranch operations in California, Arizona and Oregon. For over 30 years, he was the Chilcotts' loyal and trusted employee. By contrast, there was no evidence of any social or personal relationship between former husband and the Chilcotts. The Bramets never went out socially with the Chilcotts, and former husband never played golf or other sports with Mr. Chilcott, never took a social trip, played cards or anything of that sort with the Chilcotts. The Bramets went to the Chilcotts' house once to attend the wedding of the Chilcotts' oldest daughter, and one time former husband took care of the Chilcotts' home while they were away on vacation. Otherwise, former husband never went to the Chilcotts' home socially. Mr. Chilcott testified that, except for their business relationship, he had practically no contact with former husband.

Thus, although the conveyance of the ranch interest to former husband was in the form of a gift, the evidence would support, indeed strongly suggests, that it was in whole or part a remuneratory gift in recognition of former husband's loyal and skilled efforts for and services to his employer. * * * de Funiak and Vaughn, Principles of Community Property (2d ed. 1971) § 70, pp. 157–160.) To the extent it was and to the extent the efforts and services were rendered during the marriage * * * , the ranch interest conveyed to former husband and the proceeds of its sale were community property. * * * de Funiak and Vaughn, Principles of Community Property (2d ed. 1971) § 70, pp. 157–160.)

It was error therefore to grant the nonsuit as to the cause of action to establish former wife's interest in the proceeds of sale of the ranch interest.

* * *

MORRIS, P.J., and RICKLES, J., concur.

NOTES

1.   *Deferred earnings acquired during marriage are community property.* One of the most important rule of community property characterization is that labor during marriage belongs to the community. By this rule, earnings are community property whether they are distributed during the employment period or deferred until a later date.

2.   *Earnings   are   onerously   acquired   community   property notwithstanding the way in which those earnings might be labeled by the employer.* In *Downer*, the fact that the employer labeled the ranch interest a "gift" did not decide the character of the asset as between the spouses. What decided the character of the asset was whether the property came into the

marriage onerously, which is to say by effort, or lucratively, which is to say gratuitously. Having established that husband Keith's employer did not make a true gift, wife Gloria was permitted to proceed with her community property claim to one-half of the ranch sale proceeds. To prevail, Gloria would need to show, on remand, that the ranch constituted deferred earnings acquired by effort during marriage to Gloria while husband Keith was domiciled in California.

SECTION 5. CHAPTER SUMMARY

- Community property is any property acquired during marriage by the effort of one or both spouses while domiciled in the state.

- Property acquired during marriage by effort while residing in another state is quasi-community property in a California dissolution or probate proceeding.

- Date of acquisition is key to the characterization process. Only property acquired during marriage is eligible for characterization as community property or quasi-community property.

- California uses evidentiary presumptions to assist with characterization.

- Labor belongs to the community. The housekeeper's presumption holds that both spouses contribute to the acquisition of property during marriage. The housekeeper's presumption is conclusive as a matter of policy.

- The California Family Code Section 760 general community property presumption applies to all assets that are not governed by a superseding presumption. Predictably this means that the general presumption applies to two asset categories: those that are titled in one spouse's name alone; and those that are untitled. The general presumption is rebuttable by tracing the acquisition back to a separate property source. It is also rebuttable by an agreement between the parties (Chapter 1).

- The California Family Code Section 2581 special community property presumption applies to assets that are acquired during marriage in any joint title form. Tracing is not a permitted rebuttal form. Rather the statutory joint title presumption is rebuttable only by an agreement that one or both spouses is to retain a separate property interest in the titled asset in the event of a dissolution.

- The California Probate Code Section 5305(a) special community property presumption applies to sums on deposit in any demand deposit account of a married person. The presumption is rebuttable by tracing sums back to a separate property source or by an agreement between the spouses that specific sums in a specific account are not to be community property.

- The burden to rebut a community property presumption is on the spouse who claims the property as his or her own separate property.

- Onerous title is community property in character. Lucrative title is separate property in character.

CHAPTER 3

SEPARATE PROPERTY

■ ■ ■

Separate property is defined by statute as all property owned before marriage, received during marriage by gift, and the rents, issues, and profits of either.

Earnings and accumulations after a date of separation are separate property, as are money and settlements received for designated tort claims.

SECTION 1. STATE CONSTITUTIONAL PROTECTION FOR SEPARATE PROPERTY

Separate property is protected by the state constitution.

The California Constitution of 1849 (Art. XI, Sec. 14) protected a married woman's right to own separate property. The California Constitution of 1879 (Art. XX, Sec. 8) extended separate property protection to both spouses. The 1974 amended California Constitution (Art.1, Sec. 21) adopted gender neutral language. It reads:

"Property owned before marriage or acquired during marriage by gift, will or inheritance is separate property."

SECTION 2. SEPARATE PROPERTY DEFINED

The Organic Act of 1850 adopted the community property system as part of the California Civil Code, thus recognizing a married woman's right to own separate property. As to management and control, the 1850 Organic Act named the husband the legal manager of the community property as well as of the wife's separate property. By adopting male-management the legislative goal was not to make the husband an absolute owner of the community property. It was to make him the sole legal agent for the community. This fine legal distinction proved to be illusory because its practical effect was to divest the married woman of her community and of her separate property rights during marriage.

A. EXCEPTIONS TO THE COMMUNITY PROPERTY PRINCIPLE

The tracing principle was adopted in 1860 in *George v. Ransom*, excerpted below, a case that veered California away from the traditional civil law approach. The civil law *ganancial* rule is that separate property "fruits and profits" (notice the difference in language from the contemporary "rents, issues, and profits") are community property by usufruct. The holding in *George v. Ransom, infra*, replaced the civil law approach with what is often referred to as "the American rule" on rents, issues, and profits. See California Family Code Section 770(a)(3), reproduced below.

California Family Code Section 770(b) gives a separate property owner the right to convey separate property without the consent of the person's spouse, a right also known as exclusive control.

WEST'S ANNOTATED CALIFORNIA FAMILY CODE

§ 770.   Separate property of married person

(a) Separate property of a married person includes all of the following:

(1) All property owned by the person before marriage.

(2) All property acquired by the person after marriage by gift, bequest, devise, or descent.

(3) The rents, issues, and profits of the property described in this section.

(b) A married person may, without the consent of the person's spouse, convey the person's separate property.

(Stats. 1992, c. 162 (A.B. 2650), § 10, operative Jan. 1, 1994.)

1.   Property Owned Before Marriage

Here is a simple example to illustrate California Family Code Section 770(a)(1).

Let's say that X and Y marry on January 10. On the date of the marriage X owns a car. X's date of marriage is the date that X enters into the California community property system as a married person. How does the date of marriage affect X's ownership of the car? On January 9—one day before the marriage—X's car belongs to X as individual property. On January 10—the day that X and Y marry—X's car remains X's individual property, but now, because the parties are married the car is characterized within the California community property system as X's "separate property." During marriage X can manage and control the car without Y's consent.

2. Property Acquired During Marriage by Gift

At the filing of a petition for separation, dissolution, or nullification, the petitioner and respondent are asked to inventory their community property. Each does so by declaring any community property, any quasi-community property, and by raising any potential claim to separate property (Chapter 1; see also Appendix B).

In the context of California Family Code Section 770(a)(2) notice that the phrase "after marriage" actually refers to the time during marriage. The phrase "gift, bequest, devise, or descent" means a gratuitous transfer of property from a donor to a donee. And the word "gratuitous" means that the transfer is voluntarily made outside of the context of a bargained for exchange.

The Judicial Council offers a standard property inventory form, FL160 that lists real estate first, followed by household items, and items that are often the subject of gifts: "jewelry, antiques, art, coin collections, etc." Items in these categories may be received before the marriage, sometimes as an engagement gift or a wedding gift; they may be received during the marriage, again, sometimes as a belated engagement or wedding gift; or they may be interspousal gifts that one spouse gives to the other spouse for his or her personal use. California Family Code 852(c) defines interspousal gifts as tangible items of personal property given by one spouse to the other primarily for his or her use (Chapter 1). A gift may have different values: a market value and a sentimental value. Or just a market value, as say with a nondescript car. Or just sentimental value, as say with a photograph of a long deceased relative. A family heirloom given by a family member on behalf of a fiancée or spouse to the other fiancée or spouse remains in the donor's family under the law, but only if the donor's express intent in making the gift is that it stay in the donor's family.

In short, gifts can be complex in a legal and sociological sense. Still, when it comes to gifts a few big-picture rules emerge.

First, California Family Code Section 770 defines gifts as separate property, but the common law of gifts determines if and when title has transferred.

Second, the law of gifts requires proof of three elements for a valid gratuitous transfer. Those elements are: (a) the donor communicates a present intent to make the gift; (b) the donor delivers the gift to the donee; and (c) the donee accepts the gift.

Third, the law of gifts allows a donor to put one or more conditions on title transfer. The common law justification for allowing conditional gifts is based on a clear communication rationale: If, when the gift is made (not after), the donor tells to the donee that the gift is conditional on the occurrence or nonoccurrence of an event, then the donor retains a "reversionary interest" in the gifted property. A reversionary interest is vested. It gives the donor the right to reclaim the gifted property—even after it has been delivered to the donee—if and when the donor's original condition is broken. Conditional gifts turn on disclosure by the donor to donee. Absent explicit disclosure, the donor retains no right to the gift.

Before the parties are married, any gifts either spouse receive come into the marriage as separate property. California Family Code Section 770(a)(1).

Generally, during marriage, any personal gifts that are made by a third party to one spouse are received as the donee's separate property. California Family Code Section 770(a)(2). Personal gifts made by a third party to both spouses are owned as concurrent separate property under the same code section. In the event of a dissolution the parties can permit a court to divide concurrently held separate property (Chapter 7).

The spouses, as gift recipients, have the right to contract around California Family Code Section 770 either before or during marriage (Chapter 1).

One exception exists for a gift that the spouses acquire during marriage in joint title form. During a dissolution proceeding, such a gift would be presumed community property. California Family Code Section 2581 (Chapter 2). At death, by comparison, disposition of the same asset would be controlled by the technicalities of the title form that the parties used; in this case, only joint tenancy and tenancy in common gifts would be separate in character (Chapter 9).

Cash gifts are tangible personal property.

Cash gifts that are deposited into a bank account become sums on deposit in a demand account. As such they are presumptively community property in character. California Probate Code Section 5305(a). A party has the right to confirm separate property deposits, either by tracing or by agreement (Chapter 2).

That takes care of gifts from third-party donors to one or both spouses.

What about gifts exchanged between the spouses?

Interspousal gifts fall under the separate property definition found at California Family Code Section 770(a)(2). The exception is where an interspousal gift is purchased with community property funds; in such a case the character of the gift remains community property (by tracing) unless the property is transmuted by an express declaration made by the adversely affected spouse (the donor). To transmute an interspousal gift the donor must either formally transmute the property or the gift must fall into the category of personal gifts that are exempt from transmutation formalities. Transmutation formalities appear at California Family Code

Section 852. The interspousal personal gift exemption is found at subsection (c) of that same statute (Chapter 1).

Gifts exchanged between persons who are contemplating marriage to each other come into the marriage as the recipient's separate property. If the marriage does not occur, other issues arise. The case of *Simonian v. Dinoian*, 96 Cal.App.2d 259, 215 P.2d 119 (2d Dist. 1950)—a case where gifts by the prospective groom and his mother were delivered to the prospective bride at the engagement party of a wedding that was ultimately canceled—is an example of how quickly a line can be drawn between contemplating marriage and breaking-up.

3. Separate Property Appreciation Distinguished from Rents, Issues, and Profits of Separate Property

The Spanish *ganancial* system distinguished between the underlying asset, on one hand, and that asset's appreciation and income, on the other hand. The traditional language used was "fruits and profits." Today, all U.S. community property systems distinguish between appreciation, on one hand, and rents, issues and profits, on the other hand.

Appreciation (or depreciation) is defined as a change in value between the date of purchase and some later point in time. For example, if X and Y, who are married to each other, buy a house for $100,000 in Year 1 and sell it for $600,000 in Year 10, they realize an appreciation of $500,000.

Appreciation = fair market value @ sale − contract purchase price

If an underlying property appreciates (or depreciates) the tracing rule says that the character of the underlying property legally determines the character of the appreciation (or depreciation). The rationale is that a property and its appreciation are identical in character so long as they remain unified. Once severed, a change of form occurs, but the change of form does not affect the character of the severed parts.

At sale, what was one asset—the underlying property and its unrealized appreciation—becomes two assets. The first asset is the underlying property that the parties purchased using net character contributions. The second (now distinct) asset is the appreciation that the parties realized from the original purchase (investment). When the buyer pays the married sellers, total sale proceeds are divided so as to reimburse the parties for their net character contributions to purchase. The community estate is reimbursed for its contribution. Any contributing separate property estate is reimbursed for its contribution. If there are sale proceeds remaining after the mortgage is repaid and parties' net contributions to purchase are reimbursed those proceeds represent asset appreciation.

Appreciation, if any, is owned pro rata between the estates (community or separate) that contributed to the purchase of the asset.

Contrast asset appreciation with asset income.

Asset income is a realizable (severable) during ownership. Asset appreciation can also be realizable during ownership, but hypothecation or a partial sale is required. In other words, owners must take out an equity loan to realize their equity, or else they must sell a percentage share of the asset at current market value. Asset income, by comparison, is generated by the underlying asset. A house that is rented creates an income stream. As does a patent that is licensed. A business generates profits. These are examples of assets that produce income. Notice that for each example, the underlying asset produces its own income, independent (to varying degrees) of the owner's labor or daily effort. The California community property system refers to income streams as "rents, issues, and profits."

The civil law *ganancial* rule relies on the ancient concept of usufruct to give to the community the right to use separate property rents, issues, and profits during the marriage. At dissolution rents, issues, and profits are returned to the owning spouse, sometimes subject to a reimbursement for asset maintenance expenses. In a civil law system, an owning spouse who wants to transmute the rents, issues, and profits of his or her separate property from community to separate property is required to clearly distinguish between the underlying property, which is already separate and the asset income stream which is the subject of the transmutation.

California abandoned the civil law usufruct rationale early-on when it fashioned the American rule of separate property rents, issues, and profits.

The shift occurred in *George v. Ransom*, *infra*, a case about third-party creditor rights. The rise of credit transactions made third-party creditors skeptical about the profitability of dealing with married persons. *George v. Ransom* reflects one of the first articulations of a macroeconomic worry about the role of marriage in the larger economy: the concern that if creditors lose confidence in dealing with a married person the economy might suffer harm. Creditors needed legal assurances, in the form of community property rules that give them satisfaction in the event that a married person transfers property without the other spouse's signature or defaults on a loan. The macroeconomic consequence of *George v. Ransom* which is counterintuitive given the legal outcome, was to keep credit flowing to married persons.

The civil law *ganancial* rule exposes separate property income streams to the reach of community creditors. In a system like the early California system, where the husband had the sole legal right to manage community property, community property was always reachable by the husband's creditors. In *George v. Ransom* the problem was not whether the husband's creditors could reach community property (they could). Nor was it really about the nuts and bolts question of whether the husband's creditors could reach the wife's separate property assets (they could because early California statutory law also gave the husband the legal right to manage the wife's separate property). Instead, the question in *George v. Ransom* was whether a husband's creditors could reach the dividends that were generated by a wife's separate property. For whatever reason, the creditors sought to satisfy the husband's debt with a particular cache of property that the Organic Act had not specified as within the scope of a husband's management powers.

This a far more philosophical issue than one might expect. One that implicates macroeconomic issues as well as gender relations in the family.

The creditor in *George v. Ransom* dealt with the husband as the sole legal manager of the community property and of the wife's separate property. The husband must have pledged the wife's separate property on a debt that he eventually failed to pay. The creditors attempted to reach the dividends of the wife's separate property on the theory that those dividends were community property in character during the marriage, as they would be under the civil law *ganancial* rule. The husband countered that the applicable California statute did not explicitly clothe him with the power to manage the separate property dividends at issue. Thus, for purposes of creditor satisfaction, the court was asked to decide the scope of husband legal authority to manage the wife's separate property dividends.

One can see the problem of creditor confidence in dealing with married persons starting to brew from the outset of California history. The mere the fact that the family's creditors had to go through an uncertain court process to seek satisfaction would have caused waves of worry among repeat-player creditors. If creditors *perceived* that dealings with married persons were unreasonably risky under the community property system, that perception itself could cause creditors to shy away from transacting with married persons (men). The civil law *ganancial* rule, as originally codified in California, created the perception of unreasonable risk by how it allowed the wife's separate property to be pledged for community debts incurred by the husband without also explicitly specifying if the income streams of that property were included in the original pledge. *George v. Ransom* addresses the statutory gap between separate property rents, issues, and profits, on one hand, and the husband's management rights over that property (if any) on the other.

George v. Ransom, infra, assumes that separate property is defined as the underlying asset and its income streams.

When you read the opinion, notice how the court rejects the civil law usufruct rationale (with its fruits and profits phraseology) and adopts instead a common law rationale that is more in line with a fiercely competitive extraction economy (gold mining) than with a cyclical farming economy (agriculture and ranching). To quote the court from the case reproduced below: "It is not perceived that property can be in one [person], in full and separate ownership, with a right in another [person] to control it and enjoy all of its benefits. The sole value of property is in its use; to disassociate the right of property from the use in this class of cases, would be to preserve the name—the mere shadow—and destroy the thing itself— the substance." *Id.* at 324.

California Family Code Section 770(a)(3) codifies the holding in *George v. Ransom*. It further holds that property owned before marriage or received during marriage by gift is confirmable as separate property, as are any rents, issues and profits derived from either source.

GEORGE V. RANSOM
15 Cal. 322, 76 Am.Dec. 490 (1860)

BALDWIN, J., delivered the opinion of the Court—FIELD, C.J., concurring.

This question arises from the record in this case: can a creditor of the husband subject the proceeds or dividends of the separate estate of the wife to his claim? In this case the property sought to be subjected was the dividends of certain stock purchased by the wife with her separate funds.

By the fourteenth section of article eleven of the Constitution, it is provided: "All property, both real and personal, of the wife, owned or claimed by her before marriage, and that acquired afterward by gift, devise, or descent, shall be her separate property; and laws shall be passed, more clearly defining the rights of the wife, in relation as well to her separate property as to that held in common with her husband. Laws shall also be passed, providing for the registration of the wife's separate property."

By section nine of the act regulating the relation of husband and wife, (Wood's Dig. 488) it is enacted: "The husband shall have the entire management and control of the common property, with the like absolute power of disposition, as of his own separate estate; and the rents and profits of the separate estate of either husband or wife shall be deemed common property, unless, in the case of the separate property of the wife, it shall be provided by the terms of the instrument whereby such property may have been bequeathed, devised, or given to her, that the rents and profits thereof shall be applied to her sole and separate use—in which case, the entire management and disposal of the rents and profits of such property shall belong to the wife, and shall not be liable for the debts of the husband."

We think the Legislature has not the Constitutional power to say that the fruits of the property of the wife shall be taken from her, and given to the husband or his creditors. If the Constitutional provision be not a protection to the wife against the exercise of this authority, the anomaly would seem to exist, of a right of property in one, divested of all beneficial use—the barren right to hold in the wife, and the beneficial right to enjoy in the husband. One object of the provision was, to protect the wife against the improvidence of the husband; but this object would wholly fail, in many instances, if the estate of the wife were reduced to a mere reversionary interest, to be of no avail to her except in the contingency of her surviving her husband.

It has been seen that the provision of the Constitution is, that the property acquired by the wife by devise, bequest, etc., shall be her separate property. This term "separate property" has a fixed meaning in the common law, and had in the minds of those who framed the Constitution, the large majority of whom were familiar with, and had lived under that system. By the common law, the idea attached to separate property in the wife, and which forms a portion of its definition, is, that it is an estate, held as well in its use as in its title, for the exclusive benefit and advantage of the wife. The common law recognized no such solecism as a right in the wife to the estate, and a right in someone else to use it as he pleased, and to enjoy all the advantages of its use. It is not perceived that property can be in one, in full and separate ownership, with a right in another to control it and enjoy all of its benefits. The sole value of property is in its use; to disassociate the right of property from the use in this class of cases, would be to preserve the name—the mere shadow—and destroy the thing itself—the substance. It would be to make the wife the trustee for the husband, holding the legal title, while he held the fruits of that title. This could no more be done, in consistency with our ideas of property, during the lifetime of the wife, than for all time.

This was the view taken by the Judge below, and his judgment is affirmed.

NOTES

1. *What makes the American rule so, well, American?* American-rule states adopt a common law based tracing rule. In the civil law tradition tracing was historically limited to land-for-land exchanges and reinvestments of separate property land sale proceeds in land. William O. Huie, *Some Principles of Texas Community Property, in* COMPARATIVE STUDIES IN COMMUNITY PROPERTY LAW 116–117 (Jan. P Charmatz and Harriet S. Daggett eds., 1955). The Huie essay cites WILLIAM Q. DE FUNIAK, PRINCIPLES OF COMMUNITY PROPERTY 2D 142 (1943), which translates Spanish commentaries like Gutierrez and Matienzo. *William A. Reppy, Jr., Major Events in the Evolution of American Community Property Law,* 23 FAMILY LAW QUARTERLY 163, 172 (1989).

Practical consequences of the tracing rule are that it creates a large implied category of separate property within the definition of California Family Code Section 770, namely property acquired in exchanged for separate property. Like California, the statutes of U.S. community property states, other than Louisiana and Wisconsin, do not mention the category of separate property that traces back to separate property. The idea is recognized by judicial decisions that adopt the tracing rule, and by the doctrine of precedent which perpetuates the idea.

2.   *What makes the civil law rule so civil?* A community property system is a code-based system, the idea being that the code provides a default answer to property questions that might arise between two spouses during and at the end of marriage. Idaho, Louisiana, Texas, and Wisconsin (by statute) follow the civil law rule that characterizes separate property rents, issues and profits as community property. Cyclical efforts to amend the Texas Constitution to replace the civil law rule with the American rule are evident in Texas's constitutional history. The civil law uses the concept of usufruct to explain why a property owner might have to share property with the community during marriage. Usufruct does not split title, as a common law trust would. It functions more like a license. Under a usufruct justification, the community gets to use separate property income during the marriage unless the parties exclude that specific income stream by agreement.

3.   *What Did Ida Hoe?* In 1955, the late W.J. Brockelbank, a professor at the University of Idaho School of Law, wrote about a specific type of complexity that arose when Idaho fused civil and common law legal methods. *See*, W.J. Brockelbank, *The Creditor and the Community in Idaho*, COMPARATIVE STUDIES IN COMMUNITY PROPERTY LAW 26–49 (Jan P. Charmatz and Harriet S. Daggett eds., 1955).

Some background: Idaho is a U.S. community property state that follows the Spanish *ganancial* income rule, as included in IDAHO CODE SECTION 32–906: "Property acquired after marriage by either spouse is community property." IDAHO CODE SECTION 32–912 provides that either spouse can manage and control community property, which includes the income of either or both spouse's separate property. Spouses can agree to transmute separate property income (from community to separate), but they must do so by specific reference to the income itself. Once transmuted, the owning spouse regains exclusive management and control of the separate property income and, more to the point, creditors are barred from reaching that income for "the debts of the other member of the community." In the absence of a transmutation agreement, a creditor can reach separate property income obtained during marriage because it is characterized under the civil law *ganancial* system adopted by Idaho state law as community in character. In his article, Professor Brockelbank sets out to meticulously point out the clear civil law rule and the gaps that Idaho case law has created as to three issues in particular: (a) the character of separate property income; (b) whether and when separate property can be reached by third-party creditors; and (c) what inferential gaps persist despite judicial and legislative efforts to clarify the law.

Idaho also has a long history of statutes and precedents that extend special protection to a married woman's separate property and any income that it might produce during marriage. The explicitly gender specific statutes were on the books until very recently. For example, IDAHO CODE SECTION 11–204. Exemption in favor of a married person read (past tense): "All real and personal estate belonging to any *married woman* at the time of her marriage, or to which she subsequently becomes entitled in her own right, and all the rents, issues and profits thereof, and all compensation due or owing for her personal services is exempt from execution against *her husband*." (Italics added.) The code section was declared unconstitutional because it arbitrarily treated married persons differently based on their gender. In *Credit Bureau of E. Idaho, Inc. v. Lecheminant*, 149 Idaho 468, 235 P.3d 1188 (2010) the arbitrary, treatment was held not to be substantially related to the objective of community property legislation. Explicitly gender biased legislation was repealed and enacted anew in 2011. IDAHO CODE SECTION 11–204. "Exemption in favor of a married person" now reads (present tense): "All real and personal property of any *married person* at the time of *his or* her marriage, or which *he or* she subsequently *acquires as separate property*, and all *noncommunity* rents, issues and profits thereof, * * * are exempt from execution * * * for any separate debts incurred by his or her spouse." (Added amended language is in italics.)

In 1976, the Idaho Supreme Court decided *Williams v. Paxton*, 98 Idaho 155, 559 P.2d 1123 (1976), a case that incorporates federal equal protection principles into Idaho community property law. (Specifically, *Williams* restored to the married woman in Idaho her capacity to enter into contracts during marriage.) But it was a long time (thirty-five years) from the decision in *Williams* to the repeal and enactment of the gender neutral revised version of IDAHO CODE SECTION 11–204.

Professor Brockelbank catalogues other interpretive fusions/gaps that arose; many in the context of the Idaho law on creditors' rights. Many gaps were caused by historical practices around credit (many of those practices were gender specific). Others by Idaho's unique settler history—Idaho did not have a strong Spanish presence; instead, many of Idaho's original white settlers were adherents of Mormonism. Others by legal realities and events like (i) the civil law income rule; (ii) the transition from male management to equal management and control; (iii) the decision in *Williams* recognizing a married woman's right to enter into contracts; (iv) general creditor's rights rules (i.e., creditors can reach whatever property the debtor has the legal right to control), and now (v) repeal of the gender unequal legislation that had been on the books. The resulting "gaps" (Professor Brockelbank's word) complicated the Idaho community property system certainly by the 1950s, the era in which Professor Brockelbank published his article, and probably continue to do so today.

What counteracts the gaps? What calms the fusions?

In the U.S. community property states statutory gaps and fusions inevitably arise. When they do they are resolved or eased by code sections and cases. Additionally, the English, now American, common law doctrine of precedent is used to reconcile, distinguish, and sometimes even overrule case precedents. Case precedent is applied as if it supersedes code provisions, even in a (code-based) community property system. The result is that adherence to the doctrine of precedent in a community property system is a practice that can (and does) make family code provisions a bit encrusted with implied meaning. That may be at least one reason why state legislatures are ever busy revising the family code statutes. It is unusual for a state to take thirty-five years to correct a statute; Idaho did, but perhaps it was because Idaho lawmakers knew that federal equal protection law had been incorporated into the family law by a 1976 case (*Williams*).

California typically does not tarry in amending its family code statutes. Once there is a change in understanding, culture, mores, federal rules, political signs and so forth the California Legislature tends to revise the family code to reflect the change. The idea is to keep the law updated in a state (California) that is exceedingly diverse and complex culturally, legally, politically, and geographically (Chapter 1).

But if some complexity can improve the delivery of justice, too much can add to the expense of delivering justice. A solution to addressing over-complexity is not to jettison the community property system because it is no longer "pure." The solution is to understand how the system has become complex, to remove what is hyper-complex or no longer useful and to do it quickly. Legislating for clarity and if possible simplicity improves justice for married persons, their families, and third parties.

Community property systems have twisted and turned over long, long periods of historical time. This doesn't mean they should be bowed to. Nor does it mean that they are old fashioned and ready for repeal. What it means, if anything, is that community property works. More to the point, the community property sharing principle, which has been around since ancient time, works.

To some up the conversation of gaps and complexity: One recognizes a *ganancial*-based community property system by the fact that both spouses are vested in the property that they acquire during marriage while domiciled in the jurisdiction. Vesting takes place regardless of gender, earning ability, educational level, physical ability, or any other personal or individual difference between the spouses. The community property system, or at least the California community property system, has envisioned the family as a firm, a firm that forms the basic unit of the economy, a firm that is entitled to clear and useful rules about property, liabilities, and duties.

4.   *The civil law, the common law, and the postcolonial state.* Mauritius is an island nation in the Indian Ocean. Like Louisiana, Mauritius was a French colony (1715 to 1810). While Louisiana became an American territory, Mauritius become a British colony (1810 to 1968). In its history Mauritius has based its legal system on, among other traditions, French civil law; it has relied on English common law; and it has developed a Mauritian law of its own. Mauritian law, much like the community property law of California (and of the

other U.S. community property states) is a code-based system in which individual code provisions can be superseded by case law (precedent).

In H. Narsinghen, *Reception of the Doctrine of Precedent in a Mixed Law Jurisprudence*, XXVII DELHI LAW REV. 26 (2005), Narsinghen describes the Mauritius system as a "mixed law jurisdiction" (not a mixed model) and he goes on to identify how the Mauritian code and precedent interact. Narsinghen's description is not radically unlike how one might describe California's community property system. *See e.g.*, JO CARRILLO, UNDERSTANDING CALIFORNIA COMMUNITY PROPERTY LAW 3–16 (2015).

As a postcolonial nation, Mauritius transitioned from French to English control by a treaty that protected the inhabitants' existing property rights. So too did California enter the U.S. with a promise to protect the property rights of the Mexican citizens who found themselves suddenly in U.S. territory. The Treaty of Guadalupe Hidalgo (1848) protected the property rights of the Mexican citizens who opted for U.S. citizenship.

Back to Mauritius: in that system courts act in accordance with the nation's history. According to Professor Narsinghen:

"... Mauritian law does not borrow blindly from English law and French law. In fact, in many areas of private law, family law, property law, the Mauritian judges have provided original solutions." Narsinghen, *supra.* p. 27.

Narsinghen's observation is that Mauritian solutions are original echoes of individualized national histories. They are not simply "mixed models." The view of original fusion is supported by the theoretical work of comparative law scholars who object to the use of "mixed model" to describe postcolonial legal systems.

In light of the above, was *George v. Ransom* a mistake? Or was it an original legal solution to one or more reoccurring problems?

Most contemporary comparative law scholars likely would not view *George v. Ransom* as a mistake. *See e.g.*, Pierre Legrand, *The Same and Different, in* COMPARATIVE LEGAL STUDIES: TRADITIONS AND TRANSITIONS 240–277 (Pierre Legrand and Munday, eds., 2003). These scholars might argue instead that the lines between types of legal systems are not set in stone. History shows that it is possible for a civil law system to incorporate common law principles that lead to new outcomes. For example: What happens when a state supreme court incorporates the doctrine of precedent into a community property state's jurisprudence? Does the community property system, which has its origin in the civil law, develop its own precedent, meaning its own common law, over time? If so, does the code provision supersede the case precedent? Or is it the other way around?

California's legal history is unique among the U.S. community property states principally because of the social and legal conditions that were set in motion by the Gold Rush. Once gold was discovered there was an exponential increase in the state's population. Legal disputes arose; and they were decided.

The state's first court reporter wrote that there were no law libraries (they had been destroyed by an earthquake, fires, and rain), and thus early California judges and lawyers, most of whom had been trained in the common law, had to rely on their training. There were (evidently) not too many experts on Romanized Spanish law in early California. Spanish California was part of New Spain's outback, so to speak; and Mexican California handled all but the rarest marriage matters through its localized *alcalde* system, a system that originated in Arabic (Moorish) Spain but that in Mexican California, was administered not by judges, but by Catholic parish priests.

SECTION 3. PERSONAL INJURY CLAIMS, MONEY, AND PROPERTY

A personal injury cause of action can arise when one person is injured by another person. The claim may result in the receipt of money or property as settlement, but the claim itself is not an "accumulation" as that term is used within the community property system. The rationale for restricting the definition of a personal injury claim has to do with the theoretical difference between a personal right and a property right. A personal right exists apart from any object or property; it is not proprietary and, therefore, it is not tradable, as a property right is.

A property right—evoked by the word *accumulation*—gives its owner the legal ability *to exclude* others. Likewise, a reasonable expectation of privacy gives its holder the right to control matters related to his or her body. And yet, one's body is not a "thing" in the way the term is typically used in property law.

Moore v. UC Regents, 51 Cal.3d 120, 271 Cal.Rptr. 146, 793 P.2d 479 (Cal. 1990) (in bank) is a case on point. In that case, the California Supreme Court dismissed the conversion claim of a plaintiff whose excised diseased organ had been used by medical researchers to create a patented cell-line. The court held that the human source did not retain a property interest in excised biological materials. The court acknowledged that a person enjoys property rights in attached body parts, but once removed biological material is effectively abandoned. Additionally, as a matter of policy, the source is precluded, by public health policy from claiming excised biological materials. Abandonment in this context does not mean thrown away; it means, absent an agreement otherwise, that the source has relinquished ownership and possession over the biological materials, either factually (excision) or as a matter of law (public health law and policy). Because conversion requires proof of a property interest (ownership or possession), and because a property interest in the excised materials is exactly what the source has relinquished, the source lacks a factual basis upon which to base a conversion claim.

In a personal injury case—say, for example, where a spouse loses a limb due to the adjudged negligence of another person—legal negotiations must eventually turn to the topic of how to value the lost body part. Still, the personal injury claim itself does not arise because the limb is "property." It arises because the plaintiff's significant *personal* right to be free of harm was been violated by the defendant.

A. PERSONAL INJURY CLAIMS

Neither California Family Code Section 780 nor Section 781 characterize personal injury claims as property. Instead, each speaks of money or property received in settlement of personal injury claims.

California Family Code Section 780 is a special community property provision. It characterizes as community property money and property received for a personal injury cause of action that arose *during* marriage. It also excludes personal injury settlements from the reach of California Family Code Section 760. Settlements are subject to the reach of California Family Code Section 2603, a mandatory assignment rule whose purpose, at dissolution, is to confirm any money or property received for a personal injury claim that arose during marriage as the injured spouse's separate property.

California Family Code Section 781(a) confirms as separate property money and property received for a personal injury cause of action that arose before or after the injured person's marriage.

California Family Code Section 780(b) provides a right of reimbursement for expenses that were paid on behalf of the injured spouse by either the community property or the separate property of the noninjured spouse.

California Family Code Section 780(c) confirms as the injured spouse's separate property any property or money received for a personal injury claim brought by one spouse against the other spouse.

A personal injury cause of action against a third party that arose during marriage must be pursued during marriage in order to produce Section 780 community property. If the injured party does not sue the tortfeasor before a dissolution petition is filed, then the cause of action is left to the control of the injured spouse. Out of fairness to the injured party, any marital settlement agreement that attempts to structure the personal injury cause of action itself (like putting an unpursued cause of action into a trust) will be unenforceable as a matter of policy. The reasoning is that if money and property received in settlement of a personal injury claim are assigned at dissolution to the injured spouse as separate property, so too would an unpursued personal injury claim that arose during marriage. See California Family Code Section 781 reproduced below.

WEST'S ANNOTATED CALIFORNIA FAMILY CODE

§ 780.   Community property

Except as provided in Section 781 and subject to the rules of allocation set forth in Section 2603, money and other property received or to be received by a married person in satisfaction of a judgment for damages for personal injuries, or pursuant to an agreement for the settlement or compromise of a claim for such damages, is community property if the cause of action for the damages arose during the marriage.

(Stats. 1992, c. 162 (A.B. 2650), § 10, operative Jan. 1, 1994.)

§ 781.   Separate property

(a) Money or other property received or to be received by a married person in satisfaction of a judgment for damages for personal injuries, or pursuant to an agreement for the settlement or compromise of a claim for those damages, is the separate property of the injured person if the cause of action for the damages arose as follows:

   (1) After the entry of a judgment of dissolution of a marriage or legal separation of the parties.

   (2) While either spouse, if he or she is the injured person, is living separate from the other spouse.

(b) Notwithstanding subdivision (a), if the spouse of the injured person has paid expenses by reason of the personal injuries from separate property or from the community property, the spouse is entitled to reimbursement of the separate property or the community property for those expenses from the separate property received by the injured person under subdivision (a).

   (c) Notwithstanding subdivision (a), if one spouse has a cause of action against the other spouse which arose during the marriage of the parties, money or property paid or to be paid by or on behalf of a party to the party's spouse of that marriage in satisfaction of a judgment for damages for personal injuries to that spouse, or pursuant to an agreement for the settlement or compromise of a claim for the damages, is the separate property of the injured spouse.

(Stats. 1992, c. 162 (A.B. 2650), § 10, operative Jan. 1, 1994.)

B. NO IMPUTED CONTRIBUTORY NEGLIGENCE AS A MATTER OF LAW

An early civil law community property approach was based on a claim (settlement) apportionment theory. By that theory, personal injury damages were characterized at dissolution on the basis of the nature of the money or settlement received. In other words, personal injury money that compensated for lost wages or lost earning ability traced back to community property labor. Money that compensated for pain and suffering or for lost future earnings (because the marriage was ending) traced back to separate property.

California did not adopt the claim apportionment theory of personal injury damages. Instead, over the years, the California legislature and courts adopted other classification approaches. Most of the adoptions made along the way were intended to offset characterization problems caused by the state's adoption of the imputed contributory negligence doctrine. What follows is a brief legal history of that doctrine as it has been understood over time to interact with the community property system.

Before 1957, personal injury damages recovered during marriage were characterized as community property. The courts modified this rule by the adoption of the imputed negligence doctrine in two cases: *Zaragosa v. Craven,* 33 Cal.2d 315, 202 P.2d 73 (1949) and *McFadden v. Santa Ana, O. & T. St. Ry. Co.,* 87 Cal. 464, 25 P. 681 (1891), both now superseded on this issue. The modifying doctrine worked like this: If an injury was proximately caused by a third-party tortfeasor *and* by the injured party's spouse, the negligence of the tortfeasor spouse was imputed to the injured spouse who was then barred from obtaining a tort recovery.

Justice Traynor explained the policy behind the imputed negligence doctrine in (the now superseded) *Keslar v. Pabst,* 43 Cal.2d 254, 273 P.2d 257 (1954). On one hand Justice Traynor wrote, it is state policy to permit injured persons to recover from tortfeasors. On the other hand, a tortfeasor should not profit from an injury that they proximately cause. According to Justice Traynor, when a spouse is negligently injured by the other spouse and a third person, it is far worse—as a policy matter—for the contributorily negligent spouse to profit from a tort recovery, that is community property in character, than it is to prevent the injured spouse from obtaining a recovery in the first place. Justice Traynor was careful to limit the holding in *Keslar* to the legislative fact that California community property law at the time gave the husband exclusive legal management and control rights over tort awards. Nevertheless, the issue of how to strike a fair balance between permitting or barring recovery remained unsettled because of how the Vehicle Code imputed negligence to married vehicle "owners." Under the Vehicle Code, the husband—as the sole legal agent for management and control of community property—was imputed with negligence in any accident that involved the family vehicle.

The problems with the pre-1957 regime soon became evident as the number of traffic accidents increased. The imputed contributory negligence doctrine penalized spouses, but not friends, nonmarried cohabitants, or other family members. So, (sometime before 1957) if a wife was injured by a negligent third party while driving the family car her husband was adjudged contributorily negligent for that accident as a matter of law, even if he was not present in the vehicle when the accident occurred. The husband's contributory negligence was then imputed to the wife, who was barred from recovering at all.

Imputed contributory negligence was the law, but it proved to be a controversial doctrine in a state whose very culture came to be defined by the motorized vehicle—the car, especially. As one reform minded judge put it: "[The imputed contributory negligence doctrine] prevent[s] a fictitious "profit" by committing a real injustice—denying an innocent person recovery because of the wrong of another." George Brunn, *Study on Personal Injury Damages*, 8 CAL. LAW REVISION COMM'N REP. REC. STUDIES 423 (1967), 424. See also, Comment, 9 HASTINGS L.J. 291 (1958).

The 1957 Amendments characterized tort awards as separate property. In 1957 the Legislature amended California Civil Code Section 163.5 to provide: "All damages, special and general, awarded to a married person in a civil action for personal injuries, are the separate property of such married person."

The stated rationale behind recharacterizing personal injury settlements as separate property was to neutralize the imputed negligence doctrine. The 1957 change defined *any* and all damages recovered in personal injury actions as the separate property of the injured spouse. Calling tort awards separate property raised other issues, all noted by the California Law Review Commission:

- The future earnings of the injured spouse become separate property in contravention of the community property system;

- The community property is not entitled to a reimbursement if it pays for injury expenses;

- Damages can be disposed of by the injured spouse by will or gift without limitation;

- If the injured spouse dies intestate, depending on whether the decedent died survived by issue, parents or siblings, the non-injured spouse might get a smaller share of the (now) separate property award;

- Commingling can lead to gift tax liability; and

- A separate property characterization can lead to unfavorable gift and inheritance tax consequences.

See, *Whether Damages for Personal Injury to a Married Person Should be Separate or Community Property*, 8 CAL. LAW REVISION COMM'N REP. REC. STUDIES 408 (1967).

The 1968 amendments returned to characterizing tort awards as community property. In 1967, the California Law Revision Commission reported on the undesirable effects of the 1957 legislation and recommended that personal injury damages once again be re-characterized as community property. Based on the Commission's recommendations, the legislature amended the law in two key ways: (1) personal injury recoveries once again became community property; and (2) the interspousal imputed contributory negligence doctrine was *explicitly* eliminated from the California community property system. The 1968 legislation was carried over into the Family Law Act of 1969. Today it appears in California Family Code Section 780 (reproduced above) and California Family Code Section 783 (reproduced below).

California Family Code Section 783 requires its own explanation. Prior to 1957, imputed negligence was the law, as discussed above. Multiple tortfeasors were relieved from having to pay a personal injury award in order to prevent a married one of them, namely the injured claimant's spouse, from profiting from the wrong. From 1957 to 1968, the legislature reversed course and placed the burden of loss entirely on the third-party tortfeasor. The reversal caused unfairness by how it gave the injured spouse the option to exonerate a contributorily negligent spouse (simply) by not naming the tortfeasor spouse in a personal injury lawsuit. California Family Code Section 783—the result of the 1968 amendments—attempts to reallocate the burdens of liability more fairly.

To that end, California Family Code Section 783 states a general rule and exception. The rule is that a third-party tortfeasor cannot raise the contributory negligence of the other (unnamed) spouse as a defense in a personal injury action brought by an injured spouse. The exception is that a third-party tortfeasor can establish a right of contribution when the defendant cross-claims against the other spouse—the spouse whom the plaintiff opted not to name as a defendant—*and* the issue of the other spouse's contributory negligence is adjudicated.

Where an injured spouse (the plaintiff) sues a third party (the named defendant) but not the other spouse (an adjudged proximate cause of the injury), the defendant has a right to obtain a contribution from the unnamed contributorily negligent spouse. (A negligent spouse has the same right to seek a contribution against a contributorily negligent third party as well.) Once the other spouse is determined to be a contributing proximate cause of the harm suffered by the plaintiff-spouse, the California Code of Civil Procedure provisions on joint tortfeasors come into play. The procedural provisions are outside the scope of this casebook.

What matters here is that an award to which the torfeasor spouse contributes becomes commingled. Any percentage received from the third party is California Family Code Section 780 community property and subject to the California Family Code Section 2603 mandatory assignment rule in the event of dissolution. Any percentage traceable to the contributorily negligent spouse is subject to California Family Code Section 781, which characterizes that percentage of the settlement as separate property of the injured spouse upon receipt.

WEST'S ANNOTATED CALIFORNIA FAMILY CODE

§ 783.   Injuries to married person by third party; extent concurring negligence of spouse allowable as defense

If a married person is injured by the negligent or wrongful act or omission of a person other than the married person's spouse, the fact that the negligent or wrongful act or omission of the spouse of the injured person was a concurring cause of the injury is not a defense in an action brought by the injured person to recover damages for the injury except in cases where the concurring negligent or wrongful act or omission would be a defense if the marriage did not exist.

(Stats. 1992, c. 162 (A.B. 2650), § 10, operative Jan. 1, 1994.)

C.   PERSONAL INJURY SETTLEMENTS: MONEY AND PROPERTY

As discussed above, California Family Code Section 780 creates a special community property category that *shall* be assigned to the injured spouse as separate property at dissolution. There are two exceptions to the mandatory assignment rule of California Family Code Section 2603.

The first exception has to do with commingling. If California Family Code Section 780 *special* community property becomes confused with Family Code Section 760 *ordinary* community property, the 780 community property is transmuted into 760 community property by operation of law. Ordinary community property is not subject to the assignment rule in California Family Code Section 2603.

The second exception has to do with fairness. California Family Code 2603 authorizes a court to divide California Family Code Section 780 community property at dissolution only if justice requires. The exception is not an invitation to a factfinder to routinely treat California Family Code Section 780 community property as divisible at dissolution. Nor is it a right of reimbursement. It is a narrow grant of discretion that, if exercised, mandates an award of at least one-half of the settlement to the injured person.

WEST'S ANNOTATED CALIFORNIA FAMILY CODE

§ 2603.   Community estate personal injury damages; assignment

(a) "Community estate personal injury damages" as used in this section means all money or other property received or to be received by a person in satisfaction of a judgment for damages for the person's personal injuries or pursuant to an agreement for the settlement or compromise of a claim for the damages, if the cause of action for the damages arose during the marriage but is not separate property as described in Section 781, unless the money or other property has been commingled with other assets of the community estate.

(b) Community estate personal injury damages shall be assigned to the party who suffered the injuries unless the court, after taking into account the economic condition and needs of each party, the time that has elapsed since the recovery of the damages or the accrual of the cause of action, and all other facts of the case, determines that the interests of justice require another disposition. In such a case, the community estate personal injury damages shall be assigned to the respective parties in such proportions as the court determines to be just, except that at least one-half of the damages shall be assigned to the party who suffered the injuries.

(Stats. 1992, c. 162 (A.B. 2650), § 10, operative Jan. 1, 1994.)

D. TRACING PERSONAL INJURY SETTLEMENTS

Marriage of Devlin, excerpted below, applies the tracing principle to California Family Code Section 780 community property.

In *Devlin*, the spouses used personal injury settlement money to buy a residence that was subsequently accommodated to meet the needs of the injured (paraplegic) spouse. Applying California Family Code Section 2603, the court assigned the residence to the injured spouse as separate property. The noninjured spouse appealed. As to the law she argued (1) the word "damages" is limited to money received for the injury, not to purchases made with the money received for the injury; (2) if not, a purchase that traces back to community property damages is community property; and (3) if not, the trial court's decision to assign the entirety of the personal injury award to the injured spouse was inequitable, especially given that the noninjured spouse quit her job to care for her husband.

The court of appeal rejected the noninjured spouse's arguments. The court interpreted the word "damages" in California Family Code Section 2603(b) to mean money received or purchases made with money received. It held that California Family Code Section 2603 effectively supersedes ordinary rules concerning joint form title purposes (although the special joint form presumption was not yet operative the court's holding can be understood broadly.) Finally, the court of appeal upheld the trial court's exercise of discretion to assign the house purchased with the personal injury settlement entirely to the injured spouse despite the wife's equitable arguments. The substantial evidence standard was met, in other words, where the record showed that the injured spouse was paraplegic, the house had been modified for his injuries, he would live out his life at or below poverty level, and the noninjured spouse had "the education and ability with which to secure gainful employment and be self-supporting." *Id.* at 811.

MARRIAGE OF DEVLIN
138 Cal.App.3d 804, 189 Cal.Rptr. 1 (3d Dist. 1982)

EVANS, ASSOCIATE JUSTICE.

The question presented is whether the trial court erred in awarding the bulk of the parties' community property to husband on the basis that the property was acquired with husband's personal injury proceeds.

The parties were married in July 1975, and separated in May 1977. At that time, wife initiated proceedings to dissolve the marriage, but the parties reconciled prior to the entry of a final judgment of dissolution. The couple remained together until May 1981, and wife later filed the instant action to dissolve the marriage.

Prior to the time the parties first separated, husband was severely injured in an automobile accident, rendering him a paraplegic. The personal injury damages, totaling at least $175,000, were received by husband sometime after the parties reconciled.

At trial, the evidence demonstrated that all of the personal injury damages had been spent, and that all of the property of the community at the time of separation was purchased with the personal injury proceeds. Most of this property consists of equity in real property and a mobile home placed thereon and used as the family residence. The mobile home has been specially equipped and adapted for husband's benefit.

The trial court determined that all of the community property was traceable to husband's personal injury proceeds and awarded the bulk of the property (i.e., the realty and the mobile home) to husband. Wife was awarded some miscellaneous personal property "needed for her to get a new start." Wife appeals.

Discussion

Personal injury damages received or to be received from a cause of action arising during marriage are community property. ([currently Family Code Section 780] * * *) Upon dissolution or separation, however, [current Family Code Section 2603(b)] provides that these proceeds, labeled "community property personal injury damages," are to be assigned to the injured spouse unless the court, considering the facts of the case, determines the interests of justice require another disposition. In such case, the community property personal injury damages are assigned to the respective parties in such proportions as the court determines to be fair, except that at least one-half of such damages must be assigned to the spouse who suffered the injuries. [Section 2603(b).] "Community property personal injury damages" are thus a species unique to the Family Law Act; they are held as community property during marriage, but upon dissolution such damages are subject to special assignment rules. * * *

[Section 2603(b)], specifies that "community property personal injury damages shall be assigned to the party who suffered the injuries unless the court, after taking into account the economic condition and needs of each party, the time that has elapsed since the recovery of the damages or the accrual of the cause of action, and all other facts of the case, determines that the interests of justice require another disposition. In such case, the community property personal injury damages shall be assigned to the respective parties in such proportions as the court determines to be just, except that at least one-half of such damages shall be assigned to the party who suffered the injuries * * * ." Thus, [Section 2603(b)], not only recognizes the special nature of community property personal injury damages, but also vests discretion in the trial court in distributing these damages upon dissolution of the marriage. (See 8 Cal.Law Revision Commission (1967) pp. 1392–1393, 1396–1397 (hereafter Law Revision Report).)

Wife does not take issue with the foregoing discussion. It is her position, however, that community property personal injury damages encompass only that money or other property which is *received* from a cause of action arising during marriage. She contends that as the property divided herein was *purchased* with community property personal injury damages, such property is not subject to division pursuant to provisions of [Section 2603(b)]. We disagree.

Such a narrow interpretation of [Section 2603(b)] defeats the purpose of the statute. To accept this interpretation would require that community property personal injury damages be placed in a bank account and never utilized, lest all, or at least that part of the damages spent and converted in form (i.e., into a house, car, iron lung) be treated upon dissolution as ordinary community property. The fallacy in such reasoning is that often at least some portion, and possibly all, of the community property personal injury damages must be spent, both on the needs of the community and on needs unique to the injured spouse. Using community property personal injury damages to purchase an artificial limb, iron lung, specially adapted home or car, etc., may be essential to alleviate the pain and suffering of the injured spouse and to allow the injured spouse to function as normally as possible. Under wife's analysis, because the iron lung and artificial limb do not constitute money or property received, but are instead products purchased with community property personal injury damages, these assistive devices are subject to division just as any ordinary community property. Obviously, the Legislature did not intend such an unjust and absurd result. It is clear the mere conversion of community property personal injury damages from money into a different form does not, standing alone, remove the items purchased from the purview of [Section 2603(b)]. (See Law Revision Report, *supra*, at p. 1397 ("Subdivision (c) applies even though money recovered for personal injury damages has been invested in securities or other property"); * * *) Ordinarily, "community property personal injury damages" lose their character only if irretrievably "commingled with other community property." [Ed. note: Section 2603(b) does not contain this language].)

Wife contends however that the fact that the parties took title to both of these items in joint tenancy requires they be treated as ordinary community property. She seeks to transmute community property personal injury damages into ordinary community property. Wife notes that when a spouse uses separate property to purchase a family residence and title is taken in joint tenancy or by community property, the residence will be deemed to be community property in the absence of a showing of any agreement to the contrary. [Section 2581] * * * There is no reason, wife argues, why a family residence purchased during marriage with community property personal injury damages should not be subject to these same principles of law. Because there was no evidence presented regarding any agreement or understanding between the parties concerning their respective interests in the residence and realty, wife asserts the trial court was required to treat these items as ordinary community property, irrespective of the source used to purchase them. Again, we disagree.

The point missed in wife's argument is that the rules regarding the transmutation of separate property to community property do not apply to community property personal injury damages. Separate property is subject to the complete control of the spouse owning that property. * * *

The inferences that can be drawn, however, when separate property is voluntarily used for community purposes cannot be applied to community property personal injury damages. These damages *are* community property and are subject to the management and control of *both* spouses [Section 1100(a)]. Aside from immediately dissolving the marriage, the injured spouse has no right to segregate community property personal injury damages from the other community property of the marriage. Because community property personal injury damages are community property, it is to be expected that when the parties buy a residence with such proceeds they will take title in joint tenancy or as community property. Thus, the form of title in which property is taken when purchased with community property personal injury damages is not determinative as to how such property should be divided upon dissolution. * * *

In light of this analysis, the only time proceeds from a personal injury award lose their character as community property personal injury damages is, in the absence of an express agreement, when such proceeds have been "commingled" with other community property and it is impossible to trace the source of the property or funds. Generally, "commingling" is a word of art, used to connote the mixture of separate property or funds with community property or funds. * * * As used in [Section 2603(a)] "commingling" clearly refers to the mixture of community property personal injury damages with *other* community property into one undistinguishable, amorphous mass.

In this case there is no issue of commingling. Although the community property personal injury damages were initially deposited in the couple's joint bank account, the property purchased with the community property personal injury damages was easily traced as the evidence demonstrated, and the parties agree, there was no *other* community property with which these damages could be commingled.

We thus examine the award in this case. Having traced all of the parties' community property to the community property personal injury damages, the trial court was required to award this property to husband unless it determined the interests of justice mandated a different disposition. [Section 2603(b)]. The court noted husband has suffered injuries from which in all likelihood he will never recover. The court also considered that the mobile home has been specially adapted for husband's benefit and that even with the award of the realty and mobile home, husband, for the rest of his life, will probably exist at or below the poverty level. In contrast, wife has both the education and ability with which to secure gainful employment and be self-supporting. Exercising its discretion, the court determined the bulk of the community property (the mobile home and realty) should be awarded to husband, and awarded the remaining community property (some miscellaneous personal property) to wife. This award was a proper exercise of the court's discretion and will not be disturbed on appeal. * * *

Wife's other assertions have been considered and are without merit.

The judgment is affirmed.

NOTES

1. *Ability.* Should the wife's attorney have presented evidence about the effect of the husband's injuries on her economic wellbeing? In an economic and emotional sense, the wife was also a victim of the accident. Consider that in response to her husband's need for care she quit her job, cared for her husband at home, and helped make the physical structure of the home accessible for her husband's post-accident physical abilities. Both parties lived at or near the poverty level, and yet the judge assigned the house to the husband for two reasons: the purchase funds for the house traced back to the husband's personal injury award and the wife was (theoretically) educated and able enough to find work. Is it persuasive to say that a spouse who is impoverished

but able can find work? What of any emotional trauma that the wife may have endured as a result of the accident? As a result of giving up her pre-accident activities to care for her husband? Did it promote fairness between these particular parties to rule that the physically able spouse would leave the marriage with no financial resources?

Could the wife's attorney have brought a reimbursement claim against the husband's separate property estate? Would reimbursement be in the form of a quantum meruit claim? Would the benchmark value of wife's caregiving labor determine the amount of the reimbursement? Would a claim for reimbursement include wife's lost opportunity costs? Or, would such a claim be denied on the theory that the a spouse owes the other spouse support (Chapters 1 and 6) no matter the circumstances of the marriage?

Was the noninjured spouse's story adequately told? What social perils are posed from conceptualizing an accident as something that befalls only the injured spouse?

2. *No right of offset.* In *Marriage of Morris*, 139 Cal.App.3d 823, 189 Cal.Rptr. 80 (4th Dist. 1983), the trial court divided the California Family Code Section 760 community property equally, but awarded California Family Code Section 780 personal injury settlement funds entirely to the injured spouse. On appeal, the noninjured spouse argued that the trial court erred in failing to award him some amount of ordinary community property as an offset to equalize the division. In other words, the husband argued that he was entitled to a greater percentage of the ordinary community property (California Family Code Section 760) since all of the special community property (California Family Code Section 780) had been mandatorily assigned to the injured spouse (California Family Code Section 2603). The appellate court rejected the noninjured spouse's offset argument. It held that the legislature intended California Family Code Section 2603 to be an exception to the equal division mandate; therefore equal division does not factor into the assignment of personal injury money and property at dissolution. The equal division mandate is discussed in Chapter 7. See also *Marriage of Mason*, 93 Cal.App.3d 215, 155 Cal.Rptr. 350 (5th Dist. 1979).

3. *Mandatory assignment supersedes ordinary characterization rules.* In *Devlin*, the spouses used personal injury money to acquire a residence during marriage. They took title in both their names. *Devlin* was decided before the special joint title community property presumption (now California Family Code Section 2581) was enacted, which is why there is no discussion in the opinion of the interplay between the special joint title presumption and California Family Code Section 2603. In light of *Morris* if California Family Code Section 2603 is an exception to the equal division mandate, it likely also supersedes community property presumptions that try to achieve equal division at dissolution. Until the legislature says otherwise, any asset that can be traced to California Family Code Section 780 community property shall be assigned to the injured spouse notwithstanding whether it is titled in one spouse's name alone or in both spouses' names together.

California Family Code Section 2581 applies in a dissolution proceeding only.

At death, California Family Code Section 780 property is community in character. As such, it descends to the surviving spouse (Chapter 9).

In light of the contract modification principle (Chapter 2), would it be useful for parties to contract over the characterization of possible personal injury claims before marriage? After the injury? Before the settlement? At dissolution?

4. *Wrongful death awards.* It appears that even money and damages recovered by one spouse for the wrongful death of a relative during marriage would fall under California Family Code Section 780—they are classified as community property during the marriage but subject to assignment as separate property in a dissolution proceeding. The line of precedent that characterize money and property received as settlement for a wrongful death claim as the equivalent of any other personal injury claim (regardless of whether both spouses were related to the third-party decedent or not) appears to begin with *McFadden v. Santa Ana, O. & T. T. Ry Co., supra. See e.g.,* William A. Reppy, Jr., *Can Wrongful Death Damages Recovered by a Married Person be Separate Property Under California Law?*, 39 PEPPERDINE L.REV. 865 (2012).

E. PERSONAL INJURY CLAIMS AGAINST THE OTHER SPOUSE

A personal injury recovery received from a spouse is the injured spouse's separate property. The issue of how to characterize recovery from a spouse can arise in one of two broad circumstances.

The first is where one spouse is injured by a negligent third party, but the other spouse is also found to be the proximate contributory cause of the personal injury, as discussed in California Family Code Section 783, reproduced above. When this happens, any money or property received in satisfaction by the injured spouse for the injury is defined as separate property from the date of receipt.

The second situation is where one spouse is injured by the other spouse's violence. When this happens, money or property received by the injured spouse as a settlement for a personal injury claim against the battering spouse is confirmed as the separate property of the injured spouse. The confirmation holds no matter when the claim arose and no matter what character of money was used to ultimately satisfy the claim. California Family Code Section 782, reproduced below.

If a person is convicted of "Attempted murder or soliciting the murder of a spouse," the spouse who is the target of the crime is statutorily entitled to retain the entirety of his or her retirement and pension benefits as against the convicted spouse, as in the statute below. Other forfeiture-type provisions appear throughout the Family Code (Chapter 6).

The California Domestic Violence Prevention Act is discussed in Chapter 6.

WEST'S ANNOTATED CALIFORNIA FAMILY CODE

§ 782.   Injuries to married person by spouse; primary resort to separate property; consent of injured spouse to use of community property; indemnity

(a)   Where an injury to a married person is caused in whole or in part by the negligent or wrongful act or omission of the person's spouse, the community property may not be used to discharge the liability of the tortfeasor spouse to the injured spouse or the liability to make contribution to a joint tortfeasor until the separate property of the tortfeasor spouse, not exempt from enforcement of a money judgment, is exhausted.

(b)   This section does not prevent the use of community property to discharge a liability referred to in subdivision (a) if the injured spouse gives written consent thereto after the occurrence of the injury.

(c)   This section does not affect the right to indemnity provided by an insurance or other contract to discharge the tortfeasor spouse's liability, whether or not the consideration given for the contract consisted of community property.

(Stats. 1992, c. 162 (A.B. 2650), § 10, operative Jan. 1, 1994.)

§ 782.5. Attempted murder or soliciting the murder of a spouse; remedies; community property interests

In addition to any other remedy authorized by law, when a spouse is convicted of attempting to murder the other spouse, as punishable pursuant to subdivision (a) of Section 664 of the Penal Code, or of soliciting the murder of the other spouse, as punishable pursuant to subdivision (b) of Section 653f of the Penal Code, the injured spouse shall be entitled to an award to the injured spouse of 100 percent of the community property interest in the retirement and pension benefits of the injured spouse.

As used in this section, "injured spouse" has the same meaning as defined in Section 4324.

(Added by Stats. 1995, c. 364 (A.B. 16), § 2. Amended by Stats. 2010, c. 65 (A.B. 2674), § 1.)

§ 2603.5. Civil damages in a domestic violence action; enforcement or judgment

The court may, if there is a judgment for civil damages for an act of domestic violence perpetrated by one spouse against the other spouse, enforce that judgment against the abusive spouse's share of community property, if a proceeding for dissolution of marriage or legal separation of the parties is pending prior to the entry of final judgment.

(Added by Stats. 2004, c. 299 (A.B. 2018), § 1.)

SECTION 4. EARNINGS AND ACCUMULATIONS WHILE LIVING SEPARATE AND APART

Marriage marks a starting point at which a community property estate can acquire any property. Separation marks the end point for purposes of acquiring earnings and other accumulations.

A. THE BARE STATUTE

California Family Code Section 771 confirms that "the earnings and accumulations of a spouse . . . after the date of separation of the spouses, are the separate property of the spouse."

Date of separation marks the point after which the community is unable to *acquire* earnings and accumulations. The date of separation rule is consistent with the acquisition rule (California Family Code Section 760), which characterizes as community only property *acquired during* marriage (Chapters 1, 2, and 7).

Notwithstanding the application of California Family Code Section 771, the spouses continue to *own* (hold) any community property that they acquired during their marriage. Thus community property management and control rules for already-acquired property are in full force even after a date of separation (Chapter 6).

WEST'S ANNOTATED CALIFORNIA FAMILY CODE

§ 771.   Earnings and accumulations during period of separation

(a) The earnings and accumulations of a spouse and the minor children living with, or in the custody of, the spouse, after the date of separation of the spouses, are the separate property of the spouse.

(b) Notwithstanding subdivision (a), the earnings and accumulations of an unemancipated minor child related to a contract of a type described in Section 6750 shall remain the sole legal property of the minor child.

(Stats. 1992, c. 162 (A.B. 2650), § 10, operative Jan. 1, 1994. Amended by Stats. 1999, c. 940 (S.B. 1162), § 1; Stats. 2016, c. 114 (S.B. 1255), § 2, eff. Jan. 1, 2017.)

§ 772. Earnings or accumulations after entry of judgment of legal separation

After entry of a judgment of legal separation of the parties, the earnings or accumulations of each party are the separate property of the party acquiring the earnings or accumulations.

(Stats. 1992, c. 162 (A.B. 2650), § 10, operative Jan. 1, 1994.)

––––––––

The phrase "living separate and apart from the other spouse" appeared (past tense) in California Family Code Section 771.

On July 25, 2016, the Legislature *abrogated* the decision in *Marriage of Davis*, 61 Cal.4th 846, 352 P.3d 401 (2015) and in *Marriage of Norviel*, 102 Cal.App.4th 1152, 126 Cal.Rptr.2d 148 (6th Dist. 2002) with California Family Code Section 70, reproduced below.

Consider the comparative context. Before confirming earnings and accumulations some U.S. community property states require a spouse to present a formal petition of separation. Other states require a spouse to provide documentary proof from a third party—typically a lease or real estate purchase contract—proving that a separate residence has been established. Yet other states allow a spouse to present any evidence relevant to the issue of whether earnings and accumulations are confirmable as separate property due to the parties' separation.

California was and again is in the third category of states. As this casebook goes to press it is too early to answer questions about the retroactivity of California Family Code Section 70. Is the statute retroactive? Would it be retroactive given that vested property rights may be involved between the date of the decision in *Davis* (July 20, 2015) and the effective date of the new statute (January 1, 2017)? Retroactivity issues are discussed below (Chapter 4).

Prior to July 25, 2016, California followed the *Hardin-Manfer* test. *Marriage of Hardin,* 38 Cal.App.4th 448, 451, 45 Cal.Rptr.2d 308 (4th Dist. 1995) states the test. *Marriage of Manfer,* 144 Cal.App.4th 925, 50 Cal.Rptr.3d 785 (4th Dist. 2006) clarifies and applies it. Parties both in *Hardin* and in *Manfer* established separate residences. Nevertheless a date of separation issue arose in each case. It is not uncommon for date of separation issues to arise after one party establishes a separate residence. Life is complicated. Relationships are unique. Sometimes a couple will separate and even move into separate residences while still working on their marriage. Therefore, moving out of the marital home does not necessarily signal the end of a marriage.

Hardin and *Manfer* ruled that a party could produce any evidence—subjective or objective—on the issue of whether he or she thought the marriage was over. The factfinder was to consider that evidence "objectively." The cases also provided that it would be reversible error for the factfinder to *require* so-called "objective" evidence, meaning evidence showing that third parties understood the spouses to be living separate and apart.

Davis changed the state's historical approach by requiring parties to establish separate residences in order to be considered living separate and apart for purposes of California Family Code Section 771. After *Davis*, a separate property claimant invoking California Family Code Section 771 needed proof of a separate residence, a new lease for example, to establish date of separation. The rationale in *Davis* was problematic; it returned California to a past where the word of third parties weighed more heavily in deciding date of separation than did the perceptions of the parties themselves. Plus, in a state with the highest or near highest cost of housing *Davis* attempted to draw a bright line rule ostensibly to reduce legal costs and, astonishingly, to make it easier for lawyers. Notwithstanding the fact that a marriage may continue even after one spouse moves out of the marital home, as discussed above, establishing a separate residence in order to have proof of date of separation is no easy financial task for a great number of couples. Parties would likely need available cash to pay their current rent or mortgage *plus* more cash to pay move-in costs for a spouse to establish a separate residence (first and last month rent, security deposit, utility start-up costs, parking, and so on).

Davis was decided on July 20, 2015. Senate Bill 1255 was introduced by Senator Moorlach on February 18, 2016. It was amended in the Senate on May 5, 2016. It passed the Assembly on June 1, 2016. On July 25, 2016, S.B. 1255 was approved by the Governor and chaptered by the Secretary of State to add a new section— Section 70—to the California Family Code to clarify the meaning of "date of separation."

As per California Family Code Section 70, date of separation now means the date that "a complete and final break in the marital relationship has occurred." Evidence of intent or conduct can be subjective or objective. "[I]n determining the date of separation, the court shall take into consideration all relevant evidence."

WEST'S ANNOTATED CALIFORNIA FAMILY CODE

§ 70.   Dissolution of marriage: date of separation

(a) "Date of separation" means the date that a complete and final break in the marital relationship has occurred, as evidenced by both of the following:

    (1)   The spouse has expressed to the other spouse his or her intent to end the marriage.

(2)   The conduct of the spouse is consistent with his or her intent to end marriage

(b)   In determining the date of separation, the court shall take into consideration all relevant evidence.

(c)   It is the intent of the Legislature in enacting this section to abrogate the decisions in In re Marriage of Davis (2015) 61 Cal.4th 846 and In re Marriage of Norviel (2002) 102 Cal.App.4th 1152.

(Added by Stat. 2016, c. 114 (S.B. 1255), § 1, eff. Jan. 1, 2017).

B.   PERCEPTION, INTENTION, CONDUCT— THE *HARDIN-MANFER* TEST

Marriage of Manfer illustrates the fine line that can exist between what the spouses think about their own marriage (subjective evidence) and what other people think about their marriage (so-called objective evidence). California Family Code Section 70, above, continues this understanding. For that reason, in my opinion, the case law on living separate and apart (the previous standard) continues to be relevant to the issues of how an expression of *intent* to end marriage is made and what *conduct* is consistent with the expressed intent.

In *Manfer* the record showed that husband Samuel moved out of the marital home in 2004. At that time, after 31 years of marriage, wife Maureen decided that the marriage was over. She communicated as much to Samuel, but out of concern for their children Samuel and Maureen agreed to keep their separation a secret until after the winter holidays. Over the next year, Samuel and Maureen did not engage in sexual relations, commingle property, or financially support each other. But they did maintain social contact for holiday celebrations and they took family pictures together. To the world, it appeared that their marriage was intact, but between them it was clear that the marriage was over. The trial court made an inconsistent ruling. It decided that the date of separation by a preponderance of the evidence was 2004, the date that Samuel moved out of the marital home, but it ruled that the date of separation for purposes of California Family Code Section 771 was 2005, the date that third parties first became aware of Samuel and Maureen's breakup. Maureen appealed.

The court of appeal used a de novo standard of review to reverse and remand on the ground that the trial court reached its decision "by expressly utilizing an 'objective test' standard, i.e., '[W]ould society at large consider the couple separated?' "[1] The court of appeal explained that the law does not require so-called "objective" evidence; and it iterated the understanding that there is no objective test for California Family Code Section 771. The

---

[1]   Court's footnote: *Manfer, supra* at 928, citing *Marriage of Hardin*, 38 Cal.App.4th 448, 451, 45 Cal.Rptr.2d 308 (Cal.App.Ct., 4th Dist. 1995).

court explained that what decides a date of separation is entirely subjective, and entirely between spouses. In other words, a spouse decides when a marriage is over for purposes of confirming his or her earnings and accumulations as separate property; the spouse expresses this to the other spouse; and the spouse acts in line with that expression.

The *Manfer* decision cited *Marriage of Hardin* as "most helpful" in understanding the fine-line distinction between subjective and objective perceptions of when the parties begin to live separate and apart for purposes of California Family Code Section 771. The clear benefit of the *Hardin-Manfer* test gives spouses, not third parties, the right to determine the date of their separation. Even creditors are unconcerned about date of separation since the Family Code protects creditors if and when earnings become separate due to a spouse's decision to end the marriage (Chapter 6).

The *Hardin-Manfer* test appears to be reflected if not codified in California Family Code Section 70, above.

C. LIVING APART AS ROOMMATES: APPLYING CALIFORNIA FAMILY CODE SECTION 70

What happens in a case where the parties transition from spouses to roommates? By abrogating the California Supreme Court decision in *Davis* one might look to the court of appeal decision for instruction. *See, Davis,* 220 Cal.App 4th 1109, 163 Cal.Rptr.3d 695 (1st Dist. 2013).

There, wife Sheryl expressed to husband Xavier that it was her intent to end the marriage. Although Sheryl did not leave the family home, her conduct was consistent with her expression: she separated the couple's finances by handing Xavier a ledger and she established a part of the house (however small in square footage) that was exclusively her space.

The trial court exercised its discretion in favor of Sheryl's 2006 date of separation. Xavier appealed. The First District Court of Appeal, using the substantial evidence standard, affirmed. The court of appeal also approved of the trial court's reliance on *Marriage of Manfer*, and it disapproved any reliance on *Marriage of Norviel,* 102 Cal.App.4th 1152, 126 Cal.Rptr.2d 148 (6th Dist. 2002).

Under Family Code Section 70, Sheryl would have prevailed on her date of separation claim.

First, Sheryl expressed (many times) to Xavier her intent to end her marriage with him. The fact that he failed to grasp that point would not diminish Sheryl's claim. The new statute requires only that Sheryl have expressed her intent to Xavier, which she did, not that he also have understood or agreed. In the California community property system, an expression is not an agreement (a two-way communication) but a declaration (a one-way communication).

Second, Sheryl's conduct of moving to her own space in the home, constructing and producing a ledger for household expenses, delivering that ledger to Xavier, and maintaining the system set out in the ledger was clearly conduct consistent with Sheryl's intent to end the marriage.

What about the fact that Sheryl refused to establish a separate residence? How would that weigh into the analysis?

The statute provides that the court shall take into consideration all relevant evidence. Relevant to Sheryl's decision to live as a roommate with Xavier was that the house was as much her's as his. Also, Sheryl wanted to be present in the daily life of her children. In the context of Bay Area life these claims are entirely plausible. The family was a middle class family. At times they lived on one income. Their mortgage costs kept monthly shelter costs steady. To establish a second residence would have taken a massive amount of cash and could have left Sheryl geographically distant from her children. Sheryl already had a long commute for her job. The record shows that she was trying to consolidate her time and resources while still establishing a date of separation from Xavier.

The abrogated California Supreme Court decision in *Davis* proved to be out of touch with the daily financial realities faced by the middle class Davis family.

NOTES

1. *Historical approaches.* Under the Spanish community property system, a spouse who, in violation of marital obligations, separated from the other spouse lost any claim to have new acquisitions during the period of separation. Under some circumstances, that spouse even forfeited any claim to share in accumulations as of the time of separation. The aggrieved spouse, on the other hand, continued to benefit from new acquisitions of the guilty spouse. All American community property states have departed from any fault-based application of such a rule. WILLIAM Q. DE FUNIAK & MICHAEL J. VAUGHN, PRINCIPLES OF COMMUNITY PROPERTY §§ 189–190 (2d ed. 1971).

California statutes originally provided that the wife's earnings while living separate and apart from her husband were her separate property. The rule applied even if the wife was living separate and apart from her husband "through her own fault." *Spreckels v. Spreckels*, 116 Cal. 339, 342, 48 P. 228, 229 (1897). There was no comparable provision controlling the earnings and accumulations of a married man living separate from his wife. His earnings continued to be community property. The fact that the husband was the sole agent for the community estate factored into this outcome. The husband was personally responsible for the debts, including any that went to support the wife in her own residence. Without this rule, how could a woman leave a marital home? With no control of property during marriage, a married woman had no practical right to enter into contracts, since she had no property to pledge. Plus, she had no real ability to acquire borrowed funds, again because she had no right to pledge property as collateral. If a wife left a martial home, it was her husband who had the primary duty to support her. Nevertheless, a married woman could only gain legal management and control of her separate property if she physically left the marital home.

In 1971, the legislature amended California Family Code Section 771 to be gender neutral. Given the legislative change, do you find it problematic that the California Supreme Court relied on law that was explicitly gender-biased on its face and in its history and rationale without so much as a cursory explanation or comment?

2. *More precedent.* The phrase "living separate and apart" appears in California Family Code Section 771 until January 1, 2017, see discussion above. Early on, California courts rejected the claim that the statutory phrase should be read literally. *Tobin v. Galvin*, 49 Cal. 34 (1874), cited by the abrogated *Davis* opinion, held that that phrase "living separate and apart" does not cover cases involving a temporary separation short of a family breakdown.

In *Makeig v. United Security Bank & Trust Co.*, 112 Cal.App. 138, 296 P. 673 (1st Dist. 1931), husband and wife did not live together during their 14-year marriage due to economic and health considerations. The court held that they were married; saying there was no final break in their marriage notwithstanding that it was a long distance relationship. Therefore earnings and accumulations continued to be community property under California Family Code Section 760:

> "Living separate and apart . . . does not apply to a case where a man and wife are residing temporarily in different places due to economic or social reasons, but applies to a condition where the spouses have come to a parting of the ways and have no present intention of resuming the marital relations and taking up life together under the same roof." *Id.* at 143.

In *Kerr v. Kerr*, 182 Cal.App.2d 12, 18, 5 Cal.Rptr. 630, 634 (3d Dist. 1960), the court reached a similar conclusion: "In the instant case the evidence shows that there was no parting of the ways nor an intention not to resume marital relations and take up life together under the same roof until January 1, 1956, when appellant refused to permit respondent's return to their home. It is clear that respondent left for New Mexico [before that date] because of his fear of being reincarcerated in the Stockton State Hospital. That did not mean that he was running away from his wife."

On the other hand, *Marriage of Peters*, 52 Cal.App.4th 1487, 61 Cal.Rptr.2d 493 (3d Dist. 1997), indicates that a party's testimony that he or she intended to sever the relationship completely may not be sufficient evidence of living separate and apart "if the concomitant conduct does not support the stated subjective intention." *Id.* at 1493. The court affirmed that the date of separation is and should be established by a preponderance of the evidence, rather than by the higher clear and convincing standard. The rationale being that in a marital dissolution, the economic interests of parties are *opposite but equal*. The lower standard is additionally appropriate because it furthers the principle of no-fault dissolution. Imposing a higher burden may be what the abrogated *Davis* opinion did (in error); if so, the abrogated *Davis* opinion functionally demonstrated a preference for Xavier's interests over Sheryl's thus engaging in unconscious gender bias. By giving Xavier the benefit of the law, the court ratified Xavier's claim that he thought that the relationship was (merely) dysfunctional, not over. At the same time the court disregarded Sheryl's claim that she clearly communicated the end of the marriage to Xavier even though she chose to put the interests of her children before her own by not moving out of the family home.

3.   *What did lawmakers intend in 1870?* The abrogated *Davis* opinion notes that the California system is inherited from Spain, but then goes on to interpret the phrase living separate and apart based on what it thinks California lawmakers in 1870 intended. Is this line of reasoning persuasive? Lawmakers in 1870 had markedly different ideas of how men and women should conduct themselves in marriage. Men were the legal managers of property. Women still had only contingent rights in community property. As explained above, a woman had to move out of the home in order to obtain legal control of her own earnings or separate property, otherwise those resources would go to the very husband she was trying to separate from.

4.   *Analogizing to the Uniform Marriage and Divorce Act.* Comments to the Uniform Marriage and Divorce Act Section 302 distinguish between "living separate and apart" and terms such as "irretrievably broken" (a term used in UMDA 302), "irremediable breakdown" (a standard for dissolution adopted in California Family Code Section 2333 (Chapter 7)), "irremediable rift" (Oklahoma), and "breakdown of the marriage relationship . . . no reasonable likelihood that the marriage can be preserved" (Iowa). These terms signal a final break, the end of a marriage. They are standards upon which legislatures give courts the power to enter a decree of marriage dissolution.

"Living separate and apart" is not defined in the UMDA, but it is one of the two guidelines "set up for evidence sufficient to support a finding that the marriage is irretrievably broken. The guidelines are: (i) that the parties have lived separate and apart for more than 180 days next preceding the commencement of the proceeding for dissolution; (ii) that there exists 'serious marital discord adversely affecting the attitude of one or both of the parties toward the marriage.' " The UMDA comment goes on to make the key point regarding how "living separate and apart" gets defined:

> These [(i) and (ii) in the preceding paragraph] satisfy the desire of those who wish to have specific guidelines to assist the court in determining what is irretrievable breakdown. *At the same time*, the second provision retains *all the judicial discretion to weigh all the evidence* bearing upon the death of the marriage. . . ." Uniform

Marriage and Divorce Act (U.L.A.) Section 302 Comments. (Italics added.)

This may have been the direction that the abrogated decision in *Davis* was trying to steer the state in. But even if this standard seems plausible for a low housing-cost geographical area, can it really work in high housing-cost areas?

In the San Francisco Bay Area, at this time, rent for a modest studio apartment can be in the $3,000 and above per month range, with move-in costs of first and last month's rent and a security deposit required up front ($3,000 + $3,000 + $3,000 = $9,000). Monthly parking costs in the urban areas appear to be hovering in the $275 to $500 range. Thus a move by one spouse from the family home (already expensive on a monthly basis) to a modest separate residence (requiring approximately $9,000 move-in costs plus moving costs, plus transportation costs, plus parking costs) can be outside the reach of many families. Less expensive areas of the Bay Area are an option; but a move to an outlying area may significantly increase a person's commute time.

Hence the wisdom of a law like California Family Code Section 70, which gives the individual spouse the option to arrange his or her living situation in a period of separation as he or she sees fit.

5.   *Evidence of conduct that contradicts the public record.* Ordinarily, the fact that a spouse has moved out of the family home and filed a petition for dissolution of marriage is sufficient evidence to establish a separate property claim within the meaning of California Family Code Section 771. However, *Marriage of Marsden*, 130 Cal.App.3d 426, 181 Cal.Rptr. 910 (1st Dist. 1982) tests the assumption.

Marsden was cited but not reconciled or otherwise explained by the abrogated opinion in *Davis*, an unfortunate explanatory oversight. *Marsden* held that the parties were not living separate and apart for purposes of California Family Code Section 771 even though they had established separate residences, and one of them (the wife) had filed a petition for dissolution. The wife testified that yes she filed a petition for dissolution, but no she did not file it because she wanted a divorce. She filed it to get her husband's attention so that the parties' could work on their marriage.

In the language of the *Hardin-Manfer* test, the wife perceived a break in the marriage (proof of Element #1), but her intention was to repair that break (absence of proof as to Element #2), notwithstanding the fact that she filed for a petition for dissolution. Indeed, the fact that the wife filed for dissolution with intent to get the husband to repair the marriage was deemed an absence of proof of conduct intended to effect a separation (Element #3).

Contradicting the wife's evidence of physical separation was her testimony that the spouses continued to have sex together, see a marriage counselor together, and even travel together—as spouses.

6.   *Defining earnings and accumulations.* The term "earnings and accumulations" used in California Family Code Section 771 has caused less

difficulty than the phrase "living separate and apart." Earnings has a standard meaning. Accumulations is the more problematic word.

In a case involving the predecessor statute to California Family Code Section 771, the California Supreme Court held that the acquisition of title by adverse possession is an "accumulation" within the meaning of the statute. *Union Oil Co. v. Stewart*, 158 Cal. 149, 110 P. 313 (Cal. 1910). The word "accumulation" was interpreted as follows:

> " * * * When one speaks generally of accumulation of property, he is understood to refer to any property which a person acquires and retains, without regard to the means by which it is obtained. Of course if it were acquired by the wife by purchase with community funds, or in exchange for other community property, it would not be accumulated in the sense here involved. Such an acquisition would be a mere exchange and it would have the character possessed by that given in exchange for it. But where the wife, while living separate from her husband, through her own industry, labor, skill, or efforts of any kind, obtains property and holds it in possession, it is what would ordinarily be called an accumulation of property, and, under the rules stated in section 169, it would be a part of her separate estate." *Id.* at 156.

Likewise, in *Marriage of Wall,* 29 Cal.App.3d 76, 105 Cal.Rptr. 201 (2d Dist. Cal. 1972), proceeds of an Irish Sweepstakes Ticket purchased with support payments received after a date of separation were defined as a separate property "accumulation" within the meaning of California Family Code Section 771.

7.   *Does the date of separation have legal effects on more than just property issues?* In *Jurcoane v. Superior Court*, 93 Cal.App.4th 886, 896, 113 Cal.Rptr.2d 483 (2d Dist. 2001), a criminal defendant's wife sought to invoke the marital privilege not to testify in her husband's trial for murder, even though she had not lived with her husband for seventeen years, her husband had been living with another woman, and she had had no contact with her husband for seven years. The prosecutor argued that the privilege was intended to preserve intact marriages, which the Jurcoane spouses no longer had. The magistrate agreed, and concluded that the wife could not claim the marital testimonial privilege. The appellate court reversed. The rationale was that couple had never been divorced and the statutes defining the marital privilege (California Evidence Code Sections 970—972) do not include exceptions to the privilege where a still legally intact marriage is "moribund," "abandoned," or "no longer viable."

SECTION 5. CHAPTER SUMMARY

- The right to own separate property during marriage is protected by the California Constitution.

- Separate property is defined by statute as property owned before marriage, received during marriage by gift, and the rents, issues, and profits of either.

- The burden to confirm property as separate is on the spouse who makes the separate property claim.

- The American rule for characterizing separate property income streams as themselves separate property in character originated with a California Supreme Court case, *George v. Ransom*. In that case California broke from the civil law community property usufruct tradition on the issue of separate property rents, issues, and profits.

- Today a majority of U.S. community property systems and some foreign jurisdictions follow the American rule that separate property rents, issues, and profits are separate property.

- A minority of U.S. community property systems follow the civil law *ganancial* rule that separate property fruits and profits are community property during marriage by usufruct. Of these jurisdictions some retain the "fruits and profits" phraseology of the historical system while others adopt the contemporary "rents, issues, and profits" language.

- A personal injury recovery from a third party is confirmable at dissolution as the injured spouse's separate property if the claim arose before the marriage or after a date of separation.

- A personal injury recovery for a claim that arose during the marriage against a third party results in a special type of community property that shall be confirmed at divorce as the separate property of the injured spouse. There are two exceptions to the mandatory assignment rule:

  o The personal injury recovery has been commingled with ordinary community property (presumably to the point of confusion);

  o The interests of justice require that the personal injury recovery be apportioned between the spouses, with the injured spouse be awarded no less than one-half.

- One spouse's personal injury recovery against the other spouse is confirmable as separate property even if the cause of action arose during the marriage.

- Earnings and accumulations obtained after a date of separation are confirmable as separate property. A married person, not a third party, determines date of separation.

CHAPTER 4

LIMITS OF THE CALIFORNIA COMMUNITY PROPERTY SYSTEM

■ ■ ■

Any property can be community property under California Family Code Section 760 (Chapter 2). The California community property system characterizes real or personal property, vested or contingent, property situated in or out of the state. There are, however, limitations to the community property principle. Some types of property and, by their own choice, some persons are excluded.

But what does limiting the community property system accomplish?

Assume two people contract a marriage. Their marriage has many meanings. From a legal perspective, a marriage might be considered a way to do away with intimate partner contracting problems because, once married, the parties have access to a full array of default property rules that govern partnership formation, duties, liabilities, and termination. There is very little contracting, if any, that the parties must engage in to arrange their property matters during the course of their marriage. Most issues are governed by the California Family Code, a comprehensive system in which outcomes are dependent on fairness, not on the relative bargaining positions of the parties. The parties also can choose to contract customized terms if they so desire (Chapter 1).

As to property, the basic term of the default partnership (the marriage) agreement is that all property acquired during marriage is presumptively community property. There are exceptions for items that are too personal to the holder, or too speculative to practicably value at dissolution.

Now assume intimate partners who live without marriage. As to persons excluded from the system the philosophical issues are trickier. Persons who choose to form an intimate relationship but not to marry are excluded from the community property system (in theory) by their own choice. The nonexistence of a valid marriage restricts such partners to general law claims. Their personal arrangements with each other are determined by contract, partnership, or property law; all areas where outcomes are determined by the relative bargaining position of the parties.

Finally, what of persons who believe in good faith that they are married when in fact they are not? These couples fall into a category all their own. They are not validly married, but upon upon proof of a reasonable subjective good faith in the validity of their void or voidable marriage one or both persons may seek to be declared a putative spouse by a court. A putative spouse can opt for dissolution in accordance with Family Code rules. Because they are not married the parties are deemed to have acquired quasi-marital property during their union.

Quasi-marital property is property that would have been classified as community property or quasi-community property had the marriage been valid.

Quasi-community property is property that would have been community property had it been acquired while the acquiring party or parties were domiciled in the state.

A further introductory note about property acquired out of state. California community property can be used to acquire property in another state. If so, the acquisition falls within the California community property system by the tracing principle.

Married parties who are not domiciled in the state do not acquire California community property. Nor, for Constitutional reasons, does their property become California community property by the sole act of moving into the state. Rather one or both parties must first file a petition in a California court to give a judge authority to bring a domiciled resident's out of state property into the California community property system either as quasi-community property or as separate property.

SECTION 1. PROPERTY OUTSIDE THE CALIFORNIA COMMUNITY PROPERTY SYSTEM

Asset categories can be removed from the California community property system in four general ways.

The first is by agreement of the parties (Chapter 1).

The second is by operation of the basic separate property definition found at California Family Code Section 770 (Chapter 3). By this definition property owned before marriage, property acquired during marriage by gift, and the rents, issues, and profits of either are separate property.

The third method of removal is by operation of law and specifically by special legislation. California Family Code 2641 reproduced below and discussed in Section 1 is an example.

The fourth is by the courts on a case by case basis, as discussed in Section 4 below.

Value does not include or remove something from the community property system. An asset with no market value can fall within the system (Chapter 2), while an asset of great potential value may be excluded. On the date of graduation, for example, a professional education represents potential value for its holder. But in order to realize that value the degree holder must first develop a professional practice, earn a salary, and so on. Before that happens, what value does a degree have? Likewise, a talented person possesses something of value. But can talent be separated from the person who exhibits it?

The general rule is that any property can fall into the system no matter the form the property takes. Vested and contingent interests fall into the community property system. A mere expectancy, however, does not fall into the system because an expectancy is not (yet) property.

The next Section discusses two valuable assets that are excluded from the system. The first is an education that enhances its holder's earning capacity. The second is talent.

A. EDUCATION THAT SUBSTANTIALLY ENHANCES ITS HOLDER'S EARNING CAPACITY

A professional degree is not a mere expectancy; it is contingent upon entry into the educational program and it vests upon graduation. A newly minted professional degree represents future earnings, which may or may not take the form of an expectancy depending on the student's employment situation upon graduation. For that reason, a professional degree is excluded from the system on the theory that its future value is too speculative to quantify. The degree is property. It belongs to its holder. But neither the professional degree nor the future stream of income it might one day produce are property within the California community property system. Therefore an unrealized professional degree is not subject to characterization as community property.

A threshold marriage is defined as follows: one spouse works so that the other spouse can attend school. The working spouse foregoes opportunities with the expectation that the community will benefit from the student spouse's education. The problem occurs if and when the marriage is dissolved before the community can reap the benefit of its contribution to the student spouse's enhanced earning capacity.

In effect, a legal problem arises because the community expended its capital on the education of one spouse, at the expense of itself and the other spouse, but got nothing in return. It invested in the human capital of one spouse, at the expense of the other spouse, with the idea that the investment would benefit both spouses. At dissolution, because the community has not realized the benefit of its human capital investment, there are no community property assets to speak of; no retirement investments, no real estate, no business start-ups. Instead, what the parties have is one degree, in the name of the student spouse alone, and (more often than not) educational debt and foregone opportunities.

Early cases—now superseded by the Family Law Act of 1969 and, more specifically, by California Family Code Section 2641—pointed out the inequity of the threshold marriage situation.

One such case, *Aarons v. Brasch*, 229 Cal.App.2d 197, 40 Cal.Rptr. 153 (1st Dist. 1964) tells the story of an unrealized professional degree.

In *Aarons* the trial court awarded wife Rose $7,500 for the years that she supported her husband Zelwyn while he pursued extensive academic studies. The court relates that the costs of Zelwyn's education meant that Rose lived in deprivation in the hope that Zelwyn would someday practice medicine. That day never came. Rose sought dissolution. The trial court ordered Zelwyn to compensate Rose in 1947, again in 1948, and again in a final judgment on March 9, 1962. Just before the final order was issued, Zelwyn filed a petition for bankruptcy in which he claimed that whatever he owed Rose was a division of property, and therefore dischargeable in bankruptcy. Rose countered that Zelwyn's education was not property as it had no value to Rose, to Zelwyn, or on the market generally. As Rose saw it the trial court's award was in the form of spousal support and hence not dischargeable. Rose won. The case is interesting for how it delineates the parties failed expectations about their efforts on Zelwyn's behalf. The hope was that the community's human capital investment in Zelwyn would pay off. The reality was that it never did.

What about a realized professional degree? It too is excluded from the system, not because it is speculative, but because earnings from it trace to earnings and accumulations that take the form of community property. The general rule is that the law prefers to divide the assets of a marriage, not the degree.

Todd v. Todd, 272 Cal.App.2d 786, 78 Cal.Rptr. 131 (3d Dist. 1969) illustrates how a community realizes the economic value of a professional degree. Alice married Leo Todd in 1947. In the first few years of marriage, Leo graduated from law school, passed the bar exam, and started a law practice. At that time, the community assets "other than [Leo's] license to practice law, were practically nil." (*Id.* p. 789) Nearly twenty years later, when Leo and Alice sought dissolution, at which point they owned over $200,000 in divisible community property assets. The trial court awarded Alice $111,500.97 of those assets, and Leo $89,116.35. Leo's law practice was inventoried as an asset, as was its goodwill. Both assets (law practice and law practice goodwill) were adjudged divisible community property. Alice argued that Leo's law degree was also divisible community property. To that end, she hired an expert who valued Leo's education at $308,000. Alice showed that her community earnings paid the direct costs of Leo's law school education whenever Leo's veteran benefits were insufficient. She also proved that she supported the family while Leo was in law school.

The trial court valued Leo's law degree at $0. Alice appealed. The appellate court affirmed, saying

> "It should be pointed out that the assets of the community were the results of defendant's legal education and that in a sense plaintiff realized the value therefrom in the award to her of a value of $111,500.97 in those assets." *Id.* at 791.

In other words, Leo's law earnings allowed the parties to buy divisible assets (house, car and so on). Hence the community realized the benefit of its human capital investment in Leo. At dissolution Alice got her community property share of the dividends from Leo's law firm earnings.

NOTES

1. *Professional degrees are outside of the community property system.* Community contributions to a student spouse's income enhancing education do not give the working spouse a right to claim a share of the student spouse's future earnings. Instead, the community is reimbursed, with interest, for its direct contributions to the education as set out in the reimbursement statute below. The community reimbursement is a statutory right, not a matter of judicial discretion; and the reimbursement belongs to the community, not to only to the nonstudent spouse. For that reason, the community reimbursement is owned by the spouses by halves.

2. *Absent a court order the postdissolution efforts of a divorced person are outside of the community property system.* One early rationale for excluding a student spouse's degree from the community property system in a threshold marriage was that dividing the student spouse's future earnings would require a court to award postdissolution earnings.

Marriage of Aufmuth, 89 Cal.App.3d 446, 152 Cal.Rptr. 668 (1st Dist. 1979) relied on the rationale:

> "The value of a legal education lies in the potential for increase in the future earning capacity of the acquiring spouse made possible by the law degree and innumerable other factors and conditions which contribute to the development of a successful law practice. A determination that such an 'asset' is community property would require a division of post-dissolution earnings to the extent that they are attributable to the law degree, even though such earnings are by definition the separate property of the acquiring spouse. As the court observed in *In re Marriage of Fortier* (1973) 34 Cal.App.3d 384, 388, 109 Cal.Rptr. 915, 918: 'Since the philosophy of the community property system is that a community interest can be acquired only during the time of the marriage, it would then be inconsistent with that philosophy to assign to any community interest the value of the post-[dissolution] efforts of either spouse.' " *Id.* at 461.

3.　*Division of property is preferred to a reimbursement for education.* The California Family Code Section 2641(c) reimbursement expires when the community realizes its investment in the student spouse's education. California Family Code Section 2641(c) sensitizes courts to the potential turning point between losing the value of a human capital investment and realizing it.

California Family Code Section 2641(c) lists three mandatory offsets for the reimbursement it creates. A court "shall" reduce or modify a community reimbursement if: one, the community has substantially benefitted from the education; two, the community contributed to the education of both spouses; and three, the community's contribution reduces the student spouses need for spousal support. The list is noninclusive.

California Family Code Section (c)(1) uses two rebuttable presumptions to help identify if a degree has realized its economic value. Both presumptions affect the burden of proof.

The first presumption is that "the community has not substantially benefited from community contributions to the education or training made less than 10 years before the commencement of the proceeding." (Here, the burden is on student spouse to prove otherwise.)

The second presumption is that "the community has substantially benefited from community contributions to the education or training made more than 10 years before the commencement of the proceeding." (Here, the burden is on the community to prove otherwise.)

4.　*Example rulings from other jurisdictions.* Washington, a community property state, has allowed the unequal division of community property in the dissolution of a marriage where the community contributed to one spouse's professional education. See *Washburn v. Washburn*, 101 Wash.2d 168, 677 P.2d 152 (1984) (en banc). Keep in mind, however, that in a threshold marriage (defined above), there is typically nothing to divide, which means that an unequal division will not address the plain inequities of the situation.

New York and Michigan authorize the classification of a professional degree as property divisible at divorce. In *O'Brien v. O'Brien*, 66 N.Y.2d 576, 498 N.Y.S.2d 743, 489 N.E.2d 712 (1985), the court applied N.Y. Domestic Relations Law Section 236, which orders the court to consider:

> " . . . (6) any equitable claim to, interest in, or direct or indirect contribution made to the marital property by the party not having title, including joint efforts or expenditures and contributions and services as a spouse, parent, wage earner and homemaker, and to the career and career potential of the other party [and] . . . (9) the impossibility or difficulty of evaluating any component asset or any interest in a business, corporation or profession."

In *Postema v. Postema*, 189 Mich.App. 89, 471 N.W.2d 912 (1991), the court stated: "where an advanced degree is the end product of a concerted family effort, involving the mutual sacrifice, effort, and contribution of both spouses, there arises a 'marital asset' subject to distribution, wherein the interest of the nonstudent spouse consists of an 'equitable claim' regarding the degree."

The clear majority of American jurisdictions, however, conclude that a professional degree and the increased earning capacity it promises should not be treated as marital property divisible upon divorce. Three rationales are typically given. One, the community invested in one spouse's education alone knowing the risks. Two, even if the parties had an enforceable implied agreement that the community would benefit from the student spouse's education, the degree is too speculative to value. Three, even if a value can be placed on the degree, proportional division does not address the inequities of the threshold marriage, it simply reverses them by mortgaging the student spouse's future to favor the working spouse.

Marriage of Graham, 194 Colo. 429, 574 P.2d 75 (1978) a well-known case, cites *Todd v. Todd*. In *Graham*, the Colorado Supreme Court declined to characterize a newly minted professional degree as property, but held that it was proper to consider the working spouse's expenditures toward the student spouse's degree as a factor in awarding alimony or spousal support. In other words, reimbursement was based on a future showing of need by the working spouse. In practical effect the ruling resulted in no monetary award to the the nonstudent spouse because she was the one who financially supported the family through her husband's M.B.A. program and, therefore, she could not establish that she was in need of alimony. *Marriage of Olar*, 747 P.2d 676 (Colo. 1987) (en banc) disapproves of *Graham*.

Mahoney v. Mahoney, 91 N.J. 488, 453 A.2d 527 (1982), yet another well-known case, allowed for something called "reimbursement alimony." Reimbursement alimony is not the same as alimony or spousal support. Rather, reimbursement alimony is based on the idea that a court should have discretion to reimburse the working spouse for any contributions that were made to the student spouse's professional education. Proof is based on a (past) contribution made to the student spouse's education, not on a showing of (future) need by the working spouse. Even a highly employed nonstudent spouse is entitled to reimbursement alimony.

5. *California's many rationales for reimbursing the community for contributing to certain types of education.* In 1984, the California Legislature responded directly to the threshold marriage problem by enacting California Family Code Section 2641, reprinted below.

Under the statute, the community is entitled to reimbursement for "community contributions to education or training of a party that substantially enhances the earning capacity of the party." This standard is discussed in *Marriage of Graham*, *infra*. Spousal support consideration is given for indirect contributions; see California Family Code Section 4320 in the Statutory Appendix.

In recommending the enactment of this provision, the California Law Revision Commission set forth several policy reasons in support of then former Civil Code Section 4800.3, today found at California Family Code Section 2641:

> "The Commission does not believe that it would be either practical or fair to classify the value of the education, degree, or license, or the enhanced earning capacity, as community property and to divide the value upon marriage dissolution. Classification of these items as community property would create problems involving management and control, creditor's rights, taxation, and disposition at death, not to mention the complexities involved in valuation at dissolution. The complexities are exacerbated in the typical case where part of the student spouse's education is received before marriage and part during marriage. Moreover, to give the working spouse an interest in half the student spouse's increased earnings for the remainder of the student spouse's life because of the relatively brief period of education and training received during marriage is not only a windfall to the working spouse but in effect a permanent mortgage on the student spouse's future. Such an approach would certainly discourage the student spouse from marriage until his or her education is complete. And, if the student spouse desired further education during marriage, such a rule would force the student spouse and working spouse to arrive at a fair determination of their rights by means of a marital agreement and might encourage a dissolution of the marriage. Such a rule—one that most people would think is unfair and the effect of which they would try to avoid—should not be codified in the law.

> All factors considered, a more equitable solution, in the Commission's judgment, is to require the student spouse to reimburse the community for the community expenditures for his or her education and training. This solution in effect gives the working spouse the same amount the student spouse was given for the education. The working spouse can use the money for his or her own education or any other purpose. It puts the parties on equal footing without generating a windfall for the working spouse or permanently impairing the student spouse's future. It takes from the student spouse only what was actually given and restores to the working spouse only what he or she actually lost. It addresses the basic inequity with a minimum of disruption to the community property system."

Recommendations Relating to Family Law, 17 CAL.L.REVISION COMM'N REPORTS 201, 234–235 (1984).

WEST'S ANNOTATED CALIFORNIA FAMILY CODE

§ 2627. Educational loans; liabilities for death or injuries; assignment

Notwithstanding Sections 2550 to 2552, inclusive, and Sections 2620 to 2624, inclusive, educational loans shall be assigned pursuant to Section 2641 and liabilities subject to paragraph (2) of subdivision (b) of Section 1000 shall be assigned to the spouse whose act or omission provided the basis for the liability, without offset.

(Stats. 1992, c. 162 (A.B. 2650), § 10, operative Jan. 1, 1994.)

§ 2641. Community contributions to education or training

(a) "Community contributions to education or training" as used in this section means payments made with community or quasi-community property for education or training or for the repayment of a loan incurred for education or training, whether the payments were made while the parties were resident in this state or resident outside this state.

(b) Subject to the limitations provided in this section, upon dissolution of marriage or legal separation of the parties:

(1) The community shall be reimbursed for community contributions to education or training of a party that substantially enhances the earning capacity of the party. The amount reimbursed shall be with interest at the legal rate, accruing from the end of the calendar year in which the contributions were made.

(2) A loan incurred during marriage for the education or training of a party shall not be included among the liabilities of the community for the purpose of division pursuant to this division but shall be assigned for payment by the party.

(c) The reimbursement and assignment required by this section shall be reduced or modified to the extent circumstances render such a disposition unjust, including, but not limited to, any of the following:

(1) The community has substantially benefited from the education, training, or loan incurred for the education or training of the party. There is a rebuttable presumption, affecting the burden of proof, that the community has not substantially benefited from community contributions to the education or training made less than 10 years before the commencement of the proceeding, and that the community has substantially benefited from community contributions to the education or training made more than 10 years before the commencement of the proceeding.

(2) The education or training received by the party is offset by the education or training received by the other party for which community contributions have been made.

(3) The education or training enables the party receiving the education or training to engage in gainful employment that substantially reduces the need of the party for support that would otherwise be required.

(d) Reimbursement for community contributions and assignment of loans pursuant to this section is the exclusive remedy of the community or a party for the education or training and any resulting enhancement of the earning capacity of a party. However, nothing in this subdivision limits consideration of the effect of the education, training, or enhancement, or the amount reimbursed pursuant to this section, on the circumstances of the parties for the purpose of an order for support pursuant to Section 4320.

(e) This section is subject to an express written agreement of the parties to the contrary.

(Stats. 1992, c. 162 (A.B. 2650), § 10, operative Jan. 1, 1994.)

NOTES

1. *Community contributions to direct expenses of education.* "Community contributions" are defined in California Family Code Section 2641(a) as "payments made with community or quasi-community property." The payments must be for education or training, or for the repayment of a loan incurred for education or training.

For purposes of the statute it is irrelevant whether the contributions were made while the parties were domiciled in the state or outside this state. What matters is that they have filed a petition for dissolution in California. Obviously, proof of contributions in the form of receipts is required.

2. *The community is entitled to a reimbursement for direct contributions to one spouse's income enhancing education.* Contributions are discussed in Note 1 above and Note page 214 below.

3. *The community is entitled to a reimbursement for loan principal repayments.* California Family Code Section 2641(b)(2) creates a community reimbursement for contributions made to the repayment of educational loans whether they were incurred during or before marriage.

In *Weiner v. Weiner*, 105 Cal.App.4th 235, 240, 129 Cal.Rptr.2d 288 (4th Dist. 2003), husband Michael graduated from medical school in 1991. He and Kelly married two years later. During the marriage Michael and Kelly paid down approximately $12,200 on educational loans Michael incurred before the marriage. The trial court refused to consider the community reimbursement issue, saying that California Family Code Section 2641 does not govern premarital educational loans. The appellate court reversed. It held that the statute is intended to cover all educational costs paid with community funds, even when the education occurs before marriage.

4. *Reimbursement is the community's exclusive remedy.* California Family Code Section 2641(d) makes reimbursement the exclusive remedy for professional education or training received during marriage. The subsection precludes further litigation on the question of whether a professional education and concomitant enhanced earning capacity are susceptible of classification and division as community property.

5. *Contractual modification of the reimbursement statute is permitted.* California Family Code Section 2641(e) provides that the parties can contractually modify the terms of the statute with a written agreement between them. As the agreement represents a transaction between the parties, California Family Code Section 721(b) applies (Chapter 6).

6. *Burden of proof.* Two elements of proof establish the community's right to reimbursement.

- The education substantially enhanced the student spouse's earning capacity; and

- Community or quasi-community property contributions were made to the direct expenses (including loan principal repayments) of one spouse's education or training.

The next case, explores the California Family Code Section 2641(b)(1) phrase "substantially enhances the earning capacity of the party."

Jeffrey and Katherine Graham were married in 1992. Jeffrey, a police detective, started law school in 1994. Jeffrey filed a petition for dissolution in 1999. Katherine claimed a community reimbursement in the amount of $12,000 for Jeffrey's law school education. She submitted proof that Jeffrey's degree was a J.D., and that the community made contributions to Jeffrey's tuition, obviously a direct contribution. Jeffrey countered that Katherine had not met her burden of proof because she offered no proof that Jeffry's J.D. substantially enhanced Jeffrey's earning capacity. Katherine countered that some degrees—law, medical, dental, and accounting—should *presumptively* meet the substantial income enhancement requirement for purposes of California Family Code Section 2641. The judge rejected Katherine's argument.

MARRIAGE OF GRAHAM
109 Cal.App.4th 1321, 135 Cal.Rptr.2d 685 (4th Dist. 2003)

MOORE, J.

While Katherine and Jeffrey Graham were married, Jeffrey enrolled in and nearly completed law school. During the marital dissolution proceedings, Katherine requested reimbursement to the community for funds spent on Jeffrey's legal education. * * * The court denied Katherine's request for reimbursement * * * .

Katherine appeals. We agree with the trial court that whether Jeffrey's eventual graduation from law school might have the effect of substantially enhancing his earning capacity is speculative, making reimbursement for education costs unavailable. * * *

Facts

Katherine and Jeffrey were married in 1992. They had two children during the course of their marriage. Jeffrey enrolled as a student at Western State University College of Law (Western State) in 1994. During Jeffrey's enrollment, the couple spent over $12,000 for tuition and related expenses.

In June 1999, Jeffrey filed a petition for dissolution of marriage. At the time of trial in September 2000, Jeffrey had one remaining semester in law school, and did not have plans to take the California bar examination. His cumulative grade point average was approximately 2.2. While in law school, Jeffrey was employed as a police officer by the Costa Mesa Police Department. At the time of trial, he was making over $4,400 per month. * * *

The judgment on reserved issues denied Katherine's request for reimbursement with respect to the law school expenses, stating that the court found "no substantive enhanced earning capacity of [Jeffrey] due to said schooling." * * *

Katherine now appeals. She contends that the court erred in denying her claim for reimbursement for law school expenses * * * .

Discussion

A. Request for Reimbursement of Law School Expenses

Katherine contends the trial court erred when it denied her claim for reimbursement of the money spent on Jeffrey's law school tuition and related expenses during the marriage. Moreover, she urges this court to rule that legal, medical, dental, and accounting degrees will be presumed to result in a substantially enhanced earning capacity as a matter of law.

Family Code section 2641, subdivision (b)(1), provides in pertinent part, "Subject to the limitations provided in this section, upon dissolution of marriage or legal separation of the parties: (1) The community shall be reimbursed for community contributions to education or training of a party that substantially enhances the earning capacity of the party." Because both parties argue this appeal based upon the tacit assumption that the tuition was paid from community funds, our sole consideration with respect to the reimbursement issue is whether Jeffrey's legal education substantially enhanced his earning capacity within the meaning of section 2641, subdivision (b)(1).

As Jeffrey mentions in his reply brief, there are very few cases that discuss what is meant by substantial enhancement of the earning capacity of a student spouse. The primary source of guidance regarding the substantial enhancement of earning capacity standard is the Law Revision Commission comment following section 2641. The comment states that "[s]ection 2641 provides authority for reimbursement of educational expenses that have benefited primarily one party to the marriage." (Cal. Law Revision Com. com., 29D West's Ann. Fam. Code (1994 ed.) foll. § 2641, p. 143.) Specifically, the substantial enhancement requirement is a "limitation * * * intended to restrict litigation by requiring that the education or training must demonstrably enhance earning capacity and to implement the policy of the section to redress economic inequity." (*Ibid.*)

In the instant case, Jeffrey attained a grade point average of 2.2 at Western State, and, at the time of trial, had no plans to take the bar examination. Jeffrey testified that he went to law school to further his education, but did not necessarily have any plans to become an attorney. He explained that, when he was in college, he had partied and played football, but had wasted the opportunity to get an education. When he realized that in retrospect, he wanted to make up for the lost opportunity, by furthering his education at that time. He went to law school in pursuit of that objective, not for the purpose of financial gain. Furthermore, Jeffrey was already working at the Costa Mesa Police Department while going to law school, and he argued that his earning potential might well be greater if he remained at that place of employment, rather than pursuing a legal career.

The evidence does not support a conclusion that Jeffrey's legal education had either substantially or demonstrably enhanced his earning capacity. To the contrary, the facts support the trial court's finding that any enhanced earning capacity was questionable. The trial court summed up the situation well by stating: "It's too speculative . . . to try to figure out whether he is going to make more money in the future, and he may or he may not. [¶] He may or may not pass the bar. He may or may not do anything with the law degree. He may decide that he wants to stay in the police department and go for a higher position. . . . [¶] He might find that what he can make there looks pretty good compared with trying to scratch out a living in the legal field. [¶] A law degree is not a ticket to prosperity. Some people are very good at it and make money, and other people become disillusioned and they don't make any money. [¶] So, . . . it's all on the come. It may happen, it may not. . . ."

While Katherine requests us to declare that a law degree results in a substantial enhancement of earning capacity as a matter of law, we cannot do so. This is a perfect case to demonstrate the fallacy of the proposed rule. * * *

WE CONCUR: SILLS, P.J., and BEDSWORTH, J.

———

In the next case, wife Elaine requested a community reimbursement, however she could only produce evidence that the community paid ordinary living expenses during David's education; Elaine lacked proof that the community contributed to the direct costs of husband David's education. The trial court denied the reimbursement claim. Elaine appealed. The question was whether the court was mandated to order a reimbursement for community contributions to indirect expenses of education, meaning ordinary living expenses.

MARRIAGE OF WATT
214 Cal.App.3d 340, 262 Cal.Rptr. 783 (1st Dist. 1989)

I.   Background

The parties married on June 17, 1972, and separated nine and one-half years later on December 15, 1981. In 1974 they moved to Hawaii so David could continue his studies there. The couple had no children.

David was a full-time student for the entire nine and one-half years of the marriage, advancing from an undergraduate program to postgraduate studies and finally medical school; he received his medical degree five months after separation. Elaine worked full time during the marriage, using all of her income for family expenses.

For the years 1975 through 1981 (exclusive of 1977, for which we have no information), the parties' combined gross income was $81,779.92, of which Elaine contributed $66,923.92 in earnings and David contributed $14,856. David's student loans for the same period totaled $26,642. David used at least $3,000 in loan funds for direct educational expenses (tuition, books, fees), leaving approximately $23,642 for the couple's living expenses.

For the past 17 years Elaine has worked for Kaiser Foundation Hospital (Kaiser), first as a pharmacy clerk and, since 1979, as a pharmacy technician. Following separation, Elaine held two part-time jobs, working sometimes 60 hours per week to meet monthly living expenses. In 1986 she assumed a full-time position at Kaiser.

Elaine became interested in nutrition and culinary arts and started taking cooking classes in 1981. She testified that during their marriage, she talked with David about the possibility of attending school after he finished his education and stated, "that's when I decided I would like to go into culinary arts." Shortly after the couple separated, Elaine borrowed $500 from David's mother to pursue a junior college education in the field of nutrition. After two semesters she abandoned that effort because she could not "make it" working part time or being on call, and had to take another job. She later repaid the loan.

At trial Elaine explained she would like to enroll in the 16-month program at the California Culinary Academy in San Francisco. Her aspiration is to start her own catering business.

David now is an anesthesiologist with the Permanente Medical Group. In 1987 his annual salary was approximately $94,000. With overtime, his actual income has been much higher. * * * "

II.   The Trial Court Decision

The trial court issued a detailed statement of decision which included the following findings pertinent to this appeal: (1) the extent to which Elaine contributed to David's attainment of an education, training, career position or license "was minimal to the point of 'de minimis non curat lex' "; (2) Elaine evidenced no need for spousal support, retraining or education to obtain more marketable skills/employment; and (3) the couple's standard of living during the marriage did not exceed Elaine's present standard of living.

The court also found that Elaine's gross income was higher than the income she indicated was "achievable" as a chef and concluded, "a need to change [jobs] has not been shown. * * * " [Elaine is] self-supporting, beyond the standard of living attained by the parties while married, and in no need of support. * * * "

On the matter of reimbursement for the expenses of David's education, the court determined there were no community contributions which should be reimbursed. Finally, the court ordered David to assume full responsibility for repayment of all student loans (nothing had been repaid during the marriage).

III.   Elaine's Appeal

On appeal Elaine contends the trial court abused its discretion in denying spousal support and erred in ruling that the community made no reimbursable contributions to David's education.

Elaine's arguments concern interpretation of amendments to the Family Law Act which the Legislature enacted in 1984 to provide for (1) reimbursement of the community's contributions for the education or training of a spouse under specified circumstances and (2) consideration of the nonstudent spouse's contributions to the attainment of that education or training when awarding spousal support. * * * "

[In Section A of the opinion, the court discusses Elaine's request for spousal support. Elaine was employed, but she wanted to retrain for a different field. The trial court denied her request for spousal support, essentially for lack of need. Elaine appealed. The appellate court reversed.]

B. Reimbursement for Contribution to His Education

Elaine's second attack concerns the trial court's ruling that there were no reimbursable community contributions to David's education. The record reveals that direct education expense were paid from loan and grant funds. Elaine asserts that section 4800.3 [now California Family Code Section 2641] does not limit "payments made with community property for education or training" to direct costs, and should be construed broadly with its remedial purpose in mind to include living expenses over the nine and one-half years of marriage.

Section 4800.3 [California Family Code Section 2641] remedies the injustice that often occurred when a couple separated on the eve of, or shortly after, a spouse's graduation or other educational accomplishment, long before that education could benefit the community. (*In re Marriage of Slivka* (1986) 183 Cal.App.3d 159, 167, 228 Cal.Rptr. 76.) Prior to its enactment, there was no right of the community to reimbursement for expenditures made for education or training. The new remedy, however, is not unlimited.

The CLRC comment to section 4800.3 [California Family Code Section 2641] explains that the purpose of the provision is to authorize reimbursement of community expenditures for educational expenses that have benefited primarily one party to the marriage. It goes on to state: "Subdivision (a) does not detail the expenditures that might be included within the concept of 'community contributions.' These expenditures would at least include cost of tuition, fees, books and supplies, and transportation." (CLRC com., West's Ann.Code, § 4800.3 (1989 pocket supp.) p. 95.)

From this comment, as well as the definition of community contributions to education or training, it is evident that the thrust of section 4800.3 [California Family Code Section 2641] is to require reimbursement for expenses that are related to the education experience itself. The married couple would incur ordinary living expenses regardless of whether one spouse is attending school, staying home, or working.

Elaine has pursued her reimbursement claim on the theory that section 4800.3 [California Family Code Section 2641] entitles the community to full reimbursement for *all* its contributions to living expenses over the nine and one-half-year period. She has failed to show what expenses, if any, were specially connected to David's education. There was no evidence produced at trial that the community paid for any education-related expenses, such as tuition, fees, or special living expenses incurred because of the education experience. Based upon such a lack of evidence, we conclude the trial court correctly ruled that the community made no reimbursable contributions pursuant to section 4800.3 [California Family Code Section 2641].

Elaine further argues that unless we construe section 4800.3 [California Family Code Section 2641] as encompassing reimbursement for all living expenses "it must be declared unconstitutional." In that event, she urges us to characterize the professional degree as community property, subject to valuation and distribution.

Elaine maintains that anything short of her proposed interpretation leads to due process and equal protection violations. Not so. There is no constitutionally recognized property interest in the form of a right to reimbursement for community property earnings which a spouse voluntarily spends for the couple's living expenses during marriage. Nor, as Elaine argues, does our construction of section 4800.3 [California Family Code Section 2641] impermissibly treat spouses differently according to whether the community benefits financially from the education or not. Whether the community benefits economically from the educated spouse's enhanced opportunities depends on the parties and the timing of career development relative to the date of separation, not on section 4800.3 [California Family Code Section 2641]. Furthermore, section 4800.3 [California Family Code Section 2641] by its terms mandates a more favorable result for the nonstudent spouse when the community reaps *no* advantage from the education. Where the community has already benefited substantially from the education of one spouse, section 4800.3 [Fam. Code Sec. 2641(c)] requires the court to *reduce or modify* reimbursement as necessary to prevent an unjust disposition.

Finally, we reject Elaine's suggestion that this court declare David's medical degree community property. Section 4800.3, subdivision (d) [California Family Code Section 2641], makes it abundantly clear that reimbursement is the *only* remedy in California. The CLRC Comment further explains: "Although the education, degree or license or the resulting enhanced earning capacity is not 'property' subject to division, community expenditures for them are properly subject to reimbursement." (CLRC com., West's Annotated Code, § 4800.3 (1989 pocket supp.) p. 95.) * * *

V. Conclusion

The judgment is affirmed in part and reversed in part, with directions to conduct further proceedings consistent with this opinion. David to pay costs on appeal.

CHANNELL and PERLEY, JJ., concur.

NOTE

Mutual obligations during marriage. During marriage California Family Code Section 720 provides that parties contract mutual obligations of support. Elaine and David, in other words, had a duty to support each other with respect to ordinary living expenses. That explains why contributions to general family expenses while one spouse is in an educational program are not reimbursable.

In a case where a party can prove that he or she supported a student spouse during a period of education, California Family Code Section 4320(b)(2) provides for the possibility of a spousal support award to the extent that the non-student spouse "*contributed* to the attainment of an education, training, a career position, or a license."

California Family Code Section 4320(b) includes living expenses. It also includes direct contributions to educational programs that, because of the nature of the education, do not give rise to a right of reimbursement under California Family Code Section 2641. To qualify for a statutory reimbursement the education must be one that will substantially enhance the student spouse's earning capacity (if the dissolution takes place during the educational period) or one that does in fact enhance the degree holder's pre- and post-education earning capacity (if the dissolution takes place after the educational period). In *Aarons v. Brasch*, discussed above, Zelwin had a potentially lucrative medical education, but he was not able to use it to enhance his earning capacity in fact.

The idea of direct contributions means out-of-pocket payments for tuition, fees, books, and other necessary items and expenses of education. Does it also include opportunity costs for the student spouse like, for example, the costs of a non-paying internship that might offer future career advancement? What about lost opportunity costs for the nonstudent spouse? Are these lost opportunity costs "contributions" within the ambit of California Family Code Section 2641? What about expenses that help the student spouse manage the pace or stress of an educational program—gym memberships, yoga classes, time management classes, therapy sessions, and the like? Are these expenses directly related to education in the sense that they address stress and health, which can affect performance? Are professional licensure materials and classes (bar materials for law students) qualifying contributions? What about appearance related expenses for special educational events like moot court— are a new suit, new shoes, pre-event salon treatments (haircut, styling, color, manicure, etc.) direct expenses of the educational program? Does it matter that moot court is a program designed, in part, to teach professional presentation?

The distinction between educational expenses and ordinary living expenses is, in some ways, determined by creditors' rights. Student loans, incurred to pay educational expenses, are assigned at dissolution to the student spouse; they are not included among the community's liabilities. Other forms of debt, incurred to pay ordinary living expenses, are generally assignable to both spouses at dissolution; they are included among the community's liabilities at dissolution (Chapter 6). The community is not liable for loans incurred to pay for educational expenses. Does the way in which debts are assigned at dissolution make it fair that the community's reimbursement be limited to direct contributions?

What effect does a narrow interpretation of Section 2641(b)(1)—reimbursement to the community for direct out-of-pocket educational expenses only—have on the educational loan assignment provision of Section 2641(b)(2)? When a student loan is used solely or primarily to pay direct educational expenses like tuition, books and student fees, then the loan "shall not be included among the liabilities of the community . . . but shall be assigned for payment by the party." That statement seems fair for how it is consistent with the idea that an education belongs to its holder. But is the statement still fair if the student spouse uses the loan to cover community living expenses? One stated reason for adding California Family Code Section 2641 to the Family Code was to prevent the mortgaging of the student spouse's future earnings. Is that policy concern relevant when it comes to debt assignment? If yes, how might the statute be amended?

B. THE HUNT FOR A COLORFUL MONTH: TALENT

Is *talent* property divisible at dissolution? Or is talent excluded from the community property system as something uniquely personal to its holder and thus not subject to division.

Husband John McTiernan was an A-list director whose accomplishments included *Predator* (1987)—released before marriage to Donna Dubrow—*Hunt for Red October* (1990), *Die Hard* (1995), the *Thomas Crown Affair* (1999), released during marriage to Dubrow.

The issue of John's talent arose when he and Donna sought dissolution.

The trial court found that McTiernan possessed elite professional standing, and it attached a goodwill value of $1.5 million to that standing. John cited a number of California cases to argue that skill, reputation and experience are not community property; and that goodwill does not attach to a person's talent, even if that talent leads to an expectation that the person, once having attained elite professional status, will be called upon by others to work. John argued was that while goodwill of a business is transferable property under California Business & Professions Code, § 14102, talent is not.

MARRIAGE OF MCTIERNAN & DUBROW
133 Cal.App.4th 1090, 35 Cal.Rptr.3d 287 (2d Dist. 2005)
Review Denied Jan. 25, 2006

FLIER, J.

John McTiernan (husband) and Donna Dubrow (wife) both appeal from a judgment in the dissolution of their marriage. * * * Husband primarily challenges the trial court's determination that there existed goodwill in his business as a motion picture director, and that all of the $1.5 million of goodwill constituted community property. * * *

We find merit in husband's contention that there is no goodwill in his career as a motion picture director. * * *

FACTS

The parties were married in November 1988. They separated in July 1997, and husband commenced this proceeding the following month. The matter was extensively litigated, including 21 days of trial, conducted between June 1999 and June 28, 2000. The court's 34-page statement of decision was filed August 23, 2000, and the judgment under review was entered on August 28, 2002. At that time, husband was 51 years old and wife was 59.

The evidence showed that, during and after the marriage and to some extent before, husband was a very successful motion picture director, commanding six-to high seven-figure compensation per film, and having to his credit such blockbusters as Die Hard (20th Century Fox 1988), The Hunt for Red October (Paramount Pictures 1990), and The Thomas Crown Affair (Metro-Goldwyn-Mayer 1999). Wife also pursued a career in motion picture production, and before the marriage she was earning $195,000 a year as a production company executive. She produced several films during the marriage, while accompanying husband in his directorial pursuits. The trial court found that during the eight and three-quarter years of marriage before separation, husband had earned approximately $15 million, and wife had earned about $1 million. Predictably, the parties' community estate was substantial, as was the scale of their lifestyle.

Because the issues raised on these appeals largely involve distinct factual and legal bases, we will state the facts relevant to each issue in conjunction with its discussion. We proceed to consideration of the issues.

I.   Husband's Appeal

A.   Professional Goodwill

1.   The Trial Court's Ruling and Husband's Contention on Appeal

The trial court found that husband "is a motion picture director who has achieved exceptional success in that field. His success is dependent upon his personal skill, experience and knowledge, and the Court finds that, in that respect, the profession which he practices is similar to that of an attorney, physician, dentist, accountant, editor, architect, or any other professional who has established a successful professional practice, with quantifiable expectation of future patronage, based upon his or her personal skill, experience and knowledge."

The finding that husband has achieved exceptional success as a motion picture director is based for the most part on testimony presented by Arthur De Vany, Ph.D., an economist who is a professor in the Department of Economics of the Institute of Mathematics and Behavioral Sciences at the University of California, Irvine. The trial court found that the "evidence presented by Dr. De Vany was persuasive . . . that Petitioner [husband] has developed an earning capacity and reputation in his profession as a motion picture director which greatly exceeds that of most persons involved in that profession and that Petitioner commands a premium for his services. In addition, the evidence established that Petitioner can reasonably expect to continue to enjoy said premium. In other words, he has expectation of continued patronage at his prior level of compensation."

The trial court detailed the facts upon which these conclusions were based. Among these facts are that husband is ranked No. 13 among 1,058 motion picture directors in cumulative box office revenues during 1985–1996, No. 8 in terms of gross domestic revenues produced by movies he directed, and No. 1 in terms of production budgets entrusted to his control. Husband does not contest the trial court's conclusion that all of this boils down to the fact that he has, in the trial court's words, "elite professional standing."

The trial court determined the value of husband's goodwill by means of the "excess earnings" approach. It has been noted that the "excess earnings" method is a method that is commonly used to determine the value of the goodwill in a professional practice. (Hogoboom & King, Cal. Practice Guide: Family Law (The Rutter Group 2005) ¶ 8:1445, p. 8–350.) Broadly put, the excess earnings approach is predicated on a comparison of the earnings of the professional in question with that of a peer whose performance is "average." Using this method with some modifications, the trial court determined that husband's goodwill at the time of separation was $1.5 million.

Husband contends that he does not possess an asset that can be properly classified as goodwill. Relying on *In re Marriage of Rives* (1982) 130 Cal.App.3d 138, 153, 181 Cal.Rptr. 572, and *In re Marriage of Aufmuth* (1979) 89 Cal.App.3d 446, 460–462, 152 Cal.Rptr. 668, among other cases, husband points out that skill, reputation and experience are not community property. Husband contends that the goodwill found to exist in this case is in reality nothing other than his skill, reputation and experience.

2. *The Issue Defined*

The trial court found that husband has a "quantifiable expectation of future patronage." Future, or continued, public patronage is one essential aspect of goodwill. "The 'good will' of a business is the expectation of continued public patronage." (Bus. & Prof.Code, § 14100.) However, there is more to goodwill than expectation of continued patronage. "The good will *of a business* is property and is transferable." (Bus. & Prof.Code, § 14102, italics added.)

Since the goodwill *of a business* is property (Bus. & Prof.Code, § 14102), the question is: What is the meaning of "a business" in the definition of goodwill?

There are two possible answers.

One answer is that the term "a business" also includes "a person doing business." This is the interpretation that the trial court adopted in this case.

The other answer is that "a business" refers to a professional, commercial or industrial enterprise with assets, i.e., an entity other than a natural person.

There are three reasons why the second answer is the better one. First, it conforms to the historical understanding of goodwill. Second, the plain text of Business and Professions Code sections 14100 and 14102, which, in this respect, have not been amended since their enactment in 1872, speaks of "a business," and not of natural persons. Third, interpreting the term "a business" as it appears in Business and Professions Code sections 14100 and 14102 to refer to a professional, commercial or industrial enterprise with assets ensures that the interest that is divided as goodwill is "property," as "property" is defined by law.

3.   The Historical Understanding of "a Business"

The precursors of Business and Professions Code sections 14100 and 14102 were Civil Code sections 992 and 993, which were enacted in 1872 as part of the Civil Code. Contemporaneously with the enactment of the California Civil Code in 1872, and as of the closing decades of the 19th century, the courts spoke of goodwill as an incident of an existing business; goodwill did not exist in the abstract, apart from a business. "Undoubtedly, goodwill is in many cases a valuable thing, although there is difficulty in deciding accurately what is included under the term. It is tangible only as an incident, as connected with a going concern or business having locality or name, and is not susceptible of being disposed of independently." (*Metropolitan Bank v. St. Louis Dispatch Co.* (1893) 149 U.S. 436, 446, 13 S.Ct. 944, 37 L.Ed. 799.)

California decisions echoed this view, rejecting that goodwill attaches to the shares of stock. "It would be strange to predicate good-will as pertaining to or extending to an abstraction, to an 'artificial being, invisible, intangible, and existing only in contemplation of law.' " (*Spring Valley W.W. v. Schottler* (1882) 62 Cal. 69, 118, cited with approval in *Merchants' Ad-Sign Co. v. Sterling* (1899) 124 Cal. 429, 432, 57 P. 468.) The courts spoke of the fact that goodwill was not separable from the physical assets of the business that generated the goodwill. (E.g., *Russell v. Russell* (1918) 39 Cal.App. 174, 176–177, 178 P. 307; *Ward-Chandler Bldg. Co. v. Caldwell* (1935) 8 Cal.App.2d 375, 378, 47 P.2d 758.) This led text writers to state that goodwill cannot be sold independently of the business or the physical elements or assets to which it is incident (35 Cal.Jur.3d (1988) Good Will, § 5, at fn. 43), which is a view supported by the court in *Metropolitan Bank v. St. Louis Dispatch Co., supra,* 149 U.S. 436, 446, 13 S.Ct. 944, 37 L.Ed. 799.

One of the classic definitions of goodwill in our case law appears in *In re Lyons* (1938) 27 Cal.App.2d 293, 297–298, 81 P.2d 190. This definition, which is the same as offered in *Metropolitan Bank v. St. Louis Dispatch Co., supra,* 149 U.S. at page 446, 13 S.Ct. 944 predicates the existence of goodwill on the operations of a business entity with assets separate and distinct from the person or persons who operate, own or manage the business.

In this respect, nothing had changed since these early cases were decided. No California case has held that a natural person, apart and distinct from a "business," can create or generate goodwill. In the instance of professionals, the courts have spoken of "the nature and duration of his business as a sole practitioner" (*In re Marriage of Lopez* (1974) 38 Cal.App.3d 93, 109–110, 113 Cal.Rptr. 58) and of the value of a "professional practice" (*Golden v. Golden* (1969) 270 Cal.App.2d 401, 405, 75 Cal.Rptr. 735; see also *Todd v. Todd* (1969) 272 Cal.App.2d 786, 792, 78 Cal.Rptr. 131). It is the business, i.e., the practice, that generates goodwill, even if the practice is conducted by a sole practitioner, as was the case in *Golden* and *Todd.* (See Annot. (1990) 76 A.L.R.4th 1025; Annot. (1990) 79 A.L.R.4th 171.)

4. Business and professions Code Sections 14100 and 14102 Endow a Business, and Not a Person, with the Capacity to Generate Goodwill

"There is order in the most fundamental rules of statutory interpretation if we want to find it. The key is applying those rules in proper *sequence.* [¶] First, a court should examine the actual language of the statute. * * * [¶] In examining the language, the courts should give to the words of the statute their ordinary, everyday meaning. * * * [¶] If the meaning is without ambiguity, doubt, or uncertainty, then the language controls." * * *

There is no doubt about the "ordinary, everyday meaning" of the term "a business," nor is the term ambiguous or uncertain. In the term "a business," the word "business" is a noun, and means a professional, commercial or industrial enterprise with assets. It is also clear that "a business" is not a natural person.

It may be asked whether the term "a business" should be read to include "a person doing business," in which event Business and Professions

Code section 14102 would effectively read: "The good will of a business *or of a person doing business* is property and is transferable."

It is not within the powers of a court to amend the statute in such a fashion. And there is no doubt that this would be an amendment of the statute. It would enlarge the scope of the statute beyond the traditional understanding of goodwill, which anchors goodwill to a business establishment with assets. Nor can it be said that business" is logically included in the term "a business." In the ordinary, everyday sense, "a business" refers to an establishment, a thing, and not a person. With deference to our dissenting colleague, expanding Business and Professions Code section 14102 to state "[t]he good will of a business *or of a person doing business* is property and is transferable" should be left to the Legislature, especially since such an expansion involves considerations of social policy, as appears in the following paragraph.

Endowing "a person doing business" with the capacity to create goodwill, as opposed to limiting goodwill to "a business," has wide ramifications. "A person doing business" includes much of the working population. Notably, there would be no principled distinction between husband in this case, who is a director, and actors, artists and musicians, all of whom could be said to be "persons doing business." Thus, all such persons who would have the "expectation of continued public patronage" would possess goodwill. This would create a substantial liability, as in this case, without a guaranty that the liability would be funded. It is clear that, from an economic perspective, the "goodwill" in this case is based on earnings, and that "goodwill" is an expression of husband's earning capacity. However, there is no guaranty, especially in the arts, that earnings will not decline or even dry up, even though expectations were to the contrary. In such an event, a person would find him—or herself saddled with a massive liability without the means of satisfying it. Putting it another way, endowing directly persons with the ability to create goodwill would create an "asset" predicated on nothing other than predictions about earning capacity.

5.   Interpreting the Term "a Business" As It Appears in Business and Professions Code Sections 14100 and 14102 To Refer to a Professional, Commercial or Industrial Enterprise with Assets Ensures That the Interest That Is Divided As Goodwill Is "Property."

The trial court found that husband "has developed an earning capacity and reputation in his profession as a motion picture director which greatly exceeds that of most persons involved in that profession and that [husband] commands a premium for his services." In order for this to be divisible as community property, it must be, in the first place, property, and, in the second place, it must have been acquired during marriage. "Except as otherwise provided by statute, all property, real or personal, wherever situated, acquired by a married person during the marriage while domiciled in this state is community property." (Fam. Code, § 760.)

Since every kind of property that is not real is personal (Civ. Code, § 663), the property interest in this case, if it exists, must be personal. Personal property may be incorporeal (*King v. Goetz* (1886) 70 Cal. 236, 240, 11 P. 656), i.e., without tangible substance, and it may be intangible in the sense that it is a right rather than a physical object. (*Navistar Internat. Transportation Corp. v. State Bd. of Equalization* (1994) 8 Cal.4th 868, 875, 35 Cal.Rptr.2d 651, 884 P.2d 108.) But, even if incorporeal or intangible, property must be capable of being transferred. "[I]t is a fundamental principle of law that one of the chief incidents of ownership in property is the right to transfer it." (*Bias v. Ohio Farmers Indemnity Co.* (1938) 28 Cal.App.2d 14, 16, 81 P.2d 1057.) "A common characteristic of a property right, is that it may be disposed of, transferred to another." (*Douglas Aircraft Co. v. Byram* (1943) 57 Cal.App.2d 311, 317, 134 P.2d 15.)

Husband's "earning capacity and reputation in his profession as a motion picture director which greatly exceeds that of most persons involved in that profession" or, in the trial court's shorthand, his "elite professional standing," cannot be sold or transferred. His high standing among other motion picture directors is entirely personal to him. He cannot confer on another director his standing as No. 13 in cumulative box office revenues during 1985–1996. He cannot sell this standing to another, because a buyer would not be John McTiernan, no matter how much the buyer was willing to pay. For the same reason, and unlike a law or medical practice, husband cannot transfer his "elite professional standing." That standing is his, and his alone, and he cannot bestow it on someone else. Thus, an essential aspect of a property interest is absent.

The fact that husband's "elite professional standing" is not transferable effectively refutes the trial court's conclusion that husband's "practice" as a motion picture director is like the "practice" of an attorney or physician. The practice of an attorney, physician, dentist, or accountant is transferable, but husband's "elite professional standing" is his alone, and not susceptible to being transferred or sold.

That husband's "elite professional standing" is not a property interest is also reflected by the trial court's calculation of husband's "goodwill." Under the excess earnings method, the court must deduct from the average net pretax earnings of the business being valued the "fair return" on the "net tangible assets used by the business." No such deduction was made in this case, and the comparison was between husband's pretax net income, and that of a motion picture director who is compensated at minimum levels. Thus, the trial court's calculation of "goodwill" demonstrates that there was no business—there were no assets—that would qualify as property.

Were we to construe the goodwill *of a business* as the trial court did in this case, we would be faced with a conflict between Business and Professions Code section 14102 (the goodwill of a business is property) and the fundamental concept that property is transferable. Under section 14102, we would call "property" something that is not transferable, and therefore is not property. Instead, we anchor goodwill to "a business," as the statute requires. This ensures that goodwill is attached to property that is transferable, as a professional, commercial or industrial enterprise is transferable.

In sum, adhering to the rule that property, in order to qualify as property, must be transferable is not a theoretical exercise. Something that cannot be transferred or sold has no value on the market. Dividing such a nontransferable quantity as community property therefore creates an obligation without ensuring that that obligation can be funded. However, when "a business" with assets is divided, there is some assurance that the obligation created by the division can and will be met.

6.   *Respondent's Arguments in Support of the Trial Court's Finding of Goodwill Are Without Merit*

Respondent contends that the "existence of a business in the traditional sense is not a prerequisite to finding professional goodwill." The contrary is true. As we have seen, the plain text of Business and Professions Code sections 14100 and 14102, as well as its predecessors, refers to the "good will of a business." As we have shown, this is a reference to a professional, commercial or industrial enterprise with assets.

Respondent contends that since there is substantial evidence that husband has an expectation of continued public patronage, husband has goodwill. This begs the question. It is true that "[t]he 'good will' of a business is the expectation of continued public patronage." (Bus. & Prof. Code, § 14100.) However, the "expectation of continued public patronage" must be generated by "a business." A business is a professional, commercial or industrial enterprise with assets; "a business" is not earning capacity or professional reputation.

Finally, the fact that the trial court was able to, and did, apply the "excess earnings" method to calculate goodwill does not mean that there is goodwill in this case. Boiled down to its essentials, the excess earnings method is a comparison of husband's earnings with that of an "average" peer. The fact that this calculation can be performed, as it was performed, does not convert husband's skill and reputation into "a business," and does not transmute unique and idiosyncratic talents into property that can be transferred or sold.

We conclude that the trial court erred in finding that there was goodwill in husband's practice or career as a motion picture director. Accordingly, the judgment must be modified to eliminate $1.5 million in assets that are subject to division. As noted in the text, *post,* this affects the calculation of attorney's fees under the formula crafted by the trial court. * * *

DISPOSITION

* * * The judgment is to be modified by deleting $1.5 million in assets, denominated as goodwill, from property that is subject to division. * * *

BOLAND, J., Concurring.

I concur in the judgment and write separately to state the rationale I believe justifies the conclusion that, as a matter of law, John McTiernan's work as a movie director is not a business or professional practice to which goodwill may attach.

Let me begin with several points on which there is no dispute.

First, goodwill may exist in a professional practice or in a business which is founded upon personal skill or reputation. (*In re Marriage of Foster* (1974) 42 Cal.App.3d 577, 582, fn. 2, 117 Cal.Rptr. 49.)

Second, the goodwill of a business is property and is transferable. (Bus. & Prof.Code, § 14102.) Otherwise stated, goodwill is an asset of a business or professional practice, and where the business or professional practice is community property, it is a community asset. (*Golden v. Golden* (1969) 270 Cal.App.2d 401, 405, 75 Cal.Rptr. 735.)

Third, "[a]lthough the goodwill of a business may be the result of the personal skill, talent, experience, or reputation of an individual connected with the business, it may attach to and continue with the business even after the separation of the individual on whom it was founded." (*Smith v. Bull* (1958) 50 Cal.2d 294, 302, 325 P.2d 463.)

Fourth, "[w]hen goodwill attaches to a business, its value is a question of fact." (*In re Marriage of King* (1983) 150 Cal.App.3d 304, 309, 197 Cal.Rptr. 716.)

From these well-settled points, two other principles seem clear:

- Goodwill, as a divisible asset, does not exist apart from the business or professional practice to which it attaches.

- Because it is property, any business or professional practice (along with any goodwill attached to it) is and must be, at least in legal theory, transferable from one person or entity to another. (See *Yuba River Power Co. v. Nevada Irr. Dist.* (1929) 207 Cal. 521, 523, 279 P. 128 [citing a definition of the term "property" as "sufficiently comprehensive to include every species of estate, real and personal, and everything which one person can own and transfer to another"]; see also *Douglas Aircraft Co. v. Byram* (1943) 57 Cal.App.2d 311, 317, 134 P.2d 15["[a] common characteristic of a property right, is that it may be disposed of, transferred to another"]; *Bias v. Ohio Farmers Indemnity Co.* (1938) 28 Cal.App.2d 14, 16, 81 P.2d 1057 ["it is a fundamental principle of law that one of the chief incidents of ownership in property is the right to transfer it"].)

Accordingly, in the first instance, the question is whether McTiernan—or, more properly, the marital community—owned a business or a professional practice to which goodwill could attach. In my view, the answer is no, because McTiernan cannot—even in theory—sell or otherwise transfer his "professional practice" or "business" to a third party. This is not because there is no market for the business, but for the more fundamental reason that nothing exists to sell. McTiernan has only his talent as a director, and he cannot transfer it to anyone else. In this, he is no different from any other artist, entertainer or athlete with a talent that commands high compensation. While the occupations of these individuals, like most other occupations, are in common parlance denominated "professions," they are neither businesses nor professional practices that can be expanded beyond the individual in whom the talent resides. Unlike a doctor, lawyer, accountant or other business person, McTiernan cannot hire someone else to direct a movie he has been hired to direct. He cannot expand his "practice" or "business" because he has only his own artistic talent to offer. Whatever we may call it—talent, occupation, livelihood or profession—the creative processes of a movie director, like that of any other artist, cannot be bought, sold or given away, and therefore do not fit within any recognized definition of property. Consequently, no business or professional practice constituting property exists in McTiernan's case, within the meaning of current statutory or case law. Goodwill as statutorily defined, as merely an intangible asset of a business or professional practice, necessarily cannot exist in the absence of a business or professional practice.

The conclusion that, as a matter of law, McTiernan has no business or professional practice to which goodwill could attach is not a departure from California precedents on professional goodwill. Our dissenting colleague concludes that *In re Marriage of Watts* (1985) 171 Cal.App.3d 366, 217 Cal.Rptr. 301 and *In re Marriage of Foster, supra,* 42 Cal.App.3d 577, 117 Cal.Rptr. 49 teach that "professional goodwill" need not be susceptible to transfer to another in order to be a divisible community asset. I do not so read either case. Both *Foster* and *Watts* involved medical practices, and there is no question that medical practices, including sole proprietorships, can be and are bought and sold. * * *

A few additional observations are in order.

First, I recognize that the existence and value of goodwill in a business are questions for the trier of fact. (*Smith v. Bull, supra,* 50 Cal.2d at p. 306, 325 P.2d 463 ["whether the business possessed a goodwill is also a question of fact"]; see *In re Marriage of Rosen* (2002) 105 Cal.App.4th 808, 817, 130 Cal.Rptr.2d 1 [no goodwill existed in husband's law practice; the trial court's finding that law practice was worth $60,500, of which $42,000 constituted goodwill, was reversed with instructions to assign a goodwill value of $0].) In this case, however, transferable goodwill, by statute, exists only in a business or professional practice, and McTiernan, as a matter of law, has no goodwill because he has no transferable business or professional practice.

Second, I likewise understand that some cases recognize the goodwill a lawyer possesses as an individual, even though the lawyer practices as a partner in a firm, and by agreement holds no entitlement to the goodwill of the law firm. (*In re Marriage of Iredale and Cates* (2004) 121 Cal.App.4th 321, 329, 16 Cal.Rptr.3d 505; see also *In re Marriage of Fenton* (1982) 134 Cal.App.3d 451, 461, 184 Cal.Rptr. 597 [value of the goodwill in husband's law corporation was not controlled by the amount a shareholder in the corporation was entitled to receive on withdrawal or termination].) These cases merely recognize that the form in which a professional practice is carried on does not control the valuation of the goodwill that attaches to the individual's professional practice, which would exist "whether he stays with his firm or strikes out on his own." (*Fenton, supra,* 134 Cal.App.3d at p. 463, 184 Cal.Rptr. 597; see also *In re Marriage of Nichols* (1994) 27 Cal.App.4th 661, 673, fn. 4, 33 Cal.Rptr.2d 13 [husband with shareholder interest in law firm "has personal goodwill regardless of whether he remains with the firm, and this goodwill cannot be eliminated by a recital in the stock purchase agreement"].) These cases do not suggest that any individual, regardless of occupation, possesses transferable goodwill simply because he or she is highly compensated in comparison with his or her peers. In each case, the underlying professional practice or business in which the individual is engaged is susceptible in legal and economic theory of being changed in form, expanded, bought and sold. None of those attributes adhere to McTiernan's activity as a movie director.

Finally, I return to the words of *Smith v. Bull, supra,* 50 Cal.2d at page 302, 325 P.2d 463, which plainly demonstrate that goodwill is not a divisible asset unless it can be transferred from the person who created it. As the Supreme Court observed, "[a]lthough the goodwill of a business may be the result of the personal skill, talent, experience, or reputation of an individual connected with the business, it may attach to and continue with the business even after the separation of the individual on whom it was founded." (*Ibid.*) In this case, McTiernan cannot be separated from his "business," either practically or theoretically.

In short, the Legislature has defined goodwill as property only in connection with a business, and it has specified that the goodwill of a business is transferable. Where there is no transferable business, there is no property to divide, and there is necessarily no goodwill. The Legislature, of course, is at liberty to define goodwill in a more expansive manner, so that it would include the ability of an artist or entertainer to generate excess earnings by virtue of his or her talent and the resulting encomium of a receptive public. It has not yet done so, and it was therefore error for the trial court to conclude that McTiernan possessed professional goodwill that was a divisible community asset.

COOPER, P.J., Concurring and Dissenting.

I concur in the lead opinion and in the judgment with respect to all issues but one. I respectfully dissent from my colleagues' conclusion that husband has no divisible goodwill. The facts found by the trial court establish that husband possesses valuable goodwill, as traditionally recognized by California case law. In holding otherwise as a matter of law, the majority apply restrictive concepts that disregard established family law precedent. Moreover, even under this legal revision, substantial evidence still supports the trial court's findings that husband possessed goodwill in his professional business, in which wife was entitled to share.

Business and Professions Code section 14102 declares the goodwill of a business to be property, albeit intangible. Section 14100 of the same code compactly defines goodwill as "the expectation of continued public patronage." The United States Supreme Court has similarly stated, "Although the definition of goodwill has taken different forms over the years, the shorthand description of goodwill as 'the expectancy of continued patronage' [citation] provides a useful label with which to identify the total of all the imponderable qualities that attract customers to the business." (*Newark Morning Ledger Co. v. United States* (1993) 507 U.S. 546, 555–556, 113 S.Ct. 1670, 123 L.Ed.2d 288.)

In California, spousal goodwill[1] is uniformly recognized as subject to assessment and award in proceedings for division of community property. (See 11 Witkin, Summary of Cal. Law (9th ed. 1990) Community Property, § 69, pp. 461–462.) "Although community goodwill is usually associated with a professional practice, it may exist in any business which is founded upon personal skill or reputation." (*Id.* at p. 461.) Both the existence and the value of goodwill in a particular case are questions of fact, and their determination is reviewed on appeal under the substantial evidence test. (E.g., *Smith v. Bull* (1958) 50 Cal.2d 294, 306, 325 P.2d 463; *Mueller v. Mueller* (1956) 144 Cal.App.2d 245, 252, 301 P.2d 90 (*Mueller*); *In re Marriage of Slivka* (1986) 183 Cal.App.3d 159, 162, 228 Cal.Rptr. 76.)

---

[1] Editorial note: Cooper P.J. does not define the term "spousal goodwill." Nor is the term regularly used in Family Code case law.

Previous decisions have attributed goodwill to a variety of professional individuals and situations, including an attorney who worked at home on appointed criminal appeals (*In re Marriage of Rosen* (2002) 105 Cal.App.4th 808, 130 Cal.Rptr.2d 1), a computer consultant who worked at home or at his clients' facilities, with "no plant, no commercial location, no employees and [no] office" (*In re Marriage of King* (1983) 150 Cal.App.3d 304, 310, 197 Cal.Rptr. 716), and a law firm partner who was found to possess professional goodwill as an individual (*In re Marriage of Iredale & Cates* (2004) 121 Cal.App.4th 321, 16 Cal.Rptr.3d 505; accord, *In re Marriage of Fenton* (1982) 134 Cal.App.3d 451, 463, 184 Cal.Rptr. 597; see *In re Marriage of Nichols* (1994) 27 Cal.App.4th 661, 673, fn. 4, 33 Cal.Rptr.2d 13).

In the present case, husband's business and profession were that of a motion picture director. The trial court found, after assessing extensive evidence, that husband possessed professional goodwill of a value of $1.5 million. Because all of this value had developed during the parties' marriage, wife was entitled to a compensatory payment of $750,000.

The majority now set aside these findings by superimposing on the concept of marital goodwill a novel set of elements. In brief, the majority opine that a professional individual such as husband may not possess goodwill without having a "business" (which husband supposedly did not have), and that there can be no goodwill unless it, or the accompanying business, can be sold (which husband's allegedly cannot). These artificial restrictions are legally unfounded and factually inaccurate; moreover, even were they correct, they would provide no cause for reversing the award of goodwill in this case as a matter of law.

The lead opinion's effort to limit goodwill to a "business" as opposed to an individual is semantic. Any professional who independently practices his or her profession, for profit—be it lawyer, doctor, computer consultant, or film director—thereby conducts a business, within the lead opinion's own unattributed definition, as well as more traditional ones. It is therefore neither factually nor legally correct to say that only a business, and not a natural person, may generate or possess goodwill. When the consultant in *In re Marriage of King, supra,* 150 Cal.App.3d 304, 197 Cal.Rptr. 716, and the lawyers in *In re Marriage of Rosen, supra,* 105 Cal.App.4th 808, 130 Cal.Rptr.2d 1, and *In re Marriage of Iredale and Cates, supra,* 121 Cal.App.4th 321, 16 Cal.Rptr.3d 505, generated goodwill while practicing their professions, they did so as individuals.

But whichever view one takes of this issue, it cannot properly oust husband and wife of the palpable, valuable goodwill that the trial court found husband had developed. By any realistic understanding, husband earned his professional compensation, and developed an expectation of continued patronage, while practicing a business, of directing motion pictures. This business comprised not just husband's talent, but a series of corporations, one of which owned an airplane, which husband used to travel to and scout film locations. Husband had as much a "business" as the professionals in the cases last cited. * * *

In this case the trial court properly determined the existence and extent of husband's goodwill, in accord with substantial evidence and with California law, as consistently expounded for half a century. Even under the majority's refashioning of that law, those determinations remain sustainable. I respectfully dissent.

NOTES

1.   *If both education and talent are personal to their holders, what distinguishes the two?* Often professionals are compensated and sought after because of their talent. What is the difference between an attorney and a talented attorney? A director and a talented director? Is educational skill more reproducible than talent in the market place? Are talented lawyers easier to come by than talented directors, or novelists, or musicians? When it comes to directors, is there only one director with John McTiernan's POV, or with Sofia Coppola's POV?

2.   *What distinguishes goodwill from talent? Aufmuth* excludes professional education from the community property system. *Todd* includes law practice goodwill within the system. In *McTiernan & Dubrow,* Cooper P.J. uses the term "spousal goodwill." Given the cases that Cooper P.J. cites, what does "spousal goodwill" refer to?

3.   *What is goodwill?* The most common evidence or example of goodwill can come up in the sale of an on-going business. Goodwill, an intangible asset, is deemed to exist when a company acquires another firm and pays more than the acquiree's net worth, as measured by book value. The difference between the price paid and the book value of the acquiree is entered onto the acquirer's balance sheet as "goodwill."

To understand why goodwill is treated as an asset, bear in mind that a willing buyer normally does not pay more than what he, she, or it assesses the acquisition is worth. The acquired business may have few tangible assets that are reflected in the book value, but as a counterbalance, it may have an excellent customer base, a great reputation, proprietary knowledge, all past acquisitions that are used to predict continued patronage in the future. In other words, goodwill is an assurance that the business will carry on, even if there is a change in ownership. A dental practice is sold. If the former dentist's patients continue to seek treatment at the dental office (now under new management) the continued patronage is the result of goodwill. A bakery is sold; customers still line up for the yummies despite the change in ownership. Another example of goodwill.

But how can goodwill be established and valued in contexts other than the sale of a business? If John McTiernan signs a contract to direct a film, but then sells that right to Sofia Coppola, will the originally envisioned film be produced? McTiernan could argue that Coppola obviously knows how to complete film projects. What if, instead of selling his rights to an established and likewise elite director, McTiernan sells the rights to an upstart director whose ability to deliver the product is an unknown?

And as for goodwill, what happens to its value when the A-list director is convicted of a federal crime for wiretapping his former spouse during dissolution proceedings? Does it matter that the charge results in a federal prison sentence? Or that the director files for bankruptcy?

The *McTiernan & Dubrow* case was criticized by family law practitioners:

"There can be no doubt that husband is a top-tier director able to find scripts and projects based on his name alone. There can also be no doubt that his track record enables him to command a seven figure salary. And what enables him to do this? His reputation which was made during the marriage . . . and yet husband has no goodwill. Why? Because he wasn't involved in a business and had no business assets. Suppose he hired himself out through a corporation of which he was the sole owner and suppose that the corporation had desks, computers and telephones? Wouldn't that qualify as a business?

What really drove the opinion and required the court to make the distinction it did is contained in the following sentence: "Notably, there would be no principled distinctions between husband in this case, who is a director, and actors, artists and musicians, all of whom could be said to be 'persons doing business.'" The court simply could not abide the thought of goodwill being considered in thousands of dissolutions where today it is not.

By so defining goodwill, the court undermined the concept of professional goodwill. The court distinguishes professional goodwill (law or medical practice) because husband in the instant case cannot bestow his standing on someone else. Therefore, the court found that he could not have goodwill because the essential definition of property is something which is transferable. But can a doctor or lawyer of note transfer his reputation? Is there any difference between the husband here and anyone else who has attained stature in his or her occupation? Obviously not. I think that the court's distinction that goodwill exists only when there is a business to transfer it is ripe for reconsideration." Hugh T. Thompson, December 2005 CALIFORNIA FAMILY LAW MONTHLY 332 (LexisNexis Matthew Bender)."[2]

4.   *If the existence of goodwill is established, it shall be valued.* It has been stated that "[b]ecause many factors affect goodwill, there appear to be almost as many formulas as there are accountants," and California courts have utilized a wide variety of valuation techniques. Carol S. Bruch, *The Definition and Division of Marital Property in California: Towards Parity and Simplicity,*

---

[2]   Fair use.

33 HASTINGS L.J. 769, 810–12 (1982). Some cases indicate that because it is impermissible to classify post-separation earnings as community property, the value of goodwill must be established without reference to the future, that is to the potential or continuing net income of the professional practitioner. See, e.g., *Marriage of Fortier*, 34 Cal.App.3d 384, 109 Cal.Rptr. 915 (2d Dist. 1973); *Marriage of Foster*, 42 Cal.App.3d 577, 117 Cal.Rptr. 49 (1st Dist. 1974). *Marriage of King*, 150 Cal.App.3d 304, 309–310, 197 Cal.Rptr. 716, 719–720 (2d Dist. 1983): "[A] proper means of arriving at the value of goodwill contemplates any legitimate method of evaluation that measures its present value by taking into account some past result. . . . To some degree, goodwill always [contemplates the future (*Foster, supra.*), however] continuity of a business being assumed does *not* mean that the post-separation results of husband's efforts can, or should, be included in the goodwill formula. . . ."

5.   *Can the right of publicity be analogized to goodwill if one spouse is a celebrity?* Consider the following excerpt from Miller, *Divorce in the Entertainment Industry—Some Special Problems,* 5 COMM/ENT.L.J. 43, 54–57 (1982):

"Consider the following hypothetical situation. An unmarried actor works for a local television station in Los Angeles, performing the principal role in a 'soap opera.' After two years of broadcasts, the show and the actor have developed a substantial local following. The actor is hired for a national television version of the show aired from Los Angeles by CBS Television. He marries. Within three months the show begins to enjoy increasing national popularity. An enterprising businessman identifies the actor as a rising television 'star' and uses the actor's likeness on a 'celebrity calendar.' No consent for the use is secured. Sales of the calendar are phenomenal, and the profits are substantial. The actor immediately sues in the Los Angeles Superior Court, and a $200,000 settlement is negotiated. At the same time the actor and his wife agree that their short marriage has been a mistake and seek a dissolution of the marriage. The question presented in the divorce is whether the proceeds of the settlement are community property or simply separate property of the actor. If community property, the proceeds are subject to equal division in the proceeding for dissolution of the marriage.

A threshold question regarding the nature of the right of publicity must be asked. What is the nature of the right? Is it a property right or one grounded in tort law? The question has evoked different answers over the years.

* * *

If the nature of the interest in protecting and exploiting name and likeness is derived solely from the notion of 'privacy,' then it would appear to be an interest grounded in tort law. If so, under California law, such characterization would likely have as a consequence that money received as compensation for an *invasion* of such privacy right would (except in limited cases) be awarded solely to the 'injured' spouse upon a divorce. No equivalent award of property would be made to the other spouse. On the other hand, if the right of publicity is proprietary in character, that is, if its essence is 'property,' then to the extent that such property is generated as a result of the efforts of a spouse during marriage, it should be divisible upon a divorce as community property.

* * *

Is the 'right of publicity' more evanescent than 'goodwill'? Perhaps. The hypothetical example posed at the beginning of this section avoids a valuation issue by presenting the asset as having an established settlement value. But suppose there were no such benchmark. Suppose the celebrity had not yet succeeded in exploiting his 'right' at the time of the divorce, or suppose the celebrity recoiled from *ever* exploiting his or her fame and simply wanted to be left alone. Must he or she be judicially forced to buy back from the other spouse his or her community interest in a right never exercised or to be exercised? It has been suggested that there are a number of ways to evaluate this asset, with the most readily adaptable being a market value determination without deduction for any restraints on exploitation which the celebrity might impose.

The hypothetical example also suggests yet another problem. How does one determine whether the asset had its source in separate or community origins? The example suggests that there may have to be a tracing or allocation of some kind between the premarital (separate property) component and that resulting from the marital (community property) efforts. That exercise is bound to present formidable difficulties, not the least of which is persuading a trial court that there is a credible basis for making such an allocation."[3]

Given the number of celebrities residing in California and the state's divorce statistics, it is surprising that few California cases deal directly with the issue of celebrity goodwill. Law and law review analysis is also surprisingly scant. New York and New Jersey courts have considered the question and concluded that goodwill based on celebrity status could be treated as a marital asset subject to equitable distribution. See *Piscopo v. Piscopo*, 232 N.J.Super. 559, 557 A.2d 1040 (1989); *Golub v. Golub*, 139 Misc.2d 440, 527 N.Y.S.2d 946 (1988).

6. *Intellectual property.* In a dissolution proceeding, are parties interested in the intellectual property right or in the income stream generated by the intellectual property? To quote a great bard: That is the question.

In *Marriage of Worth*, 195 Cal.App.3d 768, 241 Cal.Rptr. 135 (1st Dist. 1987), the husband wrote and published books during marriage. At dissolution, the parties sparred over the classification of the husband's copyright because

---

[3]   Reprinted by permission of University of California Hastings College of the Law.

of their more acute concern over the division of any income from the books. The court stated: "[T]he conclusion is inescapable that such literary works constituted community property . . . If the artistic work is community property, then it must follow that the copyright itself obtains the same status."

The conclusion deemed inescapable in *Worth* was deftly escaped from in *Enovsys LLC v. NexTel Communications*, 614 F.3d 1333 (9th Cir. 2010). Mundi Fomukong was married to Fonda Whitfield when he and a co-inventor filed a GPS patent application that was later issued (the '159 patent). Two years later the co-investors filed a second application (the '461 patent).

Subsequently husband Mundi and wife Fonda sought summary dissolution in California. They certified under penalty of perjury that they had no community property. After their dissolution was final, the '461 patent was issued. Mundi formed Enovsys; in that process he and his co-inventor assigned their rights to Enovsys, one among them being the right to sue for past infringement.

Enovsys sued Sprint NexTel asserting infringement claims relevant to patents '159 and '461, Sprint Nextel moved to dismiss. Sprint NexTel—having already swung around to obtain Fonda's assignment of whatever community property interest she might have had in the patents— argued that Enovsys's case should be dismissed because Fonda had not been joined as a party. Circuit Judge Prost ruled that any community property presumption as to the patent was overcome by Mundi and Fonda's joint petition for summary dissolution, which formed the basis of the final judgment of dissolution of their marriage.

Attention in the federal action turned to the final California dissolution judgment, which was found to preclude dismissal for at several reasons. Mundi's and Fonda's final judgment of dissolution had a preclusive effect in the subsequent federal lawsuit as determined by the full faith and credit statute (28 U.S.C. § 1738); barred relitigation by the doctrine of collateral estoppel; and was entitled to res judicata effect. And, never mind that Sprint was in privity with Fonda and thus barred from relitigating whether Fonda had a property interest in the patents. Outcome: due to the final California divorce decree, Fonda had no property rights in the GPS patents, Enovsys had standing to bring and maintain its lawsuit; and the issue of whether a spouse obtains a one-half community property interest in their spouse's patented inventions was left for another day and for another court, or perhaps (bet yet) for Congress.

7.   *Accumulations.* The general rule is that all property, including earnings and accumulations, are within the community property system. Accumulations can require significant intellectual expenditures to manifest.

For example, in *Marriage of Biddle*, 52 Cal.App.4th 396, 60 Cal.Rptr.2d 569 (1st Dist. 1997), the court held that the wife had a community property interest in a qui tam action prosecuted by her former husband. A qui tam action is a type of private attorney general lawsuit; it allows an individual to sue to enforce a public statutory right and to retain a portion of any damages recovered. In *Biddle*, the husband was employed by the federal government as a contract administrator at Stanford University. He became aware of questionable billing practices involving substantial sums of money ("many millions of dollars"). In 1991 he filed the qui tam action. While the action was pending, he and his wife divorced. The court stated:

> "The cause of action may not be 'property' in the strict sense that it can be owned without restriction by a qui tam plaintiff, but the money generated by the cause of action which ends up in the plaintiff's hands clearly is property. The realization of that is dependent upon at least two contingencies—a judicial action must be initiated by the qui tam plaintiff, and the defendant must part with the money after trial or settlement. If these contingencies are satisfied, the plaintiff's entitlement to a cash recovery is, to all intents and purposes, established. This situation is indistinguishable from that of a married producer who starts work on a movie and, after separating from her husband, completes the movie which becomes a smash hit; the contingency of success results in a divisible community asset. (*See In re Marriage of Zaentz*, 218 Cal.App.3d 154, 267 Cal.Rptr. 31 (1st 1990); see also *In re Marriage of Kilbourne*, 232 Cal.App.3d 1518, 284 Cal.Rptr. 201 (1991), [holding contingent future interests in the form of unpaid contingency fees potentially owed to attorney spouse to be community property over which trial court could reserve jurisdiction])." *Id.* at 399–400.

The court also noted that a qui tam cause of action may be analogized to a lottery ticket. California courts have treated the ticket itself as property, as well as any winnings the ticket may contingently signify.

Client books may be extremely significant and valuable. See *Marriage of Finby* (Chapter 5).

SECTION 2. PERSONS OUTSIDE THE SYSTEM

Of people who marry, many manage to contract a valid marriage: they give consent to marry, they obtain a license, they engage in a solemnization process. Of those, many then file the license, which becomes a marriage certificate. The legal business of the wedding ceremony complete, the celebration begins.

But there are those who fail to maneuver through the requirements for a valid marriage. Sometimes the parties are too closely related. Sometimes one or the other is still married to someone else. Sometimes the wedding is religious, not civil. Sometimes there is factual issue that vitiates a party's consent. And so on. Most flaws can be corrected with consent; some cannot.

If the parties discover that they are not legally married, a party has grounds to request that the union be treated as if it had been legally contracted. If so, the petitioner's state of mind comes into question. Did the petitioner believe in good faith that the parties were contracting a valid marriage?

If the answer is yes, then California Family Code Section 2251 helps the petitioner gain a liminal status of "putative spouse." The status is important because it permits the person whose marriage turned out to be void or voidable to request that dissolution of the union proceed under the default Family Code.

California Family Code Section 2251 codifies the putative spouse doctrine. A party petitions a court for putative spouse status upon proof of a good faith belief in the validity of the marriage. Must the good faith belief be objective? Reasonable? Can it be subjective?

The policy behind California Family Code Section 2251 is to protect the innocent party or parties, including third parties, who may have relied on the validity of a marriage that turns out to be void. One protection comes in the form of a property classification: property obtained during the union is labeled quasi-marital property if it would have been community or quasi-community property had the marriage been valid.

The quasi-marital property statute is clearly stated. It is also becoming increasingly important in a jurisdiction where parties come from all over the world to establish a new domicile. A church or religious wedding in another country may be valid in that jurisdiction, but it is not a valid civil marriage under California law. Informal divorce may be recognized somewhere in the world, but informal dissolution is not valid in California (or any other U.S. jurisdiction); by definition, any marriage contracted after an informal divorce is bigamous and therefore void.

The world is diverse. People have different customs. People make mistakes. The quasi-marital property system incorporates some flexibility into the fabric of the California community property system.

A. VALID, VOID, AND VOIDABLE MARRIAGE

The requirements for a valid marriage are set out in California Family Code Section 300.

As for putative marriages, there are multiple ways for a marriage to be deemed invalid, meaning flawed as far as legal requirements go. Some flaws render a marriage void from the beginning; a void marriage never comes into existence and, technically, never acquires community property. Other flaws render a marriage voidable; this leaves it to the parties to decide, once a legal flaw is discovered, whether they want to correct the flaw (thus validating the marriage), or nullify the marriage. A nullified marriage does not, technically, acquire community property.

WEST'S ANNOTATED CALIFORNIA FAMILY CODE

§ 300. Consent; issuance of license and solemnization; marriage license and marriage certificate—*supra* at 11.

§ 301. Adults; capability to consent to and consummate marriage

Two unmarried persons 18 years of age or older, who are not otherwise disqualified, are capable of consenting to and consummating marriage.

(Stats. 1992, c. 162 (A.B. 2650), § 10, operative Jan. 1, 1994. Amended by Stats. 2014, c. 82 (S.B. 1306), § 3, eff. Jan. 1, 2015.)

§ 302. Minors, capability of consenting to and consummating marriage; court order and parental consent; filing

(a) An unmarried person under 18 years of age is capable of consenting to and consummating marriage upon obtaining a court order granting permission to the underage person or persons to marry.

(b) The court order and written consent of the parents of each underage person, or of one of the parents or the guardian of each underage person shall be filed with the clerk of the court, and a certified copy of the order shall be presented to the county clerk at the time the marriage license is issued.

(Stats. 1992, c. 162 (A.B. 2650), § 10, operative Jan. 1, 1994. Amended by Stats. 2006, c. 816 (A.B. 1102), § 2, operative Jan. 1, 2008; Stats. 2014, c. 82 (S.B. 1306), § 4, eff. Jan 1. 2015.)

§ 305. Proof of consent and solemnization

Consent to and solemnization of marriage may be proved under the same general rules of evidence as facts are proved in other cases.

(Stats. 1992, c. 162 (A.B. 2650), § 10, operative Jan. 1, 1994.)

§ 2200. Incestuous marriages

Marriages between parents and children, ancestors and descendants of every degree, and between siblings of the half as well as the whole blood, and between uncles or aunts and nieces or nephews, are incestuous, and void from the beginning, whether the relationship is legitimate or illegitimate.

(Stats. 1992, c. 162 (A.B. 2650), § 10, operative Jan. 1, 1994. Amended by Stats. 2014, c. 82 (S.B. 1306), § 23, eff. Jan. 1, 2015.)

§ 2201. Bigamous and polygamous marriages; exceptions; absentees

(a) A subsequent marriage contracted by a person during the life of his or her former spouse, with a person other than the former spouse, is illegal and void unless:

(1)   The former marriage has been dissolved or adjudged a nullity before the date of the subsequent marriage.

(2)   The former spouse (A) is absent, and not known to the person to be living for the period of five successive years immediately preceding the subsequent marriage, or (B) is generally reputed or believed by the person to be dead at the time the subsequent marriage was contracted.

(b)   In either of the cases described in paragraph (2) of subdivision (a), the subsequent marriage is valid until its nullity is adjudged pursuant to subdivision (b) of Section 2210.

(Stats. 1992, c. 162 (A.B. 2650), § 10, operative Jan. 1, 1994. Amended by Stats. 2014, c. 82 (S.B. 1306), § 24, eff. Jan. 1, 2015.)

§ 2210. Annulment, causes for

A marriage is voidable and may be adjudged a nullity if any of the following conditions existed at the time of the marriage:

(a)   The party who commences the proceeding or on whose behalf the proceeding is commenced was without the capability of consenting to the marriage as provided in Section 301 or 302, unless, after attaining the age of consent, the party for any time freely cohabited with the other as his or her spouse.

(b)   The spouse of either party was living and the marriage with that spouse was then in force and that spouse (1) was absent and not known to the party commencing the proceeding to be living for a period of five successive years immediately preceding the subsequent marriage for which the judgment of nullity is sought or (2) was generally reputed or believed by the party commencing the proceeding to be dead at the time the subsequent marriage was contracted.

(c)   Either party was of unsound mind, unless the party of unsound mind, after coming to reason, freely cohabited with the other as his or her spouse.

(d)   The consent of either party was obtained by fraud, unless the party whose consent was obtained by fraud afterwards, with full knowledge of the facts constituting the fraud, freely cohabited with the other as his or her spouses.

(e)   The consent of either party was obtained by force, unless the party whose consent was obtained by force afterwards freely cohabited with the other as his or her spouse.

(f)   Either party was, at the time of marriage, physically incapable of entering into the marriage state, and that incapacity continues, and appears to be incurable.

(Stats. 1992, c. 162 (A.B. 2650), § 10, operative Jan. 1, 1994. Amended by Stats. 2014, c. 82 (S.B. 1306), § 25, eff. Jan. 1, 2015.)

§ 2251. Status of putative spouse; division of community or quasi-community property

(a) If a determination is made that a marriage is void or voidable and the court finds that either party or both parties believed in good faith that the marriage was valid, the court shall:

(1) Declare the party or parties, who believed in good faith that the marriage was valid, to have the status of a putative spouse.

(2) If the division of property is in issue, divide, in accordance with Division 7 (commencing with Section 2500), that property acquired during the union that would have been community property or quasi-community property if the union had not been void or voidable, only upon request of a party who is declared a putative spouse under paragraph (1). This property is known as "quasi-marital property."

(b) If the court expressly reserves jurisdiction, it may make the property division at a time after the judgment.

(Stats. 1992, c. 162 (A.B. 2650), § 10, operative Jan. 1, 1994. Amended by Stats. 2015, c. 196 (A.B. 380), § 1, eff. Jan. 1, 2016.)

§ 2252. Liability of quasi-marital property for debts of parties

The property divided pursuant to Section 2251 is liable for debts of the parties to the same extent as if the property had been community property or quasi-community property.

(Stats. 1992, c. 162 (A.B. 2650), § 10, operative Jan. 1, 1994.)

§ 2254. Order for support; putative spouse

The court may, during the pendency of a proceeding for nullity of marriage or upon judgment of nullity of marriage, order a party to pay for the support of the other party in the same manner as if the marriage had not been void or voidable if the party for whose benefit the order is made is found to be a putative spouse.

(Stats. 1992, c. 162 (A.B. 2650), § 10, operative Jan. 1, 1994.)

§ 2255. Grant of attorney's fees and costs

The court may grant attorney's fees and costs in accordance with Chapter 3.5 (commencing with Section 2030) of Part 1 in proceedings to have the marriage adjudged void and in those proceedings based upon voidable marriage in which the party applying for attorney's fees and costs is found to be innocent of fraud or wrongdoing in inducing or entering into the marriage, and free from knowledge of the then existence of any prior marriage or other impediment to the contracting of the marriage for which a judgment of nullity is sought.

(Stats. 1992, c. 162 (A.B. 2650), § 10, operative Jan. 1, 1994. Amended by Stats. 1993, c. 219 (A.B. 1500), § 108.5.)

NOTES

1.   *The putative spouse declaration gives a person the right to opt for a division of property acquired during the relationship in accordance with the California Family Code.* Following a putative spouse declaration, the declarant (the innocent party who believed in good faith that the marriage was valid) has the option to request dissolution under default Family Code rules. Alternatively, the declarant can decide to proceed under the Civil Code or, depending on the facts, the Corporations Code (Chapter 6). Only a declarant has the option to decide.

The effect of choosing a dissolution within the parameters of the Family Code is that the putative spouse acknowledges the putative marriage while also accepting that a putative marriage produced quasi-marital property.

Quasi-marital property is defined by California Family Code Section 2251(a)(2) as "property acquired during the union that would have been community property or quasi-community property if the union had not been void or voidable."

California Family Code Section 2251 is an equitable protection because it allows a declared putative spouse to opt for the many evidentiary, substantive, and procedural protections of the Family Code. If these protections are invoked, both partners in a putative marriage (not just the innocent one) own a vested one-half interest in quasi-marital property, on an asset by asset basis, as of the date of acquisition. Since the Family Code option precludes any fault-based division, it would be reversible error for a court to award a putative spouse a larger percentage of quasi-marital property relative to a non-putative spouse. Unequal division is not, repeat not, the way to account for any wrongdoing that led to the invalid marriage.

The California Family Code offers other protective non-fault based actions, but the alternatives are also no-fault in that they do not address the fact that one person misled or deceived another person into contracting a void or voidable marriage. What they do is protect the declared putative spouse's past, present or future one-half interest in quasi-marital property from dissipation or impairment (Chapter 6). A hair-line but well-settled distinction (Chapter 7).

2.   *The putative spouse rule pre-codification.* The putative spouse doctrine was codified in the California Civil Code in 1969. It was part of the first Family Code of 1992, which became operative on January 1, 1994. Before 1969, California followed the "equitable community doctrine" as developed in *Coats v. Coats*, 160 Cal. 671, 118 P. 441 (1911).

In *Coats*, husband Lee successfully annulled a marriage of eighteen years on the ground that partner Ida lacked physical capacity. Afterwards, Lee argued that since the marriage was annulled, there could be no community property. The court looked at cases from common law jurisdictions. It also took note of Ida's good faith belief in the validity of the marriage. From there, the court used its equitable powers to deem Ida a putative spouse and to affirm the award to her of some property from her long life with Lee, the person she thought in good faith to be her legal husband. In the court's language:

> "The argument of appellant in this connection is that, while a voidable marriage is valid, unless annulled, yet, where there has been a decree of annulment, the decree determines that no marriage ever existed, and renders it void ab initio. Accordingly, upon the making of the decree, the children become illegitimate (except for statutory provisions, like section 84 of our Civil Code), and property rights of either party in so far as they depend upon marriage, are at an end. There is ample authority supporting the proposition that the effect of a decree of nullity is to declare that the marriage was void from the beginning. . . . So, too, it is generally held that when a marriage is annulled property rights dependent upon the existence of the marriage, such as dower and curtesy, are terminated and annulled. . . . But these decisions, and others cited by the appellant, deal with the rights of one of the parties in property owned by the other. An interest in such property, dependent solely upon marriage, cannot exist after an adjudication that there has been no marriage. If, as is suggested by the appellant, the annulment is to be treated as analogous to a rescission, it should properly enough be accompanied by a restoration to the parties of what they respectively had before marriage, and what they would have had in the absence of a marriage.

> Here, however, the question is a different one. The controversy is, not over the property owned by the defendant prior to marriage, or acquired by him alone thereafter, but has to do with the acquisitions of the two parties after marriage, and before annulment. If both have contributed to such acquisitions, each has an interest which did not exist at the time of the marriage. The status quo could not be restored upon annulment, without making some provision for the equitable division of this property. In the absence of fraud or other ground affecting the right to claim relief, there can be no good reason for saying that either party should by reason of the annulment, be vested with title to all of the property acquired during the existence of the supposed marriage.

> * * * Even though it may be true that, strictly speaking, there is no "community property" where there has not been a valid marriage (Chapman v. Chapman, 11 Tex.Civ.App. 392, 32 S.W. 564; see 68 Am.St.Rep. p. 376, note), the courts may well, in dividing gains made by the joint efforts of a man and a woman living together under a

voidable marriage which is subsequently annulled, apply, by analogy, the rules which would obtain with regard to community property, where a valid marriage is terminated by death of the husband or by divorce. The apportionment of such property between the parties is not provided by any statute. It must therefore be made on equitable principles. In the absence of special circumstances, such as might arise through intervening claims of third persons, we can conceive of no more equitable basis of apportionment than an equal division. Until the making of the annulment decree, the marriage was valid, and the property in question was impressed with the community character. Upon annulment, such property, even though it be no longer community property, should be divided as community property would have been upon a dissolution of the marriage by divorce or the death of the husband.

If these views be sound, it is entirely immaterial that the bulk of the property was acquired between the years 1900 and 1906, and that the plaintiff's services in its accumulation were "of no monetary value." She is not suing to recover for services rendered under a contract for labor, nor to establish the value of her interest in a business partnership. What she did, she did as a wife, and her share of the joint accumulations must be measured by what a wife would receive out of community property on the termination of the marriage. "The law will not inquire * * * whether the acquisition was by the joint efforts of the husband and wife, or attempt to adjust their respective rights in proportion to the amount each contributed thereto. The law will not concern itself with such an inquiry, but will leave the parties to share in the property in the same proportion as though the marriage contract was what the wife had every reason to believe it to be, i.e., a valid marriage." *F.W. & R.G.R. Co. v. Robertson, supra*. If then, the facts would have justified an allotment to the wife of one-half of the property acquired by the parties, there can be no complaint of the allowance of $10,000 which was much less than one-half.

The judgment is affirmed." *Id.* at 675–676, 678–680.

See also *Schneider v. Schneider*, 183 Cal. 335, 191 P. 533, 11 A.L.R. 1386 (1920).

The court in *Coats* stressed the equitable character of the doctrine, not only as to the innocent putative spouse but also as to innocent third parties like creditors (Chapter 6). The court cautioned that the putative spouse doctrine should not apply where its application would deprive third persons of vested property rights.

Aside from this qualification, the division of equitable community property (now called "quasi-marital property") is analogous to the division of community and quasi-community property.

The equitable community doctrine quickly spiraled wide until it was codified. It is accepted knowledge that codification was not meant to restrict the doctrine's applicability, as explained in a recent influential putative spouse cases, *Ceja v. Rudolph & Sletten, Inc.,* 56 Cal. 4th 1113, 158 Cal.Rptr.3d 21, 302 P.3d 211 (2013), a wrongful death case.

3. *A putative spouse is defined as a person who has a* subjective *good faith belief in the validity of the marriage.* The term "good faith belief" is a legal term of art that is tested by a subjective standard after *Ceja.* Often both parties are innocent in their belief that a void or voidable marriage is valid. Sometimes only one party believes in good faith that the marriage is valid.

Before California Family Code Section 2251, court decisions held that a declaration of putative spouse status was to be based on the alleged putative spouse's subjective belief. The following cases illustrates.

Marriage of Monti, 135 Cal.App.3d 50, 185 Cal.Rptr. 72 (2d Dist. 1982) used a subjective standard where the parties entered into a valid marriage, then split up, then petitioned for dissolution. Sometime during the formal dissolution proceeding, the parties informally reconciled and lived together. Eleven years later, one party filed for dissolution, only to discover that she was already divorced. She petitioned for a declaration of putative spouse status saying that she had relied on the other party's statement, made eleven years earlier, that their pending dissolution would not become final unless he physically appeared in court. Since he did not appear in court, she believed their original marriage had not been dissolved. This was the party's subjective belief. But was it a reasonable belief? Would a hypothetical reasonable person believe that informally getting back together stops a formal dissolution proceeding from resulting in a court judgment?

Subsequently, a court of appeal changed the standard from a subjective good faith belief to an objective good faith belief in the case of *Marriage of Vryonis,* 202 Cal.App.3d 712, 248 Cal.Rptr. 807 (2d Dist. 1988). There Speros and Fereshteh, participated in a religious ceremony that the court refers to as a " 'Muta' marriage." No civil formalities were complied with. After the religious ceremony, Speros and Fereshteh lived apart, did not hold themselves out as married, dated other people, kept separate financial lives, and so on. Speros announced that he was going to marry a third party, at which point Fereshteh petitioned for a putative spouse declaration. The appellate court was skeptical about Fereshteh's petition as a matter of law. It ruled that good faith should be judged by an objective standard. As the court defined it, the issue was: Would the facts presented by the petition cause a hypothetical reasonable person to harbor a good faith belief in the existence of a valid marriage? The court rationalized its ruling by reference to criminal and contract cases, not family law cases.

Vryonis was the first California case to require an objective standard for determining putative spouse status. And it was persuasive enough to develop its own progeny. *Marriage of Xia Guo and Xiao Hua Sun,* 186 Cal.App.4th 1491, 112 Cal.Rptr.3d 906 (2d Dist. 2010) applied the objective standard, yet ruled that only an innocent party could be declared a putative spouse. So did *Marriage of Ramirez*, 165 Cal.App.4th 751, 81 Cal.Rptr.3d 180 (4th 2008). But how to reconcile the concept of "innocence" with "objective good faith?"

Ceja, supra, addresses the problem by returning the definition of good faith to one of subjective belief. In *Ceja,* Robert and Nancy hosted a large wedding in September 2003. At that time, Robert had not yet obtained a final judgment of dissolution of his prior marriage. He refused to talk with Nancy about his past, but on December 31, 2003, a final judgment of dissolution issued to Robert and his first spouse. That judgment was mailed to Robert and Nancy's home where Nancy came into possession of it. Nancy and Robert continued to live together as married persons, with Nancy testifying that she innocently believed that her marriage to Robert was valid under California law. After Robert was killed in a work accident, Nancy filed a wrongful death action. She asserted standing as Robert's legal wife under California Code of Civil Procedure Section 377.60, below. The Defendant successfully moved for summary judgment on the ground that Nancy was not married to Robert when he died, nor was she his putative spouse. The Defendant argued that Nancy had come into possession of legal documents (Robert and Nancy's September 2003 wedding certificate and the December 2003 final dissolution judgment for Robert's prior marriage) that were sufficiently date-inconsistent to put a hypothetical reasonable person on notice that Robert could not contract a marriage to Nancy in September 2003 because he was already married to someone else. Nancy appealed. She argued that she and Robert exchanged vows before a large audience and they lived and held themselves out as a married couple until Robert's death. Therefore—notwithstanding the various legal forms that came into her possession—it was Nancy's subjective belief that she and Robert were validly married. The court of appeal reversed. The Defendant sought review. The California Supreme Court affirmed the appellate court judgment.

The California Supreme Court's opinion in *Ceja* disapproves *Vryonis* and its progeny, including *Marriage of Guo & Sun, supra,* and *Marriage of Ramirez. Ceja* holds that the correct standard for putative spouse declaration is a subjective one, and the subjective standard carries over to wrongful death claims. Here is a summary of the court's rationale: One, the equitable putative spouse doctrine, which the state followed before its codification in the Family Code, defined "good faith" as a subjective belief in the validity of the marriage. Two, the legislature intended to and did continue the subjective good faith belief standard when it added the putative spouse doctrine into the Family Code as California Family Code Section 2251 in1992. Three, California Civil Procedure Code Section 377.60 uses the same language and codifies the same equitable principle as California Family Code Section 2251. Four, *Vryonis* wrongly states the policy underlying the putative spouse doctrine. The policy is not punitive it is protective of innocent parties, like Nancy, who believe they are married when they are not. Therefore, the correct standard for determining good faith for purposes of a putative spouse declaration is a subjective one.

After *Ceja,* "good faith" for purposes of California Family Code Section 2251 is judged on a case-by-case basis. The trial court is to take into account all relevant subjective facts, like whether there was a wedding ceremony, a marriage license, a marriage certificate (all indicate an innocent good faith belief in the validity of the marriage), the alleged putative spouse's background, education, language proficiency, experience, and any other circumstances that surround the marriage. Objective evidence of the marriage's invalidity is also admissible, particularly if it is relevant to the issue of the reasonableness of the alleged putative spouse's subjective belief. A court's ultimate goal, according to the *Ceja* opinion, is to use "the totality of the circumstances [to determine] whether the [petitioner's] belief was genuinely and honestly held." *Id.* at 1120.

4.   *Once a person is declared a putative spouse, that person has the option to seek division of property under the Family Code.* If the option is exercised the court shall divide the property of the putative marriage. California Family Code Section 2251 was amended in 2015, effective on January 1, 2016, to clarify that once a putative spouse opts for a Family Code dissolution, the court "shall" divide quasi-marital property but "[o]nly upon request of a party who is declared a putative spouse."

Marriage of Tejada, 179 Cal.App.4th 973, 102 Cal.Rptr.3d 361 (6th Dist. 2009), discussed below, had the declarant asking: if putative spouse statutes are intended to protect innocent parties, then why does a guilty party (the person who knew of the impediment in the marriage) still get one-half of the quasi-marital property?

The reason is that the option to seek dissolution under the Family Code belongs to the putative spouse. The spouse who knew about the impediment in the marriage does not have the same option. Therefore it is the putative spouse's choice to seek division under Family Code rules or under general Civil Code rules. If the putative spouse requests property division under the Family Code, division is mandatory and must proceed on a no-fault basis using quasi-marital property as a proxy for community property and quasi-community property.

The facts of *Tejada* are illustrative. Pablo and Petra enjoyed a Las Vegas, Nevada civil marriage ceremony in 1973. At the time Petra did not know that Pablo was married to another woman, Margarita. Pablo, of course, was aware that he was still married to Margarita because he had not yet dissolved his marriage to her on the date he purported to contract marriage to Petra. In fact, Pablo did not did obtain a final judgment of dissolution in the Pablo-Margarita marriage until 1976, three years after the exchange of vows with Petra. Like Speros and Fereshteh in *Vryonis, supra,* Pablo and Petra participated in a religious wedding ceremony in which no civil formalities were met. Unlike Speros and Fereshteh, however, Pablo and Petra lived together for thirty years as a married couple and had children together. When Pablo filed a petition for dissolution, Petra, having discovered the details of Pablo's marital status at their wedding, filed her own petition for dissolution. She later amended it to a petition for nullification on the ground of Pablo's bigamy. She requested a ruling on property issues. Rather than use the Civil Code, Petra's argued that all property acquired during the time she lived with Pablo should be confirmed as her separate property under the Family Code. The Superior Court of Santa Cruz County entered a judgment of nullity; but it ruled that the property of the Pablo-Petra marriage was quasi-marital property of the union, with Pablo and Petra each entitled to a one-half share. Petra appealed; she thought it unfair that Pablo could exit the union with one-half of the quasi-marital property given that he knew from the start the marriage was void.

The Sixth District Appellate Court analyzed the case under California Family Code Section 2551. The excerpt below, by McAdams, J., is important for how it identifies the purpose of the putative spouse statute as protective, not as fault-based:

> "The Statutory Language:
>
> The language of the governing statute is clear and unambiguous.
>
> Section 2251 requires two predicate findings: that the "marriage is void or voidable" and "that either party or both parties believed in good faith that the marriage was valid. . . ." (§ 2251, subd. (a).) If the predicate findings are made, "the court shall" do these two things: "(1) Declare the party or parties to have the status of a putative spouse" and (2) divide any quasi-marital property as if it were community property. (*Ibid.*)
>
> For purposes of this provision, "shall" is mandatory. (§ 12; *Estate of DePasse, supra,* 97 Cal.App.4th at p. 102, 118 Cal.Rptr.2d 143.)
>
> Putative Spouse Determination:
>
> Upon a finding that the marriage is invalid, the statute requires the court to declare any party with the requisite good faith belief to be a putative spouse.
>
> As Petra observes, "the status is not automatically applied to both parties, only those with a good faith belief in the validity of the marriage." In the words of one court: "The status of 'putative spouse' requires innocence or good faith belief." (*In re Marriage of Recknor* (1982) 138 Cal.App.3d 539, 544, 187 Cal.Rptr. 887; see *Estate of Vargas, supra,* 36 Cal.App.3d at p. 717, 111 Cal.Rptr. 779.)
>
> What Petra fails to acknowledge, however, is that once either party is a putative spouse, the union is a *putative marriage.* "By definition, a putative marriage is a union in which at least one partner believes in good faith that a valid marriage exists. As in this case, the couple conducts themselves as husband and wife throughout the period of their union." (*Estate of Leslie, supra,* 37 Cal.3d at p. 197, 207 Cal.Rptr. 561, 689 P.2d 133.) Thus, even where only one party has the requisite good faith belief in the validity of the marriage, thereby qualifying as the sole putative spouse, the court's declaration of his

or her status operates as a declaration that the union itself is a putative marriage.

Property Division:

The statute commands the court to divide the quasi-marital property as if it were community property, using these words: "If the division of property is in issue," the court shall "divide, in accordance with Division 7 (commencing with Section 2500), that property acquired during the union which would have been community property or quasi-community property if the union had not been void or voidable." (§ 2251, subd. (a)(2).) Division 7 governs the division of property; section 2550 generally requires the court to "divide the community estate of the parties equally."

Nothing in the language of section 2251's property division mandate suggests that it is limited to cases where both parties are putative spouses. To the contrary, read in combination with the preceding sentence—the grant of putative spouse status to "the party or parties"—it plainly compels division of the quasi-marital property regardless of whether both parties have been declared putative spouses. (§ 2251, subd. (a)(1).)

This reading is consistent with long-standing decisional law, which holds that "property acquired during the void or voidable union . . . is divided as community property would be divided upon the dissolution of a valid marriage." (*Estate of Hafner, supra,* 184 Cal.App.3d at p. 1384, 229 Cal.Rptr. 676.) "There is no reason to believe that the Legislature * * * intended to change those principles." (*Ibid.*)"

5. *Intestacy rights and the putative spouse.* California Family Code Section 2251 is dissolution focused. But what about termination of the union by death? Should the putative spouse be accorded the rights of a spouse with respect to other types of property or claims? Suppose that one party to the putative marriage dies intestate, leaving substantial separate property in addition to quasi-marital property. The putative spouse has a right to the decedent's one-half of the quasi-marital property. But should the putative survivor receive an intestate share of the decedent's separate property? The same share as a legal spouse? A greater share than the decedent's children? California Family Code Section 2254 provides that a putative spouse may also be deemed a "surviving spouse" for purposes of intestate distribution, but how should an equitable division be made?

In *Estate of Anderson*, 60 Cal.App.4th 436, 70 Cal.Rptr.2d 266 (1st Dist. 1997), an undivorced bigamous spouse was prevented from asserting his statutory inheritance rights as a surviving spouse against the intestate estate of his legally recognized first spouse. The facts showed that the plaintiff and decedent had been legally married in 1955. They separated in 1958, but never obtained a divorce. Shortly after separating, the plaintiff began cohabiting with a woman. They had five children, and ultimately "married" in 1993. At the time of the decedent's death, this second relationship was still intact. The decedent was survived by the plaintiff and by her mother. The trial court ruled that the plaintiff should be equitably estopped from asserting inheritance rights in the decedent's separate property. The appellate court affirmed, stating that the plaintiff "should not be allowed to 'blow hot and cold' by renouncing his marriage to decedent by swearing that the marriage never existed in order to remarry and then, after a thirty-eight year separation from decedent, seek a judicial declaration that he is decedent's surviving spouse for the purpose of inheriting an interest in assets acquired during the deceased's second marriage." *Id.* at 442.

The California Supreme Court answered the question of whether a putative spouse can claim intestate succession rights to a decedent's separate property in the affirmative in *Estate of Leslie,* 37 Cal.3d 186, 207 Cal.Rptr. 561, 689 P.2d 133 (1984).

The facts of *Estate of Leslie* are that on April 22, 1972, William Garvin and Fay Reah Leslie were married in Tijuana, Mexico. The marriage was invalid because it was never recorded, as is required by Mexican law. However, Garvin believed that he and Fay were validly married. The couple lived together for almost nine years until Fay's death in 1981, believing and holding themselves out to be married. Throughout this period, they resided in a house in Mira Loma. The house had been purchased by Fay, her former husband, and a son from a prior marriage who lived next door. On, February 6, 1981, Fay Leslie died intestate, she was survived by Garvin, her son Smith, and three other adult children from a prior marriage.

Smith filed a petition for letters of administration in the estate of his deceased mother. Garvin, Leslie's putative surviving spouse, objected to Smith's petition, filed his own petition for letters of administration, and sought a determination of who was entitled to distribution of the estate. The trial court found that a putative marriage had existed between Garvin and Fay, but then denied Garvin's petition for letters of administration, and determined that he was not entitled to any of Fay's separate property.

The California Supreme Court examined a long list of Court of Appeal decisions supporting the conclusion that a putative spouse is entitled to succeed to a share of the decedent's separate property. The court also considered other areas where the putative spouse is recognized as a surviving spouse: Public Employees' Retirement Law; workers' compensation death benefits; the civil service retirement statute (5 U.S.C. § 8341; the Longshoremen's and Harbor Workers' Compensation Act (33 U.S.C. § 901 et seq.); and the Social Security Act (42 U.S.C. § 416). Based on its research, the court explained:

> "The foregoing authority compels but one conclusion: a surviving putative spouse is entitled to succeed to a share of his or her decedent's separate property. This result is inherently fair. By definition, a putative marriage is a union in which at least one partner believes in good faith that a valid marriage exists. As in this

case, the couple conducts themselves as husband and wife throughout the period of their union. Why should the right to separate property accorded to legal spouses be denied to putative spouses?

Further, to deny a putative spouse the status of surviving spouse for the purposes of succeeding to a share of the decedent's separate property would lead to anomalous and unjust results. For example, where the decedent is survived by a putative spouse and children of the putative marriage, such a rule would deny the spouse succession rights to separate property even though the children are accorded such rights. Such a rule would also deny succession rights to a putative spouse who lived with the decedent for many years, while according these rights to the legal spouse, even if that spouse's partner died the day the couple were married. (Laughran & Laughran, *Property and Inheritance Rights of Putative Spouses in California: Selected Problems and Suggested Solutions* (1977) 11 Loyola L.A.L.Rev. 45, 68.) Surely, the Legislature never intended such results.

To accord a surviving putative spouse rights to the decedent's separate property honors rather than disregards the statutory scheme governing intestate succession. (Laughran & Laughran, *op. cit. supra,* 11 Loyola L.A.L.Rev. at p. 67; but see *Levie, supra,* 50 Cal.App.3d at p. 577, 123 Cal.Rptr. 445.) Since the right to succession is not an inherent or natural right, but purely a creature of statute (*Estate of Simmons* (1966) 64 Cal.2d 217, 221, 49 Cal.Rptr. 369, 411 P.2d 97), a surviving legal spouse inherits a decedent's separate property "only because the statutes provide that a person having the status of 'surviving spouse' takes a certain share." (Laughran & Laughran, *op. cit. supra,* 11 Loyola L.A.L.Rev. at p. 67.) To accord a surviving putative spouse the status of "surviving spouse" simply recognizes that a good faith belief in the marriage should put the putative spouse in the same position as a survivor of a legal marriage. (*Id.,* at p. 68.)" *Id.* at 197, 199.

6. *Overlapping relationships.* Some putative spouse situations are downright complicated. For example, in *Estate of Vargas*, 36 Cal.App.3d 714, 111 Cal.Rptr. 779 (2d Dist. 1974), Juan Vargas lived a double life as a husband and father to two different families, neither of which knew of the other's existence. This dual-family situation lasted for 24 years, ending only when Juan died intestate. Both of Juan's partners asserted the right to succeed to Juan's estate as his surviving spouse; both attempted to block the other from succeeding to any estate property. The trial court decided it fairest to divide the estate equally between the legal spouse and the putative spouse since both were in an ongoing marital relationship with the decedent when he died. The appellate court affirmed:

"In the present case, depending on which statute or legal theory is applied, both Mildred, as legal spouse, and Josephine, as putative spouse, have valid or plausible claims to at least half, perhaps three-quarters, possibly all, of Juan's estate. The court found that both wives contributed in indeterminable amounts and proportions to the accumulations of the community. (*Vallera v. Vallera*, 21 Cal.2d 681, 683, 134 P.2d 761.) Since statutes and judicial decisions provide no sure guidance for the resolution of the controversy, the probate court cut the Gordian knot of competing claims and divided the estate equally between the two wives, presumably on the theory that innocent wives of practicing bigamists are entitled to equal shares of property accumulated during the active phase of the bigamy. No injury has been visited upon third parties, and the wisdom of Solomon is not required to perceive the justice of the result." *Id.* at 719.

Estate of Vargas involved Juan's two intimate partners each of whom claimed status as Juan's surviving spouse under the Probate Code—the proverbial Gordian knot. By comparison, *Estate of Leslie* involved a simpler problem of a decedent who was survived by (only) one putative spouse and an adult son. For that reason the California Supreme Court declined to speculate about whether the division in *Vargas* was correct.

The Gordian knot problem came up yet again in *Estate of Hafner*, 184 Cal.App.3d 1371, 229 Cal.Rptr. 676 (2d Dist. 1986)—there the issue was how to divide the decedent's approximately half-million dollar estate between his long abandoned surviving legal spouse and four children, on the one hand, and his surviving putative spouse, on the other.

7.   *The Gordian knot. Hafner* involved a legal spouse and a putative spouse, both of whom sought a share of the decedent's estate. *Hafner* is an opinion with literary qualities because of the way that it analyzes the problem from each participant's perspective. The court turns the facts over and over, looking for an answer to how to weigh the equities in a case where the decedent left a trail of innocent survivors.

> "Joan Hafner (Joan) and the decedent Charles J. Hafner (Charles) were married on June 12, 1954, in the State of New York; it was the first marriage for each of them. Following their marriage they took up residence in College Point, New York. Joan has continued to live in or near College Point ever since. The marriage between Joan and Charles produced three daughters, all of whom are now living: Catherine Kotsay, born December 25, 1955; Lillian Mayorga, born November 18, 1956; and Dorothy Hafner, born November 16, 1957.
>
> In February or March of 1956 Joan learned that she was pregnant with her second child and told Charles. In April or May of 1956 Charles left Joan, without prior notice and without letting her know where he would be. At that time their first child, Catherine, was sick and Joan moved back to her parents, who supported her; she received no support from Charles.

Joan and Charles were reunited briefly in early 1957. Charles left Joan for the last time in February 1957. Joan, then pregnant with their third child, encountered Charles on the street in New York in May 1957. He told her, "I hear you are going to have another baby", and asked her whether she would like to go to California. Joan replied, "What guarantees would I have that you won't leave me pregnant again?" Charles replied, 'There's no guarantees.'

In 1956 and 1958, Joan filed support proceedings against Charles in the New York family court. In 1956, she obtained a $12 per week child support order and in 1958 she obtained a similar order for $20 per week. Charles made four support payments in 1958 but never made any other payments. In 1958, Joan consulted an attorney in New York on the support matters, but, because of the expense required to locate Charles in California, she did not pursue the matter. In 1961, Joan abandoned any further efforts to obtain support warrants in the New York family court because such efforts caused her to lose time on her job.

Joan last saw Charles in the New York family court in 1958 when he was brought before the court on a support warrant. Shortly after that appearance, an acquaintance told Joan that Charles had gone to California. From 1958 until his death in 1982, Joan and Charles never saw or communicated with each other again. Joan knew that Charles was in California but did not know where in California.

Beginning in 1961, and continuously thereafter, Joan considered her marriage to Charles for all practicable purposes to have ended and that they would never reconcile or even see each other again.

Except for short intervals to have their babies, Joan was employed at all times following her marriage to Charles, and was so employed at the time of the trial below. She reared the three daughters of herself and decedent.

In August, 1953, shortly after graduating from high school, Joan commenced working at a magazine company and continued until August, 1955, when she left because she was pregnant with her first daughter. In April, 1957, she went to work on the assembly line of a rubber company, on a machine putting snaps on baby pants. Except for a three-month lay-off to have her third baby she stayed on that machine for about 12 years, when the company moved away. She started at the minimum wage and later became a piece worker. After two weeks of unemployment she went to work for a glove manufacturing company, starting as an order picker, filling orders, and later as a stock supervisor, making sure that the orders were picked and sent out. She was still so employed at the time of the trial of the within action and had then been working at the glove factory for 14 and a half years.

Joan never sought a divorce from Charles; it is unclear whether she did not seek a divorce because of religious convictions, the lack of financial resources, or a lack of interest. At no time from their marriage in 1954 until his death on December 25, 1982, did Charles ever file proceedings to dissolve his marriage to Joan. Their marriage was still in full force and effect at the time of Charles' death.

Respondent Helen L. Hafner (Helen) met Charles in 1962 when he was a patron at a beer bar where she was working as a barmaid. Helen had separated from her second husband, Eldon Pomeroy, in November, 1961.

Charles told Helen that he had divorced his wife, Joan, in New York on charges of adultery, that he had three children of that marriage with Joan, and that he had given up an interest in a house in lieu of child support. Charles further stated that the divorce records had been destroyed in a fire in New York. Helen, in good faith, relied on these representations and believed them to be true continuously thereafter; she had no actual knowledge or reasonable grounds to believe otherwise.

In July 1962, Helen and Charles went to Tijuana, Mexico, to enable Helen to obtain a divorce from Pomeroy and to participate in a marriage ceremony with Charles. Both of those objectives were accomplished. Helen, in good faith, believed that both the divorce and marriage were valid. Following their return from Tijuana in 1962, Helen and Charles lived as husband and wife.

Helen's second husband, Pomeroy, was killed in an accident on June 21, 1963. In June 1963, Helen consulted an attorney and was advised that her Mexican divorce from Pomeroy was invalid in California. Following Pomeroy's death Helen and Charles went to Las Vegas, Nevada, and participated in a marriage ceremony. After that marriage ceremony, on October 14, 1963, Helen and Charles returned to the Los Angeles area where they lived and held themselves out as husband and wife until Charles' death. They had one child, Kimberly Hafner, born December 10, 1964.

On September 27, 1973, Charles was seriously injured in an automobile accident which left him with permanent physical disabilities and brain damage that rendered him incapable of employment. During the nine months in the hospital and his subsequent recovery period, Helen faithfully attended to his needs as his wife and continued to do so for some nine years until his death.

Charles and Helen accumulated approximately $69,000 in hospital and doctor bills as a result of the accident. Those bills were not paid until Charles' personal injury action was settled for $900,000, in 1975, which netted decedent $600,000 after attorney's fees. Helen and her attorney, Charles Weldon, were appointed as

Charles' co-conservators in 1975. The personal injury settlement was placed in conservatorship accounts and administered under court supervision. The conservatorship assets were subsequently transferred to Charles' probate administrator following Charles' death.

Charles Hafner died intestate on December 25, 1982, leaving an estate appraised at $416,472.40; his entire probate estate consists of the remainder of the proceeds of his personal injury settlement. * * *

Helen filed a petition for determination of entitlement to estate (former § 1080), claiming to be the surviving wife of Charles and seeking to have the probate court determine the persons entitled to share in the distribution of Charles' estate.

Appellants (Joan and the three daughters) filed a response to the petition and a statement of interest, asserting their respective claims to a share of Charles' estate, as his surviving spouse and children, pursuant to section 221. Kimberly Hafner, a child of Charles, also filed a statement of interest in the state.

Appellants claimed that they, together with Kimberly, should succeed to Charles' entire estate under section 221, and that even if Helen were found to be a good faith putative spouse the court should, under equitable principles, divide the estate among them. * * *

Helen's petition came on for a nonjury trial on January 12, 1984. Following the conclusion of the trial, the court rendered its statement of decision, on February 1, 1984, in which it concluded that Helen had a legal right to succeed to Charles' entire estate as his surviving spouse under Probate Code section 201. The court also concluded that Helen was Charles' good faith putative spouse and that it would be inequitable to deny her Charles' entire estate." *Id.* at 1377–1381.

Relying on pre-1969 decisional law, the court found that Charles' property should be awarded one-half to his putative spouse, Helen, and the other half to his legal and surviving spouse, Joan, and his four children, Catherine, Lillian, Dorothy and Kimberly, in accordance with of the intestacy provisions in the Probate Code.

Presiding Acting Justice Lui dissented, reasoning that intestate succession in California is governed exclusively by statute. The basic flaw in the majority's analysis, according to Justice Lui, is that it attempts to apply equitable principles to distribute the whole of Charles's estate instead of following the statutory scheme, as is required. Lui said that in codifying the putative spouse doctrine [now California Family Code Section 2251], the Legislature established the vested legal right of a surviving *putative* spouse (in this case Helen), to the quasi-marital property of her union with Charles. In the case of dissolution, wrote Lui, "each spouse is entitled to one-half of the quasi-marital property." *Id.* at 1401. Likewise, in the case of intestacy, a surviving putative spouse (in this case Helen) is entitled to the decedent's one-half of the quasi-marital property. That right is vested in the surviving putative spouse, and thus not subject to the claims of any other person, including the decedent's legal spouse (in this case Joan). Lui concludes:

> "The proper legal distribution of the decedent's estate in this case should result in the surviving putative spouse taking one-half of the decedent's entire estate pursuant to section 4452 [California Family Code Section 2251] as her quasi-marital property. As to the remainder of the decedent's estate, following the mandate in *Leslie*, the putative and legal spouses should be treated equally. Therefore, under former Probate Code section 221, the proper legal distribution of the remainder of the decedent's estate should be as follows: one-third of that portion of the estate should be divided equally between the surviving putative and legal spouses; the remaining two-thirds should be distributed in equal shares to the decedent's four children by both relationships." *Id.* at 1403.

One question for Justice Lui: is the putative spouse's right to quasi-marital property vested upon being legally declared a putative spouse by a court? Or, upon the declarant formally opting for a Family Code based disposition?

8.   *Nonmarried cohabitants are precluded from asserting claims under the putative spouse doctrine, but they may assert* Marvin *claims. Velez v. Smith,* 142 Cal.App.4th 1154, 48 Cal.Rptr.3d 642 (1st Dist. 2006). A *Marvin* claim is a civil action, not a family court dissolution, brought between nonmarried intimate cohabitants. *Marvin v. Marvin* is reprinted below.

9.   *Wrongful death.* California Code of Civil Procedure 377.50(a) permits a wrongful death action to be asserted by the decedent's surviving spouse, as defined by California Probate Code Section 78. Additionally, California Code of Civil Procedure 377.50(b) permits a dependent putative spouse to bring a wrongful death action and defines "putative spouse" identically to the California Family Code 2251 definition.

WEST'S ANNOTATED CALIFORNIA
CODE OF CIVIL PROCEDURE

§ 377.60. Persons with standing

A cause of action for the death of a person caused by the wrongful act or neglect of another may be asserted by any of the following persons or by the decedent's personal representative on their behalf:

(a) The decedent's surviving spouse, domestic partner, children, and issue of deceased children, or, if there is no surviving issue of the decedent, the persons, including the surviving spouse or domestic partner, who would be entitled to the property of the decedent by intestate succession.

(b) Whether or not qualified under subdivision (a), if they were dependent on the decedent, the putative spouse, children of the putative spouse, stepchildren, or parents. As used in this subdivision, "putative spouse" means the surviving spouse of a void or voidable marriage who is found by the court to have believed in good faith that the marriage to the decedent was valid.

* * *

(f)(1) For the purposes of this section "domestic partner" means a person who, at the time of the decedent's death, was the domestic partner of the decedent in a registered domestic partnership established in accordance with subdivision (b) of Section 297 of the Family Code.

* * *

(Added by Stats. 1992, c. 178 (S.B. 1496), § 20. Amended by Stats. 1996, c. 563 (S.B. 392), § 1; Stats. 1997, c. 13 (S.B. 449), § 1, eff. May 23, 1997; Stats. 2001, c. 893 (A.B. 25), § 2; Stats. 2004, c. 947 (A.B. 2580), § 1.)

B. INTIMATE NONMARRIED COHABITANTS

After marriage equality (*Obergefell*, Chapter 1) California retains three distinct options for intimate partners. Marriage. Domestic partnership for age eligible couples. Nonmarriage.

Who are nonmarried cohabitants? What is nonmarried cohabitancy? Often the phrase is defined by analogy to marriage. The view holds that nonmarried cohabitants are two people who are not married, know they are not married, and live together as if they were married. No doubt some nonmarried cohabitants approve of the analogy, while others do not. For some people, marriage is not an institution they want to have any part of.

Aside from the empirical question of personal preference, nonmarried cohabitancy raises broader social and legal issues. Should a marriage analogy be applied to intimate partners who have specifically opted to reject marriage for the relationship in question? Does the use of a marriage analogy make an implicit normative claim that status as a married person is preferable to status as a single person? If so, what gender unfairness lurks in the marriage analogy? Does the assumption that nonmarried partners are waiting to marry fling us back to a time when cohabitation was disapproved of, covered up, or otherwise illegal? Would the legal adoption of the term "living together as a couple" do away with imbedded normative or sexist assumption of the marriage analogy?

Would a family analogy be more or less problematic than a marriage analogy? Does a family analogy sidestep concerns about gender unfairness? Does it elevate status as a parent over status as a person without legal parental obligations? Would a legal definition that links nonmarried cohabitants to family be legally practicable? What is a family? When does it come into being? When do family obligations end, if ever? Does a single definition of family hold in a jurisdiction as diverse as California? Can it?

One perhaps useful definition of nonmarried cohabitants is that they are people, presumably two but not necessarily two, who live together intimately, without also contracting a civil marriage. They may reject marriage altogether. They may reject civil marriage but embrace religious marriage. They may be contemplating marriage (see Chapter 3). They may be engaged. They may approve of marriage, but one or both may still be married to someone else. And the possibilities go on.

The nonmarried cohabitants (again, I'm presuming two persons) in the above categories have two things in common. One, they live together knowing that they are not married, which precludes them from seeking putative spouse status. Two, if they break up or one dies, their claims against each other cannot be brought under the Family Code or various family protection sections of the Probate Code (Chapter 9).

Nonmarried intimate cohabitants, in other words, form intimate personal, physical and financial lives together, without the rights or obligations of the Family Code as their default contract. The couples must arrange their affairs by general contract, property, trust, or partnership law. Some do so with intentionality. Others consider the impact of their intertwined lives only from the point of a break-up or a death, leaving one partner to lump it (walk away with less than they are legally entitled to, assuming proof of their claims against the other) or else rely on contract remedies, implied trust remedies, resulting and constructive thrust theories, proprietary estoppel, fraud, and other heavily fact based (and therefore time consuming and expensive to litigate) theories for asserting a claim upon which relief can be granted.

Here is an often-cited early case on the issue of adjudicating the property claims of intimate partners who live together knowing that they are not married.

VALLERA V. VALLERA
21 Cal.2d 681, 134 P.2d 761 (1943)

TRAYNOR, JUSTICE.

Plaintiff brought this action for separate maintenance and for a division of community property, which she alleged was worth at least $60,000.

* * * The trial court found that plaintiff and defendant did not on December 16, 1938, or at any other time contract a common law marriage in Michigan or elsewhere; that they did not at any time enter into or attempt to enter into an agreement to take each other as husband and wife; that beginning in May, 1936, and for at least three years thereafter, plaintiff cohabited * * * with defendant; that between January, 1933, and December 15, 1938, defendant was married to Ethel Chippo Vallera; that

plaintiff knew from the beginning of her relationship with defendant that he was married and under a legal disability to enter into a marriage contract with her; that while the marriage between defendant and Ethel Chippo Vallera was dissolved on December 15, 1938, neither plaintiff nor defendant learned of its dissolution until November, 1939; and that on July 6, 1940, defendant entered into a valid marriage with Lido Cappello. The court concluded that plaintiff and defendant had never been husband and wife; that plaintiff was not entitled to maintenance; and that there was no community property. It held, however, that all property acquired by the parties between December 16, 1938, and July 6, 1940, except such property as either might have acquired by gift, devise, bequest, or descent, was held by them as tenants in common, each owning an undivided one-half thereof, and defendant has appealed from this part of the judgment. He contends that since there was no marriage, no attempt to contract marriage, no belief in the existence of a valid marriage, no evidence of any agreement between the parties as to their property rights, and no evidence concerning the accumulation of property or contributions by the parties thereto, plaintiff could not acquire the rights of a cotenant in property acquired by him during the period of illicit cohabitation.

It is well settled that a woman who lives with a man as his wife in the belief that a valid marriage exists is entitled upon termination of their relationship to share in the property acquired by them during its existence. [Citations omitted.] The proportionate contribution of each party to the property is immaterial in this state (Coats v. Coats, supra; Macchi v. La Rocca, 54 Cal.App. 98, 201 P. 143), for the property is divided as community property would be upon the dissolution of a valid marriage. * * *

The essential basis of a putative marriage, however, is a belief in the existence of a valid marriage. Flanagan v. Capital Nat. Bank, 213 Cal. 664, 3 P.2d 307; see Evans, Property Interests Arising from Quasi-Marital Relations, 9 Corn.L.Q. 246; 20 Cal.L.Rev. 453. * * * The controversy is thus reduced to the question whether a woman living with a man as his wife but with no genuine belief that she is legally married to him acquires by reason of cohabitation alone the rights of a co-tenant in his earnings and accumulations during the period of their relationship. It has already been answered in the negative. Flanagan v. Capital Nat. Bank, 213 Cal. 664, 3 P.2d 307. Equitable considerations arising from the reasonable expectation of the continuation of benefits attending the status of marriage entered into in good faith are not present in such a case.

Plaintiff's lack of good faith in alleging the belief that she had entered into a valid marriage would not, however, preclude her from recovering property to which she would otherwise be entitled. If a man and woman live together as husband and wife under an agreement to pool their earnings and share equally in their joint accumulations, equity will protect the interests of each in such property. [Citations omitted.] Even in the absence of an express agreement to that effect, the woman would be entitled to share in the property jointly accumulated, in the proportion that her funds contributed toward its acquisition. Hayworth v. Williams, supra; Delamour v. Roger, 7 La.Ann. 152. There is no evidence that the parties in the present case made any agreement concerning their property or property rights. The meager evidence with respect to the accumulation of the alleged community property can support only the inference that the property consisted of defendant's earnings during the period in question, and there is no contention to the contrary. There is thus no support in the record for the trial court's finding that the parties each owned an undivided one-half of the property acquired by either of them between December 16, 1938, and July 5, 1940.

* * *

The part of the judgment appealed from is reversed.

CURTIS, JUSTICE (dissenting in part). * * * In the absence of any proof of any cash or property contribution by the plaintiff, the holding of the trial court that she owned a one-half interest in the property accumulated must have been based upon the conclusion that the value of her services as a housekeeper, cook, and homemaker was of sufficient value to warrant an equal division of the property. The majority opinion substitutes its own appraisal of the value of her services in the home as being of no more value than the cost of maintenance of herself and her two children. The holding of the trial court seems to me more reasonable. * * *

————

In the intervening years, California courts heard numerous cases involving parties who were presumably contemplating a marriage that never occurred. The contemplating marriage cause of action required use of the marriage analogy. It obviously also included within its ambit persons who were cohabitating as intimate partners with no serious intention of ever marrying. At break-up, a cause of action accrued if property had been exchanged and proof of some contemplation, however, minor could be offered. Socially, these cases were dealt with behind the façade of "contemplating marriage," a personal status that allowed the plaintiff to invoke civil code statutes to seek return of property exchanged with a former intimate partner (Chapter 3).

Then, in 1976, the California Supreme Court decided *Marvin v. Marvin*, a case often included on lists of the most important cases of the twentieth century. Justice Tobriner wrote the opinion in which he took note of important social changes. Up until the mid-twentieth century, cohabitation was outright illegal in some (Western) countries and jurisdictions. Or it was hidden behind the "contemplating marriage" façade. But by the time Michelle Triolla sued her intimate cohabitant Lee

Marvin for breach of contract, the Summer of Love had occurred, cohabitation was on the rise (it still is), and social mores were changing to the point that it would have been laughable to press charges or otherwise bring legal penalties to bear against consenting adults who made the choice to live together without being married.

The policy issue for the Marvin court was not whether nonmarried cohabitation was acceptable. At the time it already was. The issue was whether a nonmarried cohabitant could enforce a verbal agreement for property division and support in a civil court. In deciding that issue the court established the following framework:

- The distribution of property acquired during a nonmarital relationship is not governed by the Family Law Act;

- Nonmarital partners can enforce agreements between them except to the extent that those agreements explicitly exchange sex for property or support;

- Absent an express written agreement, the courts can and should inquire into the conduct of the parties to determine whether it demonstrates an implied agreement, an agreement of partnership or joint venture, or some other tacit understanding between the parties;

- If there is no express, implied, or tacit agreement between the parties, and the facts of the case warrant, the courts may also employ the doctrine of quantum meruit, or other equitable remedies such as constructive or resulting trusts.

NOTE

California law does not recognize informal marriage; no U.S. jurisdiction recognizes informal dissolution.

The phrase "common law" marriage is often misused to refer to intimate nonmarried cohabitants. When a state does not permit informal marriage contracts, cohabitants are just that, cohabitants; even if they hold each other out as spouse and spouse.

When a state permits informal marriage, as Texas does, an informal marriage can be recognized as a valid marriage in California. A marriage is valid in California if it is valid where contracted.

The etymology of the phrase "common law marriage" is gender biased against women in the extreme. It appears in older common law state cases to refer to a woman who, for whatever reason (from the male partner's point of view), is not eligible (read suitable) for marriage. So too the term "meretricious relationship." Far more fanciful, but still conveying the same deeply biased attitude toward the female or non-wage earning partner.

Despite problems with terminology, the term "meretricious relationship" still appears in the case law about nonmarried intimate cohabitants.

The next case, *Marvin v. Marvin*, was brought by Michelle Triolla (1932–2009), a graduate of UCLA, and an actress who worked in the late 1950s through the 1990s. Michelle lived with Lee Marvin, a wealthy and elite-talent celebrity. She was his intimate partner from 1965 to 1970. Upon her break up with Lee, Michelle sued him for one-half of the $3.6 million he had earned while the two lived together.

Michelle's civil complaint alleged that she and Lee had an oral agreement that they would work together, earn together, and share any and all property accumulated as a result of their efforts whether individual or combined.

Michelle's civil complaint also alleged that Lee had verbally promised to support Michelle. The terms of support agreement were that the parties would hold themselves out in public as husband and wife, which would require Michelle to be a companion, homemaker, housekeeper and cook to Lee. Lee in exchange promised to support Michelle for the rest of her life, in consideration for her giving up her own career. The housekeeping services were not sexual in nature, though of course Michelle and Lee also had sex. They were intimate partners, after all.

Neither agreement was in writing.

At the time that Lee and Michelle moved in together. Lee was married to wife Betty. What about Betty? An important point to remember is that the existence of a valid marriage does not shield a person from the civil claims of a nonmarried cohabitant. Had Michelle prevailed, Lee would have been obligated notwithstanding his existing marriage to Betty or any subsequent marriage.

In the end, Michelle was unable to prove either a property or a support agreement.

MARVIN V. MARVIN
18 Cal.3d 660, 134 Cal.Rptr. 815, 557 P.2d 106 (1976)

TOBRINER, JUSTICE.

During the past 15 years, there has been a substantial increase in the number of couples living together without marrying. Such nonmarital relationships lead to legal controversy when one partner dies or the couple separates. Courts of Appeal, faced with the task of determining property rights in such cases, have arrived at conflicting positions: two cases (In re Marriage of Cary (1973) 34 Cal.App.3d 345, 109 Cal.Rptr. 862; Estate of Atherley (1975) 44 Cal.App.3d 758, 119 Cal.Rptr. 41) have held that the Family Law Act (Civ.Code, § 4000 et seq.) requires division of the property according to community property principles, and one decision (Beckman v. Mayhew (1975) 49 Cal.App.3d 529, 122 Cal.Rptr. 604) has rejected that holding. We take this opportunity to resolve that controversy and to declare the principles which should govern distribution of property acquired in a nonmarital relationship.

We conclude: (1) The provisions of the Family Law Act do not govern the distribution of property acquired during a nonmarital relationship; such a relationship remains subject solely to judicial decision. (2) The courts should enforce express contracts between nonmarital partners except to the extent that the contract is explicitly founded on the consideration of meretricious sexual services. (3) In the absence of an express contract, the courts should inquire into the conduct of the parties to determine whether that conduct demonstrates an implied contract, agreement of partnership or joint venture, or some other tacit understanding between the parties. The courts may also employ the doctrine of quantum meruit, or equitable remedies such as constructive or resulting trusts, when warranted by the facts of the case.

In the instant case plaintiff and defendant lived together for seven years without marrying; all property acquired during this period was taken in defendant's name. When plaintiff sued to enforce a contract under which she was entitled to half the property and to support payments, the trial court granted judgment on the pleadings for defendant, thus leaving him with all property accumulated by the couple during their relationship. Since the trial court denied plaintiff a trial on the merits of her claim, its decision conflicts with the principles stated above, and must be reversed.

1.   The Factual Setting of This Appeal

* * *

Plaintiff avers that in October of 1964 she and defendant "entered into an oral agreement" that while "the parties lived together they would combine their efforts and earnings and would share equally any and all property accumulated as a result of their efforts whether individual or combined." Furthermore, they agreed to "hold themselves out to the general public as husband and wife" and that "plaintiff would further render her services as a companion, homemaker, housekeeper and cook to * * * defendant."

Shortly thereafter plaintiff agreed to "give up her lucrative career as an entertainer [and] singer" in order to "devote her full time to defendant * * * as a companion, homemaker, housekeeper and cook;" in return defendant agreed to "provide for all of plaintiff's financial support and needs for the rest of her life."

Plaintiff alleges that she lived with defendant from October of 1964 through May of 1970 and fulfilled her obligations under the agreement. During this period the parties as a result of their efforts and earnings acquired in defendant's name substantial real and personal property, including motion picture rights worth over $1 million. In May of 1970, however, defendant compelled plaintiff to leave his household. He continued to support plaintiff until November of 1971, but thereafter refused to provide further support.

On the basis of these allegations plaintiff asserts two causes of action. The first, for declaratory relief, asks the court to determine her contract and property rights; the second seeks to impose a constructive trust upon one half of the property acquired during the course of the relationship.

* * *

2.   Plaintiff's Complaint States a Cause of Action
for Breach of an Express Contract

In Trutalli v. Meraviglia (1932) 215 Cal. 698, 12 P.2d 430 we established the principle that nonmarital partners may lawfully contract concerning the ownership of property acquired during the relationship. We reaffirmed this principle in Vallera v. Vallera (1943) 21 Cal.2d 681, 685, 134 P.2d 761, 763, stating that "If a man and woman [who are not married] live together as husband and wife under an agreement to pool their earnings and share equally in their joint accumulations, equity will protect the interests of each in such property."

In the case before us plaintiff, basing her cause of action in contract upon these precedents, maintains that the trial court erred in denying her a trial on the merits of her contention. Although that court did not specify the ground for its conclusion that plaintiff's contractual allegations stated no cause of action, defendant offers some four theories to sustain the ruling; we proceed to examine them.

Defendant first and principally relies on the contention that the alleged contract is so closely related to the supposed "immoral" character of the relationship between plaintiff and himself that the enforcement of the contract would violate public policy. He points to cases asserting that a contract between nonmarital partners is unenforceable if it is "involved in" an illicit relationship [Citations omitted.] A review of the numerous California decisions concerning contracts between nonmarital partners, however, reveals that the courts have not employed such broad and uncertain standards to strike down contracts. The decisions instead disclose a narrower and more precise standard: a contract between nonmarital partners is unenforceable only *to the extent* that it *explicitly* rests upon the immoral and illicit consideration of meretricious sexual services.

* * *

Although the past decisions hover over the issue in the somewhat wispy form of the figures of a Chagall painting, we can abstract from those decisions a clear and simple rule. The fact that [two people] live together without marriage, and engage in a sexual relationship, does not in itself invalidate agreements between them relating to their earnings, property, or expenses. Neither is such an agreement invalid merely because the parties may have contemplated the creation or continuation of a nonmarital relationship when they entered into it. Agreements between nonmarital partners fail only to the extent that they rest upon a consideration of meretricious sexual services. Thus the rule asserted by defendant, that a contract fails if it is "involved in" or made "in contemplation" of a nonmarital relationship, cannot be reconciled with the decisions.

* * *

The principle that a contract between nonmarital partners will be enforced unless expressly and inseparably based upon an illicit consideration of sexual services not only represents the distillation of the decisional law, but also offers a far more precise and workable standard than that advocated by defendant. Our recent decision in In re Marriage of Dawley (1976) 17 Cal.3d 342, 551 P.2d 323, offers a close analogy. Rejecting the contention that an antenuptial agreement is invalid if the parties contemplated a marriage of short duration, we pointed out in *Dawley* that a standard based upon the subjective contemplation of the parties is uncertain and unworkable; such a test, we stated, "might invalidate virtually all antenuptial agreements on the ground that the parties contemplated dissolution * * * but it provides no principled basis for determining which antenuptial agreements offend public policy and which do not." (17 Cal.3d 342, 352, 551 P.2d 323, 329.)

Similarly, in the present case a standard which inquires whether an agreement is "involved" in or "contemplates" a nonmarital relationship is vague and unworkable. Virtually all agreements between nonmarital partners can be said to be "involved" in some sense in the fact of their mutual sexual relationship, or to "contemplate" the existence of that relationship. Thus defendant's proposed standards, if taken literally, might invalidate all agreements between nonmarital partners, a result no one favors. Moreover, those standards offer no basis to distinguish between valid and invalid agreements. By looking not to such uncertain tests, but only to the consideration underlying the agreement, we provide the parties and the courts with a practical guide to determine when an agreement between nonmarital partners should be enforced.

Defendant secondly relies upon the ground suggested by the trial court: that the 1964 contract violated public policy because it impaired the community property rights of Betty Marvin, defendant's lawful wife. Defendant points out that his earnings while living apart from his wife before rendition of the interlocutory decree were community property under 1964 statutory law (former Civ.Code, §§ 169, 169.2) and that defendant's agreement with plaintiff purported to transfer to her a half interest in that community property. But whether or not defendant's contract with plaintiff exceeded his authority as manager of the community property (see former Civ.Code, § 172), defendant's argument fails for the reason that an improper transfer of community property is not void *ab initio,* but merely voidable at the instance of the aggrieved spouse. (See Ballinger v. Ballinger (1937) 9 Cal.2d 330, 334, 70 P.2d 629; Trimble v. Trimble (1933) 219 Cal. 340, 344, 26 P.2d 477.)

In the present case Betty Marvin, the aggrieved spouse, had the opportunity to assert her community property rights in the divorce action. (See Babbitt v. Babbitt (1955) 44 Cal.2d 289, 293, 282 P.2d 1.) The interlocutory and final decrees in that action fix and limit her interest. Enforcement of the contract between plaintiff and defendant against property awarded to defendant by the divorce decree will not impair any right of Betty's, and thus is not on that account violative of public policy.

Defendant's third contention is noteworthy for the lack of authority advanced in its support. He contends that enforcement of the oral agreement between plaintiff and himself is barred by Civil Code section 5134, which provides that "All contracts for marriage settlements must be in writing * * * ." A marriage settlement, however, is an agreement in contemplation of marriage in which each party agrees to release or modify the property rights which would otherwise arise from the marriage. (See Corker v. Corker (1891) 87 Cal. 643, 648, 25 P. 922.) The contract at issue here does not conceivably fall within that definition, and thus is beyond the compass of section 5134.

Defendant finally argues that enforcement of the contract is barred by Civil Code section 43.5, subdivision (d), which provides that "No cause of action arises for * * * [b]reach of a promise of marriage." This rather strained contention proceeds from the premise that a promise of marriage impliedly includes a promise to support and to pool property acquired after marriage (see Boyd v. Boyd (1964) 228 Cal.App.2d 374, 39 Cal.Rptr. 400) to the conclusion that pooling and support agreements not part of or accompanied by promise of marriage are barred by the section. We conclude that section 43.5 is not reasonably susceptible to the interpretation advanced by defendant, a conclusion demonstrated by the fact that since section 43.5 was enacted in 1939, numerous cases have enforced pooling agreements between nonmarital partners, and in none did court or counsel refer to section 43.5.

In summary, we base our opinion on the principle that adults who voluntarily live together and engage in sexual relations are nonetheless as competent as any other persons to contract respecting their earnings and property rights. Of course, they cannot lawfully contract to pay for the performance of sexual services, for such a contract is, in essence, an agreement for prostitution and unlawful for that reason. But they may agree to pool their earnings and to hold all property acquired during the relationship in accord with the law governing community property; conversely they may agree that each partner's earnings and the property acquired from those earnings remains the separate property of the earning partner. So long as the agreement does not rest upon illicit meretricious consideration, the parties may order their economic affairs as they choose, and no policy precludes the courts from enforcing such agreements.

In the present instance, plaintiff alleges that the parties agreed to pool their earnings, that they contracted to share equally in all property acquired, and that defendant agreed to support plaintiff. The terms of the contract as alleged do not rest upon any unlawful consideration. We therefore conclude that the complaint furnishes a suitable basis upon which the trial court can render declaratory relief. (See 3 Witkin, Cal.Procedure (2d ed.) pp. 2335–2336.) The trial court consequently erred in granting defendant's motion for judgment on the pleadings.

3.   Plaintiff's Complaint Can Be Amended to State a Cause of Action Founded Upon Theories of Implied Contract or Equitable Relief

As we have noted, both causes of action in plaintiff's complaint allege an express contract; neither assert any basis for relief independent from the contract. In In re Marriage of Cary, supra, 34 Cal.App.3d 345, 109 Cal.Rptr. 862, however, the Court of Appeal held that, in view of the policy of the Family Law Act, property accumulated by nonmarital partners in an actual family relationship should be divided equally. Upon examining the *Cary* opinion, the parties to the present case realized that plaintiff's alleged relationship with defendant might arguably support a cause of action independent of any express contract between the parties. The parties have therefore briefed and discussed the issue of the property rights of a nonmarital partner in the absence of an express contract. Although our conclusion that plaintiff's complaint states a cause of action based on an express contract alone compels us to reverse the judgment for defendant, resolution of the *Cary* issue will serve both to guide the parties upon retrial and to resolve a conflict presently manifest in published Court of Appeal decisions.

Both plaintiff and defendant stand in broad agreement that the law should be fashioned to carry out the reasonable expectations of the parties. Plaintiff, however, presents the following contentions: that the decisions prior to *Cary* rest upon implicit and erroneous notions of punishing a party for his or her guilt in entering into a nonmarital relationship, that such decisions result in an inequitable distribution of property accumulated during the relationship, and that *Cary* correctly held that the enactment of the Family Law Act in 1970 overturned those prior decisions. Defendant in response maintains that the prior decisions merely applied common law principles of contract and property to persons who have deliberately elected to remain outside the bounds of the community property system. *Cary,* defendant contends, erred in holding that the Family Law Act vitiated the force of the prior precedents.

As we shall see from examination of the pre-*Cary* decisions, the truth lies somewhere between the positions of plaintiff and defendant. The classic opinion on this subject is Vallera v. Vallera, supra, 21 Cal.2d 681, 134 P.2d 761. Speaking for a four-member majority, Justice Traynor posed the question: "whether a woman living with a man as his wife but with no genuine belief that she is legally married to him acquires by reason of cohabitation alone the rights of a cotenant in his earnings and accumulations during the period of their relationship." (21 Cal.2d at p. 684, 134 P.2d at p. 762.) Citing Flanagan v. Capital Nat. Bank (1931) 213 Cal. 664, 3 P.2d 307, which held that a nonmarital "wife" could not claim that her husband's estate was community property, the majority answered that question "in the negative." (21 Cal.2d pp. 684–685, 134 P.2d 761.) *Vallera* explains that "Equitable considerations arising from the reasonable expectation of the continuation of benefits attending the status of marriage entered into in good faith are not present in such a case." (P. 685, 134 P.2d p. 763.) In the absence of express contract, *Vallera* concluded, the woman is entitled to share in property jointly accumulated only "in the proportion that her funds contributed toward its acquisition." (P. 685, 134 P.2d p. 763.) Justice Curtis, dissenting, argued that the evidence showed an implied contract under which each party owned an equal interest in property acquired during the relationship.

The majority opinion in *Vallera* did not expressly bar recovery based upon an implied contract, nor preclude resort to equitable remedies. But Vallera's broad assertion that equitable considerations "are not present" in the case of a nonmarital relationship (21 Cal.2d at p. 685, 134 P.2d 761) led the Courts of Appeal to interpret the language to preclude recovery based on such theories. (See Lazzarevich v. Lazzarevich (1948) 88 Cal.App.2d 708, 719, 200 P.2d 49; Oakley v. Oakley (1947) 82 Cal.App.2d 188, 191–192, 185 P.2d 848.)

Consequently, when the issue of the rights of a nonmarital partner reached this court in Keene v. Keene (1962) 57 Cal.2d 657, 21 Cal.Rptr. 593, 371 P.2d 329, the claimant forwent reliance upon theories of contract implied in law or fact. Asserting that she had worked on her partner's ranch and that her labor had enhanced its value, she confined her cause of action to the claim that the court should impress a resulting trust on the property derived from the sale of the ranch. The court limited its opinion accordingly, rejecting her argument on the ground that the rendition of services gives rise to a resulting trust only when the services aid in acquisition of the property, not in its subsequent improvement. (57 Cal.2d at p. 668, 21 Cal.Rptr. 593, 371 P.2d 329.) Justice Peters, dissenting, attacked the majority's distinction between the rendition of services and the contribution of funds or property; he maintained that both property and services furnished valuable consideration, and potentially afforded the ground for a resulting trust.

This failure of the courts to recognize an action by a nonmarital partner based upon implied contract, or to grant an equitable remedy, contrasts with the judicial treatment of the putative spouse. Prior to the enactment of the Family Law Act, no statute granted rights to a putative spouse. The courts accordingly fashioned a variety of remedies by judicial decision. Some cases permitted the putative spouse to recover half the property on a theory that the conduct of the parties implied an agreement of partnership or joint venture. (See Estate of Vargas (1974) 36 Cal.App.3d 714, 717–718, 111 Cal.Rptr. 779; Sousa v. Freitas (1970) 10 Cal.App.3d 660, 666, 89 Cal.Rptr. 485.) Others permitted the spouse to recover the reasonable value of rendered services, less the value of support received. (See Sanguinetti v. Sanguinetti (1937) 9 Cal.2d 95, 100–102, 69 P.2d 845.) Finally, decisions affirmed the power of a court to employ equitable principles to achieve a fair division of property acquired during putative marriage. (Coats v. Coats (1911) 160 Cal. 671, 677–678, 118 P. 441; Caldwell v. Odisio (1956) 142 Cal.App.2d 732, 735, 299 P.2d 14.)

Thus in summary, the cases prior to *Cary* exhibited a schizophrenic inconsistency. By enforcing an express contract between nonmarital partners unless it rested upon an unlawful consideration, the courts applied a common law principle as to contracts. Yet the courts disregarded the common law principle that holds that implied contracts can arise from the conduct of the parties. Refusing to enforce such contracts, the courts spoke of leaving the parties "in the position in which they had placed themselves" (Oakley v. Oakley, supra, 82 Cal.App.2d 188, 192, 185 P.2d 848, 850), just as if they were guilty parties "in pari delicto."

Justice Curtis noted this inconsistency in his dissenting opinion in *Vallera,* pointing out that "if an express agreement will be enforced, there is no legal or just reason why an implied agreement to share the property cannot be enforced." (21 Cal.2d 681, 686, 134 P.2d 761, 764; see Bruch, Property Rights of De Facto Spouses Including Thoughts on the Value of Homemakers' Services (1976) 10 FAMILY LAW QUARTERLY 101, 117–121.) And in Keene v. Keene, supra, 57 Cal.2d 657, 21 Cal.Rptr. 593, 371 P.2d 329, Justice Peters observed that if the man and woman "were not illegally living together * * * it would be a plain business relationship and a contract would be implied." (Diss. opn. at p. 672, 21 Cal.Rptr. at p. 602, 371 P.2d at p. 338.)

Still another inconsistency in the prior cases arises from their treatment of property accumulated through joint effort. To the extent that a partner had contributed *funds* or *property,* the cases held that the partner obtains a proportionate share in the acquisition, despite the lack of legal standing of the relationship. (Vallera v. Vallera, supra, 21 Cal.2d at p. 685, 134 P.2d at 761; see Weak v. Weak, supra, 202 Cal.App.2d 632, 639, 21 Cal.Rptr. 9.) Yet courts have refused to recognize just such an interest based upon the contribution of *services.* As Justice Curtis points out "unless it can be argued that a woman's services as cook, housekeeper, and homemaker are valueless, it would seem logical that if, when she contributes money to the purchase of property, her interest will be protected, then when she contributes her services in the home, her interest in property accumulated should be protected." (Vallera v. Vallera, supra, 21 Cal.2d 681, 686–687, 134 P.2d 761, 764 (diss. opn.); see Bruch, op. cit. supra, 10 Family L.Q. 101, 110–114; Article, Illicit Cohabitation: The Impact of the Vallera and Keene Cases on the Rights of the Meretricious Spouse (1973) 6 U.C. Davis L.Rev. 354, 369–370; Comment (1972) 48 Wash.L.Rev. 635, 641.)

Thus as of 1973, the time of the filing of In re Marriage of Cary, supra, 34 Cal.App.3d 345, 109 Cal.Rptr. 862, the cases apparently held that a nonmarital partner who rendered services in the absence of express contract could assert no right to property acquired during the relationship. The facts of *Cary* demonstrated the unfairness of that rule.

Janet and Paul Cary had lived together, unmarried, for more than eight years. They held themselves out to friends and family as husband and wife, reared four children, purchased a home and other property, obtained credit, filed joint income tax returns, and otherwise conducted themselves as though they were married. Paul worked outside the home, and Janet generally cared for the house and children.

In 1971 Paul petitioned for "nullity of the marriage." Following a hearing on that petition, the trial court awarded Janet half the property acquired during the relationship, although all such property was traceable to Paul's earnings. The Court of Appeal affirmed the award.

Reviewing the prior decisions which had denied relief to the homemaking partner, the Court of Appeal reasoned that those decisions rested upon a policy of punishing persons guilty of cohabitation without marriage. The Family Law Act, the court observed, aimed to eliminate fault or guilt as a basis for dividing marital property. But once fault or guilt is excluded, the court reasoned, nothing distinguishes the property rights of a nonmarital "spouse" from those of a putative spouse. Since the latter is entitled to half the "quasi marital property" (Civ.Code, § 4452), the Court of Appeal concluded that, giving effect to the policy of the Family Law Act, a nonmarital cohabitator should also be entitled to half the property accumulated during an "actual family relationship." (34 Cal.App.3d at p. 353, 109 Cal.Rptr. 862.)

Cary met with a mixed reception in other appellate districts. In Estate of Atherley, supra, 44 Cal.App.3d 758, 119 Cal.Rptr. 41, the Fourth District agreed with *Cary* that under the Family Law Act a nonmarital partner in an actual family relationship enjoys the same right to an equal division of property as a putative spouse. In Beckman v. Mayhew, supra, 49 Cal.App.3d 529, 122 Cal.Rptr. 604, however, the Third District rejected *Cary* on the ground that the Family Law Act was not intended to change California law dealing with nonmarital relationships.

If *Cary* is interpreted as holding that the Family Law Act requires an equal division of property accumulated in nonmarital "actual family relationships," then we agree with Beckman v. Mayhew that *Cary* distends the act. No language in the Family Law Act addresses the property rights of nonmarital partners, and nothing in the legislative history of the act suggests that the Legislature considered that subject. The delineation of the rights of nonmarital partners before 1970 had been fixed entirely by judicial decision; we see no reason to believe that the Legislature, by enacting the Family Law Act, intended to change that state of affairs.

But although we reject the reasoning of *Cary* and *Atherley,* we share the perception of the *Cary* and *Atherley* courts that the application of former precedent in the factual setting of those cases would work an unfair distribution of the property accumulated by the couple. Justice Friedman in Beckman v. Mayhew, supra, 49 Cal.App.3d 529, 535, 122 Cal.Rptr. 604, also questioned the continued viability of our decisions in *Vallera* and *Keene;* commentators have argued the need to reconsider those precedents. We should not, therefore, reject the authority of *Cary* and *Atherley* without also examining the deficiencies in the former law which led to those decisions.

The principal reason why the pre-*Cary* decisions result in an unfair distribution of property inheres in the court's refusal to permit a nonmarital partner to assert rights based upon accepted principles of implied contract or equity. We have examined the reasons advanced to justify this denial of relief, and find that none have merit.

First, we note that the cases denying relief do not rest their refusal upon any theory of "punishing" a "guilty" partner. Indeed, to the extent that denial of relief "punishes" one partner, it necessarily rewards the other by permitting him to retain a disproportionate amount of the property. Concepts of "guilt" thus cannot justify an unequal division of property between two equally "guilty" persons.

Other reasons advanced in the decisions fare no better. The principal argument seems to be that "[e]quitable considerations arising from the reasonable expectation of * * * benefits attending the status of marriage * * * are not present [in a nonmarital relationship]." (Vallera v. Vallera, supra, 21 Cal.2d at p. 685, 134 P.2d 761, 763.) But, although parties to a nonmarital relationship obviously cannot have based any expectations upon the belief that they were married, other expectations and equitable considerations remain. The parties may well expect that property will be divided in accord with the parties' own tacit understanding and that in the absence of such understanding the courts will fairly apportion property accumulated through mutual effort. We need not treat nonmarital partners as putatively married persons in order to apply principles of implied contract, or extend equitable remedies; we need to treat them only as we do any other unmarried persons.

The remaining arguments advanced from time to time to deny remedies to the nonmarital partners are of less moment. There is no more reason to presume that services are contributed as a gift than to presume that funds are contributed as a gift; in any event the better approach is to presume, as Justice Peters suggested, "that the parties intend to deal fairly with each other." (Keene v. Keene, supra, 57 Cal.2d 657, 674, 21 Cal.Rptr. 593, 603, 371 P.2d 329, 339 (dissenting opn.); see *Bruch,* op. cit., supra, 10 Family L.Q. 101, 113.)

The argument that granting remedies to the nonmarital partners would discourage marriage must fail; as *Cary* pointed out, "with equal or greater force the point might be made that the pre-1970 rule was calculated to cause the income producing partner to avoid marriage and thus retain the benefit of all of his or her accumulated earnings." (34 Cal.App.3d at p. 353, 109 Cal.Rptr. at p. 866.) Although we recognize the well-established public policy to foster and promote the institution of marriage (see Deyoe v. Superior Court (1903) 140 Cal. 476, 482, 74 P. 28), perpetuation of judicial rules which result in an inequitable distribution of property accumulated during a nonmarital relationship is neither a just nor an effective way of carrying out that policy.

In summary, we believe that the prevalence of nonmarital relationships in modern society and the social acceptance of them, marks this as a time when our courts should by no means apply the doctrine of the unlawfulness of the so-called meretricious relationship to the instant case. As we have explained, the nonenforceability of agreements expressly provided for meretricious conduct rested upon the fact that such conduct, as the word suggests, pertained to and encompassed prostitution. To equate the nonmarital relationship of today to such a subject matter is to do violence to an accepted and wholly different practice.

We are aware that many young couples live together without the solemnization of marriage, in order to make sure that they can successfully later undertake marriage. This trial period, preliminary to marriage, serves as some assurance that the marriage will not subsequently end in dissolution to the harm of both parties. We are aware, as we have stated, of the pervasiveness of nonmarital relationships in other situations.

The mores of the society have indeed changed so radically in regard to cohabitation that we cannot impose a standard based on alleged moral considerations that have apparently been so widely abandoned by so many. Lest we be misunderstood, however, we take this occasion to point out that the structure of society itself largely depends upon the institution of marriage, and nothing we have said in this opinion should be taken to derogate from that institution. The joining of the man and woman in marriage is at once the most socially productive and individually fulfilling relationship that one can enjoy in the course of a lifetime.

We conclude that the judicial barriers that may stand in the way of a policy based upon the fulfillment of the reasonable expectations of the parties to a nonmarital relationship should be removed. As we have explained, the courts now hold that express agreements will be enforced unless they rest on an unlawful meretricious consideration. We add that in the absence of an express agreement, the courts may look to a variety of other remedies in order to protect the parties' lawful expectations.

The courts may inquire into the conduct of the parties to determine whether that conduct demonstrates an implied contract or implied agreement of partnership or joint venture (see Estate of Thornton (1972) 81 Wash.2d 72, 499 P.2d 864), or some other tacit understanding between the parties. The courts may, when appropriate, employ principles of constructive trust (see Omer v. Omer (1974) 11 Wash.App. 386, 523 P.2d 957) or resulting trust (see Hyman v. Hyman (Tex.Civ.App.1954) 275 S.W.2d 149). Finally a nonmarital partner may recover in quantum meruit for the reasonable value of household services rendered less the reasonable value of support received if he can show that he rendered services with the expectation of monetary reward. (See Hill v. Estate of Westbrook, supra, 39 Cal.2d 458, 462, 247 P.2d 19.)

Since we have determined that plaintiff's complaint states a cause of action for breach of an express contract, and, as we have explained, can be amended to state a cause of action independent of allegations of express contract, we must conclude that the trial court erred in granting defendant a judgment on the pleadings.

The judgment is reversed and the cause remanded for further proceedings consistent with the views expressed herein.

WRIGHT, C.J., and MCCOMB, MOSK, SULLIVAN and RICHARDSON, JJ., concur.

CLARK, JUSTICE (concurring and dissenting).

The majority opinion properly permits recovery on the basis of either express or implied in fact agreement between the parties. These being the issues presented, their resolution requires reversal of the judgment. Here, the opinion should stop.

This court should not attempt to determine all anticipated rights, duties and remedies within every meretricious relationship—particularly in vague terms. Rather, these complex issues should be determined as each arises in a concrete case.

The majority broadly indicates that a party to a meretricious relationship may recover on the basis of equitable principles and in quantum meruit. However, the majority fails to advise us of the circumstances permitting recovery, limitations on recovery, or whether their numerous remedies are cumulative or exclusive. Conceivably, under the majority opinion a party may recover half of the property acquired during the relationship on the basis of general equitable principles, recover a bonus based on specific equitable considerations, and recover a second bonus in quantum meruit.

The general sweep of the majority opinion raises but fails to answer several questions. First, because the Legislature specifically excluded some parties to a meretricious relationship from the equal division rule of Civil Code section 4452 [now California Family Code Section 2251], is this court now free to create an equal division rule? Second, upon termination of the relationship, is it equitable to impose the economic obligations of lawful spouses on meretricious parties when the latter may have rejected matrimony to avoid such obligations? Third, does not application of equitable principles—necessitating examination of the conduct of the parties—violate the spirit of the Family Law Act of 1969, designed to eliminate the bitterness and acrimony resulting from the former fault system in divorce? Fourth, will not application of equitable principles reimpose upon trial courts the unmanageable burden of arbitrating domestic disputes? Fifth, will not a quantum meruit system of compensation for services—discounted by benefits received—place meretricious spouses in a better position than lawful spouses? Sixth, if a quantum meruit system is to be allowed, does fairness not require inclusion of all services and all benefits regardless of how difficult the evaluation?

When the parties to a meretricious relationship show by express or implied in fact agreement they intend to create mutual obligations, the courts should enforce the agreement. However, in the absence of agreement, we should stop and consider the ramifications before creating economic obligations which may violate legislative intent, contravene the intention of the parties, and surely generate undue burdens on our trial courts.

By judicial overreach, the majority perform a nunc pro tunc marriage, dissolve it, and distribute its property on terms never contemplated by the parties, case law or the Legislature.

NOTES

1. *Marriage resolves contracting problems.* The Family Code is a collection of default rules on partnership formation, termination, duties, and liabilities. Once married, parties gain the many default protections of the Family and Probate Codes. For a chart comparing marriage to nonmarriage, see JO CARRILLO, UNDERSTANDING CALIFORNIA COMMUNITY PROPERTY LAW 319 (2015).

2. *California rejects the equitable marriage doctrine.* Intimate nonmarried cohabitants face contracting problems precisely because they are precluded from relying on the California community property system. *Cary, supra,* was interpreted, *Marvin* says wrongly, as holding that the Family Law Act required an equal division of property accumulated in nonmarital "actual family relationships" where the nonmarried cohabitants had a long term relationship and were parenting children together. *Marvin* goes on to state that if *Cary* was interpreted as adopting some version of an equitable marriage doctrine, then the interpretation is incorrect because it "distends" the Family Law Act: "No language in the Family Law Act addresses the property rights of nonmarital partners, and nothing in the legislative history of the act suggests that the Legislature considered that subject. The delineation of the rights of nonmarital partners before 1970 had been fixed entirely by judicial decision; we see no reason to believe that the Legislature, by enacting the Family Law Act, intended to change that state of affairs." *Marvin, supra* at 681.

3. *No rehabilitation award is permitted absent an enforceable contract.* Upon remand following the Supreme Court's decision in *Marvin,* the trial court found that no express contract was reached between the parties, nor were there any implied agreements. On remand, the judge concluded that Michelle should be awarded $104,000 for "rehabilitation purposes so that she may have the economic means to re-educate herself . . . and so that she may return from her status as a companion of a motion picture star to a separate, independent but perhaps more prosaic existence." The appellate court struck down this award on the ground that the issue of rehabilitation had not been raised in the pleadings and that there was no legal or equitable basis for awarding a nonmarried cohabitant something akin to spousal support. *Marvin v. Marvin,* 122 Cal.App.3d 871, 176 Cal.Rptr. 555 (1981).

A similar result was obtained in *Taylor v. Polackwich,* 145 Cal.App.3d 1014, 1021, 194 Cal.Rptr. 8, 13 (2d Dist. 1983), where the appellate court overturned a rehabilitative award, stating: "[W]hile a rehabilitative award is a proper means of enforcing rights which cannot otherwise be adequately enforced, an equitable remedy may not be employed to grant rehabilitation to one who has no underlying right to relief on any theory."

Proof of cohabitation is required for enforcing a contract for continuing support obligations. Suppose that a couple never actually resided together, but that there was mutual financial and emotional support in the context of an intimate relationship. Could an implied contract give rise to continuing support obligations? In *Bergen v. Wood,* 14 Cal.App.4th 854, 18 Cal.Rptr.2d 75

(2d Dist. 1993), the appellate court indicated that such an agreement would be "unenforceable because the parties did not cohabit and therefore no consideration ... existed apart from the sexual relationship. ... [i]f cohabitation were not a prerequisite to recovery, every dating relationship would have the potential for giving rise to such claims, a result no one favors." *Id.* at 858. Compare *Milian v. De Leon*, 181 Cal.App.3d 1185, 226 Cal.Rptr. 831 (4th Dist. 1986).

4. *A surviving nonmarried cohabitant is not an heir for purposes of intestacy, nor does he or she have standing to bring a wrongful death action.* In the event that the nonmarital cohabitation relationship is terminated by the death of one of the parties, would the surviving nonmarital cohabitant have any rights in the property earned or accumulated by the decedent during the relationship? Presumably the survivor could file a creditor's claim against the estate, but currently the survivor is not an heir under the intestate succession statutes or statutory protective provisions.

California Civil Procedure Code Section 377.60, reproduced above, limits standing to bring a wrongful death claim to a spouse, a registered domestic partner, a putative spouse, or the decedent's executor or estate administrator. In other words, in order to devise property to each other at death, nonmarried cohabitants must engage in estate planning. See also, *Aspinall v. McDonnell Douglas Corp.*, 625 F.2d 325 (9th Cir.1980), *Harrod v. Pacific Southwest Airlines, Inc.*, 118 Cal.App.3d 155, 173 Cal.Rptr. 68 (4th Dist. 1981); *Matuz v. Gerardin Corporation*, 204 Cal.App.3d 128, 228 Cal.Rptr. 442 (2d Dist. 1986).

5. *Does a nonmarital intimate partner have standing to bring a loss of consortium claim?* Suppose that one partner in a nonmarital cohabitation relationship sustains serious personal injuries due to the negligence of a third person. Should the non-injured partner be permitted to maintain a cause of action for loss of consortium? The California Supreme Court addressed this and related questions in *Elden v. Sheldon*, 46 Cal.3d 267, 250 Cal.Rptr. 254, 758 P.2d 582 (1988) (in bank). The court held that a person may not recover damages for loss of consortium or negligent infliction of emotional distress caused by the injury or death of his or her nonmarital cohabitant. The Court recognized that there has been a significant increase in the number of couples who live together without marriage, and that such relationships may offer complete affection and emotional support. But, the court concluded, the strong policy favoring the marriage relationship and the projected increase in litigation mitigate against allowing such lawsuits. For a critical discussion of the *Elden* case, see Cavanaugh, *A New Tort in California: Negligent Infliction of Emotional Distress (For Married Couples Only)*, 41 HASTINGS L.J. 447 (1990).

6. *Express, implied, and tacit agreements between nonmarried partners may be enforceable.* Generally speaking, the Family Code gives married persons (and RDPs) default rights that they can modify by contract. Nonmarried cohabitants, because their claims are brought under the California Civil Code, do not have the same default rights. They must sue each

other in civil court to enforce express, implied, or tacit agreements about their intimate life together. Minnesota enacted legislation requiring that intimate partner cohabitation agreements be in writing, but the Minnesota Supreme Court severely restricted the scope of the statute by holding it applicable only where the sole consideration for the contract is the contemplation of sexual relations. *In re Estate of Eriksen*, 337 N.W.2d 671 (Minn.1983); Prince, *Public Policy Limitations on Cohabitation Agreements: Unruly Horse or Circus Pony?* 70 MINN.LAW REV. 163, 200 (1985).

So what is the benefit of bringing a civil claim against an intimate partner with whom a person has cohabitated?

7. *Title acquired during the cohabitancy in one partner's name alone.* Where title to property is held solely in the name of one nonmarried cohabitant, any contractual claim of the other cohabitant concerning the property must be proved by "clear and convincing" evidence rather than merely by a preponderance of the evidence. *Tannehill v. Finch*, 188 Cal.App.3d 224, 232 Cal.Rptr. 749 (4th Dist. 1986).

8. *Are nonmaried partners in a joint venture?* In the *Marvin* case, the court indicated that the cohabitation relationship could possibly be analogized to a joint venture (Chapter 6). Presumably this analogy is applicable only to assess the parties' rights and liabilities inter se. In *Planck v. Hartung*, 98 Cal.App.3d 838, 159 Cal.Rptr. 673 (3d Dist. 1979), the court held that nonmarital partners living together as a family were not engaged in a joint venture so as to permit the negligence of one to be imputed to the other.

9. *Property agreements between cohabitants may be enforceable despite a contrary record title. Byrne v. Laura*, 52 Cal.App.4th 1054, 60 Cal.Rptr.2d 908 (1st Dist. 1997). Gladys (Flo) Byrne and Donald (Skip) Lavezzo lived together for the five years prior to Skip's death. Skip proposed to Flo prior to their cohabitation and many times during the course of their time together. Flo declined to marry Skip because she had two children with physical limitations from a previous marriage, Flo was concerned that her children would lose insurance coverage if she were to remarry. When Flo moved in with Skip, he told her it "was our home," promised to take care of Flo for the rest of her life in exchange for her services as homemaker, and assured her that she would always have a roof over her head. Skip repeatedly told Flo that he would change everything into her name but procrastinated and had yet to amend the legal title when he died unexpectedly.

After Skip's death, Flo brought suit against the administrator of Skip's estate to enforce the couple's oral support and property agreement. The trial court granted summary judgment for the estate on all but Flo's quantum meruit claim, reasoning that there was an oral joint tenancy agreement which was unenforceable as a matter of law. The appellate court reversed, finding that there were triable factual issues. Skip's promises to Flo that she would receive his property and Flo's reliance on those promises could reasonably be treated as a *Marvin*-type agreement; and if so, the agreement was breached, albeit unintentionally, by Skip's failure to execute steps to change the record title of the house. The case was remanded for a trial to determine whether the evidence of the agreement was sufficiently strong to meet the clear and convincing standard "to command the unhesitating assent of every reasonable mind." *Id.* at 1073. For a discussion of proving implied-in-fact agreements, see *Maglica v. Maglica*, 66 Cal.App.4th 442, 78 Cal.Rptr.2d 101 (4th Dist. 1998).

C. THE DOMICILE REQUIREMENT

The California Organic Act of 1850 established the community property system in California. It provided that the system was to apply to the property of persons who contracted marriage in the state and to property acquired within the state by persons who were married elsewhere but moved to California. No evidence has been found of any attempt to use this provision to tie the operation of the system to the marriage contract. Rather the courts have consistently declared that marital property rights are to be controlled by the law of the domicile of the married person at the time the property is acquired.

Starting in 1917, the legislature attempted to modify the community property system to protect married persons who had established a domicile in California after living in and acquiring property in other states. The early legislation came up with the idea of quasi-community property to refer to property brought into the state by a married person; this definition of quasi-community was ruled unconstitutional under federal law (takings).

Following the failed attempt to define the term a second attempt was made. Subsequent legislation resulted in the development of the quasi-community property concept that the state relies on today. Parties domiciled in the state acquire community property. Parties who were previously domiciled in another state hold their property under the laws of the jurisdiction where it was acquired unless and until a petition for dissolution or probate is filed in a California court (Chapter 7). At that time, property that would have been community property, had it been acquired in California, is characterized as quasi-community property.

The constitutionality of the quasi-community property legislation was eventually upheld by the California Supreme Court. In the next case it is established that property acquired in North Dakota by the husband was purchased with California community property funds. Application of the tracing principle requires that the North Dakota property be characterized as California community property.

ROZAN V. ROZAN
49 Cal.2d 322, 317 P.2d 11 (1957)

TRAYNOR, JUSTICE.

Plaintiff brought this action against her husband, Maxwell M. Rozan, for divorce, support, custody of their minor child, and division of their community property. * * *

The first finding essential to the division of the property is that plaintiff and defendant "established their residence and domicile in California in May, 1948, and in any event not later than July, 1948" and "that ever since they have been and still are residents of and domiciled in the State of California." A determination of the domicile is essential, for marital interests in movables acquired during coverture are governed by the law of the domicile at the time of their acquisition. . . . Moreover, the interests of the spouses in movables do not change even though the movables are taken into another state or are used to purchase land in another state. Tomaier v. Tomaier, 23 Cal.2d 754, 759, 146 P.2d 905 * * *

Defendant contends that there is no evidence that he was ever in California before July of 1948 and that sending his pregnant wife to California to make a home there in May of 1948 did not establish his domicile in California. * * * It is unnecessary to determine whether defendant was domiciled in this state prior to July 1948, for all the property involved was acquired subsequent to that date.

[The court found that the evidence supported the finding of domicile not later than July, 1948.]

The next essential finding on which the division of property depends is "that after plaintiff and defendant became domiciled in California, as a result of defendant's work, efforts, ability, and skills as an oil broker and operator, they acquired some money and property but that in the latter part of 1948 and in any event before May 1949 they lost everything so acquired by them from the latter part of 1948 until May 1949 and had none thereof and that sometime between December 1948 and May 1949, Rozan was obliged to apply to the Veterans' Administration for a pension in order to furnish plaintiff and Rozan their necessary living expenses and necessities of life." This finding is substantiated by the testimony of plaintiff as well as that of defendant, who stated "At that time I was hard pressed. I had properties but no income."

The last finding on which the division of property depends is that the North Dakota properties "were acquired with community property and community property money." It is undisputed that these properties were acquired after 1949, at which time plaintiff and defendant had no funds. Defendant's testimony supports the finding that these properties were purchased with movables for he testified that he made a lot of money on his Canadian ventures as an oil operator and that it was with this money that the North Dakota properties were purchased. Both plaintiff's and defendant's testimony supports the finding that at the time of trial they still owned everything that they owned when they left Colorado in May of 1948, except two parcels that defendant transferred to a trust for his son and an interest that plaintiff sold. Plaintiff accounted for the expenditure of the proceeds received from the sale of that interest. It thus appears that the purchase money for the North Dakota properties was acquired by the efforts and skill of defendant as an oil operator subsequent to the establishment of the California domicile and was therefore community property. . . . Moreover there is a presumption that in the absence of evidence of gift, bequest, devise or descent, all property acquired by the husband after marriage is community property. * * * Wilson v. Wilson, 76 Cal.App.2d 119, 125–126, 172 P.2d 568. There is no evidence that the purchase money was acquired by gift, bequest, devise, or descent. There is, therefore, substantial evidence to sustain the trial court's finding that the North Dakota properties were purchased with community property funds. It follows that the trial court could properly declare that the plaintiff was entitled to 65 per cent of such property as against the husband, for it was within the sound discretion of the trial court to assign the community property to the respective parties in such proportions as it deems just when a divorce is granted on the ground of extreme cruelty (Civ.Code, § 146).

NOTE

Community property is a characterization of property, not an assertion of jurisdiction over property in another jurisdiction. After *Rozan*, the North Dakota court accorded full faith and credit to the California judgment in so far as it established that the price paid for the North Dakota land was community property, but the court refused to recognize that portion of the California judgment giving the wife a sixty-five percent interest in the property. *Rozan v. Rozan*, 129 N.W.2d 694 (N.D.1964). A quasi-community property determination does not mean that California courts can assert jurisdiction over real estate in another jurisdiction; it means that a court can characterize such property within the California community property system (Chapter 7).

California Family Code Section 2660, originally enacted in 1970, sets forth guidelines for the division of out of state real property acquired by a California domiciliary as community or quasi-community property. If possible the trial court should effect a division of the couple's community and quasi community property without changing the record title to out of state realty. If this is not possible, the section authorizes the court to require the parties to execute conveyances of the out of state realty or to award the equivalent money value of the property to the party who would have been benefitted by such conveyances. The application of these guidelines was considered by the Supreme Court in *Marriage of Fink*, 25 Cal.3d 877, 160 Cal.Rptr. 516, 603 P.2d

881 (1979), a case involving community property situated in Florida. It is also covered by statute (Chapter 7).

————

As mentioned above, one key aspect of the tracing rule is that California law applies to property in another jurisdiction that was purchased with funds earned by the married person in California.

GRAPPO V. COVENTRY FINANCIAL CORPORATION

235 Cal.App.3d 496, 286 Cal.Rptr. 714 (1st Dist. 1991)

MERRILL, ACTING PRESIDING JUSTICE.

. . .

Factual and Procedural History

Respondent Tillie D. Grappo and appellant Michael A. Grappo were married in 1974 and based on appellant's testimony the trial court found they separated in 1979. Both parties had been married previously and had families from those marriages. Appellant had retired from his 25-year career as an agent of the Internal Revenue Service. He was an active real estate investor. Since his retirement, he actively managed a large number of real estate investments. Aside from the pension he received from the Internal Revenue Service, appellant received income in the form of rents from 25 parcels of real estate which he owned in his own name. Appellant was also an attorney, an accountant, and a licensed real estate broker.

In 1977, respondent acquired three unimproved lots on Lakeshore Drive, Incline Village, Nevada, one of which was 1046 Lakeshore Drive, the property at issue in this case. She acquired this property in her own name, as her separate property, with funds obtained by her through a bank loan. Appellant was aware of the fact that the property was acquired by respondent as her separate property, and acknowledged this fact at trial.

Appellant and respondent resided together in Alameda, California, until late 1979, when respondent moved to one of her properties on Lakeshore in Incline Village. Although from time to time the parties would visit each other at their respective residences in Alameda, California, and Incline Village, Nevada, appellant testified that he and respondent never resumed residence together after 1979. Appellant filed for a dissolution of the marriage in 1983, but did not prosecute it. According to appellant, he wanted the marriage to be terminated in 1979, and considered himself separated from respondent as of that time.

Appellant testified that since the beginning of this marriage with respondent, they had kept their property segregated, in order that their separate property would remain separate and not be commingled with or transmuted to community property. It was appellant's intention, which he made clear to respondent, that all property acquired by either of them during their marriage was to remain the separate property of the person acquiring it. In addition, appellant and respondent had "an explicit understanding" that any incremental increase in value to each party's separate property attributable to their personal time and effort spent managing and supervising such property would also be separate property, and not community property. * * *

Choice of Law

Appellant next urges that in considering his claim of a community property interest the trial court erred in applying California rather than Nevada law. Appellant's argument is unpersuasive.

It is true, as appellant states, "[t]he general rule is that questions relating to interests in real property are determined by the law of the situs." (*Barber v. Barber* (1958) 51 Cal.2d 244, 247, 331 P.2d 628.) However, as is pointed out in the very Supreme Court case cited by appellant for this principle, this rule does *not* apply "where the funds used for the purchase were acquired by spouses while domiciled in another state. * * * " (*Ibid.*)

"Generally, the court looks to the domicile of the parties at the time the property was acquired to characterize the property as separate or community." (4A Powell on Real Property (1991) Community Property, ¶ 626[1], pp. 53–91–53–92, fn. omitted.) As a rule, marital interests in money and property acquired during a marriage are governed by the law of the domicile at the time of their acquisition, even when such money and property is used to purchase real property in another state. [Citations omitted.] "Property rights are not lost simply because property is transported into another state and exchanged there for other property." (*Tomaier v. Tomaier* (1944) 23 Cal.2d 754, 759, 146 P.2d 905.)

Here, the state in which appellant and respondent were domiciled during their marriage from 1974 to 1979, prior to their separation, was California. It was here that the parties were living at the time that respondent purchased the subject property. California was also the state in which appellant resided throughout the time that he supplied the money for the costs of construction of the house on the property, by means of loans to respondent of his own funds. Moreover, it is only appellant—a California resident—who has asked the court to apply Nevada law in this case. All of the individual parties to this action, with the possible exception of respondent Tillie Grappo, are also California residents. Respondent herself asks that California law be applied, and objects to the application of Nevada law. Under standard choice of law principles, it is apparent that California, and not Nevada, is the state which has the most significant relationship to the parties and issues in this case. (Rest.2d Conf. of Laws, §§ 6, 222.) In the instant case, we are not concerned with a conveyance transaction under real property law, but are determining the respective rights of married persons under family law.

Under the facts presented and the applicable choice-of-law rules, therefore, we conclude that the characterization of the parties' respective marital interests in the subject property must be determined under the community property law of California. (*Tomaier v. Tomaier, supra,* 23 Cal.2d at p. 759, 146 P.2d 905; *Haws v. Haws, supra,* 615 P.2d at pp. 980–981; 11 Witkin, Summary of Cal.Law, *op. cit. supra,* Community Property, § 16, p. 387; 4A Powell on Real Property, *op. cit. supra,* ¶ 626[4], [5], pp. 53–96–53–98; McClanahan, *Community Property Law in the United States, op. cit. supra,* § 13.12, p. 601.) Appellant himself states that his claim is not a contractual one, but is based on the fact that he was married to respondent and that he acquired a community interest as a result of his advancement of funds and his contribution of time, labor and skill to the property. Thus, the trial court's choice of California law was correct. * * *

Disposition

The judgment is affirmed.

STRANKMAN and CHIN, JJ., concur.

NOTES

1. *Tracing.* In cases involving California real property owned by non-California domiciliaries, the courts have employed the tracing doctrine voiced in *Rozan v. Rozan* to trace the California land back to its purchase funds so as to characterize the property according to the law of the domiciliary jurisdiction. In *Estate of Warner,* 167 Cal. 686, 140 P. 583 (1914), an Illinois domiciliary sent money to California for the acquisition of California real property. On his death, the court held that the property was not community property but rather separate property acquired in Illinois, a common law separate title state.

2. *California community property laws apply only to acquisitions by married persons who are domiciled in California.* Suppose that a married couple is first domiciled in another state, they acquire various items of property, and then they move to California. How should their property be classified? California has developed the concept of quasi-community property to help resolve this type of situation. Additional statutes and cases developing the quasi-community property concept are set forth in the next section.

SECTION 3. CONSTITUTIONAL LIMITATIONS

The California community property system is frequently modified by legislative amendments. Generally, statutes are prospectively applied. Sometimes the legislature indicates that a statute should be retroactively applied.

In the California community property system the principle of non-retroactivity (meaning prospective application) was first announced in the case of *Spreckels v. Spreckels*, 116 Cal. 339, 48 P. 228 (1897). There, a 1891 amendment denying the husband the right to make a gift of community property was held unconstitutional as to property acquired prior to the statute's effective date: "To deprive him of this power is certainly to divest him of a property right. . . ." Over the years the *Spreckels* rule was gradually undermined, and appeared to have been laid to rest in *In re Marriage of Bouquet,* reprinted in this section.

The constitutional question is not whether a vested right is impaired by a marital property law change. The question is whether a Family Code change is sufficiently necessary to the public welfare as to justify the impairment of a vested property right.

A. THE DUE PROCESS AND PRIVILEGES AND IMMUNITIES CLAUSES

Quasi-community property is property, real or personal, wherever situated that was acquired by either spouse "while domiciled elsewhere which would have been community property if the spouse who acquired the property had been domiciled in this state at the time of its acquisition." California Family Code Section 125, *supra* at 85 governs in a dissolution proceeding; California Probate Code Section 66 and 101, *supra* at pages 715–716 govern in the probate context.

When a married person establishes domicile in California, the property owned prior to the move is outside of the California community property system. Two general rules follow from the idea that property rights are not altered merely by moving to California.

Property acquired by a spouse while domiciled in a common-law state is separate property for purposes of the California system. And applying the tracing principle, all property later acquired in exchange for the common law separate property is also separate property. Likewise, property acquired while domiciled in another community property state is governed by the other state's community property system; all property later acquired with that community property is also community property governed by the laws of the other community property state's laws.

The concept of quasi-community property comes into play only if one or both parties establish domicile in California and subsequently file for dissolution in California. Once a petition for dissolution is filed, the state has a substantial interest to provide the parties with a fair and equitable division of property.

The next case, *Addison v. Addison,* raised the constitutionality of applying the (amended) quasi-community property statute retroactively. Prior to 1961, a spouse—typically a wife—could not reach property the other spouse had acquired while domiciled in a common law state. Dissolution awards and spousal support awards went unenforced. This led to the passage in California in 1961 of quasi-community property legislation (Stats. 1961, ch. 636, §§ 1–23, pp. 1838–1845). The gist of the legislation was to reclassify out of state property as quasi-community property if it would have been community property had a California domiciliary acquired it.

In *Addison* the issue is whether the retroactive application of the (then newly passed) quasi-community property statute is constitutional (yes). The Addisons moved to California from Illinois (a common law marital property state), established domicile, and then separated prior to the date that the new legislation became effective. The husband's vested property rights were clearly impaired in the sense that before the legislation he was the sole owner of the property he had acquired in Illinois, yet after the legislation, that same property was declared California quasi-community property for purposes of the California dissolution. *Addison* considers whether the retroactive application of the legislation was a proper exercise of the state's police power. It decided it was. The rationale given is that the state has a paramount interest in the equitable division of property that justifies the impairment of the husband's vested property rights.

ADDISON V. ADDISON
62 Cal.2d 558, 43 Cal.Rptr. 97, 399 P.2d 897 (1965)

PETERS, JUSTICE. * * *

At the time of their marriage in Illinois in 1939, Morton, having previously engaged in the used car business, had a net worth which he estimated as being between $15,000 and $20,000. Leona, however, testified that her husband's net worth was almost nothing at the time of their marriage. In 1949 the Addisons moved to California bringing with them cash and other personal property valued at $143,000 which had been accumulated as a result of Morton's various Illinois business enterprises. Since that time Morton has participated in several California businesses.

On February 20, 1961, Leona filed for divorce and requested an equitable division of the marital property. On trial, Leona asserted two theories in support of her claim of property rights. The first was based upon statements Morton allegedly made to her indicating that she had a proprietary interest in property standing in his name alone, i.e., the theory of oral transmutation. In addition, Leona attempted to apply the recently enacted quasi-community property legislation by contending that the property presently held in Morton's name was acquired by the use of property brought from Illinois and that that property would have been community property had it been originally acquired while the parties were domiciled in California.

The trial court found no oral transmutation of Morton's separate property into community property, a finding amply supported by the record, and held the quasi-community property legislation to be unconstitutional.

The sociological problem to which the quasi-community property legislation addresses itself has been an area of considerable legislative and judicial activity in this state. One commentator has expressed this thought as follows: "Among the perennial problems in the field of community property in California, the status of marital personal property acquired while domiciled in another State has been particularly troublesome. Attempts of the Legislature to designate such personalty as community property uniformly have been thwarted by court decisions." (Comment (1935) 8 So.Cal.L.Rev. 221, 222.)

The problem arises as a result of California's attempts to apply community property concepts to the foreign, and radically different (in hypotheses) common-law theory of matrimonial rights. In fitting the common-law system into our community property scheme the process is of two steps. First, property acquired by a spouse while domiciled in a common-law state is characterized as separate property. (Estate of O'Connor, 218 Cal. 518, 23 P.2d 1031, 88 A.L.R. 856.) Second, the rule of tracing is invoked so that all property later acquired in exchange for the common-law separate property is likewise deemed separate property. (Kraemer v. Kraemer, 52 Cal. 302.) Thus, the original property, and all property subsequently acquired through use of the original property is classified as the separate property of the acquiring spouse.

One attempt to solve the problem was the 1917 amendment to Civil Code section 164 which had the effect of classifying all personal property wherever situated and all real property located in California into California community property if that property would not have been the separate property of one of the spouses had that property been acquired while the parties were domiciled in California. Insofar as the amendment attempted to affect personal property brought to California which was the separate property of one of the spouses while domiciled outside this state, Estate of Thornton, 1 Cal.2d 1, 33 P.2d 1, 92 A.L.R. 1343, held the section was unconstitutional. The amendment's effect upon real property located in California was never tested but generally was considered to be a dead letter as the section was never again invoked on the appellate level.

Another major attempt to alter the rights in property acquired prior to California domicile was the passage of Probate Code section 201.5 [current California Probate Code Section 66.] This section gave to the surviving spouse one half of all the personal property wherever situated and the real property located in California which would not have been the separate property of the acquiring spouse had it been acquired while domiciled in

California. As a succession statute, its constitutionality was upheld on the theory that the state of domicile of the decedent at the time of his death has full power to control rights of succession. (In re Miller, 31 Cal.2d 191, 196, 187 P.2d 722.) In other words, no one has a vested right to succeed to another's property rights, and no one has a vested right in the distribution of his estate upon his death. Hence succession rights may be constitutionally altered. This theory was a basis of the dissent in Thornton.

In the present case, it is contended that Estate of Thornton, supra, 1 Cal.2d 1, 33 P.2d 1, is controlling and that the current legislation, by authority of Thornton, must be held to be unconstitutional. Thornton involved a situation of a husband and wife moving to California and bringing with them property acquired during their former domicile in Montana. Upon the husband's death, his widow sought to establish her community property rights in his estate * * * . The majority held the section unconstitutional on the theory that upon acquisition of the property the husband obtained vested rights which could not be altered without violation of his privileges and immunities as a citizen and also that "to take the property of A and transfer it to B because of his citizenship and domicile, is also to take his property without due process of law. This is true regardless of the place of acquisition or the state of his residence." (Estate of Thornton, supra, 1 Cal.2d 1, 5, 33 P.2d 1, 3, 92 A.L.R. 1343.)

The underlying rationale of the majority was the same in Thornton as it had been since Spreckels v. Spreckels, 116 Cal. 339, 48 P. 228, 36 L.R.A. 497, which established, by a concession of counsel, that changes in the community property system which affected "vested interests" could not constitutionally be applied retroactively but must be limited to prospective application.

The constitutional doctrine announced in Estate of Thornton, supra, has been questioned. Justice (now Chief Justice) Traynor in his concurring opinion in Boyd v. Oser, 23 Cal.2d 613, at p. 623, 145 P.2d 312, at page 318, had the following to say: "The decisions that existing statutes changing the rights of husbands and wives in community property can have no retroactive application have become a rule of property in this state and should not now be overruled. It is my opinion, however, that the constitutional theory on which they are based is unsound. [Citations.] That theory has not become a rule of property and should not invalidate future legislation in this field intended by the Legislature to operate retroactively."

* * *

Thus, the correctness of the rule of Thornton is open to challenge. But even if the rule of that case be accepted as sound, it is not here controlling. * * * The legislation under discussion * * * makes no attempt to alter property rights merely upon crossing the boundary into California. It does not purport to disturb vested rights "of a citizen of another state, who chances to transfer his domicile to this state, bringing his property with him * * * ." (Estate of Thornton, supra, 1 Cal.2d 1, at p. 5, 33 P.2d 1, at p. 3.) Instead, the concept of quasi-community property is applicable only if a divorce or separate maintenance action is filed here after the parties have become domiciled in California. Thus, the concept is applicable only if, after acquisition of domicile in this state, certain acts or events occur which give rise to an action for divorce or separate maintenance. These acts or events are not necessarily connected with a change of domicile at all.

It cannot be successfully argued that the quasi-community property legislation is unconstitutional because of a violation of the due process clause of the federal Constitution. Morton has not been deprived of a vested right without due process. As Professor Armstrong has correctly pointed out in her article, supra: "Vested rights, of course, may be impaired 'with due process of law' under many circumstances. The state's inherent sovereign power includes the so called 'police power' right to interfere with vested property rights whenever reasonably necessary to the protection of the health, safety, morals, and general well being of the people. The annals of constitutional law are replete with decisions approving, as constitutionally proper, the impairing of, and even the complete confiscation of, property rights when compelling public interest justified it.

* * *

"The constitutional question, on principle, therefore, would seem to be, not whether a vested right is impaired by a marital property law change, but whether such a change reasonably could be believed to be sufficiently necessary to the public welfare as to justify the impairment." (Armstrong, "Prospective" Application of Changes in Community Property Control—Rule of Property or Constitutional Necessity? (1945) supra, 33 Cal.L.Rev. 476, 495–496.)

Clearly the interest of the state of the current domicile in the matrimonial property of the parties is substantial upon the dissolution of the marriage relationship. This was expressly recognized by the United States Supreme Court in Williams v. State of North Carolina, 317 U.S. 287, at p. 298, 63 S.Ct. 207, at p. 213, 87 L.Ed. 279, where it was said: "Each state as a sovereign has a rightful and legitimate concern in the marital status of persons domiciled within its borders. The marriage relation creates problems of large social importance. Protection of offspring, property interests, and the enforcement of marital responsibilities are but a few of commanding problems in the field of domestic relations with which the state must deal."

In recognition of much the same interest as that advanced by the quasi-community property legislation, many common-law jurisdictions have provided for the division of the separate property of the respective spouses in a manner which is "just and reasonable" and none of these statutes have been overturned on a constitutional basis.

In the case at bar it was Leona who was granted a divorce from Morton on the ground of the latter's adultery and hence it is the spouse guilty of the marital infidelity from whom the otherwise separate property is sought by the operation of the quasi-community property legislation. We are of the opinion that where the innocent party would otherwise be left unprotected the state has a very substantial interest and one sufficient to provide for a fair and equitable distribution of the marital property without running afoul of the due process clause of the Fourteenth Amendment. For the same reasons sections 1 and 13 of article I of the California Constitution, substantially similar in language, are not here applicable.

Morton also asserts that there is an abridgment of the privileges and immunities clause of the Fourteenth Amendment citing Estate of Thornton, supra, 1 Cal.2d 1, 33 P.2d 1. As has been observed "The 'privileges and immunities' protected are only those that belong to citizens of the United States as distinguished from citizens of the States—those that arise from the Constitution and laws of the United States as contrasted with those that spring from other sources." (Hamilton v. Regents of the University of California, 293 U.S. 245, 261, 55 S.Ct. 197, 203, 79 L.Ed. 343, rehg. den. 293 U.S. 633, 55 S.Ct. 345, 79 L.Ed. 717.) Aside from the due process clause, already held not to be applicable, Thornton may be read as holding that the legislation there in question impinged upon the right of a citizen of the United States to maintain a domicile in any state of his choosing without the loss of valuable property rights. As to this contention, the distinction we have already noted between former Civil Code section 164 and quasi-community property legislation is relevant. Unlike the legislation in Thornton, the quasi-community property legislation does not cause a loss of valuable rights through change of domicile. The concept is applicable only in case of a decree of divorce or separate maintenance.

It is also argued that the legislation here under discussion may be unconstitutional under the privileges and immunities clause of section 2 of article IV of the United States Constitution. It is there provided that "The Citizens of each State shall be entitled to all Privileges and Immunities of Citizens in the several States." The argument is that under the doctrine of Spreckels v. Spreckels, supra, 116 Cal. 339, 48 P. 228, California has refused to tamper with vested marital property rights of its own citizens and must therefore accord the same treatment to citizens of other states. As the United States Supreme Court has observed, "Like many other constitutional provisions, the privileges and immunities clause is not an absolute. It does bar discrimination against citizens of other States where there is no substantial reason for the discrimination beyond the mere fact that they are citizens of other States. But it does not preclude disparity of treatment in the many situations where there are perfectly valid independent reasons for it. Thus the inquiry in each case must be concerned with whether such reasons do exist and whether the degree of discrimination bears a close relation to them. The inquiry must also, of course, be conducted with due regard for the principle that the States should have considerable leeway in analyzing local evils and in prescribing appropriate cures." (Toomer v. Witsell, 334 U.S. 385, 396, 68 S.Ct. 1156, 1162, 92 L.Ed. 1460, rehg. den. 335 U.S. 837, 69 S.Ct. 12, 93 L.Ed. 389.) In the case at bar, Leona, as a former nondomiciliary of California, is a member of a class of people who lost the protection afforded them in Illinois had they sought a divorce there before leaving that state. (See Marsh, Marital Property and Conflict of Laws (1st ed. 1952) pp. 233–234 and cases cited in fn. 22.) She has lost that protection, and is thus in need of protection from California. Hence, the discrimination, if there be such, is reasonable and not of the type article IV of the federal Constitution seeks to enjoin. * * *

It follows that the trial court was in error in refusing to apply the quasi-community property legislation to the case at bar.

TRAYNOR, C.J., and TOBRINER, PEEK, BURKE, and SCHAUER, JJ., concur.

MCCOMB, JUSTICE, dissenting.

NOTES

1. *Quasi-community property comes into existence at dissolution in California.* Quasi-community property is not identifiable unless and until a dissolution proceeding is filed in California.

2. *The state's interest develops when one or both spouses change domicile, or when a petition for dissolution is filed in California. Marriage of Roesch,* 83 Cal.App.3d 96, 147 Cal.Rptr. 586 (1st Dist. 1978) indicated that California's quasi-community property law would not be applied unless both spouses had changed their domicile and subsequent to doing so both sought dissolution. This part of the opinion is now superseded by case law (see below) and by statute. William and Helen Roesch married and were domiciled in Pennsylvania for twenty-seven years before husband William moved to California to take a job as president and CEO of Kaiser. William soon after petitioned for dissolution in a California court. The trial court characterized the Roesch's Pennsylvania assets as quasi-community property. Helen objected to the application of the quasi-community property statute. The court deemed California's interests minimal as compared to Pennsylvania's because the parties had lived in Pennsylvania for their married life, one spouse had only recently established domicile in California, the other spouse and a minor child remained in Pennsylvania, and that spouse was still entitled to protections of Pennsylvania law.

In *Marriage of Fransen,* 142 Cal.App.3d 419, 190 Cal.Rptr. 885 (mod. 143 Cal.App.3d 357H) (2d Dist. 1983), the court held that the second *Roesch* criterion is satisfied when *either* spouse initiates a legal proceeding to alter the marital status. The *Fransen* court reasoned that "[t]o require otherwise would enable one spouse to defeat a quasi-community property claim of the other spouse by merely refusing to seek a dissolution, annulment or legal separation."

Consent to jurisdiction has been held to satisfy the *Roesch* criterion as an alternative to change of domicile. *Marriage of Jacobson,* 161 Cal.App.3d 465, 472, 207 Cal.Rptr. 512, 516 (2d Dist.1984).

Recent statutes permit married person request spousal support immediately upon establishing a new domicile in California. After statutory residence requirements are met (six month in the state, three months in the county), the party can file a petition for dissolution (Chapter 7).

3. *Quasi-community property at the death of the acquiring spouse.* The quasi-community property concept also has application in cases when the marriage ends by the death of the acquiring spouse. California Probate Code Sections 66 and 101 indicate that upon the death of a spouse who had acquired property while domiciled elsewhere, such property may be denominated quasi-community property and accorded treatment similar to community property. An attempt to extend the quasi-community property concept in a case involving the death of a non-acquiring spouse was deemed unconstitutional in *Paley v. Bank of America National Trust & Savings Association,* 159 Cal.App.2d 500, 324 P.2d 35 (2d Dist. 1958).

4. *Proving domicile.* The elements of proof required to establish residence appear at California Government Code Section 244(a): a residence "is the place where one remains when not called elsewhere for labor or other special or temporary purpose, and to which he or she returns in seasons of repose."

California Government Code Section 244(g) further states: "A married person shall have the right to retain his or her legal residence in the State of California notwithstanding the legal residence or domicile of his or her spouse."

Originally the quasi-community property remedy was designed to alleviate problems that can arise when a married couple moves from a common law jurisdiction to California. Today, the California quasi-community property system may alleviate a whole set of different problems that can arise when parties change domicile from one state to another. The California community property system offers protections to the community as well as to the individuals. For individuals who change their domicile to California, upon doing so, they lose important marital law and probate code protections of their former domicile.

Conversely, when a person domiciled in Californian changes their domicile to a common law jurisdiction, similar problems can arise. For a discussion of the various approaches taken by the common law jurisdictions to this problem, see Clausnitzer, *Property Rights of Surviving Spouses and the Conflict of Law*, 18 JOURNAL OF FAMILY LAW 471, 491–497 (1979–80); Note, *Community Property and the Problems of Migrations*, 66 WASH. U.L.Q. 773 (1988). The approaches taken by other community property jurisdictions are considered in *Note, Beware, Migrating Spouses, Texas Lacks a Quasi Community Property Statute*, 3 TEXAS WESLEYAN L.REV. 113–122 (1996).

5.   *Property acquired in another country.* The applicability of California Family Code Section 125 in a split domicile situation was peripherally raised in the unpublished case of *Marriage of Ben-Yehoshua*, 91 Cal.App.3d 259, 154 Cal.Rptr. 80 (5th Dist. 1979). There the husband and wife were married and domiciled in Israel. After 13 years of marriage, the wife came to California for a visit and filed for dissolution in the state some six months later. The trial court determined that certain real and personal property located in Israel was quasi-community property, and awarded the wife a one-half interest. The appellate court sustained the classification and division of the Israel real property, stating: "In support of the judgment we interpret the decree as a mere declaration of entitlement to the property which has no direct effect on the title to the property in Israel." The propriety of applying Section 125 under choice of law principles was apparently not raised by the husband, nor addressed by the court.

6.   *A recurring bar exam question.* Cesar and Dolores are married to each other when they move from New York, where they own real property, to California. They establish domicile in California. While still married, Cesar is told that the couple's New York realty is "quasi-community property." Is this statement correct? (No.) When could the couple's New York realty be characterized as California quasi-community property? (If and when a petition for dissolution of the Cesar-Dolores marriage is filed in a California Superior Court.)

B. RETROACTIVITY PROBLEMS

Legislative intent is a key to determining retroactive application. In recent year the California Legislature has taken care to codify its intentions. See for example, California Family Code Section 2580 (Chapter 2).

The next case discusses the relationship between public interest and retroactivity.

MARRIAGE OF BOUQUET
16 Cal.3d 583, 128 Cal.Rptr. 427, 546 P.2d 1371 (1976)

TOBRINER, JUSTICE.

Harry Bouquet appeals from certain provisions of an interlocutory judgment dissolving the marriage and determining the property rights of the parties.

Harry Bouquet and Ima Nell Bouquet married on June 9, 1941, and separated on March 2, 1969. On April 20, 1971, Ima petitioned for dissolution of marriage and determination of the property rights of the spouses. After trial on May 17 and 18, 1972, the court entered an interlocutory judgment dissolving the marriage and determining the property rights of the spouses on May 26, 1972.

On March 4, 1972, after the filing of the petition but before the entry of the interlocutory judgment, Civil Code, section 5118, [Fam. Code Sec. 771] as amended in 1971, took effect. The amended legislation provides that the earnings and accumulations of *both* spouses while they live apart constitute separate property. Prior to the amendment of section 5118 [California Family Code Section 771], the earnings and accumulations of the wife while the spouses lived apart were separate property although those of the husband were community property. With the trial court's permission, the husband amended his original response and insisted at trial that his earnings and accumulations subsequent to March 2, 1969, the date of separation, were his separate property. The trial court rejected the husband's contention and held that only the earnings and accumulations he acquired after March 4, 1972, the effective date of the amendment, constituted his separate property.

This case squarely poses an issue of first impression, namely whether amended section 5118 [California Family Code Section 771] governs property rights acquired prior to the effective date of that amendment that have not been finally adjudicated by a judgment from which the time to appeal has elapsed. In resolving this question affirmatively we conclude that the amendment, properly construed, requires retroactive application and that such application does not constitute an unconstitutional deprivation of the wife's property.

We first address the issue of statutory construction: does the amendment to section 5118 [California Family Code Section 771] of the Civil Code govern property acquired prior to its effective date. Although legislative enactments are generally presumed to operate prospectively and not retroactively, (Interinsurance Exchange v. Ohio Cas. Ins. Co. (1962) 58 Cal.2d 142, 149, 23 Cal.Rptr. 592, 373 P.2d 640; DiGenova v. State Board of Education (1962) 57 Cal.2d 167, 176, 18 Cal.Rptr. 369, 367 P.2d 865), this presumption does not defy rebuttal. We have explicitly subordinated the presumption against the retroactive application of statutes to the transcendent canon of statutory construction that the design of the Legislature be given effect. (Mannheim v. Superior Court (1970) 3 Cal.3d 678, 686, 91 Cal.Rptr. 585, 478 P.2d 17.) The central inquiry, therefore, is whether the Legislature intended the amendment to section 5118 [Fam. Code Sec. 771] to operate retroactively.

The language of the amendment does little to reveal the Legislature's intent regarding the amendment's prospective or retroactive application. But the statutory language does not furnish the only resource at our disposal. In In re Estrada, supra, 63 Cal.2d 740, 48 Cal.Rptr. 172, 408 P.2d 948, we clothed an amendment to the Penal Code with retroactive effect despite the silence of its language on the issue and the presumption against retroactive application. We explain: "That rule of construction, however, is not a straightjacket. Where the Legislature has not set forth in so many words what it intended, the rule of construction should not be followed blindly in complete disregard of factors that may give a clue to the legislative intent. It is to be applied only after, *considering all pertinent factors, it is determined that it is impossible to ascertain the legislative intent.*" (63 Cal.2d 740, at p. 746, 48 Cal.Rptr. 172, at p. 176, 408 P.2d 948, at p. 952 (emphasis added); accord City of Sausalito v. County of Marin (1970) 12 Cal.App.3d 550, 557, 90 Cal.Rptr. 843.)

Consistent with *Estrada's* mandate, we must address "all pertinent factors" when attempting to divine the legislative purpose. A wide variety of factors may illuminate the legislative design, "such as context, the object in view, the evils to be remedied, the history of the times and of legislation upon the same subject, public policy, and contemporaneous construction." (Alford v. Pierno (1972) 27 Cal.App.3d 682, 688, 104 Cal.Rptr. 110, 114; Estate of Ryan (1943) 21 Cal.2d 498, 133 P.2d 626.) The issue in the present case is a close one, but we conclude that the Legislature did intend the amendment to section 5118 [California Family Code Section 771] to apply retroactively.

The husband suggests that one "pertinent factor" that supports the retroactivity of the present statute was the patent unconstitutionality of the former statute. The Legislature, the argument goes, surely intended as quickly as possible to substitute the new law for the prior constitutionally infirm law. This argument, though admittedly somewhat speculative, merits some weight in our calculus of legislative intent.

Although the constitutionality of former section 5118 [California Family Code Section 771] is not directly before us in this case, we can nonetheless observe that it would be subject to strong constitutional challenge. Prior to the amendment, section 5118 [California Family Code Section 771] blatantly discriminated against the husband during periods of separation: the earnings of the wife were her separate property while those of the husband belonged to the community. It seems doubtful that the state could conjure a rational relation between this unequal treatment and any legitimate state interest. It is even less likely that the state could sustain the greater showing required by our recognition that sex based classifications are inherently suspect. (Sail'er Inn, Inc. v. Kirby (1971) 5 Cal.3d 1, 95 Cal.Rptr. 329, 485 P.2d 529.)

The probable constitutional infirmity of the former law does lend some support to the conclusion that the Legislature intended the amendment to have retroactive effect. We assume that the Legislature was aware of judicial decisions (Buckley v. Chadwick (1955) 45 Cal.2d 183, 288 P.2d 12, 289 P.2d 242); we thus assume that the Legislature knew of the dubious constitutional stature of the sexually discriminating old law. We may reasonably infer, therefore, that the Legislature wished to replace the possibly infirm law with its constitutionally unobjectionable successor as soon as possible. While this inference is hardly conclusive, it is of some value in ascertaining the Legislature's intent.

The husband relies primarily upon a Senate resolution incorporating a letter written to the President Pro Tempore of the Senate by Assemblyman Hayes, the author of the amendment. In that letter, Assemblyman Hayes voiced his view that the amendment was intended to operate retroactively, and observed that he had so argued in obtaining passage of the bill. As we shall explain, although the letter is irrelevant to the extent that it merely reflects the personal views of Assemblyman Hayes, it is quite relevant to the extent that it evidences the understanding of the Legislature as a whole.

In construing a statute we do not consider the motives or understandings of individual legislators who cast their votes in favor of it. (In re Lavine (1935) 2 Cal.2d 324, 327, 41 P.2d 161, 42 P.2d 311; Bragg v. City of Auburn (1967) 253 Cal.App.2d 50, 54, 61 Cal.Rptr. 284.) Nor do we carve an exception to this principle simply because the legislator whose motives are proffered actually authored the bill in controversy. (Epstein v. Resor (N.D.Cal., 1969) 296 F.Supp. 214, 216); no guarantee can issue that those who supported his proposal shared his view of its compass. The understandings of Assemblyman Hayes, then, do not per se expose the Legislature's intent.

In the present case, however, the resolution incorporating the Hayes letter commands respect because it gives evidence of *more* than the personal understanding of the letter's author. First, the letter casts some light on the shrouded legislative history of the amendment. Assemblyman Hayes observed not only that he intended the bill to apply retroactively, but that he *argued* to that effect in obtaining the bill's passage. In Rich v. State Board of Optometry (1965) 235 Cal.App.2d 591, 45 Cal.Rptr. 512, the court accepted the testimony of an assemblyman as an indicator of legislative intent because the court was satisfied that the "testimony was not an expression of his own opinion * * * but a reiteration of the discussion and events which transpired in the Assembly committee hearing when the amendments * * * were under consideration." (235 Cal.App.2d 591, at p. 603, 45 Cal.Rptr. 512, at p. 520.) Although Assemblyman Hayes did articulate his personal view that the statute operated retroactively, he also alluded to the argument that he had presented in securing the passage of the amendment. Debates surrounding the enactment of a bill may illuminate its interpretation. (Sato v. Hall (1923) 191 Cal. 510, 519, 217 P. 520.) Consequently, the letter lends some support to the retroactive application of the amendment through the light it sheds upon legislative debates.

Second, the letter is relevant because it was printed pursuant to Senator Grunsky's motion to publish it as a "letter of legislative intent." The materiality of the letter is not lost merely because it was written and published after the effective date of the amendment; we may properly consider a subsequent expression of legislative intent regarding the construction of a prior statute. (California Employment Stabilization Commission v. Payne (1947) 31 Cal.2d 210, 213–214, 187 P.2d 702.) To be sure, Senator Grunsky's motion was technically a motion to print, not a motion of legislative intent. We are not prepared, however, to ignore completely his indication—clearly embodied in the resolution—that the letter be printed as a letter of legislative intent.

To say that the letter properly bears upon the issue of legislative intent is not to hold that it necessarily concludes that issue. In many cases the indicia of intent are in conflict, and the proper construction of the statute requires us to impute weight to expressions of intent in accord with their probative value. Thus, a motion to print a letter of legislative intent commands less respect than a formal resolution of legislative intent. Likewise, an individual legislator's recount of the argument preceding the passage of a bill probably merits less weight than extensive committee reports on the bill or a formal record of the legislative debates.

In the present case, however, such subtle balancing is unnecessary since we find no conflicting indicia against which to balance the probative value of the letter, the resolution adopting it, or the Legislature's appreciation of the probable unconstitutionality of the former law. While the language of the amendment does not evince a legislative desire that it operate retroactively, neither does it reveal a legislative intent that it operate prospectively only. Apart from the Hayes letter, the legislative history is silent on the issue of retroactivity. In short, the only indicators of legislative intent ascertainable in this case call for the retroactive application of the amendment.

Respondent must do more than merely point to the presumption against retroactive application as a counterweight. As *Estrada* counseled, the presumption should operate only when, looking at all the pertinent factors, we fail to detect the legislative intent. Given the Hayes letter and the absence of conflicting indicia, we cannot hold that "it is impossible to ascertain the legislative intent." (In re Estrada, ante, 63 Cal.2d 740, 746, 48 Cal.Rptr. 172, 176, 408 P.2d 948, 952.) We conclude, therefore that the

Legislature intended amended section 5118 [Fam. Code Sec. 771] to apply retroactively.

We must now determine whether the retroactive application of amended section 5118 [California Family Code Section 771] constitutes an unconstitutional deprivation of the property of the wife. The status of property as community or separate is normally determined at the time of its acquisition. (Trimble v. Trimble (1933) 219 Cal. 340, 343, 26 P.2d 477.) Consequently, the wife gained vested property rights when, prior to the effective date of amended section 5118 [Fam. Code Sec. 771], her husband earned income. The retroactive application of the amendment deprives the wife of her half share of the income that her husband had accumulated during that period. Notwithstanding the fact that it denudes the wife of certain vested property rights, we uphold the retroactive application of the amendment.

Retroactive legislation, though frequently disfavored, is not absolutely proscribed. The vesting of property rights, consequently, does not render them immutable: "Vested rights, of course, may be impaired 'with due process of law' under many circumstances. The state's inherent sovereign power includes the so called 'police power' right to interfere with vested property rights whenever reasonably necessary to the protection of the health, safety, morals, and general wellbeing of the people. * * * The constitutional question, on principle, therefore, would seem to be, not whether a vested right is impaired by a marital property law change, but whether such a change reasonably could be believed to be sufficiently necessary to the public welfare as to justify the impairment." (Addison v. Addison, supra, 62 Cal.2d at p. 566, 43 Cal.Rptr. at p. 102, 399 P.2d at p. 902; quoting Armstrong, "Prospective Application of Changes in Community Property Control—Rule of Property or Constitutional Necessity?" (1945) 33 Cal.L.Rev. 476, 495.)

In determining whether a retroactive law contravenes the due process clause, we consider such factors as the significance of the state interest served by the law, the importance of the retroactive application of the law to the effectuation of that interest, the extent of reliance upon the former law, the legitimacy of that reliance, the extent of actions taken on the basis of that reliance, and the extent to which the retroactive application of the new law would disrupt those actions. (See generally Reppy, Retroactivity of the 1975 California Community Property Reforms (1975) 48 So.Cal.L.Rev. 977, 1048–1049; Note, Retroactive Application of California's Community Property Statutes (1966) 18 Stan.L.Rev. 514, 518–519, 521–522; Hochman, The Supreme Court and the Constitutionality of Retroactive Legislation, supra, 73 Harv.L.Rev. 692; Greenblatt, Judicial Limitations on Retroactive Civil Legislation (1956) 51 Nw.U.L.Rev. 540, 559.) The parties agree that amended section 5118 [Fam. Code Sec. 771] can be applied retroactively if such a retroactive application is necessary to subserve a sufficiently important state interest. (See Addison v. Addison, supra, 62 Cal.2d 558, 43 Cal.Rptr. 97, 399 P.2d 897; see generally Boyd v. Oser (1944) 23 Cal.2d 613, 623, 145 P.2d 312 (Traynor, J., concurring).) The wife, however, contends that the retroactive application of this amendment serves no such interest. We disagree.

Addison involved a factual pattern almost identical to that of the present case; it conclusively establishes the constitutionality of applying the (amended) quasi-community property statute retroactively. Prior to 1961, a wife could not, upon obtaining a decree of divorce or separate maintenance, secure any interest in property that her husband had acquired in a common law state. California's 1961 quasi-community property legislation (Stats.1961, ch. 636, §§ 1–23, pp. 1838–1845) effectively reclassified as community property any common law separate property that would have been community property if it had been acquired by a California domiciliary. *Addison* upheld the constitutionality of applying that legislation to spouses who came to California, resided here, and then separated prior to the effective date of the legislation, so long as the trial was held subsequent to that date.

The application of the quasi-community property legislation to property acquired before its effective date clearly impaired the husband's vested property rights; prior to the enactment of the legislation he had been the sole owner of certain property and afterwards the property belonged to the community. Nevertheless, we deemed the retroactive application of the legislation a proper exercise of the police power. The state's paramount interest in the equitable distribution of marital property upon dissolution of the marriage, we concluded, justified the impairment of the husband's vested property rights. (See generally Williams v. North Carolina (1942) 317 U.S. 287, 298, 63 S.Ct. 207, 87 L.Ed. 279.)

The infringement of the wife's vested property rights in this case finds support in the same state interest that justified the retroactive application of the legislation in *Addison;* here, as in *Addison,* the Legislature reallocated property rights in the course of its abiding supervision of marital property and dissolutions. Moreover, the legislation sprang in both cases from an appreciation of the rank injustice of the former law. The calculus of the costs and benefits of the retroactive application of amended section 5118 [California Family Code Section 771], therefore, does not differ significantly from that implicit in *Addison*. This peculiar congruence between the present case and *Addison* permits us to sustain the retroactive application of amended section 5118 [Fam. Code Sec. 771] without protracted discussion. The divestiture of the wife's property rights in the instant case is no more a taking of property without due process of law than was the divestiture of the husband's property rights in *Addison*. The state's interest in the equitable dissolution of the marital relationship supports this use of the police power to abrogate rights in marital property that derived from the patently unfair former law.

In sum, we hold that amended section 5118 [California Family Code Section 771] governs all property rights, whenever acquired, that have not been finally adjudicated by a judgment from which the time to appeal has lapsed.

We reverse the judgment below and remand the case for proceedings consistent with the views expressed herein.

———

In *Heikes*, husband owned two parcels of property before marriage. During marriage he transferred both parcels to himself and his spouse in joint tenancy. At dissolution, California Family Code Section 2581 applied; the parcels were presumed community property in character subject to a written rebuttal agreement otherwise (Chapter 2). The parties had no other agreement.

Husband Norman sought a reimbursement for his contribution to the community's acquisition of the property. He argued for retroactive application of the newly added of California Family Code Section 2640 (Chapter 2). It was clear from California Family Code Section 2580 (Chapter 2) that the joint form title presumption was retroactive (though this issue was litigated). The discussion below provides historical context to considerations of the retroactivity for the special joint form title presumption at California Family Code Section 2581 (Chapter 2) and for the statutory reimbursement found at California Family Code Section 2640.

MARRIAGE OF HEIKES

10 Cal.4th 1211, 44 Cal.Rptr.2d 155, 899 P.2d 1349 (1995)

WERDEGAR, J.

Former Civil Code section 4800.2 (hereafter section 4800.2), now Family Code section 2640, provides that when community property is divided upon dissolution of the marriage, either spouse shall be reimbursed for his or her contributions of separate property to the acquisition of any property being divided as community property, unless the contributing spouse has waived the right of reimbursement in writing. That right was newly created on January 1, 1984, the effective date of section 4800.2. Before then, a spouse was entitled to reimbursement only if the parties had so agreed; otherwise, any contribution of separate property to the property being divided as community property was deemed an outright gift. (In re Marriage of Lucas (1980) 27 Cal.3d 808, 816 [166 Cal.Rptr. 853, 614 P.2d 285].)

In In re Marriage of Fabian (1986) 41 Cal.3d 440 [224 Cal.Rptr. 333, 715 P.2d 253] (Fabian), we held that in dissolution proceedings commenced before January 1, 1984, to apply section 4800.2 [see current Family Code Section 2640] retroactively, by reimbursing a spouse for making a separate property contribution to the acquisition of community property, would deprive the other spouse of a vested property right without due process of law in violation of article I, section 7, of the California Constitution. Soon after Fabian was filed, the Legislature amended the statutory scheme to provide expressly that section 4800.2 [see current Family Code Section 2640] would apply in dissolution proceedings commenced after January 1, 1984, regardless of the date on which the community property was acquired. (Former Civ. Code, § 4800.1 (hereafter section 4800.1), subd. (a)(3), now Fam. Code, § 2580, subd. (c).)

The issue in this post-1984 dissolution proceeding is whether the Constitution permits the statutorily authorized reimbursement of a husband for separate property contributions he made in 1976 to the property divided as community property in 1992. We conclude that, for the reasons stated in Fabian, supra, 41 Cal.3d 440, such reimbursement would unconstitutionally deprive the wife of a vested property right without due process of law. The only material factual distinction between this case and Fabian is that here, during the interval between the enactment of section 4800.2 [see current Family Code Section 2640] and the commencement of the dissolution proceeding, the wife theoretically could have attempted to protect her property right by requesting the husband to execute a written waiver of his new right of reimbursement. The unlikelihood that any such attempt could succeed in this or any other marriage makes its availability too insubstantial a factor to overcome the constitutional barriers to retroactivity set forth in Fabian.

1.   Facts and Procedural Background

Norman Heikes (husband) owned a home in Santa Barbara and a vacant lot near Boron, California, as his separate property. In January 1976, while married to Rose H. Heikes (wife), he conveyed both parcels to wife and himself as joint tenants. The trial court found there was no oral or written agreement preserving any interest of husband in the parcels other than the interests created by the deeds themselves.

The present dissolution proceeding appears to have been commenced in 1990. The judgment, filed December 11, 1992, classified both parcels as community property. On December 17, 1992, six days after the judgment, this court filed In re Marriage of Hilke (1992) 4 Cal.4th 215 [14 Cal.Rptr.2d 371, 841 P.2d 891], which gave retroactive effect to the presumption, applicable on dissolution of marriage, that property acquired in joint tenancy is community property (§ 4800.1) so as to defeat Mr. Hilke's claim of a nonvested survivorship interest in real property acquired in 1969. On

December 30, 1992, the present husband moved for a partial new trial, arguing that Hilke manifested a change of this court's views of the constitutional restrictions on retroactive application of sections 4800.1 and 4800.2 [see current Family Code Section 2640] previously set forth in Fabian, supra, 41 Cal.3d 440, and In re Marriage of Buol (1985) 39 Cal.3d 751 [218 Cal.Rptr. 31, 705 P.2d 354]. The trial court accepted that argument and ordered a new trial as to the parties' respective interests in the two parcels. The Court of Appeal agreed with the trial court and affirmed the new-trial order. We granted wife's petition for review.

II.   Classification of Parcels as Community Property

Husband claims a [retroactive] right of reimbursement under section 4800.2 [see current Family Code Section 2640], which applies in "the division of community property." Since the two parcels in question were conveyed by husband in 1976 to himself and his wife as joint tenants, we first examine the basis for treating them as community property. The operative principles applicable to the residence and to the unimproved parcel differ.

A.   Residence

[The court confirms that the single family residence held in joint title was subject to the 1965 version of the state joint title community property presumption. It also confirms that the husband produced no evidence to overcome that presumption. See Chapter 2 for a discussion of how 1965 version of the joint title community property presumption was limited to a single family residence.]

B.   Unimproved Parcel

[The court confirms that the unimproved parcel that husband owned prior to marriage but then conveyed to himself and wife as joint tenants in 1976 was also governed by the 1984 version of the state joint title community property presumption, today found at California Family Code Section 2581 (Chapter 2). The court follows Marriage of Hilke, 4 Cal.4th 215, 14 Cal.Rptr.2d 371, 841 P.2d 891 (1992) to confirm that 1984 version of the joint title form community property presumption, which had been expanded to apply to all joint tenancy titles, retroactively applied to the unimproved parcel even though husband conveyed the joint tenancy title seven years before the 1984 statute was amended, and eight years before the amendment went into effect. The court also confirms that the husband produced no evidence to rebut the presumption.

Discussion turns to husband's claim for retroactive application of what is currently California Family Code Section 2640.]

III. Right of Reimbursement

Husband claims reimbursement under section 4800.2 [see California Family Code Section 2640] for his conveyances of the two parcels he owned separately to his wife and himself in joint tenancy, thereby making both parcels presumptively community property for purposes of dissolution. Section 4800.2 [see California Family Code Section 2640] provided: "In the division of community property under this part unless a party has made a written waiver of the right to reimbursement or signed a writing that has the effect of a waiver, the party shall be reimbursed for his or her contributions to the acquisition of the property to the extent the party traces the contributions to a separate property source. . . ." The statute that originally added sections 4800.1 and 4800.2 to the Civil Code purported to make both sections applicable in all cases "to the extent proceedings as to the division of the property are not yet final on January 1, 1984." (Stats. 1983, ch. 342, § 4, p. 1539.)

In Fabian, supra, 41 Cal.3d 440, however, we held that "retroactive application of section 4800.2 to cases pending on January 1, 1984, impairs vested property interests without due process of law" (41 Cal.3d at p. 451). On appeal from a judgment entered in April 1982, Mr. Fabian challenged a finding that a motel acquired by the couple was community property. Enactment of section 4800.2 [see California Family Code Section 2640] while the appeal was pending raised the additional question whether he should be reimbursed for the $275,000 he had invested in the motel out of his separate property.

Affirming the judgment, we denied reimbursement, noting that "for more than 20 years prior to the enactment of section 4800.2 [see California Family Code Section 2640], it was well-established that, absent an agreement to the contrary, separate property contributions to a community asset were deemed gifts to the community. [Citations.]" (Fabian, supra, 41 Cal.3d at p. 446.) During that period, it was "[t]he basic rule . . . that the party who uses his separate property for community purposes is entitled to reimbursement from the community or separate property of the other only if there is an agreement between the parties to that effect." (See v. See (1966) 64 Cal.2d 778, 785 [51 Cal.Rptr. 888, 415 P.2d 776]; accord, Lucas, supra, 27 Cal.3d at p. 816.) Because the Fabians had no such agreement for reimbursement, we concluded that retroactive application of the reimbursement requirement of section 4800.2 [see California Family Code Section 2640] would have impaired Mrs. Fabian's vested property interest. (Fabian, supra, 41 Cal.3d at p. 448.)

We next pointed out, however, that impairment of a vested property interest does not necessarily invalidate a statute's retroactive application if the impairment does not violate due process of law. (Fabian, supra, 41 Cal.3d at p. 448.) As in Buol, supra, 39 Cal.3d at page 761, we focused on the considerations material to such violation, which are outlined in In re Marriage of Bouquet (1976) 16 Cal.3d 583 [128 Cal.Rptr. 427, 546 P.2d 1371] (Bouquet). These naturally divide themselves into two groups, as follows: First: "[T]he significance of the state interest served by the law [and] the importance of the retroactive application of the law to the effectuation of that interest." (Id. at p. 592.) Second: "[T]he extent of reliance upon the former law, the legitimacy of that reliance, the extent of actions taken on the basis of that reliance, and the extent to which the retroactive application of the new law would disrupt those actions." (Ibid.)

With respect to the relevant state interest, we concluded in Fabian that the need perceived by the Legislature to enhance fairness by complementing the strengthened presumption of community property (§ 4800.1) [now California Family Code Section 2581] with a right of reimbursement for separate property contributions (§ 4800.2 [see California Family Code Section 2640]) "does not . . . represent a sufficiently significant state interest to mandate retroactivity." (Fabian, supra, 41 Cal.3d at p. 449.) Because the former law was not patently unfair, retroactivity was not needed to effectuate the state's interest in equitable dissolution of the marital partnership. (Ibid.)

We next addressed the considerations pertaining to reliance. Even though "[t]he extent of [Mrs. Fabian's] reliance on former law is difficult to pinpoint * * * , the legitimacy of such reliance is clear." (Fabian, supra, 41 Cal.3d at p. 449.) From 1966 until "long after the couple separated and judgment of dissolution was entered by the trial court, the law was clear and straightforward: unrestricted separate property contributions to community assets were gifts to the community" (id. at p. 450). As to disruptive effect, "[i]t is difficult to imagine greater disruption than retroactive application of an about-face in the law, which directly alters substantial property rights, to parties who are completely incapable of complying with the dictates of the new law. * * * By the time the Legislature created the new right to separate property reimbursement which could be waived only by a writing, the parties' marriage had been terminated by a final judgment of dissolution. The spouse who asserted a separate property right adverse to the community could hardly be expected to then execute a writing waiving his right to the property he claimed." (Ibid.) The scope of Fabian's ultimate holding is explained in a footnote: "We hold only that application of [section 4800.2 [see California Family Code Section 2640] to cases pending on January 1, 1984, impairs vested rights without due process of law." (Id. at p. 451, fn. 12.)

The Legislature promptly reacted to this court's pronouncements in Buol, supra, 39 Cal.3d 751, and Fabian, supra, 41 Cal.3d 440, of the constitutional limitations on retroactive application of sections 4800.1 and 4800.2. In April 1986, within a month after the filing of Fabian, the Governor signed urgency legislation declaring that sections 4800.1 and

4800.2 "appl[y] to proceedings commenced on or after January 1, 1984, regardless of the date of acquisition of property subject to the proceedings or the date of any agreement affecting the property" (Stats. 1986, ch. 49, § 1, p. 115, italics added) [see California Family Code Section 2580]. The urgency statute explained that sections 4800.1 and 4800.2, as enacted in 1983, had been made applicable "immediately to all family law proceedings not yet final on January 1, 1984, [their] effective date, in order to cure a serious problem in the law governing division of assets at dissolution of marriage. * * * The Buol decision [Buol, supra, 39 Cal.3d 751] has caused confusion among family law judges and lawyers as to what law governs in a heavily litigated area in which important property rights are affected. The decision also frustrates the intent of the Legislature to correct a serious problem in the law that is causing inequitable treatment of many parties. This act is intended to resolve the confusion created by Buol and to reaffirm the need for immediately applicable legislation, to the extent constitutionally permissible, in order to assure all litigants of equitable treatment upon dissolution of marriage. Any further delay will accentuate unreasonably the current confusion and problems in this area of the law." (Stats. 1986, ch. 49, § 2 p. 115; for the full text of the urgency statute, see In re Marriage of Griffis (1986) 187 Cal.App.3d 156, 164, fn. 2 [231 Cal.Rptr. 510].)

Two Court of Appeal decisions soon thereafter held that the urgency statute's mandate to apply the reimbursement requirement of section 4800.2 [see California Family Code Section 2640] to community property acquired before January 1, 1984, was unconstitutional. In re Marriage of Griffis, supra, 187 Cal.App.3d 156, explained that the statute failed to declare any state interest in retroactive application that Fabian, supra, 41 Cal.3d 440, had not already found insufficient to satisfy due process. "We must presume the Supreme Court considered every possible state interest in Buol and Fabian, including those stated by the Legislature in the new law." (In re Marriage of Griffis, supra, 187 Cal.App.3d at p. 167.) In re Marriage of Hopkins & Axene (1987) 199 Cal.App.3d 288 [245 Cal.Rptr. 433] (review denied and publication ordered) quoted and followed Griffis and also invoked considerations of reliance. "Here, as in Griffis, Wife acquired a community property interest at a time when the only method of defeating or diminishing that right was by proof of an agreement to the contrary. By the time section 4800.2 [see California Family Code Section 2640] was enacted, Husband and Wife were already separated. Wife, therefore, had little, if any, opportunity to obtain a written waiver of Husband's right to reimbursement for his separate property contribution." (In re Marriage of Hopkins & Axene, supra, 199 Cal.App.3d at p. 293.)

Meanwhile, the Legislature amended section 4800.1 [now California Family Code Section 2581], as of January 1, 1987, by adding a new subdivision (a), codifying expanded recitals of "a compelling state interest

. . . to provide for uniform treatment of property" and providing that, regardless of the date of the property's acquisition, or of any agreement affecting title, sections 4800.1 and 4800.2 were "applicable in all proceedings commenced on or after January 1, 1984," except "property settlement agreements executed prior to January 1, 1987, or proceedings in which judgments were rendered prior to January 1, 1987" (§ 4800.1, subd. (a)(3)). The Courts of Appeal, however, held that even the expanded legislative recitals in the new version of section 4800.1 were insufficient to demonstrate the compelling state interest found lacking in Fabian, supra, 41 Cal.3d 440. Accordingly, they continued to reject claims for reimbursement under section 4800.2 [see California Family Code Section 2640] for contributions to community property made from separate property before January 1, 1984, as violative of due process, even in proceedings that had commenced after that date and had not culminated in any judgment before January 1, 1987. * * *

Apart from the case now under review, the foregoing six published decisions appear to be the only ones that have considered the constitutionality of requiring reimbursement of pre-1984 separate property contributions to community property under the post-Fabian modifications of section 4800.2 [see California Family Code Section 2640]. All six hold that retroactive application of the reimbursement requirement would violate due process. Yet, the present Court of Appeal refused to follow those decisions because of what it correctly characterized as "dictum" by this court in In re Marriage of Hilke, supra, 4 Cal.4th 215 (hereafter Hilke).

Mrs. Hilke died during dissolution proceedings that had been commenced in 1989, and Mr. Hilke claimed ownership of the family residence (acquired in 1969) as surviving joint tenant. Relying on Buol, supra, 39 Cal.3d 751, and Fabian, supra, 41 Cal.3d 440, he contended that the application to his claim of section 4800.1's [see California Family Code Section 2581] presumption, that property held in joint tenancy is community property in the absence of a contrary written instrument, would deprive him of a vested property right without due process of law. We held that Mr. Hilke's claim "fails at the threshold" because in 1983, when section 4800.1 was enacted, his survivorship interest in the residence was subject to the condition precedent of his surviving his wife and therefore was not a vested property right. (Hilke, supra, 4 Cal.4th at p. 222.) We went on to point out that Buol and Fabian were factually distinguishable not only because they involved impairment of vested property rights, but also because the judgments in those cases were already on appeal when sections 4800.1 and 4800.2 were first enacted, whereas in Hilke, the dissolution proceeding commenced after that enactment.

The present Court of Appeal declared that "the statements in Hilke concerning the limited holding of Fabian are significant. They suggest our Supreme Court would apply Civil Code sections 4800.1 and 4800.2 [see

California Family Code Section 2640] to dissolution actions brought after the January 1, 1984, effective date of those sections, regardless of the date of the property transfers. The reliance on former law by the parties in Fabian and Buol is not present here."

In fact, however, the import of our "statements in Hilke" was more limited. The pertinent statements simply recognized that Fabian's holding was confined to cases already pending on January 1, 1984 * * * , and that the constitutionality of impairing vested property rights acquired before that date by retroactively applying section 4800.2 [now California Family Code Section 2640] in proceedings commenced after that date was still an open question in this court. To that question we now turn.

The only material difference between the facts of the present case and those of Fabian is the date on which the dissolution proceeding was commenced. As in Fabian, husband here made a contribution to the community property well before January 1, 1984, (the effective date of section 4800.2), by conveying his separate property to wife and himself as joint tenants in 1976, thereby conferring upon wife a vested property right. The issue here, as in Fabian, is whether the impairment of that right through enforcement of reimbursement under section 4800.2 [see California Family Code Section 2640] would violate due process in light of the factors outlined in Bouquet, supra, 16 Cal.3d 583, pertaining to the state interest served by the law and to reliance upon the former law.

As to the relevant state interest, we concluded in Fabian that the perceived unfairness section 4800.2 was intended to correct did not amount to the kind of rank, patent injustice that might justify retroactive impairment of a vested property right. In the urgency statute (Stats. 1986, ch. 49, § 1, p. 115) and in the statute adding subdivision (a) to section 4800.1 (Stats. 1986, ch. 539, § 1, pp. 1924–1925; see fn. 8, ante), the Legislature explicitly declared that application of section 4800.2 "regardless of the date of acquisition of the property" (§ 4800.1, subd. (a)(3)) was necessary to alleviate confusion and provide for uniform treatment of property. We agree with the Courts of Appeal that have considered the matter (see ante, pp. 1220–1221) that the legislative declarations in those statutes do not manifest state interests any more compelling than the interests Fabian found insufficient to justify retroactive impairment of a vested right.

The considerations pertaining to "reliance upon the former law" are "the extent . . . [and] legitimacy of that reliance, the extent of actions taken on the basis of that reliance, and the extent to which the retroactive application of the new law would disrupt those actions." (Bouquet, supra, 16 Cal.3d at p. 592.) Those considerations warrant closer scrutiny here because of the differences in chronological relationship between January 1, 1984, the effective date of section 4800.2, and the respective dates on which the dissolution proceedings in the present case and in Fabian were commenced.

In both Fabian and this case, the legitimacy of the parties' reliance upon the prior law (which denied reimbursement for separate property contributions to community property in the absence of a specific agreement to the contrary) was unmistakably clear, at least from the time the property was acquired until the enactment of section 4800.2 [see California Family Code Section 2640]. In Fabian, however, "[b]y the time the Legislature created the new right to separate property reimbursement which could be waived only by a writing, the [Fabians'] marriage had been terminated by a final judgment of dissolution. The spouse who asserted a separate property right adverse to the community could hardly be expected to then execute a writing waiving his right to the property he claimed." (Fabian, supra, 41 Cal.3d at p. 450.) "It is difficult to imagine greater disruption than retroactive application of an about-face in the law, which directly alters substantial property rights, to parties who are completely incapable of complying with the dictates of the new law." (Ibid.)

Here, in contrast, the dissolution proceeding was commenced five or six years after section 4800.2 [see California Family Code Section 2640] took effect. (See ante, fn. 2.) Accordingly, there was an interval, prior to wife's petition for dissolution, during which the parties were on notice of the existence of a statute entitling husband to reimbursement for his contribution of separate property to the parties' joint acquisition of the two parcels unless he waived reimbursement in writing. The theoretical possibility of wife's obtaining husband's written waiver during that interval, however, is too insubstantial to offset the other factors that, as in Fabian, call for protection of her vested property right against retroactive enforcement of husband's claim to reimbursement.

Husband's deeds of his separate property to wife and himself as joint tenants, when executed in 1976, constituted unconditional gifts. As of January 1, 1984, section 4800.2 [see California Family Code Section 2640] introduced into the law a new right of reimbursement of separate property contributions to the community in the event the community property was divided upon dissolution of the marriage. Whatever the motives of generosity or otherwise that may have prompted husband to give wife her one-half interest in the property while they were married, he "could hardly be expected" (Fabian, supra, 41 Cal.3d at p. 450) to waive his newly created right to be reimbursed for his contribution in the event the marriage should break up. Short of extracting such magnanimity from her husband, there was nothing wife could do to protect her vested property right from a reimbursement claim.

Moreover, to let the retroactive application of section 4800.2 [see California Family Code Section 2640] depend upon factual variations in particular parties' actual reliance on prior law would unacceptably undermine the public interest in establishing uniform, predictable rules for the division of marital property. In In re Marriage of Craig, supra, 219 Cal.App.3d 683, the husband contributed his separate property to the parties' purchase of a residence in 1979 in the State of Washington. The parties lived there through December 1983, then moved to California. Dissolution proceedings were commenced in 1987. The husband sought reimbursement for his 1979 contribution to the residence, which was divisible on dissolution as quasi-community property. He contended that retroactive application of section 4800.2 [now California Family Code Section 2640] was proper because neither party could have relied on California law while they were living out of state. Rejecting the contention, the Court of Appeal said that the "result husband seeks would undermine the uniformity the quasi-community property laws were enacted to establish. Actual reliance on the prior law was not the only factor cited by Fabian against retroactive application of section 4800.2 [now California Family Code Section 2640]. The opinion conceded that the extent of the wife's reliance on former law was 'difficult to pinpoint.' (In re Marriage of Fabian, supra, 41 Cal.3d at p. 449.) The court then noted that '[i]n the interest of finality, uniformity and predictability, retroactivity of marital property statutes should be reserved for those rare instances when such disruption is necessary to promote a significantly important state interest.' (Id., at p. 450.)" (In re Marriage of Craig, supra, 219 Cal.App.3d at p. 686.) The reference in Fabian to the importance of "uniformity and predictability" has since been underscored by the Legislature's declaration of "a compelling state interest" to provide "uniformly and consistently" for "the allocation of community and separate interests" in marital property. (§ 4800.1, subd. (a); see ante, fn. 8.) [now California Family Code Section 2580].

Section 4800.2 [now California Family Code Section 2640] requires reimbursement for separate property contributions to the acquisition of any property that the court divides as community property. We hold that the applicability of that requirement is limited by the due process clause to property acquired on or after January 1, 1984.

IV. Conclusion

Husband's transfer in 1976 of his separate real property to the joint ownership of his wife and himself gave wife a vested property interest that cannot constitutionally be impaired through retroactive application of the reimbursement provisions of section 4800.2 [now California Family Code Section 2640] that first took effect on January 1, 1984. The trial court's ruling to the contrary, affirmed by the Court of Appeal, was in error. Accordingly, the judgment of the Court of Appeal is reversed.

LUCAS, C. J., MOSK, J., KENNARD, J., ARABIAN, J., BAXTER, J., and GEORGE, J., concur.

C. THE SUPREMACY CLAUSE

Another constitutional limitation upon the operation of the California community property system involves the supremacy clause of the U.S. Constitution and the doctrine of federal preemption. Under this doctrine, state laws must yield to any conflicting federal law for which Congress, in the proper exercise of a constitutionally granted source of power, has expressly or impliedly sought federal supremacy. One of the major issues that can arise in connection with state marital property laws is whether various types of federally created benefits, such as retirement benefits, life insurance, and Social Security benefits, are precluded from classification and division as community property by virtue of federal preemption.

With the exception of Social Security benefits, California courts have generally been reluctant to declare federal preemption of state community property law. But even when preemption is mandated, while the state courts attempt to mitigate its effects, the federal courts often do not.

WISSNER V. WISSNER
338 U.S. 655, 70 S.Ct. 398, 94 L.Ed. 424 (1950)

MR. JUSTICE CLARK delivered the opinion of the Court.

We are to determine whether the California community property law, as applied in this case, conflicts with certain provisions of the National Service Life Insurance Act of 1940; and if so, whether the federal law is consistent with the Fifth Amendment to the Constitution of the United States. The cause is here on appeal from the final judgment of a California District Court of Appeal, the Supreme Court of California having denied a hearing. Reading the opinion below as a decision that the federal statute was unconstitutional, we noted probable jurisdiction. 28 U.S.C. § 1257(1), 28 U.S.C.A. § 1257(1).

The material facts are not in dispute. Appellants are the parents, and appellee the widow, of Major Leonard O. Wissner, who died in India in 1945 in the service of the United States Army. He had enlisted in the Army in November 1942 and in January 1943 subscribed to a National Service Life Insurance policy in the principal sum of $10,000, which policy was in effect at the date of his death. The opinion below indicates that the decedent and appellee were estranged at the time he entered the Army or shortly thereafter. In January 1943 he requested his attorney to "get an insurance policy away" from appellee. After six months in the service decedent stopped the allotment to his wife, and in September 1943 expressed the wish that he "could find some way of forcing plaintiff to a settlement and a divorce." It is not surprising, therefore, that, without the knowledge or consent of his wife, the Major named his mother principal and his father contingent beneficiary under his National Service Life Insurance policy. Since his death the United States Veterans' Administration has been paying his mother the proceeds of the policy in monthly installments.

In 1947 the Major's widow brought action against the appellants in the Superior Court for Stanislaus County, State of California, alleging that under California community property law she was entitled to one-half the proceeds of the policy. Appellants answered that their designation as beneficiaries was "final and conclusive as against any claimed rights" of appellee. The court found that the decedent and his widow had been married in 1930, and until the date of Major Wissner's death had been legally domiciled there and subject to the state's community property laws. Major Wissner's army pay, which was held to be community property under California law, was the source of the premiums paid on the policy. But no claim was made for the premiums; the widow sought the proceeds of the insurance. The court concluded that, consistent with California law in the ordinary insurance case, the proceeds of this policy "were and are the community property" of the widow and the decedent, and entered judgment for appellee for one-half the amount of payments already received, plus interest, and required appellants to pay appellee one-half of all future payments "immediately upon the receipt thereof" by appellees or either thereof. The District Court of Appeal affirmed, 1949, 89 Cal.App.2d 759, 201 P.2d 837, holding that appellee had a "vested right" to the insurance proceeds, and the Supreme Court of California denied a hearing, one judge dissenting.

We are of the opinion that the decision below was incorrect. The National Service Life Insurance Act is the congressional mode of affording a uniform and comprehensive system of life insurance for members and veterans of the armed forces of the United States. A liberal policy toward the serviceman and his named beneficiary is everywhere evident in the comprehensive statutory plan. Premiums are very low and are waived during the insured's disability; costs of administration are borne by the United States; liabilities may be discharged out of congressional appropriations.

The controlling section of the Act provides that the insured "shall have the right to designate the beneficiary or beneficiaries of the insurance [within a designated class], * * * and shall * * * at all times have the right to change the beneficiary or beneficiaries * * *." 38 U.S.C. § 802(g), 38 U.S.C.A. § 802(g). Thus Congress has spoken with force and clarity in directing that the proceeds belong to the named beneficiary and no other. Pursuant to the congressional command, the Government contracted to pay the insurance to the insured's choice. He chose his mother. It is plain to us that the judgment of the lower court, as to one-half of the proceeds, substitutes the widow for the mother, who was the beneficiary Congress directed shall receive the insurance money. We do not share appellee's discovery of congressional purpose that widows in community property states participate in the payments under the policy, contrary to the express direction of the insured. Whether directed at the very money received from the Government or an equivalent amount, the judgment below nullifies the soldier's choice and frustrates the deliberate purpose of Congress. It cannot stand.

The judgment under review has a further deficiency so far as it ordered the diversion of future payments as soon as they are paid by the Government to the mother. At least in this respect, the very payments received under the policy are to be "seized," in effect, by the judgment below. This is in flat conflict with the exemption provision contained in 38 U.S.C. § 454a, 38 U.S.C.A. § 454a, made a part of this Act by 38 U.S.C. § 816, 38 U.S.C.A. § 816: Payments to the named beneficiary "shall be exempt from the claims of creditors, and shall not be liable to attachment, levy, or seizure by or under any legal or equitable process whatever, either before or after receipt by the beneficiary. * * * "

We recognize that some courts have ruled that this and similar exemptions relating to pensions and veterans' relief do not apply when alimony or the support of wife or children is in issue. See Schlaefer v. Schlaefer, 1940, 71 App.D.C. 350, 112 F.2d 177, 130 A.L.R. 1014; Tully v. Tully, 1893, 159 Mass. 91, 34 N.E. 79; Hodson v. New York City Employees' Retirement System, 1935, 243 App.Div. 480, 278 N.Y.S. 16; In re Guardianship of Bagnall, 1947, 238 Iowa 905, 29 N.W.2d 597, and cases therein cited. But cf. Brewer v. Brewer, 1933, 19 Tenn.App. 209, 84 S.W.2d 1022, 1040. We shall not attempt to epitomize a legal system at least as ancient as the customs of the Visigoths, but we must note that the community property principle rests upon something more than the moral obligation of supporting spouse and children: the business relationship of man and wife for their mutual monetary profit. See de Funiak, Community Property, § 11 (1943). Venerable and worthy as this community is, it is not, we think, as likely to justify an exception to the congressional language as specific judicial recognition of particular needs, in the alimony and support cases. Our view of those cases, whatever it may be, is irrelevant here. Further, Congress has provided in the National Service Life Insurance Act that the chosen beneficiary of the life insurance policy shall be, during life, the sole owner of the proceeds.

The constitutionality of the congressional mandate above expounded need not detain us long. Certainly Congress in its desire to afford as much material protection as possible to its fighting force could wisely provide a plan of insurance coverage. Possession of government insurance, payable to the relative of his choice, might well directly enhance the morale of the serviceman. The exemption provision is his guarantee of the complete and full performance of the contract to the exclusion of conflicting claims. The end is a legitimate one within the congressional powers over national defense, and the means are adapted to the chosen end. The Act is valid. McCulloch v. Maryland, 1819, 4 Wheat. 316, 421, 4 L.Ed. 579. And since the statute which made the insurance proceeds possible was explicit in announcing that the insured shall have the right to designate the recipient of the insurance, and that "No person shall have a vested right" to those proceeds, 38 U.S.C. § 802(i), 38 U.S.C.A. § 802(i), appellee could not, in law, contemplate their capture. The federal statute establishes the fund in issue, and forestalls the existence of any "vested" right in the proceeds of federal insurance. Hence no constitutional question is presented. However "vested" her right to the proceeds of nongovernmental insurance under California law, that rule cannot apply to this insurance. Compare W.B. Worthen Co. v. Thomas, 1934, 292 U.S. 426, 54 S.Ct. 816, 78 L.Ed. 1344, 93 A.L.R. 173; Lynch v. United States, 1934, 292 U.S. 571, 54 S.Ct. 840, 78 L.Ed. 1434. See Hines v. Lowrey, 1938, 305 U.S. 85, 59 S.Ct. 31, 83 L.Ed. 56; Norman v. Baltimore & Ohio R. Co., 1935, 294 U.S. 240, 55 S.Ct. 407, 79 L.Ed. 885, 95 A.L.R. 1352; Ruddy v. Rossi, 1918, 248 U.S. 104, 39 S.Ct. 46, 63 L.Ed. 148, 8 A.L.R. 843.

The judgment below is reversed.

MR. JUSTICE DOUGLAS took no part in the consideration or decision of this case.

MR. JUSTICE MINTON, dissenting.

MR. JUSTICE FRANKFURTER, MR. JUSTICE JACKSON, and I are unable to agree with the majority in this case. The husband's earnings are community property under § 161a, California Civil Code. The wife has a vested interest in one-half of such earnings. United States v. Malcolm, 282 U.S. 792, 51 S.Ct. 184, 75 L.Ed. 714; Bank of America Nat. Trust & Savings Ass'n v. Mantz, 4 Cal.2d 322, 49 P.2d 279; Cooke v. Cooke, 65 Cal.App.2d 260, 150 P.2d 514.

If the premiums on a policy in a private insurance company had been paid out of community property without the wife's consent, the wife could claim her proportionate share of the insurance. Grimm v. Grimm, 26 Cal.2d 173, 157 P.2d 841; Cooke v. Cooke, supra; Bazzell v. Endriss, 41 Cal.App.2d 463, 107 P.2d 49; Mundt v. Connecticut General Life Ins. Co., 35 Cal.App.2d 416, 95 P.2d 966.

It is claimed that the exemption provision of the federal statute prevents the same rule from applying here. This provision, 49 Stat. 609, 38 U.S.C. § 454a, 38 U.S.C.A. § 454a, provides:

> "Payments of benefits due or to become due * * * shall be exempt from the claims of creditors, and shall not be liable to attachment, levy, or seizure by or under any legal or equitable process whatever, either before or after receipt by the beneficiary."

What did Congress contemplate by the enactment of this provision? I think the statute presupposes that the beneficiary is the undisputed owner of the proceeds, and that a creditor has sought to reach the fund on an independent claim. Under those circumstances the remedy is denied, for the statute immunizes the fund from levy or attachment. That is not the case before us. The nature of this dispute is a claim by the wife that she is the *owner* of a half portion of these proceeds because such proceeds are the fruits of funds originally hers.

And recognition of her status as an owner glaringly reveals the irrelevancy of the choice of beneficiary provision. 54 Stat. 1010, 38 U.S.C. § 802(g), 38 U.S.C.A. § 802(g). Congress stated that the serviceman was to have the right to designate his beneficiary. When he has done so all other persons than the one selected are foreclosed from claiming the proceeds as beneficiary. No further effect has the statute. Here the wife makes no claim to rights as a beneficiary. I am not persuaded that either the choice of beneficiary or the exemption provision should carry the implication of wiping out family property rights, which traditionally have been defined by state law. Fully to respect the right which Congress gave the serviceman to designate his beneficiary does not require disrespect of settled family law and the incidents of the family relationship. As noted in the opinion of the Court, analogous occasions have found courts expressing greater reluctance to obliterate rights recognized by the states.

Even accepting the Court's view that the exemption provision applies to the wife, it was intended to protect the fund from attachment, levy, or seizure only so long as it could be identified as a fund. No attachment, levy, or seizure is attempted here. This was an action at law for a money judgment. Appellee obtained a judgment for one-half of the payments that had been collected by the beneficiaries and for one-half of those to be collected thereafter. Payments received under the policy are only the measure of the recovery.

To allow such a judgment does not interfere with the fund or the free designation of the beneficiary by the serviceman. I cannot believe that Congress intended to say to a serviceman, "You may take your wife's property and purchase a policy of insurance payable to your mother, and we will see that your defrauded wife gets none of the money." Certainly Congress did not intend to upset the long-standing community property law of the states where it was not necessary for the protection of the Government in its relation to the soldier or to the integrity of the fund from "attachment, levy, or seizure." These are words of art. They have a definite meaning and usage in the law. This usage is not present here. I find nothing in the section that prohibits the beneficiary from being sued at any time on a matter growing out of the transaction by which the soldier acquired the insurance, at least where there is no attempt to attach, levy, or seize the fund. It was the fund Congress was interested in protecting, not the beneficiary. I would affirm.

NOTES

1.   *"You may take your wife's property and purchase a policy of insurance payable to your mother, and we will see that your defrauded wife gets none of the money." Wissner, supra* at 664. Professor Reppy reports that *"Wissner* was such a jolt to community property principles that the attorneys general of California, Idaho, Nevada, Texas and Arizona filed briefs urging the granting of the wife's petition for a rehearing, but to no avail." Reppy, *Community Property in the U.S. Supreme Court—Why Such a Hostile Reception?* 10 Community Property Journal 93, 104 (1983). The California courts subsequently mitigated the adverse impact of *Wissner* on the community property system by a narrow interpretation of the preemption holding. The opening paragraph of the California Supreme Court's decision in *Marriage of Milhan*, 13 Cal.3d 129, 130–131, 117 Cal.Rptr. 809, 528 P.2d 1145 (1974), is illustrative:

> "In this case we determine the extent to which the trial court in a marriage dissolution proceeding may exercise jurisdiction over a National Service Life Insurance policy issued to one of the parties but paid for with community property funds. We conclude that, in view of federal law protecting an insured's interest in and control over such military policies, the trial court is without authority to divest the insured of such interest or control. Specifically, the court may not award the policy to the other spouse, may not deprive the insured of his right to change the beneficiary of the policy, and may not require the insured to surrender the policy in order to obtain, and thereupon divide and distribute, its cash value. We hold, however, that if sufficient community assets exist aside from the policy, the trial court may award the other spouse an amount therefrom equivalent to his or her community interest in the policy."

See also *Marriage of Fithian*, 10 Cal.3d 592, 111 Cal.Rptr. 369, 517 P.2d 449 (1974), indicating that *"Wissner* does not require community property states to classify the proceeds of National Service Life Insurance policies as separate property, but only to refrain from administering those incidents of community property law which would frustrate the congressional plan." The set-off approach developed by the California courts, whereby the dissolution court could value the community interest in the federal benefit and award the non-military spouse an equivalent amount of other community assets, was subsequently disapproved by the U.S. Supreme Court in the *Hisquierdo* and *McCarty*, discussed below.

2.   *Employee retirement benefits have long been deemed property classifiable as community property under the California community property system.* Under *Brown, infra*, pension benefits are subject to characterization whether they are matured, vested, or contingent (Chapter 5). Where the

retirement benefits were created by federal legislation, however, a question arose concerning the propriety of their characterization as community property. The assertion that the federal statutory schemes regarding military and other types of retirement benefits preempt state community property laws was decisively rejected by the California Supreme Court in *Marriage of Fithian, supra.*

The issue was revisted in federal court. It was heard by the U.S. Supreme Court. In *Hisquierdo v. Hisquierdo,* 439 U.S. 572, 99 S.Ct. 802, 59 L.Ed.2d 1 (1979), the Court ruled that California community property laws could not be applied to pensions created under the federal Railroad Retirement Act. In *McCarty v. McCarty,* 453 U.S. 210, 101 S.Ct. 2728, 69 L.Ed.2d 589 (1981), the court similarly held that military retirement benefits were outside the operation of the state community property system. The court first determined that the application of community property law would conflict with the federal military retirement scheme. It then reasoned that Congress' use of the term "personal entitlement" with respect to military retired pay and the anti-attachment provisions of the federal legislation were deemed indicative of a conflict between the state community property system and the federal law. The Court concluded that "it is manifest that the application of community property principles to military retired pay threatens grave harm to 'clear and substantial federal interests,' " thus ruling that federal law would preclude a state court from dividing military retired pay pursuant to state community property laws.

In 1982, Congress enacted the Uniformed Services Former Spouses' Protection Act. The USFSPA authorizes a state court to treat military retirement pay either as the property of the Armed Forces member or as property of the member and his spouse in accordance with the law of the jurisdiction of such court. 10 U.S.C.A. § 1408. The legislation abrogates *McCarty.*

In 1983, the holding in *Hisquierdo* was similarly abrogated by the Railroad Retirement Solvency Act (45 U.S.C.A. § 231m), which expressly authorizes a state court to divide railroad retirement benefits in dissolution proceedings under state law.

3.   *Under the Retirement Equity Act (REA), the "qualified domestic relations orders"—or QDROs—of a state dissolution court are not pre-empted by the Employee Retirement Income Security Act (ERISA).* Spendthrift provisions in ERISA, prohibit the assignment or alienation of benefits; but those provisions do not apply to payments to alternate beneficiaries named in a QDRO. The Retirement Equity Act [29 U.S.C.A. § 1056(d)] effective January 1, 1985, specifically addresses the possible preemption problems involved in the ERISA. Because ERISA governs most private pension plans, these problems were seen as particularly acute. The REA defines a QDRO to include any judgment, decree, or order, including the approval of a property settlement agreement that relates to marital property rights or support that is made pursuant to state law, including state community property law. The REA also

establishes procedures to be followed by pension plan administrators in complying with the domestic relations order.

The REA of 1984 did not resolve all ERISA preemption issues. In *Boggs v. Boggs*, below, the U.S. Supreme Court held that ERISA operated to pre-empt application of an alternate beneficiary's bequest to her adult children in Louisiana, a community property state.

BOGGS V. BOGGS

520 U.S. 833, 117 S.Ct. 1754, 138 L.Ed.2d 45 (1997)

JUSTICE KENNEDY delivered the opinion of the Court.

Isaac Boggs worked for South Central Bell from 1949 until his retirement in 1985. Isaac and Dorothy, his first wife, were married when he began working for the company, and they remained husband and wife until Dorothy's death in 1979. They had three sons. Within a year of Dorothy's death, Isaac married Sandra, and they remained married until his death in 1989.

Upon retirement, Isaac received various benefits from his employer's retirement plans. One was a lump-sum distribution from the Bell System Savings Plan for Salaried Employees (Savings Plan) of $151,628.94, which he rolled over into an Individual Retirement Account (IRA). He made no withdrawals and the account was worth $180,778.05 when he died. He also received 96 shares of AT & T stock from the Bell South Employee Stock Ownership Plan (ESOP). In addition, Isaac enjoyed a monthly annuity payment during his retirement of $1,777.67 from the Bell South Service Retirement Program.

The instant dispute over ownership of the benefits is between Sandra (the surviving wife) and the sons of the first marriage. The sons' claim to a portion of the benefits is based on Dorothy's will. Dorothy bequeathed to Isaac one-third of her estate, and a lifetime usufruct in the remaining two-thirds. A lifetime usufruct is the rough equivalent of a common-law life estate. See La. Civ.Code Ann., Art. 535 (West 1980). She bequeathed to her sons the naked ownership in the remaining two-thirds, subject to Isaac's usufruct. All agree that, absent pre-emption, Louisiana law controls and that under it Dorothy's will would dispose of her community property interest in Isaac's undistributed pension plan benefits. A Louisiana state court, in a 1980 order entitled "Judgment of Possession," ascribed to Dorothy's estate a community property interest in Isaac's Savings Plan account valued at the time at $21,194.29.

Sandra contests the validity of Dorothy's 1980 testamentary transfer, basing her claim to those benefits on her interest under Isaac's will and 29 U.S.C. § 1055. Isaac bequeathed to Sandra outright certain real property including the family home. His will also gave Sandra a lifetime usufruct in the remainder of his estate, with the naked ownership interest being held by the sons. Sandra argues that the sons' competing claim, since it is based on Dorothy's 1980 purported testamentary transfer of her community property interest in undistributed pension plan benefits, is pre-empted by ERISA. The Bell South Service Retirement Program monthly annuity is now paid to Sandra as the surviving spouse.

After Isaac's death, two of the sons filed an action in state court requesting the appointment of an expert to compute the percentage of the retirement benefits they would be entitled to as a result of Dorothy's attempted testamentary transfer. They further sought a judgment awarding them a portion of: the IRA; the ESOP shares of AT & T stock; the monthly annuity payments received by Isaac during his retirement; and Sandra's survivor annuity payments, both received and payable.

In response, Sandra Boggs filed a complaint in the United States District Court for the Eastern District of Louisiana, seeking a declaratory judgment that ERISA preempts the application of Louisiana's community property and succession laws to the extent they recognize the sons' claim to an interest in the disputed retirement benefits. The District Court granted summary judgment against Sandra Boggs. 849 F.Supp. 462 (1994). . . .

II

This case lies at the intersection of ERISA pension law and state community property law. None can dispute the central role community property laws play in the nine community property States. It is more than a property regime. It is a commitment to the equality of husband and wife and reflects the real partnership inherent in the marital relationship. State community property laws, many of ancient lineage, "must have continued to exist through such lengths of time because of their manifold excellences and are not lightly to be abrogated or tossed aside." 1 W. de Funiak, Principles of Community Property 11 (1943). The community property regime in Louisiana dates from 1808 when the territorial legislature of Orleans drafted a civil code which adopted Spanish principles of community property. Id., at 85–89. Louisiana's community property laws, and the community property regimes enacted in other States, implement policies and values lying within the traditional domain of the States. These considerations inform our pre-emption analysis. See Hisquierdo v. Hisquierdo, 439 U.S. 572, 581, 99 S.Ct. 802, 808, 59 L.Ed.2d 1 (1979).

The nine community property States have some 80 million residents, with perhaps $1 trillion in retirement plans. See Brief for Estate Planning, Trust and Probate Law Section of the State Bar of California as Amicus Curiae 1. This case involves a community property claim, but our ruling will affect as well the right to make claims or assert interests based on the law of any State, whether or not it recognizes community property. Our ruling must be consistent with the congressional scheme to assure the security of plan participants and their families in every State. In enacting ERISA, Congress noted the importance of pension plans in its findings and declaration of policy, explaining:

> "[T]he growth in size, scope, and numbers of employee benefit plans in recent years has been rapid and substantial; . . . the continued well-being and security of millions of employees and their dependents are directly affected by these plans; . . . they are affected with a national public interest [and] they have become an important factor affecting the stability of employment and the successful development of industrial relations. . . ." 29 U.S.C. § 1001(a).

ERISA is an intricate, comprehensive statute. Its federal regulatory scheme governs employee benefit plans, which include both pension and welfare plans. All employee benefit plans must conform to various reporting, disclosure and fiduciary requirements, see §§ 1021–1031, 1101–1114, while pension plans must also comply with participation, vesting, and funding requirements, see §§ 1051–1086. The surviving spouse annuity and QDRO provisions, central to the dispute here, are part of the statute's mandatory participation and vesting requirements. These provisions provide detailed protections to spouses of plan participants which, in some cases, exceed what their rights would be were community property law the sole measure.

ERISA's express pre-emption clause states that the Act "shall supersede any and all State laws insofar as they may now or hereafter relate to any employee benefit plan. * * * " § 1144(a). We can begin, and in this case end, the analysis by simply asking if state law conflicts with the provisions of ERISA or operates to frustrate its objects. We hold that there is a conflict, which suffices to resolve the case. We need not inquire whether the statutory phrase "relate to" provides further and additional support for the pre-emption claim. Nor need we consider the applicability of field pre-emption, see Fidelity Fed. Sav. & Loan Assn. v. de la Cuesta, 458 U.S. 141, 153, 102 S.Ct. 3014, 3022, 73 L.Ed.2d 664 (1982).

We first address the survivor's annuity and then turn to the other pension benefits.

III

Sandra Boggs, as we have observed, asserts that federal law pre-empts and supersedes state law and requires the surviving spouse annuity to be paid to her as the sole beneficiary. We agree.

Respondents say their state-law claims are consistent with these provisions. Their claims, they argue, affect only the disposition of plan proceeds after they have been disbursed by the Bell South Service

Retirement Program, and thus nothing is required of the plan. ERISA's concern for securing national uniformity in the administration of employee benefit plans, in their view, is not implicated. They argue Sandra's community property obligations, after she receives the survivor annuity payments, "fai[l] to implicate the regulatory concerns of ERISA." Fort Halifax Packing Co. v. Coyne, 482 U.S. 1, 15, 107 S.Ct. 2211, 2219, 96 L.Ed.2d 1 (1987).

We disagree. The statutory object of the qualified joint and survivor annuity provisions, along with the rest of § 1055, is to ensure a stream of income to surviving spouses. * * *

ERISA's solicitude for the economic security of surviving spouses would be undermined by allowing a predeceasing spouse's heirs and legatees to have a community property interest in the survivor's annuity. Even a plan participant cannot defeat a nonparticipant surviving spouse's statutory entitlement to an annuity. It would be odd, to say the least, if Congress permitted a predeceasing nonparticipant spouse to do so. Nothing in the language of ERISA supports concluding that Congress made such an inexplicable decision. Testamentary transfers could reduce a surviving spouse's guaranteed annuity below the minimum set by ERISA (defined as 50% of the annuity payable during the joint lives of the participant and spouse). In this case, Sandra's annuity would be reduced by approximately 20%, according to the calculations contained in the sons' state-court filings. There is no reason why testamentary transfers could not reduce a survivor's annuity by an even greater amount. Perhaps even more troubling, the recipient of the testamentary transfer need not be a family member. For instance, a surviving spouse's § 1055 annuity might be substantially reduced so that funds could be diverted to support an unrelated stranger.

In the face of this direct clash between state law and the provisions and objectives of ERISA, the state law cannot stand. Conventional conflict pre-emption principles require pre-emption "where compliance with both federal and state regulations is a physical impossibility, . . . or where state law stands as an obstacle to the accomplishment and execution of the full purposes and objectives of Congress." Gade v. National Solid Wastes Management Assn., 505 U.S. 88, 98, 112 S.Ct. 2374, 2383, 120 L.Ed.2d 73 (1992) (internal quotation marks and citation omitted). It would undermine the purpose of ERISA's mandated survivor's annuity to allow Dorothy, the predeceasing spouse, by her testamentary transfer to defeat in part Sandra's entitlement to the annuity § 1055 guarantees her as the surviving spouse. This cannot be. States are not free to change ERISA's structure and balance.

Louisiana law, to the extent it provides the sons with a right to a portion of Sandra Boggs' § 1055 survivor's annuity, is pre-empted. * * *

Reversed.

JUSTICE BREYER, with whom JUSTICE O'CONNOR joins, and with whom THE CHIEF JUSTICE and JUSTICE GINSBURG join except as to Part II–B–3, dissenting.

* * *

Judge Wisdom, writing for the Fifth Circuit in this case, described Louisiana's community property law as a "system" that "conceives of marriage as a partnership in which each partner is entitled to an equal share." 82 F.3d 90, 96 (1996); see also W. McClanahan, Community Property in the United States § 2:27, p. 38 (1982) (hereinafter McClanahan) (community property law views marriage "as a civil contract between two persons who ente[r] into the relationship as equals and retai[n] their individual personalities"). Recognizing "the value a spouse, though non-employed, contributes to a marriage," 82 F.3d, at 96, the state law provides that the interest in pension benefits that accrued during Isaac's marriage to Dorothy belongs both to Isaac and to Dorothy—that is, to them as a community—and not to the one any more than to the other. La. Civ.Code Ann., Art. 2338 (West 1985) (community property includes "property acquired during the existence of the legal regime through the effort, skill, or industry of either spouse"); T.L. James & Co. v. Montgomery, 332 So.2d 834, 841–844, 846 (La.1975) (pension benefits are community property even if the employee spouse makes no cash contributions to plan).

Louisiana law, like the law of other States, today allows both women and men to leave their property to their children. La. Civ.Code Ann., Art. 2346 (West 1985) ("Each spouse acting alone may manage, control, or dispose of community property unless otherwise provided by law"). Cf. 16 K. Spaht & W. Hargrave, Louisiana Civil Law Treatise, Matrimonial Regimes 1–2 (1989) (until 1980, Louisiana law considered a husband to be the " 'head and master' " and exclusive manager of community property). And we must assume, as did the Fifth Circuit, that Louisiana law would permit Dorothy's children, to whom she left her property, to obtain an accounting to determine the extent to which the stock, the IRA account, and the monthly annuity, in fact belong to them.

* * *

The state law in question concerns the ownership of benefits. I concede that a primary concern of ERISA is the proper financial management of pension and welfare benefit funds themselves, Dillingham, supra, at 326–327, 117 S.Ct., at 838–839 (citing Massachusetts v. Morash, 490 U.S. 107, 115, 109 S.Ct. 1668, 1673, 104 L.Ed.2d 98 (1989)), and that payment of benefits (which amounts to the writing of checks from those funds) is closely "connected with" that management. I also concede that state laws that affect those payments lie closer to ERISA's federal heart than do state laws that, say, affect those goods and services that ERISA benefit plans purchase, such as apprenticeship training programs, 519 U.S., at 322, 117 S.Ct., at 841–842, or medical benefits, De Buono v. NYSA-ILA Medical and Clinical Serv. Fund, ante, at 806, 117 S.Ct., at 1147. But, even so, I cannot say that the state law at issue here concerns a subject that Congress wished to place outside the State's legal reach.

My reason in part lies in the fact that the state law in question involves family, property, and probate—all areas of traditional, and important, state concern. Rose v. Rose, 481 U.S. 619, 625, 107 S.Ct. 2029, 2033–2034, 95 L.Ed.2d 599 (1987) (domestic relations law traditionally left to state regulation); Hisquierdo v. Hisquierdo, 439 U.S. 572, 581, 99 S.Ct. 802, 808, 59 L.Ed.2d 1 (1979) (same); Zschernig v. Miller, 389 U.S. 429, 440, 88 S.Ct. 664, 670–671, 19 L.Ed.2d 683 (1968) ("The several States, of course, have traditionally regulated the descent and distribution of estates"). But see ante, at 1764 (majority's effort to distinguish property interests passing at divorce from those passing by devise). When this Court considers pre-emption, it works "on the 'assumption that the historic police powers of the States were not to be superseded by the Federal Act unless that was the clear and manifest purpose of Congress.'" Dillingham, supra, at 326, 117 S.Ct., at 838 (quoting Rice v. Santa Fe Elevator Corp., 331 U.S. 218, 67 S.Ct. 1146, 91 L.Ed. 1447 (1947)).

I can find no reasonably defined relevant category of state law that Congress would have intended to displace. Obviously, Congress did not intend to pre-empt all state laws that govern property ownership. After all, someone must own an interest in ERISA plan benefits. Nor, for similar reasons, can one believe that Congress intended to pre-empt state laws concerning testamentary bequests. This is not an area like, say, labor relations, where Congress intended to leave private parties to work out certain matters on their own. See Machinists and Aerospace Workers, AFL-CIO v. Wisconsin Employment Relations Comm'n, 427 U.S. 132, 144–148, 96 S.Ct. 2548, 2555–2557, 49 L.Ed.2d 396 (1976). The question, "who owns the property?" needs an answer. Ordinarily, where federal law does not provide a specific answer, state law will have to do so.

* * *

ERISA's "anti-alienation" provision, § 1056(d)(1), says that "benefits provided under the [qualified ERISA plan] may not be assigned or alienated." We have stated that this provision reflects "a decision to safeguard a stream of income for pensioners (and their dependents * * *)." Guidry v. Sheet Metal Workers Nat. Pension Fund, 493 U.S. 365, 376, 110 S.Ct. 680, 687, 107 L.Ed.2d 782 (1990). Sandra Boggs and the Solicitor General claim that Louisiana law interferes with a significant "anti-alienation" objective, both (1) by permitting Dorothy, the nonparticipant spouse, to obtain an undivided interest in the pension of Isaac, the participant spouse; and (2) by permitting Dorothy to transfer that interest on her death to her children, who, as far as ERISA is concerned, are third parties.

The first claim—simply attacking Dorothy's possession of an undivided one-half interest in that portion of retirement benefits that accrued during her marriage to Isaac—does not attack any "assign[ment]" of an interest nor any "aliena[tion]" of an interest, for Dorothy's interest arose not through assignment or alienation, but through the operation of Louisiana's community property law itself. Thus, Sandra's claim must be that community property law's grant of an undivided one-half interest in retirement benefits to a nonparticipant wife or husband itself violates some congressional purpose. But what purpose could that be? Congress has recognized that community property law, like any other kind of property law, can create various property interests for nonparticipant spouses. See 29 U.S.C. § 1056(d)(3)(B)(ii)(II). Community property law, like other property law, can provide an appropriate legal framework for resolving disputes about who owns what. § 1056(d)(3). The anti-alienation provision is designed to prevent plan beneficiaries from prematurely divesting themselves of the funds they will need for retirement, not to prevent application of the property laws that define the legal interest in those funds. One cannot find frustration of an "anti-alienation" purpose simply in the state law's definition of property. * * *

If Dorothy had divorced Isaac, ERISA would have permitted state law to give her not only other assets, but also half of the pension itself (which would have left a later-appearing Sandra with a diminished annuity). See § 1056(d)(3)(A). Given Congress' purpose of allowing state courts to give first wives their community property share of pension assets, why would Congress have intended to include a silent implication that strips Dorothy of an asset that may be the bulk of her community property—simply because, instead of divorcing Isaac, she remained his wife until she died?

On the assumptions I have made, to find a conflict in this case, one would have to depart from what Congress actually said in ERISA and infer some more abstract general purpose, say to help a second wife at the expense of a first wife's state law-created interest in other property. But should we take anything like this latter approach, there would be no logical stopping place. Confusion and unnecessary interference with state property laws would become inevitable. Moreover, we should be particularly careful in making assumptions about the interaction of § 1055 and Louisiana law, as the courts below did not consider § 1055 as a possible ground for conflict pre-emption.

In sum, an annuity goes to Sandra, a surviving spouse; but otherwise Dorothy would remain free not only to have, but to bequeath, her share of the marital estate to her children. This reading of the relevant statutory provisions and purposes protects Sandra, limits ERISA's interference with basic state property and family law, and minimizes the extent to which ERISA would interfere with Dorothy's pre-existing property. * * *

These general reasons, as well as the specific reasons provided above, convince me that ERISA does not pre-empt the Louisiana law in question. And I would therefore affirm the judgment below.

NOTES

1.   *Preemption.* The United State Supreme Court confronted the preemption question also in *Mansell v. Mansell,* 490 U.S. 581, 109 S.Ct. 2023, 104 L.Ed.2d 675 (1989). The case involved the classification and diversion of military disability benefits elected by a spouse in lieu of retirement pay. California courts had treated such benefits as community property to the extent they represented a substitute for retirement pay. The U.S. Supreme Court held that the Uniformed Services Former Spouses Protection Act (USFSPA) retired pay provisions were not applicable, and that federal preemption was mandated by Congress's intent "both to create new benefits for former spouses and to place limits on state courts designed to protect military retirees." See Gilbert, *A Family Law Practitioner's Road Map to the Uniformed Services Former Spouses Protection Act,* 32 Santa Clara L.Rev. 61 (1992)

2.   *The preemption rationale of* Hisquierdo *and* Boggs *as applied to Social Security benefits. Marriage of Hillerman,* 109 Cal.App.3d 334, 167 Cal.Rptr. 240 (4th Dist. 1980). Several courts had previously reached the same result but on the theory that Social Security benefits were not legally cognizable property rights. See, e.g., *Marriage of Nizenkoff,* 65 Cal.App.3d 136, 135 Cal.Rptr. 189 (1st Dist. 1976); see generally, Cohen, *Federal Pension Benefits: The Reach of Preemption,* 34 HASTINGS L.J. 293 (1982).

3.   *The preemption doctrine may have application in contexts other than federally created pension and insurance benefits.* For example, under the federal bankruptcy laws, the filing of a bankruptcy vests the U.S. District Courts with exclusive jurisdiction over property of the bankruptcy estate. As a result, if one spouse files for bankruptcy, the bankruptcy court acquires exclusive jurisdiction over the community property of both spouses, even where dissolution proceedings are pending in state court. To the extent that there is any conflict between community property laws and the federal bankruptcy laws with respect to the disposition of the property, the federal laws will control under the supremacy clause. *In re Teel,* 34 B.R. 762 (Bkrtcy.App.1983).

In *Marriage of Cohen,* 105 Cal.App.3d 836, 164 Cal.Rptr. 672 (2d Dist. 1980), a trial court ruled that the husband's social security benefits were his separate property (not community property) and that the husband had no liability for his share of the community indebtedness as to which he had been discharged from liability in bankruptcy. On appeal, the ruling was affirmed as required under the U.S. supremacy clause.

In *Roosevelt v. Ray*, 220 F.3d 1032 (9th Cir. 2000), a fraudulent transfer case (11 U.S.C.A. § 548), a bankruptcy court applied California Family Code Section 2641 to determine whether a wife had a community property interest in the community reimbursement. Just before husband declared bankruptcy, the parties petitioned to dissolve their marriage. They negotiated a marriage settlement agreement in which wife Judy received from husband Steven his one-half interest in the family home and business in exchange for her one-half interest in his professional education. Evidently their idea was to shield the real estate from the reach of husband's creditors.

4.   *Copyrights: an undecided issue.* A California Court of Appeal has held that the federal Copyright Act does not preclude the characterization of a copyright as divisible community property: "We find no inconsistency between the federal Copyright Act and California's community property law so as to invoke the preemption doctrine." *Marriage of Worth*, 195 Cal.App.3d 768, 778, 241 Cal.Rptr. 135, 140 (1st Dist. 1987). *See also Enovsys LLC v. NexTel Communications*, discussed above (Section 1, Note 5).

5.   Boggs *as the rationale for ERISA preemption of state law, discussed below (*Chapter 5, Section 6A, Note 2).

SECTION 4. CHAPTER SUMMARY

Property:

- Generally all property—real or personal, vested or contingent, tangible or intangible—is included within the community property principle.

- Any type of asset can be removed from the community property principle by any one of the following.

  o   The general separate property statute;

  o   A special statute;

  o   A court decision;

  o   Contractual modification between the parties;

  o   Federal law preemption.

- The threshold marriage situation illustrates the inequities inherent in treating certain types of highly personalized assets (like an educational degree) as falling within the community property principle.

  o   When a community contributes to one spouse's income enhancing education at the expense of the other spouse, if dissolution occurs before the community can benefit from the student spouse's enhanced earning capacity, the student spouse leaves the marriage benefitted by the community's contribution to the education while the other spouse leaves adversely affected by those contributions.

o For that reason, an educational degree or training is removed from the California community property principle. The degree is property, but it is not subject to division upon dissolution. Instead, the degree belongs solely to the student spouse, even if it was acquired during marriage.

o Instead of valuing the degree, the legislature has mandated that the community be entitled to a statutory reimbursement, with interest, upon proof of the following.

▪ The education or training substantially enhances the student spouse's earning capacity.

▪ The community made contributions to the direct expenses of the education or training.

▪ There are no mandatory offsets to modify or negate the reimbursement.

o Contributions to indirect expenses are not reimbursable, but they can be considered in the determination of spousal support for the nonstudent spouse.

• Talent is removed from the reach of the California community property principle. Talent belongs solely to its holder. Here the idea is that talent, which is personal to the holder, can be exchanged on the labor market for compensation, which directly benefits the community during the period of the marriage.

Persons:

• A valid marriage or registered domestic partnership is required in order for intimate partners to have access to the default Family Code rules.

• In the case of a putative marriage, the declared putative spouse can choose whether or not to use the Family Code for purposes of dissolving the union.

o A putative spouse is a person who can prove a reasonable, subjective, good faith belief in the validity of a marriage that is in actuality void or voidable. Upon such proof the petitioner is declared a "putative spouse." At that time, the putative spouse has the statutory right to opt for the default rules of the Family Code.

o If the putative spouse chooses to proceed with a dissolution or probate under the Family Code, the property of the putative marriage is deemed "quasi-marital property."

- o   Quasi-marital property is characterized and divided as if it were community or quasi-community property.

- A nonmarried cohabitant is precluded from using the community property system for the following reasons. Therefore, dissolution of cohabitation must proceed outside of the parameters of the Family Code

  - o   An intimate nonmarried cohabitant chooses not to marry.

  - o   An intimate nonmarried cohabitant is not eligible for putative spouse status.

Property in other states:

- Marital property rights are controlled by the law of the domicile of the married person at the time the property is acquired.

- Property purchased in another state with California community property is California community property. California law applies.

- Parties who move to California hold their property under the laws of the previous domicile where the property was acquired unless and until a petition for dissolution is filed in a California court.

Community property law changes that affect property rights:

- The legislature makes every effort not to impair vested property rights.

- However, the legislature has the power to impair vested property rights when the change is sufficiently necessary to the public welfare to justify the impairment.

CHAPTER 5

COMMINGLED ASSETS

■ ■ ■

This chapter covers commingled assets.

Each section discusses a different type of asset. Proceed through the materials section by section while keeping in mind the general concepts set out in Section 1.

SECTION 1. GENERAL DEFINITIONS AND RULES

- Commingled assets are an admixture of community and separate property.

- A key principle, known as the doctrine of confusion, is that separate and community property keep their respective character when mixed together unless and until it is no longer possible to identify the separate property.

- The doctrine of confusion, now codified, holds that when commingled property is no longer traceable into its component parts, it becomes entirely community property by operation of law. Hence the importance of the tracing rules for apportioning commingled property.

- The inception of title rule generally determines an asset's original characterization.

- Contributions to purchase of a different character may change an asset's original characterization.

- Assets can be owned proportionally between the community estate and the separate property estate of either spouse.

- Generally, the duty to prove a separate property interest falls to the separate property claimant (as when a community property presumption starts the analysis). Sometimes it falls to the estate that seeks an ownership interest (as with separate property credit acquisitions where the burden to establish an ownership share falls on the community proponent). In the case of proving separate property sums on deposit the duty to keep records falls on the first spouse to commingle the account.

- A statutory reimbursement right exists for contributions to an asset of an entirely different character. The word "entirely" means one-hundred percent (100%) ownership by one estate. An "entirely" community property asset is one-hundred percent owned by the community.

Legal and historical overview. From a broad jurisprudential point of view, this chapter illustrates how accounting doctrines have developed.

The California community property system has veered from the Spanish *ganancial* system in historically key ways. Commentators in the United States tend to refer to these legal transitions as "Americanizations." For that reason several rules are identified as "American rules." An American rule indicates a shift away from a civil law process toward a common law one.

For example, there is the "American rule" on separate property rents, issues and profits (Chapter 3). It was developed by the California courts. To briefly review: the American rule on rents, issues, and profits changes the outcome of the traditional civil law. The civil law rule gives the community usufruct rights to separate property rents, issues and profits during marriage. The American rule, by contrast, characterizes separate property rents, issues, and profits as separate property, even during the marriage, thus effectively divesting the community of use and control of that income Under the American rule a person with separate property assets has no legal duty to relinquish management and control of those assets or the income from those assets to a spouse.

Another example: there is an "American rule" on community contributions made to an entirely separate property credit acquisition (Chapter 5B). It too was developed by the California courts. The traditional civil law rule allows a separate property owner to retain full ownership of an asset even if the community helps buy that asset. In exchange for its contribution the community is entitled to a dollar-for-dollar reimbursement, typically without interest. The American rule changes that outcome so that when the community helps buy a separate property asset, the community becomes a pro tanto owner of that asset. Ultimately, the community's pro tanto share is determined by actual contributions to the purchase divided by the total purchase price. A pro tanto share is not akin to an equitable right. A pro tanto share is a legal right that comes into existence with the first community contribution and grows, percentage wise, with each additional contribution. (Chapter 5B.) An equitable ownership right, by comparison, is a common law concept that gives a judge discretion to do equity based on a wide range of facts in evidence.

Commentators from other countries tend to recognize the hybridization that results from combining common law legal and civil law concepts and processes. American commentators typically (still) do not.

SECTION 2. DEMAND DEPOSIT ACCOUNTS

Before reading this Section please review California Probate Code Section 5305, reproduced in Chapter 2.

A demand deposit account is made up of two distinct assets: the account itself and sums on deposit in the account.

Disputes can arise between intimate partners over a number of demand deposit account related issues. Generally, disputes over accounts fall into one of three categories: Who has access to the account? Who owns the sums on deposit in the account on any given day? Who owns a purchase made from the sums deposited in the account on any given day?

Account access, information, and succession disputes are decided by reference to a bank deposit contract.

Beneficial ownership of sums on deposit in the account is decided by reference to the net contributions (for unmarried persons) or net *character* contributions (for married persons) present in the account on the date in question.

The character of any purchase that was made from a withdrawal of sums from a commingled account is analyzed by the presumption that applies to the type of asset (untitled, titled in one name alone, or titled in both names). Rebuttal requires date and character specific records that prove the existence of net separate property sums on deposit on the date of purchase. See Chapter 2.

Assuming the general community presumption governs the asset in question, rebuttal can be made by reference to date and character specific account records (Chapter 2).

Before discussing the ownership of sums on deposit in an account, it is first necessary to understand the issue of account access.

A. ACCOUNT ACCESS: THE CONTRACT OF DEPOSIT

California enacted the California Multiple-Party Accounts Law [CAMPAL] in 1990; at the time the former probate code was repealed and a new one enacted. CAMPAL is included in California Probate Code, Division 5, Nonprobate Transfers, Part 2, Multiple-Party Accounts, at Sections 5100 to 5107. California Probate Code Section 5305, a special community property presumption, was added to the Probate Code in 1983, and amended in 1989; it too is included in California Probate Code, Division 5, Nonprobate Transfers, Part 2, Multiple-Party Accounts, at Section 5305.

The first step toward understanding CAMPAL is to define basic terms.

California Probate Code Section 5122 defines an "account" conceptually as "a contract of deposit of funds between a depositor and a financial institution." In this model, the financial institution is the debtor that holds sums on deposit for the depositor, who is the creditor. The depositor-creditor calls on the debt by making a withdrawal from the account.

CAMPAL applies to any account, whether a depositor is married or not, or whether the account is a sole or a joint account.

As discussed in Chapter 2 and stated above, CAMPAL includes within it a special community property presumption for sums on deposit in any account of a married person. California Probate Code Section 5305(a). As to sums on deposit in any account of a married person, the special community property presumption supersedes the general community property presumption and the special presumption found at California Family Code Section 2581. Both the text of the statute and the Law Revision Commission Comments so indicate. See 23 CAL.L.REV.COMM. REPORTS (1993).

CAMPAL provides practical definitions to parse through legal issues related to the ownership of sums on deposit in the accout.

The term *account* is defined by California Probate Code Section 5122 to include: a checking account, savings account, certificate of deposit, share account, and "other like arrangement" with the financial institution and a depositor or depositors. The contract of deposit determines the named depositors' rights of withdrawal, access (to sums and information), and succession.

An account is sometimes called a "demand deposit account." The phrase indicates that the depositor is entitled to his or her sums on deposit on demand. The right to withdraw sums on demand distinguishes the demand deposit account from other types of accounts, like for example a pension account, a tax protected account, a tax-deferred account, or a trust account. Demand deposit accounts are subject to CAMPAL, but for purposes of family law, other types of accounts may or may not be, depending on the issue.

Withdrawal rights for an unmarried counterpart are determined by the initial deposit contract and the state civil code. The general CAMPAL rule for depositors who are not married to each other is that only named depositors (i.e., signatories to the bank contract) are permitted to withdraw sums on deposit, and only named depositors are permitted to claim an ownership share of sums on deposit in the account. For unmarried depositors, ownership shares are calculated by each named depositor's (actual) net contribution to the account.

Withdrawal rights for married counterparts—meaning depositors who are married to each other—are determined by general community property laws. Only the named depositor has access to the account. Yet regardless of which spouse's name is on the contract, both spouses presumptively own a vested one-half community property interest in all sums on deposit in the account. This is true whether community property sums are held in a sole account (an account in one spouse's name alone) or in a joint account (an account in both spouses' names).

Sole account. A contract of deposit between one depositor and a financial institution is called a sole account. A sole account gives the contractually named account owner access to the sums on deposit in that account. Practically and legally speaking, owning a sole account means that the financial institution is (only) authorized to deliver funds (deposits, interest, and dividends) to a depositor named in the contract, and then only during his or her lifetime. Additionally, it means that at the death of the named depositor, the financial institution is contractually bound to dispose of any sums on deposit in the sole account either through a beneficial designation clause in the deposit contract (a pay on death, P.O.D., provision) or through the deceased depositor's probate estate.

In the context of marriage, California Probate Code Section 5305(a) nonconclusively presumes that sums on deposit in a sole account are community property in character absent evidence to the contrary (Chapter 2).

Joint account. A contract of deposit between two or more depositors and a financial institution is called a joint account. A joint account is defined at California Probate Code Section 5130 as "[a]n account payable on the request to one or more of two or more parties whether or not mention is made of any right of survivorship."

The default CAMPAL joint account for unmarried counterparts is a joint account with the right of survivorship. The legal significance of this information is that the default account between unmarried counterparts results in a nonprobate transfer to the surviving depositor(s) upon the death of another depositor.

The default account for depositors who are married to each other, by comparison, is the community property account. The default community property account does not include a right of survivorship. At the death of a spouse, the decedent owns one-half of the community property sums on deposit and the survivor owns the other half (Chapter 9). The decedent's one-half is subject to probate.

Each and every named depositor in a joint account contract has access to all sums on deposit in that account.

The CAMPAL default designations reflect what most depositors probably want. When owners of a joint account are not married to each other, the presumption is that they want the sums to pass by right of survivorship at the death of one. If the owners are married to each other, the presumption is that they want to retain testamentary rights as to their community shares, unless they agree otherwise.

Despite these default rules, depositors have the right to decide for themselves, as to any given account, how they want to dispose of sums on deposit upon the death of a depositor. They do this by opting for a different title form.

For example, unmarried joint tenants can sever the rights of survivorship, in which case the account defaults to a tenancy in common account, making any sums on deposit on the death of depositor subject to probate. Married persons can opt out of community property account for a community property with the right of survivorship account or a joint tenancy account, both of which guarantee a nonprobate transfer of sums on deposit at the death of a named depositor.

Under CAMPAL California Probate Code Section 5203 the term "joint account" includes all of the following:

- *"Joint accounts with right of survivorship."* The joint tenancy is the *default* joint account under California Probate Code Sections 5301(a) and 5302(a) for unmarried counterparts, as noted above. The right of survivorship indicates that the depositors have agreed that upon the death of the first depositor, the surviving depositor is guaranteed to succeed to the account and to all sums on deposit in the account. See California Probate Code Section 5203(a)(1) for quoted language.

- *"Joint account without right of survivorship."* This opt-in account is sometimes known as a tenancy in common account. A tenancy in common account requires clear and convincing evidence of the depositors' intention not to elect survivorship, as determined by California Probate Code Section 5306. The absence of the right of survivorship guarantees that at the death of a depositor, the decedent's net contributions to the account will pass either by contractual designation (a P.O.D. in the account contract) or through the decedent's probate estate. See California Probate Code Section 5203(a)(6) for quoted language.

- *"Joint account held by [spouses] with right of survivorship that cannot be changed by will."* This account is the opt-in "community property with the right of survivorship account" authorized by California Civil Section 682.1 (Chapter 2). The title form is a community property title. Therefore it is available only to married counterparts; but it has a right of survivorship function. Spouses who decide to use the community property with the right of survivorship title form agree that at the death of one, the survivor will succeed to the account and to all community property deposits in the account. See California Probate Code Section 5203(a)(4) for quoted language.

- *"Joint account held by [spouses] that is specifically designated as a 'community property' account."* The community property account is the *default* community property account title form under California Probate Code Section 5307. Only depositors who are married to each other can use it. The account is *without* the right of survivorship. The decedent's net community property contributions and all provable net separate property contributions are disposed of either through a beneficial designation (a P.O.D. in the account contract) or through the decedent's probate estate.

California Probate Code Section 5305(a) treats all sums on deposit in any account of a married person as presumptively community in character. Therefore, no matter which account a married depositor uses, his or her spouse retains full rights of management and control over sums on deposit in the account during his or her lifetime, *and* full testamentary rights over his or her one-half (50%) of the net community property deposits. See California Probate Code Section 5203(a)(5) for quoted language. There are exceptions to the management and control rule. For example, if the account is a community property business account, then a spouse who manages the business has primary control over the sums (Chapter 7).

As applied to marriage, CAMPAL prevents impairment of a spouse's one-half community property interest in sums on deposit. The special community property presumption (Chapter 2) is the tool for doing so. The special presumption ensures that one spouse cannot diminish or otherwise impair the community property *ownership* rights of the other spouse by the simple movement of money from one account to another. Nevertheless, the movement of sums from one account to another will have consequences, most likely related to access and succession rights.

An example to illustrate what CAMPAL protects: Assume that married depositors H and W deposit earnings in an account in both of their names (a joint deposit account). Subsequently H moves $1,000 from the H-W joint account to H's sole account.

- When the funds are in the H-W joint account, both H and W have a right of access, either can withdraw sums on demand. Once H moves sums to his sole account, W is contractually barred from gaining access to those sums ($1,000) even though W owns a one-half community property interest in those transferred sums ($500). W can obtain a court order to have her name added to H's sole account under California Family Code Section 1101 (Chapter 6). But *absent such an order*, W is not contractually eligible to do any of the following: obtain information about H's sole account (is there still $1,000 in the account?); withdraw sums on deposit from H's sole account; succeed by right of survivorship to all of the sums on deposit in the event of H's death.

To conclude, what CAMPAL protects is W's ownership interest in sums on deposit, not necessarily W's access or survivorship rights once H moves money from a joint to a sole account. W continues to presumptively own one-half of the net community property deposits that were moved to H's sole account. W can ask for an equitable accounting, whether H is dead or alive. W can sue H's P.O.D. designee(s) for return of W's one-half interest. Or W can sue H's probate estate. These are all important rights. But there are interrelated ways in which W nevertheless might be harmed by H's decision to move money from a joint account to a sole account. In other words, without access or succession rights the right of ownership is compromised.

Finally, joint depositors—including spouses—are permitted to enter into a written agreement about rights of withdrawal to a joint account. Any such agreement must be in writing and signed by the parties. If the agreement effects a transmutation, it must comply with California Family Code Section 852(a) and California Family Code Section 721 to be valid.

CAMPAL (California Probate Code Sections 5401 through 5407) protects a financial institutions from misdelivery claims in disputes between joint account owners. By statute, the financial institution in which funds are deposited is not a party to any agreement (or dispute) between depositors. Additionally, account overdrafts are the joint liability of the account owners.

B. BENEFICIAL OWNERSHIP OF SUMS ON DEPOSIT

Generally, for unmarried joint account owners, sums on deposit are owned according to each depositor's net contributions to the account. The term "net contribution" is defined at California Probate Code Section 5134 as:

- "All deposits thereto made by or for the party, less all withdrawals made by or for the party that have not been paid to or applied to the use of any other party."

- "A pro rata share of any interest or dividends earned, whether or not included in the current balance."

- "Any proceeds of deposit life insurance added to the account by reason of the death of the party whose net contribution is in question."

If depositors to an account are unmarried, their net contribution is each named depositor's actual (provable) contribution to the sums on deposit in the account. "In the absence of proof otherwise, only parties who have a present right of withdrawal to an account shall be considered as having a net contribution" under the limiting language in California Probate Code Section 5134.

This means that if X and Y are unmarried, neither may assert a net contribution claim to the other's *sole* account as a matter of course. However if X and Y, still unmarried, open a *joint* account, then either person may assert a net contribution right to sums on deposit in that joint account. For both types of accounts, however, beneficial ownership is subject to proof. And what needs to be proved is that the claimant actually deposited money into the account.

In the context of marriage, the net contribution rule becomes the net *character* contribution rule.

Thus, if X and Y are married, all sums on deposit are presumed to be community property in character unless proven otherwise. See California Probate Code Section 5305(a), discussed above and in Chapter 2. Moreover, the sums on deposit in *any* of the spouses' accounts, sole or joint, are community property in character and thus owned by the spouses in one-half shares. The special community property presumption holds even if a spouse lacks access (i.e. a present right of withdrawal) to the account. For married persons, it doesn't matter which spouse makes the deposit: all deposits are presumptively community in character; and the burden to prove otherwise is on the separate property claimant.

Net *community property* deposits are owned in one-half (50%) shares by both spouses.

Provable net *separate property* contributions are owned entirely (100%) by one spouse.

X and Y are unmarried:	X and Y are married to each other:
SOLE ACCOUNT	**SOLE ACCOUNT**
Neither has an ownership claim to sums on deposit in the sole account of the other, absent a court judgment.	Each spouse has a community property ownership claim to sums on deposit in any sole account. All deposited sums are presumed to be community property in character. Separate property deposits must be established by tracing or by an agreement between the spouses as to the specific deposits and the specific account.
JOINT ACCOUNT	**JOINT ACCOUNT**
Each person has an ownership claim to sums on deposit in a joint account owned with the other. Ownership shares are computed by the account owners' actual deposits to the account less expenses.	Each spouse has a community property ownership claim to sums on deposit in the joint account. All deposits are presumed to be community property in character. Separate property deposits must be established by tracing or by an agreement between the spouses as to the specific deposits and the specific account.

C. "NET DEPOSITS" AND THE FAMILY EXPENSE PRESUMPTION

The CAMPAL community property presumption simplifies the process of characterizing purchases made with a withdrawal from a commingled account.

Presumptively, all deposits in any account of a married person are community property in character.

Rebuttal is by tracing or by providing an enforceable agreement between the spouses that the sums on deposit are not to be community property (Chapter 2).

Once an account is proven to be commingled—to hold net community property deposits *and* net separate property deposits—the focus shifts to identify beneficial ownership to the actual sums on deposit. Date and character specific account records are required to establish separate property rights to sums in an account, otherwise all sums on deposit are community in character.

Net deposits are defined as sums on deposits minus expenses. This is the case both under CAMPAL and earlier decisional law. *See v. See*, reproduced below, states a family presumption for married depositors. The family presumption holds that spouses have a mutual obligation to support each other. The authority for this presumption is found at California Family Code Section 720, *supra*, and again at California Family Code Section 914(a)(1) *infra*, which defines family expenses as "necessaries of life." Therefore, according to the family expense presumption "net" in the context of marriage means sums on deposit minus family expenses.

Net character deposits are defined as character sums on deposits minus family expenses.

Net community property deposits are community property sums on deposit minus family expenses and purchases.

Net separate property deposits are separate property sums minus family expenses, separate expenses, and purchases

The family expense presumption holds that community property funds pay family expenses. That said, when community property deposits are exhausted, family expenses become payable (deductible) from net separate property deposits.

CAMPAL allows for a general right of reimbursement. However, a CAMPAL right of reimbursement for an excess withdrawal applies only to (1) withdrawals of net separate property deposits that (2) do not benefit the separate property owner either as individual or as a member of the marital partnership. Otherwise under California community property law the use of net separate property deposits to pay for family expenses is *without reimbursement* absent a contrary agreement between the spouses. This is the outcome both under the California Family Code Section 914(a)(1), *infra*, and under CAMPAL's excess withdrawal provisions.

D. CONFIRMING SUMS AND PURCHASES AS SEPARATE PROPERTY

A successful rebuttal depends on two steps. First, it depends on rebutting the community property presumption as to the sums on deposit in the account (Chapter 2). Second, it depends on rebutting the community property presumption that governs the disputed asset purchased from the account.

The following rebuttal accounting methods only apply to assets purchased from commingled accounts. Otherwise, if an account is not commingled, the character of the sums on any given date determines the character of the asset that was purchased with those sums. Community sums buys community property. Separate sums buys separate property.

Commingled sums presumptively buy community property assets absent proof that separate property sums were used to make the purchase.

Focus thus shifts from the character of the sums to the character of the asset itself.

If the asset is untitled or titled in one spouse's name alone then the general California Family Code Section 760 community property presumption applies. Rebuttal by tracing is permitted. The question becomes what type of records are sufficient to prove that separate property sums in a commingled account were used on a particular day, for a particular item.

If the asset is titled in both spouses' names, the special California Family Code Section 2251 community property presumption applies. Rebuttal is by agreement only, as tracing is not permitted. The statutory preclusion of rebuttal means that the following rebuttal accounting methods are not relevant and therefore not admissible in a dissolution proceeding (Chapter 2).

Assuming tracing is permitted, however, there are two tracing methods for rebutting the general community property presumption (Chapter 2) as to a disputed purchase that was made from a commingled deposit account. Both methods derive from case law. The first method is known as the exhaustion method. The second method is known as the direct tracing method.

Additionally, either spouse has the legal right to manage and control community personal property. This rule applies in the context of a commingled account as well. Therefore, unless the account is tied to a community property business, either spouse can manage and control the sums on deposit pursuant to California Family Code Section 1100(a) (Chapter 6).

That said, legal rights of management and control may not necessarily align with contractual rights of access and withdrawal. For that reason, California Family Code Section 1101 includes a remedy that permits a spouse to petition to have his or her name added to the sole account of the other spouse. Once both spouses' names are on an account, legal rights of management and control are aligned with actual rights of access and withdrawal.

E. STATUTORY REIMBURSEMENT RIGHTS COMPARED WITH EXCESS WITHDRAWAL CLAIMS

Under the Family Code, an excess withdrawal from an account is difficult to make because once net community property contributions are exhausted, net separate property contributions become liable for family expenses. Therefore, a nonowning spouse with access to a commingled joint account has the right to withdraw separate property sums on deposits in order to pay family expenses. The general authority for this proposition is California Family Code Section 720, *supra*, which provides that "spouses contract toward each other obligations of mutual respect, fidelity, and support."

Likewise, CAMPAL identifies an excess withdrawal as occurring whenever a joint depositor (married to the other depositor or not) withdraws sums to which the depositor does not have a beneficial or legal ownership interest. California Probate Code Section 5301(f) defines excess withdrawal as follows:[1]

> "For purposes of this section, "excess withdrawal" means the amount of a party's withdrawal that exceeds that party's net contribution on deposit in the account immediately preceding the withdrawal."

Under both these laws, whenever a spouse withdraws the other spouse's provable separate property an authorized expense is made under California Family Code Section 914(a)(1), reproduced in Chapter 6, and an authorized "excess withdrawal" is made under CAMPAL. However, California Probate Code Section 5134(a)(1) defines net contributions as deposits minus withdrawals that are made "by *or for the party* that have not been paid to or applied to the use of any other party." (Italics added.)

The courts have not defined excess withdrawal for purposes of a dissolution proceeding. But whether the excess withdrawal provision is interpreted in line with community property law (or not) likely will depend upon how the term "by or for the other party" is defined. The definition of a net community property contribution is deposits minus withdrawals. If a nonowning spouse withdraws provable separate property sums for a family related purchase, the withdrawal is not made "by" the owning spouse, but it is authorized as one "for," meaning on behalf of, the spouse who owns the withdrawn sums.

For example, assume that married depositors H and W own a commingled account. On January 1, that account holds $1,500 in net community property deposits and $500 in provable net separate property deposits owned by H.

Joint Bank Account of H and W on January 1	
CP Deposits = $1,500	Provable SP of H Deposits = $500

Now assume that on January 2 the community spends down all of its $1,500 community property deposits to pay rent, a family expense. Once

---

[1] § 5301. Lifetime ownership; excess withdrawal; claim to recover ownership interest in excess withdrawal; P.O.D. accounts; totten trusts *(Stats. 1990, c. 79 (A.B. 759), § 14, operative July 1, 1991. Amended by Stats, 2012, c. 235 (A.B. 1624), § 1.)*

the rent is paid, as indicated in the box below, the net community deposits are $0. Net separate property deposits remain at $500.

Joint Bank Account of H and W on January 2	
CP Deposits = $1,500 − RENT = $0	Provable SP of H Deposits = $500

Subsequently, on January 3, a utility bill arrives for $100. The community property deposits have been exhausted. Either spouse can withdraw H's provable separate property deposits to pay the utility bill. Under California Family Code Section 720 the spouses contract toward each other (on the date of their marriage) "obligations of mutual ... support." This means that when the community runs out of money, if one or both spouses own provable separate property deposits, those deposits are liable for the family's expenses.

Now assume that W withdraws $100 to pay the utility bill, a family expense.

Joint Bank Account of H and W on January 3	
CP Deposits = $0	Provable SP of H Deposits = $400 $500 − $100 utility bill = $400

This leaves H with $400 of provable net separate property sums on deposit in the account.

The separate property depositor H is not entitled to a reimbursement from the community for paying the utility bill under either CAMPAL or the Family Code. In the context of CAMPAL the utility bill was paid for (meaning used on behalf of) H, who enjoyed utilities. Under the Family Code the $100 utility payment is a family expense, payment of which clearly benefits H in his or her status as a marital partner.

SECTION 3. PURCHASES FROM A COMMINGLED DEPOSIT ACCOUNT

The case law discussed in this Section was developed to rebut the community property presumption as applied to purchases from a commingled account. The case law can also be used to rebut the community property presumption as to sums on deposit in a commingled account insofar as the cases describe what sort of records are required to prove the existence of separate property sums on deposit in a commingled account. Both CAMPAL and *See v. See*, excerpted below can be helpful in characterizing purchases that are made from a commingled account.

A commingled account is defined as one that holds community property deposits and provable separate property deposits.

Separate property sums on deposit are established by use of contemporaneous character specific records, meaning records that have been kept during marriage. Records created in anticipation of a dissolution or probate proceeding are inadmissible for several reasons, including that they are not necessarily reliable and they increase the risk of perjury.

The following material has its origin in community property law. It is consistent with CAMPAL.

A. THE EXHAUSTION METHOD: REBUTTING THE GENERAL COMMUNITY PROPERTY PRESUMPTION

Suppose a spouse uses money from a commingled account to buy an asset. How is the asset characterized?

The classic case on the issue is *See v. See*, below. The case instructs parties on what type of records are admissible in court for purposes of rebutting a community property presumption as to certain purchases made from a commingled account. *See* is followed by other jurisdictions.

See and CAMPAL appear to be consistent, however *See* is superseded by CAMPAL as to some but not all issues. One clear difference between the two sources of law comes into play when a separate property contributor helps the community buy an asset. *See*, as former law, held that such a contribution is a gift from the separate property contributor to the community. California Family Code Section 2640 established a new rule that the separate property contributor is entitled to a right of reimbursement (Chapter 2 and Chapter 4).

In *See*, Justice Traynor wrote that the community property right vests at acquisition, not at dissolution. The idea is also known as the inception of title rule; it explains why any rebuttal method that treats the community property right as contingent until dissolution is not only incorrect within the logic of the California community property system, but also an unconstitutional impairment of the vested right that goes against a strong state policy to insure that the community property right is vested in both spouses at acquisition. When an asset is purchased from sums withdrawn from a commingled account, *See* holds that character-specific financial records made contemporaneously with the purchase are necessary to prove that the sums used to buy the disputed asset were in fact net separate property deposits.

Implicit in the *See* opinion is the view that a commingled account is a disputed account. The first spouse to commingle the account has the legal duty to keep specialized legal records that are sufficiently clear enough to identify net *character* contributions. Specialized records are required in two situations. The first is when a dispute arises over the character of the sums on deposit in the commingled account, as discussed in Section 2 above. The second is when a dispute arises over the character of a purchase that is governed by the general community property presumption, and made from the commingled account.

Justice Traynor details the way in which the records must be specialized in order to avoid impairing a community property interest. I call these records *See*-compliant records. Because they are consistent with CAMPAL, *See*-compliant records can also be referred to as CAMPAL compliant records.

Here are identifying elements of *See*-compliant records:

- *The financial records are character and date specific.* Deposits, withdrawals, and purchases are recorded on or near the date they are made.

- *The financial records identify* net *character deposits.*

  a. The records identify and show the balance of community property sums on deposit on the date of the disputed purchase. To "identify" means to mark sums as "community" or "separate" while they are deposited in the account. To "show" in this context means to keep a running balance of community deposits relative to separate property deposits.

  b. The records identify and show the existence of separate property sums on deposit.

  c. The records identify and debit family expenses.

  d. The records debit family expenses first from community property sums on deposit. When community property sums are exhausted the records debit family expenses from separate property sums on deposit. (The spouse who owns separate property sums on deposit is not entitled to a reimbursement for paying family expenses during marriage.)

  e. The records are contemporaneous with deposits and withdrawals. Contemporaneous means that records are compiled on a regular, ongoing, basis during the marriage. Records prepared in anticipation of dissolution are not as reliable as records that have been kept during the marriage, as they may not be as accurate, and they may create incentives for perjury. For that reason, records prepared in anticipation of litigation generally are not admissible for purposes of rebutting a community property presumption.

Once *See*-compliant records are admitted into evidence, this is the question those records help the court answer:

> Looking back over the account records that were
> maintained during marriage, were community property
> sums on deposit exhausted (spent) on the date that the
> disputed asset was purchased?

If community deposits were exhausted, meaning insufficient to make the purchase, on the date in question, an inference can be drawn that separate property sums were used to make the purchase. Applying the tracing rule, this would make the purchase separate property in character. Proportional ownership is permitted. It is the separate property proponent's burden to produce specialized records; without records, rebuttal fails.

If the community had sufficient sums on deposit to make the disputed purchase on the date it was made, the community is adjudged to have made the purchase. The conclusion is consistent with the application of the general community property presumption and with tracing rules. It is not the community property proponent's duty to produce specialized records.

The general community property presumption found at California Family Code Section 760 characterizes any property, such as earnings, cash acquisitions, loan proceeds, and so on, as community property in character. Once such earnings and accumulations are deposited, California Probate Code Section 5305(a) presumes that sum on deposit in an account are community in character unless they can be traced back to a separate property source (using specialized records) or the parties have agreed otherwise.

California Family Code Section 2581 states a specialized presumption for an asset in any joint title form. Here rebuttal is by agreement only, not by tracing. Nevertheless, specialized records may still be admissible to establish a right of reimbursement under California Family Code Section 2640.

The family expense presumption, discussed above, is articulated in *See*. The presumption is consistent with the CAMPAL presumption that character deposits minus family expenses equals *net* character deposits.

SEE V. SEE

64 Cal.2d 778, 51 Cal.Rptr. 888, 415 P.2d 776 (1966) (in bank)

TRAYNOR, CHIEF JUSTICE.

Plaintiff Laurance A. See and cross-complainant Elizabeth Lee See appeal from an interlocutory judgment that grants each a divorce. * * *

The parties were married on October 17, 1941, and they separated about May 10, 1962. Throughout the marriage they were residents of

California, and Laurance was employed by a family-controlled corporation, See's Candies, Inc. For most of that period he also served as president of its wholly-owned subsidiary, See's Candy Shops, Inc. In the twenty-one years of the marriage he received more than $1,000,000 in salaries from the two corporations.

Laurance had a personal account on the books of See's Candies, Inc., denominated Account 13. Throughout the marriage his annual salary from See's Candies, Inc., which was $60,000 at the time of the divorce, was credited to this account and many family expenses were paid by checks drawn on it. To maintain a credit balance in Account 13, Laurance from time to time transferred funds to it from an account at the Security First National Bank, hereafter called the Security Account.

The funds deposited in the Security Account came primarily from Laurance's separate property. On occasion he deposited his annual $15,000 salary from See's Candy Shops, Inc. in that account as a "reserve against taxes" on that salary. Thus there was a commingling of community property and separate property in both the Security Account and Account 13. Funds from the Security Account were sometimes used to pay community expenses and also to purchase some of the assets held in Laurance's name at the time of the divorce proceedings.

Over Elizabeth's objection, the trial court followed the theory advanced by Laurance that a proven excess of community expenses over community income during the marriage establishes that there has been no acquisition of property with community funds.

Such a theory, without support in either statutory or case law of this state, would disrupt the California community property system. It would transform a wife's interest in the community property from a "present, existing and equal interest" as specified by Civil Code section 161a [current Family Code Section 751], into an inchoate expectancy to be realized only if upon termination of the marriage the community income fortuitously exceeded community expenditures. It would engender uncertainties as to testamentary and inter vivos dispositions, income, estate and gift taxation, and claims against property.

The character of property as separate or community is determined at the time of its acquisition. * * * If it is community property when acquired, it remains so throughout the marriage unless the spouses agree to change its nature or the spouse charged with its management makes a gift of it to the other. * * * .

Property acquired by purchase during a marriage is presumed to be community property, and the burden is on the spouse asserting its separate character to overcome the presumption. * * * The presumption applies when a husband purchases property during the marriage with funds from an undisclosed or disputed source, such as an account or fund in which he has commingled his separate funds with community funds. He may trace the source of the property to his separate funds and overcome the presumption with evidence that community expenses exceeded community income at the time of acquisition. If he proves that at that time all community income was exhausted by family expenses, he establishes that the property was purchased with separate funds. * * * Only when through no fault of the husband, it is not possible to ascertain the balance of income and expenditures at the time property was acquired, can recapitulation of the total community expenses and income throughout the marriage be used to establish the character of the property. Thus, in *Estate of Ades*, 81 Cal.App.2d 334, 184 P.2d 1, relied on by plaintiff, this method of tracing was used to establish that assets discovered after the husband's death had been acquired before the marriage. The question was not presented as to the balance of income and expenditures at any specific time during the marriage. In *Estate of Arstein*, 56 Cal.2d 239, 14 Cal.Rptr. 809, 364 P.2d 33, relied on by plaintiff, the husband's skill and industry in managing his separate property was the source of all community income during the marriage. Not until the trial could a determination be made as to what proportion of the total income was attributable to the husband's skill and industry. In *Thomasset v. Thomasset, supra*, 122 Cal.App.2d 116, 264 P.2d 626, the court made clear that the time of acquisition of disputed property is decisive. "An accountant testified that at the time the various items adjudged to be defendant's separate property were purchased, there were no community funds available. * * * The evidence [showed] that at the time the property was purchased the community funds had been exhausted * * *." Anything to the contrary [in *Thomasset*] is disapproved.

A husband who commingles the property of the community with his separate property, but fails to keep adequate records, cannot invoke the burden of record keeping as a justification for a recapitulation of income and expenses at the termination of the marriage that disregards any acquisitions that may have been made during the marriage with community funds. If funds used for acquisitions during marriage cannot otherwise be traced to their source and the husband who has commingled property is unable to establish that there was a deficit in the community accounts when the assets were purchased, the presumption controls that property acquired by purchase during marriage is community property. The husband may protect his separate property by not commingling community and separate assets and income. Once he commingles, he assumes the burden of keeping records adequate to establish the balance of community income and expenditures at the time an asset is acquired with commingled property.

The trial court also followed the theory that a husband who expends his separate property for community expenses is entitled to reimbursement from community assets. This theory likewise lacks support in the statutory or case law of this state. A husband is required to support his wife and family. [Current California Family Code Section 720]. Indeed, husband and wife assume mutual obligations of support upon marriage. These obligations are not conditioned on the existence of community property or income. The duty to support imposed upon [spouses] requires the use of separate property of the parties when there is no community property. [Current California Family Code Section 914(a)(1).] There is no right to reimbursement [for family expenses that fall into the necessaries of life category] under the statutes.

Likewise a husband who elects to use his separate property instead of community property to meet community expenses cannot claim reimbursement. In the absence of an agreement to the contrary, the use of his separate property by a husband for community purposes is a gift to the community. . . . The husband has both management and control of the community property. [Current California Family Code Section 1100(a)] along with the right to select the place and mode of living * * * . His use of separate property to maintain a standard of living that cannot be maintained with community resources alone no more entitles him to reimbursement from after-acquired community assets than it would from existing community assets.

Nor can we approve the recognition of an exception, a right to reimbursement of separate funds expended for community purposes at a time when a community bank account is exhausted. * * * Although this exception was restricted to recovery from the same community account when replenished, there is no statutory basis for it, and the court that first declared it cited no authority to support it. Such an exception conflicts with the long-standing rule that a wife who uses her separate funds in payment of family expenses without agreement regarding repayment cannot require her husband to reimburse her. * * * Nor is a wife required to reimburse her husband in the converse situation, particularly since the husband has the control and management of community expenses and resources. The basic rule is that the party who uses his separate property for community purposes is entitled to reimbursement from the community or separate property of the other only if there is an agreement between the parties to that effect. * * *

Plaintiff has not met his burden of proving an excess of community expenses over community income at the times the other assets purchased during the marriage were acquired. The part of the judgment finding them to be his separate property is therefore reversed. Since the property issues were tried on the theory that the nature of the property could be determined by proving total community income and expenditures and since the parties may have additional evidence that would otherwise have been presented, plaintiff's failure to overcome the presumption that the assets are community property is not conclusive. We therefore remand the case for retrial of the property issues. Since the court considered the lack of community property a significant factor in determining the amount of the alimony award, that part of the judgment is also reversed.

NOTES

1. *Family expenses versus acquisitions. See* elaborates on the concept of family purposes. Family purposes can be broken down into family *expenses* and acquisitions. For family expenses the general rule is that the use of separate property to meet family expenses is not reimbursable absent an agreement between the spouses. Separate property contributions to the purchase of an asset, on the other hand, are reimbursable pursuant to California Family Code Section 2640 assuming the sums used are provable separate property sums. California Family Code Section 2640 supersedes *See* as to contributions to purchase.

2. *Gender neutrality. See* was written during the male-management era, hence the gender-specific references to community property management and control. The principles set forth in *See* continue to hold in gender-neutral form.

3. *The legal duty to keep records.* The first spouse to commingle a bank account has the legal duty to keep *See*-compliant records, as discussed above. Without records, all sums in the account and all purchases from the account are community property in character.

A spouse who fails to disclose the existence of a bank account to the other spouse has the legal duty to keep *See*-compliant records as to that account.

Under the right circumstances, the mere fact of commingling also may give rise to a breach of fiduciary duty claim under California Family Code Section 721. Once conduct is adjudged a breach of California Family Code Section 721, an impairment of community property claim accrues under California Family Code Section 1101 (Chapter 6).

4. *Reimbursing one spouse for paying the other spouse's living expenses during a period of separation.* A spouse is generally not entitled to reimbursement for the use of separate property funds to pay family *expenses* during marriage. *Marriage of Epstein*, 24 Cal.3d 76, 154 Cal.Rptr. 413, 592 P.2d 1165 (1979) held that *See* does not go as far as to preclude a reimbursement for post-separation expenditures. This is the so-called "Epstein credit." The rule denying reimbursement for family expenses has been based on the rationale that a spouse who uses separate property to pay expenditures that increase the family's standard of living intends to make a gift of the expenditures. But the gift rationale no longer holds when parties are living separate and apart. Thus after *Epstein*, a separate property owner may be eligible to claim a reimbursement from the community for expenses paid to maintain the family residence during separation. *Epstein* theoretically still holds; however its application is severely restricted by California Family Code Section 914(a)(2), which governs separate property liability after date of separation. Additionally, *Epstein* is superseded for purchases by California

Family Code Section 2640, discussed above, as stated in *Marriage of Walrath*, 17 Cal.4th 907, 72 Cal.Rptr.2d 856, 952 P.2d 1124 (1998).

5. See-*compliant records are kept during the marriage.* Character deposits and withdrawls minus family expenses equal net character sums on deposit on a particular date. Once deposits are made, expenses can be paid. Sums that remain in the account after expenses are paid are "net character deposits." Net character sums on deposit establish whether community property sums on deposit were exhausted on a particular date.

Assume that married depositors X and Y have a provable commingled account. On a specific date there are $10,100 total sums on deposit, with community property sums on deposit totaling $100 and X's provable separate property sums on deposit totaling $10,000. On that same date, rent of $1,000 is paid. Rent is covered by the family expense presumption. For purposes of *See*-compliant records (or net character contributions under CAMPAL), the rent payment of $1,000 is deducted first from any available community property sums on deposit ($100) and then, pursuant to California Family Code Section 720, from available separate property sums on deposit ($10,000 − $900 = $9,100).

Now assume that a few days later the commingling spouse X purchases camera equipment (untitled) for $9,000. This purchase is presumptively community property unless and until X, the separate property claimant in this scenario, can show that community property sums on deposit in the account were exhausted on the date of the camera equipment purchase. The way for X to make this showing is to produce character and date specific *See*-compliant records. *See*-compliant records, will allow X to rebut the general community property presumption as to the untitled camera equipment that was purchased with $9,000 of provable net separate property sums on deposit ($9,100 − $9,000). X has documentary proof to show that on the date the camera equipment is purchased there are $0 of net community property deposits in the account and $9,100 of net separate property deposits in the account; and after the purchase, there are $0 of community property sums and $100 of separate property sums remaining on deposit.

6. *The* See *exhaustion method is retrospective.* Other than keeping contemporaneous net character specific records, the exhaustion method of accounting does not require a declaration on the separate claimant's part.

The tracing principle sets the policy here. In the absence of a marital settlement agreement, if a spouse expects to leave the marriage with a judgment that gives him or her more property than the other spouse, the benefitted spouse must be prepared to explain—using rules of the California community property system—why an uneven distribution of property is an appropriate and just result. The separate property claimant does that, in this instance, by producing records (present tense) that he or she compiled during the marriage (past tense) to keep track of separate property sums that were commingled (past tense) with community property sums in a single account— a retrospective analysis.

7. See-*compliant records can be used at dissolution and at death.* Justice Traynor's opinion involved a dissolution proceeding. It left open the question of whether the ruling extended to a probate proceeding. *Estate of Murphy*, 15 Cal.3d 907, 919, 126 Cal.Rptr. 820, 829, 544 P.2d 956 (1976), subsequently answered that question in the affirmative. *Murphy* held that *See* does apply in the probate context:

> "Murphy [the alleged owner of separate property sums on deposit in a bank account with community property sums] had the opportunity during his lifetime to maintain adequate records for tracing the disposition of his separate income. His legatees are bound by the consequences of his failure to do so."

B. THE DIRECT TRACING METHOD OF REBUTTAL FOR THE GENERAL COMMUNITY PROPERTY PRESUMPTION

Suppose a separate property owner wants to make a dedicated separate property purchase from a commingled account? Suppose also that net community property deposits are *not* exhausted on the date of the proposed purchase? Can the separate property claimant proactively declare the intent to buy an asset from a commingled account with separate property deposits? The *Hicks-Mix* method—a direct tracing method—says yes.

The *Hicks-Mix* accounting method is used to rebut the general community property presumption as applied to a purchase made from a commingled account. Applying *Hicks-Mix*: if, on the date of purchase, *See*-compliant records show there were sufficient net community property sums on deposit *and* sufficient net separate property sums on deposit to make the purchase, the separate property claimant can rebut a community property presumption as to the disputed asset with a declaration of intent made on or near the date of purchase. The declaration of intent must be in writing, and it must be extraneous to the *See*-compliant records. The fiduciary duty applies.

In other words, *Hicks-Mix* requires four doctrinal categories of proof. One is *See*-compliant records. Two is proof, in the form of a written declaration extrinsic from the bank records. Three is proof that the separate property owner intended to use separate property sums on deposit to make the purchase, and did in fact do so. Four is disclosure to the other spouse (see Note 1 page 352).

In *Marriage of Mix*, Richard Mix (a professional musician) and Esther Mix (a lawyer) were married during the time when California followed the male management rule. From 1958 to 1968, Esther commingled her separate property income and community property earnings into a sole bank account. She used the money in that account to purchase real estate.

Esther did not keep contemporaneous records. (*See* was decided in 1966, two years before Esther and Richard sought dissolution.) Instead Esther prepared forensic account records with the assistance of an accountant in anticipation of the dissolution proceeding. Esther alone corroborated the accuracy of the records by testifying that, on the date of the purchase, it was her intent to purchase the disputed real estate with separate property sums on deposit in the commingled account. Finding Esther credible, the trial court characterized the disputed real estate purchases as her separate property. Richard appealed. The California Supreme Court deferred to the trial court's assessment of Esther's credibility on the stand. Relying on *Hicks v. Hicks*, the trial court had reasoned that Esther's forensic record were wholly inadequate to rebut the community property presumption as to the disputed real estate; but that her testimony was credible. Applying the sufficient evidence standard the trial court's finding was upheld, making the disputed assets Esther's separate property as of the date of their purchase.

Notwithstanding the decision in *Mix,* forensic account records—that is account records prepared at the end of marriage and in anticipation of a dissolution proceeding—are no longer admissible for purposes of rebutting the general presumption under the *Hicks-Mix* line of cases. *See*-compliant records are required. To restate the rationale, *See*-compliant records are more reliable than forensic records; they lower the risk of perjury in a dissolution or probate proceeding and guard against the unconstitutional impairment of vested community property rights.

MARRIAGE OF MIX
14 Cal.3d 604, 122 Cal.Rptr. 79, 536 P.2d 479 (1975) (in bank)

SULLIVAN, JUSTICE.

* * * During the marriage of Richard and Esther the law bestowed on Richard the management and control of the community personal property other than Esther's earnings and on Esther the management and control of her community property earnings and separate property rents, issues and profits, with other exceptions not here applicable * * * . Thus under the law and the undisputed facts Esther had the management and control of the commingled bank accounts at the California Bank. Because the presumption in [Fam. Code § 803] that any interest in property acquired by a married woman in writing is her separate property will have no further effect after the wife acquires joint management of all community property on January 1, 1975 * * * , it should likewise not apply when the wife had management and control of the bank account in question. Otherwise, the wife managing a commingled account could by this device insulate herself from the rules applicable to commingling. We conclude

therefore that the controlling presumption in this case is the one that property acquired during marriage is community property. * * *

The presumption that all property acquired by either spouse during the marriage is community property may be overcome. * * * Whether or not the presumption is overcome is a question of fact for the trial court. * * * Generally speaking such post-marital property can be established to be separate property by two independent methods of tracing. The first method involves direct tracing. As the court explained in *Hicks:* "[S]eparate funds do not lose their character as such when commingled with community funds in a bank account so long as the amount thereof can be ascertained. Whether separate funds so deposited continue to be on deposit when a withdrawal is made from such a bank account for the purpose of purchasing specific property, and whether the intention of the drawer is to withdraw such funds therefrom, are questions of fact for determination by the trial court." (Hicks v. Hicks, supra, 211 Cal.App.2d 144, 157 * * *). The second method involves a consideration of family expenses. It is based upon the presumption that family expenses are paid from community funds. * * * If at the time of the acquisition of the property in dispute, it can be shown that all community income in the commingled account has been exhausted by family expenses, then all funds remaining in the account at the time the property was purchased were necessarily separate funds. (See v. See, supra, 64 Cal.2d 778, 783, 51 Cal.Rptr. 888, 415 P.2d 776.)

The effect of the presumption and the two methods overcoming it are succinctly summarized in *See:* "If funds used for acquisitions during marriage cannot otherwise be traced to their source and the [spouse] who has commingled property is unable to establish that there was a deficit in the community accounts when the assets were purchased, the presumption controls that property acquired by purchase during marriage is community property." (Id. at p. 784, 51 Cal.Rptr. at p. 892, 415 P.2d at p. 780.) Throughout the marriage Esther commingled her community property earnings from her law practice with the rents, issues and proceeds from her separate property in several bank accounts. She concedes that she made no attempt to trace the source of the property by resorting to the "family expense method." We are satisfied from our review of the evidence that Esther failed to keep adequate records to show that family expenses had exhausted community funds at the time of the acquisition of any of the property here in dispute.

Esther contends, however, that she introduced sufficient evidence to trace the source of the funds used to acquire each item of disputed property to her separate property in accordance with the "direct tracing test" described in *Hicks v. Hicks*, supra * * * , and that therefore the trial court's finding to that effect is supported by substantial evidence. In *Hicks* the husband introduced evidence of separate property deposits * * * in combination with evidence showing that the questioned withdrawals were intended to purchase the disputed property as separate property, [and the reviewing court found that this] supported the trial court's finding of separate property.

Esther introduced into evidence a schedule compiled by herself and her accountant from her records which itemized chronologically each source of separate funds, each expenditure for separate property purposes, and the balance of separate property funds remaining after each such expenditure. She received $99,632.02 attributable to her separate property; expended $42,213.79 for separate property purposes leaving an excess of separate property receipts over separate property expenditures in the amount of $57,418.23 throughout the course of the marriage. Each year from 1958 to 1968, excepting the year 1961, there was an excess of separate property receipts over separate property expenditures, leaving a balance of separate funds. The 1961 deficit did not, however, exhaust the balance of separate funds carried forward from prior years. The schedule demonstrated that Esther's expenditures for separate property purposes closely paralleled in time and amount separate property receipts and thus established her intention to use only her separate property funds for separate property expenditures.

Richard contends that the schedule contains a fatal flaw in that the entries of receipts and expenditures are not tied to any bank account or bank accounts. Therefore, he argues, the schedule shows merely the availability of separate funds on the given dates but fails utterly to demonstrate the actual expenditures of those funds for the enumerated separate purposes. Esther concedes that she was unable to support the schedule by correlating each itemized deposit and withdrawal on the schedule with an entry in a particular bank account due to the unavailability of various bank records as well as to the lack of such records of her own. Richard urges that this state of the evidence demonstrates that Esther has failed to meet her burden, that she has therefore not overcome the community property presumption, and that her claims to specific property as being her separate property must fall.

We agree that the schedule by itself is wholly inadequate to * * * support the trial court's finding that Esther "identified and traced" the separate property. However, the schedule was not the only evidence introduced by Esther to effect the tracing. She personally testified that the schedule was a true and accurate record, that it accurately reflected the receipts and expenditures as accomplished through various bank accounts, although she could not in all instances correlate the items of the schedule with a particular bank account, and that it accurately corroborated her intention throughout her marriage to make these expenditures for separate property purposes, notwithstanding her use of the balance of her separate property receipts for family expenses.

The trial court evidently believed Esther. "The testimony of a witness, even the party himself, may be sufficient." * * * Viewing this evidence in the light most favorable to Esther, giving her the benefit of every reasonable inference, and resolving all conflicts in her favor, as we must under the rules of appellate review * * * , we conclude that there is substantial evidence to support the trial court's finding that Esther traced and identified the source and funds of her separate property. We are satisfied that the trial court was warranted in inferring from this evidence that the bank records if introduced would fully verify the schedule as supported by Esther's testimony to the effect that "separate funds * * * continue[d] to be on deposit when a withdrawal [was] made * * * for the purpose of purchasing specific property, and * * * the intention of the drawer * * * [was] to withdraw such funds therefrom * * * ." (Hicks v. Hicks, supra.)

Since we conclude that the judgment can be upheld on the basis of an adequate tracing of Esther's separate property, it is unnecessary for us to consider whether it can also be upheld on the independent basis of an agreement between Richard and Esther as to the separate character of the properties in controversy.

The judgment is affirmed.

C. STANDARD BANK RECORDS INSUFFICIENT FOR REBUTTAL

Standard bank records are ordinarily not *See*-compliant. Nor do standard bank records comply with the CAMPAL requirement to identify net character deposits.

When a separate property claimant seeks to admit standard bank records into evidence to rebut a community property presumption, he or she is asking the trial court to make several unsupported inferences about the timing and character of deposits, withdrawals, and family expense deductions. Case law constrains a trial court from drawing such inferences. *Marriage of Frick* illustrates.

In *Marriage of Frick*, Jerome Frick, a married person, owned the separate real property that he used to run his separate property businesses, the Mikado Hotel and Restaurant. During marriage Jerome leased his separate real property to his restaurant. He deposited the separate property rent into a commingled personal account. He then paid the monthly mortgage loan on the separate real property from that commingled bank account.

Jerome did not keep *See*-compliant records. Nor did he declare his intent to use separate property deposits to pay the mortgage for the commercial property. Instead, Jerome (only) introduced standard bank records with a plea that the court use them to draw an inference, from the timing of deposits and withdrawals, that separate property deposits had been used to pay the mortgage on the commercial real estate.

The trial court declined to draw that inference.

Jerome appealed. He argued that standard bank statements were sufficient evidence given that deposits were made more or less contemporaneously with mortgage payments. From Jerome's perspective his records may not have been contemporaneously kept (as *See* requires), but the pattern of deposits and payments was nevertheless sufficient to show that separate property sums had paid the mortgage on the commercial property.

The court of appeal affirmed the trial court ruling. The moral of the story being that standard bank records are generally not sufficient evidence with which to rebut the community property presumption as to sums on deposit or purchases made from a commingled account.

MARRIAGE OF FRICK
181 Cal.App.3d 997, 226 Cal.Rptr. 766 (2d Dist. 1986)

JOHNSON, J.

Jerome incorporated the Mikado Hotel and Restaurant in September 1978. On October 1, 1978, Jerome entered into a lease between himself as lessor/landlord and the Mikado as lessee/tenant. The original lease called for payment to Jerome of $9,166 per month. The payments were reduced to $6,666 per month at the end of 1979. He deposited this amount into his personal account. Each month he made trust deed payments on the Mikado to Transamerica out of his personal account. In 1978, these payments were $5,000 per month. By the time of trial, these payments were $5,700 per month. Jerome contends the payments to Transamerica should not have been credited to the community since they were made contemporaneously or reasonably contemporaneously with his deposit of the monthly rental charge and, as such, the payments were traceable to a separate property source. We disagree.

While it is true, rents which are received from a separate property source are considered separate property [Fam. Code § 770], Jerome commingled these funds with community property funds. As Jerome testified, the Mikado Hotels, Inc. has two accounts, a general account and a payroll account. He also has a personal account. The income from the operation of the hotel and the restaurant is first deposited into the general account. He then takes some of the money from this account and puts it into the payroll account to meet his corporate payroll needs. He deposits his salary, community property, into his personal account. It is also into this account that he deposits the rent he receives from the corporation and it is from this account that Jerome makes payments to Transamerica.

Where funds are paid from a commingled account, the presumption is that the funds are community funds. * * * In order to overcome this presumption, a party must trace the funds expended to a separate property source. * * * This issue presents a question of fact for the trial court and its finding will be upheld if supported by substantial evidence.

There are essentially two methods for tracing expended funds to a separate property source. The first method, relied upon by Jerome, is direct tracing. When separate funds deposited with community funds continue to be on deposit when the withdrawal is made and it is the intention of the drawer to withdraw separate funds specifically, the separate property status of the withdrawn funds is established. Jerome contends he satisfied this test. He received rent payments each month of either $9,166 or $6,666 per month. He paid Transamerica $5,000 or $5,700 per month out of this account. Thus, he concludes, these payments have been traced to a separate property source. However, this testimony is not enough to satisfy the requirements in this context. "[T]he burden of establishing a spouse's separate interest in presumptive community property is not simply that of presenting proof at the time of litigation but also one of keeping adequate records. 'The husband may protect his separate property by not commingling community and separate assets and income. Once he commingles, he assumes the burden of keeping records adequate to establish the balance of community income and expenditures at the time an asset is acquired with commingled property.' (*See v. See, supra,* 64 Cal.2d [778] at p. 784.)" * * * The exact amount of money allocable to separate property and the exact amount of money allocable to community property must be ascertained before it can be said the money allocable to separate property is not so commingled that all funds in the account are community property. * * *

In the case at bar, Jerome provided evidence he received a specific amount of separate property income each month which he deposited in a particular personal account. He also made loan payments from this account. However, he made no other showing of the activity that occurred in this account during this month. We are merely provided an isolated portion of the account's activity. For instance, Jerome provided no evidence of what other expenditures were made from this account, the nature of the funds used, and the time in which they were expended. * * * We are left in the dark as to the precise status and amount of separate property in Jerome's personal account at the time of these payments. As the court properly found, " * * * petitioner [Jerome] commingled community and separate funds so that no separate property funds could be found to be the source of the payments on the real estate after marriage." Moreover, we are not satisfied Jerome presented sufficient evidence to demonstrate it was his intent to use only separate property funds to make loan payments.

As such, Jerome did not meet his burden of tracing the monthly loan payments to his separate property income. * * *

NOTES

1.   *Basic elements and the duty to disclose.* Certified Family Law Specialist Stephen James Wagner counts at least three, but probably four, elements that must be established to perform a successful commingled funds tracing using the direct tracing method. "It must be shown that: (1) separate property funds were available at the time of the acquisition at issue; (2) separate funds were actually withdrawn; and (3) with the intent to acquire a separate property asset. It is likely that there is a fourth element: disclosure of the intent to use separate property rather than community property to acquire the asset. Without disclosure there may be a breach of duty and usurpation of a fiduciary (community) opportunity." Mr. Wagner also points out that preparing a proper tracing case may require a team approach. The team most often includes the family law practitioner, the accountant, and the client. Stephen James Wagner, *Tracing: Understanding the Stepchild of Family Law*, October 2005 CALIFORNIA FAMILY LAW MONTHLY 268 (LexisNexis Matthew Bender).[2]

2.   *The* de minimis *principle.* When a small amount of community property is added to an otherwise large amount of separate property, the property is technically commingled. Nonetheless, in *Estate of Cudworth*, 133 Cal. 462, 65 P. 1041 (1901), the California Supreme Court states the *de minimis* principle: if the commingling is of "a trifling sum" with a large amount of separate property, it may be "inequitable to hold that the husband's property thereby lost its separate character." The court's conclusion is further buttressed by the family expense presumption.

3.   *The reverse* de minimis *principle.* In *Marriage of Shelton*, 118 Cal.App.3d 811, 816–817, 173 Cal.Rptr. 629 (3d Dist. 1981), the husband contended that gambling proceeds obtained in a period of separation were his separate property. He argued that the income arose from his separate "skill, efforts and industry;" that this use of his talent resulted in the commingling of community property and separate property; and therefore that he should receive a fair share of the gambling profits as his separate property. The gambler's legal argument was rejected by the court of appeal:

> "Husband's 'skill, efforts, and industry' were minimal. Although perhaps involving some slight element of skill, successful gambling of the type afforded at the Lake Tahoe casinos depends mainly upon good luck. *Kershman v. Kershman* (1961) 192 Cal.App.2d 18, 21, 13 Cal.Rptr. 288, held where the community property portion in commingled community and separate property is inconsiderable compared to the separate property contribution, "then the whole will be treated as separate property." There is no reason why the reverse

---

[2]   Fair use.

should not be equally true. Here, husband's separate property contribution was the minimal skill and effort required at games of chance, an inconsiderable factor compared to the community property contribution of $10,000. The entire winnings are therefore community property and the trial court's judgment was correct."

SECTION 4. COMMINGLED CREDIT ACQUISITIONS

What if a person buys a home (or a car) during marriage? How are the loan proceeds accounted for?

What if a person buys a home (or a car) before marriage? Same outcome?

The example of real estate helps explain how appreciation is apportioned. Depreciation can also be apportioned; when it is, it may be tax deductible.

Assume the spouses buy a house during marriage. They obtain a loan. They secure the loan with the house. They use community earnings to pay down a mortgage. One spouse uses provable separate property funds as a down payment. Title is taken in the name of the separate property contributor alone. What is the character of the house?

In California, the characterization approach is that the house is presumed community property under the general presumption. It is acquired during marriage and titled in one spouse's name alone. The separate property contributor has a right to trace a percentage of the house to the separate property down payment. The house is commingled; the community property owns the house concurrently with the spouse who contributed the separate property down payment. Ownership is proportional as determined by contributions to purchase.

Now assume one spouse buys a house before marriage. She obtains a loan. The loan is secured by the house. A marriage occurs. The spouses pay the mortgage each month with community property earnings. What is the character of the house? Does it matter how far in advance of marriage the house was purchased?

For the house purchased before marriage scenario, some states answer the question about the house's character with the civil law rule that the house is separate property by application of the inception of title rule, but that the community is entitled to a reimbursement for its contribution to paying down the outstanding separate property mortgage principal.

The California approach to the second scenario was developed by the California courts. It is called the pro tanto, or sometimes the buy-in, approach. The Americanized rule recognizes that the community gains a proportional ownership right in the property as of the date of its first contribution to purchase. In this case, the date that the first community property mortgage payment reduces the outstanding separate property loan obligation. The community's ultimate percentage share of the asset will be determined by a pro rata calculation. The loan in this scenario is typically separate property because it was acquired before marriage.

A. CREDIT ACQUISITIONS DURING MARRIAGE

We start with a credit acquisition during marriage for ease of analysis.

In *Aufmuth*, excerpted below, a house was purchased during marriage with a community property loan and a separate property down payment. The separate property claimant contended that the house was entirely separate property, with a reimbursement due to the community. His theory was that separate property purchased the house because the loan, although acquired by the community, had not yet been repaid. Under this (ultimately rejected) theory, the loan was not a contribution; it was an obligation.

The community property claimant countered that the loan proceeds were in fact the community's contribution to the purchase of the house. The lender transferred the loan proceeds to the seller on behalf of the community; without the transfer, the sale contract would not have closed and the seller would not have conveyed title. Under the community proponent's theory, the loan was a community contribution, despite it also being a community debt.

The court of appeal adopted the community claimant's argument.

Aufmuth was decided before the enactment of the special joint form title presumption. Thus the house in *Aufmuth* was governed by the general community property presumption even though title was in both spouses' names. The part of *Aufmuth* that allows tracing to rebut a joint title is *superseded* by California Family Code Section 2581 (Chapter 2). So too is the part of *Aufmuth* that allows oral transmutations; today all transmutations must be made by written express declaration (Chapter 1).

Despite being superseded on two significant issues, *Aufmuth* remains good law to the extent that *Aufmuth* is affirmed by *Moore*, excerpted below: Within the California community property system, *Aufmuth* establishes that a loan obtained by the community is a community contribution to purchase. This is the case even if the loan has yet to be repaid when the parties dissolve the marriage.

MARRIAGE OF AUFMUTH

89 Cal.App.3d 446, 152 Cal.Rptr. 668 (1st Dist. 1979)

McGUIRE, J.

Marcia Aufmuth (hereinafter wife) appeals from an interlocutory judgment dissolving the parties' marriage. Lawrence Aufmuth (husband) cross-appeals from certain provisions of the judgment.

The parties were married on August 19, 1967. Husband was then a law student and part-time clerk, and wife was a teacher. * * *

In July 1971, the parties purchased a family residence for $66,500 with a down payment of $16,500. The $50,000 balance was paid from a real estate loan evidenced by a promissory note and a deed of trust executed by both parties. Title to the property was taken in both names and as community property, and all subsequent payments and costs connected with it were paid from community earnings during the marriage. The parties agreed at trial that the fair market value of the residence was $125,000, and that the balance on the house loan was $47,000, at that time. * * *

The following determinations by the trial court [relevant to the characterization of the family residence] are challenged by wife's appeal and husband's cross-appeal:

1. At the time the residence was purchased, wife had a separate property interest in it valued at $16,500 (the amount of the down payment) and the community interest in it was worth $50,000.

2. At the time of trial, wife's separate property interest in the residence was worth $31,014 and the community interest in it was worth $46,986.

The Family Residence

Wife contends that the trial court erred in failing to find that the home is her separate property, subject to the community's right of reimbursement. She argues that where, as here, the down payment on a home is made entirely with separate property of one spouse, and the balance of the purchase price was obtained through a loan secured by that property, the home is the separate property of that spouse.

On the other hand, husband contends on his cross-appeal that the trial court erred in failing to find that the equity in the home was entirely community property. He argues that wife failed to rebut the presumption that all property acquired during marriage is community property *See v. See* ((1966) 64 Cal.2d 778, 781, [current California Family Code Section 760], and that the down payment from wife's separate property should be treated as a gift to the community. Neither argument is well taken.

Character of the Down Payment: All property owned by a husband or wife before marriage, and "that acquired afterwards by gift, bequest, devise or descent, with the rents, issues, and profits thereof," is the separate property of the acquiring spouse. [Fam.Code Sec. 770] *In re Marriage of Mix* (1975) 14 Cal.3d 604, 610. Property purchased with separate property funds is likewise the separate property of the acquiring spouse. Such separate property does not change its character as a result of the marriage or of its mere use in the marital relationship. Nor does separate property lose its character as such merely because of a change in form or identity.

If property is separate at the time of its acquisition, "it remains so with the exception of such increase thereof as may have been due to the contribution of the community by virtue of capital or industry

There is a statutory presumption that property acquired by either spouse during marriage is community. This presumption is rebuttable, and it may be overcome by a preponderance of evidence. Whether or not the presumption has been rebutted is a question of fact for the trial court, and its findings must be upheld if supported by substantial evidence. The form of the instrument under which the parties hold title is not conclusive of the status of the property. (*Gudelj v. Gudelj, supra.*, at p. 212.)

The evidence established that the source of the funds for the down payment on the residence was a savings account which was held in trust for wife by her parents in another state. There was testimony that at the time these funds were used for the down payment there was no intent by the parents or wife to make a gift to the community. At that time, and at all times prior to the commencement of the dissolution proceeding, neither party communicated with the other as to the property status of the funds used. Thus, although title to the property was taken in both names as community property, there is substantial evidence to support the trial court's finding that the down payment was and continued to be a separate property interest held by wife in the residence. This finding is supported on the basis of an adequate tracing of the wife's separate property. It need not be based on any understanding between the parties as to the separate property character of the down payment. (*In re Marriage of Mix, supra* at p. 614.)

Classification of Balance of Purchase Price: The trial court was also justified in determining that the balance of the purchase price on the home, obtained with a $50,000 loan, was paid from community funds.

The character of property acquired upon credit during marriage is determined according to the intent of the lender to rely upon the separate property of the purchaser or upon a community asset. (*Gudelj v. Gudelj, supra* at 41). * * *

There is a presumption that the proceeds of a loan acquired during marriage are community property. [California Family Code Section 760].

The presumption may be overcome only by a showing that the loan *was extended on the faith of existing separate property belonging to the acquiring spouse.* In the absence of evidence tending to show this, the trial court must find in accordance with the presumption.

Although no testimony was presented concerning the intent of the real estate lender in extending credit to the parties, it is apparent that the credit was extended on the strength of the community earnings. Wife had no separate property other than the $16,500 before the purchase of the home, she was not employed, and she had no appreciable earnings. Husband was a practicing attorney at the time and his income was the sole source of support of the community. Under these circumstances, we decline to disturb the trial court's implied finding in accordance with the presumption that the proceeds of the loan were community funds.

Separate and Community Property Interests in the Family Residence: It follows that both separate and community interests in the family home were established. * * *

As noted above, wife contributed $16,500 of her separate funds for the down payment on the home while the community contributed the balance of the purchase price in the amount of $50,000. * * * .

Computation of Separate and Community Interest in the Home: The parties agree that the separate and community interests are to be computed on a pro rata basis in direct proportion to the amounts of separate and community funds invested in the property, but each contends that the trial court erred in its application of this rule.

It was stipulated that the home had a fair market value of $125,000, an increase in value of $58,500 over the original $66,500 purchase price. The mortgage balance at the date of separation was $47,000. The community contributed $50,000, and wife contributed $16,500 of her separate funds, to the original purchase price. The community interest in the property was therefore 75.19 percent ($50,000 divided by $66,500), and the remaining 24.81 percent interest was wife's separate property, when the residence was acquired.

In accordance with this formula, the trial court found that "the present value of the $16,500 initial investment in said residence is $31,014 and the present value of the joint investment is $46,986." Although not expressly stated, it is apparent that the court calculated the $31,014 figure by adding the amount of capital appreciation attributable to separate funds (24.81 percent of $58,500) to the amount of the equity paid by separate funds ($16,500); the $46,986 figure, by adding the amount of capital appreciation attributable to community funds (75.19 percent of $58,500) to the amount of equity paid by community funds ($50,000 minus $47,000).

The alternative formulas advanced by husband and wife are both incorrect. Wife would have this court conclude that the community investment in the property could not exceed the amount by which community funds increased the equity in the home, or $3,000. This position is based upon the erroneous assumption that the proceeds of the real estate loan were wife's separate property. Husband, on the other hand, would have the court distribute the *total* equity in the home in strict proportion to the amounts of separate and community funds invested in the property (including taxes, maintenance and related expenditures), without regard to the increase in its fair market value. The effect of this position would be to give the community a 75 percent interest in wife's original $16,500 investment, which would deny her its full reimbursement.

* * * The judgment is affirmed. Neither party shall recover costs on appeal.

NOTES

1.   *Here is the* Aufmuth *approved formula for use when an asset is purchased during marriage and titled in one spouse's name alone.*

$\dfrac{\text{CP loan proceeds}}{\text{Purchase Price}} = \text{CP \% ownership}$
$\dfrac{\text{SP down payment}}{\text{Purchase Price}} = \text{SP \% ownership}$

At distribution, each estate is entitled to
     (1)   a reimbursement for its contribution to purchase; and
     (2)   its percentage share of asset appreciation (or depreciation).

2.   *Loan proceeds are a contribution to purchase.* As discussed above, *Aufmuth* allows the estate that obtains the loan —in this case the community estate—to get dollar-for-dollar credit for the loan proceeds in an apportionment calculation.

3.   Aufmuth *distinguished from California Family Code Section 2640.* Aufmuth provides a case law definition of "contribution to purchase" for purposes of assessing *ownership* shares.

California Family Code Section 2640 provides a statutory definition for purposes of calculating a *reimbursement.*

Thus the difference between *Aufmuth* and California Family Code Section 2640 is the difference between ownership (with market rate appreciation) versus a (no-interest) reimbursement.

B.   CREDIT ACQUISITIONS BEFORE MARRIAGE

When a person uses credit to buy an asset before marriage, that asset comes to the marriage as separate property under California Family Code

Section 770(a)(1) (Chapter 3). That code section incorporates the inception of title rule, which sets the original character of an asset as of the date of acquisition. As for the loan, when a property is acquired before marriage, the loan contribution is brought to the marriage as well; as is the obligation. The lender's intent test identifies loan proceeds obtained before marriage as separate in character.

What happens when the community helps to repay a separate property loan during marriage? Is the community entitled to an equitable accounting (yes)? If so, what does the community gain (a pro tanto ownership share)?

Vieux is yet another classic California case.

In *Vieux*, the community helped to repay the separate property owner's contract loan. At dissolution, the separate property owner asserted that the real estate was entirely separate property under the traditional inception of title rule, although he conceded that the community was entitled to a dollar-for-dollar reimbursement for its help in repaying the outstanding contract debt. (This is the traditional civil law rule.) The community proponent argued that the community was entitled to more than a reimbursement if not because of an implied agreement, then because of fairness. The court agreed with the community proponent.

Vieux starts a line of precedent that distinguishes the California community property approach on credit acquisitions from the civil law approach.

Vieux stands for the proposition that a community property principal payment on a separate property loan gives the community a pro tanto ownership interest in the asset. The rationale for recognizing the community as an owner is twofold. Absent evidence otherwise, the law presumes that the parties agreed that the separate property owner would transfer some ownership interest to the community in exchange for its assistance in repaying the outstanding debt. The second rationale is based on property law; it is the idea that the community acquires an expectancy interest beginning with the community's first contribution to purchase. That interest grows stronger each time the community repays outstanding indebtedness.

VIEUX V. VIEUX

80 Cal.App. 222, 251 P. 640 (2d Dist. 1926)

[Prior to marriage plaintiff and defendant agreed that a certain lot should be purchased. The agreement to purchase was executed by the plaintiff who made the original payment of $280. After marriage community property in the amount of $553.68 was used to make payments on the purchase price, to pay interest and taxes. The conveyance was in the name of the plaintiff. In divorce proceedings the trial court held the lot was plaintiff's separate property. An appeal was taken.]

HOUSER, J.

* * * For the purpose of determining the respective property rights of the husband and the wife, the circumstances surrounding the purchase of the property should receive consideration. While no transcript of the evidence received on the trial of the action has been presented to this court, sufficient facts are set forth in the findings to enable this court to perceive that, prior to the marriage, the parties together viewed the property and concluded that it was desirable for community purposes. The fact that thereafter they may have used it in that manner, and applied community funds in payment of the purchase price of the property, confirms the thought that, as between the husband and the wife, the property was considered as "community" rather than "separate." The authorities are in accord that by agreement between husband and wife the status of any property owned by them may be changed from separate to community, and vice versa. While no finding of the court recites the fact that the parties were "agreed," either at the time of the purchase or at any time thereafter, that the property in question was "community," their action in the premises at least encourages the belief that before the marriage each of them considered the property as being prospectively "community" and after marriage the property was to be improved, sustained, supported and finally completely and absolutely owned by them by reason of their common and joint efforts and savings. In the circumstances here present, it requires no wild stretch of the imagination to perceive a "meeting of the minds" without the form of express words, either spoken or written, to the effect that the property in question was not considered by the parties as exclusively in the husband, with the wife having absolutely no material right, title, or interest therein; but, to the contrary, that the property was "theirs," each of the parties enjoying therein equal rights and privileges, at least as far as the community funds contributed to the payment of the purchase price thereof. In effect it was somewhat in the nature of a partnership relationship that existed between the parties—the husband on the one side, and the community consisting of the husband and the wife, on the other side.

For purposes affecting strangers, the acquisition, through an installment contract, of the right to purchase real property, may be considered as ownership of such property, in that such holding may entitle the intending purchaser to the possession and the use of the property to the exclusion of others; but, as between husband and wife, where community funds are used to a considerable extent in the payment of the purchase price, the meaning of the statute relating to the definition of separate and community property of spouses cannot be so limited. The confidential relationship existing between husband and wife forbids such a strict construction to be placed upon the statute as will destroy the probable intent of the husband and wife with reference to the manner in which the ownership of the property is enjoyed. Any other construction in these days of liberal terms, with reference to installment purchase price contracts for the sale of real property, including the possible provision of "a dollar down and a dollar per week," would permit a husband or a prospective husband, to buy or to agree to buy any reasonable quantity of lots or lands on the payment by him from his separate funds of a comparatively insignificant sum and thereafter to pay practically the entire purchase price from the community funds, and yet successfully maintain that, because in its inception the naked right to purchase, carrying with it the right of use and possession, was his separate property, it so remained. It would seem improbable that, through general definitions of terms, the intention of the law-makers was to bring about a result which, in many if not a majority of instances, would be of so disastrous and unjust a consequence. Rather should it be assumed that, when the Legislature undertook to define separate property as that owned by the husband before marriage, even though in other statutes the right of exclusive possession and use was specified as the indicia of ownership, the "ownership" in the husband through and by virtue of which the wife's interest would be entirely excluded, would necessarily be an absolute ownership, as distinguished from a limited ownership, and that, so far as community funds might participate in the acquisition or protection of vested rights, to that extent proportionally should the property be considered as "community." * * *

In passing upon the meaning of the word "owner," as contained in a provision of a city charter, the Supreme Court of this state has ruled that "the term 'owner' includes any person having a claim or interest in real property, though less than an absolute fee." * * * That authority, however, can be regarded as nothing more than a generality, so far as the facts in the instant case are concerned. Cases from other jurisdictions, particularly *Guye v. Guye*, 63 Wash. 340, 115 P. 731; *Barrett v. Franke*, 46 Nev. 170, 208 P. 435, and *Heintz v. Brown*, 46 Wash. 387, 90 P. 211, in effect hold that, in circumstances analogous to those indicated in the findings herein, to which reference has been had, a part of property involved may be regarded as community and a part as separate—depending upon conditions, not essentially on the manner in which the contract for the purchase of the property was entered into or ostensibly acquired, but rather upon the manner in which the payments were made; and, while the principle announced in such decisions has been subjected to some criticism, the administration of strict justice to the parties concerned, rather than the application to the facts of the hard rules of law, lends an appealing force to the conclusions reached in the cases to which reference has been had. The governing rule is indicated in 5 Ruling Case Law, p. 834, as follows:

"Thus property purchased by one spouse before marriage is separate property, though the deed therefor is not executed and delivered until after marriage, and this is true though a part of the purchase price is not paid until after marriage, in the absence of a showing that any part of the balance was paid with community funds. In any event it would be community property only to the extent and in the proportion that the purchase price is contributed by the community."

In the instant case, the husband having acquired an inchoate right, on compliance with certain conditions, to become an absolute owner of the property in question, and the facts showing that the required conditions were met with funds furnished by the community, aided by other funds issuing directly from the property agreed to be purchased, justice demands that the rights of the parties should be measured by the direct contributions made by the respective parties to the purchase price of the property. Accordingly, the judgment of the trial court herein should have indicated that the community interest was entitled to share in the title to the property in the same proportion as the amount contributed to the purchase price by the community, to wit, $553.68, bore to the sum of $833.86—the total amount paid by the respective parties therefor.

It is ordered that that part of the judgment from which the appeal herein is taken be and the same is reversed; and the trial court * * * directed to enter a new judgment on its findings of fact in accordance with the law as indicated by the opinion herein.

NOTES

1.   *The pro tanto interest. Vieux* involved a purchase contract; but the case has been easily and subsequently applied to the acquisition of real property financed by a purchase-money mortgage.

Community property states rely on the pro tanto concept. Equitable title (common law) states on the equitable owernship interest concept.

A pro tanto ownership interest is distinguishable from an equitable ownership interest on many grounds, one of which is timing: A pro tanto interest comes into existence during the marriage; the equitable interest not until a court recognizes it, typically in a dissolution proceeding.

2.   *The P of PITI rule.* Only principal payments to a loan (payments that actually decrease the borrower's outstanding loan principal) count as a community contribution to purchase. Interest, taxes and insurance do not. This is the P of PITI rule. Interest, taxes and insurance are properly categorized as family expenses.

Vieux included the payment of interest and taxes by the community in formulating the community's proportional share of ownership; but the inclusion of those expenses into the pro rata calculation was eventually disapproved by the California Supreme Court in *Marriage of Moore*, excerpted below.

Moore sets out a legal holding for how to calculate proportional interests between the separate property and the community property. The guiding principles for the calculation are equal division and tracing.

The "*Moore* formula" is not math. Rather it is the holding in *Moore* expressed as a formula.

MARRIAGE OF MOORE

28 Cal.3d 366, 168 Cal.Rptr. 662, 618 P.2d 208 (1980) (in bank)

MANUEL, JUSTICE.

David E. Moore appeals from an interlocutory judgment dissolving his marriage to Lydie D. Moore. He contests only the trial court's determination of the community property interest in the residence located at 121 Mira Way, Menlo Park and the finding that he deliberately misappropriated community property.

The principal issue to be decided in this case is the proper method of calculating the interest obtained by the community as a result of payments made during marriage on the indebtedness secured by a deed of trust on a residence which had been purchased by one of the parties before marriage.

Lydie purchased the house at 121 Mira Way in Menlo Park in April 1966, about eight months before the parties' marriage. The purchase price was $56,640.57. Lydie made a down payment of $16,640.57 and secured a loan for the balance of the purchase price. She took title in her name alone as "Lydie S. Doak, a single woman." Prior to the marriage she made seven monthly payments and reduced the principal loan balance by $245.18.

The parties lived in the house during their marriage and until their separation in June 1977. They made payment during this time with community funds and reduced the loan principal by $5,986.20. Lydie remained in the house and continued to make payments, reducing the principal by an additional $581.07 up to the time of trial. At that time the total principal paid on the purchase price was $23,453.02, the balance owing was $33,187.55, the market value of the house was $160,000, and the equity therein $126,812.45.

The trial court concluded that the residence was Lydie's separate property but that the community had an interest in it by virtue of the community property payments made during the course of the parties' marriage. The trial court further concluded that the community interest was to be determined according to the ratio that the reduction of principal resulting from community funds bears to the reduction of principal from separate funds. No credit was given for the amount paid for interest, taxes and insurance.

The community interest was calculated by multiplying the equity value of the house by the ratio of the community's reduction of principal to the total amount of principal reduction by both community and separate property ($5,986.20 divided by $23,453.02 equals 25.5242 percent). The amount of the community interest was thus determined to be $32,367.86. Lydie's separate property interest was calculated by multiplying the equity value of the house by the ratio of the separate property reduction of principal to the total amount of principal reduction ($17,466.82 divided by $23,453.02 equals 74.4758 percent). Lydie's separate property interest was thus determined to be $94,444.59.

The parties agree that the community has acquired an interest in the house by virtue of the community funds used to make the payments. They disagree, however, as to how the interest is to be determined. Appellant contends that the community property interest should be based upon the full amount of the payments made, which includes interest, taxes and insurance, rather than only on the amount by which the payments reduce the principal. He relies on *Vieux v. Vieux* (1926) 80 Cal.App. 222, 251 P. 640.

In *Vieux,* the husband contracted before marriage to buy certain property and paid $280 on account of the purchase price. After the parties' marriage they spent $553.68 of community funds for payment of principal, interest and taxes. The Court of Appeal held that the trial court erred in finding the property to be solely the husband's separate property and stated the rule as follows: "Thus property purchased by one spouse before marriage is separate property * * * , and this is true though a part of the purchase price is not paid until after marriage, in the absence of a showing that any part of the balance was paid with community funds. In any event it would be community property only to the extent and in the proportion that the purchase price is contributed by the community." (80 Cal.App. at p. 229, 251 P. 640.) The court concluded that "the community interest was entitled to share in the title to the property in the same proportion as the amount contributed to the purchase price by the community, to wit, $553.68 bore to the sum of $833.86 [sic]—the total amount paid by the respective parties therefor." (Ibid.)

Although the *Vieux* court included interest and taxes in its calculation, there is no indication that the issue of the propriety of doing so was presented to the court. The concern in that case was with the question of whether there should be any community interest at all. Since the *Vieux* court did not expressly consider the question of including interest and taxes in the community's interest in the property, we do not consider it to be persuasive authority on that issue.

Where community funds are used to make payments on property purchased by one of the spouses before marriage "the rule developed through decisions in California gives to the community a *pro tanto* community property interest in such property in the ratio that the payments on the purchase price with community funds bear to the payments made with separate funds." * * * This rule has been commonly understood as excluding payments for interest and taxes. For example in *Bare v. Bare*, the Court of Appeal directed the trial court to determine the increase in equity in the house during marriage and the fair market value of it before and after the marriage, stating: "the community is entitled to a minimum interest in the property represented by the ratio of the community investment to the total separate and community investment in the property. In the event the fair market value has increased disproportionately to the increase in equity the wife is entitled to participate in that increment in a similar proportion." (256 Cal.App.2d at p. 690, 64 Cal.Rptr. 335.) Decisions of other community property jurisdictions are in accord (see, e.g., *Hanrahan v. Sims* (1973) 20 Ariz.App. 313, 512 P.2d 617, 621; *Gapsch v. Gapsch* (1954), 76 Idaho 44, 277 P.2d 278, 283; *Merkel v. Merkel* (1951) 39 Wash.2d 102, 234 P.2d 857, 864), and *Vieux* apparently stands alone in suggesting a contrary rule.

Appellant argues, however, that interest and taxes should be included in the computation because they often represent a substantial part of current home purchase payments. We do not agree. Since such expenditures do not increase the equity value of the property, they should not be considered in its division upon dissolution of marriage. The value of real property is generally represented by the owners' equity in it, and the equity value does not include finance charges or other expenses incurred to maintain the investment. Amounts paid for interest, taxes and insurance do not contribute to the capital investment and are not considered part of it. A variety of expenses may be incurred in the maintenance of investment property, but such expenses are not considered in the valuation of the property except to the extent they may be relevant in determining its market value from which in turn the owners' equity is derived by subtracting the outstanding obligation. Upon dissolution, it is the court's duty to account for and divide the assets and the debts of the community. Payments previously made for interest, taxes and insurance are neither. Moreover, if these items were considered to be part of the community's interest, fairness would also require that the community be charged for its use of the property.

In summary, we find no basis for departing from the present rule which excludes amounts paid for interest, taxes, and insurance from the calculation of the respective separate and community interests. We turn to that calculation in this case.

Although many formulae have been suggested, we are not persuaded that any of them would be an improvement over a formula based on the reasoning of *In re Marriage of Aufmuth* * * * . We were there concerned with determining the respective community and separate interests in a residence purchased during marriage with a combination of community and separate funds where the community contributed the loan and subsequent payments on it and there was an agreement or understanding that the party contributing the separate property down payment was to retain a pro rata separate property interest. * * * The formula we used there recognized the economic value of the loan taken to purchase the property. In the formula postulated in *Lucas* the proceeds of the loan were treated as a community property contribution on the assumption that the loan was made on the strength of the community assets. (Id., at pp. 816–817, fn. 3, 166 Cal.Rptr. 853, 614 P.2d 285.)

In the present situation, the loan was based on separate assets and was thus a separate property contribution; the down payment was also a separate property contribution. Therefore under the *Lucas/Aufmuth* formula the proceeds of the loan must be treated as a separate property contribution. Accordingly, the formula would be applied as follows: The separate property percentage interest is determined by crediting the separate property with the down payment and the full amount of the loan less the amount by which the community property payments reduced the principal balance of the loan ($16,640.57 plus ($40,000 minus $5,986.20) equals $50,654.37). This sum is divided by the purchase price for the separate property percentage share ($50,654.37 divided by $56,640.57 equals 89.43 percent). The separate property interest would be $109,901.16, which represents the amount of capital appreciation attributable to the separate funds (89.43 percent of $103,359.43) added to the amount of equity paid by separate funds ($17,466.82). The community property percentage interest is found by dividing the amount by which community property payments reduced the principal by the purchase price ($5,986.20 divided by $56,640.57 equals 10.57 percent). The community property share would be $16,911.29, which represents the amount of capital appreciation attributable to community funds (10.57 percent of $103,359.43) added to the amount of equity paid by community funds ($5,986.20).

In this case the trial court used a different formula which appears to have been based upon a statement in *In re Marriage of Jafeman, supra,* 29 Cal.App.3d 244, 256, 105 Cal.Rptr. 483, that might be interpreted to mean that the interests are to be determined according to the proportionate equity contributions only, with no credit given for the loan contribution. This formula might be appropriate when the obligation on the property has been fully paid. To apply it in the present situation, however, when the purchase price of the amount owing on the loan has not been fully paid ignores the role of the loan and produces inconsistencies with the principles of the *Lucas/Aufmuth* formula.

Although the trial court erred in determining the parties' interests in the residence, the error was in David's favor. Since he was not prejudiced by the error and Lydie did not appeal, reversal of this portion of the judgment is unwarranted. * * *

BIRD, C.J., and TOBRINER, MOSK, CLARK, RICHARDSON and NEWMAN, JJ., concur.

NOTES

1. *The* Aufmuth/Moore *formula.* For use when tracing is permitted. This means that the formula can be used only when title to the property is in the purchasing spouse's name alone. This is usually not a problem because the property was purchased prior to marriage. So too the loan, which was acquired before marriage by a single person and thus meets the lender's intent test. The loan is secured by the asset in question.

Step #1: Determine pro tanto shares.

$$\frac{\text{SP down payment} + (\text{SP loan proceeds} - \text{CP contributions to purchase})}{\text{Historic Purchase Price}} = \text{SP \% ownership}$$

$$\frac{\text{CP contributions to purchase}}{\text{Historic Purchase Price}} = \text{CP \% ownership}$$

Step #2: Reimburse the respective estates for their equity contributions to purchase.

The SP is reimbursed for its down payment *plus* the difference between the loan proceeds minus the CP loan principal repayments.

The CP is reimbursed for its loan principal repayments.

Step #3: Apportion appreciation: use the percentages from Step #1.

Appreciation is defined as the fair market value [FMV] on the date of dissolution minus FMV on the date of purchase.

---

2. Moore *reconciles* Vieux *and* Aufmuth. *Vieux* defines debt principal repayments as the basis for a pro tanto ownership share. *Aufmuth* defines loan proceeds as a contribution to purchase. *Moore* reconciles these two approaches. Under *Moore*, the separate property gets full credit for obtaining loan proceeds, but community property principal payments are subtracted therefrom. The loan proceeds are what the separate property originally contributed to the purchase. The community property loan principal repayments are what the community contributed to purchase. The difference between the two values identifies the current loan balance:

SP loan proceeds − CP repayments to the loan = current mortgage indebtedness

3. Pro tanto *shares of asset appreciation (or depreciation) are based on contributions to purchase divided by the original (historic) purchase price. Moore* holds that at dissolution, each estate is entitled to a reimbursement for

its original contribution to purchase, plus its percentage share of the commingled asset's appreciation (or depreciation). Under *Moore* percentage shares are of total asset appreciation, not just of appreciation that occurred during marriage. The reason is that *Moore* is limited to its facts. Dispositive in *Moore* was that premarital loan repayments were *de minimis*, as was premarital asset appreciation. In other words, the asset was purchased soon enough before marriage that the mortgage indebtedness was not measurably reduced by the premarital loan repayments. Nor did the asset appreciate from the time of purchase to the time of marriage.

The next clarifying case is *Marsden*. The facts of *Marsden* are similar to those in *Moore*, with one important exception. In *Marsden* unlike in *Moore*, there was provable premarital equity build up since the time between purchase and marriage was almost a decade. Otherwise, the question for the *Marsden* court was how to account for the separate property owner's premarital equity and premarital appreciation as separate property (under California Family Code Section 770(a)(1)) within the framework of the *Moore* formula.

MARRIAGE OF MARSDEN

130 Cal.App.3d 426, 181 Cal.Rptr. 910 (1st Dist. 1982)

BARRY-DEAL, J.

. . .

Valuation of Leasehold and House

Husband concedes that there is a community interest in the leasehold and house. He contends, however, that the trial court incorrectly calculated the community interest. We agree.

The pertinent facts are as follows: in 1962, husband paid to Stanford University $6,300 for an 80-year lease of a parcel of property owned by Stanford. That same year, he had a house constructed on the property which he financed by a $2,000 cash payment and the proceeds from a $30,000 loan from Stanford. Thus, the cost of the property in 1962 was $38,300. By the time the parties were married in February 1971, husband had reduced the loan by $7,000, so the outstanding balance was $23,000. During the marriage, payments from community funds further reduced the principal due on the loan by $9,200. Between the time of separation in July 1978 and trial in February 1979, husband paid $655 on the principal.

The trial court found the fair market value (FMV) of the house and leasehold interest was $65,000 at the time of the marriage in February 1971 and $182,500 at the time of trial. It computed the appreciation as "$136,700 [*sic*; $126,700]", the difference between the equity at the time of trial ($182,500 less a loan balance of $13,800 equals $168,700) and the equity in 1971 ($65,000 less the $23,000 loan balance equals "$32,000 [*sic*; $42,000]"). It then allocated "$77,632 [*sic*; $71,953]" as the community interest based on the ratio of separate property loan payments ($7,000 or 43.21 percent) to the community property loan payments ($9,200 or 56.79 percent). This was clearly in error.

"Where community funds are used to make payments on property purchased by one of the spouses before marriage 'the rule developed through decisions in California gives to the community a *pro tanto* community property interest in such property in the ratio that the payments on the purchase price with community funds bear to the payments made with separate funds.' * * * " (*In re Marriage of Moore* (1980) 28 Cal.3d 366, 371–372 [168 Cal.Rptr. 662, 618 P.2d 208].) In clarifying the application of the rule, the Supreme Court has recently reaffirmed a formula articulated in *In re Marriage of Aufmuth* (1979) 89 Cal.App.3d 446, 454–457 [152 Cal.Rptr. 668], and approved in *In re Marriage of Lucas* (1980) 27 Cal.3d 808, 816–817 [166 Cal.Rptr. 853, 614 P.2d 285], to determine the respective community and separate interests in the property. (*In re Marriage of Moore, supra.*, 28 Cal.3d 366, 373–374.) The formula gives recognition to the economic value of any loan proceeds contributed toward the purchase of the property. Where, as in *Moore* and in the case before us, the loan was extended before marriage and was based on separate assets, it is a separate property contribution. The *Moore* court also negated the inclusion of such expenses as loan interest and taxes in the computation, thereby clearing up any ambiguity created by the holding in *Vieux v. Vieux* (1926) 80 Cal.App. 222 [251 P. 640]. (*In re Marriage of Moore, supra.*, 28 Cal.3d at p. 371.)

Under the *Moore/Lucas/Aufmuth* formula, husband's separate property percentage interest is determined by crediting the separate property with the down payments and the full amount of the loan, less the amount by which the community property payments reduced the principal balance of the loan ($8,300) plus ($30,000 less $9,200) equals $29,100). This sum is divided by the purchase price for the separate property percentage share ($29,100 divided by $38,300 equals 75.98 percent). The community property percentage interest is found by dividing the community property payments on the loan principal by the purchase price ($9,200 divided by $38,300 equals 24.02 percent).

Husband proposes a modification of the above formula. He contends, and we agree, that he should have the benefit of approximately nine years of appreciation in the value of the property before the marriage in 1971. Husband argues that his separate property percentage interest should be 85.85 percent, based on the FMV of the property at the time of marriage ($65,000), rather than the purchase price in 1962 ($38,300).

Husband does not cite any cases directly on point, and we can find none. * * *

It is clear that part of our confusion results from the use of the word "equity." It is defined as "5. [t]he amount or value of a property or properties above the total of liens or charges." (Webster's New Internat. Dict. (2d ed. 1935) p. 865.) The fair market value at or near the time of purchase is usually equivalent to the purchase price. In short, the appraised value equals the cost value. Such was the case in *Moore*, where the respondent wife had purchased the property eight months before the marriage, and thus no question of the fair market value of the home at the time of marriage was posed. (*Id.*, 28 Cal.3d at p. 370.)

Where the separate property is owned for a considerable period before marriage, the increase in value in an inflationary market, such as we have had for the past several decades, is substantial. The fair market value at the time of marriage would usually be significantly greater than the purchase price, and this is true in the case before us. We think it is equitable to credit the separate property interest with this prenuptial appreciation. Although we are bound by the *Moore/Lucas/Aufmuth* formula, and adjustments must fit within that formula, we can infer from the language in *Moore* * * * that recognition of prenuptial appreciation in the separate property estate is appropriate. As previously stated, the *Moore* court in explaining the *pro tanto* allocation rule noted the direction in *Bare* to the trial court "to determine the increase in equity in the house during marriage and the fair market value of it before and after the marriage. . . ." (*In re Marriage of Moore, supra.*, 28 Cal.3d at p. 372.)

We therefore compute the *pro tanto* community and separate property interests in the house and leasehold interest as follows:

[The court went on to calculate the husband's premarital equity reimbursement as determined by (1) premarital principal payments on the premarital (separate property) mortgage loan; and premarital equity as measured by real estate appreciation from the date of purchase to the date of marriage.]

The *Moore* formula was approved for calculating percentage ownership shares, as based on the original (historic) purchase price of the property. Each estate's proportional share was then applied to real estate appreciation that occurred between the date of marriage to the date of dissolution.

Based upon the above computation [which are available in the original opinion], the trial court should have awarded husband a separate property interest of $131,931.50, plus one-half of the community interest, or $18,711.75, for a total of $150,643.25. The wife's one-half share of the community interest is $18,711.75, and husband, of course, is responsible for the balance due on the loan.

NOTE

The Moore/Marsden *formula.* For use only when tracing is permitted. This means that this formula can be used, as in *Moore*, only when title to the property is in the purchasing spouse's name alone and the loan is separate property per the lender's intent test (Chapter 2). Typically these elements are met because the loan was obtained prior to marriage by a single person and the purchase was made prior to the marriage.

Step #1: Determine pro tanto shares using the *Aufmuth/Moore* formula.

$$\frac{\text{SP down payment} + (\text{SP loan proceeds} - \text{CP contributions to purchase})}{\text{Historic Purchase Price}} = \text{SP \% ownership}$$

$$\frac{\text{CP contributions to purchase}}{\text{Historic Purchase Price}} = \text{CP \% ownership}$$

Step #2: Reimburse the respective estates for their contributions to purchase.

Marsden authorizes a separate property reimbursement for a down payment, any *pre*marital loan repayments, and any established *pre*marital appreciation. Mortgage principal repayments made before marriage are reimbursed. Appreciation is measured by FMV on the date of marriage minus FMV on the date of purchase. Appraisal at marriage is useful, if not required, to establish premarital appreciation.

The separate property is reimbursed for its loan proceeds minus any community property principal repayments to the separate property loan.

The community property is reimbursed for its loan principal repayments.

Step #3: Apportion *marital* appreciation.

Apply the percentages in Step #1 to marital appreciation, defined as FMV on the date of dissolution minus FMV on the date of marriage.

The next case extends the *Moore/Marsden* approach to commercial real estate. The phrase "historic purchase price" comes from the *Marsden* opinion, where the court confirmed that fairness requires percentage ownership shares be calculated based not on fair market value on the date of marriage, but on the original (contract) purchase price. *Frick*, a case also excerpted in Section 3C above, adopts *Moore/Marsden* in the commercial context.

MARRIAGE OF FRICK

181 Cal.App.3d 997, 226 Cal.Rptr. 766 (2d Dist. 1986)

JOHNSON J.

Jerome owned certain real property prior to his marriage to Hiroko which he used to operate the Mikado Hotel and Restaurant. During the marriage he used community property funds to reduce the principal balance of the encumbrance on the real property." * * *

The trial court applied the [*Moore/Marsden*] formula in determining the parties' respective interests in the real property. Jerome contends, however, the trial court erred by calculating the separate and community property percentage interest based on the purchase price of the property rather than on the fair market value of the property at the time of marriage. Jerome, in essence, seeks not only to be awarded all the premarriage appreciation, but wants that appreciation to be factored in when determining the respective percentage interest in the property. We do not believe this is proper.

Under the formula described above, Jerome indisputably was entitled to all the capital appreciation which accrued prior to marriage. The community until marriage had absolutely no interest in the property and, as such, should not and did not reap any of the benefits of the prenuptial appreciation. The issue is how to divide the appreciation accruing during marriage, i.e., what percentage goes to the separate property interest and what percentage goes to the community property interest. We believe fairness dictates that the separate and community property's respective interest should be based on the ratio of capital contribution to the purchase price. It is this ratio (percentage) which best reflects the parties' respective interests in the property at the time the appreciation at issue is accruing. The community should share in the appreciation that accrues during marriage in the same proportion that its capital contribution bears to the total capital contribution required to own the property outright. This is the method of computation that has historically been followed in this state and we believe it is the appropriate one. To do as Jerome asks would give him *double* credit for premarital appreciation in the value of this property. We see no justification for this approach. Indeed it appears to fail the test of fundamental fairness.

———

What if the property is refinanced during marriage? Can the values identified by *Aufmuth*, *Moore*, and *Marsden* be traced through to a later time (yes)? Who bears the burden of proof to clarify the financial history of a refinanced property?

Marriage of Geraci pins the burden of proof on the separate property claimant who neglected to appraise the real estate on or near the date of marriage or otherwise keep clarifying records. The holding in *Geraci* is consistent with the idea that the burden to identify and record separate property interests during marriage is borne by the spouse who intends to claim a sum-specific separate property ownership interest at the end of the marriage. *Geraci* is also an illustration of the doctrine of confusion in action (Chapter 1).

MARRIAGE OF GERACI

144 Cal.App.4th 1278, 51 Cal.Rptr.3d 234 (2d Dist. 2006)

FACTS AND PROCEEDINGS BELOW

John J. Geraci and Jane Holder Geraci started living together in 1980. They lived in a house in Manhattan Beach John had acquired in a former marriage in 1973 for $43,000. In 1980 John razed the structure and built an entirely new 3,100-square-foot house in its place.[2] John and Jane married on June 18, 1983. They separated in October 2000 after a 17 year marriage. They had no children. In July 2001 Jane filed a petition for dissolution of marriage. * * *

During their marriage John and Jane routinely lived beyond their means. They incurred between $2,500 and $4,000 per month in credit card debt. They borrowed money from a friend, from Jane's father and against a pension plan originally set up through the now defunct Manhattan Video.

John and Jane regularly refinanced the Manhattan Beach house to pay off routine debts and to cover living expenses. Four months after they were married, in October 1983, John got a loan secured by the house for $149,500. In January 1985 John got another loan for $193,000. In 1989 John and Jane took out a $100,000 home equity loan in order to remodel the kitchen and bathrooms. In 1990 they again refinanced by taking out two loans totaling $600,000. In 1997 they filed for bankruptcy protection but managed to save the house. In April 2000 they took out another loan for $153,000 and used some of the proceeds to prepare the house for sale.

In October 2000 John and Jane separated and sold their residence in Manhattan Beach. The house sold for $974,000 and netted sale proceeds of $354,000. The parties split the proceeds with approximately $159,000 going to Jane and John retaining the balance of approximately $194,000.

At trial John presented expert testimony to the effect the Manhattan Beach house had a fair market value of approximately $400,000 in 1983 when John and Jane married. John presented his own mortgage/market research analysis and testimony to the same effect. John claimed he was entitled to reimbursement of this separate property interest in the house from its sales proceeds.

The matter was tried over numerous court days spanning several months in 2004. At its conclusion the court * * * ruled [that] * * * John failed to establish his separate property reimbursement claim and thus the court would enforce the parties' pretrial division of the sales proceeds from the Manhattan Beach house * * * .

John appeals from the adverse judgment.

I.   John Has Failed To Establish Division Of The Sales Proceeds From The Manhattan Beach Residence Was Erroneous.

At trial John produced evidence tending to show the Manhattan Beach house had a fair market value of approximately $400,000 when he and Jane married. Based on this evidence John claims he was entitled to all of the $354,000 net proceeds from the sale of the house as reimbursement of his separate property interest. He claims the trial court erred in failing to grant his request for reimbursement of this separate property contribution to the residence.

"Where, as here, the trial court is vested with discretionary powers, we review its ruling for an abuse of discretion. * * * As long as the court exercised its discretion along legal lines, its decision will be affirmed on appeal if there is substantial evidence to support it. * * * "

California Family Code Section 2640 authorizes reimbursement of separate property contributions in the division of property. This section provides: "(a) 'Contributions to the acquisition of property,' as used in this section, include downpayments, payments for improvements, and payments that reduce the principal of a loan used to finance the purchase or improvement of the property but do not include payments of interest on the loan or payments made for maintenance, insurance, or taxation of the property.

(b) In the division of the community estate under this division, unless a party has made a written waiver of the right to reimbursement or has signed a writing that has the effect of a waiver, the party shall be reimbursed for the party's contributions to the acquisition of property of the community property estate to the extent the party traces the contributions to a separate property source. The amount reimbursed shall be without interest or adjustment for change in monetary values and may not exceed the net value of the property at the time of the division." * * *

Of course, reimbursement only becomes an issue once a separate property asset takes on the character of community property. There are several ways in which this can occur. "When community property is used to reduce the principal balance of a mortgage on one spouse's separate property, the community acquires a *pro tanto* interest in the property. (*In re Marriage of Moore* [reproduced above]; *In re Marriage of Marsden* [reproduced above]) This well-established principle is known as 'the *Moore/Marsden* rule.' * * * The *Moore/Marsden* rule has been extended to cases involving separate commercial property. (*In re Marriage of Frick* [reproduced above]. It has also been applied where the parties refinanced a separate residential mortgage during marriage. (*In re Marriage of Branco* (1996) 47 Cal.App.4th 1621, 1625–1629, 55 Cal.Rptr.2d 493.)"

In the present case the evidence is undisputed John acquired the Manhattan Beach residence as his separate property in 1973 for $43,000.

According to John, he had an outstanding mortgage balance of some $17,000 ten years later when he married Jane in 1983. The evidence was also undisputed in 1980 (three years before their marriage) John razed the structure and built an entirely new residence in its place. The parties married in June 1983 and in October 1983 they refinanced the house and took out a loan for $149,500. The evidence also established John and Jane refinanced the house, or took out home equity loans against the house, five more times during the course of their marriage.

Missing, however, is any evidence of how the rebuilding project in 1980 was financed and any evidence of John's *equity* in the property at the time of marriage. Did John pay cash for the reconstruction from his own funds pre-marriage? If so, he would have been entitled to reimbursement under California Family Code Section 2640 for these improvements as well. Did John secure a construction loan for the rebuilding project? If so, when was the loan repaid and with whose funds? Was the loan taken out in October 1983 used to retire a possible construction loan and/or John's original mortgage? If so, the community acquired a *pro tanto* interest in the property from the very beginning. Despite all the evidence presented concerning the community's later refinancings and loan commitments there was an absence of evidence concerning the crucial issue of John's actual contributions of separate property to acquire and improve the residence in Manhattan Beach, and thus by extension, an absence of evidence of his actual equity interest in the property at the time of marriage. John's evidence of the house's fair market value around the time of their marriage was thus largely immaterial. What was crucial was evidence of his actual equity in the house at the time. If there were outstanding loan commitments (as was possibly the case given John's history of borrowing against the property) then these amounts had to be considered in assessing John's actual separate property interest.

Because of this crucial evidentiary gap the trial court found John had failed to carry his burden of identifying his separate property contributions to the property. [The property is characterized as community property subject to division by the] * * * parties' own pretrial settlement regarding the division of the house's sales proceeds as the best evidence of each side's respective interest. Under the parties' de facto agreement John received $194,000 and approximately $35,000 more than Jane. This amount, in the court's view, adequately accounted for John's separate property contribution toward acquisition of the Manhattan Beach residence based on the available evidence.

We find no abuse of the court's discretion in enforcing the parties' own pretrial agreement, similarly finding John failed to carry his burden of adequately tracing his separate property contributions.

SECTION 5. SEPARATE PROPERTY BUSINESS PROFITS

Capital versus income. The civil law rule treated capital brought to the marriage as separate property; however, it defined any rents or income from that the capital as community property for the duration of the marriage.

California veered away from this rule (Chapter 1). In California both capital and income from capital (despite being acquired during marriage) are defined as separate property (Chapter 3).

This section examines separate property businesses.

A separate property business is defined in one of two ways. It can be a business that is brought to the marriage. It can be a business that is started during the marriage with provable separate property capital.

All community property states define a separate property business in this way. Some states, however, carve out an exception for income from specific activities. Texas and Louisiana treat a mineral lease acquired during marriage with separate property as a nonbusiness activity. The lease may be separate property, but the mineral lease income is presumed to be community property subject to clear and convincing evidence otherwise. California treats taxable investment accounts brought to the marriage as a separate property business. The idea is to account for the labor that the account owner puts into managing the account during marriage.

The definition of capital versus income is important. But so too is the question of commingling. What happens when a separate property business generates profits that trace back to a non-monetized community property source such as labor?

A. SUBSTANTIAL JUSTICE: *PEREIRA* OR *VAN CAMP*?

Liquor or sea food?

In California, when a separate property business uses community property labor the community obtains the right to petition for an equitable accounting. The nature of the accounting proceeding is to decide whether business profits have become commingled. If they have, the profits themselves are apportioned. Profits that trace back to separate property capital remain, by definition, separate property under California Family Code Section 770(a)(1) and (3). Any excess profits, defined as profits that trace back to community labor, become community property under California Family Code Section 760. *Pereira v. Pereira*, 156 Cal. 1, 103 P. 488, 23 (1909).

By contrast, in Texas and Louisiana, two states that follow the civil law rule, commingled business profits are not subject to pro rata ownership; instead, those profits—even if they trace back to a separate property source—are characterized as entirely community property for the duration of the marriage. See *Norris v. Vaughan*, 260 S.W.2d 676 (Tex. 1953).

Returning to California law, precedent allows for two accounting methods. They are competing methods, so either one or the other is used; not both. Each method serves the policy goal of achieving substantial justice between the parties, depending on the circumstances of how the separate property business grew during the marriage.

Doctrinally, what determines which method is used is the quantity of community property labor that goes into the business. The rule is: if the community contributed more than a minimum amount of labor, called the minimum-plus standard, to the separate property business, *Pereira* accounting is used. *Pereira* is the method best able to identify excess business profits that are confirmable to the community. Excess profits are those that remain after the separate property capital investment has been fully accounted for, as discussed below.

Anything less than a minimum amount of labor calls for application of *Van Camp* accounting. *Van Camp v. Van Camp*, 53 Cal.App. 17, 199 P. 885 (2d Dist. 1921).

Pereira recognizes that community labor helped the business grow. This entitles the community to some, but not all, of the profits of the business; the profits the community is entitled to are labeled excess profits. *Van Camp* recognizes that the community labor did not help the business become successful. *Van Camp* protects the separate property business owner while also requiring that he or she reimburse the community for any nominal labor it may have contributed to the business enterprise. The net reimbursement is calculated by subtracting family expenses from labor contributions.

In the case of a separate property business, the operating assumption (which can be overcome with evidence) is that business profits are used to support the family during the marriage. Hence the family expense presumption applies in both methods. It applies as an implicit factor of *Pereira* through the use of simple interest, discussed below. It applies as an explicit factor in *Van Camp*, family expenses are explicitly accounted for insofar as any community reimbursement a net reimbursement.

Both *Pereira* and *Van Camp* follow the same basic principles of California Family Code Section 760 and California Family Code Section 770(a)(1) and (3). *Pereira* accounting defines the underlying business capital as separate property; it also defines any rents, issues and profits that trace to the underlying capital as separate property. This is a straight application of California Family Code Section 770(a)(1) and (3). *Pereira* also recognizes that labor is community property under California Family Code Section 760. By application of the tracing rule, rents, issues, and profits that trace back to labor are also community property. In the language of *Pereira*, the community's share of profits is whatever profits are in excess of the original separate capital contribution plus a fair rate of return on that contribution calculated at simple interest. The concept of excess profits entitles the community to a payout from the business as a creditor of the business. After *Patrick v. Alacer Corp.*, 201 Cal.App.4th 1326, 136 Cal.Rptr.3d 669 (4th Dist. 2011), it is clear that the community is not entitled to receive its excess profits in the forms of incidents of ownership that give control of the business (such as shares of stock). The reason is that the business is separate property entity during the marriage hence it leaves the marriage as separate property.

Pereira is widely cited and followed among U.S. community property and common law title jurisdictions alike.

In *Pereira*, the husband owned a successful saloon business before marriage. During marriage, he devoted a substantial amount of labor to working in the saloon. At dissolution, the wife argued that business receipts earned during marriage were community property earnings since they were traceable to the husband's labor. The husband countered that the business was separate in character as it was started with separate property capital; and therefore that all that rents, issues, and profits that flowed from the business were also separate property in character by application of the tracing rule (Chapter 3). The husband conceded that he worked long hours at the saloon. To that point, the wife argued that husband's work hours should be monetized to reflect the community's contribution to the growth of his separate property business.

The California Supreme Court agreed in part with both spouses. Labor is important; but the community is not entitled to all earnings traceable to labor, as the wife proposed. And yes, when the business is separate property in character, the community labor component is not free, as the husband proposed. Labor must be accounted for in some way or other. To strike the balance, the court ruled that the community property is entitled to excess business profits for its labor. The formula for identifying excess business profits, the court said, is the difference between the fair market value of the business on the date of dissolution and the original *separate property capital* contribution (defined by the value of the business on the date of marriage) plus *a hypothetical return on that investment* (defined as the original separate property capital investment plus simple interest for the period in which community labor is used, which in *Pereira* was the entirety of the marriage). The difference is excess profits, a value to which each spouse is entitled to a one-half community property share.

PEREIRA V. PEREIRA

156 Cal. 1, 103 P. 488 (1909)

SHAW, J.

The plaintiff obtained an interlocutory judgment of divorce on the ground of extreme cruelty. This judgment also declared that the plaintiff should have three-fifths of the community property when the divorce became final * * * , and it provided for theory that all of his gains received after marriage, from whatever sources, were to be classed as community property, and that no allowance was made in favor of his separate estate on account of interest or profit on the $15,500 invested in the business at the time of the marriage. This capital was undoubtedly his separate estate. The fund remained in the business after marriage and was used by him in carrying it on. The separate property should have been credited with some amount as profit on this capital. It was not a losing business, but a very profitable one.

It is true that it is very clearly shown that the principal part of the large income was due to the personal character, energy, ability, and capacity of the husband. This share of the earnings was, of course, community property; but without capital he could not have carried on the business. In the absence of circumstances showing a different result, it is to be presumed that some of the profits were justly due to the capital invested. There is nothing to show that all of it was due to defendant's efforts alone. The probable contribution of the capital to the income should have been determined from all the circumstances of the case, and, as the business was profitable, it would amount at least to the usual interest on a long investment well secured. * * * . We think the court erred in refusing to increase the proportion of separate property and decrease the community property to the extent of the reasonable gain to the separate estate from the earnings properly allowable on account of the capital invested.

* * *

The judgment as to the amount and value of the community property and as to the disposition thereof between the parties is reversed, and the cause is remanded for a new trial and judgment upon that issue alone. In all other particulars the judgment is affirmed.

On Rehearing

PER CURIAM. Since the filing of the opinion in this case, the plaintiff has asked that, instead of remanding the case for a new trial of the issues as to the property, the judgment be modified in regard thereto, and has filed a written consent that the defendant be allowed, as part of his separate estate, out of the cash on hand, interest at the rate of 7 per cent. on the $15,500 found to be the capital invested in his business. This removes the objection to directing a modification of the judgment. The defendant introduced no evidence to show that the capital invested was entitled to a greater return than legal interest, and, in the absence of such evidence, the burden of proof being upon him, that would be the utmost he could claim. The wife would have been entitled to an opportunity to prove, if she could, that it earned a smaller proportion of the profits than legal interest, and, she being the respondent, it was for that reason considered necessary to order a new trial for that purpose. Her consent aforesaid avoids this necessity and leaves the case in such condition that a modification of the judgment will end the litigation with justice to both parties. * * *

Interest at 7 per cent. on the $15,500 from April 19, 1900, the date of the marriage, to November 3, 1905, the time of the trial, amounts to $6,012.70. Deducting this from $12,139.03, found to be the cash on hand at the time of the trial, leaves $6,126.33, as the part of the cash belonging to the community. The plaintiff's three-fifths of this is $3,675.86, and the defendant's two-fifths is $2,450.47.

It is ordered that the judgment be modified by changing the respective statements of the shares of each in the cash on hand therein, so that the part relating to the plaintiff's share shall read as follows: "Second. The sum of three thousand six hundred and seventy-five and 86–100 dollars ($3,675.86), in cash, being three-fifths of the sum of $6,126.33 in cash found by the Supreme Court to be community property of the plaintiff and defendant; and that no interest in defendant's separate property be awarded to plaintiff." And so that the part relating to the defendant's share shall read as follows: "Second. The sum of two thousand four hundred and fifty and 47–100 dollars ($2,450.47), in cash, being two-fifths of the sum found to be community property as aforesaid." And that as so modified the judgment stand affirmed; the plaintiff to recover all costs.

Van Camp is the alternate approach to separate property business profits. The excerpt below describes the nature of the separate property business. The trial court applied Pereira. The husband appealed. The court of appeal reversed. It distinguished Fran Van Camp's case from the *Pereira* case. The two cases were similar, the court said, because but for the separate property capital there would have been no business. But the cases were different because in *Pereira*, the continued growth if not existence of the business was due to daily infusions of community property labor, whereas in Van Camp, the existence and growth of the business was not dependent upon Frank Van Camp's own labor. Frank Van Camp earned income from his separate property stock dividends; and, had he been content to do so, he could have accepted only those dividends, which themselves would have been entirely separate property under California Family Code Section 770(a)(3). But instead, Frank Van Camp also accepted employment from the corporation, at a benchmark salary rate; and he used that income to pay for community property expenses.

NOTES

1. *The* Pereira *formula.* The *Pereira* formula identifies excess business *profits*. Note that only "excess profits," as determined by the formula below, are characterized as community property. All other aspects of the business remain separate property. Excess profits are payable as a business debt, as discussed above. If the debt is not paid, a lien can be placed on the business.

Start with these values:

- FMV of the business at dissolution = x
- FMV of the business on the date of marriage (the original separate property capital investment) = y
- Hypothetical Fair Rate of Return on y (at simple interest *) for the period during which the business used community labor = z

x – (y + z) = Excess Profits

---

2. *Simple or compound interest?* As a default rule, simple interest is calculated as a way to account for the family expense presumption. The formula for simple interest is: principle multiplied by rate of interest multiplied by time. (Simple interest calculators are readily available online.) Compound interest is allowed, at the discretion of the judge, upon proof that family expenses were paid for with some source other than the business in question.

In *Marriage of Folb*, 53 Cal.App.3d 862, 126 Cal.Rptr. 306 (2d Dist. 1975), the court found that the evidence supported a twelve percent (12%) return on capital and also determined that a calculation using compound interest was not necessary. Compound interest would be appropriate if family expenses were not paid out of the business during the course of the marriage. *But absent such evidence*, the *Folb* court explained, using a compound interest formula rather than a simple interest formula to calculate the hypothetical fair rate of return under *Pereira* would overcompensate the separate property business owner.

3. *Interest rates, inflation rates, and other economic factors.* In the absence of evidence on the historical rate of interest the legal rate of interest is used when calculating a fair rate of return. Evidence on the effect of inflation and other economic factors on the disputed business is relevant. But if one or the other party neglects to introduce historical interest rate evidence, the trial court can properly disregard actual interest rates during the period in question. See *Pereira v. Pereira, supra,* 156; *Weinberg v. Weinberg,* 67 Cal.2d 557, 63 Cal.Rptr. 13, 432 P.2d 709 (1967). Cf. *Logan v. Forster,* 144 Cal.App.2d 587, 601, 250 P.2d 730 (2d Dist. 1952).

4. *Pereira is a total recap accounting method. Pereira* values are grossly determined. In other words *Pereira* accounting measures the growth of the business from the start to the end of the time when community property labor is used. (For many separate property businesses this may be the entire length of the marriage simply because the business was brought to the marriage and operated through to dissolution.) Start of marriage to end of marriage accounting has been referred to by California courts as total recapitulation—total recap for short—accounting. Divorcing counterparts sometimes argue for contemporaneous methods of assessing business profits. Thus far, California courts have tended to rule that total recap accounting is fairer for the non-owning party than more detailed contemporaneous accounting methods (year by year, quarter by quarter, or month by month) would be. The rationale is that total recap accounting requires less record keeping during marriage, fewer records, and less accounting time. The efficiencies (potentially) translates into lower legal fees for the parties. Another reason that courts have allowed total recap accounting is that it apportions profits only, not losses: The community enjoys excess profits, but because it is not an owner of the business, the community does not share in business losses.

5. *If the community is awarded a pro rata share of excess profits, does the non-owning spouse have the right to determine how those excess profits will be paid?* In *Patrick v. Alacer, supra,* says no. As discussed above, an excess profit award makes the community a creditor of the business, not a continuing part owner.

6. *A minority of community property jurisdictions in the United States follow the civil law rule that separate property rents, issues, and profits are community property during marriage.* The Spanish *ganancial* rule is followed by Louisiana, Texas, Idaho and Washington. In these states the rents, issues and profits of separate property can be used by the community property during marriage. The approach effectively makes rents, issues, and profits community property in character by a civil law concept known as usufruct. During the marriage, the community is the "usufructory" of business profits and the separate property owner is their "naked owner." The usufructory enjoys fulls rights of management, control, and therefore use. In the event of a dissolution, the business profit stream must be entirely returned by the usufructory to the naked owner, who in this case is the separate property business owner. An exception for mineral, oil, and gas income from leases or realty interests exists in Texas and Louisiana, as discussed in Section 3, Note 3 below.

———

Van Camp is the alternative way to account for a separate property business profits at dissolution. In certain cases, *Van Camp* achieves substantial justice between the parties by not overcompensating the community for what has been adjudged its minimal labor contribution. The *Van Camp* formula reimburses the community; all profits remain with the business, as discussed above.

VAN CAMP V. VAN CAMP

53 Cal.App. 17, 199 P. 885 (2d Dist. 1921)

THE COURT: This is an action for divorce. Defendant Van Camp has appealed from a decree dissolving the marital bonds, and also from that portion of the judgment awarding to the plaintiff * * * certain real and personal property.

In the year 1914 defendant Van Camp came from Indianapolis to Los Angeles. His family then consisted of a grown son. He was a man of large affairs and had been the directing head of an extensive packing establishment in Indianapolis bearing his name. He brought to California property of great value, consisting largely of cash and stock securities. After his arrival in Los Angeles he organized the Van Camp Sea Food Company. The company was capitalized with 2,000 shares of stock at a par value of $100 each. He became the president and general manager of the corporation and received up to January, 1918, a salary of $1,000 per month. This salary was increased on January 1, 1918, to $1,500 per month and so remained at all times subsequent thereto. The packing plant was located at the seaport town of San Pedro. * * * [T]he packing company organized by Van Camp was a successful venture and produced large returns. In March of 1916 defendant Van Camp married the plaintiff, who was or had been an employee in the post office at San Pedro. Plaintiff was then twenty-one years of age; the defendant was about fifty-four years old. Immediately upon the marriage, defendant purchased a home in the city of Los Angeles, expending therefor about the sum of $15,000, and the deed to the place was made to the wife. Not long thereafter defendant delivered to the wife a certificate of deposit representing a cash credit of $10,000 and a deed to a lot at San Pedro. Defendant further provided each month for the plaintiff a cash allowance for household expenses which, at the time of the commencement of this proceeding, was $450; he also provided plaintiff with an automobile. The evidence goes to show that defendant was in the main liberal in the direction of gratifying all the wishes of his wife as to things desired for her pleasure and comfort. The mother of plaintiff resided at San Pedro and received partial support, at least, from the exchequer of Van Camp. * * *

In the absence of any evidence showing a different practice, and there is none, the rule is that the community earnings of husband and wife are chargeable with the family support. Hence any amounts of money expended for such purpose by either spouse during the existence of the marital relation are presumed to have been paid out of the community estate. It appears that during such period defendant expended for the support of his family, and for income tax and premiums on policies of life insurance wherein his estate was made the beneficiary, [the court goes on to list the many ways in which the husband provided financial support to the community estate.]

It is insisted by counsel for Mrs. Van Camp that the Van Camp Sea Food Company, if not a myth, was a mere agency through which defendant conducted his business, and since its enormous income was due to the skill and ability with which defendant conducted the business, the community estate should be accredited with all the profits derived therefrom in excess of seven per cent interest upon the capital which defendant had invested therein. In support of this contention she cites *Pereira v. Pereira*, 156 Cal. 1, wherein it appeared that the husband at the time of the marriage had a separate estate of $15,500 invested in a business conducted by him. * * * In our opinion, the circumstances attending the Pereira case are not applicable to the facts involved herein. While it may be true that the success of the corporation of which defendant was president and manager was to a large extent due to his capacity and ability, nevertheless without the investment of his and other capital in the corporation he could not have conducted the business, and while he devoted his energies and personal efforts to making it a success, he was by the corporation paid what the evidence shows was an adequate salary, and for which another than himself with equal capacity could have been secured. Had such course been pursued and defendant contented himself merely with the receipt of dividends from the business, the character of the dividends as separate property could not have been questioned. Instead, however, of doing this, he entered upon the duties as manager of the corporation, gave his exclusive time and efforts thereto, for which he received first $12,000 and later $18,000 per year. The case presented is not unlike that involved in *Estate of Pepper*, 158 Cal. 619, wherein it was held that the profits and earnings made by the husband after marriage in conducting the business of a nursery upon property owned by him at the time of his marriage was his separate property, notwithstanding the success of the venture required industry, skill, and attention. "It is impossible," said the court, "to apportion the crop so as to determine what share of it has come from the soil and what share from the exertions of man. The product must be treated as a whole, and, if it is the growth of land separately owned, it is the separate property of the owner of the land," citing *Diefendorff v. Hopkins*, 95 Cal. 343. So, in the instant case, it is impossible to say what part of the enormous dividends paid by the Van Camp Sea Food Company should be apportioned to the skill and management thereof and what part should be apportioned to the investment of the capital and the favorable conditions under which the business was conducted. Furthermore, there is no merit in the contention that the corporation was a myth, or that it was a mere instrumentality through which defendant conducted his business. It was organized in June, 1914, long before defendant's marriage, with a capital of $200,000, consisting of 2,000 shares of the par value of $100 each, of which stock Van Camp at the time acquired 1,300 shares, Paul Eachus 500 shares, and F. H. Ford 200 shares, besides two shares distributed to others who, with the persons named, constituted the five directors of the corporation. Subsequently, for the sum of $20,000, defendant acquired the 200 shares of stock issued to Ford, and in March, 1915, for $35,000, he bought the stock issued to Paul Eachus. Later he sold 83 shares of his stock to Wilbur Wood, and, prior to his marriage, sold to his son 300 shares thereof for the sum of $45,000. At no time did he own more than 1,499 shares of the stock. The corporation was duly organized and constituted an entity separate and distinct from that of defendant. Even were it otherwise and, as claimed by plaintiff, a mere instrumentality for conducting defendant's business, nevertheless, in view of the fact that he was adequately paid by the corporation for his services, such compensation, * * * must be deemed the extent of his personal earnings, and the balance of the profits derived from the business accredited to the use of the capital invested therein, in the same manner as though he had not been employed by the corporation.

The judgment as entered on the divorce issues is affirmed.

The judgment as to the amount and value of the community property and as to the disposition thereof between the parties is reversed and the cause is remanded for a new trial upon that issue alone; appellant Frank Van Camp to have his costs of appeal.

A petition to have the cause heard in the supreme court, after judgment in the district court of appeal, was denied by the supreme court on July 25, 1921.

California has historically been permissive in defining a separate property business. *Austin* is an unusual but helpful case that illustrates how an unprofitable "business" was more properly considered a (dissipated) community property income stream rather than a business subject to apportionment under the *Pereira* or *Van Camp*. In *Austin*, one spouse ran a welding business. He provided services to clients, and he used community personal property (in this case welding tools) to do so. Had it not been for the husband's daily labor, no income whatsoever would have been produced by the business. At the end of the marriage, the trial court granted the business stock to the community on the theory that the husband had failed to prove the separate property nature of the business. Husband appealed. The trial court's judgment was affirmed.

NOTES

1. *The* Van Camp *formula*. The *Van Camp* holding is a reimbursement formula. The business, because it was owned before the marriage, is separate property by the basic definition of California Family Code Section 770(a)(1). Business profits, because they trace entirely back to the underlying separate property, are separate property under California Family Code Section 770(a)(3). The community is entitled to a reimbursement for the value of its labor contributions, if any, minus the cost of family expenses that were paid

out of the business over the period in which the nominal community property labor was used.

Start with these values:
- FMV of the business at dissolution = x
- Value of community property contributions to the business = a
- Family expenses paid from the business = b

$$x - (a - b) = SP$$
$$(a - b) = CP \text{ reimbursement}$$

---

2.   *Total recap accounting. Van Camp*, like *Pereira*, is a total recap accounting method. The value of the community labor is calculated over the course of the time that the business used the nominal community labor. Same with the family expenses that were paid out of the business. In the absence of business records, benchmark salary data are admissible. Family expenses can be approximated.

3.   *Linking labor to business growth.* In *Estate of Ney*, 212 Cal. App.2d 891, 28 Cal.Rptr.442 (1st Dist. 1963), discussed below in Section 5C, Note 2, the court used *Van Camp* accounting when the surviving spouse failed to show that husband's labor proximately caused the growth of the disputed separate property business. Once it is determined that a business is separate property in character, the burden of proof on the issue of apportionment or reimbursement lies with the community proponent.

4.   *Talent versus labor.* One argument made by young Mrs. Van Camp was that her husband's enormous talent for business (derived from years of experience), meant that whatever labor he lent to the business resulted in substantial earnings for that business. These earnings, said Mrs. Van Camp occurred during marriage making them community property.

The court disagreed. The Van Camp Seafood Corporation, which continues to operate today, was fully incorporated and organized so that it functioned independently of the husband on the date that he married. The husband owned shares of stock in the corporation and received "enormous dividends" from those shares, but, said the court, "it is impossible to say what part of the enormous dividends paid by the Van Camp Sea Food Company should be apportioned to the skill and management thereof and what part should be apportioned to the investment of the [husband's] capital and the favorable conditions under which the business was conducted [by its managers]." Mrs. Van Camp, in other words, did not provide sufficient evidence that, during marriage, Mr. Van Camp's labor contributed to the already up and running Van Camp Seafood Corporation. Additionally, husband countered wife's assertions with evidence that he had been (more than) adequately paid by the corporation for his labor, and that he treated this compensation as community property earnings. Husband's earnings, the court noted "must be deemed the extent of his personal earnings, and the balance of the profits derived from the business accredited to the use of the capital invested therein, in the same manner as though he had not been employed by the corporation." *Id.* at 29.

In *Marriage of McTiernan & Dubrow* (Chapter 4), husband John commanded "six- to high seven-figure compensation per film" while Donna Dubrow worked as a film production executive earning a salary of $195,000 per year. In terms of cumulative earnings, John McTiernan earned approximately $15 million dollars over the course of the marriage compared to Donna Dubrow, who earned $1 million. The couple owned divisible assets. Even so, Donna Dubrow sought a valuation of what she characterized as John McTiernan's talent.

The trial court determined that John McTiernan had indeed achieved exceptional success in his field based on his personal skill, experience and knowledge. Particularly dispositive was that John McTiernan was "ranked No. 13 among 1,058 motion picture directors in cumulative box office revenues during 1985–1986, No. 8 in terms of gross domestic revenues produced by movies he directed, and No. 1 in terms of production budgets entrusted to his control." *Id.* at 1095.

In the case of a talented separate property business owner, does the owner's elite professional standing generate business? Is elite professional standing a form of labor? If so, would it meet the minimum-plus requirement?

In *McTiernan & Dubrow* the court rejected the analogy that John McTiernan's talent was like that of a professional business practice. A professional's business can generate divisible goodwill, wrote the court, but it is the *business*, and not the person, that ultimately does so. From there, the court interpreted the term "business." The court noted that "business" as it appears in the Professions Code requires an industrial enterprise with assets; those business assets are what generate the intangible asset known as "goodwill" which, said the court, is in fact transferable "property" subject to division under California Family Code Section 760.

In the majority's opinion, what John McTiernan possessed was *talent*, which is something altogether different from a business or business goodwill. Talent is not property subject to division at dissolution, reasoned the court, because it is entirely personal to its holder; it cannot be sold or transferred no matter how much the buyer is willing to pay, and thus it lacks the essential attribute of property. The court concluded that the husband's elite professional standing—his talent—was not an asset of the marriage, meaning it was not labor belonging to the marriage. The practice of a lawyer, a physician, a dentist, or an accountant is labor of the marriage; but elite professional standing based on specialized talent is not.

Judge Cooper dissented, writing that a professional practice of any kind is transferable property, as is the goodwill of that "business." Citing *Marriage of Watts*, 171 Cal.App.3d 366, 372, 217 Cal.Rptr. 301 (5th Dist. 1985), Judge Cooper reasoned that whether or not a third party is willing to buy something is immaterial to whether it is property. "Goodwill is not a commodity in the marketplace but rather 'a portion of the professional practice as a going concern on the date of the dissolution of the marriage.' " (*Id.* at 371) With this principle in mind, Judge Cooper would have affirmed the trial court's determination that John McTiernan's elite professional status was an ongoing business concern that could be valued and divided at dissolution. Extending this reasoning to the *Pereira* or *Van Camp* analysis, Judge Cooper might have found that talent is a form of labor expended during marriage.

But if talent is not enough to prove that an enterprise is a business, what proof is required? The question is discussed next.

B. A SEPARATE PROPERTY BUSINESS DISTINGUISHED FROM AN INCOME STREAM

Pereira and *Van Camp* involved litigation over profitable businesses. Over the years, peripheral questions have come up over how to define a business.

A business is a going concern, as discussed above.

A business generates a return on investment, as discussed above.

A business generates goodwill, as discussed above.

A business is valued by standard pricing methods that require calculation.

Austin v. Austin, excerpted below, is the story of a losing business that was started during marriage. Husband argued that the business was started with separate property capital; it was also incorporated, with husband being a principle shareholder. Husband was unable to carry the burden of proof on the separate property character of the start-up funds. Nor could he show that the business required the initial capital to survive as an ongoing concern. Without proof, the "business" was downgraded— despite its corporate form—to an income stream dependent on labor and community personal property in the form of work tools. As such the corporation was characterized entirely as community property.

AUSTIN V. AUSTIN
190 Cal.App.2d 45, 11 Cal.Rptr. 593 (2d Dist. 1961)

SHINN, P. J.

Phyllis C. Austin brought suit against Jerome Ralph Austin for divorce * * * . Defendant answered and also filed a cross-complaint by which he sought annulment of his marriage to plaintiff upon the ground that at the time the same was entered into he was still the husband of a former wife, his second, notwithstanding a decree rendered in Mexico which purported to award him a divorce from his then wife. * * *

Judgment was entered awarding plaintiff a divorce * * * determining all the property of the parties * * * to be community property and making a division of the same. Defendant has appealed only from the part of the judgment respecting the ownership and the division of community property.

Admittedly the property consisted of a family residence in Arcadia, household furniture and furnishings, 298 shares of the capital stock of J. R. Austin Company, a corporation, and defendant's interest in the company, insurance policies, stocks, bonds, bank accounts and savings accounts. Defendant contends that it was established without conflict in the evidence that all said property was his separate property with the exception of the home of the parties which was in joint tenancy. * * *

The parties intermarried at Stockton, California, March 1, 1945. At that time both were in the employ of a shipyard company, plaintiff as a clerical worker, defendant as a superintendent. They continued their employment for eight months following their marriage and combined their earnings in an amount that was not disclosed by the evidence. Plaintiff had savings bonds of the value of about $200. Defendant had assets which he stated to plaintiff to be worth $8,000 and which he testified were of the value of about $11,000. In November 1945, defendant purchased a half interest in a partnership in a welding business in Pasadena for an amount which he stated at the time was $1,800 but which he testified was $2,700. The funds which the parties had accumulated after their marriage and placed in a bank in Stockton were transferred to a bank in Burbank, and from this account defendant withdrew the amount paid for the interest in the business. Both parties devoted their attention and efforts to the operation of the business for about nine months, until plaintiff gave birth to her first child. After about a year defendant's (nonmarital welding business) partner, Ava Beard, sold his interest to one Lugenbeil and in the following year defendant's father acquired Lugenbeil's interest. The business was incorporated in 1948; defendant owns 298 shares of the capital stock; his father owns 123 shares but was not shown to have been active in the business. * * * Defendant was awarded the 298 shares of corporate stock * * * .

Defendant contends that the sum paid for the interest in the business, whether $1,800 or $2,700, came from his separate funds on deposit in the Burbank bank, and that not only the stock which represents the appreciated value of the business but the property acquired from earnings are his separate property.

Plaintiff contends that the findings as to the community character of the property are sustainable upon alternate theories: * * * the funds with which the business was purchased consisted in part of defendant's separate funds which were commingled with community funds and for that reason were properly held to be property of the community; and * * * the growth of the business and its present value were due entirely to the personal services of defendant, consisting of labor, skill and management of the business, as a result of which the stock in the company constitutes community property.

It was incumbent upon defendant to produce proof which would convince the trial court that the business was purchased entirely with his separate funds. Although he testified that the money came from his account in Burbank which he maintained prior to the marriage, he produced no records respecting the same, nor any evidence as to the amount of the combined earnings of the parties which were transferred to his own account. These could well have amounted to all or a substantial part of the sum paid for the business. The parties had discussed the purchase of the business; there was no agreement that it would be purchased with defendant's funds or that he would own it as his separate property. Inasmuch as the property was acquired after marriage and was presumably community property, we cannot hold as a matter of law that it was proved beyond question that the business was acquired with the separate funds of defendant. Where separate and community funds were commingled, as they were here, in a single bank account, in undisclosed amounts, the court would have been warranted in concluding that the entire amount constituted community property. * * *

Defendant cites the case of *Van Camp v. Van Camp,* 53 Cal.App. 17 [199 P. 885], and says the facts of that case "are identical with the facts of the instant case." In *Van Camp,* the husband's interest in the business, which he owned prior to the marriage amounted to as much as $150,000 of total capital of $200,000. Although he devoted much time to the business his services were only such as could have been performed by any other person of equal ability. It was held that the husband's share of the earnings of the business, in excess of the salary he had received, were not property of the community. Defendant also relies upon *Gilmore v. Gilmore,* 45 Cal.2d 142 [287 P.2d 769], a case in which the husband's business increased in value after the marriage from $182,000 to $780,000. The wife claimed the amount of the increase as community property. The trial court rejected her claim and the judgment was affirmed. With respect to the contributions attributed to the husband's use of capital and the services he performed for the several corporations the court remarked: "Defendant's corporations were staffed by well trained personnel who were capable of carrying on the business unassisted. Defendant worked relatively short hours and took many extended vacations. There was expert testimony that the salaries he received, which were found to constitute community income, were more than ample compensation for the services he rendered." (P. 150.)

In the foregoing cases, and others which follow the same rules, the businesses which belonged to the several husbands at the time of marriage were going concerns which could not have existed or functioned without the use of the husbands' capital.

Plaintiff cites the case of *Pereira v. Pereira,* 156 Cal. 1 [103 P. 488], as the leading California case announcing the doctrine that where the separate property of a husband is invested and used in his business and without which the business could not have been carried on, he should be allowed in a division of the community property, at least interest upon the money as upon a long-term secured investment. * * * The facts in *Pereira* which were held to justify an allowance to the husband for the use of his money were that although the principal part of the large income was due to the personal character, energy, ability and capacity of the husband, which earnings were community property, the business could not have been carried on without the use of the husband's capital. This factual situation is far removed from the one we are considering. It is clear to us that the finding of the community character of the stock was the only logical conclusion to be reached from the fact that the welding business ever since it became successful has been essentially a one-man business, and that the equipment of the shop which defendant purchased, while essential to the operation of the business, did not in any real sense constitute a contribution to capital.

In the present case the welding business had no operating capital whatever except through earnings. In the beginning the business was only bringing in $7 or $8 a day, and it had no value whatever except in the equipment of a welding shop. This was all defendant purchased. Even his partner soon disposed of his interest, as did the incoming partner who bought it. Defendant worked long hours, from 7 a. m. until late in the evening, estimating or prospective jobs and managing and supervising the work. All the earnings of the business were due to his labor, skill and management. There was no one else to take his place. It is true that he was on a salary of $1,000 per month, and that in recent years he had withdrawn from the business about $27,000 per year, but it would be unrealistic to say that this was the full measure of the value of his services, and that the increase in value, or any part of it, was due to capital supplied by defendant and used in the business. The increased value of the business earned by the efforts of defendant was as clearly community property as were the sums which he had withdrawn from the business. If the value of his entire services were withdrawn from the value of the business there would be nothing left as separate property attributable to the use of capital as a contribution to the earnings and the value of the business. The situation was much the same as that of a professional man who invests in equipment of an office and library, or of an artisan who acquires the tools of his trade. As the business is developed the value it takes on is not due to the equipment itself aside from the labor, judgment and skill with which it is used. It must be presumed that the trial court concluded that the value which it placed upon the business of $100,000 was due to the personal services of defendant, and to nothing else. It is a conclusion with which we agree, and it supports the further conclusion that the stock representing defendant's interest in the business was community property. This is the only question presented on the appeal.

The judgment is affirmed.

VALLEE, J., and FORD, J., concurred.

NOTES

1.   *A business is an ongoing concern that requires capital to survive.* The courts have been quick to find a separate property business where separate property capital is necessary to the continuation of an ongoing concern. See for example *Marriage of Zaentz, supra.*

2.   *Pricing the business.* The price, or fair market value, of a business (according to the U.S. Internal Revenue Service) is what a willing buyer will pay for the business on a particular date.

Determining the fair market value of a business on a date such as a marriage or dissolution can be a complex and expensive matter. Therefore, standard pricing models that rely on benchmark data are used by business brokers.

Pricing methods require calculations—numbers, inputs, outputs. A valuation method that depends on subjective data can be biased. A separate property claimant may argue for one set of inputs; a community property proponent for an altogether different set. Radical disparity in calculations may not be helpful to the factfinder and may instead have the negative effect of increasing the ferocity, expense, and risk of further negotiation. By comparison, a pricing method that depends on objective factors may be a more reliable measure of what a willing buyer would pay for the business if it were to be sold on a particular day.

One commonly used objective standard pricing method is a percentage of sales divided by revenues. Another more targeted version of the approach is the last twelve months of sales divided by revenues. These methods are objective because inputs are not provided by the seller alone; they are corroborated by actual receipts.

An example of a subjective method of pricing is a percentage of earnings (seller's discretionary earnings, or SDE) divided by revenues. The SDE method is doubly subjective because inputs were historically discretionary to begin with; and they are now provided by the business owner in real time for purposes of the current apportionment. Preferred valuation models appear to calculate SDE using the seller's highest salary because the assumption is that the buyer will replace the seller (as business manager) after the sale of the business.

Generally, the standard pricing models do not include inventory, real estate, or accounts receivable. The price is for the operating assets of the business plus goodwill; hence the price of a business includes its goodwill unless a valuation report states otherwise. Additionally, part of valuing a business requires identifying comparable businesses. Comparables are analyzed to determine if the value arrived at for the disputed business is fairly valued for the market. Identifying comparable businesses is therefore another key element in valuing a business.

Multiples for standard pricing methods are provided by the business brokerage industry. For an example of businesses and franchises from A&W Restaurants to bars to law firms to UPS stores to a Zoo Health Club, with year-based multiples, *see,* TOM WEST, BUSINESS REFERENCE GUIDE: THE ESSENTIAL GUIDE TO PRICING BUSINESSES AND FRANCHISES (26th ed. 2016). West recommends different industry business brokerage sources and websites that compile data about types of businesses. See also Appendix C for an example page showing multiples.

C. THE MINIMUM-PLUS LABOR STANDARD

Yet another important legal distinction is drawn in *Beam v. Bank of America*, excerpted below. In *Beam*, unlike in *Austin*, the separate property business owner was able to prove that the business—a taxable investment fund—was owned before marriage; obviously his separate property business capital was necessary to the ongoing operation of earning profits and dividends. *Beam* allowed Tobriner J. to articulate two important points about California community property law. One: A taxable investment fund brought to a marriage is an enterprise that falls within the definition of a separate property business. Two: applying *Pereira* to an unprofitable business, the community receives a credit of zero ($0) since the business fails to generate any profits, much less excess profits.

In *Beam*, the husband spent his time managing a taxable separate property investment fund. Doctrinally, proof of minimum-plus labor called for application of *Pereira*. After accounting for the value of the fund on the date of marriage plus the hypothetical fair rate of return on his original capital over the life of the marriage at simple interest (a negative number, it turned out) there was nothing in excess to award to the community. The investment portfolio had been essentially run at a loss after paying for family expenses. For that reason the community property proponent requested a *Van Camp* accounting. She argued (unsuccessfully) that if a separate property business is a losing business the community should be at least entitled to a reimbursement for its labor.

BEAM v. BANK OF AMERICA

6 Cal.3d 12, 98 Cal.Rptr. 137, 490 P.2d 257 (S.Ct. 1971)

TOBRINER, J.

Mrs. Mary Beam, defendant in this divorce action, appeals from an interlocutory judgment awarding a divorce to both husband and wife * * * . The trial court determined that the only community property existing at the time of trial was a promissory note for $38,000, and, upon the husband's stipulation, awarded this note to the wife; the court found all other property to be the separate property of the party possessing it. * * *

On this appeal, Mrs. Beam attacks the judgment primarily on the grounds that the trial court (1) failed adequately to compensate the community for income attributable to the husband's skill, efforts and labors expended in the handling of his sizable separate estate during the marriage. * * * For the reasons discussed below, we have concluded that substantial precedent and evidence support the various conclusions under attack; thus we conclude that the judgment must be affirmed.

I. *The Facts.*

Mr. and Mrs. Beam were married on January 31, 1939; the instant divorce was granted in 1968, after 29 years of marriage. Prior to and during the early years of the marriage, Mr. Beam inherited a total of $1,629,129 in cash and securities, and, except for brief and insignificant intervals in the early 1940's, he was not employed at all during the marriage but instead devoted his time to handling the separate estate and engaging in private ventures with his own capital. Mr. Beam spent the major part of his time studying the stock market and actively trading in stocks and bonds; he also undertook several real estate ventures, including the construction of two hotel resorts, Cabana Holiday I at Piercy, California, and Cabana Holiday II at Prunedale, California. Apparently, Mr. Beam was not particularly successful in these efforts, however, for, according to Mrs. Beam's own calculations, over the lengthy marriage her husband's total estate enjoyed only a very modest increase to $1,850,507.33.

Evidence introduced at trial clearly demonstrated that the only moneys received and spent by the parties during their marriage were derived from the husband's separate estate; throughout the 29 years of marriage Mrs. Beam's sole occupation was that of housewife and mother (the Beams have four children). * * *

On this appeal, Mrs. Beam * * * contends that the trial court erred in failing to find any community property resulting from the industry, efforts and skill expended by her husband over the 29 years of marriage. We address this issue first. * * *

The trial court did not err in concluding that there was no net community property accumulated during the marriage from the earnings of Mr. Beam's separate property.

[California Family Code Section 770(a)(3)] provides generally that the profits accruing from a husband's separate property are also separate property. Nevertheless, long ago our courts recognized that, since income arising from the husband's skill, efforts and industry is community property, the community should receive a fair share of the profits which derive from the husband's devotion of more than minimal time and effort to the handling of his separate property. (*Pereira* v. *Pereira* (1909).) Furthermore, while this principle first took root in cases involving a husband's efforts expended in connection with a separately owned farm or business (e.g., *Pereira* v. *Pereira*; *Van Camp* v. *Van Camp* (1921) 53 Cal.App. 17, 29 [199 P. 885]) our courts now uniformly hold that "[a]n apportionment of profits is required not only when the husband conducts a commercial enterprise but also when he invests separate funds in real estate or securities. [Citations.]" . . . Without question, Mr. Beam's efforts in managing his separate property throughout the marriage were *more than minimal* * * * , and thus the trial court was compelled to determine what proportion of the total profits should properly be apportioned as community income. (Italics added.)

Over the years our courts have evolved two quite distinct, alternative approaches to allocating earnings between separate and community income in such cases. One method of apportionment, first applied in *Pereira* v. *Pereira* and commonly referred to as the *Pereira* approach, "is to allocate a fair return on the [husband's separate property] investment [as separate income] and to allocate any excess to the community property as arising from the husband's efforts." * * * The alternative apportionment approach, which traces its derivation to *Van Camp* v. *Van Camp* is "to determine the reasonable value of the husband's services . . . , allocate that amount as community property, and treat the balance as separate property attributable to the normal earnings of the [separate estate]."

"In making such apportionment between separate and community property our courts have developed no precise criterion or fixed standard, but have endeavored to adopt that yardstick which is most appropriate and equitable in a particular situation . . . depending on whether the character of the capital investment in the separate property or the personal activity, ability, and capacity of the spouse is the chief contributing factor in the realization of income and profits [citations] . . . In applying this principle of apportionment the court is not bound either to adopt a predetermined percentage as a fair return on business capital which is separate property [the *Pereira* approach] nor need it limit the community interest only to [a] salary fixed as the reward for a spouse's service [the *Van Camp* method] but may select [whichever] formula will achieve substantial justice between the parties." * * * [Citations omitted.]

The trial court in the instant case was well aware of these apportionment formulas and concluded from all the circumstances that the *Pereira* approach should be utilized. As stated above, under the *Pereira* test, community income is defined as the amount by which the actual income of the separate estate exceeds the return which the initial capital investment could have been expected to earn absent the spouse's personal management. In applying the *Pereira* formula the trial court adopted the legal interest rate of 7 percent simple interest as the "reasonable rate of return" on Mr. Beam's separate property; although the wife now attacks this 7 percent simple interest figure as unrealistically high, at trial she introduced no evidence in support of any other more "realistic" rate of return and, as we stated explicitly in *Weinberg* v. *Weinberg* (1967) 67 Cal.2d 557, 565 in the absence of such evidence "the trial court correctly adopted the rate of legal interest."

Testimony at trial indicated that, based upon this 7 percent simple interest growth factor, Mr. Beam's separate property would have been worth approximately 4.2 million dollars at the time of trial if no expenditures had been made during the marriage. Since Mrs. Beam's own calculations indicate that the present estate, plus all expenditures during marriage, would not amount to even 4 million dollars, it appears that, under *Pereira*, the entire increase in the estate's value over the 29-year period would be attributable to the normal growth factor of the property itself and, thus, using this formula, all income would be designated as separate property. * * * In other words, under the *Pereira* analysis, none of the increased valuation of the husband's separate property during the marriage would be attributable to Mr. Beam's efforts, time or skill and, as a result, no community income would have been received and, consequently, no community property could presently be in existence.

The wife concedes that the use of the *Pereira* formula does sustain the trial court's conclusion that the present remainder of the husband's estate is entirely his separate property, but she contends that, under the circumstances, the *Pereira* test cannot be said to "achieve substantial justice between the parties," and thus that the trial court erred in not utilizing the *Van Camp* approach. Although the trial judge did not explicitly articulate his reasons for employing the *Pereira* rather than the *Van Camp* analysis, we cannot under the facts before us condemn as unreasonable the judge's implicit decision that the modest increment of Mr. Beam's estate was more probably attributable to the "character of the capital investment" than to the "personal activity, ability and capacity of the spouse." In any event, however, we need not decide whether the court erred in applying the *Pereira* test because we conclude, as did the trial court, that even under the *Van Camp* approach, the evidence sufficiently demonstrates that all the remaining assets in the estate constitute separate property.

Under the *Van Camp* test community income is determined by designating a reasonable value to the services performed by the husband in connection with his separate property. At trial Mrs. Beam introduced evidence that a professional investment manager, performing similar functions as those undertaken by Mr. Beam during the marriage, would have charged an annual fee of 1 percent of the corpus of the funds he was managing; Mrs. Beam contends that such a fee would amount to $17,000 per year (1 percent of the 1.7 million dollar corpus) and that, computed over the full term of their marriage, this annual "salary" would amount to $357,000 of community income. Mrs. Beam asserts that under the *Van Camp* approach she is now entitled to one-half of this $357,000.

Mrs. Beam's contention, however, overlooks the fundamental distinction between the total community *income* of the marriage, i.e., the figure derived from the *Van Camp* formula, and the community *estate* existing at the dissolution of the marriage. The resulting community estate is not equivalent to total community income so long as there are any community *expenditures* to be charged against the community income. A long line of California decisions has established that "it is presumed that the expenses of the family are paid from community rather than separate funds [citations] [and] thus, in the absence of any evidence showing a different practice, the community earnings are chargeable with these expenses." [Citations omitted.] This "family expense presumption" has been universally invoked by prior California decisions applying either the *Pereira* or *Van Camp* formula. [Citations omitted.] Under these precedents, once a court ascertains the amount of community income, through either the *Pereira* or the *Van Camp* approach, it deducts the community's living expenses from community income to determine the balance of the community property.

If the "family expense" presumption is applied in the present case, clearly no part of the remaining estate can be considered to be community property. Both parties testified at trial that the family's *normal* living expenses were $2,000 per month, or $24,000 per year, and if those expenditures are charged against the annual community income, $17,000 under the *Van Camp* accounting approach, quite obviously there was never any positive balance of community property which could have been built up throughout the marriage. "When a husband devotes his services to and invests his separate property in an economic enterprise, the part of the profits or increment in value attributable to the husband's services must be apportioned to the community. If the amount apportioned to the community is less than the amount expended for family purposes, and if the presumption that family expenses are paid from community funds applies, all assets traceable to the investment are deemed to be the husband's separate property."

NOTES

1.   *How much labor justifies awarding the community excess business profits?* In *Beam v. Bank of America*, the court reaffirmed the *Pereira* rule that "the community should receive a fair share of the profits which derive from the husband's devotion of *more than minimal time and effort* to the handling of his separate property (italics added) (*Pereira v. Pereira*)." *Id.* at 17.

The *Beam* language cites to *Pereira*, *supra* at 7; the language is restated herein as a "minimum-plus labor" rule.

2.   *Once a business is adjudged a separate property business the community has the burden of proving its labor contribution.* In *Estate of Ney*, *supra*, decedent left a taxable stock portfolio that was used to pay family expenses over the life of the marriage. The portfolio was characterized as separate property on the basis that the decedent owned the investment account before his marriage. Upon decedent's death, the surviving spouse made a community claim for excess profits based on the decedent's trading activities over a ten year period. On the issue of the decedent's labor contribution, the surviving spouse introduced evidence to show that even though the decedent had no special stock trading ability (talent), he nevertheless visited his stock broker once a week, sold stocks on the average of once a month, and read the Wall Street Journal at home on a daily basis. The trial court declined to find that the decedent's labor had contributed to the growth of the investment portfolio. The surviving spouse appealed. The court of appeal affirmed the trial court. In the appellate court's view the surviving spouse had not explained how the decedent's investment-related activities led to an actual increase in his stock portfolio. It is not enough to show generalities. The burden of proof requires proximate cause between the decedent's business activities and business growth over the period in question.

3.   *Minerals: Rights* in situ, *leases, wells, and income.* Texas and Louisiana carve out an exception to the above rules for mineral, oil, and gas leases if "community labor, talent and funds were expended on its production and sale, thus impressing community character upon the gas." The rationale for the exception turns on the distinction between minerals, gas and oil that are still part of the realty (*in situ*) and those that have been severed from the realty. Minerals, oil and gas *in situ* are generally part of the realty, and thus they are characterized identically to the realty that contains them. Separate property real estate interests that hold minerals, oil and gas *in situ* result in a classification of the mineral and oil rights as separate property.

However, if and when the minerals, oil, and gas are removed from the realty, the analysis changes. If no community labor, talent, or funds have been expended on the extracted product (the gas or oil), then the character of the extracted product remains separate property. But, once community labor, talent, or funds are used to extract the mineral or oil from the land, then the character of those mineral extractions is independently determined.

Additionally, the value of severed minerals, oil, and gas lies in the income they produce. In the oil and gas context, income is produced from a well. It is in this context that the specific question is raised about how to characterize an oil or natural gas lease and the income that it produces. If the lease is owned before marriage or purchased during marriage with separate property, the lease is separate property. But what of the income produced by a lease during marriage? Under the general separate property business rule, that income would be—in the civil law community property system—community property by usufruct. In California, presumably, under California Family Code Section 770(a)(3), it would remain separate property, and thus subject to a *Pereira* or *Van Camp* accounting.

In *Norris v. Vaughan*, 260 S.W.2d 976 (Tex. 1953), Hal H. Vaughan owned as separate property a seven-eighths (7/8ths) determinable fee, as lessee, in seven producing gas wells, and three one-fourth (1/4th) interests in gas companies, including the Shamrock Gas Co. At the death of wife Beaulah Hunsaker, the decedent's daughter from a prior marriage claimed a share of her mother's estate. The daughter argued that her mother owned a community property share of the income produced from Hal Vaughan's oil wells. She argued: (a) if the gas remains in place, it is separate property; but "production and selling of the gas changes the status of the property from separate to community, and thus the proceeds should be classed as property acquired during marriage," and (b) "property thus classified is presumed to be community property *in the absence of a showing to the contrary*." (Italics in the original.) Hal Vaughan argued that the income had been community during marriage, by usufruct, but that upon the death of Beaulah, the oil income, because it traced back to the separate property oil lease, belonged entirely to him as separate property. Hal prevailed.

SECTION 6. WORK BENEFITS

Work benefits take many forms. Earnings are clearly community property, but so too are deferred earnings and other work related compensation.

A. DEFERRED EARNINGS

WEST'S ANNOTATED CALIFORNIA FAMILY CODE

§ 2610. Retirement plans; orders to ensure benefits

(a) Except as provided in subdivision (b), the court shall make whatever orders are necessary or appropriate to ensure that each party receives the party's full community property share in any retirement plan, whether public or private, including all survivor and death benefits, including, but not limited to, any of the following:

(1) Order the disposition of any retirement benefits payable upon or after the death of either party in a manner consistent with Section 2550.

(2) Order a party to elect a survivor benefit annuity or other similar election for the benefit of the other party, as specified by the court, in any case in which a retirement plan provides for such an election, provided that no court shall order a retirement plan to provide increased benefits determined on the basis of actuarial value.

(3) Upon the agreement of the nonemployee spouse, order the division of accumulated community property contributions and service credit as provided in the following or similar enactments:

(A) Article 2 (commencing with Section 21290) of Chapter 9 of Part 3 of Division 5 of Title 2 of the Government Code.

(B) Chapter 12 (commencing with Section 22650) of Part 13 of the Education Code.

(C) Article 8.4 (commencing with Section 31685) of Chapter 3 of Part 3 of Division 4 of Title 3 of the Government Code.

(D) Article 2.5 (commencing with Section 75050) of Chapter 11 of Title 8 of the Government Code.

(E) Chapter 15 (commencing with Section 27400) of Part 14 of the Education Code.

(4) Order a retirement plan to make payments directly to a nonmember party of his or her community property interest in retirement benefits.

(b) A court shall not make any order that requires a retirement plan to do either of the following:

(1) Make payments in any manner that will result in an increase in the amount of benefits provided by the plan.

(2) Make the payment of benefits to any party at any time before the member retires, except as provided in paragraph (3) of subdivision (a), unless the plan so provides.

(c) This section shall not be applied retroactively to payments made by a retirement plan to any person who retired or died prior to January 1, 1987, or to payments made to any person who retired or died prior to June 1, 1988, for plans subject to paragraph (3) of subdivision (a).

(Stats. 1992, c. 162 (A.B. 2650), § 10, operative Jan. 1, 1994. Amended by Stats. 1993, c. 219 (A.B. 1500), § 112; Stats. 1994, c. 670 (S.B. 1500), § 1;

Stats. 1994, c. 1269 (A.B. 2208), § 25.5; Stats. 1998, c. 965 (A.B. 2765), § 322; Stats. 2009, c. 130 (A.B. 966), § 1.)

NOTES

1. *Federal law.* Family law practitioners are experienced in the preparation and review of a document known as a qualified domestic relations order, or QDRO (pronounced phonetically as QUAD ro) for short. A QDRO is a federal law creation. It originates from the enactment of the Retirement Equity Act of 1984, REA, codified at Title 26 of the U.S. Code. REA provides the means to turn a domestic relations order (a DRO) into a qualified domestic relations order (a QDRO) for purposes of circumventing the anti-assignment/anti-alienation provision in the employee Retirement Income Security Act, ERISA. ERISA is codified in Title 29 of the U.S. Code.

A DRO (domestic relations order) is any state court judgment, decree, or order that relates to, among other issues, the marital property rights of the spouses, a former spouse, a child, or any other dependent of a pension plan participant. *See* 29 U.S.C.A. § 1056(d)(3)(B)(ii). The court order must be made under state law. The non-pension plan participant spouse who is named in the DRO as having rights to the pension plan participant spouse's benefits is called the "alternate payee." *Id.* A DRO is sent to the employee spouse's pension plan administrator for review. If the DRO meets the plan's requirements for a QDRO, the DRO is declared "qualified." At that point, the QDRO can be used to create or recognize the alternate payee's right to some or all of the pension plan participant's benefits. The employee spouse need not be in pay status for a QDRO to be declared; under state law, this means that the employee spouse's benefits need not be vested (certain) or even matured (actively being paid out from the pension plan).

2. *California Family Code Section 2610 and federal law.* What happens when an alternate payee under a QDRO dies?

Relying on *Boggs v. Boggs, Branco v. UFCW-Northern California Employers Joint Pension Plan*, 279 F.3d 1154 (C.A. 9 2002) held that California Family Code Section 2610, reproduced above, is preempted by ERISA. ERISA provides that if an alternative payee dies before starting to receive benefits from the pension plan, the alternate payee's share of the portion of the pension plan shall be restored to the participant. But there was a question as to what would happen if the alternate payee was already receiving benefits when he or she died. Further payment, it was deemed, would depend on the details about how the alternate payee had elected to be paid by the pension plan.

In *Branco*, husband Alfred's pension was split into one-half community shares between Alfred and a former wife Anna by a final judgment of dissolution. The judgment provided that Anna was to be paid "for so long as [the retirement benefits] are payable to or on behalf of [Alfred]." After the dissolution, Anna devised her share of retirement benefits to her two adult children.

Anna's devise was logical under the state equality of interest principle: She owned a vested one-half community property right to Alfred's pension under state law. A corollary to Anna's ownership right, again under state law, was that she had full rights of devise to her vested one-half. Therefore, Anna's devisees argued, it was entirely reasonable for Anna to expect that she could legally devise her share of a community property pension to a party or parties of her choosing.

Alfred disagreed. He invoked federal law to successfully challenge Anna's devise to her adult sons. Alfred argued that the adult sons were not qualified beneficiaries under the ERISA anti-alienation exception. He also challenged the pension plan's decision to pay Anna's sons based on its interpretation of a final state court dissolution judgment (a DRO). Alfred argued that the pension plan administrator's authorization of payment to Anna of her marital share of the pension was not a QDRO as far as Anna's adult sons were concerned. Therefore it was incorrect for the pension administrator to interpret Anna and Alfred's dissolution judgment as authority to qualify the sons as alternate payees.

The federal court of appeal agreed with Alfred: a state court order (a DRO) is not a QDRO unless it meets the requirements of 29 U.S.C. 1056(d)(3)(b)(ii)(I): a QDRO must "relate[ ] to the provision of child support, alimony payments, or *marital property rights to a spouse, former spouse*, child, or other dependent of a participant . . . " Based on its reading of the statute, rather than allow Anna's adult children to collect Anna's share of Alfred's pension payments after her death, the court restored to Alfred that portion of the pension that was being distributed to Anna during her life.

More to the point, *Branco* held that federal law pre-empts state law insofar as its application is inconsistent with ERISA or REA. U.S. constitution (Art. VI, cl. 2).

3.   *Court discretion.* The trial court has broad discretion to make a decision based on reasonableness under the circumstances. The trial court's division of the community property interest in retirement rights upon dissolution is not overturned on appeal absent a showing of abuse of discretion. *Marriage of Cooper*, 160 Cal.App.4th 574, 73 Cal.Rptr.3d 71 (2d Dist. 2008).

4.   *Apportioning pension payments and disability payments.* In a case where a spouse elects (opts) to receive a disability pension when he or she is also qualified for a retirement benefit based on years of service, the pension is apportioned as follows. The community property interest is comprised as all benefits earned during marriage. Any portion earned before marriage is separate property (Chapter 3). Any portion attributable to the person's disability status, even if during marriage, is assigned as separate property at dissolution (Chapter 3). *In re Smith*, 148 Cal.App.4th 1115, 56 Cal.Rptr. 3d 341 (6th Dist. 2007), involving federal law and military pensions that allegedly included disability benefits.

5. *Offsetting buy outs or in-kind division.* Upon dissolution of marriage, pension benefits must be accounted for in accordance with the equal division rule (Chapter 7). The trial court has the option to determine the present value of any community property rights, award the pension rights entirely to one spouse, and award offsetting community property to the other spouse as a "cash out." Under the buy-out model, the spouse who walks away *with* the pension benefit buys out the spouse who walks away *from* that benefit (i.e. who relinquishes rights to the pension benefit). Another option is for the trial court to award the pension benefit in-kind between the spouses, reserving jurisdiction to supervise future payments to each spouse. *Cooper, supra.*

6. *The time rule.* The standard rule for apportioning retirement benefits between pre-marital and marital deferred earnings is the time rule. By this rule, the community is entitled to deferred earnings obtained by the employee spouse during marriage divided by the total number of years employed. The employee spouse is entitled, as separate property, to deferred earnings earned before marriage and after a date of separation divided by the total number of years employed. See for example, *Marriage of Gray*, 155 Cal.App.4th 504, 66 Cal.Rptr.3d 87 (6th Dist. 2007). If an employer uses a different system to determine pension rights, that system can be used to determine pro rata shares. Different systems sometimes use points earned instead of a time employed. If so, point earned during marriage divided by total points earned equals the community property interest.

———

Marriage of Green, reproduced below, is the most recent case to outline California law on retirement benefits. At its broadest, it confirms that a pension earned before marriage is not community property, nor statutorily or constitutionally can it be. If the community should help the separate property owner maintain or enhance a premarital pension benefit, the community does not acquire marital property rights in the premarital pension; rather the community is entitled (only) to a reimbursement for direct costs related to the enhancement.

MARRIAGE OF GREEN

56 Cal.4th 1130, 158 Cal.Rptr.3d 247, 302 P.3d 562 (2013)

Opinion

CHIN, J.

Retirement benefits attributable to service rendered during a marriage are community property. In this case, the husband, a firefighter, has retirement benefits that are part community property and part his own separate property. During the time of the marriage, he exercised his right to purchase four years' worth of additional retirement credit for his premarital military service. He had to pay to obtain this additional credit, which he elected to do in installments, some of which came from community property. The value of the additional credit substantially exceeds the cost of obtaining it. We must decide how much, if any, of the value of the four additional years of credit is community property.

What matters in determining whether retirement benefits are community or separate property is the person's marital status when the services on which the benefits are based were rendered. Here the husband rendered the military service before the marriage. Accordingly, we conclude that, except for the community's contribution to the cost of obtaining the credit, the four years of additional credit are the husband's separate property.

The trial court ordered the husband to pay the wife one-half of the amount the community expended to obtain the credit plus interest. We conclude that the trial court acted within its discretion in using this method to compensate her for her share of the community's interest in the property. We reverse the judgment of the Court of Appeal, which reached a different conclusion.

I.   FACTS AND PROCEDURAL HISTORY

We draw these facts largely from the Court of Appeal opinion.

Timothy P. Green (husband) served in the United States Air Force for four years, from July 23, 1982, to May 1, 1986. On June 16, 1989, he began working as a firefighter for the Dougherty Regional Fire Authority in Dublin, which participated in the California Public Employees' Retirement System (CalPERS). At that time, husband had the right to buy up to four years of service credit towards his retirement benefits for his military service. Husband married Julie R. Green (wife) in May 1992.

In July 1997, the Dougherty Regional Fire Authority merged with the Alameda County Fire Department, which also participates in CalPERS. Husband continued to work for the Alameda County Fire Department.

On August 1, 2002, husband exercised his right to buy four years of service credit for his military service. He elected to pay for the purchase under an installment plan, paying $92.44 twice each month through payroll deductions for 15 years, scheduled to end in July 2017. Before the parties separated on October 1, 2007, $11,462.56 of community funds had been used toward the purchase of the military service credit.

Wife filed a petition for dissolution of the marriage in March 2008. The parties disputed whether to characterize husband's military service credit as separate or community property. After a trial, the trial court ordered that the military service credit portion of husband's CalPERS pension be awarded to him as his separate property. The court also ordered husband to pay wife $6,699.54, representing half of the installment payments made with community funds toward the military service credit, plus interest at the rate of 6 percent.

Wife appealed, challenging the characterization of the military service credit as husband's separate property. The Court of Appeal reversed the judgment. It concluded that, "because the military service credit was purchased with community funds during the parties' marriage, it was community property" and remanded the case to the trial court to determine the proper allocation of that property.

We granted husband's petition for review.

We recently summarized the applicable legal principles. In general, all property that a spouse acquires during marriage before separation is community property. (Fam.Code, §§ 760, 770.) Community property may include the right to retirement benefits that the employee spouse accrues as deferred compensation for services rendered. The right to retirement benefits is a property interest. To the extent that such a right derives from service during marriage before separation, it is a community asset. We review de novo the trial court's characterization of service credit as community or separate property. (*In re Marriage of Sonne* (2010) 48 Cal.4th 118, 124, 105 Cal.Rptr.3d 414, 225 P.3d 546 (*Sonne*).)

Husband is a member of CalPERS. "Members of CalPERS, once vested, participate in a defined benefit retirement plan, which supplies a monthly retirement allowance under a formula comprising factors such as final compensation, service credit (i.e., the credited years of employment), and a per-service-year multiplier. The retirement allowance consists of an *annuity* (which is funded by member contributions deducted from the member's paycheck and interest thereon) and a *pension* (which is funded by employer contributions and which must be sufficient, when added to the annuity, to satisfy the amount specified in the benefit formula)." (*Sonne, supra,* 48 Cal.4th at p. 121, 105 Cal.Rptr.3d 414, 225 P.3d 546.)

Government Code section 21024 permits those who work for an agency that elects to be subject to the section to obtain up to four years of additional credit towards their retirement allowance for "public service," which includes service in the United States military. (See *id.,* subds. (a), (c), (e), (f).) This public service is to be credited "as it would be credited if the member had been in state service during his or her public service." (Gov.Code, § 21034.) Government Code section 21024 was enacted in 1995 as part of the Public Employees' Retirement Law. (Stats.1995, ch. 379, § 2, pp. 2133–2134; see Gov.Code, § 20000.) But it is derived from an earlier statute containing similar provisions. (Gov.Code, former § 20930.3, added by Stats.1974, ch. 1437, § 1, p. 3142.)

Government Code section 21024, subdivision (b), requires those who elect to receive the additional credit for public service to contribute money in order to receive it. During the marriage, husband elected to obtain the four years of military service credit for which he was eligible and arranged to make the required contribution in installment payments, some of which came from community property. We must decide whether the credit for the military service is community property or husband's separate property.

Two recent cases from this court guide us. In *In re Marriage of Lehman* (1998) 18 Cal.4th 169, 74 Cal.Rptr.2d 825, 955 P.2d 451 (*Lehman*), the husband and wife had been married during part, although not all, of the time the husband worked and accumulated retirement benefits. At the time the husband retired, after dissolution of the marriage, his employer offered an "enhanced retirement program" to encourage early retirement. The program included "the crediting of three putative years of service." (*Lehman, supra,* at p. 175, 74 Cal.Rptr.2d 825, 955 P.2d 451.) We described these putative years as "*fictive*—they have no independent existence, but are merely a means by which the employer effects the enhancement." (*Id.* at p. 188, 74 Cal.Rptr.2d 825, 955 P.2d 451.) Although the employer offered the enhanced program only after the marriage had dissolved, we found the three years' additional credit to be, in part, community property.

We explained that, "if the right to retirement benefits accrues, in some part, during marriage before separation, it is a community asset and is therefore owned by the community in which the nonemployee spouse as well as the employee spouse owns an interest." (*Lehman, supra,* 18 Cal.4th at p. 179, 74 Cal.Rptr.2d 825, 955 P.2d 451.) "It follows that a nonemployee spouse who owns a community property interest in an employee spouse's retirement benefits owns a community property interest in the latter's retirement benefits as enhanced. That is because, practically by definition, the right to retirement benefits that accrues, at least in part, during marriage before separation underlies any right to an enhancement." (*Id.* at pp. 179–180, 74 Cal.Rptr.2d 825, 955 P.2d 451.) "[W]hat is determinative is the single concrete fact of time. To the extent—and only to the extent— that an employee spouse accrues a right to property during marriage before separation, the property in question is a community asset." (*Id.* at p. 183, 74 Cal.Rptr.2d 825, 955 P.2d 451.)

We cited with approval a New York case that had explained that a pension right owned as community property is, by its nature, subject to modification by future actions of either the employee or the employer. (*Lehman, supra,* 18 Cal.4th at pp. 183–184, 74 Cal.Rptr.2d 825, 955 P.2d 451, citing *Olivo v. Olivo* (1993) 82 N.Y.2d 202, 604 N.Y.S.2d 23, 624 N.E.2d 151. 155.) Accordingly, " 'both parties' rights are generally subject to changes in the terms of a retirement plan, as well as to circumstances largely beyond their control, such as the salary level finally achieved by the employee and used to calculate the pension benefit. *What the nonemployee spouse possesses, in short, is the right to share in the pension as it is ultimately determined.* . . . [Any] enhancement' in the amount is a 'modification of an asset not the creation of a new one.' " (*Lehman, supra,* at p. 184, 74 Cal.Rptr.2d 825, 955 P.2d 451, quoting *Olivo v. Olivo, supra,* 604 N.Y.S.2d 23, 624 N.E.2d at p. 155, italics added in *Lehman.*)

In *Sonne, supra,* 48 Cal.4th 118, 105 Cal.Rptr.3d 414, 225 P.3d 546, the husband transferred to a former wife several years of service credit that had accrued during the former marriage. The former wife exercised her right to collect a refund of the accumulated contributions in the retirement account, which permanently waived her rights to any further claim on the husband's retirement benefits. Later, the husband, then remarried, exercised his right to redeposit the same contributions into the account, thereby regaining the years of service credit he had previously transferred to the former wife. Some of the money used to redeposit the contributions was community property from the second marriage. When the second marriage was dissolved, "the question arose: What was the community's share of the service credit from the [former] marriage?" (*Id.* at p. 121, 105 Cal.Rptr.3d 414, 225 P.3d 546.) The trial court had found that, to the extent community funds from the second marriage were used for the redeposit, the service credit was the second marriage's community property. We took a different view.

We agreed with the argument of an amicus curiae "that since community funds contributed only to the annuity component of the retirement allowance, the community was entitled only to a *pro tanto* share of the annuity—and not to a share of the much larger pension component, which was funded by employer contributions." (*Sonne, supra,* 48 Cal.4th at p. 121, 105 Cal.Rptr.3d 414, 225 P.3d 546.) We explained that "a redeposit of member contributions for a prior period of service does not constitute consideration for the service credit for that period; it is merely a condition precedent to a credit for that previously rendered service. (See Gov.Code, § 20756.) The service credit (and the pension component of the retirement allowance) are more correctly described as ' "a form of deferred compensation for services rendered." ' (*In re Marriage of Skaden* (1977) 19 Cal.3d 679, 686 [139 Cal.Rptr. 615, 566 P.2d 249].) The trial court's analysis gave no weight whatsoever to the *service* Husband rendered as a deputy sheriff during those years, all of which preceded the [second] marriage." (*Id.* at p. 125, 105 Cal.Rptr.3d 414, 225 P.3d 546.)

. . .

A treatise has aptly distilled the rule derived from these cases: "Pension and retirement benefits are a form of employment compensation and thus tantamount to 'earnings.' As such, *regardless of when the benefits 'vest' or are received,* they are characterized in accordance with the employee's marital status at the time the services were rendered; i.e., the benefits are community property to the extent attributable to employment during marriage." (2 Hogoboom & King, Cal. Practice Guide: Family Law (The Rutter Group 2012) § 8:141, p. 8–43.) Here, husband rendered his military service before the marriage, making the military service credit his separate property.

Wife argues the military service credit was an enhanced retirement benefit like the one in *Lehman, supra,* 18 Cal.4th 169, 74 Cal.Rptr.2d 825, 955 P.2d 451, that we determined was partly community property. But this case is not similar to *Lehman*. In *Lehman,* the enhanced credits were based on "fictive" years (*id.* at p. 188, 74 Cal.Rptr.2d 825, 955 P.2d 451, italics omitted), not real ones, and, accordingly, were attributable in part to years of work during the marriage. Here, husband served in the military rather than as a firefighter during the time in question. Government Code section 21034 treats that military service as if it had been service as a firefighter. In that limited sense, the military credit is fictive. But in the sense we used the term in *Lehman,* the years of credited service are not fictive. Those years are attributable to specific, actual years of military service that husband rendered before the marriage.

To designate a portion of those four years of credit as community property—as did the Court of Appeal—solely due to the community's contribution towards the required payment gives no weight to husband's premarital service to his country. (See *Sonne, supra,* 48 Cal.4th at p. 125, 105 Cal.Rptr.3d 414, 225 P.3d 546.) But Government Code section 21034 specifically mandates that this military service is to be credited "as it would be credited if the member had been in state service during" that service. This demonstrates a legislative intent to fully credit persons for their military service. The four years of military service should be treated the same the way the years at issue in *Sonne* and *Lehman* were treated— basing the characterization of the credit on the marital status at the time of the service.

In *Sonne,* we were able to discern from the record that the payment from community funds went towards the annuity portion of the retirement benefits and not towards the far greater pension portion, which the employer paid. (*Sonne, supra,* 48 Cal.4th at pp. 127–128, 105 Cal.Rptr.3d 414, 225 P.3d 546.) The situation is less clear in this case. On this record, it is difficult to determine exactly how the required contribution was calculated and what it paid for. The Court of Appeal believed that, unlike the situation in *Sonne,* husband had to pay both the employee's and the employer's contribution. But it explained that obtaining the credit was nonetheless beneficial because "whatever method was used to set [husband's] contribution to purchase military service credit, he was able to purchase it based on his salary at the time of hire, but he will receive payment for the service credit based on his salary upon retirement."

Wife stated in the trial court that the credit's value was about $140,000, far more than the cost of the contributions, and husband seemed to accept that figure, although it is not clear how either arrived at it. An amicus curiae brief from the Northern California Chapter of the American Academy of Matrimonial Lawyers filed in the Court of Appeal argues that the value of the credit was far greater than the cost of obtaining it, resulting in a "significant subsidy" that someone other than husband would have to pay, "and that someone must, by default, be the employer or CalPERS." An amicus curiae brief from Certified Family Law Specialist Barbara A. DiFranza filed in this court argues that the same annuity/pension dichotomy described in *Sonne, supra,* 48 Cal.4th at pages 127–128, 105 Cal.Rptr.3d 414, 225 P.3d 546, governs this case.

Ultimately, it does not matter exactly how the contribution was calculated or what it paid for. It is clear the value of the four years of credit far exceeds the cost of obtaining it. Indeed, the difference in value is precisely what the parties are fighting over. The trial court awarded wife her share of the community's contribution plus interest, but she seeks instead a share of the four years' worth of credit itself. [P]urchasing the four years of military service "was obviously a great bargain." *Lucero, supra,* 118 Cal.App.3d at p. 841, 173 Cal.Rptr. 680.) And this bargain "was possible only as consideration for husband's service" in the United States military—service that predated the marriage. (*Ibid.*) The difference in value was not due to what the community contributed—part of the installment payments—but to what husband brought to the community— his military service. For these reasons, the difference in value between the four years' worth of credit and the cost of obtaining it is husband's separate property, subject to reimbursement for the community's contribution to the cost of obtaining the credit.

B. SIGNING BONUSES AND CLIENT BOOKS

Marriage of Finby, reproduced below, discusses whether and under what conditions a licensed professional's client book and bonuses are assets subject to division at dissolution. The case reviews important legal distinctions between talent and professional efforts, vested and contingent interests versus mere expectancies, and bonus earned for bringing value to a firm versus for continued performance at a firm.

MARRIAGE OF FINBY

222 Cal. App.4th 977, 166 Cal.Rptr. 3d 305 (4th Dist. 2013)

OPINION

RYLAARSDAM, J.

Mark Finby (husband) appeals from a judgment on reserved issues, covering child custody and support, spousal support, and division of the parties' assets. He contends the trial court erred in its characterization, valuation, and division of Rhonda Finby's (wife) bonuses conditionally received or earned from her employer before the parties separated. We find his arguments have merit and reverse the judgment.

FACTS

The parties married in 1995 and separated in February 2010. During the marriage, wife worked as a financial advisor. Before January 2009, she worked for UBS Financial Services. She developed a list of clients referred to as her "book of business." As of January 2009, the value of her clients' investments exceeded $192 million.

That month wife signed a contract with Wachovia Securities LLC, entitled "Offer Summary," agreeing to work for it as a financial advisor and its managing director of investments. (Some capitalization omitted.) Shortly thereafter, Wachovia was purchased by Wells Fargo Advisors (Wells Fargo).

The offer summary contained several compensation bonuses. The first, a transitional bonus exceeding $2.8 million, was "based on 150% of [wife's] pre-hire trailing twelve months production * * * of $1,868,631.00 * * * and pre-hire assets of $192,671,911." Her entitlement to receive the entire amount was conditioned on her remaining employed as a financial advisor by Wells Fargo for 112 months, maintaining a gross production level of over $1.12 million on each anniversary date, and remaining current on any other obligations she owes to the firm.

Wife chose to immediately receive the entire amount of the transitional bonus. Thus, payment was arranged as a loan evidenced by a promissory note whereby Wells Fargo agreed to forgive the sum of $27,687.54 each month over 112 months.

For tax purposes, Wells Fargo credited wife with an equal amount of income on each monthly pay voucher. However, to enforce the foregoing conditions, it was provided that if she stopped working for Wells Fargo, the entire unpaid balance of the loan would be due. In the event wife continued working for the firm but failed to satisfy the minimum production quota during annual reviews, Wells Fargo could "reduce the amount of [the] [m]onthly * * * [b]onus [p]ayment" credited to her.

The offer summary also provided wife could receive a deferred recruitment award bonus of $186,863. But to be eligible for it she must remain employed by Wells Fargo until January 31, 2016.

In addition, the offer summary stated wife was eligible for two production bonuses. Wells Fargo agreed to pay her a first production bonus of $373,726 if her "total gross production equal[ed] or exceed[ed] $1,494,905.00 in the best twelve months of the first fourteen month period beginning February 2009 and ending March 2010. * * * " Wife achieved this goal and received the entire amount of the bonus in April 2010. Like the transitional bonus Wells Fargo arranged the payment as a loan evidenced by a promissory note with the balance to be forgiven in equal monthly installments over a 10-year span, and crediting an equal amount as income on wife's monthly pay vouchers. In addition, Wells Fargo's forgiveness of this obligation was also subject to the same employment and production level conditions. The offer summary authorized a second production bonus if wife achieved a higher gross production level between April 2010 and March 2011. Wife failed to achieve the higher production goal and did not qualify for this bonus.

In mid-2009, Wells Fargo announced another benefit for its financial advisors, entitled a "level 4front" bonus. Wife testified that to receive it, she had to meet with clients, prepare and maintain investment profiles of them, plus follow up with each client's investment profile. She qualified for this bonus and was paid $890,000 in mid-2010. As with the foregoing bonuses, payment of the level 4front bonus was arranged as a loan evidenced by wife's promissory note with Wells Fargo agreeing to forgive the balance in equal installments over 108 months and, for tax purposes, crediting an equal amount as income to each of her pay vouchers. Wife testified this bonus was also conditioned on her remaining employed with Wells Fargo and maintaining her client's financial profiles.

Both parties presented expert testimony on wife's book of business and the character of the bonuses she received. Andrew Hunt, a certified public accountant, testified for wife. He employed the time rule to determine the character of the bonuses and accompanying loans. He described the transitional bonus as a "mixed-type asset," stating "approximately . . . 13 and a half percent of" it "on an after-tax basis was community" with the balance being wife's separate property. Hunt concluded the first production bonus and the level 4front bonus were wife's separate property because, being earned over a period of years, they were received after separation.

Wife also called Quinton Ellis, an associate with a firm providing litigation assistance to firms in the securities industry. He described the transitional bonus as a "kind of pay for the book of business . . . coming over," calculated as a "multiple of the value of * * * the [recruitee's] production credits of the trailing 12 months before they were to join your firm." The hiring firm would also expect to receive "a nine-to ten-year commitment to earn that bonus" because "you don't want to pay somebody upfront and then have them go into early retirement once they join the firm." Ellis described the production bonus as "a back-end bonus" that is a "performance-based" incentive for the "consultant to work extremely diligently in bringing their book over, as well as to continue to seek new business and continue to be successful. * * * " The level 4front bonus required wife to perform extensive analytical work and complete financial plans for her clients. David Altshuler, wife's boss, testified the level 4front bonus was a "loyalty award" created "to retain our financial advisors."

Barbara DiFranza, an attorney and certified family law specialist testified that in her opinion, the bonuses constituted community assets.

She described wife's book of business as "[t]he consideration" for the benefits contained in the offer summary.

Husband also called Howard Buchler, an attorney with previous work experience in the securities industry. Buchler agreed with Ellis that the offer summary's transitional bonus compensated wife for bringing her book of business to Wells Fargo. He stated the brokerage industry now recognizes that brokers own their book of business. Asked if a market existed for "a financial advisor * * * to sell her book of business," Buchler responded, "the market for it would be * * * [moving to] another [firm]."

Stephen Zamucen, a certified public accountant called by husband, testified the bonuses wife received were community assets. He explained the bonuses were either based on her book of business (transitional), agreed to before the parties separated, or based on wife's preseparation production (first production and level 4front).

The court issued a statement of decision and entered judgment. On wife's book of business, the court ruled it had no value and husband did not have an interest in it. In its statement of decision, the court agreed wife received a high salary from Wells Fargo because of the value of the investments held by her clients, but husband's assistance in helping wife transfer her clients to Wells Fargo "did not give * * * him an interest in the [b]ook of [b]usiness," "there was no expert testimony given as to the value of" it, and, citing *In re Marriage of McTiernan & Dubrow* (2005) 133 Cal.App.4th 1090, 35 Cal.Rptr.3d 287, found the book of business "cannot be transferred to another party for a price."

As for the bonuses, the court ruled the portion of transitional bonus earned during the first 11 months of wife's employment with Wells Fargo (slightly over $380,000) was received before separation and thus constituted community property to be divided between the parties. But it concluded the balance of that bonus and the remaining bonuses were wife's separate property because they were not paid or due until after the parties separated. In addition, the court noted wife's retention of the bonuses was subject to her continued employment and minimum production requirements enforced by the promissory notes. It found the reasoning in *In re Marriage of Doherty* (2002) 103 Cal.App.4th 895, 126 Cal.Rptr.2d 919 and *Garfein v. Garfein* (1971) 16 Cal.App.3d 155, 93 Cal.Rptr. 714 supported its findings.

DISCUSSION

1. Introduction

The issues presented in this appeal are the trial court's characterization and valuation of wife's list of clients, i.e., her book of business, and the bonuses Wells Fargo conditionally agreed to pay her.

"In general, all property that a spouse acquires during marriage before separation is community property." (*In re Marriage of Green* (2013) 56 Cal.4th 1130, 1134, 158 Cal.Rptr.3d 247, 302 P.3d 562; see Fam.Code, § 760; all further undesignated statutory references are to this code.) Cases have recognized that Family Code section 760 creates " 'a general presumption that property acquired during marriage by either spouse other than by gift or inheritance is community property unless traceable to a separate property source.' " (*In re Marriage of Rossin* (2009) 172 Cal.App.4th 725, 731, 91 Cal.Rptr.3d 427.) However, "[t]he earnings and accumulations of a spouse . . . while living separate and apart from the other spouse, are the separate property of the spouse." (Fam.Code, § 771, subd. (a).)

Under California's community property law, the characterization of "property as separate, community, or quasi-community" "is an integral part of the division of property on marital dissolution." (*In re Marriage of Haines* (1995) 33 Cal.App.4th 277, 291, 39 Cal.Rptr.2d 673.) Courts recognize several factors relevant to this task (see *In re Marriage of Rossin, supra,* 172 Cal.App.4th at p. 732, 91 Cal.Rptr.3d 427), but "the most basic characterization factor is the time when property is acquired in relation to the parties' marital status" (*In re Marriage of Haines, supra,* 33 Cal.App.4th at p. 291, 39 Cal.Rptr.2d 673). The "factual findings that underpin the characterization determination are reviewed for substantial evidence" (*In re Marriage of Rossin, supra,* 172 Cal.App.4th at p. 734, 91 Cal.Rptr.3d 427), but "[i]nasmuch as the basic 'inquiry requires a critical consideration, in a factual context, of legal principles and their underlying values,' the determination in question amounts to the resolution of a mixed question of law and fact that is predominantly one of law. [Citation.] As such, it is examined de novo" (*In re Marriage of Lehman* (1998) 18 Cal.4th 169, 184, 74 Cal.Rptr.2d 825, 955 P.2d 451).

Once the court determines the assets and liabilities of the community estate, it must value them and make an equal division of the estate. (§§ 2550–2552, 2601, 2620 et seq.; see *In re Marriage of Walrath* (1998) 17 Cal.4th 907, 924, 72 Cal.Rptr.2d 856, 952 P.2d 1124.) Issues concerning the valuation and apportionment of community property are reviewed for abuse of discretion. (*In re Marriage of Lehman, supra,* 18 Cal.4th at p. 187, 74 Cal.Rptr.2d 825, 955 P.2d 451 [apportionment]; *In re Marriage of Ackerman* (2006) 146 Cal.App.4th 191, 197, 52 Cal.Rptr.3d 744 [valuation].)

2.　*The Book of Business*

As noted, the trial court awarded wife's book of business to her. Citing *In re Marriage of McTiernan & Dubrow, supra,* 133 Cal.App.4th 1090, 35 Cal.Rptr.3d 287, it concluded since wife could not sell her client list, her book of business "has no value[,] and . . . [husband] does not have an interest in" it. On appeal, husband attacks this ruling. He argues the book of business can be valued even if there is no market for it, and in fact she sold her book of business when moving from UBS to Wells Fargo. Husband also relies on the Supreme Court's decision in *In re Marriage of Brown* (1976) 15 Cal.3d 838, 126 Cal.Rptr. 633, 544 P.2d 561 (*Brown*) and other cases following it for the proposition that rights created under an employment contract entered into during marriage, even if contingent in nature, constitute divisible community assets. Wife disagrees, arguing the trial court properly found her book of business was nontransferable, "Wells Fargo agreed to pay [her] a significant sum of money because she is successful at her job," and that her "success is primarily measured by the amount of assets she manages."

We conclude the trial court's ruling on the nature and value of wife's book of business constituted error. "[T]o qualify as community property, an asset or interest must be 'property' within the meaning of the community property laws." (*In re Marriage of Spengler* (1992) 5 Cal.App.4th 288, 297, 6 Cal.Rptr.2d 764.) Husband argues wife's status as a licensed financial advisor with the ability to induce clients to follow her when transferring to a new firm is similar to the goodwill found in the business of other professions such as lawyers and doctors.

This argument has merit. Business and Professions Code section 14100 declares "The 'goodwill' of a business is the expectation of continued public patronage." "[I]t is well established that the goodwill of a . . . professional practice as a sole practitioner" created during marriage constitutes a divisible asset of the community in an action for dissolution of marriage. (*In re Marriage of Foster* (1974) 42 Cal.App.3d 577, 582, 117 Cal.Rptr. 49; see *In re Marriage of Watts* (1985) 171 Cal.App.3d 366, 372, 217 Cal.Rptr. 301.) " '[W]here the issue is raised in a marital dissolution action, the trial court must make a specific finding as to the existence and value of the "goodwill" of a professional business as a going concern' " even if it involves the business " 'of a sole practitioner. . . .' " (*In re Marriage of Fenton* (1982) 134 Cal.App.3d 451, 460, 184 Cal.Rptr. 597.) As for the nature of a client list, in *Dairy Dale Co. v. Azevedo* (1931) 211 Cal. 344, 295 P. 10, the Supreme Court recognized "It is settled in this state that the names, addresses and requirements of an employer's customers * * * constitute part of the goodwill of the business. * * * " (*Id.* at p. 345, 295 P. 10.)

The parties have not cited, nor have we found, a California case on point concerning whether a licensed professional's list of clients is an asset subject to division in a dissolution action. But courts in other jurisdictions have generally held customer lists of licensed professionals who are employed in a business or industry constitute divisible marital property. (*Moll v. Moll* (N.Y.Supr.Ct.2001) 187 Misc.2d 770, 775, 722 N.Y.S.2d 732 [clients serviced by stockbroker constitute marital asset; "the 'thing of value' is the personal or professional goodwill of a stockbroker or financial advisor"]; *Reiss v. Reiss* (Fla.Dist.Ct.App.1995) 654 So.2d 268, 268–269 [stockbroker's " 'signing bonus' " for clients he brought with him to new securities firm is a divisible marital asset]; *Niroo v. Niroo* (Md.Ct.App.1988) 313 Md. 226, 234–235, 545 A.2d 35 [insurance agent's anticipated renewal commissions on policies sold during marriage "are type of property interest encompassed within the definition of marital property"]; *Pangburn v. Pangburn* (Ariz.Ct.App.1986) 152 Ariz. 227, 230, 731 P.2d 122 [citing *Brown,* insurance agent's "contractual right to commissions for future renewals * * * earned during coverture" includable within community estate].)

The record before us is unclear, but in this appeal husband claims, and wife apparently does not dispute, that she acquired her book of business during their marriage. Contrary to the trial court's findings, the terms of the offer summary and the testimony of the parties' experts reflect wife's book of business, i.e. list of clients, was a valuable asset. The offer summary states the transitional bonus was "based on 150% of your pre-hire trailing twelve months production, subject to and following verification of pre-hiring twelve months production of $1,868,631.00 * * * and pre-hire assets of $192,671,911," and that "[e]vidence of both assets under management and trailing twelve [month] production shall be dated within sixty days prior to your date of hire."

Both Ellis, wife's securities industry expert, and Buchler, husband's securities expert, acknowledged financial advisors are viewed as professionals. In order to work in the securities industry financial advisors must acquire and maintain one or more licenses. Wife's professional credentials include being certified as a financial planner, an investment management analyst, and a retirement planning counselor. Buchler testified the securities industry now recognizes a "financial advisor owns [his or her] book of business." Both experts agreed that industry protocol allows a financial advisor to take the names of his or her clients, plus their account and telephone numbers when changing firms.

Ellis described the transitional bonus "as kind of the up-front bonus," the purpose of which was "to aid the transition and—basically, if you would, kind of pay for the book of business as it was coming over." Buchler agreed wife received the transitional bonus as compensation for bringing her book of business to Wells Fargo. He explained the value of a financial advisor's book of business would "range . . . anywhere from one to three times the gross . . . commissions generated by the book of business." Although claiming wife would have been entitled to "some bonus based on her [previously demonstrated] production credits, her expertise, and her ability to build business," Ellis conceded that without bringing the book of business to Wells Fargo she likely would not have received a transitional bonus of $2.8 million.

Thus, wife's book of business was a valuable asset. The evidence reflects Wells Fargo agreed to pay wife $2.8 million for bringing her customers to the firm. The difficulty presented is that the transitional bonus was to be paid over several years, but wife received the entire amount in advance subject to the conditions that she continue to work as a financial advisor for the firm, maintain a minimum production level, and remain current on her other obligations to the firm. Wells Fargo enforced these terms by requiring wife to sign a promissory note for the entire amount to be forgiven in monthly installments over a nine- to 10-year period.

But the fact that wife's right to receive the bonus is subject to contingencies does not preclude it from being a divisible community asset. In *Brown,* the Supreme Court held "Pension rights, whether or not vested, represent a property interest . . . subject to division in a dissolution proceeding" where "such rights derive from employment during coverture. . . ." (*Brown, supra,* 15 Cal.3d at p. 842, 126 Cal.Rptr. 633, 544 P.2d 561.) In so ruling, *Brown* "reject[ed] th[e] theory" that merely because the right to receive pension benefits was contingent on the employee spouse's continued employment the asset could not be deemed a divisible community asset. (*Id.* at p. 846, 126 Cal.Rptr. 633, 544 P.2d 561.) "The fact that a contractual right is contingent upon future events does not degrade that right to an expectancy." (*Id.* at p. 846, fn. 8, 126 Cal.Rptr. 633, 544 P.2d 561.)

Shortly after issuing *Brown,* the Supreme Court decided *In re Marriage of Fonstein* (1976) 17 Cal.3d 738, 131 Cal.Rptr. 873, 552 P.2d 1169. *Fonstein* rejected a spouse's claim that his contractual right to withdraw from a law firm constituted "a mere expectancy with no present value. . . ." (*Id.* at p. 745, 131 Cal.Rptr. 873, 552 P.2d 1169.) "[W]ithdrawal rights are analogous to the pension rights which have been held to be community property when subject only to conditions within the control of the employee. [Citations.] * * * [C]ontractual rights, where the right to payment is earned during marriage, are community property though contingent upon future events." (*Id.* at pp. 745–746, 131 Cal.Rptr. 873, 552 P.2d 1169; see *In re Marriage of Skaden* (1977) 19 Cal.3d 679, 687, 139 Cal.Rptr. 615, 566 P.2d 249 [employment contract conditionally granting insurance agent right to receive postemployment payments based on premiums credited to him before termination constitute " 'a form of deferred compensation for services rendered' " because "these benefits 'derived from the terms of the employment contract' "].)

Here, Wells Fargo paid wife, a licensed financial advisor, $2.8 million as consideration for bringing to the firm clients owning over $192 million in investments that had produced over $1.8 million in commissions and fees in the prior year. While her right to retain the entire bonus is contingent on satisfying certain obligations, they are "conditions within [wife's] control. . . ." (*In re Marriage of Fonstein, supra,* 17 Cal.3d at p. 746, 131 Cal.Rptr. 873, 552 P.2d 1169.)

The trial court's reliance on *In re Marriage of McTiernan & Dubrow, supra,* 133 Cal.App.4th 1090, 35 Cal.Rptr.3d 287 was error since that case presented a distinguishable situation. There the husband was a successful movie director. The trial court held the husband's high status within the film industry constituted goodwill, noting he had " 'developed an earning capacity and reputation in his profession . . . which greatly exceeds that of most persons involved in that profession and that [husband] commands a premium for his services.' " (*Id.* at p. 1094, 35 Cal.Rptr.3d 287.)

After discussing the nature of what constitutes property, including the fact that "property must be capable of being transferred" (*In re Marriage of McTiernan & Dubrow, supra,* 133 Cal.App.4th at p. 1100, 35 Cal.Rptr.3d 287), the Court of Appeal reversed. "Husband's 'earning capacity and reputation in his profession as a motion picture director * * * ' or, in the trial court's shorthand, his 'elite professional standing,' cannot be sold or transferred. His high standing among other motion picture directors is entirely personal to him. He cannot confer on another director his standing. * * * He cannot sell this standing to another. * * * That standing is his, and his alone, and he cannot bestow it on someone else. Thus, an essential aspect of a property interest is absent." (*Id.* at pp. 1100–1101, 35 Cal.Rptr.3d 287.)

We do not disagree with the ruling in *In re Marriage of McTiernan & Dubrow, supra,* 133 Cal.App.4th 1090, 35 Cal.Rptr.3d 287. But, as discussed above, the terms of the offer summary and expert testimony reflect Wells Fargo did not pay wife the transitional bonus in return merely for her admittedly high standing in the securities industry. Rather, the consideration for that bonus was her ability to induce clients with significant assets and potential for producing future commissions and fees to follow her when moving to the firm.

The trial court did find the community had an interest in a portion of the transitional bonus. But it was limited to the payments wife earned during the 11 months between the date of her hire and the parties' separation. Based on the foregoing discussion, we conclude this limited valuation constituted an abuse of discretion. Wife's right to receive the bonus, and the obligation to repay it if she failed to satisfy the attached conditions, arose when she signed the offer summary, received immediate payment of the bonus, and began working for Wells Fargo. Further, the ability to satisfy the requirements entitling her to retain the entire bonus is within her control.

This does not mean the court must simply award one-half of the $2.8 million to husband. As discussed above, wife's conditional right to retain the entirety of the transitional bonus and the possibility she may be obligated to repay any unearned portion of it is similar to the nonvested and unmatured pension right at issue in *Brown* and the cases applying its reasoning to other contractually created contingent interests. *In re Marriage of Skaden, supra,* 19 Cal.3d 679, 139 Cal.Rptr. 615, 566 P.2d 249 noted "*Brown* . . . indicated [there were] two basic solutions" to the division of a community's interest in a contingent benefit. (*Id.* at p. 688, 139 Cal.Rptr. 615, 566 P.2d 249.) "[F]irst, a determination by the trial court of the present value of the rights or [obligations] adjudged to be marital property [or liability] and an equal division or adjustment of the same [citations][,] and second, 'if the court concludes that because of uncertainties affecting the vesting or maturation of [such] rights . . . it should not attempt to divide the present value . . . it can instead award [or confirm to] each spouse an appropriate portion of each . . . payment [or obligation] as it is paid [or incurred].' " (*Ibid.*)

Skaden further held "that in cases of this kind the matter of the proper division of rights [or obligations] * * * as marital property [or liability] should be left to the sound discretion of the trial court, exercised in light of the particular circumstances of the case." (*In re Marriage of Skaden, supra,* 19 Cal.3d at p. 688, 139 Cal.Rptr. 615, 566 P.2d 249.) Thus, in this case we will remand the matter to the trial court to determine the extent of the community interest or obligation in the transitional bonus and to decide the appropriate option of dividing or appropriating it.

3.   The Other Bonuses

The trial court ruled the first production bonus and level 4front bonus constituted wife's separate property and confirmed the entire amount of each payment to her. The court made no finding on the deferred recruitment bonus, but noted wife would not be eligible to receive it until 2016 and then only if she is still employed by Wells Fargo.

Husband argues these bonuses "were not compensation for future employment," but "for the book built up during marriage." He claims wife's postseparation salary fully compensated her for the obligations of remaining a Wells Fargo financial advisor in good standing and maintaining a specific production level. Wife asserts she "must continue to work and perform at a specified level in order to receive the benefits contracted for during marriage," and thus "[t]he bonuses paid to [her]" constitute "unearned income until the condition[s are] met."

We reject husband's argument concerning these bonuses. It is supported only by Buchler's testimony. Ellis, wife's securities expert, testified the consideration for wife's book of business was the transitional bonus. His testimony supports the trial court's rejection of husband's claim and, as noted, we must accept the trial court's express and implied factual findings when supported by the evidence. (*In re Marriage of Rossin, supra,* 172 Cal.App.4th at p. 734, 91 Cal.Rptr.3d 427.)

Furthermore, as for the deferred recruitment award, the offer summary provided wife's right to receive would "vest on January 31, 2016 . . . provided [she] remain[ed] actively employed with [Wells Fargo]. . . ." But, with certain exceptions, "[i]n the event that [wife's] employment is terminated by [her] or [Wells Fargo] for any reason whatsoever prior to the [v]esting [d]ate, [wife] agree[d] that [she] will not be entitled to any portion of the '[d]eferred [r]ecruitment [a]ward. . . ." Thus, while the offer summary provides for wife's receipt of a deferred recruitment bonus unless she remains a Wells Fargo employee until January 31, 2016, she will not be entitled to receive this payment. We conclude this bonus constitutes only an expectancy because prior to the vesting date wife "has no *enforceable right*" to receive it. (*In re Marriage of Brown, supra,* 15 Cal.3d at p. 845, 126 Cal.Rptr. 633, 544 P.2d 561.)

Nonetheless, much of our prior discussion concerning the characterization of the transitional bonus is also applicable to the first production bonus and the level 4front bonus. The critical question here is when wife's right to each bonus accrued, not her receipt of them. "What is determinative is . . . a single concrete fact—time. The right to [employment] benefits 'represent[s] a property interest; to the extent that such [a] right * * * derive[s] from employment' during marriage before separation, it 'comprise[s] a community asset. . . .' " (*In re Marriage of Lehman, supra,* 18 Cal.4th at p. 177, 74 Cal.Rptr.2d 825, 955 P.2d 451.)

The first production bonus was provided for in the offer summary. Wells Fargo announced the creation of the level 4front bonus in mid-2009, before the parties separated. Wife did not receive payment for either bonus until after separation. But the contractual right to receive each bonus and at least some of the effort necessary to qualify for them occurred before the couple separated.

The trial court's reliance on *In re Marriage of Doherty, supra,* 103 Cal.App.4th 895, 126 Cal.Rptr.2d 919 and *Garfein v. Garfein, supra,* 16 Cal.App.3d 155, 93 Cal.Rptr. 714 lacks merit. In *Doherty,* the wife's employer transferred her job to California and, to assist the family in making the cross-country move, "offered relocation housing benefits . . . [which] included . . . a 'mortgage buydown' or subsidy payable directly to a specified lender over 20 years." (*In re Marriage of Doherty, supra,* 103 Cal.App.4th at p. 897, 126 Cal.Rptr.2d 919.) Two years later, the couple separated and divorced. The trial court characterized the entire mortgage subsidy as a community asset, describing it as " 'a contract right that was received during the marriage, from the efforts of the community.' " (*Id.* at p. 898, 126 Cal.Rptr.2d 919.) The Court of Appeal disagreed, holding there was "no community interest in the . . . mortgage subsidy received after the parties' separation." (*Id.* at p. 900, 126 Cal.Rptr.2d 919.) "The mortgage subsidy . . . rests upon [the wife's] continued employment with [her employer] . . . and [the employer's] desire to continue paying the relocation benefit until its policy is 'changed or revoked.'" (*Id.* at p. 899, 126 Cal.Rptr.2d 919.) Thus, "[t]he housing allowance ... is a form of supplemental income to [the wife] and her separate property after separation." (*Ibid.*)

Garfein involved a divorce action where during marriage the wife, a movie actress, entered into a six-year "'play or pay' contract" with a studio. (*Garfein v. Garfein, supra,* 16 Cal.App.3d at p. 157, 93 Cal.Rptr. 714.) Under the agreement, the studio promised to pay her a specified sum of money each year in return for her promise to remain available to make at least one picture. Two years later the couple separated, but the husband argued he was entitled to one-half of the monies the wife received during the remaining four years of her contract. The Court of Appeal disagreed. "[A]ppearance in a picture was only one alternative of her obligations to her employer under the contract. . . . We hold that the wife 'earns' her agreed compensation by refraining from performing for anyone except the employer during the period of the contract, unless with the employer's consent. Since the payments made after [separation] were 'earned' after that date, they were separate property." (*Id.* at p. 159, 93 Cal.Rptr. 714, fns. omitted.)

As noted, unlike in *Doherty* and *Garfein,* wife's right to the first production and level 4front bonuses was earned, at least in part, before the parties separated. But as with the transitional bonus, she received the entire bonus in a lump-sum payment subject to certain conditions. Thus, upon remand the trial court must make a determination of the portion of each bonus earned before separation and evaluate the potential wife may fail to satisfy the conditions required to retain the advances received by her. The court will then need to choose the appropriate option of dividing or confirming the community's interest or liability in each bonus.

In wife's brief, she notes the trial court's awards of child and spousal support to husband were based on a calculation of her monthly income that included the transitional bonus income credited to her. She expresses the concern that if husband prevails in this appeal he would be allowed to "double-dip * * * " by "receiv[ing]" both her "post-separation earnings as property *and* support." However, the trial court's judgment dealt with both the division of the parties' assets and obligations, plus child and spousal support. Since we are reversing the judgment for further proceedings, the trial court will be able to adjust not only its division of the parties' community estate, but also the support obligations. Thus, at this time, the potential for "double-dipping" is speculative.

DISPOSITION

The judgment is reversed and the matter is remanded to the superior court for further proceedings consistent with the views expressed in this opinion. Appellant shall recover his costs on appeal.

WE CONCUR:

O'LEARY, P.J., IKOLA, J.

NOTES

1. *Basic principles apply.* Rhonda's client book was deemed a valuable asset. The transitional bonus Rhonda obtained from bringing that asset to her new firm was commingled. Rhonda's performance-based bonuses earned after the date of separation were her separate property.

2. *Talent or bargained for exchange?* Wells Fargo did not pay wife Rhonda a transitional bonus for her talent, elite professional standing, promise (potential), or educational pedigree. Wells Fargo paid Rhonda a $2.8 million transitional bonus for her (past) demonstrated ability. Rhonda signed clients, together owning $192 million in investments, under her management, and she induced them to follow her to Wells Fargo. Rhonda's client's investment, the court tells us, produced over $1.8 million in commissions and fees in the year before Rhonda was hired by Wells Fargo.

3. *Vested rights, contingent rights, and mere expectancies.* In *Marriage of Brown,* 15 Cal.3d 838, 842, 126 Cal.Rptr. 633, 544 P.2d 561 (1976) is discussed in most pension and work value related cases. *Brown* held that pension rights, whether vested or contingent, matured or unmatured, are property; as such, a community property component of such a right is subject to division upon dissolution. *Brown* rejects the idea that a contingent right, even one contingent on continued employment, is not a divisible community property asset.

As discussed above, a right, whether vested or contingent, is property. A mere expectancy is not property because it does not give rise to a legal claim. Property rights are divisible at dissolution. Expectancies are not.

California Family Code Section 760 states that "any property" acquired during marriage while domiciled in the state is community property. Property is a broad term that includes not only vested interests, but contingent interests as well. An employment related contract right that is contingent upon a future event does not degrade to an expectancy.

SECTION 7. CHAPTER SUMMARY

- In the context of marriage all sums on deposit in any account owned by one or both spouses are presumed to be community property.

- The CAMPAL community property presumption is rebuttable by tracing or by providing an enforceable agreement between the spouses that the sums on deposit are not to be community property, as discussed in Chapter 2.

- A purchase made from a commingled account is presumed to be community property. Depending on how the purchased asset is titled, rebuttal can either proceed by agreement (for assets in joint form title) or by tracing (for assets in one spouse's name alone and untitled assets). When the general community property presumption governs, date and character specific account records are required to trace a purchase back to net separate property sums on deposit.

- The first person to commingle an account has the legal duty to keep contemporaneous (*See-* or CAMPAL-compliant) records.

- The burden of rebuttal is (always) on the separate property proponent to produce records that can assist the court in making a finding that there are separate property sums on deposit in the commingled account.

- Records that are not sufficient to rebut a community property presumption are not entirely useless. They might be admissible for purposes of establishing a statutory reimbursement under California Family Code 2640.

- When an asset is purchased with debt that is secured by the asset, *Aufmuth*, *Moore* and *Marsden* allow a court to apportion ownership interests between the community and separate property.

- A separate property business is started with provable separate property capital that is necessary for the continuation of the ongoing concern. In accounting for a separate property business, a court has discretion to choose from between the two accounting methods, *Pereira* or *Van Camp*. The legal standard for making that choice is based on which method will achieve substantial justice between the parties.

- *Pereira* stands for this proposition: if the community contributes at least minimum-plus labor to the growth of a separate property business, the community is entitled to excess business profits as a creditor of the business. The business remains entirely separate property; the community is not entitled to indicia of ownership (like shares of stock) as a matter of right. But, the community is entitled to excess profits, meaning profits that trace back not to separate property capital, but to a community labor contribution.

- *Van Camp* stands for this proposition: if the community contributes less than minimum-plus labor to the business, the community is entitled to a reimbursement for its heretofore uncompensated labor contribution minus any family expenses paid from the business. The community is paid the reimbursement as a creditor of the business. The business remains entirely separate property. Use of benchmarks is permissible.

- All labor is owned by the community during marriage. This includes deferred labor, vested and contingent, and other work benefits such as bonuses, stock options, books of business, and the like.

- Commingling community and separate property can make both more productive. The sum can be greater than the parts. However, careful record keeping is required by the spouse who intends to assert a separate property claim when the marriage ends, whether by dissolution of death.

PART III

MANAGEMENT AND CONTROL

■ ■ ■

CHAPTER 6

COMMUNITY PROPERTY MANAGEMENT AND CONTROL

■ ■ ■

In the California community property system a marriage is a partnership, the default rules of which are found in the Family Code. As discussed in prior chapters, a marital property system balances three goals. One is to protect the spouses in their transactions with each other; a second is to protect third parties in their transaction with spouses; and a third is to protect society.

The California Family Code was enacted in 1992. It went into effect in 1994. Topics included in the new code clustered around property rights, custody and support, and domestic violence prevention.

As part of protecting each spouse's property rights the Family Code enhanced the law on the state's managerial approach.

The rules of the comprehensive system are calibrated toward the equal division principle. Outcomes are determined not by the relative bargaining positions of the parties, but by legislatively determined concepts of what is fair and just during and at the end of marriage. Married partners have access to the Family Code from the date of a valid marriage forward. They also retain contract rights—before, during, and at the end of marriage—to customize default rules. (Chapter 1). With respect to the spousal relationship the only two rules that cannot be waived or otherwise changed by contract are the duty to support one's spouse during marriage and the duty of good faith.

The Family Code protects third parties, namely creditors, who change their position in reliance on the continued existence of the marriage. Protection comes from adopting what is called *the managerial approach to community property*. According to the equal management rule, which is at the core of the managerial system, either spouse, acting alone, has the legal right to manage and control community personal property. The corollary of the equal management rule is that either spouse, acting alone, can bind the marital partnership in nearly all matters except those that are testamentary (meaning intended to dispose of property at death).

Among marital property systems the managerial approach is by far the most favorable to creditors. Default rules permit creditors to satisfy debts with any property the debtor spouse can legally manage and control.

During marriage either spouse has the legal right to control community property. Additionally, creditors are entitled to payment for family expense debt. The spouses' duty to support one another during marriage, and after a date of separation unless modified by contract, gives creditors the authority to reach the community property, the property of the debtor spouse, and the separate property of the nondebtor spouse if necessary. The nondebtor spouse's separate property is thus liable for categorical family expense debts during marriage (necessaries of life) and after a date of separation (common necessaries of life). If the creditor should satisfy a debt when other more appropriate property sources are available, the spouse who paid the debt can seek reimbursement from the community or from the other spouse.

Creditors can hedge risk on a contract debt by requiring both spouses to sign the loan contract.

In the California community property system, a marriage is its own legal entity, with its own legal personality, so to speak. The legal entity acquires community property. At the same time, each spouse retains their legal individuality for purposes of incurring debts and obligations. Although the marriage is a freestanding legal entity, it is not distinct from the partners. In practical terms this means that the community's creditors have priority standing to community property relative to the separate creditors of one spouse.

The managerial approach replaces marshaling with a system that gives creditors broad access to property that the spouses legally control. Thus generally, creditors can reach any property that a debtor has the legal right to manage and control; while spouses can settle any reimbursements due with each other.

There are four categories of management and control permitted by the Family Code. *Equal* management and control for community personal property. *Dual* management and control for community real property. *Primary* management and control for the manager of a community property business. *Exclusive* management and control in certain situations.

SECTION 1. EQUAL MANAGEMENT AND CONTROL

The ownership of property is directly related to the right to manage and control that property.

A person who owns property has the legal right to manage it.

A person who has the legal right to manage property has the legal right to control it.

Creditors can reach any property that a person has a legal right to control.

A person may have a legal right to manage and control property that he or she does not exercise in fact.

For example, X, a married person, opens a sole bank account and makes a deposit into the account. Y, X's spouse, does not have access to X's sole account; hence X has exclusive control of the account. Y does, however, have the legal right to manage and control the community property sums on deposit in X's account. The spouses have equal management and control rights to the sums on deposit in X's sole account.

A. PROPERTY OWNERSHIP IN RELATION TO MANAGEMENT AND CONTROL

Disputes about the spouses' property rights (relative to each other) generally arise in the context of dissolution and probate. Disputes can arise in other contexts as well.

Abstractly, the property right includes within it the right to use, transfer, protect and even destroy. In the context of marriage, the right to protect one's property from another person may include the right to protect property from a spouse. For example, during marriage or at dissolution a spouse can seek to protect property from another spouse by bringing a family court action or a civil action. A spouse can petition for a restraining order. Or the state can pursue a criminal action for misdemeanor or felony vandalism against a spouse who destroys community property, in or outside the home.

Additionally, the Family Code creates property related causes of action that one spouse can bring against the other spouse. Actions to avoid a transfer. Impairment actions based on a breach of fiduciary duty. Actions to compel disclosure. These are example claims available under the Family Code.

Even though statutory claims are available the California community property system does not require that one spouse allege a statutory basis to sue the other for a wrong.

B. NON-STATUTORY CLAIMS ARISING FROM THE PROPERTY RIGHT

Wilcox v. Wilcox is a civil case in which one spouse sued the other spouse to regain management of community personal property. The court allowed the claim, its rationale being that for every wrong there is a legal remedy.

Two theoretical premises are implicit in the court's rationale. The agency theory, which is that the spouse who seeks return of community property during a marriage acts as an agent for the community. And the fiduciary theory, which is that the spouse who secrets property away from the community property is liable to the community for conversion.

WILCOX V. WILCOX

21 Cal.App.3d 457, 98 Cal.Rptr. 319 (4th Dist. 1971)

COUGHLIN, ASSOCIATE JUSTICE.

Plaintiff appeals from a judgment of dismissal following an order sustaining defendant's demurrer without leave to amend.

Plaintiff's complaint alleges he and defendant are husband and wife; defendant has taken, is in exclusive possession of, and has secreted $30,000 of community funds; demand has been made upon her for this money; and she refuses to pay the same to plaintiff.

Defendant's demurrer to the complaint was upon the ground: "This Court does not have jurisdiction over the subject matter of this action, in that there is no statutory authority which allows a spouse to sue the other for mismanagement of community funds."

The court sustained the demurrer without leave to amend.

The cause of action alleged in plaintiff's complaint is not premised upon defendant's mismanagement of community funds, as stated in her demurrer, but upon defendant's violation of plaintiff's right to manage, control and dispose of community funds.

By statute a husband "has the management and control of the community personal property, with like absolute power of disposition, other than testamentary, as he has of his separate estate," subject to certain exceptions not material to the case at bench. (Civ.Code § 5125.) [Cal.Fam. Code § 1100] The right of the husband thus conferred to manage, control and dispose of community personal property is invaded by his wife when she deprives him thereof by taking, secreting and exercising exclusive control over community funds. A husband has a cause of action against his wife for such an invasion and violation of his right in the premises with attendant appropriate remedies. These conclusions are dictated by the principles stated and applied in Harris v. Harris, 57 Cal.2d 367, 370, 19 Cal.Rptr. 793, 369 P.2d 481; Odone v. Marzocchi, 34 Cal.2d 431, 437–439, 211 P.2d 297; Fields v. Michael, 91 Cal.App.2d 443, 447–449, 205 P.2d 402; Lynn v. Herman, 72 Cal.App.2d 614, 617, 165 P.2d 54; Salveter v. Salveter, 135 Cal.App. 238, 240, 26 P.2d 836; Johnson v. National Surety Co., 118 Cal.App. 227, 230, 5 P.2d 39; McAlvay v. Consumers' Salt Co., 112 Cal.App. 383, 396, 297 P. 135; and Mitchell v. Moses, 16 Cal.App. 594, 599, 117 P. 685. (See also McKay v. Lauriston, 204 Cal. 557, 564, 269 P. 519; Greiner v. Greiner, 58 Cal. 115, 121.)

The right of the husband to maintain an action against his wife to protect his property rights in community funds, including the right to manage, control and dispose of such with the incident right to possession thereof for this purpose, is not dependent upon statutory authority to sue his wife, as claimed by defendant in her demurrer. In McAlvay v. Consumers' Salt Co., supra, 112 Cal.App. 383, 396, 297 P. 135, 141, the court said: "[T]he right of a husband to maintain an action to quiet his title to community property against the wife has been frequently upheld * * * ." In Salveter v. Salveter, supra, 135 Cal.App. 238, 240, 26 P.2d 836, the court upheld the right of the husband to recover and required his wife to account for community funds which were the proceeds of community property. In neither of the foregoing cases was the right of the defendant to sue premised on statutory authority. Basic to the situation at bench is the provision of Civil Code section 3523 that: "For every wrong there is a remedy."

The order sustaining the demurrer was error.

The judgment is reversed.

NOTE

Spouse v. spouse in an ongoing marriage. Wilcox v. Wilcox is one of a few reported decisions brought by one spouse against the other in the absence of a specific statute. *Wilcox* was brought during the Family Act era, well before the state's adoption of: CAMPAL (California Probate Code Section 5305, discussed in Chapters 2 and 5); the Family Code; the statutory community property impairment provision (California Family Code Section 1101, discussed in Section 4C below) with its add-a-name remedy; and the Domestic Violence Prevention Act (discussed in Section 6D below). *Wilcox* raises a question that California has settled in the affirmative: in the absence of a statute, can one spouse bring a proprietary action against the other spouse outside of the context of dissolution? The answer is yes. But why?

————

The next case offers a perspective on why married persons and intimate partners, as joint venturers, must have the legal right to sue each other during the relationship if justice is to be served.

Meinhard is one of the most famous cases in organizational law as well as in trust law.

MEINHARD V. SALMON

164 N.E. 545, 249 N.Y. 458 (N.Y. 1928)

CARDOZO, C.J.

[Defendant Salmon leased valuable commercial real estate in Manhattan for twenty years (Lease 1); construction changes necessitating capital were planned. Salmon agreed with Plaintiff Meinhard that Meinhard would provide one-half of the capital for reconstructing and operating the buildings on the leasehold in exchange for a percentage of net profits. The parties agreed to share losses. Salmon was the managing partner of the real estate enterprise; Meinhard was not engaged in activities related to the lease. Months before the termination of Lease 1, Salmon negotiated a new lease (Lease 2) with the reversion holder of Lease 1. Salmon, deciding not to disclose information about Lease 2 to Meinhard, signed Lease 2 with the reversion holder months before the expiration of Lease 1.

Meinhard sued Salmon claiming that even if the two were not general partners, they had a joint venture, and that Salmon therefore owed Meinhard a duty to inform him about the reversion holder's offer to enter into Lease 2. Failing to meet that duty, Meinhard requested that Lease 2 be held in trust for the partnership. Trial court judgment was entered in favor of Meinhard. An appeal ensued. The judgment in favor of Meinhard was affirmed.]

The lease between Gerry and the Midpoint Realty Company was signed and delivered on January 25, 1922. Salmon had not told Meinhard anything about it. Whatever his motive may have been, he had kept the negotiations to himself. Meinhard was not informed even of the bare existence of a project. The first that he knew of it was in February when the lease was an accomplished fact. He then made demand on the defendants that the lease be held in trust as an asset of the venture, making offer upon the trial to share the personal obligations incidental to the guaranty. The demand was followed by refusal, and later by this suit. A referee gave judgment for the plaintiff, limiting the plaintiff's interest in the lease, however, to 25 per cent. The limitation was on the theory that the plaintiff's equity was to be restricted to one-half of so much of the value of the lease as was contributed or represented by the occupation of the Bristol site. Upon cross-appeals to the Appellate Division, the judgment was modified so as to enlarge the equitable interest to one-half of the whole lease. With this enlargement of plaintiff's interest, there went, of course, a corresponding enlargement of his attendant obligations. The case is now here on an appeal by the defendants.

Joint adventurers, like copartners, owe to one another, while the enterprise continues, the duty of the finest loyalty. Many forms of conduct permissible in a workaday world for those acting at arm's length, are forbidden to those bound by fiduciary ties. A trustee is held to something stricter than the morals of the market place. Not honesty alone, but the punctilio of an honor the most sensitive, is then the standard of behavior. As to this there has developed a tradition that is unbending and inveterate. Uncompromising rigidity has been the attitude of courts of equity when petitioned to undermine the rule of undivided loyalty by the "disintegrating erosion" of particular exceptions. Only thus has the level of conduct for fiduciaries been kept at a level higher than that trodden by the crowd. It will not consciously be lowered by any judgment of this court.

The owner of the reversion, Mr. Gerry, had vainly striven to find a tenant who would favor his ambitious scheme of demolition and construction. Baffled in the search, he turned to the defendant Salmon in possession of the Bristol, the keystone of the project. He figured to himself beyond a doubt that the man in possession would prove a likely customer. To the eye of an observer, Salmon held the lease as owner in his own right, for himself and no one else. In fact he held it as a fiduciary, for himself and another, sharers in a common venture. If this fact had been proclaimed, if the lease by its terms had run in favor of a partnership, Mr. Gerry [the owner of the reversion], we may fairly assume, would have laid before the partners, and not merely before one of them, his plan of reconstruction. The pre-emptive privilege, or, better, the pre-emptive opportunity, that was thus an incident of the enterprise, Salmon appropriated to himself in secrecy and silence. He might have warned Meinhard that the plan had been submitted, and that either would be free to compete for the award. If he had done this, we do not need to say whether he would have been under a duty, if successful in the competition, to hold the lease so acquired for the benefit of a venture then about to end, and thus prolong by indirection its responsibilities and duties. The trouble about his conduct is that he excluded his coadventurer from any chance to compete, from any chance to enjoy the opportunity for benefit that had come to him alone by virtue of his agency. This chance, if nothing more, he was under a duty to concede. The price of its denial is an extension of the trust at the option and for the benefit of the one whom he excluded.

No answer is it to say that the chance would have been of little value even if seasonably offered. Such a calculus of probabilities is beyond the science of the chancery. Salmon, the real estate operator, might have been preferred to Meinhard, the woolen merchant. On the other hand, Meinhard might have offered better terms, or reinforced his offer by alliance with the wealth of others. Perhaps he might even have persuaded the lessor to renew the Bristol lease alone, postponing for a time, in return for higher rentals, the improvement of adjoining lots. We know that even under the lease as made the time for the enlargement of the building was delayed for seven years. All these opportunities were cut away from him through another's intervention. * * * [T]here was nothing in the situation to give warning to any one that while the lease was still in being, there had come to the manager an offer of extension which he had locked within his breast to be utilized by himself alone. The very fact that Salmon was in control with exclusive powers of direction charged him the more obviously with the duty of disclosure, since only through disclosure could opportunity be equalized. If he might cut off renewal by a purchase for his own benefit when four months were to pass before the lease would have an end, he might do so with equal right while there remained as many years. He might steal a march on his comrade under cover of the darkness, and then hold the captured ground. Loyalty and comradeship are not so easily abjured.

Little profit will come from a dissection of the precedents. None precisely similar is cited in the briefs of counsel. What is similar in many, or so it seems to us, is the animating principle. Authority is, of course, abundant that one partner may not appropriate to his own use a renewal of a lease, though its term is to begin at the expiration of the partnership. The lease at hand with its many changes is not strictly a renewal. Even so, the standard of loyalty for those in trust relations is without the fixed divisions of a graduated scale. There is indeed a dictum in one of our decisions that a partner, though he may not renew a lease, may purchase the reversion if he acts openly and fairly (*Anderson v. Lemon*, 8 N. Y. 236). It is a dictum, and no more, for on the ground that he had acted slyly he was charged as a trustee. The holding is thus in favor of the conclusion that a purchase as well as a lease will succumb to the infection of secrecy and silence. Against the dictum in that case, moreover, may be set the opinion of DWIGHT, C., in *Mitchell v. Read*, where there is a dictum to the contrary (61 N. Y. at p. 143). * * *

We have no thought to hold that Salmon was guilty of a conscious purpose to defraud. Very likely he assumed in all good faith that with the approaching end of the venture he might ignore his coadventurer and take the extension for himself. He had given to the enterprise time and labor as well as money. He had made it a success. Meinhard, who had given money, but neither time nor labor, had already been richly paid. There might seem to be something grasping in his insistence upon more. Such recriminations are not unusual when coadventurers fall out. They are not without their force if conduct is to be judged by the common standards of competitors. That is not to say that they have pertinency here. Salmon had put himself in a position in which thought of self was to be renounced, however hard the abnegation. He was much more than a coadventurer. He was a managing coadventurer. For him and for those like him, the rule of undivided loyalty is relentless and supreme. * * * Here the subject-matter of the new lease was an extension and enlargement of the subject-matter of the old one. A managing coadventurer appropriating the benefit of such a lease without warning to his partner might fairly expect to be reproached with conduct that was underhand, or lacking, to say the least, in reasonable candor, if the partner were to surprise him in the act of signing the new instrument. Conduct subject to that reproach does not receive from equity a healing benediction

A question remains as to the form and extent of the equitable interest to be allotted to the plaintiff. The trust as declared has been held to attach to the lease which was in the name of the defendant corporation. We think it ought to attach at the option of the defendant Salmon to the shares of stock which were owned by him or were under his control. The difference may be important if the lessee shall wish to execute an assignment of the lease, as it ought to be free to do with the consent of the lessor. On the other hand, an equal division of the shares might lead to other hardships. It might take away from Salmon the power of control and management which under the plan of the joint venture he was to have from first to last. The number of shares to be allotted to the plaintiff should, therefore, be reduced to such an extent as may be necessary to preserve to the defendant Salmon the expected measure of dominion. To that end an extra share should be added to his half. * * *

ANDREWS J. (dissenting)

* * * I am of the opinion that the issue here is simple. Was the transaction in view of all the circumstances surrounding it unfair and inequitable? [No.] I reach this conclusion for two reasons. There was no general partnership, merely a joint venture for a limited object, to end at a fixed time. * * *

Were this a general partnership between Mr. Salmon and Mr. Meinhard I should have little doubt as to the correctness of this result assuming the new lease to be an offshoot of the old. Such a situation involves questions of trust and confidence to a high degree; it involves questions of good will; many other considerations. As has been said, rarely if ever may one partner without the knowledge of the other acquire for himself the renewal of a lease held by the firm, even if the new lease is to begin after the firm is dissolved. Warning of such an intent, if he is managing partner, may not be sufficient to prevent the application of this rule.

We have here a different situation governed by less drastic principles. I assume that where parties engage in a joint enterprise each owes to the other the duty of the utmost good faith in all that relates to their common venture. Within its scope they stand in a fiduciary relationship. I assume *prima facie* that even as between joint adventurers one may not secretly obtain a renewal of the lease of property actually used in the joint adventure where the possibility of renewal is expressly or impliedly involved in the enterprise. I assume also that Mr. Meinhard had an equitable interest in the Bristol Hotel lease. Further, that an expectancy of renewal inhered in that lease. Two questions then arise. Under his contract did he share in that expectancy? And if so, did that expectancy mature into a graft of the original lease? To both questions my answer is "no."

The one complaint made is that Mr. Salmon obtained the new lease without informing Mr. Meinhard of his intention. Nothing else. There is no claim of actual fraud. No claim of misrepresentation to anyone. Here was no movable property to be acquired by a new tenant at a sacrifice to its owners. No good will, largely dependent on location, built up by the joint efforts of two men.

* * * I think also that in the absence of some fraudulent or unfair act the secret purchase of the reversion even by one partner is rightful. * * * No fraud, no deceit, no calculated secrecy is found. Simply that the arrangement was made without the knowledge of Mr. Meinhard. I think this not enough.

The judgment of the courts below should be reversed and a new trial ordered, with costs in all courts to abide the event.

NOTES

1. *Compare partners, persons married to each other, joint venturers, and intimate nonmarried cohabitants.* How does *Meinhard v. Salmon* cast light on management and control rights of married partners during marriage? Of nonmarried partners during a cohabitancy? How is the joint venture in *Meinhard* the same or different from a marriage? The intimate partnership of two nonmarried persons?

2. *Partners/joint venturers.* Spouses are partners with a formal agreement. The default terms of that agreement are set forth in the California Family Code. Default terms include disclosure provisions that are incorporated by reference into the California Family Code from the California Corporations Code. The pool of partnership property is the community property. If, as Chief Justice Cardozo says joint venturers "owe one another while the enterprise continues, the duty of the finest loyalty . . . the punctilio of an honor most sensitive," then what would possibly justify holding formal partners, a category that includes persons who are married to each other, to a lower standard of care as to community property?

Married persons are not held to the fiduciary standards of a professional trustee. Specifically they are not held to account for property in writing on a quarterly basis. Nor are they held to modern portfolio theory for securities investments. But they are held to the fiduciary duty that non-marital partners would be held to. In light of California Family Code 721 and 1100(e), it is correct to understand that married persons owe each other, in Justice Cardozo's famous phrase, "the finest loyalty . . . the punctilio of an honor most sensitive."

3. *Registered Domestic Partnership, or RDPs.* Today in California, RDPs are held to the exact same rights and obligations as married partners. After

Obergefell (Chapter 1) the California Legislature must decide whether parties of any age, no matter their gender identities, can register as domestic partners or whether age restrictions continue to apply.

4.   *Intimate nonmarried cohabitants who are* also *business partners with each other.* It is not uncommon for people who are intimate partners to also be commercial business partners with each other. Intimate partners who are also business partners are entitled to claim rights and liabilities under the California Corporations Code as business partners and under the California Family Code as spouses. Business partners are governed by their partnership agreement, which is defined as an agreement that is "written, oral, or implied among the partners concerning the partnership, including amendments to the agreement" under California Corporations Code Section 16101, a section from the Uniform Partnership Act of 1994. Unless the business partners explicitly contract otherwise, they are governed by default rules found in Chapter 5 of the California Corporations Code. The Corporations Code rules cover important issues related to formation, management and control of partnership property, record keeping and access, disclosure rights and obligations, termination, and so on.

More specifically, California Corporations Code Section 16101(9) defines a "partnership" as "an association of two or more persons to carry on as coowners of a business for profit . . . ," a definition that, depending on the facts of the case, may stretch to include married persons and nonmarital intimate cohabitants who are also business partners in a specific business concern (Chapter 4).

If nonmarried persons or nonmarried cohabitants conduct business together, they can opt to have their rights and duties to each other, relative to an identified pool of assets, determined by the California Corporations Code. Married persons have the option to resolve a business related dispute between them under the California Family Code. See, e.g., California Family Code Section 1100(e), which is self-updating and thus incorporates the most recent version of California Family Code Section 721 by reference. Nonmarried business partners do not have the option of relying on the property provisions of the California Family Code.

Generally speaking, as to each other and with respect to the pool of business assets, the partners may *not* do the following (California Corporations Code Section 16103 states the following duties in the *negative*): they may not restrict access to books and records; restrict access to partnership information; contract away the duty of loyalty or the duty of good faith and fair dealing; or unreasonably reduce the duty of care.

A partnership has a two tiered ownership structure, much like a marriage does. The partners contribute to partnership assets but they do not "own" them as individuals. Instead, what partners own are rights to net financial returns generated by the partnership assets, as well as rights to manage and control partnership assets, including those that have been commingled with individually owned assets.

As to voting, half of a two-person partnership is not a majority for purposes of making a business partnership decision. But in the case of a two-person partnership, *either* partner has rights of management and control sufficient to bind the partnership. In addition to the cited California Corporations Code Sections, see Uniform Partnership Act Sections 26 and 27, Revised Uniform Partnership Act Sections 502, 503.

5.   *Intimate nonmarried cohabitants as implied business partners or joint venturers.* Establishing the existence of a business partnership does not require specialized proof. A court can find that a partnership was formed based on evidence of activity that falls short of an explicit partnership agreement. Receiving a share of profits, for example, may create a presumption of partnership under the Uniform Partnership Act. Likewise, a third-party action against an alleged partner, in tort or contract, can serve as evidence from which to infer a partnership.

Without evidence of a partnership, unmarried cohabitants are left to organize their affairs by tort, contract, property (title), equity, or under specific California Civil Code statutes. The remedies found in these areas of law may be incident-specific or asset-specific. Cases involving nonmarried partner break-ups tend not to be alleged as business breakups but rather as palimony cases, meaning cases where an express oral, implied, or tacit agreement for post-breakup support is alleged at the end of the relationship (Chapter 4).

6.   *Cohabitation agreements.* Contractual claims between cohabitants require proof of an agreement. Cohabitants are strongly advised to enter into a written cohabitation agreement. Otherwise, their claims are based on an implied agreement theory. The implied agreement theory allows for proof of the parties reasonable expectations and understandings about financial matters based on their conduct toward each other during the relationship. The only limitation on admissibility is that terms that require payment in exchange for sexual services are unenforceable, as being against public policy. Otherwise, under the vastly important ruling in *Marvin v. Marvin, supra,* adults who live together in an intimate sexual relationship have every right to enter into oral, implied or even tacit agreements between themselves about property and support (Chapter 4).

There is little precedent on what a predictably enforceable negotiated cohabitation agreement might look like.

An enforceable cohabitation agreement would certainly be in writing and signed by both parties. It might use the California Premarital Agreement Act (Chapter 1) as a template for formalities and proof of disclosure and consent. It would incorporate a host of defensive drafting positions.

At the very least, such a contract would deal specifically with agreements about:

- Support of children;

- Ownership of property acquired during the relationship;

- Management and control issues;

- Disclosure rights and obligations;

- Sanctions, attorney's fees and other penalties;

- How to handle occurrences of intimate partner violence;

- Cohabitant duties and obligations for support during the relationship;

- Cohabitant duties and obligations for support in the event that the relationship ends by a break-up or by a death;

- Debt;

- Taxes;

- Insurance, and so on.

7. *Terminating the partnership.* If nonmarried cohabitants are also business partners, what dissolves the partnership? Does removing one's property from the home dissolve both the intimate and the business partnership? Withdrawing one's money from a joint account?

The rule in *Owen v. Cohen,* 19 Cal. 2d 147, 119 P.2d 713 (1941) is instructive. The case involved two business partners who were not intimate partners. The rule of the case is that when a partner advances a sum of money to a partnership with the understanding that the sum is a loan to the business partnership to be repaid as soon as feasible, a partnership comes into existence for the term reasonably required to repay the loan (citing U.P.A. 31(1)(b)).

Page v. Page, 55 Cal.2d 192, 359 P.2d 41 (1961) (in bank) distinguishes *Owen* on its facts. In *Page,* the defendant failed to prove that the partnership was for a term or for a specific undertaking. Justice Traynor was not discussing intimate partnerships. Nevertheless his language is reminiscent of the aspirations of intimate partners who move in together: "The understanding to which defendant testified was no more than a common hope that the partnership earnings would pay for all the necessary expenses. Such a hope does not establish even by implication a 'definite term or particular undertaking' as required by U.P.A. Section 31(1)(b)." *Id.* at 196.

With the implication of a definite term, the partnership continues on until it is terminated, which returns us to the original question: how and when is a nonmarried intimate partnership legally terminated?

8. *In a transaction between partnership fiduciaries any unfair advantage raises a presumption of undue influence.* In an article predating the incorporation of certain Corporations Code Sections into the Family Code, Professor Carol S. Bruch in *Management Powers and Duties Under California's Community Property Law: Recommendations for Reform,* 34 HASTINGS L.J. 227 (1982) proposed certain basic spousal rights of community property management and control, including the right to know, the right to sound management, the right to participate, and the right to be made whole. She indicated that filing for dissolution should not be the sole method of protecting

a spouse whose community property rights are or have been infringed or impaired.

California Family Code Sections 721, 1100 and 1101 now incorporate many of Professor Bruch's suggestions, including: the recognition of a spousal duty to disclose the existence of community assets and debts; the right to seek an equitable accounting during an intact marriage; and the right to petition a court for access to community property during marriage.

In a later article, Professor J. Thomas Oldham in *Management of the Community Estate During an Intact Marriage,* 56 LAW & CONTEMPORARY PROBLEMS 99 (1993) foresaw potential problems with invoking an accounting remedy during an intact marriage unless both parties were represented by independent counsel.

> "Although at first glance, the accounting remedy seems appropriate, it could present some problems. In an accounting, the spouse is asked to list all property, and specify whether it is separate or community. It is not clear that spouses will be represented by independent counsel in such matters. It does seem possible that a spouse contemplating divorce could utilize an accounting as a means to obtain advantageous admissions from the other spouse regarding the character of property. The other spouse might not be too vigilant in scrutinizing such an accounting, being unaware that a divorce filing was imminent. If the spouse initiated the accounting to trap the other into making admissions regarding the character of property before obtaining legal advice, such behavior probably violates the duties spouses have to one another." *Id.* at 119–120.[1]

When one spouse offers an inventory or an accounting to resolve a property dispute during an intact marriage is that a "transaction between the spouses?" It is; and as such the transaction falls within the ambit of California Family Code Section 721(b).

In *Marriage of Burkle* (Chapter 2) the parties negotiated a reconciliation agreement based on inventories and accounting reports. Each spouse was represented by a team of lawyers. A deal was struck. A contract was executed. The parties reconciled and resumed the marriage. A few years later, the parties sought to dissolve the marriage. As it turned out, their agreement resulted in the husband amassing more wealth than the community or the wife. The wife argued that the arithmetic unfairness of the reconciliation contract as performed was evidence that the husband had taken unfair advantage of her during the contract negotiation process. A presumption of undue influence was raised. On appeal, the court determined that yes, the reconciliation negotiation (based as it was on financial disclosure and accounting) is a transaction between spouses for purposes of California Family Code Section 721, reproduced below; but no, a contract that is arithmetically unfair, as performed, does not necessarily constitute one spouse taking advantage of the

---

[1]   Fair use.

other spouse (constructive fraud). In this case, the fact that the wife was represented by her own team of attorneys when she negotiated and executed the contract was sufficient evidence that she entered into the agreement voluntarily and with the required disclosure. See also Chapter 1.

C. A RIGHT TO DESTROY?

The property right includes within it a right to destroy. This right is exercised by owners on a daily basis, as when something owned is discarded.

The next two excerpts, *People v. Kahanic* and *People v. Wallace*, are example cases that can be brought in response to incidents of domestic or dating violence. Some of cases are civil, but they can also be criminal. Some of the cases go to trial; many are settled.

In *Kahanic*, damage was done by a driver of a Corvette to a community property Mercedes Benz that the driver owned with her spouse. The facts of the case showed that the Defendant's spouse had driven the Mercedes Benz to a friend's house. The Defendant followed her spouse there. Defendant tossed a bottle of beer from the Corvette through the rear window of the parked Mercedes Benz. The Defendant was arrested, charged, and convicted of vandalism.

In *Wallace*, the Defendant was charged with felony vandalism and convicted in connection with damaging community property. On appeal Defendant argued that a married person cannot be guilty of vandalizing community property in the marital home. Gomes, J. disagreed in an opinion that follows *Kahanic* to outline what the judge characterized as an emerging rule. The new rule imposes criminal liability on a spouse for intentionally causing harm to property in which the other spouse has an interest, whether the property is individual or marital, or whether the harm occurs outside or inside the marital home.

PEOPLE V. KAHANIC
196 Cal.App.3d 461, 241 Cal.Rptr. 722 (5th Dist. 1987)

WOOLPERT, ACTING P. J.

While driving her silver Corvette, defendant was seen near a residence where her husband was visiting another woman. Failing to gain entry to the building, she drove away and stopped at a bar where she tried unsuccessfully to buy a bottle of beer. She acquired a bottle elsewhere. Later, a car like hers was again seen in the vicinity of where her husband was visiting. Their community property Mercedes Benz, parked by the husband, remained in front of his friend's residence. The driver tossed a bottle of beer from the Corvette. It went through the rear window of the

Mercedes. Defendant's arrest and conviction of violating Penal Code section 594, subdivision (b)(3), vandalism, followed.

This marital misadventure took place near the conclusion of dissolution proceedings involving defendant and her husband. However, the Mercedes was still community property. As her defense, defendant ultimately claimed she could not "vandalize" her own property. Defendant unsuccessfully argued her claim in the municipal and superior courts. Following proper appellate procedure, she now seeks review of her misdemeanor conviction in this court.

We are well aware that conduct of this kind may be better resolved in family law courts than by criminal prosecution. Nevertheless we conclude the community property status of the Mercedes automobile did not preclude the application of criminal law which refers to personal property "not his own," as the property damaged by the criminal act.

The vandalism statute does not distinguish between personal property of significant value, such as a Mercedes or Corvette, and property of trivial worth, as in the case of many community property items. As a result, criminal sanctions involving spousal damage to community property may appear to be disparately invoked. However, because defendant was given probation we need not consider particular penal consequences.

Section 594, subdivision (a), provides: "(a) Every person who maliciously (1) defaces with paint or any other liquid, (2) damages or (3) destroys any real or personal property *not his own*, in cases otherwise than those specified by state law, is guilty of vandalism." (Italics added.)

The phrase "not his own" has survived numerous amendments. * * * "Own" has been defined as follows: "Following the possessive, usually of a possessive pronoun, it [own] is used as an intensive to express ownership, interest, or individual peculiarity with emphasis, or *to indicate the exclusion of others*." * * * In section 594, "own" is an intensive; the section would make complete sense if "own" was omitted.

There is no dispute the Mercedes was community property * * * [current California Family Code Section 751] provides: "The respective interests of the husband and wife in community property during continuance of the marriage relation are present, existing and *equal interests*. This section shall be construed as defining the respective interests and rights of husband and wife in community property." (Italics added.)

Neither party cites a case on point, and we have found none. However, Vehicle Code section 10851 also includes "not his own" in its definition of theft and unlawful taking of an automobile. In discussing the proof of ownership required under that section, this court looked, in part, to evidence of exclusive dominion and control. (See *People v. Clifton* (1985)

171 Cal.App.3d 195, 200–201 [217 Cal.Rptr. 192].) The notion of exclusivity is helpful, especially in light of the "equal interests" definition of community property.

By way of analogy, the Attorney General directs us to *People v. Sobiek* (1973) 30 Cal.App.3d 458 [106 Cal.Rptr. 519, 82 A.L.R.3d 804], certiorari denied 414 U.S. 855 [38 L.Ed.2d 104, 94 S.Ct. 155]. In *Sobiek*, the court held a partner could be guilty of embezzling or stealing partnership property. (*Id.* at pp. 462, 468.) The court reasoned: "It is both illogical and unreasonable to hold that a partner cannot steal from his partners merely because he has an undivided interest in the partnership property. Fundamentally, stealing that portion of the partners' shares which does not belong to the thief is no different from stealing the property of any other person." (*Id.* at p. 468.)

Sobiek is now the settled law of this state * * *

It was once thought, based upon dicta from *People v. Foss* (1936) 7 Cal.2d 669 [62 P.2d 372], that since each partner owned an undivided interest in all the partnership property, a partner could not be guilty of embezzling from the partnership.

The *Sobiek* court noted the language of the Model Penal Code and its use of the phrase "property of another." (*People v. Sobiek, supra,* 30 Cal.App.3d at pp. 466–467.) Specifically, the Model Penal Code provides: " '[P]roperty of another' includes property in which any person other than the actor has an interest which the actor is not privileged to infringe, regardless of the fact that the actor also has an interest in the property and regardless of the fact that the other person might be precluded from civil recovery because the property was used in an unlawful transaction or was subject to forfeiture as contraband. Property in possession of the actor shall not be deemed property of another who has only a security interest therein, even if legal title is in the creditor pursuant to a conditional sales contract or other security agreement." (Model Pen. Code, § 223.0, subd. (7).) A similar definition is found in the arson definitions: "Property is that of another, for the purposes of this section, if anyone other than the actor has a possessory or proprietary interest therein." (Model Pen. Code, § 220.1, subd. (4).)

In Wharton's treatise on criminal law, section 594 is noted in the discussion of malicious mischief, and it appears "not his own" is treated synonymously with "of another." "To constitute malicious mischief, the property injured or destroyed must be the property of another. Property is deemed to be that of another if 'any person or government other than the actor has a possessory or proprietary interest' therein. It is not open to a defendant to challenge the validity of a victim's title or the rightfulness of his possession." (4 Wharton's Criminal Law (14th ed. 1981) Malicious Mischief, § 490, p. 96, fns. omitted.)

This logic is sound. The *Sobiek* court considered the nature of a partnership and how title to its property is held. The court recognized the occasional view that a partnership is an entity, particularly for procedural purposes, and the contrasting theory that the partnership is merely a group of individuals organized for business purposes with title to partnership property held as tenants in common. (*People v. Sobiek, supra*, 30 Cal.App.3d at pp. 466–468; cf. Corp. Code, § 15025.)

It is true *Sobiek* was concerned only with partnership interests which, though similar in some respects, are not identical to community property ownership. However, the *Sobiek* court did not condition its views on the argument that partnership property is owned by the partnership, not the partners. If it had, the court would have merely stated the embezzlement was of property owned by the partnership and that the partners' ultimate interests were of insufficient present consequence to protect the defendant against criminal prosecution.

Instead, the court emphasized the American Law Institute's view that civil law notions were irrelevant. The court noted the institute's conclusion that the effort of the criminal law is "to deter deprivations of other people's economic interests." (*Id.* at p. 466.) We agree. Whether the statute refers to property "not his own," or "property of another," the sense of the descriptive words excludes criminality only when the actor-defendant is involved with property wholly his or her own.

It is of no consequence defendant wife may have had a community property right to share possession of the Mercedes. We do not determine this issue based on the husband's possession of the car at the particular time. The criminal wrong may occur irrespective of who physically "possessed" the Mercedes when the act occurred. The essence of the crime is in the physical acts against the ownership interest of another, even though that ownership is less than exclusive. (*People v. Stanford* (1940) 16 Cal.2d 247, 251 [105 P.2d 969].) Spousal community property interests are no longer "mere expectancies," as they were for a married woman many years ago. (*People v. Swalm* (1889) 80 Cal. 46, 49.) Each community property owner has an equal ownership interest and, although undivided, one which the criminal law protects from unilateral nonconsensual damage or destruction by the other marital partner. * * *

The judgment is affirmed.

BALLANTYNE, J., and IVEY, J., concurred.

PEOPLE V. WALLACE

123 Cal. App. 4th 144, 19 Cal. Rptr.3d 790 (5th Dist. 2004)

GOMES, J.

FACTUAL AND PROCEDURAL BACKGROUND

One summer evening in Fresno, Anthony LeRoy Wallace's wife of two months, Arlissa Pointer Wallace, caught him smoking crack cocaine, called him a crack head, and told him to leave the house she had bought six or seven years before the marriage and had refinanced shortly after the marriage. [Court's Footnote 1: For clarity, later references to husband and wife will be to Wallace and Pointer, respectively.] Although she had kept the house in her name, Wallace presumably had acquired a small community property interest through mortgage payments with community property funds.

Instead of leaving, however, Wallace began tearing up the house. Frightened, Pointer kept her distance from him as she opened the living room curtains in the hope a neighbor might see and call the police. He kept breaking things. Twice she dialed 911, but twice she hung up, fearing things would get much worse if he knew she had called. He left before the police arrived. She told a police officer that the only thing he had not broken in the house was his own stereo and that everything else in the house belonged to her. A couple of hours later, alerted by a neighbor to "incredible pounding, very, very loud noise" from the house, police officers found Wallace inside the house breaking things again. Only after he challenged three armed and uniformed officers to fight, did they subdue him with a taser and arrest him.

At trial, an expert witness testified to over $9,000 of damage to the house and to over $6,000 of damage to the furniture and furnishings. A jury found Wallace guilty of felony vandalism and of two misdemeanors—being under the influence and resisting, delaying, or obstructing an officer ("resisting")—and found two assault with a deadly weapon priors true as both serious felony priors and prison term priors. (Pen.Code, §§ 148 * * * ; Health & Saf.Code, § 11550, * * * .) The court sentenced him to a 25-year-to-life term for felony vandalism, a consecutive term of one year on each of his two prison term priors, and time served on each of his two misdemeanors. (Court's Footnote 2: All subsequent statutory references are to the Penal Code except where otherwise noted.)

INTRODUCTION

Wallace argues that as a matter of law he cannot be guilty of vandalizing either community property or his spouse's separate property inside the marital home. In the published portion of our opinion, we will reject his argument and embrace the emerging rule imposing criminal liability on a spouse for intentionally causing harm to property in which the other spouse has an interest, whether the property is individual or marital, whether the harm occurs outside or inside the marital home. In the nonpublished portion of our opinion, we will address his numerous other arguments and grant relief as to two. * * *

DISCUSSION

1. Scope of Vandalism Statute

The question before us is whether a spouse can be guilty of vandalizing community property and the other spouse's separate property inside the marital home. Wallace asks us to answer that question in the negative on the basis of "the common law rule that a person's home is his or her castle" and the language in the vandalism statute (§ 594) that a vandal can deface, damage, or destroy only property that is "not his or her own." The Attorney General asks us to answer that question in the affirmative, arguing that vandalism is not a crime that threatens property rights only in a particular place, that the criminal law protects each owner's interest in community property against nonconsensual damage by the other, and that Pointer's separate property suffered most of the harm anyway.

In *People v. Kahanic* (1987) 196 Cal.App.3d 461, 241 Cal.Rptr. 722 (*Kahanic*), we held that the vandalism statute applies to community property on the rationale that the "essence of the crime is in the physical acts against the ownership interest of another, even though that ownership is less than exclusive." (*Id.* at p. 466, 241 Cal.Rptr. 722.) Citing *Kahanic*, a proposed vandalism instruction from the Judicial Council's Task Force on Jury Instructions requires proof that the accused "did not own the property" or "owned the property with someone else." (See Cal. Jud. Council, Task Force on Jury Instructions, Criminal Jury Instructions (July 5, 2004 Draft) Inst. No.1995, pp. 1–2.)

However, Wallace argues that with the vandalism in *Kahanic* occurring outside the marital home the case is inapposite to the issue here whether "the common law rule that a person's home is his or her castle" precludes criminal liability for vandalizing property in one's own home. He analogizes that issue to the question whether a person can burglarize his or her own home and notes the California Supreme Court relied on the common law rule to hold that the burglary statute applies only to "a person who has no right to be in the building." (*People v. Gauze* (1975) 15 Cal.3d 709, 714, 125 Cal.Rptr. 773, 542 P.2d 1365.) Emphasizing that "burglary and the lesser related offenses of trespass and vandalism *are* 'closely related' " * * * , he argues that as one can neither burgle nor trespass in one's own home, neither can one vandalize property in one's own home.

Wallace's argument ignores three key differences between vandalism, on the one hand, and burglary and trespass, on the other. First, one can commit vandalism anywhere (see § 594 [subdivision (a) provides: "Every person who maliciously commits any of the following acts with respect to any real or personal property not his or her own, in cases other than those specified by state law, is guilty of vandalism: (1) Defaces with graffiti or other inscribed material. (2) Damages. (3) Destroys."]), but one can commit burglary and trespass only by entering into a specific place (see §§ 459 [provides in part: "Every person who enters any house, room, apartment, tenement, shop, warehouse, store, mill, barn, stable, outhouse or other building, tent, vessel . . . , floating home . . . , railroad car, locked or sealed cargo container . . . , trailer coach . . . , any house car . . . , inhabited camper . . . , vehicle . . . when the doors are locked, aircraft . . . , or mine or any underground portion thereof, with intent to commit grand or petit larceny or any felony is guilty of burglary."], 602). Second, one cannot commit vandalism without defacing, damaging, or destroying property (see § 594 but one can commit burglary and trespass without harming any property at all (§§ 459, 602). Third, the harm that vandalism by a spouse necessarily inflicts to community property or to the other spouse's separate property ousts the other spouse of his or her ownership interest in a way that neither burglary nor trespass necessarily does. Together, those differences foil Wallace's endeavor to broaden to vandalism the rule that applies to burglary and trespass.

Instead, on the question before us, we broaden our holding in *Kahanic* to embrace the emerging rule imposing criminal liability on a spouse for intentionally causing harm to property in which the other spouse has an interest, whether the property is individual or marital, whether the harm occurs outside or inside the marital home. * * * Accordingly, we answer in the affirmative the question before us and hold that a spouse can be guilty of vandalizing community property and the other spouse's separate property inside the marital home.

Finally, on the premise that the Family Code confers on each spouse "absolute power of disposition" of community personal property until service of a reciprocal temporary restraining order to the contrary (Fam.Code, §§ 1100, 2040, subd. (a)(2)), Wallace argues that as he and Pointer were not engaging in family law litigation, but rather were cohabiting as husband and wife, he cannot as a matter of law be guilty of vandalizing community personal property. Case law from other states applies the emerging rule to spouses cohabiting and presumably not engaging in family law litigation at the time of the vandalism * * * as well as to spouses no longer cohabiting and either estranged or contemplating, if not actually engaging, in family law litigation at the time of the vandalism. * * * Wallace articulates, and we perceive, no sound reason in public policy or the law for the astounding notion that the criminal law should afford protection to some spouses but not to others. We decline to so limit our holding.

DISPOSITION

The resisting conviction is ordered stricken from the judgment, which is modified to show 269 days of presentence custody credit, 134 days of presentence conduct credit, and 403 total days of presentence credit. The matter is remanded with directions to the court to issue and forward to the appropriate persons an abstract of judgment amended accordingly. Wallace has no right to be present at those proceedings. Otherwise the judgment is affirmed.

WE CONCUR: LEVY, ACTING P.J. and CORNELL, J.

SECTION 2. COMMUNITY PERSONAL PROPERTY

The California community property system was continued in the 1849 California Constitution, and operationalized in the 1850 Organic Act. The Organic Act named the husband as the sole legal manager of community property; he was also named the legal manager of the wife's separate property. Early records provide evidence that the original legislators adopted male management and control provisions because they believed that married women required the protection of their husbands in financial matters.

In 1872, legislation awarded a married woman sole control over her separate property.

In 1951, legislation permitted a wife to shield her earnings and personal injury awards from certain of her husband's premarital creditors. To be shielded, the statute mandated that the wife's earnings be kept in a demand deposit account to which only she had access. If she commingled her earnings or personal injury awards with other community property over which her husband had legal control, or if she invested her shielded earnings in real property (necessitating her husband's joinder), the earnings shield dropped, management and control shifted to the husband, and his creditors could reach the sums on deposit in the wife's account. The 1951 legislation ushered in an era in which a married woman could opt to create parallel (but not dual) control of a slice of the community property that she herself generated.

The earnings shield is still permitted, now on a gender neutral basis. Requirements for setting up the shield are found at California Family Code Section 911.

On January 1, 1975, the era of legal male management and control of community property came to an end. From that date forward, equal management and control legislation went into effect to provide that *either* spouse, acting alone, is legally empowered to manage and control the community personal property.

An equal management regime is an immensely important step toward a gender-fair marital property system.

A. THE MANAGERIAL SYSTEM

Community property states divide roughly into those that are less favorable to creditors and those that are more favorable to creditors. States less favorable to creditors (Washington and Arizona) characterize debts as community or separate; the approach can protect the family, but that protection comes at the expense of administrative problems for creditors and spouses alike. States more favorable to creditors follow the managerial system, which treats either spouse as an agent of the community.

California is a state most favorable to creditors.

California follows the managerial system. In theory and practice the managerial system has proven itself to be sound. It conforms to decisional law (*Grolemund v. Cafferata*, 17 Cal.2d 679, 111 P.2d 641 (1941)). It is consistent with the policy that the marital community owns assets and shares family expenses. The managerial system promotes gender-fairness by ensuring access to credit not on the basis of gender, but on the basis of a spouse's legal right to manage and control property as an agent. Additionally the managerial system is consistent with the expectations of spouses and creditors by how it assures creditors that the debts of married persons will be satisfied according to a statutory scheme. And at the end of marriage the managerial system requires only that property, and not debt, be characterized.

The equal management and control rule appears in Family Code Section 1100(a), reproduced below.

WEST'S ANNOTATED CALIFORNIA FAMILY CODE

§ 1100. Community personal property; management and control; restrictions on disposition

(a) Except as provided in subdivisions (b), (c), and (d) and Sections 761 and 1103, either spouse has the management and control of the community personal property, whether acquired prior to or on or after January 1, 1975, with like absolute power of disposition, other than testamentary, as the spouse has of the separate estate of the spouse.

(b) A spouse may not make a gift of community personal property, or dispose of community personal property for less than fair and reasonable value, without the *written* consent of the other spouse. This subdivision does not apply to gifts mutually given by both spouses to third parties and to gifts given by one spouse to the other spouse.

(c)   A spouse may not sell, convey, or encumber community personal property used as the family dwelling, or the furniture, furnishings, or fittings of the home, or the clothing or wearing apparel of the other spouse or minor children which is community personal property, without the written consent of the other spouse.

(d)   Except as provided in subdivisions (b) and (c), and in Section 1102, a spouse who is operating or managing a business or an interest in a business that is all or substantially all community personal property has the primary management and control of the business or interest. Primary management and control means that the managing spouse may act alone in all transactions but shall give prior written notice to the other spouse of any sale, lease, exchange, encumbrance, or other disposition of all or substantially all of the personal property used in the operation of the business (including personal property used for agricultural purposes), whether or not title to that property is held in the name of only one spouse. Written notice is not, however, required when prohibited by the law otherwise applicable to the transaction.

Remedies for the failure by a managing spouse to give prior written notice as required by this subdivision are only as specified in Section 1101. A failure to give prior written notice shall not adversely affect the validity of a transaction nor of any interest transferred.

(e)   Each spouse shall act with respect to the other spouse in the management and control of the community assets and liabilities in accordance with the general rules governing fiduciary relationships which control the actions of persons having relationships of personal confidence as specified in Section 721, until such time as the assets and liabilities have been divided by the parties or by a court. This duty includes the obligation to make full disclosure to the other spouse of all material facts and information regarding the existence, characterization, and valuation of all assets in which the community has or may have an interest and debts for which the community is or may be liable, and to provide equal access to all information, records, and books that pertain to the value and character of those assets and debts, upon request.

(Stats. 1992, c. 162 (A.B. 2650), § 10, operative Jan 1. 1994. Amended by Stats. 1993, c. 219 (A.B. 1500), § 100.8.)

B. THE RIGHT TO AVOID

California Family Code Section 1100(b) and (c), reproduced above, limit the broad right of equal management and control found at California Family Code Section 1100(1). Statutory limitations come in the form of the nonconsenting spouse's right to avoid certain gifts or transactions made by the other spouse absent evidence of the nonconsenting spouse's prior written consent.

Items subject to the right to avoid are gifts and low value transfers (California Family Code Section 1100(b)) and market value transfers of necessary items like clothing and furniture (California Family Code Section 1100(c)).

During an intact marriage, a spouse can recover either the property transferred or one hundred percent of its value. The property can be recovered either from the transacting spouse or from the third-party transferee. The entire property is recoverable for two reasons. The first is that under the managerial system the spouse acts as an agent for the community. The second is that the community property right is undivided.

At dissolution, a spouse can recover only their one-half interest in the property transferred. Here the spouse is acting on his or her own behalf. And, since a dissolution proceeding is in effect a partition proceeding, the spouse can only obtain the one-half he or she owns.

Spreckels, excerpted below, is a classic California case on point. Claus Spreckels, a sugar magnate, owned a storied mansion in an area of San Francisco known as the "Gold Coast" or "Billionaire's Row." Claus was the patriarch of a seemingly dysfunctional family. He and wife Alma had thirteen children. Only five survived to adulthood.

To fan the flames of dysfunction, Claus made an inter vivos gift of twenty-five million dollars to two of his five children. Claus's gift dissipated the community estate, which at Claus's death was characterized by the court as "not exceeding $10,000,000 in value." (*Id.* at 778.) To throw even more fuel on the fire, Claus made the gift without his (then living) wife Anna's written consent. At Anna's death, Claus's two donees were sued by their three siblings. The overlooked children hoped to void the twenty-five million dollar gift so that all or least half of it could fall into Anna's estate where it could be distributed to them.

Claus's donees defended the validity of Claus's gift with evidence that Anna's will, made irrevocable by her death, was proof that Anna knew about Claus's gift to some but not all of the couple's five children, and that Anna ratified Claus's gift posthumously by leaving her (far less valuable) estate to the three children who had been overlooked by Claus in the first place. A winning argument, it turned out.

Spreckels was brought in an era when the husband was the legal manager of the community property. As to Claus's unilateral gift, the court interpreted the predecessor statute to California Family Code Section 1100(a), reproduced below. The predecessor statute was in the Organic Code of 1850, it remained in force until the Civil Code enactment in 1872, where it was on the books until 1891, when a provision was added so that that statute read:

"The husband has the management and control of the community property, with the like absolute power of disposition, other than testamentary, as he has of his separate estate; *provided, however, that he cannot make a gift of such community property, or convey the same without a valuable consideration, unless the wife, in writing, consent thereto.*" * * * (Italics added.)

Spreckels walks through some important conceptual alternatives. A nonmutual inter vivos gift made by one spouse to a third party without the consent of the other spouse is avoidable by the nonconsenting spouse at the death of the donor spouse. At that time, nonconsenting spouse has the option to avoid or ratify the gift, but only as to that spouse's one-half community property interest in the gifted property.

Justice Shaw held that a nonconsenting spouse's cause of action accrues when the nonmutual transfer is made. However, the Justice also noted that the statute of limitations begins to run when the nonconsenting spouse knew or should have known of the gift.

SPRECKELS V. SPRECKELS
172 Cal. 775, 158 P. 537 (1916)

SHAW, J.

* * *

We are of the opinion that the gifts did not become void at the death of the husband, but were only voidable by the wife at her option. The limitation upon his power to give is not greater in its prohibitive effect than the preceding limitation upon his testamentary power. One is as absolute as the other. Both, in terms, include all the community property, and appear to withhold power to dispose of all or any of it in the proscribed manner. Yet, as above stated, it is well settled that a husband's testamentary disposition of more than one-half of the community property is not absolutely void as to the wife, but only voidable. The limitation upon the husband's power to make a gift is even less positive than that upon the testamentary power, for it depends upon two questions of fact; the absence of a valuable consideration, and the absence of her written consent, both of which may have to be proven by collateral evidence. The gift, when made, immediately vests the property in the donee subject to her right of revocation. She may give her consent at any time during her life, and if she does, the gift becomes absolute with respect to her. The provision was manifestly intended solely for the benefit of the [non-donor spouse]. If [the non-donor spouse] seeks to assert such right, it is incumbent upon [him or] her to show that the facts exist upon which it depends. * * *

* * * It is not alleged that she did not also have full knowledge of all of the alleged gifts by her husband to the defendants. The allegations show

that she did have full knowledge of a large part of them. The fourth clause of his will, above quoted, certainly put her on inquiry as to all of them. It is alleged that she caused an inquiry to be made concerning them. In this condition of her affairs she proceeded, on August 16, 1909, seven months after the probate of her deceased husband's will, to make and execute her own will. The second clause declares: "I hereby give, devise, and bequeath all of my estate, of every kind and description" to the three children, Claus A., Rudolph and Emma C., plaintiffs herein. * * *

The words "I hereby give all *my* estate, of every kind and description" to the three other children, excluded John and Adolph [Claus's donees] from participation in her estate. At that time, and up to her death, they [John and Adoph] held the property given to them by their father out of the community property. * * * The declaration is entirely inconsistent with the existence of a purpose, desire, or intention on her part that her executors or the beneficiaries under her will should have the right to recover a half of that which she says had been "given and advanced" to them. The provision, in connection with the circumstances under which it was made, precludes all idea that she regarded the property so given to the two defendants, or any part thereof or right in regard thereto, as any part of her descendible estate, or that the other three children were to receive, by her will or otherwise, any claim to that property or right to an accounting thereof. It was equivalent to an express ratification and confirmation of said gifts, and it was a consent thereto, by her, in writing, advisedly made. This will she retained unrevoked until her death, showing that notwithstanding her alleged direction to the plaintiff, Claus A. Spreckels, soon after the death of her husband, to begin an action to recover the property so given to John and Adolph, her last and final wish and will was that they should retain it all, but should receive nothing from her.

The plaintiffs have endeavored to avoid these consequences, and prevent consideration of her testamentary confirmation of the gifts, by alleging that Anna C. Spreckels "did not, at any time during her life, consent in writing or otherwise to said gifts." The respective wills of Claus Spreckels and Anna C. Spreckels, both of which are alleged to have been duly probated, are, however, incorporated into the complaint as parts thereof. This renders the aforesaid allegation inoperative, so far as it is inconsistent with the terms of her will. When applied to the will which it is alleged she made, the allegation amounts to no more than the conclusion of the pleader that the provision of the will did not constitute a consent to the gifts, or a confirmation thereof. In our opinion they were both a consent in writing and a ratification and confirmation, and they effectually contradict and nullify the above allegation.

Upon this view of the case it is immaterial whether the gifts to John and Adolph were or were not made to prevent the wife from receiving one-half of the community property of said marriage, or with the design of excluding the other children from ultimate participation, by will or inheritance from her, in any part thereof. It is also unnecessary to consider the question whether or not the right of the widow to attack or avoid those gifts survived her death, and passed to the executors of her will, or to those to whom she devised and bequeathed her estate. During her lifetime she was the only person who had the right to gainsay these gifts. Her power in that respect was complete, so far as others were concerned, and her ratification and confirmation thereof by her will concluded all other persons, regardless of the motive that prompted the gifts or of the nature of her right to avoid them.

The judgment is affirmed.

NOTES

1. *One spouse's cause of action to revoke a nonmutual gift made by the other spouse is a property claim.* The court in *Spreckels* left open the question of whether the nonconsenting spouse's cause of action to attack or avoid the gift survives his or her death. It does. Initially such a cause of action was held to be personal, but in *Harris v. Harris,* 57 Cal.2d 367, 19 Cal.Rptr. 793, 369 P.2d 481 (1962), the California Supreme Court held that the right to set aside a nonmutual gift survives the death of the nonconsenting spouse because it rests in property, not tort. Therefore, an avoidance action may be exercised by the personal representative of the deceased spouse.

2. *The testamentary plan, before and after death.* In *Spreckels,* Anna acknowledged Claus's gift in the structure of her estate plan, as discussed above. But ratification did not come until Anna's death. This is because during Anna's life, her estate plan was ambulatory, meaning that during Anna's life she could revoke a will and execute a new will at her pleasure. An ambulatory will would not prove that Anna ratified the gift of her now deceased spouse. Only an irrevocable will could do that. Once Anna died, her will was no longer subject to change, at which point it became irrevocable; only then did it become sufficient proof of Anna's intent to posthumously ratify Claus's nonmutual gift.

3. *Consent, ratification, waiver or estoppel?* When the nonacting spouse knows that a nonmutual gift was made—as Anna Spreckels knew—and that spouse fails to object, is that a ratification of the gift? This is a critical issue because once a gift is ratified, the right to avoid terminates.

Marriage of Stephenson, 162 Cal.App.3d 1057, 209 Cal.Rptr. 383 (2d. Dist. 1984) involves nearly two-dozen Uniform Gifts to Minors Act (UGM) transactions. Husband Roy opened the UGMA accounts for his and wife Beth's children; Roy funded the UGMA accounts with community funds. Since Roy was motivated by his own tax worries, he managed the investments in the UGMA accounts. As the court makes clear all UGMA accounts were "spent, lent, and reinvested by the husband and the wife." *Id.* at 1070.

In their dissolution proceeding, Beth sought to avoid the gifted sums on deposit in the UGMA accounts.

The first issue discussed by the court was whether Roy and Beth had donative intent to make the gifts. California adopts the rule that the opening of a bank account pursuant to UGMA is prima facie evidence of donative intent to make a gift of the sums on deposit in the account unless extrinsic evidence proves otherwise. California bases its adoption on *Gordon v. Gordon*, 419 N.Y.S.2d 684 (1979) as well as on UGMA Section 1156, which provides that the donor shall put the subject of the gift in possession and control of the custodian (in this case the deposit institution), but that the donor's failure to do so does not affect the consummation of the gift itself. So, what was the legal consequence of Roy and Beth opening UGMA accounts for their children? The act of opening the UGMA accounts was prima facie proof that Roy and Beth intended to give their children the sums on deposit in the accounts. In *Stephenson*, the court of appeal affirmed the referee's rationale that the couple's UGMA gifts irrevocably and indefeasibly vested legal title to the custodial property in the UGMA donees, meaning in the Roy and Beth's children.

Once it was determined that there was proof of intent, delivery and acceptance to make the gift, the next task was to determine what specifically was given.

Beth contended that Roy funded the accounts with nonmutual gifts of community property sums that he transferred into the UGMA account without her prior written consent. She wanted to recover specific community property transfers of sums on deposit in the UGMA accounts so that those sums could be inventoried as divisible property in Roy and Beth's dissolution proceeding.

The referee's decision on this point was unclear, but the court of appeal writes that the referee thought that Beth was estopped from reclaiming the community property transfers either because she had helped open the accounts, or because she had waived her rights to avoid those transfers. The appellate court reversed, making clear that as to the transfers at issue there was no evidence that Beth knowingly waived her rights to those sums. Nor was there evidence that the children changed their position in reliance on the transfer of those sums. She therefore retained the right to avoid date-specific transfers into the UGMA account notwithstanding the fact that she helped set up the account:

> "Since 1978, section 5125, subdivision (b) [now see California Family Code Section 1100] has provided: "A spouse may not make a gift of community personal property, or dispose of community personal property without a valuable consideration, without the written consent of the other spouse.
>
> A gift made by one spouse in violation of this section is voidable by the other spouse in its entirety during the donor spouse's lifetime if the community has not yet been dissolved but if action is taken after the donor spouse's death or after the community has been dissolved, it is voidable only to the extent of one-half. (*Bank of California v.*

Connolly (1973) 36 Cal.App.3d 350, 377, 111 Cal.Rptr. 468; *Harris v. Harris* (1962) 57 Cal.2d 367, 369, 19 Cal.Rptr. 793, 369 P.2d 481.)

We deal first with those UGMA accounts opened by Roy. The record is devoid of evidence that Beth gave her written consent to the opening of those accounts with community property funds.

The referee concluded, however, that Beth 'will not now be heard to allege that the UGMA Accounts were opened without her written consent and said gifts, made with the consent and approval of both Petitioner and Respondent, are irrevocable and, when made, conveyed to the minor children indefeasibly vested legal title.'

In urging the correctness of this conclusion, Roy relies on the provisions of section 1157, subdivision (b) which states that a gift made pursuant to the UGMA is "irrevocable and conveys to the minor indefeasibly vested legal title to the custodial property * * * ." We conclude that this subdivision does not preclude a spouse from voiding a gift of community property that is otherwise voidable. (See *In re Marriage of Hopkins* (1977) 74 Cal.App.3d 591, 602, fn. 7, 141 Cal.Rptr. 597; cf. *Estate of Bray* (1964) 230 Cal.App.2d 136, 40 Cal.Rptr. 750.)

In *Bray,* the husband purchased savings bonds with community funds without the knowledge or consent of his wife. He registered those bonds jointly in the names of himself and his son. Husband subsequently died and the son contended that pursuant to statutory and case authority he was entitled to full ownership of the bonds, regardless of the community property laws. The court rejected this contention, concluding that this would result in an impermissible conversion of the wife's assets. Accordingly, the court held that the purchase of the savings bonds by husband could not defeat the community property interest of the wife.

We, too, conclude that one spouse cannot defeat the interest of the other spouse in the community property by unilaterally purporting to make a gift of it pursuant to the UGMA. Consequently, absent written consent, written ratification, waiver or estoppel, the non-donor spouse is not precluded from voiding the gift.

The referee apparently concluded that Beth is estopped or has waived her right to void the subject gifts. 'Questions of waiver and estoppel involve issues of fact for the trial court.' (*Los Angeles Fire & Police Protective League v. City of Los Angeles* (1972) 23 Cal.App.3d 67, 75, 99 Cal.Rptr. 908.) 'Estoppel applies to prevent a person from asserting a right where his conduct or silence makes it unconscionable for him to assert it.' (*In re Marriage of Recknor* (1982) 138 Cal.App.3d 539, 546, 187 Cal.Rptr. 887.) Either unjust enrichment or a change in position may be the basis of an unconscionable injury which will estop a person from asserting the requirement of a writing. (*Mintz v. Rowitz* (1970) 13 Cal.App.3d 216, 224–225, 91 Cal.Rptr. 435.)

Waiver requires a voluntary act, knowingly done, with sufficient awareness of the relevant circumstances and likely consequences. [Citation.] There must be actual or constructive knowledge of the existence of the right to which the person is entitled. [Citation.] The burden is on the party claiming a waiver to prove it by evidence that does not leave the matter doubtful or uncertain and the burden must be satisfied by clear and convincing evidence that does not leave the matter to speculation. [Citation.] This rule particularly applies to cases involving a right favored in law such as * * * the right to retain lawful property entitlement * * * ." (*In re Marriage of Moore* (1980) 113 Cal.App.3d 22, 27, 169 Cal.Rptr. 619.)

In support of the trial court's conclusion, claimants refer to evidence demonstrating that Beth had knowledge and participated in the couple's program of opening up savings accounts for their children pursuant to the UGMA.

This evidence is insufficient to support a finding of either estoppel or waiver. With regard to estoppel, the record contains neither evidence that the claimant children changed their position in a manner that will cause them to suffer an unconscionable injury should Beth void the gifts, nor evidence that Beth will be unjustly enriched in such an event. Accordingly, there is insufficient evidence to support a finding that Beth is estopped to void the subject gifts.

With regard to waiver, the evidence to which Roy refers is insufficient to demonstrate that Beth knowingly and voluntarily waived her property interest in the UGMA accounts set up by Roy or that she knowingly and voluntarily waived her right to veto such transactions by withholding her written consent.

The cases to which claimants refer in support of their assertion are distinguishable. Those cases involve situations in which a wife's participation or acquiescence in the disposition of community property to third parties induced those parties to deal with the property as if she had consented to that disposition, to the detriment of the third parties. (See *MacKay v. Darusmont* (1941) 46 Cal.App.2d 21, 26, 115 P.2d 221; *Bush v. Rogers* (1941) 42 Cal.App.2d 477, 479–480, 109 P.2d 379.) The record contains no such evidence of detrimental reliance in this case.

The amendments to section 5125, subdivision (b) [current Cal.Fam. Code § 1100(b)] clearly demonstrate the Legislature's desire to strictly regulate one spouse's ability to give away community property. This is evidenced by the 1975–1978 version of that subdivision under which a spouse was precluded from making any gift of community personal property. The re-enactment of the provision allowing for gifts of community personal property with the *written* consent of the other spouse in 1978 must be interpreted to require something more than the tacit approval of the gift by the non-donor spouse. A different interpretation would entirely vitiate the writing requirement. We decline to engage in such "doctrinal machinations." (See Bruch, *Management Powers and Duties Under California's Community Property Law: Recommendations For Reform* (1982–1983) 34 HASTINGS L.J. 227, 239–240.) While the application of this rule may be harsh in the case at bench, any change in this scheme is for the Legislature and not this court to make." *Stephenson, supra* at 1070–1073.

Marriage of Stallworth, 192 Cal.App.3d 742, 237 Cal.Rptr. 829 (1st Dist. 1987) is another case on point. There, the court interpreted California Family Code Section 1100(b) to mean that in the absence of prior written consent, written ratification, a knowing waiver, or estoppel, the non-donor spouse is not precluded from avoiding a gift made by the other spouse to a third party. By implication in the presence of written consent, ratification, a knowing waiver or estoppel, the non-donor spouse is precluded from bringing an action to avoid under the statute.

C. REIMBURSEMENT RIGHTS

In a dissolution proceeding, parties are required to produce proof in support of a separate property ownership claim (Chapter 5). Often the proof required is specialized financial records.

When financial records are called for, parties can fall short because of lack of time, ability, or the will to create records for all of the purchase and debt transactions that occur during the relevant period.

During a dissolution proceeding, more particularly, even if the parties possess the stamina and resources to recreate records of financial events that took place in the past, they will fall short. Forensic records are, admissible to prove a reimbursement claim, but they are inadmissible for purposes of asserting a separate property ownership claim to community property.

A limited number of statutory reimbursement rights are available for use when a separate property claim fails. The high evidentiary bar of *See*-compliant records (Chapter 5) is not necessary to claim reimbursement. Nevertheless, some documentary proof is required.

Reimbursement rights between spouses include:

- Separate property contributions to the purchase of an entirely (100%) community property asset—California Family Code Section 2640 (Chapter 5).

- Community property contributions to education programs that substantially enhance a student spouse's earning capacity—California Family Code Section 2641 (Chapter 4).

- Separate property expenditures to repay a debt, to satisfy a debt that a person is personally liable for, made at a time when there is available (nonexempt) community property or available separate property belonging to the person's spouse—California Family Code Section 914, reproduced below.

- Community property expenditures to satisfy a spouse's premarital support obligation at a time when the obligated spouse has sufficient separate property funds with which to pay the obligation—California Family Code Section 915, below.

Additionally, courts may recognize a right of reimbursement as part of achieving an equitable division of community property. For example, after a date of separation within the meaning of California Family Code Section 771, one spouse may have de facto exclusive physical possession of all or part of the community property. De facto control does not necessarily mean that the spouse in possession has exclusive legal management and control over the assets under his her or physical control. Nevertheless, in *Marriage of Garcia*, 224 Cal.App.3d 885, 274 Cal.Rptr. 194, 197 (3d Dist. 1990) the court ruled that if "one spouse has the exclusive use of a community asset during the period between separation and trial, that spouse may be required to compensate the community for the reasonable value of that use." For a case involving a spouse's duty to account for community property in his possession after a date of separation, see *Marriage of Valle*, 53 Cal.App.3d 837, 126 Cal.Rptr. 38 (1st Dist. 1975).

Weinberg v. Weinberg, 67 Cal.2d 557, 63 Cal.Rptr. 13, 432 P.2d 709 (1967) articulates a managerial rationale for creating a community property reimbursement right for paying the premarital support obligations of a spouse. The rule is codified in California Family Code Section 915, reproduced below. Here is the rationale:

"The policy of protecting [a spouse's] creditors outweighs the policy of protecting family income even from premarital creditors of [a spouse]. Community property is therefore available to such creditors. (Grolemund v. Cafferata, supra, 17 Cal.2d 679, 689, 111 P.2d 641 * * *) As such a creditor, a husband's first wife can levy against the community property of his second marriage for alimony payments due. * * * As manager of the community property 'with like absolute power of disposition, other than testamentary, as [over a] separate estate (Civ. Code, § 172 [now California Family Code Section 1100(a)]), [a spouse] may also voluntarily discharge such obligations from community property. * * * It does not follow, however, that the community can never claim reimbursement from [one spouse's] separate estate when community property has been used to discharge [that spouse's support] obligation. [One spouse's] legal right of management and control has long been recognized to imply correlative duties to [the other spouse]. [A spouse's] duties are analogous to those of a partner; he [or she] cannot obtain an unfair advantage from the trust placed in him as a result of the marital relationship. (Vai v. Bank of America (1961) 56 Cal.2d 329, 337–339, 15 Cal.Rptr. 71, 364 P.2d 247; Fields v. Michael (1949) 91 Cal.App.2d 443, 447–448, 205 P.2d 402.)" *Id.* at 562–563.

In the case of *Marriage of Smaltz*, 82 Cal.App.3d 568, 147 Cal.Rptr. 154 (1st Dist. 1978), a spouse, who had no separate property to speak of, used community property to pay spousal support to a former spouse. In this case, the court said, the obligated spouse could not be said to be taking any unfair advantage of his current spouse.

D. THE "OTHER THAN TESTAMENTARY" LIMITATION

California Family Code Section 1100(a) gives either spouse "[a]bsolute power of disposition, *other than testamentary*, as the spouse has of the separate estate of the spouse."

What does the phrase "other than testamentary" mean in the context of marriage?

Tyre provides an often-cited explanation. In *Tyre*, husband Luis made a change to a community property term life insurance policy. Luis named his wife Rebecca as his beneficiary, a testamentary act because it purported to dispose of community property (specifically the policy proceeds) at Luis's death. Luis also opted that Rebecca be paid a survivor's annuity (monthly payments) rather than a lump sum payout. Luis made the change without Rebecca's consent.

At Luis's death, Rebecca's health issues made it evident that the annuity option adversely affected Rebecca. Rather than receive a much needed lump sum of $20,000, the life insurance settlement method chosen by Luis indicated that Rebecca was to receive an annuity of $123 per month. Rebecca sued to avoid Luis's annuity transaction with Aetna. She argued that Luis's decision to opt for an annuity rather than as a lump sum payment constituted a testamentary act that required Rebecca's prior written consent.

TYRE V. AETNA LIFE INSURANCE CO.

54 Cal.2d 399, 6 Cal.Rptr. 13, 353 P.2d 725 (1960)

TRAYNOR, JUSTICE.

Plaintiffs, the widow and three adult daughters of the insured, appeal from a judgment for defendant in an action to recover the widow's community property interest in the proceeds of a life insurance policy.

The facts are not in dispute. Rebecca Tyre (hereafter called plaintiff) and Louis Tyre, the insured, were married in Los Angeles in 1917 and lived there as husband and wife until Mr. Tyre's death in 1957. Defendant issued its policy in the face amount of $20,000 upon the life of the insured in 1926. All the premiums were paid from community funds. The original beneficiary was the Tyre Brothers Glass Company. Upon the insured's retirement from the business in 1946, he changed the beneficiary of the policy to make it payable to plaintiff in a lump sum. In 1950 the insured exercised his option under the policy of selecting an alternate settlement. He directed that upon his death plaintiff receive an annuity based on her life expectancy at that time. If she failed to survive him by ten years, the monthly payments were to be divided among the three daughters for the balance of the ten-year period only. As so amended the policy continued in force for the remainder of the insured's life and was in effect at his death.

Plaintiff was 59 years and 8 months of age at the time her husband died. An average person of that age has a life expectancy, established by standard mortality tables, of 14 years. Under the terms of her husband's choice of settlement, plaintiff will receive $20,664 in installments of $123 per month if she lives out her full expectancy. If she fails to survive the ten-year period, defendant's total liability will be $14,760. To receive $10,000, plaintiff must survive 6.77 years. Plaintiff has suffered three heart attacks and the trial court found that her life expectancy may be less than that of an average person of her age.

The insured changed the method of payment without plaintiff's knowledge or approval. Since the policy had been in the possession of a bank as collateral security for a loan, plaintiff did not learn of the change until a few months after her husband's death. She promptly disavowed his choice and requested payment of the face amount of the original policy in cash. Defendant refused to alter the method of settlement. Plaintiff and her daughters thereupon brought this action praying for $10,000 in cash representing plaintiff's community interest and a declaration that the remaining $10,000 be paid according to the insured's selection at $61.50 per month. Defendant contends that it is not obligated to pay any sum under the policy except $123 per month for plaintiff's life or ten years, whichever is longer.

A policy of insurance on the husband's life is community property when the premiums have been paid with community funds. New York Life Ins. Co. v. Bank of Italy, 60 Cal.App. 602, 606, 214 P. 61; Blethen v. Pacific Mut. Life Ins. Co., 198 Cal. 91, 99, 243 P. 431; Grimm v. Grimm, 26 Cal.2d 173, 175, 157 P.2d 841. During the existence of the marriage the respective interests of the husband and wife in community property are present, existing, and equal (Civ.Code, § 161a [current California Family Code Section 771]), but "the husband has the management and control of the community personal property, with like absolute power of disposition, other than testamentary, as he has of his separate estate; provided, however, that he cannot make a gift of such community personal property, or dispose of the same without a valuable consideration, * * * without the written consent of the wife." Civ.Code, § 172 [current California Family Code Section 1100(a)]. When the community is dissolved by death, "one-half of the community property belongs to the surviving spouse; the other half is subject to the testamentary disposition of the decedent." Prob.Code, § 201. Both parties rely on these sections. Plaintiff contends that she became entitled, immediately upon her husband's death, to one-half of each part of the community property. Defendant contends that the insured had power to enter into the supplemental contract by virtue of his general powers of management and control and that plaintiff cannot disavow his contract.

Plaintiff could not avoid a contract entered into for a valuable consideration by her husband in the course of his lifetime management of the community personalty even though it was made without her consent and temporarily affected her control immediately following his death. * * *

In the present case, however, the husband's election to have the policy proceeds paid as an annuity instead of in a lump sum was not an exercise of his nontestamentary power of management during his lifetime, but an attempt to dispose of proceeds after his death. Until he died he could elect to have the proceeds paid as a lump sum or as an annuity actuarially worth that sum. Of course, as between the husband and defendant there was consideration for the change in method of payment. The right to an annuity was consideration for the surrender of the right to a lump sum payment. Similarly there is consideration between the insurance company and the insured when the insured changes the beneficiary from one person to another. Nevertheless, it is settled that even though the insurance contract provides that the insured husband has the right to change the beneficiary without the wife's consent when she is named as such, any such change of beneficiary without her consent and without a valuable consideration other than substitution of beneficiaries is voidable, and after the death of the husband the wife may maintain an action for her community share in the proceeds of the policy. (* * * see Spreckels v. Spreckels, 172 Cal. 775, 784–785, 158 P. 537). These cases recognize that although the payment of insurance proceeds is a matter of contract between the insured and the insurer, the insured's exercise of his unilateral right under the contract to select the beneficiary is testamentary in character. Similarly, the insured's exercise of his unilateral right under the terms of the policy to determine whether the proceeds shall be paid as a lump sum or in the form of an annuity is testamentary in character. * * * [Reversed.]

GIBSON, C.J., and PETERS, WHITE and DOOLING, JJ., concur. SCHAUER and MCCOMB, JJ., dissent.

NOTES

1.   *Acts with long term consequences versus acts effecting the distribution of property upon death.* By what rationale are testamentary acts excluded from equal management and control? If the community invests money in stock or in a partnership or in bank certificates of deposit the act could produce long term consequences once the marriage ends. And yet, the act falls within ordinary management and control powers set forth in California Family Code Section 1100(a). How is undertaking an act that has long term consequences that might not reveal themselves until the death of a spouse different from an act whose effect is testamentary? A useful definition, perhaps, is that a testamentary act is carried out with the intent to dispose of (meaning to distribute) property at death.

2.   *A duty to disclose policy changes? Tyre v. Aetna Life Insurance Co.* predates the passage of California Family Code Section 721 by thirty years. If *Tyre* had arisen today, would Rebecca, the nonacting spouse, have a claim against acting spouse Louis's estate? Would that claim be based on a theory that the acting spouse breached his duty of disclosure under California Family Code Section 721(b), and that the breach resulted in an impairment of the Rebecca's future community property interest in the life insurance proceeds? See Section 4 below.

SECTION 3. COMMUNITY REAL PROPERTY

The California Family Code distinguishes between community personal property and community real property.

The general rule for management of community real property is that consequential transactions must be joined in by both spouses. The general rule is referred to as the joinder rule, or simply as joinder.

A spouse has the right to avoid a transaction for which there is no joinder.

Marriage of Lezine, illustrates and discusses the exceedingly narrow scope of the right to avoid under California Family Code Section 1102, reproduced below.

WEST'S ANNOTATED CALIFORNIA FAMILY CODE

§ 1102. Community real property; spouse's joinder in conveyances; application of section; limitation of actions

(a) Except as provided in Sections 761 and 1103, either spouse has the management and control of the community real property, whether acquired prior to or on or after January 1, 1975, but both spouses, either personally or by a duly authorized agent, must join in executing any instrument by which that community real property or any interest therein is leased for a longer period than one year, or is sold, conveyed, or encumbered.

(b) Nothing in this section shall be construed to apply to a lease, mortgage, conveyance, or transfer of real property or of any interest in real property between spouses.

(c) Notwithstanding subdivision (b):

(1) The sole lease, contract, mortgage, or deed of the husband, holding the record title to community real property, to a lessee, purchaser, or encumbrancer, in good faith without knowledge of the marriage relation, shall be presumed to be valid if executed prior to January 1, 1975.

(2) The sole lease, contract, mortgage, or deed of either spouse, holding the record title to community real property to a lessee, purchaser, or encumbrancer, in good faith without knowledge of the marriage relation, shall be presumed to be valid if executed on or after January 1, 1975.

(d) No action to avoid any instrument mentioned in this section, affecting any property standing of record in the name of either spouse alone, executed by the spouse alone, shall be commenced after the expiration of one year from the filing for record of that instrument in the recorder's office in the county in which the land is situated.

(e) Nothing in this section precludes either spouse from encumbering his or her interest in community real property, as provided in Section 2033, to pay reasonable attorney's fees in order to retain or maintain legal counsel in a proceeding for dissolution of marriage, for nullity of marriage, or for legal separation of the parties.

(Stats. 1850, c. 103, § 9; Stats. 1853, c. 116, § 1. Civil Code former § 172a, added by Stats. 1917, c. 583, § 2, amended by Stats. 1925, c. 37, § 1; Stats. 1927, c. 488, § 1; Stats. 1959, c. 125, § 22; Stats. 1969, c. 627, § 3; Stats. 1969, c. 1609, § 4. Civil Code former § 5127, added by Stats. 1969, c. 1608, § 8, amended by Stats. 1969, § 25; Stats. 1973, c. 987, § 15; Stats. 1974, c. 1206, § 5; Stats. 1987, c. 128, § 3; Stats. 1992, c. 356, § 6. Stats. 1992, c. 162

(A.B. 2650), § 10, operative Jan 1, 1994. Amended by Stats. 1993, c. 219 (A.B. 1500), § 101; Stats. 2014, c. 82 (S.B. 1306), § 18, eff. Jan. 1, 2015.)

The original 1850 purpose of what is now California Family Code Section 1102, whose derivation is set out in detail above, was to give gender-specific protection to the wife, at her option, without the necessity of court action. In the male management era (1850–1975) the husband was the sole and exclusive legal manager of community property, as discussed above. In 1917, the legislature determined that the wife should have a legal power over conveyances of community real property that adversely affected her. The joinder requirement was added by statute as Civil Code Section 172, the underlying idea being that a wife could protect her interests in community real property by refusing to sign a real estate transaction. Consequential transactions are deeds, contracts of sale, mortgages, or leases for longer than a period of one year.

Today the joinder requirement appears at California Family Code Section 1102(a) in gender-neutral form.

The next case, *Lezine*, is a difficult case that was originally litigated at about the time that the state adopted a comprehensive Family Code (1992). The California Supreme Court opinion was published two years after the Family Code went into effect (1994). The question in the case is how to balance the rights of an innocent spouse against the rights of an (adjudged) innocent third-party creditor. Specifically, the court was asked to decide on the scope of protection that the historic language of California Family Code Section 1102 offers a wronged spouse.

LEZINE V. SECURITY PACIFIC FINANCIAL SERVICES, INC.

14 Cal.4th 56, 58 Cal.Rptr.2d 76, 925 P.2d 1002 (1996)

GEORGE, CHIEF JUSTICE.

During his marriage to plaintiff Gloria J. Lezine (plaintiff), Henry Lezine (Lezine) unilaterally transferred a security interest in community real property (the Halm Avenue property) to defendant Security Pacific Financial Services, Inc. (Security Pacific), without the knowledge or consent of plaintiff, in violation of former section 5127 of the Civil Code [current Family Code Section 1102]. By the present action, plaintiff sought to have the transfer of the security interest set aside in its entirety pursuant to the authority of former section 5127 and Droeger v. Friedman, Sloan & Ross (1991) 54 Cal.3d 26, 283 Cal.Rptr. 584, 812 P.2d 931. * * *

I

In 1974, Lezine and plaintiff, a married couple, purchased for their residence the Halm Avenue property, located in the City and County of Los

Angeles. In 1989, the Halm Avenue property was encumbered by a deed of trust in favor of San Clemente Savings and Loan Association, (San Clemente Savings), and a deed of trust in favor of Imperial Thrift. On November 8, 1989, Lezine forged plaintiff's signature on a quitclaim deed, and the signature falsely was notarized by a notary public. The quitclaim deed purported to divest plaintiff of any interest in the Halm Avenue property.

The quitclaim deed was recorded on January 26, 1990. On that same date, Lezine obtained a loan in the amount of $240,000 from Guardian Savings and Loan Association (Guardian) secured by a deed of trust executed by Lezine encumbering the Halm Avenue property. Plaintiff was unaware of the loan. Approximately $106,300 of the loan proceeds were used to repay the loan obligations secured by the deeds of trust in favor of San Clemente Savings and Imperial Thrift, as well as other community debts. The balance of the loan proceeds was not used for the benefit of the community.

On April 12, 1990, Lezine obtained a $100,000 line of credit from Security Pacific secured by a deed of trust encumbering the Halm Avenue property. Approximately $60,000 was advanced to Lezine under the line of credit. The trial court found that plaintiff was unaware of the line of credit; no conduct on the part of plaintiff misled Security Pacific as to the validity of the quitclaim deed, and no portion of the proceeds from the line of credit was used for the benefit of the community.

Thereafter, plaintiff learned of the two deeds of trust that newly encumbered the Halm Avenue property. On June 5, 1990, plaintiff filed in the superior court the present equitable action against Lezine, Guardian, and Security Pacific, seeking declaratory relief, quiet title, and cancellation of the deeds of trust. On that same date, plaintiff filed a petition for the dissolution of her marriage (in the domestic relations department of the superior court, separate from the proceedings in the present action). In the present action, Guardian and Security Pacific cross-complained against plaintiff, Lezine, and the notary public, claiming the status of bona fide encumbrancers and seeking declaratory relief, foreclosure of an equitable lien, and indemnity. On July 16, 1991, in the other proceedings, a bifurcated judgment was entered dissolving the Lezine marriage and reserving jurisdiction for the division of property.

On March 6, 1992, the trial court in the present action, following a court trial, entered judgment in favor of plaintiff on the complaint, declaring the deeds of trust void and canceled in their entirety under authority of Droeger v. Friedman, Sloan & Ross, supra, 54 Cal.3d 26, 283 Cal.Rptr. 584, 812 P.2d 931. * * * The [trial] court also entered judgment in favor of Guardian and Security Pacific on their cross-complaints, granting Guardian an equitable lien encumbering the Halm Avenue residence in the amount of $106,305.38 (the extent to which the Guardian loan retired the existing community debt), and awarding judgment in favor of Guardian and Security Pacific against Lezine personally in the amounts of $302,527.85 and $87,799.50, respectively, and against the bonding company for the notary public in the amount of $10,000 (the bond limit). Neither Guardian nor Security Pacific was awarded any relief against plaintiff personally.

On April 2, 1992, Guardian and Security Pacific recorded abstracts of their money judgment against Lezine in the Los Angeles County Recorder's Office.

Three months later, on July 1, 1992, in the marital dissolution proceedings (after a default was entered against Lezine on the reserved issues regarding the division of property), the court awarded plaintiff the Halm Avenue property as her sole and separate property, subject to the equitable lien in favor of Guardian, and assigned the debt formerly secured by the deeds of trust in favor of Guardian and Security Pacific exclusively to Lezine, pursuant to Civil Code former section 4800, subdivision (b)(2). The court awarded the community property business known as Brown Automotive to Lezine as his sole and separate property.

Thereafter, in seeking refinancing to retire the equitable lien in favor of Guardian, plaintiff discovered the two abstracts of judgment that had been recorded by Guardian and Security Pacific and that appeared as liens encumbering title to the residence. On December 11, 1992, plaintiff moved for clarification of the judgment in the present action, urging that the Droeger decision compelled a determination that the abstracts of judgment did not create judgment liens that attached to her separate property. Guardian and Security Pacific objected to the proposed amendment, arguing, among other things, that the court lacked jurisdiction to extinguish their liens upon awarding the Halm Avenue property to plaintiff.

The trial court granted plaintiff's motion, issuing an order clarifying that the abstracts of judgment "shall not constitute liens against the [Halm Avenue] real property. * * * "

Security Pacific appealed from the order clarifying the judgment (Code Civ. Proc., § 904.1, subd.(a)(2)), and from the judgment as clarified. * * *

We granted review to determine whether community real property remains liable for satisfaction of a debt after the transfer of a security interest, which secured repayment of that debt, is set aside pursuant to former section 5127.

II

Before stating the various contentions of the parties and framing the legal issues presented for our determination, we shall review the statutory schemes governing the liability of community property for marital debts, as well as the liability of real property received by the nondebtor spouse following the division of property in a dissolution proceeding. We shall then turn to former section 5127 [current Family Code Section 1102] and its purpose and underlying policies.

We consider first the applicable rules governing the liability of community property for debts incurred during the marriage (such as the loan obligation incurred by Lezine owing to Security Pacific). In general, "[e]xcept as otherwise expressly provided by statute, the community estate is liable for a debt incurred by either spouse before or during marriage, regardless of which spouse has the management and control of the property and regardless of whether one or both spouses are parties to the debt or to a judgment for the debt." (Fam.Code, § 910, subd. (a).) Thus, the liability of community property is not limited to debts incurred for the benefit of the community, but extends to debts incurred by one spouse alone exclusively for his or her own personal benefit. (See Robertson v. Willis (1978) 77 Cal.App.3d 358, 362, 143 Cal.Rptr. 523; Stratton v. Superior Court (1948) 87 Cal.App.2d 809, 197 P.2d 821.) Although a spouse may be required to reimburse the community for the misuse of community assets (see, e.g., Fam.Code, §§ 1101, 2602; In re Marriage of Czapar (1991) 232 Cal.App.3d 1308, 1318, 285 Cal.Rptr. 479; In re Marriage of Lister (1984) 152 Cal.App.3d 411, 418–419, 199 Cal.Rptr. 321), the community estate remains liable to third-party creditors for any debt incurred as a result of such misuse of assets.

Code of Civil Procedure section 695.020 addresses specifically the liability of community property for money judgments. That statute provides in pertinent part: "(a) Community property is subject to enforcement of a money judgment as provided in the Family Code. (b) Unless the provision or context otherwise requires, if community property that is subject to enforcement of a money judgment is sought to be applied to the satisfaction of a money judgment: (1) Any provision of this division that applies to the property of the judgment debtor or to obligations owed to the judgment debtor also applies to the community property interest of the spouse of the judgment debtor and to obligations owed to the other spouse that are community property."

Under these provisions, all of the community property of plaintiff and Lezine was liable for the debts incurred by Lezine during the marriage, including the loan obligations owing to Guardian and Security Pacific. Additionally, the community property, including the Halm Avenue property, was subject to enforcement of the money judgment against Lezine prior to the property division, unless some contrary rule "otherwise requires" (Code Civ. Proc., § 695.020, subd. (b)). Contrary to the contention of plaintiff, the community estate was not exempt from liability for the money judgment simply because the judgment was rendered subsequent to the "status only" judgment of dissolution, where the underlying debt arose prior to dissolution of the marriage. (See Kinney v. Vallentyne (1975) 15 Cal.3d 475, 478–479, 124 Cal.Rptr. 897, 541 P.2d 537.)

Under California's judgment lien law, a judgment creditor's recordation of an abstract of judgment creates a judgment lien that attaches to all real property situated in the county in which the judgment is recorded and that otherwise is subject to enforcement of the money judgment against the debtor. (Code Civ. Proc., §§ 697.310, 697.340.)

Finally, at the time of the present proceedings, former section 5120.160 of the Civil Code governed the liability of community property for marital debts following the division of property in a marital dissolution proceeding. That statute provided in relevant part: "(a) Notwithstanding any other provision of this article, after division of community and quasi-community property pursuant to Section 4800: (2) The separate property owned by a married person at the time of the division and the property received by the person in the division is not liable for a debt incurred by the person's spouse before or during marriage, and the person is not personally liable for the debt, unless the debt was assigned for payment by the person in the division of the property. Nothing in this paragraph affects the liability of property for the satisfaction of a lien on the property." (Italics added.) Under this provision, following the division of property, the community property awarded to one spouse no longer is liable for marital debts that are assigned to the other spouse, with the exception that the award of community real property to one spouse that is subject to a lien remains liable for satisfaction of the lien, i.e, the lien remains enforceable to satisfy the underlying debt. (See Kinney v. Vallentyne, supra, 15 Cal.3d 475, 479, 124 Cal.Rptr. 897, 541 P.2d 537.) If the property division requires one person to pay a debt, and the creditor satisfies a money judgment for that debt from the property that was awarded to the person's spouse (e.g., through the enforcement of a lien), the person's spouse has a right of reimbursement from that person to the extent of the property applied. (Civ.Code, former § 5120.160, subds. (a)(2), (b).)

Under these rules, if a valid judgment lien in favor of Security Pacific attached to the Halm Avenue property before it was awarded to plaintiff as her sole and separate property, plaintiff received the property subject to the lien, and the property remained liable for satisfaction of the lien, even though the underlying debt was assigned to Lezine. In the event Security Pacific satisfies the judgment by enforcement of the lien, plaintiff has a right of reimbursement against Lezine to the extent of the property applied.

The question before us is whether the foregoing rules and principles governing the liability of the Halm Avenue property for the loan obligations incurred by Lezine are altered or otherwise affected by former section 5127, or the circumstance that the deed of trust that formerly secured that obligation was set aside pursuant to former section 5127.

Former section 5127 [Current Family Code Section 1102] provided in pertinent part that "either spouse has the management and control of the community real property . . . but both spouses either personally or by duly authorized agent, must join in executing any instrument by which such community real property or any interest therein is leased for a longer period than one year, or is sold, conveyed, or encumbered." * * * The statutory provision requiring that both spouses join in the execution of any instrument transferring an interest in real property first appeared in former section 172a of the Civil Code (Stats.1917, ch. 583, § 2, p. 829), the predecessor to former section 5127. The enactment of former section 172a reflected the evolution of community property law in recognizing the wife's equal status, and a legislative intent to protect the innocent spouse against an unauthorized transfer of community real property by the other spouse. (See Droeger v. Friedman, Sloan, & Ross, supra, 54 Cal.3d at pp. 32–33, 283 Cal.Rptr. 584, 812 P.2d 931.) In Britton v. Hammell (1935) 4 Cal.2d 690, 52 P.2d 221, the court held that if the nonconsenting spouse challenges a unilateral gift of community real property by the consenting spouse during the marriage, the nonconsenting spouse is entitled to set aside the gift in its entirety, rather than solely the transfer of his or her one-half community share. (4 Cal.2d at p. 692, 52 P.2d 221.) The Britton decision, as well as other early cases applying former section 172a, involved the setting aside of a gift of community real property in contrast to the circumstances of the present case, involving a transfer made in exchange for consideration.

In 1969, former section 172a of the Civil Code became part of the Family Law Act as section 5127 (Stats.1969, ch. 1608, § 8, p. 3342)[current Family Code Section 1102]. In Droeger v. Friedman, Sloan, & Ross, supra, 54 Cal.3d 26, 283 Cal.Rptr. 584, 812 P.2d 931, this court, reaffirming prior decisional law, held that under former section 5127, both spouses must consent to the transfer of an interest in community real property, regardless whether the transaction is a gift or supported by consideration. Resolving a conflict among appellate decisions as to the relief that may be afforded under former section 5127, the court, citing among other authority Britton v. Hammell, supra, 4 Cal.2d 690, 52 P.2d 221, further held that when a nonconsenting spouse, during the marriage, timely challenges a transfer made in violation of former section 5127, the transfer is voidable in its entirety. (54 Cal.3d at p. 30, 283 Cal.Rptr. 584, 812 P.2d 931.) * * *

Significantly (with respect to the issue presented in this case), the court in Droeger did not address the effect of the cancellation of the deeds of trust on the underlying obligation for payment of attorney fees; in other words, the court did not hold that, as a result of the setting aside of the security for the underlying debt, the community estate no longer was liable for the payment of attorney fees, or that the attorney creditors no longer could seek to apply the community real property formerly encumbered by the deeds of trust toward satisfaction of an obligation for payment of attorney fees.

The specific issue before us is whether the trial court, in addition to setting aside Security Pacific's deed of trust encumbering the Halm Avenue property pursuant to former section 5127, had the authority to extinguish a lien that otherwise would be enforceable to satisfy a money judgment arising from the setting aside of that deed of trust. The Court of Appeal concluded that, as a result of setting aside the deed of trust pursuant to former section 5127, Security Pacific's security for the community debt was canceled but that the underlying community debt was not, and the relief afforded under former section 5127 did not alter the liability of the community real property for the underlying debt, or the enforcement of a money judgment for that debt. The Court of Appeal further concluded that, under Family Code section 916, the award of the Halm Avenue property to plaintiff as her separate property did not affect the enforceability of the judgment lien; accordingly the trial court lacked authority to extinguish the judgment lien in favor of Security Pacific.

Urging a contrary result, plaintiff maintains that when a security interest in community real property that was transferred unilaterally by a debtor spouse in violation of former section 5127 [current Family Code Section 1102] is canceled, that real property no longer is liable for satisfaction of a money judgment that previously was secured by the deed of trust. Otherwise, argues plaintiff, the nonconsenting spouse is in the same position after the security interest is set aside as he or she was in prior to the granting of relief, i.e., the property remains subject to an encumbrance in the amount of the underlying loan obligation; consequently the relief afforded under former section 5127 [current Family Code Section 1102] would be nullified, and the action to set aside the unilateral transfer will have been a futile act. Such a result, urges plaintiff, would be contrary to the legislative purpose of former section 5127 [current Family Code Section 1102].

In resolving the issue presented, we note there is scant authority pertaining to the rights and remedies, in general, of a transferee of an interest in community real property after the unauthorized transfer is set aside pursuant to former section 5127. In one early decision involving a unilateral transfer made in violation of former section 172a of the Civil Code (the predecessor to former section 5127 [current Family Code Section 1102]), the court held that, although the transfer was voidable by the nonconsenting wife, the third-party innocent purchaser, without knowledge of the marriage, was entitled to restoration of the purchase price from the community. (Mark v. Title Guar. & Trust Co. (1932) 122 Cal.App. 301, 9 P.2d 839.) In Mark, the husband had transferred to a third party the community interest in a contract for the sale of real property, without the knowledge or consent of his wife, and had retained for his own use and benefit the sale proceeds paid by the purchaser.

This court concluded that the wife was entitled to set aside the unilateral transfer, pursuant to former section 172a of the Civil Code. The court further held, however, that the bona fide purchaser, without knowledge of the marriage relationship, was entitled to restoration of the purchase price from the community. In reaching this conclusion, the court first noted "the difficulty of protecting the expectancy of the innocent wife and at the same time of safeguarding the rights of innocent purchasers. . . ." (Mark v. Title Guar. & Trust Co., supra, 122 Cal.App. at p. 311, 9 P.2d 839.) Nonetheless, the court further observed that although husband had misappropriated the sale proceeds for his own personal use and benefit, the proceeds had the character of community property and had been paid into the community estate. "The fact that the wife derived no benefit from the transaction and that the husband expended the whole of the proceeds for his own sole benefit did not change the complexion of the property. Its character was not altered because the husband, instead of conserving the money, used it for his own purposes." (Id., at p. 312, 9 P.2d 839.) The court accordingly concluded that the community was required to reimburse the purchaser for the consideration paid as a condition of the set-aside relief.

In Andrade Development Co. v. Martin (1982) 138 Cal.App.3d 330, 187 Cal.Rptr. 863, the court observed, in dicta, that in the case of a contract for the sale of community real property that is voided pursuant to former section 5127 [current Family Code Section 1102], the purchaser who acquired the contractual interest in the property, in good faith and without knowledge of the marriage relationship, might be entitled to damages for breach of contract from the community estate. (138 Cal.App.3d at pp. 337–338, 187 Cal.Rptr. 863.)

Legal commentators have noted that, in the case of a unilateral transfer that is set aside pursuant to former section 5127 [current Family Code Section 1102], the third-party transferee properly should be deprived of any interest in the real property itself, but should be permitted to assert rights as an unsecured creditor for repayment of whatever consideration was passed in exchange for the ineffective title. "This solution would entail no violation of community property management principles, as either spouse may unilaterally incur a debt for which the community is liable." (Bruch, Protecting the Rights of Spouses in Intact Marriages—The 1987 California Community Property Reform and Why It Was So Hard to Get (1990) Wis. L.Rev. 731, 743, fn. 35; see Hogoboom & King, Cal. Practice Guide: Family Law (The Rutter Group 1996) 8:687, p. 8–166 ["Arguably . . . since set-aside relief is an equitable remedy, it should be ordered subject to the return of consideration paid by the innocent purchaser who entered the transaction having no knowledge and no reason to know the transferor was married."].)

The foregoing rules and principles articulated in Mark and Andrade, and by family law commentators, are consistent with the rules generally governing the liability of community property for marital debts, as well as with equitable principles. When these rules and principles are applied to the transfer of a security interest in community real property, if the security interest is forfeited pursuant to former section 5127 [current Family Code Section 1102] the community remains liable to the formerly secured creditor for the underlying debt. The loss of the security does not extinguish the underlying debt, or the character of that unsecured debt as one for which the community estate is liable. * * *

Under the foregoing principles, a court in equity may require as a condition to the granting of equitable relief under former section 5127 [current Family Code Section 1102] the restoration of any consideration transferred by an innocent encumbrancer in exchange for the security interest, who acts without knowledge of the community status of the property. The trial court in the present case granted such relief in the form of a money judgment against Lezine. At the time of the entry of that judgment (prior to the property division in the separate marital dissolution proceedings), the community property (which included the Halm Avenue property) was liable for satisfaction of that money judgment.

The remaining question is whether former section 5127 [current Family Code Section 1102], or any policy underlying that statute, precludes a creditor such as Security Pacific from seeking to apply community real property toward satisfaction of a debt that previously was secured by that same real property but which security interest was voided under former section 5127 [current Family Code Section 1102]. The plain language of the current statute, requiring that "both spouses . . . must join in executing any instrument by which such community real property or any interest therein . . . " is transferred, reflects a legislative intent to protect an innocent spouse against an unauthorized unilateral transfer of community real property by the other spouse. Nothing in the foregoing statutory language refers to the liability of community real property for marital debts. In contrast, the Legislature has enacted a variety of statutory schemes that expressly exempt or otherwise protect the interests of a real property owner from creditor claims, such as the provisions for declared homesteads (Code Civ. Proc., §§ 704.910 et seq.) or governing home equity sales contracts (Civ.Code, § 1695.1). No part of former section 5127 [current Family Code Section 1102], however, indicates any similar intent to exempt community real property from liability for marital debts, even debts incurred unilaterally by one spouse.

Instead, as reflected in Code of Civil Procedure section 695.020, the Legislature expressly has established the liability of community real property for the satisfaction of money judgments rendered against either spouse, including the nondebtor spouse's one-half community interest. Indeed, because California law governing the enforcement of judgments and debts enables a judgment creditor of one spouse to levy execution on community real property, "[i]n effect, one spouse alone can indirectly alienate community realty by incurring an enforceable obligation and refusing to pay it." (Reppy, Debt Collection from Married Californians: Problems Caused by Transmutations, Single-Spouse Management, and Invalid Marriage (1981) 18 San Diego L.Rev. 143, 169, fn. omitted.) Thus, for example, one spouse unilaterally may incur credit card charges which, if unpaid, may be reduced to a money judgment that may be satisfied from community real property. The Legislature has not created any statutory exception—either in former section 5127 [current Family Code Section 1102] or any other statute—for money judgments reflecting a debt arising from, or formerly secured by, a unilateral transfer of community real property made in violation of former section 5127 [current Family Code Section 1102].

Thus, construing former section 5127 [current Family Code Section 1102] with reference to, and in harmony with, the various statutory schemes governing the liability of community property for marital debts, it does not appear that the purpose or effect of former section 5127 [current Family Code Section 1102] is to exempt community real property from liability for satisfaction of marital debts incurred unilaterally by one spouse, for which the community otherwise is liable. Thus, the creditor who loses its security interest under former section 5127 [current Family Code Section 1102] retains the rights of any other unsecured creditor to resort to the community real property for satisfaction of the underlying debt.

If we were to conclude, as plaintiff urges, that, after a security interest in real property is set aside pursuant to former section 5127 [current Family Code Section 1102], the formerly secured creditor no longer may resort to the property to satisfy the debt, that creditor would be placed in a position less advantageous than that of other unsecured creditors of the community estate—the formerly secured creditor, having obtained a judgment against the debtor spouse, would be precluded from establishing a judgment lien that attaches to the community real property to satisfy the judgment, while the unsecured creditor (such as the credit card issuer, for example), after obtaining a judgment against the debtor spouse, could proceed to record an abstract of judgment creating a judgment lien that attaches to the community real property. There is no principled basis for treating the formerly secured creditor, who originally obtained its security interest in good faith, less favorably than any other unsecured creditor, with respect to the ability to resort to community real property to satisfy a money judgment for which the community is liable.

For these reasons, we conclude that neither former section 5127 nor Droeger carves out an exception to the rules governing the liability of community real property for enforcement of a money judgment against a debtor spouse, or the enforceability of a judgment lien that has attached to community real property for satisfaction of a money judgment. Accordingly, a creditor who previously has forfeited a security interest in community real property under former section 5127 is placed in the position of any other unsecured creditor entitled to seek a judgment against the debtor spouse, and to enforce its money judgment against the community estate. Furthermore, the judgment creditor's recordation of an abstract of judgment creates a judgment lien that attaches to the community real property and that may be enforced to satisfy the lien.

We recognize that our holding effectively may nullify in substantial part the relief afforded under former section 5127 when the unilateral transfer is a security interest for the repayment of a debt. If the creditor obtains a judgment for the amount of the debt when the security interest is set aside and records an abstract of judgment, the security interest will be converted into a judgment lien encumbering the community real property. Nevertheless, the purpose of the statute is served—the unauthorized direct transfer is canceled, and both spouses retain full management and control of the property. Moreover, as explained above, the same result could obtain had the court set aside a unilateral sale or lease of the property and rendered judgment in favor of the purchaser or lessee for the amount of the consideration paid.

Accordingly, in the present case, after Security Pacific's deed of trust was set aside pursuant to former section 5127 [current Family Code Section 1102] and Security Pacific was awarded a money judgment against Lezine, it was placed in the position of any other judgment creditor entitled to enforce the judgment against the community estate. By recording an abstract of judgment in Los Angeles County, reflecting the money judgment against Lezine, Security Pacific created a judgment lien that attached to all real property in Los Angeles County that was subject to enforcement of the money judgment, including the Halm Avenue property. * * *

We recognize that the result we reach may appear inequitable in some respects. An institutional lender such as Security Pacific may be in a far better position than the innocent nondebtor spouse to protect against forgeries and deception by a debtor spouse such as Lezine who seeks a loan to be secured by community real property. The result we reach nevertheless is dictated by existing legislation protecting the rights of creditors.

For the foregoing reasons, we conclude that the Court of Appeal properly determined that the trial court exceeded its authority in declaring the Halm Avenue property free of any judgment lien in favor of Security Pacific. Our holding is without prejudice to the right of plaintiff to seek a reallocation of the community property as to which the court in the marital dissolution proceeding retained jurisdiction.

III

The judgment of the Court of Appeal is affirmed.

MOSK, KENNARD, BAXTER, WERDEGAR, CHIN and BROWN, JJ., concur.

NOTE

The Lezine *opinion met with consternation in the popular press.* One commentator said: "The case of Lezine v. Security Pacific Financial Services is a lesson in how California's vaunted 'community property' laws sometimes collide with a common sense understanding of right and wrong. In this case . . . the creditor's rights easily overrode those of the betrayed wife."[2] LOS ANGELES TIMES, February 15, 1997 p. A1.

Legal commentators have generally been more sanguine: "in simple terms, the lender is simply an unsecured community creditor and may enforce the judgment as such."[3] Richard Denner, February 1997 CALIFORNIA FAMILY LAW MONTHLY 28 (LexisNexis Matthew Bender). Other commentators viewed the decision as rational and logical, based as it is on the distinction between the underlying debt and how that debt ultimately got secured via a judgment lien.

Academic commentators faulted the court for not taking into account institutional lending practices: "In the real world, this guy never would have been able to borrow all this money but for the improper security," opined one academic commentator. LOS ANGELES TIMES, Feb. 15, 1997 p. A24. Keep in mind, however, that *Lezine did* arise in the "real world" and that the creditors, after being adjudged good faith, obtained a judgment that they could then place as a lien on the family home.

The dismissal of *Lezine* as an outlier has obscured the necessity of discussing domestic violence prevention issues in community property law. Financial abuse is a serious matter. To address it requires detection and fast action by the spouse who is the perpetrator's target. Time is of the essence. Domestic violence prevention is discussed in Section 6D below.

From a theoretical perspective, *Lezine* points out the limits of any marital property system, the functions of which are to protect spouses in transactions with each other, to give third parties confidence in their dealings with married persons, and to effectuate the state's compelling interest in marriage.

---

[2]   Fair use.

[3]   Fair use.

On one hand, was Gloria who, although represented by counsel, could not keep up with the brutal financial chaos and destruction that her husband rained down upon their marital community and, more to the point, upon her. On the other hand were the lenders who established that they advanced funds to the husband based on a fraud he perpetrated against them using forged and fraudulently notarized deeds.

Gloria successfully sought statutory remedies that limited her to avoiding a security interest for which there was no joinder—a security interest, in other words, that she did not sign. The creditors' response strategy was swift. Once the security interest was canceled, the creditors sued Henry personally, obtained judgments against him, and filed those judgments as liens against the Halm Avenue home, which was still community property in character.

SECTION 4. TRANSACTIONS BETWEEN THE SPOUSES

California Family Code Section 721 codifies the view that married persons are partners in a confidential relationship. The confidential nature of the relationship gives rise to general and specific fiduciary duties. Those duties include a spouse's general obligation not to take any unfair advantage of the other spouse.

The spousal duty not to take any unfair advantage of the other in a transaction between the spouses is in many ways a duty to be as transparent about the transaction as the situation requires. For that reason, disclosure rights and obligations have become an increasingly important part of the California Family Code.

A. FIDUCIARY DUTIES

Spousal fiduciary duties come into being on the date of the marriage, not before.

What protects the parties before they marry, if they choose to contract with each other over marital property rights, is the California Premarital Agreement Act (Chapter 1).

What protects the parties in transactions between themselves once they are married is California Family Code Section 721, which is incorporated by reference into California Family Code Section 1100(e). These two code sections also protect the parties during separation and dissolution. At that phase, the two basic statutes draw enforcement support from a series of additional dissolution-related code sections, chief among them California Family Code Section 2120 (Chapters 7 and 8).

Section 2 of the 2002 version of California Family Code Section 721(c). 310 (S.B. 1936) makes clear that married persons have the same rights and duties as unmarried business partners:

"SEC. 2. It is the intent of the Legislature in enacting this act to clarify that Section 721 of the Family Code provides that the fiduciary relationship between spouses includes all of the same rights and duties in the management of community property as the rights and duties of unmarried business partners in managing partnership property as provided in Sections 16403, 16404 and 16503 of the Corporations Code, and to abrogate the ruling in *In re Marriage of Duffy* (2001) 91 Cal.App.4th 923, to the extent that it is in conflict with this clarification."

WEST'S ANNOTATED CALIFORNIA FAMILY CODE

§ 721. Contracts with each other and third parties; fiduciary relationship

(a) Subject to subdivision (b), either spouse may enter into any transaction with the other, or with any other person, respecting property, which either might if unmarried.

(b) Except as provided in Sections 143, 144, 146, 16040, and 16047 of the Probate Code [which requires a trustee to manage trust assets in accordance with the prudent investor rule], in transactions between themselves, spouses are subject to the general rules governing fiduciary relationships that control the actions of persons occupying confidential relations with each other. This confidential relationship imposes a duty of the highest good faith and fair dealing on each spouse, and neither shall take any unfair advantage of the other. This confidential relationship is a fiduciary relationship subject to the same rights and duties of nonmarital business partners, as provided in Sections 16403, 16404, and 16503 of the Corporation Code, including, but not limited to, the following:

(1) Providing each spouse access at all times to all books kept regarding a transaction for the purposes of inspection and copying.

(2) Rendering upon request, true and full information of all things affecting any transaction that concerns the community property. Nothing in this section is intended to impose a duty for either spouse to keep detailed books and records of community property transactions.

(3) Accounting to the spouse, and holding as a trust any benefit or profit derived from any transaction by one spouse without the consent of the other spouse that concerns the community property.

(Stats. 1992, c. 162 (A.B. 2650), § 10, operative Jan. 1, 1994. Amended by Stats. 2002, c. 310 (S.B. 1936), § 1; Stats. 2014, c. 82 (S.B. 1306), § 12, eff. Jan. 1, 2015.)

B. DISCLOSURE WITHOUT DEMAND

The 2002 amendments to California Family Code Section 721(b), effective 2003, incorporate the corresponding 1997 Revised Uniform Partnership Act amendments to the California Corporations Code. Pertinent is Corporations Code Section 16403, which governs unmarried business partners' rights to information.

Specifically, Section 16403 gives partners rights of access to partnership books, records, and information without demand. Disclosure duties arise from the management and control of property. Therefore, partners are required to disclose information to each other about day to day matters as an ordinary course of affairs. Otherwise, disclosure is on demand.

WEST'S ANNOTATED CALIFORNIA CORPORATIONS CODE

§ 16403. Books and records; right of access

(a) A partnership shall keep its books and records, if any . . . at its chief executive office.

(b) A partnership shall provide partners and their agents and attorneys access to its books and records. It shall provide former partners and their agents and attorneys access to books and records pertaining to the period during which they were partners. . . .

(c) Each partner . . . shall furnish to a partner, and to the legal representative of a deceased partner or partner under legal disability, both of the following . . .

(1) Without demand, any information concerning the partnership's business and affairs reasonably required for the proper exercise of the partners' rights and duties under the partnership agreement or this chapter, and

(2) On demand, any other information concerning the partnership's business and affairs, except to the extent the demand or the information demanded is unreasonable or otherwise improper under the circumstances.

(Added by Stats. 1996, c. 1003 (A.B. 583), § 2. Amended by Stats. 2004, c. 254 (S.B. 1306), § 45.)

———

As discussed above (Section 4.A.), the fiduciary duty exists until such time as the assets and liabilities have been divided by the parties or by a court. The right to have access to books continues after dissolution, but only as to periods of time that occurred during the (now dissolved) marriage.

To summarize the interaction between fiduciary and disclosure duties:

For transactions on or before December 31, 2002, the right to financial information about the community is triggered by a direct request for information.

For transactions on and after January 1, 2003, the right to financial information about the community is a matter of right.

Under current law there is no requirement that a spouse ask for information about the community in order to be entitled to that information. Rather, spouses are entitled to financial information from each other as a matter of right, which means that spouse have a fiduciary duty to provide information about ordinary matters related to the management of community property. The 2002 amendments to California Family Code Section 721(b) incorporate California Corporations Code Section 16403, which require nonmarital business partners to disclose financial information concerning the partnership as a normal part of management, which is to say without demand. And, as to community personal property, California Family Code Section 1100(e), because it is self-updating, incorporates the most recent version of California Family Code Section 721.

Therefore new law imposes higher transparency standards on spouses when it comes to the management of past, present, or future community property.

Applied to spouses the legal transition places a disclosure duty on an acting spouse to provide access to existing books and records that concern the community's property, business and affairs. The access to make existing books available does not entail a duty to keep books and records; it entails only a duty to disclose any records or books that may have been kept. The absence of records is not necessarily problematic for purposes of characterizing property (Chapter 5); it simply signals that the property in question is entirely community property.

The failure to disclose information is distinct from the duty to provide the other spouse with existing books and records. Information can be provided orally or in writing; information need not be formatted in any particular way for purposes of keeping a spouse up to date on community property management. More to the point, the failure to disclose information may be the basis of a breach of impairment claim because, with the inclusion of the phrase "*including but not limited to*" in California Family Code Section 721(b) (2002), a spouse is held to standards beyond those that are explicitly enumerated in the statute. (Italics added.)

Therefore, the current version of California Family Code Section 721(b) (2002), codifies and updates the longstanding rule that spouses have fiduciary duties toward each other. Fiduciary duties are comprised of at least the following standards by statute, decisional law, or both:

(1)   the duty of good faith, or honesty in fact;

(2)   the duty of loyalty;

(3)   the duty of care (as limited by the business judgment rule);

(4)   the duty to provide access to and disclosure of information, as set forth in California Corporations Code Section 16403:

   (a)   the duty to keep accessible to the other spouse during marriage existing books and records of community property transactions;

   (b)   the duty to provide after divorce the non-acting former spouse or that spouse's agents existing books and records that pertain to all periods that occurred during marriage; and

   (c)   the duty to make full disclosure to the other spouse of all material facts and information regarding what the community owns and owes as an ordinary course of business; and

   (d)   the duty to provide any ordinary information without demand, and all other reasonable information on demand.

(5)   the duty to refrain from general mismanagement (actionable if the mismanagement stems from a breach of fiduciary duty under California Family Code Section 721(b)), from grossly negligent or reckless conduct, from intentional misconduct, or from a knowing violation of the law).

(6)   all specific statutory duties that appear in, for example, California Family Code Sections 1100 (management of community personal property), 1102 (management of community real property), and 1101 (community property impairment claims and remedies).

––––––––

California Family Code Section 721(b) applies in any transaction between spouses. It comes into play generally and specifically for purposes of California Family Code Section 1100, which applies to community personal property; California Family Code Section 1102, which applies to community real property; and California Family Code Section 1101(a), which provides a cause of action for the impairment of a community property interest due to a breach of fiduciary interest. Remedies are set out at 1101(g) or 1101(h).

C. IMPAIRMENT CLAIMS

Impairment is defined broadly under California Family Code Section 1101(a) to mean a detrimental impact to the claimant spouse's one-half community property interest.

Spouses (obviously) can disagree about whether a particular act was in fact undertaken for the benefit of the community. Similarly they (obviously) can disagree over whether an act by one spouse has impaired, is impairing, or will impair the other spouse's community property right.

What constitutes a legitimate act of management is undefined. Nevertheless, a legitimate act of spousal management—conceived broadly—is one that is disclosed, transparent, and undertaken with the marital partnership in mind. The act need not be undertaken to benefit the community; but it cannot be undertaken to gain any unfair advantage over the other spouse.

That said, even where a particular act falls within the sphere of an acting spouse's legitimate management and control rights the effect of such an act may be to give one spouse one or more benefits that diminish the other spouse's share in the community property, or that restrict the community's opportunities, as discussed by analogy in *Meinhard v. Salmon, supra*.

Resolving a breach of fiduciary duty problem might require that the adversely affected spouse request an equitable accounting from the benefitted spouse, either during marriage or at dissolution.

Or, a breach of fiduciary duty claim may be the basis upon which a presumption of undue influence is raised in favor of the adversely affected spouse. If so, the burden of proof shifts to the benefitted spouse to rebut the presumption of undue influence either with evidence that the other spouse was represented by counsel, with financial records, or with some combination of both. Evidence of representation and disclosure go to the issue of fairness and voluntary consent.

Moreover, a spouse in an intact marriage has the right to request an equitable accounting per California Family Code Section 1101(b). The transfer of community property in violation of a statutory restriction like California Family Code Section 1100(b) or (c) gives rise to an immediate action by the injured spouse, if for nothing else than to request an accounting under California Family Code Section 1101. So too does a breach of a fiduciary duty alleged under California Family Code Section 721(b) give rise to an impairment claim under California Family Code Section 1101(a).

WEST'S ANNOTATED CALIFORNIA FAMILY CODE

§ 1101. Claim for breach of fiduciary duty; court ordered accounting; addition of name of spouse to community property; limitation of action; consent of spouse not required; remedies

(a) A spouse has a claim against the other spouse for any breach of the fiduciary duty that results in impairment to the claimant spouse's present undivided one-half interest in the community estate, including, but not limited to, a single transaction or a pattern or series of transactions, which transaction or transactions have caused or will cause a detrimental impact to the claimant spouse's undivided one-half interest in the community estate.

(b) A court may order an accounting of the property and obligations of the parties to a marriage and may determine the rights of ownership in, the beneficial enjoyment of, or access to, community property, and the classification of all property of the parties to a marriage.

(c) A court may order that the name of a spouse shall be added to community property held in the name of the other spouse alone or that the title of community property held in some other title form shall be reformed to reflect its community character, except with respect to any of the following:

(1) A partnership interest held by the other spouse as a general partner.

(2) An interest in a professional corporation or professional association.

(3) An asset of an unincorporated business if the other spouse is the only spouse involved in operating and managing the business.

(4) Any other property, if the revision would adversely affect the rights of a third person.

(d)(1) Except as provided in paragraph (2), any action under subdivision (a) shall be commenced within three years of the date a petitioning spouse had actual knowledge that the transaction or event for which the remedy is being sought occurred.

(2) An action may be commenced under this section upon the death of a spouse or in conjunction with an action for legal separation, dissolution of marriage, or nullity without regard to the time limitations set forth in paragraph (1).

(3) The defense of laches may be raised in any action brought under this section.

(4) Except as to actions authorized by paragraph (2), remedies under subdivision (a) apply only to transactions or events occurring on or after July 1, 1987.

(e) In any transaction affecting community property in which the consent of both spouses is required, the court may, upon the motion of a spouse, dispense with the requirement of the other spouse's consent if both of the following requirements are met:

(1) The proposed transaction is in the best interest of the community.

(2) Consent has been arbitrarily refused or cannot be obtained due to the physical incapacity, mental incapacity, or prolonged absence of the nonconsenting spouse.

(f) Any action may be brought under this section without filing an action for dissolution of marriage, legal separation, or nullity, or may be brought in conjunction with the action or upon the death of a spouse.

(g) Remedies for breach of the fiduciary duty by one spouse, including those set out in Sections 721 and 1100 shall include, but not be limited to, an award to the other spouse of 50 percent, or an amount equal to 50 percent, of any asset undisclosed or transferred in breach of the fiduciary duty plus attorney's fees and court costs. The value of the asset shall be determined to be its highest value at the date of the breach of fiduciary duty, the date of the sale or disposition of the asset, or the date of the award by the court.

(h) Remedies for the breach of the fiduciary duty by one spouse, as set forth in Sections 721 and 1100, when the breach falls within the ambit of Section 3294 of the Civil Code shall include, but not be limited to, an award to the other spouse of 100 percent, or an amount equal to 100 percent, of any asset undisclosed or transferred in breach of the fiduciary duty.

(Stats. 1992, c. 162 (A.B. 2650), § 10, operative Jan. 1, 1994. Amended by Stats. 2001, c. 703 (A.B. 583), § 1.)

NOTE

Disclosure on demand versus disclosure in the ordinary course, an important legal transition. The legal transition from needing to ask for disclosure to having a right to be told as a matter of ordinary course is a consequence of *Marriage of Duffy,* 91 Cal.App.4th 923, 111 Cal.Rptr.2d 160 (2d Dist. 2001), the case abrogated by the new amendments to California Family Code Section 721, discussed above.

In now-abrogated *Duffy,* the spouses together opened a community property defined contribution brokerage account (an IRA) in the amount of $482,925. They opened the account in 1995, a relevant fact because the following activities took place *after* the 1992 rule requiring disclosure on demand under California Family Code Section 721 but *before* the adoption of the Revised Uniform Partnership Act in 1996, effective 1997 (incorporated by reference into California Family Code Section 721), which does not tie the duty to disclose to the other spouse's request for information.

After opening the account, husband Vincent, acting alone, selected stockbrokers who were children of family friends. At all times thereafter, Vincent continued to act alone without disclosing information about stock trades to wife Patricia. Patricia later testified that she was afraid to ask Vincent about financial matters because he would get angry. From 1995 to 1997, Vincent invested all the IRA sums on deposit ($482,925) in one volatile stock. The value of that stock rollercoastered as the share prices went from $13 per share, to a high of $26 per share, to a low of $3.75 per share. When the ride was over, the couple's IRA account had only $261,483 remaining, for a total loss of $221,442.

The legal issue in *Duffy* was whether, Vincent, the acting spouse, had a duty under California Family Code 721(b) to disclose to Patricia, the nonacting spouse relative to the particular asset, how (badly) he was managing the community property IRA. The court of appeal applied the 1992 version of California Family Code Section 721(b) to hold that an acting spouse's duty to disclose is triggered by the non-acting spouse's demand for disclosure, meaning absent a request for disclosure there is no duty to disclose.

The uproar was quick and fierce, and it led the legislature to abrogate *Duffy*.

In *Marriage of Walker*, 138 Cal.App.4th 1408, 42 Cal.Rptr.3d 325 (1st Dist. 2006), the appellate court held that the duty to disclose without demand applies only prospectively.

The next case asks whether one spouse is obligated to disclose to the other spouse a right obtained during marriage (winning the state lottery jackpot) if the winning spouse files a petition for dissolution before receiving the first benefit from the right (a lottery dispersement check).

MARRIAGE OF ROSSI

90 Cal.App.4th 34, 108 Cal.Rptr.2d 270 (2d Dist. 2001)

EPSTEIN, J.

* * *

Factual and Procedural Summary

Denise and Thomas were married in 1971. In early November 1996, Bernadette Quercio formed a lottery pool with a group of her co-workers, including Denise. Each member of the pool contributed $5 per week. Denise contributed her $5 for a short time—three weeks—but, according to her papers, on December 1, 1996 or about that date, she withdrew from the pool.

In late December 1996, Ms. Quercio called Denise to say that their group had won the lottery jackpot. The jackpot prize was $6,680,000 and Denise's share was $1,336,000, to be paid in 20 equal annual installments of $66,800 less taxes, from 1996 through 2015. According to declarations by Denise and by Ms. Quercio, Ms. Quercio told her that she wanted to give Denise a share in the jackpot as a gift. Denise explained: "I was afraid to tell [Thomas] because I knew he would try to take the money away from me. I went to the Lottery Commission office and told them I was married but contemplating divorce. They told me to file before I got my first check, which I did. I believed that the lottery winnings were my separate property because they were a gift." In early January 1997, Denise filed a petition for dissolution of marriage in the Los Angeles Superior Court. She never told Thomas about the lottery jackpot. She used her mother's address to receive checks and other information from the California Lottery because it would be safer since Thomas would not see the lottery checks.

Thomas was served with the dissolution petition in January 1997. He and Denise talked about a settlement the same day. Thomas was not represented by counsel in the dissolution proceedings. He and Denise met with Denise's attorney. According to Thomas, he was given several papers to sign to finalize the dissolution. These included a marital settlement agreement and a judgment of dissolution. There is a dispute between the parties about the actual date of separation and why the date of separation was listed as June 27, 1994.

Denise filled out a schedule of assets and debts dated January 27, 1997; a final declaration of disclosure; and an income and expense declaration dated January 30, 1997. She did not reveal the lottery winnings in any of these documents, either as community or separate property. Because Thomas did not have an attorney, Denise also filled out Thomas's schedule of assets and debts.

The marital settlement agreement was approved as part of the judgment of dissolution. Paragraph 9.1 of the marital settlement agreement is a warranty about disclosure of assets. * * *

Paragraph 9.4 of the marital settlement agreement also relates to disclosure of assets: "Each party has fairly and with candor disclosed all of the property in which either has a claim or interest, *whether or not the claim or interest is separate or joint property.* * * *

Finally, paragraph 9.7 of the marital settlement agreement provides: "The parties have no separate property other than what he or she has earned or accumulated after separation. Those items, if any, are specifically set forth in Exhibits 'A' and 'B'." The lottery winnings are not listed on the schedules attached to the marital settlement agreement. Denise testified that the lottery winnings were not listed on the schedules.

The marital settlement agreement also provided that concealment of assets was a basis to seek to set aside the agreement and that the party who was wronged by the concealment could seek payment of one-half of the concealed property or its value plus one-half of any income derived from the property. (Paragraph 9.8.)

Judgment of dissolution was entered April 7, 1997. In 1998, Thomas filed for bankruptcy. In May 1999, a letter was sent to Thomas's home address, asking if Denise was interested in a lump-sum buy-out of her lottery winnings. This was the first Thomas knew about the lottery prize. He confirmed that Denise was a winner with the California Lottery. Thomas retained counsel, who contacted Denise's attorney. According to a declaration filed by Thomas's counsel, Denise's attorney confirmed that she had won a share of a lottery prize, "however, his client was unwilling to share any 'meaningful' amount of the Lottery proceeds." * * * In July 1999, Denise withdrew $33,000 in lottery winnings to repay a loan made by her mother in 1980.

In July 1999, Thomas filed a motion to set aside the dissolution of marriage based on fraud, breach of fiduciary duty and failure to disclose; for adjudication of the lottery winnings as an omitted asset; and sought the award of 100 percent of the lottery winnings pursuant to Family Code section 1101, subdivision (h). Thomas also sought an award of his attorney's fees under section 1101, subdivision (g). * * *

In his points and authorities, Thomas asked the court to enforce the disclosure penalty provision of the judgment of dissolution. * * * In the alternative, Thomas asked the court to set aside the dissolution based on concealment and breach of fiduciary duty. Alternatively, Thomas sought an award of 100 percent of the lottery winnings pursuant to section 1101, subdivision (h), which penalizes a breach of fiduciary duty by a spouse in dissolution proceedings. As a final alternative ground, Thomas argued the lottery proceedings should be adjudicated an omitted asset pursuant to section 2556. * * *

The trial court found that Denise intentionally failed to disclose her lottery winnings in the marital settlement agreement, the judgment, and her declaration of disclosure. It found that Denise breached her fiduciary duties under sections 721, 1100, 2100, and 2101 by fraudulently failing to disclose the lottery winnings and that she intentionally breached her warranties and representations set forth in paragraphs 9.1, 9.4 and 9.7 of the Marital Settlement Agreement. The court specifically found that Denise's failure to disclose the lottery winnings constituted fraud, oppression and malice within the meaning of Civil Code section 3294 and section 1101, subdivision (h). The trial court awarded Thomas 100 percent of the lottery winnings pursuant to Provision E of the Judgment of

Dissolution, paragraph 9.1 of the Marital Settlement Agreement, and section 1101, subdivisions (g) and (h).

The trial court found that Denise's evidence that her share of the lottery winnings was a gift was not credible, and concluded that the lottery winnings were community property. Denise's motion to vacate the restraining orders and the cross motions to strike portions of declarations were denied. The court ordered each party to bear his or her own costs. Denise filed a timely notice of appeal.

Discussion

* * * The court found that Denise intentionally concealed her lottery winnings during the dissolution proceedings and that her conduct constituted fraud, oppression, and malice within the meaning of Civil Code section 3294 and section 1101, subdivision (h). On that basis, it awarded Thomas 100 percent of the winnings.

Section 721, subdivision (b) imposes a fiduciary duty on spouses in transactions between themselves: "This confidential relationship imposes a duty of the highest good faith and fair dealing on each spouse, and neither shall take any unfair advantage of the other. This confidential relationship is a fiduciary relationship subject to the same rights and duties of nonmarital business partners, as provided in * * * Corporations Code Section [16403], * * * "

Section 1101, subdivision (h) provides: "Remedies for the breach of the fiduciary duty by one spouse when the breach falls within the ambit of Section 3294 of the Civil Code shall include, but not be limited to, an award to the other spouse of 100 percent, or an amount equal to 100 percent, of any asset undisclosed or transferred in breach of the fiduciary duty."

Thomas argues that imposition of the 100 percent penalty under section 1101, subdivision (h) was mandatory, once the family court found that Denise acted with fraud, oppression or malice in concealing the lottery winnings during the dissolution proceedings.

The correctness of the family court's order awarding Thomas all of the lottery winnings was based on the finding that Denise's conduct constituted fraud within the meaning of Civil Code section 3294. Civil Code section 3294 provides in pertinent part: "(a) In an action for the breach of an obligation not arising from contract, where it is proven by clear and convincing evidence that the defendant has been guilty of oppression, fraud, or malice, the plaintiff, in addition to the actual damages, may recover damages for the sake of example and by way of punishing the defendant. [¶] . . . . [¶] (c) As used in this section, the following definitions shall apply: [¶] (1) 'Malice' means conduct which is intended by the defendant to cause injury to the plaintiff or despicable conduct which is carried on by the defendant with a willful and conscious disregard of the rights or safety of others. [¶] (2) 'Oppression' means despicable conduct that subjects a person to cruel and unjust hardship in conscious disregard of that person's rights. [¶] (3) 'Fraud' means an intentional misrepresentation, deceit, or concealment of a material fact known to the defendant with the intention on the part of the defendant of thereby depriving a person of property or legal rights or otherwise causing injury. . . ."

The evidence established that Denise filed for dissolution after learning that she had won a share of a substantial lottery jackpot; that she consulted the Lottery Commission personnel about ways in which she could avoid sharing the jackpot with her husband; that she used her mother's address for all communications with the Lottery Commission to avoid notifying Thomas of her winnings; and that she failed to disclose the winnings at any time during the dissolution proceedings, despite her warranties in the marital settlement agreement and the judgment that all assets had been disclosed. The family court expressly rejected her evidence that the winnings constituted a gift and, as such, were her separate property. The record supports the family court's conclusion that Denise intentionally concealed the lottery winnings and that they were community property.

Denise argues she committed no fraud because the statutory definition of that term "denotes conduct much more malicious and vile in nature than the failure of a physically and emotionally abused woman to disclose an asset to her husband, whose gambling and money mismanagement problems detrimentally affected her life and caused her to file for bankruptcy and caused him to threaten to kill her. In not disclosing what Denise Rossi believed was her separate property, Denise Rossi did not intend to deprive Respondent of an asset that he was entitled to because she felt it belonged to her alone. Denise Rossi did not believe that she was misappropriating a community asset, and therefore did not have the requisite fraudulent intent to deprive Respondent of a community asset."

The problem with her argument is that the court expressly found her evidence was not credible. The record supports this finding. The court put it in the following clear terms: "I believe the funds used to purchase the ticket were community. I don't believe the story about the gift." The court expressly found that Denise intentionally failed to disclose her lottery winnings in the marital settlement agreement, the judgment and her declaration of disclosure. This case presents precisely the circumstance that section 1101, subdivision (h) is intended to address. Here, one spouse intentionally concealed a significant community property asset. * * * This supports a finding of fraud within the meaning of Civil Code section 3294. The family court properly concluded that under these circumstances, Thomas was entitled to 100 percent of the lottery winnings under section 1101, subdivision (h).

* * * The strong language of section 1101, subdivision (h) serves an important purpose: full disclosure of marital assets is absolutely essential to the trial court in determining the proper dissolution of property and resolving support issues. The statutory scheme for dissolution depends on the parties' full disclosure of all assets so they may be taken into account by the trial court. A failure to make such disclosure is properly subject to the severe sanction of section 1101, subdivision (h).

In light of this conclusion, we need not consider the alternative grounds that Denise's conduct constituted malice and oppression under Civil Code section 3294. This conclusion also disposes of Denise's alternative argument that Thomas should have received only 50 percent of the concealed lottery winnings pursuant to section 1101, subdivision (g), which applies when a spouse's breach of fiduciary duty does not constitute fraud, oppression or malice under Civil Code section 3294.

We find nothing in the language of the statute to justify an exception to the penalty provision of section 1101, subdivision (h) because of the supposed unclean hands of the spouse from whom the asset was concealed. Nor are we cited to legislative history which would suggest such an exception. None of the cases cited by Denise in support of her unclean hands defense is a family law case construing section 1101. This undercuts Denise's primary argument on appeal, that she was justified in concealing the lottery winnings because of Thomas's behavior. The plain meaning of section 1101, subdivision (h) disposes of Denise's argument that there should be a "downward departure in any remedy against Denise" because, as she claims, she was battered emotionally and physically by Thomas. She cites federal law to the effect that evidence of the battered woman's syndrome is a valid basis for a discretionary downward departure of criminal penalties otherwise applicable under federal criminal sentencing guidelines, and to California criminal cases addressing this syndrome. As we have discussed, no such exception is codified into section 1101. The cases cited are off point. The statute provides that, where a spouse conceals assets under circumstances satisfying the criteria for punitive damages under Civil Code section 3294, a penalty representing 100 percent of the concealed asset is warranted. The statute is unambiguous and no exception is provided.

Denise also argues that the order must be reversed because Thomas's attorneys will receive half of the lottery proceeds. Without citation of authority, she asserts that this is counter to the purpose of section 1101. But the plain language of section 1101, subdivision (h) demonstrates legislative intent to enforce the fiduciary obligations of spouses to one another in dissolution proceedings by imposing substantial penalties for breaches of that duty. The order of the family court in this case is consistent with that intent. We find no basis to reverse the order of the family court because of Thomas's fee arrangement. * * *

Disposition

The order of the family court is affirmed. Respondent is to have his costs on appeal.

CHARLES S. VOGEL, P.J., HASTINGS, J., concur.

NOTES

1. *"The starting point is Section 721, which provides that accountability for the management of community assets is a fundamental aspect of the fiduciary duties owed between spouses."* The quote is from *Marriage of Prentis-Margulis & Margulis*, 198 Cal.App.4th 1252, 1269, 130 Cal.Rptr.3d 327 (4th Dist. 2011).

2. *Disclosing credit card transactions in the ordinary course of business.* In *Marriage of Fossum*, 192 Cal.App.4th 336, 121 Cal.Rptr.3d 195 (2d Dist. 2011), a married couple purchased a house. Originally, husband Edward's name alone was on title because his credit score was better than wife Sandra's score. After the purchase, Edward executed a quitclaim deed in favor of himself and Sandra so that both spouses' names appeared on title to the house. A refinance occurred; the lender required that title be changed back to Edward's name alone. After the refinance, Sandra asked Edward to put her name back on title. By that time (2002), however, the marriage was in trouble. Edward told Sandra that he would put her name back on title if she would be willing to " 'behave" and become a 'Godly woman and a good Christian wife,' with a 'heart . . . free of sin.' " Sandra moved out of the house, but before she did, she charged a $24,000 cash advance on a credit card and transferred the loan proceeds into her sole deposit account. Sandra used $13,500 of that money to buy a horse trailer and a car for her son. She used the remainder for necessary living expenses. Sandra did not disclose the cash advance or the purchases to Edward.

The trial court ruling characterizing the house as community property was affirmed on appeal.

Additionally, the trial court awarded Edward ($12,000) payable by Sandra. It found that Sandra breached her fiduciary duty to disclose the cash advance and purchases to Edward, a duty required of her by California Family Code Section 721. Upon breach, Edward's claim of impairment accrued under California Family Code 1101(a). Edward's remedy under the same statute entitled him to one-half of the cash advance incurred by Sandra as his separate property.

3. *Attorney fees shall be awarded upon proof of community property impairment.* The *Fossum* trial court found that Sandra breached her disclosure duties to Edward (California Family Code Section 721) by taking out an undisclosed credit card cash advance (California Family Code Section 1101(a)), as discussed above. Sandra's action impaired Edward's community property interest in the borrowed funds, yet the trial court also held that Sandra's conduct did not rise to a level of wrongdoing that required she pay sanctions in

the form of attorney's fees (California Family Code Section 1101(g)). The appellate court disagreed. It interpreted California Family Code Section 1101(g) to mean that once a breach is proven the trial court lacks discretion to deny attorney's fees. The issue of attorney's fees for Edward was reversed and remanded.

Sandra was in financial straights when she took out the cash advance. She gave half of the advance to her son and kept the other half. Who has the obligation to pay the credit card company for the advance plus interest? What about the harm that would be done to Edward's credit score if Sandra (or Edward) were to default on the cash advance repayment? In light of these concerns, was it fair to Edward for the court to use California Family Code Section 1100(g)? Would it have been fairer to Edward if the court had used California Family Code Section 1100(h) on the theory that Sandra's gift to her child constituted a theft from the community? Could Edward also sue Sandra's son for return of the percentage of the cash advance that his mother gave him, plus interest calculated by the credit card company's interest-due algorithm?

4.   *Money sanctions for failing to disclose after a formal discovery request in a dissolution proceeding.* In a marital dissolution proceeding the trial court may order the payment of sanctions and attorney's fees if one party fails to disclose relevant financial information. In *Marriage of Feldman*, 153 Cal.App.4th 1470, 64 Cal.Rptr.3d 29 (4th Dist. 2007), the husband was ordered to pay sanctions in the amount of $250,000 and attorney's fees of $140,000 for the nondisclosure of various items, including an Israeli government bond, a multimillion dollar house, a 401k retirement account, and various new business entities. *Feldman* appears in Chapter 8.

5.   *Do Family Code statutory remedies supplant tort actions for concealment?* In the context of a final dissolution judgment set-aside proceeding the answer is yes. *Dale v. Dale,* 66 Cal.App.4th 1172, 78 Cal.Rptr.2d 513 (4th Dist. 1998) held that the concealment of community property assets may also provide the basis for a tort cause of action. *Rubenstein v. Rubenstein,* 81 Cal.App.4th 1131, 97 Cal.Rptr.2d 707 (2d Dist. 2000) held otherwise.

Alan and Arteena Rubenstein began living together in 1970, they had a daughter in 1972, they were married in 1976 and they separated in 1984. Alan filed a petition for dissolution in 1986, his listed essentially no community assets. A decade or so after the final dissolution judgment was issued, Arteena learned that Alan's production company had been sued by entities that held rights to rock legend Jimi Hendrix's and psychedelic rock legend George Clinton's music; and that Alan had counterclaimed the plaintiffs in that federal action to assert his ownership rights to Jimi Hendrix's music. As it turned out, Alan's production company, valued by Alan at $1,000 for purposes of the 1986 dissolution proceeding with Arteena, now asserted a claim to Jimi Hendrix and George Clinton music valued in 1998 at an estimated $15 million.

Arteena, sued to set aside the dissolution judgment. But would she be required to bring a related tort claim too?

"We are aware that *Dale* held a defrauded spouse may bring a tort action for concealment of community assets as an alternative to moving to set aside the dissolution judgment. (*Dale v. Dale, supra*, 66 Cal.App.4th at pp. 1178–1183.) However, the *Dale* decision clearly was a major departure from existing law. Where a civil judgment is procured by extrinsic fraud, the normal remedy is to seek equitable relief from the judgment, not to sue in tort. (See, e.g., *Brink v. Brink* (1984) 155 Cal.App.3d 218, 220 [202 Cal.Rptr. 57] [aggrieved spouse brought an independent action in equity to vacate the judgment of dissolution on ground of extrinsic fraud].) Moreover, the absolute litigation privilege of Civil Code section 47, subdivision (b), bars derivative tort actions and "applies to all torts other than malicious prosecution, including fraud, negligence and negligent misrepresentation. [Citation.]" (*Harris v. King* (1998) 60 Cal.App.4th 1185, 1188 [70 Cal.Rptr.2d 790]; accord, *Edwards v. Centex Real Estate Corp.* (1997) 53 Cal.App.4th 15, 28–29 [61 Cal.Rptr.2d 518].)

In any event, leaving aside the soundness of the *Dale* decision, it is no longer operative. *Dale* itself observed, "[f]or judgments entered on or after January 1, 1993, Family Code section 2120 et seq. provides a comprehensive statutory scheme for setting aside such judgments on grounds of actual fraud, perjury, duress, mental incapacity, or mistake. (See *In re Marriage of Varner* (1997) 55 Cal.App.4th 128, 136–137. . . .)" (*Dale v. Dale, supra*, 66 Cal.App.4th at p. 1179, fn. 5.) *Dale* explained: "Because the judgment at issue here was entered in 1988, we have no occasion to address the effect of Family Code section 2120 et seq. on the viability of a tort action for concealment of community assets." (*Ibid.*) * * *

Therefore, we conclude Arteena's remedy under section 2120 et seq. is a traditional setting aside of the judgment, to the exclusion of an action in tort arising out of the underlying proceeding.

Therefore, Arteena was entitled to rely on Alan's testimony in the dissolution trial, wherein he asserted: he never had any ownership interest either in Are You Experienced? Ltd., or in the Hendrix estate and that he had never acquired any royalty or other interest in the record catalogs involving Hendrix, except for three records he produced prior to the marriage. When Arteena came across new information from the federal action, wherein Alan asserted a position that was diametrically opposed to his testimony in the dissolution matter, Arteena was entitled to seek equitable relief pursuant to section 2120 et seq. to vacate the dissolution judgment based on these new facts, which did not exist at the time the underlying matter was adjudicated." *Id.* at 1146–1148, 1151.

By setting aside the final dissolution judgment that was tainted by fraud, Arteena could begin again to rightfully recover her community property interest in activities and property that Alan had failed to disclose or properly value at dissolution. From reading the federal court counterclaim, it appears that Alan put an enormous amount of consistent effort into promoting Jimi Hendrix; and some degree of that effort was expended during Alan's marriage to Arteena. Would *Pereira* (Chapter 5) be the appropriate way to account for the community property labor that Alan put into (what appears to have been) his separate property music production company?

6.   *The involuntary forfeiture of a community property asset may give rise to an impairment claim.* In the case of *Marriage of Beltran*, 183 Cal.App.3d 292, 227 Cal.Rptr. 924 (1st Dist.1986) the husband was an Army colonel when the couple separated. While their dissolution action was pending, the husband was convicted of a felony; as a result, he was dismissed from the Army and stripped of all military benefits, including his pension and accrued leave. As part of the dissolution judgment the trial court charged the husband with receipt of the forfeited pension and leave; the trial court then ordered that the wife be reimbursed for one-half of the benefits ($59,230.50). The award to the wife was upheld on appeal:

> "In our view, wife should not be made in effect to share in a penalty imposed upon husband for his criminal conduct. We accordingly conclude as a matter of equity that criminal conduct on the part of husband which directly caused forfeiture of pension benefits justified the trial court's conclusion that wife was entitled to reimbursement for her share of such lost community property." *Id.* at 295.

When, however, the criminal or tortious conduct results in a financial benefit to the communit, the community estate may be required to bear at least a portion of the ensuing financial burden. In *Marriage of Bell*, 49 Cal.App.4th 300, 56 Cal.Rptr.2d 623 (4th Dist. 1996) the wife embezzled funds from her employer without her husband's knowledge. She settled an ensuing civil suit for $150,000 using community funds. Civil and criminal attorneys' fees and tax penalties were also incurred. The court distinguished between the civil settlement and the other costs and liabilities:

> "In the present case we have an intentional tort (as well as a crime) but we also have benefit to the community. Applying the principles of the cited cases to the facts before us, we conclude that the trial court correctly decided that Wife should be held liable for the attorney fees required for her defense in both the civil and the criminal actions, and that she should be liable also for the state and federal tax liability arising out of the embezzlement, including interest and penalties. Wife engaged in intentional tortious and criminal activity and knowingly accepted the risk that she would be caught and would have to face the consequences. Husband, who knew nothing of the risk and could do nothing to avoid it, should not in fairness bear the same burden once it did go wrong. In this regard our decision here follows the ruling in *Stitt*.
>
> As to the $150,000 civil settlement, however, we find the considerations are different. Wife was still engaged in an intentional

tort, and Husband still knew nothing about it. Here, however, there was uncontradicted testimony that the community received the benefit of the embezzlement. Even if the numbers were somewhat uncertain, it was apparent that the community had received a major infusion of funds over the years, and it was clear that all the embezzled funds had been put to community, and not separate, use. . . .

We hold that the trial court erred by allocating the entire $150,000 settlement, which had previously been paid out of community property, to Wife as part of her share of the community property distribution. The community had shared in the benefit and could properly be asked to share in the cost. Although this was not exactly the outcome in In re Marriage of Hirsch, supra, 211 Cal.App.3d 104, 259 Cal.Rptr. 39, dictum in Hirsch indicated the court there would have approved such a result in this case; the court there stated, "For example, had the wife put the embezzled funds into a community account or other community property, it would have been appropriate for the community to bear the corresponding loss." (Id., at p. 110, fn. 8, 259 Cal.Rptr. 39.)

Here we find that the trial court's resolution of this issue was not supported by the evidence presented and does not reflect a correct analysis and application of the law and we therefore reverse on this issue." *Id.* at 309–310.

7. *The concealment of community property assets may result in criminal charges.* "In a Bakersfield case reported on in the popular legal press, a couple separated. The wife obtained a restraining order to prevent any transfer of community property. The husband violated the order by withdrawing $1.9 million in community funds from two California banks. He then flew to Massachusetts and deposited the money in an account in his father's name. The husband later transferred the funds offshore, first to a bank in the Cayman Islands and finally into a Swiss bank account. The husband was eventually indicted in federal district court for the criminal charge of transmitting stolen property across state lines. The case marks "the first time in California that a husband has been charged criminally with stealing from his wife." Durstman, *Criminalizing Community Property,* CALIFORNIA LAWYER, Feb. 1995 at 23.[4]

Disclosure duties have been held not to extend to a situation where the disclosed information may expose either party to civil or criminal liability, or where state disclosure requirements are preempted by federal law. *Marriage of Reuling*, 23 Cal.App.4th 1428, 28 Cal.Rptr.2d 726 (1st Dist. 1994), presented this latter situation.

In *Reuling*, husband Irvin was the chief financial officer of ADAC Laboratories. During his marriage to Sharon he acquired 450,000 share of ADAC stock and 225,000 ADAC stock options. The couple separated in 1987.

---

[4] Fair use.

Sharon petitioned for dissolution in 1988. Prior to a dissolution trial in 1989, the value of the ADAC shares dropped approximately fifty percent in response to a class action brought against ADAC by the Securities and Exchange Commission (S.E.C.). Sharon alleged, among other issues, that Irvin had a "duty" under California Civil Code Section 5125 [now California Family Code Section § 1000(e)] to disclose "insider" information concerning the value of the stock before it lost its value.

On appeal, the court found no abuse of discretion by the trial court. The trial court held that in the absence of a written agreement or in-court stipulation by the parties to divide the assets before trial the husband was under no obligation to transfer any of the stock to the wife until the dissolution court issued its judgment dividing the community property estate. The decline in the value of the stock was not related to or triggered by the husband's conduct. Besides, said the court, if the husband had disclosed insider information and transferred shares of stock to the wife so that she could sell them before they fell in market value, he would have violated federal law. In that case the wife herself could have been subject to S.E.C. prosecution as a "tippee." The appellate court concluded that federal laws proscribing the use of insider information preempt any state statute purporting to impose a conflicting obligation of disclosure.

SECTION 5. CREDITORS' CLAIMS

How far can creditors pursue community assets to satisfy claims? Separate property assets?

An early nineteenth-century solution to partnership debt is called the jingle rule: "partnership creditors first in partnership assets, separate creditors first in separate assets."[5] The jingle rule entered into The Bankruptcy Act of 1898, but was modified by The Bankruptcy Act of 1978, Section 723. The U.P.A. adheres to the jingle rule. The R.U.P.A. diverges from it. The California Family Code adopts a managerial approach that seems consistent with the R.U.P.A. divergence.

The California managerial approach turns on the basic premise that creditors possess first priority claims to community assets *and* to each spouse's separate property assets. Debts are not characterized. Nor is there a general order of satisfaction rule. Instead, creditors of California spouses are fully protected to reach property necessary to satisfy debt, no matter its character. In turn, the community can seek reimbursement from its partners, or the partners can seek reimbursement from each other or from the community.

A few caveats are worth listing here. Creditors might be barred from reaching property kept in the sole legal control of one spouse; or certain out

---

[5] Henry Hansmann, Reinier Kraakman & Richard Squire, *The Essential Role of Organizational Law*, 110 YALE L.J. 387 (2000) and Henry Hansmann, Reinier Kraakman & Richard Squire, *Law and the Rise of the Firm*, 119 HARV. L. REV. 1333, 1381 (2006).

of state property; or liabilities for debts that are outside the scope of the necessaries of life rule. Additionally, in cases where multiple creditors want to reach the same property, secured creditors have priority over unsecured creditors as to the secured assets; and unsecured family expense creditors have priority claims to community property assets relative to one spouse's unsecured separate property creditors. The lender's intent test (Chapter 2) essentially gives lenders notice of these rules by how it requires a lender who intends to rely only on separate property in satisfying a debt to document its understanding of the consequences of doing so.

California adopted the managerial approach quite deliberately. The process started with the adoption of equal management and control; it proceeded through the enhancement of transmutation standards and the abrogation of order of satisfaction for most matters. The idea animating the transition is to protect creditors as fully as possible so as to inspire their confidence in dealing with married persons. By constrast a system that characterizes debts and allows creditors priority to one or the other character of property incentivizes married persons to engage in transmutations in order to avoid debt (Chapter 1). This leaves it to the creditor to sort out legitimate transmutations from fraudulent ones. Such a system creates obstacles and procedural difficulties for creditors of the sort that could counter-incentivize creditors to adopt practices that restrict credit to married persons generally, or to one or the other spouse more specifically.

In California today, therefore, creditors possess a priority claim to the entirety of the community property under decisional law (*Grolemund v. Cafferata, supra*). Moreover, a creditor's access to community and separate property pools is implicitly confirmed by California Family Code Section 1100, a section that codifies the managerial approach as to community personal property. Additionally, California Family Code Section 720 codifies the spouses' mutual duty to support each other during marriage, which justifies a creditor's attempt to reach either spouse's separate property during the marriage.

Here is a standard *policy* rationale for offering such broad protection to creditors.

During marriage creditors can reach what the spouses have the legal right to control; and either spouse has the legal right to control community personal property. Additionally, the spouses have a statutory obligation to support each other during marriage, which includes the obligation to use separate property for family expenses when community property is not available. The duty of support is determined by the parties' lifestyle, which is to say by the standard of living to which they are accustomed. Finally, the state has a compelling reason to provide creditors with confidence when dealing with married persons.

After a date of separation a spouse owns earnings and accumulations as separate property (California Family Code Section 771). Even so the duty to support a spouse continues, especially if the other spouse is without a sufficient income to be self-supporting (California Family Code Section 720). In the absence of available community property funds, therefore, the ongoing duty to support exposes the earning spouse's postseparation income to creditors with whom the needy spouse contracts for common necessaries of life. After a date of separation the duty of support continues but it is limited to the other spouse's basic necessities. Common necessaries of life are categorical expenditures that include contract debt, housing, food, transportation, and basic medical liabilities (California Family Code Section 914).

Here is an alternative (but still standard) *statutory* rationale for extending broad protections to creditors. It begins with a general rule (California Family Code Section 913(b)(1)). California Family Code Section 913(b)(1), reproduced below, states the rule that "[t]he separate property of a married person is not liable for a debt incurred by the person's spouse before or during marriage." The purpose of the rule is to satisfy due process concerns. California Family Code Section 914, reproduced below, subsequently carves out the massively huge exception, codified as the "necessaries of life" doctrine. The purpose of the exception is to assure creditors that they have claims to the separate property of both spouses in a broad range of situations.

Finally, creditors possess a claim to community property even in those exceptional situations where community property is under the exclusive management and control of a spouse (Section 5 below). So, for example, a bank account in one spouse's name alone does not shield the sums deposited in the account from creditors, a rule in line with the state policy to give creditors maximum protection with minimum procedural barriers or burdens.

To conclude, the managerial system that inspires confidence in creditors when dealing with a married person is the same system that protects individual spouses from overpayment by providing reimbursements. That is the theory.

A. DURING MARRIAGE

The *necessaries of life doctrine* exposes both the community property and the separate property of both spouses to liability for family expenses contracted by either spouse while living together as a married couple. The rationale for the doctrine is found at California Family Code Section 720, which provides that the spouses contract mutual obligations of support.

The doctrine is not limited to contractual debt. Rather, it includes all necessaries of life including medical care not contracted for (emergency room visits and so forth). Therefore, in situations where a debt is incurred in furtherance of the mutual obligation of support the creditor can reach community property, the separate property of the debtor spouse, and the separate property of the nondebtor spouse, regardless of whether the debt is contractual or not.

How is the phrase necessaries of life defined?

Necessaries of life, as discussed above, refers to a category of family expenses that are incurred in furtherance of the spouses' mutual duty to support each other during marriage. These expenses include debts necessary to maintain the spouses' lifestyle, their economic position, their social position, and so on. A spendthrift high-income family may count among their necessary expenditures things that seem frivolous to a frugal high-income family. For that reasons, one sees included among the necessaries of life category anything from mortgage and utility payments to private club fees, independent school tuition, equestrian training expenditures, weekly salon treatments, designer clothing, luxury car leases, vacations and so on.

B. AFTER A DATE OF SEPARATION

After a date of separation the duty of mutual support continues unless the spouses agree otherwise. Parties can, but often do not, modify the duty of mutual support by contract. Instead, it is not uncommon for parties to simply split up, each going a separate way, relying typically on wages to set up a new household.

If one spouse needs the support of the other spouse after the date of separation the *common necessaries of life doctrine* comes into play. Common necessaries of life are categorical expenses that include but are restricted to basic necessities such as housing, food, utilities, transportation, clothing, and basic medical needs. The doctrine provides that a needy spouse can contract for common necessaires of life and the creditor can extend those necessities to the debtor spouse knowing that in event of the debtor spouse's default the other (nondebtor) spouse's assets can be reached. The community property is liable for the ongoing debts since the debtor spouse owns a one-half interest in that property; the separate property of the spouse who purchased the common necessaries is liable based on contract; and the nondebtor spouse's separate property is liable because of the duty of support.

The California system permits creditors to reach the nondebtor spouse's separate property without a judgment. To have a system that otherwise blocks creditors from the nondebtor spouse in a period of separation would be to penalize the needy spouse, the spouse who cares for children in the home, the spouse who is in the process of work retraining, the spouse with disabilities, the spouse in need.

Additionally, shielding a non-debtor spouse from liability after a period of separation would violate the state policy of mutual support, a policy so strong that it is neither waivable nor subject to contractual modification *during* marriage. Therefore, the rule is that after a date of separation the community property, the separate property of the debtor spouse, and the separate property of the nondebtor spouse remain liable for debts incurred for common necessaries of life subject to a reimbursement from community property when it is available. California Family Code Section 914(b).

What are common necessaries of life?

Common necessaries of life are expenses that are necessary to sustain a basic (bare minimum) standard of living. California rejects the station in life rule during periods of separation. Therefore, while the nondebtor spouse is liable for common necessaries of life, that liability stops short of lifestyle expenses. Therefore, common necessaries of life include housing, utilities, transportation, and basic medical expenditures. They do not include lifestyle expenses or housekeeping expenses.

C. CONTRACT DEBTS FOR NON-SUPPORT RELATED EXPENSES

The creditors of a spouse's non-support related expenditures are treated as follows. These creditors possess a priority claim to the debtor spouse's separate property. For contractual debts, the lender's intent test (Chapter 2) in effect requires that the creditor evidence its understanding of this reality by confirming that the credit is extended solely on the basis of the debtor spouse's separate property assets. The lender's intent test documents the creditor's expectation to satisfy non-support related expenditures from the debtor spouse's separate property in the case of default.

They retain claims to community property too, since the debtor spouse owns a one-half interest in community property. Nevertheless, claims are subordinate to the claims of the community's creditors.

And these creditors are barred from reaching the nondebtor spouse's separate property unless the nondebtor spouse is made party to a recovery action.

D. TORT JUDGMENT CREDITORS

Tort judgments are one of the few remaining areas where California continues to rely on an order of satisfaction approach rather than on a managerial/reimbursement.

Generally, an order of satisfaction approach is no longer favored because it creates more problems than it resolves. An order of satisfaction approach does not fully protect contract creditors. Rather, it places obstacles and burdens in the creditor's path, thereby reducing creditor confidence in dealing with married persons and possibly restricting equal access to credit for married individuals.

Some of the above problems are not present in the area of tort judgment satisfaction, which is perhaps why the order of satisfaction approach, found at California Family Code Section 1000, reproduced below, continues to be used.

Tort liabilities are characterized depending on whether the tortfeasor spouse's act or omission occurred while he or she was performing an activity for the benefit of the community or not.

A tort that is a community liability is satisfied first from community property and second from the tortfeasor's separate property.

A tort that is a separate liability is satisfied first from the tortfeasor's separate property and second from that person's share of the community property.

E. LIABILITY OF QUASI-COMMUNITY PROPERTY

Property purchased while domiciled outside of the state is quasi-community property once a dissolution petition is filed (Chapter 4).

Quasi-community property is available to satisfy debts under California Family Code Section 912, reproduced below.

The section was added to prevent quasi-community property from being treated as separate property for purposes of debt satisfaction.

The current rule makes quasi-community property subject to the same rules as community property.

F. LIABILITY OF QUASI-MARITAL PROPERTY

Quasi-marital property comes into existence at the option of the person who is adjudged a putative spouse.

If the putative spouse opts for a Family Code dissolution, property and debts are divided in accordance with the rules on community and quasi-community property (Chapter 4). Creditors' rights to reach quasi-marital property to satisfy a debt are the same as if the parties had been validly married.

The rationale for the outcome is reliance. The parties held themselves out as married, since the putative spouse in good faith believed him or herself to be married. Creditors who rely to their detriment on that representation retain all rights. Here again, the state policy is to provide creditors with confidence when dealing with married persons. The fact that the parties are only putatively married does not change the policy motives that animate the managerial system.

G. LIABILITY OF COMMUNITY REAL PROPERTY LOCATED IN ANOTHER STATE

Real property acquired outside of California with community property funds is community property both in character (Chapter 2) and for purposes of debt satisfaction. It is not quasi-community property. Nor is it shielded from creditors simply by the fact that it is outside the state. A California court has personal jurisdiction to order any necessary conveyance to satisfy the claims of creditors. California Civil Procedure Code Section 708.205 states the rule. See also California Civil Procedure Code Section 708.180.

H. LIABILITY FOR PREMARITAL DEBTS

The general rule is that the community property is not liable for a spouse's (closed) premarital debt. A corollary to the rule is that at dissolution premarital debts are assigned to the debtor spouse.

The reality of revolving debt, credit cards, creates a large exception to the general rule for debts that are incurred before but recontracted during marriage.

Revolving or open debt is debt that is essentially recontracted on a periodic basis. What was premarital debt, eventually, over time, turns into a debt incurred during marriage. When that happens, the creditor obtains claims to the community property and to the nondebtor and debtor spouses' separate property, as discussed above.

I. LIABILITY FOR PREMARITAL SUPPORT OBLIGATIONS

Here the clarity of the statute, California Family Code Section 915, reflects the seriousness of the state policy toward one type of premarital obligation: the premarital support obligation to a former spouse or a child. Premarital support obligations are satisfiable out of the community property of a subsequent marriage. The rule places premarital support obligees on the same plane as any other community creditor of the subsequent marriage.

A premarital support claim is enforceable against the community property of the obligor spouse. And it is enforceable against the separate property income of the obligor spouse.

It is not generally enforceable against the earnings of the nonobligor spouse by decisional law. Of course, this limitation presumes that the nonoligor's earnings have been properly segregated under California Family Code Section 911, discussed above.

Thus if the obligor spouse uses community property of the subsequent marriage to satisfy a support obligation at a time when he or she also has separate property, the community property of the subsequent marriage is entitled to a reimbursement.

If the obligor spouse has available separate property income (for example from a trust fund), he or she is obligated to use the separate property income for a premarital support obligation. If community property is used at a time when the separate property income is available, the community is entitled to a reimbursement, from the obligor spouse, "in the amount of the separate income, not exceeding the property in the community estate so applied."

Where an obligor is a trust beneficiary, a premarital support obligee has other options as well. By decisional law, the obligee can sue the trust directly rather than be required to pursue trust income payments from the obligor-beneficiary. It would seem that the community of the subsequent marriage would also have the option to seek its reimbursement directly from the trust.

WEST'S ANNOTATED CALIFORNIA FAMILY CODE

§ 900. Construction of part

Unless the provision or context otherwise requires, the definitions in this chapter govern the construction of this part.

(Stats. 1992, c. 162 (A.B. 2650), § 10, operative Jan. 1, 1994.)

§ 902. Debt

"Debt" means an obligation incurred by a married person before or during marriage, whether based on contract, tort, or otherwise.

(Stats. 1992, c. 162 (A.B. 2650), § 10, operative Jan. 1, 1994.)

§ 903. Time debt is incurred

A debt is "incurred" at the following time:

(a) In the case of a contract, at the time the contract is made.

(b) In the case of a tort, at the time the tort occurs.

(c) In other cases, at the time the obligation arises.

(Stats. 1992, c. 162 (A.B. 2650), § 10, operative Jan. 1, 1994.)

§ 910. Community estate; liability for debts

(a) Except as otherwise expressly provided by statute, the community estate is liable for a debt incurred by either spouse before or during marriage, regardless of which spouse has the management and control of the property and regardless of whether one or both spouses are parties to the debt or to a judgment for the debt.

(b) "During marriage" for purposes of this section does not include the period after the date of separation, as defined in Section 70, and before a judgment of dissolution of marriage or legal separation of the parties.

(Stats. 1992, c. 162 (A.B. 2650), § 10, operative Jan. 1, 1994; Stats. 2016, c. 114 (S.B. 1255), § 3, eff. Jan. 1, 2017.)

§ 911. Earnings of married persons; liability for premarital debts; earnings held in deposit accounts

(a) The earnings of a married person during marriage are not liable for a debt incurred by the person's spouse before marriage. After the earnings of the married person are paid, they remain not liable so long as they are held in a deposit account in which the person's spouse has no right of withdrawal and are uncommingled with other property in the community estate, except property insignificant in amount.

(b) As used in this section:

(1) "Deposit account" has the meaning prescribed in paragraph (29) of subdivision (a) of Section 9102 of the Commercial Code.

(2) "Earnings" means compensation for personal services performed, whether as an employee or otherwise.

(Stats. 1992, c. 162 (A.B. 2650), § 10, operative Jan. 1, 1994. Amended by Stats. 1999, c. 991 (S.B. 45), § 42.5, operative July 1, 2001.)

§ 912. Quasi-community property; treatment

For the purposes of this part, quasi-community property is liable to the same extent, and shall be treated the same in all other respects, as community property.

(Stats. 1992, c. 162 (A.B. 2650), § 10, operative Jan. 1, 1994.)

§ 913. Separate property of married person; liability for debt

(a) The separate property of a married person is liable for a debt incurred by the person before or during marriage.

(b) Except as otherwise provided by statute:

(1) The separate property of a married person is not liable for a debt incurred by the person's spouse before or during marriage.

(2) The joinder or consent of a married person to an encumbrance of community estate property to secure payment of a debt incurred by the person's spouse does not subject the person's separate property to liability for the debt unless the person also incurred the debt.

(Stats. 1992, c. 162 (A.B. 2650), § 10, operative Jan. 1, 1994.)

§ 914. Personal liability for debts incurred by spouse; separate property applied to satisfaction of debt; statute of limitations

(a) Notwithstanding Section 913, a married person is personally liable for the following debts incurred by the person's spouse during marriage:

(1) A debt incurred for necessaries of life of the person's spouse before the date of separation of the spouses.

(2) Except as provided in Section 4302, a debt incurred for common necessaries of life of the person's spouse after the date of separation of the spouses.

(b) The separate property of a married person may be applied to the satisfaction of a debt for which the person is personally liable pursuant to this section. If separate property is so applied at a time when nonexempt property in the community estate or separate property of the person's spouse is available but is not applied to the satisfaction of the debt, the married person is entitled to reimbursement to the extent such property was available.

(c)(1) Except as provided in paragraph (2), the statute of limitations set forth in Section 366.2 of the Code of Civil Procedure shall apply if the spouse for whom the married person is personally liable dies.

(2) If the surviving spouse had actual knowledge of the debt prior to the expiration of the period set forth in 366.2 of the Code of Civil Procedure and the personal representative of the deceased spouse's estate failed to provide the creditor asserting the claim under this section with a timely written notice of the probate administration of the estate in the manner provided for pursuant to Section 9050 of the Probate Code, the statute of limitations set forth in Section 337 or 339 of the Code of Civil Procedure, as applicable, shall apply.

(d) For purposes of this section, "date of separation" has the same meaning as set forth in Section 70.

(Stats. 1992, c. 162 (A.B. 2650), § 10, operative Jan. 1, 1994. Amended by Stats. 1993, c. 219 (A.B. 1500), § 100.4; Stats. 2001, c. 702 (A.B. 539), § 1; Stats. 2014, c. 71 (S.B. 1304), § 53; Stats. 2016, c. 114 (S.B. 1255), § 4, eff. Jan. 1, 2017.)

§ 915. Child or spousal support obligation not arising out of marriage; reimbursement of community

(a) For the purpose of this part, a child or spousal support obligation of a married person that does not arise out of the marriage shall be treated as a debt incurred before marriage, regardless of whether a court order for support is made or modified before or during marriage and regardless of whether any installment payment on the obligation accrues before or during marriage.

(b) If property in the community estate is applied to the satisfaction of a child or spousal support obligation of a married person that does not arise out of the marriage, at a time when nonexempt separate income of the person is available but is not applied to the satisfaction of the obligation, the community estate is entitled to reimbursement from the person in the amount of the separate income, not exceeding the property in the community estate so applied.

(c) Nothing in this section limits the matters a court may take into consideration in determining or modifying the amount of a support order, including, but not limited to, the earnings of the spouses of the parties.

(Stats. 1992, c. 162 (A.B. 2650), § 10, operative Jan. 1, 1994. Amended by Stats. 1993, c. 219 (A.B. 1500), § 100.5.)

§ 916. Division of property; subsequent liability; right of reimbursement; interest and attorney's fees

(a) Notwithstanding any other provision of this chapter, after division of community and quasi-community property pursuant to Division 7 (commencing with Section 2500):

(1) The separate property owned by a married person at the time of the division and the property received by the person in the division is liable for a debt incurred by the person before or during marriage and the person is personally liable for the debt, whether or not the debt was assigned for payment by the person's spouse in the division.

(2) The separate property owned by a married person at the time of the division and the property received by the person in the division is not liable for a debt incurred by the person's spouse before or during marriage, and the person is not personally liable for the debt, unless the debt was assigned for payment by the person in the division of the property. Nothing in this paragraph affects the liability of property for the satisfaction of a lien on the property.

(3) The separate property owned by a married person at the time of the division and the property received by the person in the division is liable for a debt incurred by the person's spouse before or during marriage, and the person is personally liable for the debt, if the debt was assigned for payment by the person in the division of the property. If a money judgment for the debt is entered after the division, the property is not subject to enforcement of the judgment and the judgment may not be enforced against the married person, unless the person is made a party to the judgment for the purpose of this paragraph.

(b) If property of a married person is applied to the satisfaction of a money judgment pursuant to subdivision (a) for a debt incurred by the person that is assigned for payment by the person's spouse, the person has a right of reimbursement from the person's spouse to the extent of the property applied, with interest at the legal rate, and may recover reasonable attorney's fees incurred in enforcing the right of reimbursement.

(Stats. 1992, c. 162 (A.B. 2650), § 10, operative Jan. 1, 1994.)

§ 920. Conditions governing right of reimbursement

A right of reimbursement provided by this part is subject to the following provisions:

(a) The right arises regardless of which spouse applies the property to the satisfaction of the debt, regardless of whether the property is applied to the satisfaction of the debt voluntarily or involuntarily, and regardless of whether the debt to which the property is applied is satisfied in whole or in part. The right is subject to an express written waiver of the right by the spouse in whose favor the right arises.

(b) The measure of reimbursement is the value of the property or interest in property at the time the right arises.

(c) The right shall be exercised not later than the earlier of the following times:

(1) Within three years after the spouse in whose favor the right arises has actual knowledge of the application of the property to the satisfaction of the debt.

(2) In proceedings for division of community and quasi-community property pursuant to Division 7 (commencing with Section 2500) or in proceedings upon the death of a spouse.

(Stats. 1992, c. 162 (A.B. 2650), § 10, operative Jan. 1, 1994.)

§ 930. Liability for debts enforced on or after Jan. 1, 1985

Except as otherwise provided by statute, this part governs the liability of separate property and property in the community estate and the personal liability of a married person for a debt enforced on or after January 1, 1985, regardless of whether the debt was incurred before, on, or after that date.

(Stats. 1992, c. 162 (A.B. 2650), § 10, operative Jan. 1, 1994. Amended by Stats. 1993, c. 219 (A.B. 1500), § 100.6.)

§ 1000. Liability for injury or damage caused by spouse; property subject to satisfaction of liability; satisfaction out of insurance proceeds; limitation on exercise of reimbursement right

(a) A married person is not liable for any injury or damage caused by the other spouse except in cases where the married person would be liable therefor if the marriage did not exist.

(b) The liability of a married person for death or injury to person or property shall be satisfied as follows:

(1) If the liability of the married person is based upon an act or omission which occurred while the married person was performing an activity for the benefit of the community, the liability shall first be satisfied from the community estate and second from the separate property of the married person.

(2) If the liability of the married person is not based upon an act or omission which occurred while the married person was performing an activity for the benefit of the community, the liability shall first be satisfied from the separate property of the married person and second from the community estate.

(c) This section does not apply to the extent the liability is satisfied out of proceeds of insurance for the liability, whether the proceeds are from property in the community estate or from separate property. Notwithstanding Section 920, no right of reimbursement under this section shall be exercised more than seven years after the spouse in whose favor the right arises has actual knowledge of the application of the property to the satisfaction of the debt.

(Stats. 1992, c. 162 (A.B. 2650), § 10, operative Jan. 1, 1994. Amended by Stats. 1993, c. 219 (A.B. 1500), § 100.7.)

SECTION 6. PRIMARY AND EXCLUSIVE MANAGEMENT AND CONTROL OF COMMUNITY PROPERTY

As discussed above, there are different gradations of management and control rights in the California community property system.

Equal management and control is the rule for community personal property.

Dual management and control is required for consequential transactions involving community real property.

There are four situations prescribed by law in which community property is rightfully under the primary or exclusive management and control of one spouse but not the other.[6] *Primary* management and control pertains to community property business management. *Exclusive* control arises in the case of sole bank accounts, conservatorships, and domestic violence.

A. ONE SPOUSE HAS EXCLUSIVE ACCESS TO A SOLE BANK ACCOUNT

A married person with a bank account in his or her name alone has exclusive access to that account (Chapter 5).

Exclusive access to the account includes the exclusive right to obtain information about the account and the exclusive right to withdraw sums on deposit from the account.

Exclusive access to the bank account does not mean that the sole account owner is the separate property owner of the sums on deposit in the account (Chapters 2 and 5). All sums on deposit in any account of a married person are presumed to be community property absent contrary evidence. California Probate Code Section 5305, reproduced in Chapter 2. Both spouses have beneficial ownership to community property sums on deposit, both are legal managers of those sums, and therefore, creditors can reach the sums on deposit in a sole account to satisfy debts incurred by either spouse.

California Family Code Section 1101(c) provides a remedy specific to sole accounts: the spouse whose name does not appear on the account may petition a court for an order to add his or her name to the account.

B. ONE SPOUSE OPERATES OR MANAGES A COMMUNITY PROPERTY BUSINESS

A spouse who operates or manages a business that is all or substantially all community property has the *primary* right to manage and control the business. On a day to day basis, primary control is, effectively, exclusive control. The difference between the two concepts is subtle, but important.

California Family Code Section 1100(d) defines primary control as exclusive control ("*may act alone in all transactions*") limited by disclosure provisions for certain consequential transactions ("*but shall give prior written notice to the other spouse*")

> § 1101(d): " . . . Primary management and control means that the managing spouse *may act alone in all transactions but shall give prior written notice to the other spouse* of any sale, lease, exchange,

---

[6] The ideas herein were developed in other publications. See *e.g.*, Jo Carrillo, *Financial Interpersonal Violence: When Assets and Transactions are Weapons*, 22 DOMESTIC VIOLENCE REPORT 1 (2017).

encumbrance, or other disposition of all or substantially all of the personal property used in the operation of the business (including personal property used for agricultural purposes), whether or not title to that property is held in the name of only spouse. . . ." (Italics added.)

The statutory grant of primary management and control of a community property business in California Family Code Section 1100(e) includes disclosure responsibilities under California Family Code Section 721. These duties last during marriage and through dissolution (see Chapters 7 and 8).

Separate property businesses are not generally subject to California Family Code Section 1100(e), especially if and when the community benefits from the business. See, for example, *Marriage of Brandes*, 239 Cal.App.4th 1461, 192 Cal.Rptr.3d 1 (4th Dist. 2015), a case that ties together the basic theories for apportioning commingled assets, commingled deposit accounts, purchases from commingled deposit accounts, and management and control rights.

C. ONE SPOUSE HAS A CONSERVATOR, THE OTHER SPOUSE HAS LEGAL CAPACITY

The general rule is that management and control of community property when one or both spouses is under conservatorship is governed by the Probate Code, as indicated in California Family Code Section 1103, reproduced below.

If one spouse has a conservator the spouse with legal capacity has exclusive management and control of community property. See specifically California Probate Code Section 3051.

Here is the first instance where "exclusive" means exclusive. Not primary, as with a community property business; or exclusive as to the account but equal as to the sums on deposit in the account, as with a sole bank account.

WEST'S ANNOTATED CALIFORNIA FAMILY CODE

§ 1103. Management and control of community property; one or both spouses having conservator of estate or lacking legal capacity

(a) Where one or both of the spouses either has a conservator of the estate or lacks legal capacity to manage and control community property, the procedure for management and control (which includes disposition) of the community property is that prescribed in Part 6 (commencing with Section 3000) of Division 4 of the Probate Code.

(b) Where one or both spouses either has a conservator of the estate or lacks legal capacity to give consent to a gift of community personal property or a disposition of community personal property without a valuable consideration as required by Section 1100 or to a sale, conveyance, or encumbrance of community personal property for which a consent is required by Section 1100, the procedure for that gift, disposition, sale, conveyance, or encumbrance is that prescribed in Part 6 (commencing with Section 3000) of Division 4 of the Probate Code.

(c) Where one or both spouses either has a conservator of the estate or lacks legal capacity to join in executing a lease, sale, conveyance, or encumbrance of community real property or any interest therein as required by Section 1102, the procedure for that lease, sale, conveyance, or encumbrance is that prescribed in Part 6 (commencing with Section 3000) of Division 4 of the Probate Code.

(Stats. 1992, c. 162 (A.B. 2650), § 10, operative Jan. 1, 1994.)

WEST'S ANNOTATED CALIFORNIA PROBATE CODE

§ 3051. Community property

(a) Subject to Section 3071 [relating to joinder], the right of a spouse to manage and control community property, including the right to dispose of community property, is not affected by the lack or alleged lack of legal capacity of the other spouse.

(b) Except as provided in subdivision (c), if one spouse has legal capacity and the other has a conservator:

(1) The spouse who has legal capacity has the *exclusive* management and control of the community property including, subject to Section 3071 [joinder], the *exclusive* power to dispose of the community property.

(2) The community property is not part of the conservatorship estate.

(c) [Provides that the spouse with legal capacity may opt to have all or some of the community property be included in or managed, control, and disposed of as part of the conservatorship estate.]

. . .

(Stats. 1990, c. 79 (A.B. 759), § 14, operative July 1, 1991.) (Italics added.)

D. ONE SPOUSE OBTAINS A COURT ORDER

A spouse may petition for a restraining order as to property (Section 6D below).

The Domestic Violence Prevention Act (DVPA), which appears in the Family Code, extends the right to seek a restraining order to nonmarital and dating partners as well (Section 6D below).

In both situations a court also has the power to order whatever is necessary to effect a restraining order. Necessity may require that the respondent be restrained and, correlatively, that the petitioner be granted exclusive control over the particular asset that is the subject of the restraining order.

California has adopted an enhanced version of the Uniform Interstate Enforcement of Domestic Violence Prevention Orders Act as part of the DVPA. The uniform act makes California DVPA restraining orders substantively enforceable in eleven other adopting states, on military bases, and on tribal lands that authorize the use of protective orders. California Family Code Sections 6400 through 6409.

1.   Ex Parte Restraining Orders During Dissolution

During dissolution, a spouse may petition a court ex parte to restrain the other spouse from exercising specific management and control rights for a particular purpose, as to a particular asset, for a specific time. Depending on the circumstances, restraining one spouse's management and control rights may necessitate a grant of exclusive management and control over the same property to the petitioner.

An ex parte order may extend to community property, quasi-community property, or separate property assets.

WEST'S ANNOTATED CALIFORNIA FAMILY CODE

§ 2045. Ex parte protective orders

During the pendency of the proceeding, on application of a party in the manner provided by Part 4 (commencing with Section 240) of Division 2, the court may issue ex parte any of the following orders:

(a) An order restraining any person from *transferring, encumbering, hypothecating, concealing, or in any way disposing of any property, real or personal, whether community, quasi-community, or separate, except* in the usual course of business or *for the necessities of life,* and if the order is directed against a party, requiring that party to notify the other party of any proposed extraordinary expenditures and to account to the court for all extraordinary expenditures.

(b) A protective order, as defined in Section 6218, and any other order as provided in Article 1 (commencing with Section 6320) of Chapter 2 of Part 4 of Division 10.

(Added by Stats. 1993, c. 219 (A.B. 1500), § 106.7.) (Italics added.)

§ 242. Deadline for hearing on the petition

(a) Within 21 days, or, if good cause appears to the court, 25 days from the date that a temporary restraining order is granted or denied, a hearing shall be held on the petition. If no request for a temporary restraining order is made, the hearing shall be held within 21 days, or, if good cause appears to the court, 25 days from the date that the petition is filed.

(b) If a hearing is not held within the time provided in subdivision (a), the court may nonetheless hear the matter, but the temporary restraining order shall no longer be enforceable unless it is extended under Section 245.

(Added by Stats. 1993, c. 219 (A.B. 1500), § 85.4. Amended by Stats. 2010, c. 572 (A.B. 1596), § 7, operative Jan. 1, 2012; Stats. 2015, c. 411 (A.B. 1081), § 4, eff. Jan. 1, 2016.)

§ 245. Continuance

(a) The respondent shall be entitled, as a matter of course, to one continuance for a reasonable period, to respond to the petition.

(b) Either party may request a continuance of the hearing, which the court shall grant on a showing of good cause. The request may be in writing before or at the hearing or orally at the hearing. The court may also grant a continuance on its own motion.

(c) If the court grants a continuance, any temporary restraining order that has been issued shall remain in effect until the end of the continued hearing, unless otherwise ordered by the court. In granting a continuance, the court may modify or terminate a temporary restraining order.

(d) If the court grants a continuance, the extended temporary restraining order shall state on its face the new date of expiration of the order.

(e) A fee shall not be charged for the extension of the temporary restraining order.

(Stats. 1992, c. 162 A.B. 2650), § 10, operative Jan 1, 1994. Amended by Stats. 2010, c. 572 (A.B. 1596), § 10, operative Jan. 1, 2012; Stats. 2015, c. 411 (A.B. 1081), § 6, eff. Jan. 1, 2016.)

§ 246. Grant of denial on date petition submitted

A request for a temporary restraining order described in Section 240, issued without notice, shall be granted or denied on the same day that the petition is submitted to the court, unless the petition is filed too late in the day to permit effective review, in which case the order shall be granted or denied on the next day of judicial business in sufficient time for the order to be filed that day with the clerk of the court.

(Added by Stats. 1993, c. 148 (A.B. 1331), § 1. Amended by Stats. 2010, c. 572 (A.B. 1596), § 11, operative Jan. 1, 2012.)

2. Domestic Violence Prevention Act Restraining Orders

The Domestic Violence Prevention Act, or DVPA, was adopted in 1993 as part of the first comprehensive Family Code, which went into effect on January 1, 1994.

Found at Section 6200 et seq. the DVPA applies broadly to many types of familial and intimate relationships.

The DVPA allows a court to restrain one person from having contact with another person. A domestic violence restraining order (DVRO) can be either emergency or protective.

Here are the definitional sections from the DVPA.

WEST'S ANNOTATED CALIFORNIA FAMILY CODE

§ 6203. "Abuse" defined

(a) For purposes of this act, "abuse" means any of the following:

(1) To intentionally or recklessly cause or attempt to cause bodily injury.

(2) Sexual assault.

(3) To place a person in reasonable apprehension of imminent serious bodily injury to that person or to another.

(4) To engage in any behavior that has been or could be enjoined pursuant to 6320.

(b) Abuse is not limited to the actual infliction of physical injury or assault.

(Added by Stats. 1993, c. 219 (A.B. 1500), § 154. Amended by Stats. 1998, c. 581 (A.B. 2801), § 16; Stats. 2014, c. 635 (A.B. 2089), § 2, eff. Jan.1, 2015; Stats. 2015, c. 303 (A.B. 731), § 149, eff. Jan. 1, 2016.)

———

The terms "affinity," "cohabitant" and "dating relationship" are defined in California Family Code Sections 6205, 6209, and 6210, reproduced below.

WEST'S ANNOTATED CALIFORNIA FAMILY CODE

§ 6205. "Affinity" defined

"Affinity," when applied to the marriage relation, signifies the connection existing in consequence of marriage between each of the married persons and the blood relatives of the other.

(Added by Stats. 1993, c. 219 (A.B. 1500), § 154.)

§ 6209. "Cohabitant" defined

"Cohabitant" means a person who regularly resides in the household. "Former cohabitant" means a person who formerly regularly resided in the household.

(Added by Stats. 1993, c. 219 (A.B. 1500), § 154.)

§ 6210. "Dating relationship" defined

"Dating relationship" means frequent, intimate associations primarily characterized by the expectation of affection or sexual involvement independent of financial considerations.

(Added by Stats. 2001, c. 110 (A.B. 362), § 1.)

§ 6211. "Domestic violence" defined

"Domestic violence" is abuse perpetrated against any of the following persons:

(a) A spouse or former spouse.

(b) A cohabitant or former cohabitant, as defined in Section 6209.

(c) A person with whom the respondent is having or has had a dating or engagement relationship.

(d) A person with whom the respondent has had a child, where the presumption applies that the male parent is the father of the child of the female parent under the Uniform Parentage Act (Part 3 (commencing with Section 7600) of Division 12).

(e) A child of a party or a child who is the subject of an action under the Uniform Parentage Act, where the presumption applies that the male parent is the father of the child to be protected.

(f) Any other person related by consanguinity or affinity within the second degree.

(Added by Stats. 1993, c. 219 (A.B. 1500), § 154.)

———

A domestic violence "emergency protective order," DVEPO, process is started by the call of a law enforcement officer to a scene. A DVEPO can be issued by a judge day or night. The standard of issuance under California Family Code Section 6250 is "[i]mmediate and present danger of domestic violence, based on the person's allegation of a recent incident of abuse or threat of abuse by the person against whom the order is sought." The fact that a married person or intimate partner has left their home to avoid abuse does not preclude that person from seeking an emergency protective order. California Family Code Section 6254.

Generally economic and financial abuse cannot be addressed by the DVEPO process. The theory being that economic and financial abuse pose no immediate and present danger to the person who seeks the emergency protective order (DVEPO). To address such issues, a party must use the non-emergency protective order process.

The next few paragraphs discuss financial abuse and economic abuse. Although the two forms of abuse are to date conflated in the advocacy and law review literature they are in fact distinguishable. Financial abuse is abuse related to specific assets and transactions whereas economic abuse is behavior that threatens the other spouse's financial wellbeing in a general sense.

At its most general, financial abuse meets the DVPA standard in that it "disturbs the peace of the other party." In a specific manifestation, financial abuse may involve the other spouse or intimate partner, third-party creditors, impersonating the other spouse or forging the other spouse's or intimate partner's signature to defraud third-party transactors, or other transaction-specific acts of oppression, fraud and malice. *Marriage of Lezine* is an example of a paradigmatic financial abuse case.

3. Obtaining Exclusive Management and Control to Prevent Financial Abuse

A non-emergency protective order is issued ex parte, after notice and hearing; or it is issued in a judgment. Restraining orders can be temporary or permanent. Family Code time frames for obtaining a restraining order are expedited relative to Civil Code time frames. Additionally, Family Code protective orders are no-fee.

California Family Code Section 6300 permits a trial court to issue a (non-emergency) protective order "to restrain any person for the purpose of preventing a recurrence of domestic violence . . . " and to give the parties "a period sufficient to enable these persons to seek a resolution of the causes of the violence." California Family Code Section 6220. The policy underlying the issuance of nonemergency restraining orders is preventative; the statute makes this clear. Even so, the standard for issuance under California Family Code Section 6300 is " . . . reasonable proof of a past act or acts of abuse . . . " (By contrast, after a hearing in a

Civil Code harassment case the evidentiary standard of proof may be higher.)

A respondent named in a domestic violence restraining order (DVRO) petition has an opportunity to respond. If the respondent fails to file a response brief in the matter, the judge shall "decide the appeal on the record, the opening brief, and any oral argument by the appellant." California Rules of Court, rule 8.220(a)(2), formerly 17(a). Reversal is permitted only if prejudicial error is shown. The same understanding is incorporated into the 2014 amendments to California Family Code Section 6300, which establishes the new rule that "[t]he court may issue an order under this part based solely on the affidavit or testimony of the person requesting the restraining order." The amendment went into effect on January 1, 2015.

In short, while the policy of the DVPA non-emergency order process is to prevent future acts of domestic violence, obtaining a DVRO does not require proof of the likelihood of future abuse, nor does it require proof that great and irreparable harm would result without the restraining order. (*Compare* this DVPA standard *with* California Civil Procedure 527.6(d).) In fact such evidence might be impractical to obtain thereby increasing the risk of intimate partner violence in the present or immediate future. An emergent understanding of the legal relationship between a past act of abuse and the prevention of a future act of abuse is discussed in *Rodriguez v. Menjivar*, 243 Cal.App.4th 816, 196 Cal.Rtpr.3d 816 (2d Dist. 2015), discussed *infra*. On the same theory, the length of time since the last act of abuse does not determine whether a restraining order should be granted. Instead, the DVPA instructs the court to consider reasonable proof in light of the circumstances.

California Family Code Section 6203, reproduced below, defines the word "abuse." The definition of abuse under the DVPA " . . . is not limited to the actual infliction of physical injury or assault." California Family Code Section 6203(d) links the basic definition to yet another definition of abuse found at California Family Code Section 6320, reproduced below. Additionally, the legislature states that the California Family Code Section 6203 definition can stretch to include any behavior designed to exert coercive control and power over another person. Historical and Statutory Notes, 2014 Legislation, SECTION 1.

To that end California Family Code Section 6320 provides that a court may issue an ex parte order for a number of behaviors including those that " . . . destroy the peace of the other party . . . "

With this framework, it becomes clear that intimate partner abuse (our topic here) can include financial interpersonal violence.

A preventative measure for addressing financial interpersonal violence, therefore, would be to seek a restraining order to prevent the respondent from dissipating a particular asset, in a particular way, for a particular time. If the DVRO is granted, it may be necessary to also obtain a corollary order to vest the petitioner with (temporary) exclusive control over the same asset or assets. The grant of exclusive authority must authorize the petitioner to take whatever action is necessary to prevent dissipation of the asset for the specified time period; and may also extend to ordinary acts of management and control.

WEST'S ANNOTATED CALIFORNIA FAMILY CODE

§ 6320. Ex parte order enjoining contact; credibly or falsely impersonating; or destroying personal property; protection for companion animals

(a)   The court may issue an ex parte order enjoining a party from molesting, attacking, striking, stalking, threatening, sexually assaulting, battering, credibly impersonating as described in Section 528.5 of the Penal Code, falsely personating as described in Section 529 of the Penal Code, harassing, telephoning, including, but not limited to, making annoying telephone calls as described in Section 653m of the Penal Code, destroying personal property, contacting, either directly or indirectly, by mail or otherwise, coming within a specified distance of, or *disturbing the peace of the other party*, and, in the discretion of the court, on a showing of good cause, of other named family or household members.

(b)   On a showing of good cause, the court may include in a protective order a grant to the petitioner of the exclusive care, possession, or control of any animal owned, possessed, leased, kept, or held by either the petitioner or the respondent or a minor child residing in the residence or household of either the petitioner or the respondent. The court may order the respondent to stay away from the animal and forbid the respondent from taking, transferring, encumbering, concealing, molesting, attacking, striking, threatening, harming, or otherwise disposing of the animal.

(c)   This section shall become operative on July 1, 2014.

(Added by Stats. 1993, c. 219 (A.B. 1500), § 154. Amended by Stats. 1995, c. 598 (A.B. 878), § 1; Stats. 1996, c. 904 (A.B. 2224), § 1; Stats. 2007, c. 205 (S.B. 353), 2; Stats. 2010, c. 572 (A.B. 1596), § 16, operative Jan. 1, 2012. Added by Stats. 2013, c. 260 (A.B. 157), § 2, operative July 1, 2014.) (Italics added.)

4.   Economic Abuse

Finally, one last word about an issue raised earlier (Chapter 3). Is a domestic violence perpetrator liable for the financial consequences attendant to physical harm? Reciting a litany of harm from the hundreds of domestic and intimate partner violence cases on record, is there a financial consequence to slamming an intimate partner's face into a car dashboard to the point of unconsciousness or permanent disability? Are there financial consequences to shooting an intimate partner in the neck in an attempt to commit murder? Or running over an intimate partner with a car? Or beating an intimate partner with a belt buckle? Or stalking an intimate partner at a work place?

Arrest, conviction, and incarceration allow the state to address criminal behavior. But does incarceration assist the survivor of domestic violence who must live with the very real psychological, spiritual, emotional, physical and *economic* consequences of being assaulted, battered, permanently injured, or left unemployed?

And what of murder?

Various Family Code statutes attempt to answer the question of how to better address the economic effects of domestic, intimate partner, and dating violence for the survivor of the abuse. Intimate partner violence is becoming more visible in society, which means that the pressure is (as it should be) increasingly on state legislatures to address the problem. An intimate partner may be in fear or too impoverished to leave the family home, but how does that relieve lawmakers of their duty to address the issue? It does not, of course. For that reason, state legislatures must continues to pursue meaningful responses to the multiple layers of harm caused by domestic violence.

I have been informed by other academics that community property is not relevant except to bar takers, or that the rules on domestic violence are not relevant to the study of community property. I disagree with those assertions. The Family Code was compiled to deal with these issues: property, custody and support, and domestic violence. Not much scholarly work has been done on the relationship between property rights and intimate partner violence in the California community property system. Moreover, given that an immediate shared ownership (*ganancial*) community property system vests each spouse with a one-half community property right upon acquisition, it is imperative that academic and legislative analyists consider ways in which to both protect those rights and to empower persons who opt into the community property system via marriage.

The legislature enacts laws for persons who find themselves in fear of violence at the hands of an intimate partner. The laws exist even if any one person is unable to use them in a particular moment, or for a particular reason. Underuse may plausibly come from a lack of education; therefore, I end this brief section on financial and economic interpersonal violence by highlighting example sections that impose financial consequences on perpetrators of domestic violence. (Additional sections appear in the Statutory Appendix.)

WEST'S ANNOTATED CALIFORNIA FAMILY CODE

§ 274.   Attempted murder of a spouse; attorney's fees and costs; notice and hearing; source of funds

(a) Notwithstanding any other provision of law, if the injured spouse is entitled to a remedy authorized pursuant to Section 4324, the injured spouse shall be entitled to an award of reasonable attorney's fees and costs as a sanction pursuant to this section.

(b) An award of attorney's fees and costs as a sanction pursuant to this section shall be imposed only after notice to the party against whom the sanction is proposed to be imposed and opportunity for that party to be heard.

(c) An award of attorney's fees and costs as a sanction pursuant to this section is payable only from the property or income of the party against whom the sanction is imposed, except that the award may be against the sanctioned party's share of the community property. In order to obtain an award under this section, the party requesting an award of attorney's fees and costs is not required to demonstrate any financial need for the award.

(Added by Stats. 1995, c. 364 (A.B. 16), § 1. Amended by Stats. 2006, c. 538 (S.B. 1852), § 156.)

§ 4324. Attempted murder or soliciting the murder of spouse; prohibited awards

In addition to any other remedy authorized by law, when a spouse is convicted of attempting to murder the other spouse, as punishable pursuant to subdivision (a) of Section 664 of the Penal Code, or of soliciting the murder of the other spouse, as punishable pursuant to subdivision (b) of Section 653f of the Penal Code, the injured spouse shall be entitled to a prohibition of any temporary or permanent award for spousal support or medical, life, or other insurance benefits or payments from the injured spouse to the other spouse.

As used in this section, "injured spouse" means the spouse who has been the subject of the attempted murder or the solicitation of murder for which the other spouse was convicted, whether or not actual physical injury occurred.

(Added by Stats. 1995, c. 364 (A.B. 16), § 3. Amended by Stats. 2010, c. 65 (A.B. 2674), § 2.)

§ 4324.5.   Violent sexual felony; prohibited awards

(a) In any proceeding for dissolution of marriage where there is a criminal conviction for a violent sexual felony perpetrated by one spouse against the other spouse and the petition for dissolution is filed before five years following the conviction and any time served in custody, on probation, or on parole, the following shall apply:

(1) An award of spousal support to the convicted spouse from the injured spouse is prohibited.

(2) Where economic circumstances warrant, the court shall order the attorney's fees and costs incurred by the parties to be paid from the community assets. The injured spouse shall not be required to pay any attorney's fees of the convicted spouse out of the injured spouse's separate property.

(3) At the request of the injured spouse, the date of legal separation shall be the date of the incident giving rise to the conviction, or earlier, if the court finds circumstances that justify an earlier date.

(4) The injured spouse shall be entitled to 100 percent of the community property interest in the retirement and pension benefits of the injured spouse.

(b) As used in this section, "violent sexual felony" means those offenses described in paragraphs (3), (4), (5), (11), and (18) of subdivision (c) of Section 667.5 of the Penal Code.

(c) As used in this section, "injured spouse" means the spouse who has been the subject of the violent sexual felony for which the other spouse was convicted.

(Added by Stats. 2001, c. 718 (A.B. 1522), § 2.)

§ 4325. Temporary or permanent support to abusive spouse; rebuttable presumption disfavoring award; evidence

(a) In any proceeding for dissolution of marriage where there is a criminal conviction for an act of domestic violence perpetrated by one spouse against the other spouse entered by the court within five years prior to the filing of the dissolution proceeding, or at any time thereafter, there shall be a rebuttable presumption affecting the burden of proof that any award of temporary or permanent spousal support to the abusive spouse otherwise awardable pursuant to the standards of this part should not be made.

(b) The court may consider documented evidence of a convicted spouse's history as a victim of domestic violence, as defined in Section 6211, perpetrated by the other spouse, or any other factors the court deems just and equitable, as conditions for rebutting this presumption.

(c) The rebuttable presumption created in this section may be rebutted by a preponderance of the evidence.

(Added by Stat. 2001, c. 293 (S.B. 1221), § 3.)

The rationale behind the above statutes is straightforward. A domestic abuse survivor should not have to expend resources to assist the person who has hurt them, is hurting them, or attempts to hurt them. In that sense, during marriage and up until dissolution, these statutes and others like them give the survivor of domestic violence exclusive rights of management and control to important assets such as postseparation earnings and accumulations, insurance benefits, pension rights, the right to attorney's fees and costs in impairment and tort claims, and so forth.

NOTES

1.   *Rubberstamped restraining order denials are reversible on appeal.* Judicial discretion in ruling on a non-emergency restraining order is broad but not without limits.

Nakamura v. Parker, 156 Cal.App.4th 327, 67 Cal. Rptr. 3d 286 (1st. Dist. 2007) explains the policy and procedures underlying the DVPA. In *Nakamura*, one spouse perpetrated abuse against the other spouse by threatening to destroy separate and community property as a way to get back at the innocent spouse. The abusive spouse's conduct against the petitioner's person, her possessions, her finances, and her economic wellbeing was criminal in nature. And yet the trial court denied the DVRO request with a rubber stamp; no explanation given. The First District Court of Appeal reversed the trial court both for denying the restraining order and for denying it with no written explanation. From the appellate opinion comes an important guiding principle for the issuance of restraining orders: "judicial discretion to grant or deny an application petition for a protective order is not unfettered." *Id.* at 291.

2.   *The Family Code definition of disturbing the peace of the other party.* *Marriage of Nadkarni*, 173 Cal.App. 4th 1483, 93 Cal.Rptr.3d 723 (6th Dist. 2009) is one of the first cases to define the DVPA concept of disturbing the peace of the other party. In *Nadkarni*, a petitioner alleged that her former spouses' behavior constituted abuse under California Family Code Sections 6203 and, more specifically, under the 6320 "disturbing the peace of the other party" standard. Respondent's conduct included accessing, reading, and publicly disclosing the password-protected content of the petitioner's emails and confidential e-mails; threating to send those emails to petitioner's business contacts; and making veiled physical threats. The petitioner sought a restraining order, explaining that her former husband's conduct resulted in shock, embarrassment, fear that her business relationships would be compromised, and fear for her physical safety, among other feelings. The trial court denied the restraining order petition for failure to show cause. The court of appeal reversed, saying that proof of conduct that "destroy[s] the mental and emotional calm of another" meets the statutory standard of "disturbing the peace of the other party." *Id.* at 1497.

Burquet v. Brumbaugh, 223 Cal.App.4th 1140, 167 Cal.Rptr.3d 664 (2d Dist. 2014) applied *Nadkarni* to a permanent restraining order after a hearing. In *Burquet*, the petitioner established that after the break-up of a dating relationship, in which past acts of domestic abuse had occurred, respondent insisted on making unwelcome ongoing contact with her. The respondent acted in person (making unannounced and uninvited appearances outside of the petitioner's home) as well as electronically (sending uninvited texts) and telephonically (initiating uninvited phone calls). The respondent's alleged intent in initiating the conduct was to communicate strong emotions running the gamut from despair to anger, to expressions of "love" made with the aim of convincing petitioner to get back together with respondent, to threats. Even though the respondent's conduct caused the petitioner to feel fearful the trial court denied the petitioner's request for a protective order, saying that the DVPA definition of "disturbing the peace" is the same definition used in the penal code; and, as such, it requires proof of physical disturbance. The petitioner appealed. The court of appeal reversed. It ruled that the DVPA standard for "disturbing the peace" is different than the penal code standard of the same phrase. The DVPA disturbing the peace standard allows for disturbances that are non-physical in nature, whereas the penal code standard requires a physically violent act that incites violence. The legislature immediately updated California Family Code Section 6203 to codify the appellate court's understanding.

3. *Control.* Financial abuse can be established by the lack of control or by the presence of excessive or manipulative control. Too much control is typically indicated by the intention of one spouse to block the other's access to community resources. The absence of control is typically indicated by conduct intended to or reasonably certain to dissipate family financial resources. Often dissipation occurs because one spouse is out of control, and engaging in acts that are oppressive, malicious, or fraudulent as defined by the Penal Code. California Family Code Section 1101(h) incorporates California Penal Code Sections so as to assess how to allege and prove such situations.

Lezine, supra, the case where one spouse's acts of draining and dissipating community property home equity resulted in an impairment of the other spouse's community property interest, is a paradigmatic case of oppression, malice and fraud. The perpetrator's conduct was not only emotionally and economically abusive, it was financially abusive. As financial abuse Henry's actions led to the loss of Gloria's community property home equity as well as to a coerced debt that would haunt her for long after the dissolution. The sum total of the many acts of Henry's financial abuse caused Gloria fear and financial ruin. The marriage may have been dissolved, but Gloria, the domestic violence survivor, would be forced to deal with the consequences of Henry's devastating financial attack on her and on the community.

Additionally, the manner in which the dissolution process was conducted perpetrated harm against Gloria. Her attorney handled the case in such a way that Gloria's postdissolution earnings and accumulations became legally obligated to repay a massive debt that arose from Henry's wrongs against her and against third-party creditors. Henry forged Gloria's names on deeds and loan documents, he used the forged documents to extract community property home equity in the form of cash, he dissipated the cash, and he left the community and Gloria financially ruined.

How might you have handled Gloria's dissolution petition so as to both stop Henry from dissipating the community property? Is there a strategy through which you might have legally empowered Gloria to protect herself from financial and economic abuse and ruin? What did Gloria's attorney do to address the domestic violence, if anything? What did the attorney do to exacerbate it? After the dissolution proceeding, might Gloria have had a cause of action against her attorney for malpractice?

In *Rodriguez v. Menjivar, supra,* manipulative control was the issue. There, the perpetrator, in addition to being physically violent, sought to control the petitioner through property. The respondent used his property (his phone) to threaten and control the petitioner through her property (her phone); he did this by ongoing mental abuse that led the petitioner to keep a line open so that the respondent could "monitor" her behavior at all times. If the petitioner, a student, was in class, for example, the respondent threatened her with physical harm if she did not leave a phone line open so that he could hear her conversations with others.

4.   *Property matters.* Property matters, if not to you then to your clients. Intimate partnerships are important producers of property and wealth. But intimate partnerships can also be relationships in which domestic violence is present.

SECTION 7. CHAPTER SUMMARY

- A spouse has a right to protect community property. That right arises from the property right itself as well as from Family Code statutes.

- Management and control rights are an important part of the property right.

- Spouses have equal management and control rights to community personal property.

  - The spouses are partners who are bound by good faith and partnership level fiduciary duties.

  - A spouse does not have the right to destroy community property without the other spouse's consent.

- The California community property system is a managerial system.

- As to community personal property, equal management and control is the rule: either spouse has equal rights of management and control.

- o Equal management and control means that either spouse, acting alone, has an absolute legal right of disposition.

- o The legal right does not extend to testamentary matters. For purposes of disposing of community property at death, a spouse is limited to controlling his or her one-half interest only.

- o Gifts, low value transfers, and fair market transfers are avoidable by the spouse who has not given his or her prior written consent to the transfer.

- o A spouse who brings a claim to avoid a transfer made by the other spouse without prior written consent can recover:

  - During marriage, 100% of the asset's value, either from the spouse who made the unconsented to transfer or from the transferee.

  - Upon dissolution, 50% percent of the asset's value, either from the estate of the spouse who made the unconsented to transfer or from the transferee.

- As to community real property, dual management and control is the rule: both spouses must join in executing any consequential transaction, such as a sale, a conveyance, an encumbrance, or a term lease for longer than one year.

- Spouses have fiduciary obligations to each other in transactions between them. An impairment of community property claim accrues upon the breach of a fiduciary duty.

  - o Spouses owe each other mutual duties of respect, fidelity, and support.

  - o A spouse shall not take any unfair advantage of the other in a transaction between them.

  - o Stated positively, transparency and fidelity in financial matters is at the heart of the interspousal fiduciary duty.

  - o If an allegation of any unfair advantage is made by one spouse against the other, a rebuttable presumption of undue influence is raised to protect the adversely affected spouse. The benefitted spouse can rebut the presumption with evidence that the other spouse consented to the transaction based on full and fair disclosure and voluntarily.

  - o Spouses have a right to disclosure of information without demand. This right applies to a wide range of ordinary business matters.

- o   The fiduciary duty comes into existence on the date that the marriage is contracted. The fiduciary duty is in force until the date that the marriage terminates; and it may even extend postdissolution as to specific assets.

- The managerial system is fully protective of creditors' rights. Creditors can reach all property that a spouse has the legal right to manage and control, including community property that is outside of the spouse's de facto access. Creditors can also reach the separate property assets of both spouses with relative ease, depending on the nature of the debt or obligation.

- Primary or sometimes exclusive control over community property assets is permitted under the California Family Code in the following situations.

  - o   One spouse has a sole bank account. Here, exclusive control is over the account.

  - o   One spouse operates or manages a community property business. Here, primary control is over the assets of the business.

  - o   One spouse has a conservator, the other spouse has legal capacity. Here, exclusive control is by court order as determined by the circumstances of the conservatorship.

  - o   One spouse obtains a restraining order under the Domestic Violence Prevent Act with a corollary order granting exclusive control over a specifically identified asset or assets, as to a specifically identified act or acts, for a specifically identified time. Here, control is by court order as determined by the circumstances delineated by the court to prevent future domestic violence.

PART IV

AT MARRIAGE'S END

■ ■ ■

CHAPTER 7

DIVISION OF COMMUNITY PROPERTY AT DISSOLUTION

■ ■ ■

The Family Law Act of 1969 took effect on January 1, 1970. That Act made a number of significant changes to the law, perhaps the two most important of which were to eliminate fault as a basis for dissolution and to adopt equal management and control of community property (Chapter 6).

In 1992, the Family Law Act was replaced by a comprehensive Family Code, which went into effect in 1994 (Chapter 1). Property and support agreements are governed by the Family Code.

There are two ways to effect a division of property at dissolution. The most common way is for the parties to agree to a property settlement. The other way is to resort to litigation, a process that involves the adversarial use of public courts.

This chapter examines problems involved in negotiating a property marriage settlement agreement, or MSA. It also covers issues associated with adversarial litigation, including jurisdiction, disclosure, valuation, and the equal division requirement.

SECTION 1. DISSOLUTION, LEGAL SEPARATION, NULLITY

The legal process commonly called divorce accomplishes two goals. It restores the parties to their status as unmarried persons. California Family Code Section 2300. It also effects a partition, or division, of the community property estate.

As of January 1, 1970, there are (only) two grounds for dissolution in California: "irreconcilable differences" and "permanent legal incapacity to make decisions." California Family Code Section 2310.

Irreconcilable differences are defined as "those grounds which are determined by the court to be substantial reasons for not continuing the marriage and which make it appear that the marriage should be dissolved." California Family Code Section 2333. "Permanent legal incapacity to make decisions" requires medical proof that the incapacitated spouse lacked and remains permanently lacking the legal capacity to make decisions.

The petition for dissolution is the first formal step to terminating a marriage (Appendix B). The last step is the issuance of a final judgment of dissolution by a court. California Family Code Section 2338(c) specifies a distinction between "the entry of the judgment" and the point at which that judgment "becomes final. . . ." Until a judgment of dissolution is final the parties are not divorced. California Family Code Section 2339.

A final judgment may not be issued until the petitioner has resided in the state for at least six months and in the county where the petition is filed for at least three months. California Family Code Section 2320. The residency requirement is a way to give a court presiding over a marital dissolution action in rem jurisdiction over the "marital res." The "marital res" means the marriage. In rem jurisdiction permits a court to terminate the parties' marital status and consequently to restore each person to their status as unmarried persons. Subject matter jurisdiction give a court authority over community property. Personal jurisdiction gives a court authority over a party. For same sex partners, effective 2012, California Family Code Section 2320 includes subdivision (b), which offers protection for same-sex spouses who married in California but subsequently moved to a "jurisdiction [that] does not recognize the marriage." Subdivision permits such a couple to file a petition for dissolution in a California court, in the county where their marriage was entered into.

In a judicial proceeding under the Family Code, there is a minimum six month waiting period from the service of the petition to the final judgment of dissolution. California Family Code Section 2339. Continuances are commonly granted. California Family Code Section 2334. Default judgments are permitted. California Family Code Section 2336. Mandatory notice procedures for a default judgment are required. California Family Code Section 2338.5.

The phrase irreconcilable differences, defined above, is broad enough to offer the parties' a privacy screen; and indeed pursuant to California Family Code Section 2335, evidence of misconduct in marriage is inadmissible unless otherwise permitted. The requirement to stylize petitions as "*In re Marriage of* _____ " rather than as "*Spouse v. Spouse*," the now abandoned practice, is intended to dispel the belief of dissolution as an adversarial event. California Family Code Section 2330.[1]

Key Family Code sections relevant to the dissolution petition and judgment are reproduced below. Other sections appear in the Statutory Appendix.

---

[1]   Editorial practice for this casebook is to drop the "*In re*" tag.

WEST'S ANNOTATED CALIFORNIA FAMILY CODE

§ 2300. Effect of dissolution

The effect of a judgment of dissolution of marriage when it becomes final is to restore the parties to the state of unmarried persons.

(Stats. 1992, c. 162 (A.B. 2650), § 10, operative Jan. 1, 1994.)

§ 2310. Grounds for dissolution or legal separation

Dissolution of the marriage or legal separation of the parties may be based on either of the following grounds, which shall be pleaded generally:

(a) Irreconcilable differences, which have caused the irremediable breakdown of the marriage.

(b) Permanent legal incapacity to make decisions.

(Stats. 1992, c. 162 (A.B. 2650), § 10, operative Jan. 1, 1994. Amended by Stats. 2014, c. 144 (A.B. 1847), § 9, eff. Jan. 1, 2015.)

§ 2311. "Irreconcilable differences" defined

Irreconcilable differences are those grounds which are determined by the court to be substantial reasons for not continuing the marriage and which make it appear that the marriage should be dissolved.

(Stats. 1992, c. 162 (A.B. 2650), § 10, operative Jan. 1, 1994.)

§ 2312. Permanent legal incapacity to make decisions

A marriage may be dissolved on the grounds of permanent legal incapacity to make decisions only upon proof, including competent medical or psychiatric testimony, that the spouse was at the time the petition was filed, and remains, permanently lacking the legal capacity to make decisions.

(Stats. 1992, c. 162 (A.B. 2650), § 10, operative Jan. 1, 1994. Amended by Stats. 2014, c. 144 (A.B. 1847), § 10, eff. Jan. 1, 2015.)

§ 2320. Entry of judgment of dissolution; entry of judgment for dissolution, nullity, or legal separation of a marriage between persons of the same sex

(a) Except as provided in subdivision (b), a judgment of dissolution of marriage may not be entered unless one of the parties to the marriage has been a resident of this state for six months and of the county in which the proceeding is filed for three months next preceding the filing of the petition.

(b)(1) A judgment for dissolution, nullity, or legal separation of a marriage between persons of the same sex may be entered, even if neither spouse is a resident of, or maintains a domicile in, this state at the time the proceedings are filed, if the following apply:

(A) The marriage was entered in California.

(B) Neither party to the marriage resides in a jurisdiction that will dissolve the marriage. If the jurisdiction does not recognize the marriage, there shall be a rebuttable presumption that the jurisdiction will not dissolve the marriage.

(2) For the purposes of this subdivision, the superior court in the county where the marriage was entered shall be the proper court for the proceeding. The dissolution, nullity, or legal separation shall be adjudicated in accordance with California law.

(Stats. 1992, c. 162 (A.B. 2650), § 10, operative Jan. 1, 1994. Amended by Stats. 2011, c. 721 (S.B. 651), § 4.)

§ 2330. Petition

(a) A proceeding for dissolution of marriage or for legal separation of the parties is commenced by filing a petition entitled "In re the marriage of _____ and _____" which shall state whether it is a petition for dissolution of the marriage or for legal separation of the parties.

(b) In a proceeding for dissolution of marriage or for legal separation of the parties, the petition shall set forth among other matters, as nearly as can be ascertained, the following facts:

(1) The date of marriage.

(2) The date of separation.

(3) The number of years from marriage to separation.

(4) The number of children of the marriage, if any, and if none a statement of that fact.

(5) The age and birth date of each minor child of the marriage.

(Stats. 1992, c. 162 (A.B. 2650), § 10, operative Jan. 1, 1994. Amended by Stats. 1998, c. 581 (A.B. 2801), § 11.)

§ 2333. Irreconcilable differences; order for dissolution

Subject to Section 2334, if from the evidence at the hearing the court finds that there are irreconcilable differences which have caused the irremediable breakdown of the marriage, the court shall order the dissolution of the marriage or a legal separation of the parties.

(Stats. 1992, c. 162 (A.B. 2650), § 10, operative Jan. 1, 1994.)

§ 2335. Misconduct; admissibility of specific acts of misconduct

Except as otherwise provided by statute, in a pleading or proceeding for dissolution of marriage or legal separation of the parties, including depositions and discovery proceedings, evidence of specific acts of misconduct is improper and inadmissible.

(Stats. 1992, c. 162 (A.B. 2650), § 10, operative Jan. 1, 1994. Amended by Stats. 1993, c. 219 (A.B. 1500), § 110.)

§ 2337. Early and separate trial on dissolution; preliminary declaration; conditions; effect on retirement plan; service on plan administrator; reservation of jurisdiction; effect of party's death

(a) In a proceeding for dissolution of marriage, the court, upon noticed motion, may sever and grant an early and separate trial on the issue of the dissolution of the status of the marriage apart from other issues.

(b) A preliminary declaration of disclosure with a completed schedule of assets and debts shall be served on the nonmoving party with the noticed motion unless it has been served previously, or unless the parties stipulate in writing to defer service of the preliminary declaration of disclosure until a later time.

(c) The court may impose upon a party . . . conditions on granting a severance of the issue of the dissolution of the status of the marriage, and in case of that party's death, an order of any of the following conditions continues to be binding upon that party's estate: . . .

(Stats. 1992, c. 162 (A.B. 2650), § 10, operative Jan. 1, 1994. Amended by Stats. 1994, c. 1269 (A.B. 2208), § 24; Stats. 1997, c. 56 (A.B. 1098), § 1; Stats. 1998, c. 581 (A.B. 2801), § 14; Stats. 2007, c. 141 (A.B. 861), § 1; Stats. 2015, c. 293 (A.B. 139), § 1, eff. Jan. 1, 2016.)

§ 2338. Decisions; judgments

(a) In a proceeding for dissolution of the marriage or legal separation of the parties, the court shall file its decision and any statement of decision as in other cases.

(b) If the court determines that no dissolution should be granted, a judgment to that effect only shall be entered.

(c) If the court determines that a dissolution should be granted, a judgment of dissolution of marriage shall be entered. After the entry of the judgment and before it becomes final, neither party has the right to dismiss the proceeding without the consent of the other.

(Stats. 1992, c. 162 (A.B. 2650), § 10, operative Jan. 1, 1994.)

§ 2339. Finality of judgment; waiting period

(a) Subject to subdivision (b) and to Sections 2340 to 2344, inclusive, no judgment of dissolution is final for the purpose of terminating the marriage relationship of the parties until six months have expired from the date of service of a copy of summons and petition or the date of appearance of the respondent, whichever occurs first.

(b) The court may extend the six-month period described in subdivision (a) for good cause shown.

(Stats. 1992, c. 162 (A.B. 2650), § 10, operative Jan. 1, 1994.)

§ 2344. Death of party after entry of judgment

(a) The death of either party after entry of the judgment does not prevent the judgment from becoming a final judgment under Sections 2339 to 2343, inclusive.

(b) Subdivision (a) does not validate a marriage by either party before the judgment becomes final, nor does it constitute a defense in a criminal prosecution against either party.

(Stats. 1992, c. 162 (A.B. 2650), § 10, operative Jan. 1, 1994.)

NOTES

1. *Irreconcilable differences.* Suppose that one spouse wants a divorce and the other wants to stay married. Should the court grant a dissolution under these circumstances? (Yes.) See *Marriage of Walton*, 28 Cal.App.3d 108, 104 Cal.Rptr. 472 (4th Dist. 1972).

2. *As a practical matter, the issue of irreconcilable differences is rarely contested.* The refusal of one spouse to live with the other is generally viewed as sufficient evidence of a finding of irreconcilable differences that have caused an irremediable breakdown of the marriage. Upon such a finding, California Family Code Section 2333 mandates the court to order dissolution or separation (depending on the type of petition filed). For a historicized discussion of the transition from fault to no-fault divorce in the United States generally, see J. Major, *Termination of Marital Relationship*, CALIFORNIA FAMILY LAW SERVICE §§ 20:15–20:16 (1986), or Freed & Walker, *Family Law in the Fifty States: An Overview*, 19 FAMILY LAW QUARTERLY 331, 341 (1985).

3. *A dissolution proceeding has status and property components.* A final judgment ends the marriage of the parties, restoring each to the status of unmarried individual. A judgment also divides the community property, assigns liabilities, and awards support (if necessary) to a spouse or a child. Sometimes dissolution proceedings are bifurcated pursuant to California Family Code Section 2337. For purposes of a bifurcation motion, a court decides status issues but leaves property issues pending. If applicable, support and custody issues also can be left pending. State policy favors bifurcation for the reasons discussed in *Gionis v. Superior Court*, excerpted below.

4. *With the adoption of the Family Law Act in 1969, California became the first no-fault dissolution divorce state.* In 2016, every state in the United States permits some form of no-fault divorce. Seventeen U.S. states are complete no-fault states; thirty-three states have a no-fault option. The American Law Institute PRINCIPLES OF FAMILY DISSOLUTION (2000) argues for the total abolition of all fault-based factors either in marital property division or in the determination of spousal support. Peter Nash Swisher, *The ALI*

Principles: A Farewell to Fault—But What Remedy for the Egregious Marital Misconduct of an Abusive Spouse? 8 DUKE J. GENDER L. & POL'Y 213 (2001). The impetus underlying the widespread adoption of no-fault legislation has been the desire to reduce acrimony, hostility and perjury in divorce proceedings by eliminating nonfinancial marital misconduct as a basis for divorce.

In her book THE DIVORCE REVOLUTION, sociologist Lenore Weitzman argues that divorce law reforms have met their aim. Weitzman points out, however, that no-fault divorce has also had unintended consequences. On the basis of a ten year empirical study on the societal effects of no-fault divorce, Weitzman found that women (more so than men) lost the bargaining leverage that they once had in divorce proceedings. She attributes this loss to a number of factors, one among them being that neither spouse needs the consent of the other to end the marriage. The result, according to Weitzman, is that each spouse can expect to exit a marriage with an equal or equitable share of the marital property; but if one spouse leaves the marriage with an earning ability that the other lacks, then the law creates a new impoverished class of divorced persons, a group made up statistically of women and children. L. Weitzman, THE DIVORCE REVOLUTION (1985). The question is whether Weitzman's findings still hold thirty years later.

Susan Faludi points to discrepancies between Weitzman's empirical data and the report of the U.S. Census Bureau, which issued a study on the economic effects of divorce in 1991. Faludi argues that "the real source of divorced women's woes can be found not in the fine print of [no-fault] divorce legislation but in the behavior of husbands and judges. * * * In the end, the most effective way to correct the post-divorce inequities between the spouses is simple: correct pay inequality in the work force." SUSAN FALUDI, BACKLASH 21–25 (1991).

5.   *No-fault divorce remains controversial after its passage.* In her essay *"I Promise to Love, Honor, Obey . . . And Not Divorce You": Covenant Marriage and the Backlash Against No-Fault Divorce,* 34 FAMILY L. Q. 133 (2000), Heather Flory points out that the debate over the acrimonious and destructive aspects of divorce must be historicized in the era in which the debate occurs:

> "[W]hile many have blamed the most recent liberalization of divorce laws on the adoption of no-fault divorce in the California legislature, the process actually began long before the first Europeans settled America. For at least one tribe of Native Americans, a marriage was literally terminated when a wife placed her husband's moccasins outside the family tent. In regard to the Colonists, many came to the 'new world' in search of freedom from English tyranny, strict class based systems, and tough divorce laws. From the start, they advocated liberal divorce laws, indicating that 'the freedom to divorce was an expression of republican liberty.' " *Id.* at 135.

Criticism of the no-fault concept led some jurisdictions to develop a two-tier marriage system. In 1997, Louisiana enacted legislation that allows couples to choose between a standard form of marriage (which admits of no-fault divorce) and "covenant marriage." Couples who opt for covenant marriage agree to receive premarital counseling at the start of marriage; they also agree (at the start) to be held to more restrictive fault-based grounds that require proof of misconduct in the event that one or both spouses petition for dissolution. Grounds for divorce under a covenant marriage include adultery, a felony conviction, abandonment, physical cruelty, and child abuse. Separation for a period of two years (one year if no minor children) may also afford grounds for divorce. La. Stat. Ann. § 9:307. Arizona and Arkansas have adopted similar legislation.

Nearly thirty years after the passage of no-fault divorce legislation the American Academy of Matrimonial Lawyers surveyed its (then) over 300 members on the issue. The survey found that a majority of Academy respondents held the view that no-fault divorce laws have had a positive effect on families insofar as they reduce the costs (emotional and economic) of divorce, but the respondents also indicated that fault or egregious fault should be considered in the areas of property division, attorneys' fees and child custody. Whitehead, *Divorce California Style*, CALIFORNIA LAWYER, Jan. 1998. California has perhaps addressed the split identified by the American Academy of Matrimonial Lawyers survey by adopting legislation that acknowledges the spouses' ongoing legal duties toward each other during marriage (California Family Code Section 721), that provides remedies for the impairment of a community property interest (California Family Code Section 1101), and that gives a judge discretion, outside of a conservatorship proceeding, to issue an ex parte order that awards one spouse exclusive control of specifically defined property for an explicitly limited period of time (Chapter 6).

No-fault divorce remained controversial into the early twenty-first century, Heather Flory notes in her article: "armed with statistical data, public opinion polls and hypotheses, critics across the political spectrum have blamed no-fault divorce for rising divorce rates, child welfare, the feminization of poverty, and the downfall of family values." Flory, *I Promise to Love, Honor, Obey . . . And Not Divorce You": Covenant Marriage and the Backlash Against No-Fault Divorce*, 34 FAM. L.Q. 133, 138 (2000).

From an economic standpoint, it was posited that after roughly twenty-years in the making "a no-fault regime [proved] inefficient compared to a fault regime—on efficiency grounds too many divorces occur under no-fault, but the right number occur under fault," and therefore no-fault divorce should be eliminated "so that marriage will be preserved when it is economically efficient to do so." Martin Zelder, *The Economic Analysis of the Effect of No-Fault Divorce Law on the Divorce Rate*, 16 HARV. J. OF LAW & PUB. POL'Y 241, 259–262 (1993).

Analytic philosophical debates link property, domestic labor, wage labor, and the rights of spouses relative to each other during and at the end of marriage. Katharine B. Silbaugh's two articles, *Commodification and Women's Household Labor*, 9 YALE L.J. & FEM. 81 (1997) and *Turning Labor into Love:*

Housework and the Law, 91 N.W. U.L. REV. (1996), incorporate and extend the analytic philosophical debate into the legal scholarship literature.

6.   *Fault and property division.* California referees are prohibited from considering fault in the division of property. See for example *Askew v. Askew*, 22 Cal.App.4th 942, 28 Cal.Rptr.2d 284 (4th Dist. 1994) (wife deceived husband into marriage by representing that she loved him and was sexually attracted to him); *Smith v. Pust*, 19 Cal.App.4th 263, 23 Cal.Rptr.2d 364 (4th Dist. 1993) (husband files tort claim against the wife's therapist for commencing a sexual relationship with her).

Today, the general practice is to cite irreconcilable differences as the basis for dissolution petition. Traditional notions of fault, such as adultery, can no longer be alleged in a pure no-fault state such as California. The reason is that a dissolution petition commences the dissolution process.

SECTION 2. DIVISION BY MARRIAGE SETTLEMENT AGREEMENT

Three economic issues must be addressed at the end of marriage.

One, property rights must be adjudicated. Generally divorcing parties do not want to continue owning property together. Therefore a partition proceeding is necessary to divide community property and assign liabilities.

Two, spousal support, where necessary, is calculated. So too is child support.

Three, the parties are returned to the status of single individuals.

Each of these issues may be resolved through a negotiated agreement. In the dissolution context, negotiated agreements are variously referred to as property settlement agreements, divorce settlements, and marital settlement agreements. A negotiated agreement can be reached through mediation, private arbitration, collaborative dissolution, or adversarial litigation.

Identifying and implementing alternatives to adversarial litigation has been a strong legislative policy since 1986, the year alternative dispute resolution legislation was enacted into the California Business and Professions Code as Sections 465 and 466. Additionally, California Family Code Section 1850, which concludes Division 5, mandates that the Judicial Council implement mediation and conciliation proceedings, as well as domestic violence protocol for Family Court Services. California Family Code Division 5 is the Family Conciliation Court Law. California Family Code Division 6 applies to proceedings for nullity, separation and dissolution proceedings. California Family Code Division 10 is titled the Prevention of Domestic Violence Act (Chapter 6).

In order to dissolve their marriage, parties can opt for or else be submitted by the court for arbitration pursuant to the Code of Civil Procedure. A court has authority to order parties to arbitration "if the total value of the community and quasi-community property in controversy in the opinion of the court does not exceed fifty thousand dollars ($50,000)." California Family Code Section 2554. For purposes of this section "[t]he decision of the judge regarding the value of the community and quasi-community property . . . is not appealable." *Id.*

Legislation in Family Code Divisions 5 and 6 states and promotes the state's strong interest in conciliation and alternative dispute resolution in family law.

A. MEDIATION, ARBITRATION, DISCLOSURE STANDARDS, AND SUPPORT MODIFICATIONS

Alternative dispute resolution allows parties to dissolve the community estate outside of the public court system. Commonly used alternative dispute resolution, or ADR, methods include mediation, arbitration, and collaborative law.

Mediation is "a process in which a neutral person or persons facilitate communication between the disputants to help them reach a mutually acceptable agreement." California Evidence Code Section 1115. With mediation, the parties choose a mediator and the style of mediation. The mediator facilitates but does not decide or award (as an arbitrator or judge would). If the parties find themselves at an impasse in mediation, they can choose to litigate the divorce in a private arbitration proceeding or in public court. In a mediation, parties are free to adopt different, typically summary, disclosure standards.

Arbitration is a process whereby the parties agree to be bound by the decision of one or more private arbitrators. With arbitration, the parties choose the arbitrator(s). The parties' choice of arbitrator is an important one because the arbitrator is a factfinder who can decide and award, and whose award is generally, by agreement of the parties, not subject to appeal. Parties are entitled to modify statutory disclosure requirements for purposes of an arbitration process, as discussed below. California Code of Civil Procedure Section 1280 et seq. When parties modify disclosure requirements, they more often than not adopt summary disclosure procedures. Summary procedures value time more than the substantive protections of California Family Code Section 721(b), California Family Code Sections 2100 and 2101, or any other disclosure-related statute.

Collaborative divorce is the third often-used alternative dispute resolution method available to parties who want a dissolution. In a collaborative law process, clients permit their lawyers to work together, collaborate, to effect a dissolution. Depending on the parties' available resources, collaborative lawyers can assemble a team of professionals that includes accountants, financial advisors, psychologists, and social workers. The team assists in the characterization and dissolution of assets, liabilities, spousal and child support issues, and so on. In a collaborative process, full disclosure is a must if the collaborative process is to result in a negotiated settlement agreement. As with mediation and arbitration, if the parties find themselves at an impasse, the collaborative lawyers resign pursuant to the original agreement, which typically precludes them from participating in contested court proceedings on behalf of their respective clients. Practically speaking, this means that the clients must start the dissolution process over again, from the beginning, either with new counsel or in propria persona.

ELDEN V. SUPERIOR COURT
53 Cal. App.4th 1497, 62 Cal.Rptr.2d 322 (2d Dist.1997)

BOREN, P.J.

Petitioner, David A. Elden, seeks a writ of mandate directing the superior court to set aside its order denying his petition to confirm an arbitration award. In performing our review, we must consider the application of Family Code provisions that require parties in a marital dissolution to serve preliminary and final declarations of disclosure on each other. (Fam. Code, § 2100 et seq.)

I.   Factual and Procedural Background

Petitioner (hereafter Husband) and real party in interest, Paula Elden (hereafter Wife), are attorneys. Both are members of the State Bar of California. Each has practiced only in the area of criminal defense. They were married on November 17, 1978, and separated in either 1988 or 1989.

On August 11, 1994, Husband, in propria persona, filed a petition for dissolution of marriage. By stipulation, the matter was bifurcated and judgment of dissolution (status only) was entered on March 9, 1995.

Husband and Wife entered into a stipulation agreeing that "[t]his matter shall be tried to a final conclusion at an arbitration proceeding pursuant to California Code of Civil Procedure [section] 1280, et seq." Husband and Wife also agreed that "[t]he award of the arbitrator shall be final and shall not be subject to appeal, or attacked or set aside other than as provided in California Code of Civil Procedure [section] 1286.2." Attorney Jeffrey Weiner was appointed by the parties to conduct the arbitration. Although Weiner is licensed in Florida, he is not licensed to practice law in California. The stipulation, which was filed with the superior court, is undated.

On November 28, 1995, Weiner issued a document entitled "Decision and Award." It is clear from the content of the decision that Weiner believed that sometime after the parties separated they entered into an agreement in early 1989, which resolved all of their property issues with the exception of the disposition of the family residence, and that the agreement had been "fully performed."[3] Weiner set forth what he believed he had been asked to arbitrate. He noted that the residence had been sold in 1994 and that Husband had promised to give Wife $75,000 as her share of the proceeds from the sale. Weiner indicated he had been asked to determine "whether [Wife] is owed the sum of $75,000, or another amount, from [Husband] . . . or whether [Husband] is entitled to reimbursement and/or credit as a result of [Wife's] continued use of retail store and other credit cards in both the [Husband's] name as well as the [Wife's] name." Weiner also noted that he had been "given an alternative option with respect to resolution" of the issue involving the $75,000. Weiner noted that he had elected to "forego using the 'alternative option' and instead [would] render the Decision and Award based on the evidence presented as to each issue and beginning with the $75,000 being owed by [Husband] to [Wife] as the starting point."

Weiner then made a determination as to the "debits" and "credits" and made the following award with respect to the family residence issue: "Totalling the credits set forth in this Decision and Award, [Husband] is entitled to a credit in the amount of $79,533.25. The [Wife] is awarded a credit in the amount of $75,000 as has been agreed between the parties. From that amount, $79,533.25 will be subtracted as credits to the [Husband]. Therefore, the final monetary award in this matter is in favor of the [Husband] in the amount of $4,533.25. Said amount is due and payable immediately upon the filing of this arbitration Decision and Award."

Also contained within the award is the following language: "Although both parties have repeatedly indicated that they were fully aware of each other's finances, it is hereby ordered that within seven (7) days of the filing of this Arbitration Decision and Award, that both parties submit to each other by registered mail, with a copy to the undersigned arbitrator, financial statements sufficient under California law to satisfy each other that they are fully knowledgeable in the matters contained therein."

Husband claims that on November 29, 1995, Weiner mail-served the award on the parties by Federal Express. Wife denies this, but concedes she received a copy of the award either on or shortly after the November 29, 1995, date.

On February 7, 1996, Husband filed a petition to confirm the arbitration award. On that same date, he served on Wife his final declaration of disclosure and income and expense declaration, under section 2105, and he served and filed his declaration regarding service of final declaration of disclosure and income and expense declaration pursuant to section 2106.

Wife concedes she did not serve a declaration of disclosure. Husband claims he demanded service of Wife's disclosure declaration. Wife claims that no such demand was made.

On August 12, 1996, Wife filed a motion pursuant to Code of Civil Procedure section 473 seeking relief from the statutory time limitations for opposing the petition to confirm and for seeking vacation of the award, and seeking to vacate the award. Wife claimed, among other things, that she had been "coerced into signing a written agreement to arbitrate." She claimed that "[a]s a result of [Husband's] improper conduct, [Wife] only signed the 'Stipulation' under duress and undue influence," and that her "mental state was such that she was in no position to effectively secure representation or otherwise protect her rights during the so-called arbitration process." Wife also claimed that the arbitrator "exceeded his power," because "the entire issue of credit card balances was not to be considered," and that her rights were "substantially prejudiced by the refusal of the arbitrator to postpone the hearing upon sufficient cause to hear evidence."

On August 28, 1996, the superior court denied Husband's motion to confirm the arbitration award on the basis that the parties' failure to comply with the requirements of section 2105 precluded entry of judgment. The court ruled that Wife's Code of Civil Procedure section 473 motion was moot. Husband then filed this mandamus petition.

II. Discussion

A. *Contentions*

Husband contends that the denial of his petition to confirm the arbitration award was in excess of the superior court's jurisdiction and was a prejudicial abuse of discretion for the following reasons: (1) the "procedural disclosure provisions of . . . sections 2105 and 2106 do not apply to private arbitrations held under [Code of Civil Procedure] section * * * 1280 et seq.," (2) application of the "procedural disclosure provisions to private arbitrations defeats the purposes and provisions of [Code of Civil Procedure] section * * * 1280 et seq.," and (3) the award is "final, cannot be vacated, and must be confirmed and have judgment entered thereon."

Wife contends that the "superior court correctly determined that the mandatory disclosure requirements of [sections 2105 and 2106] prohibit entry of judgment after arbitration."

B. *Writ Review*

Wife contends an order denying a petition to confirm an arbitration award is appealable, and that writ review is therefore inappropriate. Regardless of whether the order is appealable, writ review is permissible here since the petition raises a novel issue of law. (See *Estate of Hearst* (1977) 67 Cal.App.3d 777, 781 [136 Cal.Rptr. 821].)

* * *

D. *The Family Code Provisions*

The Family Code embodies public policy designed to foster full disclosure and cooperative discovery concerning marital community and quasi-community assets and liabilities. Section 2104 requires that "each party shall serve on the other party a *preliminary declaration of disclosure,* executed under penalty of perjury" (italics added) within 60 days of the filing of a petition for dissolution. Section 2105 requires that " . . . each party . . . shall serve on the other party a *final declaration of disclosure* and a *current income and expense declaration,* executed under penalty of perjury" (italics added) when the parties enter into a property or support agreement or no later than 45 days before the first assigned trial date (if the case goes to trial). The statutes provide for the content of these declarations and specify that they be on forms prescribed by the Judicial Council.

However, "[t]he parties may stipulate to a mutual waiver of [final declarations] by execution of a waiver in a marital settlement agreement or by stipulated judgment or a stipulation entered into in open court." (§ 2105, subd. (c).) The record here does not demonstrate that the parties entered into such a waiver or stipulation.

Section 2106 provides that, aside from a waiver or stipulation or "absent good cause, no judgment shall be entered with respect to the parties' property rights without each party, or the attorney for that party in this matter, having executed and served a copy of the final declaration of disclosure and current income and expense declaration. Each party shall execute and file with the court a declaration signed under penalty of perjury stating that service of the final declaration of disclosure and current income and expense declaration was made on the other party or that service of the final declaration of disclosure has been waived pursuant to subdivision (c) of Section 2105."

Section 2107 sets forth the procedures that a complying party may employ should the other party fail to comply with these requirements. The available remedies include imposition of cost and attorney fees sanctions, and contempt, although the latter remedy is not explicitly cited in the statute.

E. *Do Sections 2104 and 2105 Apply to Private Arbitration?*

Sections 2104 and 2105 were enacted in 1993, as part of a statutory scheme designed to ensure that parties to a dissolution action meet their fiduciary duty to make full disclosure of their assets and liabilities. (§ 2100.) However, nothing contained within these statutes addresses the issue of whether parties to private arbitration are required to comply with the disclosure requirements of these provisions.

Husband and Wife submitted their dispute to an arbitrator pursuant to their written agreement. This case thus involves private or nonjudicial arbitration. (*Moncharsh v. Heily & Blase* (1992) 3 Cal.4th 1, 8 [10 Cal.Rptr.2d 183, 832 P.2d 899].) This being so, the controversy was removed from the procedures applicable to trials. (*Severtson v. Williams Construction Co.* (1985) 173 Cal.App.3d 86, 91 [220 Cal.Rptr. 400].)

"Nonjudicial arbitration proceedings are generally regulated by the procedural rules established by the arbitration agency; such proceedings are not necessarily controlled by the Code of Civil Procedure unless expressly provided by that code (Code Civ. Proc., § 1280 et seq.), by the arbitration rules, by the parties' contract, or other provisions of law regulating such nonjudicial arbitration." (* * * *Titan/Value Equities Group, Inc. v. Superior Court* (1994) 29 Cal.App.4th 482, 488–489 [35 Cal.Rptr.2d 4] [holding that the arbitrator, and not the court, decides questions of procedure and discovery: An arbitration has a life of its own outside the judicial system. The trial court may not step into a case submitted to arbitration and tell the arbitrator what to do and when to do it. Nor may it resolve procedural questions, or order discovery. It is for the arbitrator, and not the court, to resolve such questions.]; *Jordan-Lyon Productions, Ltd. v. Cineplex Odeon Corp.* (1994) 29 Cal.App.4th 1459, 1468 [35 Cal.Rptr.2d 200] [holding that the attachment law does not apply to an arbitration award].)

Wife argues that the foregoing authority is inapplicable because the requirements of the disclosure provisions are substantive rules of law rather than procedural rules or discovery provisions. Section 2100, subdivision (b) provides that "[s]ound public policy . . . favors the reduction of the adversarial nature of marital dissolution and the attendant costs by fostering full disclosure and cooperative discovery." Husband claims that the plain language of section 2100 compels the conclusion that sections 2104 and 2105 are discovery provisions rather than substantive rules of law. Looking to the purpose of the provisions, we conclude that they may well be substantive rights. This does not mean, however, that parties to an arbitration may not agree to alter the time provisions of section 2105 (as they did here). Although we recognize the public policy reasons for the disclosure sections set forth within the Family Code, we conclude that the parties to a dissolution who have agreed to engage in private arbitration of their property issues are entitled to adopt other, more summary procedures for financial disclosure. Here, for example, according to the arbitrator, the parties assured him that they had made the necessary disclosures. Under these circumstances, and because parties to private arbitrations waive a number of rights just as important as those set forth in the disclosure provisions at issue here, we conclude that the trial court erred in holding that Husband and Wife were required—prior to the arbitration—to submit the disclosure statement required by section 2105. If parties to a marital dissolution enter an agreement to settle their property or support issues by private or nonjudicial arbitration, they may do so without complying with section 2104 or 2105. Thus, Husband and Wife here could arbitrate to an award whether or not they had filed either preliminary declarations or final declarations.

Our conclusion is supported by the strong public policy in favor of arbitration as a speedy and relatively inexpensive means of dispute resolution. (See *Moncharsh v. Heily & Blase, supra,* 3 Cal.4th at p. 9; *Valsan Partners Limited Partnership v. Calcor Space Facility, Inc.* (1994) 25 Cal.App.4th 809, 816 [30 Cal.Rptr.2d 785].)

Contained within the arbitration award here, however, is the following language: "Although both parties have repeatedly indicated that they were fully aware of each other's finances, it is hereby ordered that within seven (7) days of the filing of this arbitration decision and Award, that both parties submit to each other by registered mail, with a copy to the undersigned arbitrator, financial statements sufficient under California law to satisfy each other that they are fully knowledgeable in the matters contained therein." We can only interpret this language to mean that Husband and Wife—as they were allowed to do under their private arbitration agreement—agreed to serve final declarations pursuant to section 2105 after the arbitration proceedings had ended. The parties did not specify any remedy if either party failed timely to file the final declarations. We assume, therefore, that the parties intended that the remedies provided in section 2107 (compulsion, sanction, and contempt orders) and in section 2106 (prohibiting entry of final judgment) would apply. In our view, they apply regardless of the intention of these parties.
* * *

III. Disposition

Let a writ issue directing the superior court to vacate its order denying petitioner David A. Elden's petition to confirm the arbitration award and denying Wife's Code of Civil Procedure section 473 motion as moot, and to issue a new and different order denying Wife's section 473 motion as untimely. The court may within a reasonable time thereafter permit either party to file or amend final declarations that comply with the requirements of sections 2105 and 2106 and permit any complying party to file a motion or motions pursuant to section 2107. * * *

NOTT, J., and BRANDLIN, J., concurred.

————

California has a strong public policy favoring marriage. Therefore when a contract encourages dissolution it is deemed void for public policy. However, when a marriage has broken down to such a degree that the spouses are contemplating dissolution, the spouses have the right to reach a negotiated settlement agreement. Conditioning such an agreement on a final dissolution decree is not contrary to the state public policy in favor of marriage.

In *Hill v. Hill*, 23 Cal.2d 82, 142 P.2d 417 (1943), the California Supreme Court stated:

> "Public policy seeks to foster and protect marriage, to encourage parties to live together, and to prevent separation. * * * But public policy does not discourage divorce where the relations between husband and wife are such that the legitimate objects of matrimony have been utterly destroyed. * * * In the absence of fraud, collusion or imposition upon the court, public policy does not prevent parties who have separated from entering into a contract disposing of their property rights which shall become effective only in the event one of the parties obtains a divorce, even though such a contract may be a factor in persuading a party who has a good cause for divorce to proceed to establish it." *Id.* at 93.

Negotiated marital settlement agreements can save time and money. With a negotiated agreement the parties have an opportunity to tailor their property division and support provisions to meet their needs and circumstances. Offsets, asset trades, equalizing payments, debt swaps, and so forth are not uncommon strategies for hammering out a negotiated settlement agreement. For example, one spouse might be willing to accept less than half of the community property in exchange for higher spousal support payments for a certain period of time. Another might agree to accept less than half of the community property in exchange for a waiver of spousal support. The key idea is that parties to a marriage settlement agreement are entitled to divide their property as they see fit, even if their agreement results in an arithmetically unequal division. Once an agreement is reached, it is presented to a court for confirmation.

If the parties reach an impasse, a judicial referee shall step in to divide the community and quasi-community property. In such a case, division is subject to the equal division requirement. A judge or referee has a wide grant of authority. She can order appraisals, divide assets fifty-fifty, exchange one asset for another asset; she can assign assets to one spouse conditional on an equalizing payment from the other; and generally she can do what is required to meet the equal division mandate. In a litigated dissolution there is no additional requirement that the judge take the parties' subjective preferences into consideration in reaching an equal division award. Consequently, it is critical for the parties to understand the (perhaps high) price of reaching an impasse. The parties have a right to reach their own settlement agreement; but where they cannot or choose not to, they relinquish decision making to the judge or referee. The judge or referee has a broad grant of discretion to restructure the parties' property rights.

In the case of a judicial division—so long as the parties are domiciled in California or otherwise under the jurisdiction of the court—the court can issue orders relevant to a wide scope of issues from marital status to in-state community property division to out of state community or quasi-community property division. If the respondent is domiciled in another state, as in *Muckle v. Superior Court,* excerpted below, a California court has authority to characterize property within the California community property system, which (in turn) allows the parties to negotiate over the property in a private mediation, arbitration, or collaborative process. Even if the property is community or quasi-community in character, however, the power to characterize property generally does not include the power to adjudicate rights related to the out of state property. The distinction may be important since jurisdiction over real property is required for conveyance, reconveyance, and other orders concerning title.

Additionally, the court may lack personal jurisdiction over the respondent.

Importantly, during marriage a husband and wife stand in a fiduciary relationship as a matter of law to each other with respect to the management and control of the community property. California Family Code Section 721(b) (Chapter 6). The fiduciary relationship arises from the fact of a valid marriage; it continues until the final judgment of dissolution. Additional asset specific duties may come into play, even after divorce, so long as the parties own or enjoy concurrent interests in the asset. The fiduciary duty that arises by operation of the Family Code includes an obligation to make a full disclosure of assets, debts, and any information that might result in an impairment of the other spouse's one-half community property interest. California Family Code Section 721(b) and California Family Code Section 1101(a). Moreover, a failure to disclose may be the basis for vacating an order or setting aside a final dissolution judgment (Chapter 8).

If the parties agree on how to dissolve their community estate, that agreement is binding under general principles of contract law. Often parties seek judicial approval of the agreement in connection with the dissolution proceedings. Two types of judicial actions are available: the court can (simply) approve the agreement or the agreement can be merged in the dissolution judgment. Whether an agreement is approved or merged into the final dissolution judgment depends on the parties' intent. Approved contracts are governed by contract law, which holds that a contract cause of action accrues if and when the agreement is breached. By comparison, agreements merged with the final court judgment become part of that court judgment, which means that the marriage settlement agreement is superseded by the judgment. In the latter case the agreement is enforced as a court judgment (contempt charges) not as a contract (breach).

Property division provisions in a judgment generally are not modifiable.

On the other hand, the state has a strong policy in favor of modification of spousal support agreements. The modifiability of spousal support provisions is governed by Family Code Section 3591. That said, the parties have the right to disallow modification of a spousal support award; they can do so either by agreement or by the merger of their spousal support award into a judgment. California Family Code Section 3591. Importantly, it is the act of opting out of the spousal support modification protection (policy) that precludes a family court from exercising its jurisdiction to modify the award at a later date. California Family Court Section 3651(d).

Child support provision are outside the scope of this casebook. They are governed by Family Code Section 3585. Generally, child support provisions are separate and severable from all issues, including property and spousal support. Even more to the point, child support provisions are subject to modification or revocation, at any time, at the discretion of the court.

WEST'S ANNOTATED CALIFORNIA FAMILY CODE

§ 3590. Severability of support provisions; orders based on agreements

The provisions of an agreement for support of either party shall be deemed to be separate and severable from the provisions of the agreement relating to property. An order for support of either party based on the agreement shall be law-imposed and shall be made under the power of the court to order spousal support.

(Stats. 1992, c. 162 (A.B. 2650), § 10, operative Jan. 1, 1994.)

§ 3591. Modification or termination of agreements

(a) Except as provided in subdivisions (b) and (c), the provisions of an agreement for the support of either party are subject to subsequent modification or termination by court order.

(b) An agreement may not be modified or terminated as to an amount that accrued before the date of the filing of the notice of motion or order to show cause to modify or terminate.

(c) An agreement for spousal support may not be modified or revoked to the extent that a written agreement, or, if there is no written agreement, an oral agreement entered into in open court between the parties, specifically provides that the spousal support is not subject to modification or termination.

(Stats. 1992, c. 162 (A.B. 2650), § 10, operative Jan. 1, 1994.)

§ 3650. Support order

Unless the provision or context otherwise requires, as used in this chapter, "support order" means a child, family, or spousal support order.

(Stats. 1992, c. 162 (A.B. 2650), § 10, operative Jan. 1, 1994. Amended by Stats. 1993, c. 219 (A.B. 1500), § 124.5.)

§ 3651. Powers of court; application of section

(a) Except as provided in subdivisions (c) and (d) and subject to Article 3 (commencing with Section 3680) and Sections 3552, 3587, and 4004, a support order may be modified or terminated at any time as the court determines to be necessary. . . .

. . .

(d) An order for spousal support may not be modified or terminated to the extent that a written agreement, or, if there is no written agreement, an oral agreement entered into in open court between the parties, specifically provides that the spousal support is not subject to modification or termination.

. . .

(Stats. 1992, c. 162 (A.B. 2650), § 10, operative Jan. 1, 1994. Amended by Stats. 1994, c. 1269 (A.B. 2208), § 31.4; Stats. 1997, c. 599 (A.B. 573), § 6; Stats. 2005, c. 154 (S.B. 1082), § 2, eff. Aug. 30, 2005.)

―――――

Former spouses no longer have a community between them. They are outside the community property system relative to each other. Nevertheless, an award for spousal support, to the degree that it will be payable out of post-dissolution work earnings, has the effect of assigning the supporting party's post-dissolution income to his or her supported ex-spouse for a period of time after the marriage ends.

The next case, *Marriage of Hufford*, discusses some of the pitfalls inherent in agreeing about the modifiability of a spousal support order. In *Hufford,* the parties relied on boilerplate language presumably to preclude modification. Circumstances changed after dissolution. A motion to modify the spousal support order was filed by the supporting spouse. The motion raised the legal issue of whether the boilerplate language in the parties' original marital settlement agreement was specific and unequivocal enough to preclude a later court from modifying the original support award.

MARRIAGE OF HUFFORD

152 Cal.App.3d 825, 199 Cal.Rptr. 726 (2d Dist. 1984)

THOMPSON, ASSOCIATE JUSTICE.

In this appeal we are called upon to determine whether judicial modification of spousal support is precluded by a boiler plate provision in a marital settlement agreement which merely provides that the agreement is entire and cannot be amended, altered or modified by the parties except by a writing signed by both parties. For the reasons to follow, we have concluded that such a provision does not fulfill the exception of Civil Code section 4811, subdivision (b) [current California Family Code Section 3591], to exclude judicial modification.

Guy Hufford (husband) appeals from the denial of his order to show cause for modification of spousal support of his ex-wife, Dorothy Hufford (wife).

On March 1, 1978, husband and wife filed in court a signed written "stipulation" and waiver of rights prepared by wife's counsel, covering among other things spousal support, division of property, attorney's fees and waivers. Paragraph 2 of the agreement provided for husband to pay wife spousal support of $1,200 per month for the first two years after entry of an interlocutory judgment of dissolution, and thereafter $600 per month until wife remarried or died.

Paragraph 6 recited the parties' agreement that "this court shall retain jurisdiction, after rendering the Final Judgment of Dissolution in the subject action, to determine all issues raised by this agreement and not specifically excluded from this reservation of jurisdiction."

Paragraph 10 provided: "This agreement is entire. We may not alter, amend or modify it, except by an instrument in writing executed by both of us. It includes all representations of every kind and nature made by each of us to the other. This agreement shall be binding upon and inure to the benefit of both of us, and of our heirs, administrators, executors, successors, and assigns."

On March 15, 1978, the Ventura Superior Court entered an interlocutory decree of dissolution of marriage ordering spousal support, property division, attorney's fees and execution of further documents in substantially identical language with the provisions of the stipulation. The decree did not in any way refer to the prior stipulation; nor did it contain the provisions of paragraphs 6 or 10.

On July 14, 1982, husband filed an order to show cause for modification of spousal support on grounds of alleged reduced ability to pay because of lesser income and increased obligations for a new wife and five children, coupled with ex-wife's reduced need. The wife opposed the motion on the ground that paragraph 10 of the stipulation rendered the spousal support provision nonmodifiable.

The superior court denied husband's request for modification. The court found that the order for spousal support contained in the judgment of dissolution was not modifiable because the provision in paragraph 10 of the stipulation constituted compliance with Civil Code section 4811, subdivision (b) [see current California Family Code Section 3591 and 3651(d)], as to nonmodifiability of spousal support, and the provision of paragraph 6 of the stipulation did not constitute a reservation of jurisdiction to modify spousal support.

This appeal followed.

Discussion

Civil Code section 4811, subdivision (b) [see current California Family Code Section 3591 and 3651(d)], provides in pertinent part:

"(b) The provisions of any agreement for the support of either party shall be deemed to be separate and severable from the provisions of the agreement relating to property. All orders for the support of either party based on such agreement shall be deemed law-imposed and shall be deemed made under the power of the court to make such orders. *The provisions of any agreement or order for the support of either party shall be subject to subsequent modification or revocation by court order, * * * except to the extent that any written agreement * * * specifically provides to the contrary.*" (Italics added.)

Thus, there is a general rule in favor of modifiability by the court of spousal support provisions.

"The evident purposes of Civil Code section 4811 [see current California Family Code Section 3591 and 3651(d)] *were to* dispose of the abstruse and unprofitable jurisprudence which had grown up around the concepts of integration and severability [citations] and *establish a legislatively declared social policy that contractual provisions for the support of a spouse be subject to modification by the court in the light of changed circumstances unless the parties explicitly agree to preclude such modification.* The utility of this policy is obvious. Even in the absence of inflationary distortions, the parties to a marital settlement agreement can hardly anticipate and provide for unexpected changes of circumstance which may invalidate the expectations reflected in the agreement. Despite the public interest in reserving for judicial redetermination on the basis of changed circumstances contractual provisions for support, the Legislature left it open to marital partners to preclude judicial modification by inserting in the agreement a specific provision to that effect." (*In re Marriage of Nielsen* (1980) 100 Cal.App.3d 874, 877–878, 161 Cal.Rptr. 272.) (Italics added.)

Although an agreement making spousal support nonmodifiable by the court is not contrary to public policy (*In re Marriage of Hawkins* (1975) 48 Cal.App.3d 208, 212–213, 121 Cal.Rptr. 681), "[u]nderlying section 4811 [see current California Family Code Section 3591 and 3651(d)] is the policy determination that the public interest is best served when support awards reflect changes in need or ability to pay" (*Esserman v. Esserman* (1982) 136 Cal.App.3d 572, 577, 186 Cal.Rptr. 329).

In determining whether the trial court properly found that the language in the agreement herein was legally sufficient to preclude judicial modification of spousal support under section 4811, subdivision (b) [see current California Family Code Section 3591 and 3651(d)], we first view, from an historical perspective, cases considering that issue.

In re Marriage of Smiley (1975) 53 Cal.App.3d 228, 125 Cal.Rptr. 717, held that a general provision of an agreement incorporated into the dissolution decree containing language "that this agreement is entire, indivisible, and shall constitute an integrated agreement, which is not subject to modification [and] [t]his agreement may not be amended except by an instrument in writing signed by both parties" (*id.,* at p. 231, 125 Cal.Rptr. 717) rendered spousal support nonmodifiable under section 4811, subdivision (b), [current California Family Code Section 3591] notwithstanding the language in the spousal support provision of the agreement that "the support of Wife is subject to any order, Decree or Judgment of any Court based thereon" (*id.,* at pp. 230, 233). The court held the latter language simply made it clear that contempt was a permissible method of enforcement and the former language was sufficient to satisfy the statutory requirement that written agreements specifically provide against modifiability by the court.

Forgy v. Forgy (1976) 63 Cal.App.3d 767, 134 Cal.Rptr. 75, held under former section 139 (the predecessor of section 4811) that the following language precluded later judicial modification of spousal support: " '[i]n the event that either the Husband or the Wife shall hereafter obtain a decree of absolute or limited divorce, such decree shall incorporate the provisions of this Agreement to the extent acceptable to the Court, but such decree shall in no way affect this Agreement or any of the terms, covenants, or conditions thereof, it being understood that this Agreement is absolute, unconditional and irrevocable.' " (*Id.,* at p. 770, 134 Cal.Rptr. 75.)

The *Forgy* court explained: "The word 'decree' used therein impliedly includes the orders embodied in the decree and any modification of those orders. Any other interpretation would permit the court to comply with the agreement in its 'decree' but forthwith effect noncompliance therewith by a subsequent decree or order. As thus interpreted the agreement provides, a court decree incorporating its provisions and any modification thereof shall in no way affect the spousal support provisions thereof as to which the agreement 'is absolute, unconditional and irrevocable.' A modification of those provisions certainly would 'affect' them and render nugatory the understanding of the parties the agreement was absolute and irrevocable. To comply with the nonmodifiable provisions of * * * it is not necessary the parties to a separation agreement state categorically: 'The provisions of this agreement for support are not subject to modification or revocation by court order.' To the contrary, 'no particular magic words are needed' to provide the exception to modifiability contemplated by the statute. [Citations.]" (*Id.,* at pp. 770–771.)

In re Marriage of Kilkenny (1979) 96 Cal.App.3d 617, 158 Cal.Rptr. 158, relying on *Forgy, supra,* held that the terms "absolute, unconditional and irrevocable" as intended in the agreement prohibited modification of spousal support by court decree. The *Kilkenny* court pointed out that the provision in its agreement that " '[i]t is the intention of the parties that this agreement, whether or not incorporated in any decree of divorce, shall be binding upon the parties, and shall be absolute, unconditional and irrevocable' " presented an even stronger showing of nonmodifiability than did *Forgy* because the parties more clearly stated their intent. (96 Cal.App.3d at p. 620, 158 Cal.Rptr. 158.)

Subsequently, *In re Marriage of Nielsen, supra,* 100 Cal.App.3d 874, 161 Cal.Rptr. 272, addressed the issue of what general boiler plate language in agreements, if any, was sufficient to preclude judicial modification of spousal support. The court, relying upon *Forgy, supra,* held that a provision in the final paragraph that the agreement shall not depend for its effectiveness on court approval nor be affected thereby was a specific provision rendering spousal support nonmodifiable. (*Id.,* at p. 878, 161 Cal.Rptr. 272.)

However, the *Nielsen* court also held that neither the paragraph establishing spousal support of $214 per month "continuing for the remainder of wife's life" nor the general release of rights paragraph was sufficient to prohibit judicial modification. The court explained:

> *"The paragraph of the agreement dealing with spousal support is silent on the question of modification.* The general release of rights * * * refers, among other items, to 'all claims of either party upon the other for support and maintenance * * * it being understood that this present agreement is intended to settle the rights of the parties hereto in all respects.' *So far as the contractual relations of the parties are concerned, the general release of rights would be held to express an intention that the obligation of support would be governed by agreement. [Citation.] But the release of rights provision is entirely silent with respect to the power of modification vested in the court by Civil Code section 4811* [California Family Code Section 3591 and 3651(d)]. *Therefore, * * * there was no*

specific provision in the release language *precluding modification by judicial action.* Just as parol evidence may not be received to supply a missing provision against modification, the statute cannot be avoided by drawing inferences as to the intention of the parties from a general 'release of rights' *paragraph which contains no 'specific' provision concerning judicial modification.*" (*Id.,* at p. 878, 161 Cal.Rptr. 272.) (Italics added.)

Soon thereafter, *In re Marriage of Aylesworth* (1980) 106 Cal.App.3d 869, 165 Cal.Rptr. 389, held that prefatory language in a marital settlement agreement, providing that " '[w]ith the exception of provisions relating to child custody and child support, this Agreement is intended to be a final, binding, and nonmodifiable agreement between said parties' " (*id.,* at p. 873, 165 Cal.Rptr. 389), fulfilled the exception requirement of section 4811, subdivision (b) (*id.,* at p. 874, 165 Cal.Rptr. 389).

More recently, *Fukuzaki v. Superior Court* (1981) 120 Cal.App.3d 454, 174 Cal.Rptr. 536, discussed what language in an agreement was sufficiently specific to preclude judicial modification of spousal support. The *Fukuzaki* agreement contained boiler plate provisions that (1) the purpose of the agreement was to make a final and complete settlement of all rights and obligations concerning the wife's support; (2) the agreement contained the entire agreement of the parties; (3) the agreement was to be submitted to the court for incorporation into the interlocutory judgment, and (4) mutual release of rights by both parties.

Fukuzaki held that these provisions, individually and collectively, were not sufficiently specific to avoid the power of the court to modify a spousal support agreement where the paragraph reciting the agreement for spousal support was silent on the question of modification.

The *Fukuzaki* court explained:

"The provisions for a 'final and complete' settlement coupled with a release of all obligations and a provision that the agreement is entire and binding on the parties and their heirs do not equate with the requirement of a 'specific' provision for nonmodification such as 'nonmodifiable' [citation], or 'irrevocable' [citation]. Although no particular magic words are needed to provide the exception to nonmodifiability contemplated by section 4811, subdivision (b) [current California Family Code Section 3591], some specific unequivocal language directly on the question of modification is required. The subject agreement is entirely silent with respect to the power of modification placed on the court by Civil Code section 4811 [current California Family Code Section 3591]. *The import of the statute may not be 'avoided by drawing inferences as to the intention of the parties' from general provisions of the agreement which do not contain a specific provision concerning judicial modification.* [Citation.]"

(*Fukuzaki, supra,* 120 Cal.App.3d at p. 458, 174 Cal.Rptr. 576.) (Italics added.)

Subsequently, in 1982, in *Esserman v. Esserman, supra,* 136 Cal.App.3d 572, 186 Cal.Rptr. 329, the court held that section 4811, subdivision (b) [see current California Family Code Section 3591 and 3651(d)], applies to private agreements made after entry of a final judgment of dissolution. The court pointed out that, regardless of whether support provisions in the earlier agreement and judgment were nonmodifiable, the court had authority to modify the spousal support arrangement in the later private agreement. The *Esserman* court found, citing *Fukuzaki v. Superior Court, supra,* that there was no language in the later private agreement which would meet the "test of 'specific unequivocal language directly on the question of [judicial] modification.' " (*Id.,* at p. 577, 186 Cal.Rptr. 329.)

Finally, *In re Marriage of Forcum* (1983) 145 Cal.App.3d 599, 193 Cal.Rptr. 596, is the most recent case to consider in detail what language in an agreement or order is legally sufficient to bring into play the provisions of section 4811, subdivision (b) [see current California Family Code Section 3591 and 3651(d)], that orders for spousal support are modifiable except to the extent that a written agreement of the parties "specifically provides to the contrary." (*Id.,* at p. 604, 193 Cal.Rptr. 596.) There, as in *Nielsen,* a general provision that the agreement was effective upon execution and did not depend upon court approval for effectiveness was involved. The court held that a specific provision for a dollar-a-year spousal support payments had the legal effect of retaining the court's jurisdiction to modify spousal support. The court reasoned that a specific provision would prevail over the more general *Nielsen*-type provision to permit future judicial modification (145 Cal.App.3d at pp. 601, 605, 193 Cal.Rptr. 596.)

In addition to the *Nielsen*-type provision, the *Forcum* agreement *also* provided that (1) the agreement was entire and could not be altered, amended or modified except in a writing executed by both parties, and (2) each party, except for provisions contained in the agreement, released the other from any and all liabilities, obligations and claims, including all claims of either party upon the other for support. *Forcum* pointed out that "these provisions are insufficient to cause spousal support to be nonmodifiable." (145 Cal.App.3d at p. 604, 193 Cal.Rptr. 596.)

Moreover, in an instructive observation, the *Forcum* court stressed:

"A dispute on the issue of nonmodifiability of spousal support would not arise if the provision for spousal support within the marital settlement agreement stated 'spousal support is nonmodifiable.' Section 4811, subdivision (b) [see current California Family Code Section 3591 and 3651(d)], provides that spousal support is always modifiable unless the agreement of the parties specifically provides to the contrary. Careful draftsmen preparing marital settlement agreements providing for spousal support should specifically state that spousal support is nonmodifiable, if that is the agreement of the parties." (*Ibid.*)

With this historical perspective in mind, we now turn to the agreement in this case. Paragraph 10 of the agreement is a classic example of general boiler plate language which is routinely inserted in most contracts. Such a provision is obviously intended to prohibit those kinds of oral modifications of a written contract which would otherwise be permitted under section 1698. (See 14 Cal.Jur.3d, Contracts, § 222, pp. 501–503; Timbie, *Modification of Written Contracts in California* (1972) 23 Hast.L.J. 1549, 1554–1564; see, e.g., *Mitchell v. Mitchell* (Me.1980) 418 A.2d 1140, 1142.)

Wife argues that under decisional law this paragraph precludes judicial modification of spousal support. Wife points to the "strikingly similar" language in *Smiley, supra,* 53 Cal.App.3d 228, 125 Cal.Rptr. 717, which was held sufficient to cause spousal support to be nonmodifiable. However, the provision herein more closely parallels the provision in *Forcum, supra,* 145 Cal.App.3d 599, which was deemed insufficient. Thus, insofar as *Smiley* and *Forcum* can be distinguished, *Forcum* is more on point.

Furthermore, insofar as there is a conflict between the 1975 *Smiley* decision and the 1983 *Forcum* decision, we find the rationale of the latter authority more persuasive. We agree with *Forcum* that general language that an agreement is entire and may not be altered, amended or modified is insufficient to invoke the exception to the statutory rule.

Whereas the earlier cases stressed the fact that no magic words were necessary and appeared willing to infer intent to make spousal support nonmodifiable from general language, the most recent cases have emphasized the need for specific unequivocal language directly on the issue of judicial modification. We are concerned about judicial erosion of the statutory policy in favor of modifiability of spousal support and the danger of inferring a contrary intent of the parties from seemingly-innocuous boiler plate provisions. (See Cal.Family L.Rep. (1980) p. 1304.) Since, under section 4811, subdivision (b) [see current California Family Code Section 3591 and 3651(d)], the court is vested with the power to modify spousal support unless the parties specifically agree to preclude judicial modification, draftsmen should specifically state that "spousal support is nonmodifiable" in the provision for spousal support if that is the intended agreement of the parties.

Moreover, insufficiency of this boiler plate language to specifically preclude modification by the court is even more obvious in this case than in *Forcum* because here the language merely states that "we"—that is, the parties—may not modify the document. Nowhere in the paragraph is there a limitation, even by implication, on the court's power to do so. Thus, although the paragraph expresses an intention regarding the contractual relations of the parties, it does not comply with the requirement enunciated in *Fukuzaki* and *Nielsen* that in order to foreclose the power vested in the court by section 4811 [see current California Family Code Section 3591 and 3651(d)], there must be a specific provision concerning judicial modification. (*Fukuzaki, supra,* 120 Cal.App.3d at p. 458, 174 Cal.Rptr. 536; *Nielsen, supra,* 100 Cal.App.3d at p. 878, 161 Cal.Rptr. 272.)

In addition, a contract must be read as a whole with each part helping to interpret the other. (§ 1641.) Here, paragraph 6 of the agreement expressly retains the jurisdiction of the court to determine all issues which are not specifically excluded from the reservation. Thus, this paragraph reinforces our unwillingness to infer an intent to prohibit judicial modification of spousal support from the boiler plate language in paragraph 10. We are not persuaded by wife's argument, relying on *Smiley,* that this paragraph merely makes the agreement subject to enforcement by contempt. All such orders already are. (See §§ 4811, subd. (b); 4380.) [see current California Family Code Section 3591 and 3651(d)]. Nor do we find any language in paragraph 10 that can reasonably be construed as a specific exclusion of the court's jurisdiction.

In any event, the agreement does not unequivocally exclude judicial modification and, therefore, is ambiguous on that issue. But any ambiguity must be resolved in favor of the general statutory rule of modifiability, rather than the exception (*Moyer v. Workmen's Comp. Appeals Bd.* (1973) 10 Cal.3d 222, 232, 110 Cal.Rptr. 144, 514 P.2d 1224) and against the wife whose counsel drafted the agreement (§ 1654). Accordingly, the judgment (order) denying the motion to show cause re modification is reversed, and the cause is remanded to the superior court to hold a hearing on the merits.

SCHAUER, P.J., and JOHNSON, J., concur.

NOTES

1.   Marriage of Hufford *is a frequently cited case.*

2.   *Property settlement agreements can include spousal and child support provisions where applicable.* A party may include support requests in the dissolution petition, absent an agreement not to. Statutes and decisional law are consistent in holding firm to the rule that marital fault plays no part in support orders under the current law: "In determining the need for, the amount of and duration of spousal support . . . the court is to ignore marital fault and is to base its determination solely on the circumstances of the parties, including the duration of their marriage and the ability of the supported spouse to engage in gainful employment." *Marriage of Rosan,* 24 Cal.App.3d 885, 892, 101 Cal.Rptr. 295 (4th Dist. 1972).

California Family Code Section 4320, reproduced in the Statutory Appendix, lists fourteen mandatory factors that shall be considered by a court in making a spousal support decision. Traditional notions of fault are not on the list. Domestic violence is. California Family Code Section 4320(i) provides:

"(i) Documented evidence, including a plea of nolo contendere, of any history of domestic violence, as defined in Section 6211, between the parties or perpetrated by either party against either party's child, including, but not limited to, consideration of emotional distress resulting from domestic violence perpetrated against the supported party by the supporting party, and consideration of any history of violence against the supporting party by the supported party."

The code mandates a court to consider all fourteen circumstances in granting or denying support awards, and in determining amount and duration. But the statute is drafted in such a way as to give a court broad discretion.

3. *Modifying spousal support orders.* A motion for modification of a spousal support order may only be granted if there has been a material change of circumstances since the last order. *Marriage of Smith,* 225 Cal.App.3d 469, 274 Cal.Rptr. 911 (1st Dist. 1990) discusses the major statutory factors for spousal support awards.

The court concludes:

"Determining the issue of spousal support, including its amount and duration, is one of the most difficult tasks a judge faces. Invariably parties seeking support ask for amounts which they honestly believe to be the minimum necessary for them to survive, and adverse parties propose amounts which they honestly believe to be the most they can pay and have sufficient funds left for them to survive. Our experience is that both parties often are right, and that is why this issue brings so many cases to trial. In exercising the discretion vested under section 4801, subdivision (a), to reach a fair and just result, the trial court considers the circumstances listed therein that are applicable to the case, according each its appropriate weight under the facts of the case, and issues what the judge believes to be the proper decision. It is usually a decision which satisfies neither party, and perhaps that is one measure of a fair decision. " *Id.* at 494.

With regard to child support, the controlling statutes are Family Code Sections 3600 et seq. There are now statewide guidelines governing child support awards. (California Family Code Sections 4050 et seq.). Major principles include the statements that parents' primary obligation is to support their children according to their circumstances and station in life, and that children should share in the standard of living of both parents. A child support order may therefore appropriately improve the standard of living of the custodial household to improve the lives of the children. California Family Code Section 4055(a) establishes a formula for making a child support award. Child support is always subject to judicial modification, the best interest of the child being of paramount concern. See California Family Code Sections 3650–51.

B. COLLABORATIVE LAW

The California Legislature recognizes the collaborative family law concept with the enactment of California Family Code Section 2013 effective January 1, 2007, reproduced below. The legislation provides parties with a framework for the collaborative law method. For more on collaborative law, see Andrew Schouten, *Breaking Up is* No Longer *Hard to Do: The Collaborative Family Law Act*, 38 MCGEORGE L. REV. 125 (2007). *See also*, PAULINE TESLER, & PEGGY THOMPSON, COLLABORATIVE DIVORCE: THE REVOLUTIONARY NEW WAY TO RESTRUCTURE YOUR FAMILY, RESOLVE LEGAL ISSUES, AND MOVE ON WITH YOUR LIFE (2006).

WEST'S ANNOTATED CALIFORNIA FAMILY CODE

§ 2013. Collaborative law process

(a) If a written agreement is entered into by the parties, the parties may utilize a collaborative law process to resolve any matter governed by this code over which the court is granted jurisdiction pursuant to Section 2000.

(b) "Collaborative law process" means the process in which the parties and any professionals engaged by the parties to assist them agree in writing to use their best efforts and to make a good faith attempt to resolve disputes related to the family law matters as referenced in subdivision (a) on an agreed basis without resorting to adversary judicial intervention.

(Added by Stats. 2006, c. 496 (A.B. 402), § 2.)

———

Elden, *supra*, also raises the legal issue of whether parties in a private mediation are entitled to adopt their own disclosure requirement.

SECTION 3. DIVISION BY COURT ORDER

Various issues may be encountered in a litigated division, including jurisdictional problems, the equal division requirement, valuation problems, and tax consequences.

In a proceeding under the Family Code for the dissolution of marriage or legal separation, the trial court has the jurisdiction to inquire into and make appropriate orders for the settlement of the property rights of the parties. If the court believes that the total value of the community property does not exceed $50,000, the court may submit the issues of classification, valuation and division to arbitration for resolution.

A. POWERS OF THE COURT TO DIVIDE AND DISPOSE OF PROPERTY

The California Family Code controls the disposition of property by the court in a dissolution proceeding. Select provisions, which took effect on January 1, 1994, are set forth below.

In general, a court has jurisdiction over community property and quasi-community property, but not over a spouse's separate property unless the owning spouse consents. Either spouse can ask a court to divide separate property that the spouses own concurrently.

At dissolution, assets and liabilities are identified, confirmed, and assigned to one or the other party. Reimbursements, if any, are confirmed. Property is divided, subject to family protections, spousal and child support orders, and so on. Conveyances and reconveyances are ordered. Postdissolution real property titles are recorded in the county where the property is situated.

When economically feasible, a court may issue a deferred sale of home order (Section C below). The deferred sale order awards temporary exclusive use of the family home to a custodial parent; the rationale considers the best interests of the children. California Family code 3800 et seq.

Motions to adjudicate omitted assets must be filed in a timely manner.

Once the time for motions and appeals pass, a set-aside motion may be raised on a limited number of grounds such as fraud, perjury, duress, mental incapacity, mistake, and failure to comply with disclosure. These issues are covered in Chapter 8.

WEST'S ANNOTATED CALIFORNIA FAMILY CODE

§ 63.   Community estate

"Community estate" includes both community property and quasi-community property.

(Added by Stats. 1993, c. 219 (A.B. 1500), § 79.3.)

§ 2502. Separate property

"Separate property" does not include quasi-community property.

(Stats. 1992, c. 162 (A.B. 2650), § 10, operative Jan. 1, 1994.)

§ 2550. Manner of division of community estate

Except upon the written agreement of the parties, or on oral stipulation of the parties in open court, or as otherwise provided in this division, in a proceeding for dissolution of marriage or for legal separation of the parties, the court shall, either in its judgment of dissolution of the marriage, in its judgment of legal separation of the parties, or at a later time if it expressly reserves jurisdiction to make such a property division, divide the community estate of the parties equally.

(Stats. 1992, c. 162 (A.B. 2650), § 10, operative Jan. 1, 1994.)

§ 2551. Characterization of liabilities; confirmation or assignment

For the purposes of division and in confirming or assigning the liabilities of the parties for which the community estate is liable, the court shall characterize liabilities as separate or community and confirm or assign them to the parties in accordance with Part 6 (commencing with Section 2620).

(Stats. 1992, c. 162 (A.B. 2650), § 10, operative Jan. 1, 1994.)

§ 2552. Valuation of assets and liabilities

(a) For the purpose of division of the community estate upon dissolution of marriage or legal separation of the parties, except as provided in subdivision (b), the court shall value the assets and liabilities as near as practicable to the time of trial.

(b) Upon 30 days' notice by the moving party to the other party, the court for good cause shown may value all or any portion of the assets and liabilities at a date after separation and before trial to accomplish an equal division of the community estate of the parties in an equitable manner.

(Stats. 1992, c. 162 (A.B. 2650), § 10, operative Jan. 1, 1994.)

§ 2553. Powers of court

The court may make any orders the court considers necessary to carry out the purposes of this division.

(Stats. 1992, c. 162 (A.B. 2650), § 10, operative Jan. 1, 1994.)

§ 2554. Failure to agree to voluntary division of property; submission to arbitration

(a) Notwithstanding any other provision of this division, in any case in which the parties do not agree in writing to a voluntary division of the community estate of the parties, the issue of the character, the value, and the division of the community estate may be submitted by the court to arbitration for resolution pursuant to Chapter 2.5 (commencing with Section 1141.10) of Title 3 of Part 3 of the Code of Civil Procedure, if the total value of the community and quasi-community property in controversy in the opinion of the court does not exceed fifty thousand dollars ($50,000). The decision of the court regarding the value of the community and quasi-community property for purposes of this section is not appealable.

(b) The court may submit the matter to arbitration at any time it believes the parties are unable to agree upon a division of the property.

(Stats. 1992, c. 162 (A.B. 2650), § 10, operative Jan. 1, 1994.)

§ 2555. Disposition of community estate; revision on appeal

The disposition of the community estate, as provided in this division, is subject to revision on appeal in all particulars, including those which are stated to be in the discretion of the court.

(Stats. 1992, c. 162 (A.B. 2650), § 10, operative Jan. 1, 1994.)

§ 2556. Community property or debts; continuing jurisdiction

In a proceeding for dissolution of marriage, for nullity of marriage, or for legal separation of the parties, the court has continuing jurisdiction to award community estate assets or community estate liabilities to the parties that have not been previously adjudicated by a judgment in the proceeding. A party may file a postjudgment motion or order to show cause in the proceeding in order to obtain adjudication of any community estate asset or liability omitted or not adjudicated by the judgment. In these cases, the court shall equally divide the omitted or unadjudicated community estate asset or liability, unless the court finds upon good cause shown that the interests of justice require an unequal division of the asset or liability.

(Stats. 1992, c. 162 (A.B. 2650), § 10, operative Jan. 1, 1994. Amended by Stats. 1993, c. 219, (A.B. 1500), § 111.)

§ 2600. Powers of court

Notwithstanding Sections 2550 to 2552, inclusive, the court may divide the community estate as provided in this part.

(Stats. 1992, c. 162 (A.B. 2650), § 10, operative Jan. 1, 1994.)

§ 2601. Conditional award of an asset of the community estate to one party

Where economic circumstances warrant, the court may award an asset of the community estate to one party on such conditions as the court deems proper to effect a substantially equal division of the community estate.

(Stats. 1992, c. 162 (A.B. 2650), § 10, operative Jan. 1, 1994).

§ 2602. Additional award or offset against existing property; award of amount determined to have been misappropriated

As an additional award or offset against existing property, the court may award, from a party's share, the amount the court determines to have been deliberately misappropriated by the party to the exclusion of the interest of the other party in the community estate.

(Stats. 1992, c. 162 (A.B. 2650), § 10, operative Jan. 1, 1994.)

§ 2603. Community estate personal injury damages; assignment— *supra* at 176.

§ 2604. Community estates of less than $5,000; award of entire estate

If the net value of the community estate is less than five thousand dollars ($5,000) and one party cannot be located through the exercise of reasonable diligence, the court may award all the community estate to the other party on conditions the court deems proper in its judgment of dissolution of marriage or legal separation of the parties.

(Stats. 1992, c. 162 (A.B. 2650), § 10, operative Jan. 1, 1994.)

§ 2650. Jurisdiction; division of real and personal property

In a proceeding for division of the community estate, the court has jurisdiction, at the request of either party, to divide the separate property interests of the parties in real and personal property, wherever situated and whenever acquired, held by the parties as joint tenants or tenants in common. The property shall be divided together with, and in accordance with the same procedure for and limitations on, division of community estate.

(Stats. 1992, c. 162 (A.B. 2650), § 10, operative January 1, 1994.)

§ 2660. Division of real property situated in another state

(a) Except as provided in subdivision (b), if the property subject to division includes real property situated in another state, the court shall, if possible, divide the community property and quasi-community property as provided for in this division in such a manner that it is not necessary to change the nature of the interests held in the real property situated in the other state.

(b) If it is not possible to divide the property in the manner provided for in subdivision (a), the court may do any of the following in order to effect a division of the property as provided for in this division:

(1) Require the parties to execute conveyances or take other actions with respect to the real property situated in the other state as are necessary.

(2) Award to the party who would have been benefited by the conveyances or other actions the money value of the interest in the property that the party would have received if the conveyances had been executed or other actions taken.

(Stats. 1992, c. 162 (A.B. 2650), § 10, operative Jan. 1, 1994.)

———

Family Code, Division 6, Chapter 2 was enacted in 1992, effective 1994. California Family Code Section 2010 through 2013 speak to jurisdiction.

Pursuant to California Family Code Section 2010, the court has the power to divide the community property and quasi-community property of the parties in a dissolution or legal separation proceeding. The power to divide presumes the power to characterize property as separate or community. Once characterization is determined a court has no jurisdiction over the separate property of either spouse, with two exceptions. The first is that either party can request that the court divide separate property owned concurrently between them. California Family Code Section 2650. The second is that a spouse who owns separate property can consent to the exercise of jurisdiction over that property for purposes of the proceeding.

Personal jurisdiction is required over a respondent in order to adjudicate his or her rights in community or quasi-community property. A judgment affecting property rights entered without personal jurisdiction is not entitled to full faith and credit. *Muckle v. Superior Court,* below, addresses the issue. There are a variety of bases for obtaining the requisite personal jurisdiction, including domicile, residence, and consent. See California Code of Civil Procedure § 410.10.

B. JURISDICTION TO DIVIDE PROPERTY

Another jurisdictional issue involves the power of the court to determine property rights in a default proceeding. Prior to the 1969 Family Law Act, in order to invoke the jurisdiction of the court to divide community property it was necessary to plead the existence of such property and to request a division. A general prayer would support a division if the issues of classification and division had actually been contested, but a general prayer would not support a division in default proceedings. Although terminology has changed (the divorce complaint is now a petition for dissolution), it appears that the rules about pleading the existence of property and requesting division would continue to apply. Additionally, the distinction between contested and default proceedings will continue to obtain.

During the dissolution process, a petitioner may opt to file a motion to bifurcate, or sever, the issue of marital status from property issues. The rationale for bifurcation is that the public interest is not concerned if the parties engage in property litigation, but it is concerned if the parties are forced to retain the status of married when they would prefer to be single.

Bifurcation requires disclosure with a completed schedule of assets and debts. That schedule shall be served to the nonmoving party with the motion to sever (unless disclosure has already been made). California Family Code 2337. The policy behind the bifurcation disclosure requirement is to protect the nonmoving party from adverse consequences that might result from the granting of a severance motion.

GIONIS V. SUPERIOR COURT

202 Cal.App.3d 786, 248 Cal.Rptr. 741 (4th Dist. 1988)

WALLIN, ASSOCIATE JUSTICE.

Thomas A. Gionis seeks a writ of mandate compelling the superior court to vacate its order denying his motion to bifurcate the issue of his marital status from all other issues. He claims the trial court abused its discretion by denying his motion as untimely. We agree with petitioner and issue the writ.

* * *

Aissa and Thomas Gionis were married on February 14, 1986. In June 1987 Aissa filed a petition for legal separation and a separate petition for dissolution of marriage. Both petitions requested sole custody of the parties' infant daughter as well as child and spousal support.

Thomas responded and filed a motion to change venue. The declarations supporting and opposing the motion revealed deep bitterness between the parties over the issue of child custody. The parties then stipulated to proceed with the petition for dissolution of marriage, and agreed that the court acquired jurisdiction over both parties for that purpose in June 1987.

On January 29, 1988, Thomas moved to bifurcate the issue of marital status from the issues of custody, support and property division. His declaration stated the marriage had irrevocably failed, reconciliation was not possible and although the trial of the dissolution would be brief, the remaining issues would require discovery and a more lengthy trial. He further stated he wanted his marital status resolved so he could make investments and obtain credit without having to seek quitclaim deeds from Aissa or worry that a lender might rely on community rather than separate credit. Aissa's opposition to the motion raised procedural objections; she set forth no substantive reasons why bifurcation would be against her interests.

The court denied the motion, stating there was no compelling reason to bifurcate since the petition had been on file less than a year. "I don't really find a good cause stated for proceeding after only about seven months since the filing. . . . I'll tell you one I granted. They had been separated for a couple of years, and the wife had two babies, on her husband's health insurance policy; and he was not the father of either one of them. And I thought that was good cause. And I granted that." Additionally, the judge apparently felt the parties should be required to undergo a period of sexual restraint before being permitted to dissolve their marriage. He stated twice: "Tell them to take a cold shower." Thomas filed this petition for a writ of mandate, contending the trial court abused its discretion by refusing to bifurcate the action.

Separating the termination of a marriage from controversies over spousal support, child custody and division of marital property is not a new idea. In *Hull v. Superior Court* (1960) 54 Cal.2d 139, 5 Cal.Rptr. 1, 352 P.2d 161, the Supreme Court explained the concept of "divisible divorce" as follows: "Severance of a personal relationship which the law has found to be unworkable and, as a result, injurious to the public welfare is not dependent upon final settlement of property disputes. Society will be little concerned if the parties engage in property litigation of however long duration; it will be much concerned if two people are forced to remain legally bound to one another when this status can do nothing but engender additional bitterness and unhappiness." (*Id.,* at pp. 147–148, 5 Cal.Rptr. 1, 352 P.2d 161.)

This philosophy was incorporated into the Family Law Act * * * which removed the issue of marital fault from domestic relations litigation. (*In re Marriage of Fink* (1976) 54 Cal.App.3d 357, 126 Cal.Rptr. 626.) "[T]he new Family Law Act embodied a legislative intent that the dissolution of marriage should not be postponed merely because issues relating to property, support, attorney fees or child custody were unready for decision." (*Id.,* at p. 363, 126 Cal.Rptr. 626.) Complying with that legislative intent, courts have encouraged bifurcation of marital status from other issues. (*In re Marriage of Wolfe* (1985) 173 Cal.App.3d 889, 219 Cal.Rptr. 337; *In re Marriage of Lusk* (1978) 86 Cal.App.3d 228, 150 Cal.Rptr. 63; *In re Marriage of Van Sickle* (1977) 68 Cal.App.3d 728, 137 Cal.Rptr. 568; *In re Marriage of Fink, supra,* 54 Cal.App.3d 357, 126 Cal.Rptr. 626.)

In light of the policies favoring bifurcation, the trial court was mistaken in its apparent belief that Thomas was required to justify his request with a compelling showing of need. Two previous cases in which the granting of a bifurcation motion was contested upheld the order based on declarations strikingly similar to Thomas'. In *In re Marriage of Fink, supra,* 54 Cal.App.3d 357, 126 Cal.Rptr. 626, the husband's declaration stated "that reconciliation was not possible, that the dissolution hearing would be brief, and that the other issues (ascertainment and division of community property, spousal support and attorney fees) would require a long trial preceded by extensive discovery." (*Id.,* at pp. 359–360, 126 Cal.Rptr. 626.) And in *In re Marriage of Lusk, supra,* 86 Cal.App.3d 228, 150 Cal.Rptr. 63, the husband's declaration "averred that he had no intention of reconciling with wife, that he believed it was in the best interest of all parties that the marriage be dissolved without further delay 'so that all parties may develop a new life with a reasonable degree of stability and certainty' and with the hope that 'immediate dissolution of the marriage will remove a great deal of emotional strain and pressure' from both husband and wife and 'may help facilitate a settlement regarding the other reserved issues.' " (*Id.*, at p. 231, 150 Cal.Rptr. 63.)

In his declaration Thomas maintained reconciliation was impossible and the issues other than status would require a lengthy trial. He continued with extensive personal reasons why he wanted his brief marriage to Aissa dissolved quickly. Absent a showing by Aissa why bifurcation should not be granted, Thomas' declaration provided a proper basis for the motion.

* * *

Thomas' declaration contained sufficient reasons supporting his motion to bifurcate, and the trial court abused its discretion by refusing to grant it. Consistent with the legislative policy favoring no fault dissolution of marriage, only slight evidence is necessary to obtain bifurcation and resolution of marital status. On the other hand, a spouse opposing bifurcation must present compelling reasons for denial.

* * *

SCOVILLE, P.J. and CROSBY, J., concur.

Although the court in a dissolution proceeding has no jurisdiction over the parties' separate property, it has been held that the parties may stipulate to a determination and disposition of all their property rights, and that a broad grant of consent gives a court authority to dispose of separate property.

ROBINSON V. ROBINSON
65 Cal.App.2d 118, 150 P.2d 7 (2d Dist. 1944)

W.J. WOOD, JUSTICE.

In this action to quiet title plaintiff has appealed from a judgment awarding to defendant a life interest in the real property which is the subject of the litigation.

An interlocutory decree was awarded to Theresa Robinson, defendant herein, on June 10, 1942, she having theretofore commenced an action against plaintiff for separate maintenance in which she later changed her prayer to ask for a divorce. In the divorce action she listed various properties of the parties, some of which she alleged to be community property. She specifically alleged that the real estate which is the subject of the present litigation was the separate property of the plaintiff herein,

Lewis Robinson. A cross-complaint was filed in the divorce action and the court in its interlocutory decree of divorce ordered the plaintiff herein to pay to defendant herein the sum of $12.50 per month until the further order of the court and also gave her "the right to remain in and to continue to reside and enjoy possession of the premises she now occupies at 1609 East 110th Street, Los Angeles." A part of the community property was awarded to each of the parties. In the final decree of divorce, which was entered on June 17, 1943, no reference was made to the real property involved in this action.

The present action was commenced on January 12, 1943. By its judgment entered on October 5, 1943, the court decreed that plaintiff is the owner in fee of the land described in the complaint, "subject however, to a life estate therein of defendant Theresa Robinson during her natural life to use the improvement thereon consisting of a dwelling known as 1609 East 110th Street, Los Angeles, California."

The power of the court in disposing of the property of the parties in a divorce action is limited to their community property. In such a proceeding the court has no power to dispose of the separate property of one of the parties, nor to carve out a life estate therein. Roy v. Roy, 29 Cal.App.2d 596, 85 P.2d 223. In the divorce action of the parties to the present litigation no issue was made concerning the ownership of the real estate in question, for it was specifically alleged by the wife that the realty was the separate property of the husband. The court therefore was without jurisdiction to award to the wife a life estate therein.

The judgment is reversed. The purported appeal from the order denying a motion for a new trial is dismissed.

NOTES

1.   *Jurisdiction over separate property?* For additional cases on the subject, see *Spahn v. Spahn*, 70 Cal.App.2d 791, 162 P.2d 53 (2d Dist. 1945); *Marriage of Dorris*, 160 Cal.App.3d 1208, 207 Cal.Rptr. 160 (4th Dist. 1984).

2.   *Concurrently owned* separate property *interests (joint tenancy and tenancy in common).* California Family Code Section 2650 provides that if the parties so request, a court has authority to divide "the separate property interest of the parties in real and personal property, wherever situated and whenever acquired . . . [because] it is that request that gives the court express jurisdiction over such property in a dissolution proceeding." California Family Code Section 2650 applies regardless of where the separate property is located, or when the separate property was acquired. The parties can agree to bar the application of California Family Code Section 2650. Background on the updated provision can be found at *Recommendation Relating to Dividing Jointly Owned Property Upon Marriage Dissolution*, 18 CAL. L. REVISION COMM'N REPORTS 147, 365 (1986) and 23 CAL. L. REVISION COMM'N REPORTS 1 (1993).

3. *To what extent can a dissolution judgment affect the property rights of third persons?* Clearly the rights of creditors may be affected by a dissolution judgment, but on occasion so might the rights of other third parties. In *Marriage of Davis,* 68 Cal.App.3d 294, 137 Cal.Rptr. 265 (5th Dist. 1977), for example, the wife filed a petition for dissolution in which she joined her husband's mother as an indispensable party. The wife alleged that the mother held legal title to community real property for convenience only. The mother appeared solely to argue that the family court's limited jurisdiction precluded it from trying title to property in her name. The appellate court disagreed: It held that the trial court acquires jurisdiction over the marriage and the marital property; once that jurisdiction is acquired, the " '[the family court] may bring to its aid the full equitable and legal powers with which, as the superior court it is invested' and which is necessary to the discharge of its jurisdiction of the subject matter. *Estate of Baldwin*, 21 Cal. 2d 586, 594, 134 P.2d 259, 264 (1943)." *Davis, supra* at 300.

Third-party due process concerns in a dissolution proceeding may require an analysis of a court's acquired jurisdiction. Two elements must be met to satisfy a third party's due process rights relative to a dissolution. The third party must have notice. And the third party must have an opportunity to be heard.

Muckle is a case about personal jurisdiction over a defendant who is named in a 2001 dissolution proceeding, but who has been domiciled in George since 1998.

MUCKLE V. SUPERIOR COURT
102 Cal.App.4th 218, 125 Cal.Rptr.2d 303 (4th Dist. 2002)

Huffman, J.

Andrew Muckle (Andrew) petitions for a writ of mandate commanding respondent court to vacate its order of April 4, 2002, denying his motion to quash service of summons in the action commenced by real party in interest Cassandra Burgess-Muckle (Cassandra) for dissolution of their 11-year marriage, spousal support and property division, or dismiss the action on the ground of inconvenient forum, and to enter a new and different order granting the motion. The question raised is whether, consistent with the due process clause of the United States Constitution, California can exercise personal jurisdiction over Andrew, who has been domiciled in Georgia since December 1998. Based on the record presented, we answer the question in the negative and issue a writ of mandate to prevent the court from exercising such jurisdiction.

Background and Procedure

Andrew and Cassandra met in Georgia, where Andrew lived and worked and Cassandra visited her mother. When Cassandra's mother died in 1988, she moved into her mother's house in Georgia, where she resided continuously until marrying Andrew there in 1989. During their 11-year marriage they lived at various times in Georgia and California, separating and reconciling repeatedly. The couple had no children during their marriage.

In July 1998, while the parties were living in California, Andrew purchased a home in Georgia, taking title to it in his name alone. In December 1998, Andrew returned to Georgia to live in the house. Shortly thereafter Cassandra followed, eventually moving in with Andrew. In the spring of 2000, Cassandra returned to California and lived in a trailer Andrew bought for her. At some point, she sold the trailer, keeping the proceeds, and filed her petition for dissolution.

On about August 21, 2001, Cassandra served dissolution papers on Andrew in Georgia by substituted service. In those papers Cassandra claimed as community property both the home Andrew had bought in Georgia while living in California in 1998 and another house in Georgia that had been purchased in 1985 with title in Andrew's name and that of his son Phillip Muckle.

On March 1, 2002, Andrew made a special appearance to contest jurisdiction (Code Civ. Proc., § 418.10; Cal. Rules of Court, rule 1234), moving to quash service of summons for lack of personal jurisdiction or, alternatively, to stay or dismiss the action on the ground of inconvenient forum. He argued he had insufficient minimum contacts with California for the trial court to establish personal jurisdiction over him, and, alternatively if such were found, the court should dismiss the action on the ground of forum non conveniens. (Code Civ. Proc., § 410.30.) In his supporting declaration, Andrew noted he was 65 years old, had lived in Georgia continuously since December 1998, had worked and paid taxes in Georgia, had a Georgia driver's license, was registered to vote in Georgia, had no personal or real property in California, and asserted he could not afford to travel to California to "fight this litigation [or] transport witnesses to verify [his] rights and interests in the houses [he] own[ed] in Georgia."

Cassandra countered Andrew's position, declaring he had been a resident of California from January 1998 through December 1998, that the subject property had been bought in Georgia in July 1998, thus making it community property under Family Code section 760, that Andrew had refused to submit to the court's jurisdiction to determine her community property interests in such property, and that she was "too ill to travel to Georgia to litigate this matter."

At the March 11, 2002 hearing on the matter, Cassandra's counsel conceded there were not minimum contacts for personal jurisdiction over Andrew for spousal support purposes, but argued the trial court did not need personal, only "in rem," jurisdiction over him to divide his home in Georgia because it was purchased during the marriage while he was living in California. The court took the matter under submission on the agreed upon issue of whether the court had jurisdiction to determine the rights of the parties in the Georgia property that was purchased while the parties resided in California. That same date, Andrew filed supplemental points and authorities supporting his motion to quash, arguing the same "minimum contacts" standard necessary for personal jurisdiction over a person was also required to exercise in rem or quasi in rem jurisdiction when property rights were asserted.

On March 14, 2002, Cassandra filed points and authorities in opposition to Andrew's motion to quash, arguing Andrew had maintained sufficient minimum contacts with California due to his "purposeful availment" of privileges of conducting activities in California by residing and working in California for over 10 years before returning to Georgia in 1998, by filing and receiving $150,000 on a worker's compensation claim against his Escondido employer, by using $70,000 of those funds for his down payment on the property he purchased in Georgia while the parties were married and lived in California, and by traveling from Georgia to California on numerous occasions. Cassandra asserted it was reasonable to exert jurisdiction over Andrew because of his above affirmative conduct and the facts he was in "excellent health," while she was "suffering from an attack on her auto-immune system which makes walking for her more difficult each day." She stated she had been a resident of California for over 10 years and that California had a strong public policy of equal division of community property for which she did not have an alternative forum to litigate her interests because Georgia is not a community property state. She further asserted that " 'progress in communications and transportation has made the defense of a suit in a foreign tribunal less burdensome. [Citation.]' " Cassandra filed no declaration or evidence in support of the factual allegations contained in her papers filed after the matter was taken under submission.

On April 4, 2002, the trial court issued its order on the matter, "[a]fter considering the Briefing filed by the parties, both before and after the hearing and entertaining oral argument," as follows:

> "1. The Court denies [Andrew's] companion Motion to Quash Service of Process. The factual basis for this ruling is that the parties had an 11-year marriage with no children. They met and married in Georgia and lived in both Georgia and California. The parties lived in California until at least December of 1998. While in California, [Andrew] rented an apartment in Vista from January, 1998 through December of 1998. He purchased property in Georgia while he was still a resident in California. He was a California resident for ten (10) years prior to December of 1998. He filed a worker's compensation claim against an Escondido employer while a resident of California. He received $150,000

from the worker's compensation claim while a resident in California and used $70,000 of these funds to purchase property in Georgia. [¶]

2.   Under these circumstances, the Court believes that [Andrew] has 'minimum contact with a forum state, such that maintenance of the suit does not offend traditional notions of fair play and substantial justice." [(] *In re Marriage of Lontos* (1979) 89 Cal.App.3d 61, 152 Cal.Rptr. 271 [*Lontos*], citing *International Shoe v. Washington* (1945) 326 U.S. 310, 66 S.Ct. 154, 90 L.Ed. 95 [(*International Shoe*).)]

The court also noted authority for its ability to adjudicate the rights of the parties to the property in Georgia, and stated "[t]he pivotal factor[s] for the Court in this matter in determining minimum contacts are the fact that [Andrew] lived in California and availed himself of the protections offered by this forum during his period of residency, including participation in the California Worker's Compensation program."

Andrew thereafter filed the current petition for writ of mandate, challenging the trial court's ruling denying his motion to quash service of summons. (Code Civ. Proc., § 418.10.) We issued an order to show cause why the relief requested should not be granted and set the matter for oral argument.

Discussion

In general, "jurisdiction" to adjudicate matters in a marital case involves three requirements: 1) that the court have authority to adjudicate the specific matter raised by the pleadings (subject matter jurisdiction) (see Fam.Code, § 2010); 2) that the court have "in rem" jurisdiction over the marital "res" to terminate marital status ("in rem" jurisdiction) (see *Marriage of Zierenberg* (1992) 11 Cal.App.4th 1436, 1444–1445, 16 Cal.Rptr.2d 238); and 3) that the court have jurisdiction over the parties to adjudicate personal rights and obligations (personal jurisdiction). (See Code Civ. Proc., § 410.10; *Burnham v. Superior Court* (1990) 495 U.S. 604, 110 S.Ct. 2105, 109 L.Ed.2d 631 (*Burnham*); *In re Marriage of Fitzgerald & King* (1995) 39 Cal.App.4th 1419, 1425, 46 Cal.Rptr.2d 558 (*Fitzgerald & King*).)

Once the court has met these jurisdictional requirements it may determine not only the marital status, but also the personal rights and obligations of the parties, including custody and support of minor children of the marriage, spousal support, settlement and division of the parties' property rights, and the award of costs and attorney fees. (Fam.Code, § 2010.) With regard to property rights, the court generally looks to the domicile of the parties at the time the property was acquired to characterize it as separate or community for the purposes of division upon a dissolution of the marital status. (*Grappo v. Coventry Financial Corp.*

(1991) 235 Cal.App.3d 496, 505, 286 Cal.Rptr. 714.) "[M]arital interests in money and property acquired during a marriage are governed by the law of the domicile at the time of their acquisition, even when such money and property is used to purchase real property in another state. [Citations.]" (*Ibid.*) California law provides that "[e]xcept as otherwise provided by statute, all property, real or personal, wherever situated, acquired by a married person during the marriage while domiciled in this state is community property." (Fam.Code, § 760.) It is further settled California law that " 'a court having jurisdiction of the parties [in a dissolution action] may adjudicate their rights to land located in another state and that the adjudication is res judicata and is to be accorded full faith and credit in the situs state regardless of whether the decree orders execution of a conveyance. * * * ' [Citations.]" (*In re Marriage of Economou* (1990) 224 Cal.App.3d 1466, 1479–1480, 274 Cal.Rptr. 473; see also Fam.Code, § 2660.)

Here, the parties do not contest that the California trial court has subject matter jurisdiction and in rem jurisdiction to adjudicate the status of their marriage due to Cassandra's domicile in California at the time of filing her petition for dissolution. (See *Marriage of Gray* (1988) 204 Cal.App.3d 1239, 1250, 251 Cal.Rptr. 846.) Rather the parties conflict only on whether the trial court can exercise personal jurisdiction over Andrew who is now a resident and domiciled in Georgia for purposes of adjudicating his rights in real property located in Georgia and for spousal support.

As the court in *Fitzgerald & King* noted, "[d]ue process permits the exercise of personal jurisdiction over a nonresident defendant in the following four situations: (1) where the defendant is domiciled in the forum state when the lawsuit is commenced [citation]; (2) where the defendant is personally served with process while he or she is physically present in the forum state [citation]; (3) where the defendant consents to jurisdiction [citations]; and (4) where the defendant has sufficient 'minimum contacts' with the forum state, such that the exercise of jurisdiction would not offend ' "traditional notions of fair play and substantial justice" ' [citation]." (*Fitzgerald & King, supra,* 39 Cal.App.4th at pp. 1425–1426, 46 Cal.Rptr.2d 558.) Because Andrew is not domiciled in California, was not personally served with process while present in California, and did not consent to jurisdiction, the trial court could only support its denial of his motion to quash the summons served on him in Georgia by predicating personal jurisdiction to determine any property rights of the marriage for division on Andrew having "minimum contacts" with California.

In determining whether such "minimum contacts" exist for a valid assertion of jurisdiction over a nonconsenting nonresident who is not present in the forum, a court must look at " 'the quality and nature of [the nonresident's] activity' in relation to the forum [to determine whether it] renders such jurisdiction consistent with "traditional notions of fair play and substantial justice." (*Burnham, supra,* 495 U.S. at p. 618, 110 S.Ct. 2105; *International Shoe, supra,* 326 U.S. at pp. 316, 319, 66 S.Ct. 154.) Although the existence of sufficient "minimum contacts" depends on the facts of each case, the ultimate determination generally rests on some conduct by which the nonresident has purposefully availed himself of the privilege of conducting activities within the forum state to invoke its benefits and protections, and a sufficient relationship or nexus between the nonresident and the forum state such that it is reasonable and fair to require the nonresident to appear locally to conduct a defense. (*Kulko v. Superior Court of California* (1978) 436 U.S. 84, 93–94, 96–97, 98 S.Ct. 1690, 56 L.Ed.2d 132 (*Kulko*); *Khan v. Superior Court* (1988) 204 Cal.App.3d 1168, 1175–1176, 251 Cal.Rptr. 815 (*Khan*).) This latter "fairness" finding requires a balancing of the burden or inconvenience to the nonresident against the resident plaintiff's or petitioner's interest in obtaining effective relief, and the state's interest in adjudicating the particular dispute, which ultimately turns on the nature and quality of the nonresident's forum-related activity. (*Kulko, supra,* 436 U.S. at p. 94, 98 S.Ct. 1690; see also *Khan, supra,* 204 Cal.App.3d at pp. 1179–1180, 251 Cal.Rptr. 815.)

Whereas here, in an initial family law proceeding for marriage dissolution, a nonresident moves to quash for defective personal jurisdiction on grounds he lacks minimum contacts with the forum state, the court looks at the contacts at the time of the proceeding and not on whether past minimum contacts might suffice. (*Tarvin v. Tarvin* (1986) 187 Cal.App.3d 56, 60–61, 232 Cal.Rptr. 13.) When the contacts are "substantial, continuous and systematic," general personal jurisdiction may be exercised as to any cause of action, even one unrelated to the nonresident's activities within the forum state. (*Perkins v. Benguet Consolidated Mining Co.* (1952) 342 U.S. 437, 447–448, 72 S.Ct. 413, 96 L.Ed. 485.) Even when the nonresident's contacts are not "substantial, continuous and systematic" forum-state acts, a court may still exercise "specific" personal jurisdiction limited to claims arising out of the forum-related acts. (*Burger King Corp. v. Rudzewicz* (1985) 471 U.S. 462, 472–473, 105 S.Ct. 2174, 85 L.Ed.2d 528 (*Burger King*).)

The test for whether a court may exercise "specific" personal jurisdiction requires that the nonresident purposefully directed his acts to the forum state or otherwise purposefully established contacts with the forum state, that the cause of action be related to or arise or result from the acts or contacts in the forum, and that the exercise of personal jurisdiction by the forum would be reasonable. (*Burger King, supra,* 471 U.S. at pp. 476–478, 105 S.Ct. 2174; see *Vons Companies, Inc. v. Seabest Foods, Inc.* (1996) 14 Cal.4th 434, 446–448, 58 Cal.Rptr.2d 899, 926 P.2d 1085 (*Vons*); *In re Marriage of Hattis* (1987) 196 Cal.App.3d 1162, 1173, 242 Cal.Rptr. 410 (*Hattis*).)

As the court in *Vons,* stated:

"When a [nonresident] moves to quash service of process on jurisdictional grounds, the plaintiff [or petitioner] has the initial burden of demonstrating facts justifying the exercise of jurisdiction. [Citation.] Once facts showing minimum contacts with the forum state are established, however, it becomes the defendant's burden to demonstrate that the exercise of jurisdiction would be unreasonable. [Citation.] When there is conflicting evidence, the trial court's factual determinations are not disturbed on appeal if supported by substantial evidence. [Citation.] When no conflict in the evidence exists, however, the question of jurisdiction is purely one of law and the reviewing court engages in an independent review of the record. [Citation.]" (*Vons, supra,* 14 Cal.4th at p. 449, 58 Cal.Rptr.2d 899, 926 P.2d 1085.)

In this case, Cassandra had the initial burden of establishing facts to justify the trial court's exercise of personal jurisdiction over Andrew with regard to determining the rights of the parties in the Georgia property admittedly purchased while Andrew lived in California during his marriage to Cassandra. At the time the matter was taken under submission, those were the only facts supported by evidence before the court concerning Andrew's contacts with the state of California other than the length of the marriage, that it was entered into in Georgia, that there were no children of the marriage, that the parties lived at various times in Georgia and California, separating and reconciling repeatedly during the marriage, that Andrew left California in December 1998, and that Cassandra followed him to Georgia to live with him shortly thereafter. Although there was evidence that sometime after Cassandra left Andrew in Georgia to return to California to live in the spring of 2000, he bought a trailer in California for her, there were no underlying facts established as to whether Andrew came to California at that time or merely gave Cassandra the money to use to purchase the trailer. Regardless, evidence showed that the trailer had been sold before Cassandra filed her schedule of assets and debts in the dissolution action she filed in California. Thus, at the time of the motion to quash hearing, there was no evidence of any contacts by Andrew with California at the time the dissolution action was filed by Cassandra; only past contacts with California by Andrew were shown.

The trial court, however, took into consideration unsubstantiated "alleged facts" in Cassandra's points and authorities in opposition to the motion filed after the matter was taken under submission regarding Andrew's additional past and arguably continuing contacts with California to support its denial of the motion. In addition to the court considering new material after an issue was taken under submission, there was no evidence in the record to support the assertions by Cassandra that Andrew lived and worked in California for 10 years before he departed for Georgia in December 1998, or that he received and then used money from the settlement of a California worker's compensation claim to purchase the property he bought in Georgia in July 1998. The trial court relied heavily on such facts to find that Andrew had so availed himself of the benefits of this state in the past that traditional notions of fair play and substantial justice would not be offended by making him appear in California to defend his rights to the property in Georgia. On the paucity of evidence in this record, we cannot find the trial court's finding of minimum contacts for personal jurisdiction over Andrew supported by substantial evidence. Nor does our independent review of the matter render a different conclusion.

Unlike the situation in *Lontos, supra,* 89 Cal.App.3d 61, 152 Cal.Rptr. 271, which the trial court cited as authority for finding personal jurisdiction, the parties did not meet or marry in California, they did not have any children in California, they did not live in California at the time of the separation, and there is no evidence Andrew abandoned Cassandra or failed to provide for her after the separation. In *Lontos,* the parties had met and married in California; one of their three children was born in California; they had lived continuously in California for six years before they moved to New Mexico where husband, who was in the United States Marine Corps, had been transferred. (*Lontos, supra,* 89 Cal.App.3d at pp. 64–65, 152 Cal.Rptr. 271.) The husband then abandoned his wife and three children, leaving them $10 for support; and wife and children returned to San Diego and obtained welfare assistance when husband refused to pay court-ordered support. (*Ibid.*) Based on these facts, the court in *Lontos* found that husband's contacts in California together with his abandonment of the family, which constituted "proof of a purposeful causing of an effect creating a substantial contact in California," were "of such quality and nature that it [was] 'reasonable' and 'fair' to require him to conduct his defense in California." (*Id.* at pp. 71–72, 152 Cal.Rptr. 271.)

Although "California has a manifest interest in providing effective means of redress for its residents" (*McGee v. International Life Ins. Co.* (1957) 355 U.S. 220, 223, 78 S.Ct. 199, 2 L.Ed.2d 223), we do not believe such interest coupled with the mere fact of past residency, during which a party while married purchased out of state property, is sufficient contacts of such nature and quality to entertain even "special" personal jurisdiction over Andrew consistent with "traditional notions of fair play and substantial justice." (*Burnham, supra,* 495 U.S. at p. 618, 110 S.Ct. 2105.) Andrew's contacts with California since 1998 have not been "substantial, continuous and systematic," and there is no evidence he purposefully directed any activities since that time in or toward California other than to provide some shelter for Cassandra.

However, even if we were to find that Cassandra had met her burden of showing Andrew had sufficient minimum contacts at the time she filed the dissolution action, we would find the exercise of personal jurisdiction over Andrew on this record unreasonable. Although Cassandra is purportedly of ill health, there is no evidence she is a burden on the state (as in *Lontos, supra,* 89 Cal.App.3d 61, 152 Cal.Rptr. 271 or *Hattis, supra,* 196 Cal.App.3d 1162, 242 Cal.Rptr. 410) or that she does not have financial resources to pursue her action on the division of the property and spousal support in Georgia after obtaining a dissolution of the marital status in California. As she noted in her declaration, " 'progress in communications and transportation has made the defense of a suit in a foreign tribunal less burdensome. [Citation.]' "

On the other hand, Andrew has submitted evidence to show he has been domiciled and has worked in Georgia since December 1998, has paid taxes there, has a Georgia driver's license, and only owns property in Georgia—thereby taking advantage of the benefits of that state. There is also evidence that the parties met and married in Georgia and lived in Georgia almost two years before they separated and Cassandra returned to California in 2000. Although Andrew does not mention anything about his health, he does say he is 65 years old and without much wealth, making it a financial burden to travel to California to "fight this litigation," which would entail transporting witnesses from Georgia to verify his rights and interests in the houses he owns in Georgia. Balancing these factors against those in favor of Cassandra due to her current residency in California and the state's connection to the parties marriage via her uncontested domicile here, and the fact any potential clash in the marital property laws of Georgia and California may be accommodated through application of Georgia's choice-of-law rules, we conclude it would be unreasonable or unfair to require Andrew to come to California to litigate issues of spousal support and property rights. Accordingly, a writ of mandate is proper to prevent the trial court from asserting personal jurisdiction over Andrew for purposes of determining such rights and support. (Code Civ. Proc., § 418.10, subd. (c).)

Having determined that the trial court erred in denying Andrew's motion to quash on the evidence properly before it, we need not address Andrew's additional arguments concerning judicial estoppel and forum non conveniens.

Disposition

Let a writ of mandate issue directing the Superior Court of San Diego to vacate its order of April 4, 2002, denying Andrew's motion to quash service of summons in the dissolution action and to enter a new and different order granting the motion and quashing the service of summons in such action. Costs are awarded to Andrew.

WE CONCUR: BENKE, ACTING P.J., and McCONNELL, J.

NOTE

Dissolution related forms. Marriage of Siegel, 239 Cal.App.4th 944, 191 Cal.Rptr.3d 330 (1st Dist. 2015) declined to extend *Marriage of Andresen*, 28 Cal.App.4th 873, 34 Cal.Rptr.2d 147 (5th Dist. 1994) saying that in *Andresen* the petitioner filled out the necessary dissolution-related property forms properly and consistently thus giving the respondent adequate notice, whereas in *Siegel* the petitioner (only) filled out a request for an order to disclose insurance information. The court distinguished a request from an order to divide property (*Andresen*) from a request for an order to disclose insurance information (*Siegal*).

C. POWER TO DEFER SALE OF THE FAMILY HOME

Custodial parents have an option to request that the sale of the family home be deferred. Originally the deferred sale option was available only to custodial parents of minor children. Eventually, statutes were amended, in response to decisional law, to expand the deferred sale option to custodial parents of adult children with disabilities who need continuing support.

The next case, *Stallworth*, confirms that the trial judge has broad discretion to defer the sale of the family home after weighing economic and noneconomic factors. The issue has been codified in the relevant Family Code provisions that follow the court opinion.

MARRIAGE OF STALLWORTH
192 Cal.App.3d 742, 237 Cal.Rptr. 829 (1st Dist. 1987)

KING, ASSOCIATE JUSTICE.

William Stallworth appeals from a judgment of dissolution of marriage. He asserts multiple errors in the classification and distribution of certain assets * * * .

William and Carol Stallworth were married 14 1/2 years and had one son, Robert, born November 30, 1976. They separated in October 1983, and William filed for dissolution in February 1984. The matter came to trial in April 1985. Although William filed objections to the trial court's proposed statement of decision, they were rejected.

The Family Home

It was undisputed that the Stallworth family home, the parties' major asset, was community property. The court found it had a fair market value of $138,250 with a loan balance of $16,000, for an equity of $122,250. In making its disposition of the home the court found "that the mental condition of the minor child of the parties and the financial condition of the parties require that [Carol] and the minor child be allowed to live in the family residence until the said child shall reach the age of 18 years, dies, marries, becomes otherwise emancipated, or until [Carol] remarries, discontinues her residence at said residence, or resides therein with a male with whom she is cohabiting who also resides at said residence. Upon the happening of any of the above circumstances, the residence shall be placed on the market for sale and the proceeds of said sale divided equally between the parties. [Carol] shall pay all mortgage payments, taxes, upkeep, and homeowners association payments on the said residence while she resides there." The court left title to the home in the names of the parties as joint tenants.

The testimony was uncontroverted that Robert was under a psychiatrist's care, was in a special education program at school, and attended a private reading program at the school's recommendation. These facts, standing alone, are insufficient to support an inference that a move from the family home would have an adverse social or emotional impact on Robert. There was no evidence that Robert's circumstances would be adversely affected by a move from the family home or, if so, that the effect would offset the economic detriment to William of deferring his receipt of his community share of the equity in the home for a 10-year period.

Carol testified she could not obtain equivalent housing in the same district for a comparable price ($238 a month for mortgage, taxes and insurance). The court reduced William's family support obligation by $150 in light of the low house payments on the family residence. There was no evidence as to whether and at what cost Carol could obtain comparable housing in the same neighborhood or school district, although she believed the cost would be greater. If a sale causes Carol's housing cost to increase, this increased need should result in higher support. (See fn. 1, *supra.*) Finally, Carol presented no evidence to justify continuing the family home award, if any, for 10 years, until Robert reached the age of 18. Since Civil Code section 4800.7 provides that a "family home award" means "an order that awards *temporary* use of the home," the evidence would have to justify a family home award for a 10-year period. (Emphasis added.) Even if the evidence justifies a family home award, the trial court must exercise its discretion in setting the duration of the award in accordance with the evidence on that issue.

"The trial court's authority to award the family residence to the parties as tenants-in-common and award the custodial parent exclusive possession as additional child support was first approved in *In re Marriage of Boseman* (1973) 31 Cal.App.3d 372 [107 Cal.Rptr. 232]. *Boseman* was followed in *In re Marriage of Herrmann* (1978) 84 Cal.App.3d 361 [148 Cal.Rptr. 550] [award of note reversed; house should be awarded to parties as tenants-in-common, with exclusive possession to custodial parent, when award to either party is economically unfeasible]. The third part of the trilogy, *In re Marriage of Duke* (1980) 101 Cal.App.3d 152 [161 Cal.Rptr. 444], requires that the sale of the house be deferred and that a *Boseman/Herrmann* order be made under certain designated circumstances." * * * We have previously noted our disagreement with *Duke's* limitation on the trial court's discretion by stating "*Duke* has been described as holding that deferring the sale of the family home until the youngest child of the parties reaches the age of majority must always be ordered where adverse economic, emotional and social impacts on the minor result from an immediate loss of a long-established family home and are not outweighed by the economic detriment to the out-spouse by the delay in receiving his or her share of the proceeds in the equity of the family home. We believe the better rule is that of *In re Marriage of Herrmann, supra,* 84 Cal.App.3d 361 [148 Cal.Rptr. 550], and *In re Marriage of Boseman, supra,* 31 Cal.App.3d 372 [107 Cal.Rptr. 232], that the trial judge should weigh these factors, as well as others, and be vested with broad discretion in making a disposition of the family home. * * * As a practical matter, it should be noted that the emotional attachment of a child to a home may be minimal if the child is very young and of questionable significance if the child is an older teenager. However, in the event the court exercises its discretion to order a deferral of sale of the family home, we do not agree that sale of the family home must always be deferred until the youngest child of the parties reaches the age of 18. Where such deferral would delay sale for many years the trial court has the discretion to determine an appropriate earlier time at which a sale might take place, such as when the child would naturally be changing schools to one outside of the immediate neighborhood. Additionally, we believe that the factor of economic detriment to the noncustodial parent should be broadly construed in today's economic circumstances. Given the extremely high cost of housing in urban areas in California, only the very wealthy are in a position to purchase a new home without receiving their share of a sizeable equity in an existing home. Thus, deferral of the sale of the family home would not only interfere and perhaps preclude the out-spouse from obtaining suitable housing accommodations to be able to enjoy the frequent and continuing contact with his or her children which is the public policy of California as set forth in [Civil Code] section 4600, subdivision (a) [current California Family Code Section 3020], but may well preclude obtaining adequate housing for themselves and any later family they may acquire, and limit their ability to be able to get on with living their own life in their postdivorce world. If considerable appreciation has taken place, tax factors should also be considered in reaching the decision whether or not to defer a sale, even if they are not clearly immediate and specific as would be required for accomplishing an equal division of the property. * * * If deferral of the sale would deprive the out-spouse of a deferral of tax on the gain by precluding the tax-free 24-month roll-over of equity into a new residence under Internal Revenue Code section 1034, or of the one time exclusion of gain up to $125,000 under Internal Revenue Code section 121 and Revenue and Taxation Code section

17155, it is certainly equitable to consider these factors in determining the disposition of the family home. It could be argued that the loss of the tax benefits of Internal Revenue Code sections 1034 and 121, and their California counterparts, provide sufficient economic detriment to the out-spouse so as to require, as a matter of law, an immediate, rather than a deferred, sale of the family home." (*In re Marriage of Horowitz* (1984) 159 Cal.App.3d 368, 374, fn. 6, 205 Cal.Rptr. 874.)

The trial judge has broad discretion to defer the sale of the family home after weighing the factors outlined above. The problem in the instant case is that the record discloses no evidence was presented on these factors; thus the trial court could not have weighed them. For this reason we must reverse the trial court's determination to defer the sale of the family home and remand this issue for retrial. We express no opinion as to how the trial court should exercise its discretion on this issue because of the lack of evidence in the record. [ ]

* * *

Low, P.J., concurs.

Haning, Associate Justice, concurring in part and dissenting in part.

The parties were married for nearly 15 years. The husband is a journeyman plumber earning in excess of $50,000 annually. The wife has not been employed outside the home and has no demonstrable earning capacity save for nominal income obtained through sales of Tupperware products. She has only a high school education, but has enrolled in college and is pursuing a course of study leading to a baccalaureate degree.

The minor son of the parties is suffering from psychiatric problems. He is unable to handle ordinary classroom work at school without additional help, and is attending a special educational program. The wife's assumption of her formal education is laudable, and should be encouraged. Achievement of her degree will promote her ability to become self-supporting and relieve the husband of much, if not all of his spousal support obligation. The wife's education will also inure to the child's benefit. If remaining in the family residence temporarily will accelerate or advance the wife's educational program, the trial court is acting well within its discretion to permit her to remain.

I think the child's situation speaks for itself. His circumstances and the need for continued treatment are not disputed, and the current low house payments greatly facilitate the continuation of his medical and educational needs. The trial court found that the mental condition of the child and the financial condition of the parties require that the wife and child be permitted to reside in the family residence temporarily. It reserved jurisdiction to modify their occupancy of the residence upon a sufficient change of circumstances. If the wife maintains her present educational progress she will complete school long before the child reaches 18. By that time, if not before, the child's circumstances may also have changed, and the trial court can reassess the situation.

The *possible* adverse tax consequences of the deferred sale of the residence were *not* presented to the trial court by the husband. Although he urges us to do so, we cannot speculate on appeal that such consequences exist. (See, e.g., 9 Witkin, Cal.Procedure (3d ed. 1985) Appeal, § 250.) The trial court found that the child's mental condition and the financial circumstances of the parties required that the wife and child remain in the family residence until the circumstances changed. I think its finding is supported by substantial evidence, and should be affirmed.

WEST'S ANNOTATED CALIFORNIA FAMILY CODE

§ 3800. Definitions

As used in this chapter:

(a) "Custodial parent" means a party awarded physical custody of a child.

(b) "Deferred sale of home order" means an order that temporarily delays the sale and awards the temporary exclusive use and possession of the family home to a custodial parent of a minor child or child for whom support is authorized under Sections 3900 and 3901 or under Section 3910, whether or not the custodial parent has sole or joint custody, in order to minimize the adverse impact of dissolution of marriage or legal separation of the parties on the welfare of the child.

(c) "Resident parent" means a party who has requested or who has already been awarded a deferred sale of home order.

(Stats. 1992, c. 162 (A.B. 2650), § 10, operative Jan. 1, 1994.)

§ 3801. Determination of economic feasibility of deferred sale

(a) If one of the parties has requested a deferred sale of home order pursuant to this chapter, the court shall first determine whether it is economically feasible to maintain the payments of any note secured by a deed of trust, property taxes, insurance for the home during the period the sale of the home is deferred, and the condition of the home comparable to that at the time of trial.

(b) In making this determination, the court shall consider all of the following:

(1) The resident parent's income.

(2) The availability of spousal support, child support, or both spousal and child support.

(3) Any other sources of funds available to make those payments.

(c) It is the intent of the Legislature, by requiring the determination under this section, to do all of the following:

(1) Avoid the likelihood of possible defaults on the payments of notes and resulting foreclosures.

(2) Avoid inadequate insurance coverage.

(3) Prevent deterioration of the condition of the family home.

(4) Prevent any other circumstance which would jeopardize both parents' equity in the home.

(Stats. 1992, c. 162 (A.B. 2650), § 10, operative Jan. 1, 1994.)

§ 3802. Grant or denial of order; discretion of court

(a) If the court determines pursuant to Section 3801 that it is economically feasible to consider ordering a deferred sale of the family home, the court may grant a deferred sale of home order to a custodial parent if the court determines that the order is necessary in order to minimize the adverse impact of dissolution of marriage or legal separation of the parties on the child.

(b) In exercising its discretion to grant or deny a deferred sale of home order, the court shall consider all of the following:

(1) The length of time the child has resided in the home.

(2) The child's placement or grade in school.

(3) The accessibility and convenience of the home to the child's school and other services or facilities used by and available to the child, including child care.

(4) Whether the home has been adapted or modified to accommodate any physical disabilities of a child or a resident parent in a manner that a change in residence may adversely affect the ability of the resident parent to meet the needs of the child.

(5) The emotional detriment to the child associated with a change in residence.

(6) The extent to which the location of the home permits the resident parent to continue employment.

(7) The financial ability of each parent to obtain suitable housing.

(8) The tax consequences to the parents.

(9) The economic detriment to the nonresident parent in the event of a deferred sale of home order.

(10) Any other factors the court deems just and equitable.

(Stats. 1992, c. 162 (A.B. 2650), § 10, operative Jan. 1, 1994.)

§ 3803. Contents of order

A deferred sale of home order shall state the duration of the order and may include the legal description and assessor's parcel number of the real property which is subject to the order.

(Stats. 1992, c. 162 (A.B. 2650), § 10, operative Jan. 1, 1994.)

§ 3804. Recordation of order

A deferred sale of home order may be recorded in the office of the county recorder of the county in which the real property is located.

(Stats. 1992, c. 162 (A.B. 2650), § 10, operative Jan. 1, 1994.)

§ 3806. Payment of maintenance and capital improvement costs; order

The court may make an order specifying the parties' respective responsibilities for the payment of the costs of routine maintenance and capital improvements.

(Stats. 1992, c. 162 (A.B. 2650), § 10, operative Jan. 1, 1994.)

§ 3807. Time for modification or termination of orders; exceptions

Except as otherwise agreed to by the parties in writing, a deferred sale of home order may be modified or terminated at any time at the discretion of the court.

(Stats. 1992, c. 162 (A.B. 2650), § 10, operative Jan. 1, 1994.)

§ 3808. Remarriage or other change in circumstances; rebuttable presumption

Except as otherwise agreed to by the parties in writing, if the party awarded the deferred sale of home order remarries, or if there is otherwise a change in circumstances affecting the determinations made pursuant to Section 3801 or 3802 or affecting the economic status of the parties or the children on which the award is based, a rebuttable presumption, affecting the burden of proof, is created that further deferral of the sale is no longer an equitable method of minimizing the adverse impact of the dissolution of marriage or legal separation of the parties on the children.

(Stats. 1992, c. 162 (A.B. 2650), § 10, operative Jan. 1, 1994.)

§ 3809. Reservation of jurisdiction

In making an order pursuant to this chapter, the court shall reserve jurisdiction to determine any issues that arise with respect to the deferred sale of home order including, but not limit to, the maintenance of the home and the tax consequences to each party.

(Stats. 1992, c. 162 (A.B. 2650), § 10, operative Jan. 1, 1994.)

NOTES

1.   *What is a "family home?" Marriage of Duke,* 101 Cal.App.3d 152, 161 Cal.Rptr. 444 (4th Dist. 1980) was decided before the passage of California Family Court Sections 3800 et seq. In *Duke,* the appellate court indicated factors to balance in a deferred home sale order. On one hand are quality of life factors. On the other hand are economic factors related to housing in general, and any particulars involving the deferred sale scenario at issue. *Id.* at 155–158. What justifies considering quality of life factors, the court said, is that "the value of a family home to its occupants cannot be measured solely by its value in the marketplace. The longer the occupancy, the more important these noneconomic factors become and the more traumatic and disruptive a move to a new environment is to children whose roots have become firmly entwined in the school and social milieu of their neighborhood." *Id.* The court also noted the custodial parent's "emotional attachment to a family residence of a long-time residence [as] a cognizable factor in determining disposition of property on dissolution." *Id.* at 158. Factors are to be weighed on a case-by-case basis.

The current statute makes clear that the court shall first determine whether it is economically feasible to carry the house for the period the sale of the home is deferred. Only if it is feasible does the statute direct the court to consider additional qualitative considerations, including the child's grade in school, the convenience of the house to the school or other facilities used by the child, the continued employment of the resident parent, the tax consequences, and the economic detriment to the nonresident parent, together with "any other factors the court deems just and reasonable." California Family Code Section 3802.

California Family Code Section 3807 provides a standard for the modification of a deferred sale of a family home order. Under prior law, unless the award was designated as additional child support (in which case it could be modified at any time by a showing of changed circumstances), the award would be modified only upon the occurrence of a specific contingency. The deferred sale of a family home order was not available in cases involving adult disabled children. The original version of California Family Code Section 3800 authorized the use of the family home award only where there was a duty to support minor children, with sale typically deferred until the youngest child reached majority.

Marriage of Cooper, 170 Cal.App.3d 883, 216 Cal.Rptr. 611 (2d Dist. 1985) challenged the distinction between minor children and disabled adult children in the context of deferred sale of the family home. In *Cooper,* a disabled adult who was past the age of majority but had dependency needs of a two-year old child moved to intervene in his parents' dissolution proceeding on the issue of deferring the sale of the family home. The intervenor argued that the family home should be a form of child support. Intervenor lived in the family home with his mother, who also was his full-time caretaker. The family home was the intervenor's parent's only community property asset. Neither parent was employed at the time of the dissolution proceeding. The intervenor was represented by a guardian ad litem. The intervenor argued that the rationale for deferring the sale of a family home—"to minimize the adverse impact of dissolution of marriage or legal separation of the parties on the welfare of the child" (California Family Code Section 3801)—was the same whether the case involved a minor child or an incapacitated adult child. The superior court denied the intervenor's motion; that decision was affirmed on appeal. The court of appeal explained that there is a rational basis for distinguishing between a minor well-child and an incapacitated adult child when it comes to the granting of a deferred home sales order. The minor well-child transitions to legal majority which relieves the parents of their duty of support. The incapacitated adult, by contrast, ages chronologically, possibly outlives his or her parents, and yet still needs full support. Said the court, both the courts and the legislature contemplated the deferred home sale order as a temporary award, not a permanent one.

The statute has since been amended to include disabled adult children to whom a duty of support is owed because of their inability to maintain themselves by work. One question arising under the amendment is how long the sale should be deferred in such a case.

2.   *Is a deferred sale of a family home order appropriate where the noncustodial parent possesses a substantial separate property interest in the property?* In *Marriage of Braud,* 45 Cal.App.4th 797, 53 Cal.Rptr.2d 179 (1st Dist. 1996), the trial court's decision to defer the sale of a family home in which the noncustodial parent had a separate property interest of $44,396 and the custodial parent had minimal earning potential was upheld as a valid exercise of jurisdiction by the family court. Provable commingled funds had been used to acquire the house, making it proportionally separate in character. The court of appeal's decision turned on the meaning of "family home" which is not defined in the statutory scheme. While acknowledging the limited jurisdiction of the family court over separate property, the court of appeal found the term "family home" to be consonant with "principal residence." The court of appeal explained that the legislative focus in the deferred sale statute is the economic feasibility of a deferred sale scenario balanced against the welfare of the children. This focus, with the absence of contrary indicia, is sufficient to override the traditional limitations on family court jurisdiction over separate property.

Marriage of Ficke, 217 Cal. App. 4th 10, 157 Cal.Rptr.3d 870 (4th Dist. 2013) declined to follow *Braud*, in part because there was no substantial evidence that the funds used to acquire the house were comingled.

3.   *Change of circumstances. Marriage of Katz,* 201 Cal.App.3d 1029, 247 Cal. Rptr. 562 (2d Dist. 1988) discusses the way in which changed circumstances might factor into the analysis.

D. THE EQUAL DIVISION REQUIREMENT FOR LITIGATED DECISIONS

The equal division rule holds that with certain limited exceptions the dissolution court shall divide the community and quasi-community property of the parties equally.

California Family Code Section 2501 defines the divisible community estate to include both the community and quasi-community assets and liabilities of the parties. For purposes of dividing and assigning liabilities, the court must characterize the obligations as either separate or community and assign them to the appropriate party under California Family Code Section 2551.

Various methods of division may be used to divide community and quasi-community property. For example, the court could make a division in kind, awarding the spouses different items of equal value. Or, the court can partition the property, awarding each spouse an undivided one-half interest in the particular asset or splitting the asset fifty-fifty if it is practicable to do so. Or, the court could order a particular asset sold, and the proceeds divided equally between the spouses. No one method of division is appropriate to all cases or even to all assets in a single case, which means the trial court generally has a great deal of flexibility in selecting the most suitable method of division. Certain kinds of assets have given rise to more division problems than others; these include the types of assets discussed in Chapter 5. The situation where there is only one significant community property asset can create problems, particularly where that asset is the family home and there are minor children. Finally, the division of the community estate where the liabilities exceed the value of the assets may be problematic. Statutory exceptions to equal division of community and quasi-community property also exist.

California Family Code Section 2602 creates an exception in cases where one spouse is adjudged to have misappropriated property. In such a case, the trial court may award from one spouse's share of the property any sums deliberately misappropriated by that spouse to the exclusion of the community property interest of the other spouse. This is not so much an exception to the equal division rule as it is a way of ensuring an equal division in the wake of misappropriation. The following exceptions, however, are true limitations on the equal division rule.

California Family Code Section 2604 creates an in cases where the net value of the community property estate is less than $5,000. For a small community property estate, if one party cannot be located through the exercise of reasonable diligence, the family court may award all of the property to the other spouse.

The other major statutory exception to the equal division rule involves the treatment of personal injury damage awards. Personal injury damages recovered by a spouse during marriage are classified as community property under California Family Code Section 780. At dissolution, however, California Family Code Section 2603 mandates that such personal injury damages be assigned to the injured spouse unless the court determines that the interests of justice require another disposition (Chapter 3). Factors to be considered include the economic needs and circumstances of each party and the time that has elapsed since the recovery of the damages or the accrual of the cause of action.

MARRIAGE OF TAMMEN
63 Cal.App.3d 927, 134 Cal.Rptr. 161 (1st Dist. 1976)

ELKINGTON, ASSOCIATE JUSTICE.

The instant appeal is taken by Richard W. Tammen (hereafter for convenience, "Richard") from an interlocutory judgment of dissolution of his marriage to Elizabeth L. Tammen (hereafter for convenience, "Elizabeth"). The issues relate only to the division of the parties' community property.

The community property awarded Elizabeth approximated 79 percent of the whole. To equalize the division the judgment ordered Elizabeth to execute and deliver to Richard a promissory note for $19,820.80 bearing simple interest at 7 percent, secured by a second trust deed on the major item of community property, the family residence which had been awarded to her. The note's principal, and all interest to accrue thereon, were to be payable "upon the expiration of ten years from the date thereof, upon the wife's remarriage, the sale of said real property, voluntarily refinancing by her, upon her ceasing to use or occupy the same as a family residence, or upon her death, whichever event shall first occur."

Richard contends that this arrangement is inequitable and unfair, and that the value of the promissory note is far less than that of the offsetting $19,820.80 of community property taken by Elizabeth.

We find ourselves in agreement, and for the reasons we now state.

Civil Code section 4800, subdivision (a) [Cal.Fam. Code § 2550], provides that upon dissolution of a marriage, the court shall *"divide the community property * * * of the parties * * * equally."* (Emphasis added.) Under this statute "clearly the ideal is a mathematically equal division." (In re Marriage of Juick, 21 Cal.App.3d 421, 427, 98 Cal.Rptr. 324, 329.) And to assure such an equal division the trial court must make findings of fact as to the nature and value of the specific items of community property of the parties. (In re Marriage of Lopez, 38 Cal.App.3d 93, 107, 113 Cal.Rptr. 58.)

Civil Code section 4800, subdivision (b)(1) [Cal.Fam. Code § 2601], provides that:

"(b) Notwithstanding subdivision (a), the court may divide the community property and quasi-community property of the parties as follows: (1) Where economic circumstances warrant, the court may award any asset to one party on such conditions as it deems proper to effect a substantially equal division of the property."

Under this provision it is contemplated that where a major item of community property not reasonably subject to division is awarded one party, the other shall be compensated in some manner so as to maintain the required equal division.

In the case at bench Elizabeth was awarded community property, including the family home, as a result of which she received $19,820.80 more than an equal division. In order that the division be equalized according to Civil Code section 4800 [Cal.Fam. Code § 2550], it became necessary that the court attach a condition to that award in order "to effect a substantially equal division of the [community] property." The condition decided upon was the above-mentioned promissory note.

The issue presented to us is whether, as a matter of law, the promissory note was worth substantially less than its face value of $19,820.80.

The note was a promise to pay money at a future time, which promise was secured by a deed of trust on real estate. It was "essentially a security" (Bk. of America, etc. v. Bk. of Amador Co., 135 Cal.App. 714, 719, 28 P.2d 86), and as with securities generally it had a value. That value was its "market value" (Bagdasarian v. Gragnon, 31 Cal.2d 744, 752–753, 192 P.2d 935; Bullock's, Inc. v. Security-First Nat. Bk., 160 Cal.App.2d 277, 281–282, 325 P.2d 185), which means "the price or value of the article as established or shown by sales in the way of ordinary business" (Sackett v. Spindler, 248 Cal.App.2d 220, 236, 56 Cal.Rptr. 435, 445; S.P. Mill Co. v. Billiwhack etc. Farm, 50 Cal.App.2d 79, 88, 122 P.2d 650).

It is a matter of common knowledge, subject to the judicial notice of the superior, and this, court that deeds of trust are bought and sold in the course of ordinary business. (See Evid.Code, § 451, subd. (f).)

It is observed that the promissory note of the case at bench was secured by a second deed of trust subject to a first such lien for $18,497.12. Realization of the money was long deferred. Neither its interest nor principal was payable for 10 years, except upon the uncertain contingencies that have been pointed out. There were attending considerations of probable inflation upon the value of the security, as well as the need for its owner to be alert, and able, to protect it against foreclosure of the senior deed of trust, and perhaps tax and other liens.

We have, and we are furnished with, no certain information concerning the market value of such a promissory note. But its face value would most certainly be discounted by the inferiority of its security, the long and uncertain deferment of its enjoyment, the probable effect of inflation upon it, and the concerns of its ownership. We share the common knowledge, and accordingly take judicial notice (see Evid.Code, § 451, subd. (f)), that it would at least be substantially less than its face value.

It follows that the community property of the parties was not divided equally, according to the mandate of Civil Code section 4800 [Cal.Fam.Code § 2550].

* * *

The judgment is reversed, and the superior court will take further proceedings not inconsistent with our opinion.

MOLINARI, P.J. and WEINBERGER, J., concur.

NOTE

The promise to pay in the future as an offset. The use of a note (the promise to pay in the future) as an offset was rejected in *Marriage of Herrmann,* 84 Cal.App.3d 361, 148 Cal.Rptr. 550 (2d Dist. 1978). There the trial court awarded the house and child custody to the wife; the husband was awarded a note for his one-half equity in the house. The appellate court indicated that discounting the note was not an effective solution, and instead ordered the trial court to place the house in tenancy in common with various contingencies for sale and later division of the proceeds.

If a note is used to equalize the property division, it should provide that the entire balance becomes due and payable on certain events such as the borrower's death, or the sale or refinancing of the asset. See *Marriage of Hopkins,* 74 Cal.App.3d 591, 141 Cal.Rptr. 597 (2d Dist. 1977).

Marriage of Fink, 25 Cal.3d 877, 603 P.2d 881 (1979) distinguishes *Hopkins.* In *Fink,* the husband complained that the trial court's decision to award him a note violated the equal division principle because, as a creditor, the husband's use of the loan principal was deferred and the payback was at below the prevailing interest rate. The California Supreme Court determined that the equal division principle was not violated by the award of a note especially where there was no evidence that the note was less than its face value (long term at a below market interest rate).

MARRIAGE OF EASTIS

47 Cal.App.3d 459, 120 Cal.Rptr. 861 (4th Dist. 1975)

GARDNER, PRESIDING JUSTICE.

After a childless marriage of 3 years' duration, wife filed an action for dissolution of the marriage and, after a contested trial, the court entered a judgment of dissolution.

The court found that the wife had waived spousal support. It further found that the parties had community assets totaling $5,250 and community liabilities of $6,450. The wife was awarded community assets valued at $3,500 and ordered to pay $1,000 in community obligations. Thus, the net assets awarded to the wife amounted to $2,500. The husband was awarded community assets valued at $1,750 and ordered to pay $5,450 of community obligations. This left the husband with a net deficit of $3,700.

Husband appeals from that portion of the interlocutory judgment dividing the community assets and obligations.

Rather obviously the court was in error in its division of the community property of the parties. Civil Code, § 4800 [current California Family Code Section 2550] provides that the court shall divide the community property equally. California Rules of Court define property as including "assets and obligations" (California Rules of Court, Rule 1201(d)) and further provide that the court "shall ascertain the nature and extent of all assets and obligations subject to disposition by the court * * * and shall divide such assets and obligations as provided in the Family Law Act." [ ] This was not done in the instant case. The matter must be returned to the trial court in order to effect an equal division of the meager assets. Just how that is to be done we leave to the ingenuity of the trial judge.

However, whatever the trial judge does the parties are going to be left with unpaid obligations after the division of the assets.

We thus turn to a consistent and perplexing problem facing trial judges—just what to do about the division of debts and obligations where there are either (1) no assets, only obligations, or (2) obligations remaining after the division of the assets. This is a very common situation facing the trial courts which the authors of the Family Law Act apparently did not contemplate.

It is true that the Rules of Court define property as including assets and obligations. But, realistically, in the division of property, obligations come into the picture only when there exist assets against which the obligations can be set off. This is recognized in California Marital Termination Settlements (CEB, 1971), p. 67, " * * * equal division of community * * * property under CC § 4800 [California Family Code Section 2550], requires an allocation of obligations as well as assets to each party. The obligations to be allocated are those that could be enforced against one or more assets included in the division, either because the obligation is secured by an encumbrance on the asset or because the asset could be reached on execution if the obligation were reduced to judgment."

However, when there are no assets, only obligations, an entirely different picture is presented.

Here, the husband contends that following the general philosophy of equality between the spouses contained in the Family Law Act, these obligations should be divided equally. He reaches this conclusion by arguing that such obligations are community property, referring to them as "negative property." We think that this is carrying principles of sexual egalitarianism too far. Whatever one may think of the social philosophy underlying the Family Law Act, at this point the need for absolute equality between husband and wife vanishes and certain pragmatic considerations take over.

Obligations, standing by themselves, are not property. It is not necessary to go back to Blackstone or Beowulf to observe that property is something of value. A debt is not. At this point, we are not dividing property in the usual sense of the word, we are attempting a just disposition of the responsibility for debts, liabilities and obligations which by their very nature are the complete antithesis of assets or property. Common sense would indicate that we should look to the respective abilities of the parties to pay these obligations. Thus, if one of the spouses has an earning capacity of $1,000 per month and the other has an earning capacity of $500 per month, it would be patently unjust to order the parties to pay the community debts equally. There is nothing in the Family Law Act to the contrary.

We construe the proper rule to be that if there are no assets to divide, only obligations, or after the equal division of the assets there remain obligations to be disposed of, the court has the discretion to order the payment of such obligations in a manner that is just and equitable, depending upon the respective earning capacities of the spouses and other relevant factors. When there are no assets, common sense would indicate that equal distribution of the obligations is not mandated either by Civil Code, § 4800, or California Rules of Court, Rule 1242. The definition of property as "assets and obligations" cannot be tortured to mean simply "obligations."

Judgment reversed as to that portion of the judgment purporting to divide the community property of the parties.

NOTES

1. *California Family Code Sections 2620 et seq. now specifies the method for confirmation and division of debts at dissolution.* Debts incurred by either spouse before marriage shall be confirmed without offset to the spouse who

incurred the debt. Debts incurred during marriage and prior to separation must be divided equally, but "[t]o the extent the community debts exceed total community and quasi-community assets, the excess of debt shall be assigned as the court deems just and equitable, taking into account factors such as the parties' relative ability to pay." California Family Code Section 2622(b). This latter clause appears to represent a codification of the *Eastis* holding.

2.   *Debts excluded from the equal division mandate.* In addition to pre-marriage obligations, California Family Code Sections 2623, 2624, 2625 and 2627 exclude certain other types of debts from the equal division mandate by requiring that they be confirmed without offset to the incurring party. These obligations include (1) debts incurred during marriage that were not incurred for the benefit of the community; (2) debts incurred after separation for non-necessaries; (3) debts incurred after a judgment of dissolution or legal separation. This particular statutory passage does not define the terms non-necessaries or "benefit of the community."

California Family Code Section 2641(b)(2), discussed in Chapter 4, mandatorily assigns "a loan incurred during marriage for the education or training of a [spouse]" to the student spouse:

> "A loan incurred during marriage for the education or training of a party shall not be included among the liabilities of the community for the purpose of division pursuant to this division but shall be assigned for payment by the party." The parties can alter this outcome by an agreement under California Family Code Section 2641(e).

3.   *Credits for use of post-separation earnings?* Although a spouse is generally not entitled to reimbursement for separate funds expended to meet community obligations (*See v. See*, 64 Cal.2d 778, 51 Cal.Rptr. 888, 415 P.2d 776 (1966)), the California Supreme Court has held that reimbursement may be appropriate where one spouse uses his or her postseparation earnings to pay certain pre-existing community debts, as stated in *Marriage of Epstein*, 24 Cal.3d 76, 80 154 Cal.Rptr. 413, 592 P.2d 1165 (1979) (Chapter 6).

There are two limitations on the so-called *Epstein* credit. The payor-spouse get no credit in either of these situations. One, the payment is made on a debt incurred to buy or preserve an asset that the payor spouse is using and the amount paid is not substantially in excess of the value of the use. Two, the debt payment discharges the payor's child support or spousal support obligations. *Epstein*, 24 Cal. 3d 76, 84–85.

California Family Code Section 2626 now expressly authorizes the trial court to order reimbursement in cases it deems appropriate for debts paid after separation but prior to trial.

Marriage of Warren, 28 Cal.App.3d 777, 104 Cal.Rptr. 860 (2d Dist. 1972) assigned as an asset an outstanding loan of community property funds made by the husband to his brother. The husband challenged the assignment as a violation of the equal division mandate. The court of appeal affirmed. The court found it dispositive that the husband had not made an effort to collect on the outstanding debt and the statute of limitations had not yet run.

"Appellant loaned $34,000 of community funds to his brother and took a promissory note from him in that amount dated March 15, 1962. By December 20, 1963, the note was paid down to the sum of $14,761, and a new promissory note in the amount of the balance due was drawn, dated March 23, 1964, with no interest payable for one year and a due date of March 23, 1972. The notes contain no schedule for installment payments of principal or a standard default paragraph.

Appellant contends that this debt should not be regarded as an asset because his brother has 'disappeared.' However, there is no indication in the record that appellant has made any effort whatever to collect the debt. Since the statute of limitations has not yet run, this debt is still an asset under the law.

Civil Code section 4800, subdivision (b), subsection (1) [now California Family Code Section 2601] provides: 'Where economic circumstances warrant, the court may award any asset to one party on such conditions as it deems proper to effect a substantially equal division of the property.' In view of the nature of the loan transaction, and the appellant's relationship to the debtor, the assignment made of this asset was clearly within the court's statutory discretion. There is no requirement that each asset be divided but merely that there be a mathematical equality in which the court, in its discretion, may utilize the single asset provision under the Family Law Act. (*In re Marriage of Juick*, 21 Cal.App.3d 421, 428, [98 Cal.Rptr. 324].)" *Id.* at 783.

Warren is distinguished by *Marriage of Laure*, 2005 WL 2436349, an unpublished case. The facts of *Laure* asked whether a debt exists if the parents of a spouse make a loan to their child without memorializing that loan in a promissory note. The trial court followed the rule that a promissory note is not required to establish a debt; and it was persuaded by testimony that the debt did in fact exist.

E. THE VALUATION REQUIREMENT FOR LITIGATED DIVISIONS

Unless the court can simply divide the community property assets in kind, awarding one-half to each party, it must make a determination as to the value of the property.

California Family Code Section 2105 requires that the valuation of the assets and liabilities of the parties be determined as near as practicable to the time of trial, unless one party shows good cause why a different date for valuation would be used. Value is defined as the fair market value of the property, and it is a question of fact for the trial court.

Some assets are easier to value than others. For example the value of deposit account can be ascertained by checking the balance of sums on deposit on the date of trial. The value of stocks and bonds listed on a stock exchange can be determined by checking the listed closing price for the particular security on the date of trial. By comparison, assets such as goodwill, unmatured retirement benefits, and closely held stock frequently give rise to valuation issues. The *Micalizio* case illustrates.

MARRIAGE OF MICALIZIO

199 Cal.App.3d 662, 245 Cal.Rptr. 673 (4th Dist. 1988)

DABNEY, ASSOCIATE JUSTICE.

Facts and Procedural History

Robert Micalizio (Robert) has been employed since 1960 for the J.R. Norton Company (Norton), a closely-held agricultural corporation. In June 1963, Robert purchased stock in Norton for $100,000 and financed the purchase by executing two promissory notes which called for 19 annual principal payments of $2,500 with balloon payments in the 20th year. Each note stated: "This note is secured by a pledge of shares of stock." Robert, however, retained custody of the share certificates, which were issued in his name alone.

Norton pays dividends only on its preferred stock, all of which is owned by J.R. Norton. The remainder, totaling 25 percent of all stock, is owned by Robert (15 percent) and three other vice-presidents (collectively 10 percent). After a corporate merger, the 150,000 Norton shares were reissued to Robert in January 1971. In March 1971, Robert executed a corporate buy-sell agreement which specified that the minority shareholders could not sell or transfer their stock to any third person without first offering to sell it to the corporation for the lower of the book value of the stock adjusted annually on the basis of standard accounting principles, or the amount offered by any third person.

Robert and Gerry Micalizio (Gerry) were married in June 1971. During their marriage, Robert and Gerry separated and maintained separate households at least four times for periods of six months to three years. Gerry wrote checks from a community account to make the principal payments on Robert's promissory notes. In 1974, the buy-sell agreement was modified to change the formula for determining the price of the stock in the event of a sale to the corporation.

Robert filed a petition for dissolution in May 1981. The judgment as to marital status became final in December 1981, and the court reserved jurisdiction on all other issues. A one-day court trial was held on August 16, 1984. The evidence showed that the value of the stock under the buy-sell agreements was approximately $13 per share. The 1971 buy-sell agreement and the 1974 modification were introduced as exhibits. Roger Stevenson, the secretary-treasurer of Norton, testified that if Norton were to liquidate all of its assets, its stock would be worth $25 per share. Stevenson further testified as to the history, activities, and operations of Norton.

On November 30, 1984, the court filed its "Ruling After Court Trial", which stated that the Norton stock had not been transmuted from Robert's separate property to community property. However, the court ruled that the stock should be valued "on the pro-tanto basis, allocating a portion of the value at the date of trial to the community." The court found that there was no evidence of pre-marriage appreciation in the value of the stock and found that nine annual principal installments of $2,500 on Robert's promissory notes to the Nortons had been made by the community, for a total contribution of 22.5 percent of the purchase price of the stock, or the equivalent of 33,750 shares. The court assigned a value of $13.667 per share to the stock, but directed division of the community shares in kind. The Ruling After Court Trial was never entered in the judgment book.

In June 1984, the buy-sell agreement was again amended to provide, among other things, that Norton must consent to all stock transfers, assignments, or conveyances. In addition, the amended agreement provided more favorable terms for payment to the shareholder from the corporation for shares redeemed or purchased. Robert did not advise the court or Gerry of the amendment during the trial. After learning of the amendment when she sought to have Norton issue shares in her name, Gerry filed a motion based on Code of Civil Procedure sections 657 and 473 for new trial or to set aside for fraud. Gerry claimed that the newly-discovered amendment was oppressive to her and made her shares of Norton stock unsalable. She therefore requested the court to order Robert to pay her the value of the shares of stock.

Gerry filed an "amended" motion for new trial or to set aside for fraud on April 12, 1985, in which she requested the court to order Robert to pay her the value of the shares of stock, and to fix the value at the "fair market price" rather than the contractual buy-out price. Robert submitted declarations of Norton officials stating that: (1) Norton would issue shares of stock to Gerry without the restrictions of the June 1984 agreement, and (2) as of September 30, 1984, the book value of the stock had declined to $12.04 per share because of losses incurred in the lettuce crop.

The court heard the amended motion, and on June 13, 1985, filed its ruling. The court noted that because no judgment had been entered on its earlier ruling, it would treat the amended motion as one to reopen, to reconsider, or for further argument. The court stated that the June 1984 amendment made the stock valueless to Gerry, but did not address Robert's contention that the stock would be issued to Gerry without the restrictions of that amendment. The court reconsidered its earlier valuation of the stock at the buy-back price of $13.67 per share, and concluded that its "real value" was $25 per share. The court entered judgment on April 29, 1986, incorporating its June 13, 1985 ruling. The court ordered Robert to execute a promissory note to Gerry in the amount of $421,875, amortized over 10 years, at 10 percent interest to compensate Gerry for her interest in the stock.

* * *

The Trial Court's Valuation of the Stock Was Not
Supported by Substantial Evidence

Under Civil Code section 4800, subdivision (a), [now Family Code Sections 2550 et seq.] to divide community property equally, the court must make specific findings concerning the nature and value of all community assets of the parties unless property is divided in kind. (*In re Marriage of Hewitson* (1983) 142 Cal.App.3d 874, 884, 191 Cal.Rptr. 392.) The trial court's determination of the value of a particular asset is a factual one which will be upheld on appeal if supported by substantial evidence in the record. (*Id.,* at p. 885, 191 Cal.Rptr. 392.)

The court fixed the value of the Norton stock at $25 per share. The court stated that it had considered all of the evidence bearing on the value of the stock, including "the $13.67 figure established under the old agreements," and "the $25.00 figure per Mr. Stevenson." The court also considered other testimony of Mr. Stevenson about the size, volume, and extent of Norton's operations.

Robert contends that Mr. Stevenson's testimony was not evidence of the value of Robert's minority stock holdings subject to transfer restrictions. Rather, Mr. Stevenson simply expressed an opinion on a hypothetical situation bearing no relation to the facts, and was not asked to consider liquidation costs, contingent liabilities, or similar factors. When a trial court accepts an expert's ultimate conclusion without critical consideration of his reasoning, and it appears that the conclusion was based upon improper or unwarranted matters, then the judgment must be reversed for lack of substantial evidence. (*Pacific Gas & Electric Co. v. Zuckerman* (1987) 189 Cal.App.3d, 1113, 1136, 234 Cal. Rptr. 630.) For example, in *Hewitson, supra,* 142 Cal. App.3d at pp. 885–887, 191 Cal. Rptr. 392, an expert attempted to determine the value of a closely held corporation by using the selling price/book value ratio of publicly traded companies. The appellate court held that because of differences between the two types of companies, the analogy was improper and the judgment based upon the expert's testimony was not supported by substantial evidence. Similarly, in *In re Marriage of Rives* (1982) 130 Cal. App.3d 138, 149–151, 181 Cal. Rptr. 572, the appellate court reversed valuation of a queen bee business because the trial court accepted the testimony of an expert who relied upon false assumptions and improper factors and failed to consider all of the relevant factors which established value. Here, likewise, Mr. Stevenson's testimony relied on a false assumption and did not include all of the relevant factors which establish the value of minority shares in a closely held corporation.

The basic question for the court was the value of the shares of stock held by the community at the time of trial. In *Hewitson, supra,* 142 Cal.App.3d at pp. 882–883, 191 Cal.Rptr. 392, the court recognized that the determination of the value of closely-held stock is a difficult legal problem, and urged the trial court to use the factors listed in the Internal Revenue Service's Revenue Ruling 59–60 (1959)—1 Cum.Bull. 237 in such determination, unless there is some statutory or decisional proscription against their use. In *Hewitson,* the court was faced with the valuation of a closely-held corporation wholly owned by the parties. Here, in contrast, Robert owned a mere minority interest in a closely-held corporation dominated by members of the Norton family. In a closely-held corporation, *in the absence of other influencing or determining factors,* one method for determining the value of a share of stock is by ascertaining the net market value of the property which those shares represent and by assigning to each share its proportionate worth. (*Estate of Rowell* (1955) 132 Cal.App.2d 421, 429, 282 P.2d 163.) However, as the court explained in *Hewitson,* it is incumbent on a court faced with a valuation problem to consider *each* factor which might have a bearing on the value of the shares. (*Hewitson, supra,* 142 Cal.App.3d at p. 888, 191 Cal.Rptr. 392.)

The court listed the factors which it considered in fixing the value of the stock, but did not consider either that Robert owned only a minority block of shares, or that Robert was restricted both as to the price he could obtain for his shares and as to his ability to sell them. Those restrictive agreements and the size of Robert's holdings were factors which have a bearing on the value of the shares. Section 8 of Revenue Ruling 59–60 directs consideration of agreements restricting the sale or transfer of stock. See, e.g. *Estate of Seltzer* (TC Memo 1985–519 (P-H Para. 85, 519) [When a shareholder died, her shares were sold to the corporation at the value specified in the shareholders' buy-sell agreement. The trial court held that the value under that agreement was controlling. The court explained that inasmuch as the estate was bound by the agreement, the estate's interest in the stock was by contract limited to the book value of the stock].) Moreover Revenue Ruling 59–60 directs consideration of the size of the block of stock. The comments in Revenue Ruling 59–60 state that a minority interest in an unlisted corporation's stock is more difficult to sell than a similar block of listed stock.

This court has also required consideration of restrictive agreements when valuing stock in a closely-held corporation. (*In re Marriage of Rosan* (1972) 24 Cal.App.3d 885, 101 Cal.Rptr. 295.) In *Rosan,* the husband owned

15 percent of the stock in Hudson Jewelers. An agreement between the husband and the majority shareholder provided that the husband's shares could not be sold or transferred to anyone other than the corporation or the other shareholder without prior written consent. The other shareholder could purchase such shares for the lower of their "computed value" or the price offered by a third party. "Computed value" was to be determined by a formula based primarily on the book asset value of the stock. Moreover, if the husband quit or was terminated for cause, the other shareholder could purchase the husband's stock for 70 percent of its "computed value." The trial court fixed the value of the stock for purposes of a community property division at 70 percent of its "computed value."

The wife argued that the trial court erred, first by failing to include goodwill, and second, by not valuing the stock at the entire "computed value." With respect to the first contention, this court stated that there was no evidence that the corporation planned a merger, and in the absence of such plan, the corporation or the other shareholder had the right to purchase the stock for the "computed value" if the husband offered it for sale, regardless of the existence of goodwill. (*Id.,* at p. 890, 101 Cal.Rptr. 295.)

With respect to the second contention, the court noted that for the husband to realize the full "computed value," he would have to die, become permanently disabled, be discharged from his employment without cause, or be offered at least that amount by a third person. The court stated: "An offer from a third person to purchase a minority interest in a closely held corporation paying no dividends for full 'computed value' would be an unlikely prospect," and the husband's death, disability or discharge without cause was also unlikely. (*Ibid.*)

The court concluded: "Under the circumstances disclosed by the evidence, and particularly in view of the restrictive conditions on the disposition of the stock and its resulting illiquidity, factors substantially affecting its value, the trial court was justified in assessing the value of the stock at 70 percent of its 'computed value.' Although that was its lowest value except in the event of a sale to a third person for less, it was the only value that was relatively certain." (*Id.,* at p. 891, 101 Cal.Rptr. 295.)

The Supreme Court in *In re Marriage of Fonstein* (1976) 17 Cal. 3d 738, 131 Cal. Rptr. 873, 552 P.2d 1169 approved a similar approach in a valuation problem. The husband argued that his interest in a law partnership was valueless because it was contingent on his decision to withdraw and subject to modification by agreement of his partners. The court observed that the asset being divided was the interest in the partnership, not the contractual right to withdraw. However, the court explicitly approved the trial court's valuation based on the value of the right to withdraw from the firm as provided in the partnership agreement, and rejected the wife's argument that the value should be based on a percentage of partnership assets. (*Id.,* at pp. 745–747, 131 Cal.Rptr. 873, 552 P.2d 1169.)

Gerry's counsel ignores *Fonstein* and *Rosan,* and instead cites *In re Marriage of Fenton* (1982) 134 Cal.App.3d 451, 184 Cal.Rptr. 597 and *In re Marriage of Slater* (1979) 100 Cal.App.3d 241, 160 Cal.Rptr. 686, which involved the issue of evaluating the goodwill in professional practice, in light of the rule that "[W]here the issue is raised in a marital dissolution action, the trial court must make a specific finding as to the existence and value of the 'goodwill' of a professional business as a going concern whether related to that of a sole practitioner, a professional partnership or a professional corporation." (*In re Marriage of Lopez* (1974) 38 Cal.App.3d 93, 109, 113 Cal.Rptr. 58.) Although the courts in *Fenton* and *Slater* did not rely on the restrictive terms of partnership and stock purchase contracts when making required findings of the value of goodwill in professional practices, those decisions do not provide guidance on the issue of valuing a minority block of stock in a closely-held corporation.

We conclude that there was no substantial evidence to support the trial court's determination that the value of the Norton stock was $25 per share, and the judgment must be reversed. * * *

Disposition

The judgment is reversed. The trial court is directed to consider whether the community stock should be divided in kind under the principles set forth in *Connolly, supra,* 23 Cal.3d 590, 153 Cal.Rptr. 423, 591 P.2d 911 and *Lotz, supra,* 120 Cal.App.3d 379, 174 Cal.Rptr. 618. If the court determines that an in-kind division is not appropriate, the court is directed to determine the value of the stock in light of the principles set forth in *Hewitson, supra,* 142 Cal.App.3d 874, 191 Cal.Rptr. 392, 142 Cal.App.3d 874 and *Rosan, supra,* 24 Cal.App.3d 885, 101 Cal.Rptr. 295.

CAMPBELL, P.J., and McDANIEL, J., concur.

NOTE

The relationship between valuation and record keeping. California Family Code section 2552 requires that the dissolution court value the assets and liabilities of the parties as near as practicable to the time of trial. However, the statute also authorizes the court, for good cause shown, to value the assets or liabilities "at a date after separation and before trial to accomplish an equal division of the community estate of the parties in an equitable manner."

Marriage of Nelson, 139 Cal.App.4th 1546, 44 Cal.Rptr.3d 52 (6th Dist. 2006) explores the impact of poor record keeping on valuation. In *Nelson,* the court of appeal held that trial court properly stepped up to value the wife's business at the time of separation (a legal question) when her poor record keeping made valuation at a later date impracticable (undisputed fact).

F. CONFIRMATION AND ASSIGNMENT OF LIABILITIES

The California community property system does not generally classify debts for the purposes of creditors' rights (Chapter 6). In the dissolution context, however, it may be appropriate to do so in order to allocate outstanding debts fairly between the spouses while also protecting the rights of third parties.

California Family Code Sections 2620 et seq. provide guidelines for the trial court in allocating outstanding debts.

Here is a summary of the statutory rules:

(1) Debts incurred by either spouse before the date of marriage must be confirmed without offset to the spouse incurring the debt.

(2) Community debts incurred during marriage generally should be divided equally. If the community debts exceed the community estate the court has the discretion to assign the excess debt equitably, taking into account factors such as the parties' relative ability to pay.

(3) All separate debts, including those incurred by a spouse during marriage that were not incurred for the benefit of the community, must be confirmed without offset to the spouse who incurred the debt.

(4) Debts for nonnecessaries incurred by either spouse after the date of separation and before judgment should be confirmed without offset to the spouse who incurred the debt.

(5) Debts for the common necessaries of life incurred by a spouse after the date of separation and before judgment may be confirmed to either spouse according to need and ability to pay as of the time the debt is incurred.

(6) The trial court also has jurisdiction to order reimbursement in appropriate cases for debts paid after the date of separation but before trial.

WEST'S ANNOTATED CALIFORNIA FAMILY CODE

§ 2620. Community estate debts; confirmation or division

The debts for which the community estate is liable which are unpaid at the time of trial, or for which the community estate becomes liable after trial, shall be confirmed or divided as provided in this part.

(Stats. 1992, c. 162 (A.B. 2650), § 10, operative Jan. 1, 1994.)

§ 2621. Premarital debts; confirmation

Debts incurred by either spouse before the date of marriage shall be confirmed without offset to the spouse who incurred the debt.

(Stats. 1992, c. 162 (A.B. 2650), § 10, operative Jan. 1, 1994.)

§ 2622. Marital debts incurred before the date of separation; division

(a) Except as provided in subdivision (b), debts incurred by either spouse after the date of marriage but before the date of separation shall be divided as set forth in Sections 2550 to 2552, inclusive, and Sections 2601 to 2604, inclusive.

(b) To the extent that community debts exceed total community and quasi-community assets, the excess of debt shall be assigned as the court deems just and equitable, taking into account factors such as the parties' relative ability to pay.

(Stats. 1992, c. 162 (A.B. 2650), § 10, operative Jan. 1, 1994.)

§ 2623. Marital debts incurred after the date of separation; confirmation

Debts incurred by either spouse after the date of separation but before entry of a judgment of dissolution of marriage or legal separation of the parties shall be confirmed as follows:

(a) Debts incurred by either spouse for the common necessaries of life of either spouse or the necessaries of life of the children of the marriage for whom support may be ordered, in the absence of a court order or written agreement for support or for the payment of these debts, shall be confirmed to either spouse according to the parties' respective needs and abilities to pay at the time the debt was incurred.

(b) Debts incurred by either spouse for nonnecessaries of that spouse or children of the marriage for whom support may be ordered shall be confirmed without offset to the spouse who incurred the debt.

(Stats. 1992, c. 162 (A.B. 2650), § 10, operative Jan. 1, 1994. Amended by Stats. 1993, c. 219 (A.B. 1500), § 113.)

§ 2624. Marital debts incurred after entry of judgment of dissolution or after entry of judgment of legal separation; confirmation

Debts incurred by either spouse after entry of a judgment of dissolution of marriage but before termination of the parties' marital status or after entry of a judgment of legal separation of the parties shall be confirmed without offset to the spouse who incurred the debt.

(Stats. 1992, c. 162 (A.B. 2650), § 10, operative Jan. 1, 1994.)

§ 2625. Separate debts incurred before date of separation; confirmation

Notwithstanding Sections 2620 to 2624, inclusive, all separate debts, including those debts incurred by a spouse during marriage and before the date of separation that were not incurred for the benefit of the community, shall be confirmed without offset to the spouse who incurred the debt.

(Stats. 1992, c. 162 (A.B. 2650), § 10, operative Jan. 1, 1994.)

§ 2626. Reimbursements

The court has jurisdiction to order reimbursement in cases it deems appropriate for debts paid after separation but before trial.

(Stats. 1992, c. 162 (A.B. 2650), § 10, operative Jan. 1, 1994.)

NOTE

P of PITI: Principal is a contribution to purchase; interests, taxes, and insurance are ongoing family expenses. Ordinarily, for purposes of a property settlement, only principal payments on a mortgage fall within the definition of a contribution to purchase, either for purposes of proportional ownership calculations (by case law) or for purposes of a reimbursement (under California Family Code Section 2640) (Chapter 5). The P of PITI concept may hold for other purposes according to other rationales. See e.g., *Kenney v. U.S.*, 458 F.3d 1025 (9th Cir. 2006) where, applying the de novo review standard, a federal court of appeal upheld a federal district court's exercise of discretion to deny taxpayer's husband interest on mortgage payments he made for the taxpayer on the parties' former marital residence.

G. TAX CONSEQUENCES OF DIVISION

The dissolution of a marriage and the attendant division of property are likely to trigger significant tax problems. For example, two items of community property may be of substantially equal value at the time of trial, but one may be a "high basis" asset and the other a "low basis" asset. The party receiving the low basis asset may incur substantial capital gains tax liability when and if that asset is sold.

To what extent must the court consider such tax consequences in effecting an equal division of the community?

With regard to the property division itself, it has long been established that the equal division of community property between the spouses at dissolution is not a taxable event. As a practical matter, however, many community estates are not amenable to equal division without the addition of equalizing assets, such as a promissory note. Under prior law, if the equalizing assets involved separate property, a taxable transfer was deemed to have occurred. This rule was changed by the Tax Reform Act of 1984. Under the current tax law, no gain or loss is recognized on a transfer of property between spouses (or between former spouses if the transfer was incident to the divorce). For income tax purposes, the recipient is treated as if the property were acquired by gift, so that the basis of the transferee is the same as it was in the hands of the transferor.

Finally, some mention should be made of the tax consequences of spousal and child support provisions. Spousal support payments are distinguished from payments made pursuant to a division of property. Periodic spousal support payments are generally deductible by the payor and taxable as income to the payee. Payments made in discharge of property rights are not so treated. Child support payments are also distinguished from spousal support payments. Child support payments are not deductible by the payor nor are they taxable to the person having custody of the child.

MARRIAGE OF HARRINGTON

6 Cal.App.4th 1847, 8 Cal.Rptr.2d 631 (2d Dist. 1992)

GILBERT, ASSOCIATE JUSTICE.

Husband and wife dissolve their marriage. They sell their home at a profit and divide the proceeds. The capital gains taxes due from the profits are not the same for each party. Under the facts here we hold that each party alone is liable for his or her capital gains taxes.

Wife Judith W. Harrington appeals an order denying her motion that husband Ronald G. Harrington pay one-half of the capital gains taxes recognized upon her share of profits realized from the sale of the family residence. The trial court properly decided each party alone was liable for capital gains taxes due upon his or her share of the profits. We affirm.

Facts

On January 5, 1988, Judith W. Harrington brought a petition to dissolve her nearly 25-year marriage to Ronald G. Harrington. Six months later, the Harringtons sold the family residence and realized a profit of $480,000. Husband and wife divided the $480,000 profit equally. Husband, a lawyer, then used part of his proceeds to purchase wife's community property interest in his law firm and to pay wife for her waiver of spousal support.

In court proceedings husband declared he and wife orally agreed that each of them alone would be liable for any capital gains income taxes resulting from his or her equal share of the $480,000 profit. (Int.Rev.Code, §§ 1001, 1221; Rev. & Tax.Code, § 18031.) Husband stated he and wife discussed the subject often. Husband offered his legal expertise to suggest ways in which wife could defer recognition of capital gains taxes upon her share of the proceeds. The family accountant also declared that wife acknowledged her capital gains tax obligation concerning one-half of the $480,000, or $240,000.

In contrast, wife declared she and husband had no oral agreement concerning responsibility for the capital gains taxes. Although she stated that she and husband frequently discussed methods to defer recognition of taxes, "[she] never made any agreement whatsoever [to] pay any particular portion of [the] taxes. * * * "

The parties' written marital settlement agreement stated that "[t]he Court shall retain jurisdiction over the 1988 [tax] returns and all other jointly filed returns." It said nothing about liability for capital gains taxes.

Within two years of the sale of the family home, husband acquired a replacement residence in Ventura for $251,250. By so doing, he successfully deferred recognition of capital gains tax on the $240,000 profit he realized from sale of the family residence. (Int.Rev.Code, § 1034, subd. (a); Rev. & Tax.Code, § 18031.)

Within the same two years, wife purchased a condominium in Chicago for $120,000 and invested $5,000 in condominium improvements. She thus deferred recognition of capital gains tax on only $125,000 of the $240,000 profit she realized from sale of the family home. Wife incurred a capital gains tax of $52,000, reportable and due upon husband and wife's joint 1988 federal and state tax returns.

Wife sought an order in the trial court requiring husband to pay one-half of the $52,000 capital gains taxes then due. In support of her order, wife declared she had changed occupations and was not yet self-supporting. After moving to Chicago, she abandoned her profession as a schoolteacher due to her fears for her personal safety in the schools. Her current occupation, a personnel consultant, had not afforded her any commissions after 10 months' labors. Wife stated she used her share of the community property proceeds to support herself and could not pay the mortgage payments on a more expensive residence.

The trial court denied wife's motion and found husband and wife had an agreement that each alone would be liable for any capital gains income taxes recognized after division of the community property. The court also determined husband and wife should bear the tax burdens equally, any agreement aside. Wife's appeal followed.

On appeal wife argues 1) equal division of the community liabilities requires husband to pay one-half of the $52,000 capital gains taxes, and 2) enforcement of any oral agreement between them violates Civil Code section 4800 [current California Family Code § 2550 et seq.], *In re Marriage of Maricle* (1990) 220 Cal.App.3d 55, 57–58, 269 Cal.Rptr. 204, and Code of Civil Procedure section 664.6.

Discussion

Wife contends an equal division of the assets and liabilities of the community property * * * compels equal liability for capital gains income taxes when those taxes are recognized. She argues the taxes arose because a community asset appreciated during marriage, and therefore tax liability must be shared equally. She claims burdening her with 100 percent of the $52,000 tax penalizes her for her inability to earn as much income as husband. Wife asserts she has acted responsibly and prudently in investing in a relatively inexpensive condominium to save the remainder of her separate property for her present support and future retirement.

Federal and state tax laws treat residential real property as a capital asset, yielding a taxable capital gain or profit upon sale. (Int.Rev.Code, §§ 1001, 1221; Rev. & Tax.Code, § 18031.) The tax laws also permit a postponement or deferral of income taxes upon the taxable gain if the selling taxpayer purchases, within two years of sale of the old residence, a new residence for an amount at least equal to the "adjusted sales price" of the old residence. (Int.Rev.Code, § 1034, subd. (a); Rev. & Tax.Code, § 18031.)

These deferral or postponement provisions of the federal and state tax laws obviously make it impossible to gauge what the ultimate tax gain liability will be. (*In re Marriage of Epstein* (1979) 24 Cal.3d 76, 88, 154 Cal.Rptr. 413, 592 P.2d 1165.) With successive purchase and sale of replacement residences by the taxpayer, the capital gains income taxes may be postponed for an indeterminate period of time. The trial court cannot realistically apportion tax liability because of the uncertainty as to what the ultimate tax burden will be. (*Id.,* p. 88, fn. 10, 154 Cal.Rptr. 413, 592 P.2d 1165.)

Civil Code section 4800, subdivision (a) [current Family Code Sections 2550 et seq.] requires the trial court, in dividing community assets and liabilities upon dissolution, to distribute the assets so that each party receives an equal share after deduction of community liabilities. (*In re Marriage of Fonstein* (1976) 17 Cal.3d 738, 748, 131 Cal.Rptr. 873, 552 P.2d 1169.) Once having divided the community property equally, the court is not required to speculate concerning what either party may do with his or her share, thereby incurring recognition of tax liability. (*Id.,* p. 749, 131 Cal.Rptr. 873, 552 P.2d 1169.) Whether either party could defer capital gains taxes depends upon factors unrelated to the equal division of community property. (*In re Marriage of Davies* (1983) 143 Cal.App.3d 851, 857–858, 192 Cal.Rptr. 212.) These factors include individual income two years later, individual savings, receipt of gifts or inheritance, ability to borrow money, and other circumstances not pertinent to the division of community property. (*Id.,* p. 858, 192 Cal.Rptr. 212.)

Here a taxable event—sale of residential real property—occurred during dissolution proceedings. Each party is equally liable for any income taxes incurred on his or her capital gain. The trial court was not required to account for the possibility that either spouse may or may not be able to postpone recognition of capital gains taxes by purchasing a replacement residence within two years. (*In re Marriage of Epstein, supra,* 24 Cal.3d 76, 88, fn. 10, 154 Cal.Rptr. 413, 592 P.2d 1165.) Neither is it appropriate for the trial court to retain jurisdiction to consider apportionment of tax liabilities when any capital gains taxes become recognized. (*In re Marriage of Davies, supra,* 143 Cal.App.3d 851, 858, 192 Cal.Rptr. 212.) The court's jurisdiction cannot continue on and on into the indefinite future.

Wife mistakenly relies upon *In re Marriage of Epstein, supra,* 24 Cal.3d 76, 154 Cal.Rptr. 413, 592 P.2d 1165, *In re Marriage of Davies, supra,* 143 Cal.App.3d 851, 192 Cal.Rptr. 212, and *In re Marriage of Clark* (1978) 80 Cal.App.3d 417, 145 Cal.Rptr. 602. Those decisions concerned unequal distribution of proceeds from the sale of a community asset in order to equalize the uneven division of other community assets. Under those circumstances, each party is responsible for one-half of the capital gains taxes incurred by the sale, regardless of the party's share of the sale proceeds. (*In re Marriage of Davies, supra,* 143 Cal.App.3d at pp. 856–857, 192 Cal.Rptr. 212.) Although husband used some of the proceeds arising from sale of the family residence here to buy wife's community property interest in his law firm and her waiver of spousal support, husband has not requested apportionment of his tax liability, if any.

II

Because the trial court's order imposing tax liability upon each party for his or her share of the capital gain was proper as a matter of law, we do not consider whether husband and wife had a valid oral agreement to apportion tax liability. If any applicable ground supports the trial court's order, the reviewing court will affirm the judgment. (*In re Marriage of Jacobs* (1982) 128 Cal.App.3d 273, 284, 180 Cal.Rptr. 234.)

Accordingly, the judgment is affirmed. Wife is to bear costs on appeal.

STEVEN J. STONE, P.J., and YEGAN, J., concur.

NOTE

The U.S. Internal Revenue Service. Principles of community property law are followed by the I. R. S., which maintains a state-by-state primer on the subject. See Part 25, Special Topics, Chapter 18, Community Property, which can be found at https://www.irs.gov/irm/part25/irm_25-018-001.html.

H. OMITTED ASSETS

What is the effect of a dissolution judgment settling the parties' respective community property rights? Does the judgment define the community and quasi-community property? Or, does it merely represent the adjudication of the parties' rights in the property that was specifically before the court? Historically, whenever assets were omitted from a judgment due to inadvertence, negligence, or a misunderstanding about or uncertainty in the law the issue of the judgment's effect was litigated.

California appellate courts took different approaches to this problem prior to the passage of California Family Code Section 2556, which was part of the original Family Code. Some took a broad view of the property issue, holding that the trial court's final judgment of dissolution was in fact a final determination of the extent of the community property estate and, as such, the final judgment must stand absent fraud or mistake. Others took a more restricted approach, finding that the final judgment of dissolution was binding only as to property before the court. The Supreme Court undertook to resolve the dichotomous holdings in the *Henn* case, excerpted below. Despite the adoption of a statutory solution, *Henn* is still worth reading for how it discusses the intersection of res judicata and collateral estoppel, on one hand, and the community property system on the other.

Today, California Family Code Section 2556 allows a party to invoke the court's continuing jurisdiction over assets or liabilities that have not been previously adjudicated by a judgment in the proceeding. To do this, a party files a postjudgment motion to show cause that a community estate asset or liability was omitted from the final judgment of dissolution or not adjudicated by that judgment. If the motion is granted the remedy is a postjudgment adjudication of the omitted asset or liability.

HENN V. HENN

26 Cal.3d 323, 161 Cal.Rptr. 502, 605 P.2d 10 (1980)

BIRD, CHIEF JUSTICE.

This court must determine whether a former spouse may bring an action to establish her community property interest in her ex-husband's federal military pension which was not adjudicated or distributed in the final decree of dissolution.

I

Helen and Henry Henn were married in 1945. After 25 years, Henry petitioned for dissolution of their marriage in the Superior Court for the City and County of San Francisco. An interlocutory decree was granted on February 22, 1971, and a final judgment issued on May 19, 1971. The decree incorporated a property settlement which awarded the parties specific items of the marital community as their separate property. The decree also awarded Helen $500 monthly support payments until the death of either party or her remarriage.

Neither the pleadings nor the judgment made mention of the fully matured federal military retirement pension that Henry was receiving at the time of the interlocutory decree. The pension had been partially earned during the marriage, and its existence was known to Helen at the time of the dissolution proceedings. Henry concedes that the court made no determination with respect to the pension.

On October 17, 1973, in response to a motion by Henry in the San Francisco Superior Court to reduce the amount of Helen's spousal support, Helen moved for an order to show cause why Henry's retirement pension should not be divided as community property. In support of this motion, Helen filed a short declaration setting forth the nature of her interest in the pension and alleging that she had never relinquished her community property rights in that asset. Henry opposed Helen's motion. Admitting that at the time of the interlocutory decree his pension was in part community property, he argued that the court lacked jurisdiction to modify the property settlement incorporated in the judgment of dissolution since there was no showing of extrinsic fraud or mistake. Helen's motion was denied without opinion on March 5, 1974.

Approximately two and one half years later, Helen filed the underlying complaint in the Superior Court of San Mateo County. Helen sought (1) a determination that Henry's military pension was community property to the extent earned by Henry during their marriage; (2) a full accounting of all pension payments received by Henry since March 1, 1971; and (3) a division of the community property portion of the pension. In his answer to the complaint, Henry raised the defense of res judicata based on the original decree of dissolution and the 1974 denial of Helen's motion. He also contended that these proceedings, together with Helen's recovery in settlement of a malpractice action against her former attorneys, estopped her from maintaining the present action. After a separate trial on these affirmative defenses, the trial court entered judgment on Henry's behalf. Helen appealed.

II

* * *

It is clear that Henry's entitlement to his federal military pension was fully vested and matured in 1971 at the time of the dissolution of the Henns' marriage. To the extent earned during the marriage, it was part of their community property. However, Henry argues that Helen is prevented from seeking a judicial division of her community property interest in this asset under the principles of res judicata and collateral estoppel. These defenses are grounded on the original decree of dissolution and property settlement and the subsequent denial of Helen's motion to modify the original decree to divide the military pension.

The doctrine of res judicata has long been recognized to have a dual aspect. (See Teitelbaum Furs, Inc. v. Dominion Ins. Co., Ltd. (1962) 58 Cal.2d 601, 604, 25 Cal.Rptr. 559, 375 P.2d 439; Todhunter v. Smith (1934) 219 Cal. 690, 695, 28 P.2d 916. See also 4 Witkin, Cal.Procedure (2d ed. 1971) Judgment, § 148, p. 3293.) "In its primary aspect the doctrine of res judicata operates as a bar to the maintenance of a second suit between the same parties on the same cause of action." (Clark v. Lesher (1956) 46 Cal.2d 874, 880, 299 P.2d 865, 868.) Also, the doctrine comes into play in situations involving a second suit, not necessarily between the same parties, which is based upon a different cause of action. There "[t]he prior judgment is not a complete bar, but it 'operates [against the party against whom it was obtained] as an estoppel or conclusive adjudication as to such issues in the second action as were actually litigated and determined in the first section.'" (Id., citations omitted.) Neither aspect is applicable to the original judgment of dissolution and property settlement in this case.

Under California law, a spouse's entitlement to a share of the community property arises at the time that the property is acquired. (Civ.Code, §§ 5107, 5108, 5110.) [Cal.Fam. Code §§ 770 and 760] That interest is not altered except by judicial decree or an agreement between the parties. Hence "under settled principles of California community property law, 'property which is not mentioned in the pleadings as community property is left unadjudicated by decree of divorce, and is subject to future litigation, the parties being tenants in common meanwhile.'" (In re Marriage of Brown, supra, 15 Cal.3d at pp. 850–851, 126 Cal.Rptr. at p. 641, 544 P.2d at p. 569, quoting In re Marriage of Elkins (1972) 28 Cal.App.3d 899, 903, 105 Cal.Rptr. 59. Accord Estate of Williams (1950) 36 Cal.2d 289, 292–293, 223 P.2d 248; Lewis v. Superior Court (1978) 77 Cal.App.3d 844, 847–850, 144 Cal.Rptr. 1; Irwin v. Irwin (1977) 69 Cal.App.3d 317, 320–321, 138 Cal.Rptr. 9; Kelley v. Kelley (1977) 73 Cal.App.3d 672, 676, 141 Cal.Rptr. 33.) This rule applies to partial divisions of community property as well as divorces unaccompanied by any property adjudication whatsoever.

Helen's interest in Henry's military pension arose independent of and predates the original decree of dissolution and property settlement. This interest was separate and distinct from her interest in the items of community property which were divided at the time of the dissolution. Since it is conceded that the issue of Henry's military pension was not before the court which issued the final decree, the judgment of that court cannot be said to have extinguished Helen's putative interest in that asset.

Further, Helen cannot be collaterally estopped from litigating her community property right in that pension. Henry has not asserted that Helen is relying upon some factual or legal theory which was adjudicated in the prior litigation or which would have had to have been adjudicated if it had been raised at the time. (E.g., Sutphin v. Speik (1940) 15 Cal.2d 195, 202–205, 99 P.2d 652, 101 P.2d 497.) Rather, Henry argues that Helen's failure to assert her community property right in the pension, when there was an adjudication of her entitlement to other assets of the community, should preclude her from asserting her rights to the pension now.

The doctrine of collateral estoppel cannot be stretched to compel such a result. (Gorman v. Gorman, supra, 90 Cal.App.3d at pp. 464–465, 153 Cal.Rptr. 479; Lewis v. Superior Court, supra, 77 Cal.App.3d at p. 852, fn. 2, 144 Cal.Rptr. 1.) As explained in Carroll v. Puritan Leasing Co. (1978) 77 Cal.App.3d 481, 490, 143 Cal.Rptr. 772, the rule prohibiting the raising of any factual or legal contentions which were not actually asserted but which were within the scope of a prior action, "does not mean that issues not litigated and determined are binding in a subsequent proceeding on a new cause of action. Rather, it means that once an issue is litigated and determined, it is binding in a subsequent action notwithstanding that a party may have omitted to raise matters for or against it which if asserted may have produced a different outcome." Hence, the doctrine of collateral estoppel is not applicable here because Henry failed to demonstrate that Helen is relying upon some specific factual or legal contention which could have been relevant to the adjudication of the parties' rights to the property distributed in the 1971 decree if it had been raised. [ ]

The enforcement of Helen's rights in the pension payments received by Henry since the 1971 adjudication and distribution of the community assets does not present any substantial danger of unjust enrichment. On remand, Henry may seek to limit retrospective enforcement of Helen's claim on an equitable estoppel theory by demonstrating that she in fact received additional support payments in lieu of a share in the pension. (See Civ.Code, § 4800, subds. (a), (b).) [Cal.Fam. Code § 2601].

If Helen is allowed to recover her share of the pension payments received by Henry between 1971 and the initiation of the present action, a problem may arise. It may be substantially more burdensome for Henry to account for the pension payments he has received since the 1971 division of community assets than it would have been for him to have complied with a partition effected at that time. Henry is likely to have treated the asset as his separate property and disposed of it according to his needs. The court is confident that this problem may be adequately addressed under the defense of laches. The exercise of a court's authority to so limit equitable relief will provide litigants with an additional incentive to assert all tenable community property rights in assets known to exist at the time of the initial judicial distribution of the marital community.

The judgment is reversed.

TOBRINER, MOSK, CLARK, RICHARDSON, MANUEL and NEWMAN, JJ., concur.

NOTES

1. *The* Henn *rule.* Henn is partially codified at California Family Code Section 2556, discussed above.

2. *Personal jurisdiction must reattach if a subsequent property action is filed.* The "lawsuit for division of community property is a wholly separate and independent action, not a subsequent proceeding within the original dissolution action [citations omitted]. Consequently, the trial court has no authority to render a personal judgment against defendant-husband unless jurisdiction again attaches." *Tarvin v. Tarvin*, 187 Cal.App.3d 56, 61, 232 Cal.Rptr. 13, 16 (1st Dist. 1986).

3. *Laches.* In *Simon v. Simon*, 165 Cal.App.3d 1044, 212 Cal.Rptr. 87 (2d Dist. 1985), the former wife filed an action seeking a division of the community property interest in two parcels of land purchased by the parties during marriage. The appellate court held that the wife's action, filed approximately nine years after the final dissolution judgment, was barred by the doctrine of laches. The rationale was that nothing in the record explained the wife's delay in pursuing her rights. Plus the former husband had changed his position on the reasonable belief that all legal issues concerning the parcels had been resolved in the dissolution proceedings.

4. *Default judgments.* The omitted assets problem arose in the default judgment context in *Irwin v. Irwin*, 69 Cal.App.3d 317, 138 Cal.Rptr. 9 (5th Dist. 1977). There the wife filed a petition for dissolution on the prescribed printed form. She checked the box indicating "There is no property subject to disposition by the court in this proceeding," and left blank the box requesting that rights be determined as provided by law. The husband defaulted. Although the wife testified that the husband had a military retirement pension, neither the interlocutory decree nor the final judgment mentioned property rights. Some two years later, the wife filed an action to establish a community property interest in the pension, and the trial judge entered a judgment declaring that she had such an interest. The husband appealed. The appellate court noted that under the bifurcated divorce concept, where the property is not mentioned or distributed in the judgment of dissolution the issue of property rights is not deemed adjudicated and may be the subject of a later independent action. The husband contended that this case fell within an exception because the wife herself had alleged that there was no community property and the judgment against the husband was by default. The court of appeal declined to recognize such an exception. It found that checking the box preceding the words "There is no property subject to disposition by the court in this proceeding," merely reserves the right to have the matter resolved in a later proceeding.

5. *Res judicata.* The doctrine of *res judicata* can bar an attempt to reopen a judgment. In *Marriage of Mason,* 46 Cal.App.4th 1025, 54 Cal.Rptr.2d 263 (2d Dist. 1996), the wife operated a board and care facility. She was forced to close the business for health reasons. At dissolution, she was awarded the business account and other assets of the business. The issue of goodwill associated with a business was not raised. Two months after a final dissolution judgment was entered, the husband sought to set aside the property division alleging the wife concealed income and was reopening the board and care facility. The trial court denied his motion. The husband, relying on California Family Code Section 2556, filed an order to show cause to divide the business goodwill, claiming it was an omitted asset. The court found that the business was not an omitted asset; rather it was a known asset, part of the business that was divided at trial, and that if the movant did not raise the related issue of business goodwill issue during the original dissolution proceeding, it was "his tough luck." *Id.* at 1028.

In *Smith v. Smith,* 127 Cal.App.3d 203, 179 Cal.Rptr. 492 (3d Dist. 1981), the husband's state and federal retirement benefits were not included in the division of community property in the 1967 dissolution judgment. In 1968, the wife moved to amend the final decree under California Code of Civil Procedure Section 473 on the grounds of mistake, inadvertence and excusable neglect. The motion was denied as untimely. Thereafter, the wife brought a new action, seeking either to have the dissolution decree set aside, or to partition the retirement benefits on the theory that she had not had an opportunity to litigate the issue in the dissolution proceedings as a result of her attorney's negligence. The husband's demurrer was sustained without leave to amend and the action was dismissed. The wife subsequently sued her attorney for malpractice and recovered $100,000. In 1978 the wife again brought an action against her former spouse for her community property share of his retirement benefits. The trial court sustained the husband's *res judicata* defense. The appellate court affirmed, noting that the "plaintiff has manifestly received her day in court on the substance of her underlying claim, although not against her former husband." *Id.* at 210.

6. *Judicial estoppel.* In *Levin v. Ligon,* 140 Cal.App.4th 1456, 45 Cal.Rptr.3d 560 (1st Dist. 2006), the husband and wife were originally married and domiciled in California. The wife was employed by Levi Strauss and participated in the company's retirement and savings plans. In 1994, the couple moved to England, where they divorced a year later. Both husband and wife filed applications with the English court for ancillary relief, which would adjudicate their marital property rights. In 1996 the husband remarried an English national; he subsequently learned that his remarriage had barred his claim for ancillary relief under English law. The husband commenced a malpractice action against his solicitor, which was eventually settled for approximately $330,000. This settlement was approved by the English court. In 1999 the husband returned to California to claim a community property interest in his first wife's retirement benefits. The trial court granted the wife's motion for summary judgment, ruling that under the doctrine of judicial

estoppel the husband's English malpractice action barred him from recovering any of the property at issue in the California action. The appellate court agreed, reasoning that all criteria for application of the judicial estoppel doctrine were satisfied.

The doctrine of judicial estoppel has been described as "the ultimate silver bullet in the judicial arsenal for stopping what the courts view as misuse of the process. It is entirely an equitable remedy, and [ ] requires a sense of astonishment and outrage at the litigant's behavior." James D. Allen, *Commentary,* April 2006 CALIFORNIA FAMILY LAW MONTHLY 228 (LexisNexis Matthew Bender).[2]

7. *Legal Malpractice.* In *Marriage of Klug,* 130 Cal.App.4th 1389, 31 Cal.Rptr.3d 327 (3d Dist. 2005), the reviewing court held that the trial judge properly denied a former husband's motion under California Family Code section 2556 for division of an omitted community asset. The alleged community asset was a $346,000 settlement awarded to his former wife in a legal malpractice lawsuit against the couple's former attorney. The appellate court reasoned that the wife's cause of action for legal malpractice arose after the couple's date of separation and was, therefore, her separate property. The court also held that the husband's postseparation actions in transferring large amounts of community property offshore with the attorney's aid barred him from sharing in the wife's settlement because he had benefitted from the attorney's malpractice.

To avoid the problems that can arise where an item of community property is omitted from a dissolution judgment, it has been suggested that a warranty provision be inserted in the judgment. For the nature and effect of such a provision, see *In re Marriage of Smethurst,* 102 Cal.App.3d 494, 162 Cal.Rptr. 300 (4th Dist. 1980).

The next case discusses attorney liability for omission of a potential community property asset.

ALOY V. MASH

38 Cal.3d 413, 212 Cal.Rptr. 162, 696 P.2d 656 (1985)

KAUS, JUSTICE.

Marcella G. Aloy, plaintiff in a legal malpractice action, appeals from a summary judgment for defendant Eugene A. Mash, her former attorney in a 1971 dissolution action against her husband Richard. Marcella's claim of legal malpractice is based on defendant's failure to assert a community property interest in Richard's vested military retirement pension.

Marcella employed defendant Mash in January 1971 to represent her in the dissolution action. Richard was then on active military service and was therefore not receiving a pension although he had been in the service

---

[2] Fair use.

for over 20 years and was eligible to retire. (10 U.S.C. § 8911.) Defendant failed to claim any community property interest in Richard's pension and it was not put in issue in the dissolution action. The final decree of dissolution was entered in December 1971. Richard retired sometime between 1971 and 1980.

In 1971, the California view regarding the characterization of vested federal military retirement pensions as community or separate property was unsettled. In 1974, however, we held that federal preemption did not bar treating such federal military pensions as community property. (*Marriage of Fithian, supra,* 10 Cal.3d 592, 111 Cal.Rptr. 369, 517 P.2d 449.)

In 1980, Marcella filed a complaint against defendant alleging that he negligently failed to assert her community property interest in Richard's military retirement pension, which failure prevented her from receiving any share of his gross military retirement pension benefits "from either the date of separation and/or the date of [his] retirement."

Defendant moved for summary judgment on the ground that in 1971 the law regarding the character of federal military retirement pensions was unsettled, and that he had exercised informed judgment and was therefore immune from a claim of professional negligence. He submitted a declaration stating, among other things: "2. In 1971, it was my practice to read advance sheets, particularly in the dissolution area, an area in which I have regularly practiced. I would therefore have had knowledge of specific decisions at the time they were rendered or shortly thereafter. 3. In 1971, I relied on the case of *French v. French,* 17 Cal.2d 775, 112 P.2d 235 (1941) as authority that a non-matured military pension, that is, one owned by a person on active military duty, was not subject to division upon dissolution. I was also aware that in 1971 this case had not yet been overruled. I read the decision *In re Marriage of Fithian,* 10 Cal.3d 592, 111 Cal.Rptr. 369, 517 P.2d 449 (1974) shortly after it was issued in 1974. 4. I drafted the terms of the interlocutory decree based on my research, knowledge, and understanding of the law in 1971."

Marcella opposed the motion, asserting that it was a triable issue whether defendant had made an informed decision. She submitted excerpts from her deposition testimony in which she stated that the one time she asked defendant whether she was entitled to a portion of Richard's military retirement pension, he told her she had no such right because Richard was still on active duty. Marcella also submitted excerpts from defendant's deposition testimony where he discussed his knowledge and research as follows: "MR. WATTERS: Q. Are you a regular reader of the advance sheets, say from 1971 up until now? [¶] A. I read them. I get them in the office but I can't recall when I started getting them, frankly. Whether I got them in 1971, I don't know. I used to read the advance sheets all the time but I don't know when I got them. I still skim them, review them, when I can. [¶] Q. You review the cases in your particular area of practice? [¶] A. Yes, I do. [¶] Q. That would include the domestic area, up until you stopped doing domestic work, or slowed down? [¶] A. Right. [¶] Q. As of 1971, what was your case authority for your position that when someone in the military service was on active duty that their pension was not community property, what was your authority? [¶] A. I don't know what I checked with at that time. Probably the *French* case would be the authority. [¶] Q. A 1941 case? [¶] A. Whatever the date is. [¶] Q. Sir, any other authority that you can cite me other than the *French* case for that belief that you had? [¶] * * * [¶] A. I can't recall what else, what I might have looked up at that point. Might have been something else but I don't * * * [¶] A. Well, this is again going back to my thinking, what I might have thought back then, and I'd have to say probably the same thing, that if a person has been in the military, active military duty, was not drawing his pension, that it was not an item to be divided at that time. [¶] Q. This would be true when the person was in the service over twenty years, over twenty or under twenty years? [¶] MRS. MARRISON: Q. Do you understand the question? [¶] A. I presume he is asking what was in my mind at that time and I'm not sure in this case at that time what was in my mind. I'm not sure what I would have stated at that time. If you ask me the question in 1971, is that what you're asking?"

Marcella further submitted a declaration by James J. Simonelli, which stated that he was an attorney with an extensive practice in family law since 1970, and that in 1971 attorneys in the family law field in the San Joaquin Valley uniformly claimed a community property interest in vested military retirement pensions. Simonelli further stated that had he been representing Marcella in November 1971, he would have advised her that she had some community property interest in Richard's vested military retirement pension and that the only issue as to that interest was whether federal law preempted state enforcement of such an interest.

II

The criteria on appeals from summary judgments are too familiar to need restatement. In brief, if the record discloses triable issues with respect to negligence, causation and damages, the judgment must be reversed.

In *Smith v. Lewis* (1975) 13 Cal.3d 349, 118 Cal.Rptr. 621, 530 P.2d 589—a legal malpractice case based on an attorney's 1967 failure to claim a community property interest in the husband's vested retirement benefits—we affirmed a judgment for plaintiff and rejected the defendant attorney's contention that he should not be liable for mistaken advice when well-informed lawyers in the community had entertained reasonable doubt at the time as to the proper resolution of the legal issue. We found the situation in no way analogous to that in *Lucas v. Hamm* (1961) 56 Cal.2d

583, 15 Cal.Rptr. 821, 364 P.2d 685, involving the esoteric subject of the rule against perpetuities. We conceded that in 1967 the law regarding the community character of the husband's federal pension was unsettled. We said, however: "If the law on a particular subject is doubtful or debatable, an attorney will not be held responsible for failing to anticipate the manner in which the uncertainty will be resolved. [Citation.] But even with respect to an unsettled area of the law, we believe an attorney assumes an obligation to his client to undertake reasonable research in an effort to ascertain relevant legal principles and to make an informed decision as to a course of conduct based upon an intelligent assessment of the problem." (*Id.*, 13 Cal.3d, at pp. 358–359, 118 Cal.Rptr. 621, 530 P.2d 589.)

Smith v. Lewis, supra, is obviously of little help to defendant. His motion for summary judgment was, in fact, primarily based on *Davis v. Damrell* (1981) 119 Cal.App.3d 883, 174 Cal.Rptr. 257—a similar case in which Damrell, the wife's attorney, in 1970 failed to assert a community property interest in the husband's vested federal military retirement pension. The husband retired in 1973, and the wife filed suit against Damrell sometime thereafter. The Court of Appeal affirmed the summary judgment for Damrell on the ground that he had demonstrated compliance with the *Smith v. Lewis* standards by showing a thorough, contemporaneous research effort on an issue of unsettled law. He had submitted a declaration describing his detailed knowledge of legal developments and debate in the field. He traced his familiarity with the line of cases following the earlier *French* rule (*French v. French* (1941) 17 Cal.2d 775, 112 P.2d 235 [nonvested military pension was mere expectancy not subject to division as community property]), overruled in *In re Marriage of Brown* (1976) 15 Cal.3d 838, 126 Cal.Rptr. 633, 544 P.2d 561, and recounted his special interest in the *Wissner* case (*Wissner v. Wissner* (1950) 338 U.S. 655, 70 S.Ct. 398, 94 L.Ed. 424 [establishing the supremacy of a federal statute governing disposition of the proceeds of a military service life insurance policy]), which had motivated him to follow its progress from its inception.

Defendant's reliance on *Davis v. Damrell, supra,* is ill-advised, since the differences between his professional conduct and that of the defendant in that case inexorably point to potential liability on defendant's part. In brief, in *Davis* the defendant attorney was thoroughly familiar with all the pertinent authorities, state and federal, and had reached the conclusion, based primarily on *Wissner v. Wissner, supra,* 338 U.S. 655, 70 S.Ct. 398, 94 L.Ed. 424, that vested military pension benefits were not subject to California community property rules. His decision not to claim a community property interest in the husband's military pension was not actionable, as it represented "a reasoned exercise of an informed judgment grounded on a professional evaluation of applicable legal principles." (*Id.*, 119 Cal.App.3d, at p. 888, 174 Cal.Rptr. 257.) Defendant, by contrast, relied on a single case—*French v. French* (1941) 17 Cal.2d 775, 112 P.2d 235 for the proposition that a nonmatured military pension was not subject to division on dissolution. At his deposition he never did answer the question whether he was aware that a military pension vests after 20 years of service, whether the serviceman retires or not. This would have been a vital point in his research, for in *French v. French* itself a dictum indicates that after retirement pay vests it becomes community property. (*Id.* at p. 778, 112 P.2d 235.) He thus never even gave himself a chance to consider whether his client was entitled to a community share in monthly payments which, but for the husband's election not to retire, would have been vested pension payments. (See *In re Marriage of Gillmore, supra,* 29 Cal.3d 418, 423, 174 Cal.Rptr. 493, 629 P.2d 1; *Waite v. Waite* (1972) 6 Cal.3d 461, 472, 99 Cal.Rptr. 325, 492 P.2d 13.)

In sum, this is not a case where the defendant attorney, basing his judgment on all available data, made a rational professional judgment not to claim an interest in the husband's pension. Rather, he acted—more precisely, failed to act—on an incomplete reading of a single case, without appreciating the vital difference between a member of the armed forces who has not yet served long enough to be eligible to retire and one who has but chooses to stay in the service. As far as the issue of federal preemption is concerned, the record does not show that he ever considered it.

In sum, the record on which the motion for summary judgment was argued presented a triable issue of negligence.

III

The question whether the defendant's negligence caused damage in some amount need not detain us long. Footnote 9 to *Smith v. Lewis, supra,* 13 Cal.3d at pages 360–361, 118 Cal.Rptr. 621, 530 P.2d 589, makes this an a fortiori case. (See also *Martin v. Hall* (1971) 20 Cal.App.3d 414, at pp. 423–424, 97 Cal.Rptr. 730.) Nor—the arguments based on *McCarty v. McCarty* (1981) 453 U.S. 210, 101 S.Ct. 2728, 69 L.Ed.2d 589, aside—do we understand defendant to claim otherwise.

IV

McCarty v. McCarty, supra, decided on June 26, 1981, held that the application of community property principles impermissibly conflicts with the federal military retirement scheme. This, of course, happened a decade after defendant had represented plaintiff. Nor, unlike the defendant attorney in *Davis v. Damrell, supra,* had defendant anticipated this development. Nevertheless he seeks to take advantage of *McCarty* in two ways: first, he argues that had he asserted a community property interest in Richard's pension, the United States Supreme Court case which invalidated any favorable ruling by a California court might have been *Aloy v. Aloy,* rather than *McCarty v. McCarty;* second, he argues that it simply cannot be actionable malpractice not to assert a claim which is eventually found to be invalid.

A

Defendant's first argument assumes, of course, that *McCarty v. McCarty* once and for all settled the question of Colonel McCarty's pension in his favor. Solely because we happen to know judicially that the *McCarty* controversy is far from over and do not wish to make any unnecessary statement which might affect its outcome, we shall assume defendant's hypothesis to be true.

Assuming further that it is a legitimate subject of inquiry whether, at the critical time, the early '70's, the United States Supreme Court would have granted certiorari on the issue whether states could hold military pensions to be community property, all the available evidence is negative. After we first decided in favor of the nonmember spouse in *Fithian,* certiorari was denied (*Fithian v. Fithian* (1974) 419 U.S. 825, 95 S.Ct. 41, 42 L.Ed.2d 48), as was a petition for rehearing. (*Fithian v. Fithian, supra,* 419 U.S., at p. 1060, 95 S.Ct. at p. 644, 42 L.Ed.2d 657.) Shortly thereafter we reaffirmed *Fithian* in *In re Marriage of Milhan* (1974) 13 Cal.3d 129, 117 Cal.Rptr. 809, 528 P.2d 1145. Again certiorari was denied. (*Milhan v. Milhan* (1975) 421 U.S. 976, 95 S.Ct. 1976, 44 L.Ed.2d 467.) Nothing in the *Aloy v. Aloy* litigation suggests to us that it was more likely than *Fithian* or *Milhan* to persuade the high court that the military pension issue was one whose time had come.

B

Finally we turn to the argument that the summary judgment was correct because the claim which defendant negligently failed to assert in 1971 luckily turned out to be worthless in 1981—the serendipity defense. This argument is not based on any theory that in point of fact Marcella would not have benefited financially had a community property claim to Richard's pension rights been asserted in 1971. (See pt. III, *ante.*) Rather, defendant simply asserts that he was under no "duty to secure for plaintiff benefits to which she was not legally entitled."

It is evident from the way defendant makes his point—"benefits to which she *was* not legally entitled"—that he assumes as a premise of his argument that *McCarty* has been retroactively applied and that, therefore, in a real sense *McCarty* "was" the law 10 years before it was decided, when defendant acted for Marcella.

Whatever may be said in favor of defendant's theory were this premise correct, the fact is that no case within our memory has received less retroactive application than *McCarty.* Starting with the last paragraph of the *McCarty* opinion itself, the judicial and legislative branches, state and federal, cooperated in a massive and largely successful drive to make

McCarty disappear—prospectively, presently and retroactively. Some highlights of that effort are noted below. The result is that, for most purposes, *McCarty* not only is not the law but never really was. As one Court of Appeal put it: "[T]here is no longer any *McCarty* rule to be retroactively applied." (*In re Marriage of Frederick* (1983) 141 Cal.App.3d 876, 880, 190 Cal.Rptr. 588.) It would be ironic if the chief legacy of *McCarty* were the immunization of legal malpractice by an attorney who never even pondered the issues which fathered *McCarty*'s brief life.

The judgment is reversed.

MOSK and GRODIN, JJ., and RAMSEY, J., concur.

REYNOSO, JUSTICE, dissenting.

I respectfully dissent. With the exception of the majority opinion, I know of no case which suggests that an attorney whose advice is correct may be held liable for malpractice.

Relying on the standard developed in *Smith v. Lewis* (1975) 13 Cal.3d 349, 118 Cal.Rptr. 621, 530 P.2d 589 and its progeny, the majority concludes that an attorney may face malpractice liability despite the fact that the law is ultimately resolved in accordance with the advice given. Although this application of the *Smith* standard follows logically from its emphasis on the duty of care owed a client, it nonetheless raises a troubling anomaly: where the law is unsettled, the attorney who gives advice later determined to be correct may well have committed malpractice, while the attorney whose advice turns out to be erroneous may avoid liability entirely.

The law cannot tolerate such incongruous results. As Justice Holmes so aptly observed long ago, "[t]he life of the law has not been logic: it has been experience." (Holmes, Common Law (1881) 1.) Experience now tells us that the *Smith* standard, however rational and well-suited to its original purpose, no longer makes sense. We must therefore formulate a new standard that draws a fair and reasonable distinction between culpable and nonculpable practitioners.

The defect inherent in the *Smith* standard, made ever clearer by today's majority opinion, is that the concept of legal error is confused with that of fault, converting a question of law into one of fact. Malpractice consists of four elements: duty arising out of the attorney-client relationship, breach of that duty, causation and damages. The second element breaks down further into two components: legal error and failure to use "such skill, prudence and diligence as lawyers of ordinary skill and capacity commonly possess and exercise in the performance of the tasks which they undertake." (*Lucas v. Hamm* (1961) 56 Cal.2d 583, 591, 15 Cal.Rptr. 821, 364 P.2d 685.) The first is a question of law, the second a question of fact.

The question of whether an attorney erred necessarily must be resolved before any issue of negligence arises. An attorney who renders erroneous advice may not be negligent in doing so. (See *Davis v. Damrell* (1981) 119 Cal.App.3d 883, 174 Cal.Rptr. 257.) A second attorney may fail to perform adequate research but somehow give his client accurate advice. Neither of these attorneys has committed malpractice. (See Mallen & Levit, Legal Malpractice (2d ed. 1981) § 250, p. 317.)

Where the law is settled, it is relatively easy to determine whether the attorney's advice was erroneous. Problems arise only with respect to issues of law that are unresolved or in a state of flux at the time the advice is given. In either instance, however, the question of whether the advice was wrong is a question of law.

Ironically, *Smith* itself reflects this basic approach. At the outset of the analysis the court stressed: "the crucial inquiry is whether his advice was *so legally deficient* when it was given that he may be found to have failed to use 'such skill, prudence, and diligence as lawyers of ordinary skill and capacity commonly possess and exercise in the performance of the tasks which they undertake.' [Citation.] We must, therefore, examine the indicia of the law which were readily available to defendant at the time he performed the legal services in question." (Id., 13 Cal.3d, at p. 356, 118 Cal.Rptr. 621, 530 P.2d 589.) (Emphasis added.)

Thus, *Smith* initially proposed a two-step test for determining whether an attorney has been negligent. As noted, the threshold inquiry is a legal one, whether adequate legal authority existed at the time to support the advice given. Only when this question is answered in the negative is it necessary to move to the second part of the test, the factual inquiry as to whether the attorney breached the standard of care in rendering the erroneous advice.

Applying this test to the case at bar reveals that Attorney Mash did not err in advising his client in 1971 that her husband's federal military pension was not community property. As the majority notes, "[i]n 1971, the California view regarding the characterization of vested federal military retirement pensions as community or separate property was unsettled." Ante, p. 163 of 212 Cal.Rptr., at p. 657 of 696 P.2d. In fact, Mash relied on an opinion of this court, *French v. French* (1941) 17 Cal.2d 775, 112 P.2d 235, in concluding that the pension was not divisible. As *French* remained good law, this reliance was neither unreasonable nor erroneous. Because Mash committed no error, the malpractice claim must fail.

It is imperative that a lawyer remain free to choose one of a number of reasonable and legally supportable solutions to an otherwise unsettled legal question and advise the client accordingly without facing a malpractice suit.

BIRD, C.J., and TABER, J., concur.

NOTE

Other states. McHugh v. McHugh, 115 Idaho 198, 766 P.2d 133 (1988) characterized the *Aloy* rationale as teleological. On that basis the Idaho Supreme Court declined to follow *Aloy*.

SECTION 4. CHAPTER SUMMARY

- A community property estate comes into existence on the date of marriage (Chapter 2).

- A marriage ends either by the issuance of a final judgment of dissolution or by the death of a spouse.

- The community property estate is distinct from the marriage itself.

- The California community property estate terminates at one of several possible points:

  o On a date of separation (Chapter 3);

  o When an acquiring spouse changes domicile (Chapter 4);

  o When the parties execute a marriage settlement agreement;

  o When a final judgment dissolving the estate is issued by a court.

- Dissolution is the process of ending a marriage by a court judgment. A final judgment of dissolution returns each party to the status of a single individual and memorializes the parties' division of community property.

- California is a pure no-fault divorce jurisdiction. A petition for dissolution can be based on only one of two statutory grounds: irreconcilable differences or permanent legal incapacity.

- Spouses who seek to dissolve their marriage are entitled to use alternative dispute resolution methods to negotiate a marriage settlement agreement. The most commonly used alternative dispute resolution (ADR) methods for dissolution are mediation, arbitration, and collaborative law.

- If the parties opt for a litigated settlement, a public court shall step in to divide the property in accordance with the equal division principle. A public court has jurisdiction to divide property as well as to assign liabilities. The jurisdiction to divide property includes the power to determine property valuation.

- The court is invested with continuing jurisdiction in certain cases. Upon a timely motion showing that a community asset or liability was inadvertently omitted from the final judgment for dissolution, a court can grant the remedy of postjudgment adjudication as to that asset.

CHAPTER 8

POSTDISSOLUTION REMEDIES

■ ■ ■

What if, long after the final dissolution judgment had been issued, a party were to discover, that the other party fraudulently concealed or omitted an asset? What would be the remedy if all other time limitations had run?

The California courts have held that relief is available for fraud in a dissolution proceeding. Relief comes in the form of a final judgment set aside order.

Historically, a final dissolution judgment set aside order was available for extrinsic fraud, but not for intrinsic fraud. The extrinsic-intrinsic fraud distinction proved difficult to apply in the family context. Extrinsic fraud— a basis for equitable relief—required proof that a party was deprived of the opportunity to present or defend a claim to a court, or else otherwise prevented from fully participating in a dissolution proceeding. Intrinsic fraud—not a basis for equitable relief—occurred when a party was given fair and adequate notice of a proceeding, but unreasonably neglected to present or defend a case.

SECTION 1. THE IMPORTANCE OF DISCLOSURE AT DISSOLUTION

Disclosure and cooperative discovery serve key state interests.

Those interests are set forth in California Family Code Section 2100, reproduced below.

In brief, disclosure and cooperative discovery are important to the fair dissolution of the community property estate. Both prevent the dissipation of community and quasi-community assets. Both protect creditors. Disclosure and cooperative discovery (at least in a perfect world) reduce the adversarial nature of marital dissolution proceedings; in a way, this makes community estate partition a somewhat quantitative evaluation. Finally, disclosure and cooperative discovery are intended to prevent fraud by how they protect the public policy in favor of finality of judgments. Preventing fraud enhances confidence in the legal system.

California Family Code Section 2101 disclosure standards apply to:

- Assets;

- Liabilities;

- Business and investment opportunities;

- Business activities in which the community may have an interest.

California Family Code Section 2102 provides that each party in a dissolution proceeding is subject to standards that are set forth in California Family Code Section 721 (Chapter 6). California Family Code Section 721 standards apply generally; they also apply specifically to any asset or liability under negotiation in the dissolution proceeding. California Family Code Section 721 standards go into effect at the start of the marriage, they apply during the marriage, and they continue to apply until the community estate (including any specific asset and liability) is distributed or assigned. The California Family Code Section 2100 et seq. standards (Chapter 8) do not mandate parties to divide property equally; rather, they mandate something far more subtle, namely that neither party shall take any unfair advantage of the other.

The California Family Code Section 2100 standards were part of the original Family Code. Amendments were made in 2001, effective January 1, 2002.

The effect of the amendments California Family Code Section 2102(a) was to mandate that disclosure be updated in the event of "any material changes." California Family Code Section 2102(b) and (c), were added as new provisions. California Family Code Section 2102(b) was also amended to provide that "each party is subject to standards provided in Section 721 as to all activities that affect the assets or liabilities of the other party . . . [until] a particular asset or liability has been distributed . . . " California Family Code Section 2102(c) now requires disclosure of income and expenses from the date of separation to the date of a binding resolution. Information about income and expenses must be kept updated because expenses are material to support calculations. See, for example, the spousal support considerations listed under California Family Code Section 4320 in the Statutory Appendix.

From there the statutory passage addresses other important issues such as:

- Formalities of preliminary and final disclosure declarations;

- The entry of judgments, including summary and default judgments;

- Motions to compel declarations of disclosure that comply with the statutory standards.

Preliminary and final disclosure declarations are mandatory for purposes of issuing a final judgment of dissolution.

WEST'S ANNOTATED CALIFORNIA FAMILY CODE

§ 2100. Legislative findings and declarations; disclosure of assets and liabilities

The Legislature finds and declares the following:

(a) It is the policy of the State of California (1) to marshal, preserve, and protect community and quasi-community assets and liabilities that exist at the date of separation so as to avoid dissipation of the community estate before distribution, (2) to ensure fair and sufficient child and spousal support awards, and (3) to achieve a division of community and quasi-community assets and liabilities on the dissolution or nullity of marriage or legal separation of the parties as provided under California law.

(b) Sound public policy further favors the reduction of the adversarial nature of marital dissolution and the attendant costs by fostering full disclosure and cooperative discovery.

(c) In order to promote this public policy, a full and accurate disclosure of all assets and liabilities in which one or both parties have or may have an interest must be made in the early stages of a proceeding for dissolution of marriage or legal separation of the parties, regardless of the characterization as community or separate, together with a disclosure of all income and expenses of the parties. Moreover, each party has a continuing duty to immediately, fully, and accurately update and augment that disclosure to the extent there have been any material changes so that at the time the parties enter into an agreement for the resolution of any of these issues, or at the time of trial on these issues, each party will have a full and complete knowledge of the relevant underlying facts.

(Added by Stats. 1993, c. 219 (A.B. 1500), § 107. Amended by Stats. 1993, c. 1101 (A.B. 1469), § 3, eff. Oct. 11, 1993, operative Jan. 1, 1994; Stats. 2001, c. 703 (A.B. 583), § 2.)

§ 2101. Definitions

Unless the provision or context otherwise requires, the following definitions apply to this chapter:

(a) "Asset" includes, but is not limited to, any real or personal property of any nature, whether tangible or intangible, and whether currently existing or contingent.

(b) "Default judgment" does not include a stipulated judgment or any judgment pursuant to a marital settlement agreement.

(c) "Earnings and accumulations" includes income from whatever source derived, as provided in Section 4058.

(d) "Expenses" includes, but is not limited to, all personal living expenses, but does not include business related expenses.

(e) "Income and expense declaration" includes the Income and Expense Declaration forms approved for use by the Judicial Council, and any other financial statement that is approved for use by the Judicial Council in lieu of the Income and Expense Declaration, if the financial statement form satisfies all other applicable criteria.

(f) "Liability" includes, but is not limited to, any debt or obligation, whether currently existing or contingent.

(Added by Stats. 1993, c. 219 (A.B. 1500), § 107. Amended by Stats. 1993, c. 1101 (A.B. 1469), § 4, eff. Oct. 11, 1993, operative Jan. 1, 1994; Stats. 1998, c. 581 (A.B. 2801), § 5.)

§ 2102. Fiduciary relationship; length and scope of duty; termination

(a) From the date of separation to the date of the distribution of the community or quasi-community asset or liability in question, each party is subject to the standards provided in Section 721, as to all activities that affect the assets and liabilities of the other party, including, but not limited to, the following activities:

(1) The accurate and complete disclosure of all assets and liabilities in which the party has or may have an interest or obligation and all current earnings, accumulations, and expenses, including an immediate, full, and accurate update or augmentation to the extent there have been any material changes.

(2) The accurate and complete written disclosure of any investment opportunity, business opportunity, or other income-producing opportunity that presents itself after the date of separation, but that results from any investment, significant business activity outside the ordinary course of business, or other income-producing opportunity of either spouse from the date of marriage to the date of separation, inclusive. The written disclosure shall be made in sufficient time for the other spouse to make an informed decision as to whether he or she desires to participate in the investment opportunity, business, or other potential income-producing opportunity, and for the court to resolve any dispute regarding the right of the other spouse to participate in the opportunity. In the event of nondisclosure of an investment opportunity, the division of any gain resulting from that opportunity is governed by the standard provided in Section 2556.

(3) The operation or management of a business or an interest in a business in which the community may have an interest.

(b) From the date that a valid, enforceable, and binding resolution of the disposition of the asset or liability in question is reached, until the asset or liability has actually been distributed, each party is subject to the standards provided in Section 721 as to all activities that affect the assets or liabilities of the other party. Once a particular asset or liability has been distributed, the duties and standards set forth in Section 721 shall end as to that asset or liability.

(c) From the date of separation to the date of a valid, enforceable, and binding resolution of all issues relating to child or spousal support and professional fees, each party is subject to the standards provided in Section 721 as to all issues relating to the support and fees, including immediate, full, and accurate disclosure of all material facts and information regarding the income or expenses of the party.

(Added by Stats. 1993, c. 219 (A.B. 1500), § 107. Amended by Stats. 1993, c. 1101 (A.B. 1469), § 5, eff. Oct. 11, 1993, operative Jan. 1, 1994; Stats. 2001, c. 703 (A.B. 583), § 3.)

§ 2103. Declarations of disclosure; requirements

In order to provide full and accurate disclosure of all assets and liabilities in which one or both parties may have an interest, each party to a proceeding for dissolution of the marriage or legal separation of the parties shall serve on the other party a preliminary declaration of disclosure under Section 2104, unless service of the preliminary declaration of disclosure is not required pursuant to Section 2110, and a final declaration of disclosure under Section 2105, unless service of the final declaration of disclosure is waived pursuant to Section 2105 or 2110, and shall file proof of service of each with the court.

(Added by Stats. 1993, c. 219 (A.B. 1500), § 107. Amended by Stats. 1998, c. 581 (A.B. 2801), § 6; Stats. 2015, c. 46 (S.B. 340), § 1, eff. Jan. 1, 2016.)

§ 2104. Preliminary declaration of disclosure

(a) Except by court order for good cause, as provided in Section 2107, or when service of the preliminary declaration of disclosure is not required pursuant to Section 2110, in the time period set forth in subdivision (f), each party shall serve on the other party a preliminary declaration of disclosure, executed under penalty of perjury on a form prescribed by the Judicial Council. The commission of perjury on the preliminary declaration of disclosure may be grounds for setting aside the judgment, or any part or parts thereof, pursuant to Chapter 10 (commencing with Section 2120), in addition to any and all other remedies, civil or criminal, that otherwise are available under law for the commission of perjury. The preliminary declaration of disclosure shall include all tax returns filed by the declarant within the two years prior to the date that the party served the declaration.

(b) The preliminary declaration of disclosure shall not be filed with the court, except on court order. However, the parties shall file proof of service of the preliminary declaration of disclosure with the court.

(c) The preliminary declaration of disclosure shall set forth with sufficient particularity, that a person of reasonable and ordinary intelligence can ascertain, all of the following:

(1) The identity of all assets in which the declarant has or may have an interest and all liabilities for which the declarant is or may be liable, regardless of the characterization of the asset or liability as community, quasi-community, or separate.

(2) The declarant's percentage of ownership in each asset and percentage of obligation for each liability when property is not solely owned by one or both of the parties. The preliminary declaration may also set forth the declarant's characterization of each asset or liability.

(d) A declarant may amend his or her preliminary declaration of disclosure without leave of the court. Proof of service of any amendment shall be filed with the court.

(e) Along with the preliminary declaration of disclosure, each party shall provide the other party with a completed income and expense declaration unless an income and expense declaration has already been provided and is current and valid.

(f) The petitioner shall serve the other party with the preliminary declaration of disclosure either concurrently with the petition for dissolution or legal separation, or within 60 days of filing the petition. When a petitioner serves the summons and petition by publication or posting pursuant to court order and the respondent files a response prior to a default judgment being entered, the petitioner shall serve the other party with the preliminary declaration of disclosure within 30 days of the response being filed. The respondent shall serve the other party with the preliminary declaration of disclosure either concurrently with the response to the petition, or within 60 days of filing the response. The time periods specified in this subdivision may be extended by written agreement of the parties or by court order.

(Added by Stats. 1993, c. 219 (A.B. 1500), § 107. Amended by Stats. 1993, c. 1101 (A.B. 1469), § 6, eff. Oct. 11, 1993, operative Jan. 1, 1994; Stats. 1998, c. 581 (A.B. 2801), § 7; Stats. 2009, c. 110 (A.B. 459), § 1; Stats. 2012, c. 107 (A.B. 1406), § 1; Stats. 2015, c. 46 (S.B. 340), § 2, eff. Jan. 1, 2016; Stats. 2015, c. 416 (A.B. 1519), § 1.5, eff. Jan. 1, 2016.))

§ 2105. Final declaration of disclosure of current income and expenses; execution and service; contents; waiver; perjury or noncompliance with chapter

(a) Except by court order for good cause, before or at the time the parties enter into an agreement for the resolution of property or support issues other than pendente lite support, or, if the case goes to trial, no later than 45 days before the first assigned trial date, each party, or the attorney for the party in this matter, shall serve on the other party a final declaration of disclosure and a current income and expense declaration, executed under penalty of perjury on a form prescribed by the Judicial Council, unless the parties mutually waive the final declaration of disclosure. The commission of perjury on the final declaration of disclosure by a party may be grounds for setting aside the judgment, or any part or parts thereof, pursuant to Chapter 10 (commencing with Section 2120), in addition to any and all other remedies, civil or criminal, that otherwise are available under law for the commission of perjury.

(b) The final declaration of disclosure shall include all of the following information:

(1) All material facts and information regarding the characterization of all assets and liabilities.

(2) All material facts and information regarding the valuation of all assets that are contended to be community property or in which it is contended the community has an interest.

(3) All material facts and information regarding the amounts of all obligations that are contended to be community obligations or for which it is contended the community has liability.

(4) All material facts and information regarding the earnings, accumulations, and expenses of each party that have been set forth in the income and expense declaration.

(c) In making an order setting aside a judgment for failure to comply with this section, the court may limit the set aside to those portions of the judgment materially affected by the nondisclosure.

(d) The parties may stipulate to a mutual waiver of the requirements of subdivision (a) concerning the final declaration of disclosure, by execution of a waiver under penalty of perjury entered into in open court or by separate stipulation. The waiver shall include all of the following representations:

(1) Both parties have complied with Section 2104 and the preliminary declarations of disclosure have been completed and exchanged.

(2) Both parties have completed and exchanged a current income and expense declaration, that includes all material facts and information regarding that party's earnings, accumulations, and expenses.

(3) Both parties have fully complied with Section 2102 and have fully augmented the preliminary declarations of disclosure, including disclosure of all material facts and information regarding the characterization of all assets and liabilities, the valuation of all assets

that are contended to be community property or in which it is contended the community has an interest, and the amounts of all obligations that are contended to be community obligations or for which it is contended the community has liability.

(4) The waiver is knowingly, intelligently, and voluntarily entered into by each of the parties.

(5) Each party understands that this waiver does not limit the legal disclosure obligations of the parties, but rather is a statement under penalty of perjury that those obligations have been fulfilled. Each party further understands that noncompliance with those obligations will result in the court setting aside the judgment.

(Added by Stats. 1993, c. 219 (A.B. 1500), § 107. Amended by Stats. 1993, c. 1101 (A.B. 1469), § 7, eff. Oct. 11, 1993, operative Jan. 1, 1994; Stats. 1995, c. 233 (A.B. 806), § 1; Stats. 1996, c. 1061 (S.B. 1033), § 7; Stats. 1998, c. 581 (A.B. 2801), § 8; Stats. 2001, c. 703 (A.B. 583), § 4.)

§ 2106. Entry of judgment; requirement of execution and service of declarations; exceptions; execution and filing of declaration of execution and service or of waiver

Except as provided in subdivision (d) of Section 2105, Section 2110, or absent good cause as provided in Section 2107, no judgment shall be entered with respect to the parties' property rights without each party, or the attorney for that party in this matter, having executed and served a copy of the final declaration of disclosure and current income and expense declaration. Each party, or his or her attorney, shall execute and file with the court a declaration signed under penalty of perjury stating that service of the final declaration of disclosure and current income and expense declaration was made on the other party or that service of the final declaration of disclosure has been waived pursuant to subdivision (d) of Section 2105 or in Section 2110.

(Added by Stats. 1993, c. 219 (A.B. 1500), § 107. Amended by Stats. 1993, c. 1101 (A.B. 1469), § 8, eff. Oct. 11, 1993, operative Jan. 1, 1994; Stats. 1995, c. 233 (A.B. 806), § 2; Stats. 1996, c. 1061 (S.B. 1033), § 8; Stats. 1998, c. 581 (A.B. 2801), § 9; Stats. 2001, c. 703 (A.B. 583), § 5; Stats. 2002, c. 1008 (A.B. 3028), § 15; Stats. 2009, c. 110 (A.B. 459), § 2.)

§ 2107. Noncomplying declarations; requests to comply; remedies

(a) If one party fails to serve on the other party a preliminary declaration of disclosure under Section 2104, unless that party is not required to serve a preliminary declaration of disclosure pursuant to Section 2110, or a final declaration of disclosure under Section 2105, or fails to provide the information required in the respective declarations with sufficient particularity, and if the other party has served the respective declaration of disclosure on the noncomplying party, the complying party may, within a reasonable time, request preparation of the appropriate declaration of disclosure or further particularity.

(b) If the noncomplying party fails to comply with a request under subdivision (a), the complying party may do one or more of the following:

(1) File a motion to compel a further response.

(2) File a motion for an order preventing the noncomplying party from presenting evidence on issues that should have been covered in the declaration of disclosure.

(3) File a motion showing good cause for the court to grant the complying party's voluntary waiver of receipt of the noncomplying party's preliminary declaration of disclosure pursuant to Section 2104 or final declaration of disclosure pursuant to Section 2105. The voluntary waiver does not affect the rights enumerated in subdivision (d).

(c) If a party fails to comply with any provision of this chapter, the court shall, in addition to any other remedy provided by law, impose money sanctions against the noncomplying party. Sanctions shall be in an amount sufficient to deter repetition of the conduct or comparable conduct, and shall include reasonable attorney's fees, costs incurred, or both, unless the court finds that the noncomplying party acted with substantial justification or that other circumstances make the imposition of the sanction unjust.

(d) Except as otherwise provided in this subdivision, if a court enters a judgment when the parties have failed to comply with all disclosure requirements of this chapter, the court shall set aside the judgment. The failure to comply with the disclosure requirements does not constitute harmless error. If the court granted the complying party's voluntary waiver of receipt of the noncomplying party's preliminary declaration of disclosure pursuant to paragraph (3) of subdivision (b), the court shall set aside the judgment only at the request of the complying party, unless the motion to set aside the judgment is based on one of the following:

(1) Actual fraud if the defrauded party was kept in ignorance or in some other manner was fraudulently prevented from fully participating in the proceeding.

(2) Perjury, as defined in Section 118 of the Penal Code, in the preliminary or final declaration of disclosure, in the waiver of the final declaration of disclosure, or in the current income and expense statement.

(e) Upon the motion to set aside judgment, the court may order the parties to provide the preliminary and final declarations of disclosure that were exchanged between them. Absent a court order to the contrary, the disclosure declarations shall not be filed with the court and shall be returned to the parties.

(Added by Stats. 1993, c. 219 (A.B. 1500), § 107. Amended by Stats. 1993, c. 1101 (A.B. 1469), § 9, eff. Oct. 11, 1993, operative Jan. 1, 1994; Stats. 2001, c. 703 (A.B. 583), § 6; Stats. 2009, c. 110 (A.B. 459), § 3; Stats. 2015, c. 46 (S.B. 340), § 3, eff. Jan. 1, 2016.)

§ 2108. Liquidation of community or quasi-community assets to avoid market or investment risks; authority of court

At any time during the proceeding, the court has the authority, on application of a party and for good cause, to order the liquidation of community or quasi-community assets so as to avoid unreasonable market or investment risks, given the relative nature, scope, and extent of the community estate. However, in no event shall the court grant the application unless, as provided in this chapter, the appropriate declaration of disclosure has been served by the moving party.

(Added by Stats. 1993, c. 219 (A.B. 1500), § 107.)

§ 2109. Summary dissolution of marriage; required disclosures

The provisions of this chapter requiring a final declaration of disclosure do not apply to a summary dissolution of marriage, but a preliminary declaration of disclosure is required.

(Added by Stats. 1993, c. 1101 (A.B. 1469), § 11, eff. Oct. 11, 1993, operative Jan. 1, 1994.)

§ 2110. Default judgments; declarations of disclosure

In the case of a default judgment, the petitioner may waive the final declaration of disclosure requirements provided in this chapter, and shall not be required to serve a final declaration of disclosure on the respondent nor receive a final declaration of disclosure from the respondent. However, a preliminary declaration of disclosure by the petitioner is required unless the petitioner served the summons and petition by publication or posting pursuant to court order and the respondent has defaulted.

(Added by Stats. 1993, c. 1101 (A.B. 1469), § 12, eff. Oct. 11, 1993, operative Jan. 1, 1994. Amended by Stats. 1994. c. 146 (A.B. 3601), § 41; Stats. 1998, c. 581 (A.B. 2801), § 10; Stats. 2015, c. 46 (S.B. 340), § 4, eff. Jan. 1, 2016.)

§ 2111. Attorney work product privilege; protective orders

A disclosure required by this chapter does not abrogate the attorney work product privilege or impede the power of the court to issue protective orders.

(Added by Stats. 1993, c. 1101 (A.B. 1469), § 13, eff. Oct. 11, 1993, operative Jan. 1, 1994.)

§ 2112. Forms

The Judicial Council shall adopt appropriate forms and modify existing forms to effectuate the purposes of this chapter.

(Added by Stats. 1993, c. 1101 (A.B. 1469), § 14, eff. Oct. 11, 1993, operative Jan. 1, 1994.)

§ 2113. Application of chapter

This chapter applies to any proceeding commenced on or after January 1, 1993.

(Formerly § 2109, added by Stats. 1993, c. 219 (A.B. 1500), § 107. Renumbered § 2113 and amended by Stats. 1993, c. 1101 (A.B. 1469), § 10, eff. Oct. 11, 1993, operative Jan. 1, 1994.)

SECTION 2. MONEY SANCTIONS IN AN ONGOING DISSOLUTION PROCEEDING

California Family Code Section 2107, reproduced above, is important in many respects, not the least of which is that it outlines consequences, including the use of money sanctions, for nondisclosure. In a dissolution proceeding, nondisclosure means the failure to comply with statutory requirements for preliminary and final declarations. Section 2107 was amended in 2015, effective January 1, 2016.

Money sanctions are an important tool for deterring future lapses in disclosure. According to California Family Code Section 2107(c):

> "(c) If a party fails to comply with any provision of this chapter, the court *shall*, in addition to any other remedy provided by law, impose money sanctions against the noncomplying party. Sanctions *shall* be in an amount sufficient to *deter* repetition of the conduct or comparable conduct, and *shall* include reasonable attorney's fees, costs incurred, or both, *unless* the court finds that the noncomplying party acted with substantial justification or that other circumstances make the imposition of the sanction unjust." (Italics added.)

Marriage of Feldman, reproduced below, states the rationale for money sanctions. In *Feldman*, wife Elena filed a motion for monetary sanctions against husband Aaron citing his pattern of nondisclosure throughout the dissolution proceeding. The trial court imposed sanctions, plus reasonable attorney's fees and costs. Aaron appealed generally arguing that Elena had suffered no past harm. Irion J. affirmed the trial court's order.

The *Feldman* appellate opinion is a complex case. The assets are discussed one by one. Several legal issues are raised. And the entirety of the record requires the appellate court to apply several standards of review in concert.

The court applied the *abuse of discretion standard* to review the trial court's award of the sanction. (The abuse of discretion is applied to review family court decisions to deny or grant sanctions and attorney's fees; see *Marriage of Tharp*, 188 Cal. App.4th 1295, 116 Cal.Rptr.3d 375 (5th Dist. 2010) for the general discussion of the review standard.) It applied the *de novo standard* to review the trial court's interpretation of the law. And it applied the *substantial evidence standard* to review the factual record in a light most favorable to the trial court's decision to impose sanctions.

MARRIAGE OF FELDMAN

153 Cal.App.4th 1470, 64 Cal.Rptr.3d 29 (4th Dist. 2007)

IRION, J.

In this marital dissolution proceeding, Aaron Feldman appeals from the trial court's order requiring him to pay sanctions and attorney fees based on his nondisclosure of financial information to respondent Elena Feldman. As we will explain, we conclude that the appeal lacks merit, and accordingly we affirm.

I

FACTUAL AND PROCEDURAL BACKGROUND

Aaron and Elena were married in 1969 and separated after 34 years of marriage. Elena filed a petition for dissolution of marriage in August 2003.

During the marriage Aaron created a large number of privately held companies referred to as Sunroad Enterprises (the Sunroad entities). The Sunroad entities are devoted to, among other things, investing in and developing real estate and owning auto dealerships. According to Aaron, his assets are worth in excess of $50 million. The characterization of the Sunroad entities as either separate or community property is an issue in the dissolution proceeding.

As the litigation proceeded, Elena served interrogatories and a request for production of documents on Aaron and conducted depositions of Aaron and employees of the Sunroad entities. Aaron provided responses to interrogatories and a schedule of assets and debts (the Schedule) on November 24, 2003. He subsequently provided updates to the Schedule at the request of Elena's attorney. Aaron also produced a significant number of documents in response to the request for production.

On September 2, 2004, Elena filed an application for an order (1) imposing monetary sanctions against Aaron for a violation of his fiduciary duty to make financial disclosures to her during the dissolution proceedings, and (2) requiring Aaron to pay her attorney fees (the sanctions motion). The sanctions motion was based on Family Code sections 1101, subdivision (g), 2107, subdivision (c), and 271, subdivision (a), which collectively give the trial court authority to order sanctions and the payment of attorney fees for breach of a party's fiduciary duty of disclosure and for conduct which frustrates the policy of promoting settlement.

Elena's declaration in support of the sanctions motion alleged that Aaron had failed to disclose several different financial transactions, including the purchase of a personal residence through one of his companies, the purchase of a $1 million bond, the existence of a 401(k) account, and the existence of several of the Sunroad entities.

The sanctions motion was taken off calendar while the parties pursued mediation. When the mediation was unsuccessful, Elena renoticed the sanctions motion and submitted a supplemental declaration, which described additional instances of nondisclosure.

Following full briefing and a hearing, the trial court ruled that Aaron breached his fiduciary duty to disclose financial information to Elena, and it ordered Aaron to pay sanctions in the amount of $250,000 and attorney fees of $140,000. As part of its ruling, the trial court found that Aaron intentionally had sought to circumvent the disclosure process and that his conduct had frustrated the policy of promoting settlement. Aaron appeals from the trial court's order.

II

DISCUSSION

Our analysis of Aaron's appeal requires us (1) to review the duty of disclosure that applies to spouses involved in dissolution proceedings and (2) to apply those principles to the several instances of nondisclosure alleged by Elena and cited by the trial court in support of its sanctions order.

A. *Applicable Statutory Provisions*

We first examine the fiduciary obligations of disclosure that govern the relationship between spouses involved in a dissolution proceeding and the sanctions available for the breach of such obligations.

The fiduciary obligations of spouses to each other are set forth in section 721, and are made specifically applicable during dissolution proceedings by section 1100, subdivision (e). "Each spouse shall act with respect to the other spouse in the management and control of the community assets and liabilities in accordance with the general rules governing fiduciary relationships which control the actions of persons having relationships of personal confidence as specified in Section 721, until such time as the assets and liabilities have been divided by the parties or by a court. This duty includes the obligation to make full disclosure to the other spouse of all material facts and information regarding the existence, characterization, and valuation of all assets in which the community has or may have an interest and debts for which the community is or may be liable, and to provide equal access to all information, records, and books that pertain to the value and character of those assets and debts, upon request." (§ 1100, subd. (e).)

Consistent with these fiduciary obligations, section 2100, subdivision (c) provides that "a full and accurate disclosure of all assets and liabilities in which one or both parties have or may have an interest must be made in the early stages of a proceeding for dissolution of marriage or legal separation of the parties, regardless of the characterization as community or separate, together with a disclosure of all income and expenses of the parties." This disclosure duty is ongoing, as section 2100 provides that *"each party has a continuing duty to immediately, fully, and accurately update and augment that disclosure to the extent there have been any material changes* so that at the time the parties enter into an agreement for the resolution of any of these issues, or at the time of trial on these issues, each party will have a full and complete knowledge of the relevant underlying facts." (§ 2100, subd. (c), italics added.)

To implement the disclosure obligation, the Family Code requires the service of a preliminary and final declaration of disclosure "[i]n order to provide full and accurate disclosure of all assets and liabilities in which one or both parties may have an interest. . . ." (§ 2103.) Specifically, "the preliminary declaration of disclosure shall set forth with sufficient particularity," to the extent that "a person of reasonable and ordinary intelligence can ascertain [them]," "[t]he identity of all assets in which the declarant has or may have an interest and all liabilities for which the declarant is or may be liable, regardless of the characterization of the asset or liability as community, quasi-community, or separate." (§ 2104, subd. (c)(1).) It also shall include "[t]he declarant's percentage of ownership in each asset and percentage of obligation for each liability where property is not solely owned by one or both of the parties." (§ 2104, subd. (c)(2).)

Section 2107, subdivision (c) requires the trial court to impose monetary sanctions and award reasonable attorney fees if a party fails to comply with any portion of the chapter of the Family Code that deals with a spouse's fiduciary duty of disclosure during dissolution proceedings, i.e., sections 2100 to 2113. The statute provides, "If a party fails to comply with any provision of this chapter, the court shall, in addition to any other remedy provided by law, impose money sanctions against the noncomplying party. Sanctions shall be in an amount sufficient to deter repetition of the conduct or comparable conduct, and shall include reasonable attorney's fees, costs incurred, or both, unless the court finds that the noncomplying party acted with substantial justification or that other circumstances make the imposition of the sanction unjust." (§ 2107, subd. (c).)

Similarly, section 271, subdivision (a) provides the trial court with authority to order the opposing party to pay attorney fees and costs in the nature of a sanction when "the conduct of each party or attorney . . . frustrates the policy of the law to promote settlement of litigation." Specifically the statute provides: "Notwithstanding any other provision of this code, the court may base an award of attorney's fees and costs on the extent to which the conduct of each party or attorney furthers or frustrates the policy of the law to promote settlement of litigation and, where possible, to reduce the cost of litigation by encouraging cooperation between the parties and attorneys. An award of attorney's fees and costs pursuant to this section is in the nature of a sanction. In making an award pursuant to this section, the court shall take into consideration all evidence concerning the parties' incomes, assets, and liabilities. The court shall not impose a sanction pursuant to this section that imposes an unreasonable financial burden on the party against whom the sanction is imposed. In order to obtain an award under this section, the party requesting an award of attorney's fees and costs is not required to demonstrate any financial need for the award." (§ 271, subd. (a).) Section 271 "advances the policy of the law 'to promote settlement and to encourage cooperation which will reduce the cost of litigation.' " (*In re Marriage of Petropoulos* (2001) 91 Cal.App.4th 161, 177, 110 Cal.Rptr.2d 111 (*Petropoulos*).)

B. *Standard of Review*

"A sanction order under . . . section 271 is reviewed under the abuse of discretion standard. ' "[T]he trial court's order will be overturned only if, considering all the evidence viewed most favorably in support of its order, no judge could reasonably make the order." ' " (*In re Marriage of Burgard* (1999) 72 Cal.App.4th 74, 82, 84 Cal.Rptr.2d 739.) "In reviewing such an award, we must indulge all reasonable inferences to uphold the court's order." (*In re Marriage of Abrams* (2003) 105 Cal.App.4th 979, 991, 130 Cal.Rptr.2d 16.) Although no case law discusses which standard of review we should apply to an order awarding sanctions under section 2107, subdivision (c), because the sanction is similar to that imposed under section 271 as well as similar to a sanction for civil discovery abuses (which are reviewed for abuse of discretion), we will apply an abuse of discretion standard to an order for sanctions under section 2107, subdivision (c). (*See American Home Assurance Co. v. Société Commerciale Toutélectric* (2002) 104 Cal.App.4th 406, 435, 128 Cal.Rptr.2d 430 ["The court's discretion to impose discovery sanctions is broad, subject to reversal only for manifest abuse exceeding the bounds of reason"].)

To the extent that we are called upon to interpret the statutes relied on by the trial court to impose sanctions, we apply a de novo standard of review. (See *In re Marriage of Hokanson* (1998) 68 Cal.App.4th 987, 992, 80 Cal.Rptr.2d 699.) We review any findings of fact that formed the basis for the award of sanctions under a substantial evidence standard of review. (*In re Marriage of Rossi* (2001) 90 Cal.App.4th 34, 40, 108 Cal.Rptr.2d 270.) " ' " 'In reviewing the evidence on . . . appeal all conflicts must be resolved in favor of the [prevailing party], and all legitimate and reasonable inferences indulged in [order] to uphold the [finding] if possible.' " ' " (*Ibid.*)

C. *Aaron's Argument Concerning Statutory Interpretation Issues*

Before discussing the particular instances of nondisclosure at issue in this case, we pause to address some of Aaron's arguments concerning the applicable statutory standards.

1. *No Injury to the Other Party Is Required for the Trial Court to Impose Sanctions*

Aaron argues that sanctions may not be imposed on a spouse who breaches his fiduciary duty of disclosure if the other party fails to establish any *harm* resulting from the breach. We disagree.

According to Aaron, "[t]hematic to the . . . statutes is the presence of some injury to the complaining party as a prerequisite to the remedy." However, we conclude that this argument finds no support in the language of the relevant statutes that authorize the imposition of sanctions here, i.e., sections 2107, subdivision (c) and 271, subdivision (a). Neither statute sets forth any requirement of separate injury to the complaining spouse as a precondition to the imposition of sanctions.

Section 2107, subdivision (c) indicates that sanctions are to be imposed to effectuate *compliance with the laws* that require spouses to make disclosure to each other. (See § 2107, subd. (c) [referring to sanctions imposed to "deter repetition" of conduct that "fails to comply" with the disclosure requirements].) The statute is not aimed at redressing an actual injury. Section 271, subdivision (a) authorizes sanctions to advance the *policy* of promoting settlement of litigation and encouraging cooperation of the litigants. This statute, too, does not require any actual injury.

Indeed, as expressed in section 2100, subdivision (b), the Legislature has indicated that "[s]ound public policy . . . favors the reduction of the adversarial nature of marital dissolution and the attendant costs by fostering full disclosure and cooperative discovery." In light of this legislatively expressed intention, the authority to impose sanctions for nondisclosure is plainly aimed at effectuating the goal of reducing the adversarial nature of marital dissolution rather than at redressing any *actual harm* inflicted on the complaining spouse.

In addition to relying on the purported "thematic" approach of the applicable statutes, Aaron attempts to rely on case law for his argument that *harm* is a prerequisite to the imposition of sanctions. However, the cases that Aaron cites are not applicable here because they address a different issue—whether a party must show prejudice *when seeking to vacate a judgment of dissolution* on the ground that the other party did not comply with disclosure obligations. (See *In re Marriage of Jones* (1998) 60 Cal.App.4th 685, 695, 70 Cal.Rptr.2d 542 [denying relief to party who sought to have a dissolution judgment vacated for failure of the opposing party to formally comply with certain disclosure requirements because "[s]he failed to show how she was prejudiced"]; *Brewer* (2001) 93 Cal.App.4th 1334, 1345, 113 Cal.Rptr.2d 849 (*Brewer*) [in a case where one party sought to vacate the judgment because the other party did not comply with disclosure obligations, the court cited the principle, established by § 2121, subd. (b), that a party seeking relief from a judgment of dissolution must show that " 'the facts alleged as the grounds for relief materially affected the original outcome' "].) Elena did not seek to vacate a judgment of dissolution; she sought to impose sanctions aimed at deterring future misconduct in the *ongoing* dissolution proceedings. Thus neither the case law that Aaron cites, nor the statutory authority relied on by those cases, apply here.

Because there is no requirement that Elena show harm as a prerequisite to an award of sanctions, we need not and do not analyze whether Elena was harmed by Aaron's failure to disclose.

2. *The Imposition of Sanctions Does Not Require Additional Procedural Prerequisites*

Aaron argues that sanctions may not be imposed under section 2107, subdivision I unless the complaining party first makes a request for the information that has not been disclosed and then brings either (1) a motion to compel further response or (2) a motion to preclude evidence on the nondisclosed issue. His argument is based on a misreading of section 2107, and we reject it.

The initial portion of section 2107 provides as follows:

"(a) If one party fails to serve on the other party a preliminary declaration of disclosure under Section 2104 or a final declaration of disclosure under Section 2105, or fails to provide the information required in the respective declarations with sufficient particularity, and if the other party has served the respective declaration of disclosure on the noncomplying party, the complying party may, within a reasonable time, request preparation of the appropriate declaration of disclosure or further particularity.

"(b) If the noncomplying party fails to comply with a request under subdivision (a), the complying party may do either or both of the following:

"(1) File a motion to compel a further response.

"(2) File a motion for an order preventing the noncomplying party from presenting evidence on issues that should have been covered in the declaration of disclosure."

Independent of these remedies, section 2107, subdivision I states that "[i]f a party fails to comply with any provision of this chapter [i.e., sections 2100 to 2113], the court shall, in addition to any other remedy provided by law, impose money sanctions against the noncomplying party." The terms of the statute simply do not require that before seeking sanctions for nondisclosure a party (1) seek further disclosure and (2) bring a motion to either compel further responses or preclude evidence.

Thus, sanctions were available here despite the fact that Elena did not avail herself of the remedies set forth in subdivisions (a) and (b) of section 2107.

D. *Aaron's Nondisclosures*

We next review the nondisclosures that Elena alleged as the basis for the sanctions motion and that the trial court relied on in ordering sanctions.

1. *The Israeli Bond*

On November 24, 2003, Aaron served the Schedule. It is undisputed that the Schedule failed to list a $1 million bond that Aaron personally had purchased from the Israeli government in October 2003 (the Israeli bond).

Aaron signed the agreement to acquire the Israeli bond on July 10, 2003, the bond was issued on October 8, 2003, and Aaron was notified of that fact by a letter dated October 27, 2003. Thus Aaron clearly knew about the Israeli bond when he served the Schedule, but he did not list it as one of his assets.

Further, the bond was purchased with borrowed funds. According to Aaron, he "borrowed $1,000,000 from Bank Leumi, USA; purchased an Israeli bond with the proceeds; and, in turn, assigned to Bank Leumi USA as collateral for the loan." Aaron also did not disclose the loan from Bank Leumi on the Schedule as one of his debts.

Not only did Aaron fail to disclose the Israeli bond and the Bank Leumi loan on the Schedule, he also did not timely produce *documents* about the transaction. Although Elena served Aaron with a request for production asking for all bond certificates and any documents evidencing loans, Aaron produced no documents concerning the Israeli bond or the corresponding loan from Bank Leumi either in his initial October 2003 production or in his supplemental production in January 2004. In addition, during his January 28, 2004 deposition, in response to a direct question on the subject, Aaron stated that he had no personal loans from Bank Leumi.

Elena's attorney sent a letter to Aaron's attorney on February 20, 2004, requesting that Aaron update the Schedule. Aaron replied on February 27, 2004, with a notice of correction to the Schedule. Among other things, the corrections identified the Israeli bond, which Aaron claimed was acquired in December 2003, and the $1 million loan payable to Bank Leumi. On March 1, 2004, Aaron produced documents relating to the Israeli bond and the Bank Leumi loan.

In her sanctions motion Elena argued that Aaron's failure to disclose the Israeli bond and the Bank Leumi loan in the Schedule, his failure to produce corresponding documents, and his failure to disclose the Bank Leumi loan during his deposition was a breach of his duty under section 2102, subdivision (a)(1), which requires "[t]he accurate and complete disclosure of all assets and liabilities in which the party has or may have an interest or obligation and all current earnings, accumulations, and expenses, including an immediate, full, and accurate update or augmentation to the extent there have been any material changes." The trial court agreed, concluding that the nondisclosure of the Israeli bond was part of a "clear pattern that [Aaron] has no intentions of complying with the policy . . . that this information is to be shared from the very beginning." The trial court also found that Aaron's conduct was intentional, that he was "trying to circumvent the process, hide the ball," and it stated that "[g]o fish, you figure it out, is not acceptable."

On appeal Aaron argues that "[a]s the bond was purchased with Bank Leumi *loan* proceeds and as the loan was to be paid off with the *bond* proceeds, the bond and loan were a self-contained, symbiotic package with *zero* effect on Aaron's net worth." He argues that "[g]iven the off-setting relationship [, he] forgot to list either the bond or the debt on his November 24, 2003 Schedule of Assets and Debts." Aaron also claims that he "misspoke" when he stated at his deposition that he had no personal debt to Bank Leumi.

To the extent that Aaron is attempting, through these statements, to excuse his nondisclosure, we conclude that Aaron's position lacks merit. The statutory policy in favor of disclosure contains no exception for debts and assets that offset each other, and Aaron has cited no authority to support such an exception. Instead, Aaron was required to provide a "complete disclosure of all assets and liabilities." (§ 2102, subd. (a)(1).) Further, the trial court explained that in light of the other nondisclosures detailed in the sanctions motion, it was rejecting Aaron's explanation that the failure to disclose the Israeli bond and the Bank Leumi loan was a mere oversight. The trial court's inference is reasonable, and in light of the standard of review we will not disturb it.

2. *The Calumet Avenue Property*

The next nondisclosed item identified in the sanctions motion was Aaron's acquisition in early 2004, through a newly created business entity, of a multi-million dollar home that became his personal residence.

The factual background to this issue begins with a letter sent by Elena's attorney to Aaron's attorney on March 1, 2004, specifically asking "whether [Aaron] has acquired, or is in the process of acquiring, any interest in any assets or incurred any obligations. . . ." This letter followed up on a February 20, 2004 letter, which asked "if there have been any financial changes with regard to [Aaron], including the acquisition of any new interests in properties, either personal or business in nature. . . ."

On April 1, 2004, Aaron's attorney sent a letter stating that "[Aaron], along with his son Dan, recently moved to a residence on Calumet Street [*sic*] in the Birdrock area of La Jolla. [Aaron] is leasing the residence for $15,000 a month. Otherwise, we are not aware of any substantial changes that warrant an update of [Aaron's] Income and Expense Declaration or further corrections to his Schedule of Assets and Debts."

However, the next day, April 2, 2004, in response to questions asked during the deposition of Frederick Tronboll, a senior vice president for Sunroad Holding, Inc. (Sunroad Holding), Elena learned that an entity created by Sunroad Holding—Calumet Real Estate Holdings, LLC—had purchased a residence on Calumet Avenue in La Jolla in a cash transaction for $5,797,500.

The contract to purchase was signed on February 3, 2004, and the transaction closed on March 12, 2004. Calumet Real Estate Holdings, LLC is 100 percent owned by Sunroad Holding, which in turn is 100 percent owned by Aaron. The funds for the purchase were originally provided by Sunroad Auto Holding, which is 100 percent owned by Sunroad Holding, and thus ultimately 100 percent owned by Aaron. Aaron pays a monthly lease of $15,000 to Calumet Real Estate Holdings, LLC, which transfers the funds to Sunroad Holding, which in turn repays Aaron's company Sunroad Auto Holding for the funds used to purchase the property. In his September 2004 income and expense declaration, Aaron disclosed for the first time that he *personally* pays the property taxes, insurance and maintenance on the Calumet Avenue property.

In short, Aaron caused one of the Sunroad entities to buy the Calumet Avenue property, he made the property into his personal residence, and he funded the purchase with funds that because they came from one of the Sunroad entities, could possibly be characterized as community property. However, Aaron told Elena in the April 1, 2004 letter only that he was leasing a residence for $15,000 per month.

Elena argued that Aaron's selective disclosure of the nature of the transaction involving the Calumet Avenue property was inconsistent with Aaron's fiduciary obligation toward her. The trial court agreed, citing the transaction involving the Calumet Avenue property as one example of Aaron's pattern of nondisclosure.

Aaron argues that he complied with his fiduciary obligation because he "disclosed the acquisition of the Calumet Avenue property within one month of the close of escrow." We disagree. Significantly, Aaron did *not* disclose the transaction; instead Elena stumbled upon the fact of the transaction while deposing Tronboll. Indeed, Elena may never have found out about the transaction had her attorney not asked the appropriate question of Tronboll. Based on the content of the April 1, 2004 letter, the trial court could reasonably conclude that contrary to his fiduciary duty of disclosure, Aaron was attempting to *hide* or *delay* Elena's discovery of the fact that he had used possible community property assets to buy a house in which he was residing. Indeed, the trial court could reasonably assume that absent Elena's discovery of the true facts, Aaron intended to maintain that he was merely leasing his residence from an unrelated third party. Aaron's conduct was inconsistent with his duty under section 1100, subdivision I, which gave him an obligation "to make full disclosure to the other spouse of all material facts and information regarding the existence, characterization, and valuation of all assets in which the community has or may have an interest."

In at least two separate respects, the transaction involving the Calumet Avenue property was a "material fact," giving Aaron a duty to disclose it under section 1100, subdivision I.

First, Elena is claiming that the Sunroad entities are community assets. In order for Elena to trace those community assets, she needs to obtain information about whether, postseparation, Aaron used any of those alleged community assets to capitalize new companies. Thus, the fact that Aaron took approximately $6 million from one of the other Sunroad entities and used it to capitalize Calumet Real Estate Holdings, LLC (and to purchase a personal residence in the name of that company) is a material fact concerning the community assets. Aaron accordingly had a duty of candor regarding that transaction.

Second, in the division of community property, Elena may attempt to claim reimbursement for any postseparation benefit that Aaron obtained from the use of community property. (See *In re Marriage of Watts* (1985) 171 Cal.App.3d 366, 374, 217 Cal.Rptr. 301.) The knowledge that Aaron is living in a house that was bought with alleged community assets would be material information to Elena because it would allow her to evaluate whether, postseparation, Aaron has used community property for his personal benefit under circumstances that would give rise to an obligation to reimburse the community.

In light of the facts in the record, we conclude that the trial court did not abuse its discretion in concluding that Aaron's lack of candor about the transaction involving the Calumet Avenue property was part of a pattern of nondisclosure that warranted the imposition of sanctions.

3.   *401(k) Account*

In the Schedule, Aaron stated that he did not have any retirement or pension assets. In response to Elena's request for production of documents relating to Aaron's pension plans and retirement and investment programs, Aaron produced no responsive documents, either in his initial production or in his January 2004 supplemental production. Similarly, in response to form interrogatories propounded by Elena, Aaron stated in November 2003 that he had no interest in any retirement plan.

However, during a July 23, 2004 deposition, when Aaron was asked why, according to his disclosures, he did *not* participate in the Sunroad entities' 401(k) plan, Aaron stated that he probably *did* participate. At Elena's request, Aaron subsequently produced information about his 401(k) account, showing that he had an account in the amount of $8,679.20.

In the sanctions motion, Elena argued that Aaron's failure to disclose his 401(k) account was a breach of his fiduciary duty to disclose his assets. Aaron conceded that he had not disclosed the 401(k) account and that he did indeed receive statements for the account, but he explained that he did not review the statements and that no contribution had been made to the account for 12 years. The trial court agreed with Elena that the failure to disclose the 401(k) account was another instance of Aaron's breach of his duty of disclosure, and it cited the omission of the 401(k) account as part of Aaron's pattern of misconduct.

On appeal Aaron argues that he did not breach his fiduciary duty to Elena by not disclosing the 401(k) account, because Elena had been secretly copying financial documents during their marriage and as a result she had copies of certain account statements from 1998 through 2000 for the 401(k) account, which she produced to Aaron on April 29, 2004.

We do not view this fact as in any way exonerating of Aaron's failure to disclose the information about the 401(k) account on the Schedule or to produce documents concerning the account in response to Elena's request for production. The 401(k) account is clearly one of Aaron's assets and may be community property. He was thus required to disclose it in the Schedule and to disclose it upon request from Elena. (See §§ 2102, subd. (a)(1), 2104, subd. (c)(1), 1100, subd. I, 721, subd. (b)(2).) "[A] spouse who is in a superior position to obtain records or information from which an asset can be valued and can reasonably do so must acquire and disclose such information to the other spouse" and should not expect the spouse who is not in a superior position to search for the information. (*Brewer, supra,* 93 Cal.App.4th at p. 1348, 113 Cal.Rptr.2d 849.) If Elena had not, without Aaron's knowledge, obtained statements from the 401(k) account, Elena may *never* have found out about the account, and her attorney may not have known to ask Aaron about this asset during the deposition.

We note that in November 2003 when Aaron omitted the 401(k) account from the Schedule, and in January 2004 when he omitted the account statements from his supplemental document production, Aaron likely did *not* know that Elena had any account statements. In contrast, at the time of his deposition in July 2004 when he admitted to the 401(k) account, Aaron *did* know that Elena had the documents, as she had produced them in April 2004. The trial court might reasonably have inferred that Elena's demonstrated knowledge of the 401(k) account was what prompted Aaron to finally admit to the existence of the asset and that Aaron's conduct was not consistent with his fiduciary duty of disclosure.

In sum, Aaron had a fiduciary duty to disclose the existence of the 401(k) account on the Schedule in the first place without prodding from Elena and to produce relevant documents upon Elena's request. The trial court reasonably concluded that Aaron breached that duty by not disclosing the existence of the 401(k) account until July 2004 in response to an inquiry during his deposition.

4. *The Addition of New Companies*

As another basis for its conclusion that Aaron had engaged in a pattern of nondisclosure, the trial court cited "the addition of new companies." Although the trial court could have been more clear about the transactions to which it was referring, our review of the record reveals several instances of documented nondisclosure of new Sunroad entities that the trial court reasonably could have relied upon to support its decision to order sanctions.

a. *Inmobiliaria Camino del Sol*

Two of the Sunroad entities owned by Aaron created the Mexican subsidiary Inmobiliaria Camino del Sol, S de R.L. de C.V. (Inmobiliaria) at some point in 2003. Inmobiliaria was formed to own land for an auto dealership in Mexico City. Sunroad Auto Holding Corporation loaned $2.52 million to Inmobiliaria, evidenced by an October 23, 2003 promissory note signed by Aaron.

In October 2003 and January 2004, Aaron responded to Elena's request for production which sought, among other things, (1) articles of incorporation and similar documents for the Sunroad entities and (2) evidence of any loans to the Sunroad entities. Aaron did not produce any documents concerning Inmobiliaria.

In February 2004, Elena's attorney asked "if there have been any financial changes with regard to [Aaron], including the acquisition of any new interests in properties, either personal or business in nature." In June 2004, Elena's attorney asked if there had been "any changes to [Aaron's] income or assets, whether personally or through Sunroad Holding Corporation or any other subsidiary corporation" and whether "[Aaron] has created any new corporations or subsidiary corporations." Despite these requests, Aaron did not disclose the existence of Inmobiliaria or the loan to it.

Further, until he produced a copy of the promissory note in August 2004, Aaron did not produce documents concerning Inmobiliaria or evidencing the $2.52 million loan to it. The existence of Inmobiliaria was also not disclosed on the organizational chart of the Sunroad entities that Aaron produced in December 2003, even though it clearly existed at that time.

Thus, the trial court could reasonably conclude that by failing to disclose the information about Inmobiliaria when specifically requested to do so by Elena, Aaron breached his duty under section 1100, subdivision I "to make full disclosure to the other spouse of all material facts and information regarding the existence, characterization, and valuation of all assets in which the community has or may have an interest." As we have explained, Elena had an interest in ascertaining and valuing all of the Sunroad entities, and in tracing any transfer of capital from the Sunroad entities to newly created entities. Because Aaron failed to disclose the existence of Inmobiliaria and the $2.52 million loan made to it by another Sunroad entity, Aaron did not comply with his duty of disclosure.

b. *Entities Appearing on Later Organizational Charts*

In Elena's July 2005 supplemental declaration in support of the sanctions motion, she described several new Sunroad entities that she had learned of in January 2005, although they were formed several months earlier.

On January 25, 2005, Aaron produced corporate organizational charts for the Sunroad entities dated December 31, 2004. Despite the fact that Aaron has admitted that new organizational charts are created on a quarterly basis, this was Aaron's first production of organizational charts since December 2003, when he produced organizational charts dated September 30, 2003.

Upon reviewing the new charts, Elena noticed that nine new entities were listed. Several rounds of correspondence between Elena's and Aaron's attorneys followed between January 28, 2005, and May 16, 2005, as Elena attempted to obtain detailed information about the new entities. Like Inmobiliaria, several of the companies were associated with automobile dealerships in Mexico. Another two of the new entities owned real property in Chula Vista, and still another owned land in San Diego. Six of the companies were incorporated in June or July 2004, one was incorporated in August 2004, one was incorporated in January 2005, and one was still in the process of being incorporated as of February 2005.

Thus, several of these new entities had been in existence for several months before Aaron disclosed their existence by producing updated organizational charts in January 2005.

As we have explained, Aaron was under a duty, among other things, to give "an immediate, full, and accurate update or augmentation to the extent there have been any material changes" as to his assets and liabilities (§ 2102, subd. (a)(1)). Under section 1100, subdivision I, Aaron had an obligation "to make full disclosure to the other spouse of all material facts and information regarding the existence, characterization, and valuation of all assets in which the community has or may have an interest." (See also § 721, subd. (b)(2) [requiring a spouse to provide upon request "true and full information . . . affecting any transaction which concerns the community property"].) Further, based on the inquiry of Elena's attorneys in June 2004 as to whether "[Aaron] has created any new corporations or subsidiary corporations," Aaron knew that Elena was interested in receiving updates concerning the creation of any new Sunroad entities.

On these facts, the trial court was within its discretion to conclude that Aaron's tardy disclosure of the new entities was another instance of Aaron's pattern of noncompliance with the statutory policy of disclosure.

Aaron argues that he was not required to disclose the existence of Inmobiliaria, the $2.52 million loan, or the creation of the new entities, because they were "standard business transaction[s]." Specifically, Aaron disputes that "every transaction" of a business must be reported under section 2102, "even when the transactions are within the 'ordinary course of business' of the reported asset."

Aaron relies on section 2102 for his argument. That section provides:

"(a) From the date of separation to the date of the distribution of the community or quasi-community asset or liability in question, each party is subject to the standards provided in Section 721, as to all activities that affect the assets and liabilities of the other party, including, but not limited to, the following activities:

"(1) The accurate and complete disclosure of all assets and liabilities in which the party has or may have an interest or obligation and all current earnings, accumulations, and expenses, including an immediate, full, and accurate update or augmentation to the extent there have been any material changes.

"(2) The accurate and complete written disclosure of any investment opportunity, business opportunity, or other income-producing opportunity that presents itself after the date of separation, but that results from any investment, significant business activity outside the ordinary course of business, or other income-producing opportunity of either spouse from the date of marriage to the date of separation, inclusive. The written disclosure shall be made in sufficient time for the other spouse to make an informed decision as to whether he or she desires to participate in the investment opportunity, business, or other potential income-producing opportunity, and for the court to resolve any dispute regarding the right of the other spouse to participate in the opportunity. In the event of nondisclosure of an investment opportunity, the division of any gain resulting from that opportunity is governed by the standard provided in Section 2556.

"(3) The operation or management of a business or an interest in a business in which the community may have an interest.

"(b) From the date that a valid, enforceable, and binding resolution of the disposition of the asset or liability in question is reached, until the asset or liability has actually been distributed, each party is subject to the standards provided in Section 721 as to all activities that affect the assets or liabilities of the other party. Once a particular asset or liability has been distributed, the duties and standards set forth in Section 721 shall end as to that asset or liability."

Despite Aaron's argument to the contrary, this statute does not contain an exception that exempts a spouse from having to disclose transactions "in the ordinary course of business." Aaron points out that section 2102, subdivision (a)(2) refers to disclosures that must be made only when "outside the ordinary course of business." However, that provision describes the circumstances in which one spouse must disclose a postseparation business opportunity to the other spouse *prior* to the transaction so that the spouse may decide whether to participate in the opportunity. Under the statute, a spouse is required to give *prior* written disclosure with respect to a "significant business activity *outside the ordinary course of business.*" (*Ibid.,* italics added.)

The issue here is not whether Aaron was required to disclose the various activities of Sunroad Holdings *before* they occurred. Elena's motion for sanctions is not based on Aaron's failure to disclose business opportunities *before* the Sunroad entities took advantage of them. Instead, the request for sanctions was warranted because he failed, even when Elena made it clear that she desired the information, "to make full disclosure to the other spouse of all material facts and information regarding the existence, characterization, and valuation of all assets in which the community has or may have an interest." (§ 1100, subd. I.) As the spouse involved in running the Sunroad entities, Aaron was in a superior position to obtain information about those entities and was thus obligated to disclose material information regarding them to Elena.

We agree with Aaron that as a matter of common sense, a spouse who runs a business is not under a duty to sua sponte update every *insignificant* occurrence in the operation of a business. We note as well that the statutes refer to the immediate disclosure of "material changes" and "material facts and information." (§§ 2100, subd. I, 2102, subd. (a), 1100, subd. I.) However, as we will explain, the facts here clearly justify the trial court's exercise of its discretion to conclude that the existence of Inmobiliaria, the $2.52 million loan, and the creation of the entities shown on the December 31, 2005 organizational chart were items that Aaron had a duty to promptly disclose.

Significantly, with respect to the creation of the new entities, because Elena specifically asked about the creation of any new corporations or subsidiary corporations in June 2004, Aaron was on notice that the creation of the entities reflected on the December 31, 2004 organizational charts was a significant event that he should promptly disclose. Further, any spouse seeking to ascertain the value of a community business and to trace community assets would reasonably need to know of the existence of all of the business entities existing at the time of separation and the creation of any new postseparation entities. With respect to Inmobiliaria, Elena served a request for production seeking documents that encompassed evidence of the creation of new Sunroad entities and any loans made by those entities. These requests put Aaron on notice that he had a duty to disclose the information.

5.   *Other Instances of Nondisclosure Not Cited by the Trial Court*

In support of the sanctions motion, Elena cited several other alleged instances of nondisclosure. On appeal the parties have briefed whether those alleged nondisclosures warranted the imposition of sanctions. However, because the trial court did not cite those items as the basis on which it was exercising its discretion to impose sanctions, we do not analyze whether they support the trial court's ruling. Instead, we have limited our analysis to whether, under the applicable standard of review, the instances of nondisclosure cited by the trial court support its order requiring Aaron to pay sanctions and attorney fees.

E.   *Attorney Fees*

We next discuss Aaron's challenges to the trial court's attorney fee award.

1. *The Award of Fees Under Section 271 Prior to the Conclusion of the Litigation*

As we have explained, attorney fees are statutorily authorized in this case either under (1) section 2107, subdivision I in connection with the imposition of sanctions for violation of disclosure obligations; or (2) section 271, subdivision (a), based on the trial court's finding that Aaron's acts of nondisclosure frustrated the statutory policy to promote settlement.

Aaron contends that to the extent the award of attorney fees was premised on section 271, subdivision (a), that award was improper because attorney fees may not be ordered under section 271, subdivision (a) until the end of the lawsuit.

In support of his argument, Aaron cites *In re Marriage of Freeman* (2005) 132 Cal.App.4th 1, 6, 33 Cal.Rptr.3d 237, and *In re Marriage of Quay* (1993) 18 Cal.App.4th 961, 970, 22 Cal.Rptr.2d 537. *Quay* concerned the predecessor statute to section 271 (former Civ.Code, § 4370.6). In the context of rejecting an argument that the attorney fee sanction was improper because "the only attorney's fees before the court were incurred after [the party's] wrongful conduct," *Quay* stated that "[t]he statute, we think, contemplates assessing a sanction at the end of the lawsuit, when the extent and severity of the party's bad conduct can be judged." (*Quay,* at p. 970, 22 Cal.Rptr.2d 537.) In the course of deciding that a trial court could require the payment of attorney fees incurred on appeal under section 271, *Freeman* quoted this language from *Quay*. (*Freeman,* at p. 6, 33 Cal.Rptr.3d 237.)

Thus, neither *Quay* nor *Freeman* dealt with the issue that we consider here, i.e., whether a trial court must wait until the end of the lawsuit to assess attorney fees as sanctions under section 271. We accordingly do not rely on those authorities in assessing Aaron's argument. Instead, in conducting our analysis we rely on the language of the statute.

The text of section 271 contains no requirement that the trial court impose the sanction at the end of the lawsuit. Indeed, the only procedural requirement in the statute is that an award of attorney fees and costs as a sanction may be imposed "only after notice to the party against whom the sanction is proposed to be imposed and opportunity for that party to be heard." (§ 271, subd. (b).) Further, as we have stated, section 271 is meant to "advance[ ] the policy of the law 'to promote settlement and to encourage cooperation which will reduce the cost of litigation.'" (*Petropoulos, supra,* 91 Cal.App.4th at p. 177, 110 Cal.Rptr.2d 111.) As a matter of logic, to promote cooperation a trial court must be able to apply sanctions *during the course of the litigation* when the uncooperative conduct arises in order to encourage better behavior as the litigation progresses.

We accordingly conclude that based on the statutory language and the express purpose of section 271, a trial court may impose sanctions under section 271 before the end of the lawsuit.

2. *Aaron Has Waived the Argument that Elena's Attorney Fees Were Not Reasonable and Necessary*

Aaron argues that the trial court abused its discretion in setting the amount of attorney fees at $140,000, because those fees were not shown to be "reasonable and necessary."

We reject Aaron's argument because he failed to raise a timely objection in the trial court. Elena submitted a series of declarations in support of her request for attorney fees as part of the sanctions motion. Although Aaron had ample opportunity to do so prior to or during the hearing on the sanctions motion, Aaron did not object to the amount of the fees that Elena was seeking. He did not argue that Elena had failed to show that the fees were reasonable or necessary, and he raised no other objection to the amount of the fees sought or to the documentation that Elena submitted in support of her fee request. " 'An appellate court will not consider procedural defects or erroneous rulings where an objection could have been, but was not, raised in the court below.' " (*Children's Hospital & Medical Center v. Bonta* (2002) 97 Cal.App.4th 740, 776, 118 Cal.Rptr.2d 629; see also *Robinson v. Grossman* (1997) 57 Cal.App.4th 634, 648, 67 Cal.Rptr.2d 380 [party that failed to object to the trial court that the opposing party's attorney fees were not sufficiently documented waived the right to object on appeal to the amount of the fee award].) We accordingly reject Aaron's challenge to the amount of the fees awarded to Elena.

F. *The Trial Court Was Not Required to Issue a Statement of Decision*

At the conclusion of the trial court's oral ruling, Aaron made a request for a statement of decision under Code of Civil Procedure section 632. The trial court stated at the conclusion of the hearing that it did not think that Aaron was entitled to a statement of decision. In a minute order issued several days later, the trial court clarified that it was denying the request for a statement of decision because "[s]tatements of decision are not required for orders made after hearing on motions or orders to show cause."

In subsequent correspondence with the trial court, Aaron's attorney stated that "[Aaron] agrees that a statement of decision is not required," but he nevertheless asked the court to "exercise its discretion to issue a formal statement of decision." The trial court thereafter issued a six-page ruling, entitled "Findings and Order After Hearing," but it did not formally issue a statement of decision.

As Aaron properly concedes, the trial court was not required to issue a statement of decision. (See *Mechanical Contractors Assn. v. Greater Bay*

Area Assn. (1998) 66 Cal.App.4th 672, 678, 78 Cal.Rptr.2d 225 ["The general rule is that a trial court need not issue a statement of decision after a ruling on a motion"]; see also *Maria P. v. Riles* (1987) 43 Cal.3d 1281, 1294, 240 Cal.Rptr. 872, 743 P.2d 932.) Aaron argues, however, that even though a statement of decision was not required in this case, the trial court erred by refusing to exercise its *discretion* to issue a statement of decision. In support of his argument, Aaron points out that the trial court has the *discretion* to issue a statement of decision even in instances where it is not *required* to do so. (See *Khan v. Superior Court* (1988) 204 Cal.App.3d 1168, 1173, 251 Cal.Rptr. 815, fn. 4 ["[Code of Civil Procedure s]ection 632 and [the corresponding rule of court] are directed to situations where a statement of decision is required; they do not limit situations where a statement of decision can be permitted"].)

We reject Aaron's argument. He has cited no authority *requiring* the trial court to exercise its discretion to issue a statement of decision in any specific instance. Further, we find no basis in statute or case law for a rule requiring the trial court to exercise its discretion to issue a statement of decision in instances where Code of Civil Procedure section 632 does not require it. Accordingly, we conclude that the trial court did not err in refusing to issue a statement of decision when it was not required by statute to do so.

DISPOSITION

The trial court's order is affirmed.

WE CONCUR: O'ROURKE, ACTING P.J., and AARON, J.

NOTES

1.   *The purpose of sanctions is to deter future noncompliance.* Sanctions promote the public policy of full disclosure and cooperative discovery. As such, sanctions do not compensate for past harm. They deter future noncompliance.

California Family Code Subsection 2100, subdivision (b) expresses the Legislative view that "[s]ound public policy . . . favors the reduction of the adversarial nature of marital dissolution and the attendant costs by fostering full disclosure and cooperative discovery." California Family Code Subsection 2107(c) says that in addition to "any other remedy provided by law" a court "shall" impose money sanctions against the noncomplying party. The statute also mandatorily imposes reasonable attorney's fees and costs incurred in bringing a successful sanction motion.

2.   *Who has the obligation to disclose?* Any asset in which the declarant may have an interest, regardless of its characterization, must be disclosed. California Family Code Section 2104(c)(1). In *Feldman*, wife Elena made copies of Aaron's 401k account statements, but the fact that Elena had copies of the account statements did not exonerate Aaron from having to disclose. The account was *potentially* community property in character, therefore, it was

Aaron's statutory obligation under California Family Code Sections 721(b), 1100(e), 2100 et seq. and particularly 2104 to disclose the existence of the account and to offer information to Elena about its value. Factually, the duty to disclose also fell to Aaron: the account was in Aaron's name alone meaning that Aaron had exclusive access to the account (Chapter 6). Thus, Aaron not only had a duty to disclose information about the account to Elena, he was also in a superior position to obtain records and information about the account from the financial institution. As the court concluded, as a matter of law, it was not Elena's duty to ask, it was Aaron's duty to tell.

3.   *Sworn financial disclosure statements are not mandatory in cases where the parties intend to resume the marriage.* Statutes, like California Family Code Section 2104, that require service of sworn financial disclosure statements do not apply in some cases where a postmarital reconciliation agreement is executed after a date of separation. *Marriage of Burkle*, 139 Cal.App.4th 712, 43 Cal.Rptr.3d 181 (2d Dist. 2006) involved parties who, though separated, were still married and therefore still in a confidential relationship when they decided to reconcile (Chapter 1). As part of the reconciliation process, they negotiated and executed a post-marital (after the date of marriage) agreement concerning their property rights going forward in the marriage. Each spouse was represented by counsel. The parties' executed the agreement with the intent to resume the marriage; the parties did in fact resume the marriage for four more years; and no dissolution activity occurred until six years after the post-marital agreement had been executed. On these facts, the reviewing court held that the parties' duty to disclose to each other under California Family Code Section 721(b) was in effect at the time that the post-marital reconciliation contract was signed. Even so, the court also held that the parties were not statutorily obligated at contract execution to serve each other with sworn financial disclosure statements under California Family Code Section 2104.

Marriage of Evans, 229 Cal.App.4th 374, 177 Cal.Rptr.3d 256 (5th Dist. 2014) adds that no violation of California Family Code Section 2104 occurs when the spouses enter into a negotiated marriage settlement agreement before filing a petition for dissolution. In *Evans* the parties signed a property settlement agreement two years before filing a petition for dissolution. The court held that the absence of disclosure declarations at the time that their pre-dissolution property settlement agreement was signed was not a basis for invalidating that agreement. The rationale was that during the agreement negotiation process the parties were still married and, more to the point, still intending to continue on in the marriage.

4.   *Assets with no or low value must still be disclosed. Marriage of Moore*, 226 Cal.App.4th 92, 171 Cal.Rptr.3d 762 (3d Dist. 2014) involved a highly contentious dissolution over retirement benefits (Chapter 5). Wife Leslie filed a motion for sanctions against husband Terry for his failure to disclose a retiree medical reimbursement account in either his preliminary or final declarations of disclosure. The account, called a "medical trust," was described as something related to a defined contribution benefit of Terry's retirement package.

Husband Terry argued that he had no obligation to disclose the medical trust because it had no value. The trial court agreed with Terry and reserved jurisdiction to divide and value the trust at later date, when it presumably would have value; the trial court also declined to hear Leslie's motion for sanctions.

On appeal, the medical trust was deemed to be all or partially community in character, and the trial court's decision to reserve jurisdiction over the medical trust was upheld. However, the appellate court remanded on the issue of sanctions. Citing California Family Code Sections 2104(c)(1) and 2107(c), the court of appeal interpreted these statutes to require a hearing on the sanctions motion: "If a party fails to comply with disclosure requirements, the trial court 'shall . . . impose money sanctions against the noncomplying party . . . unless the court finds that the noncomplying party acted with substantial justification or that other circumstances make the imposition of the sanction unjust.' " *Id.* at 101.

5.   *Disclosure requirements and alternative dispute resolution.* When parties opt for a private dispute resolution proceeding, they are legally entitled to alter statutory disclosure standards for purposes of that proceeding (Chapter 7). *Marriage of Woolsey*, 220 Cal.App.4th 881, 163 Cal.Rptr.3d 551 (3d Dist. 2013), the parties mediated a marriage settlement agreement in which they declared that they "agree that they have fully disclosed all financial matters." As it turned out, the husband failed to disclose information. He subsequently filed a motion to prevent the public court from issuing a final dissolution judgment; the factual basis for his motion was that the parties had not met their statutory disclosure obligations. The court noted that if parties reach a negotiated marriage settlement agreement in which they agree to modify statutory disclosure standards, and if they subsequently present that agreement to a California family court as the basis for a final dissolution judgment, the court can rely on declarations in the marriage settlement agreement.

In other words, if parties want to adopt summary disclosure standards for the purposes of alternative dispute resolution, they can (Chapter 7).

6.   *Disclosure standards and adversarial litigation.* Spouses are mandated to meet statutory disclosure requirements during a public dissolution proceeding. The disclosure requirements cannot be waived. Nondisclosure in such a case implicates California Family Code Subsection 2104 and 2107, as discussed above.

7.   *2009 and 2015 Amendments to California Family Code Subsection 2107.* In 2009, the following amendments were made to California Family Code Subsection 2107, *supra* page 630. The words *"one or more"* were substituted for "either or both" in subdivision (b). Subdivision (b)(3) was added. And subdivision (d) was rewritten to include "*if a court enters a judgment when the parties have failed to comply with all disclosure requirements of this chapter, the court shall set aside the judgment. The failure to comply with the disclosure*

requirements does not constitute harmless error." (Italicized text indicates amendments.)

Six years later, in 2015, the phrase "*unless that party is not required to serve a preliminary declaration of disclosure, pursuant to Section 2110,*" was inserted into subdivision (a).

In *Feldman*, Irion, J. explains that it is not an abuse of discretion to award sanctions without proof of actual harm. The reason is that "the authority to impose sanctions for nondisclosure is plainly aimed at effectuating the goal of reducing the adversarial nature of marital dissolution rather than at redressing any actual harm inflicted on the complaining spouse." *Feldman, supra* at 1480.

Notice, however, that the amendments to California Family Code Section 2107, and especially subdivision (d), make it clear that the failure to comply with disclosure requirements is an actual harm in and of itself.

SECTION 3. POSTJUDGMENT SET-ASIDE ORDERS

The California Family Code sets forth procedures and standards for setting aside final judgments of dissolution in cases of fraud or mistake.

The original statutory approach sought to achieve several important goals, including:

- To provide a remedy for a judgment tainted by fraud by codifying the court's power to set aside final dissolution judgments for certain grounds.

- To extinguish, or at least minimize, harsh application of the traditional (doctrinal) distinction between extrinsic and intrinsic fraud.

- To expand the definition of fraud to include related concepts like perjury, duress, mental incapacity, and mistakes of law or fact.

California Family Code Section 2120, reproduced below, identifies the state policy in favor of finality of judgments. It goes on to mandate that the policy in favor of final judgments be balanced against two public interests: the proper division of community property and fair spousal and child support awards.

California Family Code Section 2121, reproduced below, gives a court authority to adjudicate the division of property or support awards even after the six-month time limit of California Code of Civil Procedure Section 473 has run, "based on the grounds and within the time limits, provided [in California Family Code Section 2120 et seq.]."

California Family Code Section 2122(a) through (f), reproduced below, provide particular time limits, based on the discovery rule, for actual fraud, perjury, duress, mental incapacity, judgments stipulated to by mistakes of law or fact, and failure to comply with disclosure requirements.

California Family Code Section 2123 codifies two decisional rules. The first is that a court may not set aside a final dissolution judgment "simply because the court finds that [the judgment] was inequitable when made, ..." The second is that a court cannot set aside a final dissolution judgment because "subsequent circumstances caused the division of assets or liabilities to become inadequate . . ." In other words, a court has the power to set aside a final judgment of dissolution if it has been tainted by fraud, and then only if the motion to set aside has been timely filed.

WEST'S ANNOTATED CALIFORNIA FAMILY CODE

§ 2120. Legislative findings and declarations; public policy

The Legislature finds and declares the following:

(a)   The State of California has a strong policy of ensuring the division of community and quasi-community property in the dissolution of a marriage as set forth in Division 7 (commencing with Section 2500), and of providing for fair and sufficient child and spousal support awards. These policy goals can only be implemented with full disclosure of community, quasi-community, and separate assets, liabilities, income, and expenses, as provided in Chapter 9 (commencing with Section 2100), and decisions freely and knowingly made.

(b)   It occasionally happens that the division of property or the award of support, whether made as a result of agreement or trial, is inequitable when made due to the nondisclosure or other misconduct of one of the parties.

(c)   The public policy of assuring finality of judgments must be balanced against the public interest in ensuring proper division of marital property, in ensuring sufficient support awards, and in deterring misconduct.

(d)   The law governing the circumstances under which a judgment can be set aside, after the time for relief under Section 473 of the Code of Civil Procedure has passed, has been the subject of considerable confusion which has led to increased litigation and unpredictable and inconsistent decisions at the trial and appellate levels.

(Added by Stats. 1993, c. 219 (A.B. 1500), § 108.)

§ 2121.   Authority of court to provide relief

(a)   In proceedings for dissolution of marriage, for nullity of marriage, or for legal separation of the parties, the court may, on any terms that may be just, relieve a spouse from a judgment, or any part or parts thereof, adjudicating support or division of property, after the six-month time limit of Section 473 of the Code of Civil Procedure has run, based on the grounds, and within the time limits, provided in this chapter.

(b) In all proceedings under this chapter, before granting relief, the court shall find that the facts alleged as the grounds for relief materially affected the original outcome and that the moving party would materially benefit from the granting of the relief.

(Added by Stats. 1993, c. 219 (A.B. 1500), § 108.)

§ 2122. Grounds for relief; limitation of actions

The grounds and time limits for a motion to set aside a judgment, or any part or parts thereof, are governed by this section and shall be one of the following:

(a) Actual fraud where the defrauded party was kept in ignorance or in some other manner was fraudulently prevented from fully participating in the proceeding. An action or motion based on fraud shall be brought within one year after the date on which the complaining party either did discover, or should have discovered, the fraud.

(b) Perjury. An action or motion based on perjury in the preliminary or final declaration of disclosure, the waiver of the final declaration of disclosure, or in the current income and expense statement shall be brought within one year after the date on which the complaining party either did discover, or should have discovered, the perjury.

(c) Duress. An action or motion based upon duress shall be brought within two years after the date of entry of judgment.

(d) Mental incapacity. An action or motion based on mental incapacity shall be brought within two years after the date of entry of judgment.

(e) As to stipulated or uncontested judgments or that part of a judgment stipulated to by the parties, mistake, either mutual or unilateral, whether mistake of law or mistake of fact. An action or motion based on mistake shall be brought within one year after the date of entry of judgment.

(f) Failure to comply with the disclosure requirements of Chapter 9 (commencing with Section 2100). An action or motion based on failure to comply with the disclosure requirements shall be brought within one year after the date on which the complaining party either discovered, or should have discovered, the failure to comply.

(Added by Stats. 1993, c. 219 (A.B. 1500), § 108. Amended by Stats. 1993, c. 1101 (A.B. 1469), § 15, eff. Oct. 11, 1993, operative Jan. 1, 1994; Stats. 2001, c. 703 (A.B. 583), § 7.)

§ 2123. Restrictions on grounds for relief; inequitable judgments

Notwithstanding any other provision of this chapter, or any other law, a judgment may not be set aside simply because the court finds that it was inequitable when made, nor simply because subsequent circumstances caused the division of assets or liabilities to become inequitable, or the support to become inadequate.

(Added by Stats. 1993, c. 219 (A.B. 1500), § 108.)

SECTION 4. GROUNDS TO SET ASIDE A FINAL JUDGMENT OF DISSOLUTION

California Family Code Section 2122, reproduced above, lists the "failure to comply with the disclosure requirements of Chapter 9" as grounds for a motion to set aside a final judgment. Chapter 9, concerns the disclosure of assets and liabilities.

Full disclosure is key to ensuring that parties have the opportunity to make decisions based on relevant and accurate information. The California community property system links disclosure (full and accurate information) with voluntariness. Full disclosure supports a person's right to make voluntary decisions, what California Family Code Section 2120 calls "decisions freely and knowingly made." From within the dissolution disclosure framework, nondisclosure becomes a form of coercion.

A. THE PRE-STATUTORY DOCTRINE

Marriage of Baltins was decided before the Family Code was enacted. In *Baltins*, the appellate court applied the substantial evidence standard to examine fraud and duress in the context of marriage dissolution. The effect of the decision was to acknowledge concepts that would become the basis for later code sections.

Generally, the lack of counsel, without more, is not sufficient to claim fraud or mistake. More is needed. *Baltins* is a lesson in the subtle differences between extrinsic fraud, intrinsic fraud, intrinsic mistake, undue influence, and duress, each of which is problematic because each goes to the issue of consent. Consent, as discussed above, determines voluntariness.

In *Baltins*, what the trial court and later the reviewing court was asked to decide is whether threats and misrepresentations constitute coercion. The answer was a resounding yes.

MARRIAGE OF BALTINS

212 Cal.App.3d 66, 260 Cal.Rptr. 403 (1st Dist. 1989)

BARRY-DEAL, ASSOCIATE JUSTICE.

Aldis Baltins (Husband) appeals from the order granting the motion of Deanna Baltins (Wife) to set aside the property and support provisions of the interlocutory and final judgments of dissolution of marriage on the grounds of duress and extrinsic fraud or mistake. He contends that the order was not supported by the evidence and was contrary to the law, and that the court erred in refusing to prepare a statement of decision. Husband also challenges a subsequent order granting Wife's motion for modification of support, claiming that the marital settlement agreement provided for nonmodifiable support * * * . We affirm both orders.

I.   *Factual and Procedural History*

Husband and Wife were married on June 7, 1969, and separated on January 7, 1982, a period of 12 years and 7 months; they had one adopted child, born October 31, 1978. At the time of their marriage, Husband was in his senior year in medical school, and Wife was working as a secretary; following Husband's internship, they moved several times while he completed his residency in orthopedics. In 1975, the couple moved to Ukiah, where Husband became board certified in orthopedic surgery and began his private practice. Until 1978 when their child was born, Wife worked at home for Husband's medical partnership, doing the payroll, making deposits, and paying the bills.

After the couple's separation in January 1982, Wife, represented by Attorney G. Scott Gaustad, filed a petition for dissolution of marriage in action No. 45543. She discharged Gaustad in March and dismissed the action in January of 1983. During April of 1982, Husband and Wife executed a marital settlement agreement, handwritten by Husband, providing for custody of their child, support, and a division of property. (This agreement was the basis for a later agreement incorporated into the interlocutory judgment of April 11, 1983, in action No. 47523, the subject of this appeal.)

On March 30, 1983, Husband, acting in propria persona, filed a petition for dissolution of the marriage in a new action, No. 47523, alleging that all community assets and obligations had been disposed of by written agreement and requesting that custody of the minor child be awarded to Wife. Husband prepared a summons and a notice and acknowledgment of receipt of summons, as well as an appearance, stipulation, and waivers. The latter provided that the cause could be tried as an uncontested matter without notice. Without advice of counsel, Wife signed the documents on April 9, 1983. Two days later, Husband had her default entered, and an uncontested hearing that same day resulted in the court's granting an interlocutory judgment of dissolution of marriage. The court approved and incorporated into the judgment a typed property settlement agreement, which had been executed by both parties on December 22, 1982; the agreement was substantially the same as the handwritten agreement executed by the parties in April 1982. Wife did not appear at the hearing. Six months later, on October 12, 1983, the court entered the final judgment on Husband's request.

On April 6, 1984, Wife filed her motion to set aside those portions of the interlocutory and final judgments dividing the community property of the parties and providing for support. The matter was heard over a two-day period in June, and on July 16, 1984, the court filed its "Ruling on Motion," setting aside the judgment. Husband requested a statement of decision on July 25, and Wife filed a timely objection.

On August 16, 1984, the court filed its order setting aside the interlocutory and final judgments, and declining to file a statement of decision on the ground that no request for a statement was made before submission of the "one-day" case as required by Code of Civil Procedure section 632. Husband appealed from this order.

Meanwhile, Wife noticed a motion to modify support which was heard on August 31. Her motion was granted, and the court filed its order increasing spousal and child support and awarding her fees and costs. Husband filed an amended notice of appeal to include this order.

II.   *Hearing on the Motion to Set Aside Judgments*

At the full, evidentiary hearing on Wife's motion to set aside the judgments, the court took judicial notice of her prior action for dissolution of the marriage. (See Evid.Code, § 452, subd. (d).)

Wife testified in her own behalf about the history of the parties' relationship as set out above and her circumstances from the time she first consulted an attorney in April 1981. In addition, she presented the testimony of two friends and of three attorneys with whom she had consulted during the course of the proceedings. She also introduced into evidence financial statements and income tax returns of the parties. We view this evidence in the light most favorable to Wife. * * *

Wife first consulted with Attorney Scott Gaustad in April 1981 when Husband physically abused her and she was frightened about losing custody of their child if she left. The parties separated in January 1982, and Wife moved out of the family home. Gaustad represented her that month when she filed her petition for dissolution of the marriage in action No. 45543. Gaustad had issued an order to show cause for temporary restraining and support orders, which was set for hearing a short time later. The order to show cause was not heard because the parties were talking and Wife did not want anything to happen; she told Gaustad to take no action. I n either March or April of 1982, Husband became furious with Gaustad for mentioning to another attorney in a public place that he had seen bruises on Wife which had been inflicted by Husband. Husband threatened to sue Gaustad and demanded that Wife fire him, which she did.

Gaustad testified that Husband called him at home on a Saturday morning, upset and angry about the conversation over Wife's bruises, and that Wife discharged him afterwards. (A substitution of attorney was not filed, however, until July 1982.)

After discharging Gaustad, Wife signed a property settlement agreement in Husband's handwriting dated April 25, 1982. Although Gaustad was still her attorney of record, she did not consult with him before signing. At the time, Wife believed she was getting less than 50 percent of the community property. She signed the agreement because for many years Husband had told her that she had not worked for it and was not entitled to one-half of the community property. He threatened that if she did not sign, he would declare bankruptcy and thereby avoid paying anything to her or their creditors. Husband further told Wife that his medical practice was his business and that she had nothing to do with it. "He was the one who was the doctor."

Wife admitted that she knew of all the parties' assets. She assisted Husband in preparing a financial statement in June 1981. This statement, showing total community assets of $1,306,515 and a net worth of $720,302, was admitted into evidence. Most of the assets and liabilities were acquired after the parties moved to Ukiah. Less than a year after this statement, under the April 1982 agreement, Wife received a rental residence, a 1977 Mercedes-Benz automobile, and some household furnishings, at a total net value of about $63,000. Husband received the balance of the assets, which included his medical practice, an interest in a medical building, a 30-acre ranch (with improvements including a remodeled ranch house, vineyard, and vineyard equipment), two condominiums at Lake Tahoe, his Keogh Plan, a 1977 Porsche, ranch machinery, household furnishings, miscellaneous bank accounts, and life insurance policies. He also assumed various unsecured debts of about $103,400, in addition to the secured debts on assets assigned to him. Thus Husband received community property with an approximate net value of $507,700.

Under the April 1982 agreement, Wife would receive $1,000 per month for 24 months and child support of $300 per month. Both spousal and child support would terminate if Wife cohabited with someone or remarried. Wife testified that the support provision was a compromise because Husband at first did not want to pay her anything. She said, " . . . I felt I just wanted to get enough money to get on my feet, to get a job and support myself." Husband's 1982 federal income tax return showed gross income from his medical practice was over \$282,000. He testified that his net that year was \$150,000.

In July 1982, Wife consulted with Attorney Susan Jordan, who filed a substitution of attorney so Gaustad was no longer attorney of record. Wife was told by Jordan that the handwritten agreement was unfair to her.

Attorney Jordan testified that Wife was in her office three or four times. Wife did not seem to hear what Jordan was saying and frequently cried. Wife was emotionally upset and incapable of asserting herself or of explaining why she would accept an unfair agreement. She expressed fears that Husband would not visit the child and that the child would be disrupted if she fought for any additional property. Jordan felt that Wife was acting under Husband's will and that she was "terrified," afraid of the power he held over the property, her life, and her daughter.

On August 3, 1982, the parties amended the handwritten agreement to increase spousal support to \$1,200 a month for 45 months, but did not change the property division. Wife would not allow Jordan to discuss the marital agreement with Husband or engage in discovery proceedings because she felt that it would make him angry and make things more difficult for Wife. Jordan did telephone Husband once to suggest that the terms of the agreement needed clarification and that it should be typed; Husband was adamant that the agreement should be submitted to the court without change.

On September 2, 1982, the day before a scheduled default hearing based upon the handwritten agreement, Jordan was upset and could not sleep. She knew that Wife was not acting in her own best interest, but Wife would not allow Jordan to assist her. After worrying all night, Jordan felt that she could not go through with the hearing in good conscience and telephoned each party to that effect early on the morning of the hearing. Jordan felt this way because the properties had not been evaluated and she did not believe that the handwritten agreement was fair.

After Jordan substituted out of the case, Wife went to see Attorney Pano Stephens. Stephens testified that after his first meeting with Wife, in October 1982, Husband called him at home on a Saturday morning. Husband was talking loudly and asked Stephens what he was doing getting involved in the case. Husband told Stephens that Husband had been talking with Stephens's partner, Burgess Williams, about the divorce and that Stephens had a conflict. Thereafter, Stephens told Wife that there was enough of a suggestion of a conflict and that he could not get involved in an adversary proceeding.

Stephens testified that Wife said Husband was threatening to file bankruptcy and to have no contact with their child. Stephens told Wife that certain agreements she told him to prepare did not reflect an equal division of property and that the child and spousal support were not reasonable.

Nevertheless, Stephens did have two proposed agreements typed which included the provisions of the April handwritten agreement, as modified in August, in more formal language. He also eliminated the condition providing for termination of child support if Wife cohabited with or remarried someone and included standard "boilerplate" paragraphs.

In December 1982, Husband had a typed marital settlement agreement prepared, using the format of the Stephens agreements as a model. Wife testified that when she signed this agreement on December 22, she was unrepresented by an attorney. She signed it because she was emotionally unable to continue dealing with Husband on the issue. She tried to talk to him about the unfairness of the agreement, but he was not willing to talk about it, and he continued to threaten her. He also told her that if it was not settled soon, she would get nothing, because he was receiving credit for all the payments he was making on the properties as well as for the support payments.

The December marital settlement agreement made substantially the same division of property as had the handwritten agreement of April 1982 and the amendment of August 1982, both prepared by Husband. In January 1983, Wife dismissed action No. 45543, which is referred to in the marital settlement agreement, because she hoped the dismissal would give them more time to talk with each other about the possibility of getting back together.

People who knew Wife well during the period of her separation and dissolution testified regarding her emotional state. Jamie Deckoff, M.D., a friend of Wife's, testified that during this time Wife was emotionally unable to fight. She was frequently crying. She told Dr. Deckoff that Husband would not discuss anything with a lawyer, but would deal only with her directly. She was emotionally unable to confront Husband.

Minda Kamp, with whom Wife shared a house for about 11 months, testified that in December 1982, Wife was extremely depressed and distraught. She observed that Wife was having trouble coping with day-to-day things and was crying nearly every day. Ms. Kamp frequently witnessed Wife in tears and very upset following communication with Husband.

Testifying that he had been unrepresented by counsel in the proceedings, Husband admitted that he had had some casual conversations with a friend, Burgess Williams, who was an attorney, and that he had questioned Williams about a possible conflict of interest if Williams's partner, Pano Stephens, represented Wife. Husband also had sought the assistance of his current counsel on the mechanics of filing a dissolution action and in preparing the necessary forms.

Husband acknowledged feeling that he had contributed much more to the marriage emotionally, psychologically, and financially than Wife. He told her that she was not putting into the marriage what he was and that she was not an equal partner.

According to Husband, Wife received more than one-half of the community assets under the December 1982 agreement. In working out this allegedly equal division, Husband took credit for all the payments he made on the community obligations, including monthly mortgage payments and taxes on the house in which he was living and other assets which he retained. He also credited himself with all support paid and to be paid in the future and payments to be made on the debts up to the time the final judgment could be entered. Husband did not assign any value to the goodwill of his medical practice because in his opinion it had no goodwill. When questioned about the seeming inequity even after his adjustments, Husband answered that in his mind another equalizing factor was that Wife had custody of their minor child.

In a written ruling, the court granted Wife's motion to set aside the judgments on the grounds of duress and extrinsic fraud or mistake. It found that the evidence, particularly the testimony of Dr. Deckoff and the three attorneys, amply supported the grounds. Another fact compelling the court's ruling was that Wife received only 10 percent to 15 percent of the community assets. The court was apparently troubled about the possibility of Husband's having had legal counsel, as it included a statement that Husband, "after consulting his attorney, the details of which did not come up in the evidence, prepared and had the decree entered."

III. *Statement of Decision*

* * *

The Legislature has established some exceptions to [the] traditional rule [that a statement of decision is required before issuance of an order on a motion for equitable relief from a judgment, citing California Civ. Pro. Section 632]. For instance, a statement of decision is now required, if requested, after an order modifying or revoking a previous order for spousal support. [ ] We can find no case creating an exception for an order made after a motion to set aside the judgment on equitable grounds. Although a statement of decision would assist the reviewing court, we see no compelling reason for creating an exception to the traditional rule. Therefore, rather than inquire into the sufficiency of a statement of decision, our review is governed by the substantial evidence test. The trial court having found duress and extrinsic fraud or mistake, we begin with an examination of those concepts as they apply in the family law context.

IV. *Relief Against Judgment*

Husband contends that the evidence reflected only intrinsic fraud, which under the case law is not sufficient to set aside the judgments, and that there was no evidence to support a finding of duress.

Trial Court's Discretion. Even after the time for direct attack on the judgment has elapsed, the trial court has inherent power to set aside a judgment where it " ' . . . was obtained . . . through fraud, mistake, or accident, or where the defendant in the action, having a valid legal defense on the merits, was prevented in any manner from maintaining it by fraud, mistake, or accident, and there had been no negligence, laches, or other fault on his [or her] part. . . . The ground for the exercise of this jurisdiction is that there has been no fair adversary trial at law. (Citations.) The court may do so in an independent action in equity or, as here, in a motion in the original action. (Citations.)

"Legal discretion has been defined as an impartial discretion taking into account all relevant facts, together with legal principles essential to an informed and just decision. (Citations.) In the case before us, those essential legal principles include the command to weigh competing public policies, one favoring the finality of judgments, and the other favoring a fair adversary trial on the merits. The court can only exercise such inherent power "when the circumstances of the case are sufficient to overcome the strong policy favoring the finality of judgments." (Citations.)

Grounds for Relief in General. The most common ground used to justify such equitable relief is extrinsic fraud. "Fraud is extrinsic where the defrauded party was deprived of the opportunity to present his or her claim or defense to the court, that is, where he or she was kept in ignorance or in some other manner, other than from his or her own conduct, fraudulently prevented from fully participating in the proceeding." (*In re Marriage of Stevenot, supra,* 154 Cal.App.3d at p. 1068, 202 Cal.Rptr. 116.) By way of contrast, fraud is labeled intrinsic and not a ground for relief "if a party has been given notice of the action and has not been prevented from participating therein, that is, if he or she had the opportunity to present his or her case and to protect himself or herself from any mistake or fraud of his or her adversary, but *unreasonably* neglected to do so." (*Id.,* at p. 1069, 202 Cal.Rptr. 116, emphasis added.)

While it is relatively simple to state the general principles, it is a more difficult task to determine whether the facts which have been shown constitute "extrinsic" fraud, which will justify the granting of relief, or, as urged by Husband, "intrinsic" fraud, which will not. (*In re Marriage of Brennan* (1981) 124 Cal.App.3d 598, 603, 177 Cal.Rptr. 520.) Justice King, speaking for Division Five of this District, has called this distinction "the most repetitively troublesome issue in the family law field over the last 40 years." (*In re Marriage of Stevenot, supra,* 154 Cal.App.3d at p. 1056, 202 Cal.Rptr. 116.) And Judge Donald E. Smallwood has made a persuasive case for abolishing the extrinsic fraud rule. (See Smallwood, *Vacating Judgments in California: Time to Abolish the Extrinsic Fraud Rule* (1985) 13 Western St.U.L.Rev. 105–127 [hereafter cited as Smallwood]; see also Comment, *Seeking More Equitable Relief from Fraudulent Judgments:*

Abolishing the Extrinsic-Intrinsic Distinction (1981) 12 Pacific L.J. 1013.) The Restatement Second of Judgments (1982) does not distinguish between extrinsic and intrinsic fraud (§ 68). The distinction has also been abandoned in rule 60(b) of the Federal Rules of Civil Procedure (28 U.S.C.), which permits a court to relieve a party from a final judgment by motion made within a reasonable time not to exceed one year for "(1) mistake, inadvertence, surprise, or excusable neglect; (2) newly discovered evidence . . . [or] (3) fraud (*whether heretofore denominated intrinsic or extrinsic*), misrepresentation, or other misconduct of an adverse party. . . ." (Emphasis added.) Under rule 60(b), no time limit is imposed when an independent action is based on the ground of fraud on the court.

Although California courts continue to rely primarily on the extrinsic-intrinsic fraud analysis, they have also recognized that "[e]xtrinsic fraud is a broad concept that 'tend[s] to encompass almost any set of extrinsic circumstances which deprive a party of a fair adversary hearing.' [Citation.]" (*In re Marriage of Modnick* (1983) 33 Cal.3d 897, 905, 191 Cal.Rptr. 629, 663 P.2d 187; *Estate of Sanders* (1985) 40 Cal.3d 607, 614, 221 Cal.Rptr. 432, 710 P.2d 232; cf. *In re Marriage of Brockman* (1987) 194 Cal.App.3d 1035, 1047, 240 Cal.Rptr. 96.) And, in some cases, "the ground of relief is not so much the fraud or other misconduct of the [other party] as it is the excusable neglect of the [moving party] to appear and present his [or her] claim or defense. If such neglect results in an unjust judgment, *without a fair adversary hearing,* the basis for equitable relief is present, and is often called 'extrinsic mistake.' (Citations.)

Duress has also been recognized as a ground justifying relief from a final judgment. [ ] see Rest.2d Judgments, §§ 68, 70.) We have found no cases which state that they are granting relief from the judgment *solely* on the ground of duress, but this is probably because duress is often characterized as fraud. (See *Leeper, supra,* 53 Cal.2d at p. 205, 1 Cal.Rptr. 12, 347 P.2d 12 ["Duress is a species of fraud. [Citation.]"]; cf. *O'Neil v. Spillane* (1975) 45 Cal.App.3d 147, 158, 119 Cal.Rptr. 245 [undue influence a species of constructive fraud]; *Griffith v. Bank of New York* (2d Cir.1945) 147 F.2d 899, 901–902; Rest.2d Judgments, § 68.)

In addition to being grounds for setting aside a final judgment, both duress and fraud are statutory grounds for attacking the validity of a contract. Civil Code section 1567 provides that an apparent consent is not "real or free" when obtained through duress, menace, fraud, undue influence, or mistake. These same grounds are relevant in determining whether consent to entry of a default judgment, such as the one under consideration here, has been voluntary. Facts sufficient to set aside a contract, however, are not automatically sufficient to set aside a judgment. (Citations [mutual mistake not sufficient]; but see Rest.2d Judgments, § 71.) Each case will depend on whether the circumstances are sufficiently egregious to justify departing from the policy favoring the finality of judgments.

Duress. We next examine Husband's assertions on appeal in light of these general principles. Husband contends that there was no evidence he intentionally exercised duress to force Wife into an unequal agreement. We disagree.

The stringent definition of duress contained in Civil Code section 1569, codifying the early common law rule, has been relaxed. (*In re Marriage of Gonzalez, supra,* 57 Cal.App.3d at pp. 743–744, 129 Cal.Rptr. 566; *Rich & Whillock, Inc. v. Ashton Development, Inc.* (1984) 157 Cal.App.3d 1154, 1158–1159, 204 Cal.Rptr. 86 [economic compulsion].) Under the modern rule, " '[d]uress, which includes whatever destroys one's free agency and constrains [her] to do what is against [her] will, may be exercised by threats, importunity or any species of mental coercion [citation]. . . .' " (*Gonzalez, supra,* 57 Cal.App.3d at p. 744, 129 Cal.Rptr. 566.) It is shown where a party "intentionally used threats or pressure to induce action or nonaction to the other party's detriment. [Citing *Gonzalez.*]" (*In re Marriage of Stevenot, supra,* 154 Cal.App.3d at p. 1073, fn. 6, 202 Cal.Rptr. 116; see Rest.2d Contracts (1981) §§ 175, 176.) The coercion must induce the assent of the coerced party, who has no reasonable alternative to succumbing. (*Rich & Whillock, Inc. v. Ashton Development, Inc., supra,* 157 Cal.App.3d at pp. 1158–1159, 204 Cal.Rptr. 86.)

To determine whether a contract (or a default judgment) was the product of duress, the courts look not so much to the nature of the threats, but to their effect on the state of the threatened person's mind. (*In re Marriage of Gonzalez, supra,* 57 Cal.App.3d at p. 744, 129 Cal.Rptr. 566; Rest.2d Contracts, § 175, com. c.) This the trial court did. In its ruling, it cited as particularly persuasive the "overwhelming" testimony of Dr. Deckoff, and of Attorneys Gaustad, Stephens, and Jordan, to the effect that Wife was "very emotional, upset and distraught to the point that . . . she was acting under her husband's will." To show lack of consent, it was unnecessary to establish that she lacked the capacity to contract, only that she was in such a mentally weakened condition due to anxiety and emotional anguish or exhaustion that she was unable to protect herself against Husband's demands. (*O'Neil v. Spillane, supra,* 45 Cal.App.3d at p. 155, 119 Cal.Rptr. 245; *Smalley v. Baker* (1968) 262 Cal.App.2d 824, 834–835, 69 Cal.Rptr. 521.)

The testimony here graphically portrays an emotionally distraught wife who is unable to deal with her spouse on an arms-length basis and who is so intimidated by him that she is unable to take advantage of legal advice. It further reveals that her concerns about confronting Husband were well-founded. He actively interfered with her obtaining legal assistance and conducted himself in a manner calculated to deprive Wife of representation by counsel. He told Wife that he would not discuss anything with a lawyer, but would only deal with her directly. Ultimately, when Wife signed the agreement from which the trial court granted her relief, she was not represented by counsel. Nor was she represented when she signed the earlier handwritten agreement and the documents required for the default hearing.

Lack of independent advice, standing alone, is not sufficient to support a finding that Wife's consent was obtained through coercion. (*Smith v. Lombard* (1927) 201 Cal. 518, 524, 258 P. 55 [undue influence]; *Marsiglia v. Marsiglia* (1947) 78 Cal.App.2d 701, 705, 178 P.2d 478 [undue influence].) But, it " ' . . . is a fact to be weighed by the trial court in determining whether [that party] acted voluntarily and with a complete understanding of the transaction. [Citations.]' " (*Roeder v. Roeder* (1953) 118 Cal.App.2d 572, 581, 258 P.2d 581.) Here, the evidence shows Husband's active interference with Wife's attempts to obtain legal assistance. Under the circumstances of this case, lack of independent advice is persuasive evidence in support of the court's ruling.

Lack of independent advice is not the only indicia of duress present here. Perhaps the most significant mark is Wife's consent to a grossly unfair agreement by which she received only 10 to 15 percent of the community property and inadequate support for herself and the minor child. (See Rest.2d Contracts, § 208 [unconscionable contracts].) The evidence reveals no consideration for such an unequal agreement in the way of economic or psychological benefit to Wife or the child. Husband's assurance to Wife that his taking the bulk of the assets would save her the burden of debt financing has a hollow ring. He failed to consider that liquidation of assets or an adequate support award would have reduced or eliminated any such burden.

Husband made threats and misrepresentations. He threatened Wife with bankruptcy and urged her immediate action to prevent dissipation of her share of the property through credits to him of all payments for debts and support. He represented that she had no interest in his medical practice, telling her that she had not worked for it and that she was not an equal partner in the marriage. He aimed at her most vulnerable spot when he threatened not to see their child.

Husband argues that his claim to credits was an accurate statement of the law. His claim is only partly sustainable. Our Supreme Court in *In re Marriage of Epstein* (1979) 24 Cal.3d 76, 80, 154 Cal.Rptr. 413, 592 P.2d 1165, held that a spouse may claim reimbursement for amounts paid after separation on preexisting community debts. But the court also recognized that reimbursement would be inappropriate where the payment was made on a debt incurred for the acquisition or preservation of an asset the spouse was using and the amount paid was not substantially in excess of the value of the use, or where the payment constituted a discharge of the spouse's duty to pay child or spousal support. (*Id.*, at pp. 84–85, 154 Cal.Rptr. 413, 592 P.2d 1165; *In re Marriage of Reilley* (1987) 196 Cal.App.3d 1119, 1123, 242 Cal.Rptr. 302.) Here, Husband had possession and use of most of the community assets, and his right to reimbursement was uncertain even if he could establish that payments were made from his separate income rather than community accounts payable and were in excess of the value of the use of the various assets. Absent agreement, he was not entitled to credits for support payments. And it is possible that he might be required to reimburse the community for his use of the assets. (*In re Marriage of Watts* (1985) 171 Cal.App.3d 366, 374, 217 Cal.Rptr. 301.)

Upon dissolution of the marriage, the community property must be divided equally between the spouses, absent a contrary agreement. *In re Marriage of Fonstein* (1976) 17 Cal.3d 738, 748, 131 Cal.Rptr. 873, 552 P.2d 1169.) Husband's medical practice, including goodwill, was a community asset; his representations were false. (*In re Marriage of Watts, supra,* 171 Cal.App.3d at p. 372, 217 Cal.Rptr. 301.) His statement that Wife had no interest in his medical practice was not mere opinion on character or value. Rather, it was couched in terms to reinforce her feeling of inadequacy and lack of equality.

After Wife's hope for reconciliation disappeared, she reasonably believed that she had no alternative to compliance with Husband's demands and that her only recourse was to salvage the assets assigned to her and to use the meager support to develop her self-sufficiency.

It is seldom possible to show intent by direct evidence; usually it must be shown by the totality of the circumstances. From the evidence we have set out, the court could infer that Husband intentionally used coercion to induce Wife's consent to an unconscionable contract and a default judgment dissolving the marriage. (*In re Cheryl E.* (1984) 161 Cal.App.3d 587, 601, 207 Cal.Rptr. 728; *Estate of Hannam* (1951) 106 Cal.App.2d 782, 786, 236 P.2d 208.)

In summary, the evidence shows that Wife's consent to the agreement and entry of a default judgment was procured by duress practiced on her by Husband and that his acts were intentional. She was effectively deprived of independent counsel; she was in a distraught and weakened condition emotionally and unable to confront Husband; he undermined her psychologically by repeatedly telling her she had not contributed as much as he to the marriage and was not an equal partner; he made threats and misrepresentations and pressured her into taking immediate action; she agreed to an unconscionable contract; and she had no reasonable alternative. Thus, through the "extrinsic" factor of duress, she was denied a fair adversary hearing.

[See Chapter 6 for the court's discussion of the failure to disclose issue.]

Other Equitable Considerations. Husband argues that Wife should have been denied relief because of laches. "[T]he affirmative defense of laches requires unreasonable delay in bringing suit 'plus either acquiescence in the act about which [the moving party] complains or prejudice to [the other party] resulting from the delay.' [Citation] [ ] Husband offered evidence of Wife's acquiescence to the marital settlement agreement, but that, of course, was the very issue to be resolved in Wife's motion. He offered no evidence of prejudice to himself caused by her delay in seeking relief. In fact, he raised the issue of laches for the first time in his post-hearing trial brief.

Laches, strictly speaking, is not an appropriate doctrine, because it shifts to the opposing party the burden of proving that the complaining party has unreasonably delayed in seeking relief. [ ] The opposing party is not required to prove the affirmative defense of laches. Rather, a party seeking relief from a judgment has the burden of showing reasonable diligence in discovering the grounds for relief and, after discovery, in seeking relief. * * *

"In determining whether reasonable diligence has been exercised the court will consider the same factors as are considered in determining whether [the judgment] was secured by excusable extrinsic mistake [fraud, or duress]. . . ." (*McCreadie v. Arques* (1967) 248 Cal.App.2d 39, 46, 56 Cal.Rptr. 188; *In re Marriage of Wipson* (1980) 113 Cal.App.3d 136, 144, 169 Cal.Rptr. 664.) Lack of prejudice is one of the factors that the trial court may properly consider in determining whether the moving party has acted diligently. "[T]he greater the prejudice, the more timely must be the relief sought." (*McCreadie, supra,* 248 Cal.App.2d at p. 47, 56 Cal.Rptr. 188.)

In this case, the interlocutory judgment was entered on April 11, 1983, and the final judgment was entered on October 12, 1983. Wife moved to set them aside on April 6, 1984, and her motion was granted in July 1984.

When Wife left in January 1982, she took $6,000 from a savings account, but gave $4,800 back to Husband because he said he needed it to pay taxes. She had a checking account with approximately $600 in it, plus the $1,300 monthly support Husband was paying. The court could infer that, contrasted with her former standard of living, she was economically insecure. More importantly, five witnesses attested to her fragile emotional condition and her inability to confront Husband. Wife testified that it took her a long time to realize that she had been a full partner in the marriage. At the time of the hearing, Wife was living with the minor child in San Francisco and attending college, financed by the sale of the 1977 Mercedes-Benz assigned to her. This evidence is sufficient to support the trial court's implied findings that one year was not an unduly long time for Wife to regain her emotional stability and that she was reasonably diligent in asserting her claim.

Policy Favoring Finality of Judgments. The trial court here struck a proper balance between the policy favoring a trial on the merits and that favoring the finality of judgments. The evidence that Husband coerced Wife's consent to an unfair agreement and default judgment is compelling. A court applying equitable principles should not compound the miscarriage of justice by immunizing such a judgment from attack. That is not to say that every instance of pressure on a spouse should establish grounds for later attack on a judgment. It is not unusual in marital contract negotiations to find pressure exerted by one or both spouses and uninformed opinions on the law asserted as fact. But, unless the circumstances of the case are egregious, as they are here, the policy favoring finality should prevail.

The policy favoring finality is mandated primarily by the need for confidence in the judicial system. (See fn. 4, *ante.*) Judicial economy is, of course, another important factor for our overburdened courts. The average default hearing, however, usually takes less than 10 minutes. At such a hearing the court seldom has sufficient data to determine whether the agreement is fair to the nonappearing spouse, and thus judicial approval of a submitted agreement is often perfunctory. Where little judicial time and effort have been expended, " ' . . . the factor of judicial economy which otherwise weighs in favor of finality is less strong, and the equitable considerations of fair hearing and of penalizing fraud weigh more compellingly.' [Citation.]" (*In re Marriage of Brennan, supra,* 124 Cal.App.3d at pp. 604–605, 177 Cal.Rptr. 520; *Los Angeles Airways, Inc. v. Hughes Tool Co.* (1979) 95 Cal.App.3d 1, 7, 156 Cal.Rptr. 805; see Rest.2d Judgments, § 68, com. c.)

Conclusion. "In assessing the sufficiency of evidence on appeal, we must view the evidence in the light most favorable to the trial court's determination, drawing all reasonable inferences and disregarding all contradictory evidence. [Citation.]" (*In re Marriage of Adkins, supra,* 137 Cal.App.3d at p. 75, 186 Cal.Rptr. 818; *Shamblin v. Brattain* (1988) 44 Cal.3d 474, 479, 243 Cal.Rptr. 902, 749 P.2d 339.) From our review of the record, we find that the evidence is sufficient to support the trial court's express finding that Wife was prevented by fraud, mistake, and duress from having a fair adversary hearing and its (sic) implied finding that Wife's delay in seeking relief was reasonable. We also think that the court's implied finding that the circumstances of this case were sufficient to overcome the strong policy favoring finality of judgments was amply supported by the evidence.

[ ]

VI. *Disposition*

We find no abuse of discretion. The order setting aside the interlocutory and final judgments, including the marital settlement agreement, is affirmed. The order for temporary spousal support, child support, and attorney fees is affirmed. Husband shall pay Wife's costs on appeal.

WHITE, P.J., and MERRILL, J., concur.

NOTES

1.   *Threats and misrepresentations.* In finding substantial evidence of duress, *Baltins* characterized prior doctrine to instruct that "the courts look not so much to the nature of the threats, but to their effect on the state of the threatened person's mind."

The evidence showed that Deanna had retained and discharged one attorney, and consulted two others before deciding not to retain an attorney. The evidence also showed, however, that Aldis actively interfered with Deanna's efforts to obtain counsel. He threatened her with financial harm (bankruptcy), he made misstatements about community property law, and he threatened to cut off Deanna's contact with their child. Eventually, Aldis obtained a default final judgment of dissolution. One year later, Deanna moved to vacate the judgment. Aldis objected. One among many of Aldis's arguments was that just because Deanna felt duress did not mean that Aldis intended to apply duress; therefore absent proof of intent to apply duress, Deanna's actions were voluntary. The court flat out rejected that argument.

Baltins starts with the general rule that the lack of independent legal advice, without more is not sufficient evidence to prove that consent was obtained through coercion. Deanna did not have an attorney, not necessarily a problem in and of itself. But what was highly problematic was that Aldis obstructed Deanna's efforts to obtain counsel. Consequently, the court went on to offer a legal structure for how to analyze the interaction between the two. The judge stated that the task was not to understand the alleged coercer's demands; rather, it was to understand what impact those demands had on the other spouse's state of mind. Regardless of Aldis's intent, the impact of his "active interference with [Deanna's] attempts to obtain legal assistance" met the substantial evidence standard as to the trial court's finding of duress. Consequently, the absence of counsel led Deanna to stipulate to an agreement that was "grossly unfair" to her, and for which there was "no consideration given" her by Aldis.

There were additional facts in support of the finding that Aldis's conduct was coercive. Aldis threated Deanna with bankruptcy if she didn't follow his plan for the dissolution process. He misrepresented the law, such as for example, when he told Deanna that she had no property interest in the medical practice built during their marriage (she did), or when he told her that the goodwill of the medical practice was not a divisible community property asset (it is). These assertions, were not only inaccurate, wrote the court, they were "couched [by Aldis] in terms to reinforce [Deanna's] feeling of inadequacy and lack of equality." On review, the evidence offered to prove coercion, taken together, was adjudged not merely sufficient, but compelling. It showed that Aldis "intentionally used coercion to induce [Deanna's] consent to an unconscionable contract and a default judgment dissolving the marriage." *Id.* at 87.

In the end, the reviewing court found that Aldis had engaged in fraud, mistake, and duress. There is seldom direct evidence of duress, the court wrote, so other facts must go toward proving it. This record "graphically portrays an emotionally distraught wife who is unable to deal with her spouse on an arms-length basis and who is so intimidated by him that she is unable to take advantage of legal advice." *Id.* at 85. This sentence states the prior law— spouses negotiate at arm's length during a marital dissolution proceeding— while nodding to a competing understanding that was also present in prior case law, one expressed for example in *Gregory v. Gregory*, 92 Cal.App.2d 343, 206 P.2d 1122 (1st Dist. 1949)—married persons do not negotiate at arm's length given the state's strong interest in marriage.

Today, the codification of California Family Code 721, 1100(e) and 2100 et seq., incorporates California Family Code 721 by reference into the dissolution process. Spouses are fiduciaries, not arm's length contractors. As fiduciaries, spouses owe each other duties up until the final judgment is issued (generally) and up until a division of assets or assignment of liability is finalized (specifically).

2. *The burden of proof is on the party who seeks relief from the judgment.* Aldis raised a defense of laches, arguing that Deanna had acquiesced to the marital settlement agreement and unreasonably delayed in seeking a set-aside order. On review, the court noted that laches is "not an appropriate doctrine [in a dissolution judgment set aside case] because [laches] shifts to the opposing party the burden of proving that the complaining party has unreasonable delayed in seeking relief." *Id.* at 92. The burden of proof does not change; it remains on the party who seeks relief from the judgment.

Marriage of Kieturakis, reproduced below, is a mediation case that raises the legal question about burden shifting: Does equity demand that the burden of proof shift from the party who claims duress to the party who defends against the claim of duress? And, if it does, should the shift occur by applying the presumption of undue influence found at California Family Code Section 721(b)? *Kieturakis*, citing *Bonds* (Chapter 1), came down on the side of *Baltins* to hold that the burden of proof does not shift away from the party who claims duress to the party who is accused of duress. Nor should it shift. The court reasoned that because the state policy of encouraging mediated settlements is strong, the burden of proof must remain on the party who seeks to set the final judgment aside.

3. *Waiver of statutory rights.* Unless otherwise indicated by statute or case law, a party can waive statutory protections. Waiver must be proved by

clear and convincing evidence. Due to the many public policies that statutory protections support, when in doubt, a court should decide against a waiver. See *Marriage of Fell*, 55 Cal.App.4th 1058, 64 Cal.Rptr.2d 522 (2d Dist. 1997).

4. *Balancing the policy in favor of finality of judgments against the policy in favor of the equal division of community and quasi-community.* The policy in favor of finality of judgments encourages confidence in the judicial system. It also encourages judicial economy. These are important public policies. Even so, as the *Baltins* court notes, these policies should not be used as a shield against equity. To place too much weight on the policy of finality of judgments, particularly in a case where the evidence of coercion is compelling (as it was in *Baltins*), is to "compound the miscarriage of justice by immunizing such a judgment from attack." *Id.* at 93.

B. THE CURRENT STATUTORY FRAMEWORK

The current statutory framework does away with the extrinsic/intrinsic fraud distinction. It greatly expands the definition of fraud to include perjury, duress and even mistakes of law and fact. And it incorporates the discovery rule for statute of limitations purposes.

The general rule, recall, is that when parties opt to reach a private negotiated marital settlement agreement, MSA, they are not required to reach an equal division. Relatedly, when a court approves a negotiated MSA for purposes of issuing a final judgment of dissolution, the court is not empowered, much less required, to scrutinize the MSA to make sure that it effects an equal division.

A trial court is only authorized to set aside a final judgment for the grounds stated in California Family Code Section 2122, reproduced above. The trial court's exercise of discretion is subject to the abuse of discretion standard on appeal.

Marriage of Varner was decided after the Family Code was enacted. *Varner* considers the interpretation of the statutory phrase "actual fraud" in the effort to better define the concept of how incomplete or inaccurate disclosure can cause the other party to make a mistake of law or fact. The court elaborates on fixed legal principles with examples of extrinsic fraud. It names as active instances of fraud: concealment of the existence of a community property asset; failure to give notice of the action to the other party; and convincing the other party not to obtain counsel because the matter will not proceed to court. Additionally, the court of appeal sets forth a guide for use by a trial court in deciding motions to vacate a final judgment of dissolution. According to that guide, the trial court is to apply fixed legal principles, it is to conform to the spirit of the law, and it is to reach an outcome that serves rather than impedes or defeats substantial justice between the parties. The trial court decision is subject to reversal only if a reviewing court finds an abuse of discretion.

MARRIAGE OF VARNER

55 Cal.App.4th 128, 63 Cal.Rptr.2d 894 (4th Dist. 1997)

RAMIREZ, PRESIDING JUSTICE.

Former wife Kim Denise Varner (wife) appeals from a trial court order denying her motion to set aside the judgment of dissolution of her marriage to her former husband Stephen Varner (husband). The judgment of dissolution had divided the community property of the parties pursuant to a stipulation of the parties. On appeal wife contends, among other things, that husband had failed to disclose to her the extent or the value of the community property at the time she signed the stipulation, and she contends that the trial court erred by refusing to set the judgment aside.

Facts

The parties started living together when wife was 15 years old and husband, who had previously been married and divorced, was 24. The parties married in 1977, when wife was 17, and their first child was born in 1978. In 1984 they separated, and wife filed a petition for dissolution. By this time they had three children. The matter was repeatedly continued and was finally taken off calendar in October 1985 when the parties reconciled.

In September of 1989 the parties again separated; by then two more children had been born to the parties. Wife's counsel withdrew, and wife continued for a short period without representation. By January 1990, wife had new counsel. In February 1992 counsel for wife filed a 30-day notice asking the court to value numerous business assets as of September 30, 1989, or April 30, 1990, rather than at the time of trial.

In May of 1992 wife filed an amended petition for dissolution. In that petition wife included a list of 32 items of community property assets of the parties that she wished to have disposed of by the court. Included among these were five parcels of real property, seven investment or bank accounts, four businesses, three partnerships, a business center, a note receivable, a life insurance policy, five vehicles, three boats, assets in a Varner Family Trust, and other property unknown to wife.

In May of 1993 a hearing was held on a motion by counsel for wife to withdraw, and on the reasonableness of the fees charged by her attorney to that time. The court permitted counsel for wife to withdraw, but declined to rule on the motion to confirm attorney fees.

The hearing on the dissolution was held July 13, 1993. At that time wife told the court she would like to continue the matter because she had no lawyer. The court denied her request. Before calling husband to the stand, counsel for husband stated "a certain discomfort" in representing husband against wife who was not represented. Counsel then went on to state that "The Court has made its ruling, and obviously made the ruling because she had an absolutely outstanding lawyer in Mr. Harding, and probably the finest, if not one of the finest forensic accountants, Mrs. Alexander, working for her.

"It is my understanding that the judgment that's going to become relevant in these proceedings, a draft judgment was, in fact, deemed by the experts whom she had employed to be a fair resolution of the issues between the parties. I have indicated to her that, in my opinion, my client has offered to her a proposal that is much better than what she would get if we have to proceed to trial. We are now proceeding to trial, and my intention would be to simply work from the draft judgment, establish the amounts that are involved, and let the court make the order that it makes."

Husband was then called as a witness and testified to the jurisdictional facts relevant to the dissolution. Counsel then presented husband with the draft judgment and asked, "[D]id that judgment, in fact, provide for an unequal division of community property and debts to your disadvantage? . . . " to which husband replied, "This one does, yes."

Husband then testified that his monthly income was about $8,000. He stated that his business was not good the way it had been, and that he was now taking smaller jobs. He testified that wife wanted the parties' house in Riverside, which was about 5,000 square feet in size, on 2 1/2 acres. Husband stated that wife's attorney had the house appraised at $500,000 or $550,000, but that he thought it was worth between $600,000 and $700,000, and that it had a debt on it of $160,000. Husband stated that $650,000 was a fair value for the house, resulting in a net value to wife of $490,000 for the house.

Husband then testified to the value of four parcels of real property owned by the parties, properties that were to be awarded to him: A condominium in Laughlin, with a net value after tax liability of $60,000 less the cost of sale; a Bullhead condominium with an equity value of $45,000, also subject to substantial tax liability; a house in Big Bear with a realistic sales price of $300,000, and a debt of $240,000, which would be subject to about $80,000 in tax liability if it were sold, plus the costs of the sale, with the result that it was really a $45,000 liability rather than an asset; and the Brown Street property on which Varner Construction, Inc., operated, which husband testified was worth about $200,000.

Husband testified that he owned all the stock in a business called Varner Construction, Inc., and that he was a 60-percent partner in Pipeline Specialties, Inc. He also testified that he had an interest in Varner/Clendenen which owned some land, as well as Group Equity Fund VI. Husband testified that he owned Varner Construction, Inc., prior to his marriage, and that the net value of the business was about zero. He stated that Pipeline Specialties, Inc., had a negative value of about $300,000. He valued Varner/Clendenen at about $40,000 to $50,000, and Group Equity

Fund VI had a value of $7,000. Husband testified that the totality of the various business entities in which he had an interest equaled about zero. He stated that there were several notes receivable from Varner Construction that had no value because they were owed by Varner Construction to Varner Construction, and, similarly, his life insurance policies were "right at the break-even point" and had zero value. Husband then listed the value of several vehicles owned by the parties and the household furnishings, and represented that the total value of the assets to be allocated to wife was $544,830.

Totaling the value of the assets to be awarded to husband, counsel for husband stated that husband would receive assets of a value of $281,000. Spousal support under the agreement was based on wife's having zero income. Counsel for husband stated that although under the agreement wife would owe husband an equalization payment of roughly $150,000, husband had offered to let wife keep everything she had and had also agreed to pay off the $160,000 that was owed on the house.

At the end of the hearing the court stated to wife: "Ma'am, I am not your attorney, and I really can't tell you what to do, but that is a very good disposition in this case if the figures that were given to me are correct.

"Now, I have no idea. You may have some other figures that you feel are appropriate, but assuming that they are correct and backed up by appraisals and that sort of thing, even if they are incorrect a little bit, this is still—... were it me, I would take the deal, but that's your business."

The hearing was continued for a week. When the matter was again called, counsel for husband stated that the parties had signed the settlement agreement. Under questioning by counsel for husband, each of the parties testified to having voluntarily signed the agreement. On that date, July 20, 1993, the stipulated agreement was entered as a judgment of the court.

The judgment awarded custody and visitation of the children; retained jurisdiction over spousal and child support; and ordered husband to pay wife $6,000 per month as unallocated family support. The judgment then divided the community property of the parties, although no values were attached to the items of property in the judgment. Wife was awarded nine items of property; husband was awarded twenty-one items of property, including all the real property and assets related to the businesses of the parties. Husband also agreed to pay the $160,000 obligation on the house awarded to wife.

On December 10, 1993, wife's present attorney was substituted in the place of wife and began his vigorous representation of wife. On January 13, 1994, within six months of entry of the judgment, wife filed a motion to set aside the stipulation for judgment and the judgment on three grounds: First, Code of Civil Procedure section 473; second, the inherent equitable power of the court to set aside judgments obtained through fraud, duress and overreaching; and, finally, Family Code sections 2120, 2121 and 2122 "which effectively extinguish the distinction between extrinsic and intrinsic fraud, in dissolution proceedings, and greatly expand fraud to include non-disclosure, misconduct and perjury, as well as mental incapacity of the disadvantaged spouse."

In anticipation of a hearing on the motion wife submitted a psychological evaluation indicating that wife had an intelligence quotient of 75. The report went on to state that "On the surface, the behavior of this woman is characterized by submissiveness, dependency, and the seeking of affection, attention, and security. A fear of abandonment often compels her to be overly compliant and obliging. She may be quite naive about interpersonal matters. . . ."

Wife submitted to the court an appraisal of two business properties awarded to husband in the judgment which indicated the two properties had a combined value of $1,060,000. Wife also filed a preliminary appraisal of Varner Construction, Inc., that concluded that the "fair market value of Varner Construction, Inc., as of fiscal year end, April 30, 1993, is in the range of $2,000,000.00 to $2,750,[000.00]" rather than the zero testified to by husband. The report also indicated that the true value of Pipeline Specialties, Inc., was in the range of $300,000 to $600,000; the 60-percent interest of the parties in Pipeline Specialties, Inc., was therefore $180,000 to $360,000. The report indicated that Varner Construction, Inc., was incorporated in 1984 and the stock in the corporation was entirely owned by the parties. The corporation reached its highest levels of revenue and profit in 1989 at which time gross revenues exceeded $11.5 million, and profit exceeded $500,000. The appraiser indicated that the preliminary report was made without a complete record of the history of the businesses or of the other business entities in which the parties might have had an ownership interest.

Submitted to the court along with the motion to set aside the judgment was a declaration by a neighbor of wife's who stated that wife had come to her in tears after the dissolution hearing and had told her she sensed that her husband was not telling the truth but she did not know how to prove it, and that even the judge at the hearing had told her she should take what her husband was offering. The neighbor stated it was she who had helped wife get the appraiser and the lawyer representing wife at this point in the proceedings, and that wife had said that for the first time she felt that her views were being heard and her interests looked out for.

Wife further submitted to the court a declaration by the accountant who had been hired by counsel for wife to appraise the community property in 1990. The accountant submitted a declaration stating that she had had difficulty in obtaining from husband the documents necessary to complete her analysis, and she attached a declaration from October 1991 in which she had outlined those difficulties. The 1994 declaration stated that the accountant had been forced to rely on the representations of husband and his attorney in preparing her valuation of the community property.

Counsel for each party submitted excellent briefing on the issues raised by the motion to set aside, and each party submitted documentary evidence in support of its position. A hearing on the motion to set aside the judgment was held in May 1994, and the matter was taken under submission. On June 22, 1994, the court denied, by minute order, the motion to set aside the judgment. * * *

On August 22, 1994, wife filed a notice of appeal from the June 22, 1994, order denying her motion to set aside the judgment.

Discussion

I. Statutory Basis for Setting Aside the Stipulated Judgment

The notice of appeal cited the order denying wife's motion to set aside the stipulated judgment as the basis of the appeal, and that is the central issue we will address. In the trial court wife argued alternative theories under which the judgment should have been set aside, but in this court she argues only that the judgment should have been set aside under Family Code section 2120 et seq.—chapter 10 of the Family Code, entitled "Relief from Judgment."

The new provisions governing the setting aside of the division of community property in a dissolution judgment were enacted in 1992, prior to enactment of the Family Code, as section 4800.11 of the Civil Code. [ ]

Family Code section 2120 sets forth the legislative findings with regard to the "strong policy of ensuring the division of community and quasi-community property in the dissolution of a marriage . . . and of providing for fair and sufficient child and spousal support awards." (*Id.,* subd. (a).) The section goes on to state that "These policy goals can only be implemented with full disclosure of community, quasi-community, and separate assets, liabilities, income, and expenses, . . . and decisions freely and knowingly made." (*Id.,* subd. (a).) Section 2120, subdivision (b), acknowledges that "It occasionally happens that the division of property or the award of support, whether made as a result of agreement or trial, is inequitable when made due to the nondisclosure or other misconduct of one of the parties."

Section 2120 goes on to recognize the need to balance the "policy of assuring finality of judgments" against the "public interest in ensuring proper division of marital property," the award of sufficient support, and deterrence of misconduct. (*Id.,* subd. (c).) The section then acknowledges that "The law governing the circumstances under which a judgment can be set aside, after the time for relief under Section 473 of the Code of Civil

Procedure has passed, has been the subject of considerable confusion" leading to unpredictable and inconsistent decisions. (§ 2120, subd. (d).) The clear implication is that the chapter is intended to address these problems.

Section 2121 provides that a court may relieve a spouse from a judgment, "based on the grounds, and within the time limits, provided in this chapter," even beyond the six-month time limitation provided in Code of Civil Procedure section 473. (§ 2121, subd. (a).) A prerequisite to the grant of relief under the chapter is a finding by the court that "the facts alleged as the grounds for relief materially affected the original outcome" and that the grant of relief would materially benefit the moving party. (*Id.,* subd. (b).)

Section 2122 contains the substance of the chapter—the grounds for setting aside a judgment. That section provides, in summary, that a judgment may be set aside for actual fraud within one year of discovery of the fraud; for perjury, within one year of discovery of the perjury; for duress, within two years of entry of judgment; for mental incapacity, within two years of entry of the judgment; and, finally, "(e) As to stipulated or uncontested judgments or that part of a judgment stipulated to by the parties, mistake, either mutual or unilateral, whether mistake of law or mistake of fact. An action or motion based on mistake shall be brought within one year after the date of entry of judgment." It is this latter provision which we find applicable to the present case.

A.   *Standard of Review*

We recognize that the trial court's exercise of discretion in refusing to set aside a judgment under section 2122 is subject to reversal on appeal only if we find an abuse of that discretion. We also recognize that this court must not merely substitute its own view as to the proper decision: "[T]he showing on appeal is wholly insufficient if it presents a state of facts . . . which . . . merely affords an opportunity for a difference of opinion. An appellate tribunal is neither authorized nor warranted in substituting its judgment for the judgment of the trial judge." (*Brown v. Newby* (1940) 39 Cal.App.2d 615, 618, 103 P.2d 1018.) The trial court's exercise of discretion must be guided, however, by fixed legal principles, and must "be exercised in conformity with the spirit of the law and in a manner to subserve and not to impede or defeat the ends of substantial justice." (*Bailey v. Taaffe* (1866) 29 Cal. 422, 424.)

[ ]

B.   *Traditional Grounds for Setting Aside a Judgment*

Since this chapter has not previously been the subject of judicial opinions we look not to direct precedent in interpreting the language of the statute but instead to decisions under analogous authority. We begin by looking at other statutes which authorize the setting aside of a judgment.

Code of Civil Procedure section 473, subdivision (b), provides, in relevant part, that "The court may, upon any such terms as may be just, relieve a party . . . from a judgment, dismissal, order, or other proceeding taken against him or her through his or her mistake, inadvertence, surprise or excusable neglect." In *In re Marriage of Jacobs* (1982) 128 Cal.App.3d 273, 180 Cal.Rptr. 234, the trial court granted wife's motion under Code of Civil Procedure section 473 to set aside a stipulated judgment of dissolution under a theory of mistake. Husband in *Jacobs* was an accountant and a partner in an accounting firm. Throughout the marriage "husband used his financial expertise as an accountant to manipulate the parties' money." (128 Cal.App.3d at p. 278, 180 Cal.Rptr. 234.) The dissolution judgment referred to $250,000 in "trust" for the benefit of the children (*id.,* at p. 279, 180 Cal.Rptr. 234), but there was no trust instrument, and by the time of the motion to set aside the judgment all but $44,000 of the " 'children's money' " had been spent by husband (*id.,* at p. 285, 180 Cal.Rptr. 234). This court affirmed the trial court's order setting aside the judgment.

In *Hansen v. Hansen* (1961) 190 Cal.App.2d 327, 12 Cal.Rptr. 44, the appellate court affirmed a trial court decision to set aside a judgment dividing the community property of the parties. Husband had agreed to withdraw his answer to wife's petition and to allow the matter to proceed as a default after having been told by his lawyers that " 'you won't get any more if you take it into court, this is what the judge decided, and this is it.' " (*Id.,* at p. 329, 12 Cal.Rptr. 44.) In reversing, the appellate court noted that "It is clear in this case that the [husband] entered into the stipulation under a misguided belief which goes to the very heart of the administration of justice. The [husband] was told in effect that the judge had already made up his mind and that the lawsuit was over so far as he was concerned." (*Id.,* at p. 331, 12 Cal.Rptr. 44.)

In *Gregory v. Gregory* (1949) 92 Cal.App.2d 343, 206 P.2d 1122, the appellate court affirmed the setting aside of a divorce judgment under Code of Civil Procedure section 473. Wife, who was not represented by counsel, signed an agreement under which husband got the house of the parties, the family car, his life insurance policies, and most of the household furnishings. Wife received $1,000, a typewriter, a sewing machine, and all of the linens. Wife waived her rights in her Social Security benefits. (92 Cal.App.2d at p. 347, 206 P.2d 1122.) Husband's attorney, who had assured wife "he would not take part in something which was not fair and just," (*ibid.*) did not tell wife that it was her privilege to have independent counsel, and did not tell her that there was going to be a hearing in open court (*id.,* at p. 348, 206 P.2d 1122).

In affirming the order setting aside the judgment the court noted, " 'The rules of practice applicable to divorce actions differ in many respects from those which govern other actions. In an action for divorce, upon very slight showing the court will set aside a default, if application for relief be made in due time. . . . The law is at all times very solicitous to preserve the integrity of the marriage relation. That relation is the basis of the family, the foundation of society. . . . An action for divorce concerns not only the parties immediately interested, but also the state. . . . It is the duty of the court, representing the state, in accordance with the letter and policy of the law, to guard strictly against fraud, collusion, or imposition when the husband or wife seeks to dissolve the bonds that bind them together.'" (*Gregory v. Gregory, supra,* 92 Cal.App.2d at p. 345, 206 P.2d 1122.)

Courts have also been held to have inherent power to set aside a judgment, even after the six-month period of Code of Civil Procedure section 473 has passed, if the parties have been deprived of the opportunity to litigate their claim. Thus, one court has stated the applicable rules as follows: "After six months when relief is no longer available under section 473 of the Code of Civil Procedure for mistake, inadvertence, surprise, or excusable neglect, an otherwise valid judgment may only be set aside for extrinsic fraud or mistake." (*In re Marriage of Stevenot* (1984) 154 Cal.App.3d 1051, 1068, 202 Cal.Rptr. 116. . . .) Extrinsic fraud occurs when a party is deprived of his opportunity to present his claim or defense to the court, where he was kept in ignorance or in some other manner fraudulently prevented from fully participating in the proceeding. (*Ibid.*) Examples of extrinsic fraud are: concealment of the existence of a community property asset, failure to give notice of the action to the other party, convincing the other party not to obtain counsel because the matter will not proceed (and it does proceed). (*Id.* at p. 1069, 202 Cal.Rptr. 116.) A party's representation of the value of an asset, favorable to himself, does not constitute extrinsic fraud. (*Id.* at p. 1070, 202 Cal.Rptr. 116.) Extrinsic mistake involves the excusable neglect of a party. (*Kulchar v. Kulchar* (1969) 1 Cal.3d 467, 471, 82 Cal.Rptr. 489, 462 P.2d 17. . . .) When this neglect results in an unjust judgment, without a fair adversary hearing, and the basis for equitable relief is present, this is extrinsic mistake. (*Ibid.*) Reliance on an attorney who becomes incapacitated, or incompetence of the party without appointment of a guardian ad litem, are examples of extrinsic mistake. (*Id.* at pp. 469–470, 82 Cal.Rptr. 489, 462 P.2d 17.)

"Fraud is intrinsic and not a valid ground for setting aside a judgment when the party has been given notice of the action and has had an opportunity to present his case and to protect himself from any mistake or fraud of his adversary, but has unreasonably neglected to do so. (*In re Marriage of Stevenot, supra,* 154 Cal.App.3d at p. 1069, 202 Cal.Rptr. 116.) Such a claim of fraud goes to the merits of the prior proceeding which the moving party should have guarded against at the time. Where the defrauded party failed to take advantage of liberal discovery policies to fully investigate his or her claim, any fraud is intrinsic fraud. (*Ibid.*)" (*In*

re Marriage of Melton (1994) 28 Cal.App.4th 931, 937–938, 33 Cal.Rptr.2d
761.)

Cases in which a court has set aside a judgment beyond the time
allowed for doing so under Code of Civil Procedure section 473 include *In
re Marriage of Grissom* (1994) 30 Cal.App.4th 40, 35 Cal.Rptr.2d 530
[affirming grant of order setting aside default judgment obtained by
husband following reconciliation of the parties and after husband had
assured wife he would not proceed with the dissolution]; and *In re Marriage
of Brennan v. Brennan* (1981) 124 Cal.App.3d 598, 177 Cal.Rptr. 520
[reversing denial of motion to set aside dissolution judgment in which wife
failed to hire a lawyer following assurances by husband and his lawyer that
they would be "over fair" with her, and testimony by husband that book
value of stock in business was zero; wife later discovered stock was worth
a minimum of $250,000].

C.   *Recent Statutory Changes*

The addition of chapter 10 to the Family Code is not the only change
that has affected decisions in this area of the law. In 1991, former sections
5103, 5125, and 5125.1 of the Civil Code were amended to alter the duty of
care owed between spouses to "the general rules governing fiduciary
relationships" in place of the obligation to "act in good faith with respect to
the other spouse" as had been required up to that time. (Former Civil Code
§ 5125, subd. (e); Stats.1991, ch. 1026, § 3; see now Fam.Code, § 1100.) One
court discussing these statutory changes has noted the difficulty of
attempting to "draw a bright line distinction between the two duties. As
many writers have observed, 'good faith' is an amorphous phrase, having
no definite meaning of its own and usually illustrated in the negative by
what it is not." (*In re Marriage of Reuling* (1994) 23 Cal.App.4th 1428, 1438,
28 Cal.Rptr.2d 726.)

The court went on to observe that "A fiduciary relationship has been
defined as 'any relation existing between parties to a transaction wherein
one of the parties is [ ] duty bound to act with the utmost good faith for the
benefit of the other party. Such a relation ordinarily arises where a
confidence is reposed by one person in the integrity of another, and in such
a relation the party in whom the confidence is reposed, if he voluntarily
accepts or assumes to accept the confidence, can take no advantage from
his acts relating to the interest of the other party without the latter's
knowledge or consent.' [ ] Commenting on the changes to former Civil Code
section 5125, that court noted that "Given a stated judicial distinction
between the two standards and the subsequent change in the statutory
language from 'good faith' to 'fiduciary duty,' we may reasonably infer that
the Legislature intended by the 1991 amendments to replace a lesser
standard with one deemed higher." (23 Cal.App.4th at p. 1439, 28
Cal.Rptr.2d 726.) The court in *Reuling* did not determine the effect of the

statutory changes on the facts before it, however, because the court concluded that the Legislature did not intend to have the amended statute apply to conduct that had occurred before the amendments were enacted. (*Ibid.*)

The intent of the Legislature with regard to the duty of disclosure owed between spouses was made more explicit by the enactment in 1992, effective January 1, 1993, of what was then Civil Code section 4800.10, now chapter 9 of the Family Code, sections 2100 through 2113. (Former Civ.Code, § 4800.10, added by Stats.1992, ch. 37, § 1.)

Civil Code section 4800.10 [now California Family Code Sections 2100 through 2113] was added to specify that, from the date of separation to the date of distribution of the assets of the community, each party to a marriage dissolution is subject to the general rules governing the actions of persons occupying confidential relations with each other. Before it even took effect, Civil Code section 4800.10 was amended to expand the activities to which the higher standard should apply; by the time it became effective January 1, 1993, the higher standard of care now found in Family Code section 721 applied to "all activities that affect the property rights of the other party," (Stats. 1993, ch. 219, § 10) including, but not limited to, the activities enumerated in what is now Family Code section 2102.

Section 721 provides, in relevant part, that "in transactions between themselves, a husband and wife are subject to the general rules governing fiduciary relationships which control the actions of persons occupying confidential relations with each other. This confidential relationship imposes a duty of the highest good faith and fair dealing on each spouse, and neither shall take any unfair advantage of the other." This is the standard that had been applicable to spouses during a marriage and prior to separation; by the various statutory amendments in 1991 and 1992, this standard had been extended to apply to spouses between the time the parties separate and the time the marital property is divided.

Section 2102, outlining the fiduciary duties owed from one spouse to the other under the amended standard, provides in part that each spouse has a fiduciary obligation as to "The accurate and complete disclosure of all assets and liabilities in which the party has or may have an interest or obligation and all current earnings, accumulations, and expenses," and also has such an obligation with regard to "The operation or management of a business or an interest in a business in which the community may have an interest." (§ 2102, subds. (a), (c).)

D.   *Application of Present Law*

[ ] It is under the amended statutes that we must evaluate the present case. At the outset, it is clear that section 2122 now provides that a motion to set aside a stipulated judgment may be brought within one year after

the date of entry of judgment, and it is equally clear that wife's motion was timely under that statute.

Less clear is the meaning and the nature of the "mistake" which permits the setting aside of a judgment. As we have discussed above, there have been several cases which have permitted an applicant to set aside a dissolution judgment for mistakes comparable to the mistake of wife in the present case. (See, e.g., *In re Marriage of Brennan, supra,* 124 Cal.App.3d 598, 177 Cal.Rptr. 520.) Such relief, however, is not automatic. (See, e.g., *Caldwell* v. *Methodist Hospital of Southern California* (1994) 24 Cal.App.4th 1521, 29 Cal.Rptr.2d 894 [denying relief from court's dismissal of the case when neither party appeared at a hearing because counsel for both parties were mistaken on the hearing date].)

In the context of the case before us we find that the relationship between the parties and the higher duty of disclosure to which the parties are held under section 2102 regarding the community property of the marriage is relevant to our determination that the mistake in the present case warrants setting aside the judgment.

The facts submitted to this court on appeal compel a finding that husband breached his duty to provide an "accurate and complete disclosure of all assets and liabilities" of the parties at the time of the negotiations surrounding the stipulated judgment. Wife contends that husband failed to disclose the true value of the assets accumulated by the parties during the marriage. Wife has supported her argument by submitting valuations of the property prepared by her experts, and even by husband's experts, and comparing them to husband's testimony at trial regarding the value of the community property. Wife has also provided loan applications submitted to banks by husband near to the time of the testimony showing dramatically higher values given to the properties on the loan applications than were testified to by husband at trial.

Husband's failure to comply with the requirements of section 2102 regarding "accurate and complete" disclosure of assets is further shown by the declaration of wife's first accountant who stated that she had been unable to obtain information documenting the value of the property of the parties and that she had had to rely on the representations of husband and husband's attorney in valuing the property. Although wife was not represented by counsel at the time of trial, husband and his attorney had indicated to the court that the stipulated judgment had been approved by wife's previous attorney and by wife's previous accountant. In light of the declaration subsequently filed with the court, it appears that any approval by wife's attorney or accountant was necessarily made in reliance on the representations made to her, which were subsequently shown to be questionable. The court, in turn, recommended to wife that she accept the judgment, but made that recommendation with the caveat "if the figures that were given to me are correct." The record before us contains nothing but husband's testimony to support those figures. The evidence that the figures were not correct includes declarations by both of wife's accountants, loan applications prepared by husband, and appraisals by independent appraisers. Even husband's own appraiser stated values for the community property that were greater than those he testified to at trial.

It appears that wife was a difficult client near the time of the trial, as indicated by the fact that her attorney and her accountant asked to be relieved. The fact remains, however, that wife was not represented at the time of the trial, that she asked the court to continue the matter so that she could get representation, and that the court denied her request. Under the stringent "extrinsic mistake" standard that would have applied in the absence of the recent statutory changes, the facts before us might not have been sufficient to warrant a reversal by this court on abuse of discretion grounds.

Under the newly-enacted requirements of full disclosure, however, the analysis is different. Husband's failure to disclose the values of the assets, or even to give wife's accountants access to the information from which the value could be derived, would constitute a violation of section 2105, subdivision (b)(2), which states that a final declaration of disclosure must include, among other things, "All material facts and information regarding the valuation of all assets that are contended to be community or in which it is contended the community has an interest." Section 2105, subdivision (a), provides that "The commission of perjury on the final declaration of disclosure may be grounds for setting aside the judgment, or any part or parts thereof. . . ."

Quite reasonably, the remedy of setting aside a judgment is not offered for failure to disclose the existence or the value of assets; there would presumably be no judgment entered if there was a failure to disclose. The Legislature has provided, however, that the remedy of setting aside a judgment is available for violation of this chapter. Like perjury, the failure to disclose would induce the other spouse to stipulate to a judgment on the basis of incomplete or inaccurate information. We conclude that the failure of a spouse to disclose the existence or the value of a community asset, as occurred in the present case, constitutes a basis for setting aside a judgment on the grounds of mistake under section 2122.

II. *Husband's Separate Property Contention*

Husband argued extensively below, and maintains in this court, that the value of property awarded to him in the stipulated judgment is largely irrelevant because the property was not community property but was in reality his separate property which he had acquired prior to the marriage. He argues that the substantial assets acquired by the time of the dissolution of the marriage reflected primarily the enhanced value attributable to the business he owned before the marriage, and that any increase in value arising from his community property skill or effort had already been given to the community during the course of the marriage, as shown by the comfortable life of the parties during the marriage and the substantial community property awarded to wife.

Again, the record before us cannot be construed to support this contention. The only indication in the record of the business assets owned by husband at the time of the marriage in 1977 is the judgment of dissolution of his prior marriage in 1976 in which husband was awarded his home and furnishings, a 1965 Chevrolet pickup truck, a 1970 Yamaha motorcycle, and a 1962 Wabco earth mover. His former wife was awarded $2,000 in cash "as and for her share of the community property" and a 1967 Plymouth automobile. The only asset directly related to his business is the earth mover, and it strains credulity to argue that the substantial business that existed at the time of the property division in the present marriage reflects only the enhanced value attributable to that earth mover. There may be facts which do not appear before this court, but on the record before us we do not find that the stipulated judgment can be sustained under this theory. * * *

Disposition

The judgment is reversed. Costs on appeal to be borne by husband.

RICHLI and MCDANIEL JJ., concur.

NOTE

Valuation mistakes due to lack of disclosure versus *fully disclosed valuations that lead to unfair settlement agreements.* Here again, one sees the general principle stated. The parties are free to reach an imbalanced negotiated settlement agreement, which is to say an agreement that does not equally divide the community estate. *Mejia v. Reed*, 31 Cal.4th 657, 3 Cal.Rptr.3d 390, 74 P.3d 166 (2003). What matters is that the agreement is consensual, meaning knowingly made. Making a decision knowingly requires disclosure.

Brewer v. Federici, 93 Cal.App.4th 1334, 113 Cal.Rptr.2d 849 (2d Dist. 2001) gives yet another example of mistake. In *Brewer*, the parties signed a marital settlement agreement and stipulated to a dissolution judgment. The husband later moved to set aside the property division portion of the judgment on the ground that significant assets (including the wife's pension) had not been valued at the time he signed the agreement. The appellate court applied the substantial evidence standard to hold that the husband's unilateral mistake as to the value of community assets was material to his decision to agree to the division, and therefore was grounds for the trial court to set aside the judgment under California Family Code Section 2122. Cf. with *Kuehn v. Kuehn*, 85 Cal.App.4th 824, 102 Cal.Rptr.2d 743 (2d Dist. 2000).

In *Marriage of Heggie*, 99 Cal.App.4th 28, 120 Cal.Rptr.2d 707 (4th Dist. 2002) the wife sought to set aside a stipulated judgment, alleging that a postjudgment increase in the value of the stock awarded the husband resulted in an unfair imbalance of community property. The trial court granted the wife's set aside motion. The appellate court reversed after applying the substantial evidence standard. It wrote:

> "In the final analysis, all that supported the trial court's decision * * * was an imbalance in the division of community property attributable to a run-up in stock values subsequent to the filing of the judgment. Not only is such an imbalance not enough to support s motion to set aside a judgment under section 473 of the Code of Civil Procedure [citation omitted], but section 2123 of the Family Code is plain that if a set aside motion is supported only by an imbalance in the division of community property, the trial court *cannot* grant the motion." *Id.* at 29–30.

Marriage of Rosevear, 65 Cal.App.4th 673, 76 Cal.Rptr.2d 691 (1st Dist. 1998) is a case where a motion to set aside a final judgment of dissolution was denied. On appeal, applying the abuse of discretion standard, the appellate court upheld the trial court ruling. Facts cited were these: the property division was not inequitable; the support award was not inequitable; the claimant spouse was represented by counsel; and she had substantial financial documentation prior to the bench-bar settlement conference that resulted a stipulated final judgment.

Considered together, these cases cast light on the exceedingly fine distinction between a deal that is fair but arithmetically unequal, and a deal that is unfair due to coercion or nondisclosure. The former is not an appropriate basis for setting aside a final dissolution judgment. The latter is.

———

The mediation privilege may prevent the subsequent application of the substantial evidence standard due to the absence of an evidentiary record.

In *Kieturakis* the parties' negotiation process was confidential due to a mediation privilege. *Kieturakis* was decided after the Family Code was adopted. The case raises two important questions about mediation. The first is whether there is an exception to the mediation privilege that would allow a mediator or reporting party to release information about what has gone on in the mediation process. The second is whether California Family Code Section 721, and particularly the presumption of undue influence, applies or should apply in a mediation context in which the parties have reached an imbalanced agreement.

MARRIAGE OF KIETURAKIS

138 Cal.App.4th 56, 41 Cal.Rptr.3d 119 (1st Dist. 2006)

REARDON, ACTING P.J.

Anna Kieturakis appeals from the order denying her motion to set aside the parties' marital settlement agreement and the judgment incorporating that agreement. * * *

The marital settlement agreement was reached in a mediation, and Anna sought to undo the property division on grounds of fraud, duress, and lack of disclosure. Anna refused to waive the mediation privilege to allow disclosure of what transpired in the mediation, and thereby sought to prevent Maciej from defending himself against her allegations-charges on which the trial court found, based on the presumption of undue influence attaching to unequal marital transactions, Maciej bore the burden of proof. The trial court avoided that unacceptable result by admitting evidence from the mediation over Anna's objection, including evidence from the mediator over the mediator's objection. The mediation evidence, in large measure, defeated Anna's case. She contends on appeal that the evidence was wrongly admitted.

We hold, for a number of reasons, that Maciej should not have been made to bear the burden of proof on Anna's motion. In this regard, the presumption of undue influence in marital transactions must yield to the policies favoring mediation and finality of judgments. In view of this conclusion and in the particular circumstances of this case, any error in admitting evidence from the mediation was harmless.

Marital Settlement Agreement

A.   Statutory Background

(1)   The Mediation Privilege

Admission of evidence of what has transpired in a mediation is restricted by Evidence Code section 1115 et seq. Section 1119, subdivision (c) provides that all communications, negotiations, or settlement discussions among participants in the course of a mediation or a mediation consultation are to remain confidential. A "mediation consultation" means "a communication between a person and a mediator for the purpose of initiating, considering, or reconvening a mediation or retaining the mediator." (§ 1115, subd. (c).) Section 1119, subdivisions (a) and (b) direct that, except as otherwise permitted in these statutes, no "evidence of anything said or any admission made," or "writing . . . that is prepared," for "the purpose of, in the course of, or pursuant to, a mediation or a mediation consultation, is admissible or subject to discovery," and disclosure of such evidence or writings "shall not be compelled, in any arbitration, administrative adjudication, civil action, or other noncriminal proceeding in which, pursuant to law, testimony can be compelled to be given."

These prohibitions do not apply if all those conducting or participating in the mediation expressly agree to waive them (§ 1122, subd. (a)(1)), and limited exceptions to the prohibitions are afforded for, among other things, signed settlement agreements reached in mediation that are binding by their terms (§ 1123). In addition, to "prevent[ ] parties from using a mediation as a pretext to shield materials from disclosure" (27 Cal. Law Revision Com. Rep. (1997) p. 601), section 1120, subdivision (a) provides that "[e]vidence otherwise admissible or subject to discovery outside of a mediation or a mediation consultation shall not be or become inadmissible or protected from disclosure solely by reason of its introduction or use in a mediation or a mediation consultation."

Unless all parties to the mediation expressly agree otherwise, no "report, assessment, evaluation, recommendation, or finding of any kind by the mediator" concerning the mediation can be submitted to, or considered by, a court (§ 1121), and section 703.5 provides, with certain exceptions, that mediators are not "competent to testify, in any subsequent civil proceeding, as to any statement, conduct, decision, or ruling, occurring at or in conjunction with" the mediation.

(2)   Grounds for Setting Aside the Judgment

Family Code section 2122, as it formerly read, provided the following grounds for setting aside a judgment: "(a) Actual fraud where the defrauded party was kept in ignorance or in some other manner, other than his or her own lack of care or attention, was fraudulently prevented from fully participating in the proceeding. An action or motion based on fraud shall be brought within one year after the date on which the complaining party either did discover, or should have discovered, the fraud. [P] (b) Perjury. An action or motion based on perjury in the preliminary or final declaration of disclosure or in the current income and expense statement shall be brought within one year after the date on which the complaining party either did discover, or should have discovered, the perjury. [P] (c) Duress. An action or motion based upon duress shall be brought within two years after the date of entry of judgment. [P] (d) Mental incapacity. An action or motion based on mental incapacity shall be brought within two years after the date of entry of judgment. [P] (e) As to stipulated or uncontested judgments or that part of a judgment stipulated to by the parties, mistake, either mutual or unilateral, whether mistake of law or mistake of fact. An action or motion based on mistake shall be brought within one year after the date of entry of judgment."

B.   Evidence

The parties began their relationship in high school in Poland, were married in 1984, and had one child, Maximilian, born in 1991. Maciej is a surgeon and an inventor of surgical devices. While residing in Poland, Anna obtained the equivalent of a master's degree in English, was active in the Solidarity movement, and served as an administrative assistant to Lech Walesa. In the United States, Anna had been a waitress, travel agent, Polish language lecturer at Stanford, and partner in a business that translated books into Polish and published them in Poland.

Anna petitioned to dissolve the marriage in October 1998. The parties filed income and expense declarations on July 15, 1999, showing monthly income of $14,325 and expenses of $18,410 for Maciej, and monthly income of zero and expenses of $10,912 for Anna. A judgment of dissolution was filed on July 23, 1999, which incorporated a marital settlement agreement (MSA) executed by the parties on June 23, 1999, that was reached through mediation with mediator Anne Lober.

The MSA provided that Maciej would pay Anna $8,500 per month in family support, and that spousal support would terminate on June 1, 2007. The amount of support was made modifiable "upon good cause appearing," "upon a change of circumstances, and as provided by law." In the property division under the MSA, Maciej received among other things all interest in "the intellectual property described as [the] 'balloon dissector, a surgical device.'" The parties acknowledged in the MSA that the law "impose[s] a fiduciary duty on married persons regarding the accurate and complete disclosure of all assets, liabilities, and investment opportunities that were acquired, contracted or arose or may have arisen during the course of the marriage." The parties each affirmed service to the other of a declaration of disclosure and an income and expense declaration. The parties averred that they were "fully aware of the contents, legal effect and consequences of [the MSA] and its provisions," and that the agreement had been "entered into voluntarily, free from duress, fraud, undue influence, coercion or misrepresentation of any kind."

Nearly two years later, on June 26, 2001, Anna filed an order to show cause to set aside the judgment and MSA, and to modify the support she was receiving. * * *

C. Discussion

(1) Case Law on the Mediation Privilege

To put the issues before us in perspective, we begin with a review of some of the key cases that have dealt with the mediation privilege. * * *

The issue in * * * *Foxgate, supra,* 26 Cal.4th 1, 108 Cal.Rptr.2d 642, 25 P.3d 1117, was whether to recognize an exception to the mediation privilege for disclosure of conduct and communications concerning sanctionable behavior during a court-ordered mediation. The plaintiff moved for sanctions on the ground that the defendant had failed to participate in the mediation in good faith. Over the defendant's objection, the court considered declarations of the plaintiff's counsel and the mediator regarding conduct and statements of defense counsel in the mediation. The Court of Appeal recognized that confidentiality was essential to effective mediation and thus worthy of protection, but reasoned that "unless the parties and their lawyers participate in good faith in mediation, there is little to protect." (*Id.* at p. 9, 108 Cal.Rptr.2d 642, 25 P.3d 1117.) The Court of Appeal therefore carved out an exception to the mediation privilege for information "reasonably necessary to describe sanctionable conduct and place that conduct in context." (*Ibid.*) This exception permitted "reporting to the court not only that a party or attorney has disobeyed a court order governing the mediation process, but also that the mediator or reporting party believes that a party has done so intentionally with the apparent purpose of derailing the court-ordered mediation and the reasons for that belief." (*Id.* at p. 11, 108 Cal.Rptr.2d 642, 25 P.3d 1117.)

The Supreme Court concluded, contrary to the Court of Appeal, that there were "no exceptions" to the confidentiality of mediation communications (§ 1119), or the statutory limits on the content of mediator's reports (§ 1121). (*Foxgate, supra,* 26 Cal.4th at p. 4, 108 Cal.Rptr.2d 642, 25 P.3d 1117.) The court noted the strong legislative policy of promoting mediation and other alternatives to judicial dispute resolution, and found that the applicable statutes "unqualifiedly bar[ ] disclosure of communications made during mediation absent an express statutory exception." (*Id.* at p. 15, 108 Cal.Rptr.2d 642, 25 P.3d 1117, fn. omitted.) Sections 1119 and 1121 are "clear and unambiguous" (*id.* at p. 14, 108 Cal.Rptr.2d 642, 25 P.3d 1117), and while those sections allow a party to reveal noncommunicative conduct in a mediation (*id.* at p. 18, fn. 14, 108 Cal.Rptr.2d 642, 25 P.3d 1117), they preclude disclosure of mediation communications or a mediator's assessment of a party's conduct (*id.* at p. 17, 108 Cal.Rptr.2d 642, 25 P.3d 1117). The sections reflect a legislative decision that parties should be able to frankly express their views during mediation without fear of being sanctioned on the ground that those views evidenced bad faith failure to participate in the mediation. (*Ibid.*) Whether the benefits of mediation confidentiality were outweighed by a policy that might have better encouraged good faith participation in the mediation process was a matter for the Legislature to determine. (*Ibid.*) * * *

(2) *Presumption of Undue Influence*

With that background, we turn to Maciej's argument that he was erroneously required to bear the burden of proof in defending the MSA and the judgment. The court determined that Maciej had the burden of dispelling a presumption that he exercised undue influence in procuring the agreement.

Family Code section 721, subdivision (b) provides in part that "in transactions between themselves, a husband and wife are subject to the general rules governing fiduciary relationships which control the actions of persons occupying confidential relations with each other. This confidential relationship imposes a duty of the highest good faith and fair dealing on each spouse, and neither shall take any unfair advantage of the other." In view of this fiduciary relationship, "[w]hen an interspousal transaction advantages one spouse, '[t]he law, from considerations of public policy, presumes such transactions to have been induced by undue influence.'" (*In re Marriage of Haines* (1995) 33 Cal.App.4th 277, 293, 39 Cal.Rptr.2d 673.) "Generally, a fiduciary obtains an advantage if his position is improved, he obtains a favorable opportunity, or he otherwise gains, benefits, or profits." (*In re Marriage of Lange* (2002) 102 Cal.App.4th 360, 364, 125 Cal.Rptr.2d 379.) The spouse advantaged by the transaction has the burden of dispelling the presumption of undue influence. (*In re Marriage of Haines, supra,* 33 Cal.App.4th at p. 297, 39 Cal.Rptr.2d 673.) The presumption can be dispelled by evidence that the disadvantaged spouse entered into the transaction "freely and voluntarily . . . with a full knowledge of all the facts and with a complete understanding of the effect of the [transaction]." (*In re Marriage of Mathews* (2005) 133 Cal.App.4th 624, 630, 35 Cal.Rptr.3d 1.)

Our Supreme Court indicated in *In re Marriage of Bonds* (2000) 24 Cal.4th 1, 27, 99 Cal.Rptr.2d 252, 5 P.3d 815, that the presumption of undue influence applies to marital settlement agreements. At issue in that case was the enforceability of a premarital agreement, and an argument that such agreements are to be enforced under the standards applicable to marital settlement agreements. The court explained that this argument was untenable in part because the presumption of undue influence that arises with respect to unequal agreements between spouses does not attach to premarital agreements, however one-sided. (*Ibid.*) In thus distinguishing between unequal premarital agreements and unequal marital settlement agreements, the court confirmed that the presumption *would* attach to the latter, a conclusion consistent with applicable statutes. (Fam.Code, §§ 1100, subd. (e), 2102, subds. (a), (b) [fiduciary duties continue until assets are divided and distributed].)

Here, there is no dispute that the MSA favored Maciej. We nevertheless hold, for three independently sufficient reasons, that the presumption of undue influence cannot properly be applied to the agreement and judgment in this case.

First, we conclude that the presumption of undue influence cannot be applied to marital settlement agreements reached through mediation. "Voluntary participation and self-determination are fundamental principles of mediation. . . ." (Advisory Com. com. to Cal. Rules of Court, rule 1620.3; see also, e.g., *Travelers Casualty & Surety Co. v. Superior Court* (2005) 126 Cal.App.4th 1131, 1139, 24 Cal.Rptr.3d 751 [concept of self-determination is critical to mediation process]; *Saeta v. Superior Court* (2004) 117 Cal.App.4th 261, 270, 11 Cal.Rptr.3d 610 [same].) It can thus be expected that most mediators would, as Lober said at the hearing on Anna's motion, consider it their duty to attempt to determine whether the parties are "acting under their own free will" in the mediation. "[P]ower imbalance[s] between spouses" are a recognized concern when family matters are mediated. (Knight et al., Cal. Practice Guide: Alternative Dispute Resolution (The Rutter Group 2004) P 3:516, p. 3–81 (rev. #1 1996) [spouse who is overbearing or dominates conversation may have advantage].) Therefore, "[d]ivorce mediators generally work to balance the negotiating power between the parties. This tends to produce agreements that are more fair and voluntary, rather than coerced." (Roth et al., The Alternative Dispute Resolution Practice Guide (2005) § 31:5, p. 31–5.) Thus, while mediation is no guarantee against the exercise of undue influence, it should help to minimize unfairness in the process by which a marital settlement agreement is reached.

Even more importantly, to apply the presumption of undue influence to mediated marital settlements would severely undermine the practice of mediating such agreements. Application of the presumption would turn the shield of mediation confidentiality into a sword by which any unequal agreement could be invalidated. We do not believe that the Legislature could have intended that result when it provided for spousal fiduciary duties on the one hand and for mediation confidentiality on the other.

It is apparent from our review of the statutes and cases that the mediation privilege is broadly framed and strictly construed. Mediation communications are generally shielded from disclosure unless all participants expressly agree otherwise. (§§ 1119, 1121, 1122.) This " 'supermajority' requirement . . . effectively creates a 'super privilege'— impenetrable by public policies favoring disclosure. . . ." (Scallen, *Relational and Informational Privileges and the Case of the Mysterious Mediation Privilege* (2004) 38 Loyola L.A. L.Rev. 537, 588.) There is no good cause exception to the privilege *Rojas v. Superior Court, supra,* 33 Cal.4th at pp. 423–424, 15 Cal.Rptr.3d 643, 93 P.3d 260), and no exception to the privilege can be implied (*Eisendrath, supra,* 109 Cal.App.4th at pp. 362– 363, 134 Cal.Rptr.2d 716). Thus, in the case of a mediated marital settlement agreement to which the presumption of undue influence attached, the disadvantaged party could claim, for example, to have acted under duress, refuse to waive the privilege, and thereby prevent the other party from introducing the evidence required to carry the burden of proving that no duress occurred. (See Comment, *The Mediation Privilege and Its Limits* (2000) 5 Harv. Negot. L.Rev. 383, 395 [observing that "an iron-clad confidentiality rule could encourage unfounded claims of duress"].) All unequal mediated agreements would, in effect, be conclusively presumed to be invalid.

This result would, in our view, substantially diminish the incentive to mediate marital property settlements. While there are a number of reasons why parties may opt for mediation (see Knight et al., Cal. Practice Guide: Alternative Dispute Resolution, *supra,* P 3:13 et seq., p. 3–5 et seq. (rev. #1 2004) [listing numerous advantages of mediation over litigation, including speed, flexibility, and cost savings]), such parties, like anyone entering into negotiations (CJER Bench Handbook: Judges Guide to ADR (CJER 2004) § 4.5, p. 28 [mediation has been characterized as "assisted negotiation"]), can be expected to pursue their best interests and strive for an advantageous bargain. If, by virtue of the mediation privilege and the presumption of undue influence, any such favorable bargain could, as we have posited, be set aside at the option of the disappointed party, the effectiveness of mediation as a method of settling marital property disputes would be greatly impaired. Many mediated settlements might be jeopardized because relatively few of them, upon close scrutiny, would likely be found to have been perfectly equal.

To countenance that result would contravene the strong legislative and judicial policies favoring mediation and settlement. (Code Civ. Proc., § 1775, subd. (c) [mediation may help reduce courts' caseload; public interest dictates that mediation "be encouraged and used where appropriate by the courts"]; Bus. & Prof.Code, § 465, subd. (b) [greater use of mediation should be encouraged]; *Rojas v. Superior Court, supra,* 33 Cal.4th at p. 415, 15 Cal.Rptr.3d 643, 93 P.3d 260 [policy favoring mediation]; *Stewart v. Preston Pipeline Inc., supra,* 134 Cal.App.4th at p. 1583, 36 Cal.Rptr.3d 901 [policies favoring mediation and settlement]; *In re Marriage of Friedman* (2002) 100 Cal.App.4th 65, 72, 122 Cal.Rptr.2d 412 [it is "well settled that property settlement agreements occupy a favored position in California"].) The damage to those policies would be especially severe if marital property mediations were impaired, because mediation is recognized as a particularly appropriate means of dispute resolution in that context. (See Knight et al., Cal. Practice Guide: Alternative Dispute Resolution, *supra,* P 3:511, p. 3–79 (rev. #1 2004) [mediation is especially appropriate for domestic relations matters], P 3:40, p. 3–10 (rev. #1 2001) [mediation has become widely used in marital and family disputes].)

The presumption of undue influence must therefore yield when a marital settlement agreement is achieved through mediation. We recognize that this conclusion places parties defending mediated marital settlements at an advantage. Those parties can refuse to waive the privilege and thereby prevent their settlements from effectively being challenged. That result can be criticized. (See Deason, *Enforcing Mediated Settlement Agreements: Contract Law Collides With Confidentiality* (2001) 35 U.C. Davis L.Rev. 33, 102 [opining that, "[g]iven the importance of both confidentiality and full consent to mediated settlements, an inflexible rule in favor of ensuring one but not the other of these values is inappropriate"].) However, if there is a price to be paid in fairness to preserve mediation confidentiality, the cases have required that it be paid by parties challenging, not defending, what transpired in the mediation. (See *Eisendrath, supra,* 109 Cal.App.4th at p. 365, 134 Cal.Rptr.2d 716 [discussing *Foxgate, supra,* 26 Cal.4th at p. 17, 108 Cal.Rptr.2d 642, 25 P.3d 1117, and acknowledging "substantial measure of control" party defending mediated support agreement would have over other party's ability to present evidence in support of motion to correct agreement].) In choosing between a rule that may allow some unfair agreements to stand and a rule that jeopardizes all unequal agreements, "[w]e must not lose sight of the fact that 'California has a strong policy encouraging settlements' [citation]. . . ." (*Stewart v. Preston Pipeline Inc., supra,* 134 Cal.App.4th at p. 1583, 36 Cal.Rptr.3d 901.) Given that strong policy, the rule that promotes certainty and finality must govern.

Second, the presumption of undue influence should not apply in a case like this where the influence is alleged with respect to a judgment that has long been final. The presumption is asserted here in a motion under Family Code section 2122, part of the "Relief from Judgment" chapter of the Family Code. (*In re Marriage of Heggie* (2002) 99 Cal.App.4th 28, 32, 120 Cal.Rptr.2d 707 [referring to Fam. Code, §§ 2120–2129].) Within six months after a marital dissolution judgment is taken, relief from the judgment can be sought under Family Code section 2122 or Code of Civil Procedure section 473. (*In re Marriage of Heggie, supra,* 99 Cal.App.4th at p. 32, 120 Cal.Rptr.2d 707.) Family Code section 2122 specifies "the exclusive grounds and time limits for an action or motion to set aside a marital dissolution judgment" (*In re Marriage of Rosevear* (1998) 65 Cal.App.4th 673, 684, 76 Cal.Rptr.2d 691), after the six-month deadline under Code of Civil Procedure section 473 has passed (Fam. Code, § 2121, subd. (a)).

As we noted at the outset, under former Family Code section 2122 the potential grounds for setting aside the judgment in this case were fraud, perjury, duress, mental incapacity, and mistake. We will assume for purposes of this opinion that the concept of "undue influence" in spousal transactions is broad enough to subsume all of the grounds for relief Anna advanced under Family Code section 2122. Anna alleged that Maciej exerted great pressure on her to reach a settlement, and prevented her from obtaining counsel or otherwise protecting her interests, conduct characterized as both "duress" and "undue influence" in *In re Marriage of Baltins* (1989) 212 Cal.App.3d 66, 84–85, 260 Cal.Rptr. 403. Anna alleged that Maciej misrepresented his rights to future royalty payments and concealed payments he was receiving. Such breaches of the duty of disclosure Maciej owed Anna by virtue of their fiduciary relationship would constitute undue influence (see *In re Marriage of Bonds, supra,* 24 Cal.4th at p. 27, 99 Cal.Rptr.2d 252, 5 P.3d 815), and provide grounds for setting aside the judgment under Family Code section 2122 for fraud, perjury, and mistake (see *Brewer v. Federici* (2001) 93 Cal.App.4th 1334, 1345, 113 Cal.Rptr.2d 849). Whether the presumption of undue influence would apply to Anna's claims to have been mistaken about her community property rights presents a closer question, but the presumption could at least arguably extend to those claims as well. (See *In re Marriage of Mathews, supra,* 133 Cal.App.4th at p. 630, 35 Cal.Rptr.3d 1 [presumption is dispelled if, among other things, disadvantaged spouse had full knowledge of facts and completely understood effect of transaction]; *In re Marriage of Friedman, supra,* 100 Cal.App.4th at p. 72, 122 Cal.Rptr.2d 412 [evidence showed that wife understood scope and purpose of postnuptial agreement; husband carried burden of showing that wife did not enter into postnuptial agreement through mistake].)

Nevertheless, there is no precedent for applying the presumption in the context of a Family Code section 2122 motion, and those seeking to set aside judgments have always borne the burden of proof. Prior to the enactment of Family Code section 2122 and its predecessor statute, marital dissolution judgments could be set aside in equity, after expiration of the Code of Civil Procedure section 473 deadline, on the grounds of extrinsic fraud or mistake. (See *In re Marriage of Varner* (1997) 55 Cal.App.4th 128, 136, 139–140, 63 Cal.Rptr.2d 894). Where relief from a judgment is sought on Code of Civil Procedure section 473 or equitable grounds, the moving party bears the burden of proof. (See, e.g., *Schwab v. Southern California Gas Co.* (2004) 114 Cal.App.4th 1308, 1319, 8 Cal.Rptr.3d 627 [moving party bears burden under Code Civ. Proc., § 473]; *Aheroni v. Maxwell* (1988) 205 Cal.App.3d 284, 291, 252 Cal.Rptr. 369 [party seeking equitable relief from judgment must make stronger showing than is required under Code Civ. Proc., § 473]; see also *Estudillo v. Security Loan etc. Co.* (1906) 149 Cal. 556, 564, 87 P. 19 [burden of proof "rests upon no one more heavily" than one alleging that judgment was procured by fraud].) We take it that the burden of proof would rest where it has always rested, with the moving party, when a Family Code section 2122 challenge is made against a judgment entered after trial. In that event, there would be no "transaction" that could give rise to a burden-shifting presumption of undue influence. (See *In re Marriage of Mathews, supra,* 133 Cal.App.4th at p. 629, 35 Cal.Rptr.3d 1 [presumption applies if "(1) there exists an interspousal transaction; and (2) one spouse has obtained an advantage over the other"].) The question of burden shifting arises only if the judgment is reached via a settlement.

We have found no case other than our decision in *In re Marriage of Rosevear, supra,* 65 Cal.App.4th 673, 76 Cal.Rptr.2d 691, that has addressed the burden of proof under Family Code section 2122. There, a motion to set aside a stipulated judgment was made on the grounds of mistake and duress. In addressing the mistake allegation, we wrote: "Under [Family Code] section 2123, a trial court may not set aside a dissolution judgment on the *sole* grounds the judgment is inequitable or the support ordered is inadequate. As discussed, a party seeking to set aside a dissolution judgment must first establish the existence of at least one of the five exclusive grounds for relief enumerated in [Family Code] section 2122 (fraud, perjury, duress, mental incapacity, or mistake), and additionally that the presence of this element 'materially affected the original outcome' in such a way 'that the moving party would materially benefit from the granting of the relief,' as required by section 2121, subdivision (b). In other words, the moving party must establish *both* the presence of at least one of the five factors listed in section 2122, and that this resulted in material disadvantage to the moving party." (*Id.* at p. 685, fn. 11, 76 Cal.Rptr.2d 691.) The thrust of this discussion is that the moving party would bear the burden of proving grounds for relief under Family Code section 2122, even if that party were disadvantaged by a marital settlement, i.e., in a situation where a presumption of undue influence would arise. *Rosevear,* however, is inconclusive on the issue because the agreement there was an equitable one between the parties, and the case did not address the undue influence presumption. (*Ginns v. Savage* (1964) 61 Cal.2d 520, 524, fn. 2, 39 Cal.Rptr. 377, 393 P.2d 689 [opinions are not authority for propositions they do not consider].)

It is thus evidently a question of first impression whether Maciej was properly required to bear the burden of proof on Anna's Family Code section 2122 motion. Since marital settlement agreements are routinely incorporated into judgments, it can be argued that incorporating such an agreement into a judgment should not automatically dispel the presumption of undue influence. On the other hand, after some passage of time, the presumption bumps up against the policy favoring finality of judgments. As the court stated in *In re Marriage of Stevenot* (1984) 154 Cal.App.3d 1051, 1071, 202 Cal.Rptr. 116, "[m]arital settlement agreements, once incorporated into a judgment, are no longer mere contracts. . . . [T]hey become a hybrid, more like a judgment than a contract. . . ." "Once relief is no longer available under section 473, the public policy in favor of finality of judgments predominates, and the power to set aside valid final judgments and marital settlement agreements incorporated therein should be exercised only when exceptional circumstances require that the consequences of res judicata be denied. Thus, during the period when relief under section 473 is available, there is a strong public policy in favor of granting relief and allowing the requesting party his or her day in court. Beyond this period there is a strong public policy in favor of the finality of judgments and only in exceptional circumstances should relief be granted." (*Ibid.*)

While *Stevenot* was decided before Family Code section 2122 was enacted, at a time when spouses were not considered to owe each other fiduciary duties and were deemed to deal at arms' length after separating or petitioning for dissolution (*In re Marriage of Stevenot, supra,* 154 Cal.App.3d at p. 1071, 202 Cal.Rptr. 116), the policy favoring the finality of judgments has not changed. That policy militates strongly in favor of keeping the burden of proof under Family Code section 2122 with the moving party, at least where, as here, relief is sought after the time to act under Code of Civil Procedure section 473 has expired. (*Ibid.*) Family Code section 2120 et seq., reflect a balancing of the "public policy of assuring finality of judgments" and "the public interest in ensuring proper division of marital property." (Fam.Code, § 2120, subd. (c).) Nothing in these statutes suggests any intent to alter the burden of proof that has long been placed on parties challenging marital dissolution judgments. Accordingly, we conclude that a party seeking relief from a judgment that incorporates an unequal marital settlement agreement must bear the burden of proof under Family Code section 2122, at least where the judgment, as in this case, is at least six months old.

Third, the presumption of undue influence should not attach in this case because the parties acknowledged in the MSA that no undue influence was exercised. In the MSA, the parties stated that they were cognizant of the fiduciary duties they owed each other in their financial affairs, had exchanged the requisite disclosures, and were "fully aware of the contents, legal effect and consequences of this agreement and its provisions." They affirmed that they had entered into the MSA "voluntarily, free from duress, fraud, undue influence, coercion or misrepresentation of any kind." While such avowals might themselves be the product of undue influence, we think that they should count for something, at least where, as here, the parties' capacity is not in question.

" 'A presumption is an assumption of fact that the law requires to be made from another fact or group of facts found or otherwise established in the action.' (§ 600, subd. (a).) The trier of fact is required to assume the existence of the presumed fact 'unless and until evidence is introduced which would support a finding of its nonexistence, in which case the trier of fact shall determine the existence or nonexistence of the presumed fact from the evidence and without regard to the presumption.' (§ 604.)" (*In re Marriage of Haines, supra,* 33 Cal.App.4th at pp. 296–297, 39 Cal.Rptr.2d 673.) The MSA was by its terms intended to be a complete and binding settlement of all custody, support, and property issues, and there is no dispute that the agreement itself was admissible. (§ 1123, subd. (b) [written settlement achieved in mediation is admissible if it "provides that it is enforceable or binding or words to that effect"].) The MSA strongly "support[ed] a finding of [the] nonexistence" of the presumed undue influence and thereby negated that presumption. (§ 604.) That did not mean Anna could not show that undue influence was exerted, only that she had the burden of proof in so doing.

(3) Evidence From the Mediation

We now turn to Anna's argument that evidence from the mediation was wrongly admitted on her motion to set aside the MSA and judgment. We conclude that any such error was harmless under the circumstances here. * * *

Conclusion

The orders on the motion to set aside the marital settlement agreement, and on the motion for modification of support and for attorney fees, are affirmed. The parties will bear their own costs on appeal.

SEPULVEDA and RIVERA, JJ., concur.

NOTE

Mediation is a form of assisted negotiation in which the parties engage a neutral third party (commonly but not necessarily a professional mediator) to help them in their process of reaching a marital settlement agreement. A mediator is not authorized to impose a decision on the parties. Rather, a mediator strives to help the parties reach a consensus on marriage settlement issues. Despite any practical difficulties in obtaining postjudgment relief to a mediated marriage settlement agreement, mediation can be less expensive and time consuming than adversarial divorce litigation. It is also less burdensome to the judicial system than litigation. For these and other reasons, there is a statutory protection for the confidentiality of mediation proceedings.

For more on the mediation privilege, see generally, Laura A. Miles, Absolute Mediation Privilege: Promoting or Destroying Mediation by Rewarding Sharp Practice and Driving Away Smart Lawyers, 25 WHITTIER L. REV. 617 (2004).

C. TIMELY FILING

The next case arose against the backdrop of a story about an attorney, his contingency fee agreement, the valuation of his contingency fee, his law firm's successful suit against Enron, and his own marital dissolution. Focusing on the dissolution, the court of appeals instructs on how the California Family Code Section 2122 statute of limitations works.

MARRIAGE OF GEORGIOU & LESLIE

218 Cal.App.4th 561, 160 Cal.Rptr.3d 254 (4th Dist. 2013)

Opinion

McCONNELL, P.J.

More than three years after entry of judgment, Maria Leslie filed an action under Family Code section 1101, alleging her former husband, Byron Georgiou, breached his fiduciary duty to her during the dissolution proceedings by not disclosing the true value of a community asset divided in the marital settlement agreement (MSA), his prospective referral fee in federal class action securities litigation against Enron Corporation (Enron). The family court granted Georgiou's motion for summary adjudication, determining section 1101 does not authorize a postjudgment action, and alternatively, the action was untimely under the statute's three-year statute of limitations (§ 1011, subd. (d)(1)). Leslie challenges the order, contending both rulings are incorrect.

We conclude section 1101 does not authorize Leslie's action, and thus we are not required to address the alternative ruling. Because the prospective referral fee was not concealed, but rather the parties litigated the issue and the judgment fully adjudicated the asset, Leslie's recourse was an action to set aside the judgment, or a portion thereof, within the one-year limitations period specified in the relevant portion of section 2122, subdivision (f). Because her action was untimely, the court lacked jurisdiction over the matter. We affirm the order.

FACTUAL AND PROCEDURAL BACKGROUND

Leslie and Georgiou married in 1985 and separated in 2003. Georgiou filed for dissolution that year, and a bifurcated judgment terminated the marital status in 2005.

Georgiou is an attorney, and in 2000 he entered into an "of counsel" relationship with Milberg Weiss Bershad Hynes & Lerach LLP (Milberg Weiss), that entitled him to a referral fee of 10 percent in class action litigation in which Georgiou secured the plaintiff and the firm was designated lead counsel.

In 2002 Milberg Weiss entered into a contingency fee agreement with the Regents of the University of California (the Regents), which was ultimately designated the lead plaintiff in federal class action securities litigation against Enron. On a sliding scale, the agreement authorized attorney fees of between 8 and 10 percent of the recovery.

In February 2007 Leslie and Georgiou entered into an MSA. Before signing it, Leslie knew of Georgiou's referral fee agreement with Milberg Weiss that the firm had thus far recovered approximately $7.2 billion in settlement funds, the largest recovery to date in a class action, and the firm would be submitting a request for attorney fees in federal district court under its fee agreement with the Regents. It is undisputed that Georgiou did not give Leslie a copy of the fee agreement.

Leslie deposed Darren J. Robbins, a Milberg Weiss partner designated most knowledgeable about Georgiou's relationship with the firm. Her attorney questioned Robbins on whether the firm had a fee agreement with the Regents, but he did not ask Robbins what percentage of fees the Regents had agreed to pay the firm, nor did he ask for a copy of the agreement. In any event, Robbins testified the federal district court must approve a fee award based on a variety of factors, and it is not bound by a fee agreement.

Robbins also testified Georgiou was entitled to a referral fee from Milberg Weiss in the Enron litigation, but there was a dispute as to the amount of the fee. Robbins said, "I would not imagine any scenario under which [Georgiou] would receive less than three percent." Robbins also said the firm hoped to obtain attorney fees substantially exceeding the largest securities class action fee award to date of $330 million, as that award was based on a much smaller recovery than that achieved in the Enron litigation. Robbins estimated Milberg Weiss would obtain fees by the end of 2008.

In a settlement conference brief, Leslie gleaned that Georgiou's referral fee may be between $9 and $33 million, presumably based on a potential fee award to Milberg Weiss of $330 million. She acknowledged, however, that the firm intended to seek "far more than $330 million," and that Georgiou intended to "vigorously argue" he was entitled to a full 10 percent referral fee.

The MSA divided the prospective referral fee unequally. Leslie agreed to accept 10 percent of the fee, in exchange for approximately $7 million in other assets and debt relief. She received the family home, even though it was Georgiou's separate property, eight townhomes that produced net monthly income, a Roth IRA and retirement accounts. He received 90 percent of his referral fee, life insurance policies, loan receivables, business interests, and substantial credit card and other debt. According to Georgiou, Leslie "was taking everything that was certain."

The MSA was incorporated in a judgment of dissolution entered on December 12, 2007. About a month later, Milberg Weiss submitted its fee application to the federal district court in the Enron case, requesting 9.52 percent of the ultimate recovery of approximately $7.2 billion, pursuant to the terms of its fee agreement with the Regents. In September 2008 the federal district court issued a lengthy order granting the request as reasonable and awarding Milberg Weiss $688 million in fees.

Milberg Weiss then negotiated a 9 percent referral fee with Georgiou. In September 2008 Georgiou paid Leslie $4 million for her 10 percent share of the fee, which caused her to realize his fee exceeded the top range of $33 million she anticipated when she entered into the MSA. In November 2009 she learned she was entitled to an additional $1.56 million.

Leslie retained a new attorney, and in November 2009 she filed a motion under section 2122, subdivision (d), to set aside the judgment of dissolution based on her mental incapacity. A motion under this provision must be filed within two years after the date of entry of judgment. (*Ibid.*) She argued her former attorney insisted that she enter into the MSA so he could get paid, and implied she was under duress because she had not been taking psychotropic medications as prescribed by her physicians. In September 2010 after retaining yet another attorney, Leslie dismissed the motion.

On December 13, 2010, however, Leslie filed this action under section 1101 for Georgiou's breach of his fiduciary duty of disclosure. The gist of the action was that Georgiou deceived her into believing his potential referral fee would be between $9 and $33 million, by not providing her with a copy of the fee agreement between Milberg Weiss and the Regents and inventing or exaggerating a dispute with the firm over the amount of his referral fee. She argued that had she known the terms of the fee agreement, she could have calculated that Milberg Weiss stood to obtain a $688 fee award. Leslie sought either 50 percent or 100 percent of the referral fee pursuant to section 1101, subdivisions (g) and (h).

Georgiou moved for summary adjudication, arguing her action was untimely because she did not file it within three years from the date she had "actual knowledge that the transaction or event for which the remedy is being sought occurred." (§ 1101, subd. (d)(1).) Leslie argued her action did not accrue until September 2008 when she learned the amount of Georgiou's referral fee and realized he had understated his potential fee in breach of his fiduciary duty.

The court determined, sua sponte, that relief for breach of fiduciary duty under section 1101 "is not legally available in a post-marital dissolution judgment action." The court interpreted section 1101 to authorize an action in only three instances: (1) during an intact marriage; (2) in conjunction with a dissolution proceeding; or (3) after the death of a spouse.

The court also found that section 2122, subdivision (e), under which a judgment may be set aside for mistake, provided Leslie's sole recourse, but such an action was not viable because the statute's one-year limitations period was long expired. Alternatively, the court determined that even if section 1101 applied, her action was barred by the statute's three-year limitations period since she knew when she signed the MSA that she did not have a copy of Milberg Weiss's fee agreement with the Regents.

DISCUSSION

I

Standard of Review

Leslie contends the court erred by granting summary adjudication. She asserts the court misinterpreted section 1101 to authorize an independent action for breach of fiduciary duty only in an intact marriage.

A defendant meets his or her burden in a summary adjudication motion "by negating an essential element of the plaintiff's case, or by establishing a complete defense, or by demonstrating the absence of evidence to support the plaintiff's case." (*Rubenstein v. Rubenstein* (2000) 81 Cal.App.4th 1131, 1142, 97 Cal.Rptr.2d 707; see Code Civ. Proc., § 437c, subd. (f)(1) [party may move for summary adjudication as to "one or more affirmative defenses"].) "We review questions of law as well as orders granting summary adjudication under the de novo standard of review." (*Lafferty v. Wells Fargo Bank* (2013) 213 Cal.App.4th 545, 556, 153 Cal.Rptr.3d 240.) Likewise, the interpretation of a statute presents a legal question we review independently. (*Ibid.*)

II

Applicable Law / Analysis

A

Fiduciary Duties During Dissolution Proceedings

Spouses have fiduciary duties to each other as to the management and control of community property. §§ 721, subd. (b), 1100, subd. (e). "[I]n transactions between themselves, a husband and wife are subject to the general rules governing fiduciary relationships which control the actions of persons occupying confidential relations with each other. This confidential relationship imposes a duty of the highest good faith and fair dealing on each spouse, and neither shall take any unfair advantage of the other." § 721, subd. (b).

The fiduciary duties expressly extend throughout dissolution proceedings. §§ 2100, subd. (c), 2102–2107. "From the date of separation to the date of the distribution of the community or quasi-community asset or liability in question, each party is subject to the standards provided in Section 721, as to all activities that affect the assets and liabilities of the other party. . . ." § 2102, subd. (a). "[A] full and accurate disclosure of all [the parties'] assets and liabilities . . . must be made in the early stages of a proceeding for dissolution of marriage. . . ." § 2100, subd. (c). "It reasonably follows that a spouse who is in a superior position to obtain records or information from which an asset can be valued and can reasonably do so must acquire and disclose such information to the other spouse." (*Brewer v. Federici* (2001) 93 Cal.App.4th 1334, 1348, 113 Cal.Rptr.2d 849.)

Further, "each party has a continuing duty to immediately, fully, and accurately update and augment that disclosure to the extent there have been any material changes. . . ." § 2100, subd. (c). The final declaration of disclosure shall include "[a]ll material facts and information regarding the valuation of all assets that are contended to be community property." § 2105, subd. (b)(2). "The formulation of a marital settlement agreement is not an ordinary business transaction, resulting from an arm's-length negotiation between adversaries. Rather, it is the result of negotiations between fiduciaries required to openly share information." (*Brewer v. Federici, supra,* 93 Cal.App.4th at p. 1344, [113 Cal.Rptr.2d 849].)

B

Postjudgment Remedies for Breach of Fiduciary Duty

1

There are, of course, postjudgment remedies for breach of the fiduciary duty of full disclosure during dissolution proceedings. Within the first six months after entry of judgment, the court has discretion to set aside a judgment under Code of Civil Procedure section 473, subdivision (b) on the grounds of "mistake, inadvertence, surprise, or excusable neglect." (See *In re Marriage of Varner* (1997) 55 Cal.App.4th 128, 138, 63 Cal.Rptr.2d 894.) Historically, "[c]ourts have also been held to have inherent power to set aside a judgment, even after the six-month period of Code of Civil Procedure section 473 has passed, if the parties have been deprived of the opportunity to litigate their claim." (*Id.* at p. 139, 63 Cal.Rptr.2d 894.)

Further, "[i]n 1993, a chapter entitled Relief From Judgment was added to the Family Code. (§§ 2120–2129, added by Stats.1993, ch. 219, § 108, pp. 1615–1617.) In adopting this chapter, the Legislature found '[t]he law governing the circumstances under which a judgment can be set aside, after the time for relief under Section 473 of the Code of Civil Procedure has passed, has been the subject of considerable confusion which has led to increased litigation and unpredictable and inconsistent decisions at the trial and appellate levels.' (§ 2120, subd. (d).)" (*Rubenstein v. Rubenstein, supra,* 81 Cal.App.4th at p. 1143, 97 Cal.Rptr.2d 707.)

Section 2120, subdivision (a), acknowledges that California's strong public policy of ensuring the fair division of community property can only be implemented with full disclosure of community property. Section 2120 also provides: "(b) It occasionally happens that the division of property . . . , whether made as a result of agreement or trial, is inequitable when made due to the nondisclosure or other misconduct of one of the parties. [¶] (c) The public policy of *assuring finality of judgments* must be balanced against the public interest in *ensuring proper division of marital property,* . . . and in deterring misconduct." (Italics added.) Section 2120 et seq. apply to dissolution judgments adjudicating support or division of property entered on or after January 1, 1993, and as to such judgments all prior law on "equitable" set-aside relief is preempted. (See §§ 2121, subd. (a).)

"Section 2122 sets out the *exclusive grounds and time limits* for an action or motion to set aside a marital dissolution judgment." (*In re Marriage of Rosevear* (1998) 65 Cal.App.4th 673, 684, 76 Cal.Rptr.2d 691, italics added.) "Unlike traditional equitable set-aside law where 'laches' is the only time limit on relief . . . , [section] 2120 et seq. accommodates the public policy interest in putting an end to litigation and ensuring the 'finality' of family law judgments by setting *absolute deadlines* on obtaining a post-[judgment] set-aside. Once the statutorily-prescribed period expires ([§ 2122]), set-aside relief is *not available* and the judgment is effectively *final for all purposes*."

Under section 2122, there are six grounds to set aside a judgment, or portion thereof, including actual fraud, perjury, duress, mental incapacity, mistake, and the failure to fully disclose the value of assets under section 2100 et seq. (§ 2122, subds.(a)(f).) "Upon vacating the judgment, in whole or in part, a trial court is empowered to make an unequal distribution of the concealed assets, in the interests of justice. (§ 2126.)" *(Rubenstein v. Rubenstein, supra,* 81 Cal.App.4th at p. 1146, 97 Cal.Rptr.2d 707.)

Subdivision (e) of section 2122 states that "[a]s to stipulated or uncontested judgments or that part of a judgment stipulated to by the parties," a set aside motion may be based on "mistake, either mutual or unilateral, whether mistake of law or mistake of fact." Here, the family court determined Leslie's action was controlled by subdivision (e) of section 2122, based on opinions holding that a judgment of dissolution may be set aside under that provision for the breach of the fiduciary duty of full disclosure. (*In re Marriage of Varner, supra,* 55 Cal.App.4th at pp. 143–144, 63 Cal.Rptr.2d 894; *Brewer,* supra, 93 Cal.App.4th 1334, 1344, 113 Cal.Rptr.2d 849.) These opinions, however, were based on a previous iteration of section 2122. In 2001, the Legislature amended section 2122 to specify as a ground for relief the "[f]ailure to comply with the disclosure requirements of Chapter 9 (commencing with Section 2100)." (§ 2122, subd. (f).)

Leslie, however, waited too long to pursue relief under section 2122. An action based on the failure to disclose "shall be brought within one year after the date on which the complaining party either discovered, or should have discovered, the failure to comply." (§ 2122, subd. (f).) Likewise, a set-aside action for actual fraud is subject to a limitations period of one year from the date of actual or implied discovery. (§ 2122, subd. (a).) Leslie discovered in September 2008 that Georgiou obtained a referral fee substantially higher than she alleges he suggested was possible and she did not file her action until December 2010.

2

With the applicable section 2122 limitations period expired, Leslie relied on section 1101. Subdivision (a) of section 1101 provides: "A spouse has a claim against the other spouse for any breach of the fiduciary duty that results in impairment to the claimant spouse's present undivided one-half interest in the community estate, including, but not limited to, a single transaction or a pattern or series of transactions, which transaction or transactions have caused or will cause a detrimental impact to the claimant spouse's undivided one-half interest in the community estate."

Section 1101, subdivision (d)(1), provides that a claim for breach of fiduciary duty "shall be commenced within three years of the date a petitioning spouse had actual knowledge that the transaction or event for which the remedy is being sought occurred." Section 1101, subdivision (d)(2), provides that "[a]n action may be commenced under this section upon the death of a spouse or in conjunction with an action for legal separation, dissolution of marriage, or nullity without regard to the time limitations set forth in paragraph (1)." Leslie claimed this is an independent action subject to the three-year limitations period, rather than an action brought in conjunction with the dissolution proceeding.

The family court determined section 1101 authorizes an independent action only during an intact marriage. Subdivision (f) of section 1101 provides: "Any action may be brought under this section *without filing an action for dissolution of marriage,* legal separation, or nullity, or may be brought in conjunction with the action or upon the death of a spouse." (Italics added.) While California allows interspousal actions, section 1101 does not expressly preclude postjudgment actions. As a commentator observes, "spouses are not apt to sue each other while happily married." (Hogoboom, *supra,* ¶ 8:638, p. 8–158.10. (rev. #1, 2012.))

The court also noted section 1101 is part of division 4, part 4 of the Family Code, entitled "Management and Control of Marital Property," and the "language throughout Division 4 uses the terms 'spouse,' 'husband and wife' and 'married person.'" (See § 700 et seq.) In contrast, section 2122 appears in division 6, part 1 of the Family Code, entitled "Nullity, Dissolution, and Legal Separation," and division 6 "switches to the term 'party.'" (See § 2000 et seq.) Leslie asserts labels are immaterial, because section 11 explains that in the Family Code, a "reference to 'husband' and 'wife,' 'spouses,' or 'married persons,' or a comparable term, includes persons who are lawfully married to each other and persons who were previously lawfully married to each other, as is appropriate under the circumstances of the particular case."

Leslie also cites *In re Marriage of Rossi* (2001) 90 Cal.App.4th 34, 108 Cal.Rptr.2d 270 (*Rossi*), as authority for the applicability of section 1101 to her action. In *Rossi,* judgment on an MSA was entered in April 1997, and in May 1999 the former husband learned for the first time that his former wife had received lottery winnings during the marriage. In July 1999 he filed an action against her under section 1101. The family court determined the wife committed fraud within the meaning of Civil Code section 3294 by concealing the winnings, and it penalized her by awarding the husband 100 percent of the winnings under section 1101, subdivision (h). (*Rossi, supra,* at p. 39, 108 Cal.Rptr.2d 270.) The appellate court affirmed the ruling, concluding, "This case presents precisely the circumstance that . . . section 1101, subdivision (h) is intended to address." (*Id.* at p. 42, 108 Cal.Rptr.2d 270.)

Relying on *Rossi,* Hogoboom indicates section 1101 may provide a postjudgment remedy for breach of fiduciary duty in proper circumstances. Chapter 16, which is entitled "Challenging the Judgement Motions, Appeals & Writs," states that while section 2120 et seq. preempt a tort remedy arising out of a dissolution proceeding, "remedies otherwise authorized by law, are not preempted by [section] 2120 et seq. [¶] For instance, subject to statutory time limitations, a spouse alleging intentional *nondisclosure or concealment* of marital property in violation of statutory duties of disclosure may pursue alternative remedies of a set-aside based on concealment and breach of fiduciary duty *or* an award of 50% or 100% of the concealed property" pursuant to section 1101, subdivisions (g) and (h). (Hogoboom, *supra,* ¶ 16:103.2, pp. 16–30 to 16–31, (rev. #1, 2012), some italics added, citing *Rossi, supra,* 90 Cal.App.4th at pp. 38–39, 108 Cal.Rptr.2d 270.)

In *Rossi, supra,* 90 Cal.App.4th 34, 108 Cal.Rptr.2d 270, however, there was no contention that section 1101 is inapplicable to postjudgment proceedings. "[A] case is not authority for a proposition not therein considered. . . ." (*Fait v. New Faze Development, Inc.* (2012) 207 Cal.App.4th 284, 301, 143 Cal.Rptr.3d 382.)

Moreover, the facts of *Rossi* are readily distinguishable from those here. In *Rossi,* the lottery winnings were concealed and not addressed in the judgment of dissolution. Thus, the winnings could be divided in a postjudgment action under section 1101, pursuant to its harsh 100 percent penalty provision (§ 1101, subd. (h)), without affecting the judgment's division of other community property. In other words, the section 1101 action did not violate the strong public policy of ensuring the finality of judgments within the one-year limitations period of section 2122.

Here, Georgiou not only disclosed his prospective referral fee in the Enron litigation, it was a major factor during negotiations on the MSA and the subject of discovery by Leslie's attorneys. The judgment fully adjudicated the issue, with the MSA awarding Leslie 10 percent of the fee and Georgiou 90 percent of the fee, and dividing the remainder of the community assets and debts to reflect the disparity.

" 'A court must, where reasonably possible, harmonize statutes, reconcile seeming inconsistencies in them, and construe them to give force and effect to all of their provisions. [Citations.] This rule applies although one of the statutes involved deals generally with a subject and another relates specifically to particular aspects of the subject.' " (*Pacific Palisades Bowl Mobile Estates, LLC v. City of Los Angeles* (2012) 55 Cal.4th 783, 805, 149 Cal.Rptr.3d 383, 288 P.3d 717.) " ' "The courts are bound, if possible, to maintain the integrity of both statutes if the two may stand together." ' " (*In re Greg F.* (2012) 55 Cal.4th 393, 407, 146 Cal.Rptr.3d 272, 283 P.3d 1160.) "We . . . construe the words in context, keeping in mind the statutory purpose . . . relating to the same subject, both internally and with each other, to the extent possible." (*Outfitter Properties, LLC v. Wildlife Conservation Bd.* (2012) 207 Cal.App.4th 237, 244, 143 Cal.Rptr.3d 312.)

Sections 2122 and 1101 pertain to the same subject matter, as they both provide remedies for breach of the fiduciary duty of disclosure. In Leslie's view, the remedies are interchangeable, and if a party misses the one-year deadline for an action under subdivision (f) of section 2122, he or she may bring an action under section 1101, subdivision (d)(1), within the three-year limitations period.

Section 2120 et seq. take precedence, however, "when either party is seeking to 'undo' a property division judgment that *adjudicated* particular assets and/or liabilities. By contrast, those statutes have *no* effect on proceedings to determine community interests in assets and liabilities that were *unadjudicated* or *omitted* from the judgment." ([ ] see *In re Marriage of Melton* (1994) 28 Cal.App.4th 931, 939, 33 Cal.Rptr.2d 761 ["property left unadjudicated by a divorce decree is subject to future litigation, the parties being tenants in common in the meantime"]; see also § 2556 ["the court has continuing jurisdiction to award community estate assets or community estate liabilities to the parties that have not been previously adjudicated by a judgment in the proceeding"].) "The mere mention of an asset in the judgment is not controlling. [Citation.] '[T]he crucial question is whether the benefits were actually litigated and divided in the previous proceeding.' " (*In re Marriage of Thorne & Raccina* (2012) 203 Cal.App.4th 492, 501, 136 Cal.Rptr.3d 887.)

We are not required to determine the propriety of the court's finding that section 1101 *never* authorizes a postjudgment action for breach of fiduciary duty. Rather, we conclude section 1101 does not authorize a postjudgment action in these circumstances, because the referral fee cannot be disposed of without upsetting the judgment, or at least a portion of it. The judgment divided Georgiou's referral fee unequally, and divided the remainder of community assets and debts based on the disparity. Leslie cannot take the benefits of the judgment and also obtain 50 percent or 100 percent of the referral fee under section 1101, subdivision (g) or (h). To interpret section 1101 as Leslie urges, we would have to ignore section 2120 et seq. and the strong public policy of assuring finality in judgments within a reasonable time (§ 2120, subd. (b)).

The court correctly found Leslie's exclusive remedy was a set-aside action under section 2122. Because she did not file her action within the one-year limitations period of subdivision (f) of section 2122, the family court lacked jurisdiction over the matter and summary adjudication was proper. (*In re Marriage of Thorne & Raccina, supra*, 203 Cal.App.4th at p. 500, 136 Cal.Rptr.3d 887.)

DISPOSITION

The order is affirmed. Georgiou is entitled to costs on appeal.

WE CONCUR:

BENKE, J.

O'ROURKE, J.

SECTION 5. CHAPTER SUMMARY

- California Family Code, Division 5, governs conciliation proceedings.

- California Family Code, Division 6, governs nullity, dissolution and legal separation proceedings (Chapter 7).

  o Division 6, Part I is comprised of general provisions that apply to proceedings for dissolution, nullity, and legal separation of the parties.

  o Division 6, Part 2 covers judicial determinations of void or voidable marriage.

  o Division 6, Part 3 covers the effect of and grounds for dissolution of marriage or legal separation.

- California Family Code Section 2100 through 2113 set forth standards for the disclosure of assets and liabilities in a dissolution, separation, or nullity proceeding.

  o California Family Code Section 2100 articulates state policies related to disclosure and cooperative discovery.

  o California Family Code Section 2102 incorporates the California Family Code Section 721(b) by reference. That section recognizes that married persons are in a confidential relationship from the start to end of marriage. The fiduciary duty may continue on after dissolution, on an asset/ liability specific basis.

  o California Family Code Section 2104 and 2105 mandate the service of preliminary and final declarations of disclosure.

  o California Family Code Section 2107 sets out consequences of noncomplying declarations, namely mandatory money, sanctions, reasonable attorney's fees, and costs.

- California Family Code Section 2200 through 2129 provide for relief from a final dissolution judgment.

o   California Family Code Section 2120 articulates state policies related to setting aside a final dissolution judgment.

o   California Family Code Section 2121 identifies the authority by which a court can set-aside a final dissolution judgment as equitable in nature.

o   California Family Code Section 2122 states the grounds for relief as actual fraud, perjury, duress, mental incapacity, and (as to stipulated agreements and judgments) mistake. The statute includes time limits for filing a motion as to each ground.

CHAPTER 9

DISTRIBUTION OF COMMUNITY PROPERTY AT DEATH

■ ■ ■

The death of a spouse terminates a marriage.

On the death of a married person various problems may arise involving succession rights to the decedent's property and the use of community property to pay debts and expenses. These issues can be complex. They are generally covered in courses dealing with decedent estate administration.

During life, a married person domiciled in California has the power of testamentary disposition over his or her one-half of the community property and the quasi-community property. California Family Code Section 1100(a) adopts the equal management and control rule for all matters involving community personal property that are not testamentary (Chapter 6). With respect to testamentary matters a married person has the right to control only his or her one-half of the community property (California Family Code Section 1100), and all of his or her separate property (California Family Code Section 770(b)).

For purposes of property distribution, if a married person dies testate, which is to say with a valid will or estate plan, that plan controls. In such a case, the married person's property, including his or her one-half of the community property, is distributed in accordance with his or her estate plan. But if a married person dies without a will, or if the person's will does not distribute the entirety of the decedent's estate, then the state intestacy statutes mandate the order of succession as well as guide debt allocation, estate liability, and any derivative liability of the surviving spouse.

The structure of the California Probate Code offers a clear glimpse of a complicated subject. This is how the Probate Code is organized.

- Preliminary provisions
- General provisions (Section 1 below)
- Guardianship, conservatorship, and other protective proceedings
- Nonprobate transfers (Section 2 below)
- Wills
- Intestate succession (Section 3 below)

- Administration (Section 4 below)
- Disposition of estate without administration (Section 5 below)
- Trust law
- Taxes
- Construction of wills, trusts and other instruments

This chapter give an overview of some of the community property problems that can come up in the probate administration process. Covered are basics of the characterization of property at death, nonprobate transfers, and intestate succession. The chapter concludes with a short section on creditors' rights.

SECTION 1. COMMUNITY AND QUASI-COMMUNITY PROPERTY

California Probate Code Section 6401 distinguishes community and quasi-community property from separate property of the decedent. What follows are definitional probate statutes that pertain to the distribution of a married decedent's one-half community property and quasi-community property interest.

A. PROBATE CODE BASICS

The following statutes apply when a person dies without a will. They may also be intentionally incorporated into a valid will or estate plan for definitional purposes.

WEST'S ANNOTATED CALIFORNIA PROBATE CODE

§ 28.   Community property

"Community property" means:

(a) Community property heretofore or hereafter acquired during marriage by a married person while domiciled in this state.

(b) All personal property wherever situated, and all real property situated in this state, heretofore or hereafter acquired during the marriage by a married person while domiciled elsewhere, that is community property, or a substantially equivalent type of marital property, under the laws of the place where the acquiring spouse was domiciled at the time of its acquisition.

(c) All personal property wherever situated, and all real property situated in this state, heretofore or hereafter acquired during the marriage by a married person in exchange for real or personal property, wherever situated, that is community property, or a substantially equivalent type of marital property, under the laws of the place where the acquiring spouse was domiciled at the time the property so exchanged was acquired.

(Stats. 1990, c. 79 (A.B. 759), § 14, operative July 1, 1991.)

§ 66.   Quasi-community property

"Quasi-community property" means the following property, other than community property as defined in Section 28:

(a) All personal property wherever situated, and all real property situated in this state, heretofore or hereafter acquired by a decedent while domiciled elsewhere that would have been the community property of the decedent and the surviving spouse if the decedent had been domiciled in this state at the time of its acquisition.

(b) All personal property wherever situated, and all real property situated in this state, heretofore or hereafter acquired in exchange for real or personal property, wherever situated, that would have been the community property of the decedent and the surviving spouse if the decedent had been domiciled in this state at the time the property so exchanged was acquired.

(Stats. 1990, c. 79 (A.B. 759), § 14, operative July 1, 1991.)

§ 78.   Surviving spouse

"Surviving spouse" does not include any of the following:

(a) A person whose marriage to the decedent has been dissolved or annulled, unless, by virtue of a subsequent marriage, the person is married to the decedent at the time of death.

(b) A person who obtains or consents to a final decree or judgment of dissolution of marriage from the decedent or a final decree or judgment of annulment of their marriage, which decree or judgment is not recognized as valid in this state, unless they (1) subsequently participate in a marriage ceremony purporting to marry each to the other or (2) subsequently live together as husband and wife.

(c) A person who, following a decree or judgment of dissolution or annulment of marriage obtained by the decedent, participates in a marriage ceremony with a third person.

(d) A person who was a party to a valid proceeding concluded by an order purporting to terminate all marital property rights.

(Stats. 1990, c. 79 (A.B. 759), § 14, operative July 1, 1991.)

§ 100.   Community property

(a) Upon the death of a married person, one-half of the community property belongs to the surviving spouse and the other half belongs to the decedent.

(b) Notwithstanding subdivision (a), a husband and wife may agree in writing to divide their community property on the basis of a non pro rata division of the aggregate value of the community property or on the basis of a division of each individual item or asset of the community, or partly on each basis. Nothing in this subdivision shall be construed to require this written agreement in order to permit or recognize a non pro rata division of community property.

(Stats. 1990, c. 79, § 14 (A.B. 759), operative July 1, 1991. Amended by Stats. 1998, c. 662 (A.B. 2069), § 2.)

§ 101. Quasi-community property

(a) Upon the death of a married person domiciled in this state, one-half of the decedent's quasi-community property belongs to the surviving spouse and the other half belongs to the decedent.

(b) Notwithstanding subdivision (a), [the spouses] may agree in writing to divide their quasi-community property on the basis of a non pro rata division of the aggregate value of the quasi-community property, or on the basis of a division of each individual item or asset of quasi-community property, or partly on each basis. Nothing in this subdivision shall be construed to require this written agreement in order to permit or recognize a non pro rata division of quasi-community property.

(Stats. 1990, c. 79 (A.B. 759), § 14, operative July 1, 1991. Amended by Stats. 1998, c. 682 (A.B. 2069), § 3.)

§ 102. Transfer of quasi-community property; restoration of decedent's estate; requirements

(a) The decedent's surviving spouse may require the transferee of property in which the surviving spouse had an expectancy under Section 101 at the time of the transfer to restore to the decedent's estate one-half of the property if the transferee retains the property or, if not, one-half of its proceeds or, if none, one-half of its value at the time of transfer, if all of the following requirements are satisfied:

(1) The decedent died domiciled in this state.

(2) The decedent made a transfer of the property to a person other than the surviving spouse without receiving in exchange a consideration of substantial value and without the written consent or joinder of the surviving spouse.

(3) The transfer is any of the following types:

(A) A transfer under which the decedent retained at the time of death the possession or enjoyment of, or the right to income from, the property.

(B) A transfer to the extent that the decedent retained at the time of death a power, either alone or in conjunction with any other person, to revoke or to consume, invade, or dispose of the principal for the decedent's own benefit.

(C) A transfer whereby property is held at the time of the decedent's death by the decedent and another with right of survivorship.

(b) Nothing in this section requires a transferee to restore to the decedent's estate any life insurance, accident insurance, joint annuity, or pension payable to a person other than the surviving spouse.

(c) All property restored to the decedent's estate under this section belongs to the surviving spouse pursuant to Section 101 as though the transfer had not been made.

(Stats. 1990, c. 79 (A.B. 759), § 14, operative July 1, 1991.)

§ 103. Simultaneous death; community or quasi-community property

Except as provided by Section 224, if [spouses] die leaving community or quasi-community property and it cannot be established by clear and convincing evidence that one spouse survived the other:

(a) One-half of the community property and one-half of the quasi-community property shall be administered upon or distributed, or otherwise dealt with, as if one spouse had survived and as if that half belonged to that spouse.

(b) The other half of the community property and the other half of the quasi-community property shall be administered upon or distributed, or otherwise dealt with, as if the other spouse had survived and as if that half belonged to that spouse.

(Stats. 1990, c. 79 (A.B. 759), § 14, operative July 1, 1991.)

§ 240. Division into equal shares

If a statute calls for property to be distributed or taken in the manner provided in this section, the property shall be divided into as many equal shares as there are living members of the nearest generation of issue then living and deceased members of that generation who leave issue then living, each living member of the nearest generation of issue then living receiving one share and the share of each deceased member of that generation who leaves issue then living being divided in the same manner among his or her then living issue.

(Stats. 1990, c. 79 (A.B. 759), § 14, operative July 1, 1991.)

§ 6101. Property which may be disposed of by will

A will may dispose of the following property:

(a) The testator's separate property.

(b) The one-half of the community property that belongs to the testator under Section 100.

(c) The one-half of the testator's quasi-community property that belongs to the testator under Section 101.

(Stats. 1990, c. 79 (A.B. 759), § 14, operative July 1, 1991.)

B. THE SURVIVING SPOUSE'S EXALTED STATUS

California law does not require that a married person devise his or her one-half interest in community property to the other spouse. Thus a married person retains testamentary rights as to one-half of the community property.

Nevertheless a surviving spouse, as defined in accordance with California Probate Code Section 78, reproduced above, has a protected status under the intestacy statutes.

Additionally, the Probate Code provides family protections for the surviving spouse; protections are covered in a course on estates. The surviving spouse is named administrator of the decedent's estate absent a valid will that instructs otherwise.

Requirements for the execution of a valid will are set out in California Probate Code Section 6110, below.

WEST'S ANNOTATED CALIFORNIA PROBATE CODE

§ 6110. Necessity of writing; other requirements

(a) Except as provided in this part, a will shall be in writing and satisfy the requirements of this section.

(b) The will shall be signed by one of the following:

(1) By the testator.

(2) In the testator's name by some other person in the testator's presence and by the testator's direction.

(3) By a conservator pursuant to a court order to make a will under Section 2580.

(c)(1) Except as provided in paragraph (2), the will shall be witnessed by being signed, during the testator's lifetime, by at least two persons each of whom (A) being present at the same time, witnessed either the signing of the will or the testator's acknowledgment of the signature or of the will and (B) understand that the instrument they sign is the testator's will.

(2) If a will was not executed in compliance with paragraph (1), the will shall be treated as if it was executed in compliance with that paragraph if the proponent of the will establishes by clear and convincing evidence that, at the time the testator signed the will, the testator intended the will to constitute the testator's will.

(Stats. 1990, c. 79 (A.B. 759), § 14, operative July 1, 1991. Amended by Stats. 1996, c. 563 (S.B. 392), § 20; Stats. 2008, c. 53 (A.B. 2248), § 1.)

————

The 2013 case of *Estate of Ben-Ali*, below, underscores the rule that a person's right to dispose of property at death and the way in which that right is exercised by will is determined entirely by the state legislature. In other words, to effect the disposition of property at death a person must comply with statutory rules for will execution. Otherwise the property decends to the decedent's intestate heirs, chief among them being the surviving spouse. The right to devise belongs to the property owner; the right to descent belongs to the property owner's intestate heirs.

Ben-Ali also illustrates the all too common tensions that can arise between a surviving spouse and the decedent's other beneficiaries and heirs.

The statutory requirements for a valid will are as follows. One, the will must be in writing. Two, the will must be signed by the testator, or else by some other person in the testator's presence and by the testator's direction. Three, the will must be witnessed by at least two witnesses who are present at the same time, together. The witnesses must have observed the signing of the will by the testator, or the testator's acknowledgment of his or her signature or of the will; and the witnesses must understand that the instrument they are witnessing is a will. To understand that a will execution is being witnessed implies that the witnessing parties also understand that they may be called upon to testify about the circumstances surrounding the will's execution. California Probate Code Section 6110(a) and (b), reproduced above, state the necessary elements of will execution.

What if a document presented as a will does not comply with the above requirements? Modern probate law provides that a will can be adjudged compliant with the state statutory requirements if the will proponent establishes "by clear and convincing evidence that, at the time the testator signed the will, the testator intended the will to constitute the testator's will." California Probate Code Section 6110(c)(2). This is the issue in *Ben-Ali*.

Taruk Ben-Ali died at the age of 34 survived by his wife Wendelyn (Wendy) Wilburn, a minor child, and his father Hassan Ben-Ali. A document purporting to be Taruk's will surfaced. That document devised Taruk's personal property to wife Wendy and his real property to father Hassan. The record showed that Hassan had transferred an apartment building on Ashby Avenue in Berkeley, California to Taruk in 1993, when Taruk was in his early twenties. The transfer deed was executed "perhaps to avoid [Hassan] losing the property to the IRS." *Id.* at 1029. Hassan died several years after Taruk. At Hassan's death, Taruk's will proponents argued that Taruk's will was a valid devise of the apartment building to Hassan, who devised it to his former wife. Taruk's surviving spouse Wendy challenged the validity of Taruk's purported will. Relying on California Probate Code Section 6401 and 6402, Wendy argued for an intestate distribution that would distribute Taruk's separate property real estate one-half to her and one-half to Taruk's only child from a prior union.

To decide whether Taruk died testate or intestate, the court was called on to analyze the execution of Taruk's purported will.

ESTATE OF BEN-ALI

216 Cal.App.4th 1026, 157 Cal.Rptr.3d 353 (1st Dist. 2013)

Opinion

MARGULIES, ACTING P.J.

The intestate heirs of decedent Taruk Joseph Ben-Ali appeal from a judgment admitting the decedent's will to probate. Appellants contend there was insufficient evidence of due execution under Probate Code[1] section 6110. We agree, and reverse the judgment.

I.   BACKGROUND

A. *The Parties*

Taruk, born in 1968, was the only biological child of Hassan Ben-Ali and Ann Jackson. Hassan and Jackson were married in 1973 and divorced in 1974, but maintained a relationship over the next 34 years. Hassan also had a son from a different relationship, D'Artagnan Lloyd, with whom Hassan had little contact before 2006. According to Hassan's attorney, respondent Ivan Golde, Hassan was a very shrewd and savvy real estate investor who had owned a lot of properties over the years and had also gone through financial problems, including tax problems. One of Hassan's properties was an apartment building at 2235 Ashby Avenue in Berkeley (hereafter Ashby property or Ashby building), which Hassan had transferred to Taruk in approximately 1993, perhaps to avoid losing the property to the IRS.

In 1995, Jackson moved into an apartment in the Ashby building. Hassan lived in the building on and off during that time period and, according to Jackson, continued to handle all aspects of managing the property despite title being in their son's name. On August 3, 2002, Taruk married appellant Wendelyn Wilburn. According to Wilburn, Hassan opposed the marriage, believed Wilburn just wanted to obtain a portion of the Ashby property, and persisted in trying to talk Taruk out of marrying her down to the day of their wedding. At the time of the marriage, Taruk had a young daughter from a previous relationship, appellant Brittany Desmond, and Wilburn had a son. Wilburn was aware when she married Taruk that he had spent time in prison and had a history of drug problems. According to Wilburn, drugs were not an issue for Taruk during their relationship and marriage until sometime in early 2004, when he relapsed into using drugs.

B. *Decedent's Disappearance and Death*

Wilburn was on a business trip in Las Vegas on June 8, 2004, when she communicated with Taruk by telephone for the last time. Over the next two days, Wilburn repeatedly tried to call Taruk from Las Vegas, but got no answer. When she returned from her trip, she called Hassan to find out if he knew where Taruk was. Hassan told her Taruk had decided to leave her and start a new life somewhere else. He told similar stories to Jackson and others who inquired about Taruk's whereabouts. Wilburn testified she did not believe Hassan, and made attempts to locate Taruk, but neither Wilburn nor anyone else reported Taruk's disappearance to the police. Between June 2004 and December 2008, Hassan continued to manage Taruk's apartment building in Taruk's name, collected rents, forged Taruk's name on checks drawn against Taruk's bank accounts, and refinanced the property in the amount of $600,000 by forging Taruk's signature and the signature of a notary.

In November 2008, Hassan called Golde and asked to meet with him. Hassan informed Golde that Taruk had in fact died in 2004. Hassan explained he had found Taruk dead of a drug overdose in a hotel room. Not wanting to report the death for fear of losing the Ashby property, he had taken Taruk's body to the property and hidden it in the wall of a storage area of the building. Hassan further informed Golde that a person who had assisted him in the removal and concealment of Taruk's body was extorting substantial sums of money from him by threatening to reveal what had happened.

Hassan committed suicide on December 15, 2008, while Berkeley police officers were visiting the property. Two days later, Taruk's body was discovered on the premises. Police believed Taruk had died four and half years earlier, in June 2004. Hassan left a will, not contested in this proceeding, in which he named his former spouse, Ann Jackson, as the sole beneficiary of his estate.

C. *Decedent's Will*

Among Hassan's possessions, police found a purported will of Taruk, bearing the apparent signatures of Taruk and two attesting witnesses. The typewritten document was dated August 16, 2002, two weeks after Taruk and Wilburn were married, and the day before they were to leave town for a honeymoon in Hawaii. It recited that Taruk had one living child, Brittany Desmond. The document provided Taruk's "wife," who was the only person not referred to by name in it, was to receive all of Taruk's personal property, and his father, Hassan Ben-Ali, was to receive all other assets. It further stated Desmond "has been provided for by a life insurance policy on my life, which is held in trust for her by my father, Hassan Ben-Ali." Hassan was identified as executor of the estate in the document, and "Attorney Ivan Gold" was named as the alternate executor.

The purported will contained an attestation clause stating it was signed by Taruk in the presence of two witnesses who also signed in the presence of each other and that Taruk declared to them the document was his "Last Will and Testament." One of the witness signatures was of "Wendy Ben-Ali" with an address of "2235 Ashby #201 Berkeley, Ca." The handwritten name and address of the second purported witness were illegible, and the identity of that person has never been determined.

D. *Probate Court Proceedings*

Wilburn filed a petition for appointment and for letters of administration. Lloyd filed a separate petition for appointment and for probate of the will. Golde filed a petition to be appointed the executor of Taruk's will, and for probate of the will. Wilburn and Desmond objected to the petitions filed by Lloyd and Golde, and filed contests to the validity of the purported will. The question of the validity of Taruk's purported will of August 16, 2002, was tried to the court. The primary issues were whether the will was duly executed according to the requirements of section 6110, subdivision (c)(1) or, if not, whether the will's proponents proved by clear and convincing evidence under subdivision (c)(2) that Taruk intended the instrument to constitute his will when he signed it.

Respondent's forensic document expert, David Moore, testified he believed with a high degree of certainty Taruk's signature on the will was authentic based on comparing it with known signatures of Taruk. He further believed Wilburn's signature was "probably" genuine based on comparison with one known signature by Wilburn in which she signed as "Wendy Ben-Ali." Appellants' forensic document expert, James Blanco, opined it was "highly probable" the signatures of Taruk and Wilburn on the will were not genuine. Wilburn denied witnessing or signing the will, although she acknowledged the "Wendy" portion of the signature looked like "something [she] would write." She testified Hassan asked her to sign something in 2004, which he told her was a medical release needed in case Taruk required medical attention. Wilburn further testified she never lived at the Ashby building, and did not use or sign documents with the surname "Ben-Ali," except for one application she filled out with Taruk on August 2, 2002.

E. *Probate Court Decision*

The probate court rejected expert Blanco's analysis of Taruk's and Wilburn's signatures and accepted the testimony of expert Moore that both signatures were genuine. The court found these conclusions were bolstered by circumstantial evidence including (1) the common understanding that wills are often executed in anticipation of taking a trip, (2) the fact Taruk and Wilburn were flying to Hawaii the morning after the will was executed, (3) a reasonable inference Taruk wanted to be certain his testamentary intentions were made clear before embarking on that journey, and (4) the reasonable inference Taruk would want to make clear after his marriage that his father would receive the Ashby property rather than his intestate heirs. The court also noted Wilburn's interests were adverse to the will and her testimony accordingly had to be evaluated with caution.

With respect to the signature of the unknown witness, the court held the regular and complete attestation clause on the signature page of the will was prima facie evidence of the validity of the unknown signature. Further, the court held its findings regarding the validity of Taruk's and Wilburn's signatures, and the expert opinion and circumstantial evidence supporting those findings, by reasonable inference, lent credibility to the unknown signature. The court noted the evidence against the validity of the unknown signature derived from Wilburn's testimony that she did not sign the will, and by inference that the unknown signature and attestation must also be fictitious. The court found Wilburn's testimony unreliable for the following reasons: (1) she had a financial interest in having the will invalidated; (2) her testimony that she chose not to use the Ben-Ali last name during her marriage was contradicted by her use of it just two weeks before the date of the will; and (3) her testimony regarding what she may have signed, and when, was vague and equivocal, and her memory seemed selective. The court found the evidence in favor of the validity of the unknown signature outweighed the evidence against its validity. The court found it unnecessary to determine if there was clear and convincing evidence under section 6110, subdivision (c)(2) that Taruk intended the will to be his testamentary instrument, but observed such evidence "far outweighs the evidence to the contrary."

The court denied Wilburn's petition for letters, denied the will contest, granted the petitions for probate of the will, and made its own appointment of an administrator in view of an express waiver by Golde of his right to appointment.

This timely appeal followed.

II. DISCUSSION

Appellants contend (1) the trial court erred in applying a presumption of due execution since the proponents failed to establish the genuineness of the signatures of both witnesses, and (2) the proponents failed to establish by clear and convincing evidence the decedent intended the contested document to be his will.

A. *Standard of Review*

The question of due execution of a will is one of fact, and the probate court's finding will not be reversed on appeal if there is any substantial evidence to sustain it. (*Estate of Fletcher* (1958) 50 Cal.2d 317, 320, 325 P.2d 103.) In this case, however, the probate court relied on a rebuttable presumption of due execution which it found arose as a matter of law from the regular and complete attestation clause on the signature page of the will, buttressed by evidence of the genuineness of the signatures of Taruk and Wilburn. Thus, as a threshold matter, we are confronted with a question of law: In the face of contrary evidence, is evidence of the genuineness of the signatures of the testator and one of two subscribing witnesses on the signature page of a will containing a regular and complete attestation clause sufficient to establish due execution for purposes of section 6110, subdivision (c)(1)? This is a purely legal issue—the interpretation of a statute—that is subject to de novo review. (*People ex rel. Lockyer v. Shamrock Foods Co.* (2000) 24 Cal.4th 415, 432, 101 Cal.Rptr.2d 200, 11 P.3d 956.)

If the proponents' evidence was insufficient to establish compliance with section 6110, subdivision (c)(1), we must address whether the proponents nonetheless proved by clear and convincing evidence under section 6110, subdivision (c)(2) that Taruk intended the document in issue to be his will. The probate court made no finding on this issue to which this court must defer. We may therefore decide as a matter of law whether a reasonable fact finder could determine the evidence of Taruk's intent was clear and convincing. (See, e.g., *In re Henry V.* (2004) 119 Cal.App.4th 522, 530, 14 Cal.Rptr.3d 496; *City of Santa Cruz v. Pacific Gas & Electric Co.* (2000) 82 Cal.App.4th 1167, 1180, 99 Cal.Rptr.2d 198; *Aquino v. Superior Court* (1993) 21 Cal.App.4th 847, 860, 26 Cal.Rptr.2d 477.)

B. *Proof of Due Execution*

Relying on *Estate of Pitcairn* (1936) 6 Cal.2d 730, 59 P.2d 90 (*Pitcairn*), the trial court held the regular and complete attestation clause on the signature page of the will was prima facie evidence of the validity of the unknown witness signature.

For the reasons discussed below, we believe the trial court misread *Pitcairn*. It did not hold a regular and complete attestation clause could establish the genuineness of an unknown signature, but the converse—proof of the genuineness of the subscribing witnesses' signatures is sufficient to create a presumption of due execution notwithstanding an irregular or incomplete attestation clause.

Preliminarily, we note the power to make a will is conferred solely by statute: "The power to dispose of one's property by will and the mode by which it may be exercised are matters under legislative control, and the mode prescribed by the statute must be followed, or there is no will." (*Estate of Manchester* (1917) 174 Cal. 417, 419–420, 163 P. 358.) When due execution of a will is contested, the proponents of the will have the burden of proving it. (§ 8252, subd. (a).) Section 8253 specifies how execution may be proven: "At the trial, each subscribing witness shall be produced and examined. If no subscribing witness is available as a witness within the meaning of Section 240 of the Evidence Code, the court may admit the evidence of other witnesses to prove the due execution of the will."

Pitcairn was an appeal from a judgment admitting a contested will to probate. (*Pitcairn, supra,* 6 Cal.2d at p. 731, 59 P.2d 90.) The only ground of contest was that the will was not executed with the formalities required by statute. (*Ibid.*) There was no dispute the will was signed by the testatrix or that it was subscribed by two witnesses, both of whom testified at the trial. (*Ibid.*) However, one of the subscribing witnesses testified she was not present in the room when the testatrix signed and that she was asked to sign a piece of paper without being told it was a will. (*Ibid.*) There was some evidence of an adverse attitude and untrustworthy recollection on the part of the witness. (*Id.* at pp. 731–732, 59 P.2d 90.) Further, the attestation clause was incomplete and merely recited it was " 'Signed & witnessed' " by the witnesses. (*Id.* at p. 731, 59 P.2d 90.) The trial court found in favor of the proponents, and the issue before the reviewing court was whether there was substantial evidence to support its findings and judgment. (*Ibid.*) The court described the issue more particularly as follows: "We have, then, a case *where the signatures of the testatrix and subscribing witnesses are genuine*; the will is attested, but lacks a formal attestation clause reciting the steps in execution; the attesting witnesses, seemingly adverse but uncontradicted on the essential issues, testify to a technical failure to comply with the formalities of execution. In such a case, may the trial court admit the will to probate?" (*Id.* at p. 732, 59 P.2d 90, italics added.)

The Supreme Court concluded the trial court could admit the will to probate on those facts. First, the court noted the rule that a regular and complete attestation clause makes out a prima facie case of due execution. (*Pitcairn, supra,* 6 Cal.2d at p. 732, 59 P.2d 90.) This rule came about because if the witnesses are dead, unavailable, or unable to testify or recollect, or are adverse or corrupt, it is necessary to rely on other evidence of the sufficiency of the instrument. (*Ibid.*) However, the court rejected the suggestion that it is the specific recitals in the clause that furnish the basis for the presumption. (*Ibid.*) Instead, it found "[t]he foundation of the presumption is the proof of genuineness of the signatures, for the instrument is then on its face a valid will." (*Ibid.*) The recitals in an attestation clause may add to the weight or force of the presumption, but they do not in themselves create the logical basis for it. (*Id.* at pp. 732–733, 59 P.2d 90.) The *Pitcairn* court cited two earlier California cases also standing for the proposition that the presumption of due execution, when it exists, depends upon proof of the genuineness of the subscribing witnesses' signatures. (See *Estate of Kent* (1911) 161 Cal. 142, 143–145, 118 P. 523 (*Kent*) [testimony of a single subscribing witness authenticating signatures of both witnesses validates will lacking any attesting clause]; *Estate of Tyler* (1898) 121 Cal. 405, 406–409, 53 P. 928 (*Tyler*) [will upheld notwithstanding an incomplete attestation clause where the evidence established the genuineness of the testatrix's and both subscribing witnesses' signatures].)

Respondent cites *Estate of Gerst* (1957) 153 Cal.App.2d 528, 315 P.2d 49. The relevant facts in *Gerst* were stated as follows: "The signatures of both witnesses are genuine. One witness . . . predeceased testatrix; and the other . . . had absolutely no recollection of the circumstances surrounding the execution of the will or the affixing of his own signature thereto." (*Id.* at p. 534, 315 P.2d 49.) In *Gerst,* the court merely applied the rule stated in *Pitcairn, Kent,* and *Tyler* that " '*where a will bears the genuine signatures of the testator and attesting witnesses,* the presumption exists on the death of the witnesses or failure of their memory that all of the requirements of Probate Code, Section 50 [section 6110's predecessor statute], proof of which depends on the recollection of the witnesses, were duly observed.' " (*Gerst,* at p. 535, 315 P.2d 49, citing *Tyler* and other cases, italics added.)

Estate of Burdette (2000) 81 Cal.App.4th 938, 97 Cal.Rptr.2d 263, also cited by respondent, is inapposite. It merely held the will's proponents need not produce live testimony from both subscribing witnesses in order to support a presumption of due execution as long as there is other evidence the decedent's signature and the signatures of the subscribing witnesses are genuine. (*Id.* at p. 946, 97 Cal.Rptr.2d 263.) It was critical to the result in *Burdette* that one of the subscribing witnesses testified he observed the decedent sign the contested will and he identified his signature *and that of the other subscribing witness* on the will. (*Id.* at pp. 941–942, 97 Cal.Rptr.2d 263.) Under those circumstances, no testimony from the other witness was held to be necessary. (*Id.* at p. 946, 97 Cal.Rptr.2d 263; see also *Estate of Cecala* (1949) 92 Cal.App.2d 834, 838, 208 P.2d 436 [proponents entitled to presumption of due execution where signatures of at least two subscribing witnesses were shown to be genuine].)

We have found no California case in which evidence of the genuineness of the decedent's signature and of the signature of *only one* subscribing witness was held to be sufficient to establish the genuineness of *another* witness's signature, or to create a presumption or prima facie evidence of due execution. Such evidence was found insufficient for that purpose in *Estate of Wood* (1934) 153 Misc. 128, 274 N.Y.S. 461. (See also *Estate of Cann* (1928) 136 Misc. 428, 240 N.Y.S. 840 [proof of signatures of both subscribing witnesses required]; *Estate of Speers* (Okla.2008) 179 P.3d 1265, 1272–1273 [will denied probate where there was no competent evidence establishing unavailability of second witness or genuineness of her signature].)

In short, the rule in California and elsewhere is that proof of the signatures of the decedent and the witnesses makes out a prima facie case of due execution. (*Pitcairn, supra,* 6 Cal.2d at p. 732, 59 P.2d 90.) Proof of the signature of the decedent and of only one of the witnesses does not. Respondent complains that under this rule if both witnesses are deceased, or the sole available witness has a financial motive to defeat the will, it can never be admitted to probate over objection. Not so. The Evidence Code specifically provides the testimony of a subscribing witness is not required to authenticate a writing. (Evid.Code, §§ 1411, 1412.) Witness signatures can be authenticated by a variety of means including eyewitness testimony (Evid.Code, § 1413), lay opinion testimony by a person familiar with the writer's handwriting (*id.,* § 1416), comparison by the trier of fact (*id.,* § 1417), and expert testimony (*id.,* § 1418). No such evidence was produced in this case regarding the signature of the unidentified purported witness. There was therefore no adequate evidentiary basis for determining the illegible entry on the signature page of the will was in fact a signature and, if so, that it was made by a person distinct from the testator who was competent, present during the execution, and understood the instrument to be a will.

The probate court erred in admitting the will to probate on the basis of section 6110, subdivision (c)(1).

C. *Evidence of Testator's Intent*

A will not executed in compliance with section 6110, subdivision (c)(1) may nonetheless be admitted to probate if the proponent establishes by clear and convincing evidence the testator intended the instrument to constitute his will at the time he signed it. (§ 6110, subd. (c)(2).) The clear and convincing standard " 'requires a finding of high probability. . . .' 'so clear as to leave no substantial doubt'; 'sufficiently strong to command the unhesitating assent of every reasonable mind.' " ' " (*Lackner v. North* (2006) 135 Cal.App.4th 1188, 1211–1212, 37 Cal.Rptr.3d 863.) In our view, no reasonable trier of fact could find that standard has been reached on the record before us.

Taruk was only 34 years old when he allegedly executed his will. No witness in this case knew anything about the will or the circumstances of its execution. There was no evidence Taruk had spoken about his testamentary intentions with anyone, or that Wilburn ever mentioned the will to anyone between 2002 and its discovery in 2008—despite the fact that her husband's decision not to provide for her in his will would presumably have been a topic of some interest to her. There was also no testimony as to how the typewritten will had been prepared, who had drafted it, or who Taruk might have consulted about its terms or phrasing. Significantly, no original or copy of the will was found at Taruk's residence or among his belongings. The will was found among the belongings of Taruk's father, Hassan. The evidence showed Hassan was a man willing to go to extremes of fraud and dishonesty in order to protect his financial interests and, in particular, to retain control of the Ashby property—which was both his residence and a major source of his income. Before taking his own life, Hassan had hidden his son's body behind a wall, perpetrated a callous fraud on Taruk's mother, spouse, and friends about Taruk's fate, and had impersonated Taruk and forged his name to multiple documents, all apparently for financial reasons connected to the property. At the same time, no convincing theory was offered to explain how Hassan's decision to conceal the death for financial reasons was consistent with the existence of a valid will passing Taruk's property to him. There was vague testimony about possible tax concerns, but no competent evidence of Hassan's tax situation in 2004 was admitted. On the other hand, Hassan would have had an obvious financial motive for concealing Taruk's death if a will leaving the building to Hassan did not in fact exist when Taruk died. The will document itself was far from self-authenticating. In the will, Taruk referred to Wilburn as "my wife" rather than mentioning her by name, even though they had just been married two weeks earlier. Whoever signed Wilburn's name used the Ashby property as her address even though Wilburn had never lived there. Both the signature and address of the second witness were completely indecipherable. The life insurance policy for Brittany Desmond referenced in the will has never been found, and no evidence was produced of any premiums paid for such a policy. Taruk's signature on the will—the only real evidence of Taruk's intent to make a will—was primarily authenticated by the proponents' document examiner who was not told about or shown any of the known documents on which Hassan had forged Taruk's signature.

By highlighting circumstances casting doubt on the will's provenance, we do not discount the other circumstances and evidence that persuaded the trial court Taruk did in fact sign the document in issue, and intend it as his will. But in light of the many unusual events surrounding the document, and the paucity of evidence Taruk had discussed his testamentary intent with others, we do not believe a reasonable fact finder could conclude those facts were proven by clear and convincing evidence.

Accordingly, we reverse the judgment and remand for further proceedings consistent with the views expressed herein. We make no judgment about the reappointment of a special administrator, but leave that to the probate court's discretion.

III. DISPOSITION

The judgment is reversed and the matter is remanded to the probate court for the entry of a new judgment upholding appellants' contest of the will based on insufficient evidence of due execution, denying admission of the will to probate, and providing for the administration of the estate in a manner consistent with those determinations.

We concur:

DONDERO, J., BANKE, J.

NOTE

The surviving spouse's status. One important principle applies to wills and intestate distributions: the decedent's surviving spouse has an exalted status relative to the decedent's other beneficiaries or heirs.

In the context of wills, the surviving spouse may petition for family protections.

In the context of intestacy, family protections are available for the surviving spouse who also succeeds to a significant portion of the decedent's property.

As to community property, the decedent's one-half interest descends to the surviving spouse.

The decedent's separate property decends either entirely or proportionally to the surviving spouse depending on how many other heirs survive the decedent, and whether those heirs are the children of the decedent and the surviving spouse.

The surviving spouse takes all of the the decedent's separate property if the decedent's children are also children of the surviving spouse. The rationale for distributing the decedent's separate property to a surviving spouse with whom decedent has children is that those children will inherit from their surviving parent when he or she dies.

The surviving spouse takes a percentage of the decedent's separate property if the decedent's children are not also children of the surviving spouse. The rationale for this outcome is that the decedent's children from a prior union are not the natural bounty of the surviving spouse; therefore, they take their share of their deceased parent's separate property at that parent's death.

SECTION 2. BASICS OF NONPROBATE TRANSFERS

Nonprobate transfers are widely used by married persons. A nonprobate transfer is typically made by a valid instrument like a joint tenancy title, a community property with the right of survivorship title, a transfer on death title or instrument, or a trust.

A nonprobate transfer works like this. Upon death, the decedent spouse's one-half interest vests in the surviving spouse without the necessity of probate administration.

What follows are basics on nonprobate transfers. Keep in mind that written consent for a nonprobate transfer may require the signature of both spouses, or at least of the spouse who is consenting to the other spouse's nonprobate transfer. That written consent may or may not be a transmutation. To effect a transmutation it is also necessary for the written consent to meet the standards set forth in California Family Code Section 852(a) and 721 (Chapters 1 and 6).

WEST'S ANNOTATED CALIFORNIA PROBATE CODE

§ 5010. Written consent

As used in this chapter, "written consent" to a provision for a nonprobate transfer of community property on death includes a written joinder in such a provision.

(Added by Stats. 1992, c. 51 (A.B. 1719), § 6.)

§ 5011. Rights of parties in nonprobate transfers; application of chapter

Notwithstanding any other provision of this part, the rights of the parties in a nonprobate transfer of community property on death are subject to all of the following:

(a) The terms of the instrument under which the nonprobate transfer is made.

(b) A contrary state statute specifically applicable to the instrument under which the nonprobate transfer is made.

(c) A written expression of intent of a party in the provision for transfer of the property or in a written consent to the provision.

(Added by Stats. 1992, c. 51 (A.B. 1719), § 6.)

A. JOINT TENANCY AT THE DEATH OF A SPOUSE

At death, the presumption is that the form of title controls character. Common law titles—the joint tenancy and the tenancy in common—are characterized as concurrent separate property titles.

Estate of Levine was decided a few years before the requirement that transmutations be in writing, therefore (only) the part of the opinion that would have enforced an oral transmutation is superseded by California Family Code Section 852(a). Otherwise, the decision stands.

ESTATE OF LEVINE

125 Cal.App.3d 701, 178 Cal.Rptr. 275 (2d Dist. 1981)

HASTINGS, ASSOCIATE JUSTICE.

This case illustrates one of the pitfalls of "how to avoid probate." The appeal concerns a family residence held in joint tenancy although one of the spouses, secretly as it turned out, considered it community property. The court held the property to be joint tenancy and this appeal followed.

Phillip and Estelle Levine were married on January 1, 1974. They had been neighbors for 20 years on Saturn Avenue in Los Angeles, and their respective spouses had predeceased them by several years. Both had children from their prior marriages, all of whom were adults at the time Phillip and Estelle married.

In April of 1975, Phillip and Estelle purchased a home on Lindbrook Avenue in Los Angeles ("the Lindbrook home"), taking title as joint tenants.

Phillip died on November 26, 1977. His will named as co-executors his attorney, Samuel Leemon, and his son Murray Levine. Murray filed a petition in the probate court seeking to have the Lindbrook home declared to be community property of Phillip and Estelle. After hearing testimony, the court determined that the home was joint tenancy property, and denied the petition.

At the hearing, attorney Leemon testified in support of the petition. His testimony was as follows: He and Phillip were cousins and lifelong acquaintances, and he had handled Phillip's legal affairs in recent years. Shortly after he married Estelle in January of 1974, Phillip came to Leemon and asked him to prepare a will. Since Phillip planned to sell his home on Saturn Avenue and purchase a new home with the proceeds, he wanted his will to reflect his intention with respect to the character of the property: the new home was to be considered community property, but would be held in joint tenancy for convenience only. The reason for this was twofold. First, Phillip wanted to be able to devise his one-half of the house to his children, Murray and Iris, which he would be able to do if the home were community property. However, if Estelle predeceased him he also wanted to prevent Estelle from devising her one-half of their community property to her children and wanted to avoid a lengthy probate administration, both of which he could accomplish by holding the property in joint tenancy. Phillip's banker advised him that he could achieve what he wanted by holding the new home in joint tenancy but calling it community property. Leemon advised against this, and told Phillip that unless he had some agreement with Estelle that the home was to be community property, it would be considered joint tenancy property and would pass to Estelle if Phillip predeceased her. Phillip was adamant, however, and said there was no problem because he and Estelle had such an agreement. Accordingly, the will was drafted with the following language:

> "FIFTH: I hereby declare that I am selling my home at 9707 Saturn, Los Angeles, California, and will use part of the proceeds of sale to purchase a new home.

> "The new home is to be considered community property although of record, for convenience only, the title will be shown and taken in Joint Tenancy."

After Leemon drafted the will, he did not have any further contact with Phillip before the Lindbrook home was purchased, and did not know what agreement, if any, Phillip and Estelle had with regard to the character of the property.

Estelle testified that she never had any discussions with Phillip as to what would happen to their property if one of them died, and Phillip never told her that he wanted his half to go to his children. She never knew Phillip had a will until after he died. When questioned about her knowledge of the meaning of "joint tenancy," she said that she had a joint will with her former husband, they held their home on Saturn Avenue in joint tenancy, and the house passed to her upon his death. She thought that joint tenancy was the only way title to property could be held, and never doubted that she would get the Lindbrook home if Phillip died first.

Estelle also testified that when she and Phillip bought the Lindbrook home, they met with the bank escrow officer and Phillip instructed that the deed should be prepared showing Phillip and Estelle as joint tenants. They had a similar conversation with the real estate broker who handled the sale. She said that Phillip made the down payment and mortgage payments, while she contributed approximately $10,000 towards remodeling the home.

In rebuttal, Murray testified that he had four separate conversations with his father alone in which Phillip told him that Murray and his sister Iris would inherit half the proceeds of the Saturn Avenue house upon Phillip's death.

Based upon the testimony presented at the hearing, the court concluded that, although Phillip intended that the Lindbrook home be considered community property, he never disclosed his intention to Estelle. Accordingly, the court found that the Lindbrook home was joint tenancy property, and denied the petition. Murray, the appellant, contends that the court's finding was not supported by substantial evidence.

The law on the issue before us is quite clear. For the purpose of determining the character of real property upon the death of a spouse, there is a rebuttable presumption that the character of the property is as set forth in the deed. (*Schindler v. Schindler*, 126 Cal.App.2d 597, 601–602, 272 P.2d 566.) The presumption still applies where the property was purchased with the separate funds of one spouse. * * * The burden is on the party seeking to rebut the presumption to establish that the property is held in some other way; this may be done by a showing that the character of the property was changed or affected by an agreement or common understanding between the spouses. * * * However, there must be an agreement of some sort; the presumption may not be overcome by testimony about the hidden intention of one spouse, undisclosed to the other spouse at the time of the conveyance. Whether the presumption is rebutted is a question of fact for resolution by the trial court, and we are bound by that court's finding if it is supported by substantial evidence. * * *

The crucial question, therefore, was whether Phillip communicated his intention to Estelle, and whether they had some agreement or understanding that the property would be other than a joint tenancy. Aside from Phillip's statement to his lawyer that "there wouldn't be any problem," the only evidence presented concerning any such agreement was Estelle's testimony that there wasn't one. It was Murray's burden to show that the character of the property was as Phillip intended; absent such an agreement, Murray cannot meet his burden and overcome the presumption created by the deed that the Lindbrook home was joint tenancy property.

Murray contends that the above rule of law unfairly deprives Phillip's children of part of their inheritance. He suggests that we adopt the statutory law applied in marriage dissolution cases where the single family residence acquired during marriage and held in joint tenancy is presumed to be community property. [Current California Family Code Section 2581.] This argument, however, should be directed to our Legislature, since it specifically limited the presumption * * * to division of such property in dissolution of marriage or legal separation cases only.

The judgment is affirmed.

NOTES

1. *Joint tenancy characterization at death.* Suppose that Alpha and Zeta, who are recently married, use community property funds to purchase a parcel of real property during marriage. Each spouse wants their respective children to take their one-half share of the property at death; the spouses have no children together. Alpha and Zeta are unaware of the characterization implications of taking title joint tenancy, but they are convinced by a non-

attorney third party that it is in their best interest to avoid probate. Assume Alpha dies first. Alpha leaves a will purporting to devise Alpha's "one-half community property interest" in the parcel to children from a former marriage. What result?

2. *Recordation of a severance is required by statute.* In *Estate of England*, 233 Cal.App.3d 1, 6, 284 Cal.Rptr. 361, 364 (2d Dist. 1991) the husband died leaving a holographic (handwritten) will. The will expressly attempted to sever husband's interest in residential property that he owned with his wife in joint tenancy; the severing instrument was not recorded. The husband changed his mind prior to death; he severed the joint title in order to (instead) devise his one-half community property interest in the residence to his child. That severing document was not recorded either. Upon the husband's death, his heirs argued that the joint tenancy between the husband and the wife had been severed. The trial court disallowed the severance. The court of appeal affirmed, stating that California Civil Code Section 683.2, subdivision (c), requires that a document unilaterally severing a joint tenancy shall be recorded so as to give the other joint tenant constructive notice of the severance and to avoid fraud. Accordingly, the inclusion of the phrase "other means" to sever a joint tenancy in California Civil Code Section 683.2, subdivision (a) may not be read to include a will which has not been recorded as required by subdivision (c).

In *Dorn v. Solomon*, 57 Cal.App.4th 650, 67 Cal.Rptr.2d 311 (4th Dist. 1997), Donald and Dixie Dorn purchased a home in 1981. At that time, they took title as "husband and wife, as joint tenants." In 1992, the couple separated, and Dixie moved out. A few months after the separation Dixie discovered that she had a terminal illness. On her deathbed, Dixie executed a quitclaim deed transferring the family home to an irrevocable trust that named her daughter from a previous marriage as the sole beneficiary. The deed was executed on September 20, 1993. Dixie died the following day, on September 21, 1993.

On September 30, 1993 Donald—as Dixie's joint tenant—recorded an "Affidavit-Death of Joint Tenant" with the county recorder. On October 25, 1993, Dixie's trustee recorded the quitclaim deed that Dixie had signed to sever the Donald-Dixie joint tenancy. Donald brought an action for declaratory relief, to quiet title to the property, and to cancel the quitclaim deed. He (correctly) argued that the California Family Code Section 2581 special presumption is not applicable when a joint tenant dies and thus that the property was his by right of survivorship.

Summary judgment was granted in favor of Donald. The rationale, as discussed above, was that California Family Code Section 2581 does not arise *unless* the property division is for purposes of legal separation or marriage dissolution (Chapter 2). When property division occurs due to the death of a joint tenant, joint tenancy property passes in accordance with its title, which for Donald and Dixie's property was by right of survivorship. Wife Dixie's trustee could have legally severed title by filing Dixie's severing quitclaim deed, but she would have had to do so within seven days after Dixie's death. However, since the trustee did not file the quitclaim deed until over a month after Dixie's death, Donald succeed by right of survivorship to the entirety of the property.

California Civil Code Section 683.2 allows for a seven-day window after the death of a severing joint tenant in which to record a severing deed.

3.   *Unilateral severance.* Generally unilateral creation and unilateral severance are permitted in California, although unilateral severance may create some problems for a married person. Unilateral severance occurs when a joint tenant severs the joint tenancy without the other person's participation.

For example, assume Alpha and Zeta, who are not married to each other, own property as joint tenants by right of survivorship. A rule allowing unilateral severance would allow Alpha to convey Alpha's one-half interest to Alpha's own self. Such a deed would destroy the right of survivorship between Alpha and Zeta. After severance the property would be owned by Alpha and Zeta as tenants in common. One important consequence of the severance would be that upon the death of either tenant in common, his or her one-half interest would pass not by right of survivorship, but by will or intestacy.

Now assume that Alpha and Zeta are married to each other. California Family Code Section 1102 requires that both spouses join (sign) on any consequential transaction; plus, failure to do so gives the nonjoining spouse the power to avoid the instrument that lacks joinder (Chapter 6). The destruction of a right of survivorship is a consequential transaction. Under the Civil Code, Alpha has the power to unilaterally sever the joint tenancy; but under the Family Code, Zeta has the statutory right to avoid Alpha's severing deed within a certain period of time (Chapter 6).

4.   *Income tax consequences of characterization.* At death, the character of property owned jointly between the spouses may result in significantly different tax obligations for the surviving spouse. Consider the following two examples. In the first example, the California property is titled in joint tenancy and, ultimately, characterized as separate property. In the second example, the California property is titled in community property and, ultimately, characterized as community property.

Separate property characterization, the decedent spouse's one-half gets a step-up in basis:

Assume that during marriage tech engineers Alpha and Zeta are domiciled in California. They purchase a house in Palo Alto for $1,000,000. They take title as *"Alpha and Zeta as joint tenants."* Alpha dies. Also assume these two facts: in the year of Alpha's death the Palo Alto house is appraised at $4,000,000; and Zeta in fact sells the house for $4,000,000.

At Alpha's death, Alpha's one-half share of the house gets a step-up in basis from $500,000 to $2,000,000 due to its separate property character. By contrast, Zeta's one-half share gets a new basis of

$2,500,000: $500,000 for Zeta's original basis plus $2,000,000 for Alpha's stepped-up basis.

When surviving spouse Zeta sells the house for $4,000,000, Zeta realizes taxable income of $1,500,000.

$$\$4,000,000 - \$2,500,000 = \$1,500,000$$

Community property characterization, the entire property gets a step-up in basis:

Assume that during marriage, tech engineers Alpha and Zeta are domiciled in California. They purchase a house in Palo Alto for $1,000,000. They take title as *"Alpha and Zeta as community property."* Alpha dies. Also assume these two facts: in the year of Alpha's death the Palo Alto house is appraised at $4,000,000; and Zeta in fact sells the house for $4,000,000.

At Alpha's death, the entire property gets a step-up in basis due to its community property character. Zeta's new basis is $4,000,000.

When Zeta sells the house for $4,000,000, Zeta realizes taxable income of $0.

$$\$4,000,000 - \$4,000,000 = \$0$$

B. NONPROBATE TRANSFERS AT THE DEATH OF A FORMER SPOUSE

Nonprobate transfers are widely used. Historically, however, a nonprobate transfer could be problematic if the contractual designee was a former spouse of the decedent. The California Probate Code addressed this problem most recently with two rules that went into effect on January 1, 2016.

The first rule applies to nonprobate transfers. It appears at California Probate Code Section 5040. The new rule establishes that a nonprobate transfer to a former spouse fails if, at the time of the transferor's death, the former spouse is not the transferor's surviving spouse, due to dissolution or annulment of their marriage.

The second rule applies to joint tenancy and community property with the right of survivorship titles. The rule appears at California Probate Code Section 5041. The new rule reverses the common law to establish that a joint tenancy or community property by right of survivorship that is held between a decedent and decedent's former spouse is severed if, at the time of the decedent's death, the former spouse is not the decedent's surviving spouse due to a dissolution or annulment of the marriage.

There are exceptions to both rules. California Probate Code Section 5040(b), reproduced below, lists three exceptions. *Life Insurance v. Ortiz,* applies what is now codified as California Probate Code Section 5040(b)(2).

WEST'S ANNOTATED CALIFORNIA PROBATE CODE

§ 5040. Nonprobate transfer to former spouse executed before or during marriage; failure of transfer due to dissolution or annulment of marriage; situations that do not cause a nonprobate transfer to fail; right of subsequent purchaser

(a) Except as provided in subdivision (b), a nonprobate transfer to the transferor's former spouse, in an instrument executed by the transferor before or during the marriage, fails if, at the time of the transferor's death, the former spouse is not the transferor's surviving spouse as defined in Section 78, as a result of the dissolution or annulment of the marriage. A judgment of legal separation that does not terminate the status of husband and wife is not a dissolution for purposes of this section.

(b) Subdivision (a) does not cause a nonprobate transfer to fail in any of the following cases:

(1) The nonprobate transfer is not subject to revocation by the transferor at the time of the transferor's death.

(2) There is clear and convincing evidence that the transferor intended to preserve the nonprobate transfer to the former spouse.

(3) A court order that the nonprobate transfer be maintained on behalf of the former spouse is in effect at the time of the transferor's death.

(c) Where a nonprobate transfer fails by operation of this section, the instrument making the nonprobate transfer shall be treated as it would if the former spouse failed to survive the transferor.

(d) Nothing in this section affects the rights of a subsequent purchaser or encumbrancer for value in good faith who relies on the apparent failure of a nonprobate transfer under this section or who lacks knowledge of the failure of a nonprobate transfer under this section.

(e) As used in this section, "nonprobate transfer" means a provision, other than a provision of a life insurance policy, of either of the following types:

(1) A provision of a type described in Section 5000.

(2) A provision in an instrument that operates on death, other than a will, conferring a power of appointment or naming a trustee.

(Formerly § 5600, added by Stats. 2001, c. 417 (A.B. 873), § 9, operative Jan. 1, 2002. Renumbered § 5040 and amended by Stats. 2015, c. 293 (A.B. 139), § 12, eff. Jan. 1, 2016.)

———

Life Insurance Co. v. Ortiz arose in 2008, after the initial enactment of the rule that a nonprobate transfer to the transferor's former spouse fails if two elements are met: the instrument was executed by the transferor before or during the marriage; and at the time of the transferor's death, the former spouse is not the transferor's surviving spouse because of dissolution or annulment. The federal court recognized three exceptions to the rule, but it discussed only the exception that disposes of property by a beneficial designation to a former spouse if there is clear and convincing evidence that the transferor intended to retain the beneficial designation.

The case is an emotionally difficult one.

Police Officer Jerry Ortiz died in the line of duty survived by his new spouse Graciela, and two children from a marriage with former spouse Gloria. The children were in the custody of their mother. As the record indicates, decedent Jerry Ortiz was not on good terms with his former wife. During his first marriage Officer Ortiz listed Gloria as the sole beneficial designee on his life insurance policy. At Officer Ortiz's death, Gloria was still listed on the insurance contract as Officer Ortiz's sole pay on death beneficiary.

The full caption in *Life Insurance Company v. Ortiz* is retained to illuminate the potential (long list of) claimants. The overarching issue for the court was disposition of the $500,000 policy proceeds. Were the proceeds distributable through the beneficial designation on the life insurance policy to former spouse Gloria? Or, were the proceeds to descend (by the state intestacy statutes) to new spouse Graciela and to Officer Ortiz's two children by former wife Gloria.

LIFE INSURANCE COMPANY OF NORTH AMERICA, A
PENNSYLVANIA CORPORATION, PLAINTIFF,
V.
GLORIA IRENE ORTIZ, AN INDIVIDUAL, DEFENDANT–APPELLANT,
GRACIELA ELENA ORTIZ, AN INDIVIDUAL,
DEFENDANT–APPELLEE.
LIFE INSURANCE COMPANY OF NORTH AMERICA, A
PENNSYLVANIA CORPORATION; RELIANCE STANDARD LIFE
INSURANCE COMPANY, PLAINTIFFS,
V.
GLORIA IRENE ORTIZ, AN INDIVIDUAL, DEFENDANT–APPELLANT,
GRACIELA ELENA ORTIZ, AN INDIVIDUAL,
DEFENDANT–APPELLEE, AND
J.J.O., A MINOR; JAVIER A. ORTIZ, SR.;
GRACIELA CASTANO ORTIZ, DEFENDANTS.

535 F.3d 990 (9th Cir. 2008)

PER CURIAM.

This case involves an interpleader action over the life insurance proceeds for an officer killed in the line of duty. Although Luis Gerardo Ortiz's ex-wife, Gloria Ortiz, was designated as beneficiary, Graciela Ortiz argues that divorce extinguished Gloria Ortiz's expectancy interest. The district court awarded the life insurance proceeds to the estate for intestate division among Graciela Ortiz and the decedent's two sons. We reverse and remand.

FACTUAL AND PROCEDURAL BACKGROUND

On August 2, 1998, Luis Gerardo Ortiz ("Jerry") designated his wife, Gloria Ortiz ("Gloria"), as the beneficiary of his life insurance policies with Life Insurance Company of North America and Reliance Standard. Jerry and Gloria separated in March 2002, and the Superior Court of California entered a Judgment on Reserved Issues in their divorce on December 15, 2004. The Judgment on Reserved Issues awarded "[a]ll right, title and interest in any and all of Petitioner's retirement/pension, 457(b) plans, 401(k) plans or other deferred benefits in [Jerry]'s name" to Jerry. The document also included a pre-printed notice indicating that "[i]t does not automatically cancel the rights of a spouse as beneficiary on the other spouse's life insurance policy."

In February of 2005, Jerry's divorce attorney sent an exit letter advising him to "reaffirm and/or change any beneficiaries on any . . . insurance policies." The attorney also spoke with Jerry after the divorce judgment issued and urged him to change the beneficiaries of his life insurance policies immediately. Jerry indicated that "he intended to go and look into those policies" and "again assured [her] that he would." Despite these assurances, Jerry did not attempt to change the written beneficiary designations on file with Life Insurance Company of North America and Reliance Standard.

Jerry married Graciela Ortiz ("Graciela") on May 28, 2005. Jerry did not work May 28–31 because of the marriage and the honeymoon. On June 24, 2005, Jerry died as a result of a gunshot wound to the head while on duty. The term life insurance payment that funded Jerry's coverage at the time of death was withdrawn from his May paycheck. The life insurance companies deposited life insurance and accidental death benefits totaling $518,483.13 with the clerk of the court.

The life insurance companies instituted an interpleader action naming Gloria and Graciela as defendants. The district court judge found that the life insurance policies became Jerry's separate property at the time of his divorce from Gloria. The judge also found that Jerry expressed an intent to name Graciela as his beneficiary, but he died intestate before he could make that change. Accordingly, the judge awarded the proceeds of the policies to the estate to be split equally between Graciela and Jerry's two sons. The district court denied a motion to stay the judgment pending appeal, but this court granted an unopposed application for an emergency stay order.

JURISDICTION AND STANDARD OF REVIEW

The district court derived jurisdiction from 28 U.S.C. § 1332 because the parties are diverse and the amount in controversy exceeds $75,000 exclusive of interest and costs. We find jurisdiction over this appeal of the final judgment pursuant to 28 U.S.C. § 1291.

The interpretation of a divorce judgment is a matter of law, which we review de novo. *Lowenschuss v. Selnick,* 170 F.3d 923, 929 (9th Cir.1999).

DISCUSSION

I. DIVORCE JUDGMENT

Under California law, we look to the language of the property settlement agreement to determine whether the agreement extinguishes the expectancy interests of life insurance beneficiaries. *Life Ins. Co. of N. Am. v. Cassidy,* 35 Cal.3d 599, 200 Cal.Rptr. 28, 676 P.2d 1050, 1053 (1984). "[G]eneral language in a marital settlement agreement will not be construed to include an assignment or renunciation of the expectancy interest conferred on the named beneficiary of an insurance policy or a will unless it clearly appears that the agreement was intended to deprive either spouse of such a right." *Id.* A property settlement covering all property and releasing all claims may be found to include a life insurance expectancy interest, "but where the language is not broad enough to encompass such an expectancy . . . the wife may still take as beneficiary if the policy so provides." *Thorp v. Randazzo,* 41 Cal.2d 770, 264 P.2d 38, 40 (1953).

We find that the language of the divorce judgment between Jerry and Gloria Ortiz did not extinguish Gloria's expectancy interest in Jerry's life insurance proceeds. The text of the relevant Judgment on Reserved Issues did not contain a single direct reference to life insurance policies. Although one could read the provision awarding "[a]ll right, title and interest in any and all of Petitioner's retirement/pension, 457(b) plans, 401(k) plans or other deferred benefits" to encompass life insurance policies, it was not clearly apparent that the provision encompassed beneficiary status. Unlike in *Thorp,* the judgment did not "clearly indicate * * * that the parties' attention had been directed to the expectancy of the insurance proceeds, and that it was intended that plaintiff waive all interest therein, present and future." 264 P.2d at 41. Thus the divorce judgment was insufficient to waive beneficiary status because it is not clear from the text of the agreement that such status was contemplated and intentionally waived.

Additionally, the context of the Judgment on Reserved Issues suggests that the parties did not extinguish beneficiary status. The document contained a pre-printed notice that "[i]t does not automatically cancel the rights of a spouse as beneficiary on the other spouse's life insurance policy." This notice, while not dispositive, provided information regarding the additional steps required to alter life insurance beneficiaries. We can infer that Jerry and his attorney did not expect the judgment to terminate Gloria's beneficiary status because Jerry's attorney advised him to "reaffirm and/or change any beneficiaries on any . . . insurance policies" in her exit letter. Jerry also indicated that he understood the necessity of changing his named beneficiary when he spoke with his attorney in February. The pre-printed notice on the judgment form and the record evidence regarding Jerry's state of mind support our conclusion that the divorce judgment did not extinguish Gloria's expectancy interest.

We distinguish this case from *Meherin v. Meherin,* 99 Cal.App.2d 596, 222 P.2d 305 (1950). In *Meherin,* a property settlement agreement terminated a wife's expectancy interests by assigning "all of her right, title and interest in and to said policy" and further requiring her "to execute any instrument or documents required by the husband or the * * * Insurance Company to carry out the intention of this paragraph." *Id.* at 306. Unlike the Ortiz divorce judgment, the agreement in *Meherin* specifically referenced the insurance policy. *Id.* The agreement also referenced the documentation required by the husband or the insurance company to change the beneficiary and the wife's interests in post-death recovery. *Id.* Finally, the agreement in *Meherin* was a complete settlement whereas the Ortiz document was only a Judgment on Reserved Issues. The *Meherin* agreement clearly indicated that the parties directed their attention to expectancy interests and intended to waive those interests; the Ortiz judgment did not.

For the foregoing reasons, we find that Gloria's expectancy interest survived the divorce. In light of this finding, we hold that the district court erred when it relied on Jerry's postdivorce intent to terminate Gloria's expectancy interests. In both *Cassidy* and *Thorp*, the court only looked to the decedent's post-divorce intent *after* it determined that the language of the divorce decree terminated the expectancy interest. In *Cassidy,* the agreement "waive[d] and relinquish[ed] any expectancy that was not thereafter reaffirmed," and the court looked to evidence of post-divorce intent to determine whether the failure to change the beneficiary designation constituted a reaffirmation of the expectancy interest. 200 Cal.Rptr. 28, 676 P.2d at 1055–56. In *Thorp*, the waiver of future interests in life insurance policies and post-death benefits was explicit, and the court considered intent for the limited question of whether the failure to change the beneficiary amounted to a post-divorce confirmation of the designation. 264 P.2d at 41–42. This case is distinguishable from both *Cassidy* and *Thorp*, thus the district court's reliance on post-divorce intent was misplaced.

II. CHANGE OF BENEFICIARY

As a general rule, California requires a change to a beneficiary designation to be made in accordance with the terms of the policy. "[I]f it is not, no change is accomplished, unless whatever occurred in that respect comes within one of more of the three exceptions to the rule." *Cook v. Cook,* 17 Cal.2d 639, 111 P.2d 322, 328 (1941). [Among] the three exceptions are . . . (3) when the insured has done all that he could to effect the change but dies before the change is actually made. *Id.*

[T]he third exception is potentially applicable to this case. The Supreme Court of California interpreted this third exception, stating:

> We think that where the insurer is not contesting the change the rule is not to [be] applied rigorously and where the insured makes every reasonable effort under the circumstances, complying as far as he is able with the rules, and there is a clear manifestation of intent to make the change, which the insured has put into execution as best he can, equity should regard the change as effected.

Pimentel v. Conselho Supremo De Uniao Portugueza Do Estado Da California, 6 Cal.2d 182, 57 P.2d 131, 134 (1936). Thus, one's intent to change a beneficiary designation must be clearly manifested and put into motion as much as practicable. *See Manhattan Life Ins. Co. v. Barnes,* 462 F.2d 629, 633 (9th Cir.1972) ("California demands that substantial steps be taken to actually change a beneficiary before the formal requirements of the contract may be ignored.").

In this case, both insurance companies required written notification of change of beneficiary and Jerry took no steps toward providing such notification. Jerry's lawyer stressed the necessity of changing the designation in both her exit letter and an informal meeting. Jerry indicated that he understood and intended to change the designation; however, he took no action in the four months between the finalization of the divorce and his death. At any point following the finalization of his divorce, Jerry could have named Graciela, his two sons, or anyone else as the beneficiary of his policies. Jerry's inaction does not amount to substantial steps to change his beneficiary; therefore we find that the original designation of Gloria Ortiz remained valid. Thus the district court erred by relying on intent to circumvent a valid beneficiary designation.

III. COMMUNITY PROPERTY SHARE

Although we find that the beneficiary designation naming Gloria was valid, we note that Graciela retains a community property interest of 6.45% of the life insurance proceeds. This percentage represents a one-half interest in the four days' earnings that funded the final thirty-one day term of Luis's term life insurance.

CONCLUSION

We REVERSE and REMAND for the district court to award 93.55% of the disputed life insurance proceeds to Gloria Ortiz and 6.45% to Graciela Ortiz.

KOZINSKI, CHIEF JUDGE, dissenting:

The majority reaches a senseless, unjust and cruel result by awarding half a million dollars to the former wife of a peace officer felled in the line of duty, leaving the officer's widow and children out in the cold. We don't need to do this. The law, the facts, the equities, common sense and the district court's findings all support the just result here: giving the proceeds of the service life insurance policies meant to protect the officer's loved ones to the people he actually loved.

The majority pettifogs its way through the California caselaw, finding ways to distinguish this case and that, but loses sight of the key facts that support the district court's judgment: Gloria Ortiz—the woman who will get the windfall under the majority's stilted reasoning—had given up all interest in the policies at the time of her divorce from Deputy Ortiz. She had no interest in the policies anyway because they were for *term* insurance and thus built up no cash value. Every month's coverage was paid for by premiums deducted that month from Deputy Ortiz's paycheck. After the divorce, Gloria had no interest in the deputy's income. To award Gloria the proceeds, one must believe that Deputy Ortiz meant to spend a chunk of his salary buying insurance for the benefit of his estranged wife instead of his wife and sons.

Breadwinners buy life insurance to provide financial security for their dependents. Deputy Ortiz had no reason to provide financial security for a woman who wasn't his dependent and whom, by all accounts, he despised. Which is what the district court found after a trial. It's true that Deputy Ortiz had not yet changed the beneficiary designation on his policies when he was killed. But the delay wasn't very long, and certainly doesn't compel a finding that Deputy Ortiz meant to leave Gloria a pot of gold and his wife and sons a lump of coal.

The delay was, in any event, entirely understandable. While the deputy could have changed the beneficiary designation after his divorce in February, he prudently waited for Graciela to become his wife. The two wedded at the end of May and, after a short honeymoon, Deputy Ortiz returned to work. He didn't rush to change the beneficiary designation on his policies, probably because he didn't imagine he'd be killed three weeks later. Deputy Ortiz, like the rest of mankind, must have believed that he had plenty of time. Imprudent, perhaps, but very human. Who amongst us hasn't put off dealing with wills or other unpleasantries that remind us of our mortality? Is this the kind of mistake that should deprive Deputy Ortiz's wife and children of the insurance he maintained for their security? Surely not—at least not in California today.

The California courts have dealt with very similar situations for over half a century and have invariably awarded policy proceeds as intended by the decedent. *Thorp v. Randazzo,* 41 Cal.2d 770, 264 P.2d 38 (1953), is typical. The decedent was divorced from his former wife who, through a consent decree, gave up "all claims to any benefits that she may have at present, or which may hereafter be derived from the . . . life insurance policies upon the life of [the husband]." *Id.* at 39. The former wife was the beneficiary of two policies; the husband changed the beneficiary on one but not the other. The former wife sought the proceeds "as the named beneficiary on the policy at the time of deceased's death." *Id.* at 40. The trial court ruled against her and awarded the proceeds to the husband's estate.

The California Supreme Court recognized that "[t]he failure of the husband to exercise his power to change the beneficiary ordinarily indicates that he does not wish to effect such a change." *Id.* (citations omitted). Nevertheless, it *affirmed* the trial court because "each case must be decided upon its own facts." *Id.* (citations omitted). *Thorp* presented a much closer case than ours because the husband there *did* change the beneficiary on one policy but not the other. The most plausible inference would have been that he wanted the ex-wife to remain as beneficiary of the policy he didn't change. Even so, the trial court found that he did intend to change the beneficiary, and the state supreme court deferred to that finding.

Thorp distinguished *Grimm v. Grimm,* 26 Cal.2d 173, 157 P.2d 841 (1945), which had reached the opposite result. The only material difference between the cases was that the trial court in *Grimm* found that the decedent hadn't intended to change the beneficiary, while the trial court in *Thorp* found that he had. In each case, the state supreme court deferred to the trial court's findings.

Thorp was followed two decades later by *Life Ins. Co. of N. Am. v. Cassidy,* 35 Cal.3d 599, 200 Cal.Rptr. 28, 676 P.2d 1050 (1984), where the California Supreme Court again affirmed a trial court judgment in favor of the estate and against the former wife. The court ruled:

> We have concluded that the designation of appellant as beneficiary was superseded as of the date the parties entered into a marital settlement agreement which comprehensively disposed of all the rights and obligations between them. By terms of the agreement each waived all rights to take any property whatsoever at the death of the other unless such right was conferred by an instrument executed after the date of the agreement. *The evidence produced at trial clearly shows that the fact appellant remained the named beneficiary of the subject insurance policy was not the result of an intent by the deceased to make a new gift of the benefits of the policy to his former spouse, but was contrary to his expressed intent that she be removed as beneficiary of all insurance policies on his life.* We therefore affirm the judgment of the trial court.

Id. at 1051 (emphasis added). As the underscored language makes clear, the dispositive issue in *Cassidy* was the decedent's intent, with the beneficiary designation constituting but one indication of that intent, and not even a very significant one.

Chief Justice Bird dissented in *Cassidy* because she thought the evidence that the decedent intended to cut off the former wife's rights under the policy was very weak. Bird emphasized that "Mr. Cassidy's executor failed to offer *any* evidence as to Mr. Cassidy's intentions during the lengthy period between July of 1975 and Mr. Cassidy's death in December of 1976." *Id.* at 1059. The Chief Justice's dissent makes it very clear that the record in *Cassidy* was far flimsier than the record here: Deputy Ortiz made his statement about intending to remove his former spouse from the policies more forcefully and far closer to his untimely death than did Mr. Cassidy. Yet the *Cassidy* court upheld the finding of the trial court in favor of the estate and against the named beneficiary, while my colleagues reverse.

The California intermediate appellate courts have been even more forgiving of human frailty. In *Meherin v. Meherin,* 99 Cal.App.2d 596, 222 P.2d 305 (1950), a case the majority is at pains to distinguish, the ex-wife waived "all of her right, title and interest in and to said policy and the interest and benefits therein." *Id.* at 306. Here, Gloria gave up "all right, title and interest" in Deputy Ortiz's retirement plans and "other deferred benefits." No one, not even Gloria, claims that her interest in the policies survived the divorce; she relies entirely on the fact that Deputy Ortiz didn't change the beneficiary designation. The majority nitpicks at factual distinctions between our case and *Meherin,* but none of them matter because the trial court in both cases found that the decedent intended to change the beneficiary. If we were the triers of fact, we could make whatever findings we pleased. But we're not, so we must accept the district court's finding that Deputy Ortiz did not intend for Gloria to be the beneficiary of his life insurance policies. This makes our case materially indistinguishable from *Meherin,* and yet my colleagues reach the opposite result.

Finally, the California Court of Appeal in *Snyder v. Snyder,* 197 Cal.App.3d 6, 242 Cal.Rptr. 597 (1987), reached the same result on a surprisingly thin record. *Snyder* involved a contribution savings plan with the deceased husband's employer, Rockwell. The husband "never changed the beneficiary designation of the Rockwell savings plan," which named his former spouse. *Id.* at 598. Nor did the husband even *say* that he intended to make a change. The trial court nonetheless found against the ex-wife and in favor of the estate. In affirming that finding, the appeals court acknowledged:

> [There is] no testimony ... with respect to[the husband's] intention to change the beneficiary designation. There is, however, documentary evidence of his intent to supersede the original beneficiary designation: his will. Furthermore, *we can see no reason why [the husband] would have wanted to make a gift to [his ex-wife] of the plan's proceeds.* From a practical standpoint, any desire to retain [her] as beneficiary could have been implemented by submitting a postdivorce designation to that effect.

Id. at 600 (emphasis added). As the opinion makes clear, however, the will made no mention of the savings plan; it merely designated the new wife as the estate's residuary legatee. *Id.* at 598. *Snyder* thus relied only on the court's own sense of what the husband probably wanted, not on anything he actually said. Indeed, the court found that his *failure* to redesignate the former wife as beneficiary was sufficient proof that he didn't intend for her to take the savings plan.

There are two important things to note about the California cases, both of which my colleagues overlook. The first is that the designation of a beneficiary in a life insurance or similar plan is not very significant when there's been an intervening divorce. The California courts seem to understand, as the majority here does not, that a divorce rearranges all property relationships and, as to property acquired after the divorce, what really matters is how the deceased intended to distribute it. Every single case, including *Grimm,* and Chief Justice Bird's dissent in *Cassidy,* treats the decedent's intent as the dispositive question. In this case, Deputy Ortiz was killed in the line of duty right after his wedding, leaving him virtually no time to make the change; even Chief Justice Bird—who dissented in *Cassidy* largely because 20 months elapsed between the divorce and the husband's death—would be persuaded that Deputy Ortiz meant to leave the policy proceeds to his estate. Second, every one of the majority opinions affirms the judgment of the trial court, even on a paper-thin record. We are seriously out of step with the California cases by reversing the district court here.

What does the majority offer against this cavalcade of contrary authority? There is, of course, the fact that Deputy Ortiz was warned by his lawyer to change the beneficiary designations on his policies. But so what? Most of the decedents in the California cases knew that they should change the beneficiary designation. *See, e.g., Thorp,* 264 P.2d at 39 ("[D]eceased had discussed with his attorney his intention to change the policy so as to make it payable to his estate."); *Cassidy,* 200 Cal.Rptr. 28, 676 P.2d at 1051 ("Both parties were fully advised by their own counsel."). Had they taken the most sensible and prudent course of action, we wouldn't be reading about them in the opinions of the California courts. Here too, the advice given by Deputy Ortiz's lawyer was sound; had he followed it, he would have saved his family a great deal of aggravation, uncertainty and money.

But this doesn't mean—as the majority claims "that [Deputy Ortiz] and his attorney did not expect the judgment to terminate Gloria's beneficiary status." Maj. op. at 993–94. Setting aside the fact that inferences about the parties' state of mind are the province of the trial court, the majority is simply wrong: Deputy Ortiz and his lawyer may well have believed that the divorce settlement did cut off Gloria's interest in the policy—as it surely was meant to—and yet thought it prudent to change the beneficiary designation so as to avoid the delay, expense and grief of the current situation. The majority overreaches by reading anything more into their conversation.

The majority's reliance on the divorce decree's pre-printed notice is a makeweight. The notice was not part of the decree—it appeared below the judge's signature line—and could have had no legal effect on the relationship between the parties. It was good advice, and one wishes Deputy Ortiz had taken it. But a boilerplate notice in fine print at the bottom of a two page form can't possibly undermine the finding that Deputy Ortiz was not insuring his life for Gloria's benefit.

The majority tries to make something of the fact that Deputy Ortiz had a partial settlement, whereas the settlement in some California cases, such as *Meherin,* was "complete." Maj. op. at 993–94. This may be a distinction, but it makes no difference. The settlement here covered "all remaining issues" of property between Deputy Ortiz and Gloria. It was partial only because it didn't deal with child "custody, visitation, [and] * * * support," which the parties left for a separate consent decree. Why this should matter, the majority does not explain.

Finally, the majority cites to a series of cases which hold that a beneficiary designation is binding, unless the deceased complied with the insurer's terms for changing the designation or was unable to do so. Maj. op. at 994–95 (citing *Manhattan Life Ins. Co. v. Barnes,* 462 F.2d 629 (9th Cir.1972); *Cook v. Cook,* 17 Cal.2d 639, 111 P.2d 322 (1941); *Pimentel v. Conselho Supremo De Uniao Portugeuza Do Estado Da California,* 6 Cal.2d 182, 57 P.2d 131 (1936)). These cases are inapposite because none of them deals with the effect of a divorce decree. Were the cases the majority relies on in this section applicable to a situation such as ours, they would conflict with *Thorp, Cassidy, Meherin* and *Snyder.*

I might understand my colleagues' herculean efforts to swim against the current of California caselaw if they were straining to avoid an irrational and unjust result. But what sense is there in spinning fine distinctions to perpetrate an injustice? The wife of a man who put his life on the line to protect us will lose the protection he thought he had provided for her; his children will be left with nothing. As his lawyer predicted, I fully expect we'll hear Deputy Ortiz yelling from his grave when the majority issues its opinion.

After trial, the district court made clear findings and reached a just result that fulfilled Deputy Ortiz's fair expectations and protected his wife and children. Only a procrustean attachment to legal formalism could lead my colleagues to overturn the district court and reach an unconscionable result. Deputy Ortiz, and the family he intended to support, deserve better. Sadly, I must dissent.

NOTES

1. *Nonprobate transfers to a former spouse.* The prior rule, referenced in *Life Insurance Co. v. Ortiz,* was that a nonprobate transfer to a former spouse determined the disposition of the property. California Probate Code Section 5041(a), formerly Section 5600, reversed that rule. Subdivision (a) establishes the new general rule that "[e]xcept as provided in subdivision (b), ..." a nonprobate transfer to a former spouse fails if, at the time of the transferor's death, the former spouse is not the transferor's surviving spouse. Subdivision (b) sets out three exceptions. The new rule only applies in the case of dissolution or annulment, not in the case of separation. The term surviving spouse is defined in California Probate Code Section 78.

2. *Separated spouses. Estate of McDaniel,* 161 Cal. App. 4th 458, 73 Cal.Rptr.3d 907 (3d Dist. 2008) involved parties who were separated, had

petitioned for dissolution, but had not yet reached a settlement when soon to be ex-husband Troy died in a motorcycle accident. Marie stepped forward as Troy's surviving spouse to claim the insurance proceeds; so too did Troy's parents. As to insurance proceeds, said the court, even though Troy and Marie were still married persons by legal status, Marie was not Troy's surviving spouse for purposes of probate.

California Probate Code Section 78, reproduced above, defines what a surviving spouse is *not*, but it does not clearly state how to categorize a person who dies while in the process of obtaining a dissolution judgment. Thus the ruling in *Estate of McDaniel*, which followed *Estate of Lahey*, 76 Cal.App.4th 1056, 91 Cal.Rptr.2d 30 (1st Dist. 1999), helps clarify the issue: until the Legislature says otherwise, a separated spouse is not a "surviving spouse" for purposes of the Probate Code.

3.   *The* old *rule on joint tenancy with the right of survivorship after dissolution.* Under the common law rule, dissolution or annulment did not sever a joint tenancy. *Estate of Layton v. Pulliam*, 44 Cal.App.4th 1337, 52 Cal.Rptr.2d 251 (6th Dist.1996) illustrates. The case is about Roy and Angelina Layton, who separated in 1973 after 29 years of marriage. A final judgment of dissolution restored the parties to the status of single individuals in 1983, but that judgment reserved jurisdiction for the court to make a disposition of the community property at a later date. At dissolution, the couple owned a house titled in joint tenancy. Angelina continued to live in the residence after the divorce. In the decade following the final judgment of dissolution, the parties did not change the title to the disputed property, they did not sever the joint tenancy, and they did not ask the family law court to exercise its reserved jurisdiction to sever the joint tenancy. When Roy died in 1992, his will disposed of his estate to James Layton, one of his several children. At Angelina's subsequent death, her will disposed of her estate to her and Roy's two children and to her four children from a previous marriage.

A probate dispute ensued between James Layton, as executor of Roy's estate, and Linda Pulliam, as executor of Angelina's estate. James argued that the family law court's reserved jurisdiction authorized the probate court to divide community property at Roy's death; and, therefore, that the probate court erred when it failed to recognize that the effect of the status-only dissolution judgment was to sever the joint tenancy. Linda countered that title to the residence was in joint tenancy, the spouses knew it, they took no action to sever the joint tenancy—all evidence of their intent to have the survivor own the entire property at the death of the first.

Linda's legal argument was that the probate court was correct to decide the case by recognizing that California Family Code Section 802 precludes the use of any community property presumption—including the special joint title community property presumption of California Family Code Section 2581— when a marriage is dissolved more than four years prior to the death of the claimant's decedent (Chapter 2). The court agreed with this argument. It held (applying the old rule) that the joint tenancy was not severed by the dissolution. Hence the last surviving joint tenant (in this case Angelina) came into ownership of the residence at the other joint tenant's death (in this case James) by right of survivorship. The court indicated that the joint tenancy had not been severed by either former spouse despite ample motive and opportunity to do so.

> "We recognize that it may be illogical that divorcing parties, 'awaiting the court's division of property acquired during marriage, would envision or desire the operation of [joint tenancy] survivorship. An untimely death results in a windfall to the surviving spouse, a result neither party presumably intends or anticipates.' * * * But this is not invariably so. In this case, for instance, after passage of nearly a decade (from the dissolution judgment until Roy's death) neither Roy nor Angelina invoked the family court's reserved jurisdiction to declare the residence community property and divide it as such. Nor did either take measures to unilaterally sever the joint tenancy. These facts strongly suggest that Roy and Angelina envisioned or desired the operation of joint tenancy survivorship." *Id.* at 1343–1344.

4. *California Probate Code Section 5042, formerly Section 5601 establishes the* new *general rule that dissolution severs a joint tenancy.* The new rule is that a joint tenancy held between a decedent and decedent's former spouse, is severed if, at the time of the decedent's death, the former spouse is not the decedent's surviving spouse due to a dissolution or annulment of the marriage. This rule applies also to community property with the right of survivorship titles.

The rule does not apply in cases of separation. The term "surviving spouse" is defined in negative terms in California Probate Code Section 78, as discussed above. A joint tenancy severance is different from a disposition of funds by beneficial designation, as in an insurance policy. A separated spouse can take a joint tenancy by right of survivorship because the transfer does not depend on the joint tenant's marital status. Whereas a separated spouse would be barred from asserting surviving spouse status for purposes of obtaining life insurance proceeds, as discussed in *McDaniel,* see Note 2 above. That said, once the final judgment of dissolution is obtained, the joint tenancy is severed by operation of law. It defaults to a tenancy in common; and a decedent's share passes not by right of survivorship, but by will or intestacy.

The new rule applies to real and personal property. However, it does not affect U.S. Savings Bonds, which are controlled by federal law. See *Conrad v. Conrad,* 66 Cal.App.2d 280, 284–285, 152 P.2d 221 (4th Dist. 1944) for California's treatment of the issue.

In the case of a joint tenancy involving three or more joint tenants, severance by Section 5042 converts the decedent's interest into a tenancy in common, but does not sever the joint tenancy as between the other joint tenants. This is a favorite problem of first year property casebooks. So for example, Lake and Ocean, a married couple, own a residence as joint tenants with friend Bay. (Because the interst is a joint tenancy, shares are equal under the equality of interest rule.) Lake and Ocean obtain a final judgment of dissolution. The joint tenancy is severed by operation of law, but only as to the ex-spouse's two-thirds, not as to Bay's one-third. After severance, Lake owns one-third of the property as a tenant in common relative to Ocean, who also owns one-third; the couple own their two-third shares as joint tenants with Bay, who owns an undivided one-third. Now assume ex-spouse Lake predeceases ex-spouse Ocean while friend Bay is still alive. At Lake's death, Lake's one-third share is subject to probate administration. After that process the property is owned as follows: Ocean and the person who is Lake's successor own two-thirds as tenants in common; but they own their share in joint tenancy with Bay. The point of this twisty-turning story is that divorce severs Lake and Ocean's joint tenancy, but not their joint tenancy with Bay. Bay alone has the authority to sever the joint tenancy as to her one-third interest.

Court orders or binding agreements can prohibit the severance of the joint tenancy by the decedent. Such instruments supersede the application of California Probate Code Section 5042.

Third parties, and specifically subsequent good faith purchasers and encumbrancers are protected by California Probate Code Section 5042(c), which states: "nothing in this section affects the rights of a subsequent purchaser or encumbrancer for value in good faith who relies on an apparent severance under this section or who lacks knowledge of a severance under this section."

Importantly, joint form property acquired during marriage is presumed to be community property for purposes of dissolution under California Family Code Section 2581 (Chapter 2). The special joint title community property presumption can be applied after the death of a former spouse if—*and only if*— the court entered a judgment of dissolution prior to the former spouse's death, reserved jurisdiction over property matters, and the decedent died within four years of filing for dissolution. See *Marriage of Hilke*, 4 Cal. 4th 215, 841 P.2d 891, 14 Cal.Rptr. 2d 371 (1992) (Chapter 4). Otherwise, California Probate Code Section 5042 does not affect the community property presumption found at California Family Code Section 2581 or 802 (Chapters 2 and 9 above).

Renumbered Section 5042 was amended by Stats. 2015, c. 293 (A.B. 139), § 13, eff. Jan. 1, 2016.

SECTION 3. BASICS OF INTESTATE DISTRIBUTION AND ADMINISTRATION

When a married person dies intestate (without a valid will), intestacy law mandates that the decedent's one-half interest in community property pass to the surviving spouse by intestate succession. The surviving spouse already owns a one-half interest in any community or quasi-community property asset. Therefore, upon succeeding to the decedent's one-half interest, the surviving spouse steps into ownership of the entirety of the asset in question. The disposition of quasi-community property is substantially similar to that of community property.

The disposition of the decedent's separate property depends upon which consanguineous (blood) relatives survive the decedent. This is especially the case when a decedent is survived by biological or adopted children who are not also the children of the surviving spouse.

So for example, if the decedent is survived by a surviving spouse and *one* child (or the issue of one deceased child) who is not also the child of the surviving spouse, the surviving spouse and the decedent's child share the decedent's separate property by halves. If the decedent is survived by a surviving spouse and *two or more* children who are not also the children of the surviving spouse, the surviving spouse shares the decedent's separate property with the decedent's children. The surviving spouse receives one-third of the decedent's separate property; the children split the remaining two-thirds.

What if the decedent leaves no biological or adopted descendants?

Here again the surviving spouse may be required to share the decedent spouse's separate property with the decedent's ancestors (parents and grandparents) or collateral heirs (siblings and their issue). So, for example, if the decedent is survived by a surviving spouse, but no children (or issue of children) who are not also the children of the surviving spouse, then the decedent's parents or siblings have a right of descent. The surviving spouse succeeds to a one-half share of the decedent's separate property; the decedent's ancestors or collaterals split the other half.

Only in the case where the decedent dies without descendants, ancestors, or collateral heirs does the decedent's separate property descend entirely to the surviving spouse.

Because of the substantial difference in succession rights to community property as compared to separate property characterization of property is frequently at issue in probate proceedings.

Probate administration is essentially a three-fold process. One, it collects and inventories the decedent's assets. Two, it allocates and directs the payment of debts and taxes. Three, it distributes any remaining property, after debts and family protections are set aside, to the beneficiaries under the decedent's will or to the decedent's heirs under the laws of intestacy.

Not all property in which the decedent had an interest is subject to probate administration. Nonprobate property passes without the necessity of probate. Therefore, property held by the decedent and another in joint tenancy is not included in the probate estate. Likewise property held in community property with the right of survivorship is not included in the decedent spouse's probate estate.

Proceeds of life insurance policies are normally not included in the probate estate.

With some limited exceptions, a decedent's separate property is subject to probate administration, as discussed above.

If the deceased spouse died intestate leaving property passing to the surviving spouse under the intestate succession laws, or if the decedent died testate and by will bequeathing all or part of the decedent's property to the surviving spouse, the surviving spouse may use an abbreviated "set aside" procedure in lieu of the regular probate process. This set aside procedure is now available with respect to both community and separate property owned by the decedent. Even though probate administration is not required, death taxes, if any, must be paid and title to the property must be cleared. To resolve these problems, there is a special statutory procedure for the determination and confirmation of the property to the surviving spouse. This procedure is faster and less costly than regular probate administration. The surviving spouse need not avail himself or herself of the set-aside procedure, and may elect to have the property administered in the decedent's probate estate. The set aside procedure is available only to the surviving spouse. If the decedent left separate property or an interest in the community property to someone other than the surviving spouse, probate administration most likely would be required.

A problem that may arise in connection with probate or property set-aside proceedings involves the payment of the decedent's debts. Where the decedent's estate consists of both community and separate property, should the debts simply be apportioned between the two estates ratably according to their relative sizes? Or should the debts be classified, with community debts chargeable against the community property and separate debts payable out of separate property?

The California Probate Code currently provides that the allocation of liability is to be based on the rules applicable to liability of community and separate property for debts during marriage (Chapter 6). The test determines allocation based on the liability that the deceased spouse would have had for the debt if the death had not occurred.

WEST'S ANNOTATED CALIFORNIA PROBATE CODE

§ 6400. Property subject to intestacy provisions

Any part of the estate of a decedent not effectively disposed of by will passes to the decedent's heirs as prescribed in this part.

(Stats. 1990, c. 79 (A.B. 759), § 14, operative July 1, 1991.)

§ 6401. Surviving spouse; intestate share; community or quasi-community property; separate property

(a) As to community property, the intestate share of the surviving spouse is the one-half of the community property that belongs to the decedent under Section 100.

(b) As to quasi-community property, the intestate share of the surviving spouse is the one-half of the quasi-community property that belongs to the decedent under Section 101.

(c) As to separate property, the intestate share of the surviving spouse is as follows:

(1) The entire intestate estate if the decedent did not leave any surviving issue, parent, brother, sister, or issue of a deceased brother or sister.

(2) One-half of the intestate estate in the following cases:

(A) Where the decedent leaves only one child or the issue of a deceased child.

(B) Where the decedent leaves no issue, but leaves a parent or parents or their issue or the issue of either of them.

(3) One-third of the intestate estate in the following cases:

(A) Where the decedent leaves more than one child living.

(B) Where the decedent leaves one child living and the issue of one or more deceased children.

(C) Where the decedent leaves issue of two or more deceased children.

(Stats. 1990, c. 79 (A.B. 759), § 14, operative July 1, 1991. Amended by Stats. 2002, c. 447 (A.B. 2216), § 1, operative July 1, 2003; Stats. 2014, c. 913, (A.B. 2747), § 32, eff. Jan. 1, 2015.)

§ 6402. Intestate estate not passing to surviving spouse

Except as provided in Section 6402.5, the part of the intestate estate not passing to the surviving spouse under Section 6401, or the entire intestate estate if there is no surviving spouse, passes as follows:

(a) To the issue of the decedent, the issue taking equally if they are all of the same degree of kinship to the decedent they take equally, but if of unequal degree, then those of more remote degree take in the manner provided in Section 240.

(b) If there is no surviving issue, to the decedent's parent or parents equally.

(c) If there is no surviving issue or parent, to the issue of the parents of either of them, the issue taking equally if they are all of the same degree of kinship to the decedent, but if of unequal degree those of more remote degree take in the manner provided in Section 240.

(d) If there is no surviving issue, parent or issue of a parent, but the decedent is survived by one or more grandparents or issue of grandparents, to the grandparent or grandparents equally, or to the issue of such grandparents if there is no surviving grandparent, the issue taking equally if they are all of the same degree of kinship to the decedent, but if of unequal degree those of more remote degree take in the manner provided in Section 240.

(e) If there is no surviving issue, parent or issue of a parent, grandparent or issue of a grandparent, but the decedent is survived by the issue of a predeceased spouse, to that issue, the issue taking equally if they are all of the same degree of kinship to the predeceased spouse, but if of unequal degree those of more remote degree take in the manner provided in Section 240.

(f) If there is no surviving issue, parent or issue of a parent, grandparent or issue of a grandparent, or issue of a predeceased spouse, but the decedent is survived by next of kin, to the next of kin in equal degree, but where there are two or more collateral kindred in equal degree who claim through different ancestors, those who claim through the nearest ancestor are preferred to those claiming through an ancestor more remote.

(g) If there is no surviving next of kin of the decedent and no surviving issue of a predeceased spouse of the decedent, but the decedent is survived by the parents of a predeceased spouse or the issue of those parents, to the parent or parents equally, or to the issue of those parents if both are deceased, the issue taking equally if they are all of the same degree of kinship to the predeceased spouse, but if of unequal degree those of more remote degree take in the manner provided in Section 240.

(Stats. 1990, c. 79 (A.B. 759), § 14, operative July 1, 1991. Amended by Stats. 2002, c. 447 (A.B. 2216), § 2, operative July 1, 2003; Stats. 2014, c. 913 (A.B. 2747), § 32.5, eff. Jan. 1, 2015)

§ 6402.5. Predeceased spouse; portion of decedent's estate attributable to decedent's predeceased spouse

(a) For purposes of distributing real property under this section if the decedent had a predeceased spouse who died not more than 15 years before the decedent and there is no surviving spouse or issue of the decedent, the portion of the decedent's estate attributable to the decedent's predeceased spouse passes as follows:

(1)   If the decedent is survived by issue of the predeceased spouse, to the surviving issue of the predeceased spouse; if they are all of the same degree of kinship to the predeceased spouse they take equally, but if of unequal degree those of more remote degree take in the manner provided in Section 240.

(2)   If there is no surviving issue of the predeceased spouse but the decedent is survived by a parent or parents of the predeceased spouse, to the predeceased spouse's surviving parent or parents equally.

(3)   If there is no surviving issue or parent of the predeceased spouse but the decedent is survived by issue of a parent of the predeceased spouse, to the surviving issue of the parents of the predeceased spouse or either of them, the issue taking equally if they are all of the same degree of kinship to the predeceased spouse, but if of unequal degree those of more remote degree take in the manner provided in Section 240.

(4)   If the decedent is not survived by issue, parent, or issue of a parent of the predeceased spouse, to the next of kin of the decedent in the manner provided in Section 6402.

(5)   If the portion of the decedent's estate attributable to the decedent's predeceased spouse would otherwise escheat to the state because there is no kin of the decedent to take under Section 6402, the portion of the decedent's estate attributable to the predeceased spouse passes to the next of kin of the predeceased spouse who shall take in the same manner as the next of kin of the decedent take under Section 6402.

(b)   For purposes of distributing personal property under this section if the decedent had a predeceased spouse who died not more than five years before the decedent, and there is no surviving spouse or issue of the decedent, the portion of the decedent's estate attributable to the decedent's predeceased spouse passes as follows:

(1)   If the decedent is survived by issue of the predeceased spouse, to the surviving issue of the predeceased spouse; if they are all of the same degree of kinship to the predeceased spouse they take equally, but if of unequal degree those of more remote degree take in the manner provided in Section 240.

(2)   If there is no surviving issue of the predeceased spouse but the decedent is survived by a parent or parents of the predeceased spouse, to the predeceased spouse's surviving parent or parents equally.

(3)   If there is no surviving issue or parent of the predeceased spouse but the decedent is survived by issue of a parent of the

predeceased spouse, to the surviving issue of the parents of the predeceased spouse or either of them, the issue taking equally if they are all of the same degree of kinship to the predeceased spouse, but if of unequal degree those of more remote degree take in the manner provided in Section 240.

(4)   If the decedent is not survived by issue, parent, or issue of a parent of the predeceased spouse, to the next of kin of the decedent in the manner provided in Section 6402.

(5)   If the portion of the decedent's estate attributable to the decedent's predeceased spouse would otherwise escheat to the state because there is no kin of the decedent to take under Section 6402, the portion of the decedent's estate attributable to the predeceased spouse passes to the next of kin of the predeceased spouse who shall take in the same manner as the next of kin of the decedent take under Section 6402.

(c)   For purposes of disposing of personal property under subdivision (b), the claimant heir bears the burden of proof to show the exact personal property to be disposed of to the heir.

(d)   For purposes of providing notice under any provision of this code with respect to an estate that may include personal property subject to distribution under subdivision (b), if the aggregate fair market value of tangible and intangible personal property with a written record of title or ownership in the estate is believed in good faith by the petitioning party to be less than ten thousand dollars ($10,000), the petitioning party need not give notice to the issue or next of kin of the predeceased spouse. If the personal property is subsequently determined to have an aggregate fair market value in excess of ten thousand dollars ($10,000), notice shall be given to the issue or next of kin of the predeceased spouse as provided by law.

(e)   For the purposes of disposing of property pursuant to subdivision (b), "personal property" means that personal property in which there is a written record of title or ownership and the value of which in the aggregate is ten thousand dollars ($10,000) or more.

(f)   For the purposes of this section, the "portion of the decedent's estate attributable to the decedent's predeceased spouse" means all of the following property in the decedent's estate:

(1)   One-half of the community property in existence at the time of the death of the predeceased spouse.

(2)   One-half of any community property, in existence at the time of death of the predeceased spouse, which was given to the decedent by the predeceased spouse by way of gift, descent, or devise.

(3) That portion of any community property in which the predeceased spouse had any incident of ownership and which vested in the decedent upon the death of the predeceased spouse by right of survivorship.

(4) Any separate property of the predeceased spouse which came to the decedent by gift, descent, or devise of the predeceased spouse or which vested in the decedent upon the death of the predeceased spouse by right of survivorship.

(g) For the purposes of this section, quasi-community property shall be treated the same as community property.

(h) For the purposes of this section:

(1) Relatives of the predeceased spouse conceived before the decedent's death but born thereafter inherit as if they had been born in the lifetime of the decedent.

(2) A person who is related to the predeceased spouse through two lines of relationship is entitled to only a single share based on the relationship which would entitle the person to the larger share.

(Stats. 1990, c. 79 (A.B. 759), § 14, operative July 1, 1991.)

SECTION 4. ALLOCATING DEBT/ CREDITORS' RIGHTS

California Probate Code Section 11444 states that each debt shall first be characterized by the court as separate or community in accordance with the laws applicable to marital dissolution proceedings. Separate debts of either spouse shall be allocated to the spouse's separate property assets; community debts shall be allocated to the spouses' community property assets.

The interplay between the creditors' rights provisions of the Family Code and those of the California Probate Code is explored in *Dawes v. Rich* and *Collection Bureau of San Jose v. Rumsey*, excerpted below.

WEST'S ANNOTATED CALIFORNIA PROBATE CODE

§ 11440. Petition to allocate debt

If it appears that a debt of the decedent has been paid or is payable in whole or in part by the surviving spouse, or that a debt of the surviving spouse has been paid or is payable in whole or in part from property in the decedent's estate, the personal representative, the surviving spouse, or a beneficiary may, at any time before an order for final distribution is made, petition for an order to allocate the debt.

(Stats. 1990, c. 79 (A.B. 759), § 14, operative July 1, 1991.)

§ 11441. Contents of petition

The petition shall include a statement of all of the following:

(a) All debts of the decedent and surviving spouse known to the petitioner that are alleged to be subject to allocation and whether paid in whole or part or unpaid.

(b) The reason why the debts should be allocated.

(c) The proposed allocation and the basis for allocation alleged by the petitioner.

(Stats. 1990, c. 79 (A.B. 759), § 14, operative July 1, 1991.)

§ 11442. Value of separate and community property affecting allocation where no inventory and appraisal provided; show cause order

If it appears from the petition that allocation would be affected by the value of the separate property of the surviving spouse and any community property and quasi-community property not administered in the estate and if an inventory and appraisal of the property has not been provided by the surviving spouse, the court shall make an order to show cause why the information should not be provided.

(Stats. 1990, c. 79 (A.B. 759), § 14, operative July 1, 1991.)

§ 11444. Allocation of debt

(a) The personal representative and the surviving spouse may provide for allocation by agreement and, on a determination by the court that the agreement substantially protects the rights of interested persons, the allocation provided in the agreement shall be ordered by the court.

(b) In the absence of an agreement, each debt subject to allocation shall first be characterized by the court as separate or community, in accordance with the laws of the state applicable to marital dissolution proceedings. Following that characterization, the debt or debts shall be allocated as follows:

(1) Separate debts of either spouse shall be allocated to that spouse's separate property assets, and community debts shall be allocated to the spouses' community property assets.

(2) If a separate property asset of either spouse is subject to a secured debt that is characterized as that spouse's separate debt, and the net equity in that asset available to satisfy that secured debt is less than that secured debt, the unsatisfied portion of that secured debt shall be treated as an unsecured separate debt of that spouse and allocated to the net value of that spouse's other separate property assets.

(3)   If the net value of either spouse's separate property assets is less than that spouse's unsecured separate debt or debts, the unsatisfied portion of the debt or debts shall be allocated to the net value of that spouse's one-half share of the community property assets. If the net value of that spouse's one-half share of the community property assets is less than that spouse's unsatisfied unsecured separate debt or debts, the remaining unsatisfied portion of the debt or debts shall be allocated to the net value of the other spouse's one-half share of the community property assets.

(4)   If a community property asset is subject to a secured debt that is characterized as a community debt, and the net equity in that asset available to satisfy that secured debt is less than that secured debt, the unsatisfied portion of that secured debt shall be treated as an unsecured community debt and allocated to the net value of the other community property assets.

(5)   If the net value of the community property assets is less than the unsecured community debt or debts, the unsatisfied portion of the debt or debts shall be allocated equally between the separate property assets of the decedent and the surviving spouse. If the net value of either spouse's separate property assets is less than that spouse's share of the unsatisfied portion of the unsecured community debt or debts, the remaining unsatisfied portion of the debt or debts shall be allocated to the net value of the other spouse's separate property assets.

(c)   For purposes of this section:

(1)   The net value of either spouse's separate property asset shall refer to its fair market value as of the date of the decedent's death, minus the date-of-death balance of any liens and encumbrances on that asset that have been characterized as that spouse's separate debts.

(2)   The net value of a community property asset shall refer to its fair market value as of the date of the decedent's death, minus the date-of-death balance of any liens and encumbrances on that asset that have been characterized as community debts.

(3)   In the case of a nonrecourse debt, the amount of that debt shall be limited to the net equity in the collateral, based on the fair market value of the collateral as of the date of the decedent's death, that is available to satisfy that debt. For the purposes of this paragraph, "nonrecourse debt" means a debt for which the debtor's obligation to repay is limited to the collateral securing the debt, and for which a deficiency judgment against the debtor is not permitted by law.

(d)   Notwithstanding the foregoing provisions of this section, the court may order a different allocation of debts between the decedent's estate and the surviving spouse if the court finds a different allocation to be equitable under the circumstances.

(e)   Nothing contained in this section is intended to impair or affect the rights of third parties. If a personal representative or the surviving spouse incurs any damages or expense, including attorney's fees, on account of the nonpayment of a debt that was allocated to the other party pursuant to subdivision (b), or as the result of a debt being misallocated due to fraud or intentional misrepresentation by the other party, the party incurring damages shall be entitled to recover from the other party for damages or expense deemed reasonable by the court that made the allocation.

(Stats. 1990, c. 79 (A.B. 759), § 14, operative July 1, 1991. Amended by Stats. 2001, c. 72 (S.B. 668), § 1.)

§ 11445.   Payment of allocated shares; court order

On making a determination as provided in this chapter, the court shall make an order that:

(a)   Directs the personal representative to make payment of the amounts allocated to the estate by payment to the surviving spouse or creditors.

(b)   Directs the personal representative to charge amounts allocated to the surviving spouse against any property or interests of the surviving spouse that are in the possession or control of the personal representative. To the extent that property or interests of the surviving spouse in the possession or control of the personal representative are insufficient to satisfy the allocation, the court order shall summarily direct the surviving spouse to pay the allocation to the personal representative.

(Stats. 1990, c. 79 (A.B. 759), § 14, operative July 1, 1991.)

§ 11446.   Last illness and funeral expenses

Notwithstanding any other statute, funeral expenses and expenses of last illness shall be charged against the estate of the decedent and shall not be allocated to, or charged against the community share of, the surviving spouse, whether or not the surviving spouse is financially able to pay the expenses and whether or not the surviving spouse or any other person is also liable for the expenses.

(Stats. 1990, c. 79 (A.B. 759), § 14, operative July 1, 1991.)

§ 13550.   Personal liability for debts chargeable against property

Except as provided in Sections 11446, 13552, 13553, and 13554, upon the death of a married person, the surviving spouse is personally liable for the debts of the deceased spouse chargeable against the property described in Section 13551 to the extent provided in Section 13551.

(Stats. 1990, c. 79 (A.B. 759), § 14, operative July 1, 1991.)

§ 13551. Limitation of liability

The liability imposed by Section 13550 shall not exceed the fair market value at the date of the decedent's death, less the amount of any liens and encumbrances, of the total of the following:

(a) The portion of the one-half of the community and quasi-community property belonging to the surviving spouse under Sections 100 and 101 that is not exempt from enforcement of a money judgment and is not administered in the estate of the deceased spouse.

(b) The portion of the one-half of the community and quasi-community property belonging to the decedent under Sections 100 and 101 that passes to the surviving spouse without administration.

(c) The separate property of the decedent that passes to the surviving spouse without administration.

(Stats. 1990, c. 79 (A.B. 759), § 14, operative July 1, 1991.)

§ 13553. Exemption from liability

The surviving spouse is not liable under this chapter if all the property described in paragraphs (1) and (2) of subdivision (a) of Section 13502 is administered under this code.

(Stats. 1990, c. 79 (A.B. 759), § 14, operative July 1, 1991.)

§ 13554. Enforcement of debt against surviving spouse

(a) Except as otherwise provided in this chapter, any debt described in Section 13550 may be enforced against the surviving spouse in the same manner as it could have been enforced against the deceased spouse if the deceased spouse had not died.

(b) In any action based upon the debt, the surviving spouse may assert any defense, cross-complaint, or setoff which would have been available to the deceased spouse if the deceased spouse had not died.

(c) Section 366.2 of the Code of Civil Procedure applies in an action under this section.

(Stats. 1990, c. 79 (A.B. 759), § 14, operative July 1, 1991. Amended by Stats. 1990, c. 140 (S.B. 1855), § 18.1, operative July 1, 1991; Stats. 1992, c. 178 (S.B. 1496), § 43.)

§ 13650. Petition for order of administration not necessary

(a) A surviving spouse or the personal representative, guardian of the estate, or conservator of the estate of the surviving spouse may file a petition in the superior court of the county in which the estate of the deceased spouse may be administered requesting an order that administration of all or part of the estate is not necessary for the reason that all or part of the estate is property passing to the surviving spouse. The petition may also request an order confirming the ownership of the surviving spouse of property belonging to the surviving spouse under Section 100 or 101.

(b) To the extent of the election, this section does not apply to property that the petitioner has elected, as provided in Section 13502, to have administered under this code.

(c) A guardian or conservator may file a petition under this section without authorization or approval of the court in which the guardianship or conservatorship proceeding is pending.

(Stats. 1990, c. 79 (A.B. 759), § 14, operative July 1, 1991.)

§ 13651. Petition for order of administration not necessary—see Statutory Appendix.

§ 13656. Order; determination of property passing to surviving spouse

(a) If the court finds that all of the estate of the deceased spouse is property passing to the surviving spouse, the court shall issue an order describing the property, determining that the property is property passing to the surviving spouse, and determining that no administration is necessary. The court may issue any further orders which may be necessary to cause delivery of the property or its proceeds to the surviving spouse.

(b) If the court finds that all or part of the estate of the deceased spouse is not property passing to the surviving spouse, the court shall issue an order (1) describing any property which is not property passing to the surviving spouse, determining that that property does not pass to the surviving spouse and determining that that property is subject to administration under this code and (2) describing the property, if any, which is property passing to the surviving spouse, determining that that property passes to the surviving spouse, and determining that no administration of that property is necessary. If the court determines that property passes to the surviving spouse, the court may issue any further orders which may be necessary to cause delivery of that property or its proceeds to the surviving spouse.

(c) If the petition filed under this chapter includes a description of the interest of the surviving spouse in the community or quasi-community property, or both, which belongs to the surviving spouse pursuant to Section 100 or 101 and the court finds that the interest belongs to the surviving spouse, the court shall issue an order describing the property and confirming the ownership of the surviving spouse and may issue any further orders which may be necessary to cause ownership of the property to be confirmed in the surviving spouse.

(Stats. 1990, c. 79 (A.B. 759), § 14, operative July 1, 1991.)

§ 13657. Conclusive nature of order

Upon becoming final, an order under Section 13656(1) determining that property is property passing to the surviving spouse or (2) confirming the ownership of the surviving spouse of property belonging to the surviving spouse under Section 100 or 101 shall be conclusive on all persons, whether or not they are in being.

(Stats. 1990, c. 79 (A.B. 759), § 14, operative July 1, 1991.)

———

In *Dawes v. Rich*, a married couple owned a community property interest in Western Land & Development Company (Western), a general partnership. Western owned a trailer park and leased out trailers. Litigation was brought by the tenants against the general partnership and against husband, David Dawes. Wife Dorothy was not named in the litigation.

Before the litigation resolved, David and Dorothy transferred their community property to a revocable inter vivos trust called the "A Trust." Upon Dorothy's death in 1990, the A Trust transferred what had been her community property share to two other trusts, imaginatively named "the B and C" trusts. The B and C trusts were irrevocable. Dawes's children were trustees of the B and C trust, surviving spouse David was named the life estate beneficiary, and the children and living issue of one deceased child were remainderpersons.

On November 17, 1992, two years after Dorothy's death, a judgment in favor of the park tenants and against David Dawes was entered in one of the three actions. In 1993 and 1996 additional judgments in favor of the tenants were entered against David Dawes in the other two pending actions.

Shortly after the first 1992 judgment was entered in the tenants' favor, David Dawes filed bankruptcy petitions on his own behalf and on behalf of Western, the general partnership. The bankruptcy court determined, among other matters, that it did not have jurisdiction over the B and C trusts. Additionally, the probate court found that upon the death of Dorothy Dawes the assets in the A trust transferred to the B and C trusts. The consequence of the transfer was that the trust assets lost their community property character; as such the properties in the trust were evidently no longer reachable by the tenants, who were now judgment creditors of David Dawes.

The tenants appealed on two issues. One, were the assets in the B and C trusts reachable to satisfy their judgments against David Dawes? And two, had the action against the trusts been brought in a timely manner?

DAWES V. RICH

60 Cal.App.4th 24, 70 Cal.Rptr.2d 72 (4th Dist. 1997)

BENKE, ACTING PRESIDING JUSTICE.

Under our system of community property law, the marital community is liable for debts incurred by either spouse before or during marriage. The first question we confront in this case is whether, upon the death of one spouse, such liability continues. The second question we confront is whether, if such liability attaches to a deceased spouse's estate, the Legislature limited the time in which such liability may be asserted. We answer both questions in the affirmative and affirm the judgments of the trial court in favor of trustees of the estate of a deceased spouse.

I

Factual and Procedural Background

At all relevant times the Rancho Carlsbad mobile home park was owned by Western Land & Development Company (Western), a general partnership consisting of David F. Dawes and Ronald S. Schwab. Commencing in 1980 the tenants of the Rancho Carlsbad park engaged in litigation against Western, Dawes and Schwab with respect to rent increases Western attempted to impose on the tenants. Eventually, the tenants brought three actions in which Dawes was named as a defendant. In those actions, the tenants sought to rescind rent increases imposed in 1981 and 1982 and damages.

In 1983, many years prior to any final resolution of the tenants' litigation, Dawes and his wife, Dorothy L. Dawes, transferred their community property to an inter vivos trust. Among other goals, the trust was designed to minimize the amount of federal gift and estate tax which might be payable upon the death of either spouse. The trust instrument provided that during the lifetimes of the settlors, the community property would remain community property and the trust would be revocable. The trust instrument further provided that upon death, the community property would be divided into three subsidiary trusts. The first trust, the so-called A trust, would be funded with the survivor's one-half share of the community property and would be revocable by the survivor.

The second trust, the so-called B trust, would be in the maximum amount allowable under the federal gift and estate tax marital deduction and would be funded from the decedent's one-half share of the community property. The third trust, or so-called C trust, would contain any residue from the decedent's one-half of the community property. The B and C trusts would be irrevocable. The surviving spouse was entitled to the income from the B and C trusts during his or her lifetime, and upon his or her death the corpus of the trust would pass to the Dawes's children and the children of their deceased daughter. The trustees of the trust were the Daweses' two surviving children, defendants and respondents David Alan Dawes and Stuart E. Dawes.

Dorothy Dawes died in January 1990 and the terms of the trust instrument became operative. Her one-half of the community property estate passed to the B and C trusts and David F. Dawes's one-half share passed to the A trust.

On November 17, 1992, a judgment in favor of the tenants and against David F. Dawes was entered in one of the three actions. Thereafter, in 1993 and 1996 additional judgments in the tenants' favor were entered in the other two actions they had brought against Western, David F. Dawes and Schwab.

Shortly after the first judgment was entered in the tenants' favor, David F. Dawes filed bankruptcy petitions on his own behalf and on behalf of Western. The bankruptcy court determined, among other matters, that it did not have jurisdiction over the B and C trusts.

On December 29, 1995, the tenants levied writs of execution on defendants and respondents David Alan Dawes and Stuart E. Dawes as trustees of the B and C trusts. The trustees then filed a petition in probate court seeking a determination trust assets were not subject to execution on the tenants' judgment. On August 5, 1996, before judgment on the trustees' probate petition was entered, the tenants filed two complaints against the trustees seeking a declaration the assets in the B and C trusts were subject to the judgment entered in the tenants' favor. The trustees demurred to the complaints.

The probate court entered judgment in favor of the trustees. The probate court found that upon the death of Dorothy Dawes, the assets transferred to the B and C trusts lost their community property character and their liability for David F. Dawes's debts. In the alternative, the probate court found the tenants' attempts to execute against trust assets were time barred. Finally, the probate court found that due process did not permit execution of judgment against trust assets where neither Dorothy Dawes nor the trustees had been named as defendants.

The trial court hearing the trustees' demurrers sustained them on the grounds the tenants' complaints were untimely and judgments in favor of the trustees were entered. The tenants filed notices of appeal from the order of the probate court and the judgments dismissing their complaints. We consolidated the appeals.

II

Issues

On appeal the tenants contend that, notwithstanding Dorothy Dawes's death, the assets held in the B and C trusts are liable for the judgments entered against David F. Dawes and that the liability of the assets was asserted in a timely manner.

III

Discussion

A. *Post-Mortem Liability for Community Debts*

From the time of statehood in the middle of the last century until 1984, when the Legislature acted to alter the system, our courts held that as a matter of equity and fairness to creditors, one spouse who received community property following termination of a marriage received the community property subject to liability for community debts incurred by the other spouse during the marriage. (See Frankel v. Boyd (1895) 106 Cal. 608, 612–615, 39 P. 939; Bank of America etc. Assn. v. Mantz (1935) 4 Cal.2d 322, 327, 49 P.2d 279; Gould v. Fuller (1967) 249 Cal.App.2d 18, 24, 57 Cal.Rptr. 23; Head v. Crawford (1984) 156 Cal.App.3d 11, 18, 202 Cal.Rptr. 534, disapproved on other grounds Droeger v. Friedman, Sloan & Ross (1991) 54 Cal.3d 26, 36, 283 Cal.Rptr. 584, 812 P.2d 931.)

In Frankel v. Boyd the court held that community property a wife received in a divorce proceeding was subject to a creditor's bill brought by her former husband's creditor with respect to a debt incurred during marriage. The court relied on earlier cases which reached the same result with respect to community property received upon the death of a spouse. The court stated: "In Packard v. Arellanes, supra [17 Cal. 525 (1861)], the court, speaking through Cope, J. said: 'Our whole system by which the rights and property between husband and wife are regulated and determined is borrowed from the civil and Spanish laws, and we must look to these sources for the reasons which induced its adoption and the rules and principles which govern its operation and effect. The relation of husband and wife is regarded by the civil law as a species of partnership, the property of which, like that of any other partnership, is primarily liable for the payment of its debts. . . . It is the well-settled rule of the law that the debts of the partnership have priority of claim to satisfaction out of the community estate. [Citation.]. . . . The legislature intended to establish a similar relationship as to property as that existing in the civil law. The contracting of debts is one of the incidents of that relationship, and it would be unreasonable to suppose that the intention was to do away with so important a principle as that of the liability of the community property for their payment. We think that for all purposes connected with the administration of such property the debts of the community are to be regarded, not as the mere private and individual debts of the husband, but as obligations involving the liability of each of the members of the community.'" (Frankel v. Boyd, supra, 106 Cal. at pp. 613–614, 39 P. 939.)

As will become evident in the second part of this opinion, it bears emphasis that a spouse's post-marital liability for debts incurred by a former or deceased spouse is based on one spouse's receipt of property which in fairness should have been applied to the other spouse's debts. (See Frankel v. Boyd, supra, 106 Cal. at pp. 611–612, 39 P. 939; Gould v. Fuller, supra, 249 Cal.App.2d at p. 21, 57 Cal.Rptr. 23.) Such liability is not based on any legal interest the creditor has in the particular property transferred. As the court in Frankel v. Boyd explained: "That the [creditor] has no specific lien upon the property sought to be held liable for the satisfaction of his debt may be conceded.

"Had his judgment or execution established such lien there would have been no necessity for this action.

"The nature and purpose of a creditor's bill is to enable the creditor to apply to the payment of his debt property of the judgment debtor which, by its nature, cannot be taken in an execution at law, or to convert the holder of a legal estate into a trustee and call for a conveyance, or to have it sold in satisfaction of his claim, or to aid the creditor in reaching property of his debtor by removing fraudulent judgments or conveyances which defeat his remedy at law." (Frankel v. Boyd, supra, 106 Cal. at p. 611, 39 P. 939; see also Gould v. Fuller, supra, 249 Cal.App.2d at p. 21, 57 Cal.Rptr. 23.) Significantly, given the nature of the creditor's claim, the court in Gould v. Fuller held that the three-year limitation period which governed fraudulent transfers, Code of Civil Procedure section 338, governed the action against the transferee spouse. (249 Cal.App.2d at p. 32, 57 Cal.Rptr. 23.)

In 1984 the Legislature materially altered the post-marital liability of spouses. The Legislature determined that, under most circumstances, after a marriage has ended, it is unwise to continue the liability of spouses for community debts incurred by former spouses. Accordingly, the Legislature enacted former Civil Code section 5120.160, subdivision (a)(2), which provided that upon division of the community estate by way of dissolution: "The separate property owned by a married person at the time of the division and the property received by the person in the division is not liable for a debt incurred by the person's spouse before or during marriage, and the person is not personally liable for the debt, unless the debt was assigned for payment by the person in the division of the property. Nothing in this paragraph affects the liability of property for the satisfaction of a lien on the property." (Stats.1984, ch. 1671, § 9.) In 1992 former Civil Code section 5120.160 was enacted without substantive change as Family Code section 916.

The Law Revision Commission Comment to Family Code section 916 states: "When enacted in 1984 (as former Civil Code Section 5120.160), subdivisions (a)(2)–(3) reversed the former case law rule that a creditor may seek enforcement of a money judgment against the former community property in the hands of a nondebtor spouse after dissolution of the marriage. See e.g., Bank of America N.T. & S.A. v. Mantz, 4 Cal.2d 322, 49 P.2d 279 (1935).

"Subdivision (a)(2) makes clear that former community estate property received by the nondebtor spouse at division is liable only if the nondebtor spouse is assigned the debt in division."

Importantly, however, "[w]hen the Legislature enacted [former Civ.Code, § 5120.160], it was contemplated that '[i]n allocating the debts to the parties, the court in the dissolution proceeding should take into account the rights of creditors so there will be available sufficient property to satisfy the debt by the person to whom the debt is assigned, provided the net division is equal.'" (Lezine v. Security Pacific Fin. Services, Inc. (1996) 14 Cal.4th 56, 75, 58 Cal.Rptr.2d 76, 925 P.2d 1002, quoting Recommendation Relating to Liability of Marital Property for Debts (Jan.1983) 17 Cal. Law Revision Com. Rep. (1984) pp. 23–24, fn. omitted.)

When a community estate is terminated by way of the death of a spouse, community debts are treated somewhat differently. Under Probate Code section 11444, the surviving spouse, the personal representative or an interested party may petition the probate court for an allocation of debts between the surviving spouse and the estate of the deceased spouse. Under section 11444, subdivision (a), the personal representative and the surviving spouse may agree to an allocation subject to a determination by the probate court that the agreement substantially protects the rights of interested persons. In the absence of such an agreement, the probate court is required to apportion the debt between the surviving spouse and the estate on the same basis it would be required to employ during marriage. (Prob.Code, § 11444, subd. (b).)

In contrast to the provisions of Probate Code section 11444, when a deceased spouse's property is not subject to any administration but passes directly to the surviving spouse, the surviving spouse's liability for debts incurred by the deceased spouse is governed by Probate Code sections 13550 et seq. Under section 13550, the surviving spouse who receives community property without probate administration "is personally liable for the debts of the deceased spouse chargeable against the property described in Section 13551 to the extent provided in Section 13551." (Italics added.) Probate Code section 13551 in turn provides that the liability created by Probate Code section 13550 shall not exceed the fair market value of the community property and the decedent's separate property which passed to the survivor without administration. Claims against a surviving spouse under Probate Code section 13550 must be brought within one year of the death of the deceased spouse. (Prob.Code, § 13554, subd. (c); Code Civ. Proc., § 366.2, subd. (a)(1).)

The problem posed here—the liability of a deceased spouse's estate for community debts incurred by a surviving spouse—is apparently not the subject of any directly applicable substantive statute. The marriage was not terminated by way of dissolution and a judicially approved division of the community property; thus, the substantive bar to liability created by Family Code section 916 has no application. Moreover, there was no judicially approved allocation of debts between the trustees and David F. Dawes which arguably might protect the trustees from the tenants' claim under Probate Code section 11444.

Although the trustees suggest that we do so, we are not inclined to create a bar to substantive liability by way of analogy to the dissolution and allocation provisions set forth in Family Code section 916 or Probate Code section 11444, subdivision (b). Aside from important considerations of stare decisis and separation of powers, the principal difficulty we face in doing so in this case is the lack of any judicial supervision over the allocation of assets and liabilities of the community estate. Our Supreme Court has expressly found that judicial supervision was a condition contemplated by the Legislature in revoking the pre-existing rule of continuing liability for community debts. (See Lezine v. Security Pacific Fin. Services, Inc., supra, 14 Cal.4th at p. 75, 58 Cal.Rptr.2d 76, 925 P.2d 1002.) The express continuation of a surviving spouse's liability set forth in Probate Code section 13550 is further evidence the Legislature's desire to eliminate post-mortem liability for community debts was closely connected to the availability of judicial supervision over the allocation of community debts.

In sum then, we agree with the tenants insofar as they argue the trustees did not receive Dorothy Dawes's share of the community estate entirely free from liability for debts incurred by David F. Dawes during the Daweses' marriage.

B.   Statute of Limitations

As we have noted, in at least one case a claim based upon receipt of community property and growing out of debts incurred by a former spouse was treated as a fraudulent conveyance subject to the three-year statute of limitations set forth in Code of Civil Procedure section 338. (See Gould v. Fuller, supra, 249 Cal.App.2d at p. 32, 57 Cal.Rptr. 23.) Arguably, the tenants' claims in this case are also in the nature of a fraudulent conveyance action and, in the absence of any other more directly applicable statute, would be governed by either Code of Civil Procedure section 338 or Civil Code section 3439.09, the statute of limitations for claims under the recently enacted Uniform Fraudulent Transfer Act.

However, as the trustees point out, the Legislature has adopted a more directly applicable statute. In 1990 the Legislature amended former Code of Civil Procedure section 353 to shorten the time in which claims against decedents may be asserted. In particular, the Legislature added subsections (b), (c) and (d) to former Code of Civil Procedure section 353. As enacted, former Code of Civil Procedure section 353, subdivision (b), stated in pertinent part: "Except as provided in subdivisions (c) and (d), if a person against whom an action may be brought on a liability of the person, whether arising in contract, tort, or otherwise, dies before the expiration of the time limited for the commencement thereof, and the cause of action survives, an action may be commenced within one year after the date of death, and the time otherwise limited for the commencement of the action does not apply. Subject to Chapter 8 (commencing with Section 9350) of Part 4 of Division 7 of the Probate Code, the time provided in this subdivision for commencement of an action is not tolled or extended for any reason." (Stats.1990, ch. 140, § 1.) Subsection (b) of Code of Civil Procedure section 353 was enacted without substantive change as Code of Civil Procedure section 366.2 in 1992.

Subsection (d) of former Code of Civil Procedure section 353, which would be applicable to Dorothy Dawes's estate, stated: "If a person against whom an action may be brought died on or after July 1, 1988, and before January 1, 1991, and before the expiration of the time limited for the commencement of the action, and the cause of action survives, an action may be commenced before the earlier of the following times:

"(1) January 1, 1992.

"(2) One year after the issuing of letters testamentary or of administration, or the time otherwise limited for the commencement of the action, whichever is the later time." (Stats.1990, ch. 140, § 1.)

The repeal of former Code of Civil Procedure section 353 and adoption of Code of Civil Procedure section 366.2 did not have any effect on cases to which Civil Procedure section 353, subdivision (d), applied. (23 Cal.L.Rev. Comm. 895 (1992).)

The statute was enacted because of concern the four-month claims period which governed probated estates was not constitutionally sound if applied to creditors who did not have actual notice of a probate administration. The Law Revision Commission believed a one-year statute running from death would pass constitutional muster because "it allows a reasonable time for the creditor to discover the decedent's death, and it is an appropriate period to afford repose and provide a reasonable cutoff for claims that soon would become stale." (Recommendation Relating to Notice to Creditors in Estate Administration (1990) 20 Cal.L.Rev. Comm. Reports 507, 513, fn. omitted.)

By its terms, former Code of Civil Procedure section 353, subdivision (d), bars the tenants' attempts to recover from the trustees. The levies of execution they served on the trustees and their declaratory relief action were actions within the meaning of the statute. (See Code Civ. Proc., §§ 21, 363.) Moreover, those actions were commenced after January 1, 1992.

The tenants contend former Code of Civil Procedure section 353, subdivision (d), does not apply to their claims against the trustees because they believe the claims are not "based upon a liability of the person" within the meaning of former Code of Civil Procedure section 353, subdivision (b), and current Code of Civil Procedure section 366.2. The tenants argue that because the judgments they are attempting to enforce are for debts incurred by David F. Dawes and since their ability to recover on those debts is limited to the amount of community property the trustees received, the debts are not based upon any personal liability of Dorothy Dawes within the meaning of the statute. We disagree.

By its terms, the statute speaks of a "liability of the person, whether arising in contract, tort, or otherwise." (Former Code Civ. Proc., § 353, subd. (b), current Code Civ. Proc., § 366.2, subd. (a)(1), italics added.) Thus the principle question we must consider is the nature of the claims the tenants are asserting against the trustees. In doing so, we must bear in mind that the drafters of former Code of Civil Procedure section 353 and current Code of Civil Procedure section 366.2 believed the limitation period the statute imposes serves "the strong public policies of expeditious estate administration and security of title for distributees, and is consistent with the concept that a creditor has some obligation to keep informed of the status of the debtor." (Recommendation Relating to Notice to Creditors in Estate Administration, supra, 20 Cal.L.Rev. Comm. Reports at p. 512.)

First, we note that when a surviving spouse is asked to pay debts incurred by a deceased spouse, the Legislature has expressly determined the survivor is "personally liable" for debts incurred by the deceased spouse but that the extent of such personal liability is limited to the value of the community property received or held by the surviving spouse. (Prob.Code, §§ 13550, 13551.) Significantly, such claims are expressly made subject to the time limitations set forth in Code of Civil Procedure section 366.2.

Plainly, enactment of Probate Code section 13550 et seq. raises a question of fairness to the respective interests of surviving and deceased spouses. It is difficult to discern any reason for providing a surviving spouse greater protection from claims incurred during a marriage than is afforded to his or deceased spouse's estate. Indeed, given the need to promptly resolve claims against a decedent's estate and distribute its assets, it does not seem likely that the Legislature would intend that third-party distributees would be exposed to claims against community assets for a longer period of time than an actual surviving member of the marital community. Given these circumstances, what we discern from enactment of Probate Code section 13550 is that it is less a prescription of law than a description of what the law otherwise imposes: personal liability upon the receipt of assets which in fairness should be devoted to meeting the debts of the transferor.

Our conclusion about the descriptive nature of Probate Code section 13550 is consistent with the cases which have treated post-marital liability as transferee liability which arises as a result of receiving property which should be applied to the transferor's debt. (See Frankel v. Boyd, supra, 106 Cal. at pp. 613–614, 39 P. 939, Gould v. Fuller, supra, 249 Cal.App.2d at p. 21, 57 Cal.Rptr. 23.) Importantly, we are aware of no case in which the need to prevent injustice has ever been so great that in addition to creating liability on behalf of a transferee spouse, creditors have been provided anything in the nature of a lien against or title to particular property the transferee spouse received upon termination of a marriage. Indeed, the authority we have discovered appears to have flatly rejected the notion the creditor has any legal interest in a transferee spouse's report. (See Frankel v. Boyd, supra, 106 Cal. at p. 611, 39 P. 939 [conceded that creditor has no specific lien on transferee spouse's property].) Rather, as under Probate Code section 13550, the cases have merely found that the underlying personal liability of the transferor spouse is limited to the value of property received. (See e.g., Gould v. Fuller, supra, 249 Cal.App.2d at p. 21, 57 Cal.Rptr. 23.)

It is also helpful to recognize this treatment of post-marital liability is in no sense unique. Indeed, it is quite similar in fundamental respects to the liability imposed on transferees under California's version of the Uniform Fraudulent Transfer Act (UFTA), Civil Code section 3439 et seq. In particular we note that where a transfer is voidable under UFTA, "the creditor may recover judgment for the value of the asset transferred . . . or the amount necessary to satisfy the creditor's claim, whichever is less. The judgment may be entered against the following: (1) The first transferee of the asset or the person for whose benefit the transfer was made. (2) Any subsequent transferee other than a good faith transferee who took for value or from any subsequent transferee." (Civ.Code, § 3439.08, subd. (b).) The liability of a transferee spouse for community debts is much the same: a judgment against the transferee is limited to the value of the property received. (See Prob.Code, § 13550.)

Accordingly, we find that any liability growing of the transfer of community property upon the death of Dorothy Dawes was a personal liability subject to the time limitations set forth in former Code of Civil Procedure section 353, subdivision (d). Because the levies of execution and declaratory relief action were not filed within those time limits, the probate court and the trial court did not err in entering judgments in favor of the trustees.

We appreciate that given the protracted nature of the litigation which they pursued against David F. Dawes, the tenants believe application of former Code of Civil Procedure section 353, subdivision (d), is particularly unfair to them. However, in adopting the limitation period in the statute, the Legislature plainly recognized the risk that in unusual circumstances creditors would not be able to bring an action within one year of death. In rejecting any longer limitation period, the drafters of the statute stated: "Even under the existing four-month claim period it is unusual for an unpaid creditor problem to arise. A year is usually sufficient time for all debts to come to light. Thus, it is sound public policy to limit potential liability to a year; this will avoid delay and procedural complication of every probate proceeding for the rare claim that might arise more than a year after the decedent's death." (Recommendation Relating to Notice Creditors, supra, 20 Cal.L.Rev. Comm. Reports at p. 513.) Given this drafting history we are in no position to relieve tenants from operation of the statute.

Order and judgments affirmed.

HALLER and MCINTYRE, JJ., concur.

NOTES

1. *The 1991 version of California Probate Code Section 11444.* Under this section, liability was based on the (then current) rules applicable to the liability for community property for debts during marriage. *Dawes* was decided in 1997, before significant amendments were made to California Probate Code Section 11444. *Dawes* holds that wife Dorothy's one-half share of the community property, even though transferred into irrevocable Trusts B and C upon her death, was subject to the timely claims of husband David's creditors. Unfortunately, however, the creditor's claims were brought too late—they were time barred.

2. *The 2001 version of California Probate Code Section 11444.* The amended version of the statute, the personal representative and the surviving spouse may provide for allocation of debts by agreement and, after a court determines that the allocation protects the rights of interested persons, "the allocation provided in the agreement shall be ordered by the court." The quoted language is part of the original 1991 statute.

The 2001 amendments to the statute are extensive. They direct a court, "in the absence of an agreement," to do the following for "each debt . . . .":

- Characterize the debt "in accordance with the laws of the state applicable to marital dissolution proceedings" (11444(b));
- Allocate the debt by treating it, subject to statutory value guidelines, as:
  - According to its character—community property debts are paid by community property; separate property debts are paid by separate property;

    o   As an unsecured debt of one or the other spouse's separate property;

    o   As a debt of one or the other spouse's one-half share of the community property assets.

The statute is long and involved, but rest assured that if there is an issue, prepared forms assist parties in inventorying, ordering and allocating debts for purposes of obtaining a judicial order to allocate debts. *See*, West's California Code Forms, Probate § 11440 Form 1, Petition to Allocate Debts When There is No Agreement Between Personal Representative and Surviving Spouse. *See also*, Rutter, Cal. Practice Guide: Enforcing Judgments/Debts Ch. 3-A, A. Evaluating the Claim.

Dawes adjudicates the surviving spouse's judgment creditors' right to reach community property that has lost its character due to the operation of an estate plan.

What about debts of a deceased spouse? Can the creditor reach the assets of a surviving spouse to satisfy claims against the deceased spouse?

The general rule is that upon the death of a married person, the surviving spouse is personally liable for the debts of the deceased spouse. The survivor's one-half community property interest is not part of the decedent's administered estate, but neither is the survivor's one-half interest exempt from the reach of the decedent's creditors.

The general rule of *derivative liability*, in a broad sense, may appear to contradict the rule in California Family Code Section 1100(a). For example, consider a case where a spouse, with a terminal illness takes on debt knowing that he or she will not be alive to satisfy creditors' claim. Has that spouse exercised management and control over community property in a testamentary way? The answer is no for several reasons.

One, there is a definitional rationale for how California Family Code Section 1100(a) is consistent with the general rule of derivative liability. California Family Code Section 1100(a) provides that during marriage a spouse has the right to legal management and control of the community personal property in all matters nontestamentary (Chapter 6). Testamentary, in this context, means an action designed to dispose of property through an instrument that becomes effective at death, something like a valid will or a nonprobate transfer.

Two, there is a marshaling rationale. When a person dies *testate*, as in *Dawes* the decedent's estate is collected by an executor. The executor is directed to pay the decedent's debts according to a pre-established plan; debts are paid before any distributions of property are made. Additionally, as was the case in *Dawes*, in the absence of a private plan to pay the decedent's debts, there is a statutory rubric for how to classify and allocate the decedent's debts.

Three, there is an administrative rationale. When a married person dies *intestate*, there is no pre-established plan for how to pay off the decedent's debts. Additionally, depending on the size of the estate, there may or may not be a probate administration. Therefore, the purpose of holding the surviving spouse personally (derivatively) liable for the debts of an intestate decedent spouse is twofold. Derivative liability protects third-party creditors from stale claims by ensuring the payment of debts that were incurred by the decedent spouse *during the marriage*. California Probate Code Section 13550. The surviving spouse pays from the (former) community property or, if available, from separate property that passes to the survivor.

One sometimes hears that the surviving spouse essentially steps into the shoes of the decedent spouse. This folk-wisdom about derivative liability has a legal parallel in California Probate Code Section 13554, which provides that "... any debt described in California Probate Code Section 13550 may be enforced against the surviving spouse in the same manner as it could have been enforced against the deceased spouse if the deceased spouse had not died." Derivative liability actions are currently governed by California Code of Civil Procedure 366.2 if a decedent "[d]ies before the expiration of the applicable limitations period, and the cause of action survives ... " the death of the decedent. The statute of limitations is one year.

The next case, *Rumsey* for short, illustrates.

Rumsey is a tale of competing statutes of limitation. Wife Jean died intestate leaving a hospital bill of over $100,000. The Collection Bureau of San Jose waited four years to bring an action against Jean's husband Donald. The Bureau (successfully) argued on appeal that Jean's hospital expenses were a necessary of life as under California Family Code Section 914, and as such Donald, as Jean's spouse, was independently (not derivatively) liable for her debt; the Bureau then cited California Civil Code Section 337, which provides a four year statute of limitations for independent claims.

Donald countered that the debt was incurred by Jean, not by Donald. Given the fact of Jean's death the creditor was permitted to sue either Jean's estate directly or Donald derivatively. For a derivative suit against Donald, pursuant to California Probate Code Section 13554, the applicable statute of limitations was one year, as set forth in former California Code of Civil Procedure Section 353, now California Code of Civil Procedure Section 366.2.

COLLECTION BUREAU OF SAN JOSE V. RUMSEY
24 Cal.4th 301, 99 Cal.Rptr.2d 792, 6 P.3d 713 (2000)

BAXTER, J.

In this case we determine which statute of limitations governs an action by a collection agency against a surviving spouse for recovery of the hospital and medical expenses of a deceased spouse's last illness.

Code of Civil Procedure former section 353 * * * [now California Code of Civil Procedure 366.2], applicable at all relevant times to this case, specified a one-year limitations period for surviving causes of action on the liabilities of decedents. Subject to certain exceptions and limitations, Probate Code section 13550 prescribes the manner and extent to which a surviving spouse remains personally liable for the debts of a deceased spouse. Probate Code section 13554, as worded at all times relevant herein, clarified that these debts may be enforced against the surviving spouse in the same manner as they could have been enforced against the deceased spouse if he or she had not died, and are subject to the same "defense[s], cross-complaint[s] or setoff[s]" that would have been available to the deceased spouse if the deceased spouse had not died. Most importantly, subdivision (c) of Probate Code section 13554 expressly and specifically provided that the one-year limitations period of Code of Civil Procedure former section 353 (it now refers to Code Civ. Proc., § 366.2) is applicable to actions against a deceased debtor spouse, or derivatively, against the surviving spouse, for debts remaining unpaid upon the death of the debtor spouse.

The trial court found these statutory provisions controlling and concluded that because plaintiff collection agency had failed to file suit within one year of the death of the debtor spouse, its suit against the surviving spouse for recovery of the expenses of the debtor spouse's last illness was barred by the limitations period of Code of Civil Procedure former section 353.

The Court of Appeal reversed, concluding that although the collection agency's suit against the estate of the deceased debtor spouse, or derivatively against Donald Rumsey as the surviving spouse, was barred by the one-year limitations period of Code of Civil Procedure former section 353, an entirely separate and independent cause of action for recovery of the debt from the surviving spouse existed by virtue of Family Code section 914, which makes spouses personally liable for each other's debts incurred for "necessaries of life." The Court of Appeal went on to reason that the action pursuant to section 914 would be governed by the four-year limitations period of Code of Civil Procedure section 337 generally applicable to open book accounts, and that because the accounts receivable for the medical and hospital bills here in question qualify as open book accounts, the collection agency's action against the surviving spouse, although filed only a few days shy of four years after the debtor spouse's death, was nonetheless timely.

For the reasons to be explained, we conclude the provisions of sections 13550 and 13554 of the Probate Code exclusively control here, expressly making the one-year limitations period of Code of Civil Procedure former section 353 applicable to actions of this nature. We shall therefore reverse the judgment of the Court of Appeal.

Facts and Procedural Background

Jean Rumsey (hereafter sometimes deceased spouse) died on November 4, 1990, in El Camino Hospital in Santa Clara County after a prolonged battle with cancer, leaving behind hospital bills totaling $103,715.95. The accounts were ultimately assigned for collection to respondent Collection Bureau of San Jose (CBSJ). The accounts receivable for medical expenses were technically open book accounts as set forth in Code of Civil Procedure section 337. (See *County of Santa Clara v. Vargas* (1977) 71 Cal.App.3d 510, 516–517 [139 Cal.Rptr. 537] [bill for medical expenses is a book account].) Generally, there is a four-year statute of limitations period applicable to claims on open book accounts. (Code Civ. Proc., § 337.) CBSJ filed its original complaint in this action against Mr. Donald Rumsey (hereafter sometimes Mr. Rumsey or surviving spouse) just three days shy of four years after Jean Rumsey's death.

Mr. Rumsey demurred to the original complaint on the ground that sections 13550 and 13554 of the Probate Code together made the one-year statute of limitations period of Code of Civil Procedure former section 353 applicable to CBSJ's action against him, rendering the suit time-barred. The trial court agreed, sustaining the demurrer with leave to amend. CBSJ filed a first amended complaint; Mr. Rumsey demurred to the amended complaint on the same ground, and a second trial judge agreed with him, sustaining the demurrer with leave to amend. CBSJ then filed a second amended complaint; Mr. Rumsey demurred yet again on the ground that the one-year limitations period of former section 353 controlled and barred the action against him. This time, because the superior court judge who had heard the second demurrer was unavailable to hear the matter for the third time, it was heard by a retired justice of the Court of Appeal sitting as a temporary judge of the superior court. Mr. Rumsey's previously twice-sustained demurrer was overruled and the matter set for trial.

By stipulation, trial was to the court on the sole legal issue of which statute of limitations properly applied. At the conclusion of trial, the court agreed with Mr. Rumsey, ruling that Probate Code section 13554 and the one-year limitations period of Code of Civil Procedure former section 353 controlled, rendering CBSJ's action against him time-barred on its face. The court issued a statement of decision explaining its ruling on the dispositive statute of limitations issue. It also made factual findings in support of its further ruling, rejecting CBSJ's claim that Mr. Rumsey should be estopped from demurring to the complaint on statute of limitations grounds because he had lulled CBSJ into not filing suit earlier, on the representation he could obtain payment of the owed amounts directly from his deceased wife's medical insurer.

CBSJ appealed. The Court of Appeal reversed in an unpublished opinion. The appellate court explained why the court *agreed* with Mr.

Rumsey's position that "the limiting provisions of [Code of Civil Procedure former] section 353 and Probate Code section 13554 applied to any action against Jean Rumsey that survived her death. CBSJ therefore had until January 1, 1992 to bring an action to enforce Jean Rumsey's debts." But then, in a final single paragraph, the court set forth its rationale for reversing the judgment: "CBSJ also had a separate cause of action against [Mr. Rumsey] under Code of Civil Procedure section 337, because Family Code section 914 (formerly Civ. Code, § 5120.140) made him personally responsible for obligations incurred for his wife's necessaries of life. . . . [T]his was an *independent*, not derivative, basis of [Mr. Rumsey's] liability. Code of Civil Procedure section 337 allowed CBSJ four years to file an action against [Mr. Rumsey] for the balance due on his wife's hospital expenses, which [Mr. Rumsey] concedes were incurred for the necessaries of life. Although Jean Rumsey's death altered the period in which a suit could be brought to enforce her debt, [Mr. Rumsey's] own personal liability for these expenses remained. Since the last entry on the hospital bill was November 4, 1990, and CBSJ's original complaint was filed November 1, 1994, the action against [Mr. Rumsey] was timely filed." (Fn. omitted.)

We granted review to determine whether the one-year limitations period of Code of Civil Procedure former section 353, specifically applicable to surviving causes of action on the liabilities of decedents, or the four-year limitations period of Code of Civil Procedure section 337, generally applicable to open book accounts, controls on these facts.

Discussion

Subject to certain exceptions and limitations, Probate Code sections 13550 and 13551 make a surviving spouse personally liable for the debts of the deceased spouse, but only to the extent such debts are chargeable against the community property of both spouses and the separate property of the deceased spouse passing to the surviving spouse without formal probate administration.

Probate Code section 13550 provides: "Except as provided in Sections 11446, 13552, 13553, and 13554, upon the death of a married person, the surviving spouse is personally liable for the debts of the deceased spouse chargeable against the property described in Section 13551 to the extent provided in Section 13551."

Probate Code section 13551 in turn delineates the sources from which the surviving spouse's liability may be satisfied, as follows: "The liability imposed by Section 13550 shall not exceed the fair market value at the date of the decedent's death, less the amount of any liens and encumbrances, of the total of the following: [¶] (a) The portion of the one-half of the community and quasi-community property belonging to the surviving spouse under Sections 100 and 101 that is not exempt from enforcement of a money judgment and is not administered in the estate of the deceased spouse. [¶] (b) The portion of the one-half of the community and quasi-community property belonging to the decedent under Sections 100 and 101 that passes to the surviving spouse without administration. [¶] (c) The separate property of the decedent that passes to the surviving spouse without administration."

Probate Code section 13554 then clarifies that these debts may be enforced against the surviving spouse in the same manner as they could have been enforced against the deceased spouse if he or she had not died. (*Id.*, § 13554, subd. (a).) At all times relevant to this case, former section 13554 provided: "(a) Except as otherwise provided in this chapter, any debt described in Section 13550 may be enforced against the surviving spouse in the same manner as it could have been enforced against the deceased spouse if the deceased spouse had not died. [¶] (b) In any action or proceeding based upon the debt, the surviving spouse may assert any defense, cross-complaint or setoff which would have been available to the deceased spouse if the deceased spouse had not died. [¶] (c) *Section 353 of the Code of Civil Procedure applies in an action under this section.*" (Stats. 1990, ch. 79, § 14, p. 922, italics added.)

Code of Civil Procedure former section 353, expressly made applicable to this case by Probate Code section 13554, subdivision (c), provided in relevant part: "(b) Except as provided in subdivisions (c) and (d), if a person against whom an action may be brought on a liability of the person, whether arising in contract, tort, or otherwise, dies before the expiration of the time limited for the commencement thereof, and the cause of action survives, an action may be commenced within one year after the date of death, and the time otherwise limited for the commencement of the action does not apply. . . . [¶] . . . [¶] (d) If a person against whom an action may be brought died on or after July 1, 1988, and before January 1, 1991, and before the expiration of the time limited for the commencement of the action, and the cause of action survives, an action may be commenced before the earlier of the following times: [¶] (1) January 1, 1992. [¶] (2) One year after the issuing of letters testamentary or of administration, or the time otherwise limited for the commencement of the action, whichever is the later time." (Stats. 1990, ch. 140, § 1, p. 1172.)

The overall intent of the Legislature in enacting Code of Civil Procedure former section 353 was to protect decedents' estates from creditors' stale claims. (*Dawes v. Rich* (1997) 60 Cal.App.4th 24, 34, fn. 4 [70 Cal.Rptr.2d 72]; see Recommendation Relating to Notice to Creditors in Estate Administration (Dec. 1989) 20 Cal. Law Revision Com. Rep. (1990) p. 507.) "[T]he drafters of former Code of Civil Procedure section 353 and current Code of Civil Procedure section 366.2 believed the limitation period the statute imposes serves 'the strong public policies of expeditious estate administration and security of title for distributees, and is consistent with the concept that a creditor has some obligation to keep informed of the status of the debtor.' (Recommendation Relating to Notice to Creditors in Estate Administration, *supra*, 20 Cal. Law Revision Com. Rep. (1990) p. 512.)" (*Dawes v. Rich, supra*, 60 Cal.App.4th at p. 34.)

The December 1989 California Law Revision Commission recommendation on the proposed legislation amending Code of Civil Procedure former section 353 explained that "the one year statute of limitations is intended to apply *in any action on a debt of the decedent*, whether against the personal representative under Probate Code Sections 9350 to 9354 (claim on cause of action), *or against another person, such as* a distributee under Probate Code Section 9392 (liability of distributee), *a person who takes the decedent's property and is liable for the decedent's debts under Sections* 13109 (affidavit procedure for collection or transfer of personal property), 13156 (court order determining succession to real property), 13204 (affidavit procedure for real property of small value), and *13554 (passage of property to surviving spouse without administration)*, or a trustee." (Recommendation Relating to Notice to Creditors in Estate Administration, *supra*, 20 Cal. Law Revision Com. Rep., *supra*, at p. 515, italics added.) It thus appears that when the amendments to former section 353 were enacted, they were done so with the clear understanding and intent that such provisions would govern and apply to "any action on a debt of the decedent," regardless of whom the action was brought against, and specifically including the surviving spouse.

Read together, sections 13550, 13551, and 13554 of the Probate Code, and former section 353 of the Code of Civil Procedure, thus provided that Mr. Rumsey was "personally liable" (Prob. Code, § 13550) for the debts left behind by his deceased spouse, including the hospital and medical bills here in issue, to the extent of his own share of the community property, and those portions of his deceased spouse's share of the community property and her separate property that passed to him without formal administration. And under the limitations period of Code of Civil Procedure former section 353, expressly made applicable by Probate Code section 13554, creditors had one year from the date of Jean Rumsey's death (actually 14 months in this instance, given the specially controlling dates that applied during 1991–1992; see fn. 3, *ante*) within which to file an action against her estate, or against Mr. Rumsey derivatively, seeking to collect any such unpaid debts.

Although the Court of Appeal recognized that "the limiting provisions of [Code of Civil Procedure former] section 353 and Probate Code section 13554 applied to any action against Jean Rumsey that survived her death," the court did not scrutinize the manner in which those limiting provisions circumscribe a surviving spouse's personal liability for a deceased spouse's debts, as described above. Instead, the Court of Appeal concluded that CBSJ had an entirely separate and independent cause of action against Mr. Rumsey under Family Code section 914, which made him personally liable for debts incurred for his wife's "necessaries of life" and provided that his separate property could be applied to satisfy such category of debts, and to which, the Court of Appeal further concluded, the four-year statute of limitations for open book accounts (Code Civ. Proc., § 337) applied.

Family Code section 914 provides, in pertinent part: "(a) Notwithstanding Section 913, a married person is personally liable for the following debts incurred by the person's spouse during marriage: [¶] (1) *A debt incurred for necessaries of life of the person's spouse while the spouses are living together. . . .* [¶] (b) The separate property of a married person may be applied to the satisfaction of a debt for which the person is personally liable pursuant to this section. If separate property is so applied at a time when nonexempt property in the community estate or separate property of the person's spouse is available but is not applied to the satisfaction of the debt, the married person is entitled to reimbursement to the extent such property was available." (Italics added.) Section 914 is an exception to the general rule that a married person's separate property is not liable for debts incurred by his or her spouse during marriage. (See Fam. Code, § 913, subd. (b)(1) [separate property of married person not liable for debt incurred by spouse before or during marriage].)

In seeking to determine which statute of limitations was intended to govern on facts such as those before us, our goal is to discern the probable intent of the Legislature so as to effectuate the purpose of the laws in question. (*California Teachers Assn. v. Governing Bd. of Rialto Unified School Dist.* (1997) 14 Cal.4th 627, 632 [59 Cal.Rptr.2d 671, 927 P.2d 1175].) We examine the statutes in their context and with other legislation on the same subject. (*Id.* at p. 642.) If they conflict on a central element, we strive to harmonize them so as to give effect to each. If conflicting statutes cannot be reconciled, later enactments supersede earlier ones (*Orange Unified School Dist. v. Rancho Santiago Community College Dist.* (1997) 54 Cal.App.4th 750, 757 [62 Cal.Rptr.2d 778]), and more specific provisions take precedence over more general ones (*People v. Vargas* (1985) 175 Cal.App.3d 271, 277 [220 Cal.Rptr. 720]). Absent a compelling reason to do otherwise, we strive to construe each statute in accordance with its plain language. (*Samuels v. Mix* (1999) 22 Cal.4th 1, 7 [91 Cal.Rptr.2d 273, 989 P.2d 701].)

Applying these basic principles of statutory construction to this case, we must, first and foremost, give effect to the plain and express language of Probate Code section 13554. As explained, subdivision (c) of that section specifically provides that the one-year limitations period of Code of Civil Procedure former section 353 (now Code Civ. Proc., § 366.2) is applicable to actions against a deceased debtor spouse, or derivatively, against the surviving spouse, for "any debt" (Prob. Code, § 13554) remaining unpaid upon the death of the debtor spouse. To our minds the Legislature's intent could not be any clearer, and it must be given effect. (*Samuels v. Mix, supra,* 22 Cal.4th at p. 7.)

Second, ignoring for sake of argument the Legislature's clear and express command in Probate Code section 13554, that the one-year limitations period of Code of Civil Procedure former section 353 apply to actions on "any debt" remaining unpaid upon the death of the debtor spouse, and assuming the statutory schemes of Probate Code section 13550 et seq. and Family Code section 914 are indeed in conflict on the facts of this case, the Probate Code provisions still must be found to control as they are clearly the more specific. (*People v. Vargas, supra,* 175 Cal.App.3d at p. 277.) Those provisions specifically address the liability of a married person for the debts incurred by the other spouse *upon the death of that spouse,* whereas Family Code section 914 merely addresses the general liability of a spouse for the debts of the other spouse incurred during marriage. Moreover, the one-year statute of limitations of Code of Civil Procedure former section 353, expressly made applicable by Probate Code section 13554, is the more specific limitations provision, as it prescribes the limitations period for *surviving causes of action on the liabilities of decedents,* whereas Code of Civil Procedure section 337 merely sets forth a four-year limitations period generally applicable to all open book accounts. In both instances, the more specific statutory provisions control.

Third, if the statutory schemes of Probate Code section 13550 et seq. and Family Code section 914 are in conflict, then the former controls, as it is the later enactment. (*Orange Unified School Dist. v. Rancho Santiago Community College Dist., supra,* 54 Cal.App.4th at p. 757.) Although Family Code section 914 was enacted in 1992, its substantive language was transferred in its entirety from Code of Civil Procedure former section 5120.140, without any change in wording. Former section 5120.140 was enacted in 1984. (Stats. 1984, ch. 1671, § 9, p. 6020.) Probate Code section 13554 was enacted in 1990, some six years later. (Stats. 1990, ch. 79, § 14, p. 922.) Probate Code section 13554 is therefore both the more specific and the more recent legislation. Since the Legislature was aware of the provisions of Code of Civil Procedure former section 5120.140 (now Fam. Code, § 914) when it enacted Probate Code section 13554—the more specific provision insofar as it specifically addresses the liability of a *surviving* spouse for debts left behind by a *deceased* spouse—the latter statute controls here.

Most importantly, however, the Court of Appeal's conclusion that Family Code section 914 (and the four-year limitations period of Code Civ. Proc., § 337, applicable to debts under that section in the form of an open book account) should take precedence over Probate Code section 13554 (and the one-year limitations period of Code Civ. Proc., former § 353, applicable to actions against surviving spouses for the debts of a deceased spouse) in circumstances where, as here, the debts are those of a *deceased* spouse, would lead to conflicting results that could not possibly have been envisioned or intended by the Legislature. Family Code section 914 was not drafted with an eye toward governing creditors' claims made after the community estate is terminated by the death of one spouse; as noted, its substance was enacted (in Code Civ. Proc., former § 5120.140) well before Probate Code section 13554 became law. Section 914 is instead, on its face, addressed to a particular category of debts incurred during marriage—those for "necessaries of life," and further deals with only one aspect of a nondebtor spouse's liability for such debts—the availability of his or her *separate property* to satisfy those debts.

If the holding of the Court of Appeal below were to become law, then a creditor's suit that looks to a surviving spouse's separate property for recovery of a *deceased* spouse's debt for necessaries of life incurred during the marriage would lead to the following anomalous results.

First, under Probate Code sections 13550, 13551, and 13554, and Code of Civil Procedure former section 353, the surviving spouse's own share of the community property, and the share of the deceased spouse's community and separate property which the surviving spouse stands to receive without formal probate administration, would be subject to the applicable one-year statute of limitations, whereas his or her *separate property* would be "on the risk" for the debt for a period of four years under Family Code section 914. It has been observed that "a spouse's postmarital liability for debts incurred by a former or deceased spouse is based on one spouse's receipt of property which in fairness should have been applied to the other spouse's debts. [Citations.]" (*Dawes v. Rich, supra,* 60 Cal.App.4th at p. 29.) The holding of the Court of Appeal in this case would turn that fundamental principle on its head-by permitting a creditor to elect to look to a surviving spouse's *separate property* for a period of four years to satisfy the debt. Such a result would contravene the strong public policy of expeditious estate administration evidenced in Probate Code section 13554's incorporation of a one-year statute of limitations for suit to recover on "any debt" of a deceased debtor-spouse. (Prob. Code, § 13554.)

Second, Family Code section 914, by its own terms, creates a right of reimbursement for a creditor-spouse whose separate property is applied to satisfy a debt of his or her spouse for "necessaries of life" (*id.*, § 914, subd. (b)), and Family Code section 920, subdivision (c), in turn provides that "The right shall be exercised not later than the earlier of the following times: [¶] (1) Within three years after the spouse in whose favor the right arises has actual knowledge of the application of the property to the satisfaction of the debt. [¶] (2) In proceedings for division of community and quasi-community property . . . *or in proceedings upon the death of a spouse.*" (Italics added.) A conclusion that an action can be brought pursuant to Family Code section 914 for up to four years against a *surviving spouse* to recover on a *deceased spouse's* debt for necessaries of life would stand in patent conflict with the surviving spouse's right of reimbursement, and the prescribed periods in which that right must be exercised, under Family Code section 920. If a four-year limitations period applied to actions against a *surviving* spouse under Family Code section 914, and the creditor waited more than one year before bringing the action, the surviving spouse's right of reimbursement provided for in Family Code section 920 would be defeated, for subdivision (c) of section 920 expressly provides that where the debtor spouse has died, such right of reimbursement must be exercised "in proceedings upon the death of [the] spouse," which proceedings, pursuant to the Probate Code provisions discussed herein, will generally transpire within a year after the deceased spouse's death.

We agree that Family Code section 914, subdivision (a) (1), on its face, made Mr. Rumsey "personally liable" for any debts incurred by Mrs. Rumsey for "necessaries of life," and the parties do not contest that expenses of last illness are a subcategory of such debts. We further agree that, pursuant to Family Code section 914, subdivision (b), Mr. Rumsey's separate property could be applied to satisfaction of that debt, subject to his right of reimbursement spelled out in that subdivision (and any applicable limits set forth in Prob. Code, § 13551; see *ante*, at p. 307). We disagree that the four-year statute of limitations *generally* applicable to open book accounts (Code Civ. Proc., § 337) applied in this case, as we disagree with the Court of Appeal's conclusion that, in a case such as this, where the debtor spouse is *deceased*, suit on such a debt brought against the surviving spouse pursuant to Family Code section 914 states an independent, rather than a derivative, cause of action. Although section 914 makes a married person personally liable for such category of debts of his or her spouse, that liability is plainly derivative of the marital relationship between the two.

The provisions of Probate Code section 13554, making the one-year limitations period of Code of Civil Procedure former section 353 applicable to proceedings on "any debt" (Prob. Code, § 13554) of a deceased spouse, and the provisions of Family Code sections 914 and 920, making a married person liable for, and his or her separate property available to satisfy, such a debt, but also creating a right of reimbursement in the creditor-spouse, and further expressly requiring that such right be exercised "in proceedings upon the death of a spouse" (Fam. Code, § 920, subd. (c)(2))— together reflect the Legislature's intent that *in cases where the debtor spouse has died*, a one-year limitations period applies to actions brought under either statute.

We conclude that Probate Code section 13554 controls in this case, expressly making the one-year limitations period of Code of Civil Procedure former section 353 applicable to CBSJ's action against Mr. Rumsey.

Conclusion

The judgment of the Court of Appeal is reversed, and the matter remanded to that court for further proceedings consistent with the views expressed herein.

GEORGE, C. J., MOSK, J., KENNARD, J., CHIN, J., and BROWN, J., concurred.

WERDEGAR, J., dissenting.

The result the majority reaches in this case, by effectively shortening the period within which creditors may sue a surviving spouse on obligations incurred for necessaries of life, may be desirable from a policy standpoint as contributing to prompt resolution of such claims and a sense of closure for parties who have suffered the loss of a spouse. Be that as it may, the policy choice the majority has effectuated is properly one for the Legislature alone to articulate, and—unlike the majority—I do not read the relevant statutes as doing so. Accordingly, I dissent.

The Court of Appeal in the present case correctly concluded Donald Rumsey was independently liable for the expenses of his wife's hospitalization pursuant to Family Code section 914, and that the four-year statute of limitations for open book accounts governed such liability (Code Civ. Proc., § 337). As the majority acknowledges, Family Code section 914 addresses a married person's liability for debts incurred during marriage. (Fam. Code, § 914, subd. (a).) Nothing in the statute suggests, nor does Mr. Rumsey even argue, that the liability so incurred somehow vanishes, or transmutes into a liability that is merely "derivative," at the moment of the spouse's death.

Underlying the majority's opinion appears to be the premise that the liabilities created by Family Code section 914 and Probate Code section 13550, respectively, are functionally identical. The latter liability is one of the deceased spouse, *not* the survivor, and may be the subject of a distinct cause of action brought against the personal representative, or the surviving spouse as distributee, of the decedent's estate. The sources of recovery in an action under Probate Code section 13550, moreover, are limited in ways that an independent action under Family Code section 914 are not. (See Prob. Code, § 13551 [referring to the surviving spouse's one-half and the decedent's one-half of the community and quasi-community property, and the separate property of the decedent].) Family Code section 914, in contrast, describes the liability of the married person's *separate* property, but only for his or her spouse's necessaries of life. These differences, apparent on the face of the statutes, compel the conclusion that the two types of actions are not coextensive, but, rather, independent.

In maintaining a contrary view, the majority relies on the "strong public policy of expeditious estate administration evidenced in Probate

Code section 13554's incorporation of a one-year statute of limitations for suit to recover on 'any debt' of a deceased debtor-spouse." (Maj. opn., *ante*, at p. 312.) This policy, however, is not jeopardized—or even implicated—by the Court of Appeal's decision, to which I would adhere. Plainly, an action of the kind with which we are concerned in this case, once recognized as independent of the deceased spouse's own obligation and as seeking satisfaction against the surviving spouse personally, in no way interferes with the administration of the decedent's estate. Indeed, in the present case no proceedings were ever instituted for the administration of Mrs. Rumsey's estate; hence, the policy is unaffected by any ruling in this case.

The majority also relies, in support of its conclusion, on the existence of a married person's right to reimbursement for payment of his or her spouse's necessaries of life and the time limitations on that right: reimbursement must be sought within three years after the person has actual knowledge that his or her separate property has been applied to the debt, or in proceedings upon dissolution of the marriage or the death of the spouse, whichever occurs first, whereas open book accounts are governed generally by a four-year limitations period. (See Fam. Code, § 914, subd. (b); *id.*, § 920, subd. (c)(1); Code Civ. Proc., § 337, subd. 2.) The majority fails, however, to specify any basis in the statutory language for its conclusion that the married person's right to reimbursement delimits the *creditor's* right to satisfaction of the obligation. Nor does the majority acknowledge the conditional nature of the married person's reimbursement right. By limiting the right to those times "when nonexempt property in the community estate or separate property of the person's spouse is available but is not applied to the satisfaction of the debt" (Fam. Code, § 914, subd. (b)), the Legislature apparently understood there might be times when no other property—either nonexempt community property or separate property of the spouse—is available.

As the California Law Revision Commission essentially recognized, the remedy of reimbursement is not favored in the law. Reimbursement generates difficult accounting and proof problems, and is "inimical to sharing principles during marriage." (Recommendation Relating to Liability of Marital Property for Debts (Jan. 1983) 17 Cal. Law Revision Com. Rep. (1984) pp. 16–17 [because of discovery and proof problems and the risk of erroneous determinations, the reimbursement right "should be strictly limited to a period of three years after application of the property to the satisfaction of the debt"].) Because the death of a spouse can only tend to exacerbate discovery and proof problems, questions of the availability of reimbursement should not govern our interpretation of the statutes at issue here.

The rule the majority announces will have unanticipated consequences. Its reasoning logically must apply to other, analogous, so-called derivative obligations, such as loans to decedents cosigned by surviving spouses. That such a result will upset parties' settled expectations goes without saying. I therefore dissent.

NOTE

Death, debts, and statutes of limitation. In 2001 the Legislature amended California Family Code Section 914 to add the following provisions:

"(c)(1) Except as provided in paragraph (2), the statute of limitations set forth in Section 366.2 of the Code of Civil Procedure shall apply if the spouse for whom the married person is personally liable dies.

(2) If the surviving spouse had actual knowledge of the debt prior to the expiration of the period set forth in 366.2 and the personal representative of the deceased spouse's estate failed to provide the creditor asserting the claim under this section with a timely written notice of the probate administration of the estate pursuant to Section 9050 of the Probate Code, the statute of limitations set forth in Section 337 or 339, as applicable, shall apply."

The California Code of Civil Procedure Section 366.2 statutory period is one year. The California Code of Civil Procedure Section 337 period is four years. The California Code of Civil Procedure Section 339 statutory period is two years.

SECTION 5. CHAPTER SUMMARY

- Death terminates a marriage.

- At the death of a spouse the California Probate Code governs.

- The Probate Code contains its own definitions of "community property," "quasi-community property," and "surviving spouse."

- During life, a married person has full testamentary rights over his or her one-half of the community property.

- During life, a married person has full testamentary rights over his or her separate property.

- If a married person dies intestate, the decedent's one-half of the community property and one-half of the quasi-community property (if any) descend by statute to the surviving spouse.

- If a married person dies intestate, the decedent's separate property (if any) is shared by the surviving spouse and other of the decedent's eligible heirs. The decedent spouse takes all of the decedent's separate property only if the decedent has no other eligible intestate heirs.

- A nonprobate transfer passes at the decedent's death without the necessity of probate.

- At the death of a spouse, creditors are entitled to bring personal claims against the decedent's estate or derivative claims against the decedent's surviving spouse. Time limits apply.

APPENDIX A

STATUTORY APPENDIX

■ ■ ■

The California Family Code

DIVISION 1.   PRELIMINARY PROVISIONS AND DEFINITIONS [1–185]

DIVISION 2.   GENERAL PROVISIONS [200–295]

DIVISION 2.5. DOMESTIC PARTNER REGISTRATION [297–299.6]

DIVISION 3.   MARRIAGE [300–536]

DIVISION 4.   RIGHTS AND OBLIGATIONS DURING MARRIAGE [700–1620]

DIVISION 5.   CONCILIATION PROCEEDINGS [1800–1852]

DIVISION 6.   NULLITY, DISSOLUTION, AND LEGAL SEPARATION [2000–2452]

DIVISION 7.   DIVISION OF PROPERTY [2500–2660]

DIVISION 8.   CUSTODY OF CHILDREN [3000–3465]

DIVISION 9.   SUPPORT [3500–5700.905]

DIVISION 10. PREVENTION OF DOMESTIC VIOLENCE [6200–6409]

DIVISION 11. MINORS [6500–7143]

DIVISION 12. PARENT AND CHILD RELATIONSHIP [7500–7961]

DIVISION 13. ADOPTION [8500–9340]

DIVISION 14. FAMILY LAW FACILITATOR ACT [10000–10015]

DIVISION 17. SUPPORT SERVICES [17000–17804]

DIVISION 20. PILOT PROJECTS [20000–20043]

SELECT CALIFORNIA STATUTES

WEST'S ANNOTATED CALIFORNIA FAMILY CODE

§ 63.   Community estate

"Community estate" includes both community property and quasi-community property.

(Added by Stats. 1993, c. 219 (A.B. 1500), § 79.3.)

§ 70.   Dissolution of marriage: date of separation

(a) "Date of separation" means the date that a complete and final break in the marital relationship has occurred, as evidenced by both of the following:

(1) The spouse has expressed to the other spouse his or her intent to end the marriage.

(2) The conduct of the spouse is consistent with his or her intent to end marriage

(b) In determining the date of separation, the court shall take into consideration all relevant evidence.

(c) It is the intent of the Legislature in enacting this section to abrogate the decisions in In re Marriage of Davis (2015) 61 Cal.4th 846 and In re Marriage of Norviel (2002) 102 Cal.App.4th 1152.

(Added by Stat. 2016, c. 114 (S.B. 1255), § 1, eff. Jan. 1, 2017).

§ 125.   Quasi-community property

"Quasi-community property" means all real or personal property, wherever situated, acquired before or after the operative date of this code in any of the following ways:

(a) By either spouse while domiciled elsewhere which would have been community property if the spouse who acquired the property had been domiciled in this state at the time of its acquisition.

(b) In exchange for real or personal property, wherever situated, which would have been community property if the spouse who acquired the property so exchanged had been domiciled in this state at the time of its acquisition.

(Stats. 1992, c. 162 (A.B. 2650), § 10, operative Jan. 1, 1994.)

§ 240.   Application of part

This part applies where a temporary restraining order, including a protective order as defined in Section 6218, is issued under any of the following provisions:

(a) Article 2 (commencing with Section 2045) of Chapter 4 of Part 1 of Division 6 (dissolution of marriage, nullity of marriage, or legal separation of the parties).

(b) Article 3 (commencing with Section 4620) of Chapter 3 of Part 5 of Division 9 (deposit of assets to secure future child support payments).

(c) Article 1 (commencing with Section 6320) of Chapter 2 of Part 4 of Division 10 (Domestic Violence Prevention Act), other than an order under Section 6322.5.

(d) Article 2 (commencing with Section 7710) of Chapter 6 of Part 3 of Division 12 (Uniform Parentage Act).

(Added by Stats. 1993, c. 219 (A.B. 1500), § 85.1. Amended by Stats. 1998, c. 511 (A.B. 1900), § 1.)

§ 242.   Deadline for hearing on the petition

(a) Within 21 days, or, if good cause appears to the court, 25 days from the date that a temporary restraining order is granted or denied, a hearing shall be held on the petition. If no request for a temporary restraining order is made, the hearing shall be held within 21 days, or, if good cause appears to the court, 25 days from the date that the petition is filed.

(b) If a hearing is not held within the time provided in subdivision (a), the court may nonetheless hear the matter, but the temporary restraining order shall no longer be enforceable unless it is extended under Section 245.

(Added by Stats. 1993, c. 219 (A.B. 1500), § 85.4. Amended by Stats. 2010, c. 572 (A.B. 1596), § 7, operative Jan. 1, 2012; Stats. 2015, c. 411 (A.B. 1081), § 4, eff. Jan. 1, 2016.)

§ 245.   Continuance

(a) The respondent shall be entitled, as a matter of course, to one continuance for a reasonable period, to respond to the petition.

(b) Either party may request a continuance of the hearing, which the court shall grant on a showing of good cause. The request may be in writing before or at the hearing or orally at the hearing. The court may also grant a continuance on its own motion.

(c) If the court grants a continuance, any temporary restraining order that has been issued shall remain in effect until the end of the continued hearing, unless otherwise ordered by the court. In granting a continuance, the court may modify or terminate a temporary restraining order.

(d) If the court grants a continuance, the extended temporary restraining order shall state on its face the new date of expiration of the order.

(e) A fee shall not be charged for the extension of the temporary restraining order.

(Stats. 1992, c. 162 (A.B. 2650), § 10, operative Jan. 1, 1994. Amended by Stats. 2010, c. 572 (A.B. 1596), § 10, operative Jan. 1, 2012; Stats. 2015, c. 411 (A.B. 1081), § 6, eff. Jan 1, 2016.)

§ 246.   Grant of denial on date petition submitted

A request for a temporary restraining order described in Section 240, issued without notice, shall be granted or denied on the same day that the petition is submitted to the court, unless the petition is filed too late in the day to permit effective review, in which case the order shall be granted or denied on the next day of judicial business in sufficient time for the order to be filed that day with the clerk of the court.

(Added by Stats. 1993, c. 148 (A.B. 1331), § 1. Amended by Stats. 2010, c. 572 (A.B. 1596), § 11, operative Jan. 1, 2012.)

§ 274. Attempted murder of a spouse; attorney's fees and costs; notice and hearing; source of funds

(a) Notwithstanding any other provision of law, if the injured spouse is entitled to a remedy authorized pursuant to Section 4324, the injured spouse shall be entitled to an award of reasonable attorney's fees and costs as a sanction pursuant to this section.

(b) An award of attorney's fees and costs as a sanction pursuant to this section shall be imposed only after notice to the party against whom the sanction is proposed to be imposed and opportunity for that party to be heard.

(c) An award of attorney's fees and costs as a sanction pursuant to this section is payable only from the property or income of the party against whom the sanction is imposed, except that the award may be against the sanctioned party's share of the community property. In order to obtain an award under this section, the party requesting an award of attorney's fees and costs is not required to demonstrate any financial need for the award.

(Added by Stats. 1995, c. 364 (A.B. 16), § 1. Amended by Stats. 2006, c. 538 (S.B. 1852), § 156.)

§ 300. Consent; issuance of license and solemnization; marriage license and marriage certificate

(a) Marriage is a personal relation arising out of a civil contract between two persons, to which the consent of the parties capable of making that contract is necessary. Consent alone does not constitute marriage. Consent must be followed by the issuance of a license and solemnization as authorized by this division, except as provided by Section 425 and Part 4 (commencing with Section 500).

(b) For purposes of this part, the document issued by the county clerk is a marriage license until it is registered with the county recorder, at which time the license becomes a marriage certificate.

(Stats. 1992, c. 162 (A.B. 2650), § 10, operative Jan. 1, 1994. Amended by Stats. 1993, c. 219 (A.B. 1500), § 88; Stats. 2006, c. 816 (A.B. 1102), § 1, operative Jan. 1, 2008; Stats. 2014 c. 82 (S.B. 1306), § 2, eff. Jan 1. 2105.)

§ 301. Adults; capability to consent to and consummate marriage

Two unmarried persons 18 years of age or older, who are not otherwise disqualified, are capable of consenting to and consummating marriage.

(Stats. 1992, c. 162 (A.B. 2650), § 10, operative Jan. 1, 1994. Amended by Stats. 2014, c. 82 (S.B. 1306), § 3, eff. Jan. 1, 2015.)

§ 302. Minors, capability of consenting to and consummating marriage; court order and parental consent; filing

(a) An unmarried person under 18 years of age is capable of consenting to and consummating marriage upon obtaining a court order granting permission to the underage person or persons to marry.

(b) The court order and written consent of the parents of each underage person, or of one of the parents or the guardian of each underage person shall be filed with the clerk of the court, and a certified copy of the order shall be presented to the county clerk at the time the marriage license is issued.

(Stats. 1992, c. 162 (A.B. 2650), § 10, operative Jan. 1, 1994. Amended by Stats. 2006, c. 816 (A.B. 1102), § 2, operative Jan. 1, 2008; Stats. 2014, c. 82 (S.B. 1306), § 4, eff. Jan 1. 2015.)

§ 305. Proof of consent and solemnization

Consent to and solemnization of marriage may be proved under the same general rules of evidence as facts are proved in other cases.

(Stats. 1992, c. 162 (A.B. 2650), § 10, operative Jan. 1, 1994.)

§ 720. Mutual obligations

Spouses contract toward each other obligations of mutual respect, fidelity, and support.

(Stats. 1992, c. 162 (A.B. 2650), § 10, operative Jan. 1, 1994. Amended by Stats. 2014, c. 82 (S.B. 1306), § 11, eff. Jan. 1, 2015.)

§ 721. Contracts with each other and third parties; fiduciary relationship

(a) Subject to subdivision (b), either spouse may enter into any transaction with the other, or with any other person, respecting property, which either might if unmarried.

(b) Except as provided in Sections 143, 144, 146, 16040, and 16047 of the Probate Code [which requires a trustee to manage trust assets in accordance with the prudent investor rule], in transactions between themselves, spouses are subject to the general rules governing fiduciary relationships that control the actions of persons occupying confidential relations with each other. This confidential relationship imposes a duty of the highest good faith and fair dealing on each spouse, and neither shall take any unfair advantage of the other. This confidential relationship is a fiduciary relationship subject to the same rights and duties of nonmarital business partners, as provided in Sections 16403, 16404, and 16503 of the Corporation Code, including, but not limited to, the following:

(1) Providing each spouse access at all times to all books kept regarding a transaction for the purposes of inspection and copying.

(2) Rendering upon request, true and full information of all things affecting any transaction that concerns the community property. Nothing in this section is intended to impose a duty for either spouse to keep detailed books and records of community property transactions.

(3) Accounting to the spouse, and holding as a trust any benefit or profit derived from any transaction by one spouse without the consent of the other spouse that concerns the community property.

(Stats. 1992, c. 162 (A.B. 2650), § 10, operative Jan. 1, 1994. Amended by Stats. 2002, c. 310 (S.B. 1936), § 1; Stats. 2014, c. 82 (S.B. 1306), § 12, eff. Jan. 1, 2015.)

§ 750. Methods of holding property

Spouses may hold property as joint tenants or tenants in common, or as community property, or as community property with a right of survivorship.

(Stats. 1992, c. 162 (A.B. 2650), § 10, operative Jan. 1, 1994. Amended by Stats. 2001, c. 754 (A.B. 1697), § 2; Stats. 2014, c. 82 (S.B. 1306), § 13, eff. Jan. 1, 2015.)

§ 751. Community property; interests of parties

The respective interests of each spouse in community property during continuance of the marriage relation are present, existing, and equal interests.

(Stats. 1992, c. 162 (A.B. 2650), § 10, operative Jan. 1, 1994. Amended by Stats. 2014, c. 82 (S.B. 1306), § 14, eff. Jan. 1, 2015.)

§ 760. Community property defined

Except as otherwise provided by statute, all property, real or personal, wherever situated, acquired by a married person during the marriage while domiciled in this state is community property.

(Stats. 1992, c. 162 (A.B. 2650), § 10, operative Jan. 1, 1994.)

§ 770. Separate property of married person

(a) Separate property of a married person includes all of the following:

(1) All property owned by the person before marriage.

(2) All property acquired by the person after marriage by gift, bequest, devise, or descent.

(3) The rents, issues, and profits of the property described in this section.

(b) A married person may, without the consent of the person's spouse, convey the person's separate property.

(Stats. 1992, c. 162 (A.B. 2650), § 10, operative Jan. 1, 1994.)

§ 771. Earnings and accumulations during period of separation

(a) The earnings and accumulations of a spouse and the minor children living with, or in the custody of, the spouse, after the date of separation of the spouses, are the separate property of the spouse.

(b) Notwithstanding subdivision (a), the earnings and accumulations of an unemancipated minor child related to a contract of a type described in Section 6750 shall remain the sole legal property of the minor child.

(Stats. 1992, c. 162 (A.B. 2650), § 10, operative Jan. 1, 1994. Amended by Stats. 1999, c. 940 (S.B. 1162), § 1; Stats. 2016, c. 114 (S.B. 1255), § 2, eff. Jan. 1, 2017.)

§ 772. Earnings or accumulations after entry of judgment of legal separation

After entry of a judgment of legal separation of the parties, the earnings or accumulations of each party are the separate property of the party acquiring the earnings or accumulations.

(Stats. 1992, c. 162 (A.B. 2650), § 10, operative Jan. 1, 1994.)

§ 780. Community property

Except as provided in Section 781 and subject to the rules of allocation set forth in Section 2603, money and other property received or to be received by a married person in satisfaction of a judgment for damages for personal injuries, or pursuant to an agreement for the settlement or compromise of a claim for such damages, is community property if the cause of action for the damages arose during the marriage.

(Stats. 1992, c. 162 (A.B. 2650), § 10, operative Jan. 1, 1994.)

§ 781. Separate property

(a) Money or other property received or to be received by a married person in satisfaction of a judgment for damages for personal injuries, or pursuant to an agreement for the settlement or compromise of a claim for those damages, is the separate property of the injured person if the cause of action for the damages arose as follows:

(1) After the entry of a judgment of dissolution of a marriage or legal separation of the parties.

(2) While either spouse, if he or she is the injured person, is living separate from the other spouse.

(b) Notwithstanding subdivision (a), if the spouse of the injured person has paid expenses by reason of the personal injuries from separate property or from the community property, the spouse is entitled to reimbursement of the separate property or the community property for those expenses from the separate property received by the injured person under subdivision (a).

(c) Notwithstanding subdivision (a), if one spouse has a cause of action against the other spouse which arose during the marriage of the parties, money or property paid or to be paid by or on behalf of a party to the party's spouse of that marriage in satisfaction of a judgment for damages for personal injuries to that spouse, or pursuant to an agreement for the settlement or compromise of a claim for the damages, is the separate property of the injured spouse.

(Stats. 1992, c. 162 (A.B. 2650), § 10, operative Jan. 1, 1994.)

§ 782. Injuries to married person by spouse; primary resort to separate property; consent of injured spouse to use of community property; indemnity

(a) Where an injury to a married person is caused in whole or in part by the negligent or wrongful act or omission of the person's spouse, the community property may not be used to discharge the liability of the tortfeasor spouse to the injured spouse or the liability to make contribution to a joint tortfeasor until the separate property of the tortfeasor spouse, not exempt from enforcement of a money judgment, is exhausted.

(b) This section does not prevent the use of community property to discharge a liability referred to in subdivision (a) if the injured spouse gives written consent thereto after the occurrence of the injury.

(c) This section does not affect the right to indemnity provided by an insurance or other contract to discharge the tortfeasor spouse's liability, whether or not the consideration given for the contract consisted of community property.

(Stats. 1992, c. 162 (A.B. 2650), § 10, operative Jan. 1, 1994.)

§ 782.5. Attempted murder or soliciting the murder of a spouse; remedies; community property interests

In addition to any other remedy authorized by law, when a spouse is convicted of attempting to murder the other spouse, as punishable pursuant to subdivision (a) of Section 664 of the Penal Code, or of soliciting the murder of the other spouse, as punishable pursuant to subdivision (b) of Section 653f of the Penal Code, the injured spouse shall be entitled to an award to the injured spouse of 100 percent of the community property interest in the retirement and pension benefits of the injured spouse.

As used in this section, "injured spouse" has the same meaning as defined in Section 4324.

(Added by Stats. 1995, c. 364 (A.B. 16), § 2. Amended by Stats. 2010, c. 65 (A.B. 2674), § 1.)

§ 783. Injuries to married person by third party; extent concurring negligence of spouse allowable as defense

If a married person is injured by the negligent or wrongful act or omission of a person other than the married person's spouse, the fact that the negligent or wrongful act or omission of the spouse of the injured person was a concurring cause of the injury is not a defense in an action brought by the injured person to recover damages for the injury except in cases where the concurring negligent or wrongful act or omission would be a defense if the marriage did not exist.

(Stats. 1992, c. 162 (A.B. 2650), § 10, operative Jan. 1, 1994.)

§ 802. Property acquired during marriage terminated by dissolution more than four years prior to death

The presumption that property acquired during marriage is community property does not apply to any property to which legal or equitable title is held by a person at the time of the person's death if the marriage during which the property was acquired was terminated by dissolution of marriage more than four years before the death.

(Stats. 1992, c. 162 (A.B. 2650), § 10, operative Jan. 1, 1994.)

§ 850. Transmutation by agreement or transfer

Subject to Sections 851 to 853, inclusive, married persons may by agreement or transfer, with or without consideration, do any of the following:

(a) Transmute community property to separate property of either spouse.

(b) Transmute separate property of either spouse to community property.

(c) Transmute separate property of one spouse to separate property of the other spouse.

(Stats. 1992, c. 162 (A.B. 2650), § 10, operative Jan. 1, 1994.)

§ 851. Transmutation subject to fraudulent transfer laws

A transmutation is subject to the laws governing fraudulent transfers.

(Stats. 1992, c. 162 (A.B. 2650), § 10, operative Jan. 1, 1994.)

§ 852. Requirements

(a) A transmutation of real or personal property is not valid unless made in writing by an express declaration that is made, joined in, consented to, or accepted by the spouse whose interest in the property is adversely affected.

(b) A transmutation of real property is not effective as to third parties without notice thereof unless recorded.

(c) This section does not apply to a gift between the spouses of clothing, wearing apparel, jewelry, or other tangible articles of a personal nature that is used solely or principally by the spouse to whom the gift is made and that is not substantial in value taking into account the circumstances of the marriage.

(d) Nothing in this section affects the law governing characterization of property in which separate property and community property are commingled or otherwise combined.

(e) This section does not apply to or affect a transmutation of property made before January 1, 1985, and the law that would otherwise be applicable to that transmutation shall continue to apply.

(Stats. 1992, c. 162 (A.B. 2650), § 10, operative Jan. 1, 1994.)

§ 853. Characterization of property in will; admissibility in proceedings commenced before death of testator; waiver of right to joint and survivor annuity or survivor's benefits; written joinders or consent to nonprobate transfers of community property

(a) A statement in a will of the character of property is not admissible as evidence of a transmutation of the property in a proceeding commenced before the death of the person who made the will.

(b) A waiver of a right to a joint and survivor annuity or survivor's benefits under the federal Retirement Equity Act of 1984 (Public Law 98–397) is not a transmutation of the community property rights of the person executing the waiver.

(c) A written joinder or written consent to a nonprobate transfer of community property on death that satisfies Section 852 is a transmutation and is governed by the law applicable to transmutations and not by Chapter 2 (commencing with Section 5010) of Part 1 of Division 5 of the Probate Code.

(Stats. 1992, c. 162 (A.B. 2650), § 10, operative Jan. 1, 1994. Amended by Stats. 1993, c. 219 (A.B. 1500), § 100.)

§ 900. Construction of part

Unless the provision or context otherwise requires, the definitions in this chapter govern the construction of this part.

(Stats. 1992, c. 162 (A.B. 2650), § 10, operative Jan. 1, 1994.)

§ 902. Debt

"Debt" means an obligation incurred by a married person before or during marriage, whether based on contract, tort, or otherwise.

(Stats. 1992, c. 162 (A.B. 2650), § 10, operative Jan. 1, 1994.)

§ 903. Time debt is incurred

A debt is "incurred" at the following time:

(a) In the case of a contract, at the time the contract is made.

(b) In the case of a tort, at the time the tort occurs.

(c) In other cases, at the time the obligation arises.

(Stats. 1992, c. 162 (A.B. 2650), § 10, operative Jan. 1, 1994.)

§ 910. Community estate; liability for debts

(a) Except as otherwise expressly provided by statute, the community estate is liable for a debt incurred by either spouse before or during marriage, regardless of which spouse has the management and control of the property and regardless of whether one or both spouses are parties to the debt or to a judgment for the debt.

(b) "During marriage" for purposes of this section does not include the period after the date of separation, as defined in Section 70, and before a judgment of dissolution of marriage or legal separation of the parties.

(Stats. 1992, c. 162 (A.B. 2650), § 10, operative Jan. 1, 1994; Stats. 2016, c. 114 (S.B. 1255), § 3, eff. Jan. 1, 2017.)

§ 911. Earnings of married persons; liability for premarital debts; earnings held in deposit accounts

(a) The earnings of a married person during marriage are not liable for a debt incurred by the person's spouse before marriage. After the earnings of the married person are paid, they remain not liable so long as they are held in a deposit account in which the person's spouse has no right of withdrawal and are uncommingled with other property in the community estate, except property insignificant in amount.

(b) As used in this section:

(1) "Deposit account" has the meaning prescribed in paragraph (29) of subdivision (a) of Section 9102 of the Commercial Code.

(2) "Earnings" means compensation for personal services performed, whether as an employee or otherwise.

(Stats. 1992, c. 162 (A.B. 2650), § 10, operative Jan. 1, 1994. Amended by Stats. 1999, c. 991 (S.B. 45), § 42.5, operative July 1, 2001.)

§ 912.   Quasi-community property; treatment

For the purposes of this part, quasi-community property is liable to the same extent, and shall be treated the same in all other respects, as community property.

(Stats. 1992, c. 162 (A.B. 2650), § 10, operative Jan. 1, 1994.)

§ 913.   Separate property of married person; liability for debt

(a) The separate property of a married person is liable for a debt incurred by the person before or during marriage.

(b) Except as otherwise provided by statute:

(1) The separate property of a married person is not liable for a debt incurred by the person's spouse before or during marriage.

(2) The joinder or consent of a married person to an encumbrance of community estate property to secure payment of a debt incurred by the person's spouse does not subject the person's separate property to liability for the debt unless the person also incurred the debt.

(Stats. 1992, c. 162 (A.B. 2650), § 10, operative Jan. 1, 1994.)

§ 914.   Personal liability for debts incurred by spouse; separate property applied to satisfaction of debt; statute of limitations

(a) Notwithstanding Section 913, a married person is personally liable for the following debts incurred by the person's spouse during marriage:

(1) A debt incurred for necessaries of life of the person's spouse before the date of separation of the spouses.

(2) Except as provided in Section 4302, a debt incurred for common necessaries of life of the person's spouse after the date of separation of the spouses.

(b) The separate property of a married person may be applied to the satisfaction of a debt for which the person is personally liable pursuant to this section. If separate property is so applied at a time when nonexempt property in the community estate or separate property of the person's spouse is available but is not applied to the satisfaction of the debt, the married person is entitled to reimbursement to the extent such property was available.

(c)(1) Except as provided in paragraph (2), the statute of limitations set forth in Section 366.2 of the Code of Civil Procedure shall apply if the spouse for whom the married person is personally liable dies.

(2) If the surviving spouse had actual knowledge of the debt prior to the expiration of the period set forth in 366.2 of the Code of Civil Procedure and the personal representative of the deceased spouse's

estate failed to provide the creditor asserting the claim under this section with a timely written notice of the probate administration of the estate in the manner provided for pursuant to Section 9050 of the Probate Code, the statute of limitations set forth in Section 337 or 339 of the Code of Civil Procedure, as applicable, shall apply.

(d) For purposes of this section, "date of separation" has the same meaning as set forth in Section 70.

(Stats. 1992, c. 162 (A.B. 2650), § 10, operative Jan. 1, 1994. Amended by Stats. 1993, c. 219 (A.B. 1500), § 100.4; Stats. 2001, c. 702 (A.B. 539), § 1; Stats. 2014, c. 71 (S.B. 1304), § 53; Stats. 2016, c. 114 (S.B. 1255), § 4, eff. Jan. 1, 2017.)

§ 915. Child or spousal support obligation not arising out of marriage; reimbursement of community

(a) For the purpose of this part, a child or spousal support obligation of a married person that does not arise out of the marriage shall be treated as a debt incurred before marriage, regardless of whether a court order for support is made or modified before or during marriage and regardless of whether any installment payment on the obligation accrues before or during marriage.

(b) If property in the community estate is applied to the satisfaction of a child or spousal support obligation of a married person that does not arise out of the marriage, at a time when nonexempt separate income of the person is available but is not applied to the satisfaction of the obligation, the community estate is entitled to reimbursement from the person in the amount of the separate income, not exceeding the property in the community estate so applied.

(c) Nothing in this section limits the matters a court may take into consideration in determining or modifying the amount of a support order, including, but not limited to, the earnings of the spouses of the parties.

(Stats. 1992, c. 162 (A.B. 2650), § 10, operative Jan. 1, 1994. Amended by Stats. 1993, c. 219 (A.B. 1500), § 100.5.)

§ 916. Division of property; subsequent liability; right of reimbursement, interest and attorney's fees

(a) Notwithstanding any other provision of this chapter, after division of community and quasi-community property pursuant to Division 7 (commencing with Section 2500):

(1) The separate property owned by a married person at the time of the division and the property received by the person in the division is liable for a debt incurred by the person before or during marriage and the person is personally liable for the debt, whether or not the debt was assigned for payment by the person's spouse in the division.

(2)   The separate property owned by a married person at the time of the division and the property received by the person in the division is not liable for a debt incurred by the person's spouse before or during marriage, and the person is not personally liable for the debt, unless the debt was assigned for payment by the person in the division of the property. Nothing in this paragraph affects the liability of property for the satisfaction of a lien on the property.

(3)   The separate property owned by a married person at the time of the division and the property received by the person in the division is liable for a debt incurred by the person's spouse before or during marriage, and the person is personally liable for the debt, if the debt was assigned for payment by the person in the division of the property. If a money judgment for the debt is entered after the division, the property is not subject to enforcement of the judgment and the judgment may not be enforced against the married person, unless the person is made a party to the judgment for the purpose of this paragraph.

(b)   If property of a married person is applied to the satisfaction of a money judgment pursuant to subdivision (a) for a debt incurred by the person that is assigned for payment by the person's spouse, the person has a right of reimbursement from the person's spouse to the extent of the property applied, with interest at the legal rate, and may recover reasonable attorney's fees incurred in enforcing the right of reimbursement.

(Stats. 1992, c. 162 (A.B. 2650), § 10, operative Jan. 1, 1994.)

§ 920.   Conditions governing right of reimbursement

A right of reimbursement provided by this part is subject to the following provisions:

(a)   The right arises regardless of which spouse applies the property to the satisfaction of the debt, regardless of whether the property is applied to the satisfaction of the debt voluntarily or involuntarily, and regardless of whether the debt to which the property is applied is satisfied in whole or in part. The right is subject to an express written waiver of the right by the spouse in whose favor the right arises.

(b)   The measure of reimbursement is the value of the property or interest in property at the time the right arises.

(c)   The right shall be exercised not later than the earlier of the following times:

(1)   Within three years after the spouse in whose favor the right arises has actual knowledge of the application of the property to the satisfaction of the debt.

(2) In proceedings for division of community and quasi-community property pursuant to Division 7 (commencing with Section 2500) or in proceedings upon the death of a spouse.

(Stats. 1992, c. 162 (A.B. 2650), § 10, operative Jan. 1, 1994.)

§ 930.   Liability for debts enforced on or after Jan. 1, 1985

Except as otherwise provided by statute, this part governs the liability of separate property and property in the community estate and the personal liability of a married person for a debt enforced on or after January 1, 1985, regardless of whether the debt was incurred before, on, or after that date.

(Stats. 1992, c. 162 (A.B. 2650), § 10, operative Jan. 1, 1994. Amended by Stats. 1993, c. 219 (A.B. 1500), § 100.6.)

§ 1000.   Liability for injury or damage caused by spouse; property subject to satisfaction of liability; satisfaction out of insurance proceeds; limitation on exercise of reimbursement right

(a)   A married person is not liable for any injury or damage caused by the other spouse except in cases where the married person would be liable therefor if the marriage did not exist.

(b)   The liability of a married person for death or injury to person or property shall be satisfied as follows:

(1)   If the liability of the married person is based upon an act or omission which occurred while the married person was performing an activity for the benefit of the community, the liability shall first be satisfied from the community estate and second from the separate property of the married person.

(2)   If the liability of the married person is not based upon an act or omission which occurred while the married person was performing an activity for the benefit of the community, the liability shall first be satisfied from the separate property of the married person and second from the community estate.

(c)   This section does not apply to the extent the liability is satisfied out of proceeds of insurance for the liability, whether the proceeds are from property in the community estate or from separate property. Notwithstanding Section 920, no right of reimbursement under this section shall be exercised more than seven years after the spouse in whose favor the right arises has actual knowledge of the application of the property to the satisfaction of the debt.

(Stats. 1992, c. 162 (A.B. 2650), § 10, operative Jan. 1, 1994. Amended by Stats. 1993, c. 219 (A.B. 1500), § 100.7.)

§ 1100. Community personal property; management and control; restrictions on disposition

(a) Except as provided in subdivisions (b), (c), and (d) and Sections 761 and 1103, either spouse has the management and control of the community personal property, whether acquired prior to or on or after January 1, 1975, with like absolute power of disposition, other than testamentary, as the spouse has of the separate estate of the spouse.

(b) A spouse may not make a gift of community personal property, or dispose of community personal property for less than fair and reasonable value, without the *written* consent of the other spouse. This subdivision does not apply to gifts mutually given by both spouses to third parties and to gifts given by one spouse to the other spouse.

(c) A spouse may not sell, convey, or encumber community personal property used as the family dwelling, or the furniture, furnishings, or fittings of the home, or the clothing or wearing apparel of the other spouse or minor children which is community personal property, without the written consent of the other spouse.

(d) Except as provided in subdivisions (b) and (c), and in Section 1102, a spouse who is operating or managing a business or an interest in a business that is all or substantially all community personal property has the primary management and control of the business or interest. Primary management and control means that the managing spouse may act alone in all transactions but shall give prior written notice to the other spouse of any sale, lease, exchange, encumbrance, or other disposition of all or substantially all of the personal property used in the operation of the business (including personal property used for agricultural purposes), whether or not title to that property is held in the name of only one spouse. Written notice is not, however, required when prohibited by the law otherwise applicable to the transaction.

Remedies for the failure by a managing spouse to give prior written notice as required by this subdivision are only as specified in Section 1101. A failure to give prior written notice shall not adversely affect the validity of a transaction nor of any interest transferred.

(e) Each spouse shall act with respect to the other spouse in the management and control of the community assets and liabilities in accordance with the general rules governing fiduciary relationships which control the actions of persons having relationships of personal confidence as specified in Section 721, until such time as the assets and liabilities have been divided by the parties or by a court. This duty includes the obligation to make full disclosure to the other spouse of all material facts and information regarding the existence, characterization, and valuation of all assets in which the community has or may have an interest and debts for which the community is or may be liable, and to provide equal access to all information, records, and books that pertain to the value and character of those assets and debts, upon request.

(Stats. 1992, c. 162 (A.B. 2650), § 10, operative Jan 1. 1994. Amended by Stats. 1993, c. 219 (A.B. 1500), § 100.8.)

§ 1101. Claim for breach of fiduciary duty; court ordered accounting; addition of name of spouse to community property; limitation of action; consent of spouse not required; remedies

(a) A spouse has a claim against the other spouse for any breach of the fiduciary duty that results in impairment to the claimant spouse's present undivided one-half interest in the community estate, including, but not limited to, a single transaction or a pattern or series of transactions, which transaction or transactions have caused or will cause a detrimental impact to the claimant spouse's undivided one-half interest in the community estate.

(b) A court may order an accounting of the property and obligations of the parties to a marriage and may determine the rights of ownership in, the beneficial enjoyment of, or access to, community property, and the classification of all property of the parties to a marriage.

(c) A court may order that the name of a spouse shall be added to community property held in the name of the other spouse alone or that the title of community property held in some other title form shall be reformed to reflect its community character, except with respect to any of the following:

(1) A partnership interest held by the other spouse as a general partner.

(2) An interest in a professional corporation or professional association.

(3) An asset of an unincorporated business if the other spouse is the only spouse involved in operating and managing the business.

(4) Any other property, if the revision would adversely affect the rights of a third person.

(d)(1) Except as provided in paragraph (2), any action under subdivision (a) shall be commenced within three years of the date a petitioning spouse had actual knowledge that the transaction or event for which the remedy is being sought occurred.

(2) An action may be commenced under this section upon the death of a spouse or in conjunction with an action for legal separation, dissolution of marriage, or nullity without regard to the time limitations set forth in paragraph (1).

(3) The defense of laches may be raised in any action brought under this section.

(4) Except as to actions authorized by paragraph (2), remedies under subdivision (a) apply only to transactions or events occurring on or after July 1, 1987.

(e) In any transaction affecting community property in which the consent of both spouses is required, the court may, upon the motion of a spouse, dispense with the requirement of the other spouse's consent if both of the following requirements are met:

(1) The proposed transaction is in the best interest of the community.

(2) Consent has been arbitrarily refused or cannot be obtained due to the physical incapacity, mental incapacity, or prolonged absence of the nonconsenting spouse.

(f) Any action may be brought under this section without filing an action for dissolution of marriage, legal separation, or nullity, or may be brought in conjunction with the action or upon the death of a spouse.

(g) Remedies for breach of the fiduciary duty by one spouse, including those set out in Sections 721 and 1100 shall include, but not be limited to, an award to the other spouse of 50 percent, or an amount equal to 50 percent, of any asset undisclosed or transferred in breach of the fiduciary duty plus attorney's fees and court costs. The value of the asset shall be determined to be its highest value at the date of the breach of fiduciary duty, the date of the sale or disposition of the asset, or the date of the award by the court.

(h) Remedies for the breach of the fiduciary duty by one spouse, as set forth in Sections 721 and 1100, when the breach falls within the ambit of Section 3294 of the Civil Code shall include, but not be limited to, an award to the other spouse of 100 percent, or an amount equal to 100 percent, of any asset undisclosed or transferred in breach of the fiduciary duty.

(Stats. 1992, c. 162 (A.B. 2650), § 10, operative Jan. 1, 1994. Amended by Stats. 2001, c. 703 (A.B. 583), § 1.)

§ 1102. Community real property; spouse's joinder in conveyances; application of section; limitation of actions

(a) Except as provided in Sections 761 and 1103, either spouse has the management and control of the community real property, whether acquired prior to or on or after January 1, 1975, but both spouses, either personally or by a duly authorized agent, must join in executing any instrument by which that community real property or any interest therein is leased for a longer period than one year, or is sold, conveyed, or encumbered.

(b) Nothing in this section shall be construed to apply to a lease, mortgage, conveyance, or transfer of real property or of any interest in real property between spouses.

(c) Notwithstanding subdivision (b):

(1) The sole lease, contract, mortgage, or deed of the husband, holding the record title to community real property, to a lessee, purchaser, or encumbrancer, in good faith without knowledge of the marriage relation, shall be presumed to be valid if executed prior to January 1, 1975.

(2) The sole lease, contract, mortgage, or deed of either spouse, holding the record title to community real property to a lessee, purchaser, or encumbrancer, in good faith without knowledge of the marriage relation, shall be presumed to be valid if executed on or after January 1, 1975.

(d) No action to avoid any instrument mentioned in this section, affecting any property standing of record in the name of either spouse alone, executed by the spouse alone, shall be commenced after the expiration of one year from the filing for record of that instrument in the recorder's office in the county in which the land is situated.

(e) Nothing in this section precludes either spouse from encumbering his or her interest in community real property, as provided in Section 2033, to pay reasonable attorney's fees in order to retain or maintain legal counsel in a proceeding for dissolution of marriage, for nullity of marriage, or for legal separation of the parties.

Historical Derivation: *(Stats. 1850, c. 103, § 9; Stats. 1853, c. 116, § 1. Civil Code former § 172a, added by Stats. 1917, c. 583, § 2, amended by Stats. 1925, c. 37, § 1; Stats. 1927, c. 488, § 1; Stats. 1959, c. 125, § 22; Stats. 1969, c. 627, § 3; Stats. 1969, c. 1609, § 4. Civil Code former § 5127, added by Stats. 1969, c. 1608, § 8, amended by Stats. 1969, c. 1609, § 25; Stats. 1973, c. 987, § 15; Stats. 1974, c. 1206, § 5; Stats. 1987, c. 128, § 3; Stats. 1992, c. 356, § 6. Stats. 1992, c. 162 (A.B. 2650), § 10, operative Jan. 1, 1994. Amended by Stats. 1993, c. 219 (A.B. 1500), § 101; Stats. 2014, c. 82 (S.B. 1306), § 18, eff. Jan. 1, 2015.)*

§ 1103. Management and control of community property; one or both spouses having conservator of estate or lacking legal capacity

(a) Where one or both of the spouses either has a conservator of the estate or lacks legal capacity to manage and control community property, the procedure for management and control (which includes disposition) of the community property is that prescribed in Part 6 (commencing with Section 3000) of Division 4 of the Probate Code.

(b)   Where one or both spouses either has a conservator of the estate or lacks legal capacity to give consent to a gift of community personal property or a disposition of community personal property without a valuable consideration as required by Section 1100 or to a sale, conveyance, or encumbrance of community personal property for which a consent is required by Section 1100, the procedure for that gift, disposition, sale, conveyance, or encumbrance is that prescribed in Part 6 (commencing with Section 3000) of Division 4 of the Probate Code.

(c)   Where one or both spouses either has a conservator of the estate or lacks legal capacity to join in executing a lease, sale, conveyance, or encumbrance of community real property or any interest therein as required by Section 1102, the procedure for that lease, sale, conveyance, or encumbrance is that prescribed in Part 6 (commencing with Section 3000) of Division 4 of the Probate Code.

(Stats. 1992, c. 162 (A.B. 2650), § 10, operative Jan. 1, 1994.)

§ 1500.   Effect of premarital agreements and other marital property agreements

The property rights of spouses prescribed by statute may be altered by a premarital agreement or other marital property agreement.

(Stats. 1992, c. 162 (A.B. 2650), § 10, operative Jan. 1, 1994. Amended by Stats. 2014, c. 82 (S.B. 1306), § 19, eff. Jan. 1, 2015.)

§ 1600.   Short title

This chapter may be cited as the Uniform Premarital Agreement Act.

(Stats. 1992, c. 162 (A.B. 2650), § 10, operative Jan. 1, 1994.)

§ 1601.   Effective date of chapter

This chapter is effective on and after January 1, 1986, and applies to any premarital agreement executed on or after that date.

(Stats. 1992, c. 162 (A.B. 2650), § 10, operative Jan. 1, 1994.)

§ 1610.   Definitions

As used in this chapter:

(a)   "Premarital agreement" means an agreement between prospective spouses made in contemplation of marriage and to be effective upon marriage.

(b)   "Property" means an interest, present or future, legal or equitable, vested or contingent, in real or personal property, including income and earnings.

(Stats. 1992, c. 162 (A.B. 2650), § 10, operative Jan. 1, 1994.)

§ 1611. Form and execution of agreement; consideration

A premarital agreement shall be in writing and signed by both parties. It is enforceable without consideration.

(Stats. 1992, c. 162 (A.B. 2650), § 10, operative Jan. 1, 1994.)

§ 1612. Subject matter of premarital agreements

(a) Parties to a premarital agreement may contract with respect to all of the following:

(1) The rights and obligations of each of the parties in any of the property of either or both of them whenever and wherever acquired or located.

(2) The right to buy, sell, use, transfer, exchange, abandon, lease, consume, expend, assign, create a security interest in, mortgage, encumber, dispose of, or otherwise manage and control property.

(3) The disposition of property upon separation, marital dissolution, death, or the occurrence or nonoccurrence of any other event.

(4) The making of a will, trust, or other arrangement to carry out the provisions of the agreement.

(5) The ownership rights in and disposition of the death benefit from a life insurance policy.

(6) The choice of law governing the construction of the agreement.

(7) Any other matter, including their personal rights and obligations, not in violation of public policy or a statute imposing a criminal penalty.

(b) The right of a child to support may not be adversely affected by a premarital agreement.

(c) Any provision in a premarital agreement regarding spousal support, including, but not limited to, a waiver of it, is not enforceable if the party against whom enforcement of the spousal support provision is sought was not represented by independent counsel at the time the agreement containing the provision was signed, or if the provision regarding spousal support is unconscionable at the time of enforcement. An otherwise unenforceable provision in a premarital agreement regarding spousal support may not become enforceable solely because the party against whom enforcement is sought was represented by independent counsel.

(Stats. 1992, c. 162 (A.B. 2650), § 10, operative Jan. 1, 1994. Amended by Stats. 2001, c. 286 (S.B. 78), § 1.)

§ 1613. Effective date of agreements

A premarital agreement becomes effective upon marriage.

(Stats. 1992, c. 162 (A.B. 2650), § 10, operative Jan. 1, 1994.)

§ 1614. Amendment or revocation of agreements

After marriage, a premarital agreement may be amended or revoked only by a written agreement signed by the parties. The amended agreement or the revocation is enforceable without consideration.

(Stats. 1992, c. 162 (A.B. 2650), § 10, operative Jan. 1, 1994.)

§ 1615. Unenforceable   agreements;   unconscionability; voluntariness

(a) A premarital agreement is not enforceable if the party against whom enforcement is sought proves either of the following:

(1) That party did not execute the agreement voluntarily.

(2) The agreement was unconscionable when it was executed and, before execution of the agreement, all of the following applied to that party:

(A) That party was not provided a fair, reasonable, and full disclosure of the property or financial obligations of the other party.

(B) That party did not voluntarily and expressly waive, in writing, any right to disclosure of the property or financial obligations of the other party beyond the disclosure provided.

(C) That party did not have, or reasonably could not have had, an adequate knowledge of the property or financial obligations of the other party.

(b) An issue of unconscionability of a premarital agreement shall be decided by the court as a matter of law.

(c) For the purposes of subdivision (a), it shall be deemed that a premarital agreement was not executed voluntarily unless the court finds in writing or on the record all of the following:

(1) The party against whom enforcement is sought was represented by independent legal counsel at the time of signing the agreement or, after being advised to seek independent legal counsel, expressly waived, in a separate writing, representation by independent legal counsel.

(2) The party against whom enforcement is sought had not less than seven calendar days between the time that party was first presented with the agreement and advised to seek independent legal counsel and the time the agreement was signed.

(3) The party against whom enforcement is sought, if unrepresented by legal counsel, was fully informed of the terms and basic effect of the agreement as well as the rights and obligations he or she was giving up by signing the agreement, and was proficient in the language in which the explanation of the party's rights was conducted and in which the agreement was written. The explanation of the rights and obligations relinquished shall be memorialized in writing and delivered to the party prior to signing the agreement. The unrepresented party shall, on or before the signing of the premarital agreement, execute a document declaring that he or she received the information required by this paragraph and indicating who provided that information.

(4) The agreement and the writings executed pursuant to paragraphs (1) and (3) were not executed under duress, fraud, or undue influence, and the parties did not lack capacity to enter into the agreement.

(5) Any other factors the court deems relevant.

(Stats. 1992, c. 162 (A.B. 2650), § 10, operative Jan. 1, 1994. Amended by Stats. 2001, c. 286 (S.B. 78), § 2.)

§ 1616. Void marriage, effect on agreement

If a marriage is determined to be void, an agreement that would otherwise have been a premarital agreement is enforceable only to the extent necessary to avoid an inequitable result.

(Stats. 1992, c. 162 (A.B. 2650), § 10, operative Jan. 1, 1994.)

§ 1617. Limitations of actions; equitable defenses including laches and estoppel

Any statute of limitations applicable to an action asserting a claim for relief under a premarital agreement is tolled during the marriage of the parties to the agreement. However, equitable defenses limiting the time for enforcement, including laches and estoppel, are available to either party.

(Stats. 1992, c. 162 (A.B. 2650), § 10, operative Jan. 1, 1994.)

§ 1620. Contracts altering legal relations of spouses; restrictions

Except as otherwise provided by law, spouses cannot, by a contract with each other, alter their legal relations, except as to property.

(Stats. 1992, c. 162 (A.B. 2650), § 10, operative Jan. 1, 1994. Amended by Stats. 2014, c. 82 (S.B. 1306), § 21, eff. Jan 1, 2015.)

§ 2013. Collaborative law process

(a) If a written agreement is entered into by the parties, the parties may utilize a collaborative law process to resolve any matter governed by this code over which the court is granted jurisdiction pursuant to Section 2000.

(b) "Collaborative law process" means the process in which the parties and any professionals engaged by the parties to assist them agree in writing to use their best efforts and to make a good faith attempt to resolve disputes related to the family law matters as referenced in subdivision (a) on an agreed basis without resorting to adversary judicial intervention.

(Added by Stats. 2006, c. 496 (A.B. 402), § 2.)

§ 2045. Ex parte protective orders

During the pendency of the proceeding, on application of a party in the manner provided by Part 4 (commencing with Section 240) of Division 2, the court may issue ex parte any of the following orders:

(a) An order restraining any person from transferring, encumbering, hypothecating, concealing, or in any way disposing of any property, real or personal, whether community, quasi-community, or separate, except in the usual course of business or for the necessities of life, and if the order is directed against a party, requiring that party to notify the other party of any proposed extraordinary expenditures and to account to the court for all extraordinary expenditures.

(b) A protective order, as defined in Section 6218, and any other order as provided in Article 1 (commencing with Section 6320) of Chapter 2 of Part 4 of Division 10.

(Added by Stats. 1993, c. 219 (A.B. 1500), § 106.7.)

§ 2100. Legislative findings and declarations; disclosure of assets and liabilities

The Legislature finds and declares the following:

(a) It is the policy of the State of California (1) to marshal, preserve, and protect community and quasi-community assets and liabilities that exist at the date of separation so as to avoid dissipation of the community estate before distribution, (2) to ensure fair and sufficient child and spousal support awards, and (3) to achieve a division of community and quasi-community assets and liabilities on the dissolution or nullity of marriage or legal separation of the parties as provided under California law.

(b) Sound public policy further favors the reduction of the adversarial nature of marital dissolution and the attendant costs by fostering full disclosure and cooperative discovery.

(c) In order to promote this public policy, a full and accurate disclosure of all assets and liabilities in which one or both parties have or may have an interest must be made in the early stages of a proceeding for dissolution of marriage or legal separation of the parties, regardless of the characterization as community or separate, together with a disclosure of all income and expenses of the parties. Moreover, each party has a continuing duty to immediately, fully, and accurately update and augment that disclosure to the extent there have been any material changes so that at the time the parties enter into an agreement for the resolution of any of these issues, or at the time of trial on these issues, each party will have a full and complete knowledge of the relevant underlying facts.

(Added by Stats. 1993, c. 219 (A.B. 1500), § 107. Amended by Stats. 1993, c. 1101 (A.B. 1469), § 3, eff. Oct. 11, 1993, operative Jan.1, 1994; Stats. 2001, c. 703 (A.B. 583), § 2.)

§ 2101. Definitions

Unless the provision or context otherwise requires, the following definitions apply to this chapter:

(a) "Asset" includes, but is not limited to, any real or personal property of any nature, whether tangible or intangible, and whether currently existing or contingent.

(b) "Default judgment" does not include a stipulated judgment or any judgment pursuant to a marital settlement agreement.

(c) "Earnings and accumulations" includes income from whatever source derived, as provided in Section 4058.

(d) "Expenses" includes, but is not limited to, all personal living expenses, but does not include business related expenses.

(e) "Income and expense declaration" includes the Income and Expense Declaration forms approved for use by the Judicial Council, and any other financial statement that is approved for use by the Judicial Council in lieu of the Income and Expense Declaration, if the financial statement form satisfies all other applicable criteria.

(f) "Liability" includes, but is not limited to, any debt or obligation, whether currently existing or contingent.

(Added by Stats. 1993, c. 219 (A.B. 1500), § 107. Amended by Stats. 1993, c. 1101 (A.B. 1469), § 4, eff. Oct. 11, 1993, operative Jan. 1, 1994; Stats. 1998, c. 581 (A.B. 2801), § 5.)

§ 2102. Fiduciary relationship; length and scope of duty; termination

(a) From the date of separation to the date of the distribution of the community or quasi-community asset or liability in question, each party is subject to the standards provided in Section 721, as to all activities that affect the assets and liabilities of the other party, including, but not limited to, the following activities:

(1) The accurate and complete disclosure of all assets and liabilities in which the party has or may have an interest or obligation and all current earnings, accumulations, and expenses, including an immediate, full, and accurate update or augmentation to the extent there have been any material changes.

(2) The accurate and complete written disclosure of any investment opportunity, business opportunity, or other income-producing opportunity that presents itself after the date of separation, but that results from any investment, significant business activity outside the ordinary course of business, or other income-producing opportunity of either spouse from the date of marriage to the date of separation, inclusive. The written disclosure shall be made in sufficient time for the other spouse to make an informed decision as to whether he or she desires to participate in the investment opportunity, business, or other potential income-producing opportunity, and for the court to resolve any dispute regarding the right of the other spouse to participate in the opportunity. In the event of nondisclosure of an investment opportunity, the division of any gain resulting from that opportunity is governed by the standard provided in Section 2556.

(3) The operation or management of a business or an interest in a business in which the community may have an interest.

(b) From the date that a valid, enforceable, and binding resolution of the disposition of the asset or liability in question is reached, until the asset or liability has actually been distributed, each party is subject to the standards provided in Section 721 as to all activities that affect the assets or liabilities of the other party. Once a particular asset or liability has been distributed, the duties and standards set forth in Section 721 shall end as to that asset or liability.

(c) From the date of separation to the date of a valid, enforceable, and binding resolution of all issues relating to child or spousal support and professional fees, each party is subject to the standards provided in Section 721 as to all issues relating to the support and fees, including immediate, full, and accurate disclosure of all material facts and information regarding the income or expenses of the party.

(Added by Stats. 1993, c. 219 (A.B. 1500), § 107. Amended by Stats. 1993, c. 1101 (A.B. 1469), § 5, eff. Oct. 11, 1993, operative Jan. 1, 1994; Stats. 2001, c. 703 (A.B. 583), § 3.)

§ 2103. Declarations of disclosure; requirements

In order to provide full and accurate disclosure of all assets and liabilities in which one or both parties may have an interest, each party to a proceeding for dissolution of the marriage or legal separation of the parties shall serve on the other party a preliminary declaration of disclosure under Section 2104, unless service of the preliminary declaration of disclosure is not required pursuant to Section 2110, and a final declaration of disclosure under Section 2105, unless service of the final declaration of disclosure is waived pursuant to Section 2105 or 2110, and shall file proof of service of each with the court.

(Added by Stats. 1993, c. 219 (A.B. 1500), § 107. Amended by Stats. 1998, c. 581 (A.B. 2801), § 6; Stats. 2015, c. 46 (S.B. 340), § 1, eff. Jan. 1, 2016.)

§ 2104. Preliminary declaration of disclosure

(a) Except by court order for good cause, as provided in Section 2107, or when service of the preliminary declaration of disclosure is not required pursuant to Section 2110, in the time period set forth in subdivision (f), each party shall serve on the other party a preliminary declaration of disclosure, executed under penalty of perjury on a form prescribed by the Judicial Council. The commission of perjury on the preliminary declaration of disclosure may be grounds for setting aside the judgment, or any part or parts thereof, pursuant to Chapter 10 (commencing with Section 2120), in addition to any and all other remedies, civil or criminal, that otherwise are available under law for the commission of perjury. The preliminary declaration of disclosure shall include all tax returns filed by the declarant within the two years prior to the date that the party served the declaration.

(b) The preliminary declaration of disclosure shall not be filed with the court, except on court order. However, the parties shall file proof of service of the preliminary declaration of disclosure with the court.

(c) The preliminary declaration of disclosure shall set forth with sufficient particularity, that a person of reasonable and ordinary intelligence can ascertain, all of the following:

(1) The identity of all assets in which the declarant has or may have an interest and all liabilities for which the declarant is or may be liable, regardless of the characterization of the asset or liability as community, quasi-community, or separate.

(2) The declarant's percentage of ownership in each asset and percentage of obligation for each liability when property is not solely owned by one or both of the parties. The preliminary declaration may also set forth the declarant's characterization of each asset or liability.

(d) A declarant may amend his or her preliminary declaration of disclosure without leave of the court. Proof of service of any amendment shall be filed with the court.

(e) Along with the preliminary declaration of disclosure, each party shall provide the other party with a completed income and expense declaration unless an income and expense declaration has already been provided and is current and valid.

(f)   The petitioner shall serve the other party with the preliminary declaration of disclosure either concurrently with the petition for dissolution or legal separation, or within 60 days of filing the petition. When a petitioner serves the summons and petition by publication or posting pursuant to court order and the respondent files a response prior to a default judgment being entered, the petitioner shall serve the other party with the preliminary declaration of disclosure within 30 days of the response being filed. The respondent shall serve the other party with the preliminary declaration of disclosure either concurrently with the response to the petition, or within 60 days of filing the response. The time periods specified in this subdivision may be extended by written agreement of the parties or by court order.

(Added by Stats. 1993, c. 219 (A.B. 1500), § 107. Amended by Stats. 1993, c. 1101 (A.B. 1469), § 6, eff. Oct. 11, 1993, operative Jan. 1, 1994; Stats. 1998, c. 581 (A.B. 2801), § 7; Stats. 2009, c. 110 (A.B. 459), § 1; Stats. 2012, c. 107 (A.B. 1406), § 1; Stats. 2015, c. 46 (S.B. 340), § 2, eff. Jan. 1, 2016; Stats. 2015, c. 416 (A.B. 1519), § 1.5, eff. Jan. 1, 2016.)

§ 2105. Final declaration of disclosure of current income and expenses; execution and service; contents; waiver; perjury or noncompliance with chapter

(a)   Except by court order for good cause, before or at the time the parties enter into an agreement for the resolution of property or support issues other than pendente lite support, or, if the case goes to trial, no later than 45 days before the first assigned trial date, each party, or the attorney for the party in this matter, shall serve on the other party a final declaration of disclosure and a current income and expense declaration, executed under penalty of perjury on a form prescribed by the Judicial Council, unless the parties mutually waive the final declaration of disclosure. The commission of perjury on the final declaration of disclosure by a party may be grounds for setting aside the judgment, or any part or parts thereof, pursuant to Chapter 10 (commencing with Section 2120), in addition to any and all other remedies, civil or criminal, that otherwise are available under law for the commission of perjury.

(b)   The final declaration of disclosure shall include all of the following information:

(1)   All material facts and information regarding the characterization of all assets and liabilities.

(2)   All material facts and information regarding the valuation of all assets that are contended to be community property or in which it is contended the community has an interest.

(3) All material facts and information regarding the amounts of all obligations that are contended to be community obligations or for which it is contended the community has liability.

(4) All material facts and information regarding the earnings, accumulations, and expenses of each party that have been set forth in the income and expense declaration.

(c) In making an order setting aside a judgment for failure to comply with this section, the court may limit the set aside to those portions of the judgment materially affected by the nondisclosure.

(d) The parties may stipulate to a mutual waiver of the requirements of subdivision (a) concerning the final declaration of disclosure, by execution of a waiver under penalty of perjury entered into in open court or by separate stipulation. The waiver shall include all of the following representations:

(1) Both parties have complied with Section 2104 and the preliminary declarations of disclosure have been completed and exchanged.

(2) Both parties have completed and exchanged a current income and expense declaration, that includes all material facts and information regarding that party's earnings, accumulations, and expenses.

(3) Both parties have fully complied with Section 2102 and have fully augmented the preliminary declarations of disclosure, including disclosure of all material facts and information regarding the characterization of all assets and liabilities, the valuation of all assets that are contended to be community property or in which it is contended the community has an interest, and the amounts of all obligations that are contended to be community obligations or for which it is contended the community has liability.

(4) The waiver is knowingly, intelligently, and voluntarily entered into by each of the parties.

(5) Each party understands that this waiver does not limit the legal disclosure obligations of the parties, but rather is a statement under penalty of perjury that those obligations have been fulfilled. Each party further understands that noncompliance with those obligations will result in the court setting aside the judgment.

(Added by Stats. 1993, c. 219 (A.B. 1500), § 107. Amended by Stats. 1993, c. 1101 (A.B. 1469), § 7, eff. Oct. 11, 1993, operative Jan. 1, 1994; Stats. 1995, c. 233 (A.B. 806), § 1; Stats. 1996, c. 1061 (S.B. 1033), § 7; Stats. 1998, c. 581 (A.B. 2801), § 8; Stats. 2001, c. 703 (A.B. 583), § 4.)

§ 2106. Entry of judgment; requirement of execution and service of declarations; exceptions; execution and filing of declaration of execution and service or of waiver

Except as provided in subdivision (d) of Section 2105, Section 2110, or absent good cause as provided in Section 2107, no judgment shall be entered with respect to the parties' property rights without each party, or the attorney for that party in this matter, having executed and served a copy of the final declaration of disclosure and current income and expense declaration. Each party, or his or her attorney, shall execute and file with the court a declaration signed under penalty of perjury stating that service of the final declaration of disclosure and current income and expense declaration was made on the other party or that service of the final declaration of disclosure has been waived pursuant to subdivision (d) of Section 2105 or in Section 2110.

(Added by Stats. 1993, c. 219 (A.B. 1500), § 107. Amended by Stats. 1993, c. 1101 (A.B. 1469), § 8, eff. Oct. 11, 1993, operative Jan. 1, 1994; Stats. 1995, c. 233 (A.B. 806), § 2; Stats. 1996, c. 1061 (S.B. 1033), § 8; Stats. 1998, c. 581 (A.B. 2801), § 9; Stats. 2001, c. 703 (A.B. 583), § 5; Stats. 2002, c. 1008 (A.B. 3028), § 15; Stats. 2009, c. 110 (A.B. 459), § 2.)

§ 2107. Noncomplying declarations; requests to comply; remedies

(a) If one party fails to serve on the other party a preliminary declaration of disclosure under Section 2104, unless that party is not required to serve a preliminary declaration of disclosure pursuant to Section 2110, or a final declaration of disclosure under Section 2105, or fails to provide the information required in the respective declarations with sufficient particularity, and if the other party has served the respective declaration of disclosure on the noncomplying party, the complying party may, within a reasonable time, request preparation of the appropriate declaration of disclosure or further particularity.

(b) If the noncomplying party fails to comply with a request under subdivision (a), the complying party may do one or more of the following:

(1) File a motion to compel a further response.

(2) File a motion for an order preventing the noncomplying party from presenting evidence on issues that should have been covered in the declaration of disclosure.

(3) File a motion showing good cause for the court to grant the complying party's voluntary waiver of receipt of the noncomplying party's preliminary declaration of disclosure pursuant to Section 2104 or final declaration of disclosure pursuant to Section 2105. The voluntary waiver does not affect the rights enumerated in subdivision (d).

(c)   If a party fails to comply with any provision of this chapter, the court shall, in addition to any other remedy provided by law, impose money sanctions against the noncomplying party. Sanctions shall be in an amount sufficient to deter repetition of the conduct or comparable conduct, and shall include reasonable attorney's fees, costs incurred, or both, unless the court finds that the noncomplying party acted with substantial justification or that other circumstances make the imposition of the sanction unjust.

(d)   Except as otherwise provided in this subdivision, if a court enters a judgment when the parties have failed to comply with all disclosure requirements of this chapter, the court shall set aside the judgment. The failure to comply with the disclosure requirements does not constitute harmless error. If the court granted the complying party's voluntary waiver of receipt of the noncomplying party's preliminary declaration of disclosure pursuant to paragraph (3) of subdivision (b), the court shall set aside the judgment only at the request of the complying party, unless the motion to set aside the judgment is based on one of the following:

(1)   Actual fraud if the defrauded party was kept in ignorance or in some other manner was fraudulently prevented from fully participating in the proceeding.

(2)   Perjury, as defined in Section 118 of the Penal Code, in the preliminary or final declaration of disclosure, in the waiver of the final declaration of disclosure, or in the current income and expense statement.

(e)   Upon the motion to set aside judgment, the court may order the parties to provide the preliminary and final declarations of disclosure that were exchanged between them. Absent a court order to the contrary, the disclosure declarations shall not be filed with the court and shall be returned to the parties.

(Added by Stats. 1993, c. 219 (A.B. 1500), § 107. Amended by Stats. 1993, c. 1101 (A.B. 1469), § 9, eff. Oct. 11, 1993, operative Jan. 1, 1994; Stats. 2001, c. 703 (A.B. 583), § 6; Stats. 2009, c. 110 (A.B. 459), § 3; Stats. 2015, c. 46 (S.B. 340), § 3, eff. Jan. 1, 2016.)

§ 2108. Liquidation of community or quasi-community assets to avoid market or investment risks; authority of court

At any time during the proceeding, the court has the authority, on application of a party and for good cause, to order the liquidation of community or quasi-community assets so as to avoid unreasonable market or investment risks, given the relative nature, scope, and extent of the community estate. However, in no event shall the court grant the application unless, as provided in this chapter, the appropriate declaration of disclosure has been served by the moving party.

(Added by Stats. 1993, c. 219 (A.B. 1500), § 107.)

§ 2109. Summary dissolution of marriage; required disclosures

The provisions of this chapter requiring a final declaration of disclosure do not apply to a summary dissolution of marriage, but a preliminary declaration of disclosure is required.

(Added by Stats. 1993, c. 1101 (A.B. 1469), § 11, eff. Oct. 11, 1993, operative Jan. 1, 1994.)

§ 2110. Default judgments; declarations of disclosure

In the case of a default judgment, the petitioner may waive the final declaration of disclosure requirements provided in this chapter, and shall not be required to serve a final declaration of disclosure on the respondent nor receive a final declaration of disclosure from the respondent. However, a preliminary declaration of disclosure by the petitioner is required unless the petitioner served the summons and petition by publication or posting pursuant to court order and the respondent has defaulted.

(Added by Stats. 1993, c. 1101 (A.B. 1469), § 12, eff. Oct. 11, 1993, operative Jan. 1, 1994. Amended by Stats. 1994, c. 146 (A.B. 3601), § 41; Stats. 1998, c. 581 (A.B. 2801), § 10; Stats. 2015, c. 46 (S.B. 340), § 4, eff. Jan. 1, 2016.)

§ 2111. Attorney work product privilege; protective orders

A disclosure required by this chapter does not abrogate the attorney work product privilege or impede the power of the court to issue protective orders.

(Added by Stats. 1993, c. 1101 (A.B. 1469), § 13, eff. Oct. 11, 1993, operative Jan. 1, 1994.)

§ 2112. Forms

The Judicial Council shall adopt appropriate forms and modify existing forms to effectuate the purposes of this chapter.

(Added by Stats. 1993, c. 1101 (A.B. 1469), § 14, eff. Oct. 11, 1993, operative Jan. 1, 1994.)

§ 2113. Application of chapter

This chapter applies to any proceeding commenced on or after January 1, 1993.

(Formerly § 2109, added by Stats. 1993, c. 219 (A.B. 1500), § 107. Renumbered § 2113 and amended by Stats. 1993, c. 1101 (A.B. 1469), § 10, eff. Oct. 11, 1993, operative Jan. 1, 1994.)

§ 2120. Legislative findings and declarations; public policy

The Legislature finds and declares the following:

(a) The State of California has a strong policy of ensuring the division of community and quasi-community property in the dissolution of a marriage as set forth in Division 7 (commencing with Section 2500), and of providing for fair and sufficient child and spousal support awards. These policy goals can only be implemented with full disclosure of community, quasi-community, and separate assets, liabilities, income, and expenses, as provided in Chapter 9 (commencing with Section 2100), and decisions freely and knowingly made.

(b)   It occasionally happens that the division of property or the award of support, whether made as a result of agreement or trial, is inequitable when made due to the nondisclosure or other misconduct of one of the parties.

(c)   The public policy of assuring finality of judgments must be balanced against the public interest in ensuring proper division of marital property, in ensuring sufficient support awards, and in deterring misconduct.

(d)   The law governing the circumstances under which a judgment can be set aside, after the time for relief under Section 473 of the Code of Civil Procedure has passed, has been the subject of considerable confusion which has led to increased litigation and unpredictable and inconsistent decisions at the trial and appellate levels.

(Added by Stats. 1993, c. 219 (A.B. 1500), § 108.)

§ 2121.   Authority of court to provide relief

(a)   In proceedings for dissolution of marriage, for nullity of marriage, or for legal separation of the parties, the court may, on any terms that may be just, relieve a spouse from a judgment, or any part or parts thereof, adjudicating support or division of property, after the six-month time limit of Section 473 of the Code of Civil Procedure has run, based on the grounds, and within the time limits, provided in this chapter.

(b)   In all proceedings under this chapter, before granting relief, the court shall find that the facts alleged as the grounds for relief materially affected the original outcome and that the moving party would materially benefit from the granting of the relief.

(Added by Stats. 1993, c. 219 (A.B. 1500), § 108.)

§ 2122.   Grounds for relief; limitation of actions

The grounds and time limits for a motion to set aside a judgment, or any part or parts thereof, are governed by this section and shall be one of the following:

(a)   Actual fraud where the defrauded party was kept in ignorance or in some other manner was fraudulently prevented from fully participating in the proceeding. An action or motion based on fraud shall be brought within one year after the date on which the complaining party either did discover, or should have discovered, the fraud.

(b)   Perjury. An action or motion based on perjury in the preliminary or final declaration of disclosure, the waiver of the final declaration of disclosure, or in the current income and expense statement shall be brought within one year after the date on which the complaining party either did discover, or should have discovered, the perjury.

(c)   Duress. An action or motion based upon duress shall be brought within two years after the date of entry of judgment.

(d)   Mental incapacity. An action or motion based on mental incapacity shall be brought within two years after the date of entry of judgment.

(e)   As to stipulated or uncontested judgments or that part of a judgment stipulated to by the parties, mistake, either mutual or unilateral, whether mistake of law or mistake of fact. An action or motion based on mistake shall be brought within one year after the date of entry of judgment.

(f)   Failure to comply with the disclosure requirements of Chapter 9 (commencing with Section 2100). An action or motion based on failure to comply with the disclosure requirements shall be brought within one year after the date on which the complaining party either discovered, or should have discovered, the failure to comply.

(Added by Stats. 1993, c. 219 (A.B. 1500), § 108. Amended by Stats. 1993, c. 1101 (A.B. 1469), § 15, eff. Oct. 11, 1993, operative Jan. 1, 1994; Stats. 2001, c. 703 (A.B. 583), § 7.)

§ 2123.   Restrictions on grounds for relief; inequitable judgments

Notwithstanding any other provision of this chapter, or any other law, a judgment may not be set aside simply because the court finds that it was inequitable when made, nor simply because subsequent circumstances caused the division of assets or liabilities to become inequitable, or the support to become inadequate.

(Added by Stats. 1993, c. 219 (A.B. 1500), § 108.)

§ 2200.   Incestuous marriages

Marriages between parents and children, ancestors and descendants of every degree, and between siblings of the half as well as the whole blood, and between uncles or aunts and nieces or nephews, are incestuous, and void from the beginning, whether the relationship is legitimate or illegitimate.

(Stats. 1992, c. 162 (A.B. 2650), § 10, operative Jan. 1, 1994. Amended by Stats. 2014, c. 82 (S.B. 1306), § 23, eff. Jan. 1, 2015.)

§ 2201. Bigamous and polygamous marriages; exceptions; absentees

(a) A subsequent marriage contracted by a person during the life of his or her former spouse, with a person other than the former spouse, is illegal and void unless:

> (1) The former marriage has been dissolved or adjudged a nullity before the date of the subsequent marriage.

> (2) The former spouse (A) is absent, and not known to the person to be living for the period of five successive years immediately preceding the subsequent marriage, or (B) is generally reputed or believed by the person to be dead at the time the subsequent marriage was contracted.

(b) In either of the cases described in paragraph (2) of subdivision (a), the subsequent marriage is valid until its nullity is adjudged pursuant to subdivision (b) of Section 2210.

(Stats. 1992, c. 162 (A.B. 2650), § 10, operative Jan. 1, 1994. Amended by Stats. 2014, c. 82 (S.B. 1306), § 24, eff. Jan. 1, 2015.)

§ 2210. Annulment, causes for

A marriage is voidable and may be adjudged a nullity if any of the following conditions existed at the time of the marriage:

(a) The party who commences the proceeding or on whose behalf the proceeding is commenced was without the capability of consenting to the marriage as provided in Section 301 or 302, unless, after attaining the age of consent, the party for any time freely cohabited with the other as his or her spouse.

(b) The spouse of either party was living and the marriage with that spouse was then in force and that spouse (1) was absent and not known to the party commencing the proceeding to be living for a period of five successive years immediately preceding the subsequent marriage for which the judgment of nullity is sought or (2) was generally reputed or believed by the party commencing the proceeding to be dead at the time the subsequent marriage was contracted.

(c) Either party was of unsound mind, unless the party of unsound mind, after coming to reason, freely cohabited with the other as his or her spouse.

(d) The consent of either party was obtained by fraud, unless the party whose consent was obtained by fraud afterwards, with full knowledge of the facts constituting the fraud, freely cohabited with the other as his or her spouses.

(e) The consent of either party was obtained by force, unless the party whose consent was obtained by force afterwards freely cohabited with the other as his or her spouse.

(f) Either party was, at the time of marriage, physically incapable of entering into the marriage state, and that incapacity continues, and appears to be incurable.

(Stats. 1992, c. 162 (A.B. 2650), § 10, operative Jan. 1, 1994. Amended by Stats. 2014, c. 82 (S.B. 1306), § 25, eff. Jan. 1, 2015.)

§ 2251. Status of putative spouse; division of community or quasi-community property

(a) If a determination is made that a marriage is void or voidable and the court finds that either party or both parties believed in good faith that the marriage was valid, the court shall:

(1) Declare the party or parties, who believed in good faith that the marriage was valid, to have the status of a putative spouse.

(2) If the division of property is in issue, divide, in accordance with Division 7 (commencing with Section 2500), that property acquired during the union that would have been community property or quasi-community property if the union had not been void or voidable, only upon request of a party who is declared a putative spouse under paragraph (1). This property is known as "quasi-marital property."

(b) If the court expressly reserves jurisdiction, it may make the property division at a time after the judgment.

(Stats. 1992, c. 162 (A.B. 2650), § 10, operative Jan. 1, 1994. Amended by Stats. 2015, c. 196 (A.B. 380), § 1, eff. Jan. 1, 2016.)

§ 2252. Liability of quasi-marital property for debts of parties

The property divided pursuant to Section 2251 is liable for debts of the parties to the same extent as if the property had been community property or quasi-community property.

(Stats. 1992, c. 162 (A.B. 2650), § 10, operative Jan. 1, 1994.)

§ 2254. Order for support; putative spouse

The court may, during the pendency of a proceeding for nullity of marriage or upon judgment of nullity of marriage, order a party to pay for the support of the other party in the same manner as if the marriage had not been void or voidable if the party for whose benefit the order is made is found to be a putative spouse.

(Stats. 1992, c. 162 (A.B. 2650), § 10, operative Jan. 1, 1994.)

§ 2255. Grant of attorney's fees and costs

The court may grant attorney's fees and costs in accordance with Chapter 3.5 (commencing with Section 2030) of Part 1 in proceedings to have the marriage adjudged void and in those proceedings based upon voidable marriage in which the party applying for attorney's fees and costs is found to be innocent of fraud or wrongdoing in inducing or entering into the marriage, and free from knowledge of the then existence of any prior marriage or other impediment to the contracting of the marriage for which a judgment of nullity is sought.

(Stats. 1992, c. 162 (A.B. 2650), § 10, operative Jan. 1, 1994. Amended by Stats. 1993, c. 219 (A.B. 1500), § 108.5.)

§ 2300. Effect of dissolution

The effect of a judgment of dissolution of marriage when it becomes final is to restore the parties to the state of unmarried persons.

(Stats. 1992, c. 162 (A.B. 2650), § 10, operative Jan. 1, 1994.)

§ 2310. Grounds for dissolution or legal separation

Dissolution of the marriage or legal separation of the parties may be based on either of the following grounds, which shall be pleaded generally:

(a) Irreconcilable differences, which have caused the irremediable breakdown of the marriage.

(b) Permanent legal incapacity to make decisions.

(Stats. 1992, c. 162 (A.B. 2650), § 10, operative Jan. 1, 1994. Amended by Stats. 2014, c. 144 (A.B. 1847), § 9, eff. Jan. 1, 2015.)

§ 2311. "Irreconcilable differences" defined

Irreconcilable differences are those grounds which are determined by the court to be substantial reasons for not continuing the marriage and which make it appear that the marriage should be dissolved.

(Stats. 1992, c. 162 (A.B. 2650), § 10, operative Jan. 1, 1994.)

§ 2312. Permanent legal incapacity to make decisions

A marriage may be dissolved on the grounds of permanent legal incapacity to make decisions only upon proof, including competent medical or psychiatric testimony, that the spouse was at the time the petition was filed, and remains, permanently lacking the legal capacity to make decisions.

(Stats. 1992, c. 162 (A.B. 2650), § 10, operative Jan. 1, 1994. Amended by Stats. 2014, c. 144 (A.B. 1847), § 10, eff. Jan. 1, 2015.)

§ 2320. Entry of judgment of dissolution; entry of judgment for dissolution, nullity, or legal separation of a marriage between persons of the same sex

(a) Except as provided in subdivision (b), a judgment of dissolution of marriage may not be entered unless one of the parties to the marriage has been a resident of this state for six months and of the county in which the proceeding is filed for three months next preceding the filing of the petition.

(b)(1) A judgment for dissolution, nullity, or legal separation of a marriage between persons of the same sex may be entered, even if neither spouse is a resident of, or maintains a domicile in, this state at the time the proceedings are filed, if the following apply:

  (A) The marriage was entered in California.

  (B) Neither party to the marriage resides in a jurisdiction that will dissolve the marriage. If the jurisdiction does not recognize the marriage, there shall be a rebuttable presumption that the jurisdiction will not dissolve the marriage.

  (2) For the purposes of this subdivision, the superior court in the county where the marriage was entered shall be the proper court for the proceeding. The dissolution, nullity, or legal separation shall be adjudicated in accordance with California law.

(Stats. 1992, c. 162 (A.B. 2650), § 10, operative Jan. 1, 1994. Amended by Stats. 2011, c. 721 (S.B. 651), § 4.)

§ 2330. Petition

(a) A proceeding for dissolution of marriage or for legal separation of the parties is commenced by filing a petition entitled "In re the marriage of _____ and _____" which shall state whether it is a petition for dissolution of the marriage or for legal separation of the parties.

(b) In a proceeding for dissolution of marriage or for legal separation of the parties, the petition shall set forth among other matters, as nearly as can be ascertained, the following facts:

  (1) The date of marriage.

  (2) The date of separation.

  (3) The number of years from marriage to separation.

  (4) The number of children of the marriage, if any, and if none a statement of that fact.

  (5) The age and birth date of each minor child of the marriage.

(Stats. 1992, c. 162 (A.B. 2650), § 10, operative Jan. 1, 1994. Amended by Stats. 1998, c. 581 (A.B. 2801), § 11.)

§ 2333. Irreconcilable differences; order for dissolution

Subject to Section 2334, if from the evidence at the hearing the court finds that there are irreconcilable differences which have caused the irremediable breakdown of the marriage, the court shall order the dissolution of the marriage or a legal separation of the parties.

(Stats. 1992, c. 162 (A.B. 2650), § 10, operative Jan. 1, 1994.)

§ 2335. Misconduct; admissibility of specific acts of misconduct

Except as otherwise provided by statute, in a pleading or proceeding for dissolution of marriage or legal separation of the parties, including depositions and discovery proceedings, evidence of specific acts of misconduct is improper and inadmissible.

(Stats. 1992, c. 162 (A.B. 2650), § 10, operative Jan. 1, 1994. Amended by Stats. 1993, c. 219 (A.B. 1500), § 110.)

§ 2337. Early and separate trial on dissolution; preliminary declaration; conditions; effect on retirement plan; service on plan administrator; reservation of jurisdiction; effect of party's death

(a) In a proceeding for dissolution of marriage, the court, upon noticed motion, may sever and grant an early and separate trial on the issue of the dissolution of the status of the marriage apart from other issues.

(b) A preliminary declaration of disclosure with a completed schedule of assets and debts shall be served on the nonmoving party with the noticed motion unless it has been served previously, or unless the parties stipulate in writing to defer service of the preliminary declaration of disclosure until a later time.

(c) The court may impose upon a party . . . conditions on granting a severance of the issue of the dissolution of the status of the marriage, and in case of that party's death, an order of any of the following conditions continues to be binding upon that party's estate: . . .

(Stats. 1992, c. 162 (A.B. 2650), § 10, operative Jan. 1, 1994. Amended by Stats. 1994, c. 1269 (A.B. 2208), § 24; Stats. 1997, c. 56 (A.B. 1098), § 1; Stats. 1998, c. 581 (A.B. 2801), § 14; Stats. 2007, c. 141 (A.B. 861), § 1; Stats. 2015, c. 293 (A.B. 139), § 1, eff. Jan. 1, 2016.)

§ 2338. Decisions; judgments

(a) In a proceeding for dissolution of the marriage or legal separation of the parties, the court shall file its decision and any statement of decision as in other cases.

(b) If the court determines that no dissolution should be granted, a judgment to that effect only shall be entered.

(c) If the court determines that a dissolution should be granted, a judgment of dissolution of marriage shall be entered. After the entry of the judgment and before it becomes final, neither party has the right to dismiss the proceeding without the consent of the other.

(Stats. 1992, c. 162 (A.B. 2650), § 10, operative Jan. 1, 1994.)

§ 2339. Finality of judgment; waiting period

(a) Subject to subdivision (b) and to Sections 2340 to 2344, inclusive, no judgment of dissolution is final for the purpose of terminating the marriage relationship of the parties until six months have expired from the date of service of a copy of summons and petition or the date of appearance of the respondent, whichever occurs first.

(b) The court may extend the six-month period described in subdivision (a) for good cause shown.

(Stats. 1992, c. 162 (A.B. 2650), § 10, operative Jan. 1, 1994.)

§ 2344. Death of party after entry of judgment

(a) The death of either party after entry of the judgment does not prevent the judgment from becoming a final judgment under Sections 2339 to 2343, inclusive.

(b) Subdivision (a) does not validate a marriage by either party before the judgment becomes final, nor does it constitute a defense in a criminal prosecution against either party.

(Stats. 1992, c. 162 (A.B. 2650), § 10, operative Jan. 1, 1994.)

§ 2502. Separate property

"Separate property" does not include quasi-community property.

(Stats. 1992, c. 162 (A.B. 2650), § 10, operative Jan. 1, 1994.)

§ 2550. Manner of division of community estate

Except upon the written agreement of the parties, or on oral stipulation of the parties in open court, or as otherwise provided in this division, in a proceeding for dissolution of marriage or for legal separation of the parties, the court shall, either in its judgment of dissolution of the marriage, in its judgment of legal separation of the parties, or at a later time if it expressly reserves jurisdiction to make such a property division, divide the community estate of the parties equally.

(Stats. 1992, c. 162 (A.B. 2650), § 10, operative Jan. 1, 1994.)

§ 2551. Characterization of liabilities; confirmation or assignment

For the purposes of division and in confirming or assigning the liabilities of the parties for which the community estate is liable, the court shall characterize liabilities as separate or community and confirm or assign them to the parties in accordance with Part 6 (commencing with Section 2620).

(Stats. 1992, c. 162 (A.B. 2650), § 10, operative Jan. 1, 1994.)

§ 2552. Valuation of assets and liabilities

(a) For the purpose of division of the community estate upon dissolution of marriage or legal separation of the parties, except as provided in subdivision (b), the court shall value the assets and liabilities as near as practicable to the time of trial.

(b) Upon 30 days' notice by the moving party to the other party, the court for good cause shown may value all or any portion of the assets and liabilities at a date after separation and before trial to accomplish an equal division of the community estate of the parties in an equitable manner.

(Stats. 1992, c. 162 (A.B. 2650), § 10, operative Jan. 1, 1994.)

§ 2553. Powers of court

The court may make any orders the court considers necessary to carry out the purposes of this division.

(Stats. 1992, c. 162 (A.B. 2650), § 10, operative Jan. 1, 1994.)

§ 2554. Failure to agree to voluntary division of property; submission to arbitration

(a) Notwithstanding any other provision of this division, in any case in which the parties do not agree in writing to a voluntary division of the community estate of the parties, the issue of the character, the value, and the division of the community estate may be submitted by the court to arbitration for resolution pursuant to Chapter 2.5 (commencing with Section 1141.10) of Title 3 of Part 3 of the Code of Civil Procedure, if the total value of the community and quasi-community property in controversy in the opinion of the court does not exceed fifty thousand dollars ($50,000). The decision of the court regarding the value of the community and quasi-community property for purposes of this section is not appealable.

(b) The court may submit the matter to arbitration at any time it believes the parties are unable to agree upon a division of the property.

(Stats. 1992, c. 162 (A.B. 2650), § 10, operative Jan. 1, 1994.)

§ 2555. Disposition of community estate; revision on appeal

The disposition of the community estate, as provided in this division, is subject to revision on appeal in all particulars, including those which are stated to be in the discretion of the court.

(Stats. 1992, c. 162 (A.B. 2650), § 10, operative Jan. 1, 1994.)

§ 2556. Community property or debts; continuing jurisdiction

In a proceeding for dissolution of marriage, for nullity of marriage, or for legal separation of the parties, the court has continuing jurisdiction to award community estate assets or community estate liabilities to the parties that have not been previously adjudicated by a judgment in the proceeding. A party may file a postjudgment motion or order to show cause in the proceeding in order to obtain adjudication of any community estate asset or liability omitted or not adjudicated by the judgment. In these cases, the court shall equally divide the omitted or unadjudicated community estate asset or liability, unless the court finds upon good cause shown that the interests of justice require an unequal division of the asset or liability.

(Stats. 1992, c. 162 (A.B. 2650), § 10, operative Jan. 1, 1994. Amended by Stats. 1993, c. 219 (A.B. 1500), § 111.)

§ 2580. Legislative findings and declarations; public policy

The Legislature hereby finds and declares as follows:

(a) It is the public policy of this state to provide uniformly and consistently for the standard of proof in establishing the character of property acquired by spouses during marriage in joint title form, and for the allocation of community and separate interests in that property between the spouses.

(b) The methods provided by case and statutory law have not resulted in consistency in the treatment of spouses' interests in property they hold in joint title, but rather, have created confusion as to which law applies to property at a particular point in time, depending on the form of title, and, as a result, spouses cannot have reliable expectations as to the characterization of their property and the allocation of the interests therein, and attorneys cannot reliably advise their clients regarding applicable law.

(c) Therefore, a compelling state interest exists to provide for uniform treatment of property. Thus, former Sections 4800.1 and 4800.2 of the Civil Code, as operative on January 1, 1987, and as continued in Sections 2581 and 2640 of this code, apply to all property held in joint title regardless of the date of acquisition of the property or the date of any agreement affecting the character of the property, and those sections apply in all proceedings commenced on or after January 1, 1984. However, those sections do not apply to property settlement agreements executed before January 1, 1987, or proceedings in which judgments were rendered before January 1, 1987, regardless of whether those judgments have become final.

(Added by Stats. 1993, c. 219 (A.B. 1500), § 111.6. Amended by Stats. 1993, c. 876 (S.B. 1068), § 15.2, eff. Oct. 6, 1993, operative Jan. 1, 1994.)

§ 2581. Division of property; presumptions

For the purpose of division of property on dissolution of marriage or legal separation of the parties, property acquired by the parties during marriage in joint form, including property held in tenancy in common, joint tenancy, or tenancy by the entirety, or as community property, is presumed to be community property. This presumption is a presumption affecting the burden of proof and may be rebutted by either of the following:

(a) A clear statement in the deed or other documentary evidence of title by which the property is acquired that the property is separate property and not community property.

(b) Proof that the parties have made a written agreement that the property is separate property.

(Added by Stats. 1993, c. 219 (A.B. 1500), § 111.7.)

§ 2600. Powers of court

Notwithstanding Sections 2550 to 2552, inclusive, the court may divide the community estate as provided in this part.

(Stats. 1992, c. 162 (A.B. 2650), § 10, operative Jan. 1, 1994.)

§ 2601. Conditional award of an asset of the community estate to one party

Where economic circumstances warrant, the court may award an asset of the community estate to one party on such conditions as the court deems proper to effect a substantially equal division of the community estate.

(Stats. 1992, c. 162 (A.B. 2650), § 10, operative Jan. 1, 1994.)

§ 2602. Additional award or offset against existing property; award of amount determined to have been misappropriated

As an additional award or offset against existing property, the court may award, from a party's share, the amount the court determines to have been deliberately misappropriated by the party to the exclusion of the interest of the other party in the community estate.

(Stats. 1992, c. 162 (A.B. 2650), § 10, operative Jan. 1, 1994.)

§ 2603. Community estate personal injury damages; assignment

(a) "Community estate personal injury damages" as used in this section means all money or other property received or to be received by a person in satisfaction of a judgment for damages for the person's personal injuries or pursuant to an agreement for the settlement or compromise of a claim for the damages, if the cause of action for the damages arose during the marriage but is not separate property as described in Section 781, unless the money or other property has been commingled with other assets of the community estate.

(b) Community estate personal injury damages shall be assigned to the party who suffered the injuries unless the court, after taking into account the economic condition and needs of each party, the time that has elapsed since the recovery of the damages or the accrual of the cause of action, and all other facts of the case, determines that the interests of justice require another disposition. In such a case, the community estate personal injury damages shall be assigned to the respective parties in such proportions as the court determines to be just, except that at least one-half of the damages shall be assigned to the party who suffered the injuries.

(Stats. 1992, c. 162 (A.B. 2650), § 10, operative Jan. 1, 1994.)

§ 2603.5. Civil damages in a domestic violence action; enforcement or judgment

The court may, if there is a judgment for civil damages for an act of domestic violence perpetrated by one spouse against the other spouse, enforce that judgment against the abusive spouse's share of community property, if a proceeding for dissolution of marriage or legal separation of the parties is pending prior to the entry of final judgment.

(Added by Stats. 2004, c. 299 (A.B. 2018), § 1.)

§ 2604. Community estates of less than $5,000; award of entire estate

If the net value of the community estate is less than five thousand dollars ($5,000) and one party cannot be located through the exercise of reasonable diligence, the court may award all the community estate to the other party on conditions the court deems proper in its judgment of dissolution of marriage or legal separation of the parties.

(Stats. 1992, c. 162 (A.B. 2650), § 10, operative Jan. 1, 1994.)

§ 2610. Retirement plans; orders to ensure benefits

(a) Except as provided in subdivision (b), the court shall make whatever orders are necessary or appropriate to ensure that each party receives the party's full community property share in any retirement plan, whether public or private, including all survivor and death benefits, including, but not limited to, any of the following:

(1) Order the disposition of any retirement benefits payable upon or after the death of either party in a manner consistent with Section 2550.

(2) Order a party to elect a survivor benefit annuity or other similar election for the benefit of the other party, as specified by the court, in any case in which a retirement plan provides for such an election, provided that no court shall order a retirement plan to provide increased benefits determined on the basis of actuarial value.

(3) Upon the agreement of the nonemployee spouse, order the division of accumulated community property contributions and service credit as provided in the following or similar enactments:

(A) Article 2 (commencing with Section 21290) of Chapter 9 of Part 3 of Division 5 of Title 2 of the Government Code.

(B) Chapter 12 (commencing with Section 22650) of Part 13 of the Education Code.

(C) Article 8.4 (commencing with Section 31685) of Chapter 3 of Part 3 of Division 4 of Title 3 of the Government Code.

(D) Article 2.5 (commencing with Section 75050) of Chapter 11 of Title 8 of the Government Code.

(E) Chapter 15 (commencing with Section 27400) of Part 14 of the Education Code.

(4) Order a retirement plan to make payments directly to a nonmember party of his or her community property interest in retirement benefits.

(b) A court shall not make any order that requires a retirement plan to do either of the following:

(1) Make payments in any manner that will result in an increase in the amount of benefits provided by the plan.

(2) Make the payment of benefits to any party at any time before the member retires, except as provided in paragraph (3) of subdivision (a), unless the plan so provides.

(c) This section shall not be applied retroactively to payments made by a retirement plan to any person who retired or died prior to January 1, 1987, or to payments made to any person who retired or died prior to June 1, 1988, for plans subject to paragraph (3) of subdivision (a).

(Stats. 1992, c. 162 (A.B. 2650), § 10, operative Jan. 1, 1994. Amended by Stats. 1993, c. 219 (A.B. 1500), § 112; Stats. 1994, c. 670 (S.B. 1500), § 1; Stats. 1994, c. 1269 (A.B. 2208), § 25.5; Stats. 1998, c. 965 (A.B. 2765), § 322; Stats. 2009, c. 130 (A.B. 966), § 1.)

§ 2620. Community estate debts; confirmation or division

The debts for which the community estate is liable which are unpaid at the time of trial, or for which the community estate becomes liable after trial, shall be confirmed or divided as provided in this part.

(Stats. 1992, c. 162 (A.B. 2650), § 10, operative Jan. 1, 1994.)

§ 2621. Premarital debts; confirmation

Debts incurred by either spouse before the date of marriage shall be confirmed without offset to the spouse who incurred the debt.

(Stats. 1992, c. 162 (A.B. 2650), § 10, operative Jan. 1, 1994.)

§ 2622. Marital debts incurred before the date of separation; division

(a) Except as provided in subdivision (b), debts incurred by either spouse after the date of marriage but before the date of separation shall be divided as set forth in Sections 2550 to 2552, inclusive, and Sections 2601 to 2604, inclusive.

(b) To the extent that community debts exceed total community and quasi-community assets, the excess of debt shall be assigned as the court deems just and equitable, taking into account factors such as the parties' relative ability to pay.

(Stats. 1992, c. 162 (A.B. 2650), § 10, operative Jan. 1, 1994.)

§ 2623. Marital debts incurred after the date of separation; confirmation

Debts incurred by either spouse after the date of separation but before entry of a judgment of dissolution of marriage or legal separation of the parties shall be confirmed as follows:

(a) Debts incurred by either spouse for the common necessaries of life of either spouse or the necessaries of life of the children of the marriage for whom support may be ordered, in the absence of a court order or written agreement for support or for the payment of these debts, shall be confirmed to either spouse according to the parties' respective needs and abilities to pay at the time the debt was incurred.

(b) Debts incurred by either spouse for nonnecessaries of that spouse or children of the marriage for whom support may be ordered shall be confirmed without offset to the spouse who incurred the debt.

(Stats. 1992, c. 162 (A.B. 2650), § 10, operative Jan. 1, 1994. Amended by Stats. 1993, c. 219 (A.B. 1500), § 113.)

§ 2624. Marital debts incurred after entry of judgment of dissolution or after entry of judgment of legal separation; confirmation

Debts incurred by either spouse after entry of a judgment of dissolution of marriage but before termination of the parties' marital status or after entry of a judgment of legal separation of the parties shall be confirmed without offset to the spouse who incurred the debt.

(Stats. 1992, c. 162 (A.B. 2650), § 10, operative Jan. 1, 1994.)

§ 2625. Separate debts incurred before date of separation; confirmation

Notwithstanding Sections 2620 to 2624, inclusive, all separate debts, including those debts incurred by a spouse during marriage and before the date of separation that were not incurred for the benefit of the community, shall be confirmed without offset to the spouse who incurred the debt.

(Stats. 1992, c. 162 (A.B. 2650), § 10, operative Jan. 1, 1994.)

§ 2626. Reimbursements

The court has jurisdiction to order reimbursement in cases it deems appropriate for debts paid after separation but before trial.

(Stats. 1992, c. 162 (A.B. 2650), § 10, operative Jan. 1, 1994.)

§ 2627. Educational loans; liabilities for death or injuries; assignment

Notwithstanding Sections 2550 to 2552, inclusive, and Sections 2620 to 2624, inclusive, educational loans shall be assigned pursuant to Section 2641 and liabilities subject to paragraph (2) of subdivision (b) of Section 1000 shall be assigned to the spouse whose act or omission provided the basis for the liability, without offset.

(Stats. 1992, c. 162 (A.B. 2650), § 10, operative Jan. 1, 1994.)

§ 2640. Contributions to the acquisition of the property of the community property estate; waivers; amount of reimbursement

(a) "Contributions to the acquisition of property," as used in this section, include downpayments, payments for improvements, and payments that reduce the principal of a loan used to finance the purchase or improvement of the property but do not include payments of interest on the loan or payments made for maintenance, insurance, or taxation of the property.

(b) In the division of the community estate under this division, unless a party has made a written waiver of the right to reimbursement or has signed a writing that has the effect of a waiver, the party shall be reimbursed for the party's contributions to the acquisition of property of the community property estate to the extent the party traces the contributions to a separate property source. The amount reimbursed shall be without interest or adjustment for change in monetary values and may not exceed the net value of the property at the time of the division.

(c) A party shall be reimbursed for the party's separate property contributions to the acquisition of property of the other spouse's separate property estate during the marriage, unless there has been a transmutation [ ] or a written waiver of the right to reimbursement. The amount reimbursed shall be without interest or adjustment for change in monetary values and may not exceed the net value of the property at the time of the division.

(Stats. 1992, c. 162 (A.B. 2650), § 10, operative Jan. 1, 1994. Amended by Stats. 1993, c. 219 (A.B. 1500), § 114.5; Stats. 2004, c. 119 (S.B. 1407), § 1.)

§ 2641. Community contributions to education or training

(a) "Community contributions to education or training" as used in this section means payments made with community or quasi-community property for education or training or for the repayment of a loan incurred for education or training, whether the payments were made while the parties were resident in this state or resident outside this state.

(b) Subject to the limitations provided in this section, upon dissolution of marriage or legal separation of the parties:

(1) The community shall be reimbursed for community contributions to education or training of a party that substantially enhances the earning capacity of the party. The amount reimbursed shall be with interest at the legal rate, accruing from the end of the calendar year in which the contributions were made.

(2) A loan incurred during marriage for the education or training of a party shall not be included among the liabilities of the community for the purpose of division pursuant to this division but shall be assigned for payment by the party.

(c) The reimbursement and assignment required by this section shall be reduced or modified to the extent circumstances render such a disposition unjust, including, but not limited to, any of the following:

(1) The community has substantially benefited from the education, training, or loan incurred for the education or training of the party. There is a rebuttable presumption, affecting the burden of proof, that the community has not substantially benefited from community contributions to the education or training made less than 10 years before the commencement of the proceeding, and that the community has substantially benefited from community contributions to the education or training made more than 10 years before the commencement of the proceeding.

(2) The education or training received by the party is offset by the education or training received by the other party for which community contributions have been made.

(3) The education or training enables the party receiving the education or training to engage in gainful employment that substantially reduces the need of the party for support that would otherwise be required.

(d) Reimbursement for community contributions and assignment of loans pursuant to this section is the exclusive remedy of the community or a party for the education or training and any resulting enhancement of the earning capacity of a party. However, nothing in this subdivision limits consideration of the effect of the education, training, or enhancement, or the amount reimbursed pursuant to this section, on the circumstances of the parties for the purpose of an order for support pursuant to Section 4320.

(e) This section is subject to an express written agreement of the parties to the contrary.

(Stats. 1992, c. 162 (A.B. 2650), § 10, operative Jan. 1, 1994.)

§ 2650. Jurisdiction; division of real and personal property

In a proceeding for division of the community estate, the court has jurisdiction, at the request of either party, to divide the separate property interests of the parties in real and personal property, wherever situated and whenever acquired, held by the parties as joint tenants or tenants in common. The property shall be divided together with, and in accordance with the same procedure for and limitations on, division of community estate.

(Stats. 1992, c. 162 (A.B. 2650), § 10, operative Jan. 1, 1994.)

§ 2660. Division of real property situated in another state

(a) Except as provided in subdivision (b), if the property subject to division includes real property situated in another state, the court shall, if possible, divide the community property and quasi-community property as provided for in this division in such a manner that it is not necessary to change the nature of the interests held in the real property situated in the other state.

(b) If it is not possible to divide the property in the manner provided for in subdivision (a), the court may do any of the following in order to effect a division of the property as provided for in this division:

(1) Require the parties to execute conveyances or take other actions with respect to the real property situated in the other state as are necessary.

(2) Award to the party who would have been benefited by the conveyances or other actions the money value of the interest in the property that the party would have received if the conveyances had been executed or other actions taken.

(Stats. 1992, c. 162 (A.B. 2650), § 10, operative Jan. 1, 1994.)

§ 3590. Severability of support provisions; orders based on agreements

The provisions of an agreement for support of either party shall be deemed to be separate and severable from the provisions of the agreement relating to property. An order for support of either party based on the agreement shall be law-imposed and shall be made under the power of the court to order spousal support.

(Stats. 1992, c. 162 (A.B. 2650), § 10, operative Jan. 1, 1994.)

§ 3591. Modification or termination of agreements

(a) Except as provided in subdivisions (b) and (c), the provisions of an agreement for the support of either party are subject to subsequent modification or termination by court order.

(b) An agreement may not be modified or terminated as to an amount that accrued before the date of the filing of the notice of motion or order to show cause to modify or terminate.

(c) An agreement for spousal support may not be modified or revoked to the extent that a written agreement, or, if there is no written agreement, an oral agreement entered into in open court between the parties, specifically provides that the spousal support is not subject to modification or termination.

(Stats. 1992, c. 162 (A.B. 2650), § 10, operative Jan. 1, 1994.)

§ 3650. Support order

Unless the provision or context otherwise requires, as used in this chapter, "support order" means a child, family, or spousal support order.

(Stats. 1992, c. 162 (A.B. 2650), § 10, operative Jan. 1, 1994. Amended by Stats. 1993, c. 219 (A.B. 1500), § 124.5.)

§ 3651. Powers of court; application of section

(a) Except as provided in subdivisions (c) and (d) and subject to Article 3 (commencing with Section 3680) and Sections 3552, 3587, and 4004, a support order may be modified or terminated at any time as the court determines to be necessary. . . .

. . .

(d) An order for spousal support may not be modified or terminated to the extent that a written agreement, or, if there is no written agreement, an oral agreement entered into in open court between the parties, specifically provides that the spousal support is not subject to modification or termination.

(Stats. 1992, c. 162 (A.B. 2650), § 10, operative Jan. 1, 1994. Amended by Stats. 1994, c. 1269 (A.B. 2208), § 31.4; Stats. 1997, c. 599 (A.B. 573), § 6; Stats. 2005, c. 154 (S.B. 1082), § 2, eff. Aug. 30, 2005.)

§ 3800. Definitions

As used in this chapter:

(a) "Custodial parent" means a party awarded physical custody of a child.

(b) "Deferred sale of home order" means an order that temporarily delays the sale and awards the temporary exclusive use and possession of the family home to a custodial parent of a minor child or child for whom support is authorized under Sections 3900 and 3901 or under Section 3910, whether or not the custodial parent has sole or joint custody, in order to minimize the adverse impact of dissolution of marriage or legal separation of the parties on the welfare of the child.

(c) "Resident parent" means a party who has requested or who has already been awarded a deferred sale of home order.

(Stats. 1992, c. 162 (A.B. 2650), § 10, operative Jan. 1, 1994.)

§ 3801. Determination of economic feasibility of deferred sale

(a) If one of the parties has requested a deferred sale of home order pursuant to this chapter, the court shall first determine whether it is economically feasible to maintain the payments of any note secured by a deed of trust, property taxes, insurance for the home during the period the sale of the home is deferred, and the condition of the home comparable to that at the time of trial.

(b) In making this determination, the court shall consider all of the following:

(1) The resident parent's income.

(2) The availability of spousal support, child support, or both spousal and child support.

(3) Any other sources of funds available to make those payments.

(c) It is the intent of the Legislature, by requiring the determination under this section, to do all of the following:

(1) Avoid the likelihood of possible defaults on the payments of notes and resulting foreclosures.

(2) Avoid inadequate insurance coverage.

(3) Prevent deterioration of the condition of the family home.

(4) Prevent any other circumstance which would jeopardize both parents' equity in the home.

(Stats. 1992, c. 162 (A.B. 2650), § 10, operative Jan. 1, 1994.)

§ 3802. Grant or denial of order; discretion of court

(a) If the court determines pursuant to Section 3801 that it is economically feasible to consider ordering a deferred sale of the family home, the court may grant a deferred sale of home order to a custodial parent if the court determines that the order is necessary in order to minimize the adverse impact of dissolution of marriage or legal separation of the parties on the child.

(b) In exercising its discretion to grant or deny a deferred sale of home order, the court shall consider all of the following:

(1) The length of time the child has resided in the home.

(2) The child's placement or grade in school.

(3) The accessibility and convenience of the home to the child's school and other services or facilities used by and available to the child, including child care.

(4) Whether the home has been adapted or modified to accommodate any physical disabilities of a child or a resident parent in a manner that a change in residence may adversely affect the ability of the resident parent to meet the needs of the child.

(5) The emotional detriment to the child associated with a change in residence.

(6) The extent to which the location of the home permits the resident parent to continue employment.

(7) The financial ability of each parent to obtain suitable housing.

(8) The tax consequences to the parents.

(9) The economic detriment to the nonresident parent in the event of a deferred sale of home order.

(10) Any other factors the court deems just and equitable.

(Stats. 1992, c. 162 (A.B. 2650), § 10, operative Jan. 1, 1994.)

§ 3803. Contents of order

A deferred sale of home order shall state the duration of the order and may include the legal description and assessor's parcel number of the real property which is subject to the order.

(Stats. 1992, c. 162 (A.B. 2650), § 10, operative Jan. 1, 1994.)

§ 3804. Recordation of order

A deferred sale of home order may be recorded in the office of the county recorder of the county in which the real property is located.

(Stats. 1992, c. 162 (A.B. 2650), § 10, operative Jan. 1, 1994.)

§ 3805. Inoperative

§ 3806. Payment of maintenance and capital improvement costs; order

The court may make an order specifying the parties' respective responsibilities for the payment of the costs of routine maintenance and capital improvements.

(Stats. 1992, c. 162 (A.B. 2650), § 10, operative Jan. 1, 1994.)

§ 3807. Time for modification or termination of orders; exceptions

Except as otherwise agreed to by the parties in writing, a deferred sale of home order may be modified or terminated at any time at the discretion of the court.

(Stats. 1992, c. 162 (A.B. 2650), § 10, operative Jan. 1, 1994.)

§ 3808. Remarriage or other change in circumstances; rebuttable presumption

Except as otherwise agreed to by the parties in writing, if the party awarded the deferred sale of home order remarries, or if there is otherwise a change in circumstances affecting the determinations made pursuant to Section 3801 or 3802 or affecting the economic status of the parties or the children on which the award is based, a rebuttable presumption, affecting the burden of proof, is created that further deferral of the sale is no longer an equitable method of minimizing the adverse impact of the dissolution of marriage or legal separation of the parties on the children.

(Stats. 1992, c. 162 (A.B. 2650), § 10, operative Jan. 1, 1994.)

§ 3809. Reservation of jurisdiction

In making an order pursuant to this chapter, the court shall reserve jurisdiction to determine any issues that arise with respect to the deferred sale of home order including, but not limit to, the maintenance of the home and the tax consequences to each party.

(Stats. 1992, c. 162 (A.B. 2650), § 10, operative Jan. 1, 1994.)

§ 4300. Individual's duty of support

Subject to this division, a person shall support the person's spouse.

(Stats. 1992, c. 162 (A.B. 2650), § 10, operative Jan. 1, 1994.)

§ 4301. Support of spouse from separate property

Subject to Section 914, a person shall support the person's spouse while they are living together out of the separate property of the person when there is no community property or quasi-community property.

(Stats. 1992, c. 162 (A.B. 2650), § 10, operative Jan. 1, 1994.)

§ 4302. Support of spouse living separate by agreement

A person is not liable for support of the person's spouse when the person is living separate from the spouse by agreement unless support is stipulated in the agreement.

(Stats. 1992, c. 162 (A.B. 2650), § 10, operative Jan. 1, 1994.)

§ 4303. Enforcement of duty of support; reimbursement of county

(a) The obligee spouse, or the county on behalf of the obligee spouse, may bring an action against the obligor spouse to enforce the duty of support.

(b) If the county furnishes support to a spouse, the county has the same right as the spouse to whom the support was furnished to secure reimbursement and obtain continuing support. The right of the county to reimbursement is subject to any limitation otherwise imposed by the law of this state.

(c) The court may order the obligor to pay the county reasonable attorney's fees and court costs in a proceeding brought by the county under this section.

(Stats. 1992, c. 162 (A.B. 2650), § 10, operative Jan. 1, 1994.)

§ 4320. Determination of amount due for support; considerations

In ordering spousal support under this part, the court shall consider all of the following circumstances:

(a) The extent to which the earning capacity of each party is sufficient to maintain the standard of living established during the marriage, taking into account all of the following:

(1) The marketable skills of the supported party; the job market for those skills; the time and expenses required for the supported party to acquire the appropriate education or training to develop those skills; and the possible need for retraining or education to acquire other, more marketable skills or employment.

(2) The extent to which the supported party's present or future earning capacity is impaired by periods of unemployment that were incurred during the marriage to permit the supported party to devote time to domestic duties.

(b) The extent to which the supported party contributed to the attainment of an education, training, a career position, or a license by the supporting party.

(c) The ability of the supporting party to pay spousal support, taking into account the supporting party's earning capacity, earned and unearned income, assets, and standard of living.

(d) The needs of each party based on the standard of living established during the marriage.

(e) The obligations and assets, including the separate property, of each party.

(f) The duration of the marriage.

(g) The ability of the supported party to engage in gainful employment without unduly interfering with the interests of dependent children in the custody of the party.

(h) The age and health of the parties.

(i) Documented evidence, including a plea of nolo contendere, of any history of domestic violence, as defined in Section 6211, between the parties or perpetrated by either party against either party's child, including, but not limited to, consideration of emotional distress resulting from domestic violence perpetrated against the supported party by the supporting party, and consideration of any history of violence against the supporting party by the supported party.

(j) The immediate and specific tax consequences to each party.

(k) The balance of the hardships to each party.

(l) The goal that the supported party shall be self-supporting within a reasonable period of time. Except in the case of a marriage of long duration as described in Section 4336, a "reasonable period of time" for purposes of this section generally shall be one-half the length of the marriage. However, nothing in this section is intended to limit the court's discretion to order support for a greater or lesser length of time, based on any of the other factors listed in this section, Section 4336, and the circumstances of the parties.

(m) The criminal conviction of an abusive spouse shall be considered in making a reduction or elimination of a spousal support award in accordance with Section 4324.5 or 4325.

(n) Any other factors the court determines are just and equitable.

(Stats. 1992, c. 162 (A.B. 2650), § 10, operative Jan. 1, 1994. Amended by Stats. 1996, c. 1163 (S.B. 509), § 1; Stats. 1999, c. 284 (A.B. 808), § 1; Stats. 1999, c. 846 (A.B. 391), § 1.5; Stats. 2001, c. 293 (S.B. 1221), § 2; Stats.

2012, c. 718 (A.B. 1522), § 1; Stats. 2013, c. 455 (A.B. 681), § 1; Stats. 2015, c. 137 (S.B. 28), § 1, eff. Jan 1, 2016.)

§ 4321. Denial of support from separate property of the other party; grounds

In a judgment of dissolution of marriage or legal separation of the parties, the court may deny support to a party out of the separate property of the other party in any of the following circumstances:

(a) The party has separate property, or is earning the party's own livelihood, or there is community property or quasi-community property sufficient to give the party proper support.

(b) The custody of the children has been awarded to the other party, who is supporting them.

(Stats. 1992, c. 162 (A.B. 2650), § 10, operative Jan. 1, 1994. Amended by Stats. 1993, c. 219 (A.B. 1500), § 141.5.)

§ 4322. Childless party has or acquires a separate estate sufficient for support; prohibition on order or continuation of support

In an original or modification proceeding, where there are no children, and a party has or acquires a separate estate, including income from employment, sufficient for the party's proper support, no support shall be ordered or continued against the other party.

(Stats. 1992, c. 162 (A.B. 2650), § 10, operative Jan. 1, 1994.)

§ 4323. Cohabitation with nonmarital partner; rebuttable presumption of decreased need for support; modification or termination of support

(a)(1) Except as otherwise agreed to by the parties in writing, there is a rebuttable presumption, affecting the burden of proof, of decreased need for spousal support if the supported party is cohabiting with a nonmarital partner. Upon a determination that circumstances have changed, the court may modify or terminate the spousal support as provided for in Chapter 6 (commencing with Section 3650) of Part 1.

(2) Holding oneself out to be the spouse of the person with whom one is cohabiting is not necessary to constitute cohabitation as the term is used in this subdivision.

(b) The income of a supporting spouse's subsequent spouse or nonmarital partner shall not be considered when determining or modifying spousal support.

(c) Nothing in this section precludes later modification or termination of spousal support on proof of change of circumstances.

(Stats. 1992, c. 162 (A.B. 2650), § 10, operative Jan. 1, 1994. Amended by Stats. 1993, c. 935 (A.B. 145), § 3; Stats. 2014, c. 82 (S.B. 1306), § 36, eff. Jan. 1, 2015.)

§ 4324. Attempted murder or soliciting the murder of spouse; prohibited awards

In addition to any other remedy authorized by law, when a spouse is convicted of attempting to murder the other spouse, as punishable pursuant to subdivision (a) of Section 664 of the Penal Code, or of soliciting the murder of the other spouse, as punishable pursuant to subdivision (b) of Section 653f of the Penal Code, the injured spouse shall be entitled to a prohibition of any temporary or permanent award for spousal support or medical, life, or other insurance benefits or payments from the injured spouse to the other spouse.

As used in this section, "injured spouse" means the spouse who has been the subject of the attempted murder or the solicitation of murder for which the other spouse was convicted, whether or not actual physical injury occurred.

(Added by Stats. 1995, c. 364 (A.B. 16), § 3. Amended by Stats. 2010, c. 65 (A.B. 2674), § 2.)

§ 4324.5. Violent sexual felony; prohibited awards

(a) In any proceeding for dissolution of marriage where there is a criminal conviction for a violent sexual felony perpetrated by one spouse against the other spouse and the petition for dissolution is filed before five years following the conviction and any time served in custody, on probation, or on parole, the following shall apply:

(1) An award of spousal support to the convicted spouse from the injured spouse is prohibited.

(2) Where economic circumstances warrant, the court shall order the attorney's fees and costs incurred by the parties to be paid from the community assets. The injured spouse shall not be required to pay any attorney's fees of the convicted spouse out of the injured spouse's separate property.

(3) At the request of the injured spouse, the date of legal separation shall be the date of the incident giving rise to the conviction, or earlier, if the court finds circumstances that justify an earlier date.

(4) The injured spouse shall be entitled to 100 percent of the community property interest in the retirement and pension benefits of the injured spouse.

(b) As used in this section, "violent sexual felony" means those offenses described in paragraphs (3), (4), (5), (11), and (18) of subdivision (c) of Section 667.5 of the Penal Code.

(c) As used in this section, "injured spouse" means the spouse who has been the subject of the violent sexual felony for which the other spouse was convicted.

(Added by Stats. 2012, c. 718 (A.B. 1522), § 2.)

§ 4325. Temporary or permanent support to abusive spouse; rebuttable presumption disfavoring award; evidence

(a) In any proceeding for dissolution of marriage where there is a criminal conviction for an act of domestic violence perpetrated by one spouse against the other spouse entered by the court within five years prior to the filing of the dissolution proceeding, or at any time thereafter, there shall be a rebuttable presumption affecting the burden of proof that any award of temporary or permanent spousal support to the abusive spouse otherwise awardable pursuant to the standards of this part should not be made.

(b) The court may consider documented evidence of a convicted spouse's history as a victim of domestic violence, as defined in Section 6211, perpetrated by the other spouse, or any other factors the court deems just and equitable, as conditions for rebutting this presumption.

(c) The rebuttable presumption created in this section may be rebutted by a preponderance of the evidence.

(Added by Stat. 2001, c. 293 (S.B. 1221), § 3.)

§ 4338. Enforcement of order; order of resort to property

In the enforcement of an order for spousal support, the court shall resort to the property described below in the order indicated:

(a) The earnings, income, or accumulations of either spouse after the date of separation, as defined in Section 70, which would have been community property if the spouse had not been separated from the other spouse.

(b) The community property.

(c) The quasi-community property.

(d) The other separate property of the party required to make the support payments.

(Stats. 1992, c. 162 (A.B. 2650), § 10, operative Jan. 1, 1994; Stats. 2016, c. 114 (S.B. 1255), § 5, eff. Jan. 1, 2017.)

§ 6203. "Abuse" defined

(a) For purposes of this act, "abuse" means any of the following:

(1) To intentionally or recklessly cause or attempt to cause bodily injury.

(2) Sexual assault.

(3) To place a person in reasonable apprehension of imminent serious bodily injury to that person or to another.

(4) To engage in any behavior that has been or could be enjoined pursuant to 6320.

(b) Abuse is not limited to the actual infliction of physical injury or assault.

(Added by Stats. 1993, c. 219 (A.B. 1500), § 154. Amended by Stats. 1998, c. 581 (A.B. 2801), § 16; Stats. 2014, c. 635 (A.B. 2089), § 2, eff. Jan.1, 2015; Stats. 2015, c. 303 (A.B. 731), § 149, eff. Jan. 1, 2016.)

Editor's note: The terms "affinity," "cohabitant" and "dating relationship" are defined in California Family Code Sections 6205, 6209, and 6210, which is reproduced below.

§ 6205. "Affinity" defined

"Affinity," when applied to the marriage relation, signifies the connection existing in consequence of marriage between each of the married persons and the blood relatives of the other.

(Added by Stats. 1993, c. 219 (A.B. 1500), § 154.)

§ 6209. "Cohabitant" defined

"Cohabitant" means a person who regularly resides in the household. "Former cohabitant" means a person who formerly regularly resided in the household.

(Added by Stats. 1993, c. 219 (A.B. 1500), § 154.)

§ 6210. "Dating relationship" defined

"Dating relationship" means frequent, intimate associations primarily characterized by the expectation of affection or sexual involvement independent of financial considerations.

(Added by Stats. 2001, c. 110 (A.B. 362), § 1.)

§ 6211. "Domestic violence" defined

"Domestic violence" is abuse perpetrated against any of the following persons:

(a) A spouse or former spouse.

(b) A cohabitant or former cohabitant, as defined in Section 6209.

(c) A person with whom the respondent is having or has had a dating or engagement relationship.

(d) A person with whom the respondent has had a child, where the presumption applies that the male parent is the father of the child of the female parent under the Uniform Parentage Act (Part 3 (commencing with Section 7600) of Division 12).

(e) A child of a party or a child who is the subject of an action under the Uniform Parentage Act, where the presumption applies that the male parent is the father of the child to be protected.

(f) Any other person related by consanguinity or affinity within the second degree.

(Added by Stats. 1993, c. 219 (A.B. 1500), § 154.)

§ 6320. Ex parte order enjoining contact, credibly or falsely impersonating, or destroying personal property; protection for companion animals

(a) The court may issue an ex parte order enjoining a party from molesting, attacking, striking, stalking, threatening, sexually assaulting, battering, credibly impersonating as described in Section 528.5 of the Penal Code, falsely personating as described in Section 529 of the Penal Code, harassing, telephoning, including, but not limited to, making annoying telephone calls as described in Section 653m of the Penal Code, destroying personal property, contacting, either directly or indirectly, by mail or otherwise, coming within a specified distance of, or *disturbing the peace of the other party*, and, in the discretion of the court, on a showing of good cause, of other named family or household members.

(b) On a showing of good cause, the court may include in a protective order a grant to the petitioner of the exclusive care, possession, or control of any animal owned, possessed, leased, kept, or held by either the petitioner or the respondent or a minor child residing in the residence or household of either the petitioner or the respondent. The court may order the respondent to stay away from the animal and forbid the respondent from taking, transferring, encumbering, concealing, molesting, attacking, striking, threatening, harming, or otherwise disposing of the animal.

(c) This section shall become operative on July 1, 2014.

(Added by Stats. 1993, c. 219 (A.B. 1500), § 154. Amended by Stats. 1995, c. 598 (A.B. 878), § 1; Stats. 1996, c. 904 (A.B. 2224), § 1; Stats. 2007, c. 205 (S.B. 353), 2; Stats. 2010, c. 572 (A.B. 1596), § 16, operative Jan. 1, 2012. Added by Stats. 2013, c. 260 (A.B. 157), § 2, operative July 1, 2014.) (Italics added.)

§ 6325.5.   Ex parte order regarding insurance coverage

(a) The court may issue an ex parte order restraining any party from cashing, borrowing against, canceling, transferring, disposing of, or changing the beneficiaries of any insurance or other coverage held for the benefit of the parties, or their child or children, if any, for whom support may be ordered, or both.

(b) This section shall become operative on July 1, 2014.

(Added by Stats. 2013, c. 261 (A.B. 161), § 1, operative July 1, 2014.)

§ 6400.   Short title

This part may be cited as the Uniform Interstate Enforcement of Domestic Violence Protection Orders Act.

(Added by Stats. 2001, c. 816 (A.B. 731), § 3.)

[Editor's note: The UIEODVPOA has been adopted by twelve states including California. The uniform act provides that an adopting state shall enforce the terms of the order, including terms that provide relief, even if the tribunal would otherwise lack the power to do so under state law. This allows California courts to enforce the substantive provisions from the other eleven adopting states as well as protective orders from military bases, and tribal areas in California. The California UIEODVPOA defines "state" to mean "a state of the United States, the District of Columbia, Puerto Rico, the United States Virgin Islands, or any territory or insular possession subject to the jurisdiction of the United States. The term includes an Indian tribe or band, or any branch of the United States military, that has jurisdiction to issue protection orders."]

WEST'S ANNOTATED CALIFORNIA CIVIL CODE

§ 682.1. Community property of [spouses]; subject to express declaration in transfer documents; application and operation of section

(a)   Community property of [the spouses], when expressly declared in the transfer document to be community property with right of survivorship, and which may be accepted in writing on the face of the document by a statement signed or initialed by the grantees, shall, upon the death of one of the spouses, pass to the survivor, without administration, pursuant to the terms of the instrument, subject to the same procedures, as property held in joint tenancy. Prior to the death of either spouse, the right of survivorship may be terminated pursuant to the same procedures by which a joint tenancy may be severed. * * *

(b)   This section does not apply to a joint account in a financial institution to which Part 2 (commencing with Section 5100) of Division 5 of the Probate Code applies.

(c) This section shall become operative on July 1, 2001, and shall apply to instruments created on or after that date.

(Added by Stats. 2000, c. 645 (A.B. 2913), § 1, operative July 1, 2001.)

§ 683. Joint tenancy; definition; method of creation

(a) A joint interest is one owned by two or more persons in equal shares, by a title created by a single will or transfer, when expressly declared in the will or transfer to be a joint tenancy, or by transfer from a sole owner to himself or herself and others, or from tenants in common or joint tenants to themselves or some of them, or to themselves or any of them and others, or from [spouses], when holding title as community property or otherwise to themselves or to themselves and others or to one of them and to another or others, when expressly declared in the transfer to be a joint tenancy, or when granted or devised to executors or trustees as joint tenants. A joint tenancy in personal property may be created by a written transfer, instrument, or agreement.

(b) Provisions of this section do not apply to a joint account in a financial institution if Part 2 (commencing with Section 5100) of Division 5 of the Probate Code applies to such an account.

(Enacted 1872. Amended by Stats. 1929, c. 93, p. 172, § 1; Stats. 1931, c. 1051, p. 2205, § 1; Stats. 1935, c. 234, p. 912, § 1; Stats. 1955, c. 178, p. 645, § 1; Stats. 1983, c. 92, § 1, operative July 1, 1984; Stats. 1989, c. 397, § 1, operative July 1, 1990; Stats. 1990, c. 79, (A.B. 759), § 1, operative July 1, 1991.)

WEST'S ANNOTATED CALIFORNIA CORPORATIONS CODE

§ 16403. Books and records; right of access

(a) A partnership shall keep its books and records, if any . . . at its chief executive office.

(b) A partnership shall provide partners and their agents and attorneys access to its books and records. It shall provide former partners and their agents and attorneys access to books and records pertaining to the period during which they were partners. . . .

(c) Each partner . . . shall furnish to a partner, and to the legal representative of a deceased partner or partner under legal disability, both of the following . . .

(1) Without demand, any information concerning the partnership's business and affairs reasonably required for the proper exercise of the partners' rights and duties under the partnership agreement or this chapter, and

(2) On demand, any other information concerning the partnership's business and affairs, except to the extent the demand or the information demanded is unreasonable or otherwise improper under the circumstances.

(Added by Stats. 1996, c. 1003 (A.B. 583), § 2. Amended by Stats. 2004, c. 254 (S.B. 1306), § 45.)

WEST'S ANNOTATED CALIFORNIA PROBATE CODE

§ 28.   Community property

"Community property" means:

(a) Community property heretofore or hereafter acquired during marriage by a married person while domiciled in this state.

(b) All personal property wherever situated, and all real property situated in this state, heretofore or hereafter acquired during the marriage by a married person while domiciled elsewhere, that is community property, or a substantially equivalent type of marital property, under the laws of the place where the acquiring spouse was domiciled at the time of its acquisition.

(c) All personal property wherever situated, and all real property situated in this state, heretofore or hereafter acquired during the marriage by a married person in exchange for real or personal property, wherever situated, that is community property, or a substantially equivalent type of marital property, under the laws of the place where the acquiring spouse was domiciled at the time the property so exchanged was acquired.

(Stats. 1990, c. 79 (A.B. 759), § 14, operative July 1, 1991.)

§ 66.   Quasi-community property

"Quasi-community property" means the following property, other than community property as defined in Section 28:

(a) All personal property wherever situated, and all real property situated in this state, heretofore or hereafter acquired by a decedent while domiciled elsewhere that would have been the community property of the decedent and the surviving spouse if the decedent had been domiciled in this state at the time of its acquisition.

(b) All personal property wherever situated, and all real property situated in this state, heretofore or hereafter acquired in exchange for real or personal property, wherever situated, that would have been the community property of the decedent and the surviving spouse if the decedent had been domiciled in this state at the time the property so exchanged was acquired.

(Stats. 1990, c. 79 (A.B. 759), § 14, operative July 1, 1991.)

§ 78.   Surviving spouse

"Surviving spouse" does not include any of the following:

(a) A person whose marriage to the decedent has been dissolved or annulled, unless, by virtue of a subsequent marriage, the person is married to the decedent at the time of death.

(b) A person who obtains or consents to a final decree or judgment of dissolution of marriage from the decedent or a final decree or judgment of annulment of their marriage, which decree or judgment is not recognized as valid in this state, unless they (1) subsequently participate in a marriage ceremony purporting to marry each to the other or (2) subsequently live together as husband and wife.

(c) A person who, following a decree or judgment of dissolution or annulment of marriage obtained by the decedent, participates in a marriage ceremony with a third person.

(d) A person who was a party to a valid proceeding concluded by an order purporting to terminate all marital property rights.

(Stats. 1990, c. 79 (A.B. 759), § 14, operative July 1, 1991.)

§ 100.   Community property

(a) Upon the death of a married person, one-half of the community property belongs to the surviving spouse and the other half belongs to the decedent.

(b) Notwithstanding subdivision (a), a husband and wife may agree in writing to divide their community property on the basis of a non pro rata division of the aggregate value of the community property or on the basis of a division of each individual item or asset of the community, or partly on each basis. Nothing in this subdivision shall be construed to require this written agreement in order to permit or recognize a non pro rata division of community property.

(Stats. 1990, c. 79 (A.B. 759), § 14, operative July 1, 1991. Amended by Stats. 1998, c. 682 (A.B. 2069), § 2.)

§ 101.   Quasi-community property

(a) Upon the death of a married person domiciled in this state, one-half of the decedent's quasi-community property belongs to the surviving spouse and the other half belongs to the decedent.

(b) Notwithstanding subdivision (a), [the spouses] may agree in writing to divide their quasi-community property on the basis of a non pro rata division of the aggregate value of the quasi-community property, or on the basis of a division of each individual item or asset of quasi-community property, or partly on each basis. Nothing in this subdivision shall be construed to require this written agreement in order to permit or recognize a non pro rata division of quasi-community property.

(Stats. 1990, c. 79 (A.B. 759), § 14, operative July 1, 1991. Amended by Stats. 1998, c. 682 (A.B. 2069), § 3.)

§ 102. Transfer of quasi-community property; restoration of decedent's estate; requirements

(a) The decedent's surviving spouse may require the transferee of property in which the surviving spouse had an expectancy under Section 101 at the time of the transfer to restore to the decedent's estate one-half of the property if the transferee retains the property or, if not, one-half of its proceeds or, if none, one-half of its value at the time of transfer, if all of the following requirements are satisfied:

(1) The decedent died domiciled in this state.

(2) The decedent made a transfer of the property to a person other than the surviving spouse without receiving in exchange a consideration of substantial value and without the written consent or joinder of the surviving spouse.

(3) The transfer is any of the following types:

(A) A transfer under which the decedent retained at the time of death the possession or enjoyment of, or the right to income from, the property.

(B) A transfer to the extent that the decedent retained at the time of death a power, either alone or in conjunction with any other person, to revoke or to consume, invade, or dispose of the principal for the decedent's own benefit.

(C) A transfer whereby property is held at the time of the decedent's death by the decedent and another with right of survivorship.

(b) Nothing in this section requires a transferee to restore to the decedent's estate any life insurance, accident insurance, joint annuity, or pension payable to a person other than the surviving spouse.

(c) All property restored to the decedent's estate under this section belongs to the surviving spouse pursuant to Section 101 as though the transfer had not been made.

(Stats. 1990, c. 79 (A.B. 759), § 14, operative July 1, 1991.)

§ 103. Simultaneous death; community or quasi-community property

Except as provided by Section 224, if [spouses] die leaving community or quasi-community property and it cannot be established by clear and convincing evidence that one spouse survived the other:

(a) One-half of the community property and one-half of the quasi-community property shall be administered upon or distributed, or otherwise dealt with, as if one spouse had survived and as if that half belonged to that spouse.

(b) The other half of the community property and the other half of the quasi-community property shall be administered upon or distributed, or otherwise dealt with, as if the other spouse had survived and as if that half belonged to that spouse.

(Stats. 1990, c. 79 (A.B. 759), § 14, operative July 1, 1991.)

§ 240. Division into equal shares

If a statute calls for property to be distributed or taken in the manner provided in this section, the property shall be divided into as many equal shares as there are living members of the nearest generation of issue then living and deceased members of that generation who leave issue then living, each living member of the nearest generation of issue then living receiving one share and the share of each deceased member of that generation who leaves issue then living being divided in the same manner among his or her then living issue.

(Stats. 1990, c. 79 (A.B. 759), § 14, operative July 1, 1991.)

§ 3051. Community property

(a) Subject to Section 3071 [relating to joinder], the right of a spouse to manage and control community property, including the right to dispose of community property, is not affected by the lack or alleged lack of legal capacity of the other spouse.

(b) Except as provided in subdivision (c), if one spouse has legal capacity and the other has a conservator:

(1) The spouse who has legal capacity has the *exclusive* management and control of the community property including, subject to Section 3071 [joinder], the *exclusive* power to dispose of the community property.

(2) The community property is not part of the conservatorship estate.

(c) [Provides that the spouse with legal capacity may opt to have all or some of the community property be included in or managed, control, and disposed of as part of the conservatorship estate.]

. . .

(Stats. 1990, c. 79 (A.B. 759), § 14, operative July 1, 1991.) (Italics added.)

§ 5010. Written consent

As used in this chapter, "written consent" to a provision for a nonprobate transfer of community property on death includes a written joinder in such a provision.

(Added by Stats. 1992, c. 51 (A.B. 1719), § 6.)

§ 5011. Rights of parties in nonprobate transfers; application of chapter

Notwithstanding any other provision of this part, the rights of the parties in a nonprobate transfer of community property on death are subject to all of the following:

(a) The terms of the instrument under which the nonprobate transfer is made.

(b) A contrary state statute specifically applicable to the instrument under which the nonprobate transfer is made.

(c) A written expression of intent of a party in the provision for transfer of the property or in a written consent to the provision.

(Added by Stats. 1992, c. 51 (A.B. 1719), § 6.)

§ 5040. Nonprobate transfer to former spouse executed before or during marriage; failure of transfer due to dissolution or annulment of marriage; situations that do not cause a nonprobate transfer to fail; right of subsequent purchaser

(a) Except as provided in subdivision (b), a nonprobate transfer to the transferor's former spouse, in an instrument executed by the transferor before or during the marriage, fails if, at the time of the transferor's death, the former spouse is not the transferor's surviving spouse as defined in Section 78, as a result of the dissolution or annulment of the marriage. A judgment of legal separation that does not terminate the status of husband and wife is not a dissolution for purposes of this section.

(b) Subdivision (a) does not cause a nonprobate transfer to fail in any of the following cases:

(1) The nonprobate transfer is not subject to revocation by the transferor at the time of the transferor's death.

(2) There is clear and convincing evidence that the transferor intended to preserve the nonprobate transfer to the former spouse.

(3) A court order that the nonprobate transfer be maintained on behalf of the former spouse is in effect at the time of the transferor's death.

(c)   Where a nonprobate transfer fails by operation of this section, the instrument making the nonprobate transfer shall be treated as it would if the former spouse failed to survive the transferor.

(d)   Nothing in this section affects the rights of a subsequent purchaser or encumbrancer for value in good faith who relies on the apparent failure of a nonprobate transfer under this section or who lacks knowledge of the failure of a nonprobate transfer under this section.

(e)   As used in this section, "nonprobate transfer" means a provision, other than a provision of a life insurance policy, of either of the following types:

(1)   A provision of a type described in Section 5000.

(2)   A provision in an instrument that operates on death, other than a will, conferring a power of appointment or naming a trustee.

(Formerly § 5600, added by Stats. 2001, c. 417 (A.B. 873), § 9, operative Jan. 1, 2002. Renumbered § 5040 and amended by Stats. 2015, c. 293 (A.B. 139), § 12, eff. Jan. 1, 2016.)

§ 5042.   Joint tenancy created before or during marriage severed if former spouse not decedent's surviving spouse; situations where joint tenancy is not severed

(a)   Except as provided in subdivision (b), a joint tenancy between the decedent and the decedent's former spouse, created before or during the marriage, is severed as to the decedent's interest if, at the time of the decedent's death, the former spouse is not the decedent's surviving spouse as defined in Section 78, as a result of the dissolution or annulment of the marriage. A judgment of legal separation that does not terminate the status of husband and wife is not a dissolution for purposes of this section.

(b)   Subdivision (a) does not sever a joint tenancy in either of the following cases:

(1)   The joint tenancy is not subject to severance by the decedent at the time of the decedent's death.

(2)   There is clear and convincing evidence that the decedent intended to preserve the joint tenancy in favor of the former spouse.

(c)   Nothing in this section affects the rights of a subsequent purchaser or encumbrancer for value in good faith who relies on an apparent severance under this section or who lacks knowledge of a severance under this section.

(d)   For purposes of this section, property held in "joint tenancy" includes property held as community property with right of survivorship, as described in Section 682.1 of the Civil Code.

(Formerly § 5601, added by Stats. 2001, c. 417 (A.B. 873), § 9, operative Jan. 1, 2002. Renumbered § 5042 and amended by Stats. 2015, c. 293 (A.B. 139), § 13, eff. Jan. 1, 2016.)

§ 5044. Rights of purchaser or encumbrancer of real property who relies on affidavit or declaration

(a) Nothing in this chapter affects the rights of a purchaser or encumbrancer of real property for value who in good faith relies on an affidavit or a declaration under penalty of perjury under the laws of this state that states all of the following:

(1) The name of the decedent.

(2) The date and place of the decedent's death.

(3) A description of the real property transferred to the affiant or declarant by an instrument making a nonprobate transfer or by operation of joint tenancy survivorship.

(4) Either of the following, as appropriate:

(A) The affiant or declarant is the surviving spouse of the decedent.

(B) The affiant or declarant is not the surviving spouse of the decedent, but the rights of the affiant or declarant to the described property are not affected by Section 5040 or 5042.

(b) A person relying on an affidavit or declaration made pursuant to subdivision (a) has no duty to inquire into the truth of the matters stated in the affidavit or declaration.

(c) An affidavit or declaration made pursuant to subdivision (a) may be recorded.

(Formerly § 5602, added by Stats. 2001, c. 417 (A.B. 873), § 9, operative Jan. 1, 2002. Renumbered § 5044 and amended by Stats. 2015, c. 293 (A.B. 139), § 14, eff. Jan. 1, 2016.)

§ 5046. Court authority to order dissolution or annulment of marriage to maintain former spouse as beneficiary or preserve joint tenancy

Nothing in this chapter is intended to limit the court's authority to order a party to a dissolution or annulment of marriage to maintain the former spouse as a beneficiary on any nonprobate transfer described in this chapter, or to preserve a joint tenancy in favor of the former spouse.

(Formerly § 5603, added by Stats. 2001, c. 417 (A.B. 873), § 9, operative Jan. 1, 2002. Renumbered § 5046 and amended by Stats. 2015, c. 293 (A.B. 139), § 15, eff. Jan. 1, 2016.)

§ 5048. Operative date and application

(a) This chapter, formerly Part 4 (commencing with Section 5600), is operative on January 1, 2002.

(b) Except as provided in subdivision (c), this chapter applies to an instrument making a nonprobate transfer or creating a joint tenancy whether executed before, on, or after the operative date of this chapter.

(c) Sections 5040 and 5042 do not apply, and the applicable law in effect before the operative date of this chapter applies, to an instrument making a nonprobate transfer or creating a joint tenancy in either of the following circumstances:

(1) The person making the nonprobate transfer or creating the joint tenancy dies before the operative date of this chapter.

(2) The dissolution of marriage or other event that terminates the status of the nonprobate transfer beneficiary or joint tenant as a surviving spouse occurs before the operative date of this chapter.

(Formerly § 5604, added by Stats. 2001, c. 417 (A.B. 873), § 9, operative Jan. 1, 2002. Renumbered § 5048 and amended by Stats. 2015, c. 293 (A.B. 139), § 16, eff. Jan. 1, 2016.)

§ 5305. Married parties; community property; presumptions; rebuttal; change of survivorship right, beneficiary, or payee by will

(a) Notwithstanding Sections 5301 to 5303, inclusive, if parties to an account are married to each other, whether or not they are so described in the deposit agreement, their net contribution to the account is presumed to be and remain their community property.

(b) Notwithstanding Sections 2581 and 2640 of the Family Code, the presumption established by this section is a presumption affecting the burden of proof and may be rebutted by proof of either of the following:

(1) The sums on deposit that are claimed to be separate property can be traced from separate property unless it is proved that the married persons made a written agreement that expressed their clear intent that the sums be their community property.

(2) The married persons made a written agreement, separate from the deposit agreement, that expressly provided that the sums on deposit, claimed not to be community property, were not to be community property.

(c) Except as provided in Section 5307, a right of survivorship arising from the express terms of the account or under Section 5302, a beneficiary designation in a Totten trust account, or a P.O.D. payee designation, may not be changed by will.

(d) Except as provided in subdivisions (b) and (c), a multiple-party account created with community property funds does not in any way alter community property rights.

(Stats. 1990, c. 79 (A.B. 759), § 14, operative July 1, 1991. Amended by Stats. 1992, c. 163 (A.B. 2641), § 131, operative Jan. 1, 1994; Stats. 1993, c. 219 (A.B. 1500), § 224.7.)

§ 5610. "Real property" defined

"Real property" means any of the following:

(a) Real property improved with not less than one nor more than four residential dwelling units.

(b) A condominium unit, including the limited common elements allocated to the exclusive use thereof that form an integral part of the condominium unit.

(c) A single tract of agricultural real estate consisting of 40 acres or less that is improved with a single-family residence.

(Added by Stats. 2015, c. 293 (A.B. 139), § 17, eff. Jan. 1, 2016. Repealed as of January 1, 2021, pursuant to Section 5600 "unless a later enacted statute . . . deletes or extends that date.")

§ 5612. "Recorded" defined

"Recorded" has the meaning provided in Section 1170 of the Civil Code.

(Added by Stats. 2015, c. 293 (A.B. 139), § 17, eff. Jan. 1, 2016. Repealed as of January 1, 2021, pursuant to Section 5600 "unless a later enacted statute . . . deletes or extends that date.")

§ 5614. "Revocable transfer on death deed" defined

(a) "Revocable transfer on death deed" means an instrument created pursuant to this part that does all of the following:

(1) Makes a donative transfer of real property to a named beneficiary.

(2) Operates on the transferor's death.

(3) Remains revocable until the transferor's death.

(b) A revocable transfer on death deed may also be known as a "revocable TOD deed."

(Added by Stats. 2015, c. 293 (A.B. 139), § 17, eff. Jan. 1, 2016. Repealed as of January 1, 2021, pursuant to Section 5600 "unless a later enacted statute . . . deletes or extends that date.")

§ 5620. Who may make revocable transfer on death deed

An owner of real property who has the capacity to contract may make a revocable transfer on death deed of the property.

(Added by Stats. 2015, c. 293 (A.B. 139), § 17, eff. Jan. 1, 2016. Repealed as of January 1, 2021, pursuant to Section 5600 "unless a later enacted statute . . . deletes or extends that date.")

§ 5622. Identification of beneficiary

The transferor shall identify the beneficiary by name in a revocable transfer on death deed.

(Added by Stats. 2015, c. 293 (A.B. 139), § 17, eff. Jan. 1, 2016. Repealed as of January 1, 2021, pursuant to Section 5600 "unless a later enacted statute . . . deletes or extends that date.")

§ 5624. Signature, date and acknowledgment

A revocable transfer on death deed is not effective unless the transferor signs and dates the deed and acknowledges the deed before a notary public.

(Added by Stats. 2015, c. 293 (A.B. 139), § 17, eff. Jan. 1, 2016. Repealed as of January 1, 2021, pursuant to Section 5600 "unless a later enacted statute . . . deletes or extends that date.")

§ 5626. Recording; delivery to beneficiary not required; acceptance by beneficiary not required

(a) A revocable transfer on death deed is not effective unless the deed is recorded on or before 60 days after the date it was executed.

(b) The transferor is not required to deliver a revocable transfer on death deed to the beneficiary during the transferor's life.

(c) The beneficiary is not required to accept a revocable transfer on death deed from the transferor during the transferor's life.

(Added by Stats. 2015, c. 293 (A.B. 139), § 17, eff. Jan. 1, 2016. Repealed as of January 1, 2021, pursuant to Section 5600 "unless a later enacted statute . . . deletes or extends that date.")

§ 5628. Effect of multiple recordings for same property

(a) If a revocable transfer on death deed is recorded for the same property for which another revocable transfer on death deed is recorded, the later executed deed is the operative instrument and its recordation revokes the earlier executed deed.

(b) Revocation of a revocable transfer on death deed does not revive an instrument earlier revoked by recordation of that deed.

(Added by Stats. 2015, c. 293 (A.B. 139), § 17, eff. Jan. 1, 2016. Repealed as of January 1, 2021, pursuant to Section 5600 "unless a later enacted statute . . . deletes or extends that date.")

§ 5630. Who may revoke revocable transfer on death deed

A transferor who has the capacity to contract may revoke a revocable transfer on death deed at any time.

(Added by Stats. 2015, c. 293 (A.B. 139), § 17, eff. Jan. 1, 2016. Repealed as of January 1, 2021, pursuant to Section 5600 "unless a later enacted statute . . . deletes or extends that date.")

§ 5632. Execution and recording of revocation

(a) An instrument revoking a revocable transfer on death deed shall be executed and recorded before the transferor's death in the same manner as execution and recordation of a revocable transfer on death deed.

(b) Joinder, consent, or agreement of, or notice to, the beneficiary is not required for revocation of a revocable transfer on death deed.

(Added by Stats. 2015, c. 293 (A.B. 139), § 17, eff. Jan. 1, 2016. Repealed as of January 1, 2021, pursuant to Section 5600 "unless a later enacted statute . . . deletes or extends that date.")

§ 6101. Property which may be disposed of by will

A will may dispose of the following property:

(a) The testator's separate property.

(b) The one-half of the community property that belongs to the testator under Section 100.

(c) The one-half of the testator's quasi-community property that belongs to the testator under Section 101.

(Stats. 1990, c. 79 (A.B. 759), § 14, operative July 1, 1991.)

§ 6110. Necessity of writing; other requirements

(a) Except as provided in this part, a will shall be in writing and satisfy the requirements of this section.

(b) The will shall be signed by one of the following:

(1) By the testator.

(2) In the testator's name by some other person in the testator's presence and by the testator's direction.

(3) By a conservator pursuant to a court order to make a will under Section 2580.

(c)(1) Except as provided in paragraph (2), the will shall be witnessed by being signed, during the testator's lifetime, by at least two persons each of whom (A) being present at the same time, witnessed either the signing of the will or the testator's acknowledgment of the signature or of the will and (B) understand that the instrument they sign is the testator's will.

(2) If a will was not executed in compliance with paragraph (1), the will shall be treated as if it was executed in compliance with that paragraph if the proponent of the will establishes by clear and convincing evidence that, at the time the testator signed the will, the testator intended the will to constitute the testator's will.

(Stats. 1990, c. 79 (A.B. 759), § 14, operative July 1, 1991. Amended by Stats. 1996, c. 563 (S.B. 392), § 20; Stats. 2008, c. 53 (A.B. 2248), § 1)

§ 6400. Property subject to intestacy provisions

Any part of the estate of a decedent not effectively disposed of by will passes to the decedent's heirs as prescribed in this part.

(Stats. 1990, c. 79 (A.B. 759), § 14, operative July 1, 1991.)

§ 6401. Surviving spouse; intestate share; community or quasi-community property; separate property

(a) As to community property, the intestate share of the surviving spouse is the one-half of the community property that belongs to the decedent under Section 100.

(b) As to quasi-community property, the intestate share of the surviving spouse is the one-half of the quasi-community property that belongs to the decedent under Section 101.

(c) As to separate property, the intestate share of the surviving spouse is as follows:

(1) The entire intestate estate if the decedent did not leave any surviving issue, parent, brother, sister, or issue of a deceased brother or sister.

(2) One-half of the intestate estate in the following cases:

(A) Where the decedent leaves only one child or the issue of a deceased child.

(B) Where the decedent leaves no issue, but leaves a parent or parents or their issue or the issue of either of them.

(3) One-third of the intestate estate in the following cases:

(A) Where the decedent leaves more than one child living.

(B) Where the decedent leaves one child living and the issue of one or more deceased children.

(C) Where the decedent leaves issue of two or more deceased children.

(Stats. 1990, c. 79 (A.B. 759), § 14, operative July 1, 1991. Amended by Stats. 2002, c. 447 (A.B. 2216), § 1, operative July 1, 2003; Stats. 2014, c. 913, (A.B. 2747), § 32, eff. Jan. 1, 2015.)

§ 6402. Intestate estate not passing to surviving spouse

Except as provided in Section 6402.5, the part of the intestate estate not passing to the surviving spouse, under Section 6401, or the entire intestate estate if there is no surviving spouse, passes as follows:

(a) To the issue of the decedent, the issue taking equally if they are all of the same degree of kinship to the decedent, but if of unequal degree those of more remote degree take in the manner provided in Section 240.

(b) If there is no surviving issue, to the decedent's parent or parents equally.

(c) If there is no surviving issue or parent, to the issue of the parents of either of them, the issue taking equally if they are all of the same degree of kinship to the decedent, but if of unequal degree those of more remote degree take in the manner provided in Section 240.

(d) If there is no surviving issue, parent or issue of a parent, but the decedent is survived by one or more grandparents or issue of grandparents, to the grandparent or grandparents equally, or to the issue of such grandparents if there is no surviving grandparent, the issue taking equally if they are all of the same degree of kinship to the decedent, but if of unequal degree those of more remote degree take in the manner provided in Section 240.

(e) If there is no surviving issue, parent or issue of a parent, grandparent or issue of a grandparent, but the decedent is survived by the issue of a predeceased spouse, to that issue, the issue taking equally if they are all of the same degree of kinship to the predeceased spouse, but if of unequal degree those of more remote degree take in the manner provided in Section 240.

(f) If there is no surviving issue, parent or issue of a parent, grandparent or issue of a grandparent, or issue of a predeceased spouse, but the decedent is survived by next of kin, to the next of kin in equal degree, but where there are two or more collateral kindred in equal degree who claim through different ancestors, those who claim through the nearest ancestor are preferred to those claiming through an ancestor more remote.

(g) If there is no surviving next of kin of the decedent and no surviving issue of a predeceased spouse of the decedent, but the decedent is survived by the parents of a predeceased spouse or the issue of those parents, to the parent or parents equally, or to the issue of those parents if both are deceased, the issue taking equally if they are all of the same degree of kinship to the predeceased spouse, but if of unequal degree those of more remote degree take in the manner provided in Section 240.

(Stats. 1990, c. 79 (A.B. 759), § 14, operative July 1, 1991. Amended by Stats. 2002, c. 447 (A.B. 2216), § 2, operative July 1, 2003; Stats. 2014, c. 913 (A.B. 2747), § 32.5, eff. Jan. 1, 2015)

§ 6402.5. Predeceased spouse; portion of decedent's estate attributable to decedent's predeceased spouse

(a) For purposes of distributing real property under this section if the decedent had a predeceased spouse who died not more than 15 years before the decedent and there is no surviving spouse or issue of the decedent, the portion of the decedent's estate attributable to the decedent's predeceased spouse passes as follows:

(1) If the decedent is survived by issue of the predeceased spouse, to the surviving issue of the predeceased spouse; if they are all of the same degree of kinship to the predeceased spouse they take equally, but if of unequal degree those of more remote degree take in the manner provided in Section 240.

(2) If there is no surviving issue of the predeceased spouse but the decedent is survived by a parent or parents of the predeceased spouse, to the predeceased spouse's surviving parent or parents equally.

(3) If there is no surviving issue or parent of the predeceased spouse but the decedent is survived by issue of a parent of the predeceased spouse, to the surviving issue of the parents of the predeceased spouse or either of them, the issue taking equally if they are all of the same degree of kinship to the predeceased spouse, but if of unequal degree those of more remote degree take in the manner provided in Section 240.

(4) If the decedent is not survived by issue, parent, or issue of a parent of the predeceased spouse, to the next of kin of the decedent in the manner provided in Section 6402.

(5) If the portion of the decedent's estate attributable to the decedent's predeceased spouse would otherwise escheat to the state because there is no kin of the decedent to take under Section 6402, the portion of the decedent's estate attributable to the predeceased spouse passes to the next of kin of the predeceased spouse who shall take in the same manner as the next of kin of the decedent take under Section 6402.

(b) For purposes of distributing personal property under this section if the decedent had a predeceased spouse who died not more than five years before the decedent, and there is no surviving spouse or issue of the decedent, the portion of the decedent's estate attributable to the decedent's predeceased spouse passes as follows:

(1) If the decedent is survived by issue of the predeceased spouse, to the surviving issue of the predeceased spouse; if they are all of the same degree of kinship to the predeceased spouse they take equally, but if of unequal degree those of more remote degree take in the manner provided in Section 240.

(2) If there is no surviving issue of the predeceased spouse but the decedent is survived by a parent or parents of the predeceased spouse, to the predeceased spouse's surviving parent or parents equally.

(3) If there is no surviving issue or parent of the predeceased spouse but the decedent is survived by issue of a parent of the predeceased spouse, to the surviving issue of the parents of the predeceased spouse or either of them, the issue taking equally if they are all of the same degree of kinship to the predeceased spouse, but if of unequal degree those of more remote degree take in the manner provided in Section 240.

(4) If the decedent is not survived by issue, parent, or issue of a parent of the predeceased spouse, to the next of kin of the decedent in the manner provided in Section 6402.

(5) If the portion of the decedent's estate attributable to the decedent's predeceased spouse would otherwise escheat to the state because there is no kin of the decedent to take under Section 6402, the portion of the decedent's estate attributable to the predeceased spouse passes to the next of kin of the predeceased spouse who shall take in the same manner as the next of kin of the decedent take under Section 6402.

(c) For purposes of disposing of personal property under subdivision (b), the claimant heir bears the burden of proof to show the exact personal property to be disposed of to the heir.

(d) For purposes of providing notice under any provision of this code with respect to an estate that may include personal property subject to distribution under subdivision (b), if the aggregate fair market value of tangible and intangible personal property with a written record of title or ownership in the estate is believed in good faith by the petitioning party to be less than ten thousand dollars ($10,000), the petitioning party need not give notice to the issue or next of kin of the predeceased spouse. If the personal property is subsequently determined to have an aggregate fair market value in excess of ten thousand dollars ($10,000), notice shall be given to the issue or next of kin of the predeceased spouse as provided by law.

(e) For the purposes of disposing of property pursuant to subdivision (b), "personal property" means that personal property in which there is a written record of title or ownership and the value of which in the aggregate is ten thousand dollars ($10,000) or more.

(f) For the purposes of this section, the "portion of the decedent's estate attributable to the decedent's predeceased spouse" means all of the following property in the decedent's estate:

(1) One-half of the community property in existence at the time of the death of the predeceased spouse.

(2) One-half of any community property, in existence at the time of death of the predeceased spouse, which was given to the decedent by the predeceased spouse by way of gift, descent, or devise.

(3) That portion of any community property in which the predeceased spouse had any incident of ownership and which vested in the decedent upon the death of the predeceased spouse by right of survivorship.

(4) Any separate property of the predeceased spouse which came to the decedent by gift, descent, or devise of the predeceased spouse or which vested in the decedent upon the death of the predeceased spouse by right of survivorship.

(g) For the purposes of this section, quasi-community property shall be treated the same as community property.

(h) For the purposes of this section:

(1) Relatives of the predeceased spouse conceived before the decedent's death but born thereafter inherit as if they had been born in the lifetime of the decedent.

(2) A person who is related to the predeceased spouse through two lines of relationship is entitled to only a single share based on the relationship which would entitle the person to the larger share.

(Stats. 1990, c. 79 (A.B. 759), § 14, operative July 1, 1991.)

§ 11440. Petition to allocate debt

If it appears that a debt of the decedent has been paid or is payable in whole or in part by the surviving spouse, or that a debt of the surviving spouse has been paid or is payable in whole or in part from property in the decedent's estate, the personal representative, the surviving spouse, or a beneficiary may, at any time before an order for final distribution is made, petition for an order to allocate the debt.

(Stats. 1990, c. 79 (A.B. 759), § 14, operative July 1, 1991.)

§ 11441. Contents of petition

The petition shall include a statement of all of the following:

(a) All debts of the decedent and surviving spouse known to the petitioner that are alleged to be subject to allocation and whether paid in whole or part or unpaid.

(b) The reason why the debts should be allocated.

(c) The proposed allocation and the basis for allocation alleged by the petitioner.

(Stats. 1990, c. 79 (A.B. 759), § 14, operative July 1, 1991.)

§ 11442. Value of separate and community property affecting allocation where no inventory and appraisal provided; show cause order

If it appears from the petition that allocation would be affected by the value of the separate property of the surviving spouse and any community property and quasi-community property not administered in the estate and if an inventory and appraisal of the property has not been provided by the surviving spouse, the court shall make an order to show cause why the information should not be provided.

(Stats. 1990, c. 79 (A.B. 759), § 14, operative July 1, 1991.)

§ 11444. Allocation of debt

(a) The personal representative and the surviving spouse may provide for allocation by agreement and, on a determination by the court that the agreement substantially protects the rights of interested persons, the allocation provided in the agreement shall be ordered by the court.

(b) In the absence of an agreement, each debt subject to allocation shall first be characterized by the court as separate or community, in accordance with the laws of the state applicable to marital dissolution proceedings. Following that characterization, the debt or debts shall be allocated as follows:

(1) Separate debts of either spouse shall be allocated to that spouse's separate property assets, and community debts shall be allocated to the spouses' community property assets.

(2) If a separate property asset of either spouse is subject to a secured debt that is characterized as that spouse's separate debt, and the net equity in that asset available to satisfy that secured debt is less than that secured debt, the unsatisfied portion of that secured debt shall be treated as an unsecured separate debt of that spouse and allocated to the net value of that spouse's other separate property assets.

(3) If the net value of either spouse's separate property assets is less than that spouse's unsecured separate debt or debts, the unsatisfied portion of the debt or debts shall be allocated to the net value of that spouse's one-half share of the community property assets. If the net value of that spouse's one-half share of the community property assets is less than that spouse's unsatisfied unsecured separate debt or debts, the remaining unsatisfied portion of the debt or debts shall be allocated to the net value of the other spouse's one-half share of the community property assets.

(4) If a community property asset is subject to a secured debt that is characterized as a community debt, and the net equity in that asset available to satisfy that secured debt is less than that secured debt, the unsatisfied portion of that secured debt shall be treated as an unsecured community debt and allocated to the net value of the other community property assets.

(5) If the net value of the community property assets is less than the unsecured community debt or debts, the unsatisfied portion of the debt or debts shall be allocated equally between the separate property assets of the decedent and the surviving spouse. If the net value of either spouse's separate property assets is less than that spouse's share of the unsatisfied portion of the unsecured community debt or debts, the remaining unsatisfied portion of the debt or debts shall be allocated to the net value of the other spouse's separate property assets.

(c) For purposes of this section:

(1) The net value of either spouse's separate property asset shall refer to its fair market value as of the date of the decedent's death, minus the date-of-death balance of any liens and encumbrances on that asset that have been characterized as that spouse's separate debts.

(2) The net value of a community property asset shall refer to its fair market value as of the date of the decedent's death, minus the date-of-death balance of any liens and encumbrances on that asset that have been characterized as community debts.

(3) In the case of a nonrecourse debt, the amount of that debt shall be limited to the net equity in the collateral, based on the fair market value of the collateral as of the date of the decedent's death, that is available to satisfy that debt. For the purposes of this paragraph, "nonrecourse debt" means a debt for which the debtor's obligation to repay is limited to the collateral securing the debt, and for which a deficiency judgment against the debtor is not permitted by law.

(d)   Notwithstanding the foregoing provisions of this section, the court may order a different allocation of debts between the decedent's estate and the surviving spouse if the court finds a different allocation to be equitable under the circumstances.

(e)   Nothing contained in this section is intended to impair or affect the rights of third parties. If a personal representative or the surviving spouse incurs any damages or expense, including attorney's fees, on account of the nonpayment of a debt that was allocated to the other party pursuant to subdivision (b), or as the result of a debt being misallocated due to fraud or intentional misrepresentation by the other party, the party incurring damages shall be entitled to recover from the other party for damages or expense deemed reasonable by the court that made the allocation.

(Stats. 1990, c. 79, (A.B. 759), § 14, operative July 1, 1991. Amended by Stats. 2001, c. 72 (S.B. 668), § 1.)

§ 11445. Payment of allocated shares; court order

On making a determination as provided in this chapter, the court shall make an order that:

(a)   Directs the personal representative to make payment of the amounts allocated to the estate by payment to the surviving spouse or creditors.

(b)   Directs the personal representative to charge amounts allocated to the surviving spouse against any property or interests of the surviving spouse that are in the possession or control of the personal representative. To the extent that property or interests of the surviving spouse in the possession or control of the personal representative are insufficient to satisfy the allocation, the court order shall summarily direct the surviving spouse to pay the allocation to the personal representative.

(Stats. 1990, c. 79 (A.B. 759), § 14, operative July 1, 1991.)

§ 11446. Last illness and funeral expenses

Notwithstanding any other statute, funeral expenses and expenses of last illness shall be charged against the estate of the decedent and shall not be allocated to, or charged against the community share of, the surviving spouse, whether or not the surviving spouse is financially able to pay the expenses and whether or not the surviving spouse or any other person is also liable for the expenses.

(Stats. 1990, c. 79 (A.B. 759), § 14, operative July 1, 1991.)

§ 13550. Personal liability for debts chargeable against property

Except as provided in Sections 11446, 13552, 13553, and 13554, upon the death of a married person, the surviving spouse is personally liable for the debts of the deceased spouse chargeable against the property described in Section 13551 to the extent provided in Section 13551.

(Stats. 1990, c. 79 (A.B. 759), § 14, operative July 1, 1991.)

§ 13551. Limitation of liability

The liability imposed by Section 13550 shall not exceed the fair market value at the date of the decedent's death, less the amount of any liens and encumbrances, of the total of the following:

(a) The portion of the one-half of the community and quasi-community property belonging to the surviving spouse under Sections 100 and 101 that is not exempt from enforcement of a money judgment and is not administered in the estate of the deceased spouse.

(b) The portion of the one-half of the community and quasi-community property belonging to the decedent under Sections 100 and 101 that passes to the surviving spouse without administration.

(c) The separate property of the decedent that passes to the surviving spouse without administration.

(Stats. 1990, c. 79 (A.B. 759), § 14, operative July 1, 1991.)

§ 13553. Exemption from liability

The surviving spouse is not liable under this chapter if all the property described in paragraphs (1) and (2) of subdivision (a) of Section 13502 is administered under this code.

(Stats. 1990, c. 79 (A.B. 759), § 14, operative July 1, 1991.)

§ 13554. Enforcement of debt against surviving spouse

(a) Except as otherwise provided in this chapter, any debt described in Section 13550 may be enforced against the surviving spouse in the same manner as it could have been enforced against the deceased spouse if the deceased spouse had not died.

(b) In any action or proceeding based upon the debt, the surviving spouse may assert any defense, cross-complaint, or setoff which would have been available to the deceased spouse if the deceased spouse had not died.

(c) Section 366.2 of the Code of Civil Procedure applies in an action under this section.

(Stats. 1990, c. 79 (A.B. 759), § 14, operative July 1, 1991. Amended by Stats. 1990, c. 140 (S.B. 1855), § 18.1, operative July 1, 1991; Stats. 1992, c. 178 (S.B. 1496), § 43.)

§ 13650. Petition for order of administration not necessary

(a) A surviving spouse or the personal representative, guardian of the estate, or conservator of the estate of the surviving spouse may file a petition in the superior court of the county in which the estate of the deceased spouse may be administered requesting an order that administration of all or part of the estate is not necessary for the reason that all or part of the estate is property passing to the surviving spouse. The petition may also request an order confirming the ownership of the surviving spouse of property belonging to the surviving spouse under Section 100 or 101.

(b) To the extent of the election, this section does not apply to property that the petitioner has elected, as provided in Section 13502, to have administered under this code.

(c) A guardian or conservator may file a petition under this section without authorization or approval of the court in which the guardianship or conservatorship proceeding is pending.

(Stats. 1990, c. 79 (A.B. 759), § 14, operative July 1, 1991.)

§ 13651. Contents of petition

(a) A petition filed pursuant to Section 13650 shall allege that administration of all or a part of the estate of the deceased spouse is not necessary for the reason that all or a part of the estate is property passing to the surviving spouse, and shall set forth all of the following information:

(1) If proceedings for the administration of the estate are not pending, the facts necessary to determine the county in which the estate of the deceased spouse may be administered.

(2) A description of the property of the deceased spouse which the petitioner alleges is property passing to the surviving spouse, including the trade or business name of any property passing to the surviving spouse that consists of an unincorporated business or an interest in an unincorporated business which the deceased spouse was operating or managing at the time of death, subject to any written agreement between the deceased spouse and the surviving spouse providing for a non pro rata division of the aggregate value of the community property assets or quasi-community assets, or both.

(3) The facts upon which the petitioner bases the allegation that all or a part of the estate of the deceased spouse is property passing to the surviving spouse.

(4) A description of any interest in the community property or quasi-community property, or both, which the petitioner requests the court to confirm to the surviving spouse as belonging to the surviving spouse pursuant to Section 100 or 101, subject to any written agreement between the deceased spouse and the surviving spouse providing for a non pro rata division of the aggregate value of the community property assets or quasi-community assets, or both.

(5) The name, age, address, and relation to the deceased spouse of each heir and devisee of the deceased spouse, the names and addresses of all persons named as executors of the will of the deceased spouse, and the names and addresses of all persons appointed as personal representatives of the deceased spouse, which are known to the petitioner.

Disclosure of any written agreement between the deceased spouse and the surviving spouse providing for a non pro rata division of the aggregate value of the community property assets or quasi-community property assets, or both, or the affirmative statement that this agreement does not exist. If a dispute arises as to the division of the community property assets or quasi-community property assets, or both, pursuant to this agreement, the court shall determine the division subject to terms and conditions or other remedies that appear equitable under the circumstances of the case, taking into account the rights of all interested persons.

(b) If the petitioner bases the allegation that all or part of the estate of the deceased spouse is property passing to the surviving spouse upon the will of the deceased spouse, a copy of the will shall be attached to the petition.

(c) If the petitioner bases the description of the property of the deceased spouse passing to the surviving spouse or the property to be confirmed to the surviving spouse, or both, upon a written agreement between the deceased spouse and the surviving spouse providing for a non pro rata division of the aggregate value of the community property assets or quasi-community assets, or both, a copy of the agreement shall be attached to the petition.

(Stats. 1990, c. 79 (A.B. 759), § 14, operative July 1, 1991. Amended by Stats. 1998, c. 682 (A.B. 2069), § 6.)

§ 13656. Order; determination of property passing to surviving spouse

(a) If the court finds that all of the estate of the deceased spouse is property passing to the surviving spouse, the court shall issue an order describing the property, determining that the property is property passing to the surviving spouse, and determining that no administration is necessary. The court may issue any further orders which may be necessary to cause delivery of the property or its proceeds to the surviving spouse.

(b) If the court finds that all or part of the estate of the deceased spouse is not property passing to the surviving spouse, the court shall issue an order (1) describing any property which is not property passing to the surviving spouse, determining that that property does not pass to the surviving spouse and determining that that property is subject to administration under this code and (2) describing the property, if any, which is property passing to the surviving spouse, determining that that property passes to the surviving spouse, and determining that no administration of that property is necessary. If the court determines that property passes to the surviving spouse, the court may issue any further orders which may be necessary to cause delivery of that property or its proceeds to the surviving spouse.

(c) If the petition filed under this chapter includes a description of the interest of the surviving spouse in the community or quasi-community property, or both, which belongs to the surviving spouse pursuant to Section 100 or 101 and the court finds that the interest belongs to the surviving spouse, the court shall issue an order describing the property and confirming the ownership of the surviving spouse and may issue any further orders which may be necessary to cause ownership of the property to be confirmed in the surviving spouse.

(Stats. 1990, c. 79 (A.B. 759), § 14, operative July 1, 1991.)

§ 13657. Conclusive nature of order

Upon becoming final, an order under Section 13656(1) determining that property is property passing to the surviving spouse or (2) confirming the ownership of the surviving spouse of property belonging to the surviving spouse under Section 100 or 101 shall be conclusive on all persons, whether or not they are in being.

(Stats. 1990, c. 79 (A.B. 759), § 14, operative July 1, 1991.)

§ 13658. Unincorporated businesses; list of creditors; order to protect interests

If the court determines that all or a part of the property passing to the surviving spouse consists of an unincorporated business or an interest in an unincorporated business which the deceased spouse was operating or managing at the time of death, the court shall require the surviving spouse to file a list of all of the known creditors of the business and the amounts owing to each of them. The court may issue any order necessary to protect the interests of the creditors of the business, including, but not limited to, the filing of (1) an undertaking and (2) an inventory and appraisal in the form provided in Section 8802 and made as provided in Part 3 (commencing with Section 8800) of Division 7.

(Stats. 1990, c. 79 (A.B. 759), § 14, operative July 1, 1991.)

§ 13659. Inventory and appraisal

Except as provided in Section 13658, no inventory and appraisal of the estate of the deceased spouse is required in a proceeding under this chapter. However, within three months after the filing of a petition under this chapter, or within such further time as the court or judge for reasonable cause may allow, the petitioner may file with the clerk of the court an inventory and appraisal made as provided in Part 3 (commencing with Section 8800) of Division 7. The petitioner may appraise the assets which a personal representative could appraise under Section 8901.

(Stats. 1990, c. 79 (A.B. 759), § 14, operative July 1, 1991.)

§ 13660. Attorney's fees

The attorney's fees for services performed in connection with the filing of a petition and obtaining of a court order under this chapter shall be determined by private agreement between the attorney and the client and are not subject to approval by the court. If there is no agreement between the attorney and the client concerning the attorney's fees for services performed in connection with the filing of a petition and obtaining of a court order under this chapter and there is a dispute concerning the reasonableness of the attorney's fees for those services, a petition may be filed with the court in the same proceeding requesting that the court determine the reasonableness of the attorney's fees for those services. If there is an agreement between the attorney and the client concerning the attorney's fees for services performed in connection with the filing of a petition and obtaining a court order under this chapter and there is a dispute concerning the meaning of the agreement, a petition may be filed with the court in the same proceeding requesting that the court determine the dispute.

(Stats. 1990, c. 79 (A.B. 759), § 14, operative July 1, 1991.)

WEST'S ANNOTATED CODE OF CIVIL PROCEDURE

§ 377.60.   Persons with standing

A cause of action for the death of a person caused by the wrongful act or neglect of another may be asserted by any of the following persons or by the decedent's personal representative on their behalf:

(a) The decedent's surviving spouse, domestic partner, children, and issue of deceased children, or, if there is no surviving issue of the decedent, the persons, including the surviving spouse or domestic partner, who would be entitled to the property of the decedent by intestate succession.

(b) Whether or not qualified under subdivision (a), if they were dependent on the decedent, the putative spouse, children of the putative spouse, stepchildren, or parents. As used in this subdivision, "putative spouse" means the surviving spouse of a void or voidable marriage who is found by the court to have believed in good faith that the marriage to the decedent was valid.

* * *

(f)(1) For the purposes of this section "domestic partner" means a person who, at the time of the decedent's death, was the domestic partner of the decedent in a registered domestic partnership established in accordance with subdivision (b) of Section 297 of the Family Code.

. . .

(Added by Stats. 1992, c. 178 (S.B. 1496), § 20. Amended by Stats. 1996, c. 563 (S.B. 392), § 1; Stats. 1997, c. 13 (S.B. 449), § 1, eff. May 23, 1997; Stats. 2001, c. 893 (A.B. 25), § 2; Stats. 2004, c. 947 (A.B. 2580), § 1.)

APPENDIX B

JUDICIAL COUNCIL FORMS

∎ ∎ ∎

FL-100

ATTORNEY OR PARTY WITHOUT ATTORNEY *(Name, State Bar number, and address)*:	FOR COURT USE ONLY
TELEPHONE NO.: FAX NO.:	
E-MAIL ADDRESS:	
ATTORNEY FOR *(Name)*:	

SUPERIOR COURT OF CALIFORNIA, COUNTY OF
STREET ADDRESS:
MAILING ADDRESS:
CITY AND ZIP CODE:
BRANCH NAME:

PETITIONER:

RESPONDENT:

PETITION FOR ☐ AMENDED	CASE NUMBER:
☐ **Dissolution (Divorce) of:** ☐ Marriage ☐ Domestic Partnership	
☐ **Legal Separation of:** ☐ Marriage ☐ Domestic Partnership	
☐ **Nullity of:** ☐ Marriage ☐ Domestic Partnership	

1. **LEGAL RELATIONSHIP** *(check all that apply)*:
   a. ☐ We are married.
   b. ☐ We are domestic partners and our domestic partnership was established in California.
   c. ☐ We are domestic partners and our domestic partnership was NOT established in California.

2. **RESIDENCE REQUIREMENTS** *(check all that apply)*:
   a. ☐ Petitioner ☐ Respondent   has been a resident of this state for at least six months and of this county for at least three months immediately preceding the filing of this *Petition*. *(For a divorce, at least one person in the legal relationship described in items 1a and 1c must comply with this requirement.)*
   b. ☐ We are the same sex and were married in California but are not residents of California. Neither of us lives in a state or nation that will dissolve the marriage. This case is filed in the county in which we married.
      Petitioner's residence *(state or nation)*:   Respondent's residence *(state or nation)*:
   c. ☐ Our domestic partnership was established in California. Neither of us has to be a resident or have a domicile in California to dissolve our partnership here.

3. **STATISTICAL FACTS**
   a. ☐ (1) Date of marriage *(specify)*:   (2) Date of separation *(specify)*:
      (3) Time from date of marriage to date of separation *(specify)*:   Years   Months
   b. ☐ (1) Registration date of domestic partnership with the California Secretary of State or other state equivalent *(specify below)*:
      (2) Date of separation *(specify)*:
      (3) Time from date of registration of domestic partnership to date of separation *(specify)*:   Years   Months

4. **MINOR CHILDREN** *(children born before (or born or adopted during) the marriage or domestic partnership)*:
   a. ☐ There are no minor children.
   b. ☐ The minor children are:
      Child's name   Birthdate   Age   Sex

      (1) ☐ continued on Attachment 4b.
      (2) ☐ a child who is not yet born.
   c. If there are minor children of Petitioner and Respondent, a completed *Declaration Under Uniform Child Custody Jurisdiction and Enforcement Act (UCCJEA)* (form FL-105) must be attached.
   d. ☐ Petitioner and Respondent signed a voluntary declaration of paternity. A copy ☐ is ☐ is not   attached.

Page 1 of 3

Form Adopted for Mandatory Use	**PETITION—MARRIAGE/DOMESTIC PARTNERSHIP**	Family Code, §§ 297, 299, 2320, 2330, 3409;
Judicial Council of California	**(Family Law)**	www.courts.ca.gov
FL-100 [Rev. January 1, 2015]		

FL-100

PETITIONER:	CASE NUMBER:
RESPONDENT:	

Petitioner requests that the court make the following orders:

5. **LEGAL GROUNDS** (Family Code sections 2200–2210, 2310–2312)

    a. ☐ Divorce   or   ☐ Legal separation   of the marriage or domestic partnership based on *(check one)*:

        (1) ☐ irreconcilable differences.   (2) ☐ permanent legal incapacity to make decisions.

    b. ☐ Nullity of void marriage or domestic partnership based on:

        (1) ☐ incest.   (2) ☐ bigamy.

    c. ☐ Nullity of voidable marriage or domestic partnership based on:

        (1) ☐ petitioner's age at time of registration of domestic   (4) ☐ fraud.
            partnership or marriage.

        (2) ☐ prior existing marriage or domestic partnership.   (5) ☐ force.

        (3) ☐ unsound mind.   (6) ☐ physical incapacity.

6. **CHILD CUSTODY AND VISITATION (PARENTING TIME)**

	Petitioner	Respondent	Joint	Other
a. Legal custody of children to............	☐	☐		
b. Physical custody of children to............	☐	☐	☐	☐
c. Child visitation (parenting time) be granted to	☐	☐		☐

    As requested in: ☐ form FL-311   ☐ form FL-312   ☐ form FL-341(C)

                    ☐ form FL-341(D)   ☐ form FL-341(E)   ☐ Attachment 6c(1)

    d. ☐ Determine the parentage of children born to Petitioner and Respondent before the marriage or domestic partnership.

7. **CHILD SUPPORT**

    a. If there are minor children born to or adopted by Petitioner and Respondent before or during this marriage or domestic partnership, the court will make orders for the support of the children upon request and submission of financial forms by the requesting party.

    b. An earnings assignment may be issued without further notice.

    c. Any party required to pay support must pay interest on overdue amounts at the "legal" rate, which is currently 10 percent.

    d. ☐ Other *(specify):*

8. **SPOUSAL OR DOMESTIC PARTNER SUPPORT**

    a. ☐ Spousal or domestic partner support payable to   ☐ Petitioner   ☐ Respondent

    b. ☐ Terminate (end) the court's ability to award support to   ☐ Petitioner   ☐ Respondent

    c. ☐ Reserve for future determination the issue of support payable to   ☐ Petitioner   ☐ Respondent

    d. ☐ Other *(specify):*

9. **SEPARATE PROPERTY**

    a. ☐ There are no such assets or debts that I know of to be confirmed by the court.

    b. ☐ Confirm as separate property the assets and debts in   ☐ *Property Declaration* (form FL-160)   ☐ Attachment 9b
        ☐ the following list.   Item   Confirm to

FL-100

PETITIONER:	CASE NUMBER:
RESPONDENT:	

10. COMMUNITY AND QUASI-COMMUNITY PROPERTY

a. ☐ There are no such assets or debts that I know of to be divided by the court.

b. ☐ Determine rights to community and quasi-community assets and debts. All such assets and debts are listed

☐ in *Property Declaration* (form FL-160)   ☐ in Attachment 10b.

☐ as follows (specify):

11. OTHER REQUESTS

a. ☐ Attorney's fees and costs payable by   ☐ Petitioner   ☐ Respondent

b. ☐ Petitioner's former name be restored to (specify):

c. ☐ Other (specify):

☐ Continued on Attachment 11c.

12. I HAVE READ THE RESTRAINING ORDERS ON THE BACK OF THE SUMMONS, AND I UNDERSTAND THAT THEY APPLY TO ME WHEN THIS PETITION IS FILED.

I declare under penalty of perjury under the laws of the State of California that the foregoing is true and correct.

Date:

_____   ▶ _____
(TYPE OR PRINT NAME)   (SIGNATURE OF PETITIONER)

Date:

_____   ▶ _____
(TYPE OR PRINT NAME)   (SIGNATURE OF ATTORNEY FOR PETITIONER)

NOTICE: You may redact (black out) social security numbers from any written material filed with the court in this case other than a form used to collect child, spousal or partner support.

NOTICE—CANCELLATION OF RIGHTS: Dissolution or legal separation may automatically cancel the rights of a domestic partner or spouse under the other domestic partner's or spouse's will, trust, retirement plan, power of attorney, pay-on-death bank account, survivorship rights to any property owned in joint tenancy, and any other similar thing. It does not automatically cancel the right of a domestic partner or spouse as beneficiary of the other partner's or spouse's life insurance policy. You should review these matters, as well as any credit cards, other credit accounts, insurance polices, retirement plans, and credit reports, to determine whether they should be changed or whether you should take any other actions. Some changes may require the agreement of your partner or spouse or a court order.

FL-100 [Rev. January 1, 2015]   **PETITION—MARRIAGE/DOMESTIC PARTNERSHIP**   Page 3 of 3
(Family Law)

For your protection and privacy, please press the Clear This Form button after you have printed the form.   [Print this form] [Save this form]   [Clear this form]

FL-160

ATTORNEY OR PARTY WITHOUT ATTORNEY (Name, State Bar number, and address):	
TELEPHONE NO.: FAX NO. : E-MAIL ADDRESS: ATTORNEY FOR (Name):	
SUPERIOR COURT OF CALIFORNIA, COUNTY OF STREET ADDRESS: MAILING ADDRESS: CITY AND ZIP CODE: BRANCH NAME:	
PETITIONER: RESPONDENT: OTHER PARENT/PARTY:	

☐ **PETITIONER'S**   ☐ **RESPONDENT'S**
      ☐ **COMMUNITY AND QUASI-COMMUNITY PROPERTY DECLARATION**
      ☐ **SEPARATE PROPERTY DECLARATION**
	CASE NUMBER:

See *Instructions* on page 4 for information about completing this form. For additional space, use *Continuation of Property Declaration* (form FL-161).

A	B	C -	D =	E	F	
ITEM NO. BRIEF DESCRIPTION	DATE ACQUIRED	GROSS FAIR MARKET VALUE	AMOUNT OF DEBT	NET FAIR MARKET VALUE	PROPOSAL FOR DIVISION Award or Confirm to: PETITIONER	RESPONDENT
1. REAL ESTATE		$	$	$	$	$
2. HOUSEHOLD FURNITURE, FURNISHINGS, APPLIANCES						
3. JEWELRY, ANTIQUES, ART, COIN COLLECTIONS, etc.						
4. VEHICLES, BOATS, TRAILERS						
5. SAVINGS ACCOUNTS						
6. CHECKING ACCOUNTS						

Page 1 of 4

FL-160

A	B	C - D = E			F	
ITEM BRIEF DESCRIPTION NO.	DATE ACQUIRED	GROSS FAIR MARKET VALUE	AMOUNT OF DEBT	NET FAIR MARKET VALUE	PROPOSAL FOR DIVISION Award or Confirm to: PETITIONER	RESPONDENT
7. CREDIT UNION, OTHER DEPOSITORY ACCOUNTS		$	$	$	$	$
8. CASH						
9. TAX REFUND						
10. LIFE INSURANCE WITH CASH SURRENDER OR LOAN VALUE						
11. STOCKS, BONDS, SECURED NOTES, MUTUAL FUNDS						
12. RETIREMENT AND PENSIONS						

13. PROFIT-SHARING, IRAS,
     DEFERRED COMPENSATION,
     ANNUITIES						

14. ACCOUNTS RECEIVABLE, UNSECURED NOTES						
15. PARTNERSHIP, OTHER BUSINESS INTERESTS						
16. OTHER ASSETS						
17. ASSETS FROM CONTINUATION SHEET						
18. TOTAL ASSETS						

FL-160

A	B	C	D		
ITEM DEBTS— NO. SHOW TO WHOM OWED	DATE INCURRED	TOTAL OWING	PROPOSAL FOR DIVISION Award or Confirm to: PETITIONER　　RESPONDENT		
19. STUDENT LOANS		$	$		$
20. TAXES					
21. SUPPORT ARREARAGES					
22. LOANS—UNSECURED					
23. CREDIT CARDS					
24. OTHER DEBTS					
25. OTHER DEBTS FROM CONTINUATION SHEET					
26. TOTAL DEBTS					

☐ A *Continuation of Property Declaration* (form FL-161) is attached and incorporated by reference.

I declare under penalty of perjury under the laws of the State of California that, to the best of my knowledge, the foregoing is a true and correct listing of assets and obligations and the amounts shown are correct.

Date:

▶

_____
(TYPE OR PRINT NAME)

_____
SIGNATURE

FL-160

INFORMATION AND INSTRUCTIONS FOR COMPLETING FORM FL-160

Property Declaration (form FL-160) is a multipurpose form, which may be filed with the court as an attachment to a *Petition* or *Response* or served on the other party to comply with disclosure requirements in place of a *Schedule of Assets and Debts* (form FL-142). Courts may also require a party to file a *Property Declaration* as an attachment to a *Request to Enter Default* (form FL-165) or *Judgment* (form FL-180).

When filing a *Property Declaration* with the court, do not include private financial documents listed below.

Identify the type of declaration completed
1. Check "Community and Quasi-Community Property Declaration" on page 1 to use *Property Declaration* (form FL-160) to provide a combined list of community and quasi-community property assets and debts. Quasi-community property is property you own outside of California that would be community property if it were located in California.

2. Do not combine a separate property declaration with a community and quasi-community property declaration. Check "Separate Property Declaration" on page 1 when using *Property Declaration* to provide a list of separate property assets and debts.

Description of the Property Declaration chart
Pages 1 and 2
1. Column A is used to provide a brief description of each item of separate or community or quasi-community property.
2. Column B is used to list the date the item was acquired.
3. Column C is used to list the item's gross fair market value (an estimate of the amount of money you could get if you sold the item to another person through an advertisement).
4. Column D is used to list the amount owed on the item.
5. Column E is used to indicate the net fair market value of each item. The net fair market value is calculated by subtracting the dollar amount in column D from the amount in column C ("C minus D").
6. Column F is used to show a proposal on how to divide (or confirm) the item described in column A.
Page 3
1. Column A is used to provide a brief description of each separate or community or quasi-community property debt.
2. Column B is used to list the date the debt was acquired.
3. Column C is used to list the total amount of money owed on the debt.
4. Column D is used to show a proposal on how to divide (or confirm) the item of debt described in column A.

When using this form only as an attachment to a *Petition* or *Response*
1. Attach a *Separate Property Declaration* to respond to item 4. Only columns A and F on pages 1 and 2, and columns A D on page 3 are required.
2. Attach a *Community or Quasi-Community Declaration* to respond to item 5, and complete column A on all pages.

When serving this form on the other party as an attachment to *Declaration of Disclosure* (form FL-140)
1. Complete columns A through E on pages 1 and 2, and columns A through C on page 3.
2. Copies of the following documents must be attached and served on the other party:
   (a) *For real estate* (item 1): deeds with legal descriptions and the latest lender's statement.
   (b) *For vehicles, boats, trailers* (item 4): the title documents.
   (c) *For all bank accounts* (item 5, 6, 7): the latest statement.
   (d) *For life insurance policies with cash surrender or loan value* (item 10): the latest declaration page.
   (e) *For stocks, bonds, secured notes, mutual funds* (item 11): the certificate or latest statement.
   (f) *For retirement and pensions* (item 12): the latest summary plan document and latest benefit statement.
   (g) *For profit-sharing, IRAs, deferred compensation, and annuities* (item 13): the latest statement.
   (h) *For each account receivable and unsecured note* (item 14): documentation of the account receivable or note.
   (i) *For partnerships and other business interests* (item 15): the most current K-1 and Schedule C.
   (j) *For other assets* (item 16): the most current statement, title document, or declaration.
   (k) *For support arrearages* (item 21): orders and statements.
   (l) *For credit cards and other debts* (items 23 and 24): the latest statement.
3. Do not file copies of the above private financial documents with the court.

When filing this form with the court as a attachment to *Request to Enter Default* (FL-165) or *Judgment* (FL-180)
Complete all columns on the form.

For more information about forms required to process and obtain a judgment in dissolution, legal separation, and nullity cases, see http://www.courts.ca.gov/selfhelp-divorcesteps.htm.

FL-160 [Rev. July 1, 2013]   **PROPERTY DECLARATION**   Page 4 of 4
(Family Law)

For your protection and privacy, please press the Clear This Form button after you have printed the form.   [Print this form]   [Save this form]   [Clear this form]

APPENDIX C

EXAMPLE BUSINESS
VALUATION MATERIALS

■ ■ ■

FRANCHISE BUSINESS VALUATION EXAMPLES

Tom West, BUSINESS REFERENCE GUIDE: THE ESSENTIAL GUIDE TO PRICING BUSINESSES AND FRANCHISES 1–5 (26th ed. 2016), by permission of Business Brokerage Press (businessbrokeragepress.com) and Tom West.

Rules of Thumb - **A**

Franchise

A&W Restaurants (A&W Root Beer) (See also Franchises)	
Estimated Annual Sales/Unit	$290,000

SIC 5812-06	NAICS 722513	Number of Businesses/Units 1,000 +

Rules of Thumb

➢ 45 percent of annual sales plus inventory

Benchmark Data

- "Recommended square footage is between 1,500 and 2,000 square feet ..."

Resources

Websites
- www.awrestaurants.com

Franchise

AAMCO Transmission (See also Auto Transmission Centers, Franchises)	
Approx. Total Investment	$227,000 to $333,000
Estimated Annual Sales/Unit	$645,000

SIC 7537-01	NAICS 811113	Number of Businesses/Units 700+

Rules of Thumb

➢ 40 to 42 percent of annual sales plus inventory

➢ 2 to 3 times EBITDA

➢ An industry rule of thumb for AAMCO is 20 times average weekly sales for the past 16–26 weeks for a shop that has average weekly sales of less than $20,000 per week, and up to 27 times average weekly sales for shops above $20,000 per week.

Pricing Tips

- "One observation is that franchised shops who are following the model with a good manager are successful. The typical shop has three technicians, a rebuilder and two mechanics, and a manager. Most of the franchised shops have an owner who oversees but might be considered absentee.

  "The better way to analyze a business is from a well-defined proforma as opposed to tax returns and financial statements. Looking at the top line on the tax return, I sell from a proforma using market values for parts, cost and labor."

  "Detailed weekly reports provided to the franchisor are more important documents for analyzing historical performance than financial statements and tax returns, as these reports will reveal the prices charged ratio of major/minor repairs and warranty repairs."

- "Established shops with a manager in the expenses:
  Small Shops—Less than $20,000 per week

26th Edition   **1**

A - Rules of Thumb

- ✓ Sixteen to twenty (16–20) times weekly sales for the last 26 weeks—and/ or one and one half (1.5) to three (3) times adjusted earnings (EBITDA). If the seller is the manager or builder—assets plus one year's SDE.
- ✓ "Minimum sale price for an established, poorly performing, franchised transmission shop that is in a proven location which historically has been profitable but has recent sales which at least are 'breakeven' ($8,000 to $10,000 per week) is no less than the total cost it would take to put in a new franchise and reach breakeven—typically $195,000 to $225,000."

"Large Shops—$20,000 per week and higher
- ✓ Twenty to Thirty (20–30) times average weekly sales for the last 26 weeks—and/or two (2) to three (3) times adjusted earnings (EBITDA).

Expert Comments

"Typically a buyer assumes responsibility for warranty repairs. In my analysis I look at this very carefully and at the compensation to the rebuilder to see if it is too low."

"The Internet has changed the marketing and advertising model—lowering cost but making it more difficult for the small independent to compete with the franchises in the major market areas."

Benchmark Data

Expenses as a percentage of annual sales

Production labor costs	20%
Sales/Labor	08% to 10%
Occupancy	06% to 10%
Profit (estimated pretax)	10% to 20%

Percentage of Gross Sales: (where they should be):

Sales	100%

Cost of Sales:

Parts & Fluids	22%
Production Labor (All Technical Employees)	20%
Towing	1%
Misc. Production Supplies	3%
Total Cost of Sales	46%

Sales & Administration Expenses:

Salaries (Center Mgr. & Office)	10%
Rent	8%
Insurance	3%
Utilities	1%
Advertising-Yellow Pages	8%
Telephone	1%
Legal/Accounting	1%
Bank Fees/Bad Debt	1%
Training	1%
Total Sales & Administration Expenses	34%
Net Profit	20%

Seller Financing

- ▪ "50 percent down—five (5) years"

Resources

Websites
- AAMCO Franchises:www.aamcofranchises.com

Accounting Firms/CPAs (See also Accounting Firms)		
SIC 8721-01	NAICS 541211	Number of Businesses/Units 121,125

Rules of Thumb

➤ 100 to 125 percent of annual revenues plus inventory

➤ 1.8 to 3 times SDE plus inventory

➤ 2 times EBIT

➤ 2.2 times EBITDA

Pricing Tips

- "Most practices will sell for a minimum of 1 x earnings. Anywhere from 1.0 to 1.5 x sales. Profitability and location are some of the most important variables when determining asking price."
- "In Florida I find the multiples of SDE to be slightly lower than 2. Important to understand that generally speaking CPA and accounting practice sales will require the seller to stay on for at least one tax season and that there typically will include an earnout structure. It is important that purchaser has a similar style to seller to maximize client retention."
- "Premiums paid above 100% of gross revenues for above average net income (of 45%), location (major metro area), special expertise (tax, etc.), established clientele with above average fees."
- "Even distribution of revenue from tax return preparation and accounting fees is better."
- "CPAs commonly use 1 times gross although we have frequently exceeded that amount."
- "Product mix and any special areas of practice can affect selling price to the right buyer. There is always the possibility to split up a practice among two or more buyers if specialty work is involved."
- "Revenue composition is important; retail tax, write-up, monthly accounting, review work, audit, consulting, types of revenue streams—all have an effect on sale's price."
- "Generally sold based on an annual multiple of gross revenue."
- "Biggest factor is the terms and whether seller will guarantee part or all of the income."
- "SDE should be between 40% and 60% of revenue."
- "CPA buyers always want to pay 1 times gross . . . sellers tend to want more . . . terms drive price."
- "1 to 1.25 times revenue, with SDE of 30% to 60% of gross revenue."
- "Employees on non-compete will increase; composition of services, accounts receivable, pricing of client work, recovery percentages. These last few will swing price in both directions."
- "Accounting, tax, bookkeeping, EA and/or CPA firms typically sell for 100% to 135% of annual gross revenue. They tend to sell for 2–4 times SDE."

A - Rules of Thumb

- "Sale price should yield an SDE range of 40% to 60%."
- "Location is paramount. Same practice will sell for 1.3 times gross revenue in one location and 1 times gross revenue in another."
- "The composition of billings is important. The split between recurring/one time. The split among taxes/accounting/audit/consulting/other is important in determining staff composition. Labor costs are extremely important in bottom line. Accounts receivable levels may indicate problems with billings and/or clients."
- "The commonly accepted rule of thumb is one times annual gross sales. The biggest cause for variation from this (50% more or less) is location. Prices in big metro areas are seldom that low. Prices in rural areas are often not that high. Also, it is VERY important to consider the wide variation in definition of 'one times annual gross.' One definition is a total 'work out' situation paying seller 20% of collection each year for five years. On the other end of the scale is a check for all cash at closing with no seller risk regarding retention of clients. These differences in definition of 'price' can mean that actual present value can vary by as much as 100% depending on definition used. Owners (sellers) and buyers are often very confused and misled regarding these issues."
- "Sales price will be the lesser of 1.3 times gross revenues or 3 times SDE—and will include FF&E."
- "CPA firms typically sell for 100% to 130% of Annual Gross Sales. Larger firms typically demand a higher percentage. Small single CPA offices may only warrant 100%. The size, training, and qualifications of the firm's staff have an impact on pricing."
- "Earnouts are used for most do-it-yourselfers."

Expert Comments

"Buyer will need to be a CPA or have an accounting background in order to buy the business. It is a specialized and niche field. Buyers will need this education and background in order to retain the existing client base. Not everyone who wants to buy a business will be able to buy an accounting or tax practice."

"Although I don't think ease of replication is that difficult, I've found that the personality types that are drawn to CPA/accounting practices are not strong in sales, and as a result they usually need to purchase rather than start a practice. I have many CPA/accounting buyers so I would say marketability is high."

"Great buyer demand....difficult industry to grow organically."

"Most smaller CPA firms either specialize in a type of industry audit or avoid all audits. The special industry audit firm may be more difficult to sell due to small demand."

"Competition is aging and the regulating agencies are making an impact on various areas of practice, in particular taxation. Accountants are usually not very good at generating new business so acquisitions are a key growth strategy."

"The profit trend and industry trend is upward due to increased tax and government regulations on businesses and individuals. Location and facilities are located in office or upscale retail locations. A profitable, well-

Rules of Thumb - **A**

balanced CPA practice is highly marketable to those entering the profession from corporate and established firms to expand their client base. Replication or opening a practice is not difficult. Establishing a client base is the challenge for a new CPA practice."

"Although a very stable industry, current government regulations and the changes of such have put increasing demand on service. There is also a decline in numbers of people entering and staying in public accounting."

"Risk of client loss is the biggest factor in a purchase."

"The marketability of accounting firms is much greater in major metro areas but still fairly marketable even in rural areas."

"People don't leave their CPA often—so there's competition but it doesn't affect established firms much. Very low risk—very few CPAs go out of business. Profits are up although firms can be adversely affected by local trends—i.e., Silicon Valley fallout where CPAs have a concentration in a particular industry. Facilities are often Class A buildings. There's definitely a market for CPA firms but finding the right buyer is difficult. The industry is increasing while fewer people enter the profession. Replicating an existing practice is often very difficult and the reason we sell 400+ practices a year."

"The accounting/tax industry as it pertains to small privately owned locations has been steady for some years. Profitability has always been high and replication difficult, especially in the CPA field. As for risk, CPAs are the second best rated business loans to make—their default rate is very low."

Benchmark Data

Statistics (Accounting Services)

Number of Establishments	123,984
Average Profit Margin	17.8%
Revenue per Employee	$186,600
Average Number of Employees	4.5
Average Wages per Employee	$67,511

Products and Services Segmentation

Financial auditing services	34.1%
Other services	19.1%
Corporate tax preparation and representative services	13.5%
Individual tax preparation and representative services	11.1%
Tax planning and consulting services	10.4%
General accounting services	5.6%
Financial statement review services	3.4%
Other financial assurance services	2.8%

Major Market Segmentation

Other businesses	23.5%
Finance sector	20.7%
Individuals	18.0%
Manufacturing sector	12.7%
Retail sector	10.7%
Utilities and mining sector	6.6%
Nonprofit organizations	4.7%
Federal, state and local government	3.1%

LAW FIRM BUSINESS VALUATION EXAMPLE

Tom West, BUSINESS REFERENCE GUIDE: THE ESSENTIAL GUIDE TO PRICING BUSINESSES AND FRANCHISES 442–444 (26th ed. 2016), by permission of Business Brokerage Press (businessbrokeragepress.com) and Tom West.

L - Rules of Thumb

sophisticated technologies, such as remote sensing and GPS, will continue to increase the precision and productivity of these workers. Opportunities for surveyors, cartographers, and photogrammetrists should remain concentrated in engineering, surveying, mapping, building inspection, and drafting services firms."

Source: "Latest trends in the Economic Outlook for Land Surveyors," www.landsurveyor4hire.com

- "The executive director of the National Society of Professional Surveyors (NSPS) told members of a Congressional subcommittee that the U.S. Department of Labor's recent decision to categorize survey crew members as 'laborers and mechanics' was 'detrimental to the surveying profession,' and requested Congress' help in reversing DOL's decision."

Source: "Press Release from the National Society of Professional Surveyors concerning the Davis-Bacon Act," www.amerisurv.com, June 19, 2013

Resources

Trade Publications
- Professional Surveyor magazine: www.profsurv.com

Associations
- The National Society of Professional Surveyors: http://www.nsps.us.com/

		Franchise
Laptop Xchange (See also Computer Stores)		
Approx. Total Investment		$183,750 to $267,800
	NAICS 443142	Number of Businesses/Units 20

Rules of Thumb
➢ 80 to 85 percent of annual sales plus inventory

Resources

Websites
- www.laptopxchange.com

Law Firms		
SIC 8111-03	NAICS 541110	Number of Businesses/Units 468,202

Rules of Thumb
➢ 90 to 100 percent of annual fee revenue; firms specializing in estate work would approach 100 percent; may require earnout.

➢ 4 times SDE includes inventory

➢ 3.5 times EBIT

➢ 3.5 times EBITDA

Pricing Tips
- "A lot will depend upon the consultants, and how loyal they are to the firm."

Rules of Thumb - **L**

- "Whether the multiplier is in the lower or the higher level of the range depends primarily on how much repeat business is expected, the nature of the law practice, the number of clients and the transferability of client relationships. If there is a great deal of repeat business and client loyalty that can be transferred, the multiplier will be higher. In the sale of a law practice, a portion of the clients will not stay with the practice by reason of the close personal relationship usually developed between client and attorney. This must be considered when determining the multiplier. The multiplier may then be raised or lowered depending on the stability of the flow of future revenue expected."

Source: "Valuing Professional Practices and Licenses"

Expert Comments

"It is difficult to replicate, as the good businesses have reputations built over many years."

Benchmark Data

Statistics (Law Firms)

Number of Establishments	468,202
Average Profit Margin	18.1%
Revenue per Employee	$205,600
Average Number of employees	2.9
Average Wages per Employee	$77,114

Products and Services Segmentation

Commercial law services	43.6%
Other services	26.0%
Criminal law, civil negligence and personal injury	16.9%
Real estate law	8.1%
Labor and employment	5.4%

Major Market Segmentation

Business and corporate clients	66.1%
Households	29.1%
Government and not-for-profit clients	4.8%

Industry Costs

Profit	18.1%
Wages	37.7%
Purchases	1.8%
Depreciation	0.9%
Marketing	1.6%
Rent & Utilities	6.0%
Other	33.9%

Source: IBISWorld, April 2015

Enterprises by Employment Size

No. of Employees	Share %
1 to 4	88.3
5 to 9	5.6
10 to 19	2.8
20 to 99	2.1
100 to 499	0.8
500+	0.4%

Source: IBISWorld, May 2014

L - Rules of Thumb

Expenses as a percentage of annual sales

Cost of goods	0
Payroll/labor Costs	0
Occupancy	0
Profit (estimated pretax)	30%

Industry Trend

- "Consistent with past practices, firms continued to raise their rates in 2014, albeit at a fairly modest level of 3.1 percent. And, also consistent with past experience, clients continued to push back, keeping strong pressure on firm realization rates. Over this ten-year period (2005 through November 2014), firms increased their standard rates by 35.9 percent from an average of $348 per hour to $473 (or an average increase of about 3.6 percent per year). At the same time, reflecting mounting client push back to these rate hikes, the collected rates achieved by law firms increased by a somewhat more modest 28.2 percent over the ten-year period, from an average of $304 per hour to $390 (or an average increase of about 2.8 percent per year). While the market for law firm services has clearly been impacted by external factors, there has also been an important shift in the internal dynamics of the market that has become increasingly apparent in recent years. Specifically, there is now strong evidence that the U.S. legal market has segmented into discernible categories of highly successful and less successful firms, and that the performance gaps between those categories has been steadily widening."
  Source: http://www.law.georgetown.edu/academics/centers-institutes/legal-profession/upload/FINAL-Report-1-7-15.pdf

- "For practically everyone else in Big Law, the future looks chaotic. Client fee pressures will be matched by the cost overhang of the pre-recession go-go era. Young lawyers will increasingly struggle to establish a foothold. To protect their personal pocketbooks, firms are lengthening the path to partnership amid an oversupply of fresh labor. The Bureau of Labor Statistics estimates that during the decade ending in 2020, the U.S. economy will create 73,600 lawyer positions. Law schools are pumping out 25,000 graduates a year, suggesting an excess of 176,400 JDs no one really needs."
  Source: "Law firms are merging and growing like conglomerates. Sharp young minds keep flooding into law schools. But as D.C.-based Howrey discovered, Big Law is about to get small," by Paul M. Barrett, *Businessweek*

- "Fast growing. Litigation is becoming larger and larger, especially in the medical, accounting and technical fields."

Questions

- "What is their backlog? Customer concentration?"

Lawn Maintenance & Service (See also Landscaping Services)		
SIC 0782-06	NAICS 561730	Number of Businesses/Units 39,000

Rules of Thumb

- 50 to 60 percent of annual sales plus inventory
- 2 to 2.75 times SDE plus inventory
- 1.7 to 3 times EBIT
- 2 to 4 times EBITDA

INDEX

References are to Pages

ACCOUNT, *see* DEMAND DEPOSIT ACCOUNTS

ACCOUNTING
Accounting methods,
    Contemporaneous accounting, *see* DEMAND DEPOSIT ACCOUNTS
    Total recap accounting, *see* SEPARATE PROPERTY BUSINESS PROFITS
Equitable right to, *see* MANAGEMENT AND CONTROL

AGREEMENTS BETWEEN SPOUSES
    See also PREMARITAL CONTRACTS *and* TRANSMUTATIONS
Marriage settlement agreement, 3, 94, 114

AMERICAN LAW INSTITUTE, *see* EQUITABLE DISTRIBUTION STATES

"AMERICANIZED" RULES
Community property contributions to separate property credit acquisition, 358–359
Hybridity, 166
Original solutions to recurring problems, 165, 169
Separate property business profits, 376
Separate property rents, issues, and profits, 161, 324
    Distinguished from
        Appreciation, 88
        Community rents, issues, and profits, 509
        Income stream, 388
    Tracing rule, Family Code, 158

APPRECIATION
Appreciation,
    Defined, 87
Asset, defined, 87
Distinguished from rents, issues, and profits, 88

ASSET, *see* APPRECIATION

CALIFORNIA COMMUNITY PROPERTY SYSTEM
    See also CALIFORNIA CONTEXT

California Multiple-Party Accounts Law (CAMPAL), 132, 134–138, 325–334
Contractual modification principle, 33
    Legal transitions, 35
    Premarital agreement, *see* CALIFORNIA PREMARITAL AGREEMENT ACT (CPAA)
Disclosure,
    Books and records, Corporations Code, 479
Equitable doctrines, *see* NONMARITAL INTIMATE PARTNERS
    Equitable marriage doctrine, rejected, 271
    Equitable spousal support doctrine, rejected, 271
    Marvin v. Marvin (CA), 258
Management and control of community property, 8, 428
Nonmarried partners, and, 12, 257, 437–439
Ownership of community property, 8
Persons outside system, 233
Policy goals of a marital property system generally, 9, 427
Property excluded from the community property system, 198–199
    Professional degrees, 199–215
        Community contributions to education or training, 199–204, 205
        Burden of proof, 207
        California Law Revision Commission rationale, 204
        Direct costs of education, 206, 214
        Educational loans, 205, 206
        Indirect costs of education, and spousal support claim, 210, 214
        Contractual modification, and, 207
        Creditors' rights, generally, 214–215
        Educational loans, Family Code, 205
        Family expenses, Family Code, 503
    Defined, 199

Division of property, compared
    with reimbursement, 202
Domicile, and, 206, 287
Duty of support during
    marriage, and, 214
Early cases,
    Aarons v. Brash (CA), 200,
        214
    In re Marriage of
        Aufmuth (CA), 201,
        228
    Todd v. Todd (CA), 200,
        228
Loans,
    Educational loans,
        Family Code, 205
    General loans, 214, 496
Mandatory offsets, 202
Other jurisdictions, 202–203
Postdissolution efforts and
    earnings, 201
Presumption affecting the
    community, 202, 205
Professional degree,
    As community
        investment, 199,
        202, 205
    As property, 199, 201
Realization of investment, 202,
    205
Reimbursement statute, Family
    Code, 205
    Interest claimable,
        Family Code, 205
Substantial income
    enhancement, question of
    fact, 207–210
Threshold-marriage defined, 199
Talent, 215
    Character of, 228
    Distinguished from,
        Accumulations, 232
        Celebrity, 230
        Education, 228–229
        Goodwill, 229–230
        Intellectual property, 231,
            320
        Labor contribution to a
            separate property
            business, 386, 398
        Patent infringement
            claims, 232
        Qui Tam Action, 232–233
        Right of publicity, 230
    In re Marriage of McTiernan &
        Dubrow (CA), 215–228,
        387
    Transferability, 215, 228
Retroactivity, 288, 295
Sui generis system, as a, 20
Title, role of, 5

CALIFORNIA CONTEXT
    See also CALIFORNIA
        COMMUNITY PROPERTY
        SYSTEM
Constitutions and Acts,
    1849 Constitution, 7, 21
    1850 Organic Act, 7, 22–24, 34, 157,
        274
    1879 Constitution, 21
    1969 Family Law Act, 529
    1974 Amendment, 21, 157
    1992 Family Code (effective 1994),
        28, 234, 529
    Separate property protections, 157
Counties, 26
Court system, 25
    COURT STATISTICS REPORTS, annual,
        28
    Court Website, 25
    Dissolution, legal separation, nullity,
        number of petitions, 27
    Domestic violence, number of
        petitions, 27
    Domestic violence petitions relative
        to dissolution petitions, 27
    Family and Juvenile Court, 27
    Language protections, 25–26
    Structure of courts, 26
        Appellate courts and districts,
            27
        Supreme Court, 27
        Trial courts, 27
Dissolution, 529
    Informal dissolution, not recognized
        by state, 257
Divorce, *see* Dissolution
Factual context for state community
    property system, 25–29
Family Code,
    See also CALIFORNIA
        COMMUNITY
        PROPERTY SYSTEM
    Comprehensive coverage of, 28
    Origins of, 28
    Public welfare, and, 279–280
George v. Ransom (CA), 164
Hybridity, complexity in the community
    property system, 166–170
    Doctrine of precedent, 169
    Idaho example, 166–168
    Mauritius, as postcolonial system,
        168–169
    Original solutions, as, 165, 169
Male-management era, and, 157
Organic Act (1850), 7, 22–24, 34, 157, 274
Tort award characterizations, Family Code,
    172
    See also PERSONAL INJURY
        CLAIMS, MONEY, AWARDS
Tracing principle, development and
    consequences, 165
Treaty of Guadalupe Hidalgo (1848), 7

CALIFORNIA FAMILY CODE, *see* CHARACTERIZATION

CALIFORNIA MULTIPLE-PARTY ACCOUNTS LAW (CAMPAL)
See also DEMAND DEPOSIT ACCOUNTS
Community property presumption, Probate Code, 136, 325
  Rebuttal of, 337
    Agreement, Probate Code, 136
    Tracing, Probate Code, 136
Default account,
  Community property, for married depositors, 329
  Joint tenancy, for unmarried depositors, 328
Definitions,
  Access, 325
  Account, 326
  Beneficial ownership of sums on deposit in an account, 325, 330
  Community property account, 329
  Community property with the right of survivorship, 328
  Excess withdrawal, 334
  Joint account, 327
  "Net," 332
  "Net character," 5339, 333
  "Net character contribution," Probate Code, 331
  "Net character deposit" defined, 331, 333
  "Net community property" deposit, 331, 333
  "Net contribution," Probate Code, 330
  "Net deposit," 332
  Family expense presumption, and, 332, 333
  "Net separate property" deposit, provable, 331, 333
  Reimbursement right, Probate Code, 333
Excess withdrawal claims, 334
Family Code rights, compared with, 333
  Sole account, 327
  Survivorship rights, and, 328
  Withdrawal right, synonymous with access, 326
Purchase from a commingled account, *see* PRESUMPTIONS

CALIFORNIA PREMARITAL AGREEMENT ACT (CPAA)
Consent, 11
Default contract terms for marital partnership, 6, 9
Disclosure, Family Code, 42
Legal hybridity, 19–21
Legal scholarship, 24–25
"Legal transitions," chart, 35
  1985 CPAA, 34
  2001 CPAA, 35, 33–44, 508

  Pre-CPAA law, 35
Marriage, partnership model, 3, 6
Personal injury claims, 171
Personal injury settlements, money and property from third-party tortfeasor, 176–177
  Assignment at dissolution, Family Code, 176
  Community property, Family Code, 172
  Contributory negligence, between spouse and third-party, 172–176
  Separate property, Family Code, 172
  Tracing, 177–183
  Wrongful death awards, 183
Personal injury settlements, money and property, spouse versus spouse, 183–185
Spousal support waivers, *see* MARRIAGE CONTRACT
Sui generis, 20
Systemic foundations, 3, 6–12, 427
  Contractual modification principle, 20, 29, 33–76
  Equality of interest principle, 20, 29, 31–33
  General definitions and rules, for apportionment, 323–324
  Tracing principle, 20, 29–31
Third party confidence, 6
Transmutations, 44
Voluntariness, Family Code, 43

CHARACTERIZATION
See also COMMUNITY PROPERTY
Acquisition time line, 84
Community property statute, Family Code, 85
  "All . . . except" format, 86
  "All property, real or personal wherever situated . . . ," 87
  Principal rather than definition, 88
  Rents, issues, and profits included, 88
  Tracing principle, implied, 29, 88
Property, division compared with characterization, 82
Significance of, 82–84
Quasi-community property, 84, 715, 274
Quasi-marital property, 81, 238–252

CHILD CUSTODY
Family Code coverage, 8

CIVIL LAW
Code-based system, 14, 166
Mineral leases, 398
  Exceptions to civil law usufruct, 398
Reimbursement for community contribution to separate property credit purchase, 359
Separate property business profits, 376
Usufruct, 162, 166

COMMINGLED ASSETS
See also CREDIT ACQUISITIONS
    and SEPARATE PROPERTY
    BUSINESS PROFITS
Basic rules, 323
Burden of proof,
    Commingled credit acquisition
        record-keeping, 372
    Disclosure of business and
        investment opportunities, 111–
        113
    Disclosure of credit card transactions,
        491
    Proving separate property business,
        388
    See v. See (CA) compliant record-
        keeping duty, 343
Community contributions to purchase, *see*
    "AMERICANIZED" RULES
Credit acquisitions secured by the
    purchased asset, 358–359
De minimis principle, 352
    Reverse *de minimis* principle,
        compared with, 352
Defined, 29, 31, 323–324
General definition, 323
Inception of title rule, 323
Pro tanto ownership, defined, 362
    Distinguished from equitable
        ownership, 362–364
Proportional ownership, permitted, 332
Reimbursement, when available, 458
Tracing rules, general, 29, 323

COMMINGLED PROPERTY, *see*
    COMMINGLED ASSETS

COMMUNITY PROPERTY
See also CALIFORNIA
    COMMUNITY PROPERTY
    SYSTEM
Basic statute, Family Code, 85
    Understood as elastic, 88
Characterization, modes of, 83
Contract modification, 33
Date of acquisition during marriage, 81, 82,
    84
Domicile, 82, 84, 287
Elements, 82
    Acquisition during marriage, 81, 82,
        84
    Domiciled in state, 82, 84, 287
    Onerous/effort, 82, 147–156
    Valid marriage, 235
Equality of interest, Family Code, 32
General presumption,
    See also PRESUMPTIONS
    Title in one spouse's name alone, 84,
        89
    Untitled assets, 89, 96
Judicial discretion,
    To characterize property, 82

To raise general community property
    presumption, 90
Lucrative title, 148
Management and control, categories, in
    California, 508
    Equal, 428
    Exclusive,
        Conservatorship, one spouse in,
            510
        Court order, by, 511
        Restraining orders, 512–514
        See also DOMESTIC
            VIOLENCE
            PREVENTION
        Sole bank account, access, 509
        See also DEMAND
            DEPOSIT
            ACCOUNTS
    Joint, 463
    Primary, 509
Onerous title, 147
Personal property, 87
Possession,
    Compared with acquisition, 100
    Presumption, as basis for, 96–97
    Proxy for acquisition, as, 100
Real property, 87
Superseding presumptions, *see*
    PRESUMPTIONS
    Joint form title in a dissolution
        proceeding, Family Code, 125
    Sums on deposit in a demand deposit
        account, Probate Code, 136
Tracing principle, 29, 85

COMMUNITY PROPERTY
    JURISDICTIONS IN THE U.S.
Code-based classification system, as, 14
Community estate,
    Start date, 3
    Termination date, 529
Common law title approach, compared
    with, 4–5, 13–15
Deferred community property systems,
    compared with, 15
Equitable distribution systems, compared
    with, 5, 13–19
Immediate shared ownership systems,
    ganancial, 16
    Arizona, 4
    California, 4
    Idaho, 4
    Louisiana, 4
    Nevada, 4
    New Mexico, 4
    Texas, 4
    Washington, 4
Uniform Marital Property Act System state,
    Wisconsin, 4

COMMUNITY PROPERTY
    LIQUIDATION JURISDICTIONS
Puerto Rico, 4

COMMUNITY PROPERTY OPTION JURISDICTIONS IN THE U.S.
Alaska, 4
Tennessee, 4

COMPLICATING FACTORS IN AN EQUAL DIVISION
Commingling,
 Example, 5
 Tracing principle, implied, 29
Emotion, 6
Legal hybridity, 166–170

CONTRACTS, *see* MARRIAGE CONTRACT

CREDIT ACQUISITIONS
Acquisition date, 358
Appreciation, 161, 353
Burden of proof, 323, 372
Commingled, 353
Contributions to purchase, 323, 362, 367
Law restated as tracing formula,
 Aufmuth/Moore formula, 367
 Basic tracing formula, 102
  Aufmuth modification to, 358
 Moore/Marsden formula, 371
  Community property
   repayment of separate
   property loan as
   contribution, 367
 Tracing, and doctrine of confusion, 372
In re Marriage of Aufmuth (CA), loan
 proceeds as contribution to purchase,
 355
 Superseded in part, 354, 358
In re Marriage of Geraci (CA), doctrine of
 confusion applies, 373
 Doctrine of confusion, Family Code,
  45, 323, 372
In re Marriage of *Marsden* (CA), premarital
 appreciation and equity reimbursed,
 368
In re Marriage of Moore (CA), community
 loan repayments as contributions to
 purchase, 363
Inception of title rule applies, 323
Principle, interest, taxes, insurance rule
 applies, 362
Pro tanto share, 353, 362
 Distinguished from equitable
  ownership, 362
 Vieux v. Vieux (CA), 359
Tracing principle applies, 323

CREDITORS' CLAIMS
Contract obligations, after date of
 separation, 498
 Contracting spouse, liability of, 499
 Noncontracting spouse, liability of,
  498, 499
Contract obligations during marriage, 499
 Common necessaries of life,
  Doctrine, 499

Mutual obligations during
 marriage, Family Code, 33
Personal liability for debts
 incurred by spouse,
 Family Code, 505
Family expenses, 33, 498
Necessaries of life,
 Doctrine, 498
 Personal liability for debts
  incurred by spouse,
  Family Code, 505
Judgment creditors,
 Child support obligations not arising
  out of marriage, Family Code,
  505–506
 Liability for injury or damages
  caused by spouse, Family Code,
  508
 Spousal support obligations not
  arising out of marriage, Family
  Code, 505–506
 Tort judgment, order of satisfaction,
  500
Lender's intent test, 139, 500
Managerial approach, policy, 427–428,
 441–440
Partnership Act,
 Managerial approach, 497
 Meinhard v. Salmon (NY), 432
 Revised Uniform Partnership Act, 496
 Uniform Partnership Act, 496
Premarital debts,
 Earnings shield, Family Code, 504
Premarital debts, closed and open, 502
Premarital support obligations, 502–503
Quasi-community property, liability of, 501
Quasi-marital property, liability of, 501
Real property located in another state,
 liability of, 502
Rights of, 162–163
Secured creditors, compared with
 unsecured creditors, 497
Tort judgments for injury or damage
 caused by spouse, Family Code, 508
 Order of satisfaction approach
  applies, 500
 Property subject to satisfaction of
  liability, Family Code, 508
 Reimbursement right limitations,
  Family Code, 508
 Satisfaction out of insurance
  proceeds, Family Code, 508

DATE OF SEPARATION
Date of separation, formerly living separate
 and apart, 191–192
Earnings and accumulations,
 Adverse possession, 194
 Defined as separate property, Family
  Code, 185
 Defined by case law, 193–194
 Sweepstakes winnings, 194

Hardin-Manfer test, 186, 187, 188–189
Codified, Family Code, 187
Historical approach, 190
In re Marriage of Davis (CA), abrogated by
California Legislature in 2016, 186
Facts of, 189–190
Evidence on review, 190
Outcome of California Supreme Court
Decision, 187
Unconscious gender bias in, 191, 192
In re Marriage of Norviel (CA), abrogated
by California Legislature in 2016, 186
Male-management era, and, 190–191
Objective test versus subjective test, 188–
189
Other legal effects, 194
Other states, 186
Formal date of separation states, 186
Informal date of separation states, 186
Physical date of separation states, 186
Petition for dissolution, and, 193
Recent precedent, 191–192
Roommates, living as, 189
Subjective versus objective test, 188–189
Uniform Marriage and Divorce Act,
compared with, 192

DEATH
Allocation of debt, 758
Last illness and funeral expenses,
Probate Code, 761
Statutes of limitation, 788
Trust assets, 765
Income tax consequences of
characterization at death, for
surviving spouse, 735–736
Intestate distribution, Probate Code, 753
Joint form titles at death, 730
Unilateral creation, 735
Unilateral severance, 735
Nonprobate transfers,
At death of a former spouse, 76
At death of a spouse, 730
Probate Code, basics, 714
Definitions, Probate Code, 714–715
Simultaneous death, Probate Code,
717
Surviving spouse, exalted status of, 718, 729
Will requirements, Probate Code, 718–719

DEMAND DEPOSIT ACCOUNTS
Account, 325
Accounts, access, 325
Add-a-name remedy, *see*
MANAGEMENT AND
CONTROL
Accounts, default,
Community property, for married
depositors, 329
Joint tenancy, for unmarried
depositors, 328
Accounts, opt in,

Community property with right of
survivorship, for married
depositors, 328
Tenancy in common, for unmarried
depositors, 328
Beneficial ownership of sums on deposit,
325, 330
Breach of fiduciary duty, *see*
MANAGEMENT AND CONTROL
Commingled account, 337
Character of purchase, 333
Disputed as matter of law, 337
De minimis principle, 352
Reverse *de minimis* principle, 352
Disclosure, 352
See also MANAGEMENT AND
CONTROL
Excess withdrawal claim, 334
Family expense presumption, 332, 343
Net character deposits, 333
Net deposits, 332
Policy, 330
Rebuttal of community property
presumption,
General community property
presumption as to purchases,
102, 334
See v. See (CA), exhaustion
rebuttal, 337
Disclosure, *see*
MANAGEMENT
AND CONTROL
Dissolution, 345
Exhaustion of community
sums on date of
purchase, 339
Forensic records, 346
Probate, 345
Retrospective analysis,
344
See-compliant records,
elements to
establish, 338
Standard bank account
records, 349
Tracing principle applies,
344
Hicks-Mix direct tracing, 345,
352
Disclosure, *see*
MANAGEMENT
AND CONTROL
Prospective analysis, 345
See-compliant records
required, 344
Inception of title principle
applies, 323
Tracing principle applies, 323
Special community property
presumption as to sums on
deposit, 136, 333
Agreement, Probate Code, 136

Tracing, Probate Code, 136
Reimbursement rights, 334, 343
Remedies for impairment, *see*
MANAGEMENT AND CONTROL
RIGHTS AND DUTIES
Special community property presumption,
Probate Code, 136

DISSOLUTION
See also DIVISION OF
COMMUNITY PROPERTY AT
DISSOLUTION
American Law Institute, *see* EQUITABLE
DISTRIBUTION SYSTEMS
Disclosure during, 538, 623
Attorney work product privilege,
Family Code, 632
Declarations,
Noncomplying, 630
Required, Family Code, 627, 628
Definitions, Family Code, 625
Fiduciary relationship, Family code,
626
Legislative findings, Family Code, 625
Final judgment of dissolution, functions of,
12
Property inventory at end of marriage, 86,
882

**DIVISION OF COMMUNITY
PROPERTY AT DISSOLUTION**
Disclosure,
Final declarations, Family code, 628
Noncomplying declarations, Family
code, 630
Preliminary declarations, Family
Code, 627
Relation to attorney work product
privilege, 632
Dissolution statutes, Family Code, 531
Division by court order, litigation, 558
Equal division requirement applies,
586
Jurisdiction of court to divide
property, 653
Powers of court,
To defer sale of the family home,
577
To divide property, 559
Valuation requirement, 593
Effect of dissolution, Family Code, 531
Fiduciary duty, Family Code, 626
Final judgment of dissolution, Family
Code, 531
Irreconcilable differences, 534–535
Defined, Family Code, 531
Liabilities, confirmation and assignment,
600
Marriage settlement agreement, division by,
537
Arbitration, 538
Collaborative law, Family Code, 558
Mediation, 538

Mediation privilege, 688
Money sanctions, 633
Omitted assets, 607
Legal malpractice, 613
Postdissolution remedies,
Duties and breach of duties during
dissolution proceeding, 623–655
Disclosure of assets and
liabilities, Family code,
625
Importance to dissolution, 623
Mediation privilege, and, 688
Money sanctions, 633
Postjudgment set-aside orders, 655
Grounds for relief, Family
Code, 657
Current statutory
framework, 674
Pre-statutory doctrine,
658
Policy, Family Code, 656
Timely filing requirement, 700
Spousal support,
Agreements, modification or
termination, Family Code, 547
Awards, 548
Tax consequences, 602

DOMESTIC VIOLENCE PREVENTION
Definitions, Family Code, 514–515
Disturbing the peace of the other party,
Family Code, 522
Domestic Violence Prevention Act (DVPA),
Family Code, 511–512
Economic abuse, 518
Exclusive management and control of
community property order, Family
Code, 516–518
Financial abuse, 516–517, 523
Forfeiture provision examples, Family
Code, 520–522
Restraining orders, Family Code
Burden of proof, Family Code, 516
Domestic violence restraining order,
516
Disturbing the peace, 522–524
Case law, 522–524
Family Code, 518
During dissolution, 512
Emergency protective order, 515
Reasonable proof of past act or acts of
abuse standard, 516–517
Standard of review, 522

**EMOTION, *see* COMPLICATING
FACTORS IN AN EQUAL
DIVISION**

**EQUAL DIVISION MANDATE, *see*
DISSOLUTION**

EQUITABLE DIVISION SYSTEMS
American Law Institute, and, 15

Compared to community property systems, 13–19
Elkus v. Elkus (NY), 18
Equitable distribution states in U.S., forty-one total, 4–5
    By decisional law only, Mississippi, 4
    By statutory authority, forty total, 4–5, 15–19
Marital property type (court has jurisdiction over property acquired during marriage), 15
Universal property type (court has jurisdiction over property owned at end of marriage), 15
Wendt v. Wendt (CT), 16–18

FEDERAL SUPREMACY
Bankruptcy, 320
Copyrights, 320
Due Process, 280
National Life Insurance, 310
Privileges and immunities, 280
Retroactivity, relative to public interest, 288
Supremacy Clause, 305
    Employee retirement benefits, 310–311, 401
    Employee Retirement Income Security Act (ERISA), 311–312, 318
    Pension and insurance benefits, 319
    Qualified Domestic Relations Order (QDRO), 311
    Railroad Retirement Solvency Act, 311
    Retirement Equity Act, 311–312
    Retirement Plan Orders, Family Code, 399–400
    Testamentary rights, 312
    Uniformed Services Former Spouses' Protection Act, 311, 319
Patent law, 232
Preemption, 319
Social Security benefits, 319

GANANCIAL COMMUNITY PROPERTY SYSTEMS
California, 3
Equitable distribution states, compared with, 5, 13–19
Ganancial, defined, 20
Housekeeper's contribution, comparative, 15, 16–19
    During marriage, 92
Puerto Rico, 4
    "Conjugal partnership," 4
    Liquidation rather than dissolution, 5
Treaty of Guadalupe Hidalgo (1848), 7, 20, 169
Wisconsin, 4

GENDER FAIRNESS/UNFAIRNESS
Common law states, 16–19
Community property states,
    Compared with deferred community property states, 13–19

Constitution protections, 21
Contracting protections, Family Code, 41
Disclosure requirements, Family Code, 479
Equal ownership of property, 19
Equality of interest, Family Code, 32
Fiduciary duty, Family Code, 478
Protections for sums on deposit, Probate Code, 136
Tracing, 29
Community property opt-in states, 4
Deferred community property systems, 16–19
    Elkus, v. Elkus (NY), 18
    Gender unfairness, 13–15
    Separate title states, 13–19
    Title-based ownership, 14
Male-management era cases, 343
Wendt, Lorna, 16–18

GENERAL COMMUNITY PROPERTY PRESUMPTION, *see* **PRESUMPTIONS**

HOUSEKEEPER'S CONTRIBUTION, *see GANANCIAL* **COMMUNITY PROPERTY SYSTEMS**

HYBRIDITY
California, 168, 169–170
    See also CALIFORNIA COMMUNITY PROPERTY SYSTEM,
Commingled assets, *see* "AMERICANIZED" RULES
Emotion, *see* COMPLICATING FACTORS IN AN EQUAL DIVISION
Idaho, 166–167
Mauritius, 168–169

INCEPTION OF TITLE
Inception of title rule, 81, 323
Statutory application, Family Code, 158

LEGAL TRANSITIONS
Disclosure on demand to disclosure as ordinary matter, 478–479, 625
Fault to no-fault divorce, 7
Male management to equal management of community property, 7
Premarital contracting protections, and, 35
Tort award characterization, pre-1957 to today, 170–177
Written transmutations, verbal to writing requirement, 44–45

LENDER'S INTENT TEST
Basic financial terms, 132–134, 138
Borrowed funds acquired before marriage, application of test, 367
Borrowed funds acquired during marriage, general rule, 138
CAMPAL, and, 137
Community property loan proceeds, 137

Contract signatures, significance of, 147
Lender's intent rebuttal test, stated, 139
Macroeconomic function of community
      property system relative to third-
      party lenders, 146, 427
Money, *see* BASIC FINANCIAL TERMS
Personal information of spouses,
      creditworthiness, 145–146

LGBT PERSONS
Civil rights, 26
Obergefell v. Hodges (SCOTUS), 8

LIVING SEPARATE AND APART, *see*
      DATE OF SEPARATION

**MANAGEMENT AND CONTROL
      RIGHTS AND DUTIES**
Community property, management and
      control,
      Community property business, 509
      Conservatorship, 510
      Contract modification before marriage,
            508
      Court order, 511
            See also DOMESTIC
                  VIOLENCE
                  PREVENTION
      Equal management, 428
      General law, 429
      Managerial approach, 427–428, 449
      Partnership fiduciary rights and
            duties, general law, 432, 436
            Meinhard v. Salmon (NY), 432
            Presumption of undue
                  influence, and, 439
      Personal community property, 428,
            449
      Right to bring a claim against other
            spouse,
            Arising from general property
                  right, 430
            Right to destroy, limited by
                  concurrent ownership,
                  441, 445
      Sole bank account, access to, 509
Community property management, Family
      Code, 449, 464, 478, 479, 483
      Personal property, equal
            management rights, Family
            Code, 449
            "Other than testamentary"
                  limitation, Family Code,
                  460
            Reimbursement rights, 458
            Restrictions on disposition,
                  Family Code, 449
            Right to avoid, 450
      Real property, 463
            Joinder requirement, Family
                  Code, 464
Impairment remedies, Family Code, 483
      Add-a-name, Family Code, 483
      Attorney fees, Family Code, 483

Attorney fees mandatory, 491
Equitable accounting, Family Code,
      483
Involuntary forfeiture, 494
Money sanctions, 492
Remedies for breach, Family Code,
      483
Sanctions, 491
Managerial system, 427, 449
Transactions between spouses, 477
      Disclosure, Family Code, 479
            Credit card transactions, 491
            Demand for information, when
                  required, 479–481
            Financial records, Family Code,
                  479
      Impairment claims, Family Code, 482
            See also DOMESTIC
                  VIOLENCE
                  PREVENTION *and*
                  MANAGEMENT
                  AND CONTROL
            Breach of fiduciary duty, basis
                  of claim, 482
            Commingling, and right to
                  equitable accounting,
                  482–483
            Concealment of property, 495
            Presumption of undue
                  influence, when raised,
                  439, 482
            Tort actions, and, 492

MARITAL PROPERTY
Community property, Family Code, 85
Separate property, Family Code, 158
Two characters only, 81

MARITAL PROPERTY SYSTEM
      See also CREDITORS' CLAIMS
Impairment claims, Family Code, 484
Partnership fiduciary duties,
      Fiduciary relationship, Family Code,
            478
      Meinhard v. Salmon (NY), 432
      Policy goals of, general, 427
Property right,
      Agent of the community, spouse as,
            427
      Claims arising from, 429
      Destroy, right to, 441
      Fiduciary, 436–437
      Management and control,
            relationship to, 429
      Rationale, 436
      Spouse versus spouse, basis for, 429,
            431
      Wilcox v. Wilcox (CA), 430
Protecting creditors, 427
      Fixed claims, 497
      Joint venture, 436–437
      Order of satisfaction approach, when
            used, 500

Spouses as partners, 427, 436
Theoretical rationales for protection,
        428–429, 449
Right to avoid, 450
Spouses, compared with unmarried
        business partners, 477–478
Transactions between spouses, during
        marriage, 477

MARRIAGE CONTRACT
Age of consent, Family Code, 235
Annulment grounds, Family Code, 236
Children, 8
Consent, license, solemnization statute,
        Family Code, 11
Contracting barriers, Family Code, 234–
        235
    Annulment, Family Code, 236
    Putative spouse,
        Declarant's option to invoke
            Family Code dissolution,
            243–245
        Family Code rules apply
            as equitable
            protection, 238
        Liability for debts, Family
            Code, 237
        Spousal support
            allowable, Family
            Code, 237
        Declaration required, Family
            Code, 237, 238
        Intestacy rights, 245, 248–252
        Nonmarried cohabitants,
            compared with, 252
        Overlapping valid marriage and
            putative marriage, 247
        Wrongful death claims, Civil
            Code, 252
Domestic violence, 10
Domestic violence prevention, Family Code,
        511
Domicile, 274, 276, 277, 279, 287
    Quasi-community property, and, 274
    Proof required, 274, 287
Existential unknown, as a, 10
Family Code, role of, 234
Federal Constitutional right, 8
Fidelity, 10
Fiduciary rights and duties, Family Code,
        478–479
    Presumption of undue influence,
        when raised, 40, 439, 482
Gender fairness, and, 6–10, 11
General policy goals, 3
Informal divorce not recognized in any
        state, 257
Informal marriage, not recognized in
        California, 257
Marriage as partnership, *see*
        MANAGEMENT AND CONTROL
Marriage equality, 436–437
Public ritual, as, 10

Reasons for, 9–11
    Happiness, 9
    Personal empowerment, 9
    Wealth creation, 9
Restrictions on contracting a valid
        marriage, 12
Start-up entity, as, 10
State interest in, 12
Statutory requirements (consent, license,
        solemnization), Family Code, 235
Types of contracts,
    Cohabitation contract, example
        terms, 438
    Contracting, in general, 6
    Premarital contract,
        Executed before marriage, 35
        Executed before marriage and
            amended during
            marriage, 35, 40
    Marital contract, executed during
        marriage, 35
        See also MANAGEMENT AND
            CONTROL
    Marital settlement agreement,
        executed during dissolution, 537
        See also MANAGEMENT AND
            CONTROL
    Separate property sums on deposit,
        proving, Probate Code, 136
        See also MANAGEMENT AND
            CONTROL
    Spousal support modification
        contract, enforceable
        postdissolution, 547–548
        See also MANAGEMENT AND
            CONTROL
    Transmutation, changes character of
        property, 44
        See also MANAGEMENT AND
            CONTROL
Valid marriage, Family Code, 234, 235
    Distinguished from nonmarriage, 253
Void marriage, Family Code, 233–234
    Bigamous, Family Code, 235
    Incestuous, Family Code, 235
    Polygamous, Family Code, 235
Voidable marriage, Family Code, 236

MINERAL RIGHTS
Extracted, 398–399
In situ, 398–399
Leases, 376
        See also SEPARATE
            PROPERTY BUSINESS
            PROFITS
Exception states,
    Louisiana, 398–399
    Texas, 398–399

MONEY RELATED TERMS
Borrowed funds, presumptive character of,
        137
    During marriage, 137

Lender's intent test, *see*
PRESUMPTIONS
Method of distribution, significance of,
137
Pro tanto ownership, and, 146
American rule buy-in approach,
146
Civil law reimbursement
approach, 147
Rebuttal, *see* PRESUMPTIONS
Separate property, proof required for
claim, 139
Cash,
Commodity, as, 132
Gifts, 160
Tangible nature of, 132
Credit card, 133
Creditworthiness, 146–147
Loan proceeds, 133
Delivered to debtor, 133
Rebuttal, *see* LENDER'S INTENT
TEST
Transferred from lender to third
party, presumptive character,
137
Money, 132
Sums on deposit, 133
Debt enforceable against financial
institution, 133
Electronic fund transfers, drawn from,
133
Intangible nature of, 133
Loan proceeds from lender, 133

NONMARITAL INTIMATE PARTNERS
Analogy to marriage, 253–254
Cohabitation, example contract terms, 438
Cohabitation, proof of living together
required, 271
Contracts, agreements, and contracting
problems, 254, 271, 272–274, 436–439
Distinguished from,
Common law marriage, synonymous
with informal marriage, 257
Informal marriage, 257
"Meretricious relationship," 258
Putative spouse, 247
Equitable spouse doctrine, rejected by
state, 271
General laws apply, 254
Informal divorce, disallowed in all U.S.
states, 257
Informal marriage, disallowed in
California, 257
Intestacy rights, and, 272
Heir, no standing as, 272
Surviving spouse, no standing as, 272
Wrongful death, no standing as, Civil
Code, 272
Joint venture, 273–274
Legal spouse, and, 258
Loss of consortium, no standing for, 272
Marvin v. Marvin (CA), 258–270

Property agreements between nonmarried
cohabitants, 273
Terminology, 253–254
Title acquired during cohabitancy, Civil
Code, 273

OBERGEFELL v. HODGES (SCOTUS)
Significance of, 8, 253

**PARENTAGE, *see* MARRIAGE
CONTRACT**

**PERSONAL INJURY CLAIMS,
MONEY, AWARDS**
Contract modification, 183
Imputed contributory negligence doctrine,
172
Eliminated from California
community property system,
172–173
Exception, concurring negligence of
spouse allowable as defense,
Family Code, 176
Interpersonal violence, 184
Mandatory dissolution assignment rule,
Family Code, 176
Commingling with ordinary
community property, exception,
176
Fairness, exception, 176
Supersedes ordinary community
property rules, 182
Tracing rule applies, 177
Money and property received, legal
transitions in characterization, 173–
175
1849 to 1956, 173
1957 to 1967, 174
1968–on, 174–175
Personal right, distinguished from property
right, 170
Personal injury claim defined, 171
Property claim defined, 170
Right to exclude, 170
Transferability, 170, 228–229
Right of reimbursement, Family Code, 172
Quantum meruit claim, 182
Spouse versus spouse, 183
Characterizing personal injury
recovery, generally, 183
Separate property characterization,
Family Code, 172
Spouse contributes to third party's
negligence, Family Code, 176
Spouse versus third party, 171–172
Timing of injury, before, during or
after marriage, Family Code,
172
Wrongful death awards, 183

PREMARITAL CONTRACTS
Amendments, executed while spouses are
in confidential relationship, 35, 40
Disclosure defined, Family Code, 42–43

Distinguished from,
Cohabitation agreement, 438
Marital contract, 40
Transmutation, 40
Enforceability of premarital contracts,
generally, 37–38
Amendments, 35, 40
Disclosure, 37–38
Domestic violence, history of at
execution, 40
Formalities for enforceability, 36
Executed before marriage, 35
Executed before marriage and
amended during marriage, 35,
40
Gifts, contracting around, 71, 159
Original contract before marriage, 35
Recordation of, 40
Right to modify default Family Code terms
by contract, 34
Spousal support waivers, 36–37
See also MARRIAGE
CONTRACT
During marriage, void, 33
Postdissolution, potentially
enforceable, 33
Subject matter, permissible, 36
Terms, allowable
Cohabitation contract, compared with,
438
Contracting, in general, 6
Personal obligations, allowable
terms, Family Code, 41–42
Postdissolution spousal support
wavier, Family Code, 41–42
Property related terms, Family Code,
41–42
Transmutation, Family Code, 44
Voluntariness, Family Code, 42–43

PRESUMPTIONS
Acquisition-based, 89, 115
California Multiple-Party Account Law
(CAMPAL), Probate Code, 136
Application, 134
Lender's intent test, and, 138
Nonconclusive, 135
Possession based, 135
Rebuttal, by tracing or written
agreement, 135
Supersedes,
Civil Code rule on joint bank
accounts, 134
Joint form title community
property presumption,
134
Conclusive, 92
Housekeeper's presumption, 92, 96
Deceased former spouse's estate, Family
Code, 114
Disclosure, 111, 352
Evidentiary leniency, as, 89

General community property presumption,
83, 89
Acquisition-based, 96–101
Possession-based, compared
with, 100
Applicability, generally, 89, 100–101
Burden of proof, 92
California general presumption
compared with Texas general
presumption, 100
Disclosure, 93–94, 111–113
Discretion of court, by, 90
Evidentiary leniency, 89
Equality of interest, 103
Fiduciary duty, disclosure, 93, 111
Functions served, 95
Inception of title, and, 94
Management and control, and, 111
Nonconclusive, 92–93
Policy, 31, 82, 89
Equal one-half shares, 95
Equality of interest principle,
31, 92, 103
Present, existing, equal shares,
Family Code, 32
Proof required to raise, 89, 112–113
Protection for the community estate,
as, 89, 94–95
Rebuttal, 101, 102
Actual proof required to rebut,
93
Corroborating evidence, 112
Lender's intent test, by, 139
Sums on deposit in an account,
as applied to, 114
Tracing, explained, 101–102
Tracing formula, basic, 102
Standard of review, 103, 110
Superseding presumptions, effect of,
100
Title by creation, applies to, 96
Nonconclusive, 93
Possession based,
Acquisition, compared with, 100
Sums on deposit in an account, 133
Zagorski v. Zagorski (TX), 112
Same-sex marriage equality, *see*
MARRIAGE CONTRACT
Special superseding community property
presumptions, 81, 124–125, 134
Joint form title, community property
presumption, Family Code, 125
Acquisition-based, 125
Acquisition before marriage, 131
Commercial property, 129
Community property title, 116
Community property with the
right of survivorship title,
Civil Code, 117
Current legislation, 124
Dissolution proceeding, applied
in, 114, 125

General community property presumption, distinguished from, 115
Historical context, 119–125
    Early statutory version, 122–124
    Implied contract rationale, development of, 119–122
    Siberell v. Siberell (CA), 119
    Tomaier v. Tomaier (CA), 119
    Watson v. Peyton (CA), 120
Joint tenancy creation, Civil Code, 116
Nonmarried intimate partners, title controls, 132, 273
Policy, 118
Rebuttal by agreement only, Family Code, 125
Rebuttal compared with reimbursement, 128
Reimbursement right, 115, 124–126
    Amendments to reimbursement statute, Family Code, 131
    No interest, 124
    Retroactivity of reimbursement statute, 130
    Statute creating the right, Family Code, 126, 130
    Value limitations, subject to, 124
    When right arises, 124, 126
Retroactive application, 130, 295
Standard on review, example problem, 129
Sums on deposit, community property presumption for, 89, 136
Tenancy in common, 116
Termination of marriage, application,
    Applies in dissolution proceeding, 115, 125
    Not applicable in probate proceeding, 119–124
    See also DEATH
Transmutations, 131
Unilateral creation/severance, 128

PRO TANTO OWNERSHIP, *see* **COMMINGLED ASSETS**

PROPERTY OUTSIDE THE COMMUNITY PROPERTY SYSTEM
Professional degrees, 198–199
Talent, 87, 215, 386

PUTATIVE SPOUSE DOCTRINE
See also QUASI-MARITAL PROPERTY
Coats v. Coats (CA), 239–240
Defined, 81, 198
Distinguished from,
    "Common law" marriage, 247
    "Meretricious relationship," obsolete term, 258
Good faith subjective belief in validity of marriage required, 234, 241–243
Intestacy rights, 245
    Estoppel of legal spouse's claim, 245
    Overlapping claims of putative and legal spouse, 245–246, 247
    Estate of Hafner (CA), 248
    Estate of Leslie (CA), 246
    Estate of Vargas (CA), 247
    Separate property of decedent, 246–247
Liminal status, 234
No-fault division of quasi-marital property, 243–245
Nonmarital intimate partners, and, 252
Policy, 234, 238
Protections of doctrine, 238
    Option for dissolution, Family Code, 234, 238, 243–245
Quasi-marital property, 234, 237, 240
Rehabilitation (support) claim, 271
Requirements,
    Ceja v. Rudolph & Sletten, Inc. (CA), 241
    Domicile, 279, 287
    Good faith, same as subjective belief in validity of marriage, 242
    Subjective standard, 242–243
Statute governing, Family Code, 234, 237
Wrongful death, 252

QUASI-COMMUNITY PROPERTY
See also COMMUNITY PROPERTY
Creditors' rights to reach, Family Code, 501, 504
Death, 715, 287
Defined, 81, 198
Dissolution, 125
Dissolution petition, and, 286
Domicile requirement, 274, 287
Recurring bar exam topic, 288
Tracing, 279

QUASI-MARITAL PROPERTY
See also PUTATIVE SPOUSE
Creditors' rights to reach, Family Code, 501, 504
Statutory definition, Family Code, 237

REAL PROPERTY, *see* COMMUNITY PROPERTY

REIMBURSEMENT RIGHTS BY STATUTE
Contributions to purchase, for,
    Generally, 128–129, 358, 367, 458
    In re Marriage of Aufmuth (CA), 359
        Distinguished from civil law rule, 358
    Statutory right, Family Code, 126
    Retroactivity of, 295
Debt repayment, for,
    After date of separation, 459
    Separate property payments for community property debts, 459
    Statutory right, Family Code, 505
Education, direct contributions, Family Code, 205
Equitable division, in lieu of, 459
Expenses paid for personal injury expenses, Family code, 172
Premarital support obligation, Family Code, 459, 505

RENTS, ISSUES, AND PROFITS, *see* COMMUNITY PROPERTY

SEPARATE PROPERTY
American law approach, 155–158, 165
Appreciation, under American rule,
    Defined, 161
    Ownership of, under American rule, 162
    Realized at sale, 161
    Rents, issues, and profits, compared with, 162
    Severed from base asset, 162
Civil law approach, 158, 161
    Usufruct, 162, 166
Constitutional protections, 157
Definition, 157
George v. Ransom (CA), 164, 169
    Change instituted, 157–158, 162, 163
    Codification, 164
    Creditors' rights, 162–164
        See also CREDITORS' CLAIMS
    Doctrine of precedent, and, 169
    Tracing principle, and, 161, 165
Gifts, Family Code, 160
    Cash, 160
    Cash deposited into account, 160
    Character of, 160
    Conditional, 161
        Disclosure of condition requirement, 159–160
        Express condition requirement, 159
    Contemplation of marriage, made in, 161
    Contracting around, 160
    Exchanged between spouses, 160
        See also TRANSMUTATIONS

Family heirlooms, 159
Judicial Council forms, 159, 882
Law of gifts, application of, 159–160
Third-party donor, 160
Title documents, 160
    Joint title, 160
Separate property by definition, Family Code, 160
Validity, 159
Judicial Council property inventory form, 159, 882
Owned before marriage, Family Code, 160
Property owned before marriage, 160
Rents, issues, and profits, Family Code, 160
    "American" rule, 158, 161, 163
    Civil law usufruct rule, 162, 166
    Statutory tracing rule, Family Code, 158
    Tracing principle, 29, 158, 161–165
Statutory definition of, Family Code, 160

SEPARATE PROPERTY BUSINESS PROFITS
Accounting, equitable right to, 382
Burden of proof, 398
    Austin v. Austin (CA), 388
    Estate of Ney (CA), 398
Civil law rule, 377, 382
    Norris v. Vaughn (TX), 399
Definitions,
    Business, 388, 392
    Capital, 376, 378
    Excess profits, 378, 381
    Fair market value of business, 381, 392–393
        Comparable businesses, 393
        Goodwill, 393
        Multiples for standard pricing methods, examples, 393, 888–895
        Operating assets, 393
    Fair return on investment, 378, 381
    Income, 376
    Pricing methods, 392–393
    Separate property business, 376
    Willing buyer rule, stated, 392
Labor, 376
    Community property component, 378, 381, 386, 393, 398
    Minimum plus labor standard, 393, 398
    Proximate cause of business growth, and, 387, 386
    Talent, compared with, 386–387
Mineral leases, 376
Pereira v. Pereira (CA), identifies "excess profits," 379
    Economic factors, and, 381
    Excess profits, 379, 382
    Income stream, 388
    Inflation rates, and, 381
    Minimum-plus labor requirement, 398

Patrick v. Alacer (CA), community as creditor of business, 382
Pereira formula, 381
Separate property business, 388, 392
Simple interest calculation, relevance of, 381
Total recap accounting method, 382
Tracing applies, 378, 323
Profits,
    Defined, 390
    Labor stream, distinguished from, 388
Separate property business, distinguished from income stream, 388
    Austin v. Austin (CA), 388
    Capital requirement, 388, 392
    Taxable investment account, *Beam v. Bank of America* (CA), 393–394
Substantial justice between the parties, policy, 376–378
Taxable investment account, 393, 394
Van Camp v. Van Camp (CA), calculates community reimbursement, 383
    Family expenses, and, 385, 386
    Total recap accounting method, 386
    Van Camp formula, 386

SHARING PRINCIPLE
Sharing principle stated, 3
    Hypothetical application to *Wendt*, 19
Spanish law, 20, 147
Visigothic origin, 7
Unpaid housework and career facilitation work, 16

SUMS ON DEPOSIT, *see* **MONEY RELATED TERMS**

TITLE DOCUMENTS
Creation, by, 96
Documents, role of, 89
Joint form titles, 115
    At death of spouse, 731
    Before marriage, 131
    Creation statutes, Civil Code, 116, 117
    Early case law, 119–122
        Siberell v. Siberell (CA), transmutation theory, 119–120
        Tomaier v. Tomaier (CA), separate property presumption theory, 121
    Early legislative attempts to clarify, 122–124
        Any joint form title (1987 legislation), 123–124
        Any joint tenancy title (1984 legislation), 123
        Single family residence in joint form title (1965 legislation), 122
    How operates, 116–117
        Community property, 116
        Community property with the right of survivorship, 117
        Joint tenancy, 116
        Tenancy in common, 116
    Joint interest defined, 116
    Origin of, 119
    Practice problem with solution, 129
    Probate proceeding, *see* Joint form titles, early case law
    Unilateral change during marriage, 128–129
        Right to avoid, 1285
        Unilateral creation, 128
        Unilateral severance, 128

TRANSMUTATIONS
Civil Code presumptions inapplicable, 67
Common law contract exception or defenses, 70
Defined, 44–45
Exempt property, 45, 71–76
    Interspousal gifts, Family Code, 45
Express declaration, 45–76
    Definition, 67
    Statute requiring, Family Code, 45
Fiduciary duties during marriage, 69–71
    Any unfair transaction, Family Code, 70, 478
    Presumption of undue influence, *see* MANAGEMENT AND CONTROL
    Raising, 69
    Rebutting, 70
    Voluntariness, 69
Formalities, Family Code, 45–46
Premarital contracts, distinguished from, 44
Presumption of undue influence,
    See also MANAGEMENT AND CONTROL
    Any unfair advantage, prohibition on taking, 70
    Confidential relationship between spouses, 46, 69–71
    Statute imposing partnership fiduciary duties, Family Code, 46, 478, 626, 657

TREATY OF GUADALUPE HIDALGO (1848), *see* **GANANCIAL COMMUNITY PROPERTY SYSTEMS**

UNIFORM ACTS FROM THE NATIONAL CONFERENCE OF COMISSIONERS ON UNIFORM STATE LAWS
Uniform Interstate Enforcement of Domestic Violence Prevention Orders Act (UIEODVPOA), 512
Uniform Marital Property Act, 4, 16
    Wisconsin as adopter of, 4
Uniform Multiple-Party Accounts Law, 134
    California Multiple-Party Accounts Law (CAMPAL), 134–137

Uniform Premarital Agreement Act, 34
    California Premarital Agreement Act,
        see CALIFORNIA
        COMMUNITY PROPERTY
        SYSTEM

UNTITLED ASSET
Cash, 132
Creation, 96

WORK BENEFITS
    See also FEDERAL SUPREMACY
Client books, 409
Deferred earnings, 399
Federal law, 401
    Employment Retirement Income
        Security Act (ERISA), 401
        Alternate payee, 401
        Pension plan participant, 401
        Qualified Domestic Relations
            Order (QDRO), 401
    Pre-emption, 401
        See also FEDERAL
            SUPREMACY
    Retirement Equity Act (REA), 401
Retirement plan orders, Family Code, 399
Right, distinguished from expectancy, 421
Time rule, 403
    In re Marriage of Green (CA), 403
Trial court discretion, 399, 402
    In-kind division, 403
    Offsets, 403
Signing bonuses, 409
    Characterization of, 421
    Client book, 421
    In re Marriage of Finby (CA), 409